MANCHESTER CITY

THE COMPLETE RECORD 1880-2006

MANCHESTER CITY

THE COMPLETE RECORD 1880-2006

GARY JAMES

First published in Great Britain in 2006 by The Breedon Books Publishing Company Limited, 3 The Parker Centre, Derby, DE21 4SZ.

Paperback reprint in Great Britain in 2012 by The Derby Books Publishing Company Limited, 3 The Parker Centre, Derby, DE21 4SZ.

ISBN 978-1-78091-146-5

Printed and bound by CPI Group (UK) Ltd, Croydon, CRO 4YY

Contents

Acknowledgements

So many people who have helped during the production of this work, but the first thanks must go to Ray Goble and Andy Ward, the authors of the first *Manchester City Complete Record.* They laid the groundwork for this book and I know that their work has helped every City-related writer, statistician and researcher. I have always been grateful to Ray for his initial encouragement when I sought a publisher for *The Pride of Manchester* in 1991, and have always admired the quality of his statistical records. Likewise Andy Ward has been an inspirational figure throughout my writing career. He has provided me with a great deal of advice and support since we first met during my research for *Football With A Smile*, my official biography of Joe Mercer, OBE. Andy is not only a great writer but also a kind and supportive man.

Inevitably, fellow City statisticians Dennis Chapman and John Maddocks have helped me throughout my writing career, and much of their influence is evident in this work. Dennis has helped cast his expert eye over several sections of this book. Sadly John passed away a few years ago, but his influence remains strong. Another man who has helped significantly is Jean-François Maille. Despite being born in France and remaining a French resident, Jean-François is a passionate Blue with an obsession for unravelling the facts of City's birth that matches my own. His interest in Manchester's club has been encouraging.

Others who have helped include (listed in alphabetical order): Peter Barnes; Colin Bell, MBE; Graham Birch; Howard Burr; Brian Houghton; Alan Jubb; Steve Kay; Mark Kennedy; Peter Lupson; James McCann; Tommy Muir; Roger Reade; Ken Smallwood; Richard Tucker; Dave & Sue Wallace and Chris Williams. Of course, all the staff of the Manchester City Experience (award-winning museum and tour) and Manchester City Football Club need thanking, as do those from Manchester Central Library; The *Manchester Evening News*; the BFI; the newspaper archive of the British Library at Colindale and the Manchester United museum. Inevitably, hundreds of newspapers have been consulted, particularly those national and local editions produced in Manchester.

Significant support has also come from members of MCIVTA – the supporters' email news service – and the various supporters' organisations. Some have helped promote this book; others have offered encouragement; all share the desire to see City's history recorded properly and hope that City soon regain the winning ways demonstrated decade after decade pre-1983.

Club historians and fellow members of the Association of Football Statisticians have assisted. In particular I would like to thank Tony Brown for his extensive support with the statistical section of this volume. Of course the staff at Breedon, in particular Steve Caron and Susan Last, need thanking for their efforts in making this a great publication.

Edward Garvey, City's excellent official photographer, deserves great praise. The majority of modern photos come from his coverage of the Blues. Other photographs have come from the archives of the Manchester City Experience, the *Manchester Evening News*, Roland Cooke, and the author.

Finally, thanks to my family for their continuing support.

Foreword

From the moment I first arrived in Manchester I understood the passion supporters have for City. They help to make this a truly great club. Throughout my career and life I have been delighted with the support they have given me, and I am delighted I was part of the side that brought so much success to the Blues during the sixties and seventies.

City has had many great players and wonderful games over the years, but that period under Joe Mercer and Malcolm Allison, and then a little later when Tony Book was in charge, was always exciting for the players and of course the fans. During my City career there were many significant moments starting with the victory at Rotherham which guaranteed promotion in 1966 – who could have guessed how successful the side would be over the following four seasons when the League, FA Cup, League Cup and European Cup-Winners' Cup all arrived at Maine Road. Even in my last season before retirement there were still moments to make you feel immensely proud of playing for Manchester City. My last European game was the highly memorable 2–2 draw with AC Milan in the San Siro in November 1978. That night we took a two-goal lead, before they came back at us, but even the draw was significant as we became the first English side to leave AC Milan without defeat. And for supporters the night was even more remarkable as it had originally been scheduled for the previous night, but fog put the game back 24 hours and caused fans to spend an extra night away from work and their families. There were still a significant number of Blues in that stadium when the match was eventually played.

The most memorable of all City games for me, however, is not one of the great trophy-winning occasions. It's the Boxing Day 1977 League meeting with Newcastle. This was the game which saw my return to action after that terrible injury I'd struggled with for two years. It was a night that made me realise just how special City supporters are. That night as I made my way on to the pitch as substitute for Paul Power the ground erupted in a very special way. I was very touched and today, almost 29 years later, I can still feel the emotion of that night. City is a great club, but City supporters are by far the most significant aspect of this club today.

Manchester City: The Complete Record has been written by lifelong City fan Gary James and within the pages of this book he has provided pen pictures of the club's greatest stars, and written extensively on the great moments that have shaped the club we all love. He also provides a breakdown of every first-team game, including appearances and goalscorers, and quite simply has managed to make this the main reference work for first-team football at City.

This is a book supporters will refer to time after time, not just for the glory years, but for every period of the club's history. I hope you enjoy it.

Finally, I'd like to take this opportunity to thank City fans once again for their great support throughout my life.

All the best
Colin Bell MBE

INTRODUCTION

AS THE first Manchester side to win a major trophy, City has always been a major club with phenomenal support, and M*anchester City: The Complete Record* aims to become the definitive reference book on the Blues.

This book aims to put into perspective the club's entire history and allow the reader, via statistical records and entertaining narrative, to understand why the Blues have always been such an important force and a major source of local pride. Mancunians know the loyalty of City supporters well, but it's worth noting that during the last decade three of City's top five average attendances have been recorded. Incredibly, these highs come during City's longest period without a major trophy, thereby proving the loyalty further. As all fans understand, the strength of Manchester City comes from its fans, and this book helps to demonstrate that this has always been the case.

From the very beginning the club was created to represent the local community, and in 1899 City were the first Manchester side to win a national trophy when they became Second Division Champions. Five years later they won the FA Cup. An incredible homecoming parade followed, with one newspaper claiming: 'There is nothing in the annals of football that will compare with the magnificent reception which was accorded the Manchester City football team on the occasion of their return to Manchester last night in the proud position of holders of the English Cup for the first time in Manchester's career. Notwithstanding the lateness of their arrival, the whole population of the city seemed to have turned out to do them honour.' The homecoming parade started at approximately 9.30pm on a Monday night.

Manager Tom Maley summed up the importance of City to Manchester accurately when he told officials and the press: 'Perhaps love of sport had something to do with the bringing together of so great a gathering, but love of Manchester, had much more to do with it.'

Two days after City's homecoming had dominated all Mancunian activity, the *Manchester Evening Chronicle* claimed that Manchester was now the second city of the Empire. It was a bold statement, but it was directly connected with what had occurred earlier that week. Football really had changed the atmosphere for all in the world's first industrial city.

Of course, a lot has happened since 1904, but the basic principle that City is Manchester's club remains true. Since that time the Blues have found major success on a national and a European stage. In fact, when City faced Gillingham at Wembley in 1999, they equalled Arsenal's record of playing significant games at the old Wembley stadium in every decade of the club's existence (except the war-affected 1940s). This may not sound too amazing, but it does indicate that City's success, like Arsenal's, has occurred throughout their history. Many other major sides, most notably from a modern perspective Manchester United, Liverpool and Chelsea, didn't play at Wembley until after World War Two. It's also worth stating that since the Blues were first promoted in 1899 they have spent only 20 seasons outside of the top flight: unfortunately five of those have come since 1996.

The image referred to on page 14 of A.J. Balfour's visit. The two gentlemen in top hats are directors Parlby and Royle, not King Edward. The Stone Yard Stand at Hyde Road is in the background.

The details of City's successes appear throughout this book and, via a narrative outlining the club's history, significant players, managers, and memorable games, all readers should get a strong feel for how the Blues performed during every period of their existence.

Manchester City: The Complete Record follows two earlier 'Complete Records' on the Blues produced by Breedon during the 1980s and early 1990s. Those versions, written by City statistician Ray Goble and writer Andy Ward, provided an excellent record of the club, and this volume has been produced not only to bring the record up to date but also to build on the excellent work done by Goble and Ward.

With the full support of Ray Goble, the statistical areas of the book have been extended and enhanced. Meticulous research has been undertaken with specific attention paid to ensure details, such as attendance information, are accurately recorded. New reference sources have been discovered and previously unknown facts cross-checked with a variety of sources, including the records of opposition clubs and the League. Often reference sources differ. Where this has been the case the author has taken a realistic assessment of original sources. As an example, the attendance for Maine Road's first match in 1923 has often been recorded, even in official publications, as 56,993. During the old stadium's final season the author identified an official source from six days after the game which stated that the actual crowd was 58,159. This figure appeared in several newspapers at the time as a correction to the lower figure. The author therefore feels this is an accurate figure.

In some cases the records of City's opponents are more accurate than those previously held as true by City historians. Wherever doubt existed, the author has referred to non-City sources to identify their views. A good example is the 1968 Championship decider at Newcastle. The attendance has usually been recorded in City publications as 46,300. The

Action from the City-Grimsby Cup tie on 12 February 1966 with the Kippax Stand in the background.

author has always been suspicious of this rounded figure and, by consulting Football League records submitted by Newcastle United, and those documented by Newcastle historian Paul Joannou, the figure has now been accurately recorded as 46,492.

Every effort has been made to ensure that the facts and figures in this book are correct. During research for this book the author has identified significant information from the earliest years of the club which puts into question some of the 'facts' that existed about the founding fathers and mother. The correct details are documented in this version, but they do differ from every previously published work, including the author's own earlier works. It has to be stressed that research is still ongoing in many areas and readers may have information which helps. Past experience shows that new information often emerges following publication.

Should new information come to light, or indeed errors be spotted within this volume, then the author would be delighted to receive such information in writing, addressed to him care of The Manchester City Experience (museum & tour), City of Manchester Stadium, Sportcity, Manchester, M11 3FF.

Changes to previously published City information

The author has been pro-actively researching the history of City since the mid-1980s. During this time a number of published records relating to the Blues have been challenged and shown to be incorrect. This publication has incorporated these amendments.

A small selection of commonly published facts that have been shown to be incorrect are shown below as an example of this work:

• Miss G. Connell has usually been recorded as the lady who came up with the idea to form a working men's organisation during the 1870s that led to the formation of the club. Her full name has never been documented in a City work. Research for this book has proved that there were two Connell sisters, Georgina and Anna, and that the elder (Anna) was always referred to in the newspapers as Miss Connell and her younger sister was called Miss G. Connell. Georgina focussed on women's activities, while Anna came up with the idea of the working men's club. Earlier researchers believed Miss Connell and Miss G. Connell were the same person, and so Georgina was incorrectly believed to be the founding mother.

• Thomas Goodbehere has never been mentioned in earlier books, but he was one of two founding fathers of the club. By the 20th century Goodbehere was no longer a key member of the club and by the time City's history was documented for the first time those involved with the club couldn't remember his exact surname. The leading figure claimed it was Goodyeare, although one source did mention a slightly more accurate version (Goodbyere), and from that point on Goodyeare was recorded as if it was true.

• The role of St Mark's Church and the period pre-1894 has often been dismissed, or included simply as a footnote in the club's history. Why this has been played down is unclear. Many City officials and historians have focussed on 1894 (the year MCFC came into being) as the formation of the club, but this date is not the most significant, as 1880 is the year the first game was played. Using 1894 as the main date means several significant moments and seasons, including the first two seasons of League football played by the Blues, are ignored. In addition, as this book shows, several significant figures – from players to managers to directors and of course supporters – remained involved with the Blues throughout the various name changes and ground moves of the 1880s and early 1890s. The fact that St Mark's evolved into Manchester City via Ardwick and other names should never be downplayed.

Alf Wood (number five) and not George Heslop during the Grimsby tie of 1966.

• St Mark's first game is recorded as a meeting with Macclesfield Baptist Church in November 1880, and where possible, the author has identified the first names, addresses, and ages of the men who played in that game. It is worth noting that it is the author's belief that an earlier match had been played, probably in October, although so far he has been unable to identify a specific fixture.

• In earlier statistical books, and in several modern statistical records, George Heslop is recorded as playing in the 1966 FA Cup tie with Grimsby Town. He did not feature in that game and his place in the side was actually taken by Alf Wood. This was proved categorically when the author searched and found a photograph from the game showing Wood, and not Heslop, in action.

• Although in *The Pride Of Manchester* (1991) the author identified Tommy Browell as the scorer of two goals in the Manchester derby of 11 October 1919, every statistical book since that date has recorded the scorer as Horace Barnes. This version reaffirms that the scorer was Browell and that his two goals were both equalisers (City's second and third goals of the match).

• In 1933 after City lost the FA Cup Final captain Sam Cowan is reported as promising the king that City would be back the following year to win the trophy. Although this is a nice romantic story, it did not happen, as the king did not attend the 1933 Final. Significant research has identified that the story was first published in the 1950s following City's 1955 and 1956 Finals, and that in 1933 Cowan did say to reporters that he hoped City would be back to win the Cup. As with many stories, the history has been distorted.

Supporters celebrating promotion as Champions in 2002.

City pride and passion in the North Stand at Maine Road.

• Finally, the following story highlights why it is so important to check and challenge facts whenever writing or researching the history of the club. On 27 March 1920 King George V became the first reigning monarch to visit a provincial ground when he attended City's Hyde Road for a game with Liverpool. It was a landmark moment and it is highly significant that he chose to attend a City match. However, in recent years publications on the Commonwealth Games and talks on the history of Manchester by a leading non-footballing Mancunian writer have stated as a fact that King Edward attended a Hyde Road game in 1900, 20 years before King George.

This is totally untrue and comes as a result of an error included in a 1930s publication on the club. The typographical error mentioned King George's visit in 1920, but the date was mistakenly printed as 27 March 1900. It was a simple error, but several histories since that date repeated it. By the time of the Commonwealth Games, Mancunian writers were being asked to provide historical details of the City of Manchester Stadium's new tenants for an international audience and visitors to the city. Those writers and researchers took the typing error as fact, and added to it the true details of the 1920 visit to incorrectly claim that City were the first side to have two reigning monarchs visit! A photograph was even produced showing King Edward at Hyde Road – it was actually City director Joshua Parlby accompanying future Prime Minister A.J. Balfour at the ground in 1900. Clearly, none of the people involved checked the source material properly. If they had they would have found that City didn't even have a game on 27 March 1900, and would also have noted that Queen Victoria was still the reigning monarch at the time in any case.

Inevitably, mistakes will creep into this volume, but please understand that extensive work has been performed to try and ensure the information recorded is as factually correct as possible. Hopefully, you'll be pleased with the result.

The History of Manchester City FC

Unlike the majority of other clubs, Manchester City can claim that its initial formation was the result of the desire of a woman to improve the lives of ordinary working-class citizens. Anna, the daughter of Arthur Connell, the rector of St Mark's Church in West Gorton, was determined to ensure some of the ills of 19th-century Manchester were eradicated. West Gorton, like so many districts of the world's first industrial city, had developed at an alarming rate. Factories and terraced housing, in many cases of poor quality, were swallowing up almost every area of greenery surrounding the city, and areas such as Ardwick, Beswick, Bradford, Clayton and Gorton grew from relatively small villages to become densely populated districts of the city within 20 years.

In 1857 it was clear that West Gorton's development was to continue for some time, and in November a man called Jabez Ashworth issued a circular outlining plans to raise money to create facilities for religious worship. Incorrectly referring to the broader area as Gorton Brook, he described the location:

> *Gorton Brook is a thriving though somewhat isolated village in the Township of Gorton, and parish of Manchester, situate between Hyde Road and Openshaw, close to Ashbury Station. There are extensive Iron, Chemical, Cotton and Paper Manufactories in the neighbourhood. The population is about two thousand. Opportunities for public worship and instruction being much needed.*

A mere five years later another circular was issued stating plans to erect a new church. This was to become St Mark's Church and it's interesting to note from the comments how the population was still growing:

> *The parish of West Gorton is large in extent and population. It extends from near the railway arch on Hyde Road to Denton on the one part, and to Droylsden on the other part. The population is estimated at between nine and ten thousand, and is rapidly increasing. To meet the wants of this large population there is church accommodation for not more than one-twentieth part, and it is proposed to remedy the evil by erecting a New Church on Colonel Clowes's property at West Gorton, where building is daily in progress.*
>
> *Land sufficient for the Church has been kindly given by Colonel Clowes without cost, and Mr Beyer has headed the subscription list with a munificent donation of one thousand pounds.*

On 13 April 1864 a foundation stone was laid and St Mark's Church, costing £3,480, plus £400 for boundary walls, was erected. The consecration occurred on Thursday 30 November 1865, and the very first Bishop of Manchester, James Prince Lee, performed the main duties of the day. Shortly afterwards Irishman Arthur Connell became the first rector of St Mark's. The entire Connell family became involved with the parish and they spent considerable time and effort working with the local community. Anna was the oldest daughter and she assisted her father with most activities. Her younger sister Georgina became more involved as time progressed and in the late 1870s she helped create an organisation for the women of the parish. Their meetings became very popular but Anna began to worry about the male population of West Gorton. Gang warfare, known as 'scuttling' in Gorton, regularly seemed to break out between the different communities of east Manchester, with windows broken and people injured. Many residents were afraid of going out. In addition, the local newspaper carried reports of domestic violence with every issue.

Poverty, domestic violence, alcoholism, racial tension and gang warfare affected most Gortonians, and although these problems still affect many people within Manchester today, there was a feeling during the 1870s within West Gorton that something had to be done. By 1877 the population of the Gorton area was reported as being in excess of 30,000 – a figure Hyde Road-based Dr Kennedy claimed was far too high – and conditions were extremely poor. No wonder violence increased. Scuttling was often reported in the local newspaper and in May 1879 the *Gorton Reporter* revealed that over 500 had taken part in one battle alone. This was a significant number.

In January 1879 Arthur Connell set up a soup kitchen and a relief fund for the local poor. On its first day of operation 300 people queued for soup, bread and other food, and within a week over 1,500 gallons of soup, 1,000 loaves of bread and 10 tons of coal had been distributed from the church.

Anna Connell was convinced other activities could discourage the men of the parish from taking part in the drinking and violent activities, while some form of organisation could be set up to improve the racial tension. The local population of east Manchester was made up of several nationalities including Italians, Irish, Germans and Poles. There was a significant Jewish population in the city and, although it's not often considered, most English Mancunians were themselves immigrants to the city from other parts of the country. These had arrived from all over the nation looking for work on the railways and in the engineering works and cotton mills of the city. There was a real mix of accents, backgrounds, and interests. The two significant figures of authority were usually the local church, or the local employer. Anna Connell recognised this and decided to work with figures from the local ironworks to help improve the lives of Gortonians.

Alongside William Beastow and Thomas Goodbehere, two highly respected figures from Brooks' Union Ironworks (later known as Brooks & Doxey's), she set about creating a series of men's meetings. Beastow had previously tried – and failed – with a similar venture, but Anna was convinced that the concept could work. Her aim was to encourage the local men to meet regularly and discuss the major issues, both spiritual and social, of the day.

With strong support from Beastow and Goodbehere, Anna's group set up a cricket team in spring 1879 and after the side's second season William Beastow pushed to give the men something to do in the winter. With Anna's support and the backing of the rest of the committee the decision was taken to create a football team. This decision led to the creation of St Mark's (West Gorton) Church team, and the first known game took place on 13

THE CONNELL FAMILY

No history of Manchester City has ever really considered the role of the Connell family in creating the club, and as the events that led to the birth of the Blues slipped from living memory some 40–50 years ago, it has proved extremely difficult to get to grips with the true story of 1870s and 1880s Manchester. With strong investigative research from religious expert Peter Lupson, I can now pay proper respect to the Connells and their part in Manchester's history.

Prior to becoming the first rector of St Mark's Church, Irishman Arthur Connell trained in Birkenhead, becoming a priest in 1857 at the age of 35. His first appointment as a curate saw him based at Lurgan in County Down in the north of Ireland. Shortly afterwards he moved to nearby Tullyish and then in 1859 he was offered the curacy of Christ Church, Harrogate. His eldest daughter Anna was four years old at this point, and the Connell family lived in Yorkshire until 1865.

Whether Connell felt a desire to test his own abilities or not is not known, but in 1865, against the wishes of his Harrogate parishioners, he moved to a rapidly expanding and heavily industrialised West Gorton. Anna was 10 by this point and clearly she mixed with the children of the area. The family lived at 17 North Road (present day Northmoor Road) in an area known as Newton Detached, which today is more commonly known as Longsight.

As Anna grew older she became more involved with day-to-day parish activities and by the mid-1870s, together with her younger sister Georgina, she was helping organise events and activities.

In 1877 the 20-year-old Georgina Connell set up a series of Mothers' Meetings at the church. Only seven women attended the first session, but a year later her group moved into a newly-built parish hall capable of holding 100. Recognising the success, 24-year-old Anna decided to focus on activities for the more problematic men of the area. She set up Working Men's Meetings in 1879, to be held on Tuesday evenings. She then toured the parish, knocking on every door, and told the men of her aims for the group.

Despite her efforts only three people turned up on the first night. Two of these are believed to be 44-year-old church sidesman William Beastow and 37-year-old churchwarden Thomas Goodbehere. Anna persisted, however, and house-to-house visits gradually increased the attendance. Within a year the regular number of attendees averaged 65, and in January 1880 the men made a presentation to Anna to recognise her achievements. That summer the decision was taken to form a football team and the rest is history.

Anna remained an active member of the church for several years, particularly after her younger sister Georgina married in September 1889 and her mother passed away in March 1895. Anna's involvement increased and she supported her father in every area of the church. In July 1897 Arthur resigned as rector. He had been suffering for at least two years with chronic bronchitis and paralysis of a vocal chord. This prevented him from performing many of his duties.

At Arthur's farewell presentation his son-in-law, the Revd John Dixon, read a prepared farewell speech, while various local figures talked of Arthur's strengths and achievements. There was also a presentation made to Anna. In retirement Arthur moved to Southport where, it was hoped, the fresh air would improve his health. Anna, the devoted unmarried daughter, looked after him until his death in February 1899 at the age of 77.

During their time at St Mark's the Connells had between them helped to create a savings bank, a mutual improvement society, a highly popular and good-quality school, a choral society, a drum and fife band and of course the men's and women's organisations.

Interestingly, so important was Arthur to West Gorton that arrangements were made to transport his coffin from Southport to Victoria Station, and then a procession made its way to St Mark's for a funeral service. William Beastow, Thomas Goodbehere and players from the first St Mark's side attended, as did another Gorton player, Lawrence Furniss. Furniss wasn't from St Mark's first season, but he did become a sidesman at the church and at the time of the funeral he was a director of Manchester City and a former manager. If anyone had any doubts about the origin of the club, his attendance in 1899 proved the link was still in evidence.

No doubt Furniss and the others would have talked with Anna of their hopes for the club. 1899 saw City promoted for the first time and, two days before Arthur's funeral, the Blues had defeated Lincoln 3–1 at Hyde Road.

On 25 April 1902 – St Mark's Day – Anna Connell returned to West Gorton for what is believed to be the last time. Late in the evening she unveiled a marble tablet dedicated to her father at the church, and the following day City faced Newton Heath in the Final of the Manchester Cup at Hyde Road. Anna probably didn't attend the game that day, but she would certainly have seen the ground and the popularity of the club.

Anna joined her sister Georgina in Walsall shortly after her father's death, and later moved with the family to Darlaston in 1913 when Georgina's husband John accepted an appointment as rector. It was there that she was living on 21 October 1924 when she passed away due to heart problems at the age of 67. Nine years later, on 9 September 1933, Georgina died at the age of 72 in Rugby and the last family links with the birth of St Mark's had gone. Georgina did have children, Clare and May, and it is known that May (Wardrop) lived close to her father in Rugby at the time of his death in 1938. It is highly likely she knew nothing of her family's involvement with the birth of Manchester City, particularly as since the 1920s all official club literature had become confused about the facts of the club's birth.

November 1880 against the Baptist Church from Macclesfield, although this may not be the very first game played by the club. Extensive research has failed to find earlier references and so this is assumed to be the first match ever played. It does seem likely that William Beastow, Anna Connell, Thomas Goodbehere and the other key figures would have sought as many fixtures as possible, but football was still in its infancy across the country and, although the FA Cup was already in existence, League football did not exist at all. All games were friendlies and often they were cancelled at the last minute. Even the Manchester Cup didn't exist until the 1884–85 season.

Beastow and Goodbehere would have been keen to ensure the activity developed, as they knew only too well of the problems members of the Union Ironworks were having with drink and other social concerns of the period. In September 1880 their employer Samuel Brooks held a special dinner for key representatives of his 700-strong workforce to commemorate the organisation's 21st birthday. As well as talking of the company's successes he also lectured his workforce on the distractions of the area, and added: 'I would also point out to you the benefit of using your spare time and holiday times in a rational way; not in wasting your energies and robbing your wives and families by drinking.'

Prior to St Mark's first reported game, the committee had a difficult time locating a pitch and seeking opponents. Little is known about this period and certainly any records that did exist at St Mark's have long since vanished. It is known that detailed records of all activities of the parish were kept, but as the parish magazine did not exist until 1883, there is nothing publicly available other than comments in local newspapers.

The first known game was played on 13 November 1880 and was staged between sides containing 12 players each. This may have been to accommodate all those who arrived with the Macclesfield side, or it may have simply been agreed some time in advance. It doesn't really matter as it was the game itself that was important. It does show, however, that football as we know it today could not have been imagined back in 1880.

The historic first 12, with an indication of their age (based on census material) were:

Charles Beastow (18)
William Sumner (19-year-old captain)
Frederick Hopkinson (17)
Walter Chew (15)
Henry Heggs (20, born in Gloucestershire)
William Downing (19, born in Bramall)
Richard Hopkinson (20)
Edward Kitchen (18, born in Bramall)
Archibald MacDonald (20, an Iron moulder)*
John Pilkington (17)
John Beastow (18)
James Collinge (18, born in Heywood)

*This is the only member of the team living outside of the West Gorton area when the 1881 census was taken and therefore this is only assumed to be the 'A. MacDonald' who played in the first game.

Another member of the St Mark's parish, **William Hardy** (20), performed the role of umpire. There were two umpires who controlled the game, with each side providing one.

Frederick and Richard Hopkinson were brothers and their father, Richard Hopkinson Snr, was a member of the St Mark's congregation and played the organ for the church. William Beastow's son John and his stepson Charles were both key members of the side.

It is interesting to note that the majority of players were under the age of 20 and that they had, in the main, been born within east Manchester, although almost all the parents of those players had been born away from Manchester. This suggests that Anna Connell's aim of creating an organisation to help unite and develop a community spirit within the West Gorton area, and to give the young men of the parish something to focus on, was achieved to some extent with the first game.

The background of these players was varied. For example, James Collinge's parents appear to have both passed away some time between 1869 and 1881, and James's elder sister, 21-year-old Martha, took on total responsibility for the family. In 1880 it is known that three of James's siblings were aged 11, 14, and 16.

The first match report appeared in the *Gorton Reporter*, and a review of that newspaper's sports coverage makes it clear that the attempts by William Beastow and the others to stage the first game must have been great, as none of the other match reports detailed under the heading 'Football' refers to Association Football. All the other 'football' matches reported are rugby football games featuring local sides – Reddish, Failsworth Rangers, Newton Heath Rovers, Newton Heath, Blackley, Sandfield Hornets and St Mary's (Failsworth). This suggests that football was very much the minor sport and that rugby was the area's key winter activity. It also raises the question of who it was that introduced it to St Mark's.

Gorton, 1884. This is the oldest known image of the club. Players at the time wore shirts bearing the Maltese cross.

BEASTOW & GOODBEHERE

Other than Anna Connell, the two most significant founding members of St Mark's were William Beastow and Thomas Goodbehere, although Goodbehere in particular has not been particularly well remembered. In fact, his place in City's history had been lost until recent research identified his full name: earlier histories incorrectly named him Goodyeare and played down his involvement.

Both men worked at the Union Ironworks, with 38-year-old Goodbehere a mechanical draughtsman and 45-year-old Beastow a fireman for the works at the time of the football team's first game. They also were active members of the parish, with Beastow becoming a sidesman in 1879, later a churchwarden, and Goodbehere a churchwarden in 1877.

Earlier Beastow had been the key figure behind the West Gorton Working Men's Institute, which was forced to close in January 1877. He was bitterly disappointed by its failure and claimed it was because the men of the area were too focussed on drink and gambling to focus on more worthy leisure activities. While Beastow was concentrating on that organisation, Goodbehere, born in Youlgreave, Derbyshire, was becoming more involved with the church. He and his Hull-born wife Lilly had settled in the Gorton area in the early 1870s and were keen to play their part in community life. Goodbehere's earlier roots suggested a Continental background and the 1881 census shows a Swiss national lodging with the family.

Goodbehere went on to become a director of Brooks & Doxey's Union Ironworks and was also described as the manager of St Mark's School. He passed away in March 1903 at the age of 61, and was described by the *Reporter* newspaper as: 'a man who led a comparatively quiet life, he took a great interest in the social well-being of the community, and was very highly esteemed in the district'. He became involved with almost all of St Mark's worthy activities, such as the savings bank and lending library created for parishioners.

Beastow lived until he was 76, passing away in November 1912. By that time he had been a well-respected Conservative member of Manchester City Council (1898 to 1907) representing the St Mark's ward, and a justice of the peace. He was also recorded as 'overseer of the poor for the West Gorton district for over 25 years', and at the time of his death president of the National Friendly Society and one of the longest serving members of the Ashbury's Branch of Freemasons.

Which member of the working men's group knew enough about the game to suggest it? Clearly, as the opposition for the initial game was another church side, it does suggest contacts via the religious community may have helped, but one of the committee must have had some interest in what was a relatively new sport. As Beastow and Goodbehere were the two driving forces, it's likely one of these men had prior knowledge or experience of the game.

Actually, Beastow must have been a man ahead of his time, because a match report for Gorton (a later incarnation of St Mark's) against Gorton Villa in November 1885 mentioned the arrival of Association Football in Gorton: 'There was a pretty fair attendance of spectators, notwithstanding the unpropitious weather. The way in which Association games draw the Manchester public is wonderful, considering that it is not much more than three years since the dribbling code of football was introduced into this district.'

Two weeks after the first reported game in 1880, it was recorded that St Mark's had achieved a draw in Harpurhey against a side called Arcadians, and then on 19 March 1881 St Mark's achieved their first known victory as they defeated Stalybridge Clarence 3–1. Clarence, however, only had eight fit players, and three men from the crowd made up their 11-man side.

The St Mark's Church side developed rapidly that season. Captain Anstruther, the Archdeacon of Manchester, told the men of Anna Connell's Men's Meetings: 'it must be a great source of encouragement to see how the movement had been taken up, and the highest credit was due to Miss Connell for the way in which it had been carried out. No man could have done it – it required a woman's tact and skill to make it so successful.'

The following season, 1881–82, saw the side face Newton Heath (present-day Manchester United) for the first time, and play their home matches at the Kirkmanshulme Cricket Ground south of Hyde Road.

Newspaper reports from the period seemed uncertain as to what the team name was. Sometimes the side were known as St Mark's (West Gorton), sometimes as West Gorton (St Mark's). This has led to some suggesting that the church removed its patronage, or that there were concerns over the number of non-parishioners in the side. This seems unlikely, as all the key figures within the club remained significant figures at St Mark's Church itself. It seems more likely that the person submitting the reports to the local newspaper was simply inconsistent. Certainly indications are that the church was delighted with the direction of the club during its first couple of seasons.

In April 1882 a report on the opening of the cricket season highlighted that St Mark's had a good series of fxtures, and it also mentioned some of the players, most notably Chew, Kitchen, and Hopkinson. Clearly cricket and football co-existed for some time at St Mark's, though it's not clear where the cricket team played, or how long it survived.

Later that year the Kirkmanshulme CC asked the footballers to move on. They took up residence at a park off Queen's Road, further east along Hyde Road. The words St Mark's were finally dropped completely from the side's name. Also, reports suggest there was a merger with another Gorton side which, ultimately, led to friction.

By 1884 the old St Mark's men decided to break away from the merged side and reform under the name of Gorton Association Football Club. Edward Kitchen, Walter Chew, Lawrence Furniss and William Beastow – all influential figures at St Mark's Church – seemed to be the key players. Beastow was chairman, while Furniss found the club's new ground – at Pink Bank Lane (south of the Belle Vue Pleasure Gardens). Another St Mark's churchwarden, James Moores, became club President.

This move led to a more professional approach from the club, which then applied to join the newly formed Manchester County FA. William Beastow also presented the side with their first known formal kit – black shirts with a white 'Maltese-style' cross. The development of Gorton continued throughout the mid-1880s, but 1887 was to prove perhaps the most important year of the period.

The team had spent the previous couple of seasons playing at the Bull's Head in Reddish Lane, on the very edge of Gorton. This was really as far away from Clowes Street as the side could go while remaining in Gorton and so the club's identity was in danger of disappearing. Likewise Association Football was becoming more popular in the area and sides, such as Newton Heath, were beginning to move upwards, winning trophies such as the Manchester Cup. Professionalism was beginning to develop and Gorton had to decide on whether their future was to be as a good local side, like a modern-day pub team, or as a professional outfit.

The decision was taken to become a progressive and professional outfit. The committee also wanted Gorton to return to their Clowes Street roots. They recognised that this was not entirely possible – Clowes Street remained one of Manchester's most densely populated areas – but captain Kenneth McKenzie did manage to find an area of wasteland not too far away.

After a great deal of effort the pitch was ready for its first match by the end of August 1887, while steps were also taken to relaunch the club. The name of Ardwick AFC was chosen as the new ground was just within the boundaries of Ardwick and not Gorton, although it has to be stressed that this ground was closer to Clowes Street than any other Gorton venue used by the club after its first season. In addition, this area was actually part of the St Mark's parish until the erection of St Benedict's, Ardwick, in 1880. So this could truly be said to be within the boundaries of St Mark's at the time the club was initially created.

Despite the closeness of St Mark's the Hyde Road Hotel became Ardwick's headquarters. Stones from this building, demolished in 2002, now form part of the club's Memorial Garden at the City of Manchester Stadium. It's worth noting that, according to the records at Manchester Central Library, St Mark's itself was demolished in 1974 with a replacement church dedicated to Emmanuel opening in June 1975, close to another former home for the club, Gorton Park.

Gradually Ardwick increased their support and it's fair to say that by the summer of 1888 Ardwick were Manchester's most popular club, or at least on a par with Newton Heath. In 1889 Ardwick built a grandstand capable of holding 1,000 spectators.

From that point on the side grew at a rapid rate and managed to recruit several good-quality and well-known players, including new captain David Weir.

As football in Manchester developed, so did Ardwick's desire to become one of the region's elite clubs. The Manchester Cup had been established in 1884–85 and this was quickly perceived by the majority of Mancunians as the most prestigious competition around. The Football League was not in existence until 1888 and even then Manchester failed to have any representatives, while the FA Cup had been established since the 1871–72 but was not seen in a positive light by Manchester's sides. Entry into the Cup required great expense as games could be played anywhere in the United Kingdom – during the 1880s sides from Ireland competed in the FA Cup, while Scottish sides had been among the earliest supporters of the competition. The cost of travel clearly limited Ardwick's ability to play beyond the Manchester region.

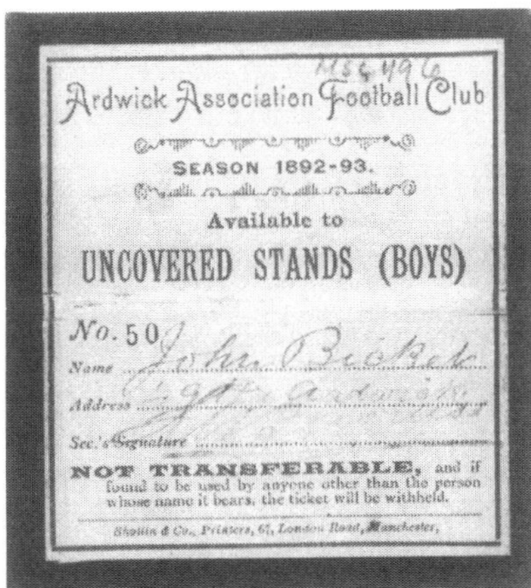

Ardwick Association Football Club

SEASON 1892-93.

Available to

UNCOVERED STANDS (BOYS)

No. 50

Name ....

Address ....

Sec.'s Signature ....

NOT TRANSFERABLE, and if found to be used by anyone other than the person whose name it bears, the ticket will be withheld.

Printers, 67, London Road, Manchester.

An Ardwick season ticket for the club's first season in the League, 1892–93.

In April 1891 Ardwick won the Manchester Cup for the first time. This was a major landmark and also resulted in the club being admitted to the Alliance League for the 1891–92 season.

The Manchester Cup had proved to be the club's major breakthrough and with their passionate support the club succeeded in the Manchester Cup again the following season, defeating Football League side Bolton Wanderers 4–1.

Joining the Football League was Ardwick's ultimate aim, as this would provide the side with the opportunity to face the elite of England's football clubs on a regular basis. It seems difficult to comprehend today, but the League was very much seen as a closed shop, with little opportunity for smaller sides to break in. In addition, those sides excluded from the League struggled to attract the best players. Often sides would give financial inducements to persuade big-name players to join the non-League sides. Ardwick certainly did this and as a result came into conflict with the League.

A life may have existed for a while outside of the League, but the committee at Ardwick knew they would not progress and develop. They saw how popular the League was becoming and they knew they had to be there. Fortunately the opportunity came in 1892.

A decision was taken in April 1892 to form a Second Division of 12 clubs and expand the First Division to 16. The additional clubs would mainly come from the Alliance, with Nottingham Forest, Wednesday and Newton Heath all applying and being accepted into the enlarged First Division. Ardwick joined Darwen, Burton Swifts, Grimsby Town, Bootle, Walsall Town Swifts, Small Heath Alliance, Crewe Alexandra, Lincoln City, Burslem Port Vale, Sheffield United and Northwich Victoria in the new Division.

Interestingly, some historians have in recent years taken the opportunity of suggesting that the Heathens' inclusion in Division One proves that United have always been a larger and more successful side than City. Clearly this is not the case.

The Heathens were admitted into Division One on the strength of their successes in the Manchester Cup over several seasons, whereas Ardwick's success had really only started during the 1890s. In terms of popularity and attendances though, Ardwick were already the

St Mark's Church seen from Clowes Street shortly before demolition.

more popular side. They were also seen by most Mancunians as the side with most potential, especially as the Heathens found life in Division One very difficult and actually finished bottom of the Division for the first two seasons. They were relegated in the end-of-season Test Matches (similar to play-offs) in 1894.

Ardwick finished fifth in Division Two during 1892–93 but then struggled in 1893–94, finishing 13th out of 15. Early in 1894, however, steps were already underway to dramatically change Manchester football for good.

1894 was one of the most important years in the history of Manchester. The Manchester Ship Canal was officially opened by Queen Victoria and the whole city felt immense pride at the achievements of its people. Manchester was, and still is, a diverse city with a population made up of many different backgrounds. The city had developed at an incredible rate during the 1800s and so this great mix of people found events such as the opening of the Ship Canal to be significant unifying moments. They may not have spent much time debating what Manchester meant to them, but they would certainly have felt great pride and joy at the achievements of the city and its people.

Some members of the Ardwick committee recognised this too, in particular Joshua Parlby. Parlby became Ardwick's secretary-manager in 1893 and was a man with a burning desire to see the side successful. He became involved with Ardwick shortly after arriving in Manchester from Stoke, and he recognised the need to build a strong identity. Perhaps because of his own arrival in the city, he wanted to establish a Mancunian identity. Most of the others on the committee, such as Matlock-born Lawrence Furniss, had arrived in Manchester at some point over the previous 30 years or so, as had many of the club's fans. Parlby also recognised that Ardwick were struggling financially to compete with the more

BLUE IS THE COLOUR

It is over 125 years since the first game played by St Mark's Church side, and one of the most important aspects of the club over the years has been the colour of City's shirts. For most of the club's history the predominant colour has been blue, or to be specific a form of sky blue, but what colour did the club originally wear? Sadly, there is no record of the colour worn for the very first match – it is highly unlikely that any formal football shirt would have been worn and regular street wear would have been the uniform of the day.

By 1881–82 it is likely a proper football shirt had been selected, but sadly there's no mention in any match reports from this period of the colour. The earliest known possible colour worn by the club was scarlet and black in 1882, although it is unclear whether the side actually wore these colours or whether these were the colours of one of the club's early rivals. According to David Williams's booklet *Famous Football Clubs – Manchester City,* published in the 1940s: 'A West Gorton club, playing in Scarlet and Black, had got going in Queen's Road, West Gorton, however, and the pitchless St Mark's men threw in their lot there.'

During the modern era some historians have incorrectly claimed that the red and black striped shirts adopted by Malcolm Allison in 1969 had their roots in this 1880s kit. This is totally untrue. It is also doubtful that scarlet and black was ever actually worn by the club as West Gorton in 1882 following the merger referred to by Williams. No other colour is mentioned in any newspaper record or report until October 1884. This was the year when a proper kit was identified for the first time.

The new colours were an interesting choice because these were black with a white 'Maltese-style' cross. Many former directors of Manchester City talk of the club as having strong links with Freemasonry and some have suggested that this version of the Maltese Cross did have significance within the Masonic community of east Manchester. The majority of historians have suggested the white cross proves the link with St Mark's was still evident, although this type of cross did not have any direct link with the local church.

Another theory is that the shirts referred to an organisation called the White Cross League, founded by a lady called Ellice Hopkins. According to David Winner, the author of *Those Feet,* the White Cross League was particularly strong in Manchester in the early 1880s and its aims were to encourage purity, self-control and chastity. Winner suggests this may have had a bearing on the use of the white cross on Gorton's shirts, but this is a total red herring as the White Cross League wasn't actually formed until 1886.

More than anything the Masonic influence seems far too strong to suggest this is co-incidence. William Beastow was known to have very strong links with Freemasonry and was a senior figure within Ashbury Masonic Lodge No.1459. Interestingly, one of Gorton's rivals, Earlestown AFC, played in white shirts with a black Maltese Cross during this same period.

By 1887 the black shirts appear to have disappeared and Ardwick AFC adopted a new identity. Some sources claim that the side wore white shirts and white – or grey – shorts, but it does appear that the colour actually adopted in 1887 was a light blue colour and that frequent washing made the colour fade to a near-white colour.

In 1892 there is a definite mention of the colour worn by Ardwick for the Manchester Cup Final against Bolton Wanderers. According to newspapers of the period, two minutes before the game was due to start the two sides entered the neutral Newton Heath pitch at North Road, only to discover that their shirts clashed. According to the report both sides were wearing white shirts and dark shorts. Again it could be that a form of light blue was too close to white for comfort – during the late 1980s City were forced to swap their home blue shirts for red and black stripes when they faced white-shirted Tottenham at Maine Road. Ardwick sent a man (probably Albert Alexander senior) in a hansom cab to fetch different colours from their Hyde Road ground. He returned 30 minutes later with a set of red and black shirts. We don't know if these were striped, hooped, quartered or another style.

White, with grey shorts, is mentioned as the club's home strip in the early 1890s, but by 1894 a form of blue was definitely the club's first choice. It is known that City have mainly played in a light blue shirt ever since they joined the League in 1892, possibly since they became Ardwick in 1887. The shade was initially referred to as Cambridge blue and then sky blue, but at times the shade has been darker. The 1926 FA Cup Final shirt, dubbed 'cornflower blue' at the time, is much darker than traditionalists would expect. However, it is a fact that City are the only side to have worn light blue consistently throughout their League history. It's worth noting that Coventry City's use of sky blue came as a direct result of a Coventry director watching the 1955 FA Cup Final and admiring City's battling spirit when they went down to 10 men. He wanted his side to show the same commitment and eventually Coventry adopted City's colours.

Why blue and white? As with the 1884 Maltese Cross shirts, there is a strong suggestion that the light blue was selected because of links with the Masonic community. The colour is used to symbolise friendship and is clearly an important colour in terms of community spirit. Even if the Masonic links are false, it is clear that the people responsible for selecting a very light shade of blue, together with virtuous white, deliberately chose the colour because of its meaning.

The official colours in 1894 were Cambridge blue shirts and white shorts, although the Association of Football Statisticians' own publications, based on League records, describe the shorts as being grey in 1894–95 and 1895–96. Again, this is probably because the shorts had become coloured in the wash. As recently as the late 1960s City used shirts and shorts for several seasons and it is clear from photographs that the Blues took to the field wearing faded kit at various times prior to 1970. It's worth noting that between 1976 and 1985 City wore blue shorts as they will do in 2006–07.

In terms of other colours adopted over the years, white was worn as an away kit in 1903 and 1907, but it is fair to say that City's main away colour has been maroon. Although it's not known exactly when City first wore maroon, it is known that the Blues were using it for some games in 1906 and most seasons after 1908.

Maroon remained City's main alternative strip until the late 1960s when Malcolm Allison's red and black stripes were adopted during 1968–69, although other colours were used at times. Since the sixties maroon has featured on a variety of City strips, and it's worth noting the fact that City's use of maroon is second only to their use of blue.

The Malcolm Allison-inspired red and black kit of the 1960s and early 70s remains an iconic image of the Mercer–Allison glory years. Often worn as a second choice since the 1970s, this is probably the away kit most often associated with City.

Another colour worn at times is yellow. During the late 50s the club adopted an away strip of yellow shirts with dark cuffs and collar. During the 1959–60 season Denis Law made his debut at Leeds United in the yellow shirt.

City have used yellow on a few occasions since 1960, with the most memorable being the striped shirt from the 1999 play-off final, although the colour was more of a day-glo affair. There was also another predominantly yellow Kappa shirt worn briefly during the late nineties.

On 14 October 1989 City took to the field for the meeting at Arsenal wearing yellow. Maroon was City's regular away kit at this time and, only days before the game, it was decided that a third strip was required to avoid a clash. In the end a basic yellow shirt was created. City lost 4–0 and the shirt was never seen again.

Since the early 1970s there have been many other 'away' shirt colours, including white, royal blue with diagonal stripes, and silver.

Interestingly, City have featured in two FA Cup Finals wearing a form of maroon (1934 and 1956); one wearing scarlet (1933); four wearing blue (1904, 1926, 1955, 1981); and one wearing red and black stripes (1969). They have also worn blue in two League Cup finals (1974 and 1976) and red and black in the 1970 League Cup Final, the 1970 ECWC Final, and the 1986 Full Members' Cup Final. Yellow and black was worn for the 1999 play-off final at Wembley.

17 October 1896, City pose prior to the game with Newcastle. Back row (left to right): Ormerod (manager), Ditchfield, Bannister, Williams, Ray, Broad (trainer). Middle: Meredith, Finnerhan, Lewis, Hill, Robinson. Front: Mann and McBride.

familiar names around the country, and he may have considered that a simple relaunch of the club might bring in new investment.

Whatever his initial motives were, it is clear that Parlby was the driving force behind the transformation of Ardwick AFC into Manchester City FC. The selection of the name was directly aimed at creating a side to represent all of Manchester and so, for perhaps the first time in the history of the region, there was to be an organisation to represent all Mancunians no matter what their social status, background, or place of birth.

This is a very important point because Manchester City can claim, quite rightly, that its name was selected because the organisers wanted a team for all citizens of Manchester, and the club has always existed to represent Manchester.

On Monday 16 April, Manchester City Football Club Limited became a registered company, with its registered address being given as 31 Halsbury Street, Stockport Road, Manchester. Making reference to the end of Ardwick AFC, the club's new motto was 'Even in our own ashes live our wonted fires'.

Parlby's first task after the formation of City was to somehow get the club accepted into the Football League. Ardwick would have had to apply for re-election, but the restructuring of the club meant that Manchester City had to apply to join the League as if they had never previously existed. At the League AGM Parlby spoke convincingly of the ambition, finances and strength of the new club, particularly the lessons learnt during their days as Ardwick. He told the committee that the two major strengths – support and the Hyde Road ground – would be utilised to make Manchester City an even stronger club. Somewhere in his logic it appears he stressed that with Newton Heath failing, the new Manchester City side would add something neither Manchester club had previously. His persuasive powers worked and City gained enough votes to force their way into the Second Division, while Parlby himself

Billy Gillespie attacking the Newton Heath goal at Hyde Road in 1898. City won the game 4–0 and Gillespie scored.

Billy Meredith taking a corner in the Boxing Day 1898 derby match with Newton Heath. Notice the boys' band ready to play.

headed the poll for a place on the League Management Committee – this was a rather cunning way to ensure that Manchester's club would receive appropriate support throughout the season by the men in control of the League. This was the start of the club's first golden age, which lasted until 1905.

Manchester City's first season saw the Blues finish ninth in Division Two, but the following season (1895–96) they managed to finish second and enter the promotion-deciding Test Matches. Sadly, a loss of form and a rather amazing organisational own-goal – the management put admission prices significantly higher for the first Test Match and fans boycotted the game as a protest – caused City to lose out. However, it did remind club officials that the very existence of the club owed everything to the people of Manchester, and the fans would always be keen to ensure the club remained theirs.

Sixth place in 1896–97 was followed by a third-place finish, then the final year of the 19th century brought real delight for the Blues. It became the foundation on which Mancunians hoped great success would be built, and it was the season of Manchester's first national success.

Throughout the year there was a belief that anything was possible. The second half of the 1898–99 season proved the direction the club was going in, especially when they defeated Darwen 10–0 at Hyde Road on 18 February. It was a thrilling game, with Fred Williams netting five and football's first true superstar Billy Meredith scoring the third of four hat-tricks that season. The leading sports newspapers of the day were quick to point out that City's success was down to a team of hardworking individuals. There were no weak links.

The Blues won their final four matches of 1898–99 with confidence, and took the Second Division title for the first time in their history. It was also the first time either Manchester club had been promoted and the people of the city celebrated. Prior to this date there had only been local sporting successes and the talking point was usually the rivalry between City and near neighbours Newton Heath. 1899 changed that, and made Mancunians realise that football could bring positive attention to the city.

Six points behind the Blues were another relatively local side, Glossop North End, and the two sides became the first to gain automatic promotion to Division One. The Test Matches had been scrapped.

When the 1899–1900 season commenced a crowd of 10,000, many travelling from Manchester, witnessed the Blues lose an exciting match to Blackburn by the odd goal in seven. The defeat had been expected, but City's approach and fighting spirit provided much hope. Seven days later a refurbished Hyde Road hosted its first Division One match. A crowd of around 22,000 welcomed Derby County – a team that possessed one of the greatest players of the period, Steve Bloomer. According to newspapers of the day it was played in front of an extremely noisy – and partisan – crowd. The attendance was significant as it was some 7,000 more than Newton Heath had enjoyed during their Division One seasons (although it was still short of City's highest crowd of the 1890s – 30,000 for a game with Liverpool in 1896), and allowed Parlby to remind the committee of his speech in 1894.

City dominated initial play, with their best chance to score coming in the 25th minute. *The Umpire* newspaper described a controversial incident:

> *Fryer saved, but the home forwards coming in a body pushed the ball through. There was apparently a doubt in the mind of the referee as to the legitimacy of the point for, on Derby protesting, he had to consult both linesmen before giving his decision in favour of the home side; and on his pointing to the centre the crowd sent a mighty roar.*

The first Hyde Road Division One goal was credited to the bustling Billy Gillespie and City eventually won the match 4–0. The first season ended with City in seventh place. Sadly, relegation followed in 1902, but the Second Division title was won again in 1903. They had played with style and conviction and when the 1903–04 season commenced they managed to maintain their wonderful form.

In the FA Cup the Blues eclipsed all previous seasons for either Manchester side by reaching the Cup Final. They faced Bolton at the Crystal Palace in London and thousands of Mancunians journeyed to the capital to witness Manchester's progress. The game itself was fairly tight, with the Blues winning 1–0 thanks to a disputed goal from captain Billy Meredith. Meredith was football's first true superstar and many neutrals had gone to the Final simply to see the great man play.

After the Final the team travelled back to Manchester with the cup. Within the city most Mancunians were keen to stage some form of celebration, but the City Council and senior figures within the constabulary were not interested. They argued that too much time had already been spent on football and that Manchester had to get back to work. Fortunately the people thought differently.

This is a very important moment in the history of Manchester and as such needs a little further explanation. The FA Cup success of City in 1904 was the first time Manchester had had reason to celebrate. Prior to City's success Lancashire CCC had found success but cricket did not appeal to the greater part of Manchester's population, and Lancashire wasn't seen as solely a Manchester institution. Other major activities occurring around the city had focussed on one-off events such as major races at the Manchester Racecourse, or festivals lasting several days. The FA Cup success was different because it was the first time a major sporting event appealing to all areas of society from the city had achieved national acclaim.

When the City side arrived back at Manchester a horsedrawn carriage, driven by Albert Alexander senior – a man who would later be vice-chairman of the Blues – took the players on the first homecoming parade the city had known. Thousands took to the streets and there was nothing the police or the City Council could do to stop them. Reports describe a wide range of people from different social classes taking to the streets while Billy Meredith lifted the trophy in celebration.

This was a great moment in the history of Manchester but didn't actually take place until two days after the Final as, incredibly, the Blues had been forced to play their crucial final match of the season on the Monday night following the Final. They travelled to Liverpool for their game over the weekend, were defeated 1–0 by Everton, then travelled back to Manchester for a Monday night homecoming. The parade started at 9.30 in the evening. Sadly, the defeat at Everton caused City to finish the season as runners-up to Sheffield Wednesday. Nevertheless, this was still Manchester's highest League position at the time.

City's development during the early years of the 20th century caused some to believe that their rapid rise could not possibly have been achieved without some form of illegal activity. There was a view among FA officials that City was a young, typically working-class northern club without a care for history, tradition and the rules of the game. This wasn't entirely true, although City, and most Mancunians, were certainly keen to challenge the Establishment.

After the Cup success the FA were keen to investigate and find out exactly how City had risen from perceived no-hopers in 1894 to FA Cup-winners and League runners-up 10

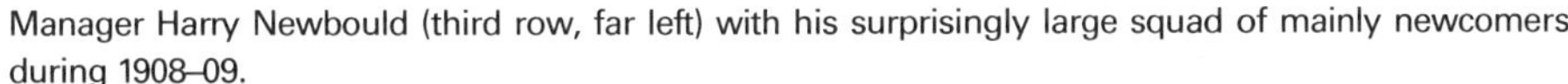
Manager Harry Newbould (third row, far left) with his surprisingly large squad of mainly newcomers during 1908–09.

years later. Officials arrived at City's Hyde Road ground with a belief that the Blues were making illegal payments. They left after finding some minor irregularities but nothing too serious. Certainly they found nothing worse than they would have found at any side.

Sadly, a year after the FA Cup success City's world fell apart when the FA had the opportunity to investigate again. The 1904–05 season saw the Blues challenge for the title again and on the very last day of the season City could have snatched the championship from eventual winners Newcastle. The Blues' final match saw them needing a victory at Aston Villa. They lost 3–2 and ended the season third, two points behind Newcastle. Had they won they could potentially have taken the title on goal average.

The Villa game was full of incident and, unfortunately, gave the FA cause to investigate once again. Alec Leake, the Villa captain, was allegedly offered £10 by Meredith to throw the game. Initially Leake laughed at those suggestions when the FA approached him, but after another man from Birmingham came forward, England international Leake changed his story. The FA, the very people who picked the England side at the time, had found the excuse they had been looking for to investigate further. What was strange, however, was that the FA chose to ignore some of the other aspects of the match. For example, City's Turnbull was, according to neutral journalists, dragged into the Villa dressing room after the game and later thrown out with cuts and bruises.

Earlier Villa's Leake had found Turnbull such a difficult player that he threw some mud at him. Turnbull responded with a two-fingered gesture (highly controversial at the time!) and Leake then gave Turnbull a 'backhander'. Yet the FA focussed on Turnbull's role and not

Dorsett, Jackson, Holford and Conlin in training prior to the 1910 FA Cup tie with Aston Villa.

Leake's. Leake was the English gentleman, while Turnbull had adopted a typically Mancunian approach to life.

City – and the other forward-looking northern sides – felt the FA's investigations were biased in favour of a side and a group of players perceived as one of football's aristocratic clubs. The Football League supported City's attempts for fairness and, considering the alleged bribery and other incidents occurred during a League game and not an FA game, it seems strange that the League was not the body in control of the investigation.

Unfortunately, the FA arrived at Hyde Road shortly after the incident and studied City's accounts and other records like never before. Meredith was initially banned for the alleged bribe, but this was eclipsed when the full FA investigations were complete. The FA found that City had been making additional payments to their players for some time, and as a result they imposed sanctions which almost killed the club. The manager, Tom Maley, and the chairman were suspended from football *sine die*, while two further directors were suspended for seven months. The most serious impact was on the playing squad. Seventeen players were suspended and fined. Basically, the entire squad that had finished as FA Cup-winners in 1904 and narrowly missed out on the Championship two years running was banned. This brought a premature end to City's first golden age.

Worse was to follow when significant pressure was placed on the Blues to transfer these players once their bans finished. Meredith, Turnbull and all the other stars were encouraged

Ernest Mangnall's 1919–20 team. Mangnall is third from left on the back row.

to join the then poor relations Manchester United. Mancunians argued that if Meredith and the others had to leave it was much better for them to join the Reds than leave the area. Those players ultimately helped United to their first FA Cup win in 1909 and to the League Championship, while City were left to start again.

There is no doubt that the southern-based FA's investigations were totally unfair as far as Manchester was concerned. No other League side has ever suffered to such an extent, regardless of tragedy or bans.

How City managed to re-establish itself as a major power in the years that followed is amazing. Not only did the Blues have to find players, but they also had to identify a manager and some directors to help move the club forward. It was not easy. Fortunately the Derby County secretary-manager Harry Newbould accepted the challenge, even though the rest of football felt that City were a dead side with no chance of resurrection.

Newbould spent the summer bringing in new players and setting a plan to avoid relegation – with so few recognisable first-team players nothing more than avoiding relegation could be expected. When Newbould joined City in July 1906, there were only 11 players of any description available.

Somehow he pulled together a side. Many of the players were of good quality, but when the season opened at home to Arsenal on 1 September 1906 no one could have predicted how Newbould's first game would develop. Due to a heat wave, City ended the match with only six players. The game ended in a 4–1 defeat, then two days later the struggling City travelled to Everton with remarkably only two changes. This match saw City suffer their heaviest defeat as Everton annihilated Newbould's side 9–1.

Despite the start of season struggles, City ended their first season following the FA bans in 17th place, five points above the relegation zone, and then the following season (1907–08) amazingly Newbould guided the Blues to third spot. Sadly, the problems following the bribe and illegal payments scandal still affected the club and relegation followed in 1909. An immediate return – as Division Two champions – came in 1909–10, but inconsistency dogged the seasons prior to World War One. City remained a top-flight side, but supporters never quite knew what to expect.

When the 1914–15 season commenced on 1 September World War One was already almost a month old. Looking back it appears rather strange that the footballing authorities had not cancelled the season, but it has to be remembered that football had never been halted for any war during the Football League's 26-year existence. Several significant conflicts, most notably the Boer War, had been fought during that time, but the authorities had never expected the conflicts to affect daily life to the extent that World War One eventually would. In addition there was a view that the war would be over by Christmas.

Despite the continuation of the game, pressure was placed on clubs to help the war effort. City were supportive from the start and under the headline 'Manchester City's Offer' *The Umpire* newspaper stated that the Blues would help any player or his dependents if that player joined the armed forces, so long as City were allowed to take attendance money. The players and officials also agreed to give five percent of their wages to the Prince of Wales' Fund.

As the 1914–15 season progressed it became increasingly difficult for the League programme to continue and at the season's end the League was suspended. City finished

A 1923–24 team, back row (left to right): Pringle, Donaldson, Mitchell, Cookson, Fletcher. Front: Sharp, Roberts, Johnson, Hamill, Barnes, Murphy.

that season in fifth place after mounting a serious challenge for much of the season.

The following season football was played on a regional basis, with the Blues winning the Lancashire Section's principal tournament.

At times during the war Hyde Road, perhaps because of its close proximity to barracks at Ardwick Green, was used for stabling and other activities connected with wartime, while many players and former players fought on the battlefields. 1904 FA Cup-winner Sandy Turnbull was killed at Arras in May 1917 while serving with the Manchester Regiment. Another former player, Jimmy Conlin – a consistent left-winger who had joined the Blues in the wake of the bribe and illegal payments scandal – was killed in action at Flanders in June 1917 while serving with the Highland Light Infantry.

By the time League football resumed in 1919 many former players, officials, and of course supporters had suffered, and there seemed to be a greater appetite for the game, perhaps as a release from the problems faced. The immediate post-war seasons saw City develop at a phenomenal rate and re-establish themselves at the level they had been prior to the 1906 scandal.

In 1919–20 City finished seventh, and had even had the pleasure of a visit from the king. In fact it was the first visit by a reigning monarch to a provincial football match. The following season they finished second to a very strong Burnley side. The Hyde Road average attendance was 31,020 – the club's highest recorded average at the time – but many games had been full houses at 40,000. Such was the pulling power of the side that the March 1921 meeting with eventual champions Burnley – which ended with a City victory – was watched by an estimated 55,000, with several thousand more in the streets outside. The official crowd was approximately 40,000, but gates were smashed down as supporters forced their way in and fans chose to sit on the roofs and stanchions to watch the match. There were also reports of fans climbing into the ground on ropes from nearby houses and there was even a suggestion that some had 'swung' into the ground on other ropes tied to the stand roofs.

WHAT'S IN A NICKNAME

In the main supporters simply refer to the team as 'City', 'the Blues', or even 'Man City' (although Kevin Keegan was told off by some supporters for using this version of the name), but a quick trawl through yearbooks and sticker albums will show that we, apparently, call our team 'the Citizens', 'the Maine Men' and other similar names. The majority of fans hardly ever – if at all – use any of those names. Clearly, names such as the Citizens may have been used principally in the 1920s, but it's highly unlikely that supporters ever utilised the name on a regular basis even then.

Looking back through time there have been many nicknames that have actually been used by fans and by the local community to talk about the side. These have included names based on the club's location, such as Gortonians (1880s), Ardwickites (late 1880s/early 1890s), and 'Hyde Roaders' (1910s), but the first and possibly most interesting nickname to gain widespread popularity was 'the Brewery Men'.

'The Brewery Men' was adopted by Ardwick during the late 1880s and survived as City's nickname into the 1900s. Its roots lie in the strong links between the club and Chester's Brewery. Chester's owned a large number of City shares, and were the main financial backers of the club for over 30 years. City's headquarters were in the Chester's public house, the Hyde Road Hotel, and many of the club's players, directors and committee men were involved with the licensed trade. Match reports, such as those from the club's first season in the Alliance League (1891–92), tended to refer to 'the Brewery Men' and the name seemed perfect for many reasons.

The move to Maine Road in 1923 ended Chester's involvement with the club and the nickname was dropped entirely.

Inevitably 'City' and 'the Blues' have dominated and most football fans around England seem to see Manchester City as 'City', whereas other sides are more often known by their city's name, such as Birmingham, Leicester and Coventry. Having said that, for several years supporters did use the term 'Sky Blues' to describe City (the term is included in popular fan songs of the 1950s) as the club were the only major side wearing sky blue at the time. However, in the modern era Coventry have adopted the nickname as their own and City have focussed more on using 'the Blues'.

Another name used by the media throughout the club's history apart from perhaps the modern era, is the name 'Manchester'. Newspaper reports and newsreel footage of City right up to the sixties, and occasionally since then, referred to the club simply as Manchester. This is simply a shortened version of the name, although it perhaps matches the perceptions of supporters who know City as Manchester's side.

King George V meeting players at Hyde Road. This was the first time a reigning monarch had attended a match in the provinces.

The 1920–21 season had also seen the Main Stand destroyed by fire, and it was clear to everyone connected to the club that a move away from Hyde Road was needed to ensure the Blues could develop further. Senior officials had been searching for a much larger venue on a frequent basis ever since the turn of the century, but the fire and City's popularity meant a move was essential or the club would stagnate.

After rejecting two sites at Belle Vue – the present-day greyhound stadium and the athletics/speedway stadium demolished in the 1980s – City settled on land on the border of Moss Side and Rusholme. This site became City's spiritual home, Maine Road. The Blues were based there from 1923 to 2003.

Huge crowds started to attend Maine Road, with over 76,000 attending a Cup match during Maine Road's first season. At the time this was the largest football crowd ever recorded in Manchester.

In terms of match action, 1923–24 saw the Blues reach the semi-final of the FA Cup. This was a significant moment and a major national news story as Billy Meredith, City's great captain from 1904, had returned and was playing well enough to be selected, at the age of 49, for first-team duty. His final match was the semi-final with Newcastle at Middlesbrough's Ayresome Park ground. Sadly, a 2–0 defeat prevented Meredith from appearing at Wembley in the FA Cup Final.

The move to Maine Road allowed larger crowds, but it also brought criticism City's way. The pitch was not of the quality fans had got used to at Hyde Road – although it must be

The king is introduced by Lawrence Furniss to the City players at the 1926 FA Cup Final. He is shaking hands with Billy Austin.

stressed that no pitch in Manchester during the 1920s was particularly great. Eleventh place in 1923–24 was the worst finish in a decade.

Ernest Mangnall, who had managed the club from 1912 and had been one of the key figures behind City's growth in popularity and the development of Maine Road, had not had his contract renewed in the summer of 1924. Some believe this was because of the problems with the Maine Road pitch itself, but it may simply be because the directors felt it was time to push the club on to another level. Whatever the reason, his departure led to a real downturn in morale and performance during 1924–25. Mangnall's replacement had been David Ashworth, who in 1921–22 had guided Liverpool to the First Division title. He seemed a good choice, but for a club that would later become famous for having high-profile charismatic figures like 'Big Mal' Allison, appointing a man with the nickname 'Little Dave' can hardly be seen in a positive light.

Under Ashworth the 1924–25 season ended with a 10th-spot finish. This was not viewed as much of an improvement, but the following season saw a significant deterioration. Only three victories in the opening 13 games caused the pressure on Ashworth to increase, but the most worrying aspect for fans and directors alike was the fact that the Blues were showing a ridiculously high level of inconsistency. Had City been totally poor it might have been relatively easy to identify the weak areas, but they were scoring plenty of goals in some

A general action image of the 1926 FA Cup Final.

An aerial image of the 1926 FA Cup Final. Notice how rural Wembley was in 1926.

THE ILLUSTRATED SPORTING AND DRAMATIC NEWS — May 1, 1926

MORE CUP-TIE SCENES AT WEMBLEY: BOLTON WANDERERS WIN THE

PYM, THE BOLTON GOALKEEPER, RUNS OUT AND PUNCHES THE BALL AWAY.

PYM DEFLECTS A SHOT.

JACK (ON ONE KNEE) SETTLES THE ISSUE BY SCORING FOR BOLTON: THE MANCHESTER CITY GOALKEEPER HAD NO CHANCE TO SAVE THIS SHOT.

BROWELL (LEFT) AND SEDDON (BOLTON'S CENTRE-HALF) IN A DUEL FOR THE BALL.

BOLTON WANDERERS KEEP UP A STRONG PRESSURE ON THE MANCHESTER CITY GOAL: SOME ANXIOUS MOMENTS FOR THE LATTER'S DEFENCE.

The Football Association Cup Competition was first instituted in 1871, and since that time there have been three all-Lancashire finals. Last Saturday's match between Bolton Wanderers and Manchester City was the third of these, the same two teams, moreover, having also supplied another of the three, for they met in that memorable final of twenty-two years ago, when Manchester City won by a goal, which has always been challenged by the Bolton supporters. But Bolton were successful this time in turning the tables on their

Scenes from the 1926 FA Cup Final between City and Bolton Wanderers.

games then conceding plenty in the next match. The best and most obvious example came in October 1925 when City defeated Burnley 8–3 at Maine Road. Two days later the Blues were on the receiving end of an 8–3 scoreline at Sheffield United. How could one side win by such a large score one day then lose by exactly the same score two days later?

Over the years City fans have grown to expect a certain level of inconsistency, but in 1925–26 this was a new phenomenon. That November, with results worsening, Ashworth resigned, although it seems more likely he was pushed. Everyone expected another man to be appointed quickly, but the City directors decided to hold back until they could find the

The 1927–28 City line-up. The players' names were handwritten by Sam Cowan, although he spelt McMullan's name incorrectly.

A late 1920s image of City travelling to an away game. Vice-chairman Albert Alexander is the bowler-hatted gentleman.

right candidate. In the meantime the directors, with vice-chairman Albert Alexander Snr taking the lead role, managed the side.

Alexander had been involved with the club since formation as Manchester City and had even driven the horsedrawn coach through Manchester at City's 1904 homecoming. He knew the club and Manchester inside out and he was also a very knowledgeable football man, although he had never played the game professionally nor had any professional experience of team management.

1933 FA Cup Final,
Cowan and Dean.

Under his leadership League form remained erratic but entertaining: a 4–3 victory at Leeds was followed in the next away game by a 5–6 defeat at Bury. In the FA Cup, however, Alexander's side proved particularly strong. Exciting victories over Corinthians (4–0), Huddersfield (4–0), Crystal Palace (11–4) and Clapton Orient (6–1) brought a semi-final meeting with Manchester United. The game was played at Bramall Lane and ended in a 3–0 City win. Incidentally, Alexander's side had earlier beaten United 6–1 at Old Trafford – this remains the record League win by either side in the Manchester derby.

At Wembley Alexander's side were defeated 1–0 by old Cup Final foes Bolton, but again City had made history by being the first Manchester side to play at the new stadium.

Back in the League City's form improved during April with four consecutive wins – three before the Final and one after – but the final match of the season ended 3–2 to Newcastle and relegation followed. A saved penalty in that match seemed to typify the season. A draw would possibly have saved the Blues on goal average.

The task of rebuilding the Blues was left to former Leicester manager Peter Hodge. Hodge finished the season with Leicester – their last game being 24 April, the same day as the Cup Final – then joined the Blues for the final two matches of their season, making Alexander's last game in charge the FA Cup Final.

Cowan introduces the Duke of York (the present Queen's father) to Matt Busby in 1933.

In Division Two Hodge's side found the consistency the side had lacked the previous term. Sure there were occasional defeats, but City were one of the Division's leaders from the start. Only a miserable run of four defeats over the Christmas period caused any real concern and, as City entered the final fortnight of the season, they were well on course for promotion. Sadly, the final three games proved to be City's undoing as a 1–1 draw at Southampton was followed by a goalless game at Chelsea. This meant the Blues not only had to win their final match at home to Bradford City, but they also had to score plenty of goals to ensure a better goal average than their main rival Portsmouth.

A tense day saw the Blues defeat Bradford 8–0, but on the south coast Portsmouth's match had kicked off 15 minutes later than City and ticker-tape – an early form of telecommunication whereby messages would be telegraphed from one part of the country to another and printed out at a receiving machine – was used to keep both City and Portsmouth's directors aware of action at the other ground. City's eight goals should have been enough, but immediately after City's game had ended Portsmouth knew they needed one more goal to win promotion and sure enough, three minutes later, that goal came. While the band were playing *Auld Lang Syne* and fans were partying on the pitch at Maine Road, the news came through that it was all over and that Portsmouth were up on the narrowest goal average margin in history. One more goal from City would have been enough to see the side promoted in second place.

Despite the agony of that day, Hodge managed to fire the Blues up for another assault on the Second Division in 1927–28. This time there were no mistakes as City ended the campaign as Second Division Champions, two points above Leeds and five points ahead of third-placed Chelsea. They were also the best supported side throughout football with an average attendance of 37,468 – a position they maintained in 1928–29.

In 1929–30 Hodge guided the Blues to third place in the League, but it wasn't until 1931–32 that his side seemed ready to seriously challenge for major honours. That season City reached the FA Cup semi-final, losing out to a goal in the final minute by Cliff Bastin. Neutrals believed City had done enough to deserve at least another chance, but the defeat meant Arsenal were through to the Final and not Hodge's City. Surprisingly, Hodge left the Blues at the end of the season to return to his first love, Leicester. The City directors had been delighted with the progress under Hodge and rather than bring a fresh man in they decided to move club secretary Wilf Wild into the role.

This may well have been seen as a temporary measure at the time, but Wild went on to manage City through to 1946, and brought about City's second golden age. In his first full season Wild's Blues went one step further than in 1931–32 by reaching the FA Cup Final. They lost to Everton, but Wild had proved his side were great Cup fighters. In addition, listening on radio at home that day was a young boy who would later have a major impact on the fortunes of the club: Malcolm Allison, who later claimed that his interest in the Blues was born that day.

City captain Sam Cowan had played in both the 1926 and 1933 FA Cup Finals and felt bitterly disappointed with each defeat. By the time of the 1933 Final Cowan was City's captain and that defeat understandably hurt him more than the earlier Final. He hated being runner-up and was determined to see the Blues triumph. He vowed to guide the Blues

The 1936–37 Championship team. Back row (left to right): McCullough, Dale, Swift, Marshall, Bray. Middle: Toseland, Herd, Tilson, Barkas, Doherty, Brook. Front: Heale, Rodgers, Clark, Percival.

to glory and promised supporters that City would be back in 1934 to win the trophy. His promise became a reality and over the years Cowan's promise has become part of City folklore, with various publications, including official City magazines and other works, claiming that Cowan had told King George V at the 1933 Final that the Blues would be back in 1934 to win the trophy. This story has become a little corrupted over the years and Cowan never did make a promise to the king. The Guest of Honour at the 1933 Final was the Duke of York, the present Queen's father and the future King George VI. He attended because King George V was too ill to make the Final.

Cowan appeared on a newsreel shortly after the 1933 Final with Everton's Dixie Dean, where both men toasted each other for the future and Cowan stated that he hoped his team, Manchester City, would win the Cup in 1934. This film was shown across the country and made it clear that Cowan wanted to return to Wembley. Today this footage is shown daily in the Manchester City Experience – the club's award winning museum and tour.

In 1934 Cowan guided City to a 2–1 FA Cup Final victory over Portsmouth. This Cup run broke many records, including record attendance figures at Maine Road and at Hillsborough, both of which still stand today, and one important scoreline record in the semi-final.

The Blues faced Cup favourites Aston Villa at Huddersfield in the semi-final. It was anticipated to be a tough game, but Cowan's City were determined to reach Wembley and they opened the scoring with a terrific shot from Ernie Toseland. After 34 minutes Fred Tilson made it 2–0, then a minute later Alec Herd scored a third.

City's fourth came almost immediately after Herd's goal, Fred Tilson netting his second as Villa became more demoralised following three goals in five minutes. Midway through the second half Tilson added a couple more to make it four goals for the striker. Four minutes from time Villa scored a consolation, although reports claimed that City were too bored to tackle by this time!

The match ended 6–1 – an FA Cup semi-final record – and was a major boost for City as they reached Wembley for the second consecutive season. Pre-match Villa had been favourites, with City travelling to Huddersfield with little chance of success according to some journalists. They left Huddersfield in high spirits for the FA Cup Final, and the victory over Portsmouth completed a terrific season.

In terms of the Sam Cowan prediction, Lawrence Furniss, the City President, told journalists immediately after the 1934 Final that Cowan had predicted that the Blues would be back after the 1933 Final, and he also suggested that Cowan had mentioned this to the Duke of York. So it's possible this comment is the one which later became adapted by journalists looking for an even better story. Apart from Furniss's comments nothing was said of a prediction by Cowan to the king or Duke of York, it was only years later that it was mentioned. In fact the first time the story was quoted appears to be in 1955 when City's fifties captain Roy Paul talked of emulating Sam Cowan by guiding City back to Wembley the following year. Books and articles from the period then made the claim that Cowan had told the king in 1933 that the Blues would return. Clearly, this was a corruption of the truth, but the story sounded great and future generations accepted this as fact.

Reaching Wembley in successive seasons was a major achievement for Cowan and his team, and today Cowan remains the only man to appear in three FA Cup Finals with City.

The Blues were without doubt one of football's glamour sides throughout the 1930s, with large crowds watching their games both home and away. In 1934 the record attendance was set at 84,569 for the FA Cup tie with Stoke then, in 1935, 79,491 watched City's League game with Arsenal. At the time, this was the highest attendance for any League match, and even today only one other League ground has held a higher attendance (Stamford Bridge, 82,905, Chelsea v Arsenal, October 1935). Manchester United attracted 83,260, including a significant proportion of City fans, for their League game with future champions Arsenal in 1948 at City's Maine Road ground.

Arsenal were always viewed as one of football's greatest opponents, and in the 1930s City were seen as the only credible opponents to the Gunners. Arsenal regularly challenged for the League, winning the title four times in five seasons, while the Blues had a great reputation as Cup fighters. As the thirties developed, City came close to winning the title on a few occasions – in 1930 they were third; 1934 fifth; 1935 fourth; and then in 1937 they won the title for the first time. The first few weeks of the season had seen mixed results for the Blues and certainly few expected this to be the club's first title-winning season. Nevertheless, Wild's side persevered and by New Year they had amassed 23 points out of a possible 44. It was still not Championship form, but enough to give them a foundation to build on.

The New Year saw City climb up the table and, by the time of their meeting with the usually dominant Arsenal in April 1937, the two sides occupied the top two positions. Arsenal had been the side to watch throughout the season and this meeting in April 1937 proved to be crucial. It ended 2–0 in City's favour before an amazing crowd of 74,918. The Blues gained the upper hand from that point onwards and ended the season five points clear of third-placed Arsenal and three points above second-placed Charlton. The last 22 matches of the campaign had brought 15 wins and seven draws, and City were worthy champions. There were several star players, including Frank Swift, Sam Barkas, Ernie Toseland, Fred Tilson, Eric Brook and Alec Herd, but for many the greatest player was Irishman Peter Doherty. Doherty was proclaimed as the greatest City player of all time, and even in the 1970s was still being described as the greatest Irish footballer of all time. He was a great goalscorer and stylish player and for many football fans there was no one better.

The 1936–37 Championship success was the high point of City's 1930s golden age. It was the first time City had won the title and Manchester celebrated like never before. It was also Coronation year and so the entire nation was celebrating during May 1937. The players and officials missed most of the celebrations, however, as they embarked on a tour of Nazi Germany.

The League Champions had been invited on a tour of Germany and, looking back at this time, it is easy to see that this was a propaganda stunt by the Germans to try to prove what their players could do against the best side in England. For this reason alone the tour is significant.

City played five games, with their best performance coming on 12 May in their third game. A German XI were defeated 3–2 at Schweinfurt – City had been two goals behind – and then came the biggest test, a match in Berlin's magnificent Olympic Stadium against a more powerful German XI. Not only was this going to be a real test, but it was also going to be a major cultural shock. The players arrived to witness hundreds of Nazi guards parading outside and it was clear the Germans wanted to put in an exceptionally good performance, especially as the game was to be filmed and distributed across Germany and the United Kingdom. The match was not merely a football friendly, it was a game of pride for the Germans. Only a few days earlier German pride had been battered when the Hindenberg airship burst into flames in one of the world's most high-profile disasters. The Germans were determined to beat City – the first English side to play at the 1936 Olympic Stadium – and regain a little self-esteem.

The players entered the arena to the cheers of over 70,000 spectators. Forward Peter Doherty described what City did next: 'We were expected to give the Nazi salute at the line-up before the match started; but we decided merely to stand to attention. When the German national anthem was played, only 11 arms went up instead of the expected 22!'

When England played Germany in the same stadium the following May, the FA encouraged the players to perform the salute; here the City men themselves decided not to bother.

Sadly the match was a difficult one and the Germans took an early lead. City then equalised, as the *Manchester Guardian* reported: 'The Germans played up strongly after this, but Swift, with his sure and capable hands, proved a stumbling block. Six minutes after scoring their first goal, the City went ahead through Brook, who scored with a hard, long shot.'

The *Guardian* reported that the Blues started the second half brightly: 'At this point Manchester City looked the better team and appeared likely winners, but after sixteen minutes the Germans equalised. Siffling, the inside-right, shot from a short distance, Swift was unable to catch the ball properly and let it slip from his grasp, and Hohmann ran up and scored.'

Jimmy Meadows being helped off the field during the 1955 FA Cup Final.

As the game progressed, Germany attacked relentlessly and 18 minutes from time Hohmann scored his second and Germany's third. The match ended 3–2 to a very powerful German side. City's final tour match was another 3–2 defeat to another German XI, this time played in Stuttgart.

Sadly, the following season City struggled in the League. No one knew exactly why, but more or less the same side that had won the Championship was relegated 12 months later. They still thrilled on occasion and managed to score more goals than any other side in the First Division, but they were relegated with two points less than Grimsby in 20th place. Had they managed a victory at Cup finalists Huddersfield on the last day of the season they would have been safe, and Huddersfield themselves would have been relegated. Instead the Yorkshiremen won 1–0 with a 78th-minute goal while City had had an earlier goal disallowed.

City finished fifth in Division Two the following season, but as the 1939–40 campaign commenced it became clear world events were going to curtail the season. World War Two caused the abandonment of the season after only three games, and League football didn't resume until 1946–47. When it did return, City were desperate to find their way back into Division One, and the first full season saw the Blues promoted as champions with Burnley second, four points behind. It had been a rather strange season, however. Poor weather during the winter months had limited the number of games played, and the season ended on 14 June 1947. This was the latest ever finish to a season, and in the final match Roy Clarke made his City debut against his home town team, while war hero George Smith netted all five goals in the 5–1 victory over Newport.

Over the following couple of seasons, the closest the Blues came to success was when they finished seventh in 1948–49. These were not great League seasons, but as always there were several great games and performances. Even in 1949–50 – a season that ended with relegation – the Blues defeated the champions Portsmouth. They also beat second-placed Wolves and did the double over third-placed Sunderland.

Promotion in 1950–51 under new manager Les McDowall brought much hope, but the Blues came close to relegation again in 1952–53. They missed the drop by a single point, and in modern football this would often result in a change of manager, but the City directors of the period kept faith with former player McDowall and that faith was repaid as the Blues embarked on their next golden era.

McDowall was a great tactical innovator and the 1954–55 season saw him launch the deep-lying centre-forward tactic which became known as the Revie Plan. Don Revie, wearing the usual centre-forward number nine shirt, would basically be positioned deep. As opposition centre-halves were always instructed to mark the number nine, confusion reigned. It sounds rather ridiculous today that simply playing a centre-forward in a deep position could confuse the opposition, but it did. The plan really became successful when the other players, not Revie, had the ball. The opposition would be totally baffled as to who they should mark, who they should watch, and where the ball would be placed. The plan revolutionised the way managers and coaches thought of the game, but for most of that 1954–55 season the opposition had no idea how to counter the plan, once of course City themselves had got used to it.

In 1955 McDowall's City reached Wembley for the FA Cup Final against Newcastle United. The Geordies were a great Cup side, having won two of the previous four finals, so this was always going to be a tough match for the Blues.

Sadly, a goal after only 45 seconds by Jackie Milburn gave Newcastle the lead and then, after only 19 minutes, City's Jimmy Meadows tore his cruciate ligaments and the Blues were down to 10 men. They fought back, with Scottish international Bobby Johnstone heading a great equaliser, but Newcastle's extra man advantage was evident in the second half and the game ended 3–1.

Afterwards, at the commemorative banquet, captain Roy Paul was bitterly disappointed with the defeat. He stood to make a speech, and as he did so he caught sight of thirties captain Sam Cowan sat nearby. He remembered Cowan's determination following defeat in 1933 and this prompted him to make a vow that he would return to Wembley to lift the Cup with City the following year.

For the 1956 FA Cup Final, City's opponents would be Birmingham City, who had finished the season in sixth place, one point behind fourth-placed Blues. It was likely to be as tough a match as the 1955 Final, but City's commanding captain Roy Paul couldn't accept failure a second time.

Fortunately, the game began much more brightly than in 1955, with City taking the lead after two minutes and 47 seconds with a left-foot drive from Joe Hayes. Despite a Birmingham equaliser City defeated Birmingham 3–1, with Bobby Johnstone becoming the first man to score in successive Wembley finals. The Final went on to become famous as a result of a serious neck injury to goalkeeper Bert Trautmann. The player played on despite the agony he felt. City held on to their lead and at full-time a proud Paul collected the trophy. In the days that followed the full extent of Trautmann's injury became clear and newspapers were full of the story of how Bert had played on with a broken neck.

The success was the highlight of the 1950s, although City did also manage to finish fourth in 1956 and fifth in 1958. Actually the 1957–58 season was a curious affair, as the Blues became the first side to both score and concede 100 goals in a season. They actually netted 104 and conceded 100 and there were many entertaining fixtures, such as the 4–3 victory over Blackpool in March 1958 and the 5–4 win at Sheffield Wednesday the previous December. Like 1925–26 this was one of those amazing seasons when supporters had no idea which City would turn out. Would it be the side that got beaten 9–2 at West Bromwich Albion, or the side that won 5–1 against Tottenham seven days later? They won more games than they lost and drew combined, but the consistency wasn't there. Some blamed McDowall as his great tactical brain searched for a new trophy-winning formula, causing various formations to be tested. In spite of everything, this season is still remembered with affection by many fans as one of great entertainment, although it was clearly also a tense and baffling time.

A few seasons of struggle followed, with the best season coming in 1961–62 when the Blues finished 12th. The great Cup Final side of the mid-fifties had broken up, and the 1962–63 season was a difficult one. Across at Old Trafford, Manchester United were also lacking form and heading for relegation, and when the two sides met in City's penultimate match of the season there was a lot more at stake than Manchester pride.

Tony Book with the Championship trophy at Maine Road in 1968.

Prior to the game, United had played 39 matches and had 31 points, while the Blues had played one more game but had only 30 points. As the game was at Maine Road, City held some advantage, but it was vital they won the match, to put the pressure on the Reds and on fellow strugglers Birmingham and Bolton.

When the game commenced both sides were a little nervous, but the Blues seemed the more determined. After a couple of near misses, City took the lead in the ninth minute when Alex Harley rifled a low shot passed United's 'keeper Gaskell.

City then dominated play and after 30 minutes Harley appeared to score City's second with another splendid drive. The referee disallowed the goal on a hair's breadth off-side decision, which mystified the City players and the 52,424 Maine Road crowd.

Arguments raged for some time and there were ugly scenes at half-time in the tunnel. United's Pat Crerand later admitted to punching City's David Wagstaffe as they walked through.

In the second half, the Blues remained in control but United became more desperate. Then luck was on their side as Wagstaffe attempted what was later seen as a suicidal 30-yard back-pass. Denis Law, playing for the Reds, closed in and tussled with City 'keeper Harry Dowd for the ball. Dowd dived at Law's feet and the United man fell while the ball ran out of play. The referee pointed to the spot and United's Quixall scored the penalty in the 86th minute.

City were disgusted with the penalty decision, with Dowd telling journalists: 'It was never a penalty. I scooped the ball away from Denis's feet and sent it out of play. I can't remember holding his feet but I did get a kick on the head. I'm sure the linesman was signalling for a corner.'

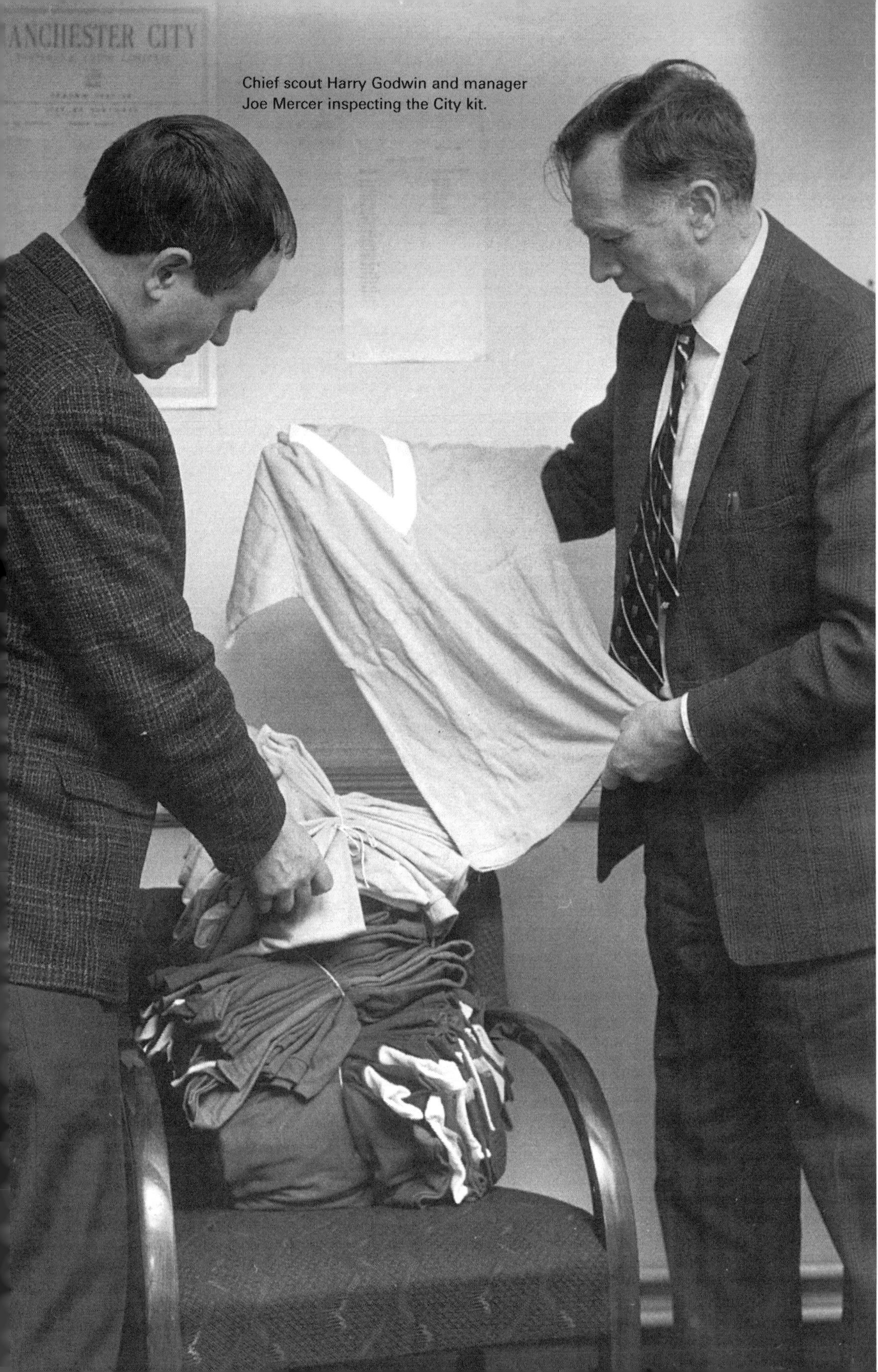

Chief scout Harry Godwin and manager Joe Mercer inspecting the City kit.

The game ended 1–1 and following a 6–1 defeat away at West Ham in their final match, the Blues were relegated and United survived with three points more than City.

Relegation in 1963 was the start of a two-year descent which culminated in what was then the all-time lowest League position as Manchester City. They had also been watched by City's lowest League crowd at Maine Road, and more than anything else a feeling of despondency had set in. There were some very talented players at the club, but the general atmosphere within Maine Road was not great. Although the late 1990s saw the Blues drop to a lower level in terms of League position, the atmosphere and negativity surrounding the club and its fans in 1965 was significantly worse than in later years. In the middle of City's decline one director even had a ridiculous idea that City and rivals United could merge. Fortunately that idea soon died, but clearly something had to be done.

By the summer of 1965 something had to change otherwise the Blues would forever become a forgotten team. The first major objective of the summer of 1965 was to find a new manager. Two years earlier Les McDowall had been replaced by his number two George Poyser, and the period 1963 to 1965 was one of confusion. City needed stability and a fresh style.

The man City's directors eventually chose as their new leader was Joe Mercer. Mercer was out of football at the time and, over the years, many writers have suggested that he was a failed manager at this point. The truth was somewhat different. After a truly successful playing career Mercer became manager of Sheffield United, where he developed a good Cup side, and then Aston Villa. At both sides Mercer had suffered relegation at the end of his first season, although he had joined Villa midway through the season and the Blades were already a struggling side. He did, however, win the Second Division Championship with Villa in 1960 and the League Cup in 1961. His Villa side were also League Cup finalists in 1963.

So two trophies, and another Final appearance in four seasons, should be seen as a very positive record. Certainly any manager delivering that today at Aston Villa, or even at City, would be a hero. During this spell at Villa there were calls for Mercer to replace Walter Winterbottom as England manager, so it is clear that he was a highly regarded football manager.

Unfortunately Mercer became ill, suffering a stroke while still at Villa, and appallingly he was dismissed while still trying to recover. A year out of the game followed before City made their approach. Mercer arrived at Maine Road not fully fit. He desperately wanted the challenge of managing a large, progressive club, but he was also advised by relatives, friends and the medical profession that he would no longer be able to play an active part in training and other physical activities. He chose to bring in a young coach, the out-of-work Malcolm Allison, to work closely with the players, and in July 1965 City's great partnership began to resurrect their own careers and the life of Manchester's football team.

Under Joe Mercer and Malcolm Allison optimism spread through the club. The 1965–66 season commenced with an important 1–1 draw at Middlesbrough. This was significant because although both men recognised that their side was still not quite the team they needed to make a real push for promotion, they knew that avoiding defeat in the first few games would give them a foundation for the rest of the season.

In the end the Mercer-Allison side went seven League games without defeat, and only suffered one loss in their opening 15 League games.

A small number of new faces were brought in as the season progressed, with Colin Bell arriving on transfer deadline day in March for the final push. He scored the goal which guaranteed promotion at Rotherham on 4 May 1966, but for many fans the real star of the season had been Mike Summerbee.

Summerbee had been Joe Mercer's second signing, arriving shortly before the start of the season, and a few days after Scottish international Ralph Brand. Summerbee was the season's only ever-present, but had impressed so much in such a short time that England manager Alf Ramsey came to watch him during the season, and there was a real feeling that Summerbee was about to be picked for the full national side. That honour didn't occur until 1968, but Summerbee was recognised nationally as City's star man in 1965–66.

For Mercer and Allison, promotion as Division Two Champions in their first season was a major triumph. It was also the start of a great era for the Blues.

Following promotion in 1966, the Blues finished 15th in Division One in 1967. They had enjoyed a good Cup run, going out to Leeds via a controversial goal in the sixth round, and had gained many admirers by playing exciting, entertaining football.

Immediately after promotion in 1966 Malcolm Allison had predicted the Blues would win the Championship in 1967. Most journalists laughed and, although Allison's prediction proved to be incorrect, when he made a similar prediction at the start of the 1967–68 season his comment was taken a little more seriously. Nevertheless, there were still many who believed City stood little chance.

As with City's 1936–37 Championship season, the first few weeks of 1967–68 gave little indication of what the Blues were ultimately to achieve as only one point – a goalless game with Liverpool – was obtained during the first three matches. Fortunately, this was followed by a five-match unbeaten run, lifting City into the top five.

Mercer and Allison were still searching to strengthen their squad. Tony Book had arrived in 1966 and was now captain, but Mercer and Allison recognised they needed more strength in attack. On 9 October they signed a man who was ultimately to become one of the greatest City players of all time, Francis Lee.

Lee's arrival coincided with a run of 11 League games without defeat. One of those – a 4–1 victory over Spurs on 9 December – was a real classic, enjoyed by around five million on the BBC's *Match Of The Day* programme, and known as the 'Ballet on Ice' due to the snowy conditions.

Despite Spurs going a goal up in the seventh minute through Jimmy Greaves, the Blues played with real style and demonstrated to the entire nation why they really were the team to watch. With snow still falling, Bell was first to score for the Blues, then Young piled on the pressure and almost gave City a first-half lead.

In the second half City took the lead. Young crossed from the left and Summerbee scored from six yards with a brilliant header. Then, in the 64th minute, Coleman scored the third when he followed up a Lee shot that had hit the left post. Young made it four with one from close range. City continued to push forward, overwhelming a Spurs side packed with internationals. Shot after shot went towards the Spurs goal, with City's forwards in outstanding form. In one attack, Coleman latched on to a pass from Bell. His shot hit the left-hand post, and then Young followed up by hitting the right-hand post. It was a game that proved the strength of the City side.

Now, at the halfway stage, City were in third position on 28 points. Liverpool were second with the same tally, while United were top with 30 points. Two defeats against West Bromwich Albion over the Christmas period caused some concern, although Francis Lee claimed: 'We lost 3–2 at their place on Boxing Day. But even then, we murdered them!'

Another good run through early 1968 set the Blues up for a 1–0 victory at Burnley on 2 March. City were in third place, four points behind leaders United. Liverpool, Leeds and Newcastle also posed a threat, and any of these teams were capable of snatching the title. Sadly, City suffered a 2–0 defeat at Leeds on 23 March and then travelled to Old Trafford for the 78th Manchester League derby.

It was a rearranged fixture, played on Wednesday 27 March. To many Reds this was to be the night when City would be taught a footballing lesson, and the opening moments reinforced those thoughts as George Best took the lead after only 38 seconds. Tony Book felt he was to blame, believing he should have stopped Best. For the first 10 minutes, life was hell being a Blue, then, just when it was needed most, Bell began to control midfield. Doyle won important tackles and City gradually gained the upper hand. After 15 minutes Bell started a right-wing move and then ran yards to reach the final pass and blast the equaliser past United 'keeper, and future City goalkeeping coach, Alex Stepney.

City, in rampant mood, dominated from then on. They pushed forward time and time again, and were appropriately rewarded with a second goal after 57 minutes. Coleman, City's loveable rogue, curled across a free-kick and centre-half Heslop scored his first goal for the Blues with a firm downward header.

Mercer and Allison were delighted as the Blues powered forward. Bell, by far the best player on display that night, raced clear and headed for goal before being dramatically hauled down by Francis Burns. Lee scored the resultant penalty, but the excellent Bell had to be carried off on a stretcher with an injured knee. One of City's most important players would miss the next four crucial games. The match ended 3–1 and City's confidence grew.

After the derby both Mercer and Allison tried to keep the momentum going. It wasn't easy. Missing Bell, City lost to Leicester and Chelsea. It looked as if the title was slipping away from them and in the first of their final five games they drew at Wolves, and then scraped a 1–0 win over Sheffield Wednesday.

Victories over Everton (2–0) and Tottenham Hotspur (3–1) followed before the final crucial match at 10th-placed Newcastle. City and United were now level on 56 points after the same number of games, but United appeared to have the upper hand as they were playing lowly Sunderland at Old Trafford. In the end City won an extremely exciting and entertaining match 4–3. It was a tremendous occasion and one which has been chronicled extensively ever since. Suffice to say, City thoroughly deserved the Championship. United lost 2–1 to Sunderland. Journalist James Mossop wrote: 'There could be no more popular, sentimental success story. For 90 minutes City, the team that has won more friends than any other in a season of imaginative attacking football, turned on the style.'

Tony Book was the club's only ever-present in the Championship season with 42

THE EVOLUTION OF THE CITY BADGE

The first known emblem to appear on the club's shirts was the white Maltese Cross featured on the 1884 Gorton shirt. This was followed by a shield proclaiming AAFC. This appeared on tickets from the early 1890s with the initials AAFC representing Ardwick Association Football Club. The only known surviving version is coloured gold and black, see photograph on page 25.

In 1894 the relaunch as Manchester City saw the club adopt the full Manchester coat of arms. This remained as the club's emblem until the 1960s, although City have worn this for every major Cup Final through time (apart from the FA Cup in 1904 and for some unknown reason the 1970 ECWC Final, when no badge was worn).

On 29 August 1970 an announcement appeared in *Shoot* magazine saying City had developed a new club badge to wear on their shirts. The announcement showed that the badge was basically the central part of the City of Manchester coat of arms – the yellow ship over a red shield with three yellow stripes emblazoned across – surrounded by two circles and the club's name. The badge had been used by the club on various occasions during the 1960s but it first appeared on shirts during the 1970–71 season.

This badge only survived until 1972 (although an illuminated version remained on the external wall of the City Social Club until the early 1990s) when the red/yellow shield was replaced by a red rose to represent the county of Lancashire. This more popular and familiar badge was first seen in the City programme of 29 January 1972, when it was described as a 'trading symbol' – similar wording today would probably make supporters assume the club were after increasing income.

City's present-day club badge was adopted during the summer of 1997 and was the final stage in the club's plan to regain control of its merchandise operation following the 1993–94 takeover of the club by Francis Lee. Prior to Lee the merchandise rights were not under the direct control of the Blues.

The new badge was designed to incorporate significant elements of Manchester life and also to try and present a new image. A Latin motto *Superbia in proelio*, meaning 'Pride in battle', was added – the English version of this motto now appears above the tunnel so that the players see this as they take to the field.

In addition the badge incorporates the ship over the three emblazoned lines from the Manchester coat of arms. Over the years many have assumed the ship represents the Manchester Ship Canal, but Manchester's coat of arms predates the Ship Canal. The ship actually represents Manchester's trading links, focusing on the canals developed during the 18th and early 19th century, such as the Bridgewater Canal. The three diagonal stripes on the

CITY'S BADGE OF HONOUR

For the first time in the club's history, Manchester City will be wearing badges on their shirts for every game they play this season, irrespective of status. Previously City have only worn badges in Cup games. Our picture (above) shows the badge The Blues will be sporting.

An illustration of the new MCFC badge, to be worn on shirts for first time in 1970.

coat of arms signify the three rivers of Manchester – the Medlock, Irwell and the Irk – and on City's 1997 badge these lines have changed from red and gold to blue and white to match City's traditional colours.

The City badge also includes a golden eagle and three gold stars. The stars are simply for styling purposes, but the eagle does have strong links with Manchester's past. It comes from the official badge of the City of Manchester, dating from 1957, and has at various times been used by other Manchester organisations in preference to the formal coat of arms. In fact United wore this bird on their shirt in the 1958 FA Cup Final, although the majority of Reds fans today believe the bird worn was a phoenix. In between the ship and the blue and white lines are the initials MCFC.

At various times during the last 40 years the club's emblems have been altered as a result of particular celebrations or events. The 50th anniversary of Maine Road in 1973 saw a circular badge with the ship and rose incorporated but no shield, and the words 'Maine Road Fifty Years' surrounding the circle. At other times the 1972 badge was amended to incorporate the season within the circles, and the League Cup appeared as the central feature on some programmes in 1976.

The modern-day emblem was altered for Maine Road's last season, with the Latin motto replaced by 'Maine Road 1923–2003'.

appearances. Top scorer was Neil Young on 19. Lee scored 16, while Bell and Summerbee both netted 14.

The following day City held a press conference. It was a light-hearted affair with Mercer, Allison and Book talking openly about City's success and their hopes for the future, in particular their first venture into Europe. Allison boasted that the European coaches were 'cowards' and said that City would 'terrify Europe to death'. The English footballing public loved his statements. He ended by saying: 'I think we will be the first team to play on Mars.' At the time nobody dared argue, but City's first venture into Europe was not a success, with the Blues going out against Turkish Champions Fenerbahce 2–1 on aggregate in the first round. Captain Tony Book had been missing for these games and his loss was clearly a major factor.

As League champions, the Blues were expected to coast through the 1968–69 season, particularly as the Charity Shield match against Cup-winners West Bromwich Albion ended in a comfortable 6–1 City victory. Unfortunately life is rarely that easy, and only one of the opening nine games ended in victory. The Blues simply could not get into the rhythm they had enjoyed the previous season. One of the reasons was the injury to Tony Book sustained during the club's pre-season tour of the US. Book was out of action until January.

Book's return did help steady City a little – Chelsea were defeated 4–1 in his first match of the season – but the Blues still couldn't move up the table too much and ended the season in 13th place. Not the position expected, but as League Champions they had been the team to beat.

Fortunately, the season proved more successful once the FA Cup run began. A third-round victory over Luton was followed by a goalless match at Newcastle, then a 2–0 City win in the replay. Alan Thompson wrote in the *Daily Express*: 'They pulverised Newcastle so completely in the first half that it was not so much a match as a massacre.'

The fifth-round draw sent City to Blackburn, although the match had to be postponed on several occasions as a result of poor weather conditions and a flu epidemic in Blackburn. When the game eventually took place, 16 days after the original date, City dominated. The first goal came in the 13th minute when Colin Bell steered a perfect pass to Lee. The forward then charged upfield and knocked the ball past Adam Blacklaw in the Blackburn goal. In the 47th minute the home side equalised, then 11 minutes later Tony Coleman restored the lead.

City went on to win the match 4–1 and then beat Tottenham 1–0 at Maine Road for the right to face Everton in the semi-final. The early moments of the semi were rather mixed, with City appearing rather nervous. Nevertheless, City, playing in their recently adopted AC Milan-style away strip, ran and fought for everything and managed to keep Everton at bay. Despite City's attacking nature, the game remained goalless right up to the last minute. Then a wonder goal by youngster Tommy Booth set the Blues up for their seventh Cup Final. The ball had been cleared by Harry Dowd and was worked upfield in a fluent passing move which started with Young. He fed the ball to Bell before running upfield. Bell accurately passed to Lee, who sent the ball to Young. Quickly, he sent an absolute screamer goalwards, only to see it rebound off the shoulders of Everton's 'keeper Gordon West. The ball went out of play, giving City a corner taken by Young. Doyle headed it down to Summerbee, who flicked it across the goalface towards the waiting Bell. Booth rushed forward and sent the ball crashing into the net. It was a great moment.

Norman Wynne, writing in *The People*, was pleased for Booth: 'The game was moving with certainty to a replay until Booth came up with his last-minute goal. It was fitting that the City centre-half should be the goalscoring hero of the day. He was the youngest player on the field, and also the best.' Allison was also full of praise for Booth: 'What can I add to what's already been said about him? He was the "man of the match" before he did what he stopped Joe Royle from doing – scoring.'

By reaching Wembley, City had equalled Arsenal's record of six Wembley Finals – a feat which made former Arsenal great Mercer immensely proud.

The Final itself was not a classic, although it did produce some fine moments. It ended 1–0 with Neil Young scoring the only goal and Leicester combined defeat with relegation, thereby emulating City's feat of 1926.

The following season saw the Blues return to European action with entry into the European Cup-Winners' Cup (ECWC), and they also progressed to the League Cup Final. The Fenerbahce experience of 1968 had been an important lesson, and one that helped City's preparations during the 1969–70 season.

The ECWC campaign began in September with a 6–3 aggregate victory over Spanish side Atletico Bilbao. In the second round SK Lierse were totally outclassed as City beat the Belgians 3–0 away and 5–0 at Maine Road in November. The third round against Portuguese side Academica Coimbra wasn't played until March, with the first leg taking place only three days before the 1970 League Cup Final. The press expected City to rest their key players, especially as their opponents were allegedly rather inexperienced students, but Mercer and Allison were keen to ensure a good result.

A grim and at times difficult match ended goalless. A whole host of travel problems followed, disrupting preparations for the 1970 League Cup Final, but all of this was forgotten when the second leg ended in a 1–0 victory thanks to a goal from Tony Towers.

City's semi-final opponents were German side Schalke 04, who in the fifties had tried to sign Bert Trautmann. Despite losing the away leg 1–0 on April Fool's Day, City won 5–2 on aggregate.

The Final against Poland's Gornik Zabrze was played in poor conditions on 29 April at the Prater Stadium, Vienna. The game ended in a 2–1 City victory.

The 1969–70 season was successful domestically as well, with glory coming in the League Cup. The run started with a 3–0 victory over Southport on 3 September 1969. A thrilling 3–2 Maine Road victory over Bill Shankly's great Liverpool side came in round three. Then goals from Colin Bell and Francis Lee ensured a 2–0 defeat of Everton in the next round.

QPR were despatched 3–0 in the quarter-final, leaving City to face Matt Busby's United in the two-legged semi-final. In the 13th minute of the first leg, Colin Bell sent a half-volley past United 'keeper Alex Stepney to open the scoring. Stepney performed exceptionally well under intense pressure from Bell, Lee and Oakes in the first half, and managed to keep the Reds in the match. In the 66th minute Bobby Charlton equalised, causing City to rue their missed chances. However, the gloom was lifted in the 88th minute when Ian Ure felled Francis Lee in the penalty area. Penalty expert Lee sent the ball low to Stepney's right to bring a 2–1 victory.

As the players left the field, George Best exchanged words with referee Jack Taylor and appeared to knock the ball out of his hands. The Irishman was fined £100 and suspended for a month as a result.

In the second leg, City youngster Ian Bowyer netted first, but the Reds fought back. Goals from Paul Edwards and former Blue Denis Law made the scores level on aggregate, but all that was to change with only eight minutes remaining. City were awarded an indirect free-kick. Francis Lee seemed to ignore the signal and fired the ball goalwards. Stepney went to catch it, but fumbled and the ball went loose. Mike Summerbee proceeded to bury it in the net. Had Stepney allowed Lee's shot to enter the net no goal would have been given. City reached their first League Cup Final by means of a 4–3 aggregate victory over their biggest rivals.

The Final, against West Bromwich Albion, was played only 36 hours after City had returned to England from the ECWC quarter-final with Coimbra. Freezing conditions had brought transport chaos and caused many to wonder if City would be in the right frame of mind for the Final, but the Blues won 2–1 in extra-time.

Success in the League Cup and ECWC made City the first English side to win a major domestic and European trophy in the same season, although it has to be remembered that Leeds United did win the Fairs Cup and League Cup in 1968, but at that time several significant English sides had refused to enter the League Cup. In fact the 1969–70 season was the first time all League clubs had entered the competition. In addition the 1968 Final of the Fairs Cup wasn't played until the start of the 1968–69 season.

City had played an incredible 61 first-team matches during 1969–70. Unsurprisingly, there wasn't a single player who appeared in every match. Mike Doyle came closest, appearing in 60 games – the only one he missed was a 3–1 League defeat at Chelsea in December. Tommy Booth appeared in 59 matches.

1970–71 brought much excitement, but sadly no actual trophy success. Defeat at Carlisle in the opening round ended City's hopes of retaining the League Cup, then Arsenal knocked the Blues out of the FA Cup at the fifth-round stage. The League campaign ended with City 11th. Only the ECWC offered City a major chance of success, but the Blues were unfortunate to draw FA Cup-winners Chelsea at the semi-final stage. Sadly both games ended in 1–0 defeats to the eventual ECWC winners. Behind the scenes a takeover battle had raged on, causing tension between Mercer, who backed the existing board, and Allison, who had been promised total control of team affairs by those seeking to gain control of the club.

Despite a 1–0 defeat by Leeds in the opening League fixture, 1971–72 was a season of excitement, with the Blues managing to mount a serious title challenge. There were several thrilling victories in the first two months, most notably the 4–0 victories over Crystal Palace and Tottenham in August. Part of the credit for this went to City's groundsman, Stan Gibson, who, under the direction of Malcolm Allison, had widened the pitch by two yards. This made it the largest playing surface in England, and gave City's team of entertainers plenty of freedom.

On 9 October a 1–0 victory at home to Everton was notable for two reasons. Firstly, it gave City fourth place in the table, and secondly it was the first time Allison had been given formal control of the side. Joe Mercer had been moved 'upstairs' into the position of general manager as part of the promises made to Allison during the club's somewhat protracted takeover. It was a move that ultimately forced the break-up of the partnership, but in October 1971 it seemed a sensible step to City's battling directors.

A few weeks later the Blues faced United in what proved to be one of the most thrilling Manchester derbies of all time. It ended 3–3 thanks to a last-gasp equaliser from Mike

Summerbee. Francis Lee proved to be a bit of a handful for the Reds, and at one point he delighted the City fans when he accused George Best of making a theatrical dive. To prove his point he demonstrated the dive several times to United men Morgan and Sadler, each time raising a cheer from the City faithful. Sadly the referee wasn't too impressed and promptly booked Lee. It was worth it though!

On 11 December Allison was presented with the Manager of the Month award prior to City's 4–0 drubbing of Bobby Robson's Ipswich as the Blues continued to progress. By mid-March they were four points clear at the top of the table. Leeds were second, although they had two games in hand. It was then that Allison made a bold move. He signed the great entertainer Rodney Marsh for £200,000. It seemed the perfect signing, but City's rhythm fell apart. Of the nine matches remaining City lost three and drew two others.

The Blues' final match was a 2–0 victory over Championship contenders Derby. It left City top of the division, but a fixture backlog meant they had to wait a further 12 days before the other sides completed their fixtures. In the end Derby won the title by a point, with Allison's City fourth, on the same points as Liverpool and Leeds.

City's top scorer was Francis Lee with 33 League goals. A record 13 of these were from the penalty spot as Lee developed something of a reputation for penalty taking. Interestingly, only six of those penalties were for fouls on Lee; two were for handball and the others were for fouls on other players. Francis Lee was also the club's only ever-present.

The inquests soon started. Was the Marsh signing to blame? Allison preferred to believe that a sterling performance from Gordon Banks, which led to a 2–1 Stoke victory on April Fool's Day, was the main cause. Others blamed the ongoing battles in the City boardroom, and the confusion over Mercer and Allison's roles.

Nevertheless it had been a thrilling season, but it was also the definite end of the Mercer–Allison era. Mercer moved to Coventry in June 1972, while Allison managed another season before he moved on. First ex-fifties star Johnny Hart was asked to fill the void left by Allison then, once Hart had resigned due to health issues, Ron Saunders became the first managerial appointment of new chairman Peter Swales. Swales famously wrote in the City programme late in 1973: 'When the appointment was made I thought, from all the candidates considered and the interviews conducted, that he was the right man. Having seen him at work I now know for sure he's the right one. If he goes down, I go with him – it's as blunt as that.'

The following Easter Saunders was dismissed, despite taking City to the 1974 League Cup Final.

The 1974 League Cup Final has become the forgotten Final in many ways. City's defeat to Wolverhampton Wanderers came four years after the significant League Cup and ECWC double success of 1970, so those successes remain significant moments, while 1974 has often been seen as a footnote in the club's history. In 2000 an official history video, *Maine Road To Glory*, was produced which included no footage at all from the game.

The Blues had defeated Walsall (a second replay played at Old Trafford was needed), Carlisle, York City (4–1 in a replay), Coventry City (4–2 in a replay) and Plymouth Argyle to reach Wembley. Although the majority of those sides were relatively small in comparison with the Blues the journey had been a difficult one, with City playing 10 games to reach the

Final to face Wolves. Sadly City lost the Final 2–1, despite dominating for most of the game.

Former captain Tony Book became City's new manager after Saunders's Easter departure, and his side began to match the great Mercer–Allison side for excitement. Eighth in 1974–75 was followed by trophy success in 1975–76. By this time the Blues were regarded as one of football's true glamour clubs. They were one of the most popular teams in the country, with almost every player known throughout the land. When defender Dave Watson arrived for £200,000 in June 1975, City were able to boast that they possessed eight international players. By the end of the season the improved form of Joe Corrigan raised that figure to nine.

The Blues' magnificent Cup run started with a tricky 1–1 draw at John Bond's Norwich City. Bond, the future City manager, complained that the Blues had been physical, and was highly critical of what he described as City's negative attitude. The Maine Road replay was drawn 2–2 and led to a second replay at neutral Stamford Bridge. The Blues won that game 6–1 (Dennis Tueart scored a hat-trick) and on 8 October they went on to face Second Division Nottingham Forest.

Unlike Bond, Forest's Brian Clough seemed pleased: 'I was praying Manchester City would beat Norwich because I wanted to play the best. City are one of the most entertaining and talented sides in the First Division. When I last came to Maine Road it was with Leeds and we lost 2–1. If we keep the score down to 2–1 tonight then I think we'll show the strides that Forest have taken.' True to form the game ended 2–1, with Bell and Royle netting for City. That result brought a home fourth-round tie with Manchester United.

The United match was, in the main, a hugely successful night for the Blues, but there was also a great deal of sadness. City dominated the game and ran out comfortable 4–0 winners, but in the first half, with the score at 1–0, Martin Buchan seriously injured Colin Bell in a tackle. The injury led to a long, difficult and ultimately futile battle to regain full fitness for the England international and, although he did return to the side the following April, his comeback was too soon. After four games he broke down again and remained out of the side until Boxing Day 1977. He was never the same player again.

Mansfield Town were defeated 4–2 in a tense quarter-final, giving City a two-legged semi-final against Jack Charlton's Middlesbrough. The first leg ended in a 1–0 defeat – Geordie Tueart was booed every time he touched the ball by the Middlesbrough fans – but a 4–0 Maine Road victory, missed by Tueart, ensured City progressed to Wembley to face Newcastle United. The Final became highly memorable, with terrific goals from Peter Barnes and Dennis Tueart in City's 2–1 victory.

In 1976–77 Book's Blues finished second to Liverpool, missing the title by a point. It was a thrilling season and many felt Colin Bell's absence through injury would have brought at least the extra point needed. The following season City were fourth, but there had also been a good League Cup run. Attendances had also increased during Book's reign and in 1976–77 they averaged 40,058 (the highest since 1947–48), then the following season the figure rose to 41,687 – a figure not matched until 2003–04.

Always perceived as a glamorous side, Book's Blues entertained and for a period they were undoubtedly one of the top three sides in the country. In 1978–79 they made a real bid for European glory with a tremendous run in the UEFA Cup. First they defeated Twente

Ged Keegan and Dave Ewing lifting the Central League trophy in 1977–78. It was the first time the reserves had won the trophy.

Enschede 4–3 on aggregate, then Standard Liège were swept aside (4–2 on aggregate), and then came a visit to AC Milan in the third round.

The game was actually scheduled for 22 November but was called off because of heavy fog, with several thousand spectators in the San Siro. Because of travel arrangements and potential fixture issues, the decision was taken to play the game the following evening. Book's Blues raced to a two-goal lead with efforts from Brian Kidd and Paul Power. Unfortunately Milan fought back and the game ended 2–2, but City were the first English side to leave the San Siro without getting beaten.

The second leg at Maine Road ended 3–0 to City and they progressed to the fourth round to face German side Borussia Moenchengladbach.

Chairman Peter Swales felt that City were on the verge of real success and believed the best way to guarantee that the Blues would be at the forefront of English and European soccer was by bringing back former coach and manager Malcolm Allison. By the time of the fourth-round tie, Allison was back and described as City's coaching overlord. He seemed determined to create a new side and almost immediately young players such as Nicky Reid were brought into the team. In fact Reid made his debut in the second-leg UEFA Cup meeting in Germany.

The first leg had been drawn 1–1, but the second leg ended in a 3–1 defeat, and the Blues failed to compete on the European stage until 2003. Many blamed the appointment of Malcolm Allison, especially as on the pitch City were enduring a rather mixed series of results in 1978–79, but worse was to follow as players of the calibre of Dave Watson (captain at the Milan victory), Peter Barnes and Gary Owen were sold in quick succession. Allison's desire to create a new City ended all possibility of success, and by October 1980 the Blues were heading for disaster.

Peter Swales realised his gamble had failed. He dismissed Allison and Book and brought in John Bond, a highly respected figure at Norwich and a former West Ham teammate of Allison. At Maine Road Bond brought a new spirit to the club.

Always flamboyant, Bond loved the Manchester atmosphere and enjoyed the first few months of his reign. His impact was immediate. He brought in experienced players Tommy Hutchison, Bobby McDonald and Gerry Gow to help steady the side and Bond's Blues started to move up the table.

The League campaign ended with the Blues in a creditable 12th place – all indications in October were that City would be relegated. Only one player managed to appear in all 42 matches and that was the captain Paul Power, who also appeared in all 15 Cup matches.

Away from the League came the real story of the season, however, as Bond's Blues managed a semi-final appearance in the League Cup, and then a Wembley appearance in the FA Cup.

It was an extremely interesting FA Cup run, particularly as the Blues defeated Malcolm Allison's Crystal Palace 4–0 and Bond's former club Norwich 6–0. The other clubs beaten were Peterborough (1–0), Everton (3–1 in a replay), and Ipswich in the semi-final. Paul Power netted the only goal of the semi, leading the City fans to sing a memorable rendition of *You'll Never Walk Alone* while raising their scarves on the Holte End. Considering Ipswich's strength under Bobby Robson at this time, that result was a major victory for the Blues.

At Wembley City faced Tottenham. The odds were stacked against them – Ossie Ardiles had a dream according to the Spurs official song; the year ended in a 1; it was the Chinese year of the cockerel... the media hype was incredible. Nevertheless, John Bond was determined City would give it their all.

During the game Bond's men did apply a great deal of pressure and Tommy Hutchison headed City into a 29th-minute lead, but in the 80th minute the same player diverted a free-kick into the net to score an own-goal. It was the most agonising moment ever witnessed in a City Final. The following Thursday the Blues lost a thrilling replay 3–2.

In the League Cup a semi-final defeat came after a controversial disallowed goal sapped City's energy and gave Liverpool the upper hand. The Blues were ultimately defeated 2–1 on aggregate.

The season after Wembley Bond signed Martin O'Neill and Trevor Francis, and the side briefly headed the League. Unfortunately, Francis missed rather too many games through injury and, according to Bond, was always intended to be the first of several major transfers that season. Other star names did not arrive.

Due to high spending in the Allison era and a commitment by Peter Swales to improve the stadium, the Blues had major financial worries. The promises made to Bond should never have been made and perhaps, had the manager known the truth, the £1 million spent on Francis might have been used to fund the purchase of two or three other men instead. A stronger all-round squad would have allowed the Blues to compete. As it was Francis was sold within a year and Bond felt more let down than ever. He wasn't the only one: attendances reduced by over 7,000 immediately after Francis's departure. That drop in support made the finances worse, so the whole Francis gamble had failed from every

Coventry's Mick Coop and future City star Tommy Hutchison chasing City's Paul Power on 9 February 1980.

perspective. His initial arrival had not increased support, but his departure was certainly a sign that the club's ambition had receded.

As well as the playing concerns, John Bond felt that some of the directors did not support him at all, making the 1982–83 season a difficult one. With pressure mounting behind the scenes, Bond left City after an embarrassing Cup defeat at Brighton in January 1983. Although the defeat was an extremely difficult one to accept for most Blues, Bond's resignation was perhaps too early. Prior to his departure the worst position City had held was mid-table; once he left the club was in freefall.

14 May 1983 became a miserable day for all Blues as Luton Town scored the only goal of a crucial relegation match, not only to preserve their status, but also to relegate City. Luton manager David Pleat did his famous celebratory jig across the pitch – running to his captain, future City manager Brian Horton – while City were left wondering what might have been. The Blues had not been placed in the relegation zone all season, so this fall was for many a very bitter moment to endure.

Millions of pounds in debt, if media hype from the period is to be believed, City were allegedly paying £1,000 a day in interest charges alone. This situation made it abundantly clear that the new manager had to be someone used to working within a tight transfer budget. The man selected was almost former Blue Alan Oakes, but instead Peter Swales chose the ex-Celtic European Cup-winning captain Billy McNeill.

McNeill's first season in charge saw many 'bargain basement' players arrive. Some of these went on to become cult figures, particularly Neil McNab and Mick McCarthy, but in their first season McNeill's side could only finish fourth. The top three places were occupied by Chelsea, Sheffield Wednesday and a Kevin Keegan-inspired Newcastle.

The following season, 1984–85, opened with the club's first League meeting at Wimbledon, who had been promoted from Division Three the previous May. City were two goals down after a 15-minute bombardment from the Dons, but a fightback including goals from Gordon Smith and Derek Parlane brought a point.

A 3–0 victory at home to Grimsby followed, but City remained as unpredictable as ever, with successive defeats to Fulham (3–2) and Wolves (2–0) in the next two games. Better fortune followed, however, and by the time City faced League leaders Blackburn on 2 March they were challenging for automatic promotion. In fact the game's solitary goal, scored by Steve Kinsey, brought chants of 'We'll be top at 5 o'clock' and, sure enough, Billy McNeill's Blues did replace Blackburn at the top of the division.

City remained top for most of March, but injuries to several influential players, most notably Graeme Baker, Clive Wilson, Jim Melrose and Gordon Smith, brought a period of instability. Defeats at Oxford (3–0), Grimsby (4–1), and at home to Leeds (2–1) left City in fifth place with only five games remaining. Sheffield United were then defeated 2–0, but McNeill viewed the away game at promotion hopefuls Portsmouth on 27 April as the crucial test – it ended in a 2–1 City victory.

Form dipped again at Oldham (0–0), and then the penultimate match of the season ended in a 3–2 defeat at Notts County. It should have been a day of celebration, but a dismal City performance in the first half and crowd disturbances during the interval caused City a whole series of headaches. Fortunately a thrilling 5–1 defeat of Charlton on the final day of the season gave City the third automatic promotion spot ahead of Alan Ball's Portsmouth on goal difference. The City scorers that day were David Phillips, Andy May, Paul Simpson and Jim Melrose.

City's joint top scorers were David Phillips and Gordon Smith with 12, while goalkeeper Alex Williams was the side's only ever-present. This was also the season when Williams kept a club record 21 clean sheets (out of 42 games) – a record that remained until the final day of the 46-game 1998–99 League campaign when Nicky Weaver passed Williams's record.

Promotion in 1985 had been achieved with a mix of experienced players and several young stars. The likes of Steve Kinsey, Jamie Hoyland and the fans' hero, Paul Simpson, were given the opportunity to shine in Division Two and so, when promotion was achieved, much was expected of these players. Supporters knew that finances were still poor and those that watched reserve and youth-team football were aware that Simpson and the others were really only the first wave of talented youngsters being groomed by former players Ken Barnes, Tony Book and Glyn Pardoe.

Paul Moulden and Steve Redmond led the second wave, both making their League debuts during the first few months of 1986, and then in April 1986 the City youth team defeated Manchester United in the FA Youth Cup Final 3–1 on aggregate. The first leg had ended 1–1, with Paul Lake scoring the City goal before 7,602 at Old Trafford, and then Moulden and Boyd made it 2–0 in the Maine Road second leg. A crowd of 18,164 – around 700 less than the attendance for the League meeting with Watford the previous month –

Billy McNeill is seen with fingers crossed, hoping for a great future, after City's promotion match against Charlton in May 1985.

created a passionate City atmosphere. Over the seasons that followed some of these players became major stars.

City spent two seasons in Division One (1985–1987), and featured at Wembley before 68,000 in the inaugural Full Members' Cup. These seasons had many exciting moments, but consistency was hard to achieve. In fact the Blues were at best treading water and, apart from the exciting prospects in the youth team, few supporters felt City would ever be in contention for any of the major trophies. The situation worsened when manager Billy McNeill was badly advised to leave Maine Road and join Aston Villa. Jimmy Frizzell took over, but in May 1987 City were relegated.

Players celebrating in bath after the Charlton promotion match of 1985.

Former Norwich man Mel Machin took over, although Jimmy Frizzell remained in a general manager role. Machin was not a particularly outgoing manager and it is fair to say that some supporters struggled to accept him. His first season in charge caused many to criticise the direction the club was taking – 'Swales Out' protests were a regular feature of life at Maine Road by this stage. The Blues finished ninth in Division Two in 1987–88, 17 points behind champions Millwall, although there had been some exciting matches – the 10–1 victory over Huddersfield remains a strong memory for most.

Promotion was achieved in 1988–89, but even then Machin's side made it difficult for themselves. Games were lost at Blackburn and at home to Barnsley during the final run-in and a memorable Maine Road match with Bournemouth ended 3–3, with the Blues throwing away a three-goal lead. Fans' favourite, and the season's highest goalscorer, Paul Moulden was substituted when City were leading despite scoring twice and being on top form. In fact he had been used sparingly – he only made 29 starts – throughout the season and Machin received a great deal of criticism as a result. That draw meant the Blues needed at least a point from their last match at Bradford.

A tense afternoon saw the Blues go behind, and the promotion dream was fading rapidly, but Trevor Morley achieved cult status by netting the equaliser four minutes from time.

After achieving promotion Machin's City embarked on the 1989–90 First Division campaign intending to consolidate. The relatively low-key City manager seemed determined to play down expectations, especially as other clubs – in particular Manchester United – were spending millions on strengthening their squad. City could not afford to spend wildly, although they did increase their overdraft by signing Clive Allen and Ian Bishop during the close season for a combined fee of around £1.75 million.

The opening day fixture – an away game against the 'team of the 80s' Liverpool – was a major test for the Blues. Despite good debuts from Allen and Bishop the game ended in a 3–1 defeat. As the City fans waited to leave Anfield a couple of melancholic Blues started to sing *Blue Moon*. It was the first time the song had been heard at a City match and, as the season progressed, it started to be adopted as the club's anthem. It typified feelings during what became an eventful season.

Another defeat followed (2–1 at home to Southampton) before the first point was gained in a 1–1 draw with Tottenham. Two games later Clive Allen netted a solitary goal against QPR to bring the first victory, but City's celebrations were short-lived as a 1–0 defeat at Wimbledon left the Blues joint bottom of the division. This would have meant bad feeling at any time, but City feared the worst as their next match was to be the 111th League Manchester derby against Alex Ferguson's multi-million-pound United.

Not only were the United players worth many millions more than City, but the Blues were also already aware that they would be missing a few of their own first-choice men – Clive Allen, Neil McNab and regular 'keeper Andy Dibble. A massacre was predicted, and sure enough one came. Except it was United who were humiliated, not City. The game ended 5–1, with goals from Oldfield (2), Hinchcliffe, Bishop and Morley.

A week later Luton were beaten 3–1 – with City 'keeper Paul Cooper saving the 56th penalty of his long career – but sadly form deteriorated. Arsenal beat the Blues 4–0 with Machin choosing to blame the peculiar yellow kit City wore for that match. A few weeks later Derby defeated City 6–0 – the biggest League defeat in 27 years. Rumours circulated that Machin was for the chop and, after a 1–1 draw with Charlton, Peter Swales dismissed his quiet, unassuming manager.

Swales eventually managed to persuade Howard Kendall to take on the job after Joe Royle had turned the Blues down. Immediately, Kendall stamped his own authority on the team. Out went heroes Bishop and Morley, and in came Peter Reid and Alan Harper. Clive Allen was used sparingly while a whole series of players arrived at Maine Road to help preserve City's Division One status. The bulk of these had connections with Everton, although the player who went on to prove the best of all Kendall's purchases was former Arsenal man Niall Quinn.

Under Kendall City moved up the table, but there always seemed the faint possibility that the former Everton man might not stay long. No one expected him to leave for another club, but some fans did feel he still fancied managing England. Talk similar to the constant media speculation in 2005–06 that Stuart Pearce would be the next England manager dogged the season. At every opportunity the media talked of Kendall as England's next man and supporters were nervous. Despite this Kendall helped City consolidate in Division One during 1989–90 and then during the summer he announced that he had no intention whatsoever of leaving City for the England job. There was a huge feeling of relief throughout the club.

Sadly, a little over a year after he arrived Kendall did walk out on City, but he returned, as he put it, to his first love, Everton. Fearing another major upheaval, the fans called for Peter Reid to be promoted to the manager's position. They believed that Reid would continue with the overall plan laid down by Kendall, and sure enough Reid was appointed.

The Blues finished fifth in consecutive seasons (1990–91 and 1991–92) under Peter Reid and re-established themselves as a force to some extent. Supporters felt real success was just around the corner, although it never actually arrived.

Manager Peter Reid photographed with his squad at the start of the 1991–92 season.

The Premier League was formed in 1992 with the first City fixture being the meeting with Queen's Park Rangers. This was played on a Monday night to accommodate Sky Television – this was the first Monday night live game. A relatively dull 1–1 draw was livened up by fireworks at the final whistle from the Platt Lane end of the ground, and pre-match fans had endured American football-style hype with dancing girls, and even a landing on the pitch by the Red Devil parachutists (who were booed because of their name). Football was certainly changing.

That first Premiership season ended with City in ninth place. This was not too bad, but not an improvement, and seeds of discontent were once again appearing at Maine Road. The frustration being felt by supporters came to a head at the 4–2 FA Cup quarter-final defeat by Tottenham Hotspur in March 1993. Supporters were becoming impatient and, after the hyperbole of the launch of the Premier League and successive top-five finishes, they were no longer satisfied when they heard the chairman talking about his hopes for the future. As far as the fans were concerned the Blues needed success. The game with Spurs had been built up as City's route to glory, and it was also the day the new Platt Lane Stand was to be opened.

Peter Swales had been particularly good at building up the hopes of supporters over the years and, although he had a large number of critics, it is fair to say he also had impressed many supporters with the fact that he was a true Blue and felt the pain in the same way they did.

The opening of the Platt Lane Stand was a disaster. Supporters invaded the pitch out of frustration and police horses were brought on, although that seemed a major over-reaction. Tottenham fans occupying some of the new corporate boxes threw items down on to the City fans below and stewarding on the whole was poor. Fences still caged in supporters on the Kippax, but fans were able to walk freely through the gates on to the pitch, while those in the new stand simply climbed over the wall watched by stewards.

As well as the on the pitch frustrations, fans felt the new stand was a clear sign – and a bad one at that – of the direction the club was heading. The stand seated around 4,200 – some 5,000 seats less than the stand it had replaced – and with terracing about to be banned there were real concerns that the Kippax redevelopment, which had to occur over the next year or so, would be a botched effort.

So the dawn of the Premier League and the move to all-seater stadia signalled the beginning of the end of Swales's reign as chairman. The end came during the 1993–94 season. The dismissal of Peter Reid, shortly after the season opened, led to a campaign by supporters to remove the chairman. Former playing hero Francis Lee launched a takeover bid, ultimately gaining control of the club midway through the season.

Lee then embarked on a bid to improve all aspects of the club. His first obvious target was income via corporate hospitality, and he ripped out the old offices in the Main Stand and transformed the area into a dining area called the Boardroom Suite. While tackling this issue he also improved the plans for the new Kippax Stand, transformed the Platt Lane training complex and restructured the merchandise operation. Basically, Lee and his team tackled all aspects of the club.

On the pitch Brian Horton had replaced Peter Reid prior to Lee arriving, and there was always the perception that Lee would appoint his own man as soon as he could. The Blues finished 16th in 1994 but Lee stuck by Horton and gave him a full season to see what he could achieve. Unfortunately City finished 17th in 1995, although a victory on the last day of the season instead of a 3–2 defeat by QPR would have lifted Horton's men to 12th, and placed them between Chelsea (11th) and Arsenal. Horton was dismissed despite fans enjoying the brand of football played under him. Uwe Rosler and Paul Walsh typified the excitement that Horton's City brought supporters.

Horton was replaced by Alan Ball, but the appointment was not a popular one. Fans had expected a proven and successful manager such as George Graham, and many, many names were mentioned, but Alan Ball was a real disappointment. Everything else since the arrival of Francis Lee had improved, but the appointment of Ball brought real concern.

On the pitch the highlight for most fans during this period was the arrival of Georgiou Kinkladze. Kinkladze arrived at City at the start of the 1995–96 season and, although he only stayed for three years, he was a major cult hero. He made his debut on 19 August 1995, the opening game of the season against Spurs, and impressed immediately with a style of play that was exciting. There were many thrilling individual moments of genius from the Georgian. One of his two goals in the 2–1 victory over Southampton in March 1996 was voted *Match of the Day*'s goal of the month and came second in the goal of the season competition.

Against Newcastle the previous month, the BBC summariser Alan Hansen raved about his all-round performance, and it was clear to all neutrals that City possessed a very talented player.

Sadly, despite Kinkladze, City struggled under Ball and at the end of his first season in control the Blues were relegated to the second tier, Division One. Worse was to follow when the 1996–97 season saw the Blues struggle further. Despite a 1–0 win over Ipswich on the opening day, two defeats followed and Ball resigned. His last game had been the 2–1 defeat at Stoke when both sides chanted 'Ball out' – Ball had led Stoke to relegation earlier in his career.

A managerial merry-go-round followed with Asa Hartford acting as caretaker. Steve Coppell was then appointed manager, but lasted a fraction over a month before he left, then Phil Neal took control as caretaker manager until late December 1996 when ex-Nottingham Forest manager Frank Clark arrived.

City's struggles continued and in February 1998 Clark was replaced by ex-Blue Joe Royle. At last it seemed as if a man who knew and understood the club would be in charge. Sadly, Royle arrived too late to seriously alter City's direction and the Blues were relegated to the third tier of English football for the first time at the end of 1997–98.

Kinkladze was now seen as an expensive luxury by manager Joe Royle, and he left the Blues that summer after a total of 121 League and Cup appearances.

Relegation to the third tier of English football was a devastating blow for the club. Although support remained high – average attendance in their relegation season was 28,196 and in Division Two increased to 28,261 (the highest average since 1982) – it was vital the Blues returned immediately to Division One. A prolonged stay in Division Two would undoubtedly have drained the club's life away.

Fortunately Joe Royle fully understood this and he worked hard to ensure his City side was equipped for the tough battle it was to face. Experienced players were brought in and the 1998–99 season saw the Blues start to fight back. It wasn't at all easy. Confidence, morale and attitude had been knocked severely under the previous managers, and Royle had an enormous task. Fortunately City's vast support rallied behind the manager and the team. In the boardroom David Bernstein had become chairman and he brought an air of respectability and confidence to the club, while changes in the day-to-day workings of the club saw PR man Chris Bird take a more significant role as the season developed. Bird, a true Blue, understood how supporters felt and it's fair to say he worked hard behind the scenes to resurrect the club. He ultimately became the managing director.

Promotion from the Second Division came in May 1999, but City being City this was never a formality. In fact the Blues had to face Gillingham in an extremely memorable and nerve-wracking match. The Blues were eventually promoted on penalties.

Twelve months later Joe Royle guided City to promotion from Division One back into the Premier League, and players such as Shaun Goater and Paul Dickov were by this time firmly established as cult heroes. Sadly the Blues were not quite ready for life back in football's elite and Royle's men were relegated at the end of the 2000–01 season. With the move to the new Commonwealth Games venue at Eastlands scheduled for 2003 it was vital City re-established themselves as a Premier League side quickly. Joe Royle was dismissed and former England manager Kevin Keegan was appointed. Although many fans were disappointed by the departure of Royle, the appointment of Keegan brought the club tremendous attention. It also encouraged a number of players, including Eyal Berkovic and Stuart Pearce, to join the side for an assault on the First Division.

A thrilling year followed with the Blues scoring plenty of goals and entertaining throughout the season. In fact at one point City played a goalless draw against Sheffield

The City players embark on their lap of honour following their 2001–02 Championship success.

Stuart Pearce, surrounded by the other players, lifts the League Championship trophy.

Chairman David Bernstein with the League Championship trophy won in 2002.

United and the *Guardian* headline read 'Keegan's City in nil-nil shock'. It summed up the season perfectly as City challenged for promotion, which was achieved on 5 April when Wolves were defeated 1–0 at Millwall on the eve of City's home game with Barnsley. Against Barnsley City won 5–1 with a hat-trick from Huckerby and a brace from Macken to secure the League Championship. With two games still left to play it was an unusual situation for the Blues, who typically would still have something to play for on the last day of the season. In fact it was the first time since 1996–97 that City were confident of the division they would play in the following season prior to the last match.

Despite the success, Keegan's City were still determined to end the season in the best way

Stuart Pearce as captain, celebrating City's promotion in the 2001–02 season.

and it quickly became apparent that a couple of records were within their grasp. City had already broken the total number of points for a season which had stood at 89 (secured in 1999–2000), but now they stood a chance of beating the record number of goals scored in a season. This record stood at 108 and was set in 1926–27 (42 games), and with Keegan's Blues known as great scorers the figure seemed within reach. After Barnsley the Blues had netted 102 and had two matches left to play. It would be tough, but was clearly something Keegan's side could aim for. In addition, Stuart Pearce was on a figure of 99 career goals and seemed keen to reach the magic 100 figure in his final season.

Against Gillingham in their penultimate game City managed a 3–1 win, then, on the final day of celebration, Howey, Goater and Macken combined to give the Blues a 3–1 win. The victory ensured City ended the campaign on a record 99 points, which also saw them equal the number of goals scored record set in 1926–27, but sadly there was no goal for Pearce despite a last-minute penalty. The popular captain took the spot-kick but somehow blasted the ball into the Platt Lane Stand. As Pearce later told the media: 'There is always a sting in the tail when Stuart Pearce does anything, and that penalty was comical. The way I missed the goal just about sums me up, but it has been a pleasure and honour to represent the clubs I have, and I am very proud to have won this Championship medal with City.'

Widespread celebrations followed City's promotion, and the following season saw the Blues perform exceptionally well in many games in the Premier League. The season became an emotional one at times as it was the last one for the nearly 80-year-old Maine Road stadium. The move to Eastlands was scheduled for August 2003 and so the club and supporters spent a great deal of time planning and preparing for the move, although Keegan understandably tried to keep himself and the players focussed on ensuring that the Blues remained in the top division. Despite a 3–0 defeat at Leeds on the opening day, Keegan's Blues soon proved more than a match for many established Premiership sides. Newcastle and Everton were defeated in the first two home games, and then in November Manchester United arrived for the last derby match at the old ground. It was vital City won the match because of its historical significance and sure enough the Reds were beaten 3–1, with a goal from summer signing Nicolas Anelka and a couple from cult hero Shaun Goater. The second Goater goal was actually his 100th City goal. Interestingly, it was the first time the Blues had ever started a game with 11 non-Englishmen.

As the season progressed some fans started to talk of qualification for Europe as only one defeat in eight games over December and January lifted the Blues to ninth place, but a run of poor results in February – the best being a 1–1 draw at Old Trafford – caused City to slip a little.

On 21 April 2003 a goal from Robbie Fowler and two from Marc-Vivien Foe gave City a 3–0 win over Sunderland. The game became significant as it was to be the last City win at Maine Road and Foe's 80th-minute goal was the last scored by a City man at the stadium. The last game of the season was Maine Road's final game and ended in a 1–0 defeat by Southampton, but City still ended the season in a creditable ninth place and also qualified for the UEFA Cup via the Fair Play League.

Sadly, the first few weeks of the close season brought much sadness to the club. Clearly the move from Maine Road was an emotional experience, but the stadium's final days were

Marc-Vivien Foe.

marked with tributes to Marc-Vivien Foe, who passed away during an international match for Cameroon. His death was a major shock and for some his loss added to the emotion of moving away from Maine Road. For many supporters leaving the old ground was the biggest emotional upset they had felt. To some Maine Road *was* Manchester City.

Despite the sadness of Foe's early death and the departure from Maine Road, the new season opened with lots of optimism. Keegan's City were competing in the UEFA Cup and established in the Premier League. They were also playing in the best stadium in the country. Unfortunately the UEFA Cup campaign was not too successful. The Blues defeated Welsh side Total Network Solutions, and Belgians Lokeren, before losing out on the away goals rule to Polish side Groclin. The League campaign was one of inconsistency. At times Keegan's City were absolutely unstoppable, such as when they beat Bolton 6–2 in October, but there were also dismal spells with the months of November through to February proving difficult. The most satisfying and entertaining game was the marvellous 4–1 defeat of Manchester United. It was absolutely vital the Blues defeated the Reds in the first game at Eastlands, and a thoroughly deserved victory saw goals from Fowler, Macken, Sinclair, and Wright-Phillips before 47,284. Sadly United had been victorious in a fifth-round FA Cup tie between the sides in February, but the best and most dramatic game of the season had been the 4–3 victory over Spurs in the FA Cup fourth round.

The first season at the new stadium ended with City in 16th place, two places above the relegation zone but eight points clear of the drop. After the final game – a 5–1 victory over Everton – the players performed a lap of honour. As always supporters gave the side a fantastic reception, prompting chairman John Wardle to say: 'It was typical City, the tag we are trying to get rid of. We got cheered to the rafters even though we've had such a bad season. You wonder what it would be like if we won something.'

Kevin Keegan was equally impressed by City's support: 'They are the greatest thing about this club and the level of support we have enjoyed throughout a very poor season has been amazing. Thirty thousand of them bought season tickets for next year without even knowing what division we would be in. What we've done to deserve this is beyond me.'

Despite the strong support, the following season commenced with fans a little downbeat. When they looked back on 2003–04 they saw several worrying aspects to the season. Paul Connolly, writing for *The Times*, seemed to catch the mood perfectly:

> *The problem with City's underperformance lies squarely with those expensive (in terms of wages) signings who just saw City as a last money-spinning opportunity before retirement. Others blame Keegan for being unable to motivate his team. While there is an element of truth in both arguments, the latter perhaps holds more water. City's best players – other than James – were three relative youngsters, Richard Dunne, Joey Barton, and Shaun Wright-Phillips. Keegan is best working with younger, more impressionable players. One only has to be reminded of his record as the coach of England to understand that his boundless enthusiasm does not work wonders on experienced, successful players.*

Connolly blamed Keegan and added: 'He exhibited poor judgement in the transfer market, then compounded his errors by showing loyalty to players who were clearly not interested in playing for City.'

The players Connolly referred to included Steve McManaman and David Seaman. Seaman, according to Connolly, cost the Blues at least eight goals in the 19 games he played in, while McManaman excelled in his first match but after that seemed disinterested. That may be a little harsh, but during the summer of 2004 supporters read reviews such as Connolly's, talked with others about the season, read fanzines, and basically reached the conclusion that City's future did lie with talented youngsters such as Wright-Phillips and Barton. Supporters wanted big names, but not those at the end of their careers.

The first victory of the season came in the fourth match when Charlton were defeated 4–0 with goals from Anelka (2), Sinclair and Shaun Wright-Phillips. Before the end of the season Anelka was to leave the club, while Wright-Phillips was often mentioned when newspapers speculated on transfers.

On the pitch another mixed season followed. The Blues were out of both cup competitions by 9 January 2005, and hovering in a mid-table position. They did become the only side to beat Chelsea in the League with a 1–0 win in October, but by the end of February City were struggling to some extent. A 3–2 win at Norwich – a game that became famous for Norwich director Delia Smith's half-time call to her team's supporters to improve the atmosphere 'Where are you?' – helped, but a 1–0 defeat at home to Bolton on 7 March led to manager Kevin Keegan leaving the club. Everyone felt the time was right for change, and Stuart Pearce, a member of the backroom staff since retiring as a player in 2002, was asked to take charge on a temporary basis. The term 'caretaker manager' was never applied (City have had enough of those over the years), but Pearce was clearly a manager-in-waiting. His side showed much commitment, as expected, in his opening game away to Spurs, but sadly they lost 2–1 to an 84th-minute effort from Keane. Apart from that match Pearce's Blues remained undefeated for the rest of the season – eight games – and almost qualified for the UEFA Cup. A last-day draw – with Robbie Fowler missing a penalty late on – against Middlesbrough allowed 'Boro to qualify. Had City won, then the situation would have been reversed. Goalkeeper David James played as a forward for the final stages of the game after Claudia Reyna was taken off and replaced by Nicky Weaver. Weaver went in the net, naturally, but James changed his shirt and tried to attack. It was actually as a result of his involvement that the Blues were awarded the penalty which could – and should – have brought European football.

Nevertheless, an eighth-place finish was respectable in the end. Prior to that final match Stuart Pearce was given the manager's job on a permanent basis and the 2005 close season was more positive than the previous one despite the departure of Shaun Wright-Phillips for a reported £21 million.

By the start of the 2005–06 season – the 125th since formation as St Mark's in 1880 – Pearce had strengthened the squad with the acquisition of former Aston Villa forward Darius Vassell and ex-United star Andy Cole. Both men made their debuts in the opening game – a goalless draw with West Bromwich Albion – and by 2 February they had scored eight and 10 first-team goals respectively. Sadly, Cole struggled with injury soon afterwards and City clearly missed his experience and expertise.

Prior to Cole's injury Pearce had guided his side into contention for a European place. In fact the Blues led the table after the third game of the season, and remained in the top six until late November. Unfortunately, four games over the Christmas period brought only one point and City dropped to ninth. Successive 3–1 victories over Scunthorpe United in the FA Cup and Manchester United in the League soon followed and everybody assumed the Christmas games had simply been a blip. Interestingly, the Scunthorpe supporters made history by bringing the largest number of away supporters to the City of Manchester stadium – 6,129 Scunthorpe fans attended, almost double the support Aston Villa brought for their FA Cup tie.

The FA Cup actually became the main focal point of the entire season and for three months it felt as if this was to be City's year. A 1–0 victory over Wigan Athletic set the Blues up for a fifth-round meeting at Aston Villa. The game saw the Blues dominate, but Villa took the lead and seemed certain to snatch the win. Then 17-year-old Micah Richards scored a thoroughly deserved equaliser in the dying seconds. His excitement was clear for all to see, particularly when television cameras were thrust in front of him seconds after the final whistle, for a somewhat entertaining natural reaction.

The replay was delayed for almost a month due to the requirements of television, and the game was staged six days before the quarter-final. City defeated Villa 2–1 with goals from Vassell and recent arrival Georgios Samaras. A 1–0 League defeat by Wigan came four days after the Villa game then, on Monday 20 March, the quarter-final tie with West Ham was staged at Eastlands. It ended in a hugely frustrating 2–1 defeat. City had been the better side and West Ham offered little, but they won and eventually went on to face Liverpool in the Final. For City though the defeat signalled an early end to the season. Some fans felt the FA's insistence that the quarter-finals be played on successive nights to enable them all to be screened on television, and so soon after the replay, had affected the result.

Sadly, apart from a 1–0 victory at Aston Villa, the rest of the season seemed to peter out. In fact defeat by European Cup finalists Arsenal in the last home game meant that City had been defeated in five consecutive home first-team games for the first time in their history.

Despite the dismal end, there were many strong signs of hope for the future. There were some very positive performances during the opening seven months of the season, and new arrivals Cole, Vassell and Samaras added some extra excitement to City's attack. The youth side, captained by Micah Richards, reached the FA Youth Cup Final and, thanks to the hard work of Jim Cassell and his staff, it's clear City's Academy continues to be one of the best in the country.

For Stuart Pearce it had been an important first full season in charge. In the last programme of the season he admitted: 'I'm disappointed with the League position as we stand. I'll learn a great deal of lessons from this season and hopefully try and drive the squad forward for next season, improve the squad and make us better and more resilient. We've lost too many matches this year for my liking and I know I've got to improve.'

For supporters Pearce's honest approach was perhaps the most positive aspect of the club's 125th season, while the continuing loyalty of Mancunians enabled the Blues to end the season as the fourth best supported side. The final League position may not have been in keeping with City's history, but the volume of support certainly was.

Manchester City Stadia

SINCE its formation as St Mark's Church side in 1880, the club is known to have played at eight different home venues. Three of these – Hyde Road, Maine Road and the City of Manchester Stadium – have hosted League football. Each of those three has accommodated crowds in excess of 40,000; each has staged representative matches; two have staged semi-finals; two have staged major pop concerts; one holds a variety of national records; and City are proud that all three of those League homes have been within the present-day boundaries of the city of Manchester.

Each of those three League venues has, at various points in its history, been regarded as a major venue and both Maine Road and the City of Manchester Stadium set new benchmarks for stadium construction when they opened. All of this, however, is a far cry from the grounds the Blues first used in the 1880s.

Home Grounds

Clowes Street/Thomas Street (1880–81)
Kirkmanshulme Cricket Club (1881–82)
Queen's Road (1882–84)
Pink Bank Lane (1884–85)
Bull's Head Hotel (1885–87)
Hyde Road/Bennett Street (1887–1923)
Maine Road (1923–2003)
City of Manchester Stadium (since 2003)

Clowes Street/Thomas Street (1880–81)

St Mark's Church was based on Clowes Street in West Gorton, and earlier histories of the Blues claim the club's first pitch was on Clowes Street itself. This seems highly unlikely, as most of the Clowes Street area was already occupied by housing and industry by 1880. This makes it extremely difficult to locate the exact site of this pitch, especially as the initial match report talks of the first reported game taking place in Longsight. This seems to be an error on the part of the writer at the time, although the St Mark's vicarage was south of Hyde Road in an area known variously as Newton Detached or Longsight. The first true clue as to where the ground could have been comes from the *Book Of Football* published in 1905. This states that the site of the first pitch had been developed between 1881 and 1905 into the Brooks & Doxey's Union Ironworks.

The ironworks was actually on Thomas Street, a road running parallel to Clowes Street, and maps from the late 1880s do show sufficient land next to the original factory for a sports field. This land next to the Union Ironworks was more or less directly north of St Mark's Church and was certainly an extremely short walk from the church, and so could easily have been the club's first pitch. It is highly likely that the players themselves would have changed in the church, or its schoolroom, and have been able to walk along William Street – the road St Mark's actually faced on to – to the land. A walk around this area in 2006 easily established the close proximity of all these locations and made it perfectly obvious that Thomas Street is the most likely site of the first pitch.

Interestingly, a newspaper report from April 1879 suggests the Thomas Street spot was used for sport and other recreational activity. It was certainly the type of space used by the young men and women of the area. It may also have been the space used by the St Mark's cricket team. Under the heading 'One lad stabbed by another at cricket', the unfortunate story was told of violence between West Gorton youngsters. A 14-year-old was stabbed by a 15-year-old on this site: 'the lads were playing at cricket along with some others in a field behind Thomas Street.'

This does prove the site was used for sport, but unfortunately, after over two decades of research, I have yet to prove conclusively that this was the first pitch. It is my opinion, however, that the ironworks' land was the club's first pitch, and two of the club's founding fathers, William Beastow and Thomas Goodbehere, may have been aware of the potential of the land from their working places within the works. As both men worked hard to ensure St Mark's developed, it seems likely they would have searched for a site, and as many of the first players were teenagers living yards from this popular 'hangout' space it does seem likely.

It has to be remembered that in 1880 this space was nothing more than rough land. Beastow and Goodbehere believed it was good enough for their purpose, however, and the fledgling club played its first reported home game on 13 November 1880, with the first opponents being the Baptist church from Macclesfield. Both teams fielded 12 players, and the pitch markings would have been questionable – reports from later in the decade suggest local residents knew about rugby but not association football – but the game itself was a major achievement.

After the initial game St Mark's are known to have played a further two home games – against Arcadians from Harpurhey on 27 November 1880 and Hurst from Ashton under Lyne on 26 February 1881. Both of these match reports talk of the ground as being in Longsight, and the Hurst report gives an indication of the quality of the ground: 'The ground was in a very sloppy state, and consequently the falls were very numerous.'

It is highly probable St Mark's played a few more matches at home that season, but records simply do not exist.

Today the site of St Mark's church is occupied by a small parade of shops and the West Gorton Working Men's Club at Gorton Villa Walk (ironically, Gorton Villa FC was one of the club's biggest rivals throughout the 1880s). Gorton Villa Walk follows the original line of Clowes Street, but Clowes Street itself has been rerouted somewhat. The street starts at a junction with Hyde Road and follows its original course for a few hundred metres before it bends around a small housing estate until it meets Wenlock Way, the street formerly known as Thomas Street. The new junction of Clowes Street and Wenlock Way is roughly situated in front of the site of the Brooks & Doxey's works entrance in 1880. The site believed to be that of the first pitch at Thomas Street is currently the car park for the Fujitsu office block a little further down Wenlock Way.

Interestingly, all of this area – in particular the houses on Gorton Villa Walk and the shopping parade occupying the St Mark's site – has been used for the Channel Four television series *Shameless*, which features a Manchester City-supporting family.

A plaque recording City's formation is positioned on the Aces public house (named after the Belle Vue Aces speedway team), but this is incorrectly placed and should be positioned on the Working Men's Club, Gorton Villa Walk, to highlight the actual site of St Mark's Church. It is particularly galling that City's history warrants only one blue plaque in the city and that even then this has been incorrectly placed, with few specific details.

Kirkmanshulme Cricket Ground (1881–82)

The original pitch was clearly not appropriate for a side keen to develop, and so St Mark's moved to a more appropriate playing surface at the Kirkmanshulme Cricket Club ground. This was positioned on the southern side of Hyde Road on Redgate Lane, midway between St Mark's Church and the rectory on North Road, and the ground gave the side terrific opportunities. This was a five-acre site and had a pavilion in one corner of the ground. There were no facilities for spectators, but this was nevertheless a major improvement.

The ground was next to Tank Row where Edward Kitchen – a key player and committee member – was known to live in 1881. It is believed Kitchen encouraged the move.

At the cricket ground, the club are known to have played five games out of 12 matches that season, including the club's first home meeting with Newton Heath (present-day Manchester United) on 4 March 1882. This attracted an attendance of around 5,000 – some 2,000 more than the away fixture the previous November – with these spectators positioned along the touchline, stood on the outer edges of the cricket pitch. It seems incredible that somewhere in the region of a sixth of Gorton's population at the time would have been able to attend a game which, at that point, was not regarded as a 'derby' or an important fixture whatsoever. However, it is clear that football was gaining popularity all the time and St Mark's, because of their roots and the work of Beastow, Goodbehere and Anna Connell, were a very worthy cause to support.

St Mark's managed to take the lead as early as the eighth minute, and then had to hold off the Heathens, who had been awarded a couple of consecutive corners. The second actually led to St Mark's second goal. James Collinge obtained possession in front of the Gorton goal then proceeded to run the full length of the pitch, before sending the ball flying between the Heathens' posts amid loud cheering. The score remained 2–0 until late in the game when, according to reports, the Heathens baffled the home 'keeper Kitchen by performing several good passes before the ball entered the goal. Exactly how baffled Kitchen was is unclear. The match ended 2–1 to St Mark's.

According to early club histories, at the end of the season Kirkmanshulme CC asked the footballers to find another ground as their playing surface had been badly damaged, or at least they felt that it was no longer the perfect pitch you would expect for a gentlemanly game of cricket. Maybe the damage had been caused by the large attendance at the Newton Heath game, West Gorton's last at the cricket ground, or maybe it was simply because of the general wear and tear on the pitch. It is possible some cricket officials were concerned that the football club was becoming more popular than the long-established cricket club.

Eventually the cricket club disappeared as the area became more industrial and the popularity of the neighbouring Belle Vue Pleasure Gardens increased. During the 1980s the site became derelict and today it is still mainly in the same state, although the ring road, which ultimately leads to the City of Manchester Stadium, cuts through the site as it makes its way from Longsight across Redgate Lane and on to Hyde Road. Some industrial buildings have been erected on part of the site.

Queen's Road 1882–84

For the start of the 1882–83 season St Mark's moved to land off Queen's Road, approximately three-quarters of a mile east of Clowes Street. The land is believed to be the present-day Gorton Park and, if this is true, it is the only actual former venue of Manchester City that is still staging football today.

At the time the local newspaper referred to the venue as Clemington Park – although this is not a name that has ever really been utilised by Gortonians – while supporters at the turn of the century were reported as calling it 'Donkey Common', although reports never referred to this name. During the 1940s a booklet called *Famous Football Clubs – Manchester City* referred to this ground: 'In later years this ground developed into a park, but it looked more "parky" than anything else in those days.'

The history of St Mark's during this period is confusing and match reports suggest only three home games were played there in 1882–83, with five the following season, and that there was a merger with another local team. However, material written during the 1930s and early 1940s – a time when some of the original founders were still around – suggests around 20 games (10 at home) were played each season.

Although little proof exists today, it is clear that this venue was the first to last more than one season, and that it was the first venue which allowed the side to play football seriously. The St Mark's connections were reducing to some extent, but the game itself was developing.

In 1884 the club split, with the original St Mark's men renaming their club Gorton Association Football Club, while the others created West Gorton Athletic. That side survived for a few years, first at Queen's Road, then near the Gorton Brook Hotel at the top end of Clowes Street, but eventually the side folded. The St Mark's men, however, saw their side grow considerably over the following years.

Pink Bank Lane 1884–85

Pink Bank Lane was initially a step backwards for the renamed Gorton AFC, and it's highly possible that the selection was one of desperation. The club became Gorton AFC in October, and it appears that the split with West Gorton Athletic came as the result of a sudden decision. Once that split had occurred a ground – any ground – had to be found. Player Lawrence Furniss was the man who identified the potential of the site and club secretary Edward Kitchen negotiated a rent of £6 a year.

Clearly, the land was not equipped for football, but it was close to the old Kirkmanshulme cricket ground and the St Mark's rectory, and it was as good as some of the homes of some of St Mark's main rivals. It was referred to as 'the Pink Bank Lane Ground' in a report of the Gorton-Gorton Villa derby match of 14 March 1885 when Gorton won 3–0.

At the end of the season, the club's first annual report stated that Gorton had played 16 matches, won seven, lost seven and drawn two. They had scored 31 goals and conceded 21.

The following season Gorton moved again. This is a strong indication that Pink Bank Lane was a short-term solution and that Gorton needed to find a better location if they truly wanted to progress.

Since Gorton's departure, Pink Bank Lane has been redeveloped a couple of times. One side of the Lane houses the Belle Vue Athletics Centre, which was utilized during the 2002 Commonwealth Games.

Bull's Head Hotel, Reddish Lane 1885–87

This venue was completely different from the club's earlier grounds as it was some distance away from their St Mark's birthplace. It was right on the edge of Gorton – in fact it was right on the border of Gorton, Reddish and Denton. The Bull's Head Hotel is roughly two miles from Clowes Street.

Despite the distance the Bull's Head, or Reddish Lane ground as it was often called, offered the club potential. The landlord charged Gorton £6 per year rent to use the ground and to change in the public house, and he also gained from improved beer sales on match days. Personally, I have always been suspicious about this venue and felt it couldn't possibly have been Gorton's home, but recently I have uncovered evidence that the ground was used for a variety of sports in the years leading up to Gorton's residence here. Reports appeared in local newspapers of various events and in one month alone, July 1882, reports mentioned rabbit coursing, pigeon shooting and quoits all occurring in the Bull's Head grounds.

The first Gorton football game to be staged at the new ground was a 1–1 draw with Earlestown on 3 October 1885. The game must have been an interesting one, as Earlestown wore a kit that was almost a negative of Gorton's – white shirts with a black Maltese Cross positioned on the right, as opposed to Gorton's black shirts with a white Maltese Cross on the left. The man who scored the Gorton equaliser was Lawrence Furniss, who four years later would become the club's manager/secretary, and in the 1920s the chairman responsible for the move to Maine Road.

Gorton stayed at this ground for two seasons, with the last known game being against Pendleton Olympic on 30 April 1887. Sadly, no report for this match exists. The reason for moving on appears to have been financial. According to early club histories the landlord asked for a rent increase. Perhaps he wasn't making as much out of beer sales as he had anticipated, or, more likely, he realised Gorton's attendances were increasing and felt he deserved a share. He also knew that his land still had a reputation for other sports and perhaps he felt he could earn more from those activities.

The present day Bull's Head was built on the site of the earlier public house in 1906, and nowadays the area is clearly seen as Reddish rather than Gorton. Terraced housing covers the immediate hinterland, while the only open space behind the public house is a playing field for a local school. Potentially, this could be the site of the old pitch, but that seems unlikely.

Hyde Road, Ardwick 1887–1923

The landlord of the Bull's Head gave Gorton another opportunity to progress, even if at the time the committee found the news a serious blow. The Bull's Head ground was never likely to see the club establish itself as one of football's elite and, although this would not have been considered at the time, Gorton's move came at a moment in history when football was about to become much more professional in its outlook. Some clubs were already paying players, and the whole game was about to go through a major change with the formation of the Football League in 1888. Gorton's move in 1887 was able to lay the foundations for the club's later move into League football.

It was actually Kenneth McKenzie, the club captain, who first discovered the potential of wasteland located close to his workplace. This land was a decent size, but wasn't used for any kind of recreational activity whatsoever at the time. McKenzie felt it offered potential nevertheless and he immediately told the leading committee members of the find. It is believed they took some convincing, as the land was uneven and riddled with polluted streams, but with few other options the Gortonians decided to take it. In addition, Lawrence Furniss and Walter Chew were both aware that this land lay closer to the club's spiritual home, St Mark's Church, than any of the previous venues other than perhaps the very first ground.

Furniss discovered that the land belonged to the Manchester, Sheffield, and Lincolnshire railway, and after some negotiation Gorton were able to rent the land for £10 for a period of seven months. Furniss, Chew and company spent a few weeks trying to level an area suitable as a pitch and by late August the ground was ready. It was still relatively basic, but it was deemed suitable for a relaunch of the club. The move to this ground caused the committee to consider changing the name of the club. As the new ground was based in the district of Ardwick, rather than Gorton, the committee felt a change was needed and Ardwick AFC was born. A circular was issued on 23 August 1887 and the inaugural meeting was held at the Hyde Road Hotel on 30 August. The Hyde Road Hotel became the headquarters of the club and was also used as dressing rooms for several years.

Within a decade the Hyde Road ground, as it became known, had grown from nothing to become a major venue. In some ways the ground developed at a similar rate to the club. In 1892 Ardwick were founder members of Division Two, then two years later the club reformed as Manchester City, and in 1896 the Blues were the third-best supported side in the League behind Everton and Aston Villa.

In 1904 a major refurbishment occurred following the FA Cup success, and the following season the venue was selected for an inter-League game between Ireland and England and the FA Cup semi-final between Newcastle and Sheffield Wednesday. The inter-League match was filmed and today the footage is believed to be the oldest surviving footage of a professional football venue in Manchester. The camera was positioned slightly in front of the Main Stand, at the Galloway corner, and film clearly shows the Popular Side, part of the Galloway End, the Main Stand, and the players' tunnel.

By this time crowds of 40,000 could be housed, although contemporary reports suggest attendances were actually higher. The stadium was often packed and it is impossible to now

These photographs show the Skircoat Road Stand roof at the Shay, Halifax, in 1987. This roof was previously erected at Hyde Road and was sold to Halifax Town shortly before Hyde Road staged its last game.

identify the actual attendances of games at this time. Journalists would state that the crowd was around 40,000, while the club appears to have downplayed the number that were actually present for financial and safety reasons. A few games, most notably a Cup tie with Sunderland in 1913 and a League game with Burnley in 1921, caused local journalists to question the club's management of safety, organisation and attendances at games at Hyde Road.

At regular intervals it was suggested that the Blues would have to move, but each time the directors looked elsewhere they would come back and announce that Hyde Road would continue to be the club's home. There was a feeling among the senior committee men that City would only move if a significantly better venue could be found.

In March 1920 Hyde Road became the first provincial ground to be visited by a reigning monarch when King George V attended City's victory over Liverpool. He did this because he knew it would be a great way to meet a large number of Mancunians, as City remained Manchester's number one club despite United's move to Old Trafford in 1910. Actually, United's development of Old Trafford caused the Blues to improve Hyde Road considerably in 1910. City decided to improve facilities for all supporters, and set plans in place to provide shelter for a total of 35,000 spectators. This would be achieved by erecting multi-span roofs on the three remaining open sides. By the start of the new season the work was complete and was a source of much pride.

These ground improvements, which meant that all four sides had cover (no other Manchester football venue could match this until the 1970s), significantly improved the facilities, but the fact was that the venue's 40,000 capacity was still far too small. The close proximity of railway lines, factories and housing prevented expansion, so the Blues continued to look for a larger site. By 1920 City were publicly planning a move to a site at Belle Vue, but in November of that year fire destroyed the club's 1890s Main Stand. The rest of the stadium survived, but a move became absolutely vital if the Blues were to capitalise on their popularity.

City should have moved immediately, but discussions with United, the owners of the only venue worth considering, proved difficult and the Blues deemed it better to soldier on at Hyde Road. In fact local newspapers were highly critical of United's terms and accused the Reds of opportunism. According to the *Athletic News* the terms were:

> *… City should take the equivalent of last season's gate in the corresponding match and that the remainder should belong to the United. As gates have increased by 30 percent at the very least in the First Division matches the Manchester City directors declined to entertain the proposal, and no wonder Manchester United did not in our opinion manifest the much-vaunted League spirit.*
>
> *They missed a great opportunity to make the club popular by a fine sporting act. The followers of Manchester City have greater affection for the old club than ever. And they have formed a just opinion of their neighbours.*

Rather than pay exorbitant rental to United the Blues patched up their ground and found enough breathing space to create magnificent plans for the future. Interestingly, City's attempts to patch up Hyde Road brought the club national attention and journalists

KENNETH McKENZIE

For several years the name 'K. McKenzie' has been a footnote in the history of City's grounds. He has often been mentioned as the man who identified the potential of the site that in 1887 became the Hyde Road ground, but other than his initial and surname little has ever been published. Now, for the first time, significant information can be revealed about McKenzie and his City connections.

Kenneth McKenzie was born in Wick, Caithness, Scotland on 14 August 1863, and was living with his parents and two brothers (Alexander and Donald) in Falkirk in 1881. It is not exactly clear when he moved to Gorton, although it is known that the whole family were living in the Gorton area during the mid-1880s. As with many of St Mark's team in 1880, it is believed the McKenzies had moved to Manchester to find work with the hope of building a more prosperous life.

Kenneth was an active young man and keen to form part of the local community, and we know that he was a Gorton player from the 1885–86 season up to the 1890s, and became captain of the side in 1886. He was a full-back and his younger brother Donald (born in Wick on 17 March 1866) also played for the side during this period. Donald was a forward and, possibly because of Ardwick AFC's connections with the brewing industry, he became a beerhouse keeper at the Nelson Inn on Grey Street. Sadly, he passed away aged 29 in 1895.

The first mention of any McKenzie came on 13 February 1886 when a match report mentioned that a player with that surname was missing from the line up. It is believed this was Kenneth and that he must have played in earlier games for them to note he was missing. It's highly possible that the involvement of the two McKenzies helped the side take on a more professional approach. Scotland was ahead of England in terms of football knowledge and tactics, and many Scottish men helped northern English sides to develop around this time.

According to old club histories, the site of the Hyde Road ground was discovered when: 'Club captain K McKenzie lived on Bennett St (Ardwick) and used to take the short cut to his work at a timber yard off Hyde Rd'. Today it's not clear where this information came from, and it does seem that this story is not entirely accurate, although there's no doubt that it was McKenzie who discovered the Hyde Road site. The timber yard was actually called Bennett's timber yard and McKenzie is believed to have been a moulder at the yard. It was positioned between Hyde Road and the railway lines, close to Devonshire Street, on the site of the present-day bus depot, and a short cut from Bennett Street would almost certainly have meant a trip across the site of the ground, although it isn't clear exactly where McKenzie was living in 1887 when he 'found' the site.

It doesn't appear he was living on Bennett Street, although he must have been living close by. We do know that he married in 1888 and, with his new wife, set up home at 50 Grey Street, close to the railway bridge on the opposite side of Hyde Road to the ground. A short cut from there would not have taken him across the site of the ground.

McKenzie was a regular player and also played in the Hyde Coal Mining Disaster charity match for Ardwick against Newton Heath (United) at Belle Vue on 26 February 1889. This match is a major landmark in Manchester history because it was played under floodlights and was staged to raise money for victims of the Hyde coal mine disaster, where 23 people died. Twenty electric lights were placed around the pitch and 10,000 attended. McKenzie was one of Ardwick's 'backs'. We also know that by 1891 his profession is given as milk dealer, so that raises some questions about the mention of his job at Bennett's.

By 1901 McKenzie, his wife and three daughters (the youngest being born in the Gorton area in 1896) were living in Warrington, where McKenzie was employed as an iron moulder, but it does appear he returned to Manchester shortly afterwards.

He passed away aged 88 in Chapel-en-le-Frith in 1952. Interestingly, his name is often recorded as MacKenzie, although match reports tended to use Mc, and his descendants use the Mac version of the surname.

Regardless of how his surname is spelt, or his exact residence in 1887, it is essential McKenzie's place in Hyde Road's early history is remembered. Without him Ardwick AFC might not have been created, and ultimately City might not have developed.

from all over the United Kingdom came to Manchester to check on City's progress. The *Glasgow Evening Times* was particularly impressed:

> *Manchester City must have some good friends. They are of course the popular club in Manchester. It was surprising to find a fine new stand, estimated to hold 6,000 spectators, rising to the height of 25 tiers on the site of the old structure. In addition, extensive new terracing had been carried out, and new dressing rooms for both teams and offices had been erected. Talk about the building of an American city!*

Inevitably, Hyde Road was unable to cope with City's continuing growth and the management realised a move was absolutely vital. During the 1921–2 season they planned to develop a new stadium – in the truest sense of the word – at Moss Side, and managed to prolong the life of Hyde Road until the start of the 1923–4 season. The last game at Hyde Road was a public practice match in August 1923. Afterwards it was dismantled and within a decade or so all trace had disappeared for ever, or so everyone believed. In the late 1990s metalwork from one of the club's multi-span roofs was rediscovered as the roof of a factory in Sale. The building has since been demolished, but another section of roof still survives today as a football stand at Halifax Town's Shay stadium. City sold the stand and a few turnstiles to Halifax for £1,000, and this stand remains a key feature of the Shay today, although since the mid-1990s redevelopment plans for the Shay have frequently predicted the demise of the stand, financial problems ensuring, however, that the stand remains.

The site occupied by the Hyde Road ground is currently used as a storage yard for containers and lorries, after several years use as a skid pan for the Hyde Road bus depot. In the main the site has not housed any form of building and so, when travelling past by railway towards Piccadilly train station, it is still possible to visualise how the venue would have looked when first found in the 1880s.

Significant Hyde Road ground information

The Main Stand

Erected in 1899 after being purchased from the Fulham Pageant for approximately £1,500. Destroyed by fire November 1920. The Main Stand had replaced an earlier 1,000-seater stand, built in 1888 by Chester's Brewery. Capacity: usually stated as 4,000, although this may in fact be the seated capacity. The stand was divided into two sections with the upper tier all seated. In front of this was a paddock, which may have held up to a further 4,000. After the 1920 fire the replacement stand was reported in several newspapers as having 25 terraced steps and holding 6,000.

The Galloway End

Roofed during the 1910 close season as part of a £3,000 refurbishment plan (an incredible sum; Huddersfield spent fractionally more than this on the creation of their state-of-the-art Main Stand the following year). This end of the ground was split in two by a railway loop line that ran into Galloway's boiler works. The area closest to the Main Stand corner became the 'Boys' Stand', but the same roof covered that and the main terracing. At the other corner, where the Galloway End met the Popular Side, the terracing was oddly shaped because terraced houses on Bennett Street cut into the terracing. Footage of the 1905 inter-League match between the English and Irish Leagues shows that large wooden screens had been erected at this end to stop those living in the houses from viewing the game. A plan of 1894 shows an earlier stand at this end of the ground. No trace of this appears on any photographs or plans post 1897. Capacity: *c.*9,000

The Stone Yard Stand

(sometimes referred to as the 'Hotel End', or Hyde Road Stand)

Roofed 1910. A large section of this irregular shaped stand was seated with a paddock in front, the rest was basic terracing. The seated section (closest to the Main Stand) was used to house the directors, press and season-ticket holders following the 1920 Main Stand fire. Despite its importance, the club were unable to erect any turnstiles at this end of the ground. Capacity: *c.*2,000 seats and 4,000 standing.

The Popular Side

Roofed in 1910. This terracing was home to City's most passionate supporters, and was usually the area where crushing occurred during big matches. Many important games saw supporters climb up on to the roof for a better view. The roof at this side only covered around three-quarters of the stand's length due to the proximity of terraced houses on Bennett Street. Footage from 1905 shows a small roof placed at the back of this terracing. It could only have covered a very small number of fans at the time. Capacity: *c.*17,000.

Turnstiles

The first pay box was erected in around 1888 at a cost of £5 15s. Due to a stone yard, the railway, Galloway's works, Bennett Street and a small area next to Galloway's Works were the only true areas available for turnstiles and entrances. This caused serious problems both before and after all major games, as the street was simply unable to cope with the large volume of people attending City's matches. At the time of Maine Road's demolition in 2003, at least 13 turnstiles were identified as being from Hyde Road, with four known to have been in place at Hyde Road in 1896, possibly earlier.

Hyde Road facts and figures

Highest official attendance: 47,500 v Burnley, First Division, 26 March 1921. Previously recorded as 40,000, it is now known City submitted an attendance of 47,500 in the days after the game. The actual attendance was probably between 50,000 to 55,000 as fans had smashed down gates to get in. Second highest attendance was recorded as 41,709 for the FA Cup tie with Sunderland on 1 February 1913.
First game: Ardwick v Hooley Hill (Denton) 17 September 1887.
First Football League game: 3 September 1892 v Bootle.
Last Football League game: 28 April 1923 v Newcastle United.
Highest average attendance: *c.*31,020, 1920–21
Hyde Road progressive capacity: 1887 – 4,000
1888 – 7,000
1891 – 10,000
1892 – 20,000
1896 – 25,000
1899 – 30,000
1904 – 40,000
1910 – 40,000 (covered accommodation for 35,000)
1920 – 45,000
1921 – 40,000

Maine Road, Moss Side 1923–2003

Regarded by many as the spiritual home of Manchester City, Maine Road opened in 1923 as the leading League ground in the country. Constructed at the same time as Wembley Stadium by the same builders, Sir Robert McAlpine, with the aim of developing an 'English Hampden', Maine Road opened in August 1923.

The Main Stand's framework as seen from the Scoreboard End corner.

The first Mancunians had heard of the new stadium was on 9 May 1922, when the Blues announced incredible plans to develop what they believed would be the greatest stadium in England. The 16.25 acre site was purchased for £5,550 and the original plans outlined that Maine Road would be developed in two phases, with the first seeing the construction of an 85,000 capacity ground with one huge seated grandstand and terracing on the other three sides. The second phase was to see the terracing extended and then roofed to provide covered accommodation for a remarkable 120,000.

The sensible capacity of Maine Road at the time of opening was probably around 80,000, though City's management felt it could hold 90,000, and *The Topical Times Sporting Annual* for 1934–35 stated a figure of 86,000.

In the main, newspaper reports of the opening match – a 2–1 victory over Sheffield United on 25 August 1923 – focussed on the stadium rather than the game with the *Manchester Guardian* particularly impressed. The newspaper provided a whole range of statistics on the venue, making note of the size of the tunnels and of the terracing, especially the Popular Side (latter day Kippax) of the ground, where there were 110 tiers of steps at its highest point. It seemed the most fantastic venue:

> *Come in and take your ease but here, inside these barriers, you stay and by these great pits and tunnels, quietly and quickly you depart. This scheme in its simplicity and*

The Main Stand being built. The base of this stand remained until Maine Road's demolition in 2003.

> *great scale suggests power and force in the way that a pyramid does, or a Babylonian tower, and there could scarcely be a better scheme to represent the passionate concentration of fifty or eighty thousand men and women on the fortunes of the field below.*

Referring to the Main Stand the article added:

> *The Grand Stand by itself is an elaborate mechanism only to be afforded by the rich town club. For long after the match was over curious crowds explored its many staircases by which the holders of all sorts of tickets are conducted without fail or confusion to their various seats. The topmost section sits aloof and remote at an incredible distance from the field. Like a squall falling suddenly from the hills, its clapping came at times in sudden gusts from far away.*

The *Manchester Guardian* reporter was particularly impressed with his initial view of the venue:

> *This ground is the last word in the provision of comfort and security for (and against) the explosive force of the great crowds that follow the League teams. There is something almost barbaric in the impression which, when it is full, it makes on the observer. As one comes on it suddenly from Claremont Road, a great rounded*

Maine Road photographed from the Platt Lane/Popular Side corner on the morning of its first game in 1923.

> *embankment towers up in front, and over it at one side looms the highly arched roof of a stand whose dim recesses cannot be discerned at all except from the ground level. Only the fresh green paint on the front of it, picked out with gold, detracts from the broad impression of size and power, giving a rather incongruous air of neatness and modernity.*

During the period since World War Two most football writers have claimed that Maine Road was designed as the Wembley of the north, and that the architect, Charles Swain, had

Blue plaque positioned on the Aces public house to commemorate the club's roots.

tried to match the London venue. In truth this is far from correct. Wembley was designed at the same time, although it did actually open a few months earlier, and because of crowd control issues at the first FA Cup Final held there Wembley did not have a good reputation in 1923. Some reports did suggest that City adjusted their plans as a result of chaos at Wembley – 'The lessons of Wembley have been taken to heart, and a feature of the ground will be six tunnels communicating with the terraces, giving easy access to all parts.'

The actual credit for the move to Maine Road must go to chairman Lawrence Furniss and manager Ernest Mangnall. At the time of opening it was suggested that the stadium should be named after Furniss, but the chairman clearly felt that no venue should bear the name of a living member of the club. Instead, the first time the name Maine Road appeared in print as the ground's name came on the morning of the game: 'The main entrances will be in Maine Road, by which name the ground will be known, for the time being at all events.'

During its first season the stadium demonstrated its worth. On 8 March 1924 a crowd of 76,166 – the highest crowd ever assembled at a football venue in Manchester at this point and still in 2006 higher than any crowd attending Old Trafford – watched the legendary Billy Meredith play for the Blues against Cardiff in the FA Cup.

A decade later the capacity was tested again when, for the first time in the history of the stadium, the gates were closed before the game. The official attendance figure was 84,569 – it remains the largest provincial attendance.

Originally only one side was roofed – the 10,000-seater Main Stand – but in 1931 the first stage of the club's development plan saw additional seating and a roof built in the Platt Lane/Main Stand corner. Four years later the second phase of the plan saw the roof extended over the rest of the Platt Lane Stand. The developments surrounding this stand actually increased the capacity of the venue as the Platt Lane Stand was extended at the back with wooden planks to square off the terracing. Assuming the record crowd of 84,569 had been the absolute maximum in 1934 (although a figure of 86,000 was more likely), it's possible that the capacity at the start of the 1936–37 season was around 88,000, or even a fraction more.

One of the myths generated by writers over the years is that Manchester City were never particularly good at making plans to redevelop Maine Road. This is simply not true. City were very good at making plans, but they were notoriously bad at turning those plans into reality. Architect Swain's original plans were to increase the size of the stadium by extending the three uncovered stands, and by roofing them in stages. The first stage was the Platt Lane corner, completed in 1931; the second was the extension of Platt Lane, completed in 1935; the third was the Main Stand/Scoreboard End corner (scheduled for 1939); the fourth phase was to cover the rest of the Scoreboard End (scheduled for 1944); and the final phase was to be the enormous extension to the Popular Side (latter day Kippax, due for development by 1950). The plans were put on hold with relegation in 1938 and then stopped altogether with the outbreak of war in 1939.

By the beginning of the 1950s Maine Road was still a major venue and continued to attract internationals and semi-finals, but the club recognized that covered accommodation and other facilities had to improve. The ground remained much the same as it had been in 1935, and then in 1953 floodlights were added.

In 1957 the Popular Side was extended slightly, roofed, and renamed the Kippax Street Stand. The extension was not as great as the one planned when the stadium first opened, but at least the roof meant the stadium provided covered accommodation for over 50,000 fans. No other Manchester venue had ever been able to match that, and few League grounds could compare.

The newly roofed Kippax soon became the home of City's more vocal fans, and supporters used to love to boast that whereas most other grounds found their more passionate support positioned behind a goal, City's occupied a full side.

In 1963 the Platt Lane Stand was seated with row after row of wooden benches. This meant that Maine Road housed more seats than any other British club – around 18,500 – something that continued throughout the 1970s and early 1980s with the development of the 8,120 capacity North Stand. Then in 1964 the floodlights were replaced with much higher – and more powerful – floodlight towers, and this was followed in 1967 by improvements to the Main Stand roof. The middle section of the roof was replaced by a rather odd looking construction which allowed an unhindered view for the directors and those in the most expensive seats, but did nothing to improve the look of the stadium.

In 1971 the original Scoreboard End was demolished and replaced by a new cantilever stand. Initially the stand was terracing, but after a year the management decided to turn this stand into a seated stand, and the North Stand was born. At the same time amazing plans to demolish the Kippax Stand and replace it with an incredible structure that would also allow vehicles to drive onto the roof of the new stand, where drivers would be able to watch the game from their own cars, were made. Former chairman Eric Alexander later revealed: 'the plans were aimed at creating a sort of private viewing area, while also improving facilities for Kippax regulars. The two big issues in the early seventies were the increasing shortage of good car parking spaces, and the lack of good quality facilities at the Kippax side of the ground. The plan would have improved both situations considerably.'

The plan was abandoned when Peter Swales became chairman in 1973. From then on Maine Road's development seemed to be piecemeal. Apart from security features such as the installation of perimeter fencing, little of note changed until in 1981 Swales announced a £6 million redevelopment of the stadium. The first phase saw the Main Stand roof replaced again, this time with a distinctive cream-coloured barrel affair.

This roof, held up by two enormous stanchions, was erected at a cost of £1 million. Relegation in 1983 caused the other redevelopment plans to be halted. This was a shame, as the second phase was due to see a much-needed new roof placed over the Kippax Stand, followed by the redevelopment of the Platt Lane Stand.

Apart from the replacement of seats in the Main Stand, the construction of a new scoreboard in the Platt Lane/Kippax corner and the increase in perimeter fencing, little obvious development occurred during the rest of the 1980s. The next significant development was the replacement of seats in the front section of the North Stand as part of £500,000-worth of alterations during the summer of 1991. The following year, the 1935 Platt Lane Stand was demolished and the rather smaller Umbro Stand was erected in its place at a reported cost of £6 million. This cost was viewed as being excessive, although it did include 48 executive boxes on two tiers. This stand was opened in March 1993 and during the summer of 1997 was renamed the Platt Lane Stand.

Maine Road in 1971 with the second Main Stand roof in place (top), and the recently completed North Stand terracing on the right.

With the Government and football's governing bodies insisting that terracing be removed at the top stadia, the Kippax Stand's days were numbered. By this time Francis Lee was chairman and he hastily set plans in place to build a new three-tier stand, housing the best facilities at any football ground in the north-west.

In April 1994, an emotional day commemorated the end of the old Kippax Stand, and immediately afterwards City demolished it and started the construction of its replacement. The new stand was completed in stages over the course of the following 18 months and Maine Road once again felt like a major venue. However, the capacity of the ground was significantly less than at any other point in its history, and was the lowest for a City venue since 1899.

The new 10,000-seater stand was officially opened by Bert Trautmann. Francis Lee's consortium had changed the plans for the new Kippax and Lee recognised that the rest of the ground needed serious improvement. He made dramatic and impressive plans to reconstruct the rest of Maine Road. His idea was to extend the other three sides of the ground to allow for a construction similar to the new Kippax, and a capacity of around 50,000. However, as the 1990s progressed Lee also became keen to negotiate with Manchester City Council and other bodies for City to become tenants of the new stadium being proposed as part of Manchester's bid to stage the Olympic Games. Three successive bids ultimately failed, but the city was awarded the 2002 Commonwealth Games.

While the bids and planning for first the Olympics and then the Commonwealth Games were occurring, Maine Road's capacity had to increase. Lee's Maine Road redevelopment plans had brought much interest from supporters, but clearly the opportunity of staging the Games meant those plans – Maine Road's last plans – were not carried out. Instead a temporary stand – nicknamed the Gene Kelly stand as fans became accustomed to 'singing in the rain' – was erected in the corner between the Kippax and the North Stand during 1997–98. This still could not satisfy the huge demand for tickets. Additional temporary seating was added in stages over the course of the following two seasons.

In May 2003 Maine Road staged its last game, and so, a mere eight years after the official opening of the new Kippax, and 10 after the Platt Lane Stand was built, Maine Road was redundant. During 2003–04 the stadium was demolished and is now in the process of being developed for housing by a company called Lowry Homes – interestingly the artist L.S. Lowry was well known for being a City supporter.

Various objects from Maine Road were salvaged by the club, including two of the mosaic signs originally positioned over exit gates. One of these has been reconstructed and currently forms part of City's memorial garden at the City of Manchester Stadium.

Maine Road was always a passionate home for City fans, but it was also a significant venue from a national perspective. As well as City's games, the stadium also hosted international matches (including the first World Cup qualifying match held in England); FA Cup semi-finals; a League Cup Final; the first European game played in England; concerts by the likes of Queen, the Rolling Stones and Oasis; religious festivals; rugby finals and even an international tennis tournament.

Significant Maine Road ground information

The Main Stand

Erected in 1923 when, at the time of construction, it had the largest roof span of any stand at any football ground in the country. Middle section of roof replaced during 1967 to provide an uninterrupted view for the Directors' Box and surrounding seats. Third roof erected in 1982, as the first phase of a £6 million redevelopment. The project was halted with relegation in 1983 and the original plan of having executive boxes suspended from the front of the roof (close to the TV gantry) was shelved. Final capacity: 8,466, original capacity: 10,000.

The Platt Lane Stand

Roofed and extended in two phases during 1931 and 1935. Seated 1963 (wooden benches). Rebuilt during 1992–93 and opened on 7 March 1993 as the Umbro Stand. Renamed the Platt Lane Stand during the 1997 close season. Final capacity: 4,548, seated capacity of old stand (*c.*1986): 9,702, highest standing capacity: *c.*20,000.

The North Stand

(originally referred to as the Scoreboard End)

Original terracing until demolition commenced in 1970. New terraced stand opened in 1971 and became seated in 1972. Final capacity: 8,527, seated capacity in 1972: 8,120, original standing capacity: *c.*18,000, standing capacity 1971–72 season: 22,000.

Above: The Kippax constructed in 1994–95. Below: The Main Stand roof is removed and the façade renovated during the summer of 1982.

The Kippax Stand

(originally known as the Popular Side)

Roofed and extended in 1957. Demolished during the 1994 close season, with the new stand opening in stages during 1994 and 1995. Final capacity: 9,882, original standing capacity: *c.*35,000, standing capacity in 1980: 26,155, standing capacity in 1990 (following the first safety recommendations after the Hillsborough disaster): *c.*22,000, final standing capacity (1994): 18,300.

Temporary stands

Temporary stands were installed from 1997 onwards, and by 2003 temporary seating existed in both Kippax corners, the tunnel between the Main Stand and Platt Lane corner,

In 1977 chairman Peter Swales headed this family photograph of the entire City staff, including players, on the forecourt in front of the Main Stand. Note: above the Manchester City sign a rectangle can just be made out. This was one of three original Manchester City FC mosaic signs. Sadly this was damaged during the mid-1970s and could not be salvaged. However, one of the others now forms part of City's memorial garden at Eastlands.

This photograph shows former manager Jimmy Frizzell and managing director Colin Barlow looking towards the Kippax Stand during the final day of the Kippax prior to the game with Chelsea in 1994.

Aerial photograph of Maine Road, April 1991, showing the 1971 North Stand (left), 1957 Kippax roof (top), 1935 Platt Lane roof (right), 1931 Platt Lane corner roof and 1982 Main Stand roof (bottom). Note also the present day site of City's Academy in the top left of the photgraph.

and behind the stadium control box above J block at the side of the Main Stand. The capacity of these sections totalled approximately 3,750.

Maine Road facts and figures

Highest attendance: 84,569 v Stoke City, FA Cup sixth round, 3 March 1934 (this remains a record for games outside London and Glasgow).

Highest League attendance: 79,491 v Arsenal, 23 February 1935 (this was the record Football League attendance at the time).

Highest average attendance: 42,725, 1947–48

Highest non-City attendance: 83,260, Manchester United v Arsenal, 17 February 1948 (this remains the record Football League attendance of all time).

First Football League game: v Sheffield United, 25 August 1923.

Last League game: v Southampton, 11 May 2003.

Other events: Maine Road has hosted many non-football events over the years from religious meetings to pop concerts. From 1939 to 1956 the ground hosted the Rugby League Championship play-off finals, with one attendance reaching the staggering figure of 75,194 (14 May 1949), and during the 1980s and 1990s Maine Road regularly held pop concerts. Some of the artists to play at the ground include David Bowie, Queen, Oasis, and the Rolling Stones.

Aerial photograph of Maine Road, 1994 close season.

Maine Road, 1995. Note how quickly the stadium changed during the early 1990s.

Aerial photograph of Maine Road, 1997.

Maine Road progressive capacity:

1923 – 84,000	1989 – 48,500
1931 – 86,000	1992 – 39,359
1935 – 88,000	1994 – 19,150*
1946 – 84,000	1995 – 31,458
1953 – 76,500	1997 – 32,147
1957 – 77,000	1999 – 34,026
1963 – 64,000	2000 – 34,421
1972 – 54,500	2002 – 35,150
1973 – 52,600	

* Note: 19,150 was the capacity for the first match of 1994–95 season; capacity increased after every game until 1995 close season figure was reached.

The City of Manchester Stadium (from 2003)

The first suggestion that City would move to a new stadium came in the late 1980s. At that time Bob Scott – a key figure behind the resurgence of the Palace and Opera House theatres – outlined an amazing plan for Manchester to stage the 1992 Olympics. Many Mancunians thought it was a crazy idea, but the *Manchester Evening News* focussed on

A classic view of the Kippax Stand during the early 1980s.

the story and eventually a front page headline – '£100m site for Blues?' – made the plan feel real. Within the article City chairman Peter Swales stated:

> *If it all happens and the stadium is built, it is something we have got to be interested in. It is at a very early stage. We have spent a lot of money at Maine Road and the new stadium would have to be something pretty special to make us move.*

The North Stand during construction of the City of Manchester Stadium in 2002–03.

The Olympic Bid committee have explained what they are trying to do and I think it is a very bold, adventurous plan to bring the Games to Manchester.

Club officials from that period have since stated that the plan was nothing more than a brief discussion, but as time moved on and Manchester's Olympic dreams grew, the idea of moving became much more serious. The only drawback was that Manchester had to get the Olympics first.

As we now know, the Olympics never did arrive in Manchester, although it's fair to say that London's successful 2012 bid was strong because of the efforts of Manchester. The bid did bring the consolation prize, if that's an appropriate phrase, of the Commonwealth Games. Francis Lee pushed to ensure City played their part in all matters relating to the stadium and, once he resigned as chairman, new chairman David Bernstein, chief operating officer Chris Bird and director Alistair Mackintosh focussed on the specifics of the stadium development and the move.

In August 1999 David Bernstein signed the legal documentation agreeing to the move and the following December Prime Minister Tony Blair laid the first stone of what was to become the City of Manchester Stadium. Considering that City had struggled on the pitch

The South Stand terracing for the lowest tier is being made during the conversion from athletics arena to football stadium.

The Platt Lane Stand awaits demolition, but the Main Stand roof has already gone. Maine Road 2003–04.

during the mid to late 1990s, and that 1999 itself had seen the Blues narrowly succeed in escaping from the third tier of English football for the first time, this was a major show of faith. Bernstein, Bird and Co. knew that City fans had remained loyal, and that Maine Road's permanent capacity of around 32,000 was woefully low, but fans feared that further struggles would see the new stadium scaled down.

By summer 2002 the stadium was a 35,000-seater athletics venue, and once the Games ended in August 2002, work commenced on reconfiguring the stadium into a football stadium. Initially the stadium had consisted of a couple of two-tier stands at the east and west sides, and a one-tier South Stand. At the northern end a large temporary uncovered structure – the new Gene Kelly Stand as City attendees at the Games dubbed it – filled the end where the running track curved beyond the boundaries of a regular football pitch.

The temporary stand was dismantled within days of the end of the Games, and work commenced on lowering the pitch. This was lowered by around 6 metres, with tons of earth removed. The lower tier was then constructed and the North Stand was erected. The capacity was raised to approximately 48,000 and, even though the Blues had only spent two of the previous seven seasons in the Premier League (City's worst ever spell on the pitch) Bernstein and Bird had committed the Blues to the move and the expense necessary to make this the leading footballing venue in the country. Behind the scenes, however, both Bernstein and Bird had resigned, with deputy chairman John Wardle replacing Bernstein and Alistair Mackintosh ultimately becoming the club's chief executive. Mackintosh in particular spent much of the 2002–03 season planning for the move.

The stadium was opened as a footballing venue on Sunday 10 August 2003, when the Blues defeated Barcelona 2–1. Nicolas Anelka scored the stadium's first goal in the 34th minute at the North Stand end, and four days later the first competitive match saw City defeat Welsh side Total Network Solutions 5–0 in the UEFA Cup qualifying round – the Blues had been awarded a UEFA Cup place via the Fair Play League.

Since those first games the stadium has continued to evolve. Seating changes have been made in many areas – the directors' box was reduced in size and additional seating has been added at the back of the second tier corners – and a television commentary box has been erected in the south-east corner of the second tier. A second television gantry was created at the front of the third tier of the West Stand as the main gantry, housed at the back of the third tier, was too high for football action, whereas it had been perfect for athletics. The West Stand has also been renamed the Colin Bell Stand after an internet vote.

Other developments include the creation of a Memorial Garden – the first of its type at a major footballing venue. The garden contains stonework from the Hyde Road Hotel, a mosaic from Maine Road and a tribute to Marc-Vivien Foe.

At the north end of the stadium the club have built a two-storey building housing the City Superstore, the City Social – a restaurant and bar open throughout the week – and the club's award-winning museum and tour, 'The Manchester City Experience'. The Experience has proved to be a highly popular attraction with visitors to Manchester and has already staged exhibitions on former players Colin Bell, Peter Barnes and Ken Barnes, and on supporters. The museum and tour are open daily, including matchdays.

The first football season at the stadium saw the Blues achieve their highest average attendance of all time, and in its first three years following the Games the stadium has staged international football, a UEFA Women's Championship game, a Rugby League international and concerts by the Red Hot Chilli Peppers, U2, Oasis, Take That and Bon Jovi. The Oasis and Take That concerts brought the largest crowds to the stadium as the size of their stage and the volume of people allowed on the playing area enabled the stadium to accommodate around 60,000. Oasis were also the first non-City organisation to play to sell-outs at both Maine Road and the new stadium.

The stadium has also won various architectural awards and remains the most awe-inspiring building in Greater Manchester.

Club secretary Bernard Halford with Gary James visit Maine Road during demolition in April 2004.

The City of Manchester Stadium as seen from the gas holder close to Phillips Park.

Significant City of Manchester Stadium information

The Colin Bell Stand

(originally known as the West Stand)

Erected in 2002 as a tier two stand for the Commonwealth Games. Basement area and dressing rooms were included in the original build below ground level. After the Games the pitch area was excavated and the tunnel was opened up and the lower tier constructed in 2003. The stand contains the club's main offices, the Boardroom and Mancunian suites, media facilities, and the Bluezone education facilities.

The North Stand

Built during 2002–03 following the Commonwealth Games. Previously a temporary stand stood at this end. Unlike the South Stand, this end contains executive boxes and the family stand.

The South Stand

Converted into a tier two stand after the Games, this end houses the Legends Lounge, away supporters and City's more vocal fans.

The East Stand

(dubbed the Kippax Stand by supporters)

A similar construction to the Colin Bell Stand as far as spectators are concerned, but corporate facilities are more extensive. The stand houses the Commonwealth, 1894, and

Citizens suites. It also is home to the Junior Blues/Live City, City In The Community, and the Development Association.

City of Manchester Stadium facts and figures:
Highest official attendance: 47,304 v Chelsea, 28 February 2004.
Highest non-football attendance: 60,000, Oasis concert, 2 July 2005.
Highest average attendance: 46,830, 2003–04 season.
First game: v Barcelona, 10 August 2003.
First competitive game: v Total Network Solutions, UEFA Cup, 14 August 2003.
First League game: v Portsmouth, 23 August 2003.

City of Manchester Stadium progressive capacity: 2002 – 38,000
2003 – 47,726

The City of Manchester Stadium during construction. The totally open end is the present day North Stand. Other landmarks include Grey Mare Lane (top left of main photograph, p106) and the gasholder next to the North car parks.

Matches to Remember

18 April 1891
Ardwick AFC 1 Newton Heath 0

Manchester Cup Final (played at West Manchester FC, Whalley Range)
The first significant trophy won by the Blues was the Manchester Senior Cup in 1891. For many sides in the Manchester area this was the most important competition of them all and, for both Ardwick and Newton Heath (present-day United), this was more important than competing in the FA Cup. Reaching the Final was a major landmark, particularly as Ardwick were still a relatively young club at this point. The competition had been established in 1884 and for the 1887–88 season a new trophy was created costing 60 guineas. That trophy is still being contested today, and in 2005 City defeated Manchester United in the Final at the City of Manchester Stadium.

Secretary-manager Lawrence Furniss saw progression in the Manchester Cup as a significant step for his side. The Cambridge Blues won the game 1–0, with a seventh-minute goal by captain David Weir. According to the *Gorton Reporter* his goal came from 'a long shot'. A short while later Ardwick were awarded an indirect free-kick after a foul on Davies. From the kick Ardwick sent the ball straight into the Heathens' net, but the referee disallowed the goal for obvious reasons, although apparently some of the Ardwick men seemed a little unsure as to why.

Both sides had opportunities in the second half, but Ardwick kept their lead and became Cup winners for the first time. Success in the competition encouraged the Brewerymen to apply to join the Football League. They were rejected of course, but this competition had helped establish a belief that Ardwick could compete at the highest level. As consolation Ardwick were admitted into the Football Alliance, ostensibly a rival to the Football League but more of an unofficial second division, and one of the Heathens' star men, Bob Milarvie, was to join the Blues a few weeks after this game. Milarvie became part of Ardwick's growth and their transformation into Manchester City.

Ardwick retained the Manchester Cup in 1892 by beating Football League side Bolton Wanderers.

Ardwick: Douglas, Robson, Bennett, Pearson, Whittle, Davidson, Davies, Weir, McColl, McWhinnie, Lambie.
Newton Heath: Slater, Felton, Clements, Doughty, Stewart, Owen, Farman, Craig, Ramsey, Milarvie, Sharpe.
Attendance: 10,000

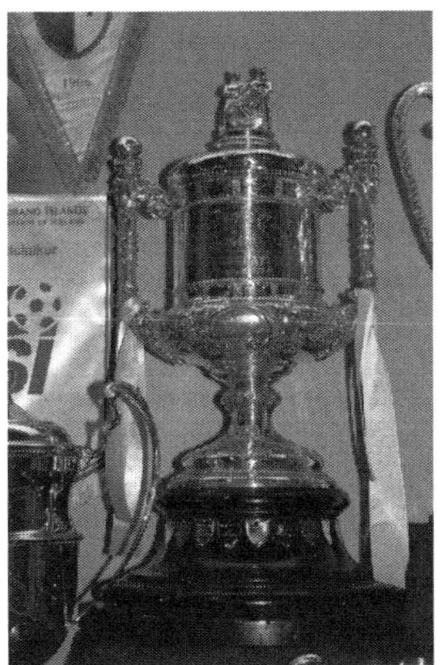

The Manchester Cup on display at City, 2005–06.

12 November 1898
Glossop North End 1 Manchester City 2

Division Two

On the face of it, a meeting between City and near neighbours Glossop may not appear a significant game in the history of the Blues, but this was an important match in the bid for promotion. Glossop had only joined the Second Division at the start of the season but their president, Samuel Hill-Wood (who later became a key figure behind the development of Arsenal and whose family still play leading roles at the Gunners), had a great deal of influence within the game. Under Hill-Wood Glossop were a decent side and a major threat to City's promotion hopes. As neither of the Manchester sides had ever been promoted it was crucial that City were first to find that success, especially as 1898–99 was to be the first season of automatic promotion.

A then record Glossop crowd of 7,000, with over half the attendance coming from Manchester according to the *Glossop Chronicle*, watched as City won 2–1. The paper reported that the game had been fairly even until the moment their player Donaldson was kicked by City's Bert Read: 'Donaldson looked dangerous when he fell near the goal. Read, in attempting to get the ball away kicked the centre-forward on the head. Donaldson was severely hurt and medical aid was at once called. Doctors Nelson and Sidebottom who were on the field at once went to the scene and it was found that Donaldson was severely cut over one of his eyes.' Glossop were down to 10 men for the rest of the game.

The score was 1–1 at half-time, with Colvin scoring for the home side and Billy Gillespie netting a goal for the Blues, described as: 'the softest I have ever seen' by the local reporter. According to the reporter: 'Williams got down to stop the ball as it rolled quietly goalwards, but he completely missed it, although it was going so slowly it hardly rolled as far as the net. A grave mistake, but Williams made up for it in the rest of the game.'

Billy Meredith netted City's winner in the second half, and at the season's end the Blues were promoted as Champions while Glossop finished second. Both sides made history as the first to gain automatic promotion.

Glossop North End: Williams, Lomax, McEwen, Colville, Evenson, Rothwell, Colvin, Gallacher, Donaldson, Pryce, Lumsden.
City: Williams, Read, Jones, Moffat, Smith, Holmes, Smith, Meredith, Gillespie, Dougal, Cowie.
Attendance: 7,000

---

23 April 1904
Manchester City 1 Bolton Wanderers 0

FA Cup Final (played at the Crystal Palace)

The 1904 FA Cup Final was the first major Final to feature a Manchester side and was

therefore a significant moment in the history of both City and of Manchester in general. Reaching the Final had not been easy, particularly as the Blues had never really made any form of impact in the Cup in previous years. In addition the sides they faced were either recognised powers in Division One, or sides heading for promotion.

Sunderland, who had ended the previous campaign in third place, were defeated 3–2 in the first round. Then came a 2–0 win at promotion-bound Woolwich Arsenal before the quarter-final with First Division Middlesbrough went to a replay, which the Blues won 3–1. Reigning champions and also eventual 1903–04 title holders the Wednesday were defeated 3–0 in the semi-final at Goodison Park.

The Final saw City face Bolton, who had been relegated the previous season and were clearly not expected to match City. To aid training the Blues spent most of the week leading up to the Final at Norbreck Hall, Blackpool, and travelled to London on the Thursday. They stayed at the Crystal Palace Hotel, West Norwood, and while they were there City's secretary-manager Tom Maley was asked by a London reporter what he thought the Blues' chances were: 'I expect we will win, but you know football is not an exact science like billiards. Look at the League. Why every team in it has been beaten by about six goals at one time or another.'

Led by influential captain Billy Meredith, City knew they could not take anything for granted. Meredith, keen to lead by example, made sure that he and his team were ready some time before the Bolton men. Meredith entered the field first, with Bolton seemingly playing catch-up, and then seemed supremely confident as he won the toss to determine the direction of play. He chose to play towards the southern end of the Crystal Palace ground, where the Boys' Band of St Joseph's was entertaining the City supporters.

The opening minutes were difficult for both sides as the surface was quite slippery, and City found it hard to cope with Bolton's bustling approach. City, playing in their traditional sky blue shirts and white shorts, were more used to a passing, stylish form of play. As a result Bolton looked more likely to score, and they tested goalkeeper Hillman on a few occasions early on. Hillman managed to protect his goal and gradually the Blues gained the upper hand. Thirty years later Herbert Burgess was asked for his memories of this Final and he focussed on the role of Hillman during this spell: 'The outstanding points of this great game to me are: the thump in the ear which Hillman gave to McMahon, knocking him senseless; and the much disputed "offside" goal. When Hillman had the ball covered he used to shout "right, boys". But on this occasion McMahon failed to get out of the way quickly enough and Hillman hit McMahon instead of the ball. And of course, there was Meredith's great goal, which never was offside.'

The Bolton 'keeper Davies was bundled over by a City attacker at one point – Billy Gillespie was a specialist at doing this and supporters loved his attempts at bundling the opposition 'keeper into the nets during almost every game – and this seemed to cause the Bolton defence to open up. After 20 minutes George Livingstone made a long, swinging pass to Meredith, who was on the right wing. Meredith seemed free to attack at will and he charged forward. From the goalkeeper's left he fired the ball diagonally across the goal out of reach of the 'keeper and it crossed the line close to the post.

In the days, weeks, and even years that followed, Bolton supporters started to complain that the goal had been offside, but on the day itself the players did not complain. They accepted the goal without comment. The *Daily Graphic* stated: 'The goal was not questioned and, to the accompaniment of loud cheers and the waving of hats and sticks, play began again. The crowds were delighted at the prospect of seeing the match definitely decided, and one of Manchester's supporters was so enthusiastic in his praise of Meredith that he left his seat and attempted to walk out to the field, apparently with the intention of embracing the Manchester captain. Two policemen reasoned with him, but he insisted on going, and at length five policemen escorted him away for a time.'

The *Athletic News* didn't even mention the incident in their main report: 'With only Davies to beat, the deed was done quietly but effectively. Bolton seemed to lag behind as Manchester played even better still, and when the interval arrived they were certainly entitled to their lead of one goal – if not more on the play.'

The second half saw no further goals, although Bolton became a little desperate as the match came close to its finish and put the Blues under real pressure for a spell.

The game ended 1–0 and Meredith became the first Manchester player to collect the trophy. Prime Minister Arthur Balfour made a speech saying how delighted he was that the game had been contested between two Lancastrian teams, and he also admitted his satisfaction at City's success. Balfour, it should be remembered, was a patron of City and had visited Hyde Road a few years earlier.

Years later trainer Jimmy Broad was asked what had been the secret of City's success: 'My lads won the Cup 'cos I gave 'em plenty of medicine and sent 'em to bed every afternoon.'

As City still had one crucial League game left, away at Everton the following Monday, arrangements had been made for them to travel straight to Liverpool after the Final. However, winning the trophy caused some to suggest they should return to Manchester immediately. They didn't and the homecoming parade was staged on the Monday night after the Everton game. Thousands took to the streets and the parade itself was the first major sporting homecoming the city had ever known.

In 1933 a newspaper article stated that the Cup Final ball was on display at Hillman's sweet shop in Burnley, but sadly the ball has not been seen since the start of World War Two.

City: Hillman, McMahon, Burgess, Frost, Hynds, Ashworth, Meredith, Livingstone, Gillespie, Turnbull, Booth.
Bolton: Davies, Brown, Struthers, Clifford, Greenhalgh, Freebairn, Stokes, Marsh, Yenson, White, Taylor.
Referee: A.J. Barker (Hanley)
Attendance: 61,374

1 September 1906
Manchester City 1   Woolwich Arsenal 4

Division One

When considering City's most important fixtures of all time, this game may not at first seem that significant. The game ended in a 4–1 defeat to a side that ended the previous campaign seven places below the Blues, and that simple statistic would make some question its importance, but the game is absolutely vital in the history of the Blues as it was the first League game following the mass suspension of City's side. Seventeen players, including several of the biggest names in football, were banned as a result of the FA's investigations into illegal payments at City, and the club was on the verge of extinction. The manager, chairman, and two directors were also suspended, causing a major overhaul of the club.

A new manager, Harry Newbould, had been found and he hastily found players to fill the gaps, with five men making their debuts in this fixture.

The game itself was to be a major test, especially as the temperature was said to be 90 degrees in the shade at kick-off. Understandably, the temperature seriously affected play.

George Dorsett in a tangle with the Arsenal 'keeper as he scores to make it 2–1, then (inset) he is being revived after collapsing.

Arsenal took the lead after 30 minutes, but shortly afterwards Irvine Thornley fell ill and spent the rest of the game lying on his back trying to recover from dehydration and sunstroke.

Shortly after Arsenal's second goal debutant Jimmy Conlin collapsed, despite wearing a knotted handkerchief on his head for most of the match – supporters seemed surprised that the typical Blackpool holiday headgear had failed to protect him.

From then on the match became desperate as City lost player after player. Robert Grieve failed to reappear at half-time, leaving the Blues missing three forwards, but Jimmy Conlin bravely staggered back onto the pitch in the 50th minute. Conlin's return seemed to give City a bit of life and George Dorsett managed to score, making it 2–1. Sadly, he collapsed almost immediately, leaving the Blues with only eight players on the pitch.

Arsenal dominated from then on and they managed to make the score 4–1. The Gunners' fourth was the last straw for the Blues and both Tommy Kelso and Jimmy Buchan were forced to leave the field as their conditions worsened. This left only six City men on the pitch, three of whom were making their debuts.

When the final whistle blew Newbould and his new players must have been relieved that the scoreline had not been worse. It was a difficult day, but more importantly it was also a sign that no matter what problems were thrown at the Blues, the club would always find a way of surviving.

City: Davies, Christie, Kelso, Steele, Buchan, Dorsett, Stewart, Thornley, Grieve, Jones, Conlin.
Woolwich Arsenal: Ashcroft, Croft, Sharp, Bigden, Sands, McEachrane, Garbutt, Coleman, Kyle, Satterthwaite, Neave.
Referee: A.J. Barker (Hanley)
Attendance: 18,000

---

29 March 1924
Newcastle United 2 Manchester City 0

FA Cup semi-final (played at St Andrew's, Birmingham)
Football's first true hero, Billy Meredith, returned to the Blues from Manchester United in July 1921 ostensibly as a coach, but the great man was always keen to play his part on the pitch, and during Maine Road's first season the 49-year-old Meredith found his way back into the first team.

Why he returned to first-team action is unclear. Some may have felt the City side was particularly weak, while others may have seen Meredith's inclusion as a cynical ploy to improve support. Clearly, Meredith's inclusion did increase crowds – the quarter-final with Cardiff attracted over 76,000 (the largest crowd for any fixture in Manchester at the time). The preferred reason for Meredith's selection is simply that the Welshman was actually playing exceptionally well and deserved to take the field at the highest level possible.

City's captain Mick Hamill shakes hands prior to the start of the 1924 FA Cup semi-final with Newcastle.

Prior to the semi-final the newspapers focussed on the possibility that Meredith was one game away from an appearance at the one-year-old Wembley Stadium, and there seemed to be a belief that all City had to do was give the ball to Meredith and City would defeat Newcastle. There was so much interest in the game that a movie company sent their news team to film the event for distribution to cinemas nationwide.

When the teams entered the field Newcastle came out first, followed by City, wearing scarlet shirts. These shirts had been deemed lucky during the season and City took every opportunity to wear the colours, although photographs of the side suggest the shirts were faded in parts after extensive washing. When Meredith came out of the tunnel the movie company and photographers concentrated on the Welshman.

This image shows Meredith taking to the field for his last game. This extremely rare photograph has only recently been discovered and this is the first time it has ever been published.

Sadly, despite the interest and hope that this would be Meredith's day, the City man hardly had a chance to impress, and his colleagues rarely had the opportunity to control the game. They did have a goal disallowed in the first half, but shortly before half-time Newcastle took the lead 1–0 with a goal from Neil Harris. According to the *Daily Dispatch*: 'Just as City were congratulating themselves on a goalless first half against the wind, he scored. Went for a wash and brush up, came back, and scored again. After which Newcastle seemed to think the spectators might like to join in, which was very inconsiderate as the City forwards got stiff necks through watching the ball go over the grandstand.'

Meredith and the other City men were frustrated with Newcastle's tactics. The Geordies were happy with a 2–0 lead and City had little chance of scoring while the ball was constantly being sent into the stands. Meredith became irritated by his lack of opportunity, and one report focussed on his impatience: 'Meredith had many idle moments, although he clapped his hands to tell his colleagues that he was still on the field.'

The semi-final may have ended in defeat but Meredith's appearance just three months short of his 50th birthday means this game remains a record-breaking match.

Newcastle United: Mutch, Hampson, Hudspeth, Mooney, Spencer, Gibson, Low, Cowan, Harris, McDonald, Seymour.
City: Mitchell, Cookson, Fletcher, Hamill, Pringle, Wilson, Meredith, Roberts, Browell, Barnes, Johnson.
Referee: Unknown
Attendance: 50,039

Jimmy McMullan is being introduced to the king by Lawrence Furniss prior to the 1926 Final.

7 May 1927
Manchester City 8 Bradford City 0

Division Two

This wonderful victory turned out to be one of City's most frustrating days. It was one of those days when supporters would use the phrase 'Typical City'. This phrase may seem rather negative to some, but supporters use this to try and find a reason for disappointments and surprise results. In many ways 'Typical City' helps to prevent fans from getting too despondent and in a sense is therapeutic. Better to blame 'Typical City' than become angry.

This game with Bradford came on the last day of the season in Division Two. City and Portsmouth were on equal points and competing for the second promotion place and, with Portsmouth having the better goal average (82 for and 48 against, with an average of 1.708 as opposed to City's 100 for, 61 against at an average of 1.639), the pressure was on the Blues to achieve a high-scoring win. The crowd for this game was officially recorded as just under 50,000, although newspapers of the period said that this was the total of those that had paid on the day and did not include season-ticket holders and others who had pre-booked. When those numbers were added the attendance was probably around 53,000.

Within six minutes of the start City took the lead through Bell, as described by the *Athletic News*: 'Bell improved upon an inspiring piece of play by Roberts and swung a ball into the goalmouth which Boot caught but failed to hold, the huge assembly was delirious with delight. The cheering was deafening. Ten minutes later another peal of thunder announced a second success, and as fine a goal as anyone could wish to see. All the time in the sweltering heat the City had been playing football of the finest quality, and at an amazing pace. Their manoeuvring was bewildering, and their forwards were as nippy and as virile as they were clever.' The second was scored with a left-foot drive by Johnson and then a third came from Hicks after 30 minutes.

At half-time City heard that the Portsmouth-Preston game had commenced 15 minutes later and that Preston were winning, so all looked well. After 52 minutes Broadhurst provided the fourth City goal via a fine long range shot. Roberts made it five six minutes later, then with 24 minutes remaining Johnson made it six. According to *The Pilgrim*: '[City] were even more dominating than they had been in the first, and one almost felt sorry for Bradford, who were metaphorically torn to ribbons. Their defence was completely disorganised. All they could do was to kick at random, and except for two occasions their forwards never got a look in.'

Everyone now believed City were home and dry although, as with so many occasions in City's history, there appeared to be confused messages coming from the other game. Some heard that Portsmouth were now leading 4–1, while others thought Preston had increased their lead.

In the 81st minute of City's game Johnson completed his hat-trick with a penalty awarded after Broadhurst was tripped, and in the final minute of the match Broadhurst made the total eight. Seconds later the whistle sounded and supporters surged onto the pitch to greet their City heroes. The police helped make a path for the players back to the dressing room as fans congratulated them on 'getting back', as the *Athletic News* put it.

The band started playing *Auld Lang Syne* and then the news came through that Portsmouth were still playing and were winning 4–1. Those that knew how to calculate goal average were frantically trying to work out what this meant, while on the south coast the Portsmouth management seemed to know that they only needed one more goal to achieve promotion. The Fratton Park crowd began singing *To Be A Farmer's Boy* – a song sung to their hero the ex-dairy farmer Willie Haines – and it wasn't long before Haines netted his fourth and Portsmouth's fifth.

A few minutes later City were officially told of the result by ticker-tape. Portsmouth were promoted by the narrowest goal average margin in history. Their average equalled 1.7755, while City's was 1.7705. One more City goal would have given the Blues that vital second promotion spot.

The *Athletic News* summed it up appropriately: 'By some infinitesimal fraction of a goal they have to go through it all again. Joy was turned to a disappointment that could be felt, but everyone's sympathy was extended to the players and the club. Never has there been such a cruel blow of fate in the history of the League.'

'More than once has goal average decided the promotion race, but never has there been a finer fight than this, and never has a club had such a distressing experience as the City. To lose their position in the First Division by their failure to convert a penalty kick in their concluding match one season, and miss promotion by such a slender margin the next, after running up such a score, is without parallel.' Typical City!

City: Gray, Cookson, McCloy, Pringle, Cowan, McMullan, Bell, Roberts, Broadhurst, Johnson, Hicks.
Bradford City: Boot, Russell, Watson, Knox, Bancroft, Poole, McMillan, Patterson, Alcock, Battes, Wright.
Referee: A. Platts (Castleford)
Attendance: 49,384

---

28 April 1934
Manchester City 2 Portsmouth 1

FA Cup Final (played at Wembley Stadium)
The 1934 Final was described as 'the greatest final ever' in the *Manchester Evening News*, while another reporter, Capel Kirby, called it 'the most amazing final ever played at Wembley'. Four City men made the headlines – goalscorer Fred Tilson, entertainer Ernie Toseland, goalkeeper Frank Swift and popular captain Sam Cowan. Swift had only made his debut the previous Christmas and was still very much learning his trade. He had been very nervous pre-match and the Final was his biggest test, but he came through with flying colours.

When the game commenced the conditions were poor. The ground was wet and players from both sides struggled in the opening minutes. Little quality football was played, then Alec

Sam Cowan as part of an advertising campaign – 'City trained on Shredded Wheat'.

Herd started to make a run. It looked as if City would get their first real chance, but Herd was fouled. According to the *Manchester Evening News*: 'Herd was bowled over and carried off amid a storm of booing, a rare happening at Wembley. Herd was placed on a stretcher and attended by an army of ambulancemen. The clever little Scot appeared to have hurt his right leg, and the booing took a louder note when a minute later Toseland was fouled.'

'Busby took the kick and fired over the bar, and before play resumed Herd returned to the field to a tempest of cheering. There was no doubting which side had the bigger following.'

As the conditions were wet, City's inexperienced 'keeper Swift was uncertain whether he should put on his gloves or not – goalkeepers tried not to wear their gloves if possible in those days as they felt that gloves actually reduced their hold on the ball. Swift noticed that the experienced Portsmouth 'keeper had chosen to keep his gloves off, so Swift felt satisfied that he didn't need to wear his. It turned out to be a big mistake and after about 30 minutes Swift blamed himself when Portsmouth took the lead. According to Swift, writing about the game 14 years later, he failed to hold the ball, but the match reports from the day tell a different story: '[Rutherford] shot wretchedly but it counted a goal. The ball was a shade to Swift's right and the goalkeeper dived full length instead of stooping. He went down, moreover too late for a comparatively simple ground shot and the ball passed under him.'

Whatever the truth of the goal, Swift certainly felt responsible. At half-time the City men realised that their 'keeper needed to lift his spirits if they were to find a way back. Fred Tilson tried to lighten the mood in the dressing room by telling Swift: 'Tha' doesn't need to worry. I'll plonk two in next half.'

In the second half City attacked as they searched for an equaliser. Ernie Toseland was in outstanding form, according to the *Manchester Evening News*: 'Toseland was indeed the prominent figure of the match and he must have despaired when he sent over a rain of centres and seen Allen and Mackie get the ball away in the face of the mildest challenges from the other Manchester forwards.'

Chance after chance came City's way as they attacked. Herd hit the crossbar and Brook came close, and then finally, about 18 minutes from time, Tilson managed to find the equaliser despite being tightly marked: 'Much of the credit for the goal went to Brook, who cut in in brilliant fashion from somewhere out on the touchline. He ran almost to the middle of the field before parting with it, and then found that Tilson, in the most intelligent

The two captains and Stanley Rous (referee) at the coin toss to start the 1934 FA Cup Final.

way possible, had run over to the left to strengthen the wing weakened by Brook leaving it. When Tilson received the ball he was far from being unmarked, however, but as he fell he shot and scored with a capital oblique drive.'

From then until the final whistle the game was almost all City's, although Frank Swift did have to pull off an amazing save as Worrall sent a powerful header goalwards. It turned out to be the save of the game.

The final five minutes saw both sides frantically battle for control, then Ernie Toseland sent a crossfield pass to Tilson. According to the *Evening News*: 'By sheer footcraft Tilson dribbled clear and a shade to the left of the penalty spot. He drove high and true with his left foot, and a better goal will never be scored.'

Tilson had scored the winner and kept his half-time promise to Swift. The young 'keeper started to feel the tension of the day and as the final seconds were counted down he began to feel drained. As the whistle blew, he turned to collect his unused gloves and fainted.

While the majority of players celebrated Cowan and trainer Alec Bell tried to bring him round, although he was still a little dazed as he collected his winners' medal from the king. Journalist Capel Kirby: 'The scenes in the Manchester City dressing room at the finish were indescribable. The players danced round and round in wild excitement except Swift, who at the sound of the final whistle collapsed from excitement and was none too steady on his feet when he reached the dressing room. Swift told me that everything went black, his legs seemed to part from his body, and the next thing he knew he was on his way to get his cherished Cup Final medal.'

The king is introduced by Sam Cowan and Albert Alexander Snr to the City players at the 1934 FA Cup Final. The king is seen here shaking hands with Alec Herd.

Another journalist, L.V. Manning, felt City were worthy winners: 'A Royal triumph for Manchester City. That is the best description of the amazing Cup Final at Wembley yesterday during which the king and 93,000 of his subjects saw the Northern team snatch the coveted trophy after Portsmouth had almost got it in their grasp. What a Final! With little more than a quarter of an hour to go City were a goal down and it was not till three minutes from time that Tilson got his second goal and won the Cup. No wonder the nervous strain was more than some could bear.'

City: Swift, Barnett, Dale, Busby, Cowan, Bray, Toseland, Marshall, Tilson, Herd, Brook.
Portsmouth: Gilfillan, Mackie, W. Smith, Nichol, Allen, Thackeray, Worrall, J. Smith, Weddle, Easson, Rutherford.
Referee: S.F. Rous (Herts)
Attendance: 93,258

---

24 April 1937
Manchester City 4 Sheffield Wednesday 1

Division One

To win their first League championship City needed two points from their final two games of the season. The first, at home to Sheffield Wednesday, was deemed the easier as Wednesday were struggling at the foot with Manchester United, and seemed certainties for relegation.

OOP FOR TA COOP.

The Cup Final this year will be remembered for three things: Everton's convincing win, the innovation of numbered shirts and poor play. There were no great thrills, though a half-hearted attempt was made to dispute Dean's goal. Neither was it a "noisy" Cup Final. There were times when the ninety-three thousand spectators voiced their approval loudly, but for the most part the play was watched keenly, but without excitement. Everton were the first to settle down and when their first goal came from Stein they became very confident and from that moment Manchester City never looked like scoring. For the second time the F.A. Cup has gone to Everton and Manchester City can console themselves with the thought that, though the trophy is not in their keeping, it will rest in a spot that is forever Lancashire. The Cup competition was this season distinguished by the early exit of favourite teams from the arena, notably the fall of Arsenal to Walsall at the outset. Still, book form was so far maintained that the two teams left in for the final at Wembley both belonged to Division 1.

Making the news: *The Illustrated Sporting and Dramatic News* featured Manchester City when they appeared in the FA Cup Final in 1933.

Despite the difference in League position, it was the visitors who dominated the early play. As the game progressed, however, the Blues started to gain control, with three goals in 12 minutes. Journalist Henry Rose, who in 1958 was to die in the Munich Air Disaster alongside City 'keeper Frank Swift, described the goals: 'The first. Percival to Doherty then a master touch by the Irishman to Brook, and that left of the wingman's seven-league boots almost broke the net.'

'The second. A "dummy" by Doherty to the Sheffield defence. A pass to Tilson, who scored with an effort that reminded me of the two he scored when the City won the Cup against Portsmouth. Then the third – the gem of the lot. I never want to see a better. Forgive me but truth must bring in Doherty's name again. He started it at the halfway line. A dribble for twenty yards, a cross pass to Tilson. Another dribble. A cross pass to Doherty. Back again, and again, and a crashing shot home by Doherty.'

That third goal had started with Swift providing one of his famous 'lofty' clearances to set the Blues up. Doherty gained possession in midfield and he and Tilson charged through the Wednesday defence with a rapid interchange of passes. They travelled well over 40 yards, and entered the Wednesday penalty area. Tilson made the final pass, then Doherty whipped it into the net. One report described it as 'one of the finest goals scored on any ground'. The players congratulated Swift for his part in such a great goal, while at half-time the crowd gave the entire team a tremendous ovation.

Wednesday managed to fight back a little in the second half and Swift was forced to make a brilliant save. Further pressure followed before Wednesday made it 3–1 with a goal from Rimmer. In the final minutes of the game Eric Brook scored the fourth. Rose: 'His second – the last of the game – was from the centre forward position from a pass by – you've guessed it – Doherty.'

At the whistle, there was a mass pitch invasion and the crowd sang, shouted, and cheered. Captain Sam Barkas, manager Wilf Wild, and chairman Bob Smith came out to make speeches, with Barkas focussing on the team's spirit: 'We have all pulled together. We have been a happy family, and that is one of the secrets of our success.'

City's first League Championship was thoroughly deserved, with the Blues going a record 22 games without defeat. Henry Rose, the most respected journalist of the period, seemed delighted: 'Manchester staged a miniature Wembley all on its own on Saturday. Excited "fans" swarmed over the field – policemen lost their helmets. Manchester City had won the championship for the first time in their history. Great stuff. And how they won it!'

Two particularly satisfied men present that day were City president Lawrence Furniss and vice-chairman Albert Alexander Snr. Furniss had been the club's first secretary-manager and a player with Gorton in the 1880s, while Alexander had been a key figure at the club from their time as Ardwick AFC. Both men knew what this success meant to Mancunians. On the same day Manchester United lost 1–0 at West Bromwich Albion and, together with City's opponents Wednesday, were relegated.

City: Swift, Clark, Barkas, Percival, Marshall, Bray, Toseland, Herd, Tilson, Doherty, Brook.
Sheffield Wednesday: Smith, Ashley, Catlin, Grosvenor, Hanford, Burrows, Luke, Robinson, Dewar, Drury, Rimmer.
Referee: R.W. Blake (Middlesbrough)
Attendance: 50,985

---

5 May 1956
Birmingham City 1 Manchester City 3

FA Cup Final (played at Wembley Stadium)
After the 1955 FA Cup Final defeat captain Roy Paul vowed City would return to Wembley in 1956, and throughout the following year he seemed determined to lead by example. Of course he was successful and the 1956 Final became a highly memorable and significant moment in the club's history.

Pre-match much of the talk had focussed on Don Revie. Revie had been in and out of favour with manager Les McDowall and wouldn't have played had Billy Spurdle been fit. In the end Revie, according to some newspapers, was by far City's best player. According to John Thickett, writing in the *Manchester Evening News*: 'Revie was the man of the match. It was his genius that steadied an erratic attack. It was he who inspired a bewildering sequence of positional changes that utterly confused a rocky Birmingham defence. It was Revie who brought the best out of a leg-troubled Johnstone and laid on that early morale-boosting goal. His class stood out as vividly as traffic-light red.'

After only two minutes and 47 seconds Joe Hayes scored with a left foot drive. Don Revie had played his part in the move. Former goalkeeper Frank Swift, writing for the *News of the World*, reported: 'Only three minutes had ticked by when Revie, in his old deep centre forward role, gave red faces to half of Manchester. The half who were against his playing in the Final! He laid the foundations of his side's convincing 3–1 win when he swept out a lovely pass to left winger Roy Clarke, raced in to collect the return and cutely backheeled a gilt edged chance for Joe Hayes. And Joey put the ball in the proper place – Birmingham's net!'

A Birmingham player bounces the ball against the wall while City players gather around manager Les McDowall for some last minute comments, 1956.

The goal rocked Birmingham for a while and four corners and another fine effort from Hayes, saved by Birmingham's Merrick, all came within 10 minutes. Despite the pressure Birmingham equalised in the 14th minute. The score remained 1–1 until the 65th minute when a throw-in by Ken Barnes reached Don Revie. Revie played the ball to Bobby Johnstone, and then rapid passes between Johnstone, Barnes and Dyson seemed to stretch Birmingham. Jack Dyson managed to force his way through before slotting the ball past an advancing Merrick. The players celebrated wildly but Paul insisted they keep their composure. Two minutes later Bobby Johnstone scored City's third and became the first player to score in successive Wembley Finals.

A Paul-inspired City managed to keep control for much of the next 10 minutes, then disaster struck. Goalkeeper Bert Trautmann was injured in a collision with Birmingham's Murphy. In the days before substitutes were allowed this gave City only two options – play with 10 men or try to keep the ball away from their in pain 'keeper. The decision was taken by Trautmann himself to stay on the field and so City tried to keep the ball away.

Scenting an opening Birmingham pushed forward, although journalist John Trickett felt they lacked punch: 'Even when Trautmann was reeling drunkenly on his goal line after a nasty knock on his head the Brum forwards never so much as took the trouble to try and pull the game around. Birmingham collapsed like a pricked balloon.'

Somehow, despite another collision, Trautmann managed to hold on until the final whistle. Journalist Eric Thornton, writing for the following Monday's *Manchester Evening News*, described his post-match discussion with the 'keeper: 'I will never forget helping

Roy Paul receiving the FA Cup from the Queen in 1956.

trainer Barnett with a dressing room massage to ease the pain in Trautmann's neck at the end of the Wembley triumph. He put both his great hands on my shoulders and said, 'The pain stabs right through me…' Came a second's pause. Then he added, 'But it's worth it. I don't care if the pain's like a red-hot poker. I know I've got that Cup medal in my wallet.' In the days that followed tests proved that Trautmann had actually seriously damaged his

The victorious 1956 team are seen about to leave London for Manchester.

Ken Barnes, Joe Hayes, Dave Ewing, Roy Paul and hidden Roy Clarke, 1956.

neck. In fact, the doctors of the period announced that he had, in effect, broken his neck.

City, wearing their stylish maroon and white shirts, won the game 3–1 and the Final, which was watched by a highly significant for the period television audience of five million, has entered folklore as the Trautmann Final, although the game was clearly won through teamwork. Swift felt it had been a great all-round performance, but two players in particular stood out: 'I thought Hayes and Dyson rose magnificently to the occasion. They may have missed a few chances between them but they were always in the right position. Never before have I seen them use the open space so intelligently. City upset the form book because Birmingham were the hottest Cup favourites in years!'

City: Trautmann, Leivers, Little, Barnes, Ewing, Paul, Johnstone, Hayes, Revie, Dyson, Clarke.
Birmingham City: Merrick, Hall, Green, Newman, Smith, Boyd, Astall, Kinsey, Brown, Murphy, Govan.
Referee: A. Bond (London)
Attendance: 100,000

---

11 May 1968
Newcastle United 3 Manchester City 4

Division One

This victory gave City their first League Championship since 1936–37, but it had been a closely fought campaign, with the Blues needing to achieve a better result than reigning champions Manchester United, and contenders Liverpool, to secure the title. Liverpool were three points behind City, but had a game in hand, to be played on 15 May at Stoke, and were at home to Nottingham Forest on the day of City's Newcastle match. Two Liverpool victories and defeats for City and United would send the title to Anfield. United were at home to lowly Sunderland. Most neutrals, when working out the possibilities and combinations, assumed the title belonged to Matt Busby's side simply because they did not expect City to beat Newcastle and United to fail on the same day.

On the face of it, it looked as if Newcastle had little to play for on this final day, but there was the possibility of a European place in the Fairs Cup (predecessor of the UEFA Cup). It was a complicated entry procedure whereby a place was allocated to the highest placed side that hadn't qualified for Europe via other means, but only one side from each city was allowed to enter. So Newcastle had an advantage over the London clubs, Manchester sides, and Merseysiders. Prior to the match it was impossible to work out all the permutations, but Newcastle knew they had to finish as high as possible to stand a chance of entry.

Malcolm Allison and Joe Mercer worked hard to ensure the players were not overawed by the occasion, and when play commenced City seemed to have a determination and spirit that few sides could hope to match. After only 13 minutes Mike Summerbee opened the scoring. Summerbee: 'The surface was good on the wings and in the middle, but it was bumpy in the goalmouths. This ball came through from the right. If it had been a flat surface, I would have struggled to score, but as Willie McFaul came out of his goal, the ball bobbled and I was able to flick it over him.'

The Geordies played with conviction and Bryan 'Pop' Robson netted an equaliser. For a spell the Geordies seemed to have the upper hand, and on 30 minutes City captain Tony Book cleared a header from Wyn Davies off the line. It had looked a certain goal, and it seemed to help City regain the initiative. Two minutes later Neil Young volleyed a glorious goal with his left foot from 22 yards out to make it 2–1. Incredibly, it was now Newcastle's turn to come back and Jackie Sinclair scored with a fine 15-yard shot. Another City goal was disallowed – Francis Lee was adjudged offside when Neil Young netted – and the score remained 2–2 at the interval.

At Anfield Liverpool were already winning 3–1, bringing them right into contention, but United were losing to Sunderland. Apparently, George Best had netted just before half time to make it 2–1. The scoreline was good, but perhaps the Best goal was the start of a fightback.

Despite the scores at the three grounds, the star City men still seemed confident. Summerbee: 'There was no way we were going to lose that game. No way! If they'd scored six, we'd score seven. That's how it was always going to go.'

Four minutes into the second half Neil Young powered home City's third. This was the moment when the fans became convinced the game would end in City victory and the 17,000 or so Mancunians started to sing as if they were stood on the Kippax Stand. Francis Lee had an effort disallowed in the 57th minute and then at 4.13pm – 27 minutes from time – the same player scored with a 12-yard shot and then raced into the crowd, arms aloft, to celebrate. The *Yorkshire Evening Press* stated: 'This was the finest goal of them all. Bell drawing the defenders and sending a through ball which Lee followed to hammer into the net.'

City still pressed forward while Malcolm Allison tried to share the excitement with the fans. Journalist Peter Gardner: 'Allison was on the touchline, clenched fist in the air in a gesture of triumph to the wailing City followers as Coleman shot just over.'

Four minutes from time John McNamee scored Newcastle's third and the final minutes were extremely tense, but City seemed keen to search for another goal. They certainly did not seem interested in wasting time and killing what time remained. This perhaps demonstrated the belief and the excitement generated by the side created by Mercer and Allison. At full-time supporters invaded the pitch to celebrate a remarkable game and a wonderful championship. The news elsewhere was that United had lost 2–1, while Liverpool had won 6–1. In the end the Liverpool scoreline didn't matter, and in their final game they lost 2–1 at Stoke – a victory would have given them second place.

The national media seemed to love City's success, with every newspaper stressing the qualities of the side and their view that the Blues were worthy champions. Frank McGhee (*Daily Mirror*): 'Even in the final match when tension was almost tangible and caution understandable they found the courage and confidence to go forward attacking.' Eric Cooper (*Daily Express*): 'It was this effort by Newcastle exceeding in skill and efficiency most of their victories this season, that made the superb merit of City's triumph all the more glorious. In such an atmosphere of fast, open football and fierce tension, mistakes were excusable, but City were never less than champions.' James Mossop (*Sunday Express*): 'A magnificent show. World champions in every sense. A credit to football. A credit to Joe Mercer.' Vince Wilson (*Sunday Mirror*): 'They were magnificent. A blue lightning speed outfit refusing to change the mood which spelled only victory. If the ideal championship winner exists at all, then this is it. It was City's championship. They did it in wonderful style.'

It was a magnificent victory for a truly great side. It's worth noting that Newcastle's defeat did not affect their chance of qualifying for Europe. Because both Manchester sides, West Bromwich Albion and Leeds had won trophies, Newcastle gained a Fairs Cup place on the 'one city one team' criterion ahead of Everton (Liverpool's third place had allowed them to qualify), Tottenham and Arsenal (Chelsea qualified in sixth place). They went on to win the trophy.

City: Mulhearn, Book, Pardoe, Doyle, Heslop, Oakes, Lee, Bell, Summerbee, Young, Coleman.
Newcastle: McFaul, Craig, Clark, Moncur, McNamee, Iley, Sinclair, Scott, Davies, B. Robson, T. Robson.
Referee: R.B. Kirkpatrick (Lewiston)
Attendance: 46,492

---

26 April 1969
Leicester City 0 Manchester City 1

FA Cup Final (played at Wembley Stadium)
This FA Cup Final appearance came midway through the glory years of Mercer and Allison. City were favourites as Leicester were struggling at the foot of the table and seemed destined for relegation, although there was also a belief that success at Wembley would spur them on in their final five League games.

Alan Oakes, Neil Young, Glyn Pardoe and Harry Dowd with the FA Cup at Wembley in 1969.

For Tommy Booth, the 19-year-old whose semi-final goal had brought this Final appearance, it was a strange feeling as he entered the field: 'My memories of the match are a bit vague because it all happened so quickly. What I can recall is how strangely quiet the older members of the team were when we were waiting in the tunnel before the match. And the deafening roar of the crowd when we walked out into the open. It really gets to you.'

The Final itself was not one of Wembley's most memorable games, although it did produce some fine moments, with attempts by Leicester's Allan Clarke, and City's Neil Young and Tony Coleman, early on. After approximately 23 minutes City took the lead.

Frank Butler, writing in the *News of the World*, described the goal: 'Summerbee rounded Woollett as he cut in along the goalline to put the perfect ball back to the unmarked Young. The inside-left just gave it everything with his left foot, and the ball was in the back of the net with goalkeeper Shilton sprawled on the ground looking a little disgusted at the hopelessness of his effort. He had no chance.'

Butler was impressed with the spirit the game was played in: 'It was a game that I am delighted to say was void of any vicious fouls. Both teams produced a good standard of skill and sportsmanship and entertainment. Special praise for Tony Book, Manchester's 34-year-old captain. He played extremely coolly throughout and produced a burst of surprising speed when necessary.'

In the end Young's goal was all that separated the two sides – something the City players knew only too well. After they had collected their medals they stood and watched Leicester collect theirs. Even in 1969 this was not a regular occurrence and the *Daily Mail* applauded City's compassion: 'The mood was equal to the match. Fear was hardly evident, bad fouls were few, and the sight of the Manchester men clapping the losers provided a warm afterglow. Manchester City are among the best Cup-winners of past decades. Leicester are far from being the worst losers.'

City embarked on the customary lap of honour and just as they started Francis Lee and Mike Summerbee paused, then shouted to assistant manager Malcolm Allison to join them. Footage of the day shows him smiling at them, then telling them to move on. Clearly the players recognised the role of Allison, and of course Mercer, and wanted to ensure full

Above: City bring home the FA Cup in 1969 and (below) the European Cup-Winners' Cup in 1970.

recognition was recorded, while Allison wanted to ensure the players enjoyed the limelight themselves. This moment said much about how the players felt about Allison.

City: Dowd, Book, Pardoe, Doyle, Booth, Oakes, Summerbee, Bell, Lee, Young, Coleman. Unused substitute: Connor.
Leicester City: Shilton, Rodrigues, Nish, Roberts, Woollett, Cross, Fern, Gibson, Lochhead, Clarke, Glover (Manley).
Referee: G. McCabe (Sheffield)
Attendance: 100,000

---

7 March 1970
Manchester City 2   West Bromwich Albion 1

League Cup Final (played at Wembley Stadium)
1969–70 was the first season when all 92 League clubs had entered the League Cup and the competition's importance had reached a new high. Success would guarantee a place in European competition, and City were determined to win their third significant trophy in as many seasons. Unfortunately, the game commenced with Albion's Jeff Astle scoring after only five minutes. City were stunned, particularly as they had opened brightly, but the conditions were extremely poor. Snow was piled up on the edge of the pitch, while the surface was appalling.

Despite the poor conditions, City thrived. Peter Gardner of the *Manchester Evening News* wrote how thrilling City were: 'Manchester City, you were magnificent! You were skilful, you were brave, you were courageous. And, above all, how you tried.'

'City attacked with the abandon of a side supremely confident it cannot lose – despite that early goal which might have wrecked lesser teams. They defended too, when the occasion demanded. Defended in depth to outplay Albion where it mattered most... in midfield.'

Gardner's view was based on City's fightback after that early goal. Attack followed attack and 14 minutes after the opening goal Francis Lee crossed to Mike Summerbee for what looked like a certain goal, but Albion's John Talbut cleared. A few moments later a corner from Glyn Pardoe was missed by Albion's 'keeper, and Lee sent a tumbling header narrowly wide.

Despite the pressure City could not find the net until the 60th minute when Summerbee, who moments earlier had been writhing in agony and was clearly injured, somehow managed to hook the ball goalwards. Bell headed to an unmarked Doyle who slid home the equaliser.

Further City attempts followed, particularly from Lee, but the game went into extra-time. Then, in the 102nd minute, Lee chipped a ball to Bell who, despite pressure from two Albion defenders, back-heeled to Glyn Pardoe. Pardoe flicked the ball over the goal-line to give City a 2–1 win. Pardoe told reporters afterwards: 'Wembley is not a bad place to score your first goal of the season!'

Lee was the most outstanding player on the day but manager Joe Mercer stressed how pleased he was with his entire team: 'This was very probably the most professional

Tony Book with the League Cup, being chaired by Francis Lee and George Heslop.

performance we have ever given. Physically, it must have been the toughest test ever. Just to play 120 minutes on a pitch that has begun to look like the biggest dump in the world was an epic performance after Cup-fighting a thousand miles away in Portugal only three days earlier. But to win in such a manner as we did was magnificent, and I cannot speak too highly in praise of the bravery of my men. We're absolutely thrilled about this League Cup triumph.' The saddest moment of the game came shortly after City's equaliser. Mike Summerbee, who had scored the semi-final winner at Old Trafford, and had achieved so much as he helped the Blues progress in both the League Cup and ECWC, became injured with an hairline fracture of the leg. Inevitably he left the field and was replaced by Ian Bowyer, but the injury was to cost him a place in the ECWC Final.

City: Corrigan, Book, Mann, Doyle, Booth, Oakes, Heslop, Bell, Summerbee (Bowyer), Lee, Pardoe.
West Bromwich Albion: Osborne, Fraser, Wilson, Brown, Talbut, Kaye, Cantello, Suggett, Astle, Hartford (Krzywicki), Hope.
Referee: V. James (York)
Attendance: 97,963

---

29 April 1970
Manchester City 2 Gornik Zabrze 1

European Cup-Winners' Cup Final (played at Prater Stadium, Vienna)
Reaching the 1970 ECWC Final was a major triumph although, incredibly, the game was not shown live on British television. Typically, even in 1970, any European Final would be broadcast, but the FA Cup Final between Leeds and Chelsea had gone to a replay, at Old Trafford, and as that was being played on the same night the BBC covered it. ITV, the only other television channel at the time, was unable to broadcast the game live, and so only highlights late in the evening were shown.

In addition to the lack of television coverage there were issues with the venue itself. The Prater Stadium was, at the time, more or less totally open, without shelter even for the directors, press and officials. As torrential rain came in bursts throughout the game it was not a pleasant night to either play or watch the game. In spite of the conditions, City were the first to make an impression and in the 12th minute Ronald Crowther described the action for the *Daily Mail*: 'When Young scored his goal it was only the culmination of 12 minutes of absolute dominance, and his breakthrough was the just reward for intelligent anticipation. Lee, playing with all the fire and fervour that will serve England well in Mexico, shook off three defenders out on the left and hammered in a shot of fearsome power. It struck the foot of the post and then cannoned off the legs of goalkeeper Kostka straight to Young, whose flick into goal was the merest of formalities.'

Four minutes later, however, Mike Doyle badly damaged an ankle tendon in a collision with Florenski and was left in agony on the pitch for two minutes as play went on around him. A reluctant referee eventually allowed trainer Dave Ewing on, and Doyle was carried

Francis Lee tries to keep hold of the ECWC he has just helped City win in Vienna, 1970.

off the pitch on his shoulders. City played on for six minutes with only 10 men as they tried in vain to get Doyle back to fitness. He was eventually replaced by Ian Bowyer.

Despite the loss of Doyle, City continued to dominate and three minutes before the interval Young broke free in the centre. As he attempted to dribble through the penalty area he was brought down in a sort of rugby tackle by the Gornik 'keeper. The Austrian referee Schiller rightly awarded a penalty and inevitably Francis Lee sent a straight, hard shot into the net via Kostka's legs.

Les Saul, a senior official in the Supporters' Club, remembers what followed: 'As it got near half-time with a lead of 2–0 we were highly contented, the lights had gone on as it started to get dark. We thought that we could feel rain drops but it got gradually heavier until it became a downpour. As there was no cover we just had to stay where we were. The second half started and the pitch started to churn up and become waterlogged. City found it hard going in the second half and after Gornik pulled one back we started to have doubts.'

Gornik's goal came in the 68th minute when a free-kick led to Oslizlo cutting in from the left. He sent a left-foot drive past Corrigan, but City remained in overall control against a team that contained seven international players. At the final whistle the City fans, who numbered some five thousand in a crowd variously reported as anything from 7,968 to around 12,000, invaded the pitch. As Gornik were a side from behind the Iron Curtain only around 300 club officials, players' wives and fans were allowed to travel to the Final.

Afterwards the players and management focussed on the support they had received. Mercer said: 'Our supporters, about 4,000 of them, stood in the pouring rain in Vienna to cheer us on. We are only sorry the rest of them were unable to watch on television.' Lee: 'We were all thrilled with the fans. But for them there would have been no game at all.'

Vice-chairman Frank Johnson announced that the Blues were thinking about pulling out of Europe the following season as they were disgusted with the choice of venue: 'This was an absolute scandal. Our fans had to travel a thousand miles to be soaked to the skin. It came close to ruining the whole thing. A European Final played before such a handful of people is ridiculous. And we're in the mood to pull out of Europe altogether if we do not get any satisfaction from UEFA.'

'We could have packed 60,000 into Maine Road for this match. But as it is we have lost money on the tie.'

At the homecoming Malcolm Allison was at his boastful best. After hearing the supporters at Manchester's Ringway airport welcoming the team with a chant of 'We won the cup' he responded with: 'We won another cup!' Later he told the fans in Albert Square: 'We are the greatest club in Manchester. I am only sorry ladies and gentlemen that we were unable to win more than two cups this year. We decided to let a London club [Chelsea, FA Cup] win something for a change!'

City: Corrigan, Book, Pardoe, Doyle (Bowyer), Booth, Oakes, Heslop, Bell, Lee, Young, Towers.
Gornik Zabrze: Kostka, Latocha, Oslizlo, Gorgan, Florenski (Deja), Szoltysik, Wilczek (Skowrone), Olek, Banas, Lubanski, Szarynbiski.
Referee: P. Schiller (Austria)
Attendance: Variously reported as anything from 7,968 to 12,000

---

3 March 1974
Wolverhampton Wanderers 2 Manchester City 1

League Cup Final (played at Wembley Stadium)
This match has become City's forgotten Final to some extent. As it came after the marvellous Mercer-Allison glory years and before Tony Book's 1976 League Cup success, its importance has often been played down, but appearing in any major Final is something to celebrate even if it is somewhat overshadowed by what follows.

City dominated the first half and seemed on course for victory as they tested Wolves' 'keeper Gary Pierce on his 23rd birthday. Despite the fine start it was Wolves who took the lead just before half-time. Kenny Hibbitt's mishit drive from the edge of the area beat City 'keeper Keith MacRae and crept in at the far post in the 43rd minute. It was clearly against the run of play, but it was a crucial time to score.

Early in the second half opportunities came City's way, but an effort from Booth was deflected off the goal-line, and a header from Lee went over. The Blues were denied again as Wolves' 'keeper Gary Pierce performed well. City were clearly the more powerful and skilful side and on the hour their persistence paid off. Rodney Marsh centred for Colin Bell to shoot the equaliser.

Later, the Wolves 'keeper was forced to make brilliant saves from Bell, Lee and Marsh as the Blues tore into Wolves, but as the game progressed the winner could not be found. Ex-City man Dave Wagstaffe was replaced with Barry Powell by Wolves and shortly afterwards John Richards fired past MacRae to give Wolves the lead in the 85th minute. According to Colin Bell it was against the run of play and partly City's own fault: 'I got the equaliser and we were never out of their half after that. Then, late on, a ball was played across our area, Rodney Marsh just got a toe to it and helped it in the direction of John Richards who scored the Wolves' winner.' Footage of this moment shows that Marsh was close to the touchline and that the ball appeared to hit the back of his foot and was diverted back out towards the edge of the penalty area, where Richards was waiting. It was an unfortunate deflection but it clearly did have an impact on the match as City were then wrong-footed.

City poured forward as they searched for an equaliser in those final five minutes but Wolves' defence was performing well and the game was over as a contest. As with their 1969 FA Cup Final appearance, the Blues proved to be good sports as, led by captain Mike Summerbee, they lined up to applaud Wolves as they collected the trophy, although Rodney Marsh felt particularly depressed by the defeat. He refused to collect his runner-up tankard and walked off, head bowed, towards the dressing room. Later, at the team's hotel, he insisted on drowning his sorrows from a paper cup he had collected in the Wembley dressing room, telling all who cared to listen that it was symbolic of City's – and his – failure. Later he sent a telegram to Wolves apologising for walking out, and later still, when he had calmed down, he admitted: 'I just felt choked. I could have prevented Wolves' winning goal, too. The ball hit my heel and went straight to John Richards, who scored.'

Wolves' 'keeper Pierce was named man of the match after his brilliant display, while all neutrals agreed that City had dominated the game. Tommy Booth: 'The reason we lost was because of their goalkeeper Gary Pierce. He was brilliant.'

The Blues had been unlucky to lose the Final but their performance deserves to be remembered as one of quality.

City: MacRae, Pardoe, Donachie, Doyle, Booth, Towers, Summerbee, Bell, Lee, Law, Marsh.
Wolverhampton Wanderers: Pierce, Palmer, Parkin, Bailey, Munro, McAlle, Sunderland, Hibbitt, Richards, Dougan, Wagstaffe (Powell).
Referee: E.D. Wallace (Crewe).
Attendance: 97,886.

---

28 February 1976
Manchester City 2 Newcastle United 1

League Cup Final (played at Wembley Stadium)
With Tony Book as manager City showed the same spirit and aptitude as they had under Mercer and Allison, and reaching Wembley in 1976 was the very least Book's side deserved. The side was a mix of youth and experience, and pre-match Book had a few selection

worries to contend with. Colin Bell was still out of action following his devastating injury in the November derby match, while centre-half Dave Watson was struggling with a slipped disc. Three hours before kick-off Book decided to take a gamble on Watson's fitness. Watson told journalists after the Final: 'At one time I thought I had no chance of playing. I slept on a board every night and I have done no training, just walking about.'

Every City player had previously played at Wembley apart from youngsters Peter Barnes and Ged Keegan. Captain Mike Doyle believed Barnes would prove to be a star: 'Peter is not only a tremendously talented player – he's got his head screwed on the right way. He just isn't the sort to get all worked up. In fact, I'll bet that he could prove the biggest success of the whole match. He's a natural. He does things superbly without having to think or worry.'

Doyle's words were prophetic as 19-year-old Barnes netted City's opener. A foul by Newcastle's Keeley on Joe Royle brought an important free-kick. Asa Hartford took the kick and sent the ball to Royle, who headed across the face of the goal. Barnes stormed in to fire a half-volley into the net to give the Blues an 11th-minute lead. The youngster, who that season won the PFA Young player of the Year award, immediately ran off the pitch towards the fans in celebration. Afterwards Barnes admitted: 'I was very nervous at the start but my

Dennis Tueart's overhead goal at Wembley in the 1976 League Cup Final.

Peter Barnes, Dave Watson and Dennis Tueart.

goal settled me down. But I am delighted for my dad (fifties hero Ken Barnes) I hope he'll let me have a drink with him tonight!'

Unfortunately, in the 35th minute Watson, Corrigan and Newcastle's Gowling all raced to collect a low centre from Macdonald, with Gowling managing to get to it first and stab home for the equaliser. It was a serious blow, but Doyle quickly marshalled his troops and all attempts by Newcastle to seize the initiative were thwarted.

After the interval City took the lead through a remarkable goal. It was an overhead kick scored by Geordie Dennis Tueart: 'Although I had my back to the net, I knew I had only to hit it right to score. That goal must be the greatest of my career. I didn't actually see it go in. But when I turned round I was mobbed. I'll be watching it on television tomorrow!'

Tueart's overhead kick proved to be the match-winner, although Joe Royle had had a goal disallowed. The victory meant that Tony Book was the first man to win the trophy as a player and as a manager: 'This was my greatest moment. It was a tremendous Final and Tueart's goal was something special... quite out of this world.'

Book added: 'Two weeks ago I met Gordon Lee (Newcastle manager) and we agreed that whoever won, it was more important for us to provide a good Final. I think we have done that.'

City: Corrigan, Keegan, Donachie, Doyle, Watson, Oakes, Barnes, Booth, Royle, Hartford, Tueart.
Newcastle United: Mahoney, Nattrass, Kennedy, Barrowclough, Keeley, Howard, Burns, Cassidy, Macdonald, Gowling, Craig.
Referee: J.K. Taylor (Wolverhampton)
Attendance: 100,000

9 May 1981
Manchester City 1 Tottenham Hotspur 1

FA Cup Final (played at Wembley Stadium)
'I was happy to settle for a draw. There were not enough passes strung together,' said Tottenham's manager Keith Burkinshaw after over two hours of exhausting football in the first match of this Final. City had been in control for much of the game and ought to have won, but Spurs seemed to have luck on their side. Pre-match the focus had been on the London side, with media hyperbole saying that City had no chance of success. There was 'Ossie's Dream' – the story that Argentinean Osvaldo Ardiles's dream was to win the FA Cup at Wembley – and the fact that the Final would be played in the Chinese Year of the Cockerel and that Spurs had won major competitions in years ending with 1 – a trend that continued in 1991. Everything seemed to focus on Spurs and City, who had enjoyed a miraculous transformation under manager John Bond, appeared to be there simply to make up the numbers.

The first half was dominated by City, with four corners coming in the opening five minutes. Hugh McIlvanney, writing for the *Observer*, felt that the Blues were more physical: 'During those nervous opening scuffles they had stirred their supporters by winning four corners in quick succession against a Tottenham defence frequently left ragged by uncertainty. The London contingent around the stadium weren't cheered by the sight of fouls by Power and McDonald on Hoddle, and Gow on Ardiles. Later, Gow was to employ his talents as a bone-cruncher on Hoddle as well.'

In the 29th minute an exciting series of passes between Dave Bennett and Kevin Reeves led to a fine centre by Ray Ranson. McIlvanney: 'What happened then will be remembered as another of the remarkable moments created by 100 FA Cup Finals. Hutchison, whose reputation has never rested on a capacity for thunderous headers, launched himself in a fierce horizontal lunge to meet the ball with great force and send it hurtling well wide of Aleksic from 12 yards out.' It was the 150th goal scored in Wembley FA Cup Finals and was thoroughly deserved, but it didn't last. Kevin Reeves: 'The game was not a classic, but I felt we deserved to win. Tommy Hutchison had scored a good goal for us and I felt it was enough to win it. Then disaster struck with Tommy's own goal – it was just one of those things and no one should be blamed for it.'

The goal Reeves referred to came 10 minutes from the end. Tottenham were awarded a free-kick 20 yards out and Osvaldo Ardiles tapped the ball to Glenn Hoddle, who curled it around the City wall. Corrigan knew he had the shot covered, but Hutchison moved. The ball hit his shoulder and was diverted past Corrigan and into the net for the equaliser. The shot would have gone wide, or at least been collected by Corrigan, had it not hit Hutchison's shoulder. Hutchison: 'It was just a freak deflection. I anticipated what Hoddle was going to do and made a run to cut it off. If I had been a fraction slower getting there, I would have taken the ball on my chest or headed it away, which was my intention. Instead, I got there too soon and was almost past it as the ball hit me.'

The game went into extra-time, but neither side could break through. Gerry Gow came

Tommy Hutchison celebrating after scoring in the 1981 FA Cup Final (with McDonald and Gow).

close in the final minutes of extra-time, but his tiredness prevented him from making the most of his opportunity. At the final whistle City felt they had lost the initiative and were certainly more disappointed with a draw than Spurs. The final statistics of the game showed that although both sides had made 14 scoring attempts over the two-hour period, City had eight corners as opposed to Spurs' five. In addition, the Blues were caught offside on 12 occasions as opposed to Tottenham's three. Everybody knew that City had been the more dominant side, but the cruel deflection off Hutchison had changed everything.

Ten years after the game Hutchison was asked if the goal still bothered him: 'It did at the time. I felt particularly sorry for big Joe Corrigan, our goalkeeper, because he was the best player on the pitch in the first game. And I was sad for Tommy Booth, who had to postpone his testimonial game the following Monday when he would have had a bumper turn out if we had won the Cup. But it has never bothered me since because I didn't go out with the intention of scoring an own goal.'

City: Corrigan, Ranson, McDonald, Reid, Power, Caton, Bennett, Gow, Mackenzie, Hutchison (Henry), Reeves.
Tottenham Hotspur: Aleksic, Hughton, Miller, Roberts, Perryman, Villa (Brooke), Ardiles, Archibald, Galvin, Hoddle, Crooks.
Referee: K. Hackett (Sheffield)
Attendance: 100,000

14 May 1981
Manchester City 2 Tottenham Hotspur 3

FA Cup Final replay (played at Wembley Stadium)
The 1981 FA Cup Final replay has become recognised as a classic, and in the opening minutes City showed their determination to succeed when Gow sent Ardiles crashing to the ground. He received a long lecture from the referee, and this time the physical approach didn't seem to work as well as it had on the Saturday. Tottenham worked well for the opening goal, which came after seven minutes from Villa, but City fought back almost immediately with a goal in the 10th minute. Ranson's free-kick was not properly cleared. Hutchison headed back to Mackenzie, who volleyed home spectacularly from about 20 yards out.

The match ended 3–2 to Spurs. Reeves: 'In the replay Steve Mackenzie scored a great volley and I netted a penalty in the 52nd minute, but Spurs had momentum and once Villa scored that goal it was clear they would win. It's nice that it's remembered as one of the great Cup Finals and it is also the greatest occasion I played in. I have to say though it is also my biggest disappointment. Losing in the FA Cup Final was devastating. There was nothing anyone could say to lift me. It's a day when you understand exactly how the fans feel.'

In the 72nd minute Garth Crooks toe-poked the Spurs equaliser and then Villa's winning goal came five minutes later.

Joe Corrigan was made the Man of the Final for his performance over the two games, but naturally he would have preferred to win the FA Cup: 'After the second match I was presented with the award by the Spurs manager Keith Burkinshaw. I remember thanking him and then saying something like 'Good luck in Europe next season' and at that very moment it hit home to me what had happened. I suddenly realised that we'd lost and that we wouldn't be playing in Europe. I was devastated. It was an awful feeling. I missed out in another way because the game went to a replay. England were playing Brazil at Wembley on the Wednesday after the Final and, although there was nothing official, I understand I was due to play, but the replay (played the following night) meant I couldn't play.'

Corrigan also felt that the game should have reached a conclusion on the Saturday: 'The FA Cup is all about the Saturday and I know we would have won had it gone to a conclusion. I never liked facing penalties – I think I only saved two – but that night we'd have won. No question. The Saturday was our day, after that it all switched.'

Paul Power, interviewed in 1985, felt that four years on it was possible to look back on the 1981 Final in a positive way: 'We lost the replay although again we were leading only to be denied at the end by that solo goal from Ricky Villa which always haunts me whenever I see it replayed on television. Steve Perryman went up to collect the trophy. I remember what our chairman, Peter Swales, had said after City had lost the 1974 League Cup Final against Wolves – 'better to have been there and lost than never to have been there at all'. That's the way I look on it now, although it was bitterly disappointing at the time.'

City: Corrigan, Ranson, McDonald (Tueart), Reid, Power, Caton, Bennett, Gow, Mackenzie, Hutchison, Reeves.
Tottenham Hotspur: Aleksic, Hughton, Miller, Roberts, Perryman, Villa, Ardiles, Archibald, Galvin, Hoddle, Crooks.
Referee: K. Hackett (Sheffield)
Attendance: 92,500

---

7 November 1987
Manchester City 10 Huddersfield Town 1

Division Two

This match has entered the record books as the highest scoring League game at Maine Road, although it was not City's highest League score. That was 11–3 when Lincoln were defeated in 1895.

Although the Blues won 10–1, it was actually Huddersfield who dominated the opening minutes. Former Blue Andy May was a member of the Huddersfield side: 'I had looked forward to my return and, like many returning players, I was given a good reception by the Kippax. Huddersfield had all the early play but we could do nothing with it. I remember Duncan Shearer having three clear cut chances and it really did feel as if it was only a matter of time. Then Neil McNab, of all people, scored against the run of play and we collapsed.

Manager Mel Machin and striker David White with cheques and the performance of the week trophy in recognition of the 10–1 victory over Huddersfield Town in 1987.

David White being presented with a match ball and champagne following City's 10–1 defeat of Huddersfield Town.

Hat-trick hero Tony Adcock celebrating during City's 10–1 defeat of Huddersfield Town.

At half-time it was 4–0 – that was bad enough – but we still felt we could do something, but the second half was much worse than the first. I know Huddersfield fans and some City fans have talked about goals being offside and so on, but none of that mattered. We were a well beaten side. And what about that horrendous yellow and black draughtboard kit we wore?'

McNab's goal came in the 12th minute and was described by Peter Gardner in the *Pink Final*: 'McNab, some 18 yards out, beat Cox with a splendid low drive following a throw-in from the right. Huddersfield shrugged off the blow, but still failed to take advantage after winning two more corners on the right. City remained prone to error and there were some anxious moments in front of Nixon.'

Tony Adcock, Paul Stewart and David White, the three hat-trick heroes in City's 10–1 victory over Huddersfield Town.

Despite the Huddersfield pressure City managed to increase the lead in the 29th minute when Paul Stewart scored a low-angled shot. Huddersfield started to fall apart. Five minutes later Tony Adcock made it three. David White scored the fourth three minutes before half-time.

As May suggested, in the second half Huddersfield had nothing to offer. Adcock scored his second with a right-foot shot in the 52nd minute, then Paul Stewart made it six after 66 minutes. A minute later Adcock scored again to complete his hat-trick.

In the 80th minute Stewart completed his hat-trick to double the half-time score, and five minutes later White made it nine. May: 'When it was 9–0 we managed to get a penalty and as the club's regular penalty taker I had to take it. Thankfully I scored, and even the City fans cheered. Then we conceded another and I think the referee blew before the scoreline got too silly! In the dressing room we were stunned. Steve Walford sat there smoking a cigar and simply stated: "looks like a bad day at the office" and there was nothing else to say.'

John Gidman had nudged David Cork to give Huddersfield the penalty and City's 10th was scored by White in the 89th minute. That meant that three City men had scored hat-tricks – the first time this had happened in the League since 1962 when Wrexham defeated Hartlepool – and caused Huddersfield to suffer their record defeat, but none of this would have been possible without McNab's determination and control early in the match.

General manager Jimmy Frizzell told reporters after the game: 'For once we gave our fans just what they wanted. They shouted for seven goals, then eight, then nine, then ten. And got them.'

City: Nixon, Gidman, Hinchcliffe, Clements, Lake, Redmond, White, Stewart, Adcock, McNab, Simpson.
Huddersfield Town: Cox, Brown, Bray, Banks, Webster, Walford, Barham, May, Shearer, Winter, Cork.
Referee: K. Breen (Maghull)
Attendance: 19,583

13 May 1989
Bradford City 1 Manchester City 1

Division Two
Desperate to gain promotion from the old Second Division – at the time the second tier of English football – City were in the second automatic promotion spot prior to the final game of the season. However, Crystal Palace were only three points behind and at this point in history the London side always seemed capable of powering their way to success. City's goal difference was better than Palace's by five goals but City couldn't afford the gamble of defeat. They had to come away from Bradford with at least a point.

Sadly, City being City they conceded a goal from Mark Ellis after only 24 minutes and for a while Bradford had control. The Blues seemed nervous and could not get back into

Goal hero Trevor Morley pressures Bradford during the crucial promotion game of May 1989.

the game until the final minutes of the first half. A little City pressure increased confidence, but when the second half started there were already rumours that Crystal Palace were winning by a big margin. The exact score somehow wasn't clear, but it was known that the Palace game had been delayed and that the London side would know the result of the City game before their own ended. This clearly gave them an advantage, but it also made everyone at Valley Parade aware that City had to ensure at least a point. They could not leave anything to chance.

As the game progressed City still found it difficult to make a break. Bradford more than matched the Blues and for the large travelling contingent of City supporters the tension was becoming too much. One fan raced on to the field and approached Paul Lake. He told him that Palace were winning 5–0 and that City needed to score. Stewards removed him from the field but it's fair to say his intervention did have an impact on what followed as the Blues charged forward at every opportunity.

With only four minutes remaining experienced goalkeeper Paul Cooper, who had been brought to the club as cover for Andy Dibble, quickly threw out to the unmarked Nigel Gleghorn, who sent the ball to cult hero Paul Moulden. Moulden passed to David White, who was racing down the wing. Trevor Morley was close to goal and seemed perfectly placed to receive the ball. Morley's memory of the moment: 'All I can remember is Whitey getting it on his left foot and clipping it in. I got goalside of the defender. The ball bobbled and I got very good contact. As soon as I did I knew it was going in.'

'I ran off and waved to the fans and as I turned round to the pitch there were none of my players near me. I suddenly got a feeling the goal wasn't allowed. I looked to the linesman and the referee for about 10 seconds. I was a bit confused why everyone wasn't jumping up and down. Then I saw a couple of the lads on the floor. It was a horrible few seconds.'

Morley's goal made it 1–1 and, although play resumed for the final minutes, on the terraces supporters celebrated wildly until the final whistle. At full-time the Bradford officials wisely allowed the City fans onto the pitch to enjoy their celebrations. These were the days when large fences penned supporters on to the terraces, but only four weeks earlier the Hillsborough disaster had made it clear that the fences themselves were a major safety concern, and Bradford had rightly taken the decision to keep the gates unlocked.

As fans and players celebrated on the pitch, the news filtered through that Palace had won 4–1, not 5–0 as many believed. Nevertheless, the result was irrelevant as City's point guaranteed promotion.

Bradford City: Tomlinson, Mitchell, Tinnion, Palin, Jackson, Evans, Campbell (Duxbury), Ellis, Leonard, Quinn, Abbott

City: Cooper, Lake, Hinchcliffe, Megson, Brightwell, Redmond, White, Moulden, Morley, McNab, Gleghorn

Referee: P.L. Wright (Northwich)

Attendance: 12,479

---

23 September 1989
Manchester City 5 Manchester United 1

Division One

This was the day when City's side of young hopefuls humiliated Alex Ferguson's expensive United side. City had been promoted the previous May, with a side dominated by players from the 1986 FA Youth Cup-winning team. Andy Hinchcliffe was one of those stars and he eagerly anticipated this match: 'All of those involved with City from childhood fully understood the derby. We were City through and through and had spent a good proportion of our life preparing for that day. Nobody needed to tell us how important the game was and I was as determined as ever to play well, however we were also very nervous. The opening 10 minutes were difficult.'

Very little actually happened in those opening minutes, until referee Neil Midgley was forced to call a halt as United fans, who had obtained tickets for the City-only North Stand, caused disturbances. The players were taken from the field for nine minutes as those United fans were transferred to the 'United only' Platt Lane Stand.

When the game recommenced any advantage those United fans had thought they could help create quickly evaporated as City seemed more determined than ever before. Hinchcliffe: 'It definitely helped us because when we returned we had the upper hand. We then started to tear into them and, I think all fans will agree, we absolutely bombarded them at times. Personally, I am thankful for TV replays because I can't remember too much about the specifics of the match.'

City were in control immediately and David Oldfield scored with a powerful 10-yard shot in the 11th minute. Less than a minute later Paul Lake and Trevor Morley tore a hole in United's defence. Leighton managed a save but Morley fired home the rebound for goal

This front cover shows Ian Bishop after scoring against Manchester United on 23 September 1989.

number two. The two City men had ripped United to shreds with ease as the expensive Pallister looked on.

United tried to get back into the game, but they simply could not cope with Bishop, White and Lake in particular. The Reds could not hold on to the ball at all as the Blues, who it has to be stressed were joint bottom of the division prior to the match, challenged. After 36 minutes Ian Bishop headed past Leighton after great work from Steve Redmond and David Oldfield, to make it 3–0.

As the players trooped off for half-time there seemed a marked difference in the attitude of both the Reds and the Blues. The City men clearly had not wanted the half to end, while United seemed relieved. Leighton in particular looked shell-shocked, although it's fair to say that one Red – Mark Hughes – seemed totally dissatisfied with his colleagues' performance. He seemed to feel the pain more than the others and when the second half started it was Hughes who briefly brought the Reds back into it. He netted a magnificent bicycle kick past Cooper to make it 3–1, but any thoughts of a Red comeback proved completely incorrect as City quickly re-established control.

What made this City dominance so special was that Alex Ferguson had spent a vast amount of money for the period on players such as Gary Pallister (£2.3 million), Paul Ince (£1.7 million), Danny Wallace (£1.2 million), and Neil Webb (£1.5 million), while the entire City side playing against United cost £1.9 million – some £400,000 less than Pallister alone. The United figures may seem small by today's rates, but the difference between United's expenditure then and the rest of football's top sides, not just City, was as large, if not larger, than the difference between Chelsea's spend in 2003–06 and the rest of the Premier League.

City's dominance continued and in the 58th minute the Blues attacked United's right flank. Anderson hesitated and Lake managed to race through and set the ball up for Oldfield to score from close range directly in front of the opposition fans in the Platt Lane

Stand. Four minutes later, as chants of 'Easy, easy' rang around the ground, a move set up on the halfway line by Bishop caught the Reds on the hop again. Bishop found White on the wing and the City youngster charged forward. He then swung over a pinpoint centre towards the centre of the penalty area, where Andy Hinchcliffe was charging forward. Hinchcliffe sent a powerful header past the desperate Leighton to make the score 5–1. Hinchcliffe: 'My goal takes some believing. I don't know why I set off when I did and when I see it I realise how great the build up by the entire team was. For me I suppose it was instinct because I still couldn't tell you why and how it happened. I don't remember heading the ball, but I do remember the feeling when it went in. It was an exhilarating experience.'

Hinchcliffe immediately held up five fingers to the United fans: 'I know that has become a defining moment to some supporters. I didn't plan it of course, but I'm glad I did it and I think it helped my relationship with supporters. I'd always been a Blue and that was my way of showing how much I cared. 5–1 is a great scoreline because the "1" proves United tried to get back into it – it wasn't as if we were playing a side incapable of attack – while the "5" shows the overall power of our own side.'

Paul Lake: 'When Andy did that he was saying what we all felt. He was showing the United fans what this game meant to us and, as a team, we'd been groomed for that day. All our lives we'd waited and hoped for that moment, and then it came. There couldn't have been a better result.'

The Platt Lane Stand quickly emptied, although the United fans did make quite a bit of noise, chanting 'Fergie Out' as they made their way to the exits, prompting Steve Bates to write in the *People*: 'They screamed "Fergie Out" after a shameful show by his £9 million team. But the horror story was a grim reminder that no matter how many millions he spends, United's defence remains one of the worst in the First Division, Fergie's stars were outplayed by City's stunning combination of skill and aggression. As goal after glorious goal flew in, Fergie sat hunched and hardly believing his stars were being so badly mauled.' The game ended 5–1 and the match entered the record books as the largest Manchester derby victory at Maine Road, although it is not the best victory in a derby match. That came in 1926 when managerless City demolished United 6–1 at Old Trafford.

Post-match Mel Machin explained that the difference in perceived individual quality didn't matter on the day as his side worked as a team: 'My players didn't really need motivating for this one. We wanted to win more than they did... that is the simple reason for our success. We never gave United an inch of room to work in, and when we had the ball we were quick to attack them. In fact, watching a video of the game, I found it hard to believe the team was going as strong at the end as they were at the beginning.'

City: Cooper, Fleming, Hinchcliffe, Bishop, Gayle, Redmond, White, Morley, Oldfield, Brightwell, Lake (Beckford).
Manchester United: Leighton, Anderson, Donaghy, Duxbury, Phelan, Pallister, Beardsmore (Sharpe), Ince, McClair, Hughes, Wallace.
Referee: N. Midgley (Bolton)
Attendance: 43,246

22 October 1994
Manchester City 5 Tottenham Hotspur 2

FA Premier League

Brian Horton was manager and Francis Lee was the new chairman as City developed a reputation for exciting and attacking play. Walsh, Rosler, Beagrie and Quinn were all popular Blues and Horton's side always seemed capable of scoring, no matter who the opposition. This match in particular seemed to highlight all that was good about the game.

The capacity of Maine Road was severely restricted as building work meant that the Kippax side of the stadium was still in the process of redevelopment, although the lower tier was fully occupied. Fortunately, the BBC's cameras were there, allowing a television audience of several million to enjoy the spectacle. Commentator John Motson, in particular, talked of this game as one of his favourites, and in 2003 when the Blues moved from Maine Road, he highlighted this as his favourite City performance at the old ground.

Although cult hero Rosler was to miss this match through injury, City still started in an attacking frame of mind. After 17 minutes they took the lead when Lomas made a run down the right before sending an impressive cross to Quinn. Campbell intercepted for Spurs, but Walsh managed to gain control and fired past 'keeper Walker.

City remained in overall control and, although Dumitrescu netted a penalty on the half hour, City seemed able to dictate play. Shortly after the equaliser Lomas passed wide to Summerbee. He then crossed to Walsh, who headed powerfully at Walker, before Quinn netted the rebound. It was that kind of commitment from City's attackers that made them such a wonderful side to watch.

Five minutes later Phelan knocked a ball to Beagrie who, after beating two Tottenham men, released the ball to Quinn to set up Walsh for the third goal.

At half-time the Blues seemed in total control, although Horton's City did have a reputation for slipping up a little in the second period. When Tottenham pulled another goal back a minute into the second half, supporters worried that this would be the start of a City collapse. Fortunately, Horton's attackers had other ideas and the goal seemed to make City stronger. In the 51st minute Walsh started a run from inside his own half. Somehow he slipped, but as he fell he managed to pass to Beagrie. Beagrie danced past Kerslake before sending an inch-perfect cross towards Lomas. He then powered home a wonderful header at the North Stand end of the ground to make it 4–2.

City remained on top and in the final 10 minutes, despite considerable pressure, Walsh made a brilliant run. He passed four Spurs men before turning and crossing to Flitcroft, who scored to make it 5–2 in the 79th minute. The victory was complete and City and Spurs had once again competed in a highly memorable game.

City: Dibble, Edghill, Phelan, Flitcroft, Curle, Brightwell, Summerbee, Walsh, Quinn, Lomas, Beagrie.

Tottenham Hotspur: Walker, Kerslake, Campbell, Scott, Edinburgh, Popescu, Dozzell, Dumitrescu, Barmby, Klinsmann, Sheringham.
Referee: D. Elleray (Harrow)
Attendance: 25,473

30 May 1999
Gillingham 2 Manchester City 2

Second Division play-off final (played at Wembley Stadium)
To say that being in the third tier of English football was a major embarrassment to City and it was vital promotion was achieved at the first attempt is a gross understatement. The game was entirely about City's survival and indeed was a crucial moment in the planning for Manchester's Commonwealth Games. Sadly, it took longer than hoped for manager Joe Royle to develop the confidence and winning ways necessary to guarantee an immediate return. Nevertheless, Royle's men did show true team spirit and as the season progressed they did begin to challenge and eventually reached the play-off final. City's opponents Gillingham were expected to be easily defeated, but the game did not go to plan, and the match became one of the most tortuous and at the same time joyous occasions ever experienced by the Blues. The entire day seemed to sum up exactly what supporting Manchester City was all about.

A slippy surface caused the Blues to struggle and only good play from 20-year-old 'keeper Nicky Weaver prevented Gillingham from taking an early lead. In the ninth minute he palmed away an effort from Galloway, and later his performance helped to bring confidence to the outfield players.

In the 26th minute a downward header from Horlock was superbly saved by Gillingham's Bartram, and this was followed by several chances for both sides. City did seem to have the better chances and should have taken the lead, especially in the 75th minute when Goater side-footed a shot against the post, but they simply could not break through. Then, in the 81st minute, Gillingham's Asaba toe-poked a shot into the roof of City's net to stun the City fans. Five minutes later future Blue Robert Taylor made it 2–0. City seemed dead and buried and many fans left the stadium for the long journey back to Manchester. They missed an amazing fight-back.

As the game entered the final seconds of the 90th minute Horlock side-footed a goal. In the stands there was a surge of excitement. It was clear that time was limited, but there was a belief that another City attack could lead to an equaliser. The clock kept on ticking and then, four and a half minutes into injury time, Dickov fired a shot into the top corner. It was an amazing moment and one which rocked the stadium. Nobody honestly felt that City could win the match prior to Horlock's goal and then suddenly everything seemed to work in City's favour. Supporters struggled to comprehend what they had witnessed. Those that had left quickly tried to make it back, while stories of fans pulling emergency cords on Underground trains and other desperate acts to get back made the newspapers in the days that followed.

Extra-time was played, with neither side managing to take the lead, and so the match went to penalties. It was another tense few minutes.

Horlock netted first, then Weaver's legs blocked Gillingham's first attempt. Dickov's kick bounced off both posts to leave the score at 1–0, but Gillingham's second went wide. Then former United man Terry Cooke calmly slotted home to make it 2–0.

Gillingham's third penalty was sent into the roof of the net by John Hodge to make it 2–1. Then Richard Edghill came up to take City's fourth. Edghill: 'When Dicky missed his penalty my thoughts were "I had to score", that was all I was concentrating on. My emotions were another aspect – they were racing. I had hot sweats, started to panic and wondered if my legs would carry me, and to add to it I thought I was deaf from the noise.' Edghill sent his kick in off the bar and then immediately kissed his shirt to show his loyalty to the club. Weaver saved Gillingham's fourth attempt and City won the penalty shoot out 3–1. Weaver went on a rather manic run across Wembley, until he was dragged to the ground by tough captain Andy Morrison and the other players.

It was claimed to be the most dramatic game City had participated in and its importance cannot be underestimated. True this was only a Second Division play-off, but had City not been successful it is highly unlikely the club would have re-established themselves as any form of power. In addition, the City of Manchester stadium would probably have not been completed, as City's position as anchor tenants would have been in doubt. This game was absolutely vital for both City and for Manchester in general.

City: Weaver, Crooks (Taylor), Edghill, Wiekens, Morrison (Vaughan), Horlock, Brown (Bishop), Whitley, Dickov, Goater, Cooke.
Gillingham: Bartram, Southall, Ashby, Smith, Butters, Pennock, Patterson (Hodge), Hessenthaler, Asaba (Carr), Galloway (Saunders), Taylor.
Referee: M. Halsey (Welwyn Garden City)
Attendance: 76,935

---

4 February 2004
Tottenham 3 Manchester City 4

FA Cup fourth round replay

As with many other City-Spurs games over the years, this match became a classic and, just like the 1999 play-off final, it was described by neutrals as the greatest comeback of all time.

The first game had ended in a 1–1 draw at the City of Manchester Stadium and Kevin Keegan's City arrived at White Hart Lane after a 2–1 defeat at Arsenal. Icelandic goalkeeper Arni Arason made his debut, but it was a difficult opening as he was beaten in the second minute by a rising, curling effort from Ledley King. Robbie Keane made it 2–0, then a minute before the interval Joey Barton was booked on the edge of the area for a foul on ex-Blue Michael Brown. Christian Ziege curled the resultant free-kick into the top corner

Arthur Cox and Kevin Keegan celebrate.

Jon Macken celebrates scoring the winner against Tottenham in 2004.

to make it 3–0 and Barton argued his case with the referee. A second yellow card was shown and City ended the half down to 10 men and losing 3–0.

As the team entered the second half ironic chants of 'We're gonna win the Cup' were sung by City fans, but it wasn't long before the game turned around and supporters sang that same song with conviction. A header from Distin in the 48th minute was followed by Paul Bosvelt scoring with a deflected shot after 61 minutes. City now searched for an equaliser, but they had to wait until 10 minutes from time when Shaun Wright-Phillips exposed a frail off-side trap to chip City level.

In the last minute Jon Macken scored the winner from a far-post header and the remarkable turnaround was complete. After the game, against the wishes of the home side, City officials managed to collect the matchball from the game and this has since been on display in City's museum.

Late in 2005 a short play written by a female Spurs fan was one of the winning entries in the Radio Five Live Short Story competition. The play tells the story of a City fan who left at half-time and didn't know the final score until visiting a pub later in the night. The play covered commitment and compared leaving the game at half-time with commitment in other relationships. It's clear the fight-back in this game was felt strongly throughout football.

Tottenham: Keller, Carr, Ziege (Jackson), Gardner, Richards, King, Brown, Dalmat, Keane, Postiga (Poyet), Davies.

City: Arason, Jihai, Tarnat, Dunne, Distin, Barton, Wright-Phillips, Bosvelt (Sibierski), Anelka (Macken), Fowler, Sinclair (McManaman).
Referee: R. Styles (Hampshire)
Attendance: 30,400

---

14 January 2006
Manchester City 3 Manchester United 1

FA Premier League

City's record in the Manchester derby since promotion under Kevin Keegan is impressive. The last meeting between the two sides at Maine Road ended in a convincing 3–1 Blue victory, while the first at the City of Manchester Stadium resulted in a 4–1 City success. This meeting was the second meeting of the sides under Stuart Pearce and followed a 1–1 draw at Old Trafford the previous September.

In the run-up to this match the Blues had struggled with one win in the previous six League games, although a 3–1 FA Cup win the previous Saturday against Scunthorpe had raised morale a little. It is correct to say, however, that the majority of fans were not entirely convinced that the Blues were ready to face a very strong United side which had not lost in the League for 11 games. As always, though, the formbook mattered little as the game commenced with the usual derby day excitement in the stands.

On the pitch there were two debutants – Spaniard Albert Riera for City and Frenchman Patrice Evra for United – but both found the atmosphere and speed of the game a little too much at times, while it was Mancunian Trevor Sinclair who netted first in the 32nd minute. The goal came as a result of a great deal of pressure and started with a Joey Barton cross

Trevor Sinclair receives treatment during the derby. He played the latter stages with a bandaged head.

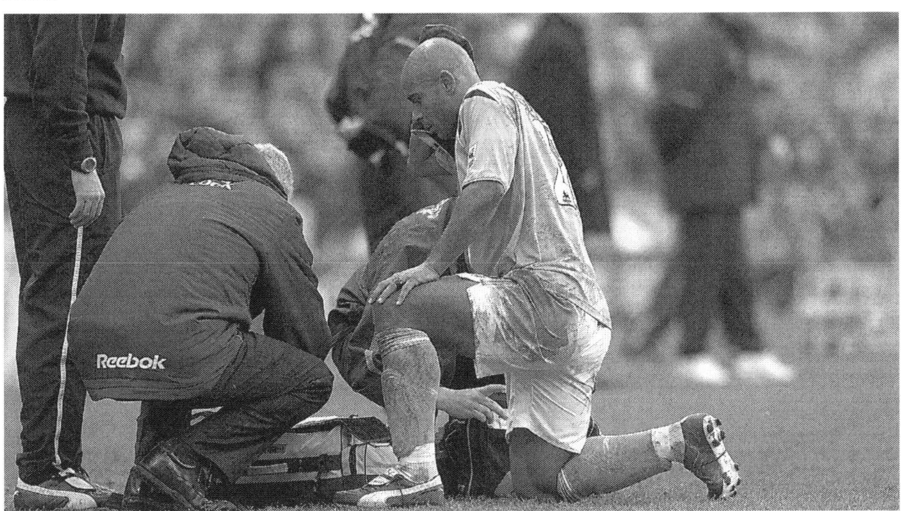

Robbie Fowler and Darius Vassell. Fowler was to score City's third.

from the right. Gary Neville headed the ball away from danger, or so he thought, but Stephen Ireland gained control and moved it quickly to Trevor Sinclair, who made a well-placed volley from 12 yards out. United claimed the effort had been offside, but Joe Lovejoy, writing in the *Sunday Times*, accurately reported: 'Darius Vassell was in an offside position when Barton played the ball in, but was not interfering when Sinclair scored.'

Mixed play followed, with David James making a good save with his legs from Rooney, but a mere seven minutes after the first goal City netted again. This time a long free-kick from James saw Sinclair beat Evra in the air. Ex-Red Andy Cole reacted quickly, leaving

A bandaged Trevor Sinclair celebrates victory over United.

England's Ferdinand behind, and passed to Vassell. Vassell moved past Silvestre quickly and easily and then scored from about eight yards out. It looked an easy goal, but in truth said a great deal about City's determination and their ability to set up attacks from the actions of goalkeeper James.

At 2–0 City had control and seemed destined to increase their lead. United still managed to look a little threatening on occasion, but City's team played as a unit while United seemed to consist of 11 stars but no team spirit. United's nasty side started to show its face as Rooney began to complain about almost every incident, leading to a booking just before the interval.

In the second half United seemed more composed, but the Blues remained the more positive side, although a 65th-minute challenge on Ronaldo by Jordan looked a little desperate. Despite protests from United the referee refused to show Jordan a yellow card and only seconds later Ronaldo decided to get his own back with a reckless lunge at Andy Cole. The tackle was appalling and occurred directly in front of the referee, and when the referee called Ronaldo to him to penalise the United man, the player challenged the referee about the previous incident. Clearly revenge had been Ronaldo's aim and so the referee had no choice but to dismiss him. Down to 10 men United actually looked more dangerous, especially when Richard Dunne became injured almost immediately after the sending-off. The player was eventually substituted in the 68th minute, and two minutes later United replaced the ineffectual Fletcher with Saha. Saha immediately started to attack in the gap left by Dunne's departure. In the 76th minute Van Nistelrooy made it 2–1 after a pass from Giggs and City fans worried, but Stuart Pearce decided to bring on Musampa and Fowler immediately. Adding the two new faces at this time helped City regain control, although Trevor Sinclair had to leave the field for some time as he had sustained a cut to his head. He returned, heavily bandaged, to a great ovation and seemingly more determined than ever to search for another goal.

Attempts were wasted to increase the lead and then the fourth official raised the board showing that there would be an additional four minutes. As usual both sides became more attacking minded, but it was City who seemed the more able and Robbie Fowler netted the third after Vassell almost lost the chance.

The 3–1 victory was fully deserved and almost every City player performed at his best. Stephen Ireland in particular impressed, while goalkeeper James proved good value for money on the occasions he was tested. Stuart Pearce was asked who was his favourite: 'I feel like a parent with a lot of children who behaved well. It's difficult to say "little Johnny was my favourite" but Trevor [Sinclair] was very good.'

City: James, Jihai, Dunne (Onuoha), Distin, Jordan, Sinclair, Barton, Ireland, Riera (Musampa), Vassell, Cole (Fowler).
United: Van der Sar, Neville, Ferdinand, Silvestre, Evra (Smith), Ronaldo, Fletcher (Saha), O'Shea (Richardson), Giggs, Van Nistelrooy, Rooney.
Referee: S.G. Bennett (Kent)
Attendance: 47,192

City's Top 100 Players

The first 77 players in the 'Top 100' (actually there are 101 players profiled) are those who have played 200 or more first-team games for the club. Unusually for a City history, the author has included wartime games, the Full Members' Cup and other similar competitions in these figures. The inclusion of these helps to provide a more appropriate record of each player's City service. Games played during the war were just as important locally as many of the peacetime games, and some players spent a considerable period of their career entertaining Mancunians during the difficulties of war.

The remaining players – listed alphabetically – have been selected by the author for their significant contribution to the history of City and the enjoyment of supporters. Inevitably, this list is subjective, although the author has endeavoured to select players from each era who had a rapport with fans or delivered consistently while at City.

Key to appearance detail:
Test Matches – the promotion-deciding test matches played during 1896
Play-off – the promotion-deciding play offs played during 1999
Charity – Charity/Community Shield games
Wartime (League and Cup) – games played in the various war leagues and war cup competitions
FL Wartime – the three games from the 1939–40 season that were expunged from the records (included here as these were initially played as first-team matches, though they do not count in official League records)
European Cup/ECWC/UEFA Cup – the three major European competitions City have competed in
AS Cup/TC Cup/AI Cup/T Cup – the Anglo-Scottish Cup; Tennent-Caledonian Cup; Anglo-Italian Cup; Texaco Cup (these games were all classed as first-team fixtures when City competed in them during 1970 to 1977)
FMC – Full Members' Cup/Zenith Data Systems/Simod Cup (City competed in this first-team competition between 1985–92)

Alan Oakes

ALAN ARTHUR OAKES (1958–1976)
Midfielder, 5ft 11in, 12st 13lb, b. Winsford, 1 September 1942
Signed from: apprentice, 8 April 1958 (Pro: 8 September 1959)
Transferred: Chester City, 17 July 1976 (player-manager, £15,000)
Career: City, Chester City, Port Vale
Debut: v Chelsea, 14 November 1959

Appearances: League: 561+3 apps, 26 gls; FA Cup: 41 apps, 2 gls; League Cup: 46+1 apps, 5 gls; European Cup: 2 apps, 0 gls; ECWC: 13 apps, 1 gl; UEFA Cup: 2 apps, 0 gls; Charity: 3 apps, 0 gls; AS Cup: 3 apps, 0 gls; AI Cup: 2 apps, 0 gls; T Cup: 3 apps, 0 gls. Total: 676+4 apps, 34 gls.

The cousin of another City hero, Glyn Pardoe, Alan Oakes is one of City's unsung heroes. He joined City in April 1958 after impressing with Mid-Cheshire Boys side and turned full-time professional in September 1959. Two months later he made his debut and was still very much a key figure with the Blues 16 years later. By that time he was City's appearance record holder and was recognised throughout football as a model professional. Don Revie and Bill Shankly were two managers who often used Oakes as an example of a true professional, and it's clear that he allowed his football to dominate. Oakes: 'I think I was a good professional. I used to simply get on with it. I was dedicated and tried to give everything for the club. I believe I was a good, honest pro. If I was asked to do an interview, I'd do it, but I never sought the headlines. Media coverage was not as it is today, so it was easier in many ways, but I would do it when needed.

Top of the tree: Alan Oakes is City's record appearance holder.

More than anything I wanted to make sure my role on the pitch spoke for me.'

The more familiar names nationally gained the headlines, but Oakes was a major influence on City throughout his career. As with Mike Doyle, Oakes was a key member of City's promotion side in 1966, Championship team of 1968, FA Cup team of 1969, ECWC and League Cup side of 1970, and League Cup winners of 1976. He also played for the English League v Scottish League, and had a great reputation as a strong, determined wing-half who possessed a brilliant left foot.

It's often forgotten that Oakes was initially included in the 1970 World Cup squad (he was also included in the famous Esso World Cup collection of 1970), although once this was whittled down to the final number who were allowed to travel he narrowly missed out.

After appearing for the Blues in City's 1976 League Cup triumph, Oakes signed for Chester City, for a fee of £15,000, where he moved into management. He was a key influence behind the career of Ian Rush, and in 1983 when City were looking to appoint a new manager Oakes was shortlisted for the post (Billy McNeill was eventually appointed).

Although the fact he is City's record appearance holder will always keep his name in the record books, it's fair to say his overall contribution to the Blues throughout a long and distinguished career also deserves to be remembered.

Joe Corrigan

JOSEPH THOMAS CORRIGAN (1966–83)

Goalkeeper, 6ft 4.5in, 14st 12lb, b. Manchester, 18 November 1948

Signed from: Sale FC as amateur, 24 September 1966 (Pro: 25 January 1967).

Transferred: Seattle Sounders, 25 March 1983 (£30,000)

Career: Sale, City, Seattle Sounders, Brighton & Hove Albion, Norwich City (loan), Stoke City (loan)

Debut: v Blackpool, 11 October 1967 (League Cup)

League debut: v Ipswich Town, 11 March 1969
Appearances: League: 476 apps, 0 gls; FA Cup: 37 apps, 0 gls; League Cup: 52 apps, 0 gls; ECWC: 14 apps, 0 gls; UEFA Cup: 13 apps, 0 gls; Charity: 3 apps, 0 gls; AS Cup: 3 apps, 0 gls; TC Cup: 2 apps; 0 gls; AI Cup: 2 apps, 0 gls; T Cup 2+1 apps, 0 gls. Total: 604+1 apps, 0 gls.

Joe Corrigan joined City as an amateur in 1966, and a mere four years later was the Blues' number one as they won the European Cup-Winners' Cup in Vienna. He was also goalkeeper for the League Cup success that season, although that perhaps disguises the fact that it was actually several years before Corrigan was recognised as a great goalkeeper. During the early seventies Corrigan was not seen as a long-term solution by the City management and at one point, in October 1973, the Blues signed expensive Scottish 'keeper Keith MacRae. Corrigan's City career seemed over, but he fought hard to get back into the side.

Inevitably, Corrigan managed to get back into the side and the mid to late seventies saw his career quickly develop. In 1976 he gained international honours when he played in the 3–2 defeat of Italy, and he went on to play nine games for England. He was on the losing side only once (1981 v Scotland), and was only kept out of the side at other times because of the strength of competition. As well as Corrigan England were blessed with quality 'keepers such as Ray Clemence and Peter Shilton, while Phil Parkes was another contender for the number one shirt.

By this time, Corrigan was a true City hero and seemed typical of the type of committed, hard-working players the supporters wanted. Throughout the late 1970s and early 1980s, as City strove to find success both at home and in Europe, Corrigan was probably the most consistent of all the squad and, as with Trautmann before him, many games were won simply because of the 'keeper's determined performances.

In 1981, when City played in the 100th FA Cup Final, Corrigan was voted Man of the Final, and he remained with the Blues until March 1983 when he moved to Seattle Sounders. He later had spells with Brighton, Norwich and Stoke, and also became goalkeeping coach at Liverpool, Stockport and a variety of other clubs.

Corrigan is unquestionably one of England's greatest post-war 'keepers, and will always remain a true Blue hero. In 2004 he became the first player to be inducted into the Manchester City Hall of Fame, and then, during 2005–06, the City magazine held a poll to find the club's greatest 'keeper. Inevitably, the age of the magazine's readers had a bearing, but it is significant that Corrigan won the poll. In historical terms the names of Swift and Trautmann may always be ahead of him, but in terms of heroes from the modern era, Corrigan is clearly a major figure.

Mike Doyle

MICHAEL DOYLE (1962–78)
Defender, 5ft 10.75in, 11st 6lb, b. Manchester, 25 November 1946
Signed from: amateur, 11 May 1962 (Pro: 26 May 1964)
Transferred: Stoke City, 5 June 1978 (£50,000)
Career: Reddish Vale School (Stockport), City, Stoke City, Bolton Wanderers, Rochdale

Debut: v Blackpool, 11 October 1967 (League Cup)
League debut: v Cardiff City, 12 March 1965
Appearances: League: 441+7 apps, 32 gls; FA Cup: 44 apps, 2 gls; League Cup: 43 apps, 4 gls; European Cup: 2 apps, 0 gls; ECWC: 16 apps, 2 gls; UEFA Cup: 5 apps, 0 gls; Charity: 4 apps, 0 gls; AS Cup: 2 apps, 0 gls; TC Cup: 2 apps, 0 gls; AI Cup: 2 apps, 0 gls; T Cup: 4 apps, 1 gl; Total: 565+7 apps, 41 gls.

Although Mike Doyle wore the number nine shirt at times during the mid-sixties, it was his time as a defender that most supporters remember him for. However, the 1970 League Cup Final programme still focussed on his earlier role and on another popular view of Doyle: 'Not just a City player, a life-long City fan who loves to hate Manchester United. Has played in the forward line where his natural aggression and heading ability were useful assets.'

The determination was a key factor in Doyle's great rapport with fans, and his commitment to the Blue cause impressed throughout the sixties and seventies when he enjoyed phenomenal success. In 1969, while City were at the height of their powers, Malcolm Allison described Doyle as the most improved player during the first few seasons of the Mercer-Allison reign. He was also recognised as a great header of the ball and for a high level of stamina.

By that time Doyle had already played for Young England against Hungary (May 1968) and eight years later he made his full England debut.

In 1976 he became only the fourth City captain (Cowan, Paul and Book being the others) to lift a major trophy at Wembley Stadium when he guided the Blues to League Cup success. He was a great example of the local boy made good. A very popular player, Doyle later played for Stoke, Bolton and Rochdale.

Bert Trautmann

BERNHARD CARL TRAUTMANN OBE
(1949–64)
Goalkeeper, 6ft 2in, 14st 5lb, b. Bremen, Germany, 22 October 1923
Signed from: amateur, 7 October 1949 (Pro: 2 November 1949).
Retired: 10 May 1964
Career: St Helens Town, City, Wellington Town
Debut: v Bolton Wanderers 19 March 1949
Appearances: League: 508 apps, 0 gls; FA Cup: 33 apps, 0 gls; League Cup: 4 apps, 0 gls. Total: 545 apps, 0 gls.
Seen by many as the greatest overseas goalkeeper ever to play in England, Bert Trautmann is a former Luftwaffe paratrooper and prisoner of war. As a youngster Trautmann, like most Germans of his age, became a member of the Hitler Youth. It enabled him to participate in many physical and sporting activities, and he became known for his athleticism. There was even talk at one point of Trautmann representing his country in the decathlon at the 1940 Olympics, but war prevented this opportunity. It did however sent him on a path which ultimately led to him becoming City's first-choice 'keeper.

Joining the Blues in 1949, Trautmann was initially met with hostility wherever he played, although his attitude and positive approach quickly impressed and he developed a good rapport with supporters and football fans in general. As time progressed his agility and bravery won him many admirers and it's fair to say his reputation was already high when the

1956 FA Cup Final approached. In fact, on the eve of the Final he was presented with the Football Writers' player of the year award. This is significant as his most famous game – the Final itself – had no bearing whatsoever on his selection.

The events of Wembley 1956 have become legendary. Trautmann, the former POW, dived at the feet of Birmingham's Murphy and received an injury that was recorded in the months that followed as a broken neck. The 'keeper bravely played on, not realising the extent of his injury. His life was in jeopardy, and as a result the significance of that day has become part of football folklore.

He continued to perform exceptionally well for the Blues for several years, and in 1964 an official crowd of 48,000 (though this is known to have been some 15,000 below those who actually attended) paid to watch his testimonial game.

A spell as manager at Stockport County followed, and he also fulfilled a variety of ambassadorial roles for the German FA, working relentlessly to use football to break down barriers. In 2004 he was deservedly awarded the OBE for services to Anglo-German relations.

Frank Swift

FRANK VICTOR SWIFT (1932–49)
Goalkeeper, 6ft 2in, 14st 0lb, b. Blackpool, 26 December 1913, d. Munich, 6 February 1958
Signed from: Fleetwood, 21 October 1932
Retired: September 1949
Career: Blackpool Corporation Gasworks, Fleetwood, City
Debut: v Derby County, 25 December 1933
Appearances: League: 338 apps, 10 gls; FA Cup: 35 apps, 0 gls; Charity: 2 apps, 0 gls; Wartime (League and Cup): 133 apps, 0 gls; FL Wartime: 3 apps, 0 gls. Total: 511 apps, 0 gls.

A great showman and entertainer, Frank Swift was a highly popular and tremendous influence on Manchester City, and indeed England, during a highly successful career. The brother of another 'keeper, Fred Swift, Blackpool-born Swift started his career with Fleetwood. In the autumn of 1932 he signed for City, with his debut coming on Christmas Day 1933. Within six months he played in his first FA Cup Final, and another three years on he was City's number one as they won the League title for the first time.

When war broke out in 1939 Swift was at the height of his career and it's clear the war robbed him of perhaps his greatest professional years. Nevertheless, he did gain international recognition during this time, and went on to make 19 full international appearances and 14 wartime international appearances. He also became the first England 'keeper of the 20th century to captain the national side.

At the end of the 1948–49 season Swift retired. He was still England's first-choice 'keeper and clearly had several seasons left in him, but he chose to go out at the top. Incredible scenes greeted his last home game of the season (v Arsenal, 27 April 1949) and a celebratory motorcade made the journey, with Swift in the lead coach, back from Huddersfield

after the last match of the season. This was not the end, however, as Swift's replacement Alec Thurlow contracted tuberculosis and Swift was asked to return to action. He agreed but insisted the Blues hasten their search for a replacement. He played four games during 1949–50 before Trautmann was rushed into action.

City, unfairly in the eyes of supporters at the time, retained Swift's registration until May 1955. In fact, during the early fifties stories appeared in the local media suggesting Trautmann was to be dropped in favour of his predecessor. Swift had no intention of playing at all and refused the advances City made, but the club's stubborn refusal to cancel his registration caused much negative publicity.

Swift died in the Munich Air Disaster while covering United's European campaign. At the time he was the Official Supporters' Club President and a very popular presence at Maine Road.

Colin Bell

COLIN BELL MBE (1966–79)
Midfielder, 5ft 12in, 11st 4lb, b. Hesleden, 26 February 1946
Signed from: Bury, 16 March 1966 (£45,000)
Retired: 21 August 1979
Career: Horden Juniors, Bury, City, San Jose Earthquakes
Debut: v Derby County, 19 March 1966
Appearances: League: 393+1 apps, 117 gls; FA Cup: 33+1 apps, 9 gls; League Cup: 40 apps, 18 gls; European Cup: 2 apps, 0 gls; ECWC: 16 apps, 7 gls; UEFA Cup: 5+1 apps, 1 gl; Charity: 4 apps, 1 gl; AI Cup: 2 apps, 0 gls; T Cup: 3 apps, 0 gls. Total: 498+3 apps, 153 gls.

In 1969 Malcolm Allison was asked how he rated Colin Bell. He said: 'In time, Colin will be among the all-time greats who have ever played in this country. Many people already compare him with another great Manchester City player in Peter Doherty. I believe Colin will be just as good… if not better.'

As time progressed Bell became recognised by the majority of supporters as the greatest City player of all time, but his early career did not start in such a positive manner. In fact ex-England star Billy Wright rejected Bell when he went for trials at Arsenal. Wright's letter to Bell includes the line: 'hope you find a side whose standards are not as high as the Arsenal.' Within four years of that letter Bell was a major star in a highly successful City side.

He joined the Blues from Bury in 1966 and immediately played his part in City's promotion under Mercer and Allison. It was Bell's goal at Rotherham that secured promotion. Inevitably he played his part in each of City's successes and became recognised for his stamina, athleticism and his good all-round skills.

Bell appeared in 48 England internationals, scoring nine goals, and remains the most capped England international while with the Blues. He also captained the side once. He was a true thoroughbred on the pitch. Sadly, his career was cut short by injury in a Manchester derby during 1975 and, although he battled

hard to regain full fitness, he eventually retired in August 1979. In between his injury and his retirement he had become the focal point of much media attention as the nation followed his bid to return to first-team action.

When he did return to action on Boxing Day 1977 he came on as substitute against Newcastle and Maine Road erupted. The player later admitted that this was the most memorable moment of his career. Undoubtedly, Bell would have made many more England appearances had it not been for the injury – he was only 29 at the time of his last cap a month before the injury.

Regardless of what impact the injury was ultimately to have on Bell's career, it is important to celebrate everything he managed to achieve by the age of 29. Since City moved to the new stadium in 2003 the main stand has been renamed the Colin Bell Stand, while Bell has also received the MBE.

Eric Brook

ERIC FRED G. BROOK (1928–39)
Forward, 5ft 9in, 11st 6lb, b. Mexborough, 27 November 1907, d. Manchester, 29 March 1965
Signed from: Barnsley, 16 March 1928 (£6,000 for Brook and Tilson)
Retired: 1940
Career: Wath Athletic, Mexborough Thursday, Barnsley, City
Debut v Grimsby Town, 17 March 1928
Appearances: League: 450 apps, 158 gls; FA Cup: 41 apps, 19 gls; Charity: 2 apps, 0 gls. Wartime (League and Cup): 4 apps, 2 gls; FL Wartime: 3 apps, 1 gl. Total: 500 apps, 180 gls.

Eric Brook was a renowned goalscorer and a very popular figure with supporters throughout the 1930s. He joined the Blues with his great friend Fred Tilson from Barnsley in 1928. His goals brought much joy to fans, with perhaps his greatest coming in the 1934 FA Cup quarter-final with Stoke, in front of a record crowd of 84,569. Brook fired home a swirling left-foot shot from the very edge of the pitch on the left wing. The ball flew past the Stoke 'keeper and entered the top corner. It was an incredible goal and brought much attention to Brook, as it was not only a quality strike, but also the match-winner.

Inevitably, Brook formed part of the great side of the 1930s. He played in both FA Cup Finals, and was one of only three ever-presents during the 1937 Championship-winning season (the others being Swift and Toseland). He also netted 20 League goals that season, including a hat-trick at Liverpool in March.

In both 1931 and 1936 he was the club's top scorer and, during his time with the Blues, he made 18 international appearances. He also played against Wales in a wartime international on 18 November 1939 and seemed destined to play a key part in those morale-boosting wartime games, when a car crash brought a premature end to his career. He did manage one more City match, but shortly afterwards the 32-year-old Brook was told he had a fractured skull. His career was over.

He later took a job as a coach driver in his native Mexborough, then for two years he became the landlord of the Albion Inn, Halifax. He returned to Manchester as a crane driver at Metrovicks, but passed away at the early age of 57 at home in Wythenshawe in 1965.

Billy Meredith

WILLIAM HENRY MEREDITH (1894–1906 and 1921–24)
Forward, 5ft 8in, 10st 7lb, b. Chirk, 30 July 1874, d. Withington, Manchester, 19 April 1958
Signed from: Chirk, 19 October 1894
Transferred: Manchester United, 5 December 1906 (free, but Meredith received 'transfer fee' of £600)
Signed from: Manchester United, 25 July 1921
Retired: 1924
Career: Black Park FC, Chirk, Wrexham, Chirk, Northwich Victoria, Chirk, City, Manchester United, City
Debut: v Newcastle United, 27 October 1894
Appearances: League: 366 apps, 146 gls; FA Cup: 23 apps, 5 gls; Wartime (League and Cup): 107 apps, 7 gls; Test Matches: 4 apps, 1 gl. Total: 500 apps, 159 gls.

While the names of most players from the earliest years of the game have faded into oblivion, almost alone Billy Meredith's name continues to be remembered and discussed by Mancunians. His name is destined to be remembered for ever as the biggest single influence in Manchester's first footballing successes.

Meredith's Manchester career lasted from 1894 until 1924 and saw him become the most talked about, most famous footballer of his generation. He joined City in 1894 and within five years he had helped them become the first Manchester side to gain promotion, and a further five years on he scored the only goal of the 1904 FA Cup Final – Manchester's first major success. He was also captain, a Welsh international, and already a major national star.

That 1904 success should have been the first of many, especially as the Blues narrowly missed out on the Championship two years running. Sadly, this possibility ended when City were investigated as a result of Meredith being accused of trying to bribe Aston Villa's England international Alec Leake. Meredith claimed he was innocent and believed he was being made the scapegoat, a view supported by City fans at the time, who were disgusted when he was banned from playing for City by the authorities. He moved to United when the ban was lifted, in a move encouraged by supporters, who felt it was better to keep him in Manchester than see him leave the region.

During World War One Meredith returned to City as a trainer and to guest in a few matches, then in peacetime he had a dispute with United and so returned to City on a permanent basis. At the age of 49 he even managed to play in a FA Cup semi-final.

In 1956 Meredith travelled to Wembley to watch City win the FA Cup, led by another great Welshman, Roy Paul, and in April 1958 he passed away at the age of 83 and was buried at Southern Cemetery.

Despite his death, his name has lived on, and during the last 30 years or so a biography has been written, television documentaries have been made, and he has been inducted into the City Hall of Fame, with his daughter Winifred collecting the award in 2004. Meredith will always be a major figure in Manchester sport.

Tommy Booth

THOMAS ANTHONY BOOTH (1965–81)
Defender/Midfielder, 6ft 1in, 11st 12lb, b. Manchester, 9 November 1949
Signed from: amateur, 11 September 1965 (Pro: 26 August 1967)
Transferred: Preston North End, 4 October 1981 (£30,000)
Career: Bishop Marshall School, City, Preston NE
Debut: v Huddersfield Town, 2 September 1968 (League Cup)
League debut: v Arsenal, 9 October 1968
Appearances: League: 380+2 apps, 25 gls; FA Cup: 27 apps, 5 gls; League Cup: 44+2 apps, 3 gls; ECWC: 14 apps, 2 gls; UEFA Cup: 11 apps, 1 gl; Charity: 3 apps, 0 gls; AS Cup: 3 apps, 0 gls; AI Cup: 1 app, 0 gls; T Cup: 4 apps, 0 gls. Total: 487+4 apps, 36 gls.

Tommy Booth made his debut in the 1–1 draw with Arsenal on 9 October 1968 and went on to feature in all but two of the remaining 30 League games that season. He also featured in all seven FA Cup ties, scoring the only goal of the semi-final at Villa Park that took the Blues to Wembley. Booth was always one of manager Joe Mercer's favourite players, and in 1969, as City prepared for the FA Cup Final, Malcolm Allison summed him up nicely as: 'The most promising centre-half in the country. He has superb control, good all-round skills, is commanding in the air and possesses two great feet – how can he be faulted?'

Booth first became noted by many fans when he captained the youth team on a successful tour of Germany in 1967–68. The Blues won the tournament and Booth impressed. At first sight he appeared tall and frail, but as his career developed he looked a much more powerful figure. As well as appearing in the 1969 Final, he featured in all City's major successes from that point. He played in the ECWC Final of 1970, three League Cup finals (1970, 1974, and 1976) and took part in City's 1981 FA Cup run. Sadly, he missed out on the 1981 Cup Final, but he did score the only goal of the fifth-round tie at Peterborough.

After his City career ended in 1981 he moved to Preston for £30,000 and he eventually moved into management for a while at Deepdale. In recent years he has been working with City's Corporate Hospitality team at the new stadium.

Eli Fletcher

ELI FLETCHER (1911–26)
Defender, 5ft 8in, 11st 7lb, b. Tunstall, 15 December 1887, d. Longsight, 6 August 1954
Signed from: Crewe Alexandra, 18 May 1911 (£300)
Transferred: Watford, 2 June 1926
Career: Elder Road Junior School, Cobridge School, Tunstall, Goldenhill Wanderers, Earlestown, Crewe Alexandra, Northwich Victoria, Hanley Swifts, Crewe Alexandra, City, Watford player-manager, Sandbach Ramblers, Ards
Debut: v Newcastle United, 23 September 1911
Appearances: League: 301 apps, 2 gls; FA Cup: 25 apps, 0 gls; Wartime (League and Cup): 133 apps, 3 gls. Total: 459 apps, 5 gls.

Full-back Eli Fletcher joined the Blues in May 1911, and went on to become the club's regular left-back. A consistent performer, Fletcher spent 15 eventful years with City and he was an important player during the transition from pre-war football at Hyde Road, to the exciting 1920s at Maine Road. Unfortunately, his career came at a time when City failed to reach a major Final, or find success in the League, but he did become captain in 1919 and managed 35 appearances when he helped City reach second place in 1921.

Cartilage problems followed in 1922, which caused him to miss much of the season, but in his bid to regain fitness he played as goalkeeper for the reserves in 11 games during 1922–23. After his return to the first team he managed a further 48 League appearances.

In June 1926 he joined Watford as player-manager and later Sandbach Ramblers and Newtonards, before returning to Manchester as coach to Manchester Central at Belle Vue.

Jackie Bray

JACKIE BRAY (1929–47)

Defender, 5ft 9in, 11st 2lb, b. Oswaldtwistle, 22 April 1909, d. Blackburn, 20 November 1982

Signed from: Manchester Central, 16 October 1929 (£1,000)

Transferred: Watford, *c.*1947

Career: St Andrews School, Clayton Olympia, Manchester Central, City, Watford player-manager

Debut: v Manchester United, 8 February 1930

Appearances: League: 257 apps, 10 gls; FA Cup: 20 apps, 0 gls; Charity: 2 apps, 0 gls; Wartime (League and Cup): 177 apps, 11 gls; FL Wartime: 3 apps, 0 gls. Total: 459 apps, 21 gls.

Signed from Manchester Central in 1929, Jackie Bray was an imaginative and speedy wing-half. Bray proved to be a good successor to the highly popular Jimmy McMullan and he became a key member of the great 1930s side. He played in both thirties Finals and made 40 appearances during the 1936–37 Championship-winning season. He even scored a couple of goals (v United, and v Chelsea in a 4–4 draw) as he helped the Blues to the title.

Bray gained six England international appearances, with the first coming on 29 September 1934 against Wales – a game which saw fellow City stars Tilson (2) and Brook score for England – and also played for the Football League.

When war broke out in 1939 Bray was still a City regular, but by the time the Football League recommenced after the war in 1946 Bray was unable to get back into the side, although he did feature throughout the war leagues, including 1945–46, and played in the reserves.

He moved to Watford as manager in March 1947, and after a brief spell there he became coach at Nelson for a while. He also opened a sportswear shop in Nelson.

Mike Summerbee

MICHAEL GEORGE SUMMERBEE (1965–75)
Forward, 5ft 11in, 11st 4lb, b. Preston, 15 December 1942
Signed from: Swindon Town, 20 August 1965 (£35,000)
Transferred: Burnley, 13 June 1975 (£25,000)
Career: Baker Street YMCA, Bristol City ground staff, Cheltenham Town, Swindon Town, City, Burnley, Blackpool, Stockport County player-manager, Mossley
Debut: v Middlesbrough, 21 August 1965
Appearances: League: 355+2 apps, 47 gls; FA Cup: 34 apps, 11 gls; League Cup: 36 apps, 8 gls; European Cup: 2 apps, 0 gls; ECWC: 13 apps, 1 gl; UEFA Cup: 1 app, 0 gls; Charity: 4 apps, 0 gls; AI Cup 1+1 apps, 0 gls; T Cup: 3 apps, 1 gl. Total: 449+3 apps, 68 gls.

One of the most famous members of the great Mercer-Allison side, Summerbee was the man who set up Neil Young to score the winner in the 1969 FA Cup Final. It was the crucial moment in the match and many newspapers commented on Summerbee's role. Leicester's Allan Clarke was voted Man of the Match, but a *Daily Mail* journalist told Summerbee it should have been him. The player summed it up nicely though when he replied: 'I'd rather have my winners' medal!'

Summerbee came from a good footballing family – his father had been a professional – and so from an early age he knew of the qualities needed to find success. He also knew the hardships that the game could present.

City signed him from Swindon, where he had made his debut at the age of 16, and he became manager Joe Mercer's second signing (Ralph Brand was first). Immediately, Summerbee impressed, with local reporters frequently describing him as the key figure behind City's 1965–66 transformation. That promotion-winning season he was the club's only ever-present and also scored eight goals. England manager Alf Ramsey came to Maine Road to watch him during the season and some claimed he was going to be called up to the national squad in time for the 1966 Finals. Sadly that didn't happen, but he did make an appearance for the Under-23 side.

His full international debut came in February 1968 against Scotland (1–1 draw) in front of 134,000 at Hampden, and he became the first member of City's great sixties side to play for England.

In 1967–68 he made 41 appearances as City won the title. Two came on the wing, the other 39 as centre-forward. At the end of the season Malcolm Allison claimed that it was this switch that brought the title to the Blues: 'I maintain his switch to centre-forward was one of the reasons for our championship success. This strong, powerful raiding winger on his day is an asset to any world-class team. He has tremendous pace and is a great crosser of the ball. He is very good in the air and feared by most full-backs.'

Inevitably Summerbee featured in every City success of the period, although injury prevented him from playing in the 1970 ECWC Final, and in 1974 he became only the sixth man to captain City in a major Final when he led the Blues at Wembley for the League Cup Final.

In June 1975 he was transferred to Burnley for £25,000 and later became Stockport's player-manager. In the mid-1990s he returned to Maine Road to work with City's commercial operations, and in 2006 he continued to be a popular presence at the City of Manchester Stadium.

Paul Power

PAUL CHRISTOPHER POWER (1974–86)
Midfield, 5ft 10in, 11st 6lb, b. Openshaw, 30 October 1953
Signed from: amateur, 11 August 1973 (Pro: 17 July 1975)
Transferred: Everton, 27 June 1986 (£65,000)
Career: St Augustine's School, Leeds Polytechnic, West Park Albion, City, Everton
Debut: v Aston Villa, 27 August 1975
Appearances: League: 358+7 apps, 26 gls; FA Cup: 28 apps, 6 gls; League Cup: 37+1 apps, 2 gls; UEFA Cup: 7+1 apps, 1 gl; FMC: 6 apps, 1 gl; TC Cup: 1+1 apps, 0 gls. Total: 437+10 apps, 36 gls.

Highly respected City scout Harry Godwin was not particularly impressed when he first watched the 13-year-old Paul Power: 'His left foot was a beauty, but there was nothing on the lad. No flesh, no height. Paul was the tiniest of tots, he made Ronnie Corbett look like a giant.' However, some time later Godwin came across Power again: 'I travelled to the CWS ground in New Moston and saw Paul play for a Manchester Under-18 team. He'd grown, the stride had lengthened and the delicate left foot was still there. I'd seen all I needed to in the first half hour of the game. He was a genuine Blue. It was a bonus that he didn't want to play for anybody else.'

He made his City debut in August 1975 and by the 1976–77 season was a first-team regular as the Blues challenged for the League title. In November 1978 he netted one of his most important goals to help the Blues achieve a 2–2 draw at AC Milan, and 11 months later Malcolm Allison appointed him captain for the first time. That game ended in a fine 1–0 victory over Nottingham Forest on 13 October 1979, and Power went on to become one of City's most popular captains.

Power was City's captain for the 1981 FA Cup Final, and he was also the scorer of the match-winner in the semi-final against Ipswich. Power was a key influence during the late seventies and early eighties as City searched for success. In 1983, following relegation, he became more determined than most to see the Blues return to Division One and to many fans his continuing commitment to the Blue cause was highly encouraging. Other players had moved on, but Power led by example. Promotion followed in 1985 and a year later Howard Kendall signed him for Everton. City fans recognised it was time for the player to move on, and the move was seen as being a step towards coaching for the model professional. In fact it brought the player a thoroughly deserved League Championship medal. He even scored at Maine Road for Everton but, ever the City Blue, Power refused to celebrate. He couldn't bear to see the club he loved suffer.

After his playing career ended he was often tipped, particularly during the mid-1990s, as a

potential City manager, but settled instead for a role behind the scenes. He continues to use his knowledge to help guide City's highly successful Academy.

Willie Donachie

WILLIAM DONACHIE (1968–80)
Defender, 5ft 10in, 11st 6lb, b. Glasgow, 5 October 1951
Signed from: amateur, 22 October 1968 (Pro: 12 December 1968)
Transferred: Portland Timbers, 19 March 1980 (£200,000)
Career: Mitchell Hill School, King's Park School, Glasgow Amateurs, City, Portland Timbers, Norwich City, Portland Timbers, Burnley, Oldham Athletic
Debut: v Nottingham Forest, 7 February 1970 (substitute)
Appearances: League: 347+4 apps, 2 gls; FA Cup: 21 apps, 0 gls; League Cup: 40 apps, 0 gls; ECWC: 3+1, 0 gls; UEFA Cup: 10 apps, 0 gls; Charity: 2 apps, 0 gls; AS Cup: 3 apps, 0 gls; TC Cup: 2 apps, 0 gls; T Cup: 5 apps, 0 gls. Total: 433+5 apps, 2 gls.

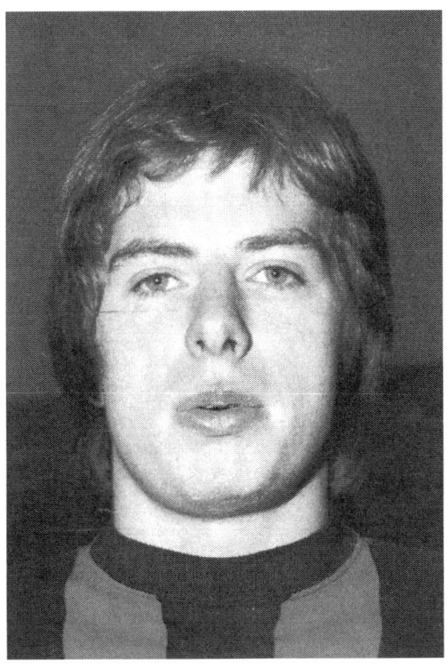

Only Colin Bell and Asa Hartford have won more caps for one of the home nations while with City than full-back Willie Donachie. Donachie, with 35 caps for Scotland as a Blue, is one appearance behind Hartford. His first international came on 26 April 1972 when Scotland defeated Peru 2–0 at Hampden Park. His final appearances came in the 1978 World Cup Finals in Argentina when, despite Scotland's ultimate disappointment in the competition, Donachie was recognised as one of Scotland's most consistent and accomplished players.

He joined City as a youngster during the Mercer-Allison era and made his League debut as substitute in February 1970. His appearances were limited until March 1971 when he appeared in the final 11 League games of the season. He also appeared in the ECWC semi-final first leg.

By 1973–74 he was a City star and in that season the stylish defender was an ever-present in all 55 first-team games played by the club – League, FA Cup and League Cup. No other player had managed to appear in every League game that year, let alone the other competitions. Inevitably, for such a key player, he was a part of the side that won the League Cup in 1976, and he was again ever-present when City missed out on the title by a single point.

Donachie moved to NASL club Portland Timbers for £200,000 in March 1980. Although he still loved City, he felt the time had come to move on. He later played for Norwich, Burnley and Oldham. While at Oldham he became Joe Royle's right-hand man and the two of them guided the Latics to Wembley in the League Cup, to 2 FA Cup semi-finals, and in 1991 to the old Second Division Championship. The partnership later moved to Everton, where they won the FA Cup, then in 1998 Donachie arrived as Royle's assistant at Maine Road.

Although Donachie and Royle arrived too late to save City from relegation to the third tier of English football, success followed with victory in the 1999 play-off final, and a second promotion 12 months later taking City back to the Premier League. Sadly, with relegation in 2001 Royle and Donachie's time came to an end, and Donachie later joined Royle at Ipswich Town.

Neil Young

NEIL JAMES YOUNG (1959–72)
Forward, 6ft 1in, 11st 3lb, b. Manchester, 17 February 1944
Signed from: amateur, 15 May 1959 (Pro: 18 July 1960)
Transferred: Preston NE, 21 January 1972 (£48,000)
Career: Rusholme School, City, Preston North End, Rochdale, Macclesfield Town
Debut: v Aston Villa, 25 November 1961
Appearances: League: 332+2 apps, 86 gls; FA Cup: 32+1 apps, 10 gls; League Cup: 28 apps, 6 gls; European Cup: 2 apps, 0 gls; ECWC: 15 apps, 5 gls; Charity: 2 apps, 1 gl; AI Cup: 2 apps, 0 gls. Total: 413+3 apps, 108 gls.

The goalscorer from the 1969 FA Cup Final and one of the scorers in the 1970 ECWC, Neil Young made the successful transition from City's youth team through to League Champions. He made his debut on the right wing in 1961 when the club was struggling to replace the great players from the fifties side. Cup Final stars Trautmann, Leivers, Ewing and Hayes were still in the side and there was clearly some quality in the team, with the likes of Peter Dobing and Bobby Kennedy playing their part, but City were not consistent, and in 1963, with Young a regular member of the side, the Blues were relegated. Such struggles so early in his career could have damaged his approach, but Young was quickly proving to be one of City's more impressive youngsters.

After the arrival of Mercer and Allison Young's career really took off and in their first season in charge he became the leading scorer with 14 goals in 35 League appearances. He led the scoring charts again in 1967–68 and in 1968–69 (shared with Lee). When asked about Young's scoring ability Allison said in 1969: 'He gets his goals despite doing a basically midfield job, but striking devastatingly.' The 1970 League Cup Final programme described him as: 'Dangerously easy to underestimate because he had greyhound speed and a marvellous left foot – the foot that won the Cup against Leicester.'

Interestingly, he almost became a Manchester United player. The Reds made an official approach to sign him two days after the Blues had signed him on amateur forms.

In 1972 Young moved on to Preston and later played for Rochdale. Over the years Young has hit the headlines several times as a result of disagreements over a promised testimonial in 1972, and in the mid-1990s following Francis Lee's return to the Blues the club supported various testimonial events organised by the fanzine *Blueprint* and supporters' groups led by Dave Cash. Sadly, in 2006 Young was forced to undergo medical treatment on his leg.

Ernie Toseland

ERNEST TOSELAND (1929–39)
Forward, 5ft 8in, 10st 4lb, b. Northampton, 17 March 1905, d. Stockport, 19 October 1987
Signed from: Coventry City, 1 March 1929
Transferred: Sheffield Wednesday, 14 March 1939

Career: Guildhall United, Higham Ferrers Town, Queens Park Rangers, Coventry City, City, Sheffield Wednesday, Droylsden, Rochdale
Debut: v Bury, 20 April 1929
Appearances: League: 368 apps, 61 gls; FA Cup: 41 apps, 14 gls; Charity: 2 apps, 0 gls; Wartime (League and Cup): 2 apps, 0 gls. Total: 413 apps, 75 gls.

Inducted into the Manchester City Hall of Fame in 2006, Ernie Toseland was a major star during the 1930s for the Blues. An exciting winger, he was given the nickname 'Twinkle Toes Toseland' by fans and supporters standing on the Popular Side (latter-day Kippax) were known to urge the defenders to get the ball to him. They also, bizarrely, used to call 'Keep chasing the pigeons Toseland' whenever he was chasing the ball. The origins of this shout are hard to identify, but it's believed it originated after he spent one particularly dull game chasing away birds from the pitch. As time moved on the shout became more popular with supporters regularly calling it to urge him to go after the ball.

Toseland played in both the 1933 and 1934 FA Cup Finals and was an ever-present when City won the League Championship in 1936–37. He also netted seven goals that season, with the most important helping City to a 2–0 victory over Championship contenders Arsenal.

In March 1939 he was transferred to Sheffield Wednesday, but war limited his appearances there. He did return to the Blues as a guest player, but only managed two appearances.

He passed away in 1987 but his widow Grace, a former Tiller girl, went on to attend functions at the City of Manchester Stadium, and she collected his Hall of Fame award in 2006.

Sam Cowan

SAMUEL COWAN (1924–1935)
Defender, 5ft 11in, 13st 0lb, b. Chesterfield, 10 May 1901, d. Haywards Heath, 4 October 1964
Signed from: Doncaster Rovers, 12 December 1924
Transferred: Bradford City, 17 October 1935 (£2,000)
Career: Adwick Juniors, Huddersfield Town, Denaby United, Bullcroft Colliery, Doncaster Rovers, City, Bradford City, Mossley player-manager
Debut: v Birmingham City, 20 December 1924
Appearances: League: 369 apps, 19 gls; FA Cup: 37 apps, 5 gls; Charity: 1 app, 0 gls. Total: 407 apps, 24 gls.

The only man to have appeared in three separate FA Cup Finals for the Blues, Sam Cowan was City's inspirational leader for the 1934 FA Cup success.

He joined the Blues in December 1924 from Doncaster Rovers and soon became renowned for his heading ability, with teammate Matt Busby later commenting: 'He could head a ball as far as most of us could kick it.' Another attribute was his man-management. As captain he often took on roles that in later years would be performed by managers and coaches, and many of City's successes came as a result of Cowan's coaxing of his players.

As well as the FA Cup appearances, Cowan also gained a Second Division Championship medal, and made three England appearances.

He also appeared for the Football League and in an England trial match before he moved on to Bradford City. City supporters were furious at the loss, but after spells at Mossley and as Brighton's trainer fans were delighted when he was appointed City manager in 1946. The rest of his career is detailed in the Managers section of this book.

Ian Brightwell

IAN ROBERT BRIGHTWELL (1986–98)
Midfielder, 5ft 10in, 11st 7lb, b. Lutterworth, 9 April 1968
Signed from: amateur, 1 July 1985 (Pro: 3 May 1986)
Transferred: Coventry City, 2 July 1998
Career: Westlands School, Midas Juniors, City, Coventry City, Walsall, Stoke City, Port Vale, Macclesfield Town
Debut: v Wimbledon, 23 August 1986
Appearances: League: 285+36 apps, 18 gls; FA Cup: 19+4 apps, 1 gl; League Cup: 29+2 apps, 0 gls; FMC: 4+3 apps, 0 gls. Total: 337+ 45 apps, 19 gls.

Of all the players from City's 1986 FA Youth Cup-winning side, Ian Brightwell is the one who went on to play most games for the Blues. He first appeared in the League at the start of the 1986–87 season, wearing the number 11 shirt, and he managed a total of 12 (plus four substitute) appearances that year and even netted a goal in the 1–1 draw at Norwich on Valentine's Day 1987.

An important member of the side throughout the seasons that followed, Brightwell helped City achieve promotion in 1989 and he also scored a wonder 25-yard goal in the February 1990 Old Trafford derby match. After the game he was asked how he scored and with schoolboy excitement he announced: 'I just wellied it!'. That phrase became part of City's 1990s folklore.

Sadly, in December 1992 Brightwell suffered a knee injury that kept him out of action for the rest of the season and most of the following

campaign, but it wasn't the end of his career and he continued to be an important Blue until 1998. After City he proved popular at Coventry, and then with first Walsall and then Stoke he helped the sides achieve promotion in the Division Two play-offs. Later he teamed up with his former City manager Brian Horton at Port Vale and then Macclesfield Town. At Macclesfield he was appointed reserve team manager in 2004, but also made League appearances for the Silkmen, including 10 starts during 2005–06.

One important fact quoted frequently throughout his career was that his parents, Robbie Brightwell and Ann Packer, were both famous athletes who had competed in the 1960 Olympics. In fact his mother's 800m gold medal was Britain's only women's track gold until Sally Gunnell's 1992 success. As well as famous parents, other members of the Brightwell family made the headlines because of sport. Ian's brother David was also a City player and on 29 February 1992 the two Brightwell brothers appeared together in the City side that beat Aston Villa 2–0.

Alec Herd

ALEC HERD (1933–48)
Forward, 5ft 8in, 11st 0lb, b. Bowhill, 8 November 1911, d. Dumfries, 21 August 1982
Signed from: Hamilton Academicals, 1 February 1933
Transferred: Stockport County, 16 March 1948 (free)
Career: Auchterderran School, Hearts o' Beath, Hamilton Academicals, City, Stockport County
Debut: v Blackpool, 4 February 1933
Appearances: League: 257 apps, 107 gls; FA Cup: 30 apps, 17 gls; Charity: 1 app, 1 gl; Wartime (League and Cup): 90 apps, 60 gls; FL Wartime: 3 apps, 0 gls. Total: 381 apps, 185 gls.

Alec Herd joined the Blues from Hamilton Academicals and made his debut on 4 February 1933. By that stage City were already progressing in the FA Cup and had reached the fifth round. Two weeks after his debut he made

his first FA Cup appearance as City beat Bolton 4–2 before 69,920 – a Burnden Park record which according to artist L.S. Lowry was the inspiration for his famous painting *Going to the Match.* As City progressed to Wembley Herd played his part in every Cup match. Sadly, City lost the Final, but 12 months later Herd returned as a member of City's successful side, although he was injured for part of the game and bravely played on. That same season he was the club's leading scorer in the League, a feat he managed again in 1938–39.

During 1936–37 he was a key member of the side that won the Championship for the first time. Herd was a terrific inside-forward with a knack for bringing the ball from deep positions before sending it to the other attackers as they charged forward.

Inevitably, wartime limited his career, but he did remain a Blue when professional football returned and he won a Second Division Championship medal in 1946–47 after scoring 11 goals in 28 appearances.

In March 1948 he joined Stockport on a free transfer and on the final day of the 1950–51 season he made history when he played alongside his son David, famous today for establishing a successful career at Manchester United, as inside-forwards for County against Hartlepool.

Glyn Pardoe

GLYN PARDOE (1961–76)
Defender, 5ft 10in, 11st 7lb, b. Winsford, 1 June 1946
Signed from: amateur, 26 July 1961 (Pro: 4 June 1963)
Retired: 30 April 1976
Career: City
Debut: v Birmingham City, 11 April 1962
Appearances: League: 303+2 apps, 17 gls; FA Cup: 30 apps, 1 gl; League Cup: 26 apps, 4 gls; European Cup: 2 apps, 0 gls; ECWC: 13 apps, 0 gls; Charity: 2 apps, 0 gls; AI Cup: 2 apps, 0 gls. Total: 378+ 2 apps, 22 gls.

Pardoe made history as City's youngest debutant. He was only 15 years and 314 days old when he made his first appearance as a centre-forward in the 4–1 defeat by Birmingham. To select a player so young suggests either desperation on the part of the club or that the player was performing at a very high level. Looking at the stories from the period and the statistics it's clear Pardoe was a player ahead of his age and was there clearly on merit. He retained his place for the following three games, and City ended that season 12th in Division One. Pardoe's selection was clearly thoroughly deserved.

Despite the early promise it took several seasons before he became established in the side. He continued to play mainly as an attacker until the arrival of Mercer and Allison and on 8 October 1966 he was converted to what became his more familiar spot, left-back. From that point on Pardoe's career blossomed, and by 1969 he was acclaimed as one of the top four left-backs in the country. The 1970 League Cup Final programme described him: 'In his early days with the club was a wonder boy centre-forward and although he was never quite sharp enough for that specialist job still retains the necessary ball skills. Looks bulky but in fact moves and tackles swiftly, something which has won him representative recognition and will win him more.' That game saw him score the winner as the Blues defeated West Bromwich Albion in extra-time to win the League Cup for the first time.

Pardoe was a highly versatile player and he could play virtually anywhere in the side. In fact, the only two positions he did not play in were goal and centre-half. Naturally right-sided, he fitted well at left-back, and was renowned for being good in the air.

Sadly, injury at Old Trafford in 1970 hampered his career – in fact he almost had to have his leg amputated so severe was the injury – but nevertheless he remained a member of the squad through to retirement in 1976, and played in the 1974 League Cup Final.

After his playing days finished he worked with Tony Book helping to develop City's great youth side of the mid-1980s and in more recent years he has provided his views on City for local radio station GMR.

Roy Clarke

ROYSTON JAMES CLARKE (1947–58)
Forward, 5ft 9in, 11st 5lb, b. Crindau, Newport, 1 June 1925, d. Manchester, 13 March 2006

Signed from: Cardiff City, 23 May 1947
Transferred: Stockport County, 19 September 1958
Career: Albion Rovers, Cardiff ATC, Cardiff City, City, Stockport County, Northwich Victoria player-manager
Debut: v Newport County, 14 June 1947
Appearances: League: 349 apps, 73 gls; FA Cup: 20 apps, 6 gls; Charity: 1 app, 0 gls. Total: 370 apps, 79 gls.

Loyal club servant Roy Clarke is a key figure in City's history. He joined the Blues in 1947 and was a popular member of the side for the following 11 years, during which time he helped the side reach successive Wembley Finals. He also appeared for Wales on 22 occasions while with City, and earlier, in 1939, he was a Welsh Schools' Baseball International.

When he first arrived some felt he was too frail for top-flight football (City were promoted from Division Two in his first match), but his appearance was deceptive. A trademark Clarke moment would often see him charge forward with his head down, looking up at the crucial moment, before body swerving an opponent and then sending in a perfect centre. Journalist Eric Todd once claimed Clarke was 'built for speed rather than comfort'.

He won an FA Cup-winners' medal in 1956 and was one of the side's more involved players, but it was his role in the 1955 semi-final against Sunderland which personally brought him the headlines. That rain-sodden day at Villa Park Clarke sent a thunderous header into the net to give City victory. Sadly, he was later injured and missed several games in the run up to Wembley. He did return to action in mid-April but suffered another injury in his third comeback game and missed the Final. It was an unfortunate blow.

After Wembley in 1956 he started to develop his interest in coaching at Maine Road, but teammate Jimmy Meadows was also keen and Clarke stepped aside, allowing him the opportunity. After a spell at Stockport County Clarke returned to Maine Road to fulfil a variety of roles. Most notably he founded the club's highly successful Development Association, and in 1966 became the first manager of the City Social club.

Together with his wife Kath, he remained the manager for almost 25 years, helping to bring success in a different field to the Blues. Arthur Hopcraft's *The Football Man* – one of football's most important literary works – paid Clarke a great tribute by devoting significant space to the importance of the City Social Club, which was the first of its kind. Roy and Kath Clarke were responsible for that success.

After retirement from that role, Clarke was a key figure behind the creation of the thriving Former Players Association, and he also became a matchday ambassador for the club. His tours of Maine Road added a wonderful touch to matchday activities.

Sadly, his later years saw him suffer with Alzheimer's, although he continued to attend games at the City of Manchester stadium as often as possible. He passed away in March 2006, as this book was in its final stages of preparation. His funeral was attended by a large number of former players, officials, and supporters.

Joe Hayes

JOSEPH HAYES (1953–65)
Forward, 5ft 7in, 10st 11lb, b. Kearsley, 20 January 1936, d. 1999
Signed from: trial, 29 August 1953

Transferred: Barnsley, 30 June 1965 (Free)
Career: Kearsley West Youth Club, Bury (trial), Bolton Wanderers (trial), City, Barnsley, Wigan Athletic, Lancaster City player-manager
Debut: v Tottenham Hotspur, 24 October 1953
Appearances: League: 331 apps, 142 gls; FA Cup: 24 apps, 9 gls; League Cup: 8 apps, 1 gl; Charity: 1 app, 0 gls. Total: 364 apps, 152 gls.

Joe Hayes was a great goalscorer for the Blues during an 11-year Maine Road career. He was only 17 when he made his debut and by the end of his first season he had made 11 appearances.

His permanent place in the side came in the latter half of the 1954–55 season and inevitably he appeared in the 1955 Final. Twelve months later he hit the headlines when he netted the opening goal of the 1956 Final in the third minute. That season he was also the club's leading League scorer with 23 goals from 42 appearances.

The 1957–58 season was another which saw Hayes making a name for himself as he netted 25 times in the League from only 40 appearances, to help the Blues achieve fifth place. Around the same time he also appeared for the England Under-23 side and for an FA XI.

Hayes continued to perform well over the years that followed and in 1961–62 he netted 16 goals in 39 games. The following season he started to drift in and out of the side, and only managed 21 appearances. Then, in September 1963, he suffered a serious knee injury at Bury. During 1964–65 he bravely made two further appearances, but he was never quite the same player again and was transferred to Barnsley during the close season. He was only 29. Had the injury not occurred it's possible he might have played a part in City's rehabilitation under Mercer and Allison.

Spells at Wigan and Lancaster followed, but his injury never really allowed him to play at his best. After his footballing career finished he worked for a finance company before moving into the greengrocery trade in his home town of Bolton. He passed away in 1999. Today, Hayes's name is not remembered as one of City's great players, but his goalscoring ratio certainly puts him high up the list of quality strikers. He deserves to be remembered as a leading City star.

Tommy Johnson

THOMAS CLARK FISHER JOHNSON (1919–30)
Forward, 5ft 10in, 12st 0lb, b. Dalton-in-Furness, 19 August 1901, d. Manchester, 28 January 1973
Signed from: amateur, February 1919 (Pro: 20 March 1919)
Transferred: Everton, 5 March 1930 (£6,000)
Career: Dalton Athletic, Dalton Casuals, City, Everton, Liverpool, Darwen player-manager
Debut: v Middlesbrough, 18 February 1920
Appearances: League: 328 apps, 158 gls; FA Cup: 26 apps, 8 gls; Wartime (League and Cup): 5 apps, 4 gls. Total: 359 apps, 170 gls.

Attacker Tommy Johnson was idolised by the City faithful throughout his career. He arrived at Hyde Road in 1919 and scored in his first senior appearance when Blackburn were defeated 5–1 in the Lancashire section of the wartime league. He didn't make his League debut until February 1920, but by the mid-1920s he was a vital member of the first team.

In 1926–27 Johnson topped City's goalscoring charts for the first time, netting 25

goals in 38 appearances. The following season he scored 19 goals in 35 appearances as City achieved promotion, but his best season was undoubtedly 1928–29 when he broke the club's goalscoring record. He scored 38 goals in 39 League appearances. Johnson was alternating from his customary inside-left position to centre-forward, and this changing emphasis helped the player, especially in his fifth game of the season when he scored five during the 6–2 victory at Everton. City had arrived late for the match, were subsequently fined, went a goal down early on, and then fought back to win by a four-goal margin. It was an amazing match, and one which brought Johnson to the attention of Everton. The next season brought 11 goals from 30 League games, but in March he was transferred to Everton. The fans were livid. They demonstrated against his departure and then voted with their feet. City's average crowd dropped by 7,000 as a result.

After great success at Goodison, including an FA Cup Final victory over City in 1933, Johnson moved across Stanley Park to Liverpool. A spell followed at Darwen. During the sixties he was a regular at Maine Road, occasionally coming to games with his old Everton teammate Dixie Dean to watch Joe Mercer's side.

In 1973 Johnson died in Monsall hospital aged 71.

Bobby Marshall

ROBERT SAMUEL MARSHALL (1928–39)
Forward, 5ft 11in, 12st 12lb, b. Hucknall, 3 April 1903, d. Chesterfield, 27 October 1966
Signed from: Sunderland, 1 March 1928
Transferred: Stockport County, 22 March 1939
Career: Hucknall Olympic, Sunderland, City, Stockport County
Debut: v Blackpool, 3 March 1928
Appearances: League: 325 apps, 70 gls; FA Cup: 30 apps, 10 gls; Charity: 1 app, 0 gls; Total: 356 apps, 80 gls.

Nottinghamshire-born Bobby Marshall was a star man at Sunderland before joining the Blues, scoring 69 goals in 198 League games at Roker Park. At Sunderland Marshall had been a fine inside-right, but by the time he was playing in City's Championship-winning side of 1936–37 he had made the centre-half position his after fulfilling the role on a needs-must basis. In between his arrival in March 1928 and that Championship season he appeared in two FA Cup Finals for the Blues, playing at inside-right.

Marshall possessed great ball control and seemed confident and capable no matter where he played – he once donned the goalkeeper's jersey in an emergency at Sunderland. His last League appearance for City came on 18 April 1938, and then 11 months later he was transferred to Stockport County. He became County manager between 1939 and February 1949 and followed this with three years in charge of Chesterfield.

Marshall passed away in 1966 at the age of 63, after collapsing while working in the public house of which he was licensee. His younger brother Harry was a forward with Nottingham Forest, Southport, Wolves, Port Vale, Spurs, and Rochdale.

Jim Goodchild

ANDREW JAMES GOODCHILD (1911–27)
Goalkeeper, 5ft 11in, 12st 7lb, b. Southampton, 4 April 1892, d. Eastleigh, 2 October 1950
Signed from: amateur: October 1911 (Pro: 15 December 1911)
Transferred: Guildford City, 18 August 1927
Career: Foundry Lane School, St Paul's Athletic, Southampton, City, Guildford City, Stoneham Nomads
Debut: v Aston Villa, 20 January 1912
Appearances: League: 204 apps, 0 gls; FA Cup: 13 apps, 0 gls; Wartime (League and Cup): 130 apps, 0 gls. Total: 347 apps, 0 gls.

Goalkeeper Jim Goodchild joined Southern League side Southampton in 1909 and made his debut in their last match of the 1909–10 season (a 3–1 win), but he only managed four games the following season. He kept clean sheets in two of those games, but his final couple of games both ended in 5–1 defeats. Inevitably, the Southampton management felt that he was never likely to be good enough to oust their regular number one, and so at the end of the season he was released.

He found employment on the Southampton docks, before Southampton scout and ex-1892–93 season Ardwick League player Jimmy Yates called his former club and told them of Goodchild's availability. The following January he made his debut and became City's first choice for the next couple of seasons. He was ousted by former first choice Walter Smith in 1913, but by the start of the 1915–16 wartime season he was back in goal.

After the war 'naughty boy' Goodchild, as he was nicknamed by fans, became a popular player and had a distinguished career. He was not a thrilling 'keeper in the mode of Trautmann, nor was he an entertainer like Swift, but he was safe and a consistent performer. He was ever-present when City finished second in 1920–21 and he was 'keeper for the 1926 FA Cup Final, although by that time he was nearing the end of his career and there was immense competition. The following year he left the Blues, moved back to Southampton and became licensee of the Royal Albert hotel, playing part-time for Guildford City. In 1941 he took over the Cricketers Arms at Eastleigh, and he remained there until his death in 1950.

Two popular stories from the early 1920s focussed on his large woollen cap that he always tried to wear and of what lay underneath. According to one story he dived to make a save in one match, his cap fell off and Goodchild

quickly dived away from the ball to get his cap and replace it before the fans could see his bald head! Similarly, when the king visited in 1920 Goodchild was reluctant to remove his cap when the king came on to the field to meet the players. Eventually he did and his lack of hair became a major talking point.

Billy Walsh

WILLIAM WALSH (1936–51)
Defender, 5ft 9in, 10st 7lb, b. Dublin, 31 May 1921
Signed from: Manchester United, 5 May 1936
Transferred: Chelmsford City player-manager, 11 April 1951 (free)
Career: St Gregory's School (Ardwick), Manchester United, City, Chelmsford City player-manager, Canterbury player-manager
Debut: v Leicester City, 31 August 1946
Appearances: League: 109 apps, 1 gl; FA Cup: 9 apps, 0 gls; Wartime (League and Cup): 229 apps, 8 gls. Total: 347 apps, 9 gls.

Dublin-born Billy Walsh moved to Manchester at the age of seven and went on to represent England at schoolboy level. He joined United as an amateur in 1935, while working with City as an office junior. The following year he joined the Blues as a player and turned professional in 1938.

Due to the outbreak of war he did not make his full League debut until 1946, but he was a key member of the wartime side. Post-war he

became an established half-back with the Blues.

While with City he hit the headlines for making international appearances for both Eire and Northern Ireland. Combined with his schoolboy appearance for England, this means Walsh played for three different countries.

The reason he appeared for both Irelands is that during his career Northern Ireland were allowed to pick players born on either side of the Irish border for Home International Championship matches, and so Walsh played five times for Northern Ireland and nine for Eire while with City.

After City he joined Chelmsford and Canterbury, and also had a spell as Grimsby Town manager. Later he emigrated to Australia where, in 2006, he still lives, although he has managed the occasional trip back to Manchester to see the Blues in recent years.

David White

DAVID WHITE (1984–93)
Forward, 6ft 1in, 12st 9lb, b. Urmston, 30 October 1967
Signed from: apprentice, 4 June 1984 (Pro: 20 October 1985)
Transferred: Leeds United, 22 December 1993 (£1,200,000 – estimated value as part of Rocastle transfer)
Career: Eccles School, Salford Boys, City, Leeds United, Sheffield United
Debut: v Leicester City, 4 October 1986
Appearances: League: 273+12 apps, 79 gls; FA Cup: 22 apps, 4 gls; League Cup: 24+1 apps, 11 gls; FMC: 9 apps, 2 gls. Total: 328+13 apps, 96 gls.

Mancunian David White signed apprentice forms on his 18th birthday, appeared in the 1986 FA Youth Cup-winning side of May 1986, then made his first team debut in a 1–0 victory at Luton on 27 September 1986, coming on as substitute for Trevor Christie. That season he appeared in 24 League games and, following relegation in 1987, the fast right-winger became a permanent fixture. One of his finest early moments came in November 1987 when he

netted a hat-trick in the 10–1 annihilation of Malcolm Macdonald's Huddersfield Town.

Fast and popular, White seemed at his best when charging towards the North Stand, urged on by those standing on the Kippax at Maine Road. Promotion came in 1989 when White only missed one of City's 46 League games, and in the top flight the winger continued to impress. In 1990–91 White was an ever-present and netted 15 goals in 38 League games. That same season he won his first England 'B' cap, and he also became the first player since Brian Kidd in January 1977 to score four in the League as Aston Villa were defeated 5–1.

Another great season followed as White became City's top scorer with 18 goals in 39 League games in 1991–92, and this led to him being called up to the full international side. On 9 September 1992 he made his England debut but, with his first kick of the match, he was presented with a great goalscoring opportunity. He failed to score and the weight of the miss seemed to affect his play. Had the chance arrived a little later in the game it is highly likely he would have scored, but no allowance was made for his inexperience and he was made the scapegoat for a 1–0 defeat by Spain. This experience seemed to affect his City career and in December 1993 he was transferred to Leeds in exchange for David Rocastle.

Tall, strong, fast and exciting, White was a great and popular member of the City side of the late eighties and early nineties. Since the move to the City of Manchester stadium, White has assisted City's hospitality department on matchdays and continues to be a popular Blue.

Billy Lot Jones

WILLIAM LOT JONES (1903–19)
Forward, 5ft 6in, 10st 7lb, b. Chirk, April 1882, d. Chirk, 13 July 1941
Signed from: Ruabon Druids, 19 January 1903
Transferred: Southend United, August 1919
Career: Chirk School, Chirk, Ruabon Druids, City, Southend United, Aberdare Athletic, Wrexham, Oswestry Town, Chirk player-manager
Debut: v West Bromwich Albion, 9 April 1904
Appearances: League: 281 apps, 69 gls; FA Cup: 20 apps, 5 gls; Wartime (League and Cup): 37 apps, 6 gls. Total: 338 apps, 80 gls.

Billy Lot Jones arrived at City in 1903 but didn't make his debut until April 1904. He only managed one League appearance that season as the Blues reached the Cup Final, but midway

through the following season he became an established member of the side. He made 12 appearances as City reached third spot in the League.

His best spell came immediately prior to World War One, but the war brought a premature end to his City League career. After the war he joined Southend and later had spells at Aberdare, Wrexham, Oswestry and Chirk, where he became player-manager.

During his City career forward Jones made 19 international appearances for Wales.

Francis Lee

FRANCIS HENRY LEE (1967–74)
Forward, 5ft 8in, 11st 8lb, b. Westhoughton, 29 April 1944
Signed from: Bolton Wanderers, 9 October 1967 (£60,000)
Transferred: Derby County, 14 August 1974 (£110,000)
Career: Bolton Wanderers, City, Derby County
Debut: v Wolverhampton Wanderers, 14 October 1967
Appearances: League: 248+1 apps, 112 gls; FA Cup: 24 apps, 7 gls; League Cup 26 apps, 14 gls; European Cup 2 apps, 0 gls; ECWC: 18 apps, 10 gls; UEFA Cup: 2 apps, 0 gls; Charity: 4 apps, 3 gls; AI Cup: 2 apps, 1 gl; T Cup: 2+1 apps, 1 gl. Total: 328+2 apps, 148 gls.

Francis Lee was described in the 1970 League Cup Final programme as: 'Chunky, stocky, strong, marvellously powerful runner, difficult to dispossess and one of the best right-footed strikers in the game. Tremendous confidence is the corner-stone of his game and this is one reason why he is and will remain a regular member of the England team.' The profile seemed to sum him up perfectly and in that game he demonstrated all those qualities and many more as the Final became one of his best City performances. He was rightly voted the supporters' player of the year that season.

Lee joined City for a fee of £60,000 in October 1967. It was a record City fee, but one that was more than repaid within his first season as he helped the Blues to the 1967–68 League Championship. Prior to Lee's arrival City had lost five of their opening 11 games and certainly did not look like champions, but with Lee they went on an 11-game unbeaten run and were only to lose a further five throughout that season. He netted 16 goals in 31 games, including the final goal of the Championship decider at Newcastle.

The final piece of the jigsaw, according to Joe Mercer, Lee's arrival set the Blues up for all the successes that followed and he certainly played his part in each triumph. A thrilling, bustling forward, Lee had many great moments with the Blues. He was also one of City's most popular England internationals. He made 27 full international appearances within a mere three years and 140 days. He also scored 10 goals from open play and featured in the 1970 World Cup Finals. In fact, although City had fielded many internationals over the years, Lee was the first City player to play for England in World Cup Finals when he faced Romania on 2 June in Mexico.

Regrettably, his City career seemed to end prematurely and, despite being the Blues'

leading scorer for each of his final five seasons with the club, he was transferred to Derby in August 1974. As if to prove how foolish City were to transfer him, he went on to win the title in his first season at Derby County.

Once his playing career came to an end he regularly made the sporting papers for his involvement in the racehorse business, while the business pages focussed on his highly successful toilet roll manufacturing company (comedian Peter Kay worked at his factory for a while) and other businesses. In 1993, with overwhelming support from fans, he mounted a takeover bid and early in 1994 he replaced Peter Swales as City's chairman. Despite significant progress off the pitch, including the development of the Kippax Stand, the Platt Lane complex, and the initial discussions and negotiations on the creation of the new stadium, Lee's City failed on the pitch. Ultimately, with relegation to Division Two on the horizon, he stepped down and was replaced by David Bernstein.

Since that time he has remained a major shareholder and attendee at City matches. He will always be a popular and important member of City's greatest side, remembered for his unrelenting determination.

Asa Hartford

RICHARD ASA HARTFORD (1974–79 and 1981–84)
Midfield, 5ft 6in, 11st 2lb, b. Clydebank, 24 October 1950
Signed from: West Bromwich Albion, 13 August 1974 (£210,000)
Transferred: Nottingham Forest, 27 June 1979 (£500,000)
Signed from: Everton, 1 October 1981 (£350,000)
Transferred: Fort Lauderdale Sun, 8 May 1984
Career: Clydebank High School, Drumchapel Amateurs, West Bromwich Albion, City, Nottingham Forest, Everton, City, Fort Lauderdale Sun, Norwich City, Bolton Wanderers player-coach, Stockport County player-manager, Oldham Athletic, Shrewsbury Town player-manager, Boston United
Debut: v West Ham United, 17 August 1974
Appearances: League: 259+1 apps, 29 gls; FA Cup: 17 apps, 2 gls; League Cup: 29 apps, 3 gls; UEFA Cup: 12 apps, 2 gls; AS Cup: 3 apps, 0 gls; TC Cup: 2 apps, 1 gl. Total: 322+1 apps, 37 gls.

Midfield dynamo Asa Hartford is second only to Colin Bell in the number of international appearances he made for the home nations while on the books of City. Hartford played 36 times for Scotland during his Maine Road career and featured in both the 1978 and 1982 World Cup Finals.

Hartford began his career with West Bromwich Albion, making over 200 appearances for them between 1967 and 1974, and he played in the 1970 League Cup Final against City. In August 1974 manager Tony Book paid Albion approximately £210,000 for the Scottish international (he had already been capped six times). Hartford rapidly became a popular member of the exciting seventies side. Inevitably, in 1976 he was part of the League Cup-winning team, and in 1976–77 the side

that finished second to the all-powerful Liverpool team.

In 1978–79 supporters voted him Player of the Year and it looked as if he would be a key City man for several years. However, he was one of the players Malcolm Allison felt no longer had a future at the club and he was sold to Nottingham Forest during the 1979 close season for £500,000. Supporters were disappointed, while the move was quickly followed by another to Everton.

In October 1981, with John Bond now in charge, Hartford was brought back to Maine Road. The supporters were delighted with the £350,000 purchase, especially as Hartford was still an international. He remained until May 1984, and then moved to Fort Lauderdale in the NASL. He later returned to England and joined Norwich, where he again proved a success, scoring the goal that beat Sunderland to lift the 1985 League Cup in his final game for the club.

After Norwich, Hartford coached in Norway, played for Bolton and became assistant manager of Portsmouth, player-manager of Stockport and manager of Shrewsbury. He also worked for Blackburn and Stoke before, in July 1995, he returned to Maine Road again. This time he was assistant manager to Alan Ball, then during 1996 he found himself acting as caretaker-manager following Ball's demise. He continued as part of City's coaching set-up until 2005.

Tony Book

ANTHONY KEITH BOOK (1966–73)
Defender, 5ft 10in, 11st 7lb, b. Bath, 4 September 1935
Signed from Plymouth Argyle, 20 July 1966 (£17,000)
Retired: 30 March 1974
Career: West Twerton School, Peasedown St John, Frome Town, Chelsea, Toronto, Bath City, Plymouth Argyle, City
Debut: v Southampton, 20 August 1966
Appearances: League: 242+2 apps, 4 gls; FA Cup: 28 apps, 0 gls; League Cup: 19+1 apps, 1 gl; ECWC: 16 apps, 0 gls; UEFA Cup: 1 app, 0 gls; Charity: 3 apps, 0 gls; AI Cup: 2 apps, 0 gls; T Cup: 1 app, 0 gls. Total: 312+3 apps, 5 gls.

Described by journalists as the 'Cinderella Man' of football, as a result of the success he found as a professional footballer late in his playing career (he made his League debut shortly before his 29th birthday), Tony Book remains one of the most influential footballers the club has ever had. Signed for £17,000, Book made his debut following promotion in 1966, and this came only two weeks before his 31st birthday. Despite his age, Book was viewed as a quick player for much of his City career. He was also a great reader of the game and a captain in every sense of the word.

Inevitably he guided City on the pitch throughout the glory years of the Mercer-Allison reign and featured in all the major successes of that time. In 1969 he was voted joint Football Writers' player of the year with Derby's Dave Mackay, although he had missed much of the season through injury. That season, as reigning champions, the Blues were under considerable pressure and it's fair to say Book's absence was felt. Nevertheless, his return coincided with the great FA Cup run and Book collected the trophy at Wembley in April. In total Book lifted four major trophies (won over three seasons) during his City playing career.

After his playing days finished he fulfilled a variety of roles at City including team manager. It was Book's side that won the League Cup in 1976. Those exploits are covered in the Managers section of this book.

All in all Book was a tremendous player and leader during a eight-year playing career at Maine Road.

Horace Barnes

HORACE BARNES (1914–24)
Forward, 5ft 8in, 11st 0lb, b. Wadsley Bridge, Sheffield, 3 January 1891, d. Clayton, 12 September 1961
Signed from: Derby County, 14 May 1914 (£2,500)
Transferred: Preston NE, 11 November 1924

Tony Book

Career: Owlerton St John, Birley Carr, Wadsley Bridge, Derby County, City, Preston NE, Oldham Athletic, Ashton National
Debut: v Bradford City, 1 September 1914
Appearances: League: 217 apps, 120 gls; FA Cup: 18 apps, 5 gls; Wartime (League and Cup): 73 apps, 73 gls. Total: 308 apps, 198 gls.

Horace Barnes had an incredible goalscoring record and combined perfectly with Tommy Browell, although these were trophy-free years. Barnes was the first City goalscorer at Maine Road, and he also scored both goals three years earlier when the king attended Hyde Road for a game with Liverpool. He ended that season as joint highest scorer (22 in 39 appearances), and in 1920–21, as City finished second to the all-powerful Burnley, Barnes was second highest scorer.

He possessed a very powerful kick and one anecdote passed through the generations tells how he once hit a 35-yard free-kick with such force that the ball broke both wrists of the opposing goalkeeper who, apparently, tried to punch it clear.

City signed Barnes from Derby for £2,500 – a record fee at the time – in 1914 and he made his debut the following September, although war took a substantial period from his career. He remained at City until November 1924 when he was transferred to Preston. His appearances had been limited during his final year or so but he still managed to be City's highest scorer in 1923–24 with 20 goals from 23 games.

After a year at Preston he moved to Oldham, then joined Cheshire League club Ashton National. His goalscoring exploits were not over, however, as in a 'Rest Of Cheshire' game against Port Vale he scored six goals in the first half hour. In addition to his footballing skills, he was also a good cricketer.

Later he took a job as a packer at Mather & Platt, close to the present-day City of Manchester Stadium. With the determination and endeavour that he always managed to show at Hyde Road and Maine Road, he continued working until he was 70. Sadly, he died aged 71 at his home in Clayton in 1961.

Sam Cookson

SAMUEL COOKSON (1918–28)
Defender, 5ft 8in, 12st 0lb, b. Manchester, 22 November 1896, d. Manchester, 17 August 1955
Signed from: Macclesfield, October 1918
Transferred: Bradford PA, 28 September 1928
Career: Ancoats Lads Club, South Salford Lads Club, Walkden, Stalybridge Celtic, Macclesfield Town, City, Bradford Park Avenue, Barnsley
Debut: v Bradford City, 1 January 1920
Appearances: League: 285 apps, 0 gls; FA Cup: 21 apps, 1 gl; Total: 306 apps, 1 gl.

Mancunian Sam Cookson joined City from Macclesfield in 1918 and went on to become a regular in the side from 1920 until the 1927–28 season. Cookson was a relatively small but heavily built player and was known as a difficult man to beat. Opposition attackers would try to rush past him, but Cookson always seemed to take control of the situation and more often than not would take the ball from his opponent. An everpresent during the 1920–21 League runners-up season, Cookson's consistency impressed many, although somehow he never managed to gain an international cap.

In 1926 he gained a FA Cup finalists' medal as City met Bolton at Wembley, but according to his family the medal was stolen during the

1930s when Cookson was attacked during his time as landlord of the Swan With Two Necks public house at Shude Hill in Manchester city centre. His shirt, however, remained in the family's possession and since 2005 this has been on display at the club's museum, The Manchester City Experience.

Cookson joined Bradford in September 1928, and also had a successful spell with Barnsley, where he won a Third Division North championship medal when he was in his 39th year. Once his playing career came to an end he moved into the brewing trade and also worked for the Co-op. He passed away in August 1955 at the relatively young age of 59.

Dave Ewing

DAVID EWING (1949–62)
Defender, 6ft 1in, 14st 9lb, b. Perth, 10 May 1929, d. Stockport
Signed from: Luncarty Juniors, 10 June 1949
Transferred: Crewe Alexandra, 7 July 1962 (free)
Career: Luncarty Juniors, City, Crewe Alexandra, Ashton United
Debut: v Manchester United, 3 January 1953
Appearances: League: 279 apps, 1 gl; FA Cup: 22 apps, 0 gls; League Cup: 1 app, 0 gls; Charity: 1 app, 0 gls. Total: 303 apps, 1 gl.

Dave Ewing made his first-team debut in January 1953, after joining the Blues in 1949, and soon established himself as a crucial member of City's defence.

He was a tall, well-built centre-half, often described as one of the toughest centre-halves in the country. Ewing was a very popular player with supporters, and was well known for his vocal encouragement, which seemed to liven up even the dullest of games. He also managed to wind up many opponents, most notably the Birmingham players in the 1956 FA Cup Final.

In 1953–54 he was ever-present in the League and went on to be one of the club's most consistent performers of the fifties. By the early sixties the bulk of the successful fifties side had moved on and inevitably Ewing left Maine Road himself in July 1962 when he joined Crewe on a free transfer.

He later returned to City as a coach during the Mercer-Allison years, and he also had coaching spells at Sheffield Wednesday, Bradford City and Crystal Palace. He was manager at Hibernian before returning to Maine Road, and in 1977–78 he guided the reserves to the Central League title for the first time.

Roy Paul

ROY PAUL (1950–57)
Half-back, 5ft 10in, 12st 10lb, b. Gelli Pentre, 18 April 1920, d. South Wales, 21 May 2002
Signed from: Swansea, 18 July 1950 (£25,000)
Transferred: Worcester City (free)
Career: Ton Pentre, Swansea Town, City, Worcester City player-manager, Brecon Corinthians player-manager, Garw Athletic player-manager
Debut: v Preston North End, 19 August 1950
Appearances: League: 270 apps, 9 gls; FA Cup: 23 apps, 0 gls; Charity: 1 app, 0 gls. Total: 294 apps, 9 gls.

The high point of Roy Paul's career must have been City's success in the 1956 FA Cup Final. The game has gone down in history as the Trautmann Final, although City's victory owes much to the entire team, but in particular to its influential captain Paul. After the game journalist Eric Thornton wrote: 'Take it from me, Paul has never played better at Wembley.'

Surprisingly, as a boy Paul wasn't rated as a footballer. He failed to make the school team and once commented: 'Nothing I have ever suffered since – not even that Cup Final defeat in 1955 – was ever quite as bad as the bitter disappointments I had at school. After these three trials, the schoolmaster sadly took me to one side and said, "You are not big enough Paul. Not quick enough and not strong enough... Just keep on trying!"' Paul did keep on trying and he went on to be one of City's greatest captains of all time and a terrific Welsh international player.

Other footballing figures recognised Paul's skills and determination. Another great Welsh player, John Charles, admitted that Paul: 'was my idol – my ideal when I was a boy'. Newcastle's successful captain Joe Harvey said: 'When I want to show a youngster how a wing-half should play I take him to see Roy Paul. He is the complete wing-half.'

Prior to joining the Blues Paul made his name at Swansea – Arsenal tried to sign him after a suggestion from another Paul fan,

Arsenal captain and future City manager Joe Mercer – and had a brief spell in South America, but he became a Blue in 1950. He made 41 appearances as City achieved promotion in his first season, but it was the mid-fifties period when the side became a force.

In 1954–55, with Paul as captain, the Blues finished seventh and reached the Cup Final. His determination helped to push the side forward and in the Final itself, after City were down to 10 men, Paul worked hard to motivate his players. Defeat was hard to take and Paul immediately vowed to lead City back to Wembley the following year. Twelve months later he did just that and the Blues were victorious. Shortly after the 1956 FA Cup win he admitted to journalists that he had almost retired following the previous season's defeat.

Hard-working Paul was one of City's most influential players of all time and his drive and determination was always evident. In 1957 he moved to Worcester on a free transfer, becoming their player-manager. He later joined Brecon Corinthians and Garw Athletic, and became a lorry driver in south Wales before passing away in 2002 aged 82.

Eric Westwood

ERIC WESTWOOD (1937–53)
Defender, 5ft 9in, 12st 8lb, b. Manchester, 25 September 1917, d. Manchester, 2001
Signed from: Manchester United, 13 November 1937
Transferred: Altrincham, 10 June 1953 (free)
Career: New Moston School, New Moston Juniors, Fairfield, Stretford Rovers, Manchester United, City, Altrincham
Debut: v Tottenham Hotspur, 5 November 1938
Appearances: League: 248 apps, 3 gls; FA Cup: 12 apps, 2 gls; Wartime (League and Cup): 29 apps, 1 gl; FL Wartime: 3 apps, 0 gls. Total: 292 apps, 6 gls.

Mancunian Eric Westwood was an amateur with United before moving to City in November 1937. He made his City debut on the same day as Bert Sproston in 1938 and seemed destined for a great career, but war broke out and it is fair to say he lost his prime playing years. Inevitably, because of his age and fitness, he did manage guest appearances for sides close to his wartime postings, most notably for Chelsea where he appeared in the 1944 War Cup (South) Final at Wembley before 85,000 fans, but he also saw military action. When football returned on a national basis Westwood played his part in the Second Division championship season of 1946–47 and by the time of Bert Trautmann's arrival in 1949 Westwood, the Normandy veteran, was City captain.

Westwood's last League appearance for the Blues came on 3 January 1953 in the 1–1 draw with United at Old Trafford. The following June, 1953, the skilful full-back was given a free-transfer and signed for Altrincham.

Steve Redmond

STEVE REDMOND (1984–92)
Defender, 5ft 11in, 12st 13lb, b. Liverpool, 2 November 1967
Signed from: Liverpool Boys, 1 July 1984
Transferred: Oldham, 5 August 1992 (complicated deal where Redmond and Pointon were swapped for Ricky Holden)
Career: Liverpool Boys, City, Oldham Athletic, Bury
Debut: v Queens Park Rangers, 8 February 1986
Appearances: League: 231+4 apps, 7 gls; FA Cup: 17 apps, 0 gls; League Cup: 24 apps, 0 gls; FMC: 11 apps, 0 gls. Total: 283+4 apps, 7 gls.

Steve Redmond made his League debut in February 1986, and then the following April he captained City to victory in the 1986 FA Youth Cup Final when Manchester United were defeated 3–1 on aggregate. Redmond himself was one of the club's most important young players of the period, as Billy McNeill's City relied on youth. Redmond was truly thrown in at the deep end and his third League game was the 2–2 Old Trafford derby on 22 March, then the following day he played at Wembley in the Full Members' Cup Final at the age of 18. This meant that prior to playing in the Youth Cup Final he had played in eight Division One matches, 21 Central League games, and 15 Lancashire League games, plus the Wembley appearance. He was also an England Youth international at this point.

In the years that followed he won the Player of the Year award and succeeded Kenny

Clements to become City's youngest-ever captain. He even went in nets for one game when Eric Nixon was sent off.

In 1988–89 he was an ever-present as City won promotion during a 46-game season, and he was the only ever-present for the following season in Division One. Sadly, in August 1992 Peter Reid felt he was no longer part of his plans and he was transferred, with Neil Pointon, to Oldham in the deal that brought Ricky Holden to Maine Road. Redmond's replacement in the first team was Michel Vonk.

Ken Barnes

KENNETH HERBERT BARNES (1950–61)
Half-back, 5ft 10in, 11st 11lb, b. Birmingham, 16 March 1929
Signed from: Stafford Rangers, 6 May 1950
Transferred: Wrexham player-manager, 4 May 1961
Career: Moor Green, Birmingham City, Stafford Rangers, City, Wrexham player-manager, Witton Albion player-manager
Debut: v Derby County, 5 January 1952
Appearances: League: 258 apps, 18 gls; FA Cup: 23 apps, 1 gl; League Cup: 2 apps, 0 gls. Total: 283 apps, 19 gls.

Awarded a Lifetime Achievement Award in 2005 for services to the club, Barnes has been a popular presence at City since the time of his arrival in May 1950. Often described as 'the best uncapped wing-half' of all time, Barnes was unfortunate not to play for England. Fellow professionals believe his non-selection was as a result of bias within the FA selection committee to players from their preferred clubs, and it is clear that Barnes was certainly equal to if not better than the majority of players featuring for England in his position during the fifties. Whatever the politics, Barnes was a consistently great City player.

His first appearance came in January 1952 but, surprisingly, he didn't get another chance to impress until the second match of the 1954–55 season. Manager Les McDowall was tinkering with his new deep-lying centre-forward tactical innovation and coach Fred Tilson and centre-forward Don Revie felt Barnes would help to make it succeed. He did, and the plan helped the Blues to consecutive FA Cup Final appearances in 1955 and 1956. Although the plan became known as the Revie Plan, all associated with the Blues recognised the contribution of all players, in particular Barnes.

On 7 December 1957 Barnes became only the third person to successfully convert three penalties in a Division One game, as City

defeated Everton 6–2. Albert Dunlop, who later became a City scout working for Barnes, was the Everton 'keeper that day and Barnes remembers facing Dunlop for each attempt: 'I stuck one to the left, one to the right and he was so confused by the time the third award arrived that I could have back-heeled it in!'

Barnes continued playing for the Blues until May 1961 when he joined Wrexham as player-manager. His later City career had seen him captain the team and his leadership qualities helped Wrexham to promotion, although Barnes's frank approach led to disagreements with his directors and he soon realised he either had to hold back his views or give up on management. Never one to hide his feelings, Barnes decided management wasn't for him. He did use his leadership qualities again, however, during the Mercer-Allison years when Joe Mercer asked him back to Maine Road in a coaching capacity. Over the years that followed he became a key member of the backroom staff and during the 1980s he helped guide the careers of youngsters Paul Lake, David White and Ian Brightwell. Barnes's influence was felt right through to the mid-1990s. A temporary exhibition at the Manchester City Experience (City's award-winning museum) in 2006 was dedicated to the career of Ken and his son Peter.

Bill Leivers

WILLIAM ERNEST LEIVERS (1953–64)
Defender, 6ft 2in, 14st 0lb, b. Bolsover, 29 January 1932
Signed from: Chesterfield, 27 November 1953 (£10,500)
Transferred: Doncaster Rovers, 10 July 1964
Career: Chesterfield, City, Doncaster Rovers player-manager, Workington Town
Debut: v Preston North End, 21 August 1954
Appearances: League: 250 apps, 4 gls; FA Cup: 20 apps, 0 gls; League Cup 11 apps, 0 gls; Charity: 1 app, 0 gls. Total: 282 apps, 4 gls.

Centre-half Bill Leivers joined City from Third Division North side Chesterfield for a fee of £10,500 in November 1953, and within two years he had played in the 1956 FA Cup-winning side. Immediately after the Final City's star forward Don Revie told journalists: 'If I must pick one man out it would be Bill Leivers. He had two pain-killing injections on his sprained ankle, yet he played the game of his life. Many of our attacking moves stemmed from his intelligent passing which switched defence on to attack.'

Leivers played as a right-back in that Final but later in his career he was moved to the number-five shirt. He remained a Blue until July 1964, and was the last of the great fifties side to appear regularly for City (Trautmann and Hayes made infrequent appearances during Leivers's last season).

After City he became player-manager of Doncaster, but resigned after guiding them to the top of the old Division Four, and followed this with a period as manager of Cambridge United when they climbed from the Southern League to Division Three. He also had spells at Chelmsford City and Cambridge City. He attended Maine Road during its last season, and around the same time he moved to Cornwall.

Kenny Clements

KENNETH HENRY CLEMENTS (1975–79 and 1985–88)
Defender, 6ft, 12st 6lb, b. Middleton, 9 April 1955
Signed from: groundstaff, 22 July 1971 (Pro: 18 July 1975)
Transferred: Oldham Athletic, 12 September 1979 (£250,000)
Signed from: Oldham Athletic, 7 March 1985 (loan, full 1 June 1985)
Transferred: Bury, 17 March 1988
Career: City, Oldham Athletic, City, Bury, Shrewsbury Town, Limerick City, Curzon Ashton
Debut: v Aston Villa, 27 August 1975
Second debut: v Middlesbrough, 9 March 1985
Appearances: League: 220+5 apps, 1 gl; FA Cup: 17 apps, 0 gls; League Cup: 26 apps, 0 gls; UEFA Cup: 6+1 apps, 0 gls; FMC: 7 apps, 1 gl. Total: 276+6 apps, 2 gls.

Kenny Clements initially joined the Blues as a member of the groundstaff in 1971. Opportunities to sign as an apprentice were limited and this, at least, guaranteed him a place within the club and the opportunity of training with the other youngsters. Initially he'd take part in training sessions and then, after the others had departed, he would stay behind and work on the pitch divots. Eventually he became a full-time player and played a key role in the 1975–76 League Cup run. Sadly he was on the substitutes bench for the Final, after injury had limited his opportunities, and never made it on to the pitch.

The following seasons saw him perform at a consistently high level as the Blues finished second to Liverpool and then fourth in 1977–78. He also played in City's key European games of the period, including the significant 2–2 draw at AC Milan.

Unfortunately, he was sold to Oldham Athletic in 1979 – a period which saw many great City stars depart – but returned to Maine Road in 1985. One of the elder statesmen of the side, he helped the Blues to promotion shortly after joining, then his experience proved invaluable as he helped the youngsters, such as Redmond, settle in during the First Division seasons of 1985–87. He was unlucky to miss a second Wembley Final while at City when in 1986 he was injured in the Manchester derby the day before City's appearance in the Full Members' Cup Final against Chelsea.

Popular with fans, Clements finally moved to Bury in March 1988. After retirement he opened a driving school in Oldham.

Tommy Browell

THOMAS BROWELL (1913–26)
Forward, 5ft 9in, 10st 11lb, b. Walbottle, 19 October 1892, d. Blackpool, 5 October 1955
Signed from: Everton, 31 October 1913 (£1,780)
Transferred: Blackpool, 15 September 1926 (£1,500)
Career: Newburn Grange, Hull City, Everton, City, Blackpool, Lytham player-coach, Morecambe
Debut: v Sheffield Wednesday, 8 November 1913
Appearances: League: 222 apps, 122 gls; FA Cup: 25 apps, 17 gls; Wartime (League and Cup): 33 apps, 18 gls. Total: 280 apps, 157 gls.

Tommy Browell signed from Everton in 1913 for a large fee of £1,780, and despite only making 27 appearances he netted 13 goals that season and was the leading City scorer. His best season was 1920–21, when he became the first Blue to score 30 or more goals in the League. His total reached 31 goals, with his 30th arriving in the 1–0 victory over Bradford on St George's Day 1921 and his 31st on the last day of the season at Newcastle. Those goals helped City to second place in the League.

He led the scoring charts again in 1921–22, and when the following season opened everyone expected more of the same. However, a serious ankle injury in September after only five games and two goals reduced his appearances. He did manage to play a further 10 matches that season, but his struggle continued into 1923–24, when he made only 14 appearances, although he did feature in the FA Cup run of 1924, scoring four goals in five matches.

Browell's determination ensured his career was resurrected, with him appearing at his best during the 1925–26 season. He scored an incredible five goals during the 8–3 demolition of Burnley on 24 October, and had earlier scored all City's goals in an amazing 4–4 draw against Everton. He also scored seven goals in five FA Cup matches, and featured in the FA Cup Final defeat to Bolton.

The following September he moved to Blackpool, where he continued to play until he was 39. Afterwards he stayed in the Blackpool area. Some sources claim he became a tram driver, but his grand-daughter explained in 2005 that he became a bus driver and that supporters would often search out Browell's bus to meet their former hero. He passed away on 5 October 1955, 14 days before his 63rd birthday.

Cliff Sear

CLIFFORD REGINALD SEAR (1955–68)
Defender, 5ft 10in, 10st 1lb, b. Rhostyllen, 22 September 1936, d. 8 July 2000
Signed from: Oswestry Town, 7 June 1955
Transferred: Chester, 25 April 1968
Career: Rhostyllen Sports Club, Oswestry Town, City, Chester
Debut: v Birmingham City, 27 April 1957
Appearances: League: 248 apps, 1 gl; FA Cup: 14 apps, 0 gls; League Cup: 17 apps, 0 gls. Total: 279 apps, 1 gl.

Stylish left-back Cliff Sear signed professional forms in January 1957, although he very nearly missed being a City player: 'I had previously been a part-timer with the club. In those days I was a 16-year-old who worked down the mines at Bershaw Colliery, near my native Wrexham, travelling over to Manchester at weekends to play for the 'B' team at Crown Point. I played regularly enough, but no one said much to me or gave advice and I didn't think I was making much progress. So I left and linked up with Oswestry Town who were then in the Cheshire League. While playing for them, City manager Les McDowall spotted me and a fee of £1,500 was agreed. Oswestry's manager in those days was Alan Ball senior and he used to bring his son with him to watch us play!'

Sear's League debut came three months later, on the last day of the season, and the following season he made 29 League appearances. He soon became established as the Blues managed the transitional period when many of the 1956 Cup side moved on or retired. Sear became a Welsh Under-23 international in 1958–59, and went on to appear for the full Wales side against England in 1962.

When Mercer and Allison arrived in 1965 Sear's opportunities were already diminishing and in April 1968 he signed for Chester City. After making almost 50 appearances for Chester he retired, becoming youth-team coach. In 1982 he succeeded ex-Blue Alan Oakes as Chester manager for a brief spell.

Dennis Tueart

DENNIS TUEART (1974–78 and 1980–1983)
Forward, 5ft 8in, 11st 4lb, b. Newcastle-upon-Tyne, 27 November 1949
Signed from: Sunderland, 11 March 1974 (£275,000)

Transferred: New York Cosmos, 13 February 1978 (£250,000)
Signed from: New York Cosmos, 31 January 1980 (£150,000)
Transferred: Stoke City, 9 July 1983 (free)
Career: Manor Park Technical Grammar School, Welbeck Juniors, Sunderland, City, New York Cosmos, City, Stoke City, Burnley, Derry City
Debut: v Manchester United, 13 March 1974
Second debut: v Norwich City, 1 March 1980
Appearances: League: 216+8 apps, 86 gls; FA Cup: 13+2 apps, 3 gls; League Cup: 27 apps, 18 gls; UEFA Cup: 3 apps, 0 gls; AS Cup: 3 apps, 0 gls; TC Cup: 2 apps, 2 gls; T Cup: 3 apps, 2 gls. Total: 267+10 apps, 111 gls.

Remembered today primarily for his spectacular overhead goal at Wembley in the 1976 League Cup Final, Dennis Tueart was always a hero with City fans. Earlier in his career he was a popular member of Sunderland's 1973 FA Cup-winning side, alongside Dave Watson, and he joined City in March 1974.

Often described by supporters as an entertaining, exciting, determined player, Tueart constantly delivered during a period when City challenged for the title in addition to the League Cup success, but in 1977–78 he became a little disenchanted and decided to move to the States to play for the New York Cosmos. He became the first 'current' England international to transfer to the US, and played alongside players such as Beckenbauer.

He remained in America for a couple of seasons before rejoining City in 1980. He netted five goals during 11 games that season, but a wrist injury during a 2–1 defeat at Stoke the following September caused Tueart to miss significant games against Manchester United, Liverpool, and Leeds. During that period the Blues struggled and the management team of Allison and Book were dismissed. New manager John Bond transformed the club, but Tueart was not given much opportunity to impress. Then, in the 1981 FA Cup Final replay, Tueart was brought on as substitute for Bobby McDonald. This brief appearance led to him appearing in 15 of the opening 18 matches of 1981–82, scoring nine goals in the process. It was a great period for him personally, but he damaged his Achilles tendon against his former team Sunderland in December and missed the rest of the season.

In 1982–83 he made 36 appearances, but relegation on the final day led to Tueart being transferred to Stoke. After his playing career finished Tueart concentrated on his sports promotions company and since the mid-1990s he has been a director of the Blues.

Fred Tilson

SAMUEL FRED TILSON (1928–1938)
Forward, 5ft 11in, 12st 0lb, b. Barnsley, 19 April 1903, d. Manchester, 21 November 1972
Signed from: Barnsley, 14 March 1928 (£6,000 – joint payment for Tilson and Brook)
Transferred: Northampton Town, 11 March 1938
Career: Regent Street Congregationals, Barnsley, City, Northampton Town, York City
Debut: v Grimsby Town, 17 March 1928
Appearances: League: 245 apps, 110 gls; FA Cup: 28 apps, 22 gls; Wartime (League and Cup): 1 app, 0 gls; Charity: 2 apps, 0 gls. Total: 276 apps, 132 gls.

One of City's most important Cup Final heroes, Yorkshireman Fred Tilson arrived at Maine Road in 1928. By the early 1930s Tilson had established himself in the first team, but became nationally famous for his part in the three significant Cup seasons between 1932 and 1934. In 1932 his hat-trick against Brentford in the fourth round and general play in the following matches helped the Blues reach the semi-final. The following season he netted six in six games as the Blues reached Wembley to face Everton. Sadly, he missed the Final and City were defeated by Everton, but in 1934 he helped bring real success as City defeated Portsmouth in the Final. During that Cup run he scored nine in eight games, including four against Aston Villa in a record-breaking semi-final, and two in the Final itself.

In 1934 he also won the first of his England caps, and kept his goalscoring touch with six goals in only four international appearances. Sadly, injury limited his international opportunities. He won a League Championship medal in 1937 and scored 15 goals in only 23 games.

In November 1938, at the age of 35, manager Wilf Wild believed it was time for Tilson to move on, and in a complicated deal, Wild brought Maurice Dunkley to Maine Road from Northampton Town in exchange for Tilson and two others. To City supporters at the time it seemed that Tilson was being sold rather cheaply regardless of his age, and supporters and even local reporters seemed mystified.

On 30 March 1940 Tilson did reappear for City when he was a wartime guest player at centre-forward in the 1–1 draw at Stockport County. Later he returned to Maine Road on a permanent basis, becoming successively coach, assistant manager and chief scout. He also acted as caretaker manager for spells in the 1960s. He remained at City into the Mercer-Allison period, before retiring in 1967. He passed away only five years later aged 69 after a short illness.

Throughout his playing career Tilson had been popular both on the pitch and in the dressing room, and many fans felt for him when injury seemed to rob him of moments of glory. Through injury he had missed most of the 1929–30 season, the 1933 Final, and a few international appearances. In fact he had been so unlucky that when Sam Cowan introduced him to King George V in 1934 the captain said: 'This is Tilson, your Majesty. He's playing today with two broken legs.'

Sam Barkas

SAMUEL BARKAS (1934–47)

Defender, 5ft 9in, 13st 7lb, b. Wardley, 29 December 1909, d. Shipley, W. Yorks, 8 December 1989

Signed from: Bradford City, 20 April 1934 (£5,000)

Transferred: Workington player-manager, May 1947

Career: Middle Dock, Thorndale, Barnes Rovers, Bradford City, City, Workington Town

Debut: v Liverpool, 2 May 1934

Appearances: League: 175 apps, 1 gl; FA Cup: 20 apps, 0 gls; Charity: 1 app, 0 gls; Wartime (League and Cup): 75 apps, 3 gls. Total: 271 apps, 4 gls.

Captain of the great 1936–37 Championship-winning side, Barkas was a stylish left-back who joined the Blues for £5,000 from Bradford City in April 1934 shortly before the FA Cup Final. Naturally, he was unable to play at Wembley, but did manage to play in the final two League games that season. In fact Barkas was to miss

only one of the first 68 League games played after his arrival as he quickly proved his value with many outstanding performances.

One of the first players to create positive play from defensive positions, Barkas became renowned for always trying to create attacking opportunities and even managed to score a goal himself – to bring a 1–1 draw on the opening day of the 1934–35 season at West Bromwich Albion.

As the decade progressed Barkas became an England international and a major figure in Manchester. Sadly, the war interrupted his career as he was in his prime – he was 29 when war broke out – and when football returned on a professional, national basis Barkas was almost 37. Nevertheless, he managed to guide the side to the Second Division title and appeared in 33 League matches during 1946–47. His last appearance came on 14 June 1947 (City's latest-ever finish) when the Blues defeated Newport County 5–1 with all goals coming from George Smith.

Barkas later became Workington Town manager and also had a spell on City's scouting staff.

Billy Dale

WILLIAM DALE (1931–38)
Defender, 5ft 9in, 11st 1lb, b. Manchester, 17 February 1905, d. Manchester, June 1987
Signed from: Manchester United, 23 December 1931
Transferred: Ipswich Town, 21 June 1938 (complicated deal where Dale and Harry Rowley were swapped for Bill Ridding plus cash)
Career: Sandbach Ramblers, Marple, Manchester United, City, Ipswich Town
Debut: v Portsmouth, 26 December 1931
Appearances: League: 237 apps, 0 gls; FA Cup: 32 apps, 0 gls: Charity: 2 apps, 0 gls. Total: 271 apps, 0 gls.

Full-back Billy Dale joined City direct from United in 1931 and made his debut three days after signing. He remained first choice for the

rest of the season and became City's preferred left-back as time progressed. Inevitably, Dale was an important member of the great 1930s side and in successive seasons he helped City progress to the semi-final (1932), FA Cup Final (1933), and finally FA Cup-winners (1934).

He made 36 appearances during the 1936–37 Championship-winning season and after 30 appearances the following season he was transferred to Ipswich Town and took part in their first season as a League club. World War Two limited his career, although he was already 34 when war broke out.

Right at the start of his career, when he appeared in a benefit match while on trial for Manchester United, the *Manchester Football Chronicle* summed him up: 'The trialist from Sandbach Ramblers kicked and tackled like a League player.' On that performance United immediately signed him up, but he only managed a total of 68 first-team appearances during six years at Old Trafford.

George Smith

GEORGE BEACHER SMITH (1938–51)
Forward, 5ft 9in, 9st 6lb, b. Fleetwood, 7 February 1921
Signed from: Salford Adelphi, *c.*1938
Transferred: Chesterfield, 18 October 1951 (£5,000)
Career: Salford Adelphi, City, Chesterfield, Mossley player-manager, Hyde United player-manager *c.*1959
Debut: v Leicester City, 31 August 1946
Appearances: League: 166 apps, 75 gls; FA Cup: 13 apps, 5 gls; Wartime (League and Cup): 90 apps, 45 gls. Total: 269 apps, 125 gls.

Forward George Smith's City career is a remarkable story of bravery and endeavour. He joined the Blues in 1938 and quickly proved his worth in the 'A' team but then war broke out. Smith joined the armed forces, but before he left Manchester he did manage to make a couple of first-team appearances in the war league.

Active service then took over and Smith went on to serve in Africa, where his life changed dramatically when he was under attack from a plane. A bullet entered his right arm above his elbow, travelled down his arm, past his elbow and came out again after travelling a good six or so inches through his flesh. Smith was in a great deal of pain, but the most shocking aspect of all of this is that the plane that shot at him was actually from the South African Air Force. This meant that Smith was on the receiving end of what would in the 21st century be described as 'friendly fire'.

He was lucky the bullet had only entered his arm, but he was desperately unlucky to have been fired at by servicemen fighting on the same side. Smith spent some time recovering in Africa before being sent home to Manchester.

The whole incident was hushed up and Smith was discouraged from talking about the specific events. In Manchester few knew the truth of what happened and, as with so many injured men, it wasn't a subject openly discussed. Even the City football guide for 1945 simply stated: 'Smith was one of the first casualties when he suffered a permanent injury to his hand sustained in manoeuvres somewhere in South Africa.'

The injury has affected Smith throughout his life and his hand and fingers have been permanently rigid in a clasping fashion, while his arm has two large indentations where the

bullet entered and exited. In addition, the path of the bullet down his arm can be seen.

Despite the disability Smith returned to football, but even then the City management insisted on him performing a number of trials. He passed them all and on 26 August 1944 he celebrated his return to the first team with a hat-trick against Tranmere in the opening match of the new season. This was his first appearance in the first team since 25 April 1942.

By the end of the war Smith was a key member of the side, although he remained a little self-conscious about his arm. Usually he would cover it up with either the sleeve of his shirt, a sock, or a glove, and for team photos and the like the arm was usually hidden either behind his back or carefully positioned behind another player.

Some thought his arm had been amputated, and understandably Smith wanted his football to do all the talking. When League football resumed Smith was a key factor behind promotion in 1946–47. He was the top scorer, and even netted five in the final game of the season.

He continued to perform exceptionally well for the following seasons and was on the verge of an England cap, but it seems his arm injury proved a factor and, to the amazement of most Mancunians, Smith was not selected for his national side.

In October 1951 he moved on to Chesterfield (scoring 97 in 250 League appearances), and was later player-manager at Mossley and Hyde United. He also managed Prestwich Heys.

Neil McNab

NEIL MCNAB (1983–90)
Midfield, 5ft 7in, 11st 0lb, b. Greenock, 4 June 1957
Signed from: Brighton & HA, 20 July 1983 (£35,000)
Transferred: Tranmere Rovers, 4 January 1990
Career: Morton, Tottenham Hotspur, Bolton Wanderers, Brighton & Hove Albion, Leeds United (loan), Portsmouth (loan), City,

Tranmere Rovers, Huddersfield Town (loan), Ayr United, Darlington, Derry City, Witton Albion
Debut: v Crystal Palace, 27 August 1983
Appearances: League: 216+5 apps, 16 gls; FA Cup: 15 apps, 1 gl; League Cup: 20 apps, 2gls; FMC: 10 apps, 0 gls. Total: 261+5 apps, 19 gls.

After playing for Morton in the early 1970s Neil McNab joined Tottenham as an amateur in February 1974 for a relatively significant fee of £40,000. When he made his League debut he was the youngest Spurs player to appear in the League, although the record has since been taken from him. The arrival of Villa and Ardiles at Spurs limited his chances and he moved on to Bolton. Spells at Brighton, Leeds, and Portsmouth followed before he became the first of an army of Scots purchased by Billy McNeill during the period 1983–86. The transfer seemed perfect as McNab thrived in Manchester. He displayed many of the characteristics fans needed from their City heroes at this time. He was tough-tackling, hard working, and seemed the perfect choice to help the Blues find their way back into the top flight.

Playing probably the best football of his career, McNab became an essential member of the side. Deservedly, he was twice voted City's Player of the Year, and he played a significant part in each of City's two promotions during the 1980s. Initially his role was to strengthen City's resolve, then during the post-McNeill period he became important as the man of experience as Mel Machin's youthful side developed.

Shortly after Christmas 1989, under new manager Howard Kendall, McNab's City career came to an end with a transfer to Tranmere Rovers for £125,000. At Prenton Park he helped Tranmere achieve promotion to Division Two via the play-offs. Later he played in non-League football for a while before returning to City in 1994 to take charge of the 'A' team. The role only lasted until 1997 when backroom changes led to his departure.

Neil McNab remains a significant Blue, however, and will always be remembered for the major part he played during the difficult 1980s.

Walter Smith

WALTER ERNEST SMITH (1906–20)
Goalkeeper, 5ft 9in, 13st 0lb, b. Leicester, 25 March 1884, d. Melton Mowbray, 6 February 1972
Signed from: Leicester Fosse, 4 July 1906 (£600)
Transferred: Port Vale, 19 October 1920
Career: Shaftesbury, Forest Rovers, Crafton Swifts, Leicester Imperial, Leicester Fosse, City, Port Vale, Plymouth Argyle, Grimsby Town
Debut: v Bolton Wanderers, 24 November 1906
Appearances: League: 232 apps, 0 gls; FA Cup: 23 apps, 0 gls; Wartime (League and Cup): 8 apps, 0 gls. Total: 263 apps, 0 gls.

Goalkeeper Walter Smith was signed for the relatively high fee of £600 with a reputation for being one of the best 'keepers in the Second Division. Manager Newbould signed him in 1906 as the Blues sought a permanent replacement for 1904 FA Cup-winner Hillman. Prior to Smith's arrival, City had used four different goalkeepers within the space of a year. In 1907–08 Smith became the club's first ever-present since Meredith in 1903–04, and even then Smith played in 44 League and Cup games as opposed to Meredith's 40.

Smith spent 14 years with City, winning two major honours when he was selected for an England XI against a Scottish team in 1914, and for the Football League against the Scottish League the following season. During World War One he guested for his old club Leicester.

After the war Smith started the first post-war League season as first choice, but after only nine games he was dropped and then transferred. His last game came in October 1919, the first post-war League meeting with United. The Reds took the lead three times before the Blues levelled at 3–3. Smith had an absolutely appalling game. For much of his City career Smith had saved the Blues with a consistently high standard of play, but for this match it seems he could do nothing right. He was heavily criticised for two of United's goals – for one he hesitated, for the other he was dispossessed while bouncing the ball in his area oblivious to the presence of United's goal-poaching star of the period Joe Spence. One newspaper report mentioned his name three times – twice for the goals and then once in the final summary: 'The City played a greatly improved game all round, and apart from Smith's mistakes, the defence was most faultless'.

Smith left Hyde Road for Port Vale, where the nightmare of the Manchester derby was rapidly eclipsed by accusations of assault on the morning of his debut. It seems that he was falsely accused of assaulting a hotel chambermaid at the Regent Hotel, South Shields, prior to his first game for Vale. He was bailed in time to play, but went through the match knowing that he was constantly being watched by a police detective. Fortunately, this was all a mistake and Smith was acquitted at Durham Assizes. He remained with Vale until 1922. At Hyde Road, despite his final appearance, Smith was remembered as a hero. Like all 'keepers he was a little eccentric – the *Athletic News* once called him: 'the only first-class goalkeeper in the country who disdains training' – but he had been a superb player for the Blues.

Nicky Reid

NICHOLAS SCOTT REID (1977-82 and 1982-87)
Defender, 5ft 10in, 12st 4lb, b. Manchester, 30 October 1960
Signed from: apprentice, 30 April 1977 (Pro: 30 October 1978)
Transferred: Seattle Sounders, 9 May 1982
Signed from: Seattle Sounders, 24 September 1982
Transferred: Blackburn Rovers, 6 July 1987 (free)
Career: Chorlton School, City, Seattle Sounders, City, Blackburn Rovers, Bristol City (loan), West Bromwich Albion, Wycombe Wanderers, Woking, Witton Albion, Bury, Sligo Rovers player-manager
Debut: v Borussia Monchengladbach, 7 March 1979 (UEFA Cup)
League debut: v Ipswich Town, 31 March 1979
Appearances: League: 211+6 apps, 2 gls; FA Cup: 17 apps, 0 gls; League Cup: 20 apps, 0 gls; UEFA Cup: 2 apps, 0 gls; FMC: 6 apps, 0 gls. Total: 256+6 apps, 2 gls.

A surprise UEFA Cup debutant at 18, Nicky Reid was one of a long line of promising local youngsters groomed by the likes of Ken Barnes and Steve Fleet. He was captain of the City FA Youth Cup Final side of 1979 and was clearly a great prospect. By the time of the 1981 FA Cup Final he was a regular in the side. Initially a defender, he was later moved into midfield by manager John Bond and whichever position he played in he was loved by the supporters.

He remained a key City player after Wembley but in July 1987 was transferred to Blackburn on a free transfer. He later became captain at Ewood as Rovers regularly challenged for a play-off place, before spells at Bristol City, West Bromwich Albion, Wycombe, Woking, Witton Albion and Bury. In 1997 he became Sligo Rovers' player-manager, and in May 2003 he was one of a number of heroes from the 1980s to be paraded around Maine Road prior to the ground's final match. He has since returned to the Blues as a member of the club's coaching staff.

Bobby Kennedy

ROBERT KENNEDY (1961–69)
Defender, 5ft 8in, 11st 5lb, b. Motherwell, 23 June 1937
Signed from: Kilmarnock, 20 July 1961 (£45,000)
Transferred: Grimsby Town, 2 March 1969
Career: Coltness United, Queen of the South (trial), Clyde (trial), Kilmarnock, City, Grimsby Town player-manager
Debut: v Leicester City, 19 August 1961
Appearances: League: 216+3 apps, 9 gls; FA Cup: 18 apps, 0 gls; League Cup 16 apps, 0 gls; European Cup 1 app, 0 gls. Total: 251+3 apps, 9 gls.

Bobby Kennedy had already overcome a serious illness, which kept him out of the game for eight months, and played in two Scottish Cup Finals and won a Scottish League Championship runners-up medal with Kilmarnock by the time he joined the Blues in 1961. It was a difficult period to arrive. The Blues had some quality players but they had sold Denis Law and another hero, Ken Barnes, had also moved on. Kennedy and Peter Dobing were the replacements and it took some time for the fans to adjust. Kennedy's commitment and approach to the game won over any doubters and they recognised that he showed the same commitment to the Blues as the fans themselves demonstrated.

In November 1962 Kennedy was given the captaincy but these pre-Mercer days were difficult and relegation came in 1963. Two years later only 8,015 paid to watch a home match with Swindon and morale was at an all time low, but Kennedy remained committed: 'In the dressing room some of the players were saying they'd had enough. They wanted to leave… saw no future etc. I didn't feel like that because, even in City's darkest hour, I still couldn't see anywhere better to go. It had been the worst day of my footballing life, but I loved Maine Road, loved the support, and I saw Manchester City as the best club in the world. Why move?'

Mercer and Allison arrived and Kennedy was an important member of the promotion side, but he gradually became more a squad member than a regular. When City won the Championship on the last day of the 1967–68 season Kennedy was the unused substitute. In March 1969 he moved to Grimsby as player-manager – Matt Busby had recommended him to the Grimsby directors – and later had spells coaching at Bradford.

After his football career ended he moved into the clothing business, but his family's involvement in football continued. His son became a coach at Bradford, while his daughter represented Scotland in women's football.

Niall Quinn

NIALL JOHN QUINN MBE (1990–96)
Forward, 6ft 4in, 12st 4lb, b. Dublin, 6 October 1966
Signed from: Arsenal, 15 March 1990 (£800,000)
Transferred: Sunderland, 15 August 1996 (£1,300,000)

Career: Drimnagh Castle School, Manortown United, Lourdes Celtic, Fulham (trial), Arsenal, City, Sunderland
Debut: v Chelsea, 21 March 1990
Appearances: League: 183+20 apps, 66 gls; FA Cup: 13+3 apps, 4 gls; League Cup: 20+2 apps, 6 gls; FMC: 3 apps, 1 gl. Total: 219+25 apps, 77 gls.

A Republic of Ireland international before he turned 20, Niall Quinn was a very popular City player from his arrival in 1989 through to his departure in 1996. A Howard Kendall signing, Quinn helped the Blues consolidate their position in the top division after his bargain £800,000 arrival in March 1990. He was a brilliant centre-forward for the Blues during the 1990s.

Quinn's arrival at Maine Road brought the perfect kick-start to his career. He scored on his debut against Chelsea and by the end of that season had scored four goals in nine appearances. The following season City finished fifth and Quinn was voted player of the year by supporters. In one match – at Crystal Palace on April Fool's Day – he netted a perfect hat-trick when he scored with both feet and his head.

At 6ft 4in opponents often thought that Quinn was simply good with his head, but the player regularly proved how skilful he was with his feet. Quinn enjoyed life under Howard Kendall and then Peter Reid and, although some supporters criticised the 'route one' style of play he adopted, Quinn emerged as the true striker of the period. When Brian Horton arrived after Reid's shock dismissal, the Blues displayed a more entertaining style of play, and some incorrectly felt Quinn wouldn't be able to adjust. When he suffered a cruciate knee injury in November 1993 it seemed as if his City career was over. He missed the World Cup Finals of 1994, but managed to regain fitness for the 1994–95 season.

His career came alive again and, despite quality competition from Rosler and Walsh, Quinn remained a firm favourite with fans and continued to impress in every game. It was clear he was a much more important player with his feet than some had suggested. He also seemed to love life at Maine Road.

Sadly, under new manager Alan Ball in 1995–96, Quinn was perceived as an expensive luxury and was not used as frequently as he should have been. Then, on the final day of the season, as City were heading for relegation from the Premier League, Quinn demonstrated to all exactly how he felt about the club. He had been substituted and, as the game neared its conclusion, he was seen running up the touchline urging the City players to get the ball out of the corner and head for goal. It seems Alan Ball was incorrectly under the impression that City's survival was certain and that the side could afford to waste time. Quinn and the fans knew the truth – the Blues needed to score. The sight of Quinn urging his colleagues to attack told supporters a great deal about the Irishman's loyalty and love of the club. Sadly, Quinn's efforts were in vain and the Blues were relegated. Inevitably, with City desperate to cut the wage bill, he was sold – against the wishes of supporters – to Peter Reid's Sunderland for £1.3 million in August 1996.

At Sunderland he scored the first League goal at the Stadium of Light – ironically against City – and he also went on to achieve cult status with a new set of fans. On the international front, Quinn was a key member of the Irish squad for over a decade, and featured in the 1990 and 2002 World Cups.

In 2004 he was one of City's inaugural entrants into the club's Hall of Fame, then in April 2006 it was reported that he was part of a consortium seeking to take over Sunderland AFC.

'Spud' Murphy

WILLIAM MURPHY (1918–26)
Forward, 5ft 7in, 10st 7lb, b. St Helens, 23 May 1895, d. Liverpool, 7 January 1962
Signed from: Alexandra Victoria, 2 February 1918
Transferred: Southampton, 18 August 1926 (£350)
Career: Peasley Cross Juniors, Liverpool, Alexandra Victoria, City, Southampton, Oldham Athletic, Tranmere Rovers, Ellesmere Port Town
Debut: v Bolton Wanderers, 13 September 1919
Appearances: League: 209 apps, 30 gls; FA Cup: 11 apps, 1 gl; Wartime (League and Cup): 23 apps, 2 gls. Total: 243 apps, 33 gls.

As a schoolboy Billy 'Spud' Murphy was a brilliant cross-country runner and it is said by some that he only took up football when his athletics club disbanded. Fortunately for the Blues it was a good move and as World War One neared its end he joined City. In 1919 he turned professional and he immediately established himself on City's left wing.

He retained many of the attributes usually found in the world of athletics and his stamina and effective use of speed made him a consistent and strong member of the City team. He scored five goals in 36 appearances during his first year, and followed this up with eight goals in 40 appearances during 1920–21. This was a highly significant season, as City finished second to Burnley, but for Murphy it was the season he made his name. Interestingly, the Irish FA were very interested in his progress and, because of his surname, they wrote to City asking if he had been born in Ireland. Manager Ernest Mangnall replied: 'He comes from St Helens, where the pills come from'.

Murphy remained an important Blue until 1926 but as City progressed to Wembley he was no longer first choice. He managed only nine League appearances during 1925–26, and the following August he was transferred to Southampton for £350. At the Dell he impressed immediately, with a local reporter describing him as: 'cute, quick and clever', but after two seasons he suffered a dramatic loss of form, and was transferred to Oldham for £100. Another move to Tranmere followed in 1930, and he ended his playing career at Ellesmere Town. He passed away on Merseyside in 1962.

Les McDowall

LESLIE JOHN MCDOWALL (1938–49)
Defender, 5ft 11in, 12st 4lb, b. Gunga Pur (India), 25 October 1912, d. Northwich, 18 August 1991
Signed from: Sunderland, 14 March 1938
Transferred: Wrexham, 11 June 1949
Career: John Neilson School, Glentyan Thistle, Kilbarchan, Sunderland, City, Wrexham player-manager
Debut: v West Bromwich Albion, 16 March 1938
Appearances: League: 117 apps, 8 gls; FA Cup: 9 apps, 0 gls; Wartime (League and Cup): 114 apps, 8 gls; FL Wartime: 3 apps, 0 gls. Total: 243 apps, 16 gls.

Les McDowall's playing career at Maine Road lasted for over 11 years, and included a spell as captain and a promotion. He arrived in March 1938 as the Blues struggled to find the form that had brought the title the previous season. Despite only making 12 League appearances and the fact that City were relegated, McDowall was viewed as a positive acquisition and the following season he was appointed captain.

Sadly, he missed four games, including the final three matches, and the Blues missed promotion by five points. Of those four games, two ended in defeat and one was a draw. Three games into the next season the League programme was abandoned as a result of the war and McDowall returned to his pre-football role as a draughtsman, working for a local aircraft factory. He continued to appear in wartime games at Maine Road and then when he was based north of the border he guested for several Scottish sides, including Rangers.

After the war he made 35 League appearances in the first full League season as the Blues won the Second Division title. In 1949 he moved to Wrexham as player-manager and a year later he was back at Maine Road as City manager. His managerial career is profiled in the Managers section of this book.

Jimmy McMullan

JAMES MCMULLAN (1926–33)
Half-back, 5ft 7in, 11st 0lb, b. Denny, 26 March 1895, d. Sheffield, 28 November 1964
Signed from: Partick Thistle, 10 February 1926 (£4,700)
Transferred: Oldham Athletic, 15 May 1933
Career: Denny Hibernian, Third Lanark, Partick Thistle, Maidstone United player-manager, Partick Thistle, City, Oldham Athletic player-manager
Debut: v Liverpool, 27 February 1926
Appearances: League: 220 apps, 10 gls; FA Cup: 22 apps, 2 gls. Total: 242 apps, 12 gls.

One of Scotland's greatest internationals of all time, left-back Jimmy McMullan was already a significant star when the Blues signed him in 1926 for £4,700. Clearly his arrival was a major talking point, especially as this was during City's

managerless period when vice-chairman Albert Alexander took on the management of the players. Alexander must have possessed a great footballing brain and must have been a terrific negotiator, as McMullan readily joined the Blues.

Within two months of his arrival McMullan was playing at Wembley in the FA Cup Final. City lost that game and were also relegated on the last day of the season, creating a new, if unwanted, record.

In 1927–28 he made 38 appearances and scored four goals as City won the Second Division title, and that same year McMullan captained Scotland to their most famous victory – a 5–1 defeat of England at Wembley. It was a highly embarrassing day for England, but a great one for the City man. He remained in the City side throughout the twenties and early thirties, and in 1933 he returned to Wembley again with the club. Sadly, his second Final also ended in defeat, and the following May he moved to Oldham as player-manager. He later had spells in charge at Aston Villa (their first

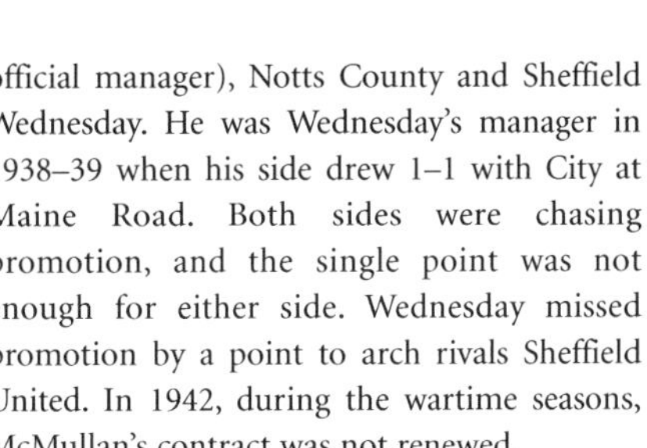

official manager), Notts County and Sheffield Wednesday. He was Wednesday's manager in 1938–39 when his side drew 1–1 with City at Maine Road. Both sides were chasing promotion, and the single point was not enough for either side. Wednesday missed promotion by a point to arch rivals Sheffield United. In 1942, during the wartime seasons, McMullan's contract was not renewed.

He passed away at the age of 69 while still living in Sheffield in 1964.

Gordon Clark

GORDON VINCENT CLARK (1936–47)
Defender, 5ft 7in, 11st 10lb, b. Gainsborough, 15 June 1914, d. Sheffield, 20 October 1997
Signed from: Denaby United, 22 January 1936
Transferred: Waterford, April 1947
Career: Highgate School, Doncaster 1925–29, Goldthorpe United, Southend United, Denaby United, City, Waterford, Hyde United player-manager
Debut: v Leeds United, 2 September 1936
Appearances: League: 55 apps, 0 gls; FA Cup: 9 apps, 0 gls; Wartime (League and Cup): 180 apps, 0 gls. Total: 244 apps, 0 gls.

Gordon Clark is often overlooked when City's longest-serving players are considered. This is because the majority of his appearances came during the war years.

Clark joined City in 1936 and made his debut in the second game of the Championship-winning season. That year he appeared in 13 League matches in defence, and was present for the final five important games of the Championship run-in. A further 22 appearances followed the next season, and 20 in 1938–39, but the arrival of Bert Sproston and the outbreak of war limited his opportunities.

During the war he joined the RAF and was able to play for City on 180 occasions, making him second to Irishman Billy Walsh in the number of appearances made during the war.

When the Football League resumed Clark missed out on playing a part in City's Second Division championship side. He joined

Waterford, then returned to the Manchester area when he became Hyde United's manager in April 1947. A great coaching career followed, with managerial spells at Aldershot, West Bromwich Albion, Sheffield Wednesday, Peterborough, Fulham and QPR. He also coached in Philadelphia and was chief scout at Arsenal.

Frank Roberts

FRANK ROBERTS (1922–29)
Forward, 5ft 8in, 12st 0lb, b. Sandbach, 3 April 1894, d. Crewe, 23 May 1961
Signed from: Bolton Wanderers, 18 October 1922 (£3,400)
Transferred: Manchester Central, 14 June 1929
Career: Sandbach Villa, Sandbach Ramblers, Crewe Alexandra, Bolton Wanderers, City, Manchester Central, Horwich RMI
Debut: v Preston North End, 21 October 1922
Appearances: League: 216 apps, 116 gls; FA Cup: 21 apps, 14 gls; Total: 237 apps, 130 gls.

Prior to joining the Blues, forward Frank Roberts had become a Bolton player in May 1914 and spearheaded their attack as they reached the FA Cup semi-final in his first season. By that time war had broken out and Roberts served in the North Lancashire Regiment. Some sources claim he made a guest appearance for City in October 1917, although this seems unlikely given his military service.

He joined City for £3,400 in October 1922 after a dispute with Bolton concerning his occupation outside of the game. Roberts had, in 1922, taken over the management of licensed premises and this was strictly against Bolton's rules. At City, despite the large outlay for the period, Roberts quickly proved value for money.

He ended his first season with 10 goals in 32 appearances, and this included the last City goal scored at the club's first League ground at Hyde Road. The following season he netted 14 goals in 41 appearances, plus four in the FA Cup run which saw City reach the semi-final. In 1924 he also earned his first England cap.

According to French sources Roberts ended his international career in goal after England's 'keeper was injured during a game at Paris in 1925, although English reports from the period claimed another England man went in nets.

Roberts scored five goals in the fifth round of the Cup in 1926 as Crystal Palace were defeated 11–4 at Maine Road, and that season he scored in every round except the Final. Inevitably, he won a finalists' medal that season, and two years later he also won a Second Division Championship medal in 1927–28 after scoring 20 goals in 26 games.

In June 1929 he was transferred to the ambitious Manchester Central, and in later life he continued his interest in the licensed trade as he became landlord of a public house.

Ray Ranson

RAYMOND RANSON (1976–84 and 1992–93)
Defender, 6ft 9in, 11st 12lb, b. St Helens, 12 June 1960
Signed from: apprentice, 15 July 1976 (Pro: 1 August 1978)
Transferred: Birmingham City, 15 November 1984 (£15,000)
Signed from: Newcastle United, 6 January 1993
Transferred: Reading, 27 July 1993
Career: Robins Lane School, City, Birmingham City, Newcastle United, City, Reading, Witton Albion player-manager
Debut: v Nottingham Forest, 23 December 1978
Second debut: v Chelsea, 9 January 1993
Appearances: League: 198+2 apps, 1 gl; FA Cup: 13 apps, 0 gls; League Cup: 22 apps, 0 gls. Total: 233+2 apps, 1 gl.

Ray Ranson became a City apprentice in July 1976 and made his League debut against Nottingham Forest in December 1978. He went on to make over 200 appearances for the Blues in two spells – the latter spell during the 1992–93 season. That second spell made Ranson the only member of the 1981 FA Cup Final side to play for the Blues in the Premier League.

The 1979–80 season was the first to see him as City's regular number two, as Malcolm Allison switched the emphasis of the side from the experienced players of Tony Book's era to one of Allison-inspired younger players. By the time Allison was dismissed in October 1980 Ranson had achieved a great deal and new manager John Bond kept him as a City regular. Inevitably he played in both the 1981 FA Cup Final and the replay that followed.

In November 1984 Ranson moved to Birmingham City after reportedly falling out with manager Billy McNeill. The fee City received was a bargain £15,000 and seemed desperately low for an FA Cup finalist who was still only 24. At St Andrew's he won promotion alongside City in 1985.

He later played for Newcastle – under Kevin Keegan for a period – and then returned to Maine Road under Peter Reid. After a spell at Reading he became Witton Albion player-manager and in later years was involved with the finance industry. Shortly after City's move to the new stadium media reports suggested Ranson was interested in buying into the Blues, then similar stories appeared linking him with a potential takeover of Aston Villa.

Charlie Williams

CHARLES ALBERT WILLIAMS (1894–1902)
Goalkeeper, 5ft 11in, 12st 0lb, b. Welling, 19 November 1886, d. Rio de Janeiro 1952
Signed from: Royal Arsenal, 5 June 1894
Transferred: Tottenham Hotspur, 2 May 1902
Career: Phoenix, Clarence, Erith, Royal Arsenal, City, Tottenham Hotspur, Norwich City, Brentford
Debut: v Bury, 1 September 1894
Appearances: League: 221 apps, 1 gl; FA Cup: 7 apps, 0 gls; Test Matches: 4 apps, 0 gls. Total: 232 apps, 1 gl.

Charlie Williams was the first League player to keep goal for the Blues under their new name of

Manchester City in 1894. As with so many of City's 'keepers Williams was a cult hero following his arrival from Woolwich Arsenal. He was also highly entertaining, although it's worth noting that he was often an erratic 'keeper. Of the 23 games he played during his opening season only three ended with clean sheets, and one game saw the Blues defeated 8–0 by Burton Wanderers. The situation improved dramatically the following season, with Williams appearing in every League game as the Blues finished second in Division Two.

In November 1897 he apppeared for the Football League against the Irish League at Hyde Road – this was a major honour at the time – and in 1898–99 Williams helped City to the Second Division Championship. On 14 April 1900 he was credited with a goal for the Blues against Sunderland. Apparently, the wind caught one of his goal kicks and the opposing 'keeper fumbled the ball into the net.

Williams remained City's first choice in Division One, but by the end of 1901 City had begun to struggle. He was replaced in January 1902 after 10 of the 15 games he played ended in defeat, and the following summer he returned to London to play for Spurs. A spell at Brentford followed before he moved into coaching. He led the Danish Olympic team to the 1908 Olympic Final, had a spell with French side Olympique (Lille), Dutch team Le Havre and eventually he settled in Brazil where he worked with Rio Grande Do Sol.

Kevin Horlock

KEVIN HORLOCK (1997–2003)
Midfield, 6ft 0in, 12st 0lb, b. Erith, 1 November 1972
Signed from: Swindon Town, 31 January 1997 (£1,250,000)
Transferred: West Ham United, August 2003 (£300,000)
Career: West Ham United, Swindon Town, City, West Ham United, Ipswich Town
Debut: v Oxford United, 2 February 1997
Appearances: League: 184+20 apps, 37 gls; FA Cup: 9 apps, 1 gl; League Cup: 15+1 apps, 3 gls; Play-off: 3 apps, 1 gl. Total: 211+21 apps, 42 gls.

Midfielder Kevin Horlock was Frank Clark's first signing and, together with Gerard Wiekens, went on to prove one of Clark's better purchases. A versatile Northern Ireland international who could play effectively in midfield and defence, Horlock was a popular player.

Prior to his £1.5 million arrival at City he had been a virtual ever-present for Swindon Town, and netted his first City goal against his former club on 22 February 1997. His most significant moment came perhaps in the 1999 play-off final when his goal was the first of City's fightback goals against Gillingham. Often overshadowed by the Dickov goal that followed, it's important to stress that Horlock's 89th-minute effort brought the hope and perhaps the momentum for what followed. Without Horlock's goal the Blues would undoubtedly have been left to struggle.

After the play-off victory Northern Ireland international Horlock was consistent in City's midfield and helped the Blues to back to back promotions. He also made 42 appearances during the 2001–02 Division One

Championship-winning season and remained a key player during Maine Road's final season, but was transferred to West Ham shortly before the start of the 2003–04 season. Sadly, unlike teammates Shaun Goater and Peter Schmeichel (who managed only one season with City), there was no public presentation made to the player to mark his contribution to the Blues.

Billy Gillespie

WILLIAM JARDINE GILLESPIE (1897–1905)
Forward, 5ft 9in, 11st 10lb, b. Strathclyde, 2 October 1873, d. Lynn, Massacheusetts (US), 1942
Signed from: Lincoln City, 7 January 1897
Emigrated: 1905
Career: Strathclyde, Lincoln City, City, General Electric (US)
Debut: v Darwen, 9 January 1897
Appearances: League: 218 apps, 126 gls; FA Cup: 13 apps, 6 gls. Total: 231 apps, 132 gls.
Perceived as the 'loveable rogue' of the 1904 FA Cup-winning team, Billy Gillespie was a tough, no-nonsense player. Supporters loved his style and his approach and he was probably the most popular member of the City side after Meredith. In many ways fans saw him as their representative on the pitch.

He joined City after scoring 16 goals in 37 League appearances for Lincoln in Division Two, where he played alongside his elder brother Matt. He played against City on three occasions, though he never managed to score, and then in November 1896 his brother joined Newton Heath, and Gillespie followed him to Manchester in January 1897 when he joined City.

From the moment he arrived the younger Gillespie became a star as he scored on his debut. An ever-present the following season, Gillespie netted 18 goals in 30 games. In 1899 he won a Second Division Championship medal – the first national success enjoyed by either Manchester side – and another Division Two Championship followed in 1903, before the biggest success of all when Gillespie helped the Blues to FA Cup success and runners-up spot in the League. This was the biggest success in Manchester's footballing history at the time.

Gillespie was unfortunate that he was unable to add a League Championship medal, but his hopes for League success failed as the FA performed investigations into illegal payments made by the club. He felt particularly aggrieved by the FA's persecution – remember the Football League and most newspapers supported City and felt the FA were angry that a non-establishment side had found success – and he chose to emigrate.

He emigrated to the US in 1905 with his Edinburgh-born wife Elizabeth, and settled in Lynn, Massacheusetts. He created a new life in the States, although football was still important to him. According to his family he coached soccer for a period at Harvard University, and he played for the American company General Electric in Lynn and in the Boston area. He was well known in the area for his soccer activities and sport became important to his family as a result.

Gillespie returned to Manchester and Glasgow on several occasions over the years, often meeting up with Billy Meredith, while newspapers in England occasionally gave information on the whereabouts of Gillespie and the other 1904 stars. These stories seemed to develop over time and supporters at Hyde Road would often talk of Gillespie searching for diamonds in Cape Town, or creating a new life in Canada. These stories were simply not true, but they did help to keep his name in the papers. Perhaps Gillespie was such a hero to Mancunians that they felt his new life had to be daring, glamorous, and perhaps a little rebellious. Who knows, but the truth is that Gillespie enjoyed a very happy family life in the States.

After he passed away his widow would wear his 1904 medal on a chain around her neck. Sadly, this was stolen from the nursing home she lived in a few years ago. Clearly, the thief could not possibly have reckoned its monetary value nor, more importantly, the sentimental value to the family. Today, the Gillespie interest in City continues. Gillespie's great-granddaughter has the middle name Meredith, while his grandson, a noted 60-and-over squash champion, aims to visit Manchester and the sites of Gillespie's Manchester life in the near future.

Incidentally, Gillespie never paid the £50 fine imposed as a result of the illegal payments investigations. He did this as a protest and this final footballing act did much to reinforce his image with City's loyal supporters. Meredith may have been City's biggest star, but Gillespie was certainly the cult figure on the terraces. For comparison purposes think of Gillespie as being a cross between Paul Dickov, Mike Doyle and Francis Lee.

Matt Busby

SIR MATTHEW WILLIAM BUSBY (1928–36)
Half-back, 5ft 10in, 11st 6lb, b. Orbiston, 26 May 1909, d. Cheadle, 20 January 1994
Signed from: Denny Hibernian, 11 February 1928
Transferred: Liverpool, 11 March 1936 (£8,000)
Career: Bellshill, Alpine Villa, Old Orbiston Celtic, Denny Hibernian, City, Liverpool, Hibernian
Debut: v Middlesbrough, 2 November 1929
Appearances: League: 202 apps, 11 gls; FA Cup: 24 apps, 3 gls; Charity: 1 app, 0 gls. Total: 227 apps, 14 gls.

It's not the type of story City fans like to mention, but the Blues were responsible for Matt Busby settling in Manchester. The Busby family were planning on emigrating to Canada and only the efforts of the City management and their development of Busby's playing career caused those plans to be cancelled. Had Busby emigrated then clearly his managerial career would not have occurred.

Obviously, Busby is most famous for his managerial work, but he was a noted player and did feature in two FA Cup Finals with City. He was also very popular with supporters.

For the Blues he featured mainly as a classy half-back during the entertaining early to mid-1930s and gained a Scottish cap in October 1933 against Wales. Further international appearances came during wartime, but by that point he had already joined Liverpool for £8,000.

Post-war his managerial career commenced at United and Busby was instrumental in

Matt Busby in training with Cowan and Brook.

creating United's first successful side for almost 40 years. His initial success came with the Reds playing at Maine Road and City supporters helped United become popular during this period as they went to games to watch Busby's side. To fans of the period Busby remained a Blue hero and City supporters were genuinely pleased to see him find success.

The fifties became United's golden era and, of course, Busby hit the headlines in 1958 following the Munich air disaster. Inevitably, stories today focus on the United players lost in the tragedy, but it's worth highlighting that many of the others killed, including the journalists, United office personnel and City's former 'keeper Frank Swift, were very good friends of Busby. Their loss is often overlooked, but for Busby losing his great friend Swift and those journalists he had known throughout his career was also significant.

Busby rebuilt United, but it should always be remembered that he was also a highly successful City star.

Peter Doherty

PETER DERMONT DOHERTY (1936–45)
Forward, 5ft 10in, 11st 6lb, b. Magharafelt, 5 June 1913, d. Blackpool, 5 April 1990.
Signed from: Blackpool, 19 February 1936 (£10,000)
Transferred: Derby County, 6 December 1945
Career: Station United, Coleraine, Glentoran, Blackpool, City, Derby County, Huddersfield Town, Doncaster Rovers player-manager
Debut: v Preston North End, 22 February 1936
Appearances: League: 119 apps, 74 gls; FA Cup: 11 apps, 5 gls; Wartime (League and Cup): 89 apps, 60 gls; FL Wartime: 3 apps, 2 gls; Charity: 1 app, 1 gl. Total: 223 apps, 142 gls.

From the 1930s through to the modern era Peter Doherty was often described as the best Irish footballer of all time, and by City supporters as the greatest City player of all time. In recent years his name has started to be forgotten as the number of people who saw him play at his peak reduces. Nevertheless, Doherty

was viewed by many as the best ever, and during the 1970s when both Irishman George Best and City star Colin Bell had passed their peak, Doherty was still being remembered as the leading Irish player and the best Blue.

Inevitably both Best and Bell's names are remembered more today, but this shouldn't diminish what Doherty achieved.

Inside-forward Doherty joined City in 1936 for a club record £10,000 – a thousand below the transfer record – and to many fans he became the star of the following season's Championship-winning side. Doherty became the third Blue to net 30 or more goals in a season that year, and the following season he netted a further 23 goals to make him top scorer again.

He was a complete footballer and an exciting attacker, but his City career was severely damaged when war broke out in 1939. The vagaries of the wartime game meant that the club came into conflict with Doherty over guest appearances for other clubs. The Blues saw Doherty as their best asset and objected to him appearing for others, although this was a perfectly acceptable part of the wartime game. By the time the Football League resumed after the war Doherty had joined Derby County. His loss was felt by all fans.

With Derby he won the FA Cup after a semi-final at Maine Road in which a crowd in excess of 80,000 included many thousands of Mancunians who had come simply to cheer on their former hero.

After his playing career ended he moved into management and in 1958 he guided Northern Ireland to the World Cup. During 1965 he was almost given the City manager's job.

Harry Dowd

HENRY 'HARRY' WILLIAM DOWD (1958–70)
Goalkeeper, 5ft 10in, 11st 10lb, b. Salford, 4 July 1958
Signed from: amateur, 10 January 1958 (Pro: 18 July 1960)
Transferred: Oldham Athletic, 1 December 1970
Career: ICI Blackley, City, Stoke City (loan), Oldham Athletic
Debut: v Blackburn Rovers, 9 December 1961
Appearances: League: 181 apps, 1 gl; FA Cup: 22 apps, 0 gls; League Cup: 16 apps, 0 gls. Total: 219 apps, 1 gl.

Goalkeeper for the 1969 FA Cup Final, Harry Dowd joined the Blues as an amateur in 1958 before turning pro in 1960. He succeeded the great Bert Trautmann as City's number one and, despite pressure from Alan Ogley and then Ken Mulhearn, he remained first choice for most of his time at Maine Road.

He was a plumber by trade and lost his place to Mulhearn in September 1967, which meant he only managed seven appearances during the 1967–68 Championship season, although he did find his way back into the side after Mulhearn was dropped following the defeat by Fenerbahce in the European Cup.

Prior to the 1969 FA Cup Final Malcolm Allison described him as: 'completely fearless. Completely unaffected by nerves.' Dowd did seem unaffected by the hype and pressure surrounding the club during this period and as a result his performances seemed steady. After victory at Wembley in 1969 he went on loan to Stoke, then joined Oldham in December 1970.

Earlier in his career he had managed to get on the scoresheet during a game with Bury on 8 February 1964. He had broken his finger and was moved to centre-forward while Matt Gray went in nets, and managed to score City's equaliser from a rebound. Incidentally, this was the game in which Colin Bell made his League debut for Bury.

Richard Dunne

RICHARD PATRICK DUNNE (2000–)
Defender, 6ft 2in, 15st 12lb, b. Dublin, 21 September 1979
Signed from: Everton, 17 October 2000 (£3,200,000)
Career: Everton, City
Debut: v Southampton, 23 October 2000
Appearances: League: 183+6 apps, 5 gls; FA Cup: 17 apps, 0 gls; League Cup: 7 apps, 0 gls; UEFA Cup: 3+1 apps, 0 gls. Total: 210+7 apps, 5 gls.

It cost Joe Royle £3.2 million to sign Richard Dunne in October 2000 and in the years that have followed Dunne has easily proved good value for money.

A Republic of Ireland international, he made his international debut in April 2000 while still at Everton. Dunne impressed immediately at Maine Road. He was a consistent performer from the start for the Blues and became noted for his exceptional speed for a defender. Clearly, the strongest aspects of his play are his defensive qualities, such as his powerful tackling and his aerial work.

A cult hero, Dunne is a tower of strength in City's defence, and is the holder of several Man of the Match and Player of the Month awards. In 2005 he became the Player of the Year and held the award again the following year after his impressive performances during the 2005–06 season. On receiving the award Dunne admitted: 'I'm really proud. It's a surprise because it's not been the best season for us, and there's a couple of other players who have done really well. Andy Cole did well before his injury; David James has been brilliant; Trevor Sinclair has done well also. So it's a really big honour and I'm totally delighted. It was really nice getting it last year and you don't expect to win it two years in a row. There are other players in the team who deserve it, some of us have all had our moments, so I'm really pleased that I have won it.'

Hugely popular with fans, Dunne was a worthy winner. He is destined to be remembered forever as one of the new century's leading defenders.

Charlie Pringle

CHARLES ROSS PRINGLE (1922–28)
Defender, 5ft 7in, 11st 7lb, b. Nitshill, 18 October 1894, d. ??
Signed from: St Mirren, 21 June 1922
Transferred: Manchester Central, June 1928
Career: Inkerman Rangers, Maryhill Juniors, St Mirren, City, Manchester Central, Bradford PA, Lincoln City, Stockport County, Zurich, Hurst, Waterford
Debut: v Sheffield United, 26 August 1922
Appearances: League: 197 apps, 1 gl; FA Cup: 19 apps, 0 gls. Total: 216 apps, 1 gl.

Charlie Pringle was already a Scottish international when he joined the Blues from St Mirren in 1922. Known as a bustling wing-half, he immediately made an impression and was an ever-present in his first season, 1922–23, the last at Hyde Road, as City finished eighth. He went on to captain City and also became known for his relationship with the great Billy Meredith's daughter Lily. Pringle became Meredith's son-in-law and the two men played alongside each other on several occasions. The last time was in Meredith's final match, the 1924 FA Cup semi-final.

During the close season of 1928, Pringle left City to become a leading figure in the development of Manchester Central FC at Belle Vue. Central were established with the aim of becoming East Manchester's replacement for City and United, and they aimed to join the Football League. Pringle was still an important figure at City – he had made 22 appearances during 1927–28 – which perhaps shows how serious a venture Manchester Central was.

He also had spells at Bradford, Stockport and Lincoln City, where he won a Third Division North championship medal, and became a coach with Zurich, Waterford and St Mirren.

Gerard Wiekens

GERARD WIEKENS (1997–2003)
Defender, 6ft 1in, 12st 9lb, b. Tolhuiswyk, Netherlands, 25 February 1973
Signed from: FC Veendam (Netherlands), 1 July 1997 (£500,000)
Released: 30 May 2003
Career: SC Vendeem, City
Debut: v Portsmouth, 9 August 1997
Appearances: League: 167+15 apps, 10 gls; FA Cup: 11+1 apps, 0 gls; League Cup: 13+2 apps, 0 gls; UEFA Cup: 1 app, 0 gls; Play-off: 3 apps, 0 gls. Total: 195+18 apps, 10 gls.
Gerard Wiekens arrived during the close season of 1997 as Frank Clark claimed to be developing a side capable of promotion from Division One to the Premier League. Sadly, Clark's claims proved false, but Wiekens was an excellent signing. He cost £500,000 from FC Veendam and marked his debut against Portsmouth with a goal.

Fast and skilful, Wiekens became an instant hero and soon established himself in the side. It has to be remembered that every season of his City career was dramatic – relegation or promotion came in every season he appeared apart from the 2002–03 season (Maine Road's last), while he also served under three managers – but Wiekens constantly delivered. Even during his final season, when he only managed six League appearances, supporters were delighted

when it was announced his first appearance would come in the Manchester derby – the last at Maine Road. This game ended in a 3–1 win and Wiekens's qualities shone. Some suggested he should have appeared more frequently.

The promotion season of 1998–99 was perhaps his best, but there were quality performances throughout the career of this enigmatic Dutchman. His last City match was a UEFA Cup-tie against Welsh side TNS at the Millennium Stadium.

Shaun Goater

SHAUN LEONARD GOATER (1998–2003)
Forward, 6ft 1in, 12st 0lb, b. Hamilton, Bermuda, 25 February 1970
Signed from: Bristol City, 26 March 1998 (£400,000)
Transferred: Reading, 4 August 2003 (£500,000)
Career: North Village (Bermuda), Manchester United, Rotherham United, Notts County (loan), Bristol City, City, Reading, Coventry City (loan), Southend
Debut: v Bradford City, 28 March 1998

Appearances: League: 164+20 apps, 84 gls; FA Cup: 9+3 apps, 9 gls; League Cup: 13 apps, 9 gls; Play-off: 3 apps, 1 gl. Total: 189+23 apps, 103 gls.

Bermudan Shaun Goater enjoyed a remarkable career with the Blues. He arrived as one of Joe Royle's signings in March 1998, and supporters were hopeful that the striker would help the Blues avoid relegation to Division Two. Although he netted three goals in the final seven matches of the season, there was actually a perception that he missed rather too many chances. Over a century of goals later, this now seems a rather silly worry, but at the time supporters were desperate to see the Blues survive and there was no time to waste. Sadly, City were relegated and when the new season commenced there was still a perception that he was still not scoring enough. This was perhaps more a frustration at City's League position than Goater's own abilities.

It wasn't long before these concerns disappeared, however, as Goater quickly turned into a major hero. By the time of the play-off final supporters had grown to love him, particularly as he had netted the only goal of the semi-final second leg. 'City Goater Wembley' proclaimed one banner at the Final, and City's top scorer with 17 League goals was an established member of the side.

These achievements were eclipsed by Shaun's performance during the 1999–2000 season, when the £500,000 signing topped the Division One goalscoring charts and played consistently well game after game. The fans were delighted and voted him player of the year, and the chant 'Feed The Goat And He Will Score' became an established Maine Road song. So much so that at the England v Portugal match during Euro 2000 a large blue banner, carefully positioned behind the goal, simply read 'Feed The Goat'. Naturally the Bermudan could not compete at Euro 2000, but those City fans that placed the banner there wanted all of football to remember their hero's name.

During 2000–01 many assumed Goater's City career was nearing its end, particularly as former world footballer of the year George Weah had been signed, but Goater's spirit,

popularity and knack for scoring ensured he managed to fight his way back into the side. Unfortunately, the season ended with relegation from the Premier League and some supporters openly argued that had Goater been given his chance from the start, instead of Weah, then City might have survived. It was a moot point, but the following season under new manager Kevin Keegan the Goat impressed again during the Division One Championship-winning season. He topped the City scoring charts for the third time and became one of the club's top 20 strikers of all time.

Back in the Premier League chances were limited, but when he appeared he was as entertaining as ever. That season he reached the 100-goal mark in his City career as he netted twice in City's thrilling 3–1 defeat of Manchester United in the last Maine Road derby match. One of those goals was extensively reported as a Gary Neville blunder, but the truth is that Neville only 'blundered' as a result of the persistence of Goater. The Bermudan pressured and challenged him and then was able to take the ball from him before scoring.

Inevitably, Goater was transferred at the end of the season, but he was given the honour of captaining the side for Maine Road's last match and was also introduced as a guest of the club prior to the opening game at the new stadium. This led to the first ever chant at the new stadium being 'Feed The Goat' in his honour.

Since City, Goater has played for Reading and been on loan at Coventry. In 2006 he announced his retirement and over 200 City supporters formed part of an organised trip to cheer him in his last match at the start of April 2006.

George Dorsett

GEORGE DORSETT (1904–12)
Forward, 5ft 8in, 11st 10lb, b. Brownhills, August 1881, d. Manchester, April 1943
Signed from: West Bromwich Albion, 8 December 1904 (£450)
Retired: *c.*1912
Career: Shireoaks Athletic, Brownhills Albion, South Bank, Darlington St Augustine, West Bromwich Albion, City
Debut: v Stoke, 7 January 1905
Appearances: League: 193 apps, 62 gls; FA Cup: 18 apps, 3 gls. Total: 211 apps, 65 gls.

Initially an outside-left, George Dorsett made his name with the Blues more as a wing-half. He joined City in December 1904 and made his debut the following month. He scored five goals in only nine appearances that season as the Blues finished third, but the club was soon to be torn apart as a result of the widespread bribery and illegal payments investigations. Fortunately Dorsett survived the purge and, during the years that followed, he became a popular City star as the Blues tried to re-establish themselves as a force.

In 1907–08 he was joint top scorer as the Blues finished third in Division One, and he led the scoring charts again in 1909–10 as City won the Second Division title. The following August his brother Joe arrived and the brothers played alongside each other on many occasions, but as Joe's career started to develop George's neared its end. An injury limited his opportunities and he retired in the 1912 close season.

Earlier in his career he had been a key player at West Bromwich Albion, and the Blues paid a then record fee of £450 for a winger in December 1904. In October 1905 he made an appearance for the Football League against the Irish League at Hyde Road. This was a major honour and footage of the game, showing Dorsett, does exist. This is believed to be the oldest surviving footage of a professional game played in Manchester.

He passed away in 1943 at the age of 62.

Jack Percival

JOHN 'JACK' PERCIVAL (1932–47)
Half-back, 5ft 8in, 11st 12lb, b. Lower Pittington, 16 May 1913, d. Rochdale, January 1976
Signed from: Durham City, 20 October 1932
Transferred: Bournemouth & Boscombe, 23 May 1947
Career: Pittington, Hetton-le-Hole, Southampton, Derby County (trial), Durham City, City, Bournemouth & Boscombe, Shotton Colliery Welfare player-coach
Debut: v Aston Villa, 21 October 1933
Appearances: League: 161 apps, 8 gls; FA Cup: 12 apps, 0 gls; Wartime (League and Cup): 37 apps, 3 gls; Charity: 1 app, 0 gls. Total: 211 apps, 11 gls.

Like so many footballers Jack Percival was a miner by trade. Maybe the hard conditions and physical nature of the job made men hungry for a life above ground, and certainly many of the attributes needed to make a good footballing career also could be found in mining communities.

After trials at Derby and Southampton Percival arrived at Maine Road in 1932 and made his League debut, replacing Matt Busby, in October 1933. He only managed five appearances that season, but it wasn't until the latter half of the 1935–36 season that he became City's first choice right-half. The following season he was an ever-present as the Blues won the League title, and the following year he only missed two matches.

By the time war broke out in 1939 there was greater competition for places, with Les McDowall in particular looking set to replace Percival, but he managed to keep his place, apart from injury and the odd spell. The wartime situation meant he wasn't always able to play at

Maine Road, and he made guest appearances at various other Lancastrian sides.

After the war Percival played in the first 16 games of the 1946–47 promotion season, but he was transferred to Bournemouth at the season's end. After football he returned to his earlier working life, and he also managed and coached colliery welfare teams, then in later life he became a lorry driver. Sadly, in 1976 he was involved in an accident when his lorry crashed with a tanker and Percival passed away a few weeks later.

Richard Edghill

RICHARD ARLON EDGHILL (1991–2002)
Defender, 5ft 9in, 11st 5lb, b. Oldham, 23 September 1974
Signed from: apprentice, 8 July 1991 (Pro: 1 July 1992)
Transferred: Wigan Athletic, 21 October 2002
Career: St Augustine's School (Oldham), Royton Town Under-17s, City, Birmingham City (loan), Wigan Athletic, Sheffield United, Queen's Park Rangers
Debut: v Wimbledon, 20 September 1993
Appearances: League: 178+3 apps, 1 gl; FA Cup: 8+1 apps, 0 gls; League Cup: 17 apps, 0 gls; Play-off 3 apps, 0 gls. Total: 206+4 apps, 1 gl.

Full-back Richard Edghill was one of those players some supporters could never take to. He did have many great moments but it's fair to say that he was always being challenged by supporters to prove himself.

His critics claimed his distribution fell below the standard required and it is obvious that at times the criticism affected his overall play. Nevertheless, he did have admirers. On local radio ex-Blue David White, among others, praised him for his ability to kill off pressure from attackers. Frequently he cut out key opponents and his supporters claimed this aspect of his play was more than enough to merit his inclusion in the side.

Early in his career he was selected to attend a senior England training session and also made appearances for the England Under-21 and 'B' teams, but his greatest City moment was when he netted the fourth penalty in the 1999 play-off final shoot-out with Gillingham. Writing in fanzine *Bert Trautmann's Helmet* Andy Noise stated: 'What a star. Never scored a goal in his life. Subject of much unjustified criticism, yet he stood up and was counted. He had the bottle.' Dickov had already missed his penalty and Edghill's goal was vital to ensure victory.

Perhaps the greatest period came when he helped guide the side to promotion to the Premier League in 2000. A spell as captain, together with his hard work, commitment and intelligent running, helped him win over many fans. Edghill moved to Wigan in 2002, although he had also had a loan spell away from City at Birmingham in 2000.

Ken Branagan

KENNETH BRANAGAN (1948–60)
Defender, 5ft 8in, 10st 9lb, b. Salford, 27 July 1930
Signed from: North Salford Youth Club, 5 November 1948
Transferred: Oldham Athletic, 1 October 1960
Career: North Salford Youth Club, City, Oldham Athletic
Debut: v Sheffield United, 9 December 1950
Appearances: League: 196 apps, 3 gls; FA Cup: 12 apps, 0 gls. Total: 208 apps, 3 gls.

As time moves on it's difficult to understand why it sometimes took players a long time to become established in the first team, but the story of full-back Ken Branagan provides an insight into life for young people in the immediate post-war period. Branagan signed for City at the age of 18 in November 1948, but he didn't manage to make his debut until December 1950. This may give the impression that Branagan took some time to establish himself, but the truth is that like the majority of young men at this time Branagan had to do a period of National Service. He spent 18 months in the Army and then when he returned he quickly established himself in the first-team squad.

He made 10 appearances during his first season, and followed this with 32 League games in 1951–52 in the number two shirt. An ever-present in 1953–54, Branagan was a consistent performer who was renowned for being rather fast for a defender. Unfortunate to miss out on the 1955 FA Cup Final – he was suffering with appendicitis and his place was occupied by Jimmy Meadows – and the 1956 Final, Branagan remained a Blue until October 1960 when he joined Oldham Athletic.

His son Jim went on to play League football with Oldham, Huddersfield and Blackburn during the 1970s and early 1980s.

Bert Sproston

BERT SPROSTON (1938–50)
Defender, 5ft 9in, 12st 2lb, b. Elworth, near Sandbach, 22 June 1915, d. 2000
Signed from: Tottenham Hotspur, 4 November 1938 (£9,500)
Transferred: Ashton United, 1950
Career: Elworth School, Sandbach School, Thurlwood, Wheelock Village, Middlewich Athletic, Sandbach Ramblers, Huddersfield Town (trial), Leeds United, Tottenham Hotspur, City, Ashton United
Debut: v Tottenham Hotspur, 5 November 1938
Appearances: League: 125 apps, 5 gls; FA Cup: 6 apps, 0 gls; Wartime (League and Cup): 74 apps, 5 gls; FL wartime: 3 apps, 0 gls. Total: 208 apps, 10 gls.

Full-back Bert Sproston was signed from Tottenham for a near £10,000 by the Blues in 1938. He made his League debut, alongside Eric Westwood, against his former side. In fact Sproston had actually been selected by Tottenham to play against City, but the player had been struggling to settle in the capital after signing for the London club only four months earlier. City negotiated with Tottenham to bring the Sandbach-born England international back

to the north-west, and the day before the game he signed. It was a strange situation and, according to some, Sproston actually travelled to Manchester on the Spurs coach.

Sproston was a highly regarded player and had earned his first England cap when he was 21 years old while at Leeds United. He won a further two England caps with City, but war was declared before his career could develop further. By the time the war ended, a crucial six-year period from his career had been taken.

After the war he played his part in City's Second Division Championship-winning season of 1946–47, and remained a key player for the following couple of seasons before retiring in 1950. He later became trainer, then scout for Bolton Wanderers.

Irvine Thornley

IRVINE THORNLEY (1904–12)

Forward, 5ft 9in, 11st 0lb, b. Hayfield, 1883, d. 24 April 1955

Signed from: Glossop North End, 7 April 1904 (£800)

Transferred: South Shields, 12 August 1912

Career: Gamesley Swifts, Glossop Villa, Glossop St James, Glossop North End, City, South Shields, Hamilton Academicals, Houghton-le-Spring

Debut: v West Bromwich Albion, 9 April 1904

Appearances: League: 195 apps, 92 gls; FA Cup: 9 apps, 1 gl. Total: 204 apps, 93 gls.

Centre-forward Irvine Thornley arrived at Hyde Road from near-neighbours Glossop shortly before the 1904 FA Cup Final. He was unable to play in the Final itself but he did feature in four of the final five League games of the season as the Blues finished as runners-up. Unfortunately, Thornley's transfer brought a little disgrace to the club as FA investigators, keen to determine why City had suddenly emerged as FA Cup-winners and League runners-up, spent the whole close season examining City's accounts, determined to find proof of illegal wages and bonuses. They found nothing significant, other than discrepancies in the transfers of Thornley and another former Glossop player, Frank Norgrove. In City's accounts were forged receipts for unusual payments that coincided with the players' transfers. The FA determined that these were actually signing-on fees far in excess of the £10 maximum then allowed. As a result of the investigations, City were fined £250, Thornley was suspended for the rest of the 1904–05 season, and Hyde Road was ordered to be closed for two games (although that doesn't appear to have occurred in the League).

Fortunately, Thornley remained a City man and survived further FA investigations the following season. He went on to become a very popular player and also captained the side in 1909. The 1909–10 season started as one of Thornley's best, as he scored 12 goals in the opening 17 games to set City up for a promotion-winning season. Sadly, injury during a 6–0 victory over Wolves caused him to relinquish the captaincy and miss most of the rest of the season, but it was his initial work which allowed 1909–10 to end with City as Second Division Championship winners.

That Easter a crowd of over 40,000 – the highest Hyde Road attendance of the season – ensured Thornley picked up a cheque for around £1,000. This League game had been selected as his benefit match and the profit was the highest ever given to a City player at the time, although the directors' report played down the amount raised (had they not learned anything from the FA's investigations?): 'The amount cannot be now stated with exactitude owing to the fact that there has to be deducted the expenses of the day, in addition to certain sums already paid and yet to be paid as compensation for accidents which occurred on the day of the match.'

Thornley had a tremendous City career and was capped by England against Wales in March 1907 and twice played for the Football League, against the Scottish and Irish Leagues. In 1912 he joined South Shields and later moved to Hamilton Academical. Interestingly, prior to joining the Blues, Thornley – a butcher by trade – was an important member of the Glossop side, and during his early career there were two other Thornleys playing for the club. It's likely these were his brothers.

Bill Eadie

WILLIAM PHILLIPS EADIE (1906–14)
Defender, 6ft 1in, 12st 6lb, b. Greenock, 1881, d. ??
Signed from: Morton, 16 August 1906
Transferred: Derby County, 30 June 1914
Career: Johnstone, St Mirren, Greenock Morton, City, Derby County
Debut: v Sheffield Wednesday, 8 September 1906
Appearances: League: 185 apps, 6 gls; FA Cup: 19 apps, 0 gls. Total: 204 apps, 6 gls.

Bill Eadie arrived at Hyde Road in 1906 following the investigations into the bribe and illegal payments scandal that had rocked the club. Virtually the entire playing squad was suspended and half-back Eadie was an important acquisition as City tried to survive.

Born in Greenock, Scotland, Eadie arrived from Morton, and took over at centre-half from the banned Tommy Hynds. He made 29 appearances and netted three goals during the 1907–08 season when, against the odds, City ended the season third, but the following year he only managed 10 appearances as the Blues plummeted towards Division Two.

In 1909–10 he made 23 appearances as City won the Second Division title, and in June 1914 he was transferred to Derby County, where he made 31 appearances as the Rams gained promotion from Division Two in 1914–15. Unfortunately, the war cut short his playing career and when the Football League was resumed after the war Eadie was well into his thirties and unable to re-establish his career.

Keith Curle

KEITH CURLE (1991–96)
Defender, 6ft 0in, 12st 0lb, b. Bristol, 14 November 1963
Signed from: Wimbledon, 6 August 1991 (£2.5 million)
Transferred: Wolverhampton Wanderers, 2 August 1996
Career: Bristol Rovers, Torquay United, Bristol City, Reading, Wimbledon, City, Wolverhampton Wanderers, Sheffield United, Barnsley, Mansfield Town
Debut: v Coventry City, 17 August 1991
Appearances: League: 171 apps, 11 gls; FA Cup: 14 apps, 0 gls; League Cup: 18 apps, 2 gls; FMC: 1 app, 0 gls. Total: 204 apps, 13 gls.

Keith Curle arrived at City for a club record of £2.5 million in the summer of 1991. The fee was also a British record for a defender and it's true to say much was expected of the central defender. Although much could be made of the cost of his signing, thinking purely of the player, Curle was a magnificent addition to the Blues.

A very fast, strong defender Curle was made captain immediately on arrival at Maine Road and he immediately toughened up City's defence. That first season he helped City to fifth place, but the Blues were not ready to challenge for the title. In 1992–93 they finished ninth, but Curle continued to impress in his role as captain. By that time he had also made three international appearances for England, with his

first cap coming in April 1992 when he appeared as substitute against the CIS – the former Soviet Union side not the Manchester-based insurance company.

After becoming City's regular penalty-taker – supporters have strong memories of his success in the April 1992 Old Trafford derby – Curle remained a fans' favourite, but in 1996 he was sold to Wolves. By that time Alan Ball was his manager and Curle was seen as one of City's more expensive players by the management, although with relegation in 1996 supporters felt Curle was exactly the kind of player needed to help the Blues challenge for promotion. Sadly that wasn't to be. He wasn't the only popular player sold during this period, as heroes Terry Phelan, Tony Coton, Garry Flitcroft and Niall Quinn were all dispensed with prematurely.

Curle later embarked on a managerial career which included three years at Mansfield Town and a spell at Chester during 2005–06.

George Heslop

GEORGE WILSON HESLOP (1965–72)
Defender, 6ft 0in, 13st 8lb, b. Wallsend, 1 July 1940
Signed from: Everton, 14 September 1965 (£25,000)
Transferred: Bury, 11 August 1972 (£3,000)
Career: Dudley Juniors, Newcastle United, Everton, City, Bury, Cape Town City, Macclesfield Town, Northwich Victoria player-manager
Debut: v Norwich City, 15 September 1965
Appearances: League: 159+3 apps, 1 gl; FA Cup: 17 apps, 1 gl; League Cup: 12 apps, 0 gls; European Cup: 2 apps, 0 gls; ECWC: 5+3 apps, 0 gls; Charity: 1 app, 0 gls; AI Cup: 1 app, 1 gl. Total: 197+6 apps, 3 gls.

Note: Earlier versions of the *Complete Record* stated Heslop played in the 12 February 1966 FA Cup-tie with Grimsby. He did not. His place was taken by Alf Wood.

Centre-half George Heslop had made League appearances for both Newcastle and Everton when he joined City, but he had rarely been given the opportunity to have a sustained period in either club's first team. At City he quickly found himself thrown into the promotion campaign of 1965–66. He made 34 appearances that season as City won the Second Division title. He remained a key member of the side for the following three seasons and then he became a useful squad member until he joined Cape Town on loan in 1971.

In 1967–68, when the Blues won the Championship, he only missed one game, and he even netted a very important goal. The goal came in the March Manchester derby and put the Blues 2–1 up against Championship rivals United, but more than that it enabled City to have the confidence to control the rest of that game. City eventually won 3–1, but Heslop's downward header had proved vital.

He spent one season in South African soccer in 1971–72 before leaving Maine Road permanently in August 1972 when he was transferred to Bury for £3,000. Later he became Northwich Victoria manager before becoming the landlord of the City Gates public house on Hyde Road. The City Gates was the original Hyde Road Hotel, the location where Ardwick became Manchester City FC. Sadly, the venture was not a success and by late 1988 the public house had closed for the last time.

The additional heroes

The remaining players – listed alphabetically – have been selected by the author for their significant contribution to the history of City and the enjoyment of supporters. Inevitably, this list is subjective, although the author has endeavoured to select players from each era who had a rapport with fans or delivered consistently while at City.

Nicolas Anelka

NICOLAS SEBASTIEN ANELKA (2002–05)
Forward, 6ft 1in, 13st 3lb, b. Versailles (France), 14 March 1979
Signed from: Paris St Germain, 6 June 2002 (£10 million)
Transferred: Fenerbahce, 30 January 2005 (£7 million)
Career: Paris St Germain, Arsenal, Real Madrid, Paris St Germain, Liverpool, Paris St Germain, City, Fenerbahce
Debut: v Leeds United, 17 August 2002
Appearances: League: 87+2 apps, 37 gls; FA Cup: 5 apps, 4 gls; League Cup: 4 apps, 0 gls; UEFA Cup: 5 apps, 4 gls. Total: 101+2 apps, 45 gls.

Signed for a club record £10 million, reported at the time as £13 million, from Paris St Germain in June 2002, Anelka was an important member of Kevin Keegan's side in their first couple of seasons back in the Premier League. A prolific scorer while with City – he quickly established himself as the Blues' highest ever goalscorer in the Premier League with 37 goals – Anelka was a firm favourite, particularly with younger supporters. Unfortunately, there was frequent speculation that Anelka would only have a brief spell with the Blues, and newspaper stories regularly focussed on rumours that he would move on. The player regularly denied these reports, but during 2004 a story in French sports paper *L'Equipe* claimed Anelka wanted to move to a 'bigger' club – again something the player denied – and the following January he was sold to Turkish side Fenerbahce for a reported £7 million.

As well as being City's highest Premiership scorer, Anelka's name also entered the record books when he became the first player to score a goal at the City of Manchester stadium. He netted after 34 minutes against Barcelona in the opening friendly on 10 August 2003, and then a month later he became the first penalty scorer and hat-trick hero as Aston Villa were defeated in City's first League win at the new stadium on 14 September 2003.

Peter Barnes

PETER SIMON BARNES (1972–79 and 1986–88)
Forward, 5ft 10in, 11st 0lb, b. Manchester, 10 June 1957
Signed from: Manchester Boys, 31 July 1972
Transferred: West Bromwich Albion, 17 July 1979
Signed from: Manchester United, 13 January 1987
Transferred: Hull City, 3 March 1988
Career: Gatley Rangers, Manchester Boys, City,

West Bromwich Albion, Leeds United, Real Betis, Leeds United, Melbourne, Coventry City, Manchester United, City, Bolton Wanderers (loan), Port Vale (loan), Hull City, Drogheda United, Sporting Farense, Bolton Wanderers, Sunderland, Tampa Bay Rowdies, Northwich Victoria, Wrexham, Radcliffe Borough, Mossley, Cliftonville
Debut: v Manchester United, 9 October 1974 (League Cup)
League debut: v Burnley, 12 October 1974
Second debut: v Liverpool, 17 January 1987
Appearances: League: 116+7 apps, 15 gls; FA Cup: 7 apps, 2 gls; League Cup: 16+5 apps, 4 gls; UEFA Cup: 9 apps, 1 gl; TC Cup: 1 app, 0 gls. Total: 149+12 apps, 22 gls.

The first City player to be awarded the PFA Young Player of The Year title, Barnes was an entertaining winger for the Blues during the mid to late 1970s. Son of fifties star Ken, Barnes was loved by supporters. Although he made his debut in October 1974, it wasn't until the following season that he really began to shine. The departure of Rodney Marsh caused manager Tony Book to reshuffle his side by moving Asa Hartford to Marsh's number 10 shirt. Barnes came in, initially as a replacement for Dennis Tueart as number 11, but eventually he took the number seven spot from Hartford.

By the end of the 1975–76 season he had appeared in 36 League and Cup games, including the League Cup Final. That Final ended in a 2–1 victory for City, with Barnes scoring the crucial opening goal after 11 minutes. He was only 19 and by the end of the season he had received the PFA award for what was seen as a remarkably good season.

Despite the promise and the popularity of the player his City career was cut short in July 1979 when he was transferred by Malcolm Allison to West Bromwich Albion. He didn't want to leave and the fans didn't want him to go, but Allison made it clear he was no longer to feature in his plans and he was off. During his final two years at the club he had appeared in 14 England internationals and seemed destined for a great international career. He went on to make 22 international appearances as he moved from West Bromwich Albion to Leeds United. A spell at Manchester United followed before he returned to City in 1987 for a brief spell during Jimmy Frizzell's period in charge. In 2006 the Manchester City Experience staged an exhibition dedicated to the careers of Peter and Ken Barnes.

Walter Bowman

WALTER W. BOWMAN (1892–1900)
Defender, b. Ontario (Canada), 1862, d. believed to be at Butte (Montana, US)
Signed from: Accrington, 25 August 1892
Released: *c.*1900
Career: Canadian XI, Accrington, Ardwick/City
Debut: v Crewe Alexandra, 18 February 1893
Appearances: League: 47 apps, 3 gls; FA Cup: 2 apps, 0 gls. Total: 49 apps, 3 gls.

Although most Mancunians were unaware at the time, one of the club's earliest League players was actually the first overseas international to play in the Football League. Walter Bowman was born in Canada during 1862, and arrived in the British Isles in August 1888 as a Canadian international.

The Canadians were playing a number of friendly fixtures against sides in Ireland,

Scotland and England, and even faced Newton Heath, winning 2–0 with Bowman scoring. Whether this appearance was witnessed by any of the Ardwick officials at the time isn't known, but Bowman returned to Canada with his teammates shortly afterwards.

A second tour followed in 1891 – including a 3–1 Ardwick victory on 12 December 1891 – and Bowman remained behind after the rest of the Canadians had returned home. He joined Accrington, making his debut in January 1892. That match made him the first overseas international to play in the League and on 25 August 1892 he signed for Ardwick. He didn't manage to make his Ardwick debut until 18 February 1893, when he scored as Crewe were defeated 3–1.

Bowman remained with the Blues until the close season of 1900, with one of his most significant matches being the 11–3 record victory over Lincoln on 23 March 1895, although Bowman failed to make the scoresheet.

After City little is known of Bowman's life. An article in April 1929 talked of a reunion in Toronto of the touring side, but Bowman did not attend. It was believed he was living in the US in a copper mining city in western Montana called Butte, but he was never traced. No matter what the final resting place of Bowman, his place as the Football League's first overseas player means his name will never be forgotten.

Tommy Caton

THOMAS STEPHEN CATON (1979–83)

Defender, 6ft 2in, 13st 0lbs, b. Liverpool, 6 October 1962, d. Oxford, 30 April 1993

Signed from: apprentice 5 July 1979 (Pro: 6 October 1979)

Transferred: Arsenal, 30 November 1983 (£500,000)

Career: St Kevin's (Kirkby), City, Arsenal, Oxford United, Charlton Athletic

Debut v Crystal Palace, 18 August 1979

Appearances: League: 164+1 apps, 8 gls; FA Cup: 12 apps, 0 gls; League Cup: 21 apps, 0 gls. Total: 197+1 apps, 8 gls.

As one of Malcolm Allison's brilliant young players, Tommy Caton made his League debut at the age of 16 and then retained his place for the entire season. This amazing arrival on the scene inevitably brought great media interest and this was followed in 1981, at the age of 18, with his appearance in the FA Cup Final. Destined to be a star for many years, City's relegation in 1983 caused Caton to assess his career. The media suggested playing in Division Two would limit his chance of playing for the full England side and, as with Shaun Wright-Phillips in 2005, a move to London seemed the perfect way of guaranteeing a great international future. Sadly for Caton, the move to London seemed to have a detrimental effect on his career and, despite joining Arsenal, his international aspirations could not be fulfilled.

After 95 League and Cup appearances with the Gunners he was transferred to Oxford for

£180,000. A move to Charlton soon followed and then a serious foot injury required repeated surgery during the early 1990s. This brought a great deal of depression to the player and early in 1993 he was forced to announce his retirement. The following April the shock news was released that he had died at the age of 30 of a suspected heart-attack. A minute's silence was held at Maine Road as supporters remembered the great moments of his early career.

Although his life and City career were extremely short, it has to be said that Caton did bring a lot of happiness to the Blues. He had been a revelation, and while at Maine Road he continually improved. Had City not been relegated in 1983 then it is unlikely he would have moved and maybe his international aspirations would have been met. After all, he had appeared for the England Under-21 side on 10 occasions while at City.

Interestingly, Caton's youngest son, Andy, has become a professional player. On the opening day of the 2004–05 season he made his debut when he came on as substitute for Swindon Town against Wrexham. He netted a consolation goal that day, and made his full debut on the final day of the season against Chesterfield. Like his father Andy made his debut at the age of 16.

Tony Coton

ANTHONY PHILLIP COTON (1990–96)
Goalkeeper, 6ft 2in, 13st 7lb, b. Tamworth, 19 May 1961
Signed from: Watford, 12 July 1990 (£1 million)
Transferred: Manchester United, 19 January 1996 (£500,000)
Career: Mile Oak Rovers, Birmingham City, Hereford United (loan), Watford, City, Manchester United, Sunderland
Debut: v Tottenham Hotspur, 25 August 1990
Appearances: League: 162+1 apps, 0 gls; FA Cup: 12 apps, 0 gls; League Cup: 16 apps, 0 gls; FMC: 3 apps, 0 gls. Total: 193+1 apps, 0 gls.

Goalkeeper Tony Coton arrived at Howard Kendall's City following a good career with First Division Watford and Second Division Birmingham. He hit the headlines from the moment he made his debut for Birmingham when, with only 54 seconds played of a 1980 meeting with Sunderland, he saved a penalty with his first touch of the ball.

Kendall signed Coton for a fee of around £1 million in July 1990 and he proved to be an excellent purchase, although some supporters took some convincing initially. The following season Coton was voted City's player of the year, and he also gained an England 'B' Cap in 1992. To many it seemed only a matter of time before a full England cap arrived but sadly it never did. Why he didn't mystified most City fans and neutrals.

In 1993–94 he was again voted City player of the year, and he remained a very popular 'keeper, providing stability during a difficult season for the club both on and off the field. Sadly injury affected him for a spell, but following Alan Ball's appointment as manager Coton seemed to be out of favour. During the summer of 1996 he was transferred to Manchester United. At the time rumours spread that Coton had sacrificed a first-team place at City for life on the bench at United, but Coton has in recent years revealed that Ball had told him that he would not be City's first choice and that the move was not sought by him.

Inevitably Coton moved into coaching while at United, but his love of City continued. The criticism he received in 1996 following his transfer is clearly not justified and it's worth stating that Coton felt he could have still achieved a great deal at Maine Road when he was transferred by Ball. This was a point proved by the fact that six months after his Old Trafford move he had a spell at Sunderland where he did play 10 Premier League matches during 1996–97.

As a key player during the reign of four managers – Kendall, Reid, Horton, and Ball – Coton proved to be a very capable 'keeper and a firm favourite with City fans. He was one of England's finest 'keepers of the nineties and should have played for the national side. The fact he didn't perhaps says a great deal about the direction of England and the FA during the immediate post-Robson period.

Johnny Crossan

JOHN ANDREW CROSSAN (1965–67)
Midfield, 5ft 8in, 11st 2lb, b. Londonderry, 29 November 1938
Signed from: Sunderland, 22 January 1965 (£40,000)
Transferred: Middlesbrough, 23 August 1967 (£30,000)
Career: Derry City, Coleraine, Sparta Rotterdam, Standard Liège, Sunderland, City, Middlesbrough, Tongren (Belgium)
Debut: v Derby County, 30 January 1965
Appearances: League: 94 apps, 24 gls; FA Cup: 14 apps, 3 gls; League Cup: 2 apps, 1 gl. Total: 110 apps, 28 gls.

Derry-born Johnny Crossan almost signed for Joe Mercer when he was manager of Sheffield United, but the deal fell through. A spell at Standard Liège, where he played in a European Cup quarter-final against Real Madrid, and Sunderland followed before he joined City towards the end of the 1964–65 season.

When Joe Mercer became manager in 1965 he was delighted to find Crossan at the club and the Irishman was captain for the promotion season of 1965–66. That season was Crossan's best at Maine Road and fans loved his playing ability and captaincy skills, while he also added a touch of humour to the dressing room.

Prior to the 1966–67 season he was involved in a car crash close to Roker Park and missed the opening game of the new season. He tried to disguise an injured knee and his form suffered. Some thought he wasn't trying, but the truth was that he was trying more than most but was simply unable to cope. He also suffered from a grumbling appendix.

In August 1967 he was transferred to Middlesbrough for £32,000 – proving that he was still a player with much to offer – and at Ayresome Park he made a total of 56 appearances and scored eight goals, but according to some sources he also had problems with insomnia.

Once his footballing career was over Crossan ran an off-licence in Derry for a while, and in 1997 was involved with a sports shop in his home town. He also played an active role in training local youngsters, and acted as a scout for the Blues. Crossan made 24 Northern Ireland international appearances (10 while with City), and proved to be a very popular Blue.

Paul Dickov

PAUL DICKOV (1996–2002)
Forward, 5ft 6in, 11st 5lb, b. Livingston, 1 November 1972
Signed from: Arsenal, 23 August 1996 (£750,000)
Transferred: Leicester City, 22 February 2002 (£150,000)
Signed from: released by Blackburn Rovers, 26 May 2006
Career: Arsenal, Luton Town (loan), Brighton & Hove Albion (loan), City, Leicester City, Blackburn Rovers
Debut: v Stoke City, 24 August 1996 (substitute)
Full debut: v Barnsley, 7 September 1996
Appearances: League: 105+51 apps, 33 gls; FA Cup: 5+4 apps, 1 gl; League Cup: 9+4 apps, 5 gls; Play-offs: 3 apps, 2 gls. Total: 122+59 apps, 41 gls.

Paul Dickov, re-signing for City in 2006.

Known as a committed kind of player, Paul Dickov proved to be one of City's cult figures following his life-saving goal in the 1999 play-off final against Gillingham. However, his contribution was considerably more than that one goal. It's worth remembering that he did score several important goals, such as in the play-off semi-final with Wigan and the promotion-clinching match at Blackburn on the last day of the 1999–2000 season.

Always known for his fighting spirit, Dickov joined City from Arsenal in August 1996 for £1 million. With the Gunners he had netted three goals in 21 appearances, but had struggled to break in to the first team. Moving to Manchester was the perfect opportunity for him to prove what he was capable of. It was a very good move and, although City struggled during his first couple of seasons, Dickov was one of the more popular players simply because he demonstrated the sort of passion and drive fans demand from their side.

He helped City to back-to-back promotions and remained a popular presence until February 2002, by which time manager Kevin Keegan felt he was no longer part of his plans. Despite his departure he remained a cult figure and at the end of the 2001–02 season he returned to Maine Road to present Keegan's side with the Division One Championship trophy. A year later he was back again as a main guest during the End of An Era Maine Road celebrations.

In the years that followed it's appropriate to say his fighting spirit and never-say-die attitude worked against the Blues, as he helped take points off City for both Leicester City and Blackburn Rovers via penalties. Those controversial goals reminded supporters of the commitment he always demonstrated but which was often lacking from other players. In the 2006 close season Dickov rejoined the Blues from Blackburn Rovers.

Sylvain Distin

SYLVAIN DISTIN (2002–)
Defender, 6ft 4in, 13st 10lb, b. Bagnolet (Guadeloupe), 16 December 1977

Signed from: Paris St Germain, 4 July 2002 (£4 million)
Career: Tours, Guegnon, Paris St Germain, Newcastle United (loan), City
Debut: v Leeds United, 17 August 2002
Appearances: League: 141 apps, 3 gls; FA Cup: 11 apps, 1 gl; League Cup: 6 apps, 0 gls; UEFA Cup 5 apps, 0 gls. Total: 163 apps, 4 gls.

A powerful left-footed centre-back, Sylvain Distin joined the Blues from Paris St Germain in July 2002 for a fee of approximately £4 million. A strong quality defender, Distin proved to be one of Kevin Keegan's quality purchases. Together with Richard Dunne, he helped the Blues build a solid base from which they could consolidate in the Premier League.

Eventually taking on the captaincy, Distin seemed most composed during the 2004–05 season, particularly when Stuart Pearce became manager. Another consistent season followed, but during the Christmas period, and again as the season neared its end, several rumours circulated that Distin would be moving on.

Paddy Fagan

FIONAN FAGAN (1953–60)
Forward, 5ft 7in, 9st 10lb, b. Dublin, 7 June 1930
Signed from: Hull City, 24 December 1953
Transferred: Derby County, 15 March 1960 (£8,000)

Career: Shamrock Rovers, Transport (Dublin), Home Park, Hull City, City, Derby County, Altrincham player-manager, Ashton United, Northwich Victoria
Debut: v Sheffield United, 26 December 1953
Appearances: League: 153 apps, 34 gls; FA Cup: 11 apps, 1 gl; Charity: 1 app, 0 gls. Total: 165 apps, 35 gls.

Fionan 'Paddy' Fagan was a versatile winger during a great career with the Blues. He won eight Republic of Ireland caps, two while with City, and was a member of the 1955 FA Cup Final side. Sadly that game ended in defeat, and he was unfortunate to miss the following year's successful Final.

Brought up in a sporting family – his father was an outside-left for Shamrock Rovers and also an Irish international – Fagan played for Irish sides Shamrock Rovers and Transport before joining Hull. He joined City from Hull City on Christmas Eve 1953, appeared for the reserves on Christmas Day, then made his League debut on Boxing Day.

In March 1960, still an international, he joined Derby County for £8,000. A spell as player-manager at Altrincham – under future City chairman Peter Swales and future FA councillor Noel White – followed. Away from football he became a driving instructor.

During the early 1990s, together with Roy Clarke, Roy Little and other fifties stars, he was a founder member of the City Former Players' Association. In 2002–03 he perhaps made history as a guest of Hull City at Boothferry Park's last game and a guest of City at Maine Road's last game. Fagan said: 'These were fantastic days. Hull's ground went first, and I didn't think anybody would remember me – it's over 50 years since I played there – but people were coming up to me to say they knew of me even if they hadn't seen me play, so that was nice. There weren't that many of my former playing colleagues left unfortunately, but I enjoyed the walk on the pitch and it brought back some good memories. The same happened at Maine Road, of course, and I do enjoy meeting supporters.'

Johnny Hart

JOHN PAUL HART (1944–63)
Forward, 5ft 10in, 10st 8lb, b. Golborne, 8 June 1928
Signed from: amateur, 8 December 1944 (Pro: 13 June 1945)
Career: Loughton Youth Club, City
Debut: v Bolton Wanderers, 10 April 1948
Appearances: League: 169 apps, 67 gls; FA Cup: 9 apps, 6 gls; Wartime (League and Cup): 4 apps, 1 gl. Total: 182 apps, 74 gls.

Johnny Hart was a skilful inside-right during a long City career, but he also suffered a few serious injuries. He was unfortunate to miss the 1955 Final due to a broken leg, and he also missed the 1956 FA Cup Final as a result of a late fitness test on Bobby Johnstone – it was later revealed that Hart himself had more or less stood aside to allow the fans' favourite to play.

Hart, a loyal Blue, may not have realised it at the time but his commitment to the City cause impressed both journalists and fans alike. In 1955 following his injury Eric Todd wrote in the *Manchester Evening Chronicle*: 'His ceaseless,

Harry Godwin and Johnny Hart.

tireless grafting has been of inestimable value. The hundreds of messages and callers he received in hospital were not only expressions of sympathy but represented a sincere tribute to a gallant footballer.'

Despite the injuries and tough competition for his place Hart still managed to head the City goalscoring charts for three seasons.

He retired in May 1963 – his last appearance had been on 3 April 1961 at Preston – and then moved in to coaching with the Blues. The rest of his career is detailed within the Managers section of this book.

Andy Hinchcliffe

ANDREW GEORGE HINCHCLIFFE (1985–90)
Defender, 5ft 10in, 12st 10lb, b. Manchester, 5 February 1969
Signed from: amateur, 1 July 1985 (Pro: 13 February 1986)
Career: William Hulme Grammar School, City, Everton, Sheffield Wednesday
Debut: v Plymouth Argyle, 15 August 1987
Appearances: League: 107+5 apps, 8 gls; FA Cup: 12 apps, 1 gl; League Cup: 11 apps, 1 gl; FMC: 4 apps, 1 gl. Total: 134+5 apps, 11 gls.

In terms of trophy success and international honours Andy Hinchcliffe is the most successful of all the members of City's 1986 FA Youth Cup-winning side, although sadly most of his major successes came away from Manchester. At Joe Royle's Everton he won an FA Cup-winner's medal and made his first England international appearance.

Hinchcliffe signed apprentice forms at Maine Road in July 1985, with his League debut coming two years later. He missed only two League games during his first season and soon proved a tremendous asset to Mel Machin's Division Two side. The following season, 1988–89, his quality shone again as he helped City to promotion, then, on 23 September 1989, the moment came that most fans tend to think of when they hear his name – his headed goal in the 5–1 massacre of Manchester United.

Defender Hinchcliffe, not known as a goalscorer, scored a wonderful fifth goal for the Blues that day.

Ten days before the United game he had appeared for the England Under–21 side in a friendly against Denmark alongside Ian Brightwell, Paul Lake and Steve Redmond. Against the wishes of supporters, Howard Kendall sold Hinchcliffe to Everton during the summer of 1990, in a deal which brought Neil Pointon to Maine Road. He was the first of City's great youth players to move on and this angered many fans, especially when Kendall himself returned to Everton only a few months later. At Goodison, Hinchcliffe continued to impress, although it took the arrival of Joe Royle and Willie Donachie to guide him towards international honours, and he later enjoyed a spell at Sheffield Wednesday.

In recent years he has been a frequent visitor to City and has embarked on a new career with local radio. It is a role he seems comfortable in.

Tommy Hutchison

THOMAS HUTCHISON (1980–82)
Midfield, 5ft 11in, 11st 2lb, b. Cardenden, 22 September 1947

Signed from: Coventry City, 22 October 1980
Transferred: Bulova (Hong Kong), 1 July 1982
Career: Oldham Athletic (trial), Dundonald Bluebell, Alloa Athletic, Blackpool, Coventry City, Seattle Sounders, City, Bulova (Hong Kong), Burnley, Swansea City player-manager, Merthyr Town
Debut: v Brighton & Hove Albion, 25 October 1980
Appearances: League: 44+2 apps, 4 gls; FA Cup: 10 apps, 1 gl; League Cup: 3+1 apps, 0 gls. Total: 57+3 apps, 5 gls.

Tommy Hutchison was the man heralded by most supporters as the key player in the 1980–81 transformation from relegation-bound side to FA Cup finalists. In 1980 new manager John Bond felt that City lacked experience and so he purchased three men – Gerry Gow, Bobby McDonald and Tommy Hutchison – with the aim of adding strength and stability to the then struggling side. The approach worked, and Hutchison became a City hero. He proved to be a dedicated, consistent, skilful professional and, considering he was 33 at the time, he was superbly fit.

City progressed to the FA Cup Final and Hutchison made history by becoming the first man to score for both sides in a Wembley FA Cup Final – this later became a Trivial Pursuit question – and his agony when the own goal went in was clear for all to see. Over the years that have followed supporters have always shared the pain of the moment without apportioning blame. All Mancunians understood that Hutchison was one of the biggest reasons why the Blues had reached Wembley, and the goal was simply an unfortunate incident, albeit a very important one.

After Wembley Hutchison continued to be a Blue but, with his main job already completed, John Bond had already started to look for a replacement. After achieving cult status with the Blues he enjoyed a long playing career with spells in Hong Kong, Burnley, Swansea and Merthyr. At the age of 43 he received a special merit award from the PFA to mark being the oldest player in League football. He later worked with Football in the Community at Swansea.

David James

DAVID BENJAMIN JAMES (2004–)
Goalkeeper, 6ft 5in, 14st 7lb, b. Welwyn Garden City, 1 August 1970
Signed from: West Ham United, 14 January 2004 (£1,300,000)
Career: Watford, Liverpool, Aston Villa, West Ham United, City
Debut: v Blackburn Rovers, 17 January 2004
Appearances: League: 93 apps, 0 gls; FA Cup: 6 apps, 0 gls; League Cup: 1 app, 0 gls. Total: 100 apps, 0 gls.

England international goalkeeper David James joined City from West Ham in January 2004 and immediately proved popular with supporters. He gained his first senior England cap against Mexico in 1997 while playing for Liverpool, and for much of the period following David Seaman's retirement he was England's first choice. By the time of the 2006 World Cup he was no longer England's regular number one, but he did make the journey to Germany after many impressive performances while at City.

At City his confidence and assured handling helped the Blues enormously during the end of

the Keegan era and the beginning of Pearce's period in charge. As with Corrigan and Swift before him, this City and England 'keeper has made the occasional slip, but his overall brilliance while with the Blues is what fans will remember as time moves on. Perhaps more than any other club, City have a terrific reputation for possessing great 'keepers and James is destined to be bracketed with Swift, Trautmann and Corrigan as one of City's greatest-ever 'keepers.

On the last day of the 2004–05 season James demonstrated another exciting aspect of his play when Pearce played him for a significant period of the second half as a striker. Substitute Nicky Weaver was brought on and went in nets while James changed his shirt and played in attack. It was an interesting and exciting period and, thanks to James's persistence, it also led to a penalty for the Blues. It was one of those crazy City moments, and James's position as one of the club's most loved players of recent years increased.

Bobby Johnstone

ROBERT JOHNSTONE (1955–59)
Forward, 5ft 5in, 11st 2lb, b. Selkirk, 7 September 1929, d. 22 August 2001
Signed from: Hibernian, 2 March 1955 (£22,000)
Transferred: Hibernian, 22 September 1959 (£7,000)
Career: Selkirk, Newtongrange Star, Newtongrange Bluebell, Hibernian, City, Hibernian, Oldham Athletic, Witton Albion
Debut: v Bolton Wanderers, 16 March 1955
Appearances: League: 124 apps, 42 gls; FA Cup: 14 apps, 9 gls; Charity: 1 app, 0 gls. Total: 139 apps, 51 gls.

Bobby Johnstone quickly established himself as a key City man after making his debut only two months before the 1955 Final. In the Cup Final City lost to Newcastle, but Johnstone scored City's only goal. The following year, as City beat

Birmingham in the 1956 Final, he netted again. This made him the first player to score in successive Wembley Finals. After the 1956 Final local journalist Eric Thornton told of how Johnstone's appearance in the Final was a major gamble: 'McDowall had taken a gamble in playing Bobby Johnstone with a weak knee and a sprained right calf muscle. But what can you do when one of your star forwards undergoes a late fitness test and then says, "I'm OK, boss." He was far from it. But I know him so well that it was easy to recognise the determination.'

Johnstone was a remarkable City player with a great goalscoring pedigree after a wonderful career with Hibernian. In addition he was a great Scottish international, making 17 appearances. In August 1955 he also played for a Great Britain XI against a Europe XI. Hugely popular with fans, Johnstone was a major 1950s star and a true blue hero during a four-year spell at Maine Road.

In September 1959 he moved back to Hibernian for a fee of £12,000, but a year later returned to the Manchester area where he joined Oldham Athletic. His debut was watched by a crowd of 17,116 – Boundary Park's highest for six and a half years – and he immediately became a hero to Latics supporters.

In addition to his footballing expertise, he also played cricket for Saddleworth. After his football playing days were over he continued to attend matches at both Boundary Park and Maine Road, and was a very popular member of City's Former Players' Association. Sadly he passed away in August 2001. Today an impressive painting of Johnstone is positioned in the Directors' Guest Lounge at City's stadium.

Georgi Kinkladze

GEORGIOU KINKLADZE (1995–98)
Midfield, 5ft 8in, 10st 9lb, b. Tbilisi, 6 July 1973
Signed from Dynamo Tbilisi, 17 August 1995 (£2 million)
Transferred: Ajax, 15 May 1998 (£5 million)
Career: Mretebi Tbilisi, Dynamo Tbilisi, Saarbrucken (loan), City, Ajax, Derby County, Anorthosis Famagusta, Rubin Kazan
Debut: v Tottenham Hotspur, 19 August 1995
Appearances: League: 105+1 apps, 20 gls; FA Cup: 9 apps, 2 gls; League Cup: 6 apps, 0 gls. Total: 120+1 apps, 22 gls.

Georgiou Kinkladze was the main highlight for most fans during the mid-nineties at Maine Road. He arrived at City at the start of the 1995–96 season and, although he only stayed for three years, he became a cult figure, recognised throughout football for his skill and artistry.

From his debut in the opening game of the 1995–96 season he demonstrated a style of play that was exciting. The *Telegraph*'s highly respected Bryon Butler became one of Kinkladze's first admirers. Within weeks of his debut Butler was making comparisons with Matthews and Best, while stating that he believed the City man had more to offer English football than Cantona, Shearer, Giggs and a whole host of other more familiar names.

There were many thrilling individual moments of genius from the Georgian. In February 1996 against Newcastle the BBC summariser Alan Hansen raved about Kinkladze's overall performance and the following month one of his two goals in the 2–1 victory over Southampton was voted *Match of the Day*'s goal of the month, and came second in the goal of the season competition. That goal was simply incredible. During the course of a

40-yard run he tore through the whole Southampton defence, allowed Dave Beasant to make his move, then delicately chipped the ball over the 'keeper's body.

Despite the excitement of the player, these were not great times on the pitch and City were relegated at the end of the Georgian's first season. Relegation to the third tier of football followed again two seasons later and, under new manager Joe Royle, a fighting, typically lower league style of play was needed. This was alien to City, but absolutely necessary, and inevitably Kinkladze was seen by Royle as an expensive luxury. A talented and gifted international was not the sort of player Royle felt could save the club, especially as the Blues seemed to lack strength and guile.

Kinkladze left the Blues in the 1998 close season, and in 2006 he helped Rubin Kazan to fourth place in the Russian League. The previous season he had played for Anorthosis as they won the Cypriot League.

Paul Lake

PAUL ANDREW GREGORY LAKE (1985–96)
Midfield, 6ft 0in, 12st 2lb, b. Manchester, 28 October 1968
Signed from: apprentice, 1 July 1985 (Pro: 1 June 1987)
Retired: January 1996
Career: St Thomas More School (Denton), Blue Star, City
Debut: v Wimbledon, 24 January 1987
Appearances: League: 106+4 apps, 7 gls; FA Cup: 9 apps, 2 gls; League Cup: 10 apps, 1 gl; FMC: 5 apps, 1 gl. Total: 130+4 apps, 11 gls.

Dentonian Paul Lake was a versatile player, making appearances for the Blues as full-back, central-defender, midfielder, and orthodox striker. For a while he was also team captain. Lake first came to prominence as a member of City's 1986 FA Youth Cup-winning team, and he also captained the side that reached the semi-finals the following season. By that time he had made his first-team debut and scored his first League goal in only his third match (City 1 Luton 1, 21 February 1987).

City's Young Player of the Year title followed in 1987–88. Lake was a regular during the 1988–89 promotion season, when he wore shirts of nine different numbers. Tragedy struck on 11 March 1989 when an accidental clash of heads during the match with Leicester resulted in Lake swallowing his tongue. Only the actions of physio Roy Bailey saved Lake from death in what was a nightmare situation.

He was talked about as one of the great England players of the future. Then injuries became all too frequent. Selected for England's 1988 Under–21 European Championships squad, he was ruled out by injury, and the first of his six Under–21 international caps did not come until September 1988, when he played against Denmark.

On the verge of a glittering England career, Lake entered the 1990–91 season full of optimism. Unfortunately he failed to make it past the third game of the season, when a knee injury sustained in a rather innocuous challenge with Aston Villa's Tony Cascarino became quite serious. For the following two years he struggled to regain fitness. He returned to action for the opening game of the 1992–93 season against QPR. He was substituted and some fans felt he had been rushed back too

soon, then two days later, after only eight minutes of action against Middlesbrough, he collapsed again. This time he had damaged his cruciate ligaments.

Determined to return to action, Lake fought a long, hard, lonely battle against injury, but sadly he was first to retire in 1996. A career looking into injuries and physiotherapy has followed and he has also teamed up with the former City manager Brian Horton at near neighbours Macclesfield.

In 2004 he was one of the inaugural inductees in the Manchester City Hall of Fame and at the ceremony Niall Quinn described him as the greatest player he had played with – that is a major recognition of the qualities Lake possessed during a frustratingly short career.

Roy Little

ROY LITTLE (1949–58)
Defender, 5ft 9in, 11st 4lb, b. Manchester, 1 June 1931
Signed from: Greenwood Victoria, 6 August 1949
Transferred: Brighton & Hove Albion, 18 October 1958
Career: Greenwood Victoria, City, Brighton & Hove Albion, Crystal Palace, Dover player-manager
Debut: v Liverpool, 17 January 1953
Appearances: League: 168 apps, 2 gls; FA Cup: 18 apps, 0 gls; Charity: 1 app, 0 gls. Total: 187 apps, 2 gls.

Mancunian Roy Little was a full-back whose defensive skills helped the Blues to successive FA Cup Finals in 1955 and 1956. Very popular in the dressing room, Little brought a light-hearted approach to life at Maine Road. In fact, whenever asked about the 1955 Final defeat by Newcastle, he talks in a light-hearted manner about the anguish he feels every Cup Final day when TV shows Jackie Milburn's opening goal. Little was the City player who almost got his head to the ball as it crossed the line. Clearly his career deserves to be remembered for much more than that moment.

Little believed the Revie Plan of 1954 was responsible for the development of his career: 'I'd missed the first game of 1954–55 when we were beat 5–0 by Preston. That was the day the Plan was first tried out, but Jimmy Meadows played at left-back. Meadows was a great player and he played well, but Bill Leivers was the number two and he seemed to get injured. It ended up that for the next match Les McDowall decided to move Meadows to number two and give me the left-back spot while Leivers was out through injury. Ken Barnes came in for McTavish and the Plan worked like a dream. Bill Leivers's injury gave me my chance and that was it.'

The 1956 Final victory was the greatest individual moment and Little was a key defender throughout that great period. In addition he managed to score two goals: 'I actually scored about eight goals – two for City and the rest own goals! It took some doing though to score past Bert Trautmann but I managed it about six times.

'The two City goals I scored both came during 1953–54 and both against Yorkshire sides. At Huddersfield I got to the halfway line and whacked the ball. The ground was rock hard and it came down just in front of the 'keeper, but the bounce sent it straight over his head and into the net. We drew that match 1–1.

'The other goal was against Sheffield Wednesday and I remember I went past the halfway line and the other players were thinking: "What's he going to do? He doesn't know what happens on that side of the pitch." Everyone was looking at me, waiting for something to happen, and I was there thinking: "What am I going to do now. I'm not supposed to be up here." So I did what I suppose most people uncertain would do, I kicked it as hard as I could. I don't know how it happened, but it flew straight towards the goal and went in. We won that match 3–2.'

After City, Little joined Brighton, Crystal Palace and became player-manager of Dover. He later returned to Manchester and spent many years working for Manchester University leisure department at Wythenshawe. He was also a significant figure behind the formation of the City Former Players' Association.

Rodney Marsh

RODNEY WILLIAM MARSH (1972–76)
Forward, 6ft 0in, 12st 0lb, b. Hatfield, 11 October 1944
Signed from: Queen's Park Rangers, 8 March 1972 (£200,000)
Transferred: Tampa Bay Rowdies, 12 January 1976 (£45,000)
Career: Alexander Boys Club, West Ham United, Fulham, Queen's Park Rangers, City, Tampa Bay Rowdies, Fulham, Tampa Bay Rowdies
Debut: v Chelsea, 18 March 1972
Appearances: League: 116+2 apps, 36 gls; FA Cup: 8 apps, 2 gls; League Cup: 16 apps, 6 gls; UEFA Cup: 2 apps, 2 gls; Charity: 2 apps, 0 gls; AS Cup 3 apps, 1 gl; T Cup: 3 apps, 0 gls. Total: 150+2 apps, 47 gls.

Rodney Marsh arrived at City as a major star and was portrayed by the media as City's answer to George Best. That was perhaps unfair on the rest of City's squad, as the Blues already possessed hugely popular and enigmatic internationals such as Mike Summerbee, Francis Lee and Colin Bell. Nevertheless, his flamboyance brought a lot of attention.

City, who had been challenging for the title prior to Marsh's arrival, seemed unsettled following Marsh's debut and the Blues missed out on the Championship. In truth Marsh wasn't to blame, but his selection did come at the wrong time. He had some great moments at City, including scoring an amazing overhead kick against QPR in September 1974.

He was also a member of the League Cup side of 1974, although he blamed himself for one of Wolves' goals and refused to collect his runners'-up tankard at the end. By the time of City's next League Cup Final in 1976 Marsh had left City for Tampa Bay Rowdies in America, although he had played in four of City's games in the competition that season.

A brief spell back at Fulham followed, where he teamed up with Bobby Moore and George Best, but for the following decade or so the lure of soccer US-style kept him in the headlines. He was seen by many as one of the most influential footballing figures in the United States.

During the 1990s he was a regular summariser on Sky Sports.

Andy Morrison

ANDREW CHARLES MORRISON
(1998–2001)
Midfield, 6ft 0in, 12st 0lb, b. Inverness, 30 July 1970
Signed from: Huddersfield Town, 29 October 1998 (£80,000)
Released: 2001
Career: Plymouth Argyle, Blackburn Rovers, Blackpool, Huddersfield Town, City, Blackpool (loan), Crystal Palace (loan), Sheffield United (loan)
Debut: v Colchester United, 31 October 1998
Appearances: League: 36+1 apps, 4 gls; FA Cup: 7 apps, 1 gl; League Cup: 3 apps, 0 gls; Play-off: 1 app, 0 gls. Total: 47+1 apps, 5 gls.

Midfielder Andy Morrison was City's no nonsense play-off final captain. Enormously popular with fans, he joined City, initially on loan, in October 1998 and impressed immediately with a goal on his debut.

Rodney Marsh puts pen to paper in the company of messrs Griffiths, Allison and Alexander.

A committed player, Morrison proved to be one of the late 1990s stars as the Blues were

brought back to life by Joe Royle. He was also an inspirational captain who seemed to know exactly what was needed game after game. In particular, he always demonstrated great leadership skills when dealing with younger or inexperienced players. His guidance, encouragement, and support helped bring success.

In 1999 he became only the fifth City captain to lift a trophy at the old Wembley stadium, and when the following season commenced his fighting spirit helped the Blues prepare for a second promotion. Sadly, injury against Port Vale at the end of October 1999 brought a premature end to his season and he missed guiding the Blues to promotion to the Premier League.

Off the pitch Morrison was a regular attendee at Supporters' Club meetings and Junior Blues events as he understood the value and importance of such activities. He also recognised the loyalty the fans had shown during the 1998–99 season, as City played at their lowest level of all time.

Morrison may not be the greatest, or most gifted player ever to wear the blue shirt, but as captain he had the common touch. He knew what made the club tick and most importantly his relationship with supporters demonstrates to all players how important City fans are to a player's career. Morrison is a cult hero because he shared the joy and the pain with supporters.

Don Revie

DONALD GEORGE REVIE, OBE (1951–56)
Forward, 6ft 0in, 12st 6lb, b. Middlesbrough, 10 July 1927, d. Edinburgh, 26 May 1989
Signed from: Hull City, 18 October 1951 (£25,000)
Transferred: Sunderland, 10 November 1956 (£24,000)
Career: Archibald Road School, Newport Boys Club, Middlesbrough Swifts, Leicester City, Hull City, City, Sunderland, Leeds United
Debut: v Burnley, 20 October 1951
Appearances: League: 162 apps, 37 gls; FA Cup: 15 apps, 4 gls; Charity: 1 app, 0 gls. Total: 178 apps, 41 gls.

In 1955 Don Revie became the first City player to win the Football Writers' Footballer of the Year Award. It was a significant accolade and was thoroughly deserved.

Revie arrived at Maine Road in 1951 but his first few seasons were not great ones for the Blues, and the player determined that 1954–55 would be his last. Fortunately, manager McDowall was also making plans for the future and the new season saw City play with a deep-lying centre-forward. Revie became that player and the new 'Revie Plan' as it was dubbed changed the club's entire approach and helped Revie's game. A 1955 FA Cup appearance followed and at the time he was described as the most talked about centre-forward in the country.

At long last Revie achieved the kind of fame and glory he deserved, but controversy followed. He fell out with manager McDowall and he was dropped from the side in 1955–56. However, he was surprisingly recalled to the side in time for the 1956 Cup Final win over Birmingham. Journalist John Trickett wrote at the time: 'Don't let's kid ourselves the club can do without Revie next season. His exceptional ability should never be wasted on the Central League and he is much too good a player to be waiting listlessly on the transfer list. Surely his differences with City can be ironed out.'

Sadly, in November 1956 Revie moved to Sunderland. He later had huge success as manager of Leeds United, although their style of play was somewhat different to the cultured approach he'd displayed as a player. Deservedly he became England manager during the 1970s but his England career ended in disgrace as he moved to secure a financial future for his family. Revie became public enemy number one in most people's eyes, and was probably the first England manager who really suffered at the hands of the British press. Unlike his peers – Busby, Shankly and Mercer – he was unable to enjoy a period of 'elder statesmanship'. He was never sought by the media to give his views on 1980s football. Instead any mention of Revie continued to bring out the negativity of the mid-1970s. That was a shame.

Revie passed away in Edinburgh on 26 May 1989 at the age of 61 after suffering from motor neurone disease. Despite the England experience it has to be stressed that Revie's time at City was successful and he was nationally one of football's major stars. He was an extremely intelligent, skilful footballer who brought honour to the club and was, without doubt, one of City's greatest players.

Uwe Rosler

UWE ROSLER (1994–98)

Forward, 6ft 1in, 11st 6lb, b. Attenburg (Germany), 15 November 1968

Signed from: Dynamo Dresden, 4 March 1994 (£500,000)

Transferred: Kaiserslautern, *c.*1998 (free)

Career: Traktor Starkenberg, Lokomotiv Leipzig, Chemie Leipzig, Magdeburg, Dynamo Dresden, Nurnberg (loan), City, Kaiserslautern, Tennis Borussia, Southampton, West Bromwich Albion (loan), Lillestrom

Debut: v Queens Park Rangers, 5 March 1994

Appearances: League: 141+11 apps, 50 gls; FA Cup: 14 apps, 9 gls; League Cup: 10+1 apps, 5 gls. Total: 165+12 apps, 64 gls.

German-born Uwe Rosler was one of English football's greatest imports. He arrived at City for a trial in March 1994 and was immediately tested in a reserve match. He scored twice before being substituted, then made his League debut a

few days later against QPR. By the end of that season he had played 12 League games and scored five goals (only one goal behind highest goalscorer Mike Sheron!). Overnight he had become a cult figure at Maine Road and over the following four seasons he was a major figure as far as the fans were concerned. Particularly remembered for his spell alongside Paul Walsh, Rosler brought a great deal of excitement to Maine Road.

For three successive seasons – 1994–95 to 1996–97 – he was City's top scorer in the League, but he also performed well in Cup competitions. In 1995 a third-round FA Cup replay against Notts County ended in a 5–2 win with four goals netted by Rosler (the other was by fellow German Maurizio Gaudino).

Sadly, the 1997–98 season was his last and he joined Kaiserslautern on a free transfer. Back in Germany he managed to appear in Champions' League football – ironically he played in Europe's top competition on the same night City faced Mansfield in the Auto-Windscreens Shield.

Later he played for Southampton, and then shortly before Maine Road's final game in 2003 it was announced that Rosler was fighting a battle against chest cancer. Supporters sent thousands of goodwill messages to him, and during the opening season at City's new stadium, Rosler made a surprise appearance prior to a game. It was a wonderful moment, and the adulation he received that day was typical of the support and interest fans have always had in his career.

Dave Watson

DAVID VERNON WATSON (1975–79)
Defender, 5ft 11in, 11st 7lb, b. Stapleford, 5 October 1946
Signed from: Sunderland, 13 June 1975 (deal valued at £275,000)
Transferred: Werder Bremen, 26 June 1979
Career: Stapleford, Notts County, Rotherham United, Sunderland, City, Werder Bremen, Southampton, Stoke City, Vancouver Whitecaps, Derby County, Fort Lauderdale Sun, Notts County player-coach, Kettering Town
Debut: v Norwich City, 16 August 1975
Appearances: League: 146 apps, 4 gls; FA Cup: 9 apps, 0 gls; League Cup: 18 apps, 1 gl; UEFA Cup: 12 apps, 1 gl; AS Cup: 3 apps, 0 gls; TC Cup: 2 apps, 0 gls. Total: 190 apps, 6 gls.

Centre-half Dave Watson was a true cult hero to City fans – tough, determined, and dedicated. Watson was City's and England's no-nonsense central defender. He was a granite-like figure who simply made it impossible for his opponents to play.

He joined the Blues in 1975 after a successful time at Sunderland where, together with Tueart, he had been an FA Cup-winner in 1973. Almost immediately he became one of City's most popular players. He was determined to see the Blues succeed and gave his all and fans enjoyed his rugged qualities and his fighting spirit. During the 1976 League Cup Final he helped City to success while blood poured from his head. In the dressing room after the game he was even interviewed by Brian Moore for ITV while having stitches. It was a great TV moment and Watson's tough guy image grew, especially when he claimed the cut was simply a scratch.

The following season saw him voted City's player of the year and the Junior Blues player of

the season. During that season one of his most popular moments came when he scored a wonder goal against fellow title-challengers Ipswich on 2 April 1977. Then the following year he became captain and continued to perform exceptionally well for both City and for England.

Despite his many abilities, Watson did not survive the Malcolm Allison purge of 1979 when Allison seemed to dispense with quality and experience as he tried to forge a new side. Watson was transferred to Werder Bremen, but shortly afterwards moved to Southampton. Spells with Stoke, Vancouver Whitecaps, Derby County, Fort Lauderdale, Notts County and Kettering Town followed.

A great City and England player, Watson's departure in 1979 affected the Blues for several years. Many fans believe City failed to find a worthy successor for at least two decades.

David Weir

DAVID WEIR (1890–93)
Forward, b. Aldershot, 1863, d. Bolton, November 1933
Signed from: Bolton Wanderers, May 1890
Transferred: Bolton Wanderers, 26 January 1893

Career: Hampton, Glasgow Thistle, Maybole, Halliwell, Bolton Wanderers, Halliwell, Bolton Wanderers, Ardwick (City), Bolton Wanderers, Maybole
Debut: v Bootle, 3 September 1892
Appearances: League: 14 apps, 8 gls; FA Cup: 2 apps, 3 gls. Total: 16 apps, 11 gls.

When David Weir joined Ardwick (City) in May 1890 he was already a significant name in football. Often described as individualistic, Weir was an England international when he arrived at Hyde Road after playing in the 6–1 victory over Ireland in March 1889 and a 3–2 defeat by Scotland the following April. Against Scotland he was credited with scoring England's second goal, although there remains some dispute as to who got the final touch.

At Ardwick Weir played as a forward, but he had previously been known for fulfilling a variety of roles, most notably centre-half. Football was still developing of course, but the key point concerning Weir's pre-Ardwick days is that he was known as a great goalscorer whatever position he played at Bolton. He'd only missed one match during Bolton's first two seasons of League football, and had netted 21 goals in 43 League games. During the 1889–90 season he scored an incredible 10 goals in only four FA Cup ties. Clearly for Weir – a player only in his late twenties – to leave League side Bolton to join a side that had yet to compete in any formal league says a great deal about the ambition of Ardwick.

At Hyde Road Weir was immediately popular and he netted two hat-tricks in his first four games. He also scored the first Ardwick goal in the FA Cup, and was a key member of the side that competed in the Alliance League in 1891–92. His career also saw him feature in the club's first season in the Football League, where he became Ardwick's top goalscorer, despite returning to Bolton midway through the season in January 1893.

In later life he became the Glossop manager in 1909 and remained with the Division Two side until April 1911, when he was approached by Stuttgart to become their coach. He passed away in November 1933 at the age of 70.

Weir was the first player associated with the Blues to be recognised as a major footballing figure. To many in football during the club's first League seasons David Weir was Ardwick.

Shaun Wright-Phillips

SHAUN CAMERON WRIGHT-PHILLIPS
Midfield, 5ft 6in, 10st 1lb, b. Greenwich, 25 October 1981
Signed from: amateur, 16 July 1998 (Pro: 25 October 1998)
Transferred: Chelsea, 18 July 2005 (£21 million)
Career: Aske's School, Ten-Em-Bee, Nottingham Forest, City, Chelsea
Debut: v Burnley, 24 August 1999 (substitute, League Cup)
League debut: v Portsmouth, 3 November 1999
Appearances: League: 130+23 apps, 26 gls; FA Cup: 8+1 apps, 1 gl; League Cup: 9+4 apps, 3 gls; UEFA Cup: 4+2 apps, 1 gl. Total: 151+30 apps, 31 gls.

A product of City's highly successful Academy, although he had previously been released by Nottingham Forest because they felt he was too small, Shaun Wright-Phillips made his debut in 1999, coming on as substitute in the League Cup. At the end of that season he was voted City's Young Player of the Year – he eventually won this four years in succession before he became too old!

From Hallowe'en 2001 he featured in every League game of the season as he helped City to the First Division Championship, and he made a total of 31 appearances during the following Premier League season.

During the first season at the City of Manchester stadium Wright-Phillips scored the second goal in a competitive match (against Welsh side TNS in the UEFA Cup) and also made history by becoming the first player sent off when he removed his shirt to celebrate scoring his second goal in the 6–2 victory over Bolton. It seemed a harsh decision.

As his career progressed, he also developed internationally with England Under–21 appearances and then in August 2004 he made his full international debut when he came on as

substitute against Ukraine. He also scored, becoming the first Blue to do so since Trevor Francis scored the only goal of the victory over Kuwait at the 1982 World Cup.

Sadly, during City's run of pre-season friendlies on the eve of the 2005–06 season, Wright-Phillips announced he'd like to speak with Chelsea about a potential move, and shortly afterwards he joined the champions for a fee in excess of £21 million. As with Tommy Caton 22 years earlier he hoped a move to London would see him find success and also improve his chances of appearing in the 2006 World Cup Finals, but his appearances for Chelsea were somewhat limited and he only made 15 starts during 2005–06. This impacted his England opportunities and in May 2006 his name was not included in the World Cup squad.

City fans loved Wright-Phillips, although some were disappointed with the nature of his departure. He had been a firm favourite with supporters throughout his career, and fans felt for him when the 2006 World Cup squad was released, although many suggested he might have been included had he remained a City man for that final season.

MANCHESTER CITY MANAGERS

Pre-League Secretaries/Managers

1880–82 Frederick Hopkinson
1882–84 unclear
1884–87 Edward Kitchen
1887–89 Walter Chew

Lawrence Furniss

Born: Matlock, 18 January 1858, died: Marple 1941

Summer 1889 – summer 1893

In all probability Manchester City Football Club would not exist at all if it hadn't been for the involvement of Lawrence Furniss. Furniss was typical of many inhabitants of West Gorton in the early 1880s in that he was born away from Manchester, in his case in Matlock, and had come to settle in the area because of work and the opportunities the world's first industrial city gave. According to the 1861 census, the three-year-old Furniss was living at Matlock railway station, where he had been born and where his father Edwin was the station master. By 1871 the family were living at Cromford station master's house and, interestingly, the former waiting room building at this station was photographed and used by City supporters Oasis on the cover of their first number one single *Some Might Say* and is now promoted as one of rock's pilgrimage sites.

Furniss himself became a railway worker – by 1881 he is recorded as being a railway clerk at Matlock – and it is believed he moved to Manchester as a result of railway opportunities. Perhaps because of his upbringing, or a desire to play his part within the local community, he became a key member of the St Mark's congregation. Eventually he became a sidesman at the church, but he also tried to play his part in many other social activities and he became a player with the church's football team, with his first known games occurring during 1884–85.

It is believed his playing career came to an end during 1886–87 following a serious knee injury, but looking at the way his life and football career developed from that point, it's clear Furniss cared passionately about the club, and he moved into a more administrative role. He also helped with the usual non-playing tasks such as upkeep of ground, search for players, paying of rents, purchase of kit etc.

Furniss clearly helped the club become focussed as it moved away from its church roots, although he himself remained a key figure at the church for many years. He was responsible for locating at least one of Gorton's grounds, and for playing a significant role in the development of Hyde Road. In later life he was also a prime mover behind the creation of Maine Road – in fact some supporters argued the stadium should be named after him.

In 1889 at the age of 31, he became Ardwick's secretary-manager. Various figures had played the lead role before, but Furniss's appointment seemed to take the club on to another level. Clearly, he wanted to see Ardwick compete with the best and with the Football League's first season occurring during 1888–89 Ardwick had something to aim for.

By the summer of 1891 Furniss had guided Ardwick to their first significant success – the Manchester Cup – and had seen his side

admitted to the Football Alliance – a league that included other progressive clubs such as Small Heath (Birmingham City) and Sheffield Wednesday – although he had tried to get his side entered into the Football League. That prize came a mere 12 months later. Furniss was only 34 years of age, making him the club's youngest League manager until the appointment of Peter Reid in 1989.

The 1892–93 season was, on the whole, a successful one for both Furniss and Ardwick. A 7–0 victory on the opening day against Bootle ensured that Ardwick led the very first Second Division table, and one defeat in the opening nine matches gave Furniss a great deal of satisfaction. Sadly, a poor run in December and January prevented the side from seriously making a Second Division title challenge, and they ended the season fifth.

Furniss had taken the club further than perhaps even he could have anticipated in 1889, and he decided to move aside for the rather more vocal and some would say dynamic Joshua Parlby. He then became a major driving force behind the scenes and is believed to have been the peacemaker in 1894 when Parlby was pushing to relaunch the club as Manchester City, while other senior figures were trying to keep Ardwick in existence. Such was his commitment to the Blue cause that he personally paid off Ardwick's debts (£70) from his own money and was forced to delay his own wedding by three years. Put simply, Manchester City could not have been allowed to compete without this commitment. Around the same time he spotted Billy Meredith and played a significant part in his arrival at City.

Furniss became a board member in 1903 and remained so until the investigations into the alleged bribe and illegal payments scandal (1906). It does not appear that he was held responsible for the club's problems and he certainly wasn't penalised, and so it seems he left the Board to pursue business interests outside of the game. It is known he moved from Longsight and joined his brother Edwin in Mellor, Stockport, as estates manager for the Roman Lakes – a significant leisure attraction of the period. He remained there for the rest of his life, although during World War One he was asked to rejoin the Manchester City board by Albert Alexander senior. In 1916 he became chairman for a brief period, then in 1921 he took the chair again.

In 1928, around the time of his 70th birthday, he stood down as chairman and three years later he was elected as the club's first President. This role was a significant ambassadorial role and was a major mark of what Furniss had achieved.

He continued to watch the Blues throughout his later years, although health issues limited his visits during World War Two. He passed away in 1941. His death ended the club's direct connections with the 1880s founding fathers – and mother Georgina Connell.

Some historians believe Furniss was secretary of Chesterfield (1906–07) during his time off the City board, but that seems unlikely due to his close involvement with the Roman Lakes at Mellor.

Joshua Parlby

Born: Longton, Staffordshire 1855, died: ??
Summer 1893 – summer 1895

Joshua Parlby was a larger than life figure with a strong commitment to promoting the activities he believed in. He came to Manchester to take over a public house and immediately, like Furniss before him, looked to get involved with the local community. Whereas Furniss had taken an interest in the church and its congregation, Parlby was more concerned with the social activities of east Mancunians. His role within the brewing community of Manchester led to his involvement with Ardwick AFC – in 1887 Ardwick's headquarters were the Hyde Road Hotel, the club was nicknamed the Brewerymen, and by 1893 Chester's Brewery played a major part in every aspect of the club's life.

According to some historians Parlby was a player and committee member with Stoke prior to arriving in Manchester, so it's possible he had some knowledge of tactics when he became Ardwick manager. This does make sense as he was born in Staffordshire, but the 1881 census claims he was a bookkeeper by profession, so how and exactly when he moved to Manchester has not yet been fully identified. It is known he was still living in Staffordshire in 1882 when he married a local girl. Whatever his background it's clear that he was always one of the more vocal members of the club. So vocal in fact that it is believed he was the man who suggested the club needed a paid secretary, someone who could focus on the team, instead of someone doing it in their spare time. His fellow committee members then proceeded to give him the new professional role and he was paid 50 shillings a week.

Ardwick were renowned for their financial struggles during their first couple of seasons in the League and Parlby became well known for his ability to 'wrangle' the club out of various financial problems. Stories of fare-dodging on the railways when travelling to away games were well known to supporters during the 1890s. It's hard to imagine any of the club's modern-day managers having to sneak his side on and off trains as the railway guards attempt to check tickets.

Parlby always wanted the club to achieve much more than this and it is clear that as his first season in charge progressed he was already planning a move to relaunch the club. He felt Ardwick AFC was very much a parochial name and not one that could appeal on the national stage. He had also seen how near neighbours Newton Heath had fared in Division One (they were accepted into an enlarged division in 1892). The Heathens were to be relegated at the end of 1893–94 but more importantly they had failed to attract sufficient support. Parlby felt that a Manchester-named side could achieve so much more.

The final season of Ardwick saw Parlby's side finish 13th out of 15 clubs, but by this time he had already sought League approval for the admittance of his new invention 'Manchester City' to replace Ardwick in the Second Division. It's not clear which of City's main committee men came up with the new name, but it is known that Parlby was the one promoting the new club. As a new arrival in the city himself, it's possible the lure of the sprawling city excited him and he may well have had more pride in Manchester and what the city stood for than many of those who had lived in the city for decades.

Parlby remained as secretary-manager and the 1894–95 season saw the Blues finish ninth out of 16 clubs in Division Two. He stood down as secretary-manager in the close season. Some have suggested this was to concentrate on a new public house he had taken over in Bolton, although it seems most likely that he felt he had achieved his main aim of re-establishing the club in a manner that would increase popularity. Whatever the truth, Parlby remained an influential committee man until 1905. Some would say too influential, as the reign of his successor Sam Ormerod was noted for the constant involvement of Parlby and others. Clearly Parlby felt the club had been his creation and he wanted others to share his vision and love for City.

Parlby was a board member until the over-zealous FA forced him out of Hyde Road, while almost killing the club, in 1905, although he wasn't named as one of the directors banned and fined. At the age of 54 in 1909 he rejoined the board and stayed an active member for three years before he moved away from the area.

Samuel Ormerod

Born: Accrington, 1848, died: 1906

Summer 1895 – July 1902

Sam Ormerod was a noted player in the Accrington area of Lancashire during the 1870s and by the early 1880s he was known to be a referee, and it is believed he was one of the key men behind the creation of Accrington FC in 1876. Accrington won the Lancashire Cup in 1881 and Ormerod appears on the team photograph with the 11 players who won the trophy. Seven years later Accrington were founder members of the Football League.

In November 1883 Ormerod refereed a game featuring Bolton Wanderers, and so appalled the home crowd that he was 'hooted on the field', according to the Lancashire FA, then followed from Bolton's Pikes Lane ground by a crowd. He was then assaulted on his way to the train station. The Football Association carried out an investigation and suggested that Bolton be expelled from the Lancashire FA. The

Lancastrians disagreed but clearly Ormerod had been badly treated.

When he was appointed City manager in 1895 Ormerod was expected to take the Blues on to a new level, and with both Lawrence Furniss and Joshua Parlby on the club committee it was difficult for him to have total control of team affairs. He still managed to achieve a great deal in his first season with City, reaching the Test Matches (equivalent of the modern day play-offs) after finishing second. Sadly, the Blues failed to gain promotion, but in the seasons that followed he continued to see City challenge. They finished sixth, third and then, in 1899, were Division Two Champions. This was the first season of automatic promotion and City, along with local rivals Glossop, became the first side to gain automatic promotion. It was also the first national success achieved by either of the Manchester sides.

Sadly, life in the top division wasn't easy and during the 1901–02 season Ormerod received more than his fair share of criticism, with the leading sports paper of the day – the *Athletic News* – attacking his team selection and organisational skills on a regular basis. In the 21st century this criticism could be seen as a normal activity, but it seems this was an early attempt to alter the views of the supporters and to then force change within the club. The *Athletic News* was owned by the high-profile press baron Edward Hulton and around this time Hulton was developing an interest in City. His newspaper empire had a significant Manchester presence and City were clearly a very popular club. Influential committee man John Allison had encouraged Hulton's involvement and the two men seemed keen to bring in a vastly more experienced football secretary-manager. They wanted a higher profile leader to help the club become a major power.

Relegation in 1902 allowed those seeking to make City a major power to act. A stormy AGM in June revealed debts of almost £1,000, and there were significant changes at board level. Ormerod resigned almost immediately. He later managed Stockport County and Clapton Orient, but passed away shortly after being dismissed from Orient in 1906.

Ormerod was a highly knowledgeable football man and had achieved a great deal throughout his footballing life. Achieving promotion in 1902 made him the first manager to find any form of national success at either Manchester side, although it has to be stressed that he was rarely given a free hand to pursue his own team selection and tactical plans at Hyde Road. Nevertheless, he helped to manage the transition from poor performing Second Division side to a team ready to match the elite.

Tom Maley

Born: Portsmouth, 8 November 1864, died: 24 August 1935

July 1902 – July 1906

Tom Maley was the first truly great Manchester manager. He arrived at Hyde Road following City's relegation in 1902 and quickly demonstrated a passion for stylish football. His footballing upbringing had come mainly in Scotland, where he played for several clubs including Partick Thistle, Third Lanark, Hibernian and Celtic, before having a spell with Preston North End in 1891. He had been a member of Celtic at formation in 1888. Nicknamed 'Handsome Tom', his time at Celtic was mainly as an administrator and as such he is recorded by Celtic historians as one of the club's most important early figures. Tom's brother Willie, who had been Celtic's manager since 1897, knew Manchester City well as he had guested for the club in 1896 and had also guested for Ardwick at Easter 1890, so the Maley family may well have known some of City's more influential figures prior to Tom's appointment.

By the time he arrived in Manchester he was known as an excellent football administrator and tactician and, by adopting the Scottish passing style, he turned City into a major force. According to a 1920s journalist, Maley built the Blues: 'It was when Tom Maley came to Hyde Road that Manchester City may be said to have entered fully into their kingdom. Under his management, he built a team for the club that was comparable with the mightiest sides in the country.

'I never happened on a greater enthusiast than Maley, nor yet a better informed man. If Maley had had average luck he would have gone down in history as one of the most successful managers the game has known. It is enough to say that so long as Maley was at the helm, the family at Hyde Road was a particularly happy one.'

At City he managed to attract great players and the club's popularity increased as a result. City's average attendance exceeded 20,000 for the first time during his reign as the Blues became Manchester's premier club, although it's fair to say Maley's first few weeks were a particularly difficult time for the Blues.

Welsh international and star player Di Jones gashed his knee during the pre-season public practice match and, despite treatment from the club doctor, within a week the wound had turned septic and the player died. Maley had to lift spirits quickly.

Maley soon brought the Blues success. His first League game ended in a 3–1 win and the Blues went on to lift the Second Division championship in his first season. This was a remarkable achievement, but more was to follow in 1903–04 when Maley's men won the FA Cup for the first time in their history. The Blues were the first Manchester side to win a major trophy and the feat had come a mere 10 years after formation as Manchester City FC.

In addition, City narrowly missed out on the double, finishing second to Sheffield Wednesday after fixture congestion forced the Blues to play five League games and the Cup Final in the space of 16 days!

Sadly, the rapid rise of City caused the southern-based FA to question whether that success was natural or whether it had been bought. Serious investigations into bribery allegations made by Aston Villa were followed up with a thorough audit of the club's accounts. Manchester City were deemed guilty of overpaying their players – something journalists of the period knew was going on at almost every club with no FA action. The Football League felt that City, being a northern side, were being made an example of, and thousands of people complained to the FA, but the result was that City suffered the worst bans and fines ever experienced.

Maley was questioned at length and admitted that he had followed what seemed like standard English practice. He claimed that if all First Division clubs were investigated, not four would come out 'scatheless'. He was right, but it was City the FA seemed determined to punish and they suspended 17 players and two directors. But the harshest sentence fell on the chairman and on Maley. They were both suspended for life.

The northern-based Football League and the footballing press supported the Blues but the FA got their way and Maley's brief but successful reign was over.

Maley suffered more than most in the unfortunate events of 1905–06, and his role in football history has been tainted forever by the FA's harsh treatment. However, in the eyes of thousands of Mancunians he is remembered as the man who brought exciting football and the FA Cup to the city for the first time. Without his period at Hyde Road, Manchester might never have found real football success. Many of his players were forced to join United after the scandal of 1905, and went on to bring the Reds their first trophy success only a few years later. Had Maley been allowed to develop those players further, who knows what success might have come City's way.

After City Maley became a headmaster in Glasgow, but in July 1910 the FA lifted his suspension and the following February he became Bradford Park Avenue's manager. The Bradford club gave him full control of team affairs – something unusual at the time – and he remained there until March 1924. During his reign the club achieved its highest position (ninth in Division One, 1914–15), and for a period played in his beloved green and white hoops. During World War One he is said to have acted like an 'amateur recruiting sergeant' and was famous for his entertaining lectures.

After Bradford he is said by some to have managed Southport between May and October 1925, and then in 1931 he temporarily took over as Celtic manager from his highly successful brother Willie during a trip to the US. It was his first visit to the States.

On 24 August 1935 he passed away at the age of 70. He should be remembered as Manchester's first great leader. Had the ban not occurred it's highly probable he would have brought the League title to Hyde Road and who knows what glories might have followed.

Henry 'Harry' J. Newbould

Born: Everton, 1861, died: April 1928

July 1906 – July 1912

Although born in Liverpool in 1861, Henry, or Harry as he became known to football fans, spent most of his young adult life in Derby. It appears his family were originally from Derbyshire but moved to Liverpool in the late 1850s, prior to Harry's birth. They moved back to Derbyshire when Harry was approximately five years of age. In his early twenties he worked as a clerk in an iron foundry and, according to later reports, he trained as an accountant. It is known that Newbould was the secretary-manager of his local League side Derby County from 1900 until his appointment at City. At Derby he guided the Rams to an FA Cup Final in 1903 and semi-finals in 1904. He was a very popular figure, even though he sold Derby's first major star Steve Bloomer to Middlesbrough.

When he arrived at City, the Blues were a desperate side. The bribe and illegal payments scandal had decimated the club from the boardroom down to the pitch, and Newbould had to quickly give direction to both the players and the administration staff. On the pitch he was left with only 11 players in the entire squad. Off the pitch the club's accounts needed to be totally legitimate and perhaps a model example of how to run a football club legally. In both areas Newbould had a lot of issues to face.

On the pitch he quickly found new players to fill the gaps left by the banning of 17 first-team players. Inevitably, some of his new signings failed, but quite a few others, most notably Bill Eadie and Jimmy Conlin, became significant stars.

As anticipated, Newbould's first season was difficult, with the Blues narrowly avoiding relegation – they finished 17th out of 20. They had also endured an embarrassing 9–1 defeat at Everton in their second game of the season. The following season (1907–08) they finished third, but Newbould's side had still not recovered from the problems of 1905–07 and inconsistency dogged 1908–09. Newbould's side were relegated in 19th place, but they immediately bounced back as Champions, and Newbould managed – just – to keep City in the First Division for the following couple of years.

In July 1912 he left the Blues and assisted Academicals (Copenhagen) for a while the following August. He also played a major role with the Manchester-based Players' Union, becoming secretary. Earlier Newbould had actually clashed with the PFA over disagreements over an alleged £500 benefit promised, according to the union, to City star Jimmy Buchan. Perhaps he joined the PFA management committee to try and build bridges between managers and players. In March 1913 he became the union's secretary, and according to the PFA's own records, Newbould's reign led to years of 'hibernation' for the PFA. One of his main acts was to move the union offices from St Peter's Square in central Manchester to his own house in Longsight. He resigned as secretary in 1915, although he actually carried on in the role during the war and by August 1919 he was being paid £7 a week plus £1 for the use of his house as offices.

He died, still the PFA's secretary, in April 1928 after a long debilitating illness.

In terms of actual trophy success, Newbould's time at Hyde Road saw him win the Second Division title, but nothing else significant. However, his reign was never likely to be judged on trophy success. His mission when he arrived at Hyde Road was to save the club, and by the time he left it is fair to say he had created a side capable of challenging, if not quite ready to win major honours, and a club that was free of scandal. For these reasons, Newbould must rank as a major influence in the history of the club.

James Ernest Mangnall

Born: Belmont, Bolton, 1866, died: 13 January 1932

9 September 1912 – July 1924

Ernest Mangnall was the first man to bring Manchester United trophy success – with a side containing the key figures in the Blues' 1904 FA Cup triumph – and was also credited with being instrumental in United's move from Clayton (roughly where the Velodrome is close to the City of Manchester Stadium) to Old Trafford. Clearly these are major moments in Manchester football, but City fans prefer to remember the achievements he made for the Blues.

Mangnall joined City in 1912, but the best thing about his arrival was the way it was carried out. Mangnall had been United's leader since 1903 and had achieved so much while there that no one could ever have expected him to move. However, Manchester City were still regarded as the region's number one club, despite the problems they had faced in the early days of Newbould's reign. City stunned the football world when they lured Mangnall from the Reds. Never before had a manager left a major club for its biggest rivals after so much success, but what made the story more of a sensation was the fact Mangnall had agreed to become City manager while still in office at Old Trafford, and that he had watched City's opening game at Notts County when he was

supposed to be with United at Arsenal. As City did not formally have a secretary-manager on that day it is believed he actually helped the directors select the side and carry out other duties. The Blues won the game 1–0 while 'his' United side drew 0–0 at Arsenal, and then five days later he was still in charge of United for the Manchester derby of 7 September 1912 at Old Trafford.

United historians dispute that Mangnall was officially their manager on the day of the derby, but leading newspapers of the period, most notably the *Umpire* and the *Daily Dispatch*, are perfectly clear that he was officially in charge. City won the Old Trafford match 1–0 despite being down to 10 men for most of the game. Mangnall, according to one report, was delighted with the City win despite, officially at least, still being a Red. 'United speeded their manager rejoicing with two points to his new club', read one article.

The following Monday Mangnall moved into his office at Hyde Road, and within a few weeks his side were looking like Championship contenders: 'Manchester City stand out boldly as the only first-class team in the two divisions of the League, the Southern and the Scottish Leagues, with the highest possible points to their credit. The Citizens of Manchester have earned every point in September. Other clubs have remained undefeated, but they have not annexed the maximum marks. Nine years have passed since Manchester City commenced a campaign in this stimulating style.'

The title didn't arrive, although Mangnall did develop a decent-looking side by the time of World War One. In fact the Blues were proving a highly popular side to watch, so much so that the ground could hardly cope. A notorious Cup match with Sunderland in February 1913 had to be abandoned due to overcrowding. Incredibly – and this is difficult to appreciate today – the team manager was also responsible for the management of the ground at this time, and so Mangnall was held responsible for all matters concerning safety and crowd control as well as picking the team and buying the players. One reporter, 'Veteran', accused Mangnall of spending too much time with the team and said: 'I am rather surprised at Mr Mangnall being caught napping, but it may be that he has been away with the team and has had little to do with the home management.'

The Blues finished fifth in Division One at the end of the 1914–15 season. During the hostilities Mangnall kept the club alive and brought some trophy success in the wartime tournaments that replaced the League.

After the war, Mangnall's side became very popular and he had to focus on ground issues as well as team matters. As secretary-manager Mangnall was held totally responsible for all activities at Hyde Road and, with the Blues filling the 40,000 capacity on a regular basis, Mangnall regularly had to face the press, the FA, the Football League, the council and the police to explain why chaotic scenes were being experienced game after game in the streets around the ground.

In 1920 fire destroyed the Main Stand and exacerbated the problems Mangnall faced. He approached United about using Old Trafford, but they met his request with terms that were ridiculed in the press. Perhaps they still felt a little aggrieved about his departure almost a decade earlier. Mangnall's view was that City had to move from Hyde Road. Its 40,000 capacity was far too small, and the manager worked with club officials, most notably another former City manager, Lawrence Furniss, to plan the development of a new ground. For many years the Blues had looked at moving to Belle Vue, and it's believed Mangnall was the man who changed the club's thinking. A move to Belle Vue would have been the safe option, but it would not have offered the club the same potential as a move to Maine Road could. At the same time as these debates, Mangnall guided the Blues to second place in the League and their popularity increased further.

By the start of 1921–22 far too many people were missing out on watching Manchester's favourite team. Together with former manager Lawrence Furniss, Mangnall set major plans in place for a move. Then in 1922 he announced that City would be creating an 'English Hampden' on the Moss Side/Rusholme border.

In 1923 City moved to Maine Road, and in Mangnall's final season (1923–24) he almost managed to guide City to the FA Cup Final. With the 49-year-old Billy Meredith back in Mangnall's side, City were defeated by Newcastle. That run was important, as it perhaps demonstrated the reason why Mangnall had been determined to join the Blues back in 1912, for his City side attracted a few magnificent attendances, including over 76,000 for a Cup tie with Cardiff. At the time this was the largest crowd for any footballing fixture played in Manchester, including two FA Cup Finals. Mangnall knew City's strengths and after 13 years in charge he must have felt a great deal of satisfaction at seeing such a large crowd in the stadium he had pushed for.

The following May the directors surprisingly decided not to renew his contract. It seems likely that he chose to step down, feeling that there was little more he could achieve at Maine Road. After leaving the Blues he became a director of his home town team, Bolton, and was a significant figure within the PFA. He died of a cerebral embolism in 1932 at St Annes.

In addition to his roles at Burnley – his first club as secretary – United, City and Bolton, he was also the man responsible for founding the Central League and the Football Managers' Association. Today, he remains one of the most influential football administrators of all time, and although most football figures talk of his time at United first, he managed City for a longer spell and, some would say, a more popular period.

Modern-day football rarely remembers men like Mangnall, but his place in the history of Manchester must always remain a significant one. He restored pride and passion to the Blues and was the key figure in City's move to Maine Road. That move enabled City to rediscover their ambition, drive, and natural position as one of England's elite.

Mangnall should always be remembered as the catalyst for City's regeneration during a difficult period. The fact that he walked out on United to take on the City challenge proves beyond doubt that Mangnall was a great Blue.

David Ashworth

Born: Blackpool, 1868, died: Blackpool, 23 March 1947

July 1924 – November 1925

The early years of David Ashworth's life have been chronicled incorrectly over the years. According to most reports he was born at Waterford in Ireland around 1868, but the 1881 census claims he was actually born in Blackpool. It does appear the Waterford line is incorrect, but the story is a little confusing as by 1881, when he was 13, David was living with his grandmother, Elizabeth Ashworth, at Newchurch, near Rawtenstall in Lancashire. The only other person living at that address was 24-year-old Elizabeth Alice Ashworth, who was described as Elizabeth's daughter. As the surname of all three residents is the same, and the two ladies were both born in Newchurch, it seems likely that David was living with his paternal grandmother and aunt.

As he grew he became interested in football and is known to have played for Newchurch Rovers. He went on to become a Football League referee before his first managerial appointment with Oldham Athletic in 1906. At Boundary Park Ashworth guided Oldham from the Lancashire Combination to the First Division within four years. Oldham's promotion in 1910 was as runners-up to City.

A spell at Stockport County followed throughout the war years, then in December 1919 he became Liverpool's manager, bringing them the title in 1921–22. The Merseysiders retained the title the following year, but midway through that season he shocked the Liverpool directors by rejoining Oldham. After only a year with the Boundary Park club he became City's manager in July 1924.

At Maine Road, his first season saw the Blues finish 10th, and Ashworth made at least one notable signing – Sam Cowan. Cowan was purchased in December 1924 from Doncaster and went on to become a major star. During the following close season he strengthened the squad further by purchasing left-back Phil McCloy from Ayr United for £3,000. It was another good signing, but the Blues struggled during 1925–26. Only two of the opening 10 games ended in victory and it was clear to all that Ashworth was finding it difficult to create the entertaining style of play the Blues had been used to.

An embarrassing 8–3 defeat at Sheffield United on 26 October brought a great deal of anguish to those associated with the club, and by 16 November, with the pressure mounting, Ashworth resigned, although it seems likely he was 'pushed'.

After City he had a brief spell with Walsall, and then managed two Welsh non-League clubs, Caernarfon and Llanelli, before returning to the English game as a scout for Blackpool before the war. He died in 1947 at the Blackpool Victoria Hospital aged 79.

Ashworth was probably the first City appointment that actually failed. Each of his predecessors had achieved some form of success and had managed to last at least two seasons, while Ashworth was only in charge for around 16 months. This was an extremely short spell at this time in football history.

Committee, led by Albert Edward Burns Alexander

16 November 1926 – 26 April 1926

Whether Ashworth's departure caught City by surprise is unknown, but it is fair to say the directors were in no rush to appoint a replacement. It's highly likely the directors felt they possessed more knowledge of the game than any of the possible replacements did. Certainly within the club there were a few knowledgeable football men – chairman Lawrence Furniss had been the club's first League secretary-manager; vice-chairman Albert Alexander has created and coached the City 'A' team, and assistant secretary Wilf Wild would ultimately become manager in his own right. In the end Albert Alexander took the lead role, and with his guidance the Blues won the first two games of December 1925, and were unbeaten in January. In fact January was an excellent month, as Manchester United were defeated 6–1 at Old Trafford – this remains the highest score in a Manchester derby – and the Blues progressed to the fifth round of the FA Cup.

Despite that optimism League form dipped, but Alexander's Blues did progress to the FA Cup Final, where City became the first Manchester side to play at Wembley. Sadly, City were defeated 1–0 by Bolton, and the following Monday City finally appointed a new manager.

Peter Hodge

Born: Dunfermline ??, died: Perth, 18 August 1934

26 April 1926 – 12 March 1932

Peter Hodge had to wait until Leicester City completed their League campaign before he could take up his appointment at Maine Road. Leicester's final game of 1925–26 was on 24 April at Bury, and the following Monday Hodge moved to Manchester as City's secretary-manager. The Blues still had two League games left to play and after victory against Leeds on 27 April, Hodge's City had the chance to survive. A victory against Newcastle would have guaranteed survival, but the game ended in a 3–2 defeat. The agony was compounded when Roberts missed a penalty which would have guaranteed survival. City were relegated by a point. Clearly Hodge had arrived too late to make a serious change to City's League season.

The following close season was spent planning for an immediate return to Division One, but 1926–27 proved to be highly dramatic and, with typical City style, the entire season came down to the final match. Sadly, City missed promotion by the tightest goal average margin in history. Their 8–0 victory over Bradford City on the final day was one goal less than the required number. It was a huge disappointment.

In 1927–28 Hodge's Blues were promoted as champions with 59 points. They were also the most watched side in England, with an average attendance of 37,468 – a figure higher than any other League side. Hodge continued to improve the side as the Blues embarked on a golden era of popularity and success during the 1930s. He had taken a team that seemed destined to struggle and created a side heading for glory. In 1929–30 the Blues reached third place in Division One, and in 1931–32 he guided City to an FA Cup semi-final where they were unfortunate to concede a goal in the final minute.

That goal ended Hodge's City career, as he had already agreed to return to his first love,

Leicester City. Leicester had announced his return to Filbert Street on 15 February 1932, but their agreement allowed Hodge to remain at Maine Road until City's FA Cup campaign came to an end. City lost the FA Cup semi-final on Saturday 12 March and Hodge is believed to have been working at Filbert Street on Tuesday 15 March.

On 30 July 1934, while visiting his mother, Hodge was admitted to Perth Infirmary and died 19 days later while still manager of Leicester City.

Wilf Wild

Born: 1893, died: 12 December 1950

14 March 1932 – 1 December 1946

Wilf Wild is a name few modern supporters will recognise, but he is clearly one of Manchester's greatest managers. He was City's longest-serving manager and the club's most successful manager of the pre-Mercer period. Wild was also the first manager to bring the League title to the Blues, and the first Manchester manager to win the FA Cup at Wembley.

He joined the Blues in 1920 as assistant secretary to Ernest Mangnall. In those days the position of manager and secretary was very much classed as one role and Mangnall was expected to shoulder the burden of ground developments as well as team selection and other managerial tasks. Understandably, Mangnall felt he needed support and so Wild assisted Mangnall, mostly on the administrative side.

Although Wild was delighted with his role, he felt the responsibility which Mangnall had was too great. Mangnall, it should be remembered, was fully occupied with the move from Hyde Road to Maine Road, and the usual club management issues such as managing the team, ticketing matters, and ground issues. Behind the scenes Wild felt he could see a more productive way for the club to develop. He was a great advocate of splitting the role of manager and secretary. When Mangnall's contract wasn't renewed in 1924 the chance came for Wild to shape the future direction of the club. He worked with the directors to encourage a new approach, and David Ashworth was appointed manager with Wild focusing purely on secretarial duties. It seems a rather obvious approach, but in 1924 this was revolutionary. It is very difficult today to understand how the club secretary could be expected to manage the side, but in 1924 this was the norm.

From then on, Wild took on the greater share of secretarial duties as David Ashworth and Peter Hodge were both allowed to focus on team issues, although, when Hodge returned to Filbert Street, it seems the directors felt the two roles could still be performed by one man, and Wild was given total responsibility for both areas.

The directors must have agreed this action during early February when they discovered that Hodge was planning on moving back to Leicester. They could have searched for a new manager, but perhaps they felt that was unnecessary after seeing the work Wild was already performing. Certainly players from the period worked well for Wild.

Wild performed exceptionally well as City's leader and in his first two seasons he guided them to consecutive FA Cup Finals. As well as the on-field success these seasons brought many challenges off the pitch, particularly as City were hitting the headlines for record crowds.

With Wild splitting his time between the two roles the club should have expected to enter a period of mediocrity, but instead Wild's side became one of the leading forces in the game. Those Finals made City a very entertaining side to watch. Wild seemed to possess a Midas touch, especially when you consider that he still had responsibility for crowd control, safety issues, ground developments – including the development of the main section of the Platt Lane Stand in 1935 – and even the control of accounts and payment of wages.

In 1936–37 Wild managed City to their first League Championship after selecting players of the calibre of Alec Herd, Sam Barkas, Matt Busby, Peter Doherty – some say the greatest Irish player of all time – and Frank Swift. Despite the success Wild was also a victim of City's peculiar unpredictable streak when, the following year, the Blues were relegated. Although it wasn't known at the time, it was a particularly bad time to enter the Second Division as war in 1939 ensured the Blues remained out of the top flight until 1947.

The pressure on Wild was immense and yet he came through it well. In fact the biggest test of all came in 1939 when he had to work closely with the club directors to ensure City survived the war years. As with all walks of life, the war brought many pressures Wild's way, but again he succeeded in the role.

Understandably, when peacetime football resumed in 1946 Wild was determined to relinquish control of the team. After 14 difficult but mainly successful years he asked the Board to bring in a new man. Former Captain Sam Cowan was recruited in December 1946 and Wild was allowed back to perform the role of secretary. From that point on the two roles were kept separate as Wild had first suggested, but even then the role of secretary was still a major one. According to former player Johnny Hart, who started working for the club as an office boy under Wild, there were only about three office staff including Wild and Hart. This seems a relatively small number to run a major football club, but this was typical of most clubs around this time.

Hart has many stories of how Wild had to cope with the dual role: 'I remember him in the dressing room giving his customary team talk – "watch the first five minutes and the last five, and don't do anything silly" – then at about twenty to three there was a knock on the door. I followed him out, we walked down the tunnel and he picked up a loud hailer. He went on to the touchline, shouting instructions to the crowd to move over, and make room for latecomers! Then he headed back to the dressing room to talk with the players a bit more. He had to share the role!'

'On another occasion I remember the Chief Scout Albert Kavanagh coming in at about 11. Wild asked him where he was going. Albert said, "I was thinking about going to watch some lads on Hough End." Wild said "No. I want you to go to Halifax." Albert pointed out the time and how difficult it would be to get there on time, but it was no use. Then he said, "I'll have no dinner", so Wild leans over. I thought he was going to get some money to give to him, but he opened up his own lunchbox, pulled out a scrappy sandwich and handed it to Albert: "Here have this. Now get off to Halifax." I couldn't believe it.'

Sadly, Wild passed away in December 1950. He was still the club's secretary at this point and his death shocked many connected with the club. His wife Betty also worked at the club and she remained a popular presence through to her retirement in the 1960s. She later moved to Lytham St Annes.

Wild brought the club success in the two major competitions of the period, and saw the ground develop in an impressive manner. He had total responsibility for events on the pitch and off it during a period when the Blues re-established themselves as a major side. Neutrals generally acknowledge that Arsenal were the team of the thirties, but Wild's City were the only other side who came close to matching them.

He may not be the first name most think of when they talk about great City managers, but Wild was the most successful of all Blues managers until the arrival of Joe Mercer in 1965.

Sam Cowan

Born: Chesterfield 10 May 1901, died: Haywards Heath, 4 October 1964

2 December 1946 – 30 June 1947

Sam Cowan

When Sam Cowan arrived as manager in December 1946 supporters and the media were delighted with the appointment. Cowan had been City's great captain during the 1930s Cup runs and according to the *Sunday People*: 'Cowan was the most popular player ever at Maine Road. If the City followers give him the same support now he will be a happy and successful manager.'

'It will not be an easy job. The team have rarely played like a promotion side this season, and there are obvious weaknesses. But if Cowan, the manager, can put into City the spirit he put into them as club captain, Newcastle and other leading Second Division clubs may be shocked.'

Although Cowan's salary, quoted as £2,000, was a substantial amount at the time, the move to Maine Road was a major gamble. He had been acting as trainer to Brighton & Hove Albion and had also set up his own physiotherapy business on the south coast. In addition, he had a young son and the family were settled in the Brighton area. Because of this City agreed that Cowan could continue to live in the south, but would be expected to be in Manchester and with the team from midweek through to after the game. It was an unusual step, but City were well aware of the progress ex-Blue Matt Busby was starting to see at United, and felt that Cowan was a much better tactician and leader of men.

Cowan's influence was felt immediately, with his first match ending in a 3–0 win at Newport County and his first Maine Road game ending 5–1 against Barnsley. After the New Year's Day 4–0 victory over Fulham journalist Tom Rudd wrote: 'Seven matches without defeat is Manchester City's fine record since Sam Cowan relinquished his post as trainer to Brighton & Hove Albion to manage the affairs of the City. Cowan seems to have altered the team's midfield tactics. On their form yesterday the City will walk into the First Division.'

Cowan's side did walk into the First Division as Division Two Champions, with only four of the 30 League and Cup games he managed ending in defeat. Sadly, behind the scenes there had been some friction. Cowan, according to journalists during the summer, had never been afraid to speak his mind and it seems he was in conflict with chairman Robert Smith as a result. One journalist stated: 'Sam took a strong line on some matters and the board viewed things in a different light. Managing big soccer clubs is one of the hardest jobs in life. Happiness and success depend largely on one's ability to recognise that directors are, after all, the bosses. Sam always practised straight talking, but often diplomacy can win greater points.'

Cowan resigned after only seven months as manager. He told the *Daily Herald* newspaper: 'Something happened, and I felt I had no option but to hand in my resignation. I don't want to implicate anyone, so rather than cause any trouble I would prefer to leave the matter there.' When he was pushed for information he added: 'The trouble had nothing to do with players, transfers, or salary. I was allowed to carry out any ideas I had up to a point and any suggestions I made were considered.' I can look back with pride on my first experience as manager. I made the winning move in the Championship race by switching McDowall from left-half to centre-half and introducing Fagan into the first team. I also created a lot of harmony among the players where there had been none previous to my coming.'

'When I came on 2 December to the Club they were fourth in the table and an indifferent side. They won 22 games on the run and made promotion to the First Division virtually safe. No matter what anybody connected with the club might say, I have not been a failure.'

During the years that followed club officials suggested that Sam's commuting from Brighton was the issue, but it's clear that performances on the pitch were not affected. Whatever the truth, it seems that City lost a very capable and well-loved manager. Cowan's departure was the first time a City manager's resignation had upset the majority of fans. They were convinced great success would come under Cowan, but his resignation, whether forced or not, caused many fans to question the direction of the club at a time when popular ex-Blue Matt Busby was guiding Maine Road's tenants Manchester United towards success. This was a testing time for supporter loyalty.

After City Cowan developed his physiotherapy business and became masseur to

Sussex CCC, and in 1962–63 he went on tour with the MCC to Australia. Earlier, in 1955, he helped Newcastle United as part of their stay on the south coast to prepare for their Cup Final meeting with City.

Cowan died at Haywards Heath while refereeing a charity match featuring television and film stars of the period, such as Tommy Steele, on 4 October 1964

Jock Thomson

Born: Thornton, Fifeshire, 6 July 1906, died: 1979

October 1947 – February 1950

Following Sam Cowan's departure, chairman Bob Smith announced that City would pay £2,000 a year to bring a top man to Maine Road. Cowan had earned less than half that figure and supporters were stunned by the high expenditure necessary to bring a recognised manager to the Blues. Sadly, it took some time to find the right man for the job.

John Ross 'Jock' Thomson became City's new manager after a highly successful career with Everton, although most sources claim he didn't actually take on the role until mid-October (Wilf Wild is believed to have reluctantly filled the gap between Cowan and Thomson). That first season saw City finish 10th, with 1948–49 showing a slight improvement as the Blues finished seventh. Considering City had been in Division Two only three seasons earlier this may have appeared satisfying, but the pressure was increasing on Thomson. Some supporters, who had loved Cowan's brief period in charge, were drifting towards Manchester United. Busby, a Blue hero, was transforming the side, and for the first time in history United were beginning to attract more fans than City. As Thomson's side seemed some way off winning a trophy, questions were beginning to be asked.

Early in the 1949 season Thomson showed exceptional bravery when he signed German prisoner-of-war Bert Trautmann. Most football managers would probably not have considered making the controversial signing at all, but Thomson made the move despite much criticism.

The 1949–50 season proved to be Thomson's make-or-break campaign and sadly, by Christmas Day, the Blues had only won three of their opening 17 matches. They were deep in relegation trouble and Thomson seemed unable to improve matters. By February City were out of the FA Cup – losing 5–3 at home to Derby – and were in further trouble in the League. Thomson's reign was over, and three months later City were relegated.

After Maine Road, Thomson returned to Scotland and managed a pub in Carnoustie until November 1974.

Les McDowall

Born: India, 25 October 1912, died: 18 August 1991

June 1950 – May 1963

It's not entirely clear who took the lead role in managing the Blues between the end of Thomson's reign and the beginning of Les McDowall's period in charge. It's possible that secretary Wilf Wild may have taken on additional responsibility, and this may have had an impact on his health as he passed away in December 1950. Members of the coaching staff, most notably 1930s stars Fred Tilson, Lawrie Barnett and Dick Neilson, carried out the bulk of training and tactical planning until McDowall arrived in June 1950 following City's relegation to the old Division Two.

McDowall had been a skilful wing-half during his City playing career of the late 1930s and the immediate post-war period, and his knowledge of both the club and its approach to the game helped him to revitalise the Blues.

Interestingly, McDowall's life could have turned out very differently had it not been for the Depression of the early 1930s. He was born in India in 1912, the son of a Scottish missionary, and trained as a draughtsman. He went on to work at a shipyard but during the Depression he became unemployed. To keep himself occupied he helped to form a football team called Glenryan Thistle while looking for work. This period was a very difficult one for him but, by chance, his life was to change completely when he was spotted by a Sunderland scout and offered a playing

contract. From then on, football became his employment, although he did return to his original profession for a while during the war.

By the time he arrived as City manager in 1950 McDowall was well known for his hard work and organisational skills as a player, and had enjoyed a brief spell as Wrexham's player-manager. Over the course of the following 13 years his achievements as a player would be eclipsed by his Maine Road managerial career.

One of his first signings was inspirational – Roy Paul. Paul proved to be one of football's greatest captains and McDowall had beaten many other clubs, including Arsenal, to sign the Swansea wing-half.

At the end of McDowall's first season the Paul-inspired Blues had achieved promotion, and the following season he added Ivor Broadis and Don Revie to the squad as the Blues became a quality side. Around this time McDowall became very famous for his tactical awareness – perhaps it was as a result of his attention to detail as a draughtsman – and he worked with his backroom staff to instigate various playing formations. The most famous of these involved a deep-lying centre-forward and was christened the 'Revie Plan' after the player who played that role in the first team. As a result of that tactic City enjoyed two Wembley appearances, winning the Cup in an entertaining manner in 1956.

McDowall brought great success and excitement to City during the fifties and he actually managed the Blues for more League seasons than any other City manager. He also had the respect of his players, and as a former player himself he worked exceptionally hard to help restore pride and bring back the glory days to Maine Road.

Unfortunately, as football moved into the 1960s McDowall's style was no longer appropriate for a major, glamorous side. McDowall was very much an old-school style of manager, working in the office, wearing a suit, rather than working on the pitch in the style that Cullis (Wolves), Busby (United) and Mercer (Villa) were finding great success with. By his final couple of seasons it seemed as if City were destined to struggle. Some great players did arrive, but when Denis Law was sold in 1960 the writing was on the wall. Not since Tommy Johnson 30 years earlier had the Blues sold one of their brightest stars and, as with Johnson's departure, supporters started to question the overall direction of the club.

The early sixties were not great for McDowall's men and with football changing it was necessary for the City directorate to replace McDowall with a man with a fresh outlook. Relegation in May 1963 ended McDowall's City career, but he still felt he had much to offer. He became Oldham Athletic manager the following month, but two years later, as Oldham were heading for relegation from Division Three, he was dismissed. He left football at this point.

Les McDowall's position in City's history is a significant one. He was a good player and a great manager. He restored pride at a time when the odds were stacked firmly against the Blues, and his tactical innovations entertained the crowd. He was a great manager at a time when tactical play increased in importance, and as a traditional office-bound leader he was excellent.

George Poyser

Born: Mansfield, 6 February 1910, died: 30 January 1995

12 July 1963 – Easter 1965

Although it was clear City needed a modern style of leader, in the mould of Cullis, Busby or

George Poyser (centre) with 1930s hero Tommy Johnson (left) and 1960s star Derek Kevan (right).

Mercer, the Board decided to promote McDowall's assistant George Poyser to the manager's chair. Poyser, over two years older than his predecessor, was clearly another office-bound manager. This may have worked well during the pre-war era, but by the 1960s this style was not appropriate. Nevertheless Poyser seemed to look forward to the challenge.

He had already been a manager with Dover Town and Notts County prior to joining City as assistant in 1957, and had managed to take County to the 1955 quarter-finals of the FA Cup. He had also been a player, most notably with Port Vale, and as part of Brentford's Second Division Championship side of 1934–35.

As City he was viewed as an exceptional scout and managed to find a number of talented players. This was perhaps his strongest skill area and perhaps if another man had been appointed instead of Poyser in 1963 he would have continued to give City many years service in this role. Sadly, McDowall's departure caused the City Board to take the easy option and Poyser was given the difficult task of bringing promotion and resurrecting the club's fortunes.

It was a task he couldn't succeed in, although his first season brought a League Cup semi-final place and a final position of sixth in the division. The League Cup run apart, Poyser's reign was one of struggle, and on 16 January 1965 a record low Maine Road League crowd of 8,015 witnessed a 2–1 defeat to Swindon. It entered folklore as City's lowest point in terms of support, but incredibly Poyser wasn't even at the ground. Instead he was away scouting – a role he seemed to love. Clearly, his absence had repercussions. At Easter, with form not improving and support remaining low (the highest crowd of the season was only 22,299 – the lowest 'highest' crowd since 1898), Poyser was dismissed.

From Easter until the end of the season City were managed by backroom staff, most notably 1934 FA Cup goalscorer Fred Tilson.

Joe Mercer, OBE

Born: Ellesmere Port, 9 August 1914, died: Hoylake, 9 August 1990
13 July 1965 – 7 October 1971
Continued as general manager until June 1972

Joe Mercer was a major footballing figure prior to joining the Blues. At Arsenal Joe was regarded as one of the greatest Gunners of all time and at times during the 1950s and early 1960s they had urged their Board to appoint him manager. Fortunately for City that never happened. As a player he won the Championship with Everton and Arsenal (twice), and also captained the Gunners to FA Cup success. He made his first England appearance shortly before the war and went on to captain his country. He was a model professional, and only stopped playing at the age of 39 when a collision resulted in a broken leg.

Naturally, for a man so in love with the game, he moved into management, firstly with Sheffield United, where he inherited a team destined for relegation. Although he was unable to turn the Blades into a promotion-winning side, he did build a very entertaining Cup fighting side.

By December 1958 Mercer realised that he had taken the Bramall Lane side just about as far as he could and he became Aston Villa's manager. Villa were a struggling side and, inevitably, another relegation followed, but Mercer was free to push forward with his ambitious plans and within two seasons his young side had been champions of Division Two and League Cup-winners.

During his time at Sheffield and at Villa he regularly hit the headlines for the bold, stylish, exciting football his sides played and many other teams showed interest in him. In the early sixties a media campaign was started to make Mercer England team manager. Mercer decided he wasn't ready for the post and chose not to apply. In the seventies he did become caretaker manager, putting the fun back into international football, but turned down a permanent appointment because of health reasons.

In the sixties 'Mercer's Minors', as Villa became known, demonstrated a very entertaining style of play and enjoyed several good Cup runs, Unfortunately, Mercer's career changed direction in 1963 when pressure increased at Villa. The Villa fans were desperate for League Championship success and, despite the great FA Cup runs and League Cup successes, they became desperate for Villa to win their first Championship since 1910. His relatively young side were still not ready for that and, as a result of the pressure, Mercer became ill. Eventually he suffered a stroke.

At Villa he had taken on too much – in addition to the playing side he was also a major player in the development of a new stand – and while he lay at home ill the Villa board decided to terminate his contract. Villa's loss was City's gain.

After a year out of the game Mercer joined the Blues in July 1965. His doctor had tried to dissuade him but admitted to Mercer's wife, Norah: 'He may as well die doing the job he loves, than sit at home and die of a broken heart.' Mercer decided to bring in a youthful coach and sought out Malcolm Allison, a young former West Ham player he had been impressed with at FA coaching sessions. Allison became Mercer's number two, and the partnership turned City into the most entertaining side of the era. Mercer said around this time: 'The chance was irresistible. I knew that people had written me off. There were doubts about my health, but I had no lack of confidence about my ability. Allison was magnificent. I knew we had a chance with Manchester City. Although they were in the Second Division they were a club with a tradition and a ready-made public.'

Promotion in 1966 – and a good FA Cup run – was followed in 1968 by the League Championship. Only Wilf Wild had managed to bring this to Maine Road prior to Mercer, but Wild's side had developed over several years, whereas Mercer's side had gone from mid-Division Two obscurity to Champions in only three seasons. The following season Mercer's side won the FA Cup and then eclipsed this by winning both the League Cup and ECWC in 1970. The Blues were a major force and were led by a very respectable footballing figure, and coached by one of the most dynamic men in Europe. For supporters it was the most exciting period ever.

Sadly, the Mercer-Allison partnership became strained and, over the course of the next couple of seasons, both men came under pressure. Allison naturally wanted full control of team affairs, Mercer understandably wanted to continue to have the final say. In addition, the boardroom battle which eventually led to Peter Swales becoming chairman forced the men into opposite camps. Mercer stuck by the established Board and as a result finished on the losing side. On 7 October 1971, two days after a League Cup defeat at Bolton, a three-hour Board meeting ended with City announcing that Allison was to be team manager, with Mercer taking on a role as general manager. It was clearly a compromise and one which never really succeeded.

In June 1972, after the new board of directors had removed his car parking space and taken away his office, Mercer felt it was time to move on. It seems he was treated appallingly by the new regime, who believed Allison had brought all the success on his own. Regardless of what the directors felt, the fans recognised Mercer's enormous contribution. Shortly after his departure the City Supporters' Club invited him to their annual ceremony and presented him with a silver tea service. It was a touching moment for Mercer, but for supporters too it was a key moment as it brought to an end the most glorious period in the club's history.

Joe Mercer was without question the most successful City manager of all time. City fans are well aware of the achievements of his reign, but so are true footballing legends. Sir Tom Finney, Preston's greatest hero, recognises this: 'Joe had great success at City – there's no question about that. They were one of the best footballing sides of all time. City had gone through some real traumas before Joe. I don't think anyone who has watched City for any length of time will ever forget that era. They will always talk about it with tremendous affection. There's no doubt

Joe Mercer (manager), Albert Alexander (chairman), and Malcolm Allison (assistant manager) clasping hands at the start of the highly successful managerial reign.

that Joe had a great influence on City and together with Malcolm Allison they put together a great side.'

After City Mercer joined Coventry with Gordon Milne, and won a manager of the month award, then in 1974 he took control of the England side on a caretaker basis. His brief period in charge helped bring new life and excitement into the national side. Entertainers such as Frank Worthington and quality players such as Kevin Keegan were given great opportunity to entertain and excite. It was a great summer, and Mercer was asked to continue on a permanent basis, but because of a painful back condition he declined, feeling that he would not give England what he felt they needed. It was a shame.

After England, he became a Coventry City director until 1981 when he returned to Merseyside to retire. He suffered from Alzheimer's in later life and passed away peacefully in his favourite armchair in August 1990 on his 76th birthday. Since the end of Peter Swales's reign as chairman the Blues have welcomed Joe's widow, Norah Mercer, to the club. At Maine Road a Joe Mercer Suite was opened, and in 2005 two outstanding mosaics of Mercer as City manager were unveiled on Joe Mercer Way at the new stadium. It is a pity, however, that the City of the 1980s never made any formal move to recognise Mercer's role during his lifetime.

Malcolm Allison

Born: Dartford, 5 September 1927

7 October 1971 – 30 March 1973

Although Malcolm Allison's two spells as City manager only saw the Blues receive one trophy – the 1972 Charity Shield – it has to be stressed that his contribution during the glory years of 1965 to 1970 was equal to that of manager Joe Mercer.

Allison arrived at Maine Road in July 1965 as assistant manager to Mercer, and by the time he left City had won almost every trophy possible. During those seven years Allison worked closely with the players and it's worth noting that this relationship fostered a great team spirit, which helped the Blues succeed. His

influence was felt throughout the club and his approach was refreshing. His charisma and style brought excitement to sixties Manchester. His 'fortune favours the brave' swashbuckling approach helped sweep aside all opposition. In fact, as the sixties progressed Allison typified a new-found Mancunian spirit, and he became a man idolised by Blues and many neutrals.

Few, if any, leading footballing figures possessed the style and charisma that oozed from him, and his dynamism was infectious. If Allison said City were going to win everybody believed him; when, following City's League success in 1968, he said City would terrify Europe no one doubted him. Of course, the comment came back to haunt him when the Blues were defeated by Fenerbahce in their first European tie, but Allison had the last laugh when City won the European Cup-Winners' Cup the following season. He later laughed: 'I said we'd terrify Europe, but I didn't say when!'

During his time at Maine Road Allison was responsible for a number of key transfers that transformed the club's fortunes. Colin Bell and Francis Lee were two signings he claimed personal credit for: 'When I signed Bell I had to pretend he was no good to put the other clubs off because we didn't have enough money and couldn't afford to get into a bidding war. With Francis Lee I told him I'd make him a great player, and when I left the room he told everyone I was an arrogant so and so! But he did join us and he was a great player, perhaps the key to the Championship success.'

Allison was also responsible for the arrival of captain Tony Book. Book brought a steadying influence to City both in defence and across the pitch, and flourished at Maine Road as a player and later as a manager.

Another great aspect of Allison's time at City was his ability to grab the headlines for the club. Prior to his arrival, City struggled to get positive coverage in the local press but, together with Joe Mercer, Allison knew how to bring attention to the club. Mercer was the all-smiling public establishment-type figure who would provide a serious story in a light-hearted way, while Allison was more boastful and always likely to make the bold statements many supporters demanded. Allison would often taunt the opposition. In December 1970 he walked up to the Stretford End prior to a League derby match and held up four fingers to indicate how many goals he expected City to score against the Reds. Understandably, the United fans hurled abuse at him, but by the end of the match the confident Allison was laughing as City won 4–1. That's why he was such an important figure. He understood what made City fans tick.

Sadly, the early seventies rift between Mercer and Allison – they supported different groups during the takeover battle – caused the partnership to fall apart. Allison became manager in his own right in October 1971 and after his first game a journalist asked him what kind of a leader he would be. He responded: 'Probably the best that ever was. And I'll tell you something else, it will be nice to walk out at Wembley ahead of the Cup Final team.'

The Blues didn't reach Wembley, but Allison's side did finish fourth, missing the title by a point. They won the Charity Shield the following year, but Allison felt he was no longer able to motivate himself in the right way. In 1993 he admitted: 'Kenny Dalglish wanted a sabbatical at Liverpool to ease the pressure the other year, and I think if I'd been offered something similar I'd have come back stronger, but in those days you either managed or left. There was no choice.'

He resigned in March 1973 and on 30 March he became Crystal Palace's new manager.

Johnny Hart

Born: Golbourne, 8 June 1928

March 1973 – 22 October 1973

Johnny Hart never really wanted to be City's manager: 'I enjoyed being a "number two", and I loved all my time as a coach. I'd loved my playing career and I felt as if Maine Road was my home. When I came to the end of my playing career I'd already started to get involved with coaching. I liked being a second in command. Management was different. I didn't really want the job, but if I'd have turned it down I'd probably have been moved on. It wasn't a job I craved at all.'

'It just wasn't the role for me. I'm quite a shy person really, and I guess management just wasn't for me. The players were terrific – I had a fantastic squad and they all wanted to play for me. Denis Law arrived back and I was very happy with the players and their motivation, but I just didn't want the role, and it all got to me. I became quite ill.'

Hart had been an office boy with the club during the war and then became a player until retirement in May 1963. An unfortunate series of injuries restricted his first-team appearances to 178. After the 1956 FA Cup Final City's star

man told journalists: 'In this hour of glory I hope the public will not forget Johnny Hart, City's inside-forward. Johnny couldn't play last year, as he had a broken leg. This time he had to watch again. It must have been sheer agony for a lad who would have given his all to have played.' Hart, despite being an important member of McDowall's side, was unlucky to miss out on two Wembley Finals.

He was a popular member of City's backroom staff during the sixties and early seventies and, following Allison's departure, he became the surprise choice as manager. Unfortunately Hart's health deteriorated during his first few months in charge and he stood down after only six months.

The feeling of most supporters was that the City Board had taken what seemed the easy option when they appointed him, and that the directors should have sought a more experienced professional.

After leaving the manager's post, Hart spent some time recuperating before finding employment at the builders Faircloughs. He still continued to attend City's games and remains a popular member of the Former Players' Association. In 2006 he was inducted into the Manchester City Hall of Fame and awarded a lifetime achievement award for services to the club.

His sons Nigel and Paul also became footballers, and Paul himself became a football manager.

Ron Saunders

Born: Birkenhead, 6 November 1932

24 November 1973 – 11 April 1974

Ron Saunders had been a player with a number of southern clubs, including Portsmouth and Watford, before moving into management with Yeovil Town. After saving them from relegation in 1968 he moved on to struggling Oxford in March 1969 and in the final months of the season he guided them to safety. The following July he became Norwich City's manager and led the Canaries into Division One for the first time in their history. He also took them to the 1973 League Cup Final.

His record of success prompted several clubs to show interest, but City's new chairman Peter Swales was determined Saunders would be the perfect man for the City job. He told journalists what he wanted Saunders to achieve: 'Put a killer instinct into the team. There's too much showbiz about City.' With his tough, no-nonsense style, he followed Swales's brief and demanded much from his players, but according to rumours circulating at the time, the more seasoned professionals did not support his approach.

Perhaps as a result of Saunders's tough approach, City started to drop down the table. Rumours even circulated that the players were on strike. Whatever the truth, Swales decided he couldn't allow his club to be relegated and according to the chairman in an interview from 1995, Saunders was sacked on Good Friday 1974 after less than six months in charge, although City played Liverpool on Good Friday and Tony Book claims he was in charge for that fixture. The football world was amazed, especially as Saunders had guided the Blues to the 1974 League Cup Final – their first Final since 1970. It is clear that Saunders's dismissal was a little harsh, especially as Swales had publicly staked his own career on his first appointment.

Saunders took control of Aston Villa the following June and brought them the success that Swales had craved. At Villa he won promotion from the Second Division, the League Cup (twice), and the League Championship. Amazingly, Saunders left Villa in February 1982 while his side were still in the European Cup. His assistant Tony Barton guided Villa through the latter stages to win their first European trophy, while Saunders joined Birmingham City. He later had a spell at West Bromwich Albion.

Tony Book

Born: Bath, 4 September 1935

12 April 1974 – July 1979

Continued as general manager until 8 October 1980

Tony Book's place in City's history had already been assured by the early 1970s thanks to his exploits as a tremendous captain and player, but his spell as City manager during the mid-seventies saw the Blues excite and entertain in another glorious period of football.

Throughout Book's time as manager City were known for flamboyance, and yet Book himself was never one to boast or to shout and scream about the team's achievements. He allowed his team to do the talking and, with star men like Dennis Tueart, Peter Barnes and Asa Hartford there was never a dull moment.

Book had been a hugely successful player during the Mercer-Allison period and was undoubtedly a key figure following his arrival in July 1966 for £17,000. Book was City's influential captain and as a result he did more than most to bring glory to the Blues.

Inevitably, after his playing career ended he moved into City's backroom and focussed on coaching. He became assistant to manager Ron Saunders in 1973, and when Saunders was dismissed Book was appointed manager. Book was given control for the final four games of the 1973–74 season with the Blues struggling. Almost immediately he transformed the club's fortunes with two victories, one draw and a defeat, ensuring City survived in Division One – they finished four points above the relegation zone, causing chairman Swales to insist he was right to dismiss Saunders. The following season Book's Blues finished eighth, and they were beginning to excite.

Supported by coach Ian MacFarlane – a former playing colleague at Bath City – Book guided City to win the 1976 League Cup Final and he made history by being the first man to win the trophy as a player and as a manager. At the time he said: 'This was my greatest moment. It was a tremendous Final and Tueart's goal was something special… quite out of this world.'

Tony Book and new signing Mike Channon, signed on 25 July 1977.

Shortly after that success MacFarlane left City for Jack Charlton's Middlesbrough, and Book was then ably supported by the impressive Bill Taylor – a coach with England as well as City. In 1976–77 the Blues missed the League title by a point, finishing second to 'team of the seventies' Liverpool.

It seemed as if nothing could stop City's progression and supporters eagerly anticipated trophy success. A fourth-place finish came in 1977–78. Glamorous football, popular players and average support exceeding 40,000 for two successive years suggested that City were a wealthy club destined for glory, but the City Board were desperate for further success. Motivated by an obsession to overtake United, the Board brought back Malcolm Allison and Book, though still City manager, found his influence diluted.

It was a major mistake by the Board and one which led to the break-up of a great City side competing in Europe. Book ultimately became general manager, but the period was an extremely difficult one. In an interview during the mid-1990s Peter Swales admitted: 'We were runners-up in the League by one point, and we had got to United on support. We averaged forty odd thousand and we almost caught them, and I thought well next year we'll win the Championship and we'll do it. That's when I made my biggest mistake – Malcolm Allison. I got talked into that!'

Swales added: 'Instead of sticking with Tony, who'd got us into second place which would make us kings today, one or two on the Board started to say "if we could just get Malcolm we could do the final push". Final bloody push all right!'

In 1980 the two men were dismissed, although Book was asked to stay on as caretaker manager for a while. Once John Bond was appointed he moved on but, after a brief period away, Bond asked him to return. He then filled a variety of positions – first team coach, youth coach, youth team manager, assistant manager, and caretaker manager (on several occasions) – and remained at Maine Road until the 1996–97 season when it was announced he was to retire. In 1997 he returned to football by joining ex-Blue Peter Reid at Sunderland in a scouting role. In 2004 he was inducted into the Manchester City Hall of Fame, and he continues to be a popular presence on match days at City.

Book's managerial reign was one of excitement and entertainment. Few other managers have succeeded in bringing the Blues that level of glamour since.

Malcolm Allison

Born: Dartford, 5 September 1927

January 1979 (as 'coaching overlord', manager from July 1979) – 8 October 1980

After his departure from City in 1973 Allison moved to Crystal Palace then, after spells at a variety of clubs, he returned to Maine Road in 1979 as a 'coaching overlord'. Despite Allison's enormous role in Manchester football it has to be stressed that his second spell at Maine Road was not a success. With hindsight Allison should never have returned, but at the time every supporter of the club was delighted with his comeback.

Sadly, Allison seemed intent on creating a new side, even though the City team of January 1979 contained at least seven international players. These players were enormously popular, but Allison quickly switched the emphasis from those well-established, quality players, to a new youthful side.

Allison's purge saw fans' favourites Brian Kidd, Dave Watson, Gary Owen, Peter Barnes, Kenny Clements and Asa Hartford leave, while Dragoslav Stepanovic, Steve Daley, Mike Robinson, Steve Mackenzie, Barry Silkman and Stuart Lee all arrived. Some of those players were of good quality, but when taken as a whole the players leaving were significantly better than those arriving. On the whole the replacements also proved to be very expensive, and ultimately caused City a number of serious financial problems over the course of the following decade, although Allison has always stated that he was appalled at the amount of money spent on Steve Daley (a staggering record amount of £1.47 million), and that he did not agree that spend.

The new City struggled and in October 1980 Allison was dismissed. He went on to manage around the world. Some locations, like his image, were exotic, others were not. Overall his managerial career has been mixed, although it has

£1 million signing Trevor Francis with John Bond, 3 September 1981.

to be stressed that he has found some real success away from City – most notably in Portugal. His last public managerial role saw him help Bristol Rovers face Ron Atkinson's Aston Villa in the FA Cup during the 1992–93 season. The media had described it as 'Big Mal v Big Ron', but Allison insisted on telling the BBC that he was the only 'Big' in football and that his opponent was 'Fat Ron'. It didn't alter the result of the game, but it gained the headlines. A few years later Allison hit the headlines again as a result of problems in his private life. Francis Lee, Mike Summerbee and other former colleagues helped him resettle in the Manchester area, and he became a regular visitor to Maine Road and then the City of Manchester Stadium.

In 2005 he stunned supporters when he visited the club's museum with his son and took part in a stadium tour with ordinary fans. Although many former greats would have sought special treatment, Allison wanted to experience the day as all City fans would.

Despite the problems of his second spell, Allison remains one of the most important figures in the history of the club and in European football. He remains a true hero.

John Bond

Born: Colchester, 17 December 1932

17 October 1980 – 29 January 1983

Former West Ham player John Bond arrived at City after a popular run as manager of Norwich City. Like his Maine Road predecessor he was known throughout the game for his flamboyance and his appointment at City seemed to give him the perfect stage. With significant media interest he focussed on improving attitude and confidence within the club. In fact his very first meeting with the players was filmed by Granada TV as part of a fly on the wall documentary and the media focussed on Bond's style of management – he wanted to be known as Boss and stressed he wanted players to show the right 'attitude' – almost 20 years later, that same scene was parodied in a one-off TV comedy called 'Bostock's Cup' starring Nick Hancock with the actor Tim Healy playing the 'Boss'.

Bond's impact was immediate: 'Attitude is important in football, and I always tried to instil the right approach in to my players. But I have to say they were great lads. They didn't have too much confidence when I arrived – we worked on that – but they did have a desire to succeed. They wanted to listen and learn. They responded well, and gave me great support. As a manager that's what you look for.'

'Don't forget I also won the manager of the month award twice for the transformation which was the talk of football. It was a great period. From Tottenham (22 October 1980) through to the middle of January we only lost two out of 15 games. I brought some players in… improved confidence… and we progressed.'

Those experienced players brought in were Tommy Hutchison, Bobby McDonald and Gerry Gow, and these men helped steady the side. Bond's Blues started to move up the table, but the real story came in both cup competitions as City progressed to the League Cup semi-final and the FA Cup Final. Bond: 'It was all a question of confidence and attitude. The young players seemed baffled when I arrived so I tried to make life simple and rebuild their confidence. It worked because we should have won the League Cup semi-final – and the whole of football knew that – and then we should have won the FA Cup. Again, the whole of football knew that as well!'

City lost the League Cup tie after a controversial disallowed goal gave Liverpool the upper hand, while the FA Cup ended in defeat against Tottenham in the replay after Tommy Hutchison had been unfortunate to score for both sides. Neither defeat should detract from what Bond had achieved in only six months.

The season after Wembley Bond signed Martin O'Neill and Trevor Francis and the side briefly headed the League. Unfortunately, Francis missed rather too many games through injury and, according to Bond, was always intended to be the first of several major transfers that season. Two players he tried to sign were Joe Jordan and Justin Fashanu, but both deals fell through at the last moment. Another player he desperately wanted to see back at Maine Road was Peter Barnes.

Due to high spending in the Allison era, City were struggling financially. Francis was sold within a year and Bond felt let down. He wasn't the only one, as attendances plummeted by almost 8,000. In addition some of the directors simply did not like Bond, although he continues to claim he always enjoyed the full support of Peter Swales.

He left City after an embarrassing Cup defeat at Brighton in 1983, but considerable rumour surrounded his departure. Events in his private life made the headlines – Bond later claimed a club director pressured him to resign by threatening to provide stories to the press – and the Brighton defeat seemed to be the final straw. Although the defeat was an extremely difficult one to accept for most Blues, Bond's resignation was too soon. Prior to his departure the worst position City had held was mid-table; once he left the club was in free fall with relegation coming in May 1983.

Always outspoken, Bond went on to Burnley, where supporters turned against him. As a summariser for Granada TV he upset City supporters in 1989 with his view that City's young side was not good enough for promotion. Some fans felt this was disloyal, Bond felt it was the truth and, as with earlier in his career, he demonstrated his belief in always saying what he thought.

In 2000 he helped John Benson, his former assistant, take Wigan to the play-off final, and in 2003 he received a terrific reception from the fans as he was one of the club's guests at Maine Road's final game: 'I was gobsmacked by their reaction! I have to be honest and say that I didn't know what reaction I would get. I didn't know if they'd be glad to see me or not, so beforehand I was very uncertain. When I came out and heard the cheering I was delighted. I loved that reaction. Afterwards I rushed home and told my family about the reception and how delighted I was with it. There were times during my management when I received fantastic support from the fans, and at Maine Road's final game I was delighted with the ovation.'

Regardless of how his managerial career progressed, it is clear that the first year or so of Bond's time at Maine Road was immensely satisfying to thousands of Blues. Gow, Hutchison and McDonald brought a real determination to the club and that, coupled with the entertainment provided by Nicky Reid, Tommy Caton and the others, meant that it was fun being a Blue again.

John Benson

Born: Arbroath, 23 December 1942

5 February 1983 – June 1983

Once John Bond had resigned Peter Swales considered the options. With City struggling financially it was not a good time to search for a new manager. Ex-player John Benson had been Bond's assistant and after a few days

Tony Book and John Benson.

deliberation he was given the manager's job. As with Johnny Hart a decade earlier, Benson felt he had to accept: 'I had no choice really. Once Bondy had left, either I had to become manager or I would, in all probability, have to move on. I had nowhere to go to, so I took the job. I kept my old wage – no increase – and tried my best. I never wanted to be manager. I was too young. Too inexperienced, and managing City is inevitably an enormous job. You have to know your strengths in football, and I know that my strength was as a number two.'

It is abundantly clear that Benson was very much a temporary manager in the eyes of Peter Swales. Had City avoided relegation in 1983 it is highly unlikely that Benson would have been in charge by the start of the 1983–84 season, so the former player really was in a difficult position. Supporters recognised this to some extent, and some even joked that Benson had only been given the job because City couldn't afford to replace the 'JB' initials on the manager's tracksuit.

Sadly, Benson's Blues plummeted down the table and were relegated in their final match of the season – a 1–0 defeat by relegation rivals Luton Town. Relegation hurt everyone enormously, including Benson: 'When relegation came I felt the pain and hurt all fans did. This was my club and I was manager when they went down. It was such a painful, horrible experience, and I still feel that hurt today.'

Benson was dismissed and rejoined Bond at Burnley – taking over the managerial reins in August 1984 after Bond's dismissal – and later became Barnsley's chief scout (under another former Norwich colleague Mel Machin). He went on to coach in non-League football, but then became manager of Wigan Athletic. Benson: 'It was another role I reluctantly accepted. I'd been working for John Deehan at Norwich, then Wigan until 1998. I was asked to take over but said no. I told them I was a good number two, but not a lucky manager. Ray Mathias took over and we finished sixth, but one thing led to another and I was asked to take over again in 1999. I kept saying no, but then I agreed, saying I would only have the job for 12 months. I was still a reluctant manager. I called Bondy up and asked him to come in and give a bit of support. It was great and I enjoyed working with him again. At the end of the season we reached the play-off final against Gillingham. They beat us 3–2 with a goal in the last desperate minutes of extra-time – this was only a year after City had beat them, so for me it felt like they'd got revenge!'

Benson later had a spell as a coach under Steve Bruce at Birmingham.

At the start of his career he had been a player at Maine Road, making 44 League appearances during 1961 to 1964, and he remains today a keen City supporter.

Billy McNeill, MBE

Born: Bellshill, Lanarkshire, 2 March 1940

June 1983 – 20 September 1986

Billy McNeill was already regarded as an all-time great player and manager at Celtic before joining City following relegation in 1983. In 1974 he received the MBE for services to the Scottish game and the following year he retired as a player. Under McNeill's captaincy the Glasgow club became the first British side to win the European Cup (1967), while his career had also seen him play in 12 Scottish Cup Finals; nine League title-winning sides and nine Scottish League Cup Finals. He also made 29 full international appearances for Scotland. All in all McNeill's time at Celtic made him a Scottish legend. The move into management was inevitable.

A brief spell at Clyde was followed by a year at Aberdeen, where he signed both Steve Archibald and Gordon Strachan. His Aberdeen side narrowly missed out on the League and the Scottish Cup that year, and some would say he laid the foundations for the success that Aberdeen were later to enjoy under Alex Ferguson.

In May 1978 McNeill took over from Jock Stein at Celtic. Stein, like Busby at United and Mercer at City, was Celtic's hugely popular and successful manager, but McNeill managed to create a Celtic side in his own image and the side continued to be successful. Then in 1983 City chairman Peter Swales saw an opportunity to bring him to England following rumours of discontent at Celtic Park. It was an appointment which proved that despite relegation, the Blues were still a major force. McNeill was the biggest name in Scottish football and it was a major coup.

McNeill and his assistant, the former Oldham manager Jimmy Frizzell, were stunned by the state of City's finances: 'City had horrendous debts in the wake of their halcyon spending sprees on players. We could hardly buy a fish supper. Jimmy and I were left with so few players we sat for days on end thinking who we could get for as close to nothing as possible.'

'We pulled players out of our memories. Derek Parlane came on a free transfer from Leeds, Jim Tolmie from Lokeren in Belgium, and Neil McNab from Brighton. I had remembered Tolmie with Morton, but was aware he could also be difficult to handle. We weren't in a position to be choosy. We got McNab from Brighton, where he had been a bit of a rebel.'

These players were brought in for bargain-basement fees, but each transfer proved inspired, demonstrating that McNeill clearly knew how to get value for money. Unfortunately, he was forced to sell the only saleable asset Tommy Caton for around £450,000 to pay off some of the debt and to fund other purchases, most notably the signing of Mick McCarthy for £200,000.

McNeill's first season brought a few high points but the Blues finished fourth behind Sheffield Wednesday, Chelsea and a Keegan-inspired Newcastle. In the mid-1980s the top three sides received automatic promotion. Had the play-offs been in force City might have scraped through, but McNeill knew promotion in 1984 would have been premature.

Promotion came the following season via a 5–1 defeat of Charlton on the last day of the season. The following March McNeill led City out at Wembley for the inaugural Full Members' Cup Final against Chelsea. Although this was not a major trophy, reaching the Final still brought satisfaction, and much needed finances, City's way.

Unfortunately, McNeill was already feeling frustrated with City's financial position and other moves behind the scenes. After the opening seven games of the 1986–87 season McNeill shocked City fans by joining Aston Villa. McNeill: 'Peter Swales didn't want me to go and he also thought Villa weren't right for me. However, upsetting influences in the background at Maine Road weren't going away.'

City supporters saw McNeill's move to Villa in an extremely negative manner, and he

Peter Swales and Billy McNeill.

received tremendous abuse – particularly when City and Villa met in the League in November – and was clearly shaken by it all. The move was a major mistake as Villa were in a similar financial position to City and the 'interference' at Villa was later revealed to be greater than that at City. McNeill eventually admitted he should never have left City but at the time he could see no other option.

At the end of the season both Villa and City were relegated. Villa's relegation was blamed totally on McNeill and resulted in his dismissal, while at Maine Road many also blamed McNeill, but that was unfair as he had only managed the side for seven games, earning seven points. City's problems came later.

McNeill returned to Celtic, managing them until May 1991. During that period he guided them to further success, breaking Rangers' eighties dominance. Since 1991 McNeill has performed media work and concentrated to some extent on his popular Glaswegian bar. In 1997 it was revealed that he had successfully undergone a triple heart bypass operation.

Although McNeill's time at City is not remembered as a successful period, it should be thought of as a time when his influence ensured City survived and regained some pride. Promotion was achieved because of the miraculous work he did in the transfer market, while he also made use of home-grown talent like Paul Simpson and Paul Moulden.

Jimmy Frizzell

Born: Greenock, 16 February 1937

21 September 1986 – May 1987

Continued as general manager until summer 1988

Jimmy Frizzell was assistant manager during McNeill's two-year reign and then was given the manager's role following McNeill's shock departure. During his first few months at City his knowledge of the local football scene and of the English Division Two helped shape McNeill's plans.

Earlier in his life he had been a utility player at Boundary Park, and had moved into coaching during the late sixties. From December 1969 through to June 1982 he was Oldham's manager and he took the Latics from the Fourth Division to the Second within four years.

When he became manager at City, supporters felt he would continue the work McNeill had

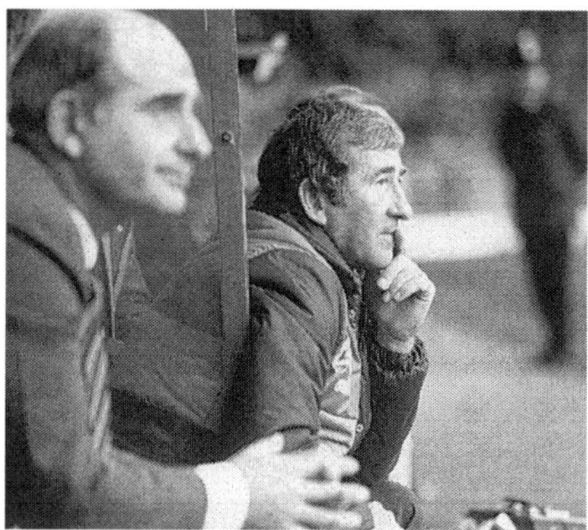

started and perhaps follow a grand plan that the two men had worked on, but Frizzell quickly made his own mark on the side. In came John Gidman, Tony Grealish and Imre Varadi to the club, almost immediately after Frizzell took office, and the exciting goalscorer Paul Stewart was signed from Blackpool shortly afterwards. Sadly, City struggled and were relegated on 39 points at the end of the season.

After relegation Frizzell was given the title of general manager, but as with McNeill in 1983 this appears to have been an attempt to help the new manager, Mel Machin, adjust to the Mancunian football scene. Frizzell remained a permanent member of staff until the mid-1990s and fulfilled a variety of roles from stadium manager to chief scout.

Mel Machin

Born: Newcastle under Lyme, 16 April 1945
May 1987 – 26 November 1989
Like Ron Saunders and John Bond before him, Mel Machin arrived at City after a productive career at Norwich. Perceived as a country bumpkin by fanzine *Blue Print* – they did a parody of his manager's notes called 'Farmer Mel' – Machin seemed the opposite of the flamboyant, high-profile style of manager many wanted. Despite this potential problem, Machin brought much joy to City and was responsible for promotion in 1989 and for several memorable results, including the 5–1 annihilation of Alex Ferguson's Manchester United in September 1989.

During his time at City he created a side that was a mixture of youth and experience. Men like Kenny Clements, Imre Varadi, and Neil McNab blended perfectly with products of the youth set up such as David White, Ian Brightwell, Andy Hinchcliffe and Paul Lake. He also signed players who went on to score memorable and important goals, including Tony Adcock and cult hero Trevor Morley.

He did, however, regularly surprise fans with bizarre team selections and formations. One player who seemed to suffer was young hero Paul Moulden: 'Remember the game at Blackburn in April when I was dropped and City lost 4–0? Mel Machin received so much abuse because he'd left me out. Naturally, I was upset we lost, but I appreciated the support I received. Then the game against Bournemouth. I'd scored twice, we were winning 3–0 and I was taken off. We ended up drawing 3–3 and everyone thought we'd blown it.'

Those games came during the 1988–89 promotion season and, although City achieved promotion on the final day, supporters had given Machin some abuse pre-match. Ironically, Machin had received criticism from supporters earlier in the season for selecting Trevor Morley, and yet Machin's belief in the player's ability was the deciding factor that gave the Blues promotion on that final day.

During the summer of 1989 he bought Ian Bishop and Clive Allen and his rapport with fans increased. The new players quickly impressed and fans were warming to Machin. Sadly, the new season in Division One saw City struggle. Seven games in the Blues were at the foot of the Division but then Machin guided his side to their greatest achievement of his reign – the 5–1 Maine Road massacre of Manchester United. That result is the one that will always be remembered as Machin's finest hour.

Sadly, Machin was dismissed by Peter Swales shortly afterwards. The Blues had been knocked out of the League Cup by Coventry and Machin was told City had to win the following League match with Charlton otherwise he would be out. Supporters travelling to the game on Supporters' Club coaches openly talked of the situation and so, when City could only manage a draw, it was clear Machin was about to leave. Swales told journalists the following Monday: 'I was forced to act quickly because I recognised the situation we had fallen into. I initially asked Mel Machin to resign. He declined – leaving me no option but to sack him.'

Swales later claimed the manager had 'no repartee' with fans. He meant rapport, but this was a rather poor excuse as, at the time, Machin was actually more popular than at any other time during his reign. Machin told journalists: 'I am surprised, disappointed and saddened by this decision. What do they want at Maine Road? If they react like this, no wonder they have remained unsuccessful for so many years.'

Machin's time at City brought some success and a few magical memories for supporters. He brought at least four influential players to the club – Trevor Morley, Ian Bishop, Clive Allen and Colin Hendry – and gave others their first chance in League football. Neil Lennon, Gerry Taggart and Michael Hughes are just three examples of players who made their debuts under Machin, although all three were to be sold by Machin's successors and went on to find success elsewhere.

Howard Kendall

Born: Ryton-on-Tyne, 22 May 1946

8 December 1989 – 5 November 1990

City fans were stunned when Mel Machin was dismissed and replaced by Howard Kendall, as rumours had circulated that Alex Ferguson was to be dismissed by United and replaced by Kendall. Some journalists suggested Swales had acted quickly to prevent the Reds from appointing a manager already known as one of Europe's most successful. Clearly, this rumour looks ridiculous today, but in 1989 it did seem perfectly plausible. In the *Manchester Evening News* immediately after Machin's dismissal City journalist Peter Gardner suggested that City would appoint Joe Royle as Howard Kendall was destined to replace the unsuccessful Alex Ferguson at United. Swales did try to bring Royle to Maine Road, but the timing was totally wrong as Swales went public on Granada TV's kick-off on the same evening that Oldham were playing at Boundary Park. Strong and passionate calls from Oldham supporters for Royle to stay caused the manager to rethink, and he publicly turned down the Maine Road

move, causing Peter Swales and the City management much embarrassment.

In the end Kendall was appointed prior to the game with Southampton on 9 December, although he played no part in selection or management for that game and left Tony Book and Ken Barnes in charge.

Kendall was the big name successful manager everyone needed to raise morale and, hopefully, he would create a side capable of challenging for the first time in a decade. Despite the excitement supporters became frustrated with his transfer activity, especially when four extremely popular players – Ian Bishop, Trevor Morley, Neil McNab and Andy Hinchcliffe – were sold and replaced by a series of former Evertonians – Alan Harper, Mark Ward, Peter Reid, Wayne Clarke and Adrian Heath. Of those recruits only Peter Reid, and to a much lesser extent Mark Ward, proved popular.

The best signing of the period came in March 1990 when Kendall bought Niall Quinn from Arsenal. Quinn's goals and all-round influence helped the Blues avoid relegation. Then, in the summer of 1990, he purchased goalkeeper Tony Coton and another ex-Evertonian, Neil Pointon, and the 1990–91 campaign started with only one defeat in the opening 11 games. By this time Kendall was a popular City manager, especially as he had turned down the chance to manage England that summer.

Sadly, just as City's future seemed bright, Kendall walked out on the club to return to his first love, Everton. Hate mail and cruel chants headed Kendall's way as supporters felt betrayed. Peter Swales was shocked and the atmosphere around Maine Road was depressing. The new Everton manager even contemplated taking Peter Reid with him to Goodison, but wisely decided against that move.

At Everton, Kendall struggled and was replaced by Mike Walker. He later managed Notts County, Sheffield United and even had a third spell at Goodison. Kendall should always be remembered as a great football manager, and a positive influence on City during 1989–90. As with McNeill in 1986, he was perhaps foolish to leave the Blues when he did as his City side probably would have evolved into a trophy-winning team.

Peter Reid

Born: Huyton, Liverpool, 20 June 1956
6 November 1990 – 26 August 1993
Almost at the insistence of supporters, Peter Reid was given the manager's job on a permanent basis following Kendall's departure. The actual appointment wasn't made permanent until after the game with Leeds on 11 November, with Reid acting as caretaker initially. Fans had grown weary of managerial changes and desperately wanted consistency, and Reid began his reign continuing the positive aspects of Kendall's tenure.

Under Reid the Blues progressed, finishing fifth in the table in consecutive seasons and making several high-profile player purchases, such as Keith Curle and Terry Phelan (for a reported £2.5 million each). Several popular players were sold, however, including Colin Hendry, Neil Pointon and Steve Redmond.

Reid kept City's momentum going for his first two seasons, but his third was more of a struggle. Nevertheless the Blues still finished ninth, although it felt as if the club had missed a great opportunity to become a dominant nineties force, especially as City were only eight points off relegation. Reid's City did reach the sixth round of the FA Cup, but a disgraceful performance was the catalyst for some supporters to invade the pitch. A 5–2 home defeat by Kendall's Everton on the final day of the League programme brought more pain.

Some suggested that the appointment of Sam Ellis as Reid's assistant had made City's style more negative and had actually reduced the opportunity of City challenging.

During the summer Reid was given an extended contract, and yet after the fourth match of the new season he was dismissed. Supporters then demonstrated against Peter Swales. The general feeling was that Swales had sacked one manager too many, and that he had obviously had doubts during the summer, yet still gave Reid a new contract. The fans kept asking 'why?'

Overall Reid's record was impressive when compared with some of his predecessors and some of those that followed. After his time at City, Reid took Sunderland to promotion to the Premier League twice, and had spells at Leeds United and Coventry City.

Brian Horton

Born: Hednesford, 4 February 1949
28 August 1993 – 16 May 1995
Brian Horton's arrival came at a difficult time, with fans demonstrating and a takeover battle about to rage between Peter Swales and Francis Lee. Nevertheless, Horton tried to focus on his role: 'I wanted to manage at City, and couldn't wait to get started. It was a perfect time in many

ways because the team had only two points from five games and were sat at the bottom of the League – I had to turn things around. That focuses your mind on the players, games, training, and results. The situation could only improve on the pitch, and whatever was happening off the pitch couldn't get in the way. The takeover hadn't started when I was given the job, so that wasn't a worry either.'

'We won the first couple of games, and then we were off. I knew I had a job to do and didn't worry. Because I'd watched games here, and knew about the club's history, I wanted to make sure we played attacking football. City has a great reputation for playing stylish and attractive football, so I wanted to encourage that. We also tried to make sure we had exciting players – Beagrie, Walshy, Uwe Rosler. I remember leaving the ground once after a game and hearing them sing 'Uwe, Uwe Rosler' down the streets ages after it finished. That was a great feeling. We also had Quinny – a great player – and then I believe my backroom staff was particularly strong.'

'We had Tony Book – I'm sure he could be still coaching somewhere today if he wanted to – David Moss, Les Chapman, Neil McNab and Colin Bell. I played with McNab at Brighton and knew his strengths and knew he was well liked here. I tried to get a good mix and because of the strong City names in there I think it was ideal.'

Horton's enthusiasm lifted some of the depression and by the end of 1993–94 he had managed to preserve City's position in the Premier League. As Francis Lee was now chairman, rumours constantly circulated suggesting Lee would eventually bring in his own manager, but Lee had told Horton to carry on and let the team's performances determine the future. Sadly, the following season saw the Blues struggle and the campaign ended with a disappointing 3–2 defeat at home to QPR. Horton was dismissed after seeing his side finish 17th. A victory on that final day would have lifted City to 12th place.

With hindsight, knowing the struggles that beset the club during the following seasons, it seems that Horton should have been given at least another season.

After City, Horton moved to Huddersfield Town, Port Vale and Macclesfield Town, and today he remains positive about his time at Maine Road: 'I loved the 20 months I was here. I loved the supporters, the players, the staff... I still live in Manchester, and I really do love this club. I'm just sorry that during my time as manager we couldn't win a trophy. We had a lot of excitement, but it would have been great to win something. Having said that we did play good, exciting football in two Premiership seasons.'

'I still get out and meet the fans. It's not always possible of course, but I always enjoy meeting them, and I'm always pleased with their reaction. I think they knew what we were trying to achieve and I think they loved the excitement of those days. I know I did.'

Alan Ball

Born: Farnworth, 12 May 1945

30 June 1995 – 26 August 1996

When Alan Ball was appointed City manager supporters were disappointed. Because of Francis Lee's own reputation as an international player and hero they felt he would be able to bring a major managerial figure to the club. Rumours of the greatest managers of the period, including George Graham and Franz Beckenbauer, circulated before Ball arrived.

Fans recognised that Ball had been a talented player who achieved success as a member of the 1966 World Cup-winning team, and as a League Championship medal-winner with Everton, but they also knew that his managerial record was not particularly inspiring. He managed Portsmouth to promotion in 1987 but they were relegated the following season. He had also endured difficult periods at Stoke City (he was dismissed in February 1991 and they ended that season in their lowest-ever position – 14th in Division Three), Exeter and Blackpool (he was dismissed after seven months after sending them hurtling towards relegation to the Fourth Division for the first time in history).

Ball's first season at City ended in relegation from the Premier League. As Peter Swales's time as chairman was marked by the number of managers he had appointed, Francis Lee was keen to ensure he at least gave his appointment time and support. That was refreshing, but Ball was simply not up to the task and the 1996–97 season commenced with supporters feeling deflated. Depressing performances and poor results brought protests from the fans. One memorable game at Stoke made the headlines because both sets of fans were chanting anti-Ball songs. It was a strange situation, but Stoke had also suffered when Ball was their leader. The game ended in a 2–1 defeat with Ball claiming: 'In terms of points we didn't come away with anything, but as the manager I got something out of the match.'

Before the next game Ball resigned, although his autobiography, *Playing Extra Time*, provides a different story to that announced at the time: 'Franny was there with secretary Bernard Halford and came straight to the point, as he always would, "Look, mate, I've got to tell you that it can't go on." I listened and some of the fight drained out of me as I told him, fine. By this time I had not really had enough but I had taken so much on my shoulders; I fielded so much flak. I had upset so many players; I had done so much of the board's dirty work that I was in danger of being bowed by worry.'

Richard Asa Hartford

(caretaker manager)

Born: Clydebank, 24 October 1950

26 August – 7 October 1996

Former player Asa Hartford was given the task of managing the Blues on a caretaker basis following Ball's departure. Anticipated to be in the role for only a couple of games, Hartford went on to guide the Blues for six League games and two League Cup matches against Third Division Lincoln City (ending in a 5–1 aggregate defeat).

Hartford did have previous experience of management at Stockport and Shrewsbury, but he was clearly not seen as City's long-term replacement. During his reign George Graham had claimed he wanted the job, then Dave Bassett accepted it but changed his mind. Meanwhile Hartford tried to focus on the role. After the appointment of Coppell, Hartford reverted to coaching roles at the club, remaining with City until 2005.

Steve Coppell

Born: Liverpool, 9 July 1955

7 October – 8 November 1996

When Steve Coppell accepted the role supporters recognised his managerial record had been better than Ball's, but inevitably some were concerned that he had made his name as a player with Manchester United. Nevertheless, his opening comments – 'I want to be here a long time' – did much to reassure fans that the Blues could now plan for the future. Sadly, Coppell lasted a month and another period of turmoil followed.

After only six matches he resigned on medical grounds. Supporters were dismayed, especially when he later returned to Crystal Palace and guided them to promotion via the play-offs.

Coppell's reign is the shortest of all City's permanent managers and he actually managed the Blues for fewer games than caretakers Asa Hartford, Phil Neal, and vice-chairman Albert Alexander senior.

Phil Neal

(caretaker manager)

Born: Irchester, 29 February 1951

8 November – 29 December 1996

The former Liverpool player had arrived at Maine Road as Steve Coppell's assistant and many neutrals felt Neal had been placed in a difficult position with Coppell's resignation. The former Bolton player-manager quickly made it clear that he wanted to stay and there was even a suggestion that he should have been given the job on a full-time basis, however it was obvious the club were still searching for a permanent replacement.

Neal managed City through 10 League games, but only two (West Bromwich Albion and Bradford City, both 3–2) ended in victory. At one point, with supporters showing dissatisfaction at performances on the pitch, Neal admitted: 'They say Steve Coppell showed courage to leave. It takes more courage to stay!'

Had results gone Neal's way then it's possible he might have been given the job full time. His last game in charge was a 2–0 defeat at Barnsley when over 6,000 fans travelled across the Pennines and, with Francis Lee in Barbados, chanted: 'I'd rather be in Barnsley than Barbados.'

Frank Clark

Born: Highfield, Gateshead, 9 September 1943
30 December 1996 – 17 February 1998
After a successful playing career with Newcastle and Nottingham Forest, Frank Clark moved into management at Leyton Orient in 1983, and in 1986 he became Orient's managing director. In June 1993 he replaced Brian Clough as Nottingham Forest manager, and stayed for three years.

His first few weeks at Maine Road were difficult, although he did start to improve performances on the pitch and make changes behind the scenes. These were not always popular – former manager Tony Book and caretaker Phil Neal were moved on, as were others with a proven Blue pedigree.

Clark's first season ended with City in their lowest-ever position at the time, yet many supporters felt it was to Clark's credit that the Blues finished that high. Had the season continued to follow the pattern set by Ball, then City would have been relegated. Sadly, Clark's improvement had only been a temporary one as the following season was one of struggle. Clark left in February 1998 claiming there was a vendetta within the club, but the truth was that City were hurtling towards relegation and something had to be done.

Clark later became more involved with the League Managers' Association and wrote his autobiography. He claimed to have been the victim of internal fighting at the club, and felt he deserved more time, but supporters believed the change should have been made a little earlier to allow his successor time to salvage the season.

Joe Royle

Born: Norris Green, Liverpool, 8 April 1949
18 February 1998 – 21 May 2001
Managing City during the 1990s and early years of the new century needed someone who understood the mechanics of the club and Mancunian life. Neither Clark, Ball nor Coppell understood what made City tick, although interestingly Brian Horton did understand. Joe Royle, Clark's replacement, was another who understood. Royle, a former City trophy-winner, had lived and breathed football in the region for most of his life and fully understood City's ambitions and role in Mancunian life.

After a successful managerial career at Oldham and Everton Royle arrived at City with the Blues at their lowest-ever point. He worked hard to try and stave off relegation, but City were relegated on the last day of the season, despite a 5–2 victory at Stoke. The generally accepted view is that had Royle's appointment come a little earlier then the Blues would have survived.

Playing in the third tier of English football for the first time, City simply had to get out of the division at the first attempt. Royle worked hard, but there were many, many problems trying to change a team that had struggled for over four consecutive seasons into one with the belief and ability to win games. Together with assistant Willie Donachie, Royle managed to turn the club's fortunes around, although they were still not the perfect side.

Promotion was achieved through the highly memorable 1999 play-off final with Gillingham, and then the momentum of Wembley enabled Royle's side to challenge in Division One. A second promotion followed, perhaps a little ahead of expectation, and Royle was able to lead the Blues into the 2000–01 season as a Premiership side. This was a major achievement, especially as it should be remembered that the City he inherited had been

on a downward spiral for a few seasons and motivation was low, while the actual size of the playing squad had been vast but not of high quality. Kinkladze had been the exception, but the Georgian was not viewed by Royle as being someone he could count on during the dark days following relegation in 1998.

Despite the resurgence under Royle, promotion in successive seasons was perhaps a step too far, and Royle's team of battlers was relegated after only one season in the top flight. Royle was dismissed at the end of the season. Contractual disagreements between the manager and club followed, but despite that negativity Royle should always be remembered as a major managerial influence on the Blues. During his reign he brought back a great deal of pride and interest, and he understood more than most what life in Manchester was all about.

Kevin Keegan, OBE

Born: Armthorpe, Doncaster, 14 February 1951
23 May 2001 – 11 March 2005
Former Liverpool, Hamburg, Southampton and Newcastle hero Kevin Keegan arrived at City after managing Newcastle, Fulham and England. Despite his pedigree, his appointment brought a mixed response from supporters and the media. Some were euphoric and considered what he had achieved in club football; others felt that putting him in charge of a club with a history of unpredictability was asking for trouble. Fortunately, Keegan's appointment brought tremendous excitement to the Blues from the start.

Clearly, Keegan's appointment reassured many that City were still a major power. Many other clubs had wanted him over the years and it was clear that Keegan, particularly after England, was only ever likely to manage a major side. Keegan came to City because he saw the potential of the move to the new stadium, and knew that, as with his time at Newcastle, Manchester fans would demonstrate their loyalty and support in a positive way.

Almost overnight Keegan transformed the Blues from the rather downbeat side relegated in 2001 into an exciting, attacking team. His side oozed talent as they charged up the Division One table with style. The title was won with the Blues equalling their record number of goals in a season (108) and creating a new record for most points in a season (99), and Keegan once again proved to his doubters in the media that he knew how to succeed.

After promotion he strengthened the Blues with several interesting signings, most notably Anelka, Schmeichel and Distin. These signings helped City establish themselves in the Premier League during Maine Road's final season as they finished ninth. The following season was a little frustrating, although Keegan did become the first manager since Tony Book to guide City into European competition. There were also a few interesting results, such as the 4–1 defeat of Ferguson's United in the first season at the new stadium. In October 2004 Keegan's Blues became

the only side to defeat eventual champions Chelsea 1–0 in the Premier League, but by the end of the season Keegan had resigned.

Many fans felt his time was nearing its end the previous season and frustration was beginning to be felt in the stands. Keegan, sensing as he did so many times in his career that it was time to move on, left the Blues in March 2005.

Overall Keegan's time at City brought great excitement. He proved to be the right man to resurrect the club and focus on the positive aspects of football when others might have chosen to grind their way to promotion and Premier League safety. Particularly between 2001 and 2003, Keegan's City entertained.

Stuart Pearce

Born: Shepherd's Bush, London, 24 April 1962
11 March 2005 –

A very popular player for several clubs including City, Stuart Pearce was a highly influential England player. As captain of the national side, Pearce gained a reputation for his commitment and determination and fans loved his never-say-die attitude.

Pearce was brought to City by Kevin Keegan to help engender the right approach on the pitch in 2001–02. He made it clear he would only play one season, but that he would be totally committed to the Blues cause. Nobody expected anything less and by the end of the season Pearce had made 38 appearances and captained the Blues to promotion as League Champions. He had developed a great rapport with fans and they were delighted when it became clear that he was to remain at the club to gain coaching experience.

Throughout 2002–03 Pearce used his influence behind the scenes and it was clear that he would ultimately turn to management at some point. It should be remembered that during 1996–97 he had been Nottingham Forest manager for a spell, although that appointment had clearly come too early in his overall development.

The media started to mention his name whenever appropriate vacancies occurred elsewhere, but in March 2005 Keegan's departure at City allowed Pearce to move into the manager's chair. Initially on a temporary basis, although the club seemed reluctant to give him the title of caretaker manager, Pearce managed City through some exciting results, and he ended the 2004–05 season with only one defeat (his first game) in nine matches. By that time his appointment had been made permanent and the 2005–06 season became his first full season. The arrival of Andy Cole and Darius Vassell added options to his selections and after three games City topped the Premier League table. Almost immediately the media started to talk of him as a potential England manager. These comments increased during January 2006 and former England star Terry Butcher claimed on Radio Five Live that Pearce should become England's manager directly after the World Cup Finals in Germany.

After the third City goal was scored in the Manchester derby of January 2006 television cameras focussed on Pearce's exuberant celebrations. He ran to the crowd and celebrated with fans, demonstrating the love he has for them and they for him.

Stuart Pearce is clearly a fans' manager. They love his attitude, commitment and humour. He seems to care passionately about the game and supporters enjoy that spirit.

1890-91

Pre-League FA Cup

Match No.	Date	Venue	Opponents	Result		Scorers	Attendance
Q1	Oct 4	H	Liverpool Stanley	W	12-0	Weir 3, Hodgetts 2, McWhinnie 2, Campbell 2, Rushton 2, Whittle	4000
Q2	22	A	Halliwell	Scratched			
							Appearances
							Goals

1891-92

Alliance League

Manager: Lawrence Furniss

Did you know that?

Ardwick finished 12th in the Alliance League.

Ardwick won the Manchester Cup for the second successive season by beating League side Bolton Wanderers 4–1 in the final.

Ardwick played a total of 30 friendly matches during 1891–92. Opposition meeting the Blues at Hyde Road included a Canadian XI international side on 12 December 1891, and established League sides Blackburn Rovers, Stoke, Sunderland, West Bromwich Albion, Bolton Wanderers, Preston North End, Notts County and Everton.

A benefit match was played against a team of internationals to raise money for captain David Weir.

Match No.	Date	Venue	Opponents	Result		Scorers	Attendance
1	Sep 12	H	BOOTLE	D	3-3	Whittle, Davies, Morris	6000
2	19	A	Lincoln City	L	0-3		2000
3	26	H	BURTON SWIFTS	W	1-0	Morris	6000
4	Oct 10	A	Newton Heath	L	1-3	Davies	4000
5	17	H	BIRM. ST. GEORGE	W	4-3	McWhinnie, Bogie 2, Morris	6000
6	Nov 7	H	WALSALL TOWN SWIFTS	W	6-0	Morris 3, Milne, Milarvie, Bogie	4500
7	14	H	NOTTM FOREST	L	1-3	Morris	11000
8	19	A	Nottingham Forest	L	0-4		2000
9	21	A	Burton Swifts	D	4-4	Bogie 3, Milarvie	2000
10	28	H	LINCOLN CITY	L	2-3	McWhinnie, Davies	12000
11	Dec 5	H	SHEFFIELD WEDNESDAY	L	0-4		6000
12	19	H	NEWTON HEATH	D	2-2	Milne 2	13000
13	25	H	GRIMSBY TOWN	W	3-1	Milarvie 2, Morris	6000
14	26	A	Sheffield Wednesday	L	0-2		12000
15	Jan 2	H	SMALL HEATH	D	2-2	Morris 2	4000
16	23	A	Bootle	L	1-2	Parry	3000
17	30	A	Grimsby Town	L	0-4		3000
18	Feb 20	A	Small Heath	L	0-4		2000
19	Mar 1	H	CREWE ALEXANDRA	W	4-0	Milne, Davies 2, Weir	5000
20	5	A	Birm. St. George	W	1-0	Milne	2000
21	26	A	Walsall Town Swifts	D	2-2	Davies, Weir	2500
22	Apr 6	A	Crewe Alexandra	D	2-2	Davies, Angus	2000
							Apps
							Goals

FA Cup

Match No.	Date	Venue	Opponents	Result		Scorers	Attendance
Q1	Oct 3		Newton Heath	L	1-5	Pearson	10000
							Apps
							Goals

Attendances

The attendances detailed within this book are in many areas significantly different from those published in earlier City reference works. This is because the figures contained here are taken primarily from those submitted as official records to the Football League. These details are taken directly from the Football League ledgers and therefore should be regarded as official and accurate. However, the League only insisted that clubs return figures from the 1925-26 season onwards, and therefore those pre-1925 are estimated based on various sources. It is also worth noting that the Football League ledgers themselves may be incorrect at times. The League attendance records have been checked and adjusted where appropriate by experts Brian Tabner and Tony Brown. They have confirmed that during production of the League records club secretaries were obliged to include season ticket holders, and (in the days when gates were shared) apportion some of the moneys they had received at the start of the season to each home game. For various reasons club officials may have reported figures differently to the media and supporters, but only the figures they have presented to the League should be regarded as accurate.

Having said that, occasionally it is clear that the figure held by the League is significantly out of character to the rest of City's attendance detail, and therefore it cannot possibly be true. Wherever doubt exists, the author has referred to as many sources as possible to identify the truth, and has assumed the figure based on the following priority order where sources disagree: Home side records submitted to the League; Home side official historians; Home side previously published material; figures quoted in reputable newspapers of the period (must be recorded in several different newspapers); Away side official historians; Away side previously published material.

Inevitably, it will always be impossible to prove some of these figures, however the attendances detailed on these pages are based on the most accurate record possible and therefore should be accepted as official MCFC figures.

Douglas W	Haydock	Robson D	Milne J	Whittle D	Simon	McWhinnie	Hodgetts	Weir	Campbell	Rushton
1	2	3	4	5	6	7	8	9	10	11
1	1	1	1	1	1	1	1	1	1	1
				1		2	2	3	2	2

Swift FV	Sproston B	Westwood E	McDowall LJ	Cardwell L	Bray J	Dunkley MEF	Herd A	Heale JA	Milsom	Doherty	Brook	Clark	Barkass	Percival	Bray	Blackshaw	Pritchard	Rudd	Wright	Walsh	Emptage	Robinson	Neilson	Smith G	Davenport	Worsley	Currier	Towsland	Burdett	McIntosh	Smith L	Tilson
1	2	9		3	4			5	6			7	8	10		11															
1	2	9		3		4		5	6			7	8	11		10															
1	2			3	10	4		5	6			7	8	9		11															
1		2		3	9	4		5	6			7		8		11					10										
1		2		3	5		4		6			7	8	10	9	11															
1		2		3	8		4	5		6		7		10	9	11															
1		2		3			4	5		6		7	8	10	9						11									
1		2		3			4	5		6		7	8	11	9	10															
1		2		3	5		4			6		7	10	8	9	11															
1		2		3	6		4			5		7	8	10	9	11															
1		2		3			4	5		6		7	8	10	9	11															
1			2	3	9		4	5		6		7		8		11	10														
1			2	3	4		6			5		7		8	9	11	10														
1			2	3	9		4	5		6		10		11		7	8														
1		4	2	3	6			5				7	10	8	9	11															
1		10	2	3	6	4		5		9		7		8			11														
1		4	2	3	6			5		9		7		8	10		11														
1		9	2		4			5			6	7		10	8	11							3									
1		8	2	3	4			5			6	7		9		10	11														
1		8	2		6						3	7	11	9		10	5							4								
1		8			6			5			4	7		10		11		3	2						9							
1		7		3	4						6	8		9		11		5	2	10												
22	3	18	9	19	18	4	10	16	5	11	5	22	11	22	11	19	7	2	2	1	1	1	1	1	1							
		2			5			1		1		7	2	10	6	4				1												

Swift FV	Sproston B	Westwood E	McDowall LJ	Cardwell L	Bray J	Dunkley MEF	Herd A	Heale JA	Milsom	Doherty	Brook	Clark	Barkass	Percival	Bray	Blackshaw	Pritchard	Rudd	Wright	Walsh	Emptage	Robinson	Neilson	Smith G	Davenport	Worsley	Currier	Towsland	Burdett	McIntosh	Smith L	Tilson
1	2			3		4		5	6			7	8	9		11										10						
1	1			1		1		1	1			1	1	1		1										1						
						1																									

League Table

	P	W	D	L	F	A	Pts
Sunderland	26	21	0	5	93	36	42
Preston N.E.	26	18	1	7	61	31	37
Bolton W	26	17	2	7	51	37	36
Aston Villa	26	15	0	11	89	56	30
Everton	26	12	4	10	49	49	28
Wolverhampton W	26	11	4	11	59	46	26
Burnley	26	11	4	11	49	45	26
Notts Co	26	11	4	11	55	51	26
Blackburn R	26	10	6	10	58	65	26
Derby Co	26	10	4	12	46	52	24
Accrington S	26	8	4	14	40	78	20
W.B.A.	26	6	6	14	51	58	18
Stoke	26	5	4	17	38	61	14
Darwen	26	4	3	19	38	112	11

1892-93

Division Two

Manager: Lawrence Furniss

Did you know that?

Match 1: Ardwick's 7–0 victory over Bootle placed them top of the first Second Division table, however the Umpire newspaper mistakenly placed them second behind Small Heath (who had won 4–1).
Match 15: Weir's last game.
Match 18: Canadian Bowman was the first overseas international to play in the Football League.

The first League game was noteworthy because Joe Davies netted the club's first League hat-trick while new captain Dave Russell took the first penalty awarded to the side. Sadly, he sent the ball straight into the hands of the Bootle 'keeper.

Match No.	Date	Venue	Opponents	Result		Scorers	Attendance
1	Sep 3	H	Bootle	W	7-0	Davies 3, Morris 2, Angus, Weir	4,000
2	10	A	Northwich Victoria	W	3-0	Russell 2, Morris	3,000
3	12	H	Burslem Port Vale	W	2-0	Angus, Weir	2,000
4	17	A	Walsall Town Swifts	W	4-2	Davies 2, Angus, Lambie	2,000
5	24	H	Northwich Victoria	D	1-1	Middleton	6,000
6	Oct 1	H	Walsall Town Swifts	W	2-0	Davies, Weir	4,000
7	8	A	Darwen	L	1-3	Davies	6,000
8	10	A	Burslem Port Vale	W	2-1	Weir 2	1,000
9	22	H	Small Heath	D	2-2	Morris, Weir	3,000
10	Nov 5	A	Grimsby Town	L	0-2		2,000
11	26	H	Burton Swifts	D	1-1	Russell	1,000
12	Dec 17	H	Darwen	W	4-2	Weir 2, Milarvie, Mooney	3,000
13	24	A	Lincoln City	L	1-2	Forrester	1,000
14	Jan 14	A	Burton Swifts	L	0-2		1,000
15	21	A	Bootle	L	3-5	Mooney 2, Middleton	800
16	30	H	Grimsby Town	L	0-3		1,000
17	Feb 4	A	Crewe Alexandra	L	1-4	Yates	1,000
18	18	H	Crewe Alexandra	W	3-1	Bowman, Milarvie, Yates	1,000
19	Mar 4	H	Sheffield United	L	2-3	Bowman, Whittle	3,000
20	25	A	Sheffield United	L	1-2	Yates	2,000
21	Apr 1	A	Small Heath	L	2-3	Carson, Yates	2,000
22	17	H	Lincoln City	W	3-1	Mooney, Morris, Yates	2,000
							Appearances
							Goals

FA Cup

PR	Sep 22	A	Fleetwood Rangers	D	1-1	Milarvie	600
rep	Oct 5	H	Fleetwood Rangers	L	0-2		2,000
							Appearances
							Goals

Douglas W	McVickers J	Robson D	Middleton H	Russell D	Hopkins W	Davies J	Morris H	Angus JW	Weir D	Milarvie R	Lambie WA	Milne J	Angus H	Forrester T	Mooney F	Yates J	Whittle D	Steele F	Turner WA	Bowman WW	Armitt GGH	Carson A	Stones H
1	2	3	4	5	6	7	8	9	10	11													
1	2	3	4	5	6	7	8	9	10	11													
1	2	3	4	5	6	7	8	9	10	11													
1	2	3	4	5	6	7	8	9		11	10												
1	2	3	4	5	6		7	9	8	11	10												
1	2	3	4	5		7	8	9	10	11		6											
1	2	3	4	5	6	7	8	9	10	11													
1	2	3	4	5	6	7	8		10	11		9											
1	2	3		5	6	7	8		10		9	4	11										
1	2	3	4	5	6	7	8		9			10	11										
1	2	3	4	5	6	7	10		9					8	11								
1	2	3	4	5	6	7	8		9	11					10								
1	2	3	4	5	6		7		9					8	10	11							
1		3	4	5	2		8		9	11		7			10		6						
1		3	4	5	2	10			7	8		11			9		6						
1		3	4	9	6					11				8	10	7	5	2					
1		3	2	5						11		4		8	10	7	6		9				
1		3	4		2		8			11		9				7	6	5		10			
1	2	3	4		6		8								10	7	5			9	11		
	2	3	4		6		8			11						7	5	9				10	1
1	2	3	4		6		8			11						7	5	9				10	
	2	3	4		6		8			11					9	7	5					10	1
20	17	22	21	17	20	12	19	7	14	17	3	8	2	4	9	8	9	4	1	2	1	3	2
			2	3		7	5	3	8	2	1			1	4	5	1			2		1	

Douglas W	McVickers J	Robson D	Middleton H	Russell D	Hopkins W	Davies J	Morris H	Angus JW	Weir D	Milarvie R	Lambie WA	Milne J	Angus H	Forrester T	Mooney F	Yates J	Whittle D	Steele F	Turner WA	Bowman WW	Armitt GGH	Carson A	Stones H
1	2	3	4	5	6	7	8	9		11										10			
1	2	3	4	5		7	8		10	11		6								9			
2	2	2	2	2	1	2	2	1	1	2		1								2			
										1													

League Table

	P	W	D	L	F	A	Pts
Small Heath	22	17	2	3	90	35	36
Sheffield United	22	16	3	3	62	19	35
Darwen	22	14	2	6	60	36	30
Grimsby Town	22	11	1	10	42	41	23
Ardwick	22	9	3	10	45	40	21
Burton Swifts	22	9	2	11	47	47	20
Northwich Victoria	22	9	2	11	42	58	20
Bootle	22	8	3	11	49	63	19
Lincoln City	22	7	3	12	45	51	17
Crewe Alexandra	22	6	3	13	42	69	15
Burslem Port Vale	22	6	3	13	30	57	15
Walsall Town Swifts	22	5	3	14	37	75	13

1893-94

Division Two

Manager: Joshua Parlby

Did you know that?

Match 8: The first own-goal scored in the club's favour.
Match 19: Alf Edge played his only game for the Blues and Billy Meredith played against City for Northwich.
Match 21: Ardwick played with only 10 men after Whittle and a reserve player missed the train.
Match 23: 10–2 remains the highest number of goals conceded by the club in the League.

On Wednesday 4 April, with two games to go, some Ardwick officials applied for a new club, Manchester City FC, to be affiliated to the Lancashire FA. On 12 April, two days before the season ended, a crowded meeting at the Hyde Road Hotel confirmed that Ardwick would become Manchester City immediately after the season ended.

Match No.	Date	Venue	Opponents	Result		Scorers	Attendance
1	Sep 2	A	Burslem Port Vale	L	2-4	Carson, Robinson	2,500
2	9	H	Middlesbro' Ironopolis	W	6-1	Morris 2, Bowman, Carson, Jones, Robinson	4,000
3	11	H	Burton Swifts	L	1-4	Morris	1,000
4	16	H	Liverpool	L	0-1		4,000
5	20	A	Burton Swifts	L	0-5		3,000
6	23	A	Middlesbro' Ironopolis	L	0-2		800
7	30	H	Small Heath	L	0-1		3,000
8	Oct 7	H	Burslem Port Vale	W	8-1	Morris 3, Middleton, Milarvie, Steele, Yates, og	4,000
9	21	H	Newcastle United	L	2-3	Morris, Yates	3,000
10	28	H	Notts County	D	0-0		4,000
11	Nov 11	A	Woolwich Arsenal	L	0-1		3,000
12	18	H	Walsall Town Swifts	W	3-0	Yates 2, Robertson	3,000
13	Dec 2	A	Liverpool	L	0-3		4,000
14	9	H	Grimsby Town	W	4-1	Bennett, Davies, Middleton, Whittle	4,000
15	26	H	Rotherham Town	W	3-2	Pickford 2, Bennett	4,000
16	30	H	Woolwich Arsenal	L	0-1		3,000
17	Jan 6	A	Newcastle United	L	1-2	Pickford	1,000
18	13	A	Grimsby Town	L	0-5		1,000
19	27	H	Northwich Victoria	W	4-2	Bennett 2, Dyer, Whittle	2,000
20	Feb 10	A	Northwich Victoria	W	4-1	Milarvie 2, Milne, Robertson	2,000
21	24	A	Crewe Alexandra	D	1-1	Bennett	1,000
22	Mar 15	A	Notts County	L	0-5		2,500
23	17	A	Small Heath	L	2-10	Bennett, Robertson	2,000
24	24	A	Lincoln City	L	0-6		1,000
25	26	A	Rotherham Town	W	3-1	Baker, Milarvie, Milne	2,000
26	31	H	Lincoln City	L	0-1		3,000
27	Apr 7	H	Crewe Alexandra	L	1-2	Spittle	2,500
28	14	A	Walsall Town Swifts	L	2-5	Forrester, Milne	1,700

Game 21 played with 10 men

Appearances

Goals

FA Cup

Match No.	Date	Venue	Opponents	Result		Scorers	Attendance
Q1	Oct 14	A	West Manchester	L	0-3		6,000

Appearances

Douglas W	Dyer F	Robson D	Middleton H	Bowman WW	Hopkins W	Yates J	Morris H	Carson A	Robinson RB	Milarvie R	Jones A	Steele F	Whittle D	Regan EJ	Saddington H	Forrester T	Pickford E	McVickers J	O'Brien J	Caine J	Bennett A	Davies J	Stones H	Robertson D	Baker J	Egan TW	Hargreaves J	Milne J	Willey W	Edge A	Stenson J	McDowell A	Hughes J	Spittle A
1	2	3	4	5	6	7	8	9	10	11																								
1	2	3	4	5	6	7	9	11	10		8																							
1	2	3	4	5	6	7	9	11	10		8																							
1		3	4	8		7		9	11			2	5	6	10																			
1	6	3	4	9		7		10		11		2	5			8																		
1	4	3		8		7		9		11		2	5	6					10															
1		3	4	6		7	9					2	5		11		8		10															
1	4	3	8			7	10			11		9	5	6				2																
1	6	3		10		7	8			11			5	9				2		4														
1		3	4	9		7	8			11			5	6				2			10													
1		3	4			7	8			11		9	5	6				2				10												
		3	4			7	8			11			5	6				2				10	1	9										
1		3	4							11			5	6	7		8	2				10				9								
1		3	4							11			5	6			7	2			8	10				9								
	10	3	4									1	5	6			7	2			8					9	11							
1	10	3	4							11			5	6			7	2			8					9								
1	2	3	4	5						11				6			7				8			9		10								
1	3			2						11			5	4			7				8					10		6	9					
	3			4						11		2	5	6			7				8		1			9				10				
	3			4						10		2	5	6							7		1	9			11	8						
	3			4						10		2		6							7		1	9			11	5						
	3			5						10		2		6	4	9					7		1				11	8						
	3			4								2	5	6	11						7		1	9			10	8						
	3			4						8			5	6	11	9							1				10	7			2			
	3			5						10				6		9							1	7	4		11	8				2		
	4			5						10			9	3		7							1		6			8				2	11	
	3			4						10			5										1	9	6			7				2	11	8
	3			4						10		1	5			9					7						11	8			6	2		
16	21	17	15	21	3	12	9	6	4	22	2	13	21	21	6	6	8	9		1	12	4	10	7	3	7	8	10	1	1	2	4	2	1
	1		2	1		4	7	2	2	4	1	1	2			1	3				6	1		3	1			3						1

Douglas W	Dyer F	Robson D	Middleton H	Bowman WW	Hopkins W	Yates J	Morris H	Carson A	Robinson RB	Milarvie R	Jones A	Steele F	Whittle D	Regan EJ	Saddington H	Forrester T	Pickford E	McVickers J	O'Brien J	Caine J	Bennett A	Davies J	Stones H	Robertson D	Baker J	Egan TW	Hargreaves J	Milne J	Willey W	Edge A	Stenson J	McDowell A	Hughes J	Spittle A
1	4	3	8			7	10			11		9	5	6				2																
1	1	1	1			1	1			1		1	1	1				1																

League Table

	P	W	D	L	F	A	Pts
Liverpool	28	22	6	0	77	18	50
Small Heath	28	21	0	7	103	44	42
Notts County	28	18	3	7	70	31	39
Newcastle United	28	15	6	7	66	39	36
Grimsby Town	28	15	2	11	71	58	32
Burton Swifts	28	14	3	11	79	61	31
Burslem Port Vale	28	13	4	11	66	64	30
Lincoln City	28	11	6	11	59	58	28
Woolwich Arsenal	28	12	4	12	52	55	28
Walsall Town Swifts	28	10	3	15	51	61	23
Middlesbro' Ironopolis	28	8	4	16	37	72	20
Crewe Alexandra	28	6	7	15	42	73	19
Ardwick	28	8	2	18	47	71	18
Rotherham Town	28	6	3	19	44	91	15
Northwich Victoria	28	3	3	22	30	98	9

1894-95

Division Two

Manager: Joshua Parlby

Did you know that?

Match 13: The first Manchester League derby and Meredith's first home game for City.
Match 25: City's record score in the League.

City failed to enter the FA Cup. It is believed this was simply an oversight.

Match No.	Date	Venue	Opponents	Result		Scorers	Attendance
1	Sep 1	A	Bury	L	2-4	Calvey, Little	8,000
2	3	H	Burton Wanderers	D	1-1	Little	2,500
3	8	H	Burslem Port Vale	W	4-1	Calvey 2, Finnerhan, Mann	3,000
4	15	A	Walsall Town Swifts	W	2-1	Finnerhan, Rowan	3,000
5	22	H	Grimsby Town	L	2-5	Little, Wallace	4,000
6	29	A	Woolwich Arsenal	L	2-4	Dyer, Rowan	5,000
7	Oct 1	A	Rotherham Town	L	2-3	Calvey 2	1,500
8	6	H	Walsall Town Swifts	W	6-1	Sharples 3, Finnerhan, Nash, Rowan	3,000
9	13	A	Notts County	W	3-1	Finnerhan, Rowan, Sharples	3,000
10	20	H	Darwen	L	2-4	Sharples, Tompkinson	6,000
11	27	A	Newcastle United	L	4-5	Sharples 2, Finnerhan, McReddie	2,000
12	Nov 3	H	Newton Heath	L	2-5	Meredith 2	6,000
13	10	A	Burton Swifts	L	1-2	Finnerhan	2,000
14	Dec 8	H	Bury	D	3-3	McReddie, Milarvie, Rowan	10,000
15	15	H	Woolwich Arsenal	W	4-1	Meredith 2, McBride, og	5,000
16	26	A	Burton Wanderers	L	0-8		2,000
17	31	A	Crewe Alexandra	W	3-2	Meredith 2, Finnerhan	450
18	Jan 1	H	Rotherham Town	W	1-0	Rowan	4,000
19	5	A	Newton Heath	L	1-4	Sharples	10,000
20	Feb 2	A	Burslem Port Vale	W	2-1	Finnerhan, McReddie	500
21	9	H	Newcastle United	W	4-0	Finnerhan 2, Meredith, Rowan	3,500
22	Mar 2	A	Lincoln City	W	2-0	Rowan 2	2,000
23	9	H	Notts County	W	7-1	Finnerhan 2, McReddie, Meredith, Rowan, Sharples, Walker	7,000
24	16	A	Leicester Fosse	L	1-3	Sharples	5,000
25	23	H	Lincoln City	W	11-3	McReddie 4, Finnerhan 2, Meredith 2, Rowan 2, Milarvie	2,000
26	30	H	Leicester Fosse	D	1-1	McReddie	3,000
27	Apr 6	A	Darwen	L	0-4		3,000
28	12	H	Crewe Alexandra	W	4-1	Dyer, Finnerhan, Meredith, Sharples	4,000
29	13	H	Burton Swifts	W	4-1	Mann, Meredith, Sharples, og	5,000
30	20	A	Grimsby Town	L	1-2	Milarvie	2,000
							Appearances
						Two own goals	Goals

FA Cup

Did not enter

Williams CA	Smith HE	Dyer F	Mann GW	Jones RS	Nash J	Wallace A	Finnerhan P	Calvey M	Sharples J	Little T	Rowan A	Ferguson A	Bowman WW	Milarvie R	Hutchinson GW	Tompkinson H	Walker J	McReddie W	Meredith WH	McBride J	Robson D
1	2	3	4	5	6	7	8	9	10	11											
1	2	3	4	5	6	7	8	9	10	11											
1	2	3	4	5	6	10	8	9		11	7										
1	2		4	5	6	10	8	7		11	9	3									
1				5	6	10	8	2		11	9	3	4	7							
	2	3	4	5	6		8	7	10	11	9				1						
		2	4	5	3	10	8	7	6	11	9				1						
	2	3	4	5	6		8		10		9			11	1	7					
	2		4	5	6		8		10		9				1	7	3	11			
	2		4		6		8		10		9		5		1	7	3	11			
	2	6	4		5		8		10		9				1		3	11	7		
	2	6	4		5		8		10		9			11	1		3		7		
1		3	4		6		8		10		5			11		7	2		9		
1	4			5			8				9			11			2	10	7	6	3
1	4			5			8		11		9						2	10	7	6	3
1				5	4		8		11		9						2	10	7	6	3
1	4			5			8		11		9						2	10	7	6	3
1	4			5			8		11		9						2	10	7	6	3
1	4			5			8		11		9						2	10	7	6	3
1			6	5			8		11		9					7	2	10		4	3
1	4			5			8		11		9						2	10	7	6	3
1			4	5			8		11		9						2	10	7	6	3
1	4						8		11		9		5				2	10	7	6	3
1	4						8		11		9		5			7	2	10		6	3
1					4		8				9		5	11			2	10	7	6	3
1			9		4		8						5	11			2	10	7	6	3
1					4		8		10				5	11			2	9	7	6	3
1		2	4				8		10		9		5					11	7	6	3
1		2	4				8		10				5	9				11	7	6	3
1		2	4				8		10				5	9				11	7	6	3
23	18	12	18	18	17	6	30	7	24	7	24	2	10	10	7	6	19	20	18	17	17
		2	2		1	1	15	5	12	3	12			3		1	1	9	12	1	

League Table

	P	W	D	L	F	A	Pts
Bury	30	23	2	5	78	33	48
Notts Co	30	17	5	8	75	45	39
Newton Heath	30	15	8	7	78	44	38
Leicester C	30	15	8	7	72	53	38
Grimsby T	30	18	1	11	79	52	37
Darwen	30	16	4	10	74	43	36
Burton W	30	14	7	9	67	39	35
Woolwich A	30	14	6	10	75	58	34
Manchester C	30	14	3	13	82	72	31
Newcastle U	30	12	3	15	72	84	27
Burton S	30	11	3	16	52	74	25
Rotherham U	30	11	2	17	55	62	24
Lincoln C	30	10	0	20	52	92	20
Walsall	30	10	0	20	47	92	20
Burslem P.V.	30	7	4	19	39	77	18
Crewe A	30	3	4	23	26	103	10

1895-96

Division Two

Manager: Sam Ormerod

Did you know that?

Match 15: The takings for the Hyde Road derby came to a club record £410.
Match 23: Maley made his only League appearance.
Match 28: Had City defeated Liverpool the Blues would have won the Second Division title. The game was Liverpool's last of the season, and the Merseyside club won the title on goal average.

Promotion was determined by a series of Test Matches, similar to modern day play-offs. The two leading sides in Division Two would compete against both the two bottom sides in Division One on a home and away basis. The two sides with the best results from their four games would play the following season in Division One. City alienated their supporters by putting prices up for the first home game, and fans stayed away as a protest.

Willie Maley, who appeared in match 23, was a founder member of Celtic and went on to become a great manager at the Scottish club. He had first appeared for Ardwick in 1890 and his game in 1896 was part of what could be described as a busman's holiday. He also played for Everton during this season.

Match No.	Date	Venue	Opponents	Result		Scorers	Attendance
1	Sep 7	A	Woolwich Arsenal	W	1-0	Meredith	6,000
2	9	H	Rotherham Town	W	2-0	Clifford, Little	3,000
3	14	H	Leicester Fosse	W	2-0	Finnerhan, Rowan	9,000
4	21	A	Grimsby Town	L	0-5		3,000
5	28	H	Woolwich Arsenal	W	1-0	Sharples	8,000
6	Oct 5	A	Newton Heath	D	1-1	Rowan	11,000
7	12	H	Darwen	W	4-1	Rowan 2, Chapman, Sharples	9,000
8	19	A	Crewe Alexandra	W	2-0	Finnerhan, Meredith	2,000
9	26	H	Grimsby Town	W	2-1	Little, Rowan	14,000
10	Nov 2	A	Darwen	W	3-2	Finnerhan, McReddie, Meredith	4,000
11	4	A	Rotherham Town	W	3-2	McReddie 2, Rowan	5,000
12	16	A	Burton Wanderers	L	1-4	Meredith	3,000
13	23	H	Burton Wanderers	D	1-1	Meredith	10,000
14	30	A	Burton Swifts	W	4-1	Morris 2, Rowan 2	3,000
15	Dec 7	H	Newton Heath	W	2-1	Hill, Meredith	17,500
16	Jan 1	A	Liverpool	L	1-3	Rowan	20,000
17	4	H	Newcastle United	W	5-2	Hill 2, Morris 2, Finnerhan	10,000
18	11	A	Lincoln City	W	2-1	Chapman, Meredith	2,000
19	Feb 1	A	Loughborough	W	4-2	Finnerhan 2, Davies, Hill	1,500
20	10	A	Burslem Port Vale	W	1-0	Davies	3,000
21	15	H	Crewe Alexandra	W	4-0	Rowan 2, Finnerhan, Meredith	5,000
22	17	H	Burslem Port Vale	W	1-0	Finnerhan	3,000
23	24	H	Loughborough	W	5-1	Morris 2, Chapman, Davies, Meredith	2,000
24	29	A	Notts County	L	0-3		3,000
25	Mar 7	H	Burton Swifts	D	1-1	Robertson	6,000
26	14	H	Lincoln City	W	4-0	Finnerhan, Meredith, Morris, Robertson	8,000
27	21	A	Newcastle United	L	1-4	Davies	12,000
28	Apr 3	H	Liverpool	D	1-1	Morris	25,000
29	4	A	Leicester Fosse	W	2-1	Meredith, Robson	5,000
30	8	H	Notts County	W	2-0	Meredith, Morris	6,000
							Appearances
							Goals

FA Cup

Withdrew

Test Matches

Date	Venue	Opponents	Result		Scorers	Attendance
Apr 18	H	West Bromwich Albion	D	1-1	Rowan	6,000
20	A	West Bromwich Albion	L	1-6	McBride	8,000
25	H	Small Heath	W	3-0	Davies, Meredith, Rowan	9,500
27	A	Small Heath	L	0-8		2,000
						Appearances
						Goals

Williams CA	Harper J	Robson D	Clifford H	Chapman T	McBride J	Meredith WH	Finnerhan P	Rowan A	McReddie W	Little T	Mann GW	Sharples J	Moffatt R	Hill R	Morris H	Dyer F	Read TH	Davies J	Bowman WW	Ditchfield JC	Espie J	Gillies A	Maley W	McCabe A	Milarvie R	Millar J	Porteous TS	Robertson J
1	2	3	4	5	6	7	8	9	10	11																		
1	2	3	6		5	7	8	9	10	11	4																	
1	2	3	4	5	6	7	8	9	11	10																		
1	2	3	4	5	6	7	8	9	11	10																		
1	2	3		5	6	7	8		11	9	4	10																
1	2	3		5	6	7	8	9	10		4	11																
1	2	3		5	6	7	8	9	10		4	11																
1	2	3		5		7	8	9		10	4	11	6															
1	2	3		5	6	7	8	9		10	4	11																
1	2	3		5	6	7	8	9	11	10	4																	
1	2	3		5	6	7	8	9	11	10	4																	
1	2	3		5	6	7	8		10		4			9	11													
1		3		5	6	7	8	9	11		4			10		2												
1	2	3		5	6	7	8	9			4			11	10													
1		3		5	6	7	8	9			4			11	10		2											
1	2	3		5	6	7	8	9			4			10	11													
1	2	3		5		7	8				4		6	9	11			10										
1	2	3		5		7	8				4			9	11			10	6									
1	2	3		5		7	8				4			9	11			10	6									
1		3		5	6	7	8	9			4				11			10									2	
1		3			6	7	8	9			4				11			10	5								2	
1		3		5	6	7	8	9			4				11			10									2	
1		3		5		7	8	9			4				11			10					6				2	
1		3		5	6		8	9										7	4					11	10		2	
1	2	3		5	6	7	8								11			10			4							9
1	2	3		5	6	7	8								11				4			10						9
1	2	3			6	7	8								11			10	5							4		9
1		3		5	6	7	8				4			9	10					2		11						
1		3		5	6	7	8	9			10								4	2		11						
1	2	3			6	7	8	9			4				10			11								5		
30	21	30	4	26	25	29	30	21	11	9	23	5	2	9	16	1	1	11	7	2	1	3	1	1	1	2	5	3
		1	1	3		12	9	11	3	2		2		4	9			4										2

Williams CA	Harper J	Robson D	Clifford H	Chapman T	McBride J	Meredith WH	Finnerhan P	Rowan A	McReddie W	Little T	Mann GW	Sharples J	Moffatt R	Hill R	Morris H	Dyer F	Read TH	Davies J	Bowman WW	Ditchfield JC	Espie J	Gillies A	Maley W	McCabe A	Milarvie R	Millar J	Porteous TS	Robertson J
1		3		5	6	7	8	9			4				11					2		10						
1	2	3		5	6	7	8				4			9	11							10						
1		3			6	7	8	9			4				11			10		2						5		
1		3			6	7	8	9			4				11			10		2						5		
4	1	4		2	4	4	4	3			4			1	4			2		3		2				2		
					1	1		2										1										

League Table

	P	W	D	L	F	A	Pts
Liverpool	30	22	2	6	106	32	46
Manchester C	30	21	4	5	63	38	46
Grimsby T	30	20	2	8	82	38	42
Burton W	30	19	4	7	69	40	42
Newcastle U	30	16	2	12	73	50	34
Newton Heath	30	15	3	12	66	57	33
Woolwich A	30	14	4	12	59	42	32
Leicester C	30	14	4	12	57	44	32
Darwen	30	12	6	12	72	67	30
Notts Co	30	12	2	16	57	54	26
Burton S	30	10	4	16	39	69	24
Loughborough T	30	9	5	16	40	67	23
Lincoln C	30	9	4	17	53	75	22
Burslem P.V.	30	7	4	19	43	78	18
Rotherham U	30	7	3	20	34	97	17
Crewe A	30	5	3	22	30	95	13

1896-97

Division Two

Manager: Sam Ormerod

Did you know that?

Match 1: Patterson's last game.
Match 6: Townley's last game.
Match 10: Ditchfield's last game.
Match 12: Tait scores his only goals for the club and McConnell plays his last game.
Match 13: Tait's last game.
Match 30: Mann, McBride, Hill and Gunn all play in their last game.

Billy Gillespie scored on his debut (v Darwen on 9 January 1897) and went on to become one of the club's leading cult heroes. Meredith was idolised for his skill, Gillespie for his rapport with ordinary supporters.

P W D L F A Pts

Match No.	Date	Venue	Opponents	Result		Scorers	Attendance
1	Sep 5	H	Woolwich Arsenal	D	1-1	Finnerhan	8,000
2	12	A	Gainsborough Trin.	D	1-1	Sharples	2,500
3	19	H	Darwen	W	4-1	Mann 2, Ditchfield, Lewis	8,000
4	21	H	Lincoln City	W	3-0	Finnerhan, Lewis, Sharples	3,000
5	26	A	Blackpool	D	2-2	Hill, Mann	4,000
6	Oct 3	H	Newton Heath	D	0-0		20,000
7	10	A	Notts County	D	3-3	Hill, Meredith, Robinson	5,000
8	17	H	Newcastle United	L	1-2	Robinson	8,000
9	24	A	Grimsby Town	L	1-3	Sharples	4,000
10	31	H	Notts County	L	1-4	Meredith	8,000
11	Nov 7	H	Blackpool	W	4-2	Bannister, Lewis, Meredith, Sharples	6,000
12	14	H	Burton Swifts	W	3-1	Tait 2, Gunn	4,000
13	23	A	Walsall	L	2-3	Finnerhan, Mann	3,000
14	28	H	Burton Wanderers	W	2-1	Gunn, Williams	2,000
15	Dec 19	H	Grimsby Town	W	3-1	Gunn, Meredith, Williams	10,000
16	25	A	Newton Heath	L	1-2	Hill	18,000
17	26	A	Burton Swifts	L	0-5		6,000
18	Jan 1	H	Small Heath	W	3-0	Bannister, Gunn, Sharples	16,000
19	6	H	Walsall	W	5-0	Lewis, Mann, Meredith, Ray, Sharples	1,000
20	9	A	Darwen	L	1-3	Gillespie	1,000
21	Feb 6	A	Newcastle United	L	0-3		9,000
22	13	A	Lincoln City	W	1-0	Gillespie	1,700
23	27	H	Gainsborough Trin.	W	4-1	Williams 2, Gillespie, Meredith	7,000
24	Mar 6	A	Burton Wanderers	D	1-1	Read	3,000
25	13	H	Leicester Fosse	W	4-0	Gillespie, Holmes, Meredith, Williams	5,000
26	17	A	Loughborough	L	0-2		1,000
27	Apr 12	A	Leicester Fosse	D	3-3	Meredith 2, og	1,000
28	16	H	Loughborough	D	1-1	Foster	2,000
29	19	A	Small Heath	L	1-3	Meredith	600
30	28	A	Woolwich Arsenal	W	2-1	Hill 2	2,000
							Appearances
						One own goal	Goals

FA Cup

R1	Jan 30	A	Preston North End	L	0-6		6,000
							Appearances

Williams CA	Ditchfield JC	Ray R	Tait D	Bannister C	McBride J	Meredith WH	Finnerhan P	Hill R	Patterson W	Townley WJ	Mann GW	Bowman WW	Platt JW	Sharples J	Lewis W	Foster HA	Robinson LG	Holmes WM	Gunn J	Harper J	McConnell T	Moffatt R	Tonge J	Gillespie WJ	Read TH	Hesham FJ	Williams F
1	2	3	4	5	6	7	8	9	10	11																	
1	2	3			6	7	8			11	4	5	9	10													
1	2	3		5	6	7	8				4			10	9	11											
1	2	3		5	6	7	8				4			10	9	11											
1	2	3		5	6	7	8	9			4				10	11											
1	2	3		5	6	7	8	9		11	4				10												
1	2	3		5	6	7	8	10			4				9		11										
1	2	3		5	6	7	8	10			4				9		11										
1	2	3		5	6	7	9				4			8	10		11										
1	2	3			6	7	8	9			4				11			5	10								
1		3	4	5	6	7								8	9				10	2	11						
1		3	4	5	6	7								8	9				10	2	11						
1		3	4	5	6	7	8				9			11					10	2							
1		3		5		7	8	9			4							6	10	2							11
1		3		5	6	7	8	9			4								10	2							11
1		3		5	6	7	8	9			4								10	2							11
1		3		5	6	7	8	9			4			11					10	2							
1		3		5	6	7	8				4			11	9				10	2							
1		3		5	6	7	8				4			11	9				10	2							
1		3		5			8				4								11	2		6	7	9			10
1		3			6													5	10			4	7	9	2	8	11
1		3			6	7	8											5	10			4		9	2		11
1		3			6	7	8											5	10			4		9	2		11
1		3			6		8											5	10			4		9	2	7	11
1		3			6	7	8											5	10			4		9	2		11
1		3			6	7	8											5	10			4		9	2		11
1		3			6	7	8											5	10			4		9	2		11
1		3			6	7	8									11		5	10			4		9	2		
1		3			6	7		8				4				11		5	10			2		9			
1		2			6	7		8			4					11		5	10			3		9			
30	10	30	4	18	28	27	25	12	1	3	18	2	1	10	12	6	3	12	21	10	2	11	2	11	8	2	11
	1	1	2	2		10	3	5			5			6	4	1	2	1	4					4	1		5

Williams CA	Ditchfield JC	Ray R	Tait D	Bannister C	McBride J	Meredith WH	Finnerhan P	Hill R	Patterson W	Townley WJ	Mann GW	Bowman WW	Platt JW	Sharples J	Lewis W	Foster HA	Robinson LG	Holmes WM	Gunn J	Harper J	McConnell T	Moffatt R	Tonge J	Gillespie WJ	Read TH	Hesham FJ	Williams F
1		3			6	7					4			8	9	11		5	10	2							
1		1			1	1					1			1	1	1		1	1	1							

League Table

	P	W	D	L	F	A	Pts
Notts Co	30	19	4	7	92	43	42
Newton Heath	30	17	5	8	56	34	39
Grimsby T	30	17	4	9	66	45	38
Small Heath	30	16	5	9	69	47	37
Newcastle U	30	17	1	12	56	52	35
Manchester C	30	12	8	10	58	50	32
Gainsborough T	30	12	7	11	50	47	31
Blackpool	30	13	5	12	59	56	31
Leicester C	30	13	4	13	59	56	30
Woolwich A	30	13	4	13	68	70	30
Darwen	30	14	0	16	67	61	28
Walsall	30	11	4	15	53	69	26
Loughborough T	30	12	1	17	50	64	25
Burton S	30	9	6	15	46	61	24
Burton W	30	9	2	19	31	67	20
Lincoln C	30	5	2	23	27	85	12

1897-98

Division Two

Manager: Sam Ormerod

Did you know that?

Match 8: The record Newton Heath crowd at the time.
Match 18: Clare, Munn and Dougal all make debuts, but Clare never plays again.
Match 26: By scoring his 16th League goal of the season, Gillespie became City's record scorer for a season.

City signed two players with the name William Smith and both made their debuts in the first game of the season. To avoid confusion officials nicknamed them after the towns they were from – so one became Buxton Smith and the other Stockport.

Match No.	Date	Venue	Opponents	Result		Scorers	Attendance
1	Sep 1	H	Gainsborough Trin.	W	3-0	Gillespie, Meredith, Williams	2,000
2	4	A	Darwen	W	4-2	Smith(S) 2, Leonard, Gillespie	1,000
3	11	H	Loughborough	W	3-0	Smith(S) 2, Gillespie	8,000
4	18	A	Blackpool	W	2-0	Smith(S), Williams	3,000
5	25	H	Woolwich Arsenal	W	4-1	Smith(S) 3, Williams	10,000
6	Oct 2	A	Loughborough	W	3-0	Williams 2, Gillespie	5,000
7	9	H	Grimsby Town	W	3-0	Gillespie, Meredith, Smith(B)	12,000
8	16	A	Newton Heath	D	1-1	Ray	20,000
9	23	H	Darwen	W	5-0	Gillespie 2, Williams 2, Whitehead	8,000
10	30	A	Burnley	L	1-3	og	10,000
11	Nov 20	H	Burnley	D	1-1	Gillespie	12,000
12	Dec 11	H	Leicester Fosse	W	2-1	Gillespie, Meredith	7,000
13	18	A	Grimsby Town	W	4-3	Leonard 2, Gillespie, Meredith	4,000
14	25	H	Newton Heath	L	0-1		23,000
15	27	A	Small Heath	W	1-0	Leonard	11,000
16	Jan 1	A	Luton Town	L	0-3		4,000
17	3	H	Walsall	W	3-2	Gillespie 2, Meredith	4,000
18	8	H	Newcastle United	D	1-1	Whitehead	15,000
19	15	A	Walsall	D	2-2	Gillespie, Smith(S)	4,000
20	24	H	Lincoln City	W	3-1	Gillespie, Meredith, og	2,000
21	Feb 5	A	Woolwich Arsenal	D	2-2	Gillespie, Holmes	12,000
22	26	A	Gainsborough Trin.	L	0-1		3,000
23	Mar 16	A	Newcastle United	L	0-2		17,000
24	19	A	Lincoln City	L	1-2	Dougal	3,000
25	26	H	Luton Town	W	2-1	Meredith 2	5,000
26	30	H	Blackpool	D	3-3	Dougal, Gillespie, Smith(S)	4,000
27	Apr 2	A	Leicester Fosse	D	0-0		6,000
28	9	A	Burton Swifts	D	0-0		3,000
29	11	H	Small Heath	D	3-3	Gillespie, Meredith, Smith(B)	2,000
30	16	H	Burton Swifts	W	9-0	Meredith 3, Whitehead 3, Smith(S) 2, Gillespie	5,000
							Appearances
						Two own goals	Goals

FA Cup

Round	Date	Venue	Opponents	Result		Scorers	Attendance
R1	Jan 29	H	Wigan County	W	1-0	Gillespie	6,000
R2	Feb 12	A	Bolton Wanderers	L	0-1		14,000
							Appearances
							Goals

The two Walter Smiths were identified as "Stockport" and "Buxton"

Williams CA	Read TH	Ray R	Moffatt R	Smith W(B)	Holmes WM	Meredith WH	Smith W(S)	Gillespie WJ	Williams F	Leonard P	Harper J	Whitehead JW	Chappell T	Wilson J	Dyer F	Foster HA	Clare T	Munn S	Dougal G	Bowman WW
1	2	3	4	5	6	7	8	9	10	11										
1	2	3	4	5	6	7	8	9	10	11										
1	2	3	4	5	6	7	8	9	10	11										
1	2	3	4	5	6	7	8	9	10	11										
1	2		4	5	6	7	8	9	10	11	3									
1	2	3	4	5	6	7	8	9	10	11										
1	2	3	4	5	6	7	8	9	10	11										
1	2	3	4	5	6	7	8	9	10	11										
1	2	3	4	5	6	7	8	9	10			11								
1	2	3	4	5	6	7	8	9	10	11										
1	2	3	4	5	6	7	8	9	11			10								
	2	3	4	5	6	7		9	11	10		8	1							
	2	3	4	5	6	7		9	11	10		8	1							
1	2	3	4	5	6	7		9	10	11		8								
1	2	3	4	5	6	7		9	10	11		8								
1		3	4	5	6	7		9	10	11	2	8								
1		3	4	5	6	7		9	10	11		8		2						
1	2	3	4	5	6	7	11	9	10			8								
1	2	3	4	5	6	7	10	9	11			8								
1	2	3	4	5	6	7	10	9	11			8								
1	2		4	5	6	7	10	9	11			8			3					
1		3	4	5	6	7	8	9	10						2	11				
1	2		4	5		7	10	9				8					3	6	11	
1	3		2	5	6	7	8	9				11						4	10	
1	3		2		6	7	8	9				10						4	11	5
	3		2		6	7	8	9				10	1					4	11	5
	3		2	5	6	7	8	9				10	1					4	11	
	3		2	5	6	7	8	9				10	1					4	11	
	3		2	5	6	7	8	9				10	1					4	11	
	3		2	5	6	7	8	9				10	1					4	11	
23	27	20	30	28	29	30	24	30	22	15	2	20	7	1	2	1	1	8	8	2
		1		2	1	12	12	18	7	4		5							2	

Williams CA	Read TH	Ray R	Moffatt R	Smith W(B)	Holmes WM	Meredith WH	Smith W(S)	Gillespie WJ	Williams F	Leonard P	Harper J	Whitehead JW
1	2	3	4	5	6	7	10	9	11			8
1	2	3	4	5	6	7	10	9		11		8
2	2	2	2	2	2	2	2	2	1	1		2
								1				

League Table

	P	W	D	L	F	A	Pts
Burnley	30	20	8	2	80	24	48
Newcastle U	30	21	3	6	64	32	45
Manchester C	30	15	9	6	66	36	39
Newton Heath	30	16	6	8	64	35	38
Woolwich A	30	16	5	9	69	49	37
Small Heath	30	16	4	10	58	50	36
Leicester C	30	13	7	10	46	35	33
Luton T	30	13	4	13	68	50	30
Gainsborough T	30	12	6	12	50	54	30
Walsall	30	12	5	13	58	58	29
Blackpool	30	10	5	15	49	61	25
Grimsby T	30	10	4	16	52	62	24
Burton S	30	8	5	17	38	69	21
Lincoln C	30	6	5	19	43	82	17
Darwen	30	6	2	22	31	76	14
Loughborough T	30	6	2	22	24	87	14

1898-99

Division Two

Manager: Sam Ormerod

Did you know that?

Match 24: Meredith becomes first City player to score 20 League goals in a season.

Match 26: Ross, a former Preston player and major star, made his debut.

Match 32: This victory guaranteed the title as the Blues went five points clear of nearest rivals Glossop.

Match 34: Both linesmen were consulted before the referee awarded City their third goal (Meredith's first of the game).

City's promotion in 1899 was the first national success of either Manchester side. It was the first time a Mancunian team had been promoted, and it was the first season of automatic promotion after the Test Matches had been dropped due to allegations of match fixing in previous seasons.

Match No.	Date	Venue	Opponents	Result		Scorers	Attendance
1	Sep 3	H	Grimsby Town	W	7-2	Gillespie 3, Meredith 3, Whitehead	5,000
2	10	A	Newton Heath	L	0-3		20,000
3	17	H	New Brighton Tower	D	1-1	Cowie	6,000
4	24	A	Lincoln City	L	1-3	Whitehead	2,000
5	Oct 1	H	Woolwich Arsenal	W	3-1	Dougal, Read, Smith(S)	8,000
6	8	A	Luton Town	W	3-0	Cowie, Meredith, Smith(S)	3,000
7	15	H	Leicester Fosse	W	3-1	Gillespie, Meredith, Smith(S)	9,000
8	22	A	Darwen	W	2-0	Meredith, Smith(S)	1,500
9	Nov 5	A	Barnsley	D	1-1	Cowie	4,000
10	12	A	Glossop	W	2-1	Gillespie, Meredith	6,000
11	19	H	Walsall	W	2-0	Gillespie, Jones	8,000
12	26	A	Burton Swifts	D	3-3	Gillespie, Meredith, Moffatt	5,000
13	Dec 3	H	Burslem Port Vale	W	3-1	Meredith 2, Dougal	8,000
14	10	A	Loughborough	W	3-1	Meredith, Smith(B), Williams	1,200
15	17	H	Loughborough	W	5-0	Meredith 3, Ray, Smith(S)	4,000
16	24	A	Blackpool	W	4-2	Moffatt 2, Gillespie, Meredith	1,000
17	26	H	Newton Heath	W	4-0	Dougal, Gillespie, Meredith, Williams	24,000
18	27	A	Small Heath	L	1-4	Dougal	10,000
19	Jan 2	H	Glossop	L	0-2		12,000
20	14	A	New Brighton Tower	W	1-0	Gillespie	10,000
21	Feb 4	H	Luton Town	W	2-0	Gillespie, Smith(S)	8,000
22	11	A	Leicester Fosse	D	1-1	Williams	10,000
23	18	H	Darwen	W	10-0	Williams 5, Meredith 3, Dougal, Smith(S)	8,000
24	22	H	Lincoln City	W	3-1	Gillespie, Smith(S), Williams	5,000
25	25	A	Gainsborough Trin.	L	1-3	Meredith	5,000
26	Mar 4	H	Barnsley	W	5-0	Meredith 3, Ross 2	12,000
27	18	A	Walsall	D	1-1	Ross	4,000
28	25	H	Burton Swifts	W	6-0	Meredith 2, Ross 2, Dougal, Moffatt	3,000
29	31	H	Gainsborough Trin.	W	4-0	Gillespie 2, Dougal, Ross	15,000
30	Apr 1	A	Burslem Port Vale	D	1-1	Meredith	12,000
31	3	A	Woolwich Arsenal	W	1-0	Gillespie	5,000
32	8	H	Small Heath	W	2-0	Williams 2	18,000
33	11	A	Grimsby Town	W	2-1	Gillespie, Meredith	500
34	22	H	Blackpool	W	4-1	Meredith 2, Gillespie, Ross	15,000
							Appearances
							Goals

FA Cup

Match No.	Date	Venue	Opponents	Result		Scorers	Attendance
R1	Jan 28	A	Small Heath	L	2-3	Gillespie, Meredith	15,399
							Appearances
							Goals

Williams CA	Read TH	Ray R	Holmes WM	Smith W(B)	Moffatt R	Meredith WH	Smith W(S)	Gillespie WJ	Whitehead JW	Cowie A	Munn S	Williams F	Bowman WW	Dougal G	Jones D	Chappell T	Ross JD
1	2	3	4	5	6	7	8	9	10	11							
1	3		4	5	2	7	8	9	10		6	11					
1	3			5	2	7	8	9	10	11	4		6				
1	2	3		5	4	7	9		8	11			6	10			
1	2	3		5	4	7	8			11		9	6	10			
1	2	6		5	4	7	8			11		9		10	3		
1	2	6		5	4	7	8	9		11				10	3		
1	2	6		5	4	7	8	9		11				10	3		
1	2		6	5	4	7	8	9		11				10	3		
1	2		6	5	4	7	8	9		11				10	3		
1	2		6	5	4	7	8	9		11				10	3		
	2		6	5	4	7	8	9		10				11	3	1	
1	2		6	5	4	7	8	9				10		11	3		
1	2		6	5	4	7	8	9				10		11	3		
1	2	8	6	5	4	7	9					10		11	3		
1		2	6	5	4	7	8	9				10		11	3		
1	2		6	5	4	7	8	9				10		11	3		
1	2	7	6	5	4		8	9				10		11	3		
1		2	6	5	4	7	8	9				10		11	3		
1		2	6	5	4	7	8	9				10		11	3		
1		2	6	5	4	7	8	9				10		11	3		
1		2	6	5	4	7	8	9				10		11	3		
1	2	3	6	5	4	7	8	9				10		11			
1	2	3		5	4	7	8	9			6	10		11			
1		2		5	4	7	8	9			6	10		11	3		
1		2		5	4	7		8			6	10		11	3		9
1		2	6	5	4	7		9				10		11	3		8
1		2	6	5	4	7		9				10		11	3		8
1		2	6	5	4	7		9				10		11	3		8
1		2	6	5	4	7		9				10		11	3		8
1	2		6	5	4	7		9				10		11	3		8
1		2	6	5	4	7		9				10		11	3		8
1		2		5	4	7		9			6	10		11	3		8
1		2	6	5	4	7		9				10		11	3		8
33	20	24	24	34	34	33	25	30	4	11	6	25	3	31	27	1	9
	1	1		1	4	29	8	17	2	3		11		7	1		7

Williams CA	Read TH	Ray R	Holmes WM	Smith W(B)	Moffatt R	Meredith WH	Smith W(S)	Gillespie WJ	Whitehead JW	Cowie A	Munn S	Williams F	Bowman WW	Dougal G	Jones D	Chappell T	Ross JD
1		2	6	5	4	7	8	9				10		11	3		
1		1	1	1	1	1	1	1				1		1	1		
						1		1									

League Table

	P	W	D	L	F	A	Pts
Manchester C	34	23	6	5	92	35	52
Glossop N.E.	34	20	6	8	76	38	46
Leicester C	34	18	9	7	64	42	45
Newton Heath	34	19	5	10	67	43	43
New Brighton	34	18	7	9	71	52	43
Walsall	34	15	12	7	79	36	42
Woolwich A	34	18	5	11	72	41	41
Small Heath	34	17	7	10	85	50	41
Burslem P.V.	34	17	5	12	56	34	39
Grimsby T	34	15	5	14	71	60	35
Barnsley	34	12	7	15	52	56	31
Lincoln C	34	12	7	15	51	56	31
Burton S	34	10	8	16	51	70	28
Gainsborough T	34	10	5	19	56	72	25
Luton T	34	10	3	21	51	95	23
Blackpool	34	8	4	22	49	90	20
Loughborough T	34	6	6	22	38	92	18
Darwen	34	2	5	27	22	141	9

1899-1900

Division One

Manager: Sam Ormerod

Did you know that?

Match 1: It was estimated that around a fifth of attendees came from Manchester.

Match 2: City's third goal will always be credited to Meredith as all newspapers and officials felt he did most of the work to earn the goal, but it was actually sent across the line by Gillespie.

Match 3: Leonard made his only appearance after rejoining City from Thames Ironworks.

Match 7: Threlfall became the first player to make his City debut in Division One.

Match 31: Goalkeeper Williams scored.

The first Division One goal at Hyde Road came after 25 minutes of the second match of the season when Billy Gillespie was credited with scoring through a crowd of players. Derby disputed the legitimacy of the goal, but it was eventually awarded after the two linesmen and the referee debated at length its validity.

Match No.	Date	Venue	Opponents	Result		Scorers	Attendance
1	Sep 2	A	Blackburn Rovers	L	3-4	Meredith, Ross, F Williams	10,000
2	9	H	Derby County	W	4-0	Meredith 2, Gillespie, Ross	19,000
3	16	A	Bury	W	4-1	Leonard, Meredith, Ross, F Williams	13,000
4	23	H	Notts County	W	5-1	Ross 2, Gillespie, Moffatt, Smith(B)	20,000
5	30	H	Wolverhampton W.	D	1-1	Ross	20,000
6	Oct 7	A	Sheffield United	L	0-3		20,000
7	14	H	Newcastle United	W	1-0	Ross	26,000
8	21	A	Aston Villa	L	1-2	F Williams	25,000
9	28	H	Liverpool	L	0-1		20,000
10	Nov 4	A	Burnley	L	0-2		6,000
11	11	H	Preston North End	W	3-1	Gillespie, Meredith, F Williams	7,000
12	25	H	Glossop	W	4-1	Dougal, Meredith, Ross, F Williams	14,000
13	Dec 2	A	Stoke	L	0-1		10,000
14	9	H	Sunderland	W	2-1	Meredith, Moffatt	20,000
15	16	A	West Bromwich Albion	D	0-0		5,000
16	23	H	Everton	L	1-2	Meredith	14,000
17	25	H	Sheffield United	L	1-2	F Williams	8,000
18	27	A	Nottingham Forest	L	0-2		6,000
19	30	H	Blackburn Rovers	D	1-1	Gillespie	10,000
20	Jan 6	A	Derby County	D	0-0		7,000
21	13	H	Bury	D	2-2	Smith(S) 2	14,000
22	20	A	Notts County	D	1-1	Gillespie	10,000
23	Feb 3	A	Wolverhampton W.	D	1-1	Meredith	3,000
24	Mar 3	A	Liverpool	L	2-5	Gillespie, Meredith	14,000
25	10	H	Burnley	W	1-0	Meredith	13,000
26	19	H	Aston Villa	L	0-2		15,000
27	31	A	Glossop	W	2-0	Davidson, Harvey	10,000
28	Apr 7	H	Stoke	W	1-0	F Williams	15,000
29	9	H	Nottingham Forest	W	2-0	Meredith 2	5,000
30	13	A	Newcastle United	D	0-0		16,000
31	14	A	Sunderland	L	1-3	C Williams	8,000
32	16	A	Preston North End	W	2-0	Dougal, Gillespie	5,000
33	21	H	West Bromwich Albion	W	4-0	Ross 2, Gillespie, Meredith	18,000
34	28	A	Everton	L	0-4		10,000
							Appearances
							Goals

FA Cup

Match No.	Date	Venue	Opponents	Result		Scorers	Attendance
R1	Jan 27	H	Aston Villa	D	1-1	Ross	22,000
rep	31	A	Aston Villa	L	0-3		20,000
							Appearances
							Goals

Williams CA	Ray R	Jones D	Moffatt R	Smith W(B)	Holmes WM	Meredith WH	Ross JD	Gillespie WJ	Williams F	Dougal G	Read TH	Leonard P	Threlfall F	Smith W(S)	Tonge J	Munn S	Harvey H	Davidson AL	Dartnell H	Cassidy J
1	2	3	4	5	6	7	8	9	10	11										
1		3	4	5	6	7	8	9	10	11	2									
1		3	4	5	6	7	8	9	10		2	11								
1		3	4	5	6	7	8	9	10	11	2									
1		3	4	5	6	7	8	9	10	11	2									
1		3	4	5	6	7	8	9	10	11	2									
1		3	4	5	6	7	8	9	10		2		11							
1		3	4	5	6	7	8	9	10	11	2									
1		3	4	5	6	7	8	9	10		2		11							
1		3	4	5	6	7	8	9	10		2			11						
1		3	4	5	6	7	8	9	10	11	2									
1		3	4	5	6	7	8	9	10	11	2									
1		3	4	5	6	7	8	9	10	11	2									
1		3	4	5	6	7	8	9	10	11	2									
1		3	4	5	6	7	8	9	10	11	2									
1		3	4	5	6	7	8	9	10	11	2									
1		3	4	5	6	7	8	9	10	11	2									
1	2	3	4	5	6		8	9		11				10	7					
1	2	3	4	5	6	7		9		10			11	8						
1	2	3		5	6	7		9	10				11	8		4				
1	2	3		5	6	7			10		4		11	8			9			
1	2	3	4	5	6	7		9	10				11				8			
1	2	3		5	6	7		9	10	11	4						8			
1	2	3		5	6	8		9	10		4		11		7					
1	2	3	4	5	6	7	8	9	10				11							
1		3	4	5	6	7	8	9		10	2		11							
1		3	4	5	6	7			10	11	2						8	9		
1		3	4	5	6	7			10	11	2						8	9		
1		3		5	6	7	8		10	11	2					4		9		
1		3		5	6	7	8		10	11	2					4		9		
1		3		5	6	7	8		10	11	2					4		9		
1		3		5	6	7	8	9	10	11	2					4				
1		3		5	6	7	8	9	10		2					4			11	
1		3	4	5	6	7	8	9	11		2									10
34	9	34	25	34	34	33	26	28	31	23	28	1	9	5	2	6	5	5	1	1
1			2	1		14	10	8	7	2		1		2			1	1		
1	2	3	4	5	6	7	8	9	10				11							
1	2	3		5	6	8		9	10		4		11		7					
2	2	2	1	2	2	2	1	2	2		1		2		1					
							1													

League Table

	P	W	D	L	F	A	Pts
Aston Villa	34	22	6	6	77	35	50
Sheffield U	34	18	12	4	63	33	48
Sunderland	34	19	3	12	50	35	41
Wolverhampton W	34	15	9	10	48	37	39
Newcastle U	34	13	10	11	53	43	36
Derby Co	34	14	8	12	45	43	36
Manchester C	34	13	8	13	50	44	34
Nottingham F	34	13	8	13	56	55	34
Stoke	34	13	8	13	37	45	34
Liverpool	34	14	5	15	49	45	33
Everton	34	13	7	14	47	49	33
Bury	34	13	6	15	40	44	32
W.B.A.	34	11	8	15	43	51	30
Blackburn R	34	13	4	17	49	61	30
Notts Co	34	9	11	14	46	60	29
Preston N.E.	34	12	4	18	38	48	28
Burnley	34	11	5	18	34	54	27
Glossop N.E.	34	4	10	20	31	74	18

1900-01

Division One

Manager: Sam Ormerod

Did you know that?

Match 5: Future Prime Minister Arthur Balfour attended.
Match 16: Davidson played last game.
Match 19: Davies played last game (made debut in match 3).
Match 22: Dartnell and Hallows played last game.
Match 23: Meechan played last game.
Match 32: Cassidy played last game.
Match 33: Dougal played last game.

When Joe Cassidy was sold for £75 in May 1901 it was the directors who made the decision against Sam Ormerod's wishes. City made a loss of £175 on the deal, but the directors were adamant Cassidy wasn't worth his £4 a week salary. Cassidy went on to be idolised at Middlesbrough and netted the club's first League goal at Ayresome Park.

Match No.	Date		Venue	Opponents	Result		Scorers	Attendance
1	Sep	1	H	Sheffield Wednesday	D	2-2	Dougal, Ross	18,000
2		8	A	Bury	L	0-4		16,000
3		15	H	Nottingham Forest	W	1-0	Cassidy	20,000
4		22	A	Blackburn Rovers	L	0-1		8,000
5		29	H	Stoke	W	2-0	Davies, Meredith	15,000
6	Oct	6	A	West Bromwich Albion	L	2-3	Holmes, Moffatt	9,000
7		13	H	Everton	W	1-0	Cassidy	20,000
8		20	A	Sunderland	L	0-3		6,000
9		27	H	Derby County	W	2-0	Williams 2	25,000
10	Nov	3	A	Bolton Wanderers	D	0-0		20,634
11		10	H	Notts County	W	2-0	Cassidy, Gillespie	16,000
12		17	A	Preston North End	W	4-0	Cassidy 2, Gillespie, Williams	6,000
13		24	H	Wolverhampton W.	W	3-2	Cassidy, Meredith, Ross	18,000
14	Dec	1	A	Aston Villa	L	1-7	Cassidy	12,000
15		8	H	Liverpool	L	3-4	Cassidy 2, Smith	15,000
16		15	A	Newcastle United	L	1-2	Williams	16,000
17		22	H	Sheffield United	W	2-1	Gillespie, Meredith	20,000
18		25	H	Sunderland	D	1-1	Gillespie	25,000
19		26	A	Sheffield United	D	1-1	Gillespie	23,341
20		29	A	Sheffield Wednesday	L	1-4	Cassidy	10,000
21	Jan	5	H	Bury	W	1-0	Cassidy	23,000
22		12	A	Nottingham Forest	L	2-4	Cassidy, Gillespie	10,000
23		19	H	Blackburn Rovers	L	1-3	Meredith	10,000
24		26	A	Stoke	L	1-2	Cassidy	3,000
25	Feb	16	A	Everton	L	2-5	Cassidy, Meredith	15,000
26		23	H	Preston North End	W	3-1	Dougal, Meredith, Williams	12,000
27	Mar	2	A	Derby County	L	0-2		5,000
28		9	H	Bolton Wanderers	D	1-1	Holmes	14,000
29		16	A	Notts County	D	0-0		6,000
30		30	A	Wolverhampton W.	L	0-1		3,000
31	Apr	5	H	West Bromwich Albion	W	1-0	Gillespie	20,000
32		13	A	Liverpool	L	1-3	Meredith	10,000
33		20	H	Newcastle United	W	2-1	Gillespie 2	24,000
34		27	H	Aston Villa	W	4-0	Scotson 2, Ross, Threlfall	16,000
								Appearances
								Goals

FA Cup

	Date		Venue	Opponents	Result		Scorers	Attendance
R1	Feb	9	A	West Bromwich Albion	L	0-1		16,000
								Appearances

Williams CA	Read TH	Jones D	Moffatt R	Smith W(B)	Holmes WM	Meredith WH	Ross JD	Davidson AL	Cassidy J	Dougal G	Gillespie WJ	Williams F	Davies J	Dartnell H	Slater P	Threlfall F	Meehan P	Hallows H	Hesham FJ	Hosie J	Harvey H	Cox W	Hunter R	Scotson J
1	2	3	4	5	6	7	8	9	10	11														
1	2	3	4	5	6	7	8			11	9	10												
1	2	3	4	5	6	7			10		9		8	11										
1	2	3	4	5	6	7			10		9	11	8											
1	2	3	4	5	6	7			9	11		10	8											
1	2	3	4	5	6	7			9	11		10	8											
1	2	3	4	5	6	7			9	11		10	8											
1	2	3	4	5	6	7			9	11		10	8											
1		3	4	5	6	7	8		9			10			2	11								
1	2	3	4	5	6	7	8		10		9	11												
1	2	3	4	5	6	7	8		10		9	11												
1	2	3	4	5	6	7	8		11		9	10												
1	2	3	4	5	6	7	8		11		9		10											
1	2	3	4	5	6	7	8		11		9	10												
1	2	3	4	5	6	7	8		11		9			10										
1	2	3	4	5	6	7	8	9	10			11												
1		3	4	5	6	7	8		11		9	10					2							
1		3	4	5	6	7	8		11		9	10					2							
1		3	4	5		7	8		11		9	10	6		2									
1		3	4	5	6	7	8		11		9	10					2							
1	5	3	4		6	7	8		10	11	9						2							
1		3	4		6	7	8		10		9			11			2	5						
1		3	4	5	6	7	8		10		9	11					2							
1	2	3	4	5	6	7	8		10		9								11					
1	2	3	4	5		7			9	11		10								6	8			
	2	3	4	5	6	7	8		9	11		10										1		
1	2	3	4	5	6	7	8		9	11		10												
1	2	3	4	5	6	7	8		9	11		10												
1	2	3		5		7	8		11		9	6									10		4	
1	2	3		5		7			8		9	6				11							4	10
1	2	3	4	5	6	7	8				9					11								10
1	2	3	4	5	6	7			10	11	9													8
1	2	3	4	5		7	8			11	9									6				10
1	2		4	5		7	8				9				3	11				6				10
33	27	33	32	32	28	34	25	2	30	13	23	23	8	3	3	4	6	1	1	3	2	1	2	5
			1	1	2	7	3		14	2	9	5	1			1								2

Williams CA	Read TH	Jones D	Moffatt R	Smith W(B)	Holmes WM	Meredith WH	Ross JD	Davidson AL	Cassidy J	Dougal G	Gillespie WJ	Williams F	Davies J	Dartnell H	Slater P	Threlfall F	Meehan P	Hallows H	Hesham FJ	Hosie J	Harvey H	Cox W	Hunter R	Scotson J
1	2	3	4	5	6	7	8		9	11		10												
1	1	1	1	1	1	1	1		1	1		1												

League Table

	P	W	D	L	F	A	Pts
Liverpool	34	19	7	8	59	35	45
Sunderland	34	15	13	6	57	26	43
Notts Co	34	18	4	12	54	46	40
Nottingham F	34	16	7	11	53	36	39
Bury	34	16	7	11	53	37	39
Newcastle U	34	14	10	10	42	37	38
Everton	34	16	5	13	55	42	37
Sheffield W	34	13	10	11	52	42	36
Blackburn R	34	12	9	13	39	47	33
Bolton W	34	13	7	14	39	55	33
Manchester C	34	13	6	15	48	58	32
Derby Co	34	12	7	15	55	42	31
Wolverhampton W	34	9	13	12	39	55	31
Sheffield U	34	12	7	15	35	52	31
Aston Villa	34	10	10	14	45	51	30
Stoke	34	11	5	18	46	57	27
Preston N.E.	34	9	7	18	49	75	25
W.B.A.	34	7	8	19	35	62	22

1901-02

Division One

Manager: Sam Ormerod

Did you know that?

Match 4: A fourth consecutive defeat brought heavy criticism on Ormerod.
Match 20: Ross's last game. He passed away later in the year.
Match 22: McOustra and Drummond made debuts.
Match 34: Jones's last game. He passed away during close season.

By match 22 Ormerod's power had effectively been taken from him. Director John Allison was signing players, while team selection was being made by committee. It seems Ormerod received the criticism, but others made the decisions.

Match No.	Date	Venue	Opponents	Result		Scorers	Attendance
1	Sep 2	A	Everton	L	1-3	Meredith	20,000
2	7	A	Sunderland	L	0-1		13,000
3	14	H	Small Heath	L	1-4	Scotson	23,000
4	21	A	Derby County	L	0-2		10,000
5	Oct 5	A	Notts County	L	0-2		12,000
6	12	H	Bolton Wanderers	W	1-0	Williams	16,000
7	19	H	Grimsby Town	W	3-0	Gillespie, Meredith, Williams	13,500
8	26	A	Wolverhampton W.	D	0-0		4,000
9	Nov 2	H	Liverpool	L	2-3	Gillespie, Williams	18,000
10	9	A	Newcastle United	L	0-3		8,000
11	23	A	Sheffield United	L	0-5		6,000
12	30	H	Nottingham Forest	W	3-1	R Jones, Meredith, Morgan	10,000
13	Dec 7	A	Bury	L	0-3		9,000
14	14	H	Blackburn Rovers	D	1-1	Meredith	8,000
15	26	A	Sheffield Wednesday	L	1-2	R Jones	12,000
16	Jan 1	A	Bolton Wanderers	D	3-3	Henderson, Meredith, Ross	20,000
17	4	H	Sunderland	L	0-3		6,000
18	11	A	Small Heath	L	0-1		20,000
19	13	A	Stoke	L	0-3		5,000
20	18	H	Derby County	D	0-0		15,000
21	Feb 1	H	Notts County	W	1-0	Threlfall	14,000
22	15	A	Grimsby Town	L	2-3	Gillespie 2	5,000
23	17	H	Aston Villa	W	1-0	Hosie	17,000
24	22	H	Wolverhampton W.	W	3-0	Gillespie 2, McOustra	21,000
25	Mar 1	A	Liverpool	L	0-4		15,000
26	8	H	Newcastle United	W	2-0	Hynds 2	20,000
27	17	H	Everton	W	2-0	McOustra, Meredith	22,000
28	22	H	Sheffield United	W	4-0	Gillespie 2, Hosie, Meredith	20,000
29	28	H	Sheffield Wednesday	L	0-3		30,000
30	29	A	Nottingham Forest	L	1-3	Hosie	8,000
31	31	A	Aston Villa	D	2-2	Drummond, Gillespie	20,000
32	Apr 5	H	Bury	W	2-0	Gillespie, Meredith	6,000
33	12	A	Blackburn Rovers	W	4-1	Gillespie 4	3,000
34	19	H	Stoke	D	2-2	Drummond, Gillespie	15,000
							Appearances
							Goals

FA Cup

R1	Jan 29	A	Preston North End	D	0-0		7,000
rep	Feb 3	A	Preston North End	W	4-2*	Smith 3, Morgan	5,000
R2	8	H	Nottingham Forest	L	0-2		16,000
							Appearances
							Goals

Note: A Round 1 tie versus Preston North End (A) on 25 Jan was abandoned in extra time.
* after extra time

Williams CA	Read TH	Slater P	Moffatt R	Smith W(B)	Hosie J	Meredith WH	Frost S	Bevan FETW	Scotson J	Hurst DJ	Jones D	Hunter R	Morgan H	Williams F	Ross JD	Orr W	Holmes WM	Gillespie WJ	Hynds T	Threlfall F	Watson LP	Jones RTW	Barrett F	Henderson J	Hillman J	McOustra W	Drummond J	Jarrett G
1	2	3	4	5	6	7	8	9	10	11																		
1	2			5	6	7		9		11	3	4	8	10														
1	2			5	6	7			10	11	3	4	9		8													
1			4	5		7	8			11	3			10		2	6	9										
1		3		5	6	7				11			8	10		2		9	4									
1			4		6	7				11	3		8	10		2		9	5									
1			4		6	7				11	3		8	10		2		9	5									
1			4		6	7					3		8	10		2		9	5	11								
1			4		6	7					3		8	10		2		9	5	11								
1			4	5	6						3		7	10	8	2		9		11								
1			4		6	7				11	3			10		2		9	5		8							
1				4	6	7				11			8			2	3	9	5			10						
1				4	6	7				11			8			2	3	9	5			10						
1				4	6	7				11	3			8		2		9	5			10						
	3			4	6	7				11					8	2			5			10	1	9				
		3		4	6	7				11					8	2			5			10	1	9				
1				4	6	7				11	3				8	2			5			10		9				
		3		4	6	7								10		2			5	11		8	1	9				
		2		4	6	7								9	8		3		5	11		10	1					
		3		4	6	7								9	8	2			5	11		10	1					
		3		4	6	7			10				8			2			5	11				9	1			
		3	4		6	7							8			2		9	5						1	10	11	
			4		6	7				11	3					2		9	5						1	8	10	
			4		6	7					3					2		9	5	11					1	8	10	
			4		6	7					3					2		9	5	11					1	8	10	
		2	4		6	7					3							9	5	11					1	8	10	
		2	4		6	7					3							9	5	11					1	8	10	
		2	4		6	7					3							9	5	11					1	8	10	
		2	4		6	7					3							9	5	11					1	8	10	
		3	4		6	7										2		9	5	11					1	8	10	
			4		6	7										2	3	9	5	11					1	8	10	
			4		6	7						2					3	9	5	11					1	8	10	
			4		6	7					3	2						9	5	11					1	8	10	
			4		6	7					3	2						9	5	11					1	8	10	
15	4	13	21	16	33	33	2	2	3	15	20	5	12	13	7	23	6	24	29	18	1	9	5	5	14	13	13	
					3	8			1				1	3	1			15	2	1		2		1		2	2	

Williams CA	Read TH	Slater P	Moffatt R	Smith W(B)	Hosie J	Meredith WH	Frost S	Bevan FETW	Scotson J	Hurst DJ	Jones D	Hunter R	Morgan H	Williams F	Ross JD	Orr W	Holmes WM	Gillespie WJ	Hynds T	Threlfall F	Watson LP	Jones RTW	Barrett F	Henderson J	Hillman J	McOustra W	Drummond J	Jarrett G
		3		4	6	7			10				8			2			5	11		9	1					
		3	4	9	6	7							8			2			5	11		10	1					
		3	4	9	6	7							8			2			5	11		10	1					
		4	2	4	4	4			1				3		1	4			4	4		4	4	1				
				3									1											1				

League Table

	P	W	D	L	F	A	Pts
Sunderland	34	19	6	9	50	35	44
Everton	34	17	7	10	53	35	41
Newcastle U	34	14	9	11	48	34	37
Blackburn R	34	15	6	13	52	48	36
Nottingham F	34	13	9	12	43	43	35
Derby Co	34	13	9	12	39	41	35
Bury	34	13	8	13	44	38	34
Aston Villa	34	13	8	13	42	40	34
Sheffield W	34	13	8	13	48	52	34
Sheffield U	34	13	7	14	53	48	33
Liverpool	34	10	12	12	42	38	32
Bolton W	34	12	8	14	51	56	32
Notts Co	34	14	4	16	51	57	32
Wolverhampton W	34	13	6	15	46	57	32
Grimsby T	34	13	6	15	44	60	32
Stoke	34	11	9	14	45	55	31
Small Heath	34	11	8	15	47	45	30
Manchester C	34	11	6	17	42	58	28

1902-03

Division Two

Manager: Tom Maley

Did you know that?

Match 3: Hosie's last game.
Match 10: Miller's last game.
Match 31: Victory guaranteed promotion.
Match 33: Orr's last game.
Match 34: Bevan's last game.

City won the Second Division title the day before their final match when Barnsley defeated second placed Small Heath 3–0, leaving City three points clear with one game each left to play.

Match No.	Date	Venue	Opponents	Result		Scorers	Attendance
1	Sep 6	H	Lincoln City	W	3-1	McOustra 2, Bevan	14,000
2	13	A	Small Heath	L	0-4		12,000
3	20	H	Leicester Fosse	W	3-1	Gillespie, Meredith, og	11,500
4	27	A	Chesterfield	W	1-0	Meredith	6,000
5	Oct 4	A	Burnley	D	1-1	Miller	4,000
6	11	H	Preston North End	W	1-0	Gillespie	18,000
7	18	A	Burslem Port Vale	W	4-1	Gillespie 2, Drummond, Meredith	5,000
8	22	A	Gainsborough Trin.	W	3-0	Gillespie 2, Miller	4,000
9	Nov 1	A	Woolwich Arsenal	L	0-1		16,000
10	8	H	Burton United	W	2-0	Gillespie, McOustra	10,000
11	15	A	Bristol City	L	2-3	Drummond, Turnbull	10,000
12	22	H	Glossop	W	5-2	Gillespie 3, Turnbull, og	6,000
13	24	H	Barnsley	W	3-2	Gillespie 2, Meredith	8,000
14	Dec 6	H	Stockport County	W	5-0	Meredith 2, Turnbull 2, Gillespie	11,000
15	13	A	Blackpool	W	3-0	Gillespie, Meredith, Turnbull	4,000
16	20	H	Woolwich Arsenal	W	4-1	Gillespie 3, Turnbull	25,000
17	25	A	Manchester United	D	1-1	Bannister	50,000
18	26	A	Preston North End	W	2-0	Drummond, Gillespie	8,000
19	27	A	Doncaster Rovers	W	2-1	Gillespie, Hynds	4,000
20	Jan 1	H	Doncaster Rovers	W	4-1	Bannister 2, Meredith, Turnbull	25,000
21	3	A	Lincoln City	L	0-1		6,000
22	17	A	Leicester Fosse	D	1-1	Threlfall	7,000
23	24	H	Chesterfield	W	4-2	Meredith 3, Turnbull	13,500
24	31	H	Burnley	W	6-0	Gillespie 2, Meredith 2, Bannister, Threlfall	13,000
25	Feb 14	H	Burslem Port Vale	W	7-1	Bannister 2, Gillespie 2, McOustra, Meredith, Turnbull	10,000
26	23	H	Small Heath	W	4-0	Meredith 2, Gillespie, Threlfall	20,000
27	28	H	Gainsborough Trin.	W	9-0	Bannister 3, Gillespie 2, Turnbull 2, Meredith, Threlfall	17,000
28	Mar 7	A	Burton United	W	5-0	Bannister 2, Gillespie 2, Meredith	5,000
29	14	H	Bristol City	D	2-2	Meredith, Threlfall	20,000
30	21	A	Glossop	W	1-0	Bannister	7,000
31	Apr 4	A	Stockport County	W	2-0	Gillespie, Turnbull	10,000
32	10	H	Manchester United	L	0-2		35,000
33	11	H	Blackpool	W	2-0	Meredith 2	8,000
34	14	A	Barnsley	W	3-0	Bannister, Gillespie, Meredith	5,500
							Appearances
						Two own goals	Goals

FA Cup

	Date	Venue	Opponents	Result		Scorers	Attendance
R1	Feb 7	A	Preston North End	L	1-3	Turnbull	8,000
							Appearances
							Goals

Hillman J	Davidson R	Holmes WM	Frost S	Hynds T	Hosie J	Meredith WH	Miller J	Bevan FETW	McOustra W	Booth F	Drummond J	Orr W	Gillespie WJ	Threlfall F	Turnbull A	Bannister J	Edmondson JH	Slater P	McMahon J	Moffatt R	Dearden R
1	2	3	4	5	6	7	8	9	10	11											
1	2	3	4	5	6	7	8		9	11	10										
1	3		4	5	6	7			8	11	10	2	9								
1	3		4	5		7	8		6	11	10	2	9								
1	3		4	5		7	8		6	11	10	2	9								
1	3		4	5		7	8		6	11	10	2	9								
1	3		4	5		7	8		6	11	10	2	9								
1	3		4	5		7	8		6		10	2	9	11							
1	3		4	5		7		8	6		10	2	9	11							
1	3		4	5		7	8		6		10	2	9	11							
1	3		4	5		7			6		10	2	9	11	8						
1	3		4	5		7			6		10	2	9	11	8						
1	3		4	5		7			6		10	2	9	11	8						
1	3		4	5		7			6			2	9	11	10	8					
1	3	2	4	5		7			6				9	11	10	8					
	3		4	5		7			6				9	11	10	8	1	2			
1	3		4	5		7			6				9	11	10	8			2		
1	3	2	4	5		7			6		10		9	11		8					
1	3		4	5		7			6		10		9	11		8			2		
1	3			5		7			6				9	11	10	8			2	4	
1	3	4		5		7			6				9	11	10	8			2		
1	3		4	5		7			6				9	11	10	8			2		
1	3		4	5		7		6					9	11	10	8			2		
1	3		4	5		7		6					9	11	10	8			2		
1	3		4	5		7			6				9	11	10	8			2		
1	3		4	5		7			6				9	11	10	8			2		
1		3	4	5		7			6				9	11	10	8			2		
1		3	4	5		7			6				9	11	10	8			2		
1		3		5		7		4	6				9	11	10	8			2		
		3	4	5		7			6				9	11	10	8	1		2		
		3	4			7			6				9	11	10	8	1		2		5
1		3	4	5		7			6				9	11	10	8			2		
1			4			7			6	11		3	9		10	8			2		5
1						7		4	6	11			9		10	8		3	2		5
31	26	11	30	31	3	34	8	6	32	9	14	13	32	25	22	21	3	2	17	1	3
				1		22	2	1	4		3		30	5	12	13					

Hillman J	Davidson R	Holmes WM	Frost S	Hynds T	Hosie J	Meredith WH	Miller J	Bevan FETW	McOustra W	Booth F	Drummond J	Orr W	Gillespie WJ	Threlfall F	Turnbull A	Bannister J	Edmondson JH	Slater P	McMahon J	Moffatt R	Dearden R
1		3	4	5		7		6				2	9	11	10	8					
1		1	1	1		1		1				1	1	1	1	1					
															1						

League Table

	P	W	D	L	F	A	Pts
Manchester C	34	25	4	5	95	29	54
Small Heath	34	24	3	7	74	36	51
Woolwich A	34	20	8	6	66	30	48
Bristol C	34	17	8	9	59	38	42
Manchester U	34	15	8	11	53	38	38
Chesterfield	34	14	9	11	67	40	37
Preston N.E.	34	13	10	11	56	40	36
Barnsley	34	13	8	13	55	51	34
Burslem P.V.	34	13	8	13	57	62	34
Lincoln C	34	12	6	16	46	53	30
Glossop N.E.	34	11	7	16	43	58	29
Gainsborough T	34	11	7	16	41	59	29
Burton U	34	11	7	16	39	59	29
Blackpool	34	9	10	15	44	59	28
Leicester C	34	10	8	16	41	65	28
Doncaster R	34	9	7	18	35	72	25
Stockport Co	34	7	6	21	39	74	20
Burnley	34	6	8	20	30	77	20

1903-04

Division One

Manager: Tom Maley

Did you know that?

Match 10: Drummond's last game.
Match 11: Lyon's last game.
Match 17: Slater's last game.
Match 25: Dennison scores two in his only game.
Match 29: Davidson's last game.
Match 33: Robinson's first and only game.
Match 34: Ashworth's last game.

Some reports mistakenly stated that City's homecoming after the 1904 FA Cup Final occurred on the Sunday after the game. The homecoming actually took place on the Monday night after City's game at Everton. The players arrived back in Manchester at approximately 9.30pm and were greeted with incredible scenes as they made their way through Manchester to Ardwick. It was the biggest sporting celebration the city had ever known.

Match No.	Date	Venue	Opponents	Result		Scorers	Attendance
1	Sep 5	A	Stoke	W	2-1	Livingstone, og	16,000
2	12	H	Derby County	W	2-1	Turnbull 2	28,000
3	19	H	Wolverhampton W.	W	4-1	Turnbull 2, Booth, Meredith	24,000
4	26	A	Notts County	W	3-0	Hynds, Meredith, Pearson	15,000
5	Oct 3	H	Sheffield United	L	0-1		28,000
6	10	A	Newcastle United	L	0-1		18,000
7	17	H	Aston Villa	W	1-0	Gillespie	30,000
8	24	A	Middlesbrough	L	0-6		12,000
9	31	H	Liverpool	W	3-2	Booth, Gillespie, Turnbull	25,000
10	Nov 7	A	Bury	W	3-1	Gillespie 2, Meredith	19,371
11	14	H	Blackburn Rovers	W	1-0	Meredith	13,000
12	21	A	Nottingham Forest	W	3-0	Frost, Gillespie, Hynds	8,000
13	28	H	Sheffield Wednesday	D	1-1	Livingstone	6,000
14	Dec 5	A	Sunderland	D	1-1	Hynds	8,000
15	12	H	West Bromwich Albion	W	6-3	Gillespie 2, Meredith 2, Livingstone, Turnbull	15,000
16	19	A	Small Heath	W	3-0	Turnbull 2, Gillespie	15,000
17	26	H	Everton	L	1-3	Gillespie	28,000
18	28	A	Sheffield United	L	3-5	Gillespie 2, Threlfall	35,000
19	Jan 1	H	Middlesbrough	D	1-1	Meredith	26,000
20	2	H	Stoke	D	2-2	Frost, Turnbull	16,000
21	9	A	Derby County	W	3-2	Gillespie 2, Meredith	12,000
22	23	H	Notts County	W	3-0	Booth, Frost, Gillespie	12,000
23	Feb 13	A	Aston Villa	W	1-0	Gillespie	12,000
24	27	A	Liverpool	D	2-2	Gillespie, Hynds	25,000
25	Mar 12	A	Blackburn Rovers	W	5-2	Dennison 2, Meredith 2, Turnbull	12,000
26	21	A	Wolverhampton W.	W	6-1	Gillespie 2, Livingstone 2, Meredith, Turnbull	6,000
27	26	A	Sheffield Wednesday	L	0-1		18,000
28	Apr 1	H	Newcastle United	L	1-3	Turnbull	25,000
29	2	H	Sunderland	W	2-1	Turnbull 2	11,000
30	9	A	West Bromwich Albion	L	1-2	Jones	10,000
31	11	H	Bury	W	3-0	Turnbull 2, Bannister	12,000
32	13	H	Nottingham Forest	D	0-0		10,000
33	16	H	Small Heath	W	4-0	Bannister 2, Moffatt 2	15,000
34	25	A	Everton	L	0-1		12,000
							Appearances
						One own goal	Goals

FA Cup

Round	Date	Venue	Opponents	Result		Scorers	Attendance
R1	Feb 6	H	Sunderland	W	3-2	Turnbull 2, Gillespie	23,000
R2	20	A	Woolwich Arsenal	W	2-0	Booth, Turnbull	30,000
R3	Mar 5	H	Middlesbrough	D	0-0		35,000
R3	9	A	Middlesbrough	W	3-1	Gillespie, Livingstone, Turnbull	33,000
SF	19	N	Sheffield Wednesday	W	3-0	Gillespie, Meredith, Turnbull	53,000
F	Apr 23	N	Bolton Wanderers	W	1-0	Meredith	61,374

SF at Goodison Park, Liverpool. Final at Crystal Palace, London

Appearances

Goals

Hillman J	McMahon J	Burgess H	McOustra W	Hynds T	Frost S	Meredith WH	Livingstone GT	Moffatt J	Turnbull A	Booth F	Ashworth SB	Gillespie WJ	Pearson F	Lyon WJ	Bannister J	Davidson R	Drummond J	Slater P	Threlfall F	Dearden R	Edmondson JH	Holmes WM	Dennison J	Thornley I	Jones W	Norgrove F	Robinson WS
1	2	3	4	5	6	7	8	9	10	11																	
1	2	3	6	5	4	7	8	9	10	11																	
1	2	3		5	4	7	8		10	11	6	9															
1	2	3		5	4	7	8		10	11	6		9														
1	2	3		5	4	7	8		10	11	6		9														
1	2	3		5		7	4		10	11		9		6	8												
1	2	3		5		7	4			11		9	10	6	8												
1	2	3		5		7	4		10	11		9		6	8												
1	2	3		5	4	7	8		10	11		9		6													
1		3		5	4	7	8			11		9		6		2	10										
1		2		5	4	7	8		10			9		6				3	11								
1	2	3		5	4	7	8		10		6	9							11								
1	2	3		5	4	7	8		10		6	9							11								
1	2	3		5	4	7	8	9	10	11	6																
1	2	3		5	4	7	8		10		6	9							11								
1	2	3		5	4	7	8		10		6	9							11								
1				5	4	7	8		10		6	9				2		3	11								
1		3		5	4	7	8		10		6	9				2			11								
1		3		5	4	7	8		10		6	9				2			11								
1		3		5	4	7	8		10		6	9				2			11								
1	2	3		5	4	7	8		10			9							11	6							
1	2	3		5	4	7	8		10	11		9								6							
1	2	3			4	7	8		10	11	6	9								5							
1	2	3		5	4	7	8		10	11	6	9															
	2			5	4	7	8		10	11										6	1	3	9				
	2	3		5	4	7	8		10	11		9									1	6					
	2	3		5	4	7	8		10	11		9									1	6					
	2	3		5	4	7	8		10	11		9									1	6					
				5	4	7			10	11		9			8	2				6	1	3					
1	2			5	4	7			10	11										6		3		8	9		
1	2			5	4	7			10	11	6				8							3		9			
	2			5	4	7			10	11	6				8						1	3		9			
1	2					7		5	10	11	6				8									9		3	4
1	2	3		5	4	7	8		10	11	6	9															
28	27	27	2	32	30	34	29	4	32	24	18	24	3	6	7	6	1	2	10	6	6	8	1	4	1	1	1
				4	3	11	5	2	16	3		18	1		3				1				2		1		

Hillman J	McMahon J	Burgess H	McOustra W	Hynds T	Frost S	Meredith WH	Livingstone GT	Moffatt J	Turnbull A	Booth F	Ashworth SB	Gillespie WJ	Pearson F	Lyon WJ	Bannister J	Davidson R	Drummond J	Slater P	Threlfall F	Dearden R	Edmondson JH	Holmes WM	Dennison J	Thornley I	Jones W	Norgrove F	Robinson WS
1	2	3		5	4	7	8		10	11	6	9															
1	2	3		5	4	7	8		10	11	6	9															
1	2	3		5	4	7	8		10	11	6	9															
	2	3		5	4	7	8		10	11		9									1	6					
1	2	3		5	4	7	8		10	11		9										6					
1	2	3		5	4	7	8		10	11	6	9															
5	6	6		6	6	6	6		6	6	4	6									1	2					
						2	1		5	1		3															

League Table

	P	W	D	L	F	A	Pts
Sheffield W	34	20	7	7	48	28	47
Manchester C	34	19	6	9	71	45	44
Everton	34	19	5	10	59	32	43
Newcastle U	34	18	6	10	58	45	42
Aston Villa	34	17	7	10	70	48	41
Sunderland	34	17	5	12	63	49	39
Sheffield U	34	15	8	11	62	57	38
Wolverhampton W	34	14	8	12	44	66	36
Nottingham F	34	11	9	14	57	57	31
Middlesbrough	34	9	12	13	46	47	30
Small Heath	34	11	8	15	39	52	30
Bury	34	7	15	12	40	53	29
Notts Co	34	12	5	17	37	61	29
Derby Co	34	9	10	15	58	60	28
Blackburn R	34	11	6	17	48	60	28
Stoke	34	10	7	17	54	57	27
Liverpool	34	9	8	17	49	62	26
W.B.A.	34	7	10	17	36	60	24

1904-05

Division One

Manager: Tom Maley

Did you know that?

Match 4: Threlfall's last game.
Match 12: Holmes's last game.
Match 21: Gillespie's last game.
Match 34: Meredith's last game of his first spell at the club.

The final match of the season was highly controversial and a City win could have brought the League title to Manchester for the first time. In the end, allegations of attempted match-fixing by City and violence by the Villa players caused the FA to investigate. The result had major implications for City as a variety of financial irregularities were uncovered. Ultimately, all the leading figures behind matters on the pitch and off it were suspended, and City was almost destroyed.

Match No.	Date	Venue	Opponents	Result		Scorers	Attendance
1	Sep 3	H	Small Heath	W	2-1	Booth, Livingstone	24,000
2	10	A	Stoke	L	0-1		12,000
3	17	A	Notts County	D	1-1	Thornley	10,000
4	24	H	Sheffield United	D	1-1	Thornley	30,000
5	Oct 1	A	Newcastle United	L	0-2		22,000
6	8	H	Preston North End	W	6-1	Livingstone 2, Turnbull 2, Booth, Gillespie	20,000
7	15	A	Middlesbrough	W	1-0	Gillespie	15,000
8	29	A	Bury	W	4-2	Booth, Gillespie, Meredith, Turnbull	18,000
9	Nov 9	H	Aston Villa	W	2-1	Booth, Turnbull	15,000
10	12	A	Blackburn Rovers	L	1-3	Turnbull	12,000
11	14	H	Wolverhampton W.	W	5-1	Booth 2, Gillespie, Livingstone, Meredith	11,000
12	19	H	Nottingham Forest	D	1-1	Booth	15,000
13	26	A	Sheffield Wednesday	L	1-2	Turnbull	8,000
14	Dec 3	H	Sunderland	W	5-2	Turnbull 3, Booth, Gillespie	12,000
15	10	A	Woolwich Arsenal	L	0-1		15,000
16	17	H	Derby County	W	6-0	Turnbull 4, Gillespie 2	23,000
17	24	A	Everton	D	0-0		24,000
18	26	A	Preston North End	W	1-0	Turnbull	17,000
19	31	A	Small Heath	L	1-3	Turnbull	15,000
20	Jan 7	H	Stoke	W	1-0	Meredith	12,000
21	14	H	Notts County	W	2-1	Dorsett, Turnbull	10,000
22	21	A	Sheffield United	W	3-0	Dorsett 2, Turnbull	8,000
23	28	H	Newcastle United	W	3-2	Dorsett, Hynds, Jones	30,000
24	Feb 11	H	Middlesbrough	W	3-2	Dorsett, Moffatt, og	20,000
25	25	H	Bury	W	3-2	Bannister 2, Meredith	14,000
26	Mar 4	A	Derby County	W	1-0	Bannister	6,000
27	11	H	Blackburn Rovers	W	2-1	Meredith, Turnbull	14,000
28	18	A	Nottingham Forest	L	1-2	Meredith	10,000
29	Apr 1	A	Sunderland	D	0-0		6,000
30	8	H	Woolwich Arsenal	W	1-0	Meredith	27,000
31	15	H	Sheffield Wednesday	D	1-1	Meredith	20,000
32	21	H	Everton	W	2-0	Hynds, Livingstone	40,000
33	24	A	Wolverhampton W.	W	3-0	Jones, Livingstone, Pearson	10,000
34	29	A	Aston Villa	L	2-3	Livingstone, Turnbull	20,000
							Appearances
						One own goal	Goals

FA Cup

R1	Feb 4	A	Lincoln City	W	2-1	Meredith, Turnbull	10,000
R2	18	H	Bolton Wanderers	L	1-2	Gillespie	39,000
							Appearances
							Goals

Hillman J	McMahon J	Burgess H	Frost S	Hynds T	McOustra W	Meredith WH	Livingstone GT	Gillespie WJ	Turnbull A	Booth F	Edmondson JH	Thornley I	Holmes WM	Dearden R	Threlfall F	Norgrove F	Bannister J	Moffatt J	Pearson F	Christie J	Dorsett G	Jones W	Buchan J
1	2	3	4	5	6	7	8	9	10	11													
	2	3	4	5	6	7	8		10	11	1	9											
1	2	3	4	5		7	8		10	11		9	6										
1	2		4	5			8		10	11		9	3	6	7								
1		3	4	5		7	8		10	11		9	2	6									
1	2	3	4	5		7	8	9	10	11				6									
1	2		4	5		7	8	9	10	11				6		3							
1	2	3	4	5		7	8	9	10	11				6									
1	2	3	4	5		7	8	9	10	11				6									
1	2	3	4	5		7	8	9	10	11				6									
1		3	4	5		7	10	9		11				6		2	8						
1	2	3	4	5		7	10	9		11			6				8						
1	2	3	4	5		7	8	9	10	11								6					
1	2	3		5		7	8	9	10	11						6		4					
1	2	3		5		7	8	9	10	11								4	6				
1	2	3	4	5		7	8	9	10	11								6					
1	2	3	4	5		7		9	10	11								6	8				
1	2	3	4	5		7	8	9	10	11								6					
1	2	3	4	5		7	8	9	10	11								6					
	2	3	4			8			10	11	1							5		6	7	9	
1	2	3	4	5		7		9	10	11								6			8		
1	2	3	4	5		7			10	11								6			8	9	
1	2	3	4	5		7			10	11								6			8	9	
1		3	4	5		7			10	11						2	8	6			9		
1	2		4	5		7			10							3	8	6			11	9	
1	2	3	4	5		7			10	11							8				6	9	
1	2		4	5		7	8		10	11						3						9	6
1	2	3	4	5		7	8		10	11												9	6
1	2	3	4	5		7	8		10	11											6	9	
1	2	3	4	5		7	10			11							8				9		6
1	2		4	5		7	8		10	11						3						9	6
1	2		4	5		7	8		10	11						3						9	6
1	2		4	5		7	8			11						3			10			9	6
1	2		4	5		7	8		10	11						3						9	6
32	31	26	32	33	2	33	26	16	30	33	2	4	4	8	1	10	6	13	3	1	9	12	7
				2		8	7	7	19	8		2					3	1	1		5	2	
1	2	3	4	5		7			10	11								6	9		8		
1	2	3		5		7		9	10	11						4		6			8		
2	2	2	1	2		2		1	2	2						1		2	1		2		
						1		1	1														

League Table

	P	W	D	L	F	A	Pts
Newcastle U	34	23	2	9	72	33	48
Everton	34	21	5	8	63	36	47
Manchester C	34	20	6	8	66	37	46
Aston Villa	34	19	4	11	63	43	42
Sunderland	34	16	8	10	60	44	40
Sheffield U	34	19	2	13	64	56	40
Small Heath	34	17	5	12	54	38	39
Preston N.E.	34	13	10	11	42	37	36
Sheffield W	34	14	5	15	61	57	33
Woolwich A	34	12	9	13	36	40	33
Derby Co	34	12	8	14	37	48	32
Stoke	34	13	4	17	40	58	30
Blackburn R	34	11	5	18	40	51	27
Wolverhampton W	34	11	4	19	47	73	26
Middlesbrough	34	9	8	17	36	56	26
Nottingham F	34	9	7	18	40	61	25
Bury	34	10	4	20	47	67	24
Notts Co	34	5	8	21	36	69	18

1905-06

Division One

Manager: Tom Maley

Did you know that?

Match 1: Pearson's last game.
Match 9: Young's first and only game.
Match 22: Frost's last game.
Match 25: Dearden's last game.
Match 31: Livingstone's last game.
Match 32: McMahon's last game.
Match 33: Booth's last game.
Match 36: Hillman, Hynds, and Moffatt all played their last game.
Match 37: Gregory and Turnbull played their last game.
Match 38: Edmondson, Burgess, Bannister and Whittaker all played their last game.

Thursday 31 May 1906 was the day when FA Commissioners Clegg, Crump and Woolfall announced the findings of their investigation into the finances of the club. A total of 17 first-team players were to be banned until January 1907 (when they would subsequently be encouraged to sign for Manchester United); Manager Maley and Chairman Forrest were to be suspended for life; and directors Allison and Davies were to be suspended for seven months. Significant fines were also placed on each person. City was more or less dead.

Match No.	Date		Venue	Opponents	Result		Scorers	Attendance
1	Sep	2	A	Sheffield Wednesday	L	0-1		17,000
2		6	A	Newcastle United	D	2-2	Dorsett, Thornley	20,000
3		9	H	Nottingham Forest	W	5-0	Dorsett 2, Booth, Jones, Livingstone	13,000
4		16	H	Wolverhampton W.	W	4-0	Jones 2, Booth, Livingstone	9,000
5		23	A	Bury	W	4-2	Thornley 2, Dorsett, Livingstone	20,000
6		30	H	Middlesbrough	W	4-0	Dorsett 2, Jones, McMahon	35,000
7	Oct	7	A	Preston North End	L	0-2		9,000
8		21	A	Aston Villa	L	1-2	Livingstone	25,000
9		28	H	Liverpool	L	0-1		25,000
10	Nov	4	A	Sheffield United	W	3-1	Dorsett, Jones, Thornley	4,000
11		11	H	Notts County	W	5-1	Thornley 2, Buchan, Dorsett, Turnbull	7,000
12		18	A	Stoke	D	0-0		8,000
13		25	H	Bolton Wanderers	W	3-1	Booth, Jones, Thornley	35,000
14	Dec	2	A	Woolwich Arsenal	L	0-2		12,000
15		9	H	Blackburn Rovers	D	1-1	Dorsett	12,000
16		16	A	Sunderland	L	0-2		15,000
17		23	H	Birmingham	W	4-1	Turnbull 2, Livingstone, Glover (og)	15,000
18		25	A	Derby County	W	2-1	Dorsett, Frost	15,000
19		26	H	Newcastle United	L	1-4	Burgess	12,000
20		30	H	Sheffield Wednesday	W	2-1	Banks, Booth	12,000
21	Jan	1	H	Everton	W	1-0	Thornley	28,000
22		6	A	Nottingham Forest	W	1-0	Thornley	8,000
23		20	A	Wolverhampton W.	W	3-2	Booth, Livingstone, Thornley	6,000
24		27	H	Bury	W	5-2	Thornley 2, Booth, Dorsett, Turnbull	13,000
25	Feb	10	H	Preston North End	D	0-0		20,000
26	Mar	3	A	Liverpool	W	1-0	Booth	30,000
27		10	H	Sheffield United	L	1-2	Bannister	15,000
28		14	H	Aston Villa	L	1-4	Dorsett	20,000
29		17	A	Notts County	L	0-3		10,000
30		24	H	Stoke	W	2-0	Dorsett, Thornley	6,000
31		31	A	Bolton Wanderers	W	3-1	Thornley 2, Livingstone	37,000
32	Apr	7	H	Woolwich Arsenal	L	1-2	Dorsett	12,000
33		13	H	Derby County	L	1-2	Dorsett	25,000
34		14	A	Blackburn Rovers	D	1-1	Turnbull	10,000
35		16	A	Everton	W	3-0	Thornley 2, Turnbull	12,000
36		17	A	Middlesbrough	L	1-6	Moffatt	15,000
37		21	H	Sunderland	W	5-1	Thornley 3, Bannister, Whittaker	20,000
38		28	A	Birmingham	L	2-3	Burgess, Thornley	3,000
								Appearances
							One own goal	Goals

FA Cup

Match No.	Date		Venue	Opponents	Result		Scorers	Attendance
R1	Jan	13	A	Sheffield United	L	1-4	Bannister	21,352
								Appearances
								Goals

Hillman J	McMahon J	Burgess H	Dearden R	Hynds T	Buchan J	Dorsett G	Livingstone GT	Jones W	Pearson F	Booth F	Norgrove F	McOustra W	Thornley I	Edmondson JH	Gregory JR	Whittaker JH	Young J	Turnbull A	Frost S	Banks W	Bannister J	Moffatt J	Christie J	Steel A
1	2	3	4	5	6	7	8	9	10	11														
1		3		5	4	7	8	9		11	2	6	10											
		3		5	4	7	8	9		11	2	6	10	1										
		3		5	4	7	8	9		11	2	6	10	1										
	2	3		5	4	7	8	9		11		6	10	1										
	2	3		5	4	7	8	9		11		6	10	1										
	2			5	4	7	8	9				6	10	1	3	11								
	2	3		5	4	7	8	9		11		6	10	1										
	2	3		5	6	7	8	9		11			10	1			4							
	2	3		5	4	7	6	9		11			8	1				10						
	2	3		5	4	7	6	9		11			8	1				10						
	2	3		5	6	7	8	9		11			10	1					4					
	2	3		5		7	6	9		11			8	1				10	4					
	2	3		5	6	7		9		11			8	1				10	4					
	2	3	6	5		11	8	9					7	1				10	4					
		3	6	5	4	7	8	9		11	2			1				10						
	2	3		5		7	8			11			9	1				10	4	6				
	2	3		5		7	8			11			9	1				10	4	6				
	2	3		5			8			11			9	1				10	4	6	7			
		3		5	4	7				11	2		9	1				10		6	8			
		3			5	7				11	2		9	1				10	4	6	8			
		3		5		7		8		11	2		9	1				10	4	6				
	2	3		5	6	11	10			7			9	1				8		4				
1	2	3		5	4	7	8			11			9					10		6				
1	2	3	5		4	7	8			11			9					10		6				
	2	3		5	4	7	8			11			9	1				10		6				
	2	3		5	4	7	8			11			9	1						6	10			
	2			5	4	11	8	7			3		9	1				10		6				
	2			5	4	11		7			3		9	1				10		6	8			
1	2				4	11	8	7			3		9					10		6		5		
1	2	3		5	4	7	8			11			9					10		6				
1	2			5	4	7				11	3		9					10		6	8			
1		3		5		7		8		11			9		2			10		6		4		
1		3		5		7							9			11		10		6	8		2	4
1		3		5				7					9			11		10		6	8		2	4
1		3		5	4			7					9			11		10			8	6	2	
					5			7					9	1	2	11		10		6	8		3	4
		3			5	7		10					9	1		11				6	8		2	4
11	25	32	4	33	29	34	26	25	1	28	11	7	36	27	3	6	1	26	9	21	11	3	5	4
	1	2			1	15	7	6		7			21			1		6	1	1	2	1		
	2	3		5		7	10			11			9	1					4	6	8			
	1	1		1		1	1			1			1	1					1	1	1			
																						1		

League Table

	P	W	D	L	F	A	Pts
Liverpool	38	23	5	10	79	46	51
Preston N.E.	38	17	13	8	54	39	47
Sheffield W	38	18	8	12	63	52	44
Newcastle U	38	18	7	13	74	48	43
Manchester C	38	19	5	14	73	54	43
Bolton W	38	17	7	14	81	67	41
Birmingham C	38	17	7	14	65	59	41
Aston Villa	38	17	6	15	72	56	40
Blackburn R	38	16	8	14	54	52	40
Stoke	38	16	7	15	54	55	39
Everton	38	15	7	16	70	66	37
Woolwich A	38	15	7	16	62	64	37
Sheffield U	38	15	6	17	57	62	36
Sunderland	38	15	5	18	61	70	35
Derby Co	38	14	7	17	39	58	35
Notts Co	38	11	12	15	55	71	34
Bury	38	11	10	17	57	74	32
Middlesbrough	38	10	11	17	56	71	31
Nottingham F	38	13	5	20	58	79	31
Wolverhampton W	38	8	7	23	58	99	23

1906-07

Division One

Manager: Harry Newbould

Did you know that?

Match 1: Infamous heatwave game.
Match 2: Heaviest defeat as Manchester City.
Match 4: Blew's first and only game.
Match 6: First victory since FA bans.
Match 7: Fisher's last game.
Match 11: Banks's last game.
Match 13: Hall's last game.
Match 15: The first Division One Manchester derby.
Match 28: Christie and Rankin's last game.
Match 31: McOustra's last game.
Match 36: The point at Stoke guaranteed City's survival.
Match 38: Hamblett and Eyres's first and only game.

After City defeated United 3–0 in the first Division One derby match on 1 December, the Hyde Road offices were the venue for the transfer negotiations for the banned players. The bans were to be lifted on 1 January 1907 and by way of a somewhat strange rule many of the players were encouraged to join United. The Daily Dispatch: 'The inexplorable laws of the FA have decreed that he [Burgess] shall not play again for City, and that he should go to Clayton.' Many of City's star men, including Meredith, were encouraged to join United, with City powerless to act.

Match No.	Date	Venue	Opponents	Result		Scorers	Attendance
1	Sep 1	H	Woolwich Arsenal	L	1-4	Dorsett	15,000
2	3	A	Everton	L	1-9	Fisher	10,000
3	8	A	Sheffield Wednesday	L	1-3	Conlin	12,000
4	15	H	Bury	D	2-2	Jones, Thornley	20,000
5	22	A	Derby County	D	2-2	Dorsett 2	6,000
6	29	A	Middlesbrough	W	3-2	Fisher, Stewart, Thornley	15,000
7	Oct 6	H	Preston North End	D	1-1	Thornley	20,000
8	13	A	Newcastle United	L	0-2		20,000
9	20	H	Aston Villa	W	4-2	Thornley 2, Conlin, Stewart	35,000
10	27	A	Liverpool	L	4-5	Thornley 2, Jones, Stewart	18,000
11	Nov 3	H	Bristol City	L	0-1		15,000
12	10	A	Notts County	D	0-0		10,000
13	17	H	Sheffield United	L	0-2		19,000
14	24	A	Bolton Wanderers	D	1-1	Thornley	20,000
15	Dec 1	H	Manchester United	W	3-0	Stewart 2, Jones	50,000
16	8	A	Stoke	L	0-3		5,000
17	15	H	Blackburn Rovers	D	0-0		15,000
18	22	A	Sunderland	D	1-1	Thornley	8,000
19	25	H	Birmingham	W	1-0	Dorsett	14,000
20	26	H	Everton	W	3-1	Jones, Steel, Thornley	24,000
21	29	A	Woolwich Arsenal	L	1-4	Thornley	15,000
22	Jan 2	H	Middlesbrough	W	3-1	Jones 2, Thornley	7,000
23	5	H	Sheffield Wednesday	L	0-1		25,000
24	19	A	Bury	L	1-3	Grieve	18,000
25	26	H	Derby County	D	2-2	Jones, Thornley	14,000
26	Feb 9	A	Preston North End	W	3-1	Dorsett, Grieve, Jones	10,000
27	16	H	Newcastle United	D	1-1	Jones	40,000
28	23	A	Aston Villa	L	1-4	Stewart	15,000
29	Mar 2	H	Liverpool	W	1-0	Grieve	30,000
30	9	A	Bristol City	L	0-2		12,000
31	16	H	Notts County	W	2-1	Grieve, Ross	18,000
32	23	A	Sheffield United	W	4-1	Dorsett 2, Grieve 2	16,000
33	29	A	Birmingham	L	0-4		16,000
34	30	H	Bolton Wanderers	D	1-1	Jones	36,000
35	Apr 6	A	Manchester United	D	1-1	Dorsett	40,000
36	13	H	Stoke	D	2-2	Jones, Stewart	12,000
37	20	A	Blackburn Rovers	L	0-4		2,000
38	27	H	Sunderland	L	2-3	Eyres, Stewart	10,000
							Appearances
							Goals

FA Cup

	Date	Venue	Opponents	Result		Scorers	Attendance
R1	Jan 12	A	Blackburn Rovers	D	2-2	Dorsett, Thornley	20,000
rep	16	H	Blackburn Rovers	L	0-1		30,000
							Appearances
							Goals

Davies F	Christie J	Kelso T	Steel A	Buchan J	Dorsett G	Stewart G	Thornley I	Grieve RB	Jones W	Conlin J	Norgrove F	Fisher AW	Hall W	Eadie WP	Baldwin W	Blew HE	Banks W	Hill P	Smith WE	Blair J	McOustra W	Farrell T	Rankin B	Ross D	Wilkinson J	Hamblett G	Eyres S
1	2	3	4	5	6	7	8	9	10	11																	
1	2		4	5	6	7		9	10	11	3	8															
		2	4	6	10	7	9			11	3		1	5	8												
			4	6		7	9		8	11	3	10	1	5		2											
		2	4	6	8	7	9			11	3	10	1	5													
		2	4	6	8	7	9			11	3	10	1	5													
		2	4	6	8	7	9			11	3	10	1	5													
		2	4		8	7	9		10	11	3		1	5			6										
		2	4		8	7	9		10	11	3		1	5			6										
		2	4		8	7	9		10	11	3		1	5			6										
	2		4		8	7	9		10	11	3		1	5			6										
			4	6	10	7	9		8	11	3		1	5				2									
		5	4	6	10	7	9		8	11	3		1					2									
				6	4	7	9		8	11	3			5				2	1	10							
				6	4	7	9		8	11	3			5				2	1	10							
				6	4	7	9		8	11	3			5				2	1	10							
				4	8	7	9			11	3			5				2	1	10	6						
		2		4	8	7	9		10	11	3			5					1		6						
		2		4	8	7	9		10	11	3			5					1		6						
		2	4	6	8	7	9		10	11	3			5					1								
		2	4	6		7	8	9	10	11	3			5					1								
			4	6		7	9	8	10	11	3			5				2	1								
			4			7		8	9	11	3			5				2	1		6	10					
		2	4	6	11	7	9	8	10		3			5					1								
				4	8	7	9		10	11	3			5				2	1		6						
					4		9	8	10	11	3			5				2	1		6		7				
					4	7		9	10	11	3			5				2	1		6	8					
	3	2			4	7	9	8						5					1		6		11	10			
1		3		6	4	7		8	9	11								2						10	5		
		3		6	4	7	9	8		11				5				2	1					10			
1		3		4		7	9	8		11				5				2			6			10			
1		3	4	6	9	7		8		11				5				2						10			
		3	4	6	9	7		8		11				5				2	1					10			
		3	4		9	7		8	10	11				5				2	1	6							
		3		4	7		9	8	10	11				5				2	1	6							
		3		4		7	9	8	10	11								2	1	6					5		
			4	5	9	7		8	10		3							2	1	6		11					
		3	4		10	7		8		11								2	1	6						5	9
5	4	24	23	28	32	36	29	19	27	35	27	5	11	31	1	1	4	21	22	9	9	3	2	6	2	1	1
			1		8	8	13	6	11	2		2												1			1
			4	6	8	7	9		10	11	3			5				2	1								
			4	6	8	7	9		10	11	3			5				2	1								
			2	2	2	2	2		2	2	2			2				2	2								
					1		1																				

League Table

	P	W	D	L	F	A	Pts
Newcastle U	38	22	7	9	74	46	51
Bristol C	38	20	8	10	66	47	48
Everton	38	20	5	13	70	46	45
Sheffield U	38	17	11	10	57	55	45
Aston Villa	38	19	6	13	78	52	44
Bolton W	38	18	8	12	59	47	44
Woolwich A	38	20	4	14	66	59	44
Manchester U	38	17	8	13	53	56	42
Birmingham C	38	15	8	15	52	52	38
Sunderland	38	14	9	15	65	66	37
Middlesbrough	38	15	6	17	56	63	36
Blackburn R	38	14	7	17	56	59	35
Sheffield W	38	12	11	15	49	60	35
Preston N.E.	38	14	7	17	44	57	35
Liverpool	38	13	7	18	64	65	33
Bury	38	13	6	19	58	68	32
Manchester C	38	10	12	16	53	77	32
Notts Co	38	8	15	15	46	50	31
Derby Co	38	9	9	20	41	59	27
Stoke	38	8	10	20	41	64	26

1907-08

Division One

Manager: Harry Newbould

Did you know that?

Match 17: Steele's last game.
Match 26: Callaghan and Baldwin's last game.
Match 26: Bannister's first and only game.
Match 28: Hill's last game.

Four of United's star men when they won the title for the first time were players transferred to the Reds following the FA's investigations. Jimmy Bannister, Herbert Burgess, Billy Meredith and top scorer Sandy Turnbull made the difference between an average side and Championship winners. Despite the loss a patched-up City still managed to finish third.

Match No.	Date	Venue	Opponents	Result		Scorers	Attendance
1	Sep 2	A	Sunderland	W	5-2	Grieve 3, Conlin, Stewart	15,000
2	7	A	Everton	D	3-3	Thornley 3	35,000
3	14	H	Sunderland	D	0-0		20,000
4	21	A	Woolwich Arsenal	L	1-2	Thornley	12,000
5	28	H	Sheffield Wednesday	W	3-2	Ross 2, Thornley	33,000
6	Oct 5	A	Bristol City	L	1-2	Thornley	12,000
7	12	H	Notts County	W	2-1	Grieve 2	13,000
8	19	H	Newcastle United	W	1-0	Thornley	32,000
9	26	A	Preston North End	W	4-2	Conlin, Dorsett, Grieve, Thornley	8,000
10	Nov 2	H	Bury	D	2-2	Jones, Wood	35,000
11	9	A	Aston Villa	D	2-2	Thornley 2	15,000
12	16	H	Liverpool	D	1-1	Dorsett	25,000
13	23	A	Middlesbrough	L	0-2		10,000
14	Dec 7	A	Chelsea	D	2-2	Buchan, Jones	20,000
15	14	H	Nottingham Forest	W	4-2	Wood 2, Eadie, Thornley	13,000
16	21	A	Manchester United	L	1-3	Eadie	35,000
17	25	A	Birmingham	L	1-2	Dorsett	12,000
18	26	H	Bolton Wanderers	W	1-0	Grieve	35,000
19	28	H	Blackburn Rovers	W	2-0	Dorsett, Thornley	20,000
20	Jan 1	A	Bolton Wanderers	L	0-2		25,000
21	4	H	Everton	W	4-2	Grieve 2, Conlin, Ross	9,000
22	18	H	Woolwich Arsenal	W	4-0	Eadie, Grieve, Jones, Wood	20,000
23	25	A	Sheffield Wednesday	L	1-5	Dorsett	10,000
24	Feb 8	A	Notts County	L	0-1		8,000
25	15	A	Newcastle United	D	1-1	Conlin	25,000
26	29	A	Bury	D	0-0		8,000
27	Mar 7	H	Aston Villa	W	3-2	Dorsett 3	25,000
28	11	H	Sheffield United	L	0-2		19,000
29	14	A	Liverpool	W	1-0	Dorsett	14,000
30	21	H	Middlesbrough	W	2-1	Thornley, Webb	32,000
31	28	A	Sheffield United	W	2-1	Conlin, Thornley	10,000
32	Apr 4	H	Chelsea	L	0-3		22,000
33	6	H	Preston North End	W	5-0	Buchan 2, Webb 2, Wilkinson	10,000
34	11	A	Nottingham Forest	L	1-3	Dorsett	5,000
35	17	H	Birmingham	W	2-1	Conlin, Jones	25,000
36	18	H	Manchester United	D	0-0		40,000
37	21	H	Bristol City	D	0-0		5,000
38	25	A	Blackburn Rovers	D	0-0		8,000
							Appearances
							Goals

FA Cup

Round	Date	Venue	Opponents	Result		Scorers	Attendance
R1	Jan 11	A	Glossop	D	0-0		6,500
rep	15	H	Glossop	W	6-0	Buchan, Conlin, Dorsett, Grieve, Jones, Wood	20,000
R2	Feb 1	H	New Brompton	D	1-1	Jones	7,000
rep	5	A	New Brompton	W	2-1	Buchan, Wood	12,000
R3	22	H	Fulham	D	1-1	Blair	25,000
rep	26	A	Fulham	L	1-3	Wood	37,000
							Appearances
							Goals

Smith WE	Hill P	Kelso T	Buchan J	Eadie WP	Blair J	Stewart G	Grieve RB	Thornley I	Jones W	Conlin J	Norgrove F	Dorsett G	Wood J	Ross D	Steel A	Buckley FC	Jackson BH	Callaghan T	Bannister E	Baldwin W	Webb C	Wilkinson J	Holford T
1	2	3	4	5	6	7	8	9	10	11													
1		2	4	5	6	7	8	9	10	11	3												
1		2	4	5	6	7		9	10	11	3	8											
1	2	3	4	5	6	7	8	9	10	11													
1	2	3	4	5	6			9		11		7	8	10									
1	2	3	4	5	6		8	9		11		7		10									
1	2	3		5	6		9			11		7	8	10	4								
1		2		5	6		8	9		11	3	7	10		4								
1		2		5	6		8	9		11	3	7	10			4							
1	4	2			6		8	9	7	11	3		10			5							
1		2			6		8	9	10	11	3	7	4			5							
1		2			6		8	9	10	11	3	7	4			5							
1	2				6			9	10	11	3	7	4	8		5							
1	2		4	5	6			9	10	11	3	7		8									
1	2		4	5	6			9		11	3	7	8	10									
1	2		4	5	6			9	10	11	3	7	8										
1	2			5	6		10	9		11	3	7	8		4								
1	2			5	6	7	10	9		11		4	8				3						
1	2			5	6	7	10	9		11		4	8				3						
1	2			5	6	7	10	9		11		4	8				3						
1	2		4	5		7	9			11		6	8	10			3						
1		2	4	5		7	9		10	11		6	8				3						
1		2	4			7	9		10	11		6	8			5	3						
1	2		5		6			9		11		4	8	10			3	7					
1		2	4	5	6			8	9	11		7		10			3						
1		2	4	5				8	10			11					3	7	6	9			
1		2	4	5	6			8		11		9	10				3				7		
1	2		4	5	6				10	11		9	8				3				7		
1		2	4	5	6			8	10	11		9					3				7		
1		2	4	5	6			8	10	11		9					3				7		
1		2	4	5	6			8	10	11		9					3				7		
1		2	4	5	6			8		11		9		10			3				7		
1		2	4		6				8	11		9				5	3				7	10	
1		2	4	5	6				10	11		9	8				3				7		
1		2	4	5	6			8	10	11		9					3				7		
1			4	5	6			8	10	11	3	9					2				7		
1			4		6			9	10	11	3	7	8				2						5
1		2	4		6			8	10	11		9					3				7		5
38	17	25	27	29	34	10	17	31	24	37	14	34	22	10	3	7	21	2	1	1	11	1	2
			3	3		1	10	14	4	6		10	4	3							3	1	
1		2	4	5	6			9		11		7	8	10			3						
1		2	4	5			8	9	10	11		7	6				3						
1		2	4	5	6		9	8	10	11		7					3						
1		2	4	5	6			9	10	11		7	8				3						
1		2	4	5	6			9	10	11		7	8				3						
1		2	4	5	6			9	10	11		7	8				3						
6		6	6	6	5		2	6	5	6		6	5	1			6						
			2		1		1		2	1		1	3										

League Table

	P	W	D	L	F	A	Pts
Manchester U	38	23	6	9	81	48	52
Aston Villa	38	17	9	12	77	59	43
Manchester C	38	16	11	11	62	54	43
Newcastle U	38	15	12	11	65	54	42
Sheffield W	38	19	4	15	73	64	42
Middlesbrough	38	17	7	14	54	45	41
Bury	38	14	11	13	58	61	39
Liverpool	38	16	6	16	68	61	38
Nottingham F	38	13	11	14	59	62	37
Bristol C	38	12	12	14	58	61	36
Everton	38	15	6	17	58	64	36
Preston N.E.	38	12	12	14	47	53	36
Chelsea	38	14	8	16	53	62	36
Blackburn R*	38	12	12	14	51	63	36
Woolwich A *	38	12	12	14	51	63	36
Sunderland	38	16	3	19	78	75	35
Sheffield U	38	12	11	15	52	58	35
Notts Co	38	13	8	17	39	51	34
Bolton W	38	14	5	19	52	58	33
Birmingham C	38	9	12	17	40	60	30

*Woolwich Arsenal & Blackburn Rovers finished in equal 14th place

1908-09

Division One

Manager: Harry Newbould

Did you know that?

Match 11: Buckley's last game.
Match 21: Wood's last game.
Match 27: Broomfield, Webb and Grieve's last game.
Match 28: Hitchcock's last game.
Match 30: Yuill and Mansfield's last game.
Match 36: Hendren's last game.
Match 38: A point would have kept City in Division One.

Patsy Hendren, who appeared in two games for City, was also a famous international cricketer. He went on to play for Middlesex and England.

Match No.	Date	Venue	Opponents	Result		Scorers	Attendance
1	Sep 1	H	Sunderland	W	1-0	Eadie	30,000
2	5	H	Blackburn Rovers	D	3-3	Thornley 2, Jones	30,000
3	12	A	Bradford City	D	0-0		30,000
4	19	H	Manchester United	L	1-2	Thornley	40,000
5	26	A	Everton	L	3-6	Thornley 3	20,000
6	Oct 3	H	Leicester Fosse	W	5-2	Grieve 2, Ross 2, Dorsett	14,000
7	10	A	Woolwich Arsenal	L	0-3		11,000
8	17	H	Notts County	W	1-0	Thornley	20,000
9	24	A	Newcastle United	L	0-2		30,000
10	31	H	Bristol City	W	5-1	Thornley 2, Buchan, Dorsett, Wood	18,000
11	Nov 7	A	Preston North End	L	0-3		10,000
12	14	H	Middlesbrough	D	0-0		18,000
13	21	A	Sheffield Wednesday	L	1-3	Thornley	12,000
14	28	A	Liverpool	W	3-1	Conlin, Dorsett, Jones	10,000
15	Dec 5	H	Bury	W	6-1	Thornley 3, Dorsett 2, Stewart	20,000
16	12	A	Sheffield United	L	0-4		12,000
17	19	H	Aston Villa	W	2-0	Dorsett, Holford	12,000
18	25	H	Chelsea	L	1-2	Dorsett	25,000
19	26	A	Chelsea	W	2-1	Jones, Ross	30,000
20	28	A	Nottingham Forest	W	2-0	Holford, Ross	10,000
21	Jan 2	A	Blackburn Rovers	L	2-3	Conlin, Wood	10,000
22	9	H	Bradford City	W	4-3	Holford 3, Conlin	11,000
23	23	A	Manchester United	L	1-3	Conlin	40,000
24	30	H	Everton	W	4-0	Holford 3, Wilkinson	20,000
25	Feb 13	H	Woolwich Arsenal	D	2-2	Buchan, Holford	23,000
26	20	A	Notts County	L	1-5	Dorsett	4,000
27	27	H	Newcastle United	L	0-2		25,000
28	Mar 11	A	Leicester Fosse	L	1-3	Thornley	8,000
29	13	H	Preston North End	W	4-1	Thornley 2, Jones, Yuill	10,000
30	20	A	Middlesbrough	L	0-3		8,000
31	27	H	Sheffield Wednesday	W	4-0	Holford 3, Jones	10,000
32	Apr 3	H	Liverpool	W	4-0	Buchan, Dorsett, Jones, Ross	15,000
33	9	A	Sunderland	L	0-2		10,000
34	10	A	Bury	L	0-1		16,000
35	13	H	Nottingham Forest	W	2-1	Conlin, Thornley	3,000
36	17	H	Sheffield United	L	1-3	Thornley	12,000
37	24	A	Aston Villa	L	1-2	Buchan	15,000
38	28	A	Bristol City	L	0-1		5,000
							Appearances
							Goals

FA Cup

Match No.	Date	Venue	Opponents	Result		Scorers	Attendance
R1	Jan 16	H	Tottenham Hotspur	L	3-4	Holford 3	20,000
							Appearances
							Goals

Smith WE	Kelso T	Jackson BH	Buchan J	Eadie WP	Blair J	Webb C	Grieve RB	Thornley I	Jones W	Conlin J	Ross D	Dorsett G	Holford T	Buckley FC	Burgess C	Bottomley W	Stewart G	Wood J	Broomfield HC	Norgrove F	Wilkinson J	Yuill JG	Hitchcock E	Brown JP	Mansfield E	Ramsey JD	Hendren EH
1	2	3	4	5	6	7	8	9	10	11																	
1	2	3	4	5	6	7	8	9	10	11																	
1	2	3	4	5	6	7	8	9	10	11																	
1	2	3	4	5	6	7		9	8		10	11															
1	2	3	4		6	7	8	9		11	10		5														
1	2	3	4	5		7	9			11	10	8		6													
1	2	3	4	5		7	9			11	10	8		6													
1		3	4		6			8	9	11	10				2	5	7										
1		3	4					8	9	11	10	6	5		2		7										
1	2		4	5		7		9	10			11		6	3			8									
1	2		4	5		7		9	10			11		6	3			8									
1		2	4			7		9	10	11		6	5		3			8									
		2	4		6		8	9		11		10	5		3		7		1								
		2	4		6			8	10	11		7	5		3			9	1								
1		2	4		6			9	8	11		10	5		3		7										
1	2		4		6			9	8	11		10	5		3		7										
1			4		6			9	8			11	5		2		7			3	10						
1			4		6			9	8			11	5		2		7			3	10						
1		2	4		6			9	8	11	10	7	5							3							
1		2	4		6					11	10	7	9					8		3	5						
1	2		4		6			9		11	10	7	5					8		3							
1		2	4		6				8	11	10	7	9							3	5						
	2		4		6			8		11	10	7	9						1	3	5						
1	2		4		6				8	11	10		9		3		7				5						
1	2		4		6			7	8	11	10		9		3						5						
1	2		4		6				8	11	10	7	9		3						5						
		3	4			7	8	9	10	11			5		2				1		6						
1		3	4		6			9			10				2						5	7	8	11			
1		3	4		6			9	8		10		5		2							7		11			
1		3	4		6			9			10		5		2							7		11	8		
1		3	4		6			7	8		10		9		2						5			11			
1		3	4		6			7	8		10	11	9		2						5						
1	3		4		6			7	8		10	11	9		2						5						
1	3		4		10			7	8	11			9		2						5					6	
1	3		4		6			7	10	11			9		2						5						8
1	3		4		6			7	8	11			9		2						5						10
1	3		4	5	6			7	8	11	10				2						9						
1	3		4	5	6			9	8	11	10	7			2												
34	21	22	38	10	31	11	8	32	29	27	22	22	26	4	26	1	8	6	4	7	17	3	1	4	1	1	2
			4	1			2	18	6	5	5	9	12				1	2			1	1					

Smith WE	Kelso T	Jackson BH	Buchan J	Eadie WP	Blair J	Webb C	Grieve RB	Thornley I	Jones W	Conlin J	Ross D	Dorsett G	Holford T	Buckley FC	Burgess C	Bottomley W	Stewart G	Wood J	Broomfield HC	Norgrove F	Wilkinson J	Yuill JG	Hitchcock E	Brown JP	Mansfield E	Ramsey JD	Hendren EH
1	2		4	5					8	11	10	6	9				7			3							
1	1		1	1					1	1	1	1	1				1			1							
													3														

League Table

	P	W	D	L	F	A	Pts
Newcastle U	38	24	5	9	65	41	53
Everton	38	18	10	10	82	57	46
Sunderland	38	21	2	15	78	63	44
Blackburn R	38	14	13	11	61	50	41
Sheffield W	38	17	6	15	67	61	40
Woolwich A	38	14	10	14	52	49	38
Aston Villa	38	14	10	14	58	56	38
Bristol C	38	13	12	13	45	58	38
Middlesbrough	38	14	9	15	59	53	37
Preston N.E.	38	13	11	14	48	44	37
Chelsea	38	14	9	15	56	61	37
Sheffield U	38	14	9	15	51	59	37
Manchester U	38	15	7	16	58	68	37
Nottingham F	38	14	8	16	66	57	36
Notts Co	38	14	8	16	51	48	36
Liverpool	38	15	6	17	57	65	36
Bury	38	14	8	16	63	77	36
Bradford C	38	12	10	16	47	47	34
Manchester C	38	15	4	19	67	69	34
Leicester C	38	8	9	21	54	102	25

1909-10

Division Two

Manager: Harry Newbould

Did you know that?

Match 4: Davies's last game.
Match 7: Swann's first and only game.
Match 11: Brown's last game.
Match 18: Chapelow's last game.
Match 19: Coupe's first and only game.
Match 30: £1,000 proceeds of this game given to Thornley as his benefit.
Match 31: Blair's last game.
Match 32: James's last game.
Match 36: Furr's last game.

By beating Leeds in their last home game of the season City guaranteed promotion, but the title was not assured. Going into the last match City had 54 points, Hull had 53, Derby 52 (but a much worse goal average), and Oldham 51. City's last-day defeat ensured a tense final day, which saw City win the title and Oldham leapfrog over the others.

Match No.	Date	Venue	Opponents	Result		Scorers	Attendance
1	Sep 2	H	Blackpool	L	1-2	Thornley	14,000
2	4	A	Leicester Fosse	W	3-1	Conlin, Ross, Stewart	9,000
3	11	H	Lincoln City	W	6-2	Jones 2, Thornley 2, Conlin, Dorsett	8,000
4	18	A	Clapton Orient	L	2-3	Dorsett, Ross	15,000
5	25	A	Blackpool	D	0-0		8,000
6	Oct 2	A	Hull City	W	2-1	Dorsett, Jones	12,000
7	9	H	Derby County	W	2-1	Conlin, Holford	20,000
8	16	A	Stockport County	W	2-1	Conlin, Eadie	12,000
9	23	H	Glossop	D	3-3	Ross 2, Holford	14,000
10	27	A	Gainsborough Trin.	W	3-1	Jones 3	4,000
11	30	A	Birmingham	D	1-1	Thornley	18,000
12	Nov 6	H	West Bromwich Albion	W	3-2	Holford 2, Thornley	24,000
13	13	A	Oldham Athletic	L	0-1		22,000
14	27	A	Fulham	D	1-1	Thornley	12,000
15	Dec 4	H	Burnley	W	4-0	Jones 2, Dorsett, Thornley	12,000
16	11	A	Leeds City	W	3-1	Thornley 2, Ross	3,000
17	18	H	Wolverhampton W.	W	6-0	Thornley 3, Dorsett 2, Ross	20,000
18	25	A	Bradford Park Avenue	L	0-2		25,000
19	27	H	Grimsby Town	W	2-0	Holford, Wynn	20,000
20	Jan 1	H	Bradford Park Avenue	W	3-1	Dorsett 2, Wynn	23,000
21	8	H	Leicester Fosse	W	2-0	Holford, Jones	25,000
22	22	A	Lincoln City	W	2-0	Conlin, Wynn	9,000
23	Feb 12	H	Hull City	W	3-0	Conlin, Holford, Wynn	30,000
24	26	H	Stockport County	W	2-1	Wynn 2	16,000
25	Mar 9	H	Barnsley	D	0-0		15,000
26	12	H	Birmingham	W	3-0	Conlin, Eadie, Jones	15,000
27	16	A	Derby County	L	1-3	Dorsett	10,000
28	19	A	West Bromwich Albion	D	0-0		10,000
29	25	A	Grimsby Town	W	1-0	Jones	6,000
30	26	H	Oldham Athletic	L	0-2		40,000
31	28	H	Gainsborough Trin.	W	3-1	Dorsett, Holford, Jones	15,000
32	Apr 2	A	Barnsley	D	1-1	Dorsett	10,000
33	6	A	Glossop	W	3-0	Conlin 2, Gould	5,000
34	9	H	Fulham	W	3-1	Holford 2, Wynn	16,000
35	13	H	Clapton Orient	W	2-1	Dorsett, Wynn	8,000
36	16	A	Burnley	D	3-3	Gould, Holford, Wynn	9,000
37	23	H	Leeds City	W	3-0	Conlin, Dorsett, Wynn	16,000
38	30	A	Wolverhampton W.	L	2-3	Conlin, Holford	10,000
							Appearances
							Goals

FA Cup

	Date	Venue	Opponents	Result		Scorers	Attendance
R1	Jan 15	A	Workington	W	2-1	Wynn 2	5,233
R2	Feb 5	A	Southampton	W	5-0	Conlin, Dorsett, Holford, Jones, Stewart	15,965
R3	19	A	Aston Villa	W	2-1	Jones, Stewart	45,000
R4	Mar 5	A	Swindon Town	L	0-2		14,429
							Appearances
							Goals

Smith WE	Kelso T	Burgess C	Buchan J	Wilkinson J	Dorsett G	Stewart G	Jones W	Thornley I	Chapelhow H	Conlin J	Jackson BH	Norgrove F	Holford T	Ross D	Davies F	Lyall J	Eadie WP	Swann JW	Brown JP	James FE	Bottomley W	Wynn GA	Coupe D	Blair J	Furr GM	Gould W
1	2	3	4	5	6	7	8	9	10	11																
1			4		6	7	8	9		11	2	3	5	10												
1			4		6	7	8	9		11	2	3	5	10												
			4		6	7	8	9		11	2	3	5	10	1											
			4		6	7	8	9		11	2	3	5	10		1										
			4		6		10	8	7	11	2	3	9			1	5									
			4		6	7	10	8		11	2	3	9			1	5									
			4		6	7	10	8		11	2	3	9				5	1								
			4		6		10	7		11	2	3	9	8		1	5									
	2		4		6	7	10	8			3		9			1	5		11							
	2		4		6	7	10	8			3					1	5		11	9						
	2		4		6	7	10	8		11	3		9			1	5									
	2		4		6	7	10	8		11	3		9			1	5									
	2				6		10	9	7	11	3			8		1	5				4					
		2			6		10	9	7	11	3			8		1	5				4					
	2				6		10	9	7	11	3			8		1	5				4					
	2				6		10	9	7	11	3			8		1	5				4					
	2				6		10		7	11	3		9			1	5				4	8				
		3			6	7	10			11			9			1	5				4	8	2			
	2				6	7	10			11	3		9			1	5				4	8				
	2				6	7	10			11	3		9			1	5				4	8				
	2				6	7	10			11	3		9			1	5				4	8				
	2				6	7	10			11	3		9			1	5				4	8				
	2		4		6	7	10			11	3		9			1	5					8				
	2		4		6	7	10			11	3		9			1	5					8				
	2		4		6	7	10	9		11	3					1	5					8				
	2		4		6	7	10			11	3		9			1	5					8				
	2		4		6	7	10	9		11	3			8		1	5									
	2		4		6	7	10	9		11	3		5			1						8				
	2	3	4		7		10	9		11			5			1						8	6			
	2			5	4		10			11	3		9			1						8	6	7		
	2			5	6					11	3		4	10		1				9		8		7		
	2			5	6		10			11	3		9			1					4	8				7
	2			5	6		10			11	3		9			1					4	8				7
	2			5	6		10			11	3		9			1					4	8				7
	2			5	6		10				3		9			1					4	8			7	11
	2			5	6		10	4		11	3		9			1						8				7
	2			5	6		10	4		11	3		9			1						8				7
3	28	4	20	9	38	22	37	23	7	35	35	8	30	11	1	33	23	1	2	2	14	20	1	2	3	6
					13	1	12	12		11			12	6			2					10				2

Smith WE	Kelso T	Burgess C	Buchan J	Wilkinson J	Dorsett G	Stewart G	Jones W	Thornley I	Chapelhow H	Conlin J	Jackson BH	Norgrove F	Holford T	Ross D	Davies F	Lyall J	Eadie WP	Swann JW	Brown JP	James FE	Bottomley W	Wynn GA	Coupe D	Blair J	Furr GM	Gould W
	2				6	7	10			11	3		9			1	5				4	8				
	2				6	7	10			11	3		9			1	5				4	8				
	2				6	7	10			11	3		9			1	5				4	8				
	2				6	7	10			11	3		9			1	5				4	8				
	4				4	4	4			4	4		4			4	4				4	4				
					1	2	2			1			1									2				

League Table

	P	W	D	L	F	A	Pts
Manchester C	38	23	8	7	81	40	54
Oldham A	38	23	7	8	79	39	53
Hull C	38	23	7	8	80	46	53
Derby Co	38	22	9	7	72	47	53
Leicester C	38	20	4	14	79	58	44
Glossop N.E.	38	18	7	13	64	57	43
Fulham	38	14	13	11	51	43	41
Wolverhampton W	38	17	6	15	64	63	40
Barnsley	38	16	7	15	62	59	39
Bradford P.A.	38	17	4	17	64	59	38
W.B.A.	38	16	5	17	58	56	37
Blackpool	38	14	8	16	50	52	36
Stockport Co	38	13	8	17	50	47	34
Burnley	38	14	6	18	62	61	34
Lincoln C	38	10	11	17	42	69	31
Clapton O	38	12	6	20	37	60	30
Leeds U	38	10	7	21	46	80	27
Gainsborough T	38	10	6	22	33	75	26
Grimsby T	38	9	6	23	50	77	24
Birmingham C	38	8	7	23	42	78	23

1910-11

Division One

Manager: Harry Newbould

Did you know that?

Match 7: Lyall and Codling's last game.
Match 9: Wilkinson's last game.
Match 26: Humphreys's last game.
Match 29: Chaplin's last game.
Match 30: Burgess's last game.
Match 36: Jackson, Buchan and Conlin's last game.
Match 37: Nelson's last game.
Match 37: Salt's first and only game.
Match 38: Stewart & Gould's last game.

When the 1910–11 season started the Blues had roofed three sides of the ground, meaning Hyde Road had covered accommodation for over 35,000 spectators. No other Manchester venue, including Old Trafford and Maine Road, could match that total until the Kippax was roofed in 1957.

Match No.	Date	Venue	Opponents	Result		Scorers	Attendance
1	Sep 1	H	Bury	W	5-1	Wynn 3, Conlin, Holford	18,000
2	3	A	Preston North End	D	1-1	Holford	12,000
3	10	H	Notts County	L	0-1		30,000
4	17	A	Manchester United	L	1-2	Jones	50,000
5	24	H	Liverpool	L	1-2	J Dorsett	25,000
6	Oct 1	A	Bury	L	2-5	G Dorsett, Wynn	20,000
7	8	H	Sheffield United	L	0-4		20,000
8	15	A	Aston Villa	L	1-2	Wall	15,000
9	22	H	Sunderland	D	3-3	G Dorsett, Norgrove, Thornley	25,000
10	29	A	Woolwich Arsenal	W	1-0	J Dorsett	12,000
11	Nov 5	H	Bradford City	L	1-3	J Dorsett	10,000
12	12	A	Blackburn Rovers	L	0-2		10,000
13	19	H	Nottingham Forest	W	1-0	Conlin	20,000
14	26	H	Oldham Athletic	W	2-0	Conlin, Thornley	20,000
15	Dec 3	A	Everton	L	0-1		10,000
16	10	H	Sheffield Wednesday	L	1-2	Thornley	15,000
17	17	A	Bristol City	L	1-2	Smith	6,000
18	24	H	Newcastle United	W	2-0	Conlin, Wynn	15,000
19	26	A	Middlesbrough	D	0-0		25,000
20	27	A	Tottenham Hotspur	D	1-1	Smith	30,000
21	31	H	Preston North End	L	0-2		27,000
22	Jan 3	H	Tottenham Hotspur	W	2-1	Jones, Ross	10,000
23	7	A	Notts County	W	1-0	Ross	10,000
24	21	H	Manchester United	D	1-1	Jones	42,000
25	28	A	Liverpool	D	1-1	Smith	12,000
26	Feb 11	A	Sheffield United	D	2-2	Ross, Smith	8,000
27	18	H	Aston Villa	D	1-1	Jones	35,000
28	25	A	Sunderland	L	0-4		8,000
29	Mar 4	H	Woolwich Arsenal	D	1-1	Thornley	15,000
30	14	A	Bradford City	L	0-1		7,000
31	18	H	Blackburn Rovers	D	0-0		30,000
32	25	A	Nottingham Forest	D	0-0		8,000
33	Apr 1	A	Oldham Athletic	D	1-1	Smith	20,000
34	8	H	Everton	W	2-1	Thornley, Wynn	30,000
35	14	H	Middlesbrough	W	2-1	Jones, Thornley	30,000
36	15	A	Sheffield Wednesday	L	1-4	Jones	9,000
37	22	H	Bristol City	L	1-2	Wynn	33,000
38	29	A	Newcastle United	D	3-3	Wynn 2, Ross	5,000
							Appearances
							Goals

FA Cup

	Date	Venue	Opponents	Result		Scorers	Attendance
R1	Jan 14	A	Stoke	W	2-1	Jones, Smith	29,000
R2	Feb 4	A	Wolverhampton W.	L	0-1		25,000
							Appearances
							Goals

Lyall J	Kelso T	Jackson BH	Bottomley W	Eadie WP	Dorsett G	Stewart G	Wynn GA	Holford T	Jones W	Conlin J	Dorsett JAH	Codling RJ	Ross D	Wilkinson J	Burgess C	Wall LJ	Smith WE	Norgrove F	Thornley I	Chaplin JF	Buchan J	Humphreys R	Smith JW	Brown HR	Nelson JH	Brooks GH	Gould W	Salt GO
1	2	3	4	5	6	7	8	9	10	11																		
1	2	3	4	5	6		8	9	10	11	7																	
1	2	3	4	5			8	9	10	11	7	6																
1	2	3	4	5				9	10	11	7	6	8															
1	2	3	4					9	10	11	7	6	8	5														
1	2	3	5		6		8		9	11	7	4	10															
1		3	4	5	11		8		10		7	6			2	9												
		2	4	5	6		8		10	11	7					9	1	3										
	2		4		6	7	8		10	11				5			1	3	9									
	2		4	5	6		8		10	11	7						1	3	9									
		2	4	5	6		8		10	11	7						1	3	9									
		2	4	5		7		9	6	11	10						1	3	8									
	2			5		7			6	11	8					10	1		9	3	4							
	2			5		7			6	11	8					10	1		9	3	4							
	2	3		5		7			6	11	8					10	1		9		4							
	2			5	6			9		11	7					10	1		8	3	4							
			4	5	8			6		11	7					10	1			3		2	9					
	2			5	4		8	6	10	11	7						1			3			9					
	2					7	8	5	10		11						1			3		4	9	6				
	2					7	8	5	6	11	10						1			3			9	4				
	2					7	8	6	10		11						1		5	3	4		9					
	2				4	7		6	10		11		8			5	1			3			9					
	2				4	7		6	10		11		8			5	1			3			9					
	2			5	4	7		6	10		11		8				1			3			9					
	2			5	4	7		6	10	11			8				1			3			9					
		3	4		6		8	5		11			10				1					2	9		7			
	2		4	5				6	10	11							1			3			9		7	8		
	2		8	5	4			6	10	11							1			3			9		7			
	2		4	5				6	10	11			8				1		9	3					7			
	2		4	5		8		6	10						3		1		9						7		11	
	2			5	4	7		6	10		11						1	3	8				9					
	2			5	4	7	8	6	10		11						1	3	9									
	2			5	4		8	6	10	11	7						1	3					9					
	2			5	4		8	6	10	11	7						1	3	9									
	2			5	4		8	6	10	11							1	3	9						7			
		2		5				6	10	11						4	1	3	9		8				7			
	2			5	4		8	6	10								1	3	9						7			11
	2		4	5		7	8	6					10				1	3	9								11	
7	31	13	19	29	23	17	20	29	34	27	26	5	10	2	2	10	31	13	18	15	6	3	14	2	8	1	2	1
					2		9	2	6	4	3		4			1		1	6				5					

Lyall J	Kelso T	Jackson BH	Bottomley W	Eadie WP	Dorsett G	Stewart G	Wynn GA	Holford T	Jones W	Conlin J	Dorsett JAH	Codling RJ	Ross D	Wilkinson J	Burgess C	Wall LJ	Smith WE	Norgrove F	Thornley I	Chaplin JF	Buchan J	Humphreys R	Smith JW	Brown HR	Nelson JH	Brooks GH	Gould W	Salt GO
	2			5	4	7		6	10		11		8				1			3			9					
	2			5	4	7		6	10	11			8				1			3			9					
	2			2	2	2		2	2	1	1		2				2			2			2					
									1														1					

League Table

	P	W	D	L	F	A	Pts
Manchester U	38	22	8	8	72	40	52
Aston Villa	38	22	7	9	69	41	51
Sunderland	38	15	15	8	67	48	45
Everton	38	19	7	12	50	36	45
Bradford C	38	20	5	13	51	42	45
Sheffield W	38	17	8	13	47	48	42
Oldham A	38	16	9	13	44	41	41
Newcastle U	38	15	10	13	61	43	40
Sheffield U	38	15	8	15	49	43	38
Woolwich A	38	13	12	13	41	49	38
Notts Co	38	14	10	14	37	45	38
Blackburn R	38	13	11	14	62	54	37
Liverpool	38	15	7	16	53	53	37
Preston N.E.	38	12	11	15	40	49	35
Tottenham H	38	13	6	19	52	63	32
Middlesbrough	38	11	10	17	49	63	32
Manchester C	38	9	13	16	43	58	31
Bury	38	9	11	18	43	71	29
Bristol C	38	11	5	22	43	66	27
Nottingham F	38	9	7	22	55	75	25

1911-12

Division One

Manager: Harry Newbould

Did you know that?

Match 3: Norgrove's last game.
Match 5: Davies and Ross' last game
Match 12: Kelso's last game.
Match 24: J. Smith and G. Dorsett's last game.
Match 25: Young and Booth's last game.
Match 26: Beeby and Keary's last game.
Match 26: Bentley's first and only game.
Match 27: Eden's first and only game.
Match 28: Brooks's last game.
Match 36: The win lifts City out of the relegation zone for first time.
Match 37: Thornley's last game.

Only minutes before the FA Cup tie with Preston goalkeeper Smith began suffering with fluid on the knee and was unable to play. The other players were already on the field as reserve 'keeper Goodchild was told he was to play, and the replacement hurriedly changed. He made it on to the pitch just in time for the kick-off.

It was an amazing game with Goodchild saving a penalty on his debut. Wynn netted an 88th-minute winner.

Match No.	Date		Venue	Opponents	Result		Scorers	Attendance
1	Sep	2	H	Manchester United	D	0-0		30,000
2		9	A	Liverpool	D	2-2	Kelso 2	22,000
3		16	H	Aston Villa	L	2-6	Holford, Jones	30,000
4		23	A	Newcastle United	L	0-1		11,000
5		30	H	Sheffield United	D	0-0		18,000
6	Oct	7	A	Oldham Athletic	L	1-4	Thornley	20,000
7		14	H	Bolton Wanderers	W	3-1	Keary, Wall, Wynn	35,000
8		21	A	Bradford City	L	1-4	Thornley	15,000
9		28	H	Woolwich Arsenal	D	3-3	Wynn 2, Thornley	25,000
10	Nov	4	A	Preston North End	L	1-2	Kelso	6,000
11		11	A	Everton	L	0-1		18,000
12		18	H	West Bromwich Albion	L	0-2		20,000
13		25	A	Sunderland	D	1-1	J Dorsett	6,000
14	Dec	2	H	Blackburn Rovers	W	3-0	Wynn 2, J Dorsett	36,000
15		9	A	Sheffield Wednesday	L	0-3		12,000
16		16	H	Bury	W	2-0	Thornley, Wynn	16,000
17		23	A	Middlesbrough	L	1-3	J Dorsett	12,000
18		25	A	Notts County	W	1-0	Young	20,000
19		26	H	Notts County	W	4-0	Fletcher, Jones, Wynn, Young	30,000
20		30	A	Manchester United	D	0-0		50,000
21	Jan	6	H	Liverpool	L	2-3	Wynn 2	10,000
22		20	A	Aston Villa	L	1-3	J Dorsett	11,760
23		27	H	Newcastle United	D	1-1	Wynn	30,000
24	Feb	10	H	Oldham Athletic	L	1-3	J Smith	28,000
25		17	A	Bolton Wanderers	L	1-2	Brooks	13,000
26		26	A	Sheffield United	L	2-6	Thornley 2	6,000
27	Mar	2	A	Woolwich Arsenal	L	0-2		15,000
28		9	H	Preston North End	D	0-0		15,000
29		16	H	Everton	W	4-0	Holford 4	22,000
30		23	A	West Bromwich Albion	D	1-1	Bottomley	6,000
31		28	H	Bradford City	W	4-0	Holford 2, Jones, Wynn	10,000
32		30	H	Sunderland	W	2-0	Holford, Wynn	20,000
33	Apr	5	H	Tottenham Hotspur	W	2-1	J Dorsett, Jones	40,000
34		6	A	Blackburn Rovers	L	0-2		20,000
35		8	A	Tottenham Hotspur	W	2-0	J Dorsett, Jones	25,000
36		13	H	Sheffield Wednesday	W	4-0	Wynn 3, Jones	28,000
37		20	A	Bury	W	2-1	Wynn 2	12,000
38		27	H	Middlesbrough	W	2-0	J Dorsett, Jones	25,000
								Appearances
								Goals

FA Cup

R1	Jan	13	A	Preston North End	W	1-0	Wynn	15,000
R2	Feb	3	H	Oldham Athletic	L	0-1		45,000
								Appearances
								Goals

	Smith WE	Kelso T	Norgrove F	Davies R	Eadie WP	Holford T	Hoad SJ	Wynn GA	Thornley I	Jones W	Dorsett JAH	Booth F	Beeby AR	Fletcher E	Wall LJ	Ross D	Smith JW	Lawrence V	Keary A	Kelly WB	Bottomley W	Henry WA	Young AS	Goodchild AJ	Dorsett G	Brooks GH	Bentley J	Eden J
	1	2	3	4	5	6	7	8	9	10	11																	
	1	2	3	4	5	6	7	8	9	10	11																	
	1	2	3	4	5	6	7	8	9	10		11																
				4	2	6	7			10		11	1	3	5	8	9											
				4	2	6	7		8			11	1	3	5	10	9											
		2			5		7		8		11		1	3	6		9	4	10									
		2				6	7	8	9		11		1	3	5			4	10									
		2				5	7	8	9	6	11		1	3				4	10									
					2	6	7	8	9		11		1	3	5			4	10									
		2			4	6	7	8		10	11		1	3	5					9								
		2		4		6	7			10	11		1	3	5				9	8								
		2					7	8		6	11		1	3	5				10	9	4							
	1				5	6	7	8	9		11			3							4	2	10					
	1				5	6	7	8	9		11			3							4	2	10					
	1				5	6	7	8	9		11			3							4	2	10					
	1				5	6	7	8	9		11			3							4	2	10					
	1				5	6	7	8		10	11			3				4				2	9					
	1				5	6	7	8		10	11			3				4				2	9					
	1				5	6	7	8		10	11			3				4				2	9					
	1				5	6	7	8		10	11			3				4				2	9					
	1				5	6		8		7	11			3				4	10			2	9					
					5	6	7	8	9		11			3				4				2	10	1				
					5	6	7	8	9		11			3				4				2	10	1				
					5	6	7							3			9	4		8		2	10	1	11			
							7					11	1	3	5			4		8	6	2	10			9		
							7	8	9		11		1	3	5				10		4	2					6	
					5	6	7		9	10	11			2						8	4			1				3
					5	6	7	8	9		11			3							4	2		1		10		
					5	9	7	8		10	11			3	6						4	2		1				
					5	9	7	8		10	11			3	6						4	2		1				
					5	9	7	8		10	11			3	6						4	2		1				
					5	9	7	8		10	11			3	6						4	2		1				
						9	7	8		10	11			3	6			5			4	2		1				
						9	7	8		10	11			3	6			5			4	2		1				
						9	7	8		10	11			3	6			5			4	2		1				
						9	7	8		10	11			3	6			5			4	2		1				
							7	8	9	10	11			3	6			5			4	2		1				
							7	8		10	11			3	6			5		9	4	2		1				
	12	9	3	6	26	32	37	31	18	24	33	4	11	35	20	2	4	19	8	7	19	25	13	15	1	2	1	1
		3				8		17	6	7	7			1	1		1		1		1		2			1		

	Smith WE	Kelso T	Norgrove F	Davies R	Eadie WP	Holford T	Hoad SJ	Wynn GA	Thornley I	Jones W	Dorsett JAH	Booth F	Beeby AR	Fletcher E	Wall LJ	Ross D	Smith JW	Lawrence V	Keary A	Kelly WB	Bottomley W	Henry WA	Young AS	Goodchild AJ	Dorsett G	Brooks GH	Bentley J	Eden J
					5	6	7	8		10	11			3				4				2	9	1				
					5	6	7	8		10	11			3				4				2	9	1				
					2	2	2	2		2	2			2				2				2	2	2				
								1																				

League Table

	P	W	D	L	F	A	Pts
Blackburn R	38	20	9	9	60	43	49
Everton	38	20	6	12	46	42	46
Newcastle U	38	18	8	12	64	50	44
Bolton W	38	20	3	15	54	43	43
Sheffield W	38	16	9	13	69	49	41
Aston Villa	38	17	7	14	76	63	41
Middlesbrough	38	16	8	14	56	45	40
Sunderland	38	14	11	13	58	51	39
W.B.A.	38	15	9	14	43	47	39
Woolwich A	38	15	8	15	55	59	38
Bradford C	38	15	8	15	46	50	38
Tottenham H	38	14	9	15	53	53	37
Manchester U	38	13	11	14	45	60	37
Sheffield U	38	13	10	15	63	56	36
Manchester C	38	13	9	16	56	58	35
Notts Co	38	14	7	17	46	63	35
Liverpool	38	12	10	16	49	55	34
Oldham A	38	12	10	16	46	54	34
Preston N.E.	38	13	7	18	40	57	33
Bury	38	6	9	23	32	59	21

1912-13

Division One

Manager: Ernest Mangnall (from 9 September 1912)

Did you know that?

Match 1: Mangnall attends.
Match 2: Webb's last game.
Match 2: Mangnall's last game as United manager.
Match 3: Mangnall's first official game as City manager.
Match 19: Lawrence's last game.
Match 22: Jobling's last game.
Match 25: Kelly's last game.

The arrival of Ernest Mangnall as City manager was one of the most amazing moments in Manchester's football history. He achieved phenomenal success at United, but prior to the derby (Match 2) it was common knowledge he would take over at City. According to reports from the period he was delighted with City's win – despite officially being United's manager!

Match No.	Date	Venue	Opponents	Result		Scorers	Attendance
1	Sep 2	A	Notts County	W	1-0	Henry	6,000
2	7	A	Manchester United	W	1-0	Wynn	38,911
3	14	H	Aston Villa	W	1-0	Wynn	32,000
4	21	A	Liverpool	W	2-1	Dorsett, Wynn	35,000
5	28	H	Bolton Wanderers	W	2-0	Hoad, Jones	33,000
6	Oct 5	A	Sheffield United	D	1-1	Wallace	20,000
7	12	H	Newcastle United	L	0-1		40,000
8	19	A	Oldham Athletic	L	1-2	Wynn	20,000
9	26	H	Chelsea	W	2-0	Jones, Taylor	8,000
10	Nov 2	A	Woolwich Arsenal	W	4-0	Taylor 2, Jones, Wynn	8,000
11	9	H	Bradford City	L	1-3	Wynn	30,000
12	16	H	Sunderland	W	1-0	Wynn	12,000
13	23	A	West Bromwich Albion	W	2-0	Jones, Wallace	10,000
14	30	H	Everton	W	1-0	Wallace	20,000
15	Dec 7	A	Sheffield Wednesday	L	0-1		20,000
16	14	H	Blackburn Rovers	W	3-1	Dorsett, Jones, Wynn	35,000
17	21	A	Derby County	L	0-2		12,000
18	25	H	Tottenham Hotspur	D	2-2	Bottomley, Wynn	25,000
19	26	A	Tottenham Hotspur	L	0-4		25,000
20	28	H	Manchester United	L	0-2		30,000
21	Jan 2	H	Notts County	W	4-0	Wynn 2, Jones, Wallace	17,000
22	4	A	Aston Villa	L	0-2		12,000
23	18	H	Liverpool	W	4-1	Howard 4	20,000
24	25	A	Bolton Wanderers	D	2-2	Howard, Wynn	25,000
25	Feb 8	H	Sheffield United	W	3-0	Howard, Jones, Wallace	16,000
26	15	A	Newcastle United	W	1-0	Wynn	30,000
27	Mar 1	A	Chelsea	L	1-2	Dorsett	30,000
28	8	H	Woolwich Arsenal	L	0-1		12,000
29	12	H	Oldham Athletic	W	2-0	Dorsett, Jones	16,000
30	15	A	Bradford City	L	1-2	Wallace	10,000
31	21	A	Middlesbrough	D	0-0		12,026
32	22	A	Sunderland	L	0-1		20,000
33	24	H	Middlesbrough	W	3-0	Howard 2, Taylor	26,000
34	29	H	West Bromwich Albion	W	2-1	Wallace 2	20,000
35	Apr 5	A	Everton	D	0-0		10,000
36	12	H	Sheffield Wednesday	D	2-2	Howard, Jones	30,000
37	19	A	Blackburn Rovers	D	2-2	Howard 2	10,000
38	26	H	Derby County	D	1-1	Wynn	14,000
							Appearances
							Goals

FA Cup

Round	Date	Venue	Opponents	Result		Scorers	Attendance
R1	Jan 11	H	Birmingham	W	4-0	Wynn 2, Hoad, Taylor	17,442
R2	Feb 5	A	Sunderland	L	0-2		27,974
							Appearances
							Goals

A R2 tie v Sunderland (H) on Feb 1 was abandoned after 60 mins because of overcrowding. The attendance was 41,709

Goodchild AJ	Henry WA	Fletcher E	Bottomley W	Eadie WP	Holford T	Hoad SJ	Wynn GA	Webb GW	Jones W	Dorsett JAH	Taylor HG	Wallace W	Kelly WB	Wall LJ	Lawrence V	Smith WE	Jobling LW	Garner W	Hughes E	Howard FJ	McGuire P
1	2	3	4	5	6	7	8	9	10	11											
1	2	3	4	5	6	7	8	9	10	11											
1	2	3	4	5	6	7	8		10	11	9										
1	2	3	4	5	6	7	8		10	11	9										
1	2	3	4	5	6	7	8		10		9	11									
1	2	3	4	5	6	7	8		10			11	9								
1	2	3	4	5	9	7	8		10	11				6							
1	2	3	4	5	6		8		10	7	9	11									
1	2	3	4	5	6	7	8		10	11	9										
1	2	3	4	5	6	7	8		10	11	9										
1	2	3	4	5	6	7	8		10	11	9										
1	2	3	4	5	6	7	8		10	11	9										
1	2	3	4	5	6				10	7	9	11	8								
1	2	3	4	5	6	7	8		10		9	11									
1	2	3	4	5	6	7	8		10		9	11									
1	2	3	4	5	6		8		10	7	9	11									
1	2	3	4	5	6		8		10	7	9	11									
1	2	3	4	5	6		8		10	7	9	11									
1	2	3	4	5	6				10	7	9	11			8						
1	2	3	4	5	9	7			10	11	8			6							
	2	3	4	5	6		8		10		9	11				1	7				
	2	3	4		6		8		10		9	11				1	7	5			
	2	3		5	6	7	8		10			11				1			4	9	
	2	3		5	6	7	8		10			11				1			4	9	
	2	3		5	6				10	7		11	8			1		4		9	
	2	3		5	6		8		10	7		11				1			4	9	
	2		4	5	6		8		10	7		11				1				9	3
	2	3	4	5	6		8		10	7		11				1				9	
	2	3	4	5	6		8		10	7		11				1				9	
		3	4		6		8		10	7		11		5		1				9	2
1	2	3	4	5	6		8		10	7		11								9	
1	2		5		6		8			7	10	11							4	9	3
1	2				6				10	7	8	11		5					4	9	3
1	2		4		6				10	7	8	11		5						9	3
1	2		4	5	6				10	7	8	11								9	3
1	2	3	4		6		8		10	7		11		5						9	
1	2	3	4		6		8		10	7		11		5						9	
1	2	3	4	5	6		8		10	7		11								9	
28	37	33	33	31	38	16	31	2	37	30	22	28	3	7	1	10	2	2	5	16	6
	1		1			1	14		9	4	4	8								11	
	2	3	4	5	6	7	8		10		9	11				1					
	2	3		5	6	7	8		10			11				1			4	9	
	2	2	1	2	2	2	2		2		1	2				2			1	1	
						1	2				1										

League Table

	P	W	D	L	F	A	Pts
Sunderland	38	25	4	9	86	43	54
Aston Villa	38	19	12	7	86	52	50
Sheffield W	38	21	7	10	75	55	49
Manchester U	38	19	8	11	69	43	46
Blackburn R	38	16	13	9	79	43	45
Manchester C	38	18	8	12	53	37	44
Derby Co	38	17	8	13	69	66	42
Bolton W	38	16	10	12	62	63	42
Oldham A	38	14	14	10	50	55	42
W.B.A.	38	13	12	13	57	50	38
Everton	38	15	7	16	48	54	37
Liverpool	38	16	5	17	61	71	37
Bradford C	38	12	11	15	50	60	35
Newcastle U	38	13	8	17	47	47	34
Sheffield U	38	14	6	18	56	70	34
Middlesbrough	38	11	10	17	55	69	32
Tottenham H	38	12	6	20	45	72	30
Chelsea	38	11	6	21	51	73	28
Notts Co	38	7	9	22	28	56	23
Woolwich A	38	3	12	23	26	74	18

1913-14

Division One

Manager: Ernest Mangnall

Did you know that?

Match 5: Abbott and Wall's last game.
Match 12: Eadie's last game.
Match 21: Spottiswood's last game.
Match 36: Holford and Wallace's last game.

City finished the season above United for the first time since the FA's insistence on players being transferred to the Reds after the illegal payments scandal. With the balance of power resumed, City would only finish lower than United on four occasions from 1913 until after World War Two.

Match No.	Date	Venue	Opponents	Result		Scorers	Attendance
1	Sep 1	A	Aston Villa	D	1-1	Taylor	10,000
2	6	H	Middlesbrough	D	1-1	Taylor	30,000
3	13	A	Sheffield United	W	3-1	Abbott, Jones, Taylor	23,500
4	20	H	Derby County	L	1-2	Abbott	30,000
5	27	A	Tottenham Hotspur	L	1-3	Jones	30,000
6	Oct 4	A	Bradford City	L	2-3	Wynn 2	15,000
7	11	H	Blackburn Rovers	L	1-2	Hughes	40,000
8	18	A	Sunderland	D	0-0		20,000
9	25	H	Everton	D	1-1	Taylor	26,000
10	Nov 1	A	West Bromwich Albion	D	0-0		12,000
11	8	H	Sheffield Wednesday	L	1-2	Browell	25,000
12	15	A	Bolton Wanderers	L	0-3		22,257
13	22	H	Chelsea	W	2-1	Browell, Wallace	25,000
14	29	A	Oldham Athletic	W	3-1	Browell, Cumming, Howard	18,000
15	Dec 6	H	Manchester United	L	0-2		36,791
16	13	A	Burnley	L	0-2		16,000
17	20	H	Preston North End	D	1-1	Browell	18,000
18	25	A	Liverpool	L	2-4	Howard 2	30,000
19	26	H	Liverpool	W	1-0	Howard	20,000
20	27	A	Middlesbrough	L	0-2		15,000
21	Jan 1	A	Newcastle United	W	1-0	Browell	25,000
22	3	H	Sheffield United	W	2-1	Browell, Taylor	25,000
23	17	A	Derby County	W	4-2	Howard 3, Taylor	8,000
24	24	H	Tottenham Hotspur	W	2-1	Cumming, Taylor	28,000
25	Feb 7	H	Bradford City	W	1-0	Browell	25,000
26	14	A	Blackburn Rovers	L	1-2	Browell	18,000
27	28	A	Everton	L	0-1		30,000
28	Mar 14	A	Sheffield Wednesday	D	2-2	Hughes, Taylor	15,000
29	18	H	Sunderland	W	3-1	Howard 2, Hindmarsh	20,000
30	21	H	Bolton Wanderers	L	0-1		30,000
31	25	H	West Bromwich Albion	L	2-3	Browell, Fairclough	18,000
32	28	A	Chelsea	L	0-1		50,000
33	Apr 4	H	Oldham Athletic	W	2-1	Jones 2	28,000
34	10	H	Aston Villa	W	3-1	Browell 2, Dorsett	20,000
35	11	A	Manchester United	W	1-0	Cumming	40,000
36	13	H	Newcastle United	L	0-1		25,000
37	18	H	Burnley	W	4-1	Browell 2, Howard, Wynn	15,000
38	25	A	Preston North End	D	2-2	Hanney, Howard	8,000
							Appearances
							Goals

FA Cup

	Date	Venue	Opponents	Result		Scorers	Attendance
R1	Jan 10	H	Fulham	W	2-0	Hindmarsh, Howard	25,345
R2	31	H	Tottenham Hotspur	W	2-1	Browell, Howard	36,256
R3	Feb 21	A	Blackburn Rovers	W	2-1	Cartwright, Howard	41,250
R4	Mar 7	H	Sheffield United	D	0-0		35,738
rep	12	A	Sheffield United	D	0-0		46,139
rep2	16	N	Sheffield United	L	0-1		23,000
							Appearances
							Goals

R4 replay 2 at Villa Park, Birmingham

Goodchild AJ	Henry WA	Fletcher E	Bottomley W	Eadie WP	Holford T	Dorsett JAH	Wynn GA	Taylor HG	Jones W	Wallace W	Wall LJ	Smith WE	Hoad SJ	Abbott JA	McGuire P	Fairclough A	Spottiswood JD	Hughes E	Howard FJ	Cartwright JE	Browell T	Garner W	Hindmarsh JL	Cumming JF	Hanney TP
1	2	3	4	5	6	7	8	9	10	11															
1	2	3	4		6	7	8	9	10	11	5														
	2	3	4		6			9	10	11	5	1	7	8											
	2	3	4		6			9	10	11	5	1	7	8											
	2	3	4		6			9	10	11	5	1	7	8											
		3	4	5	6		8		10			1	7		2	9	11								
	2	3		5	6		8		10	11		1	7					4	9						
	2	3	5		6	7	8		10			1					11	4	9						
	2		5		6			8	10	7		1			3			4	9	11					
	2	3	4	5	6			8	10	7		1							9	11					
	2	3	4	5	6	7	8		10			1								11	9				
		3	2	5	6	7		8		11		1						4	9		10				
	2	3						8		11		1						4	9		10	5	6	7	
	2	3						8		11		1						4	9		10		6	7	5
	2	3						8		11		1						4	9		10		6	7	5
		3				7		8		11		1			2			4	9		10		6		5
	2	3			9	11		8				1						4			10		6	7	5
	2	3						8				1					11	4	9		10		6	7	5
		3						8				1			2		11	4	9		10		6	7	5
		3					8	10				1			2		11	4	9				6	7	5
	2	3						8				1					11	4	9		10		6	7	5
	2	3						8				1						4	9	11	10		6	7	5
	2	3						8				1						4	9	11	10		6	7	5
	2	3						8				1						4	9	11	10		6	7	5
	2	3							8			1						4	9	11	10		6	7	5
	2	3						8				1						4	9	11	10		6	7	5
	2							8				1			3			4	9	11	10		6	7	5
	2	3						8	7	11		1						4	9		10	5	6		
	2	3				11		8				1						4	9		10		6	7	5
	2	3				11		8				1						4	9		10		6	7	5
	2	3			6	11		8				1				9		4			10			7	5
	2	3				11		8				1						4	9		10		6	7	5
	2	3				11			8			1						4	9		10		6	7	5
	2	3				11	8					1						4	9		10		6	7	5
	2	3				11	8					1						4	9		10		6	7	5
	2	3			6	11	8			7		1						4	9		10				5
	2	3				11	8					1						4	9		10		6	7	5
	2	3				11	8					1						4	9		10		6	7	5
2	33	36	11	6	15	17	12	27	14	15	4	36	5	3	6	2	6	30	29	9	27	2	24	23	24
						1	3	8	4	1				2		1		2	11		13		1	3	1

Goodchild AJ	Henry WA	Fletcher E	Bottomley W	Eadie WP	Holford T	Dorsett JAH	Wynn GA	Taylor HG	Jones W	Wallace W	Wall LJ	Smith WE	Hoad SJ	Abbott JA	McGuire P	Fairclough A	Spottiswood JD	Hughes E	Howard FJ	Cartwright JE	Browell T	Garner W	Hindmarsh JL	Cumming JF	Hanney TP
	2	3						8				1						4	9	11	10		6	7	5
	2	3						8				1						4	9	11	10		6	7	5
	2	3						8				1						4	9	11	10		6	7	5
	2	3						8				1						4	9	11	10		6	7	5
	2	3						8				1						4	9	11	10		6	7	5
	2	3						8	7	11		1						4	9		10		6		5
	6	6						6	1	1		6						6	6	5	6		6	5	6
																			3	1	1		1		

League Table

	P	W	D	L	F	A	Pts
Blackburn R	38	20	11	7	78	42	51
Aston Villa	38	19	6	13	65	50	44
Middlesbrough	38	19	5	14	77	60	43
Oldham A	38	17	9	12	55	45	43
W.B.A.	38	15	13	10	46	42	43
Bolton W	38	16	10	12	65	52	42
Sunderland	38	17	6	15	63	52	40
Chelsea	38	16	7	15	46	55	39
Bradford C	38	12	14	12	40	40	38
Sheffield U	38	16	5	17	63	60	37
Newcastle U	38	13	11	14	39	48	37
Burnley	38	12	12	14	61	53	36
Manchester C	38	14	8	16	51	53	36
Manchester U	38	15	6	17	52	62	36
Everton	38	12	11	15	46	55	35
Liverpool	38	14	7	17	46	62	35
Tottenham H	38	12	10	16	50	62	34
Sheffield W	38	13	8	17	53	70	34
Preston N.E.	38	12	6	20	52	69	30
Derby Co	38	8	11	19	55	71	27

1914-15

Division One

Manager: Ernest Mangnall

Did you know that?

Match 9: Hoad's last game.
Match 17: McGuire's last game.
Match 21: Hindmarsh's last game.
Match 35: Cumming and Gaughan's last game.
Match 36: Had City won they would probably have won the title.
Match 38: Garner's last game.
Match 38: Hall's first and only League game.

City only took two points from the final five games. Had they defeated Oldham and Everton, or had they averaged a point a game in those final weeks, they would have won the title.

Match No.	Date	Venue	Opponents	Result		Scorers	Attendance
1	Sep 1	H	Bradford City	W	4-1	Barnes, Dorsett, Howard, Taylor	12,000
2	5	A	Manchester United	D	0-0		20,000
3	12	H	Burnley	W	1-0	Howard	10,000
4	19	A	Bolton Wanderers	W	3-2	Barnes, Howard, Rowley (og)	21,658
5	26	H	Tottenham Hotspur	W	2-1	Howard, Taylor	18,000
6	Oct 3	A	Blackburn Rovers	W	1-0	Cartwright	20,000
7	10	H	Newcastle United	D	1-1	Barnes	25,000
8	17	A	Notts County	W	2-0	Howard 2	14,000
9	24	H	Middlesbrough	D	1-1	Howard	25,000
10	31	A	Sunderland	W	2-0	Howard 2	3,000
11	Nov 7	H	Sheffield United	D	0-0		25,000
12	14	A	Sheffield Wednesday	L	1-2	Taylor	20,000
13	25	H	Aston Villa	W	1-0	Howard	16,000
14	28	A	West Bromwich Albion	W	1-0	Browell	9,398
15	Dec 5	H	Liverpool	D	1-1	Howard	5,000
16	12	A	Everton	L	1-4	Howard	18,000
17	19	H	Bradford Park Avenue	L	2-3	Howard, Taylor	5,000
18	25	A	Chelsea	D	0-0		15,000
19	26	H	Chelsea	W	2-1	Howard, Taylor	25,000
20	Jan 1	A	Oldham Athletic	D	0-0		20,000
21	2	H	Manchester United	D	1-1	Howard	30,000
22	18	A	Burnley	W	2-1	Barnes, Dorsett	8,000
23	23	H	Bolton Wanderers	W	2-1	Barnes, Taylor	25,000
24	Feb 6	H	Blackburn Rovers	L	1-3	Taylor	26,000
25	13	A	Newcastle United	L	1-2	Taylor	18,000
26	22	H	Notts County	D	0-0		20,000
27	27	A	Middlesbrough	L	0-1		8,000
28	Mar 6	H	Sunderland	W	2-0	Cartwright, Ness (og)	18,000
29	13	A	Liverpool	L	2-3	Barnes, Howard	18,000
30	15	A	Tottenham Hotspur	D	2-2	Barnes, Taylor	8,000
31	20	H	Sheffield Wednesday	W	4-0	Barnes 2, Howard 2	20,000
32	29	A	Sheffield United	D	0-0		10,000
33	Apr 3	H	West Bromwich Albion	W	4-0	Barnes 2, Taylor 2	15,000
34	5	H	Oldham Athletic	D	0-0		40,000
35	6	A	Bradford City	D	0-0		15,000
36	17	H	Everton	L	0-1		30,000
37	21	A	Aston Villa	L	1-4	Barnes	15,000
38	24	A	Bradford Park Avenue	L	1-3	Jones	7,000
							Appearances
						Two own goals	Goals

FA Cup

Match No.	Date	Venue	Opponents	Result		Scorers	Attendance
R1	Jan 9	A	Preston North End	D	0-0		14,000
rep	13	H	Preston North End	W	3-0	Barnes 2, Hughes	19,985
R2	30	H	Aston Villa	W	1-0	Cartwright	29,661
R3	Feb 20	H	Chelsea	L	0-1		32,000
							Appearances
							Goals

Smith WE	Henry WA	Fletcher E	Hughes E	Hanney TP	Hindmarsh JL	Hoad SJ	Taylor HG	Howard FJ	Barnes H	Dorsett JAH	Brennan J	Cumming JF	Cartwright JE	Browell T	Gaughan WB	McGuire P	Jones W	Gartland P	Bottomley W	Fairclough A	Goodchild AJ	Wynn GA	Fairclough P	Henderson J	Garner W	Hall JE
1	2	3	4	5	6	7	8	9	10	11																
1	2	3	4	5	6	7	8	9	10	11																
1	2	3	4	5		7	8	9	10	11	6															
1	2	3	4	5			8	9	10	11	6	7														
1	2	3	4	5			8	9	10	11	6	7														
1	2	3	4	5			8	9	10	11	6		7													
1	2	3	4	5			8	9	10	11	6		7													
1	2	3	4	5		7	8	9			6			10	11											
1	2	3	4	5		7	8	9			6			10	11											
1	2	3	4	5			8	9			6	7		10	11											
1	2	3	4	5			8	9			6	7		10	11											
1	2	3	4	5			8	9	10		6	7			11											
1	2	3	4	5			8	9			6	7		10	11											
1		3	4	5			8	9			6	7		10	11	2										
1	2	3	4	5			8	9			6	7		10	11											
1		3	4	5			8	9			6	7		10	11	2										
1		3	4	5			8	9			6	7	11			2	10									
1	2	3	4	5			8	9		7	6		11				10									
1	2		4	5	6		8	9		7			11				10	3								
1	2	3		5			8	9		7	6		11				10		4							
1	2	3		5	4		8	9		7	6		11				10									
1	2	3	4	5			8	9	10	7	6		11													
1	2	3	4	5			8	9	10	7	6		11													
1	2	3	4	5			8	9	10	7			11				6									
1	2	3	4	5			8		10	7	6		11	9												
1	2	3	4	5			8		10		6	7	11	9												
1	2	3	4	5			8		10	7	6		11							9						
1	2	3	4	5			8	9	10		6		11				7									
1	2	3	4	5			8	9	10		6		11				7									
1	2	3	4	5			8	9	10		6		11				7									
	2	3	4	5			8	9	10		6		11				7				1					
1	2	3	4	5			8	9	10		6		11				7									
1	2	3	4	5			8	9	10		6		11				7									
1	2	3	4	5			8	9	10		6		11				7									
1	2	3	4	5				9	10		6	7			11		8									
1	2	3	4	5			8	9	10		6		11				7									
1	2	3	4	5					10	11	6						7					8	9			
1	2	3	4			7			10	11							8							5	6	9
37	35	37	36	37	4	6	35	33	25	18	33	12	21	10	10	3	17	1	1	1	1	1	1	1	1	1
							11	18	12	2			2	1			1									

Smith WE	Henry WA	Fletcher E	Hughes E	Hanney TP	Hindmarsh JL	Hoad SJ	Taylor HG	Howard FJ	Barnes H	Dorsett JAH	Brennan J	Cumming JF	Cartwright JE	Browell T	Gaughan WB	McGuire P	Jones W
1	2	3	4	5	6			9	10	7			11	8			
1	2	3	4	5			8	9	10	7	6		11				
1	2	3	4	5			8	9	10	7			11				6
1	2	3	4	5			9		10		6	7	11	8			
4	4	4	4	4	1		3	3	4	3	2	1	4	2			1
			1						2				1				

League Table

	P	W	D	L	F	A	Pts
Everton	38	19	8	11	76	47	46
Oldham A	38	17	11	10	70	56	45
Blackburn R	38	18	7	13	83	61	43
Burnley	38	18	7	13	61	47	43
Manchester C	38	15	13	10	49	39	43
Sheffield U	38	15	13	10	49	41	43
Sheffield W	38	15	13	10	61	54	43
Sunderland	38	18	5	15	81	72	41
Bradford P.A.	38	17	7	14	69	65	41
W.B.A.	38	15	10	13	49	43	40
Bradford C	38	13	14	11	55	49	40
Middlesbrough	38	13	12	13	62	74	38
Liverpool	38	14	9	15	65	75	37
Aston Villa	38	13	11	14	62	72	37
Newcastle U	38	11	10	17	46	48	32
Notts Co	38	9	13	16	41	57	31
Bolton W	38	11	8	19	68	84	30
Manchester U	38	9	12	17	46	62	30
Chelsea	38	8	13	17	51	65	29
Tottenham H	38	8	12	18	57	90	28

1915-16

Lancashire Selection

Match No.	Date	Venue	Opponents	Result		Scorers	Attendance
1	Sep 4	H	Stockport C	W	3-1	P.Fairclough, Wynn, Barnes	12,000
2	11	A	Liverpool	W	1-0	Cruse	15,000
3	18	H	Bury	W	5-4	Barnes 3, Cruse, Wynn	8,000
4	25	A	Manchester U	D	1-1	Barnes	20,000
5	Oct 2	H	Blackpool	W	3-0	Barnes 3	5,000
6	9	A	Southport	W	2-0	Barnes, Hughes	7,000
7	16	H	Oldham A	D	2-2-	A.Fairclough, Barnes	13,000
8	23	A	Everton	L	2-4	Barnes 2	22,000
9	30	H	Bolton W	L	1-2	Barnes	5,000
10	Nov 6	A	Rochdale	W	2-0	Barnes 2	1,000
11	13	A	Stoke	L	0-1		7,000
12	20	H	Burnley	W	1-0	Hughes	15,000
13	27	A	Preston NE	L	2-3	Howard, P.Fairclough	3,000
14	Dec 4	A	Stockport C	D	1-1	Howard	10,000
15	11	H	Liverpool	W	2-1	Howard, Barnes	3,000
16	18	A	Bury	W	3-0	Howard, Dorsett, opp own goal	2,000
17	25	H	Manchester U	W	2-1	Taylor, Barnes	20,000
18	Jan 1	A	Blackpool	L	0-2		10,000
19	8	H	Southport C	W	5-0	Taylor 3, Barnes 2	12,000
20	15	A	Oldham A	W	2-1	Taylor 2	4,000
21	22	H	Everton	W	2-1	Taylor, Barnes	20,000
22	29	A	Bolton W	L	2-4	P.Fairclough, Barnes	15,000
23	Feb 5	H	Rochdale	W	4-1	P.Fairclough, Barnes 2, Cartwright	8,000
24	12	H	Stoke	W	4-2	P.Fairclough 2, Taylor, Barnes	10,000
25	19	A	Burnley	L	1-3	P.Fairclough	12,000
26	26	H	Preston NE	W	8-0	A.Fairclough 5, Barnes 2, Cartwright	6,000
							Appearances
						1 own-goal	Goals

Subsidiary Tournament (Southern Section)

Match No.	Date	Venue	Opponents	Result		Scorers	Attendance
27	Mar 4	A	Stockport C	L	0-2		9,000
28	11	H	Liverpool	D	1-1	Barnes	10,000
29	18	A	Everton	D	1-1	Meredith	14,000
30	25	A	Manchester U	W	2-0	Taylor, Cartwright	15,000
31	Apr 1	H	Oldham A	D	4-4	Barnes 3, Cartwright	8,000
32	8	H	Stockport C	W	3-2	Brennan, Jones, Barnes	10,000
33	15	A	Liverpool	W	2-0	Taylor, Barnes	10,000
34	21	A	Oldham A	L	3-4	Taylor 2, Barnes	9,000
35	22	H	Everton	W	5-4	Barnes 2, Taylor, Jones, Meredith	24,000
36	29	H	Manchester U	W	2-1	Barnes, opp. og	18,000
							Appearances
						1 own-goal	Goals

Note: City were Champions of the Lancashire Section with a record of: P26 W16 D3 L7 F61 A35 Pts35
City were also Champions of the Subsidiary Tournament (Southern Section) with a record of: P10 W5 D3 L2 F23 A19 Pts13

Goodchild	Henry WA	Fletcher E	Hughes E	Henderson	Brennan	Broad	Taylor HG	Howard FJ	Fairclough P.	Barnes	Cartwright	Fairclough A.	Jones W.L.	Dorsett	Wynn	Bottomley	Allen	Gartland	Howe	Smith	Jones F.	Lewis	Cruse	Tomlinson	Meredith	Corcoran
1	2	3	4	5	6	7			9	10				11	8											
1	2		4	5	6	7				10				11	8		3						9			
1		3		5	6	7				10			11		8	4	2						9			
1	2	3	4	5	6	7			9	10			11		8											
1	2	3	4	5	6	7	8		9	10			11													
1	2	3	4		6	7	8			10		9	11			5										
1	2	3	4	5	6	7	8			10		9	11													
1	2	3	4	5	6	7	8			10				11										9		
	2	3	4	5	6	7	8			10				11					1				9			
1	2	3	4	5	6	7	8	9		10	11															
1		3	4	5	6	7	8	9		10	11						2									
1	2	3	4	5	6	7	8	9		10	11															
1		3	4	5	6	7	8	9	10		11							2								
1	2	3	4	5	6	7	8	9		10	11															
1	2	3	4	5	6	7	8	9		10	11															
1	2	3	4	5	6	7	8	9	10					11												
1	2	3	4	5	6	7	8		11	10						9										
1	2	3	4	5	6	7	8			10	11					9										
1	2	3	4		6	7	8		9	10	11					5										
1	2	3	4		6	7	8		9	10	11					5										
1	2	3	4	5	6	7	8		9	10	11															
1	2	3	4	5	6	7	8		9	10	11															
1	2		4	5	6	7	8		9	10	11							3								
1	2	3	4	5	6	7	8		9	10				11												
1	2	3	4	5	6	7	8		9	10			11													
1	2	3	4	5	6	7	8			10	11	9														
25	23	24	25	23	26	26	22	7	13	24	13	3	6	6	4	6	3	2	1				3	1		
			2				8	4	7	26	2	6		1	2								2			

Goodchild	Henry WA	Fletcher E	Hughes E	Henderson	Brennan	Broad	Taylor HG	Howard FJ	Fairclough P.	Barnes	Cartwright	Fairclough A.	Jones W.L.	Dorsett	Wynn	Bottomley	Allen	Gartland	Howe	Smith	Jones F.	Lewis	Cruse	Tomlinson	Meredith	Corcoran
1	2	3	4	5	6	7	8		9	10	11															
1	2		4	5	6		8			9	11		10					3							7	
1		3	4	5	6				9	10	11		8					2							7	
1		3	4	5	6	7	9			10	11		8					2								
1		3	4	5	6		8			10	11										2				7	9
1		3	4	5	6	7	9			10	11		8									2				
1		3	4	5	6	7	9			10	11		8					2								
1		3	4	5	6	7	9			10	11		8					2								
		3	4	5	6		9			10	11		8					2		1					7	
1		3	4	5	6				9	10	11				8			2							7	
9	2	9	10	10	10	5	8		3	10	10		7		1			7		1	1	1			5	1
					1		5			10	2		2												2	

1916-17

Lancashire Selection

Match No.	Date	Venue	Opponents	Result		Scorers	Attendance
1	Sep 2	A	Stoke	L	0-1		6,000
2	9	H	Southport C	D	0-0		8,000
3	16	A	Blackburn	L	1-2	P.Fairclough	3,000
4	23	H	Blackpool	W	4-0	Barnes 3, Brennan	10,000
5	30	H	Everton	W	4-1	Barnes 3, Hoare	14,000
6	Oct 7	A	Rochdale	D	2-2	Barnes, Brennan	1,000
7	14	H	Bolton W	W	1-0	P.Fairclough	8,000
8	21	A	Port Vale	W	1-0	P.Fairclough	6,000
9	28	H	Oldham A	W	2-1	Cartwright, Waldon	9,000
10	Nov 4	A	Preston NE	D	2-2	Wynn, Barnes	3,000
11	11	H	Burnley	W	2-1	Wynn, Meredith	14,000
12	18	A	Manchester U	L	1-2	Hoad	10,000
13	25	H	Liverpool	D	1-1	Barnes	10,000
14	Dec 2	A	Stockport C	D	0-0		6,000
15	9	H	Bury	D	1-1	Meredith	5,000
16	23	A	Southport C	D	0-0		1,000
17	25	H	Stoke	W	1-0	Wynn	12,000
18	30	H	Blackburn	W	8-0	Capper 5, Nelson 2, Davies	10,000
19	Jan 6	A	Blackpool	L	1-3	Cartwright	4,000
20	13	A	Everton	W	2-0	P.Fairclough, Barnes	8,000
21	20	H	Rochdale	W	2-1	Wynn, Barnes	7,000
22	27	A	Bolton W	D	2-2	Tavo, W.Newton	2,000
23	Feb 3	H	Port Vale	W	2-0	Barnes 2	6,000
24	10	A	Oldham A	L	1-2	Tyler	3,000
25	17	H	Preston NE	W	5-1	Tyler 2, Goddard 3	7,000
26	24	A	Burnley	W	1-0	Barnes	4,000
27	Mar 3	H	Manchester U	W	1-0	Barnes	15,000
28	10	A	Liverpool	L	0-3		14,000
29	17	H	Stockport C	L	1-3	Barnes	14,000
30	24	A	Bury	D	0-0		3,000
							Appearances
							Goals

Subsidiary tournament

Match No.	Date	Venue	Opponents	Result		Scorers	Attendance
31	Mar 31	H	Port Vale	W	1-0	Wynn	3,000
32	Apr 6	H	Stoke	W	1-0	McIlvenney	12,000
33	7	A	Manchester U	L	1-5	H. Newton	15,000
34	9	A	Stoke	L	0-5		8,000
35	14	A	Port Vale	D	0-0		5,000
36	21	H	Manchester U	L	0-1		15,000
							Appearances
							Goals

Note: City finished 4th in the Lancashire Section & 3rd in the Subsidiary Tournament

Goodchild	Gartland	Fletcher E	Bottomley	Tyler	Brennan	Parker	Wynn	Fairclough P.	Barnes	Cartwright	Newton H.	Jones	Scott	Newton W.	Wray	Hoad	Smith	Broad	Meredith	Davies	Nelson	Miller	Goddard	Tavo	Walden	Lomas	Armstrong	McIlvenney	Clegg	Cruse	Taylor	Hanney	Hoare	Geddes	Capper	Kite	Sheldon	Woodhouse	Hargreaves	Malone	Lee							
1	2	3	4		6				10	11		8						7		5										9																		
	2	3	4		6				10	11		8					1	7		5											9																
		3	4		5	6		9	10	11		8				7	1			2																											
1		3			5	6		9	10	11		8	4						7	2																											
1		3			4	6			10	11		8							7	2													5	9														
1		3	4		5	6	8	9	10	11									7	2																											
1		3	4	2		6	8	9	10			11							7	5																											
1		3	4	2		6	8	9	10							11			7	5																											
1	3		4	2	5		8			11		10							7	6					9																						
		3	4	2	5		8	9	10	11							1		7	6																											
		3	4	2	6	10				11					8		1		7	5		9																									
1	6	3	4	2				10		11					8	9			7	5																											
1		3	4	2	5		8		10	11									7	6					9																						
1	2	3	4	5				6		11		10			8				7				9																								
1		3	4	2	5			6	10	11					8				7															9														
1	2	3		5		6		10		11					9				7	4		8																									
1	2	3		5		6	8	10		11									7	4		9																									
1		3	4	2		6	8			11									7	5	9														10													
1	4	3		2		6	8	9		11									7	5			10																								
1	2	3	4	5		6	8	10	11										7		9																										
1	2	3	4	5			8	11	10					6					7		9																										
1	2	3	4	5				10		11				6					7		8			9																							
1	2	3	4	5			8		10	11				6					7					9																							
	2	3	4	9			8	11					5	6					7		10															1												
1	2	3		9	5		8	11					4	6					7			10																								
1	2	3	4	9		6	8		10	11			5						7																													
1	2	3		9		6	8	4	10	11			5						7																													
1	2	3	4	9		6	8		10	11			5						7																													
1	2	3	4				8	11	10				5						7	6	9																										
1	2	3	4			6		10		11			5						7			8															9											
25	19	29	23	22	12	16	18	20	18	23		8	8	5	5	3	4	2	27	18	6	4	3	2	2					1	1	1	1	1	1	1	1											
				3	2		3	4	16	2				1	1	1			2	1	2		3	1	1								1		5													

1		3		2		5	8	6		11									7							4	9		10																			
1		3		2				6			8			5					7							4	11	9	10																			
		3		2				6		11	8			5			1		7							4	9											10										
		3		2						11	8		6		10		1		7							4		9											5									
1	2	3		5		10				11	8								7							4														6	9							
1	2	3	4	9	5		8	6				10							7								11																					
4	2	6	1	6	1	2	2	4		4	4	1	1	2	1		2		6							5	4	2	2									1	1	1	1							
							1				1																	1																				

1917-18

Lancashire Selection

Match No.	Date	Venue	Opponents	Result		Scorers	Attendance
1	Sep 1	H	Stockport C	W	2-1	Tyler, Thorpe	12,000
2	8	A	Stockport C	W	1-0	opp. og	7,000
3	15	H	Oldham A	D	2-2	Thorpe, Moses	13,000
4	22	A	Oldham A	D	0-0		10,000
5	29	H	Manchester U	W	3-1	Lomas 2, Jones	20,000
6	Oct 6	A	Manchester U	D	1-1	Lomas	10,000
7	13	H	Bury	W	3-1	Lomas 2, Watson	9,000
8	20	A	Bury	W	5-2	Lomas 2, Meredith, Jones, Taylor	8,000
9	27	A	Stoke	L	3-4	Lomas 2, Watson	9,000
10	Nov 3	H	Stoke	W	1-0	Lomas	20,000
11	10	A	Liverpool	L	0-2		18,000
12	17	H	Liverpool	D	1-1	Thompson	15,000
13	24	A	Southport C	D	0-0		8,000
14	Dec 1	H	Southport C	W	5-0	Lomas 2, Tyler, Meredith, Wynn	10,000
15	8	A	Burnley	W	4-0	Lomas 3, Jones	1,000
16	15	H	Burnley	W	4-1	Tyler, Lomas, Jones, Watson	8,000
17	22	H	Blackburn R	W	1-0	Cartwright	12,000
18	29	A	Blackburn R	W	4-0	Meredith, Lomas, Cope, Cunningham	3,000
19	Jan 5	H	Rochdale	D	1-1	Tyler	9,000
20	12	A	Rochdale	W	4-1	Thompson 2, Barnes, Watson	6,000
21	19	H	Everton	L	0-2		13,000
22	26	A	Everton	D	0-0		20,000
23	Feb 2	H	Port Vale	W	5-1	Broad 2, Lomas 2, Thompson	11,000
24	9	A	Port Vale	W	2-0	Lomas, Cunningham	1,000
25	16	A	Bolton W	L	0-1		12,000
26	23	H	Bolton W	L	0-1		10,000
27	Mar 2	A	Preston NE	W	2-0	Lomas, Thompson	9,000
28	9	H	Preston NE	L	1-2	Lomas	10,000
29	16	A	Blackpool	L	0-1		9,000
30	23	H	Blackpool	D	2-2	Royle, Thompson	11,000
							Appearances
							Goals

Subsidiary Tournament

Match No.	Date	Venue	Opponents	Result		Scorers	Attendance
31	Mar 29	H	Manchester U	W	3-0	Fletcher, Royle, Mann	10,000
32	30	A	Port Vale	W	4-1	Royle 2, Thompson, P. Fairclough	8,000
33	Apr 1	A	Manchester U	L	0-2		10,000
34	6	H	Port Vale	W	1-0	Fletcher	10,000
35	13	A	Stoke	D	1-1	Fletcher	9,000
36	20	H	Stoke	W	2-0	Woodcock, opp. og.	11,000
							Appearances
						1 own-goal	Goals

Note: City finished 5th in the Lancashire Section & 3rd in the Subsidiary Tournament

Goodchild	Sugden	Fletcher	Hughes	Tyler	Fairclough P.	Jones	Murphy	Brennan	Broad	Taylor	Barnes	Royle	Parker	Sharp	Ollerenshaw	Meredith	Lomas	Moses	Thompson	Thorpe	Cunningham	Cope	Woodcock	Watson	Elliot	Mann	Gartland	Crowther	McRay	Roberts	Scott	Osmond	Hanney	Wynn	Lloyd	Cartwright	James	Hargreaves	Brierley	Allen	Brown	Wray
1	2	3		9		10		6	8							7	4			5				11																		
1	2	3		5	6	10			8							7	4							11					9												
1	2	3	4		11	10		5								7	8	9		6																						
1	2	3	4	5	6	10											7	8	9						11																		
1		3	4	5	6	10											7	8	9						11			2																
1		3	4	2	6	10		5									7	8	9						11																		
1	2	3	4	5	6	10											7	8		9					11																		
1		3	4	2	6	10		5		9						7	8							11																		
1		3	4	2	6			5									7	8		9					11						10													
1	2	3	4	5	6	10											7	9						8	11																		
1	2	3	4	5	10									6			7	8					9		11																		
1	2	3	4	5		10							6			7	9		8					11																		
1	2		4	3	11			5					6			7	8		10														9												
1		3	4	5		10											7	9							11								2	6	8								
1	2	3	4		6	10								5			7	9		8					11																		
1	2	3	4	5	6	10											7	9		8					11																		
1	2	3	4	5				6								7	9		8																	10	11						
1	2	3	4	5	6													7	9		8		10	11																			
1	2	3	4	5				6			10					7	9				8			11																		
1	2	3	4	5	6						10					7	9		8					11																		
1	2	3	4	5	6													7	9		8		10			11																		
1	2	3	4	5	6													7	8	9				11															10					
1	2	3	4	5	6		11		8							7	9		10																							
1	2	3	4	5	6		11		8							7	9				10																						
1		3	4	5			11									7	8	9	10								2												6				
1	2	3	4	5	6		11									7	8				10	9																				
	2	3	4	5	6		11								1	7	8		10										9															
			4	5	6		11		8						1	7	10																								2	3	9	
1	2	3	4	5	9		11	6									7	8		10																							
1	2	3		4	6		11					9	5			7	8		10																							
28	23	28	27	28	24	13	8	9	5	1	2	1	5	0	2	30	30	6	15	2	5	4	1	17	0	0	2	1	1	1	1	1	1	1	1	1	1	1	1	1	1	
				4		4			2	1	1	1				3	21	1	6	2	2	1		4																		

Goodchild	Sugden	Fletcher	Hughes	Tyler	Fairclough P.	Jones	Murphy	Brennan	Broad	Taylor	Barnes	Royle	Parker	Sharp	Ollerenshaw	Meredith	Lomas	Moses	Thompson	Thorpe	Cunningham	Cope	Woodcock	Watson	Elliot	Mann	Gartland	Crowther	McRay	Roberts	Scott	Osmond	Hanney	Wynn	Lloyd	Cartwright	James	Hargreaves	Brierley	Allen	Brown	Wray
1	2	3		5				6				8				7	4		10						9	11																
1	2	3		5	6							8				7	4		10						9	11																
1	2	3					11	6				9	5	8			4		10		7																					
	2	3		5	6		11					9		8	1	7	4		10																								
1	2	3		5	6							9				7	4		10		11																					8
1	2	3		5	6		11									7	4		10		8		9																				
5	6	6	0	5	4	0	3	2	0	0	0	5	1	2	1	5	6	0	6	0	3	0	1	0	2	2																1
		3			1							3							1				1			1																	

1918-19

Lancashire Selection

Match No.	Date	Venue	Opponents	Result		Scorers	Attendance
1	Sep 7	A	Stoke	L	0-3		8,000
2	14	H	Stoke	L	0-2		10,000
3	21	A	Bury	W	1-0	Moses	8,000
4	28	H	Bury	W	7-0	Browell 3, Brennan, P.Fairclough, Moses, Kenyon	12,000
5	Oct 5	A	Manchester U	W	2-0	Kenyon, Cartwright	10,000
6	Oct 12	H	Manchester U	D	0-0		15,000
7	19	A	Blackpool	W	3-0	Kenyon, Moses, Browell	9,000
8	26	H	Blackpool	W	4-0	Lievesley 2, Cartwright, Browell	15,000
9	Nov 2	H	Stockport C	W	1-0	Lievesley	12,000
10	9	A	Stockport C	D	1-1	Browell	3,000
11	Nov 16	H	Liverpool	L	0-2		25,000
12	23	A	Liverpool	L	0-2		20,000
13	30	H	Burnley	W	2-1	Lievesley, Smith	12,000
14	Dec 7	A	Burnley	L	1-2	Lievesley	9,000
15	Dec 14	H	Southport V	L	0-1		10,000
16	21	A	Southport V	L	0-2		6,000
17	28	H	Preston NE	W	2-0	Wynn, Browell	13,000
18	Jan 11	H	Rochdale	D	1-1	Lievesley	12,000
19	18	A	Rochdale	W	5-4	Barnes 2, Dorsett 2, Smith	5,000
20	Jan 25	H	Everton	W	1-0	Murphy	25,000
21	Feb 1	A	Everton	L	0-3		31,000
22	8	H	Oldham A	W	3-0	Lievesley 2, Barnes	18,000
23	15	A	Oldham A	W	3-0	Browell, Barnes, Murphy	10,000
24	22	H	Blackburn R	W	5-1	Barnes 3, Johnson, Browell	22,000
25	Mar 1	A	Blackburn R	L	1-2	Browell	8,000
26	8	H	Port Vale	W	6-1	Johnson 3, Browell 2, Barnes	14,000
27	15	A	Port Vale	W	5-1	Barnes 3, Browell, A.Fairclough	8,000
28	22	H	Bolton W	L	1-2	Browell	20,000
29	29	A	Bolton W	L	1-3	Barnes	30,000
30	Apr 10	A	Preston NE	L	1-2	Barnes	12,000
							Appearances
							Goals

Subsidiary Record

Match No.	Date	Venue	Opponents	Result		Scorers	Attendance
31	Apr 5	H	Stoke	W	1-0	A.Fairclough	25,000
32	12	A	Stoke	D	1-1	Barnes	14,000
33	18	H	Manchester U	W	3-1	Barnes 2, Wynn	35,000
34	19	A	Port Vale	W	1-0	Browell	8,000
35	21	A	Manchester U	W	4-2	Barnes 2, Browell, Lomas	35,000
36	26	H	Port Vale	W	4-1	Browell 2, Barnes 2	20,000
							Appearances
							Goals

Note: City finished 5th in the Lancashire Section & were Champions of the Subsidiary Tournament with a record of P6 W5 D1 L0 F14 A4 Pts11

Goodchild	Tyler	Brierley	Fletcher	Brennan	Fairclough P	Browell	Lievesley	Barnes	Cartwright	Murphy	Newton W	Sugden	Johnson T	Howarth	Hughes	Broad T	Jones	Blackwell	Bottomley	Wynn	Meredith	Smith AW	Moses	Kenyon	Catlow	Lingard	Lomas	Cope	Tomkins	Voysey	Spruce	Ollerenshaw	Newton H	Johnson A	Kelly	Petrie	Connor	Fairclugh A	Osmond	Duffy	Hanney	Knowles	Brown	Fielding	Royle	Wray	Dorsett
	9		3	5	6						2																	7			4	1	10	11	8												
1	5	2		6	10						3										7							8			4					9	11										
1	5	2		4	6						3										7		9	8	11				10																		
1	5	2		4	6	10				11	3										7		9	8																							
1	5	2		4	6	10			11		3					9					7			8																							
1	5	2	3	4	6	10															7		9			11			8																		
1	5	2	3	4	6	10															7		9	8		11																					
1	5		3		6	9	10		11												7	8																	2	4							
1	5	2	3		6	9	10		11												7	8			4																						
1	5	2	3	4	6	9	10		11												7						8																				
1	2		3	4	6	10															7	8	9			11															5						
1	2		3	4	6	9	10										11				7																					5	8				
1	5		3	4	6	9	10					2									7	8																						11			
1	5	2	3	4	6	9	10										8				7				11																						
1	2		3	4	6	8	10			11											7									5															9		
1	5	2	3	4	6	8		10		11						9					7																										
1	2		3	5	6	9				11										8	7				4																					10	
1	5		3	4	6	8	10			11		2									7						9																				
1	2		3	5	6	9		10		11					4							8																									7
1	2		3	5	6	8		10		11					4						7	9																									
1	2		3	5	6	8		10		11					4						7	9																									
1	2		3	4	6	8	10	9		11											7									5																	
1	2		3	5	6	8	10	9		11				4							7																										
1	2		3	5	6	8		10		11			9	4							7																										
1	2		3	5	6	8		10		11			9	4							7																										
1	2		3	5		8		10	11				9	4				6			7																										
1	2		3	5		8		10	11									6	4		7																	9									
	2		3	5	6	8		10	11				9						4		7																										
1	5			4	6	8		10	11		3	2	9								7																										
1	5		3	4	6	8		10				2				11					7																										
28	30	10	25	28	28	27	10	13	8	12	6	4	5	4	3	3	2	2	2	1	28	7	5	4	4	3	2	2	2	2	2	1	1	1	1	1	1	1	1	1	1	1	1	1	1	1	1
				1	1	14	8	13	2	2			4							1		2	3	3														1									2
1	5		3	4	6	8		10	11			2									7																	9									
1	5		3	4	6	8		10				2				11					7																	9									
1	5		3	4	6	9		10				2				11				8	7																										
1			3	4	6	8	10	9			5	2				11					7																										
1			3	5	6	9		10				2				11				8	7						4																				
1			3	5	6	9		10				2				11				8	7						4																				
6	3		6	6	6	6	1	6	1		1	6				5				3	6						2											2									
						4		7												1							1											1									

1919-20

Division One

Manager: Ernest Mangnall

Did you know that?

Match 3: Newton's last game.
Match 6: Hughes's last game.
Match 9: Smith and Hanney's last game.
Match 10: Knowles's last game.
Match 17: Henry's last game.
Match 19: A. Fairclough's last game.
Match 21: Lamph's last game.
Match 22: Henderson's last game.
Match 24: Sugden's last game.
Match 27: Howard's last game.
Match 28: Reid's last game.
Match 35: King George V attended.
Match 37: Godfrey's last game.
Match 40: Dorsett's last game.
Match 42: Fairclough's last game.

This was the first season since 1902–03 that two players had netted 20 or more goals.

Match No.	Date	Venue	Opponents	Result		Scorers	Attendance
1	Aug 30	H	Sheffield United	D	3-3	Barnes 2, Browell	25,000
2	Sep 1	A	Oldham Athletic	W	3-1	Browell 2, Cartwright	4,587
3	6	A	Sheffield United	L	1-3	Wynn	25,000
4	8	H	Oldham Athletic	W	3-1	Browell 2, Barnes	18,000
5	13	H	Bolton Wanderers	L	1-4	Crawshaw	30,000
6	20	A	Bolton Wanderers	L	2-6	Browell, Taylor	24,616
7	27	H	Notts County	W	4-1	Barnes 3, Taylor	7,000
8	Oct 4	A	Notts County	L	1-4	Barnes	14,000
9	11	H	Manchester United	D	3-3	Barnes 2, Taylor	35,000
10	18	A	Manchester United	L	0-1		50,000
11	25	H	Sheffield Wednesday	W	4-2	Browell 2, Goodwin, Taylor	20,000
12	Nov 1	A	Sheffield Wednesday	D	0-0		20,000
13	8	H	Blackburn Rovers	W	8-2	Browell 3, Barnes 2, Murphy 2, Crawshaw	25,000
14	15	A	Blackburn Rovers	W	4-1	Barnes 2, Browell 2	5,000
15	22	H	Derby County	W	3-1	Crawshaw 2, Barnes	22,000
16	29	A	Derby County	D	0-0		7,000
17	Dec 6	H	West Bromwich Albion	L	2-3	Browell 2	25,000
18	13	A	West Bromwich Albion	L	0-2		25,000
19	20	A	Sunderland	L	1-2	Reid	20,000
20	25	H	Everton	D	1-1	Barnes	20,000
21	26	A	Everton	L	0-2		28,000
22	27	H	Sunderland	W	1-0	Murphy	38,000
23	Jan 1	H	Bradford City	W	1-0	Murphy	30,000
24	3	A	Arsenal	D	2-2	Barnes, Murphy	32,000
25	17	H	Arsenal	W	4-1	Browell 3, Goodwin	25,000
26	24	H	Middlesbrough	W	1-0	Browell	30,000
27	Feb 7	H	Burnley	W	3-1	Barnes 2, Crawshaw	30,000
28	14	A	Burnley	L	0-2		20,000
29	18	A	Middlesbrough	W	2-0	Johnson 2	16,000
30	28	A	Preston North End	D	1-1	Fletcher	17,000
31	Mar 13	H	Bradford Park Avenue	W	4-1	Barnes 2, Crawshaw, Johnson	10,000
32	17	H	Preston North End	W	1-0	Godfrey	18,000
33	20	A	Liverpool	L	0-1		30,000
34	22	A	Bradford Park Avenue	L	1-2	Johnson	10,000
35	27	H	Liverpool	W	2-1	Barnes 2	32,000
36	Apr 3	A	Chelsea	L	0-1		45,000
37	5	A	Bradford City	L	0-1		23,000
38	10	H	Chelsea	W	1-0	Barnes	25,000
39	17	A	Newcastle United	L	0-3		35,000
40	24	H	Newcastle United	D	0-0		35,000
41	26	A	Aston Villa	W	1-0	Browell	45,000
42	May 1	H	Aston Villa	D	2-2	Barnes, Johnson	30,000
							Appearances
							Goals

FA Cup

Round	Date	Venue	Opponents	Result		Scorers	Attendance
R1	Jan 10	H	Clapton Orient	W	4-1	Goodwin 2, Barnes, Murphy	25,878
R2	31	A	Leicester City	L	0-3		23,041
							Appearances
							Goals

Smith WE	Henry WA	Fletcher E	Hughes E	Hanney TP	Brennan J	Broad TH	Wynn GA	Browell T	Barnes H	Cartwright JE	Tyler HE	Newton WAA	Henderson J	Crawshaw RL	Murphy W	Taylor HG	Fairclough P	Knowles F	Goodchild AJ	Scott S	Lamph T	Goodwin EW	Godfrey J	Sugden FA	Fairclough A	Lievesley EF	Reid JE	Gray G	Cookson S	Woosnam M	Dorsett JAH	Howard FJ	Sharp S	Johnson TCF	Allen AJ	Jarvis HE
1	2	3	4	5	6	7	8	9	10	11																										
1			4	5	6	7	8	9	10	11	2	3																								
1			4	5	6	7	8	9	10	11	2	3																								
1	2		4		6	7	8	9	10	11	3		5																							
1	2		4	5	6	7		9	10		3			8	11																					
1	2	3	4		6	7		9	10		5				11	8																				
1		3		5		7		9	10		2		4		11	8	6																			
1		3		5		7		9	10		2		4		11	8	6																			
1	2	3		5		7		9			4			10	11	8		6																		
	2	3				7		9	10		4				11	8		6	1	5																
	2	3						9	10		6				11	8			1	5	4	7														
	2	3						9	10		6			8	11				1	5	4	7														
	2	3						9	10		6			8	11				1	5	4	7														
	2	3						9	10		6			8	11				1	5	4	7														
	2	3						9	10		6			8	11				1	5	4	7														
	2	3						9	10		6				11				1	5	4	7	8													
	2	3						9	10		6				11				1	5	4	7	8													
		3						8			6				11				1	5	4	7		2	9	10										
		3						10			6				11				1	5	4	7		2	9		8									
		3						9	10		6			8	11				1	5	4	7		2												
		3						9	10		6			8	11				1	5	4	7		2												
		3							10		6		5	8	11				1			7		2			9	4								
		3			4			9	10		6			8	11				1			7							2	5						
					4			9	10		6			8	11				1	5		7		2					3							
		3			4			9	10		6			8	11				1			7							2	5						
		3			4			9	10		6			8	11				1										2	5	7					
		3			4	7			10		6			8	11				1										2	5		9				
		3			4	7			10		6			8	11				1								9		2	5						
		3				7			10		6				11				1				8						2	5			4	9		
		3			4	7			10		6				11				1				8						2	5				9		
		3			4	7			10		6			8	11				1										2	5				9		
		3			4	7			10		6				11				1				8					5	2					9		
		3				7			10		6				11				1				8						2	5			4	9		
		3							10		6				11				1				8						2	5	7		4	9		
		3			4				10		6			8	11				1										2	5	7			9		
		3			4				10		6			8	11				1				9						2	5	7					
		3			4				10		6			8	11				1				9						2	5	7					
		3			4			9	10		6			8	11				1										2	5	7					
					5			8	10		3				11		6		1										2		7		4	9		
								9	10		6			8	11				1										2	5	7				3	4
						7		8	10	11	6								1										2	5			4	9	3	
		3				7		8	10	11	5						6		1										2				4	9		
9	13	34	6	7	20	19	4	30	39	6	41	2	4	21	36	6	4	2	33	13	11	15	9	6	2	1	3	2	20	16	8	1	6	10	2	1
		1					1	22	22	1				6	5	4						2	1				1							5		

Smith WE	Henry WA	Fletcher E	Hughes E	Hanney TP	Brennan J	Broad TH	Wynn GA	Browell T	Barnes H	Cartwright JE	Tyler HE	Newton WAA	Henderson J	Crawshaw RL	Murphy W	Taylor HG	Fairclough P	Knowles F	Goodchild AJ	Scott S	Lamph T	Goodwin EW	Godfrey J	Sugden FA	Fairclough A	Lievesley EF	Reid JE	Gray G	Cookson S	Woosnam M	Dorsett JAH	Howard FJ	Sharp S	Johnson TCF	Allen AJ	Jarvis HE
		3			4			9	10		6			8	11				1			7							2	5						
		3			4	7		8	10		6				11				1	5									2			9				
		2			2	1		2	2		2			1	2				2	1		1							2	1		1				
									1						1							2														

League Table

	P	W	D	L	F	A	Pts
W.B.A.	42	28	4	10	104	47	60
Burnley	42	21	9	12	65	59	51
Chelsea	42	22	5	15	56	51	49
Liverpool	42	19	10	13	59	44	48
Sunderland	42	22	4	16	72	59	48
Bolton W	42	19	9	14	72	65	47
Manchester C	42	18	9	15	71	62	45
Newcastle U	42	17	9	16	44	39	43
Aston Villa	42	18	6	18	75	73	42
Arsenal	42	15	12	15	56	58	42
Bradford P.A.	42	15	12	15	60	63	42
Manchester U	42	13	14	15	54	50	40
Middlesbrough	42	15	10	17	61	65	40
Sheffield U	42	16	8	18	59	69	40
Bradford C	42	14	11	17	54	63	39
Everton	42	12	14	16	69	68	38
Oldham A	42	15	8	19	49	52	38
Derby Co	42	13	12	17	47	57	38
Preston N.E.	42	14	10	18	57	73	38
Blackburn R	42	13	11	18	64	77	37
Notts Co	42	12	12	18	56	74	36
Sheffield W	42	7	9	26	28	64	23

1920-21

Division One

Manager: Ernest Mangnall

Did you know that?

Match 5: Goodwin's last game.
Match 6: Jarvis and Edelston's last game.
Match 13: Cartwright's last game.
Match 13: Fire destroys City's Main Stand at 11pm, only hours after players return from Huddersfield.
Match 23: Scott's last game.
Match 24: Gray and Taylor's last game.
Match 33: City stop Burnley's record unbeaten run of 30 games.
Match 36: Thompson's last game.
Match 39: Browell became first City man to score 30 League goals in a season.
Match 42: Broad's last game.

City asked United if they could transfer League fixtures to Old Trafford following the fire that destroyed the club's Main Stand in November. After United demanded exorbitant terms the Blues decided to soldier on at Hyde Road, causing the Athletic News to say: 'Manchester United did not in our opinion manifest the much-vaunted League spirit. They missed a great opportunity to make the club popular by a fine sporting act. The followers of Manchester City have greater affection for the old club than ever. And they have formed a just opinion of their neighbours.'

Match No.	Date	Venue	Opponents	Result		Scorers	Attendance
1	Aug 28	A	Liverpool	L	2-4	Browell, Goodwin	30,000
2	30	H	Aston Villa	W	3-1	Browell 2, Murphy	35,000
3	Sep 4	H	Liverpool	W	3-2	Browell 3	30,000
4	6	A	Aston Villa	L	1-3	Murphy	14,000
5	11	A	Arsenal	L	1-2	Browell	40,000
6	18	H	Arsenal	W	3-1	Barnes, Browell, Murphy	38,000
7	25	A	Bolton Wanderers	L	0-3		41,317
8	Oct 2	H	Bolton Wanderers	W	3-1	Browell, Fayers, Woodcock	40,000
9	9	A	Derby County	L	0-3		20,000
10	16	H	Derby County	D	0-0		26,000
11	23	A	Blackburn Rovers	W	2-0	Johnson, Woodcock	35,000
12	30	H	Blackburn Rovers	D	0-0		30,000
13	Nov 6	A	Huddersfield Town	W	1-0	Barnes	24,000
14	13	H	Huddersfield Town	W	3-2	Browell 2, Fayers	35,000
15	20	A	Manchester United	D	1-1	Barnes	54,000
16	27	H	Manchester United	W	3-0	Barnes, Browell, Murphy	35,000
17	Dec 4	A	Bradford City	W	2-1	Browell, Murphy	18,000
18	11	H	Bradford City	W	1-0	Browell	30,000
19	18	A	Sunderland	L	0-1		25,000
20	25	H	West Bromwich Albion	W	4-0	Barnes 2, Browell 2	30,000
21	27	A	West Bromwich Albion	D	2-2	Browell 2	40,000
22	Jan 1	H	Sunderland	W	3-1	Murphy 2, Browell	35,000
23	15	A	Chelsea	L	1-2	Murphy	35,000
24	22	H	Chelsea	W	1-0	Browell	30,000
25	Feb 5	A	Everton	L	0-3		40,000
26	12	A	Tottenham Hotspur	L	0-2		35,000
27	23	H	Everton	W	2-0	Browell 2	33,000
28	26	A	Oldham Athletic	L	0-2		30,000
29	Mar 5	H	Oldham Athletic	W	3-1	Barnes, Browell, Johnson	30,000
30	9	H	Tottenham Hotspur	W	2-0	Barnes, Browell	33,000
31	12	A	Preston North End	W	1-0	Fayers	18,000
32	25	H	Middlesbrough	W	2-1	Barnes, Johnson	30,000
33	26	H	Burnley	W	3-0	Barnes 2, Johnson	47,500
34	28	A	Middlesbrough	L	1-3	Browell	20,000
35	Apr 2	A	Burnley	L	1-2	Fayers	40,000
36	9	H	Sheffield United	W	2-1	Browell, Johnson	23,000
37	16	A	Sheffield United	D	1-1	Barnes	28,000
38	20	H	Preston North End	W	5-1	Browell 3, Barnes 2	25,000
39	23	H	Bradford Park Avenue	W	1-0	Browell	18,000
40	30	A	Bradford Park Avenue	W	2-1	Barnes, Fayers	12,000
41	May 2	H	Newcastle United	W	3-1	Barnes 2, Warner	18,000
42	7	A	Newcastle United	D	1-1	Browell	30,000
							Appearances
							Goals

FA Cup

R1	Jan 8	A	Crystal Palace	L	0-2		18,000
							Appearances

Goodchild AJ	Cookson S	Fletcher E	Sharp S	Fayers FL	Edelston JH	Goodwin EW	Woodcock W	Browell T	Barnes H	Murphy W	Tyler HE	Brennan J	Jarvis HE	Woosnam M	Broad TH	Crawshaw RL	Hamill M	Johnson TCF	Cartwright JE	Leyland J	Kelly PJ	Carroll F	Scott S	Thompson J	Gray G	Taylor HG	Allen AJ	Warner J
1	2	3	4	5	6	7	8	9	10	11																		
1	2	3	4	5	6	7	8	9	10	11																		
1	2	3		5	6	7	8	9	10	11	4																	
1	2	3		5	6	7	8	9	10	11	4																	
1	2	3			4	7	8	9	10	11	5	6																
1	2	3			6			9	10	11			4	5	7	8												
1	2	3	4	6				9	10	11				5	7	8												
1	2	3		6			8	9	10	11		4		5	7													
1	2	3		4			8	9	10	11				5	7		6											
1	2	3		4				8	10	11				5	7		6	9										
1	2	3		4			8	10		11				5	7		6	9										
1	2	3		4				8	10					5	7		6	9	11									
1	2	3		4				9	10								6		11	5	7	8						
1	2	3		4				9	10	11				5			6				7	8						
1	2	3		4				9	10	11				5	7		6					8						
1	2	3		4				9	10	11				5	7		6					8						
1	2	3		4				9	10	11				5	7		6					8						
1	2	3		4				9	10	11				5	7		6					8						
1	2	3		4				9	10	11					7		6					8	5					
1	2	3		4				9	10	11				5			6				7	8						
1	2	3		4			8	9	10	11				5							7	6						
1	2	3	4	6				9	10	11				5							7	8						
1	2	3		4				9	10	11											7	6	5	8				
1	2	3		4				9	10	11				5							7				6	8		
1	2	3	6	4			8	9	10	11				5	7													
1	2	3		4			8	9	10	11				5	7		6											
1	2	3		4			8	9	10	11				5	7		6											
1	2	3		6			8	9	10	11				5	7							4						
1	2			4				8	10	11				5			6	9			7						3	
1	2	3		4				8	10	11				5			6	9			7							
1	2	3		4				8	10	11				5			6	9			7							
1	2	3		4				8	10	11				5			6	9			7							
1	2	3		4				8	10	11				5	7		6	9										
1	2	3		4				8	10	11				5			6	9			7							
1	2	3		4				8	10	11				5			6	9			7							
1	2	3		4				8	10	11				5			6	9						7				
1	2			4				8	10	11				5	7		6	9									3	
1	2			4				9	10	11				5	7		6										3	8
1	2			4				9	10	11				5	7		6										3	8
1	2			4				9	10	11				5	7		6										3	8
1	2			4				9	10	11				5	7		6										3	8
1	2			4				9	10	11				5	7		6										3	8
42	42	35	5	40	6	5	13	42	41	40	3	2	1	34	23	2	28	12	2	1	13	12	2	2	1	1	7	5
				5		1	2	31	17	8								5										1

Goodchild AJ	Cookson S	Fletcher E	Sharp S	Fayers FL	Edelston JH	Goodwin EW	Woodcock W	Browell T	Barnes H	Murphy W	Tyler HE	Brennan J	Jarvis HE	Woosnam M	Broad TH	Crawshaw RL	Hamill M	Johnson TCF	Cartwright JE	Leyland J	Kelly PJ	Carroll F	Scott S	Thompson J	Gray G	Taylor HG	Allen AJ	Warner J
1	2	3		4				9	10	11	6			5	7							8						
1	1	1		1				1	1	1	1			1	1							1						

League Table

	P	W	D	L	F	A	Pts
Burnley	42	23	13	6	79	36	59
Manchester C	42	24	6	12	70	50	54
Bolton W	42	19	14	9	77	53	52
Liverpool	42	18	15	9	63	35	51
Newcastle U	42	20	10	12	66	45	50
Tottenham H	42	19	9	14	70	48	47
Everton	42	17	13	12	66	55	47
Middlesbrough	42	17	12	13	53	53	46
Arsenal	42	15	14	13	59	63	44
Aston Villa	42	18	7	17	63	70	43
Blackburn R	42	13	15	14	57	59	41
Sunderland	42	14	13	15	57	60	41
Manchester U	42	15	10	17	64	68	40
W.B.A.	42	13	14	15	54	58	40
Bradford C	42	12	15	15	61	63	39
Preston N.E.	42	15	9	18	61	65	39
Huddersfield T	42	15	9	18	42	49	39
Chelsea	42	13	13	16	48	58	39
Oldham A	42	9	15	18	49	86	33
Sheffield U	42	6	18	18	42	68	30
Derby Co	42	5	16	21	32	58	26
Bradford P.A.	42	8	8	26	43	76	24

1921-22

Division One

Manager: Ernest Mangnall

Did you know that?

Match 2: Leyland's last game.
Match 8: Lievesley's last game.
Match 10: Albinson's last game.
Match 19: Woodcock's last game.
Match 28: Brennan's last game.
Match 33: Ford's last game.
Match 34: Royle and Pearson's last game.
Match 38: Crawshaw's last game.
Match 39: Simpson's first and only game.
Match 41: Blair and Ingham's last game.

On 9 May 1922 City announced they would build a new ground on the border of Moss Side and Rusholme. They had previously been planning to move to a venue at Belle Vue, further along Hyde Road.

Match No.	Date	Venue	Opponents	Result		Scorers	Attendance
1	Aug 27	H	Aston Villa	W	2-1	Barnes 2	35,000
2	31	A	Liverpool	L	2-3	Barnes, Murphy	27,000
3	Sep 3	A	Aston Villa	L	0-4		35,000
4	7	H	Liverpool	D	1-1	Murphy	25,000
5	10	H	Arsenal	W	2-0	Barnes, Warner	25,000
6	17	A	Arsenal	W	1-0	Barnes	35,000
7	24	H	Blackburn Rovers	D	1-1	Browell	30,000
8	Oct 1	A	Blackburn Rovers	L	1-3	Browell	25,000
9	8	H	Oldham Athletic	W	2-1	Browell, Murphy	32,000
10	15	A	Oldham Athletic	W	1-0	Browell	25,000
11	22	H	Manchester United	W	4-1	Barnes 3, Warner	20,000
12	29	A	Manchester United	L	1-3	Murphy	55,000
13	Nov 5	A	Cardiff City	W	2-0	Barnes, Browell	40,000
14	12	H	Cardiff City	D	1-1	Murphy	25,000
15	19	H	West Bromwich Albion	W	6-1	Barnes 3, Browell 2, Woosnam	23,000
16	26	A	West Bromwich Albion	L	0-2		30,000
17	Dec 3	H	Bolton Wanderers	L	2-3	Barnes, Browell	29,000
18	10	A	Bolton Wanderers	L	0-5		34,789
19	17	H	Everton	W	2-1	Browell, Murphy	15,000
20	24	A	Everton	D	2-2	Johnson 2	25,000
21	26	A	Huddersfield Town	L	0-2		25,000
22	31	H	Sunderland	W	3-0	Browell, Johnson, Murphy	25,000
23	Jan 2	H	Huddersfield Town	W	2-1	Johnson, Kelly	28,000
24	14	A	Sunderland	W	3-2	Barnes, Browell, Murphy	8,000
25	21	H	Middlesbrough	D	2-2	Barnes, Browell	20,000
26	Feb 1	A	Middlesbrough	L	1-4	Browell	20,000
27	4	H	Tottenham Hotspur	D	3-3	Barnes, Browell, Johnson	18,000
28	11	A	Tottenham Hotspur	L	1-3	Barnes	45,000
29	22	H	Bradford City	W	3-2	Barnes, Browell, Woosnam	20,000
30	25	A	Bradford City	W	2-1	Browell, Murphy	25,000
31	Mar 11	A	Preston North End	L	0-1		15,000
32	18	A	Chelsea	D	0-0		40,000
33	25	H	Chelsea	D	0-0		25,000
34	Apr 1	A	Sheffield United	L	0-1		20,000
35	5	H	Preston North End	W	2-0	Barnes, Browell	15,000
36	8	H	Sheffield United	D	2-2	Browell 2	12,000
37	14	H	Birmingham	W	1-0	Warner	35,000
38	15	A	Burnley	L	2-5	Woosnam, Meredith	15,000
39	18	A	Birmingham	L	1-3	Ashurst (og)	30,000
40	22	H	Burnley	W	2-0	Barnes, Browell	25,000
41	29	A	Newcastle United	L	1-5	Ingham	25,000
42	May 6	H	Newcastle United	W	1-0	Browell	16,000
							Appearances
						One own goal	Goals

FA Cup

Match No.	Date	Venue	Opponents	Result		Scorers	Attendance
R1	Jan 7	H	Darlington	W	3-1	Browell 3	23,686
R2	28	A	Bolton Wanderers	W	3-1	Browell 2, Kelly	66,442
R3	Feb 18	A	Tottenham Hotspur	L	1-2	Kelly	53,000
							Appearances
							Goals

Goodchild AJ	Cookson S	Fletcher E	Fayers FL	Leyland J	Hamill M	Meredith WH	Warner J	Browell T	Barnes H	Murphy W	Sharp S	Blair T	Albinson G	Johnson TCF	Woosnam M	Lievesley EF	Crawshaw RL	Woodcock W	Kelly PJ	Carroll F	Thompson F	Wilson W	Brennan J	Ford A	Allen AJ	Ingham TW	Royle S	Pearson H	Simpson A	Mulligan JA	Etherington RD
1	2	3	4	5	6	7	8	9	10	11																					
1	2	3	4	5	6	7	8	9	10	11																					
1	2	3	4		6	7	8	9	10	11	5																				
	2	3	5			7	8	9	10	11	4	1	6																		
	2	3	4		6	7	8		10	11	5	1		9																	
	2	3	5		6	7	8		10	11	4	1		9																	
	2	3	4		6	7	8	9	10	11		1			5																
	2	3	6			7	8	9		11	4	1			5	10															
	2	3				7	8	9	10	11	4	1	6		5																
	2	3				7	8	9	10	11	4	1	6		5																
	2	3	6			7	8	9	10	11	4	1			5																
	2	3	6			7	8	9	10	11	4	1			5																
	2	3	6			7	8	9	10	11	4	1			5																
	2	3	5			7	8	9	10	11	4	1					6														
	2	3	6			7	8	9	10	11	4	1			5																
	2	3	6			7	8	9	10	11	4	1			5																
	2	3	6			7	8	9	10	11	4	1			5																
	2	3	6			7		9	10	11	4	1			5			8													
	2	3	4		6	7		9	10	11		1			5			8													
	2	3	4		6			8	10	11		1		9	5				7												
	2	3			6			8	10	11	4	1		9	5				7												
	2	3	6					8	10	11		1		9	5				7	4											
	2	3	6					8	10	11		1		9	5				7	4											
	2	3	6					8	10	11		1		9	5				7	4											
	2	3	6		5			8	10	11		1		9					7	4											
		3	4		6			8	10	11		1		9	5				7		2										
		3	4					8	10	11		1		9	5				7		2	6									
		3	4					8	10	11		1		9	5				7		2		6								
	2	3	4		6			8	10	11		1		9	5				7												
	2	3	4		6			8	10	11		1		9	5									7							
	2				6			8	10	11	4	1		9	5									7	3						
	2	3			6					11	4	1		10	5				8					7		9					
	2	3			6			8	10	11	4	1		9	5									7							
	2	3			6			9	10	11	4	1			5												7	8			
	2	3			6	7		8	10	11	4	1		9	5																
	2	3			6	7		8	10	11	4	1		9	5																
	2	3			6	7	8	9		11	4	1		10	5																
	2	3	6			7	8	9		11	4	1			5		10														
	2	3	5		6	7		8		11	4	1		9															10		
	2		4		6		8	9	10	11		1			5															3	7
	2		4		6		8		10	11		1			5											9				3	7
1	2		4		6	7	8	9	10	11					5										3						
4	39	38	32	2	24	25	22	38	37	42	25	38	3	20	33	1	2	2	11	4	3	1	1	4	2	2	1	1	1	2	2
						1	3	21	20	9				5	3				1							1					

Goodchild AJ	Cookson S	Fletcher E	Fayers FL	Leyland J	Hamill M	Meredith WH	Warner J	Browell T	Barnes H	Murphy W	Sharp S	Blair T	Albinson G	Johnson TCF	Woosnam M	Lievesley EF	Crawshaw RL	Woodcock W	Kelly PJ	Carroll F	Thompson F	Wilson W	Brennan J	Ford A	Allen AJ	Ingham TW	Royle S	Pearson H	Simpson A	Mulligan JA	Etherington RD
	2	3	6					8	10	11		1		9	5				7	4											
		3	4		6			8	10	11		1		9	5				7		2										
	2	3	4		6			8	10	11		1		9	5				7												
	2	3	3		2			3	3	3		3		3	3				3	1	1										
								5											2												

League Table

	P	W	D	L	F	A	Pts
Liverpool	42	22	13	7	63	36	57
Tottenham H	42	21	9	12	65	39	51
Burnley	42	22	5	15	72	54	49
Cardiff C	42	19	10	13	61	53	48
Aston Villa	42	22	3	17	74	55	47
Bolton W	42	20	7	15	68	59	47
Newcastle U	42	18	10	14	59	45	46
Middlesbrough	42	16	14	12	79	69	46
Chelsea	42	17	12	13	40	43	46
Manchester C	42	18	9	15	65	70	45
Sheffield U	42	15	10	17	59	54	40
Sunderland	42	16	8	18	60	62	40
W.B.A.	42	15	10	17	51	63	40
Huddersfield T	42	15	9	18	53	54	39
Blackburn R	42	13	12	17	54	57	38
Preston N.E.	42	13	12	17	42	65	38
Arsenal	42	15	7	20	47	56	37
Birmingham C	42	15	7	20	48	60	37
Oldham A	42	13	11	18	38	50	37
Everton	42	12	12	18	57	55	36
Bradford C	42	11	10	21	48	72	32
Manchester U	42	8	12	22	41	73	28

1922-23

Division One

Manager: Ernest Mangnall

Did you know that?

Match 3: Doran's last game.
Match 12: Utley's first and only game.
Match 23: Mulligan's last game.
Match 25: Kelly's last game.
Match 31: Fayer's last game.
Match 37: Last victory at Hyde Road.
Match 41: Last first-team game at Hyde Road.
Match 42: Etherington's last game.

City's last victory at Hyde Road was against Sunderland, and co-incidentally 80 years later the last victory at Maine Road was also against the Black Cats.

Match No.	Date	Venue	Opponents	Result		Scorers	Attendance
1	Aug 26	A	Sheffield United	L	0-2		25,000
2	28	H	Middlesbrough	W	2-1	Barnes, Browell	25,000
3	Sep 2	H	Sheffield United	D	3-3	Browell, Doran, Murphy	25,000
4	4	A	Middlesbrough	L	0-5		15,000
5	9	H	Birmingham	L	0-1		25,000
6	16	A	Birmingham	W	1-0	Johnson	30,000
7	23	H	Huddersfield Town	W	3-1	Johnson 2, Barnes	25,000
8	30	A	Huddersfield Town	D	0-0		18,000
9	Oct 7	A	Stoke	D	1-1	Johnson	20,000
10	14	H	Stoke	W	2-1	Barnes, Johnson	30,000
11	21	A	Preston North End	W	2-0	Barnes 2	12,000
12	28	H	Preston North End	W	2-1	Barnes, Johnson	22,000
13	Nov 4	A	West Bromwich Albion	L	0-2		15,000
14	11	H	West Bromwich Albion	D	1-1	Johnson	22,000
15	18	H	Bolton Wanderers	W	2-0	Johnson, Roberts	30,000
16	25	A	Bolton Wanderers	L	1-2	Barnes	28,611
17	Dec 2	A	Blackburn Rovers	D	0-0		20,000
18	9	H	Blackburn Rovers	W	2-1	Barnes 2	15,000
19	16	A	Cardiff City	L	1-3	Barnes	20,000
20	23	H	Cardiff City	W	5-1	Barnes 3, Johnson, Roberts	16,000
21	25	A	Everton	D	0-0		35,000
22	26	H	Everton	W	2-1	Barnes, Roberts	30,000
23	30	H	Oldham Athletic	W	3-2	Johnson 2, Roberts	15,000
24	Jan 6	A	Oldham Athletic	W	3-0	Barnes 2, Roberts	20,000
25	20	A	Arsenal	L	0-1		25,000
26	27	H	Arsenal	D	0-0		25,000
27	Feb 3	A	Aston Villa	L	0-2		20,000
28	10	H	Aston Villa	D	1-1	Roberts	18,000
29	17	A	Burnley	L	0-2		10,000
30	24	H	Burnley	W	1-0	Barnes	20,000
31	Mar 3	A	Tottenham Hotspur	L	1-3	Browell	35,000
32	14	H	Tottenham Hotspur	W	3-0	Roberts 2, Johnson	23,000
33	17	H	Liverpool	W	1-0	Barnes	32,000
34	24	A	Liverpool	L	0-2		25,000
35	30	A	Sunderland	L	0-2		35,000
36	31	H	Chelsea	W	3-0	Johnson 2, Barnes	15,000
37	Apr 2	H	Sunderland	W	1-0	Barnes	30,000
38	7	A	Chelsea	D	1-1	Barnes	20,000
39	14	H	Nottingham Forest	D	1-1	Roberts	15,000
40	21	A	Nottingham Forest	L	0-2		10,000
41	28	H	Newcastle United	D	0-0		18,000
42	May 5	A	Newcastle United	L	1-3	Roberts	12,000
							Appearances
							Goals

FA Cup

Match No.	Date	Venue	Opponents	Result		Scorers	Attendance
R1	Jan 13	H	Charlton Athletic	L	1-2	Johnson	28,445
							Appearances
							Goals

Goodchild AJ	Cookson S	Fletcher E	Sharp S	Pringle CR	Hamill M	Morris H	Browell T	Doran JF	Barnes H	Murphy W	Warner J	Mitchell JF	Allen AJ	Johnson TCF	Roberts F	Utley G	Meredith WH	Thompson F	Wilson W	Calderwood JC	Mulligan JA	Kelly PJ	Etherington RD	Fayers FL	Daniels AWC
1	2	3	4	5	6	7	8	9	10	11															
1	2	3	4	5	6	7	8	9	10	11															
1	2	3	4	5	6	7	8	9	10	11															
1	2	3	4	5	6	7	9		10	11	8														
	2	3	4	6	5	7	9		10	11	8	1													
	2		4	6	5	7			10	11	8	1	3	9											
1	2		4	6	5	7			10	11	8		3	9											
	2		4	6	5	7			10	11	8	1	3	9											
	2		4	6	5	7			10	11	8	1	3	9											
	2		4	6	5	7			10	11	8	1	3	9											
	2		4	6	5	7			10	11		1	3	9	8										
	2		4	6		7			10	11		1	3	9	8	5									
	2		4	6	5				10	11		1	3	9	8		7								
	2		4	6	5	7			10	11		1	3	9	8										
	2		4	6	5	7			10	11		1	3	9	8										
1	2		4	6	5	7			10	11			3	9	8										
			4	6	5	7			10	11		1	3	9	8			2							
			4	6	5	7			10	11		1	3	9	8			2							
			4	6	5		7		10	11		1	3	9	8			2							
			4	6	5		7		10	11		1	3	9	8				2						
			4	6	5		7		10	11		1	3	9	8				2						
			4	6	5		7		10	11		1		9	8				2	3					
			4	6	5	7			10	11		1		9	8				2		3				
			4	6	5	7			10	11		1		9	8			2	3						
			4	6	5				10	11		1		9	8			2	3			7			
			4	6	5	7	8		10	11		1			9			2	3						
			4	6	5	7	8			11		1		10	9			2	3						
			4	6	5		9			11		1		10	8			2	3				7		
1			4	6	5		9			11				10	8			2	3				7		
1			4	6	5		9		10	11			3		8				2				7		
1				6	5		10						3	9	8				2				7	4	11
1	2		4	6	5				10				3	9	8								7		11
1	2		4	6	5				10				3	9	8								7		11
1	2		4	6	5				10				3	9	8								7		11
1	2		4	6	5				10				3	9	8								7		11
1	2		4	6	5	7			10				3	9	8										11
1	2		4	6	5	7			10				3	9	8										11
1	2		4	6	5	7			10				3	9	8										11
1	2		4	6	5	7			10				3	9	8										11
1	2		4	6	5	7			10					9	8					3					11
1			4	6	5				10	11			2	9	8					3			7		
1			4	6	5				10	11				9	8			2		3			7		
20	25	5	41	42	41	26	15	3	38	32	7	22	27	35	32	1	1	10	12	4	1	1	10	1	10
							3	1	21	1				14	10										

Goodchild AJ	Cookson S	Fletcher E	Sharp S	Pringle CR	Hamill M	Morris H	Browell T	Doran JF	Barnes H	Murphy W	Warner J	Mitchell JF	Allen AJ	Johnson TCF	Roberts F	Utley G	Meredith WH	Thompson F	Wilson W	Calderwood JC	Mulligan JA	Kelly PJ	Etherington RD	Fayers FL	Daniels AWC
	2		4	6	5				10	11		1		9	8				3			7			
	1		1	1	1				1	1		1		1	1				1			1			
														1											

League Table

	P	W	D	L	F	A	Pts
Liverpool	42	26	8	8	70	31	60
Sunderland	42	22	10	10	72	54	54
Huddersfield T	42	21	11	10	60	32	53
Newcastle U	42	18	12	12	45	37	48
Everton	42	20	7	15	63	59	47
Aston Villa	42	18	10	14	64	51	46
W.B.A.	42	17	11	14	58	49	45
Manchester C	42	17	11	14	50	49	45
Cardiff C	42	18	7	17	73	59	43
Sheffield U	42	16	10	16	68	64	42
Arsenal	42	16	10	16	61	62	42
Tottenham H	42	17	7	18	50	50	41
Bolton W	42	14	12	16	50	58	40
Blackburn R	42	14	12	16	47	62	40
Burnley	42	16	6	20	58	59	38
Preston N.E.	42	13	11	18	60	64	37
Birmingham C	42	13	11	18	41	57	37
Middlesbrough	42	13	10	19	57	63	36
Chelsea	42	9	18	15	45	53	36
Nottingham F	42	13	8	21	41	70	34
Stoke	42	10	10	22	47	67	30
Oldham A	42	10	10	22	35	65	30

1923-24

Division One

Manager: Ernest Mangnall

Did you know that?

Match 26: Donaldson's last game.
Match 31: Allen's last game.
Match 32: Smith's last game.
Match 33: Harper's last game and Meredith's last League game.
Match 39: Carroll's last game.
Match 39: Leslie's first and only game.
Match 41: Hamill's last game.
Match 42: Morris's last game.

When 76,166 attended the fourth-round FA Cup tie with Cardiff this was the largest footballing crowd ever seen in Manchester at the time. The figure was greater than two FA Cup Finals played in the area and every attendance at Old Trafford.

Match No.	Date	Venue	Opponents	Result		Scorers	Attendance
1	Aug 25	H	Sheffield United	W	2-1	Barnes, Johnson	60,000
2	29	A	Aston Villa	L	0-2		15,000
3	Sep 1	A	Sheffield United	L	0-3		20,000
4	5	H	Aston Villa	L	1-2	Barnes	30,000
5	8	H	Bolton Wanderers	D	1-1	Roberts	40,000
6	15	A	Bolton Wanderers	D	0-0		28,173
7	22	H	Sunderland	W	4-1	Barnes 2, Johnson, Hamill	40,000
8	29	A	Sunderland	L	2-5	Barnes 2	15,000
9	Oct 6	H	Arsenal	W	1-0	Roberts	25,000
10	13	A	Arsenal	W	2-1	Barnes 2	35,000
11	20	A	Blackburn Rovers	W	1-0	Barnes	25,000
12	27	H	Blackburn Rovers	W	3-1	Roberts 2, Barnes	35,000
13	Nov 3	H	Newcastle United	D	1-1	Barnes	20,000
14	10	A	Newcastle United	L	1-4	Murphy	28,000
15	17	H	Cardiff City	D	1-1	Murphy	20,000
16	24	A	Cardiff City	D	1-1	Roberts	30,000
17	Dec 1	H	Notts County	W	1-0	Roberts	24,000
18	8	A	Notts County	L	0-2		10,000
19	15	H	Everton	W	2-1	Barnes, Roberts	35,000
20	22	A	Everton	L	1-6	Barnes	10,000
21	26	A	Birmingham	L	0-3		35,000
22	29	H	West Bromwich Albion	D	3-3	Barnes 2, Roberts	20,000
23	Jan 1	H	Tottenham Hotspur	W	1-0	Johnson	40,000
24	5	A	West Bromwich Albion	L	1-2	Barnes	15,000
25	19	H	Liverpool	L	0-1		22,000
26	26	A	Liverpool	D	0-0		7,000
27	Feb 9	A	Nottingham Forest	W	2-1	Browell, Johnson	10,000
28	13	H	Nottingham Forest	L	1-3	Roberts	3,000
29	16	H	Burnley	D	2-2	Hicks, Roberts	25,000
30	Mar 1	H	Middlesbrough	W	3-2	Barnes 2, Roberts	15,000
31	15	A	Preston North End	L	1-4	Barnes	16,000
32	17	A	Burnley	L	2-3	Browell, Warner	3,000
33	22	H	Preston North End	D	2-2	Barnes, Johnson	25,000
34	Apr 2	A	Middlesbrough	D	1-1	Johnson	10,000
35	5	H	Chelsea	W	1-0	Johnson	15,000
36	12	A	Huddersfield Town	D	1-1	Roberts	10,000
37	18	H	Birmingham	W	1-0	Roberts	30,000
38	19	H	Huddersfield Town	D	1-1	Warner	40,000
39	21	A	Tottenham Hotspur	L	1-4	Johnson	18,000
40	26	A	West Ham United	W	2-1	Browell, Roberts	18,000
41	30	A	Chelsea	L	1-3	Browell	4,000
42	May 3	H	West Ham United	W	2-1	Johnson, Warner	12,000
							Appearances
							Goals

FA Cup

	Date	Venue	Opponents	Result		Scorers	Attendance
R1	Jan 12	H	Nottingham Forest	W	2-0	Barnes, Roberts	33,849
R2	Feb 2	H	Halifax Town	D	2-2	Hamill, Roberts	30,970
rep	6	A	Halifax Town	D	0-0e		21,590
rep2	11	N	Halifax Town	W	3-0	Roberts 2, Browell	28,128
R3	23	A	Brighton & Hove Alb.	W	5-1	Browell 2, Barnes, Meredith, Sharp	24,734
R4	Mar 8	H	Cardiff City	D	0-0		76,166
rep	12	A	Cardiff City	W	1-0e	Browell	50,000
SF	Mar 29	N	Newcastle United	L	0-2		50,039
							Appearances
							Goals

R2 replay 2 at Old Trafford. SF at St Andrews, Birmingham

Mitchell JF	Cookson S	Flatcher E	Hamill M	Woosnam M	Pringle CR	Donaldson AP	Roberts F	Johnson TCF	Barnes H	Murphy W	Sharp S	Allen AJ	Smith R	Browell T	Calderwood JC	Morris H	Daniels AWC	Goodchild AJ	Warner J	Wilson W	Harper WG	Hicks GW	Meredith WH	Thompson F	Elwood JH	Carroll F	Leslie AJ
1	2	3	4	5	6	7	8	9	10	11																	
1	2	3	5		6	7	8	9	10	11	4																
1	2		5		6	7	8	9	10	11	4	3															
1	2	3			5	7	9		10	11	4		6	8													
1	2				5	7	8	9	10	11	4		6		3												
1	2		5		6	7	8	9	10	11	4				3												
1	2		5		6		8	9	10		4				3	7	11										
		2	5		6		8	9	10		4				3	7	11	1									
1		3	5		6		9		10	11	4				2	7			8								
1			5		6		9		10	11	4	2			3	7			8								
1			5		6		9		10	11	4	2			3	7			8								
1			5				9		10	11	4	2	6		3	7			8								
1			5				9		10	11	4	2	6		3	7			8								
			5				9	10		11	4	2	6		3	7		1	8								
1	2	3	5				9	10		11	4					7			8	6							
1	2	3	5				9	10		11	4					7			8	6							
1	2	3	5		6		9	10		11	4					7			8								
1	2	3	5		6		9	10		11	4					7			8								
1	2	3	5		6		9		10	11	4					7			8								
1	2		5		6		9		10	11	4				3	7			8								
1	2		5		6		9		10	11	4			8	3	7											
1	2				5		9		10	11	4	3		8		7				6							
1	2				5		9	10		11	4	3		8		7				6							
1	2				5		8	9	10	11	4	3				7				6							
1	2		5		6		8	9	10	11	4	3				7											
1	2		5		6	7	9		10	11	4	3							8								
1	2				5		8	10		11	4	3		9		7				6							
	2				5		8	10			4	3		9		7				6	1	11					
	2	3			5		8	10			4			9		7				6	1	11					
1	2	3	5		6		8		10					9			11			4			7				
	2		5		4		8	11	10			3		9		7		1		6							
		3						10					6	9		7	11		8	4	1			2	5		
	2	3	5				8	11	10		4			9						6	1		7				
	2	3			4		9	10								7	11	1	8	6					5		
	2	3			4		9	10								7	11	1	8	6					5		
1	2	3					9	10		11						7			8	6					5	4	
1	2						9	10			4				3	7	11		8	6					5		
1	2						9	10			4				3	7	11		8	6					5		
1	2						9	10							3	7	11		8	6						4	5
1	2	3					7	10			4			9			11		8	6					5		
	2	3	5				7	10			4			9			11	1	8	6							
	2	3					9	11			4			10		7		1	8	6					5		
31	34	20	25	1	28	7	41	30	23	26	34	14	6	14	15	31	11	7	23	21	4	2	2	1	8	2	1
			1				14	9	20	2				4					3			1					

Mitchell JF	Cookson S	Flatcher E	Hamill M	Woosnam M	Pringle CR	Donaldson AP	Roberts F	Johnson TCF	Barnes H	Murphy W	Sharp S	Allen AJ	Smith R	Browell T	Calderwood JC	Morris H	Daniels AWC	Goodchild AJ	Warner J	Wilson W	Harper WG	Hicks GW	Meredith WH	Thompson F	Elwood JH	Carroll F	Leslie AJ
1	2		6	5	4		8	9	10	11		3				7											
1	2		5		6		9		10	11	4	3				7			8								
1	2		5		6		9		10	11	4	3				7			8								
1	2				5		8	10		11	4	3		9		7				6							
1	2	3	5		6		8		10		4			9			11						7				
1	2	3	5		4		8	11	10					9						6			7				
1	2	3	5		4		8	11	10					9						6			7				
1	2	3	5		4		8	11	10					9						6			7				
8	8	4	7	1	8		8	5	7	4	4	4		5		4	1		2	4			4				
			1				4		2		1			4									1				

League Table

	P	W	D	L	F	A	Pts
Huddersfield Town	42	23	11	8	60	33	57
Cardiff City	42	22	13	7	61	34	57
Sunderland	42	22	9	11	71	54	53
Bolton Wanderers	42	18	14	10	68	34	50
Sheffield United	42	19	12	11	69	49	50
Aston Villa	42	18	13	11	52	37	49
Everton	42	18	13	11	62	53	49
Blackburn Rovers	42	17	11	14	54	50	45
Newcastle United	42	17	10	15	60	54	44
Notts County	42	14	14	14	44	49	42
Manchester City	42	15	12	15	54	71	42
Liverpool	42	15	11	16	49	48	41
West Ham United	42	13	15	14	40	43	41
Birmingham	42	13	13	16	41	49	39
Tottenham Hotspur	42	12	14	16	50	56	38
West Bromwich Albion	42	12	14	16	51	62	38
Burnley	42	12	12	18	55	60	36
Preston North End	42	12	10	20	52	67	34
Arsenal	42	12	9	21	40	63	33
Nottingham Forest	42	10	12	20	42	64	32
Chelsea	42	9	14	19	31	53	32
Middlesbrough	42	7	8	27	37	60	22

1924-25

Division One

Manager: Ernest Mangnall

Did you know that?

Match 15: Barnes's last game.
Match 18: McCourt's last game.
Match 25: Woosnam's last game.
Match 33: Roberts became the second City man to score 30 League goals in a season.

Billy Meredith's testimonial match on 29 April 1925 is believed to be the oldest known surviving footage of a game at Maine Road. The importance of the player is clear as Rangers and Celtic joined together to create a side to face Meredith's XI.

Match No.	Date	Venue	Opponents	Result		Scorers	Attendance
1	Aug 30	A	Bury	W	2-0	Roberts 2	40,000
2	Sep 1	A	Arsenal	L	0-1		25,000
3	6	H	Nottingham Forest	W	4-2	Barnes 2, Murphy, Roberts	30,000
4	13	A	Liverpool	L	3-5	Roberts 2, Barnes	28,000
5	17	H	Arsenal	W	2-0	Barnes, Johnson	15,000
6	20	H	Newcastle United	W	3-1	Roberts 2, Johnson	30,000
7	27	A	Sheffield United	W	5-0	Roberts 3, Barnes, Johnson	18,000
8	Oct 4	H	West Ham United	W	3-1	Roberts 2, Barnes	45,000
9	11	A	Blackburn Rovers	L	1-3	Barnes	20,000
10	18	H	Huddersfield Town	D	1-1	Barnes	58,000
11	25	H	Bolton Wanderers	D	2-2	Johnson, Roberts	50,000
12	29	A	Everton	L	1-3	Johnson	12,000
13	Nov 1	A	Notts County	L	0-2		10,000
14	8	H	Everton	D	2-2	Austin, Roberts	30,000
15	10	A	Tottenham Hotspur	D	1-1	Roberts	15,000
16	15	A	Sunderland	L	2-3	Johnson, Murphy	20,000
17	22	H	Cardiff City	D	2-2	Roberts 2	15,000
18	29	A	Preston North End	W	3-2	Austin, Roberts, Warner	25,000
19	Dec 6	H	Burnley	D	3-3	Austin, Browell, Roberts	12,000
20	13	A	Leeds United	W	3-0	Browell, Murphy, Roberts	14,000
21	20	H	Birmingham	D	2-2	Austin, Browell	25,000
22	25	H	West Bromwich Albion	L	1-2	Browell	35,000
23	26	A	West Bromwich Albion	L	1-3	Johnson	50,000
24	Jan 3	A	Nottingham Forest	W	3-0	Johnson 2, Cowan	8,000
25	17	H	Liverpool	W	5-0	Roberts 4, Woosnam	25,000
26	24	A	Newcastle United	L	0-2		25,000
27	31	H	Bury	D	0-0		12,000
28	Feb 7	A	West Ham United	L	0-4		25,000
29	14	H	Blackburn Rovers	L	1-3	Roberts	31,000
30	21	A	Huddersfield Town	D	1-1	Roberts	18,000
31	23	H	Sheffield United	W	2-1	Roberts 2	8,000
32	28	A	Bolton Wanderers	L	2-4	Daniels, Hicks	26,769
33	Mar 7	H	Notts County	W	2-1	Roberts 2	18,000
34	21	H	Sunderland	L	1-3	Roberts	25,000
35	Apr 1	A	Cardiff City	W	2-0	Austin, Johnson	15,000
36	4	H	Preston North End	W	2-1	Browell, Warner	20,000
37	10	A	Aston Villa	L	1-2	Hicks	20,000
38	11	A	Burnley	L	0-1		13,000
39	13	H	Aston Villa	W	1-0	Warner	25,000
40	18	H	Leeds United	W	4-2	Austin, Browell, Hicks, Johnson	10,000
41	25	A	Birmingham	L	1-2	Johnson	15,000
42	May 2	H	Tottenham Hotspur	W	1-0	Warner	12,000
							Appearances
							Goals

FA Cup

Match No.	Date	Venue	Opponents	Result		Scorers	Attendance
R1	Jan 10	A	Preston North End	L	1-4	Roberts	24,536
							Appearances
							Goals

Mitchell JF	Cookson S	Fletcher E	Sharp S	McCourt J	Pringle CR	Austin SW	Roberts F	Johnson TCF	Barnes H	Murphy W	Elwood JH	Wilson W	Calderwood JC	Goodchild AJ	Daniels AWC	Browell T	Thompson F	Hicks GW	Warner J	Cowan S	Woosnam M	Benzie R
1	2	3	4	5	6	7	8	9	10	11												
1	2	3	4	5	6	7	8	9	10	11												
1	2	3	4	5	6	7	8	9	10	11												
1	2	3	4			7	8	9	10	11	5	6										
1	2		4		6	7	8	9	10	11	5		3									
1	2		4		6	7	8	9	10	11	5		3									
1	2		4		5	7	8	9	10	11		6	3									
1	2		4		6	7	8	9	10	11	5		3									
	2		4		6	7	8	9	10	11	5		3	1								
1	2	3	4		6	7	8	9	10	11	5											
1	2	3	4		6	7	8	9	10		5				11							
	2		4		6	7	8	10			5	3		1	11	9						
1			4			7	8		10	11	5	6	3			9	2					
1	2		4			7	8	9	10	11	5	6	3									
		3	4		6	7	8	9	10	11	5			1			2					
		3	4		6		8	9		11	5			1	10		2	7				
1		3	4		6		8	9		11	5				10		2	7				
1	2	3	4	5	6	7	8	10		11									9			
	2	3	4		6	7	8	10		11	5			1		9						
1	2	3	4		6	7	8	10		11	5					9						
1	2	3	4		6	7	8	10		11						9				5		
1	2	3	4		6	7	8	10							11	9				5		
1	2	3	7		4			10				6				9		11	8	5		
1		3			6	7	8	10								9	2	11		4	5	
1	2	3	4			7	9	10					6					11	8		5	
1	2	3	4			7	9	10					6					11	8	5		
1	2	3	4			7	9	10					6					11	8	5		
	2	3	4			7	9	10		11			6	1					8	5		
1	2		4		6	7	8	9		11					10		3			5		
1	2	3	8		4	7	9	10				6			11					5		
	2		8		4	7	9	10				6		1	11		3			5		
1	2	3	8		4	7		9				6			10			11		5		
1	2	3	8		4	7	9	10					6					11		5		
1	2	3	4		6	7	8	10								9		11		5		
	2	3	4		6	7		10		11				1		9			8	5		
	2	3	4		6	7		10		11				1		9			8	5		
	2	3	4		6	7	9	10						1				11	8	5		
1	2		4		6		9	10		7		3						11	8	5		
	2		4		6	7	9	11				3		1		10			8	5		
	2		4		6	7	8	10				3		1		9		11		5		
	2		4		6	7	8	10					3	1		9		11		5		
1	2				4	7	9	10					3					11	8	5		6
29	37	27	40	4	35	38	38	41	14	24	15	12	14	13	9	14	7	15	12	21	2	1
						6	31	12	8	3					1	6		3	4	1	1	

Mitchell JF	Cookson S	Fletcher E	Sharp S	McCourt J	Pringle CR	Austin SW	Roberts F	Johnson TCF	Barnes H	Murphy W	Elwood JH	Wilson W	Calderwood JC	Goodchild AJ	Daniels AWC	Browell T	Thompson F	Hicks GW	Warner J	Cowan S	Woosnam M	Benzie R
1		3	4		6	7	8	10								9	2	11			5	
1		1	1		1	1	1	1								1	1	1			1	
							1															

League Table

	P	W	D	L	F	A	Pts
Huddersfield T	42	21	16	5	69	28	58
W.B.A.	42	23	10	9	58	34	56
Bolton W	42	22	11	9	76	34	55
Liverpool	42	20	10	12	63	55	50
Bury	42	17	15	10	54	51	49
Newcastle U	42	16	16	10	61	42	48
Sunderland	42	19	10	13	64	51	48
Birmingham C	42	17	12	13	49	53	46
Notts Co	42	16	13	13	42	31	45
Manchester C	42	17	9	16	76	68	43
Cardiff C	42	16	11	15	56	51	43
Tottenham H	42	15	12	15	52	43	42
West Ham U	42	15	12	15	62	60	42
Sheffield U	42	13	13	16	55	63	39
Aston Villa	42	13	13	16	58	71	39
Blackburn R	42	11	13	18	53	66	35
Everton	42	12	11	19	40	60	35
Leeds U	42	11	12	19	46	59	34
Burnley	42	11	12	19	46	75	34
Arsenal	42	14	5	23	46	58	33
Preston N.E.	42	10	6	26	37	74	26
Nottingham F	42	6	12	24	29	65	24

1925-26

Division One

Manager: David Ashworth/Albert Alexander Snr (16 November 1926 – 26 April 1926), Peter Hodge (from 26 April 1926)

Did you know that?

Match 6: Phillips's first and only game.
Match 12: Fletcher's last game.
Match 15: Warner's last game.
Match 22: Bradford's last game.
Match 25: Calderwood's last game.
Match 26: Dennison's last game.
Match 27: The record score in a Manchester derby.
Match 29: Daniels's last game.
Match 32: Murphy's last game.
Match 39: Mitchell's last game.
Match 42: Browell's last game.

The 1925–26 season was probably the first when supporters used the phrase 'typical City' when talking of the Blues. Prior to the final match of the season City were fourth from bottom with a point advantage and a much better goal average than main rivals Burnley for the one remaining relegation spot. Sadly, City went a goal down within the first minute, then fought back to make it 1–1 at half time. In the 50th minute Newcastle took the lead again, but shortly afterwards City were awarded a penalty. Sadly, Newcastle 'keeper Wilson saved Austin's penalty and Newcastle scored again in the 60th minute. Three minutes from time Browell managed City's second but it was too late. Both relegation rivals Leeds and Burnley won 4–1 and City became the first FA Cup Finalists to be relegated in the same season.

Match No.	Date	Venue	Opponents	Result		Scorers	Attendance
1	Aug 29	H	Cardiff City	W	3-2	Austin, Johnson, Warner	42,529
2	31	A	Birmingham	L	0-1		17,560
3	Sep 5	A	Tottenham Hotspur	L	0-1		35,594
4	12	H	Manchester United	D	1-1	Cowan	62,994
5	19	H	Everton	D	4-4	Browell 4	11,393
6	23	A	West Bromwich Albion	L	1-4	Roberts	7,500
7	26	A	Huddersfield Town	D	2-2	Johnson, Warner	19,541
8	Oct 3	H	Sunderland	W	4-1	Austin 2, Browell, Warner	39,461
9	10	A	Blackburn Rovers	D	3-3	Browell 2, Roberts	25,935
10	17	A	Liverpool	L	1-2	Johnson	31,073
11	24	H	Burnley	W	8-3	Browell 5, Hicks, Johnson, Roberts	19,740
12	26	A	Sheffield United	L	3-8	Cowan, Johnson, Roberts	8,250
13	31	A	West Ham United	L	1-3	Browell	16,172
14	Nov 4	H	Sheffield United	L	2-4	Austin, Roberts	14,053
15	7	H	Arsenal	L	2-5	Browell, Warner	11,384
16	14	A	Bolton Wanderers	L	1-5	Roberts	22,326
17	21	H	Notts County	D	1-1	Coupland	16,837
18	28	A	Aston Villa	L	1-3	Dennison	21,988
19	Dec 5	H	Leicester City	W	5-1	Johnson 2, Roberts 2, Dennison	33,747
20	12	A	Leeds United	W	4-3	Bradford, Dennison, Johnson, Roberts	18,762
21	19	H	Newcastle United	D	2-2	Johnson, Murphy	28,616
22	25	A	Bury	L	5-6	Browell 2, Coupland, Johnson, Roberts	23,621
23	26	H	Bury	L	0-2		50,168
24	Jan 1	H	West Bromwich Albion	W	3-1	Austin, Dennison, Johnson	22,513
25	2	A	Cardiff City	D	2-2	Roberts 2	10,242
26	16	H	Tottenham Hotspur	D	0-0		25,244
27	23	A	Manchester United	W	6-1	Austin 2, Roberts 2, Hicks, Johnson	48,657
28	Feb 6	H	Huddersfield Town	L	1-5	Roberts	34,645
29	10	A	Everton	D	1-1	Roberts	15,067
30	13	A	Sunderland	L	3-5	Austin, Browell, Hicks	25,284
31	27	H	Liverpool	D	1-1	Browell	45,699
32	Mar 13	H	West Ham United	W	2-0	Murphy, Roberts	36,400
33	17	H	Blackburn Rovers	L	0-1		18,793
34	20	A	Arsenal	L	0-1		34,974
35	29	H	Bolton Wanderers	D	1-1	Austin	21,720
36	Apr 2	H	Birmingham	L	2-4	Austin, Hicks	49,950
37	3	A	Notts County	L	0-1		16,266
38	6	A	Burnley	W	2-1	Hicks, Johnson	19,966
39	10	H	Aston Villa	W	4-2	Austin, Browell, Johnson, Roberts	34,537
40	17	A	Leicester City	W	3-2	Roberts 2, Browell	17,702
41	27	H	Leeds United	W	2-1	Austin Johnson	43,475
42	May 1	A	Newcastle United	L	2-3	Browell, Roberts	20,262

Appearances
Goals

FA Cup

	Date	Venue	Opponents	Result		Scorers	Attendance
R3	Jan 9	A	Corinthians	D	3-3	Cookson, Hicks, Roberts	29,700
rep	13	H	Corinthians	W	4-0	Austin 2, Hicks, Johnson	42,303
R4	30	H	Huddersfield Town	W	4-0	Hicks 2, Browell, Roberts	74,799
R5	Feb 20	H	Crystal Palace	W	11-4	Roberts 5, Browell 3, Austin, Hicks, Johnson	51,630
R6	Mar 6	A	Clapton Orient	W	6-1	Johnson 3, Browell, Hicks, Roberts	24,600
SF	27	N	Manchester United	W	3-0	Browell 2, Roberts	46,450
F	Apr 24	N	Bolton Wanderers	L	0-1		91,447

SF at Bramall Lane, Final at Wembley Stadium

Appearances
Goals

Goodchild AJ	Cookson S	McCloy P	Sharp S	Cowan S	Pringle CR	Austin SW	Warner J	Roberts F	Johnson TCF	Hicks GW	Mitchell JF	Browell T	Phillips JR	Thompson F	Benzie R	Coupland CA	Bradford LJ	Fletcher E	Dennison R	Elwood JH	Murphy W	Calderwood JC	Daniels AWC	McMullan J	Appleton F
1	2	3	4	5	6	7	8	9	10	11															
	2	3	4	5	6	7	8		10	11	1	9													
	2	3	4	5	6	7	8	9	10	11	1														
	2	3	4	5	6	7	8	9	10	11	1														
	2	3	4	5	6	7		8	10	11	1	9													
		3	4	5		7		8	10	11		9	1	2	6										
		3		5		7	8		10	11	1	9		2	6	4									
		3		5		7	8		10	11	1	9		2	6	4									
		3		5		7		8	10	11	1	9		2	6	4									
	2	3		5	6	7		8	10	11	1	9				4									
	2	3		5	6			8	10	11	1	9				4	7								
1	2		4	5	6	7		8	10	11		9						3							
	2			5	4	7		8	10	11	1	9		3	6										
1	2				5	7		8		11		9		3	6	4			10						
		3	4		6	7	8	9		11	1	10		2						5					
		3		5	4	7		8	10	11	1	9		2	6										
	2	3		5	6	7		8	10		1	9				4					11				
	2	3		5	6	7			10		1	9				4			8		11				
1	2	3		5	6			9	10							4	7		8		11				
1	2	3		5	6			9	10							4	7		8		11				
1	2	3		5	6			9	10							4	7		8		11				
1	2	3		5	6			8	10			9				4	7				11				
1	2	3		5	6			8	10	7		9				4					11				
1	2			5	6	7		9	10	11						4			8			3			
1	2	3		5		7		9	10	11						4			8			6			
1		3		5	6	7		9	10					2		4			8		11				
1	2	3		5	6	7		9	10	11		8				4									
1	2	3		5	6	7		9	10	11		8				4									
1	2	3		5	6	7		9		11		8				4							10		
1	2	3		5	6	7		9	10	11		8				4									
1	2	3		5	4	7		9	10	11		8												6	
1	2			5	4	7		9		10		8									11			6	3
1	2	3		5	4	7		9	10	11		8												6	
1	2	3		5	4	7		9	10	11		8												6	
1	2	3		5	4	7		9	10	11		8												6	
1	2	3		5	4	7		9	10	11		8												6	
	2	3		5	4	7		9	10	11	1	8												6	
	2	3		9	5	7		8	10	11	1					4				6					
	2	3				7		9	10	11	1	8				4				5				6	
1	2	3			6	7		9	10	11		8				4				5					
1	2	3		5	4	7		9	10	11		8												6	
1	2	3		5	4	7		9	10	11		8												6	
24	35	37	8	38	36	36	7	38	38	35	17	32	1	9	7	23	5	1	8	4	9	2	1	10	1
				2		12	4	21	15	5		21				2	1		4		2				

Goodchild AJ	Cookson S	McCloy P	Sharp S	Cowan S	Pringle CR	Austin SW	Warner J	Roberts F	Johnson TCF	Hicks GW	Mitchell JF	Browell T	Phillips JR	Thompson F	Benzie R	Coupland CA	Bradford LJ	Fletcher E	Dennison R	Elwood JH	Murphy W	Calderwood JC	Daniels AWC	McMullan J	Appleton F
1	2			5	6	7		9	10	11						4			8			3			
1				5	6	7		9	10	11				2					8	4		3			
1	2	3		5	6	7		9	10	11		8				4									
1	2	3		5	6	7		9	10	11		8				4									
1	2			5	4	7		9	10	11		8												6	3
1	2	3		5	4	7		9	10	11		8												6	
1	2	3		5	4	7		9	10	11		8												6	
7	6	4		7	7	7		7	7	7		5		1		3			2	1		2		3	1
	1					3		9	5	6		7													

League Table

	P	W	D	L	F	A	Pts
Huddersfield T	42	23	11	8	92	60	57
Arsenal	42	22	8	12	87	63	52
Sunderland	42	21	6	15	96	80	48
Bury	42	20	7	15	85	77	47
Sheffield U	42	19	8	15	102	82	46
Aston Villa	42	16	12	14	86	76	44
Liverpool	42	14	16	12	70	63	44
Bolton W	42	17	10	15	75	76	44
Manchester U	42	19	6	17	66	73	44
Newcastle U	42	16	10	16	84	75	42
Everton	42	12	18	12	72	70	42
Blackburn R	42	15	11	16	91	80	41
W.B.A.	42	16	8	18	79	78	40
Birmingham C	42	16	8	18	66	81	40
Tottenham H	42	15	9	18	66	79	39
Cardiff C	42	16	7	19	61	76	39
Leicester C	42	14	10	18	70	80	38
West Ham U	42	15	7	20	63	76	37
Leeds U	42	14	8	20	64	76	36
Burnley	42	13	10	19	85	108	36
Manchester C	42	12	11	19	89	100	35
Notts Co	42	13	7	22	54	74	33

1926-27

Division Two

Manager: Peter Hodge

Did you know that?

Match 18: Coupland's last game.
Match 20: Finnegan's last game.
Match 22: Thompson's last League game.
Match 23: Goodchild's last League game.
Match 24: Gibson's last game.
Match 26: Wilson's last game.
Match 33: Elwood's last game.
Match 34: Benzie's last game.
Match 36: W. Cowan's last game.

Had goal difference not goal average been the deciding factor, City would have been promoted in 1926–27.

Match No.	Date	Venue	Opponents	Result		Scorers	Attendance
1	Aug 28	H	Fulham	W	4-2	Austin, Barrass, Hicks, Roberts	35,110
2	Sep 1	H	Portsmouth	W	4-0	Roberts 2, Hicks, Johnson	20,841
3	4	A	Grimsby Town	D	2-2	Johnson , Roberts	16,559
4	6	A	Oldham Athletic	W	2-1	Austin, Pringle	26,009
5	11	H	Blackpool	W	2-1	Austin, Johnson	34,885
6	18	A	Reading	L	0-1		22,399
7	22	H	Oldham Athletic	W	3-0	Hicks, Johnson, Roberts	25,676
8	25	H	Swansea Town	W	3-1	Hicks, Johnson, Roberts	24,314
9	Oct 2	A	Nottingham Forest	D	3-3	Johnson 2, W Cowan	15,121
10	9	H	Barnsley	D	1-1	Hicks	19,430
11	16	H	Southampton	L	3-4	Austin, Johnson, McMullan	34,336
12	23	A	Port Vale	W	2-0	Johnson, McMullan	14,467
13	30	H	Clapton Orient	W	6-1	Barrass 3, Roberts 2, Johnson	28,979
14	Nov 6	A	Notts County	L	0-1		5,953
15	13	H	Wolverhampton W.	W	2-1	Austin, McMullan	24,177
16	20	A	Hull City	L	2-3	Barrass, Johnson	11,582
17	27	H	South Shields	L	1-2	Barrass	20,837
18	Dec 4	A	Preston North End	W	4-2	Austin 3, Barrass	24,427
19	11	H	Chelsea	W	1-0	Bell	26,868
20	18	A	Bradford City	L	3-4	Hicks 2, Roberts	17,580
21	25	H	Middlesbrough	L	3-5	S Cowan, W Cowan, Johnson	44,077
22	27	A	Middlesbrough	L	1-2	Roberts	43,754
23	Jan 1	A	Portsmouth	L	1-2	Johnson	19,861
24	15	A	Fulham	W	5-2	Gibson 2, Austin, S Cowan, W Cowan	20,503
25	22	H	Grimsby Town	W	2-0	Hicks, Johnson	21,212
26	29	A	Blackpool	W	4-2	Hicks 2, W Cowan, Johnson	9,223
27	Feb 5	H	Reading	W	3-0	Hicks, Roberts, Evans (og)	37,286
28	12	A	Swansea Town	W	3-1	Johnson 2, Hicks	20,345
29	19	H	Nottingham Forest	D	1-1	W Cowan	48,689
30	26	A	Barnsley	D	1-1	W Cowan	16,395
31	Mar 12	H	Port Vale	W	4-1	Johnson 2, W Cowan, Hicks	34,281
32	19	A	Clapton Orient	W	4-2	Hicks 3, Austin	15,141
33	26	H	Notts County	W	4-1	W Cowan 2, Hicks 2	17,242
34	Apr 2	A	Wolverhampton W.	L	1-4	W Cowan	11,361
35	9	H	Hull City	D	2-2	Bell, W Cowan	21,508
36	15	A	Darlington	D	2-2	Broadhurst, Johnson	11,784
37	16	A	South Shields	D	2-2	Hicks, Roberts	6,543
38	18	H	Darlington	W	7-0	Broadhurst 4, Johnson 2, Bell	29,324
39	23	H	Preston North End	W	1-0	Hicks	49,343
40	25	A	Southampton	D	1-1	Roberts	5,550
41	30	A	Chelsea	D	0-0		39,995
42	May 7	H	Bradford City	W	8-0	Johnson 3, Broadhurst 2, Bell, Hicks, Roberts	49,384
							Appearances
						One own goal	Goals

FA Cup

R3	Jan 8	A	Birmingham	L	1-4	Hicks	39,503
							Appearances
							Goals

Goodchild AJ	Cookson S	McCloy P	Pringle CR	Cowan S	McMullan J	Austin SW	Barrass MW	Roberts F	Cowan WD	Hicks GW	Johnson TCF	Elwood JH	Bell PN	Sharp S	Finnigan RP	Bennett ET	Benzie R	Coupland CA	Thompson F	Wilson W	Gibson TD	Gray A	Broadhurst C	Allan J
1	2	3	4	5	6	7	8	9	10	11														
1	2	3	4	5	6	7	8	9		11	10													
1	2	3	4	5	6	7	8	9		11	10													
1	2	3	4		6	7	5	9	8	11	10													
1	2	3	4		6	7	8	9		11	10	5												
1	2	3	6				5	9	8	11	10	4	7											
1	2	3			6		5	9	8	11	10		7	4										
1	2	3			6		5	9	8	11	10		7	4										
1	2	3			6		5	9	8	11	10		7	4										
1	2	3	4		6		5	9	8	11	10		7											
1	2	3	8		6	7	5	9		11	10			4										
	2		4	5	6	7	8	9		11	10				1	3								
	2		6	5		7	8	9		11	10			4	1	3								
	2		4	5	6	7	8	9		11	10				1	3								
	2		4	5	6	7	8	9		11	10				1	3								
	2		4	5	6	7	9		8	11	10				1	3								
1	2			5	6	7	9		8	11	10					3	4							
	2			5	6	7	10	9		11			8		1	3		4						
	2		4		6	8	10	9		11			7		1	3			5					
	2				6	8	10	9		11			7		1	3			5	4				
1	2			5		7	4	9	8	11	10					3	6							
1	2					7	4	9	8	11	10					3	6		5					
1	2		4			7	8			11	10	5				3	6				9			
	2	3	4	5	6	7			8	11	10										9	1		
	2	3	4	5	6	7			8	10	9		11									1		
	2	3	4	5	6				8	10	9		11							7		1		
	2	3	4	5	6		8	9		11	10		7									1		
	2	3	4	5	6		8	9		11	10		7									1		
	2	3	4	5	6			9	8	11	10		7									1		
	2	3	4	5	6	9			8	11	10		7									1		
	2	3	4	5	6	7			8	10	9		11									1		
	2	3	4	5	6	7			8	10	9		11									1		
	2	3	6			7	4		8	10	9	5	11									1		
	2	3	4			7	5		8	10	9		11				6					1		
	2	3	4	5	6	7			8	10	9		11									1		
	2	3	4	5	6				8	11	10		7									1	9	
	2	3	5		6			8		11	10		7	4								1	9	
	2	3	4	5	6					11	10		7									1	9	8
	2	3	4	5	6					11	10		7									1	9	8
	2	3	4	5	6			8		11	10		7									1	9	
	2	3	4	5	6			8		11	10		7									1	9	
	2	3	4	5	6			8		11	10		7									1	9	
15	42	30	34	27	35	26	27	27	22	42	38	4	26	6	8	12	5	1	3	2	2	19	7	2
			1	2	3	10	7	14	11	21	25		4								2		7	

Goodchild AJ	Cookson S	McCloy P	Pringle CR	Cowan S	McMullan J	Austin SW	Barrass MW	Roberts F	Cowan WD	Hicks GW	Johnson TCF	Elwood JH	Bell PN	Sharp S	Finnigan RP	Bennett ET	Benzie R	Coupland CA	Thompson F	Wilson W	Gibson TD	Gray A	Broadhurst C	Allan J
1	2		4		6	7	8		10	11	9					3			5					
1	1		1		1	1	1		1	1	1					1			1					
										1														

League Table

	P	W	D	L	F	A	Pts
Middlesbrough	42	27	8	7	122	60	62
Portsmouth	42	23	8	11	87	49	54
Manchester C	42	22	10	10	108	61	54
Chelsea	42	20	12	10	62	52	52
Nottingham F	42	18	14	10	80	55	50
Preston N.E.	42	20	9	13	74	72	49
Hull C	42	20	7	15	63	52	47
Port Vale	42	16	13	13	88	78	45
Blackpool	42	18	8	16	95	80	44
Oldham A	42	19	6	17	74	84	44
Barnsley	42	17	9	16	88	87	43
Swansea T	42	16	11	15	68	72	43
Southampton	42	15	12	15	60	62	42
Reading	42	16	8	18	64	72	40
Wolverhampton W	42	14	7	21	73	75	35
Notts Co	42	15	5	22	70	96	35
Grimsby T	42	11	12	19	74	91	34
Fulham	42	13	8	21	58	92	34
South Shields	42	11	11	20	71	96	33
Clapton O	42	12	7	23	60	96	31
Darlington	42	12	6	24	79	98	30
Bradford C	42	7	9	26	50	88	23

1927-28

Division Two

Manager: Peter Hodge

Did you know that?

Match 12: Appleton's last game.
Match 13: Smelt's last game.
Match 19: Allan's last League game.
Match 21: Cookson's last game.
Match 23: Gorringe and Foster's last game.
Match 27: Bell's last game.
Match 33: Pringle's last game.
Match 40: Sharp's last game.

City secured the Division Two title by beating nearest rivals Leeds 1–0 in Match 40. Thousands of Mancunians travelled to the game, creating Leeds' highest League crowd of the season – over 16,000 more than their next highest attendance. City also ended the season as football's best supported side.

Match No.	Date	Venue	Opponents	Result		Scorers	Attendance
1	Aug 27	A	Wolverhampton W.	D	2-2	Hicks, McMullan	22,600
2	29	H	Swansea Town	W	7-4	Johnson 3, Bell, Broadhurst, Hicks, Roberts	34,316
3	Sep 3	H	Port Vale	W	1-0	Johnson	37,583
4	5	A	Swansea Town	L	3-5	Bell, Hicks, Johnson	17,554
5	10	A	South Shields	W	1-0	McMullan	7,623
6	17	H	Leeds United	W	2-1	Johnson 2	40,931
7	24	A	Nottingham Forest	W	5-4	Hicks 2, Johnson 2, Broadhurst	12,893
8	Oct 1	H	Oldham Athletic	W	3-1	Broadhurst 2, Johnson	25,216
9	8	H	Hull City	W	2-1	Barrass 2	42,038
10	15	A	Preston North End	L	0-1		30,590
11	22	A	Blackpool	D	2-2	Hicks, Roberts	17,013
12	29	H	Reading	W	4-1	Austin 2, Johnson, Roberts	33,717
13	Nov 5	A	Grimsby Town	L	1-4	Smelt	12,522
14	12	H	Chelsea	L	0-1		52,830
15	19	A	Clapton Orient	W	2-0	Austin, Roberts	14,129
16	26	H	Stoke City	W	4-0	Allan, Austin, Johnson, Roberts	36,456
17	Dec 3	A	Bristol City	L	0-2		23,114
18	10	H	West Bromwich Albion	W	3-1	Austin, Broadhurst, Johnson	29,747
19	17	A	Southampton	D	1-1	Broadhurst	10,013
20	24	H	Notts County	W	3-1	Broadhurst 2, Hicks	18,362
21	26	A	Barnsley	W	3-0	Broadhurst 2, Roberts	17,252
22	31	H	Wolverhampton W.	W	3-0	Johnson 2, Broadhurst	25,991
23	Jan 2	H	Barnsley	W	7-3	Austin 2, Gorringe 2, Johnson, McMullan, Roberts	38,226
24	7	A	Port Vale	W	2-1	Hicks, Roberts	14,310
25	21	H	South Shields	W	3-0	Austin, Broadhurst, Johnson	29,200
26	Feb 4	H	Nottingham Forest	D	3-3	Austin, Broadhurst, Hicks	30,037
27	11	A	Oldham Athletic	L	2-3	Bell, Broadhurst	25,426
28	25	H	Preston North End	D	2-2	Roberts 2	59,500
29	Mar 3	H	Blackpool	W	4-1	Roberts 4	40,906
30	10	A	Reading	D	1-1	Marshall	13,313
31	17	H	Grimsby Town	W	2-0	McMullan, Roberts	49,185
32	24	A	Chelsea	W	1-0	Roberts	51,813
33	31	H	Clapton Orient	W	5-3	Roberts 3, Brook, Horne	38,272
34	Apr 6	H	Fulham	W	2-1	Marshall, Roberts	50,660
35	7	A	Stoke City	L	0-2		29,455
36	9	A	Fulham	D	1-1	Tait	25,997
37	14	H	Bristol City	W	4-2	Hicks, Johnson, Marshall, Tait	31,298
38	16	A	Hull City	D	0-0		6,088
39	21	A	West Bromwich Albion	D	1-1	Brook	15,409
40	25	A	Leeds United	W	1-0	Tait	48,780
41	28	H	Southampton	W	6-1	Marshall 3, Horne, Johnson, Tait	42,361
42	May 5	A	Notts County	L	1-2	Marshall	9,907
							Appearances
							Goals

FA Cup

	Date	Venue	Opponents	Result		Scorers	Attendance
R3	Jan 14	H	Leeds United	W	1-0	Johnson	50,473
R4	28	A	Sunderland	W	2-1	Broadhurst, Hicks	38,658
R5	Feb 18	H	Stoke City	L	0-1		73,668
							Appearances
							Goals

Gray A	Cookson S	McCloy P	Pringle CR	Cowan S	McMullan J	Bell PN	Roberts F	Broadhurst C	Johnson TCF	Hicks GW	Barrass MW	Ridley JG	Gibbons S	Robertson G	Allen J	Barber LF	Appleton F	Austin SW	Smelt T	Foster CL	Gorringe FC	Bennett ET	Sharp S	Marshall RS	Horne A	Tilson SF	Brook EF	Tait T
1	2	3	4	5	6	7	8	9	10	11																		
1	2	3	4	5	6	7	8	9	10	11																		
1	2	3	4	5	6	7	8	9	10	11																		
1	2	3	4	5	6	7		9	10	11	8																	
1		3	4	5	6	7		9	10	11	8	2																
1		3	4	5	6	7		9	10	11	8	2																
1		3	4	5	6	7		9	10	11	8	2																
1		3	4		6	7		9	10	11	8	2	5															
1		3	4		6	7		9	10	11	8	2	5															
1		3	4	5		7		9		11	8	2		6	10													
1		3	4	5	6	7	8	9	10	11		2																
		3	4	5		11	9		10		6					1	2	7	8									
1		3		5	6	11	9		10			2		4				7	8									
1		3	4	5	6		9		10	11	8	2						7										
1	2	3	4	5	6		9		10	11					8			7										
1	2	3	4	5	6	11	9		10						8			7										
1	2	3	4	5	6	11	9		10						8			7										
1	2	3	4	5	6			9	10	11					8			7										
1	2	3	4		6			9	10	11	5				8			7										
1	2	3	4	5	6		8	9	10	11								7										
1	2	3		5	6		8	9	10		4							7		11								
1		3		5	6		8	9	10		4	2						7		11								
1		3		5	6		8		10		4	2						7		11	9							
1		3	4		6		8	9	10	11	5	2						7										
		3		5	6		8	9	10	11	4	2				1		7										
		3		5	6		8	9	10	11	4	2				1		7										
1		3		5	6	7	8	9	10	11	4	2																
1		3		5	6		8	9	10	11		2						7				4						
1		3	5		6		9		10	11		2						7					4	8				
1		3		5	6		9		10	11		2						7					4	8				
1		3		5	6		9					2											4	8	7	10	11	
1		3			6		9				5	2											4	8	7	10	11	
1		3	6				9				5	2											4	8	7	10	11	
1		3			6		9				5	2											4	8	7	10	11	
1					6		9				5	2										3	4	8	7	10	11	
				5	6					7	4	2				1						3		8		10	11	9
				5					10	7	6	2				1						3	4	8			11	9
					6				10	7	5	2				1						3	4	8			11	9
		3			6				10	7	5	2				1							4	8			11	9
		3			6				10	7	5	2				1							4	8			11	9
		3			6				10		5	2	4			1								8	7		11	9
		3			6				10		5	2	4			1								8	7		11	9
32	11	38	22	28	38	16	26	21	35	28	28	30	4	2	6	10	1	18	2	3	1	5	11	14	7	6	12	7
					4	3	20	14	19	10	2				1			9	1		2			7	2		2	4

Gray A	Cookson S	McCloy P	Pringle CR	Cowan S	McMullan J	Bell PN	Roberts F	Broadhurst C	Johnson TCF	Hicks GW	Barrass MW	Ridley JG	Gibbons S	Robertson G	Allen J	Barber LF	Appleton F	Austin SW	Smelt T	Foster CL	Gorringe FC	Bennett ET	Sharp S	Marshall RS	Horne A	Tilson SF	Brook EF	Tait T
1		3		5	6		8	9	10	11	4	2						7										
		3		5	6		8	9	10	11	4	2				1		7										
1		3	4		6		8	9	10	11		2	5		7													
2		3	1	2	3		3	3	3	3	2	3	1		1	1		2										
								1	1	1																		

League Table

	P	W	D	L	F	A	Pts
Manchester C	42	25	9	8	100	59	59
Leeds U	42	25	7	10	98	49	57
Chelsea	42	23	8	11	75	45	54
Preston N.E.	42	22	9	11	100	66	53
Stoke C	42	22	8	12	78	59	52
Swansea T	42	18	12	12	75	63	48
Oldham A	42	19	8	15	75	51	46
W.B.A.	42	17	12	13	90	70	46
Port Vale	42	18	8	16	68	57	44
Nottingham F	42	15	10	17	83	84	40
Grimsby T	42	14	12	16	69	83	40
Bristol C	42	15	9	18	76	79	39
Barnsley	42	14	11	17	65	85	39
Hull C	42	12	15	15	41	54	39
Notts Co	42	13	12	17	68	74	38
Wolverhampton W	42	13	10	19	63	91	36
Southampton	42	14	7	21	68	77	35
Reading	42	11	13	18	53	75	35
Blackpool	42	13	8	21	83	101	34
Clapton O	42	11	12	19	55	85	34
Fulham	42	13	7	22	68	89	33
South Shields	42	7	9	26	56	111	23

1928-29

Division One

Manager: Peter Hodge

Did you know that?

Match 8: Hick's last game.
Match 16: Broadhurst's last game.
Match 19: Gray and Horne's last game.
Match 28: Bennett's last game.
Match 29: Bacon's last game.
Match 37: Roberts's last game.

Johnson's first goal against Burnley on 30 March broke the record for the most goals scored in a season by a Blue. It was his 32nd goal, and he went on to net 38 – this remains City's record. Only one other player has netted more than 32 League goals for City – Francis Lee in 1971–72.

Match No.	Date	Venue	Opponents	Result		Scorers	Attendance
1	Aug 25	A	Birmingham	L	1-4	Tait	26,911
2	Sep 1	H	Manchester United	D	2-2	Johnson, Roberts	61,007
3	5	A	Portsmouth	L	0-1		19,873
4	8	H	Huddersfield Town	W	3-2	Johnson 2, Marshall	34,421
5	15	A	Everton	W	6-2	Johnson 5, Brook	47,871
6	22	H	Arsenal	W	4-1	Broadhurst 2, Tilson 2	36,223
7	29	A	Blackburn Rovers	D	2-2	Brook, Tilson	25,430
8	Oct 1	H	Portsmouth	W	2-1	Austin, Johnson	17,534
9	6	H	Sunderland	W	5-3	Barrass, Broadhurst, Brook, Johnson, Marshall	39,152
10	13	A	Derby County	D	1-1	Brook	25,050
11	20	A	Leeds United	L	1-4	Barrass	32,866
12	27	H	Leicester City	L	2-3	Roberts 2	33,982
13	Nov 3	A	West Ham United	L	0-3		22,572
14	10	H	Newcastle United	L	2-4	Johnson 2	19,987
15	17	A	Burnley	W	3-2	Brook, Cowan, Roberts	14,021
16	24	H	Cardiff City	D	1-1	Broadhurst	18,778
17	Dec 1	A	Sheffield United	W	3-1	Johnson 2, Roberts	21,208
18	19	A	Aston Villa	L	1-5	Roberts	8,496
19	22	H	Liverpool	L	2-3	Bacon, Johnson	19,738
20	25	A	Sheffield Wednesday	L	0-4		45,093
21	26	H	Sheffield Wednesday	D	2-2	Johnson 2	42,826
22	29	H	Birmingham	L	2-3	Johnson, Marshall	28,365
23	Jan 5	A	Manchester United	W	2-1	Austin, Johnson	42,555
24	19	A	Huddersfield Town	D	2-2	Brook, Tait	17,602
25	26	H	Everton	W	5-1	Tilson 2, Austin, Brook, Cresswell (og)	36,241
26	30	H	Bury	W	6-4	Johnson 2, Austin, Brook, Tait, Tilson	15,198
27	Feb 2	A	Arsenal	D	0-0		13,764
28	9	H	Blackburn Rovers	L	1-2	Johnson	33,801
29	16	A	Sunderland	L	1-3	Johnson	11,752
30	23	H	Derby County	L	2-3	Johnson 2	27,941
31	Mar 2	H	Leeds United	W	3-0	Brook, Johnson, Tilson	33,921
32	9	A	Leicester City	L	2-3	Johnson, Tilson	21,396
33	16	H	West Ham United	W	4-2	Brook 2, Austin, Johnson	32,157
34	23	A	Newcastle United	L	0-4		27,613
35	29	H	Bolton Wanderers	W	5-1	Johnson 3, Marshall, Tilson	45,838
36	30	H	Burnley	W	4-1	Johnson 2, Brook, Marshall	33,166
37	Apr 1	A	Bolton Wanderers	D	1-1	Marshall	21,955
38	6	A	Cardiff City	W	3-1	Johnson 2, Tilson	11,392
39	13	H	Sheffield United	W	3-1	Brook, Marshall, Tilson	25,581
40	20	A	Bury	W	2-1	Johnson, Tilson	15,428
41	27	H	Aston Villa	W	3-0	Brook, Johnson, Toseland	30,154
42	May 4	A	Liverpool	D	1-1	Johnson	8,852
							Appearances
						One own goal	Goals

FA Cup

R3	Jan 12	A	Birmingham	L	1-3	Austin	25,005
							Appearances
							Goals

Gray A	Ridley JG	McCloy P	Barrass MW	Cowan S	McMullan J	Austin SW	Marshall RS	Tait T	Johnson TCF	Brook EF	Roberts F	Tilson SF	Broadhurst C	Hicks GW	Barber LF	Bennett ET	Gibbons S	Horne A	Bacon A	Heinemann GH	Felton W	Toseland E
1	2	3	4	5	6	7	8	9	10	11												
1	2	3	4	5	6	7	8		10	11	9											
1	2	3	4	5	6	7	8	9	10	11												
1	2	3	4	5	6	7	8	9	10	11												
1	2	3	4	5	6	7	8		9	11		10										
1	2	3	4	5	6	7	8			11		10	9									
1	2	3	4	5	6	7	8		9	11		10										
1	2	3	4	5	6	7	8		9	11				10								
1	2	3	4	5	6	7	8		9	11			10									
1	2	3	4	5	6	7	8		10	11			9									
1	2	3	4	5	6	7	8		10	11			9									
		3	6	5		7	8			11	9				1	2	4	10				
1	2	3	5		6	7	4			11	9	10						8				
1	2	3	5		6	7	4		9	11	8							10				
	2	3	4	5	6	7	8		10	11	9				1							
1	2	3	4	5	6	7			10	11	9		8									
1	2	3	4	5	6	7			9	11	8	10										
1	2	3	4	5	6	7			10	11	9								8			
1	2	3	4	5	6				10	11	9							7	8			
	2	3	4	5	6	7	8		10	11	9				1							
	2	3	4	5	6	7	8		9	11					1				10			
	2	3	4	5	6	7	8		9	11					1				10			
	2	3	4	5	6	7	8		10	11	9				1							
	2	3	4	5	6	7		9	10	11	8				1							
	2	3	4	5	6	7		9	10	11		8			1							
		3	2	5	6	7		9	10	11		8			1		4					
	2	3		5	6	7		9	10	11		8			1		4					
	2		4	5	6	7		9	10	11		8			1	3						
	2	3	4		6	7	5		9	11		10			1				8			
	2	3	4	5		7	8		9	11		10			1					6		
	2	3	4	5	6	7	8		9	11		10			1							
	2	3	4		6	7	5		9	11	8	10			1							
	2		4	5	6	7	8		9	11		10			1						3	
	2		4	5	6	7	8		9	11		10			1						3	
	2		4	5	6	7	8		9	11		10			1						3	
	2		4	5	6	7	8		9	11		10			1						3	
	2		4	5		7	8		10	11	9				1					6	3	
	2		4	5	6	7	8		9	11		10			1						3	
	2		4	5		7	8		9	11		10			1					6	3	
	2		4	5	6		8		9	11		10			1						3	7
	2		4	5	6		8		9	11		10			1						3	7
	2			5	6		8		9	11		10			1					4	3	7
17	40	31	40	38	38	38	33	8	39	42	14	22	5	1	25	2	3	4	5	4	10	3
			2	1		5	7	3	38	14	6	12	4						1			1

Gray A	Ridley JG	McCloy P	Barrass MW	Cowan S	McMullan J	Austin SW	Marshall RS	Tait T	Johnson TCF	Brook EF	Roberts F	Tilson SF	Broadhurst C	Hicks GW	Barber LF	Bennett ET	Gibbons S	Horne A	Bacon A	Heinemann GH	Felton W	Toseland E
	2	3	4	5	6	7	8		10	11	9				1							
	1	1	1	1	1	1	1		1	1	1				1							
						1																

League Table

	P	W	D	L	F	A	Pts
Sheffield W	42	21	10	11	86	62	52
Leicester C	42	21	9	12	96	67	51
Aston Villa	42	23	4	15	98	81	50
Sunderland	42	20	7	15	93	75	47
Liverpool	42	17	12	13	90	64	46
Derby Co	42	18	10	14	86	71	46
Blackburn R	42	17	11	14	72	63	45
Manchester C	42	18	9	15	95	86	45
Arsenal	42	16	13	13	77	72	45
Newcastle U	42	19	6	17	70	72	44
Sheffield U	42	15	11	16	86	85	41
Manchester U	42	14	13	15	66	76	41
Leeds U	42	16	9	17	71	84	41
Bolton W	42	14	12	16	73	80	40
Birmingham C	42	15	10	17	68	77	40
Huddersfield T	42	14	11	17	70	61	39
West Ham U	42	15	9	18	86	96	39
Everton	42	17	4	21	63	75	38
Burnley	42	15	8	19	81	103	38
Portsmouth	42	15	6	21	56	80	36
Bury	42	12	7	23	62	99	31
Cardiff C	42	8	13	21	43	59	29

1929-30

Division One

Manager: Peter Hodge

Did you know that?

Match 12: Harrison's last game.
Match 28: McCloy's last game.
Match 30: Gibbons's last game.
Match 31: Johnson's last game.
Match 37: Hedley's last game.

Tommy Johnson's departure brought much criticism of the City management and caused many fans to boycott the club over the following seasons. He was a cult hero and a major loss. It took five years and two FA Cup Finals before City reached the level of support they had during Johnson's final seasons.

Match No.	Date	Venue	Opponents	Result		Scorers	Attendance
1	Aug 31	H	Burnley	D	2-2	Johnson, Marshall	21,196
2	Sep 4	H	Arsenal	W	3-1	Tilson 2, Marshall	38,458
3	7	A	Sunderland	L	2-5	Johnson, Tilson	33,869
4	11	A	Arsenal	L	2-3	Brook, McMullan	23,057
5	14	H	Bolton Wanderers	W	2-0	Brook 2	36,972
6	21	A	Everton	W	3-2	Marshall 2, Tilson	32,711
7	28	H	Derby County	W	3-0	Tilson 3	42,047
8	Oct 5	A	Manchester United	W	3-1	Brook, Johnson, Marshall	57,201
9	12	A	Portsmouth	D	2-2	Johnson, Tait	18,618
10	19	H	West Ham United	W	4-3	Tait 3, Marshall	34,568
11	26	A	Liverpool	W	6-1	Brook 2, Johnson 2, Tait 2	37,009
12	Nov 2	H	Middlesbrough	W	3-1	Harrison, Tait, Toseland	33,302
13	9	A	Grimsby Town	D	2-2	Brook, Tait	14,311
14	16	H	Newcastle United	W	3-0	Brook, Marshall, Tait	34,500
15	23	A	Sheffield United	W	2-1	Brook, Marshall	17,344
16	30	H	Huddersfield Town	D	1-1	Tait	28,746
17	Dec 7	A	Birmingham	L	0-3		15,948
18	14	H	Leicester City	W	3-2	Johnson 2, Brook	18,246
19	21	A	Blackburn Rovers	W	3-1	Marshall 3	20,483
20	25	A	Aston Villa	W	2-0	Tait 2	39,778
21	26	H	Aston Villa	L	1-2	Tait	68,704
22	28	A	Burnley	L	2-4	Cowan, Johnson	20,239
23	Jan 1	H	Sheffield Wednesday	D	3-3	Brook, Marshall, McMullan	55,930
24	4	H	Sunderland	D	2-2	Marshall 2	37,258
25	18	A	Bolton Wanderers	W	2-1	Brook, Johnson	42,543
26	Feb 1	A	Derby County	L	2-4	Brook, Tait	18,463
27	5	H	Everton	L	1-2	Marshall	24,063
28	8	H	Manchester United	L	0-1		64,472
29	22	A	West Ham United	L	0-3		21,860
30	26	H	Portsmouth	W	5-2	Tait 3, Brook, Toseland	10,907
31	Mar 1	H	Liverpool	W	4-3	Tait 2, Brook, Johnson	29,973
32	8	A	Middlesbrough	L	0-1		15,739
33	15	H	Grimsby Town	W	3-1	Tait 2, Barrass	26,462
34	22	A	Newcastle United	D	2-2	Busby, Tait	29,586
35	29	H	Sheffield United	W	2-1	Brook, Hedley	25,131
36	Apr 5	A	Huddersfield Town	D	1-1	Busby	14,180
37	12	H	Birmingham	L	1-4	Hedley	25,737
38	19	A	Leicester City	L	1-3	Tait	13,868
39	21	H	Leeds United	W	4-1	Tait 3, Ridding	23,578
40	22	A	Leeds United	L	2-3	Busby, Ridding	16,636
41	26	H	Blackburn Rovers	D	1-1	Tait	19,868
42	May 3	A	Sheffield Wednesday	L	1-5	Tait	23,293
							Appearances
							Goals

FA Cup

Round	Date	Venue	Opponents	Result		Scorers	Attendance
R3	Jan 11	A	Tottenham Hotspur	D	2-2	Cowan, Toseland	37,000
rep	15	H	Tottenham Hotspur	W	4-1	Busby 2, Marshall, Toseland	37,716
R4	25	A	Swindon Town	D	1-1	Cowan	23,697
rep	29	H	Swindon Town	W	10-1	Marshall 5, Tait 3, Brook, Johnson	46,082
R5	Feb 15	H	Hull City	L	1-2	Toseland	61,574
							Appearances
							Goals

Barber LF	Ridley JG	Felton W	Barrass MW	Cowan S	McMullan J	Toseland E	Marshall RS	Johnson TCF	Tilson SF	Brook EF	McCloy P	Robertson G	Heinemann GH	Tait T	Harrison JR	Busby MW	Gibbons S	Bray J	Wrightson FL	Hedley F	Cann ST	Ridding W
1	2	3	4	5	6	7	8	9	10	11												
1	2	3	4	5	6	7	8	9	10	11												
1	2		4	5	6	7	8	9	10	11	3											
1	2		4	5	6	7	8	9	10	11	3											
1	2		4	5	6	7	8	9	10	11	3											
1	2		4	5	6	7	8	9	10	11	3											
1		3	4	5	6	7	8	9	10	11		2										
1	2	3	4	5		7	8	9	10	11			6									
1	2	3	4	5		7	8	10		11			6	9								
1	2	3	4	5	6	7	8	10						9	11							
1	2	3	4	5	6	7	8	10		11				9								
1	2	3	4	5		7	8						6	9	11	10						
1	2	3	5			7	8	10		11			6	9			4					
1	2	3	5			7	8	10		11			6	9			4					
1	2	3	4	5		7	8	10		11			6	9								
1	2	3	4	5		7	8	10		11			6	9								
1	2	3	4	5		7	8	10		11			6	9								
1	2	3	4	5		7	8	10		11			6	9								
1	2	3	4	5		7	8	10		11			6	9								
1	2		4	5		7	8	10		11	3		6	9								
1	2		4	5		7	8	10		11	3		6	9								
1	2		4	5	6	7	8	10		11	3			9								
1	2	3	4	5	6	7	8	10		11				9								
1	2	3	4	5	6	7	8	10		11				9								
1		2	4	5		7	8	9		11	3		6			10						
1		2	4	5		7	8	10		11	3		6	9								
1		2	4	5		7	8	9	10	11	3		6									
1		2	4	5		7	8	10		11	3			9				6				
1	2	3	4	5	6	7	8	9	10	11												
1	2	3		5	6	7	8	10		11				9			4					
1	2		4	5	6	7	8	10		11		3		9								
1	2		4	5	6	7			10	11		3		9		8						
1	2	3	4	5	6	7				11				9		10			8			
1	2	3	4	5	6	7				11				9		10			8			
1	2	3	4	5	6	7				10				9					8	11		
1	2	3	4	5	6	7				11				9		10			8			
1	2	3	8	5	6	7				10				9						11	4	
1	2		4	5	6	7				11		3		9		10						8
1	2		4	5	6	7				11		3		9		10						8
1	2		4	5	6	7				11		3		9		10						8
1	2		4	5		7				11		3		9		10		6				8
1	2		4	5	6	7				11		3		9		10						8
42	37	28	41	40	25	42	31	30	11	40	11	8	15	31	2	11	3	2	4	2	1	5
			1	1	2	2	15	11	7	16				28	1	3				2		2

Barber LF	Ridley JG	Felton W	Barrass MW	Cowan S	McMullan J	Toseland E	Marshall RS	Johnson TCF	Tilson SF	Brook EF	McCloy P	Robertson G	Heinemann GH	Tait T	Harrison JR	Busby MW
1	2	3	4	5	6	7	8			11			10	9		
1		3	4	5	6	7	8	9		11		2				10
1		2	4	5		7	8	10		11	3		6	9		
1		2	4	5		7	8	10		11	3		6	9		
1	2	3	4	5	6	7	8	9	10	11						
5	2	5	5	5	3	5	5	4	1	5	2	1	3	3		1
				2		3	6	1		1				3		2

League Table

	P	W	D	L	F	A	Pts
Sheffield W	42	26	8	8	105	57	60
Derby Co	42	21	8	13	90	82	50
Manchester C	42	19	9	14	91	81	47
Aston Villa	42	21	5	16	92	83	47
Leeds U	42	20	6	16	79	63	46
Blackburn R	42	19	7	16	99	93	45
West Ham U	42	19	5	18	86	79	43
Leicester C	42	17	9	16	86	90	43
Sunderland	42	18	7	17	76	80	43
Huddersfield T	42	17	9	16	63	69	43
Birmingham C	42	16	9	17	67	62	41
Liverpool	42	16	9	17	63	79	41
Portsmouth	42	15	10	17	66	62	40
Arsenal	42	14	11	17	78	66	39
Bolton W	42	15	9	18	74	74	39
Middlesbrough	42	16	6	20	82	84	38
Manchester U	42	15	8	19	67	88	38
Grimsby T	42	15	7	20	73	89	37
Newcastle U	42	15	7	20	71	92	37
Sheffield U	42	15	6	21	91	96	36
Burnley	42	14	8	20	79	97	36
Everton	42	12	11	19	80	92	35

1930-31

Division One

Manager: Peter Hodge

Did you know that?

Match 15: Barber, Austin and Tait's last game.
Match 26: Heinemann's last game.
Match 34: Roberts'ss last game.

Top scorer Brook ended the season on 16 League goals. This was the worst seasonal highest since 1914, and even then there were four less games during the season. Fans felt Johnson's departure more than ever.

Match No.	Date	Venue	Opponents	Result		Scorers	Attendance
1	Aug 30	A	Sunderland	D	3-3	Brook, Tait, Barrass	32,892
2	Sep 3	H	Blackpool	L	2-4	Brook, Toseland	34,908
3	6	H	Leicester City	L	0-2		28,822
4	8	A	Leeds United	L	2-4	Brook 2	12,295
5	13	A	Birmingham	L	2-3	Brook, Tait	11,148
6	17	H	Leeds United	W	1-0	Brook	17,051
7	20	H	Sheffield United	L	0-4		23,260
8	27	A	Derby County	D	1-1	Tait	14,264
9	Oct 4	H	Manchester United	W	4-1	Tait 2, Marshall 2	41,757
10	11	H	Portsmouth	L	1-3	Marshall	28,602
11	18	A	Sheffield Wednesday	D	1-1	Tait	20,750
12	25	H	Grimsby Town	W	1-0	Marshall	24,770
13	Nov 1	A	Liverpool	W	2-0	Austin, Tilson	17,893
14	8	H	Middlesbrough	W	4-2	Tait 2, Marshall, Race	27,035
15	15	A	Chelsea	L	0-2		25,671
16	22	H	Bolton Wanderers	W	3-0	Halliday 2, Marshall	23,481
17	29	A	Huddersfield Town	D	1-1	Brook	14,118
18	Dec 6	H	Newcastle United	W	2-0	Tilson, Halliday	21,076
19	13	A	West Ham United	L	0-2		19,875
20	20	H	Aston Villa	W	3-1	Toseland, Halliday, Brook	29,342
21	25	H	Arsenal	L	1-4	Tilson	56,750
22	26	A	Arsenal	L	1-3	Marshall	17,624
23	27	H	Sunderland	W	2-0	Marshall, Ridding	28,696
24	Jan 1	A	Blackburn Rovers	W	1-0	Toseland	27,965
25	3	A	Leicester City	L	2-3	Halliday 2	12,998
26	17	H	Birmingham	W	4-2	Tilson, Wrightson, Brook 2	19,918
27	28	A	Sheffield United	D	2-2	Halliday, Toseland	9,418
28	31	H	Derby County	W	4-3	Halliday 2, Toseland, Roberts	14,739
29	Feb 7	A	Manchester United	W	3-1	Brook, Toseland, Halliday	39,876
30	18	A	Portsmouth	D	1-1	Halliday	6,766
31	21	H	Sheffield Wednesday	W	2-0	Halliday 2	29,822
32	28	A	Grimsby Town	W	5-3	Toseland, Marshall, Halliday, Roberts, Brook	12,611
33	Mar 7	H	Liverpool	D	1-1	Barrass	20,706
34	14	A	Middlesbrough	L	1-4	Cowan	12,661
35	21	H	Chelsea	W	2-0	Marshall, Wrightson	27,866
36	28	A	Bolton Wanderers	D	1-1	Brook	17,398
37	Apr 3	H	Blackburn Rovers	W	3-0	Brook 2, Toseland	24,392
38	4	H	Huddersfield Town	L	0-1		27,094
39	11	A	Newcastle United	W	1-0	Brook	16,097
40	18	H	West Ham United	D	1-1	Cowan	13,737
41	25	A	Aston Villa	L	2-4	Wrightson, Toseland	13,272
42	May 2	A	Blackpool	D	2-2	Toseland, Ridding	18,688
							Appearances
							Goals

FA Cup

R3	Jan 10	A	Burnley	L	0-3		25,893
							Appearances

Barber LF	Ridley JG	Felton W	Barrass MW	Cowan S	McMullan J	Toseland E	Marshall RS	Tait T	Tilson SF	Brook EF	Wrightson FL	Robertson G	Race H	Barnett LH	Heinemann GH	Bray J	Austin SW	Langford L	Halliday D	Busby MW	Ridding W	Roberts CL
1	2	3	4	5	6	7	8	9	10	11												
1	2	3	4	5	6	7	8	9	10	11												
1	2	3	4	5	6	7		9	10	11	8											
1	2		4	5	6	7	8	9	10	11		3										
1	2		4	5	6	7	8	9		11		3	10									
1	2		4		10	7		9		11			8	3	5	6						
1	2		5		6	7		9	10	11			8	3		4						
1	2	3	4	5	10	7	8	9		11						6						
1	2	3	4	5	10	7	8	9		11						6						
1	2	3	4	5	10	7	8	9		11						6						
1	2	3	4	5	10	7	8	9		11						6						
1	2	3	4	5	10		8	9		11						6	7					
1	2	3	4	5			8	9	10	11						6	7					
1	2	3	4	5			8	9		11			10			6	7					
1	2	3	4	5			8	9		11			10			6	7					
	2	3	4	5		7	8		10	11						6		1	9			
	2			5		7	8		10	11				3		6		1	9	4		
	2			5		7	8		10	11				3		6		1	9	4		
	2			5		7	8		10	11				3		6		1	9	4		
	2			5		7	8		10	11				3		6		1	9	4		
	2			5		7	8		10	11				3		6		1	9	4		
	2			5		7	8		10	11				3		6		1	9	4		
	2			5		7	8		10	11				3		6		1		4	9	
	2			5		7	8		10	11				3		6		1		4	9	
	2		4	5		7	8		10	11				3		6		1	9			
	2			5		7			10	11	8			3	6			1	9	4		
	2			5	6	7				11	8			3				1	9	4		10
	2			5	6	7	8			11				3				1	9	4		10
	2			5	6	7	8			11				3				1	9	4		10
	2			5	6	7	8			11		4		3				1	9			10
	2		4	5	6	7	8			11				3				1	9			10
	2		4	5	6	7	8			11				3				1	9			10
	2		4	5	6	7	8			11				3				1	9			10
	2		4	5	6	7	8			11				3				1	9			10
	2			5	6	7	8			11	10			3				1	9	4		
	2			5	6	7	8			11	10			3				1	9	4		
	2			5	6	7	8			11	10			3				1	9	4		
	2			5	6	7	8			11	10			3				1	9	4		
	2			5	6	7	8			11	10			3				1	9	4		
	2			5	6	7	8			11	10			3				1	9	4		
	2			5	6	7	8			11	10			3				1	9	4		
	2			5		7	8			11	10			3		6		1		4	9	
15	42	12	21	40	27	38	37	15	17	42	11	3	5	28	2	21	4	27	24	20	3	8
			2	2		10	10	8	4	16	3		1				1		14		2	2

Barber LF	Ridley JG	Felton W	Barrass MW	Cowan S	McMullan J	Toseland E	Marshall RS	Tait T	Tilson SF	Brook EF	Wrightson FL	Robertson G	Race H	Barnett LH	Heinemann GH	Bray J	Austin SW	Langford L	Halliday D	Busby MW	Ridding W	Roberts CL
	2			5		7	8		10	11				3		6		1	9	4		
	1			1		1	1		1	1				1		1		1	1	1		

League Table

	P	W	D	L	F	A	Pts
Arsenal	42	28	10	4	127	59	66
Aston Villa	42	25	9	8	128	78	59
Sheffield W	42	22	8	12	102	75	52
Portsmouth	42	18	13	11	84	67	49
Huddersfield T	42	18	12	12	81	65	48
Derby Co	42	18	10	14	94	79	46
Middlesbrough	42	19	8	15	98	90	46
Manchester C	42	18	10	14	75	70	46
Liverpool	42	15	12	15	86	85	42
Blackburn R	42	17	8	17	83	84	42
Sunderland	42	16	9	17	89	85	41
Chelsea	42	15	10	17	64	67	40
Grimsby T	42	17	5	20	82	87	39
Bolton W	42	15	9	18	68	81	39
Sheffield U	42	14	10	18	78	84	38
Leicester C	42	16	6	20	80	95	38
Newcastle U	42	15	6	21	78	87	36
West Ham U	42	14	8	20	79	94	36
Birmingham C	42	13	10	19	55	70	36
Blackpool	42	11	10	21	71	125	32
Leeds U	42	12	7	23	68	81	31
Manchester U	42	7	8	27	53	115	22

1931-32

Division One

Manager: Peter Hodge (until 12 March 1932), Wilf Wild (from 14 March 1932)

Did you know that?

Match 10: Ridding's last game.
Match 21: Wrightson's last game.
Match 32: Felton's last game.
Match 35: Walmsley's last game.

Losing a goal in the last minute of the semi-final brought a premature end to the season, and caused City's League form to suffer. Only four points were gained from the 10 League games that followed the semi. Had City's results followed a similar pattern to the previous 10 League games they would have finished in the top six.

Match No.	Date	Venue	Opponents	Result		Scorers	Attendance
1	Aug 29	H	Sunderland	D	1-1	Marshall	31,294
2	Sep 2	A	Derby County	L	1-2	Halliday	10,865
3	5	A	Leicester City	L	0-4		10,621
4	9	H	Derby County	W	3-0	Halliday 3	15,153
5	12	A	Everton	W	1-0	Halliday	32,510
6	14	A	West Bromwich Albion	D	1-1	Cowan	18,956
7	19	H	Arsenal	L	1-3	Bray	46,756
8	23	H	West Bromwich Albion	L	2-5	Cowan, Halliday	16,194
9	26	A	Blackpool	D	2-2	Wrightson, Watson (og)	25,031
10	Oct 3	H	Sheffield United	D	1-1	Marshall	27,488
11	10	A	Blackburn Rovers	D	2-2	Halliday, Tilson	12,313
12	17	H	West Ham United	L	0-1		18,310
13	24	A	Newcastle United	L	1-2	Marshall	21,772
14	31	H	Huddersfield Town	W	3-0	Halliday 2, Marshall	21,332
15	Nov 7	A	Middlesbrough	D	3-3	Halliday, Tilson, Toseland	9,142
16	14	H	Grimsby Town	W	4-1	Halliday 2, Brook, Marshall	20,352
17	21	A	Liverpool	L	3-4	Halliday, Marshall, Tilson	24,704
18	28	H	Aston Villa	D	3-3	Halliday 2, Tilson	27,334
19	Dec 5	A	Chelsea	L	2-3	Tilson, Toseland	27,509
20	12	H	Bolton Wanderers	W	2-1	Halliday, Tilson	20,283
21	19	A	Sheffield Wednesday	D	1-1	Brook	7,431
22	26	A	Portsmouth	L	2-3	Halliday, Tilson	31,759
23	Jan 1	H	Portsmouth	D	3-3	Marshall, McMullan, one og	34,623
24	2	A	Sunderland	W	5-2	Halliday 3, Rowley 2	19,689
25	16	H	Leicester City	W	5-1	Marshall 2, Brook, Halliday, Tilson	21,006
26	27	H	Everton	W	1-0	Halliday	26,363
27	30	A	Arsenal	L	0-4		39,834
28	Feb 6	H	Blackpool	W	7-1	Halliday 2, Brook 2, Cowan, Tilson, Toseland	24,739
29	15	A	Sheffield United	L	1-2	Rowley	13,073
30	20	H	Blackburn Rovers	W	3-1	Marshall 2, Brook	24,438
31	Mar 2	A	West Ham United	D	1-1	Busby	13,524
32	5	H	Newcastle United	W	5-1	Tilson 2, Brook, Marshall, Toseland	28,322
33	19	H	Middlesbrough	L	1-2	Tilson	24,114
34	26	A	Grimsby Town	L	1-2	Brook	11,481
35	28	H	Birmingham	W	2-1	Brook, Marshall	19,804
36	29	A	Birmingham	W	5-1	Halliday 3, Payne, Tilson	12,603
37	Apr 2	H	Liverpool	L	0-1		23,281
38	6	A	Huddersfield Town	L	0-1		2,963
39	9	A	Aston Villa	L	1-2	Brook	18,170
40	16	H	Chelsea	D	1-1	Rowley	20,124
41	23	A	Bolton Wanderers	D	1-1	Halliday	8,680
42	30	H	Sheffield Wednesday	L	1-2	Toseland	16,322
							Appearances
						Two own goals	Goals

FA Cup

Round	Date	Venue	Opponents	Result		Scorers	Attendance
R3	Jan 9	A	Millwall	W	3-2	Halliday 2, Toseland	32,091
R4	23	H	Brentford	W	6-1	Tilson 3, Brook 2, Halliday	56,190
R5	Feb 13	H	Derby County	W	3-0	Marshall 2, Brook	62,641
R6	27	A	Bury	W	4-3	Toseland 2, Cowan, Halliday	28,035
SF	Mar 12	N	Arsenal	L	0-1		50,337
							Appearances
							Goals

SF at Villa Park, Birmingham

Langford L	Ridley JG	Barnett LH	Busby MW	Cowan S	McMullan J	Toseland E	Marshall RS	Halliday D	Tilson SF	Brook EF	Bray J	Wrightson FL	Gregory CF	Felton W	Ridding W	Race H	Barrass MW	Dale W	Rowley HB	Walmsley C	Cann ST	Payne JF	Syme RG
1	2	3	4	5	6	7	8	9	10	11													
1	2	3	4	5	6	7	8	9	10	11													
1	2	3	4	5	6	7	8	9	10	11													
1	2	3	4	5		7		9	10	11	6	8											
1	2	3	4	5		7		9	10	11	6	8											
1	2	3	4	5		7		9	10	11	6	8											
1	2	3	4			7		9	10	11	6	8	5										
1	2	3	4	5		7		9	10	11	6	8											
1	2	3	4	5		7		9	10	11	6	8											
1	2		4	5		7	8			11	6			3	9	10							
1		3	4	5		7	8	9	10	11				2			6						
1		3	4	5		7	8	9	10	11	6			2									
1	2		4	5		7	8	9	10	11	6			3									
1	2		4	5		7	8	9	10	11	6			3									
1	2		4	5		7	8	9	10	11	6			3									
1	2		4	5		7	8	9	10	11	6			3									
1	2		4	5		7	8	9	10	11	6			3									
1	2		4	5		7	8	9	10	11	6			3									
1	2		4	5		7	8	9	10	11	6			3									
1	2		4	5		7	8	9	10	11	6			3									
1	2		4	5		7		9	10	11	6	8		3									
1			4	5	6	7	8	9	10	11				2				3					
1			4	5	6	7	8	9	10	11				2				3					
1			4	5		7	8	9		11	6			2				3	10				
1			4	5	6	7	8	9	10	11				2				3					
1			4		6	7	5	9	8	11				2				3	10				
1			4	5	6	7	8	9	10	11				2				3					
1			4	5	6	7		9	8	11				2				3	10				
1						7	5	9	8	11	6			2			4	3	10				
1			4	5	6	7	8	9	10	11				2				3					
1			4	5	6	7	8	9	10	11				2				3					
1			4	5	6	7	8	9	10	11				2				3					
1	2		4	5	6	7	8	9	10	11								3					
			4	5	6	7	8	9		11								3	10	1	2		
			4		6	7	5	9	8	11								3	10	1	2		
1			4				5	9	8	11	6							3	10		2	7	
1			4		6		8	9		11			5					3	10		2	7	
1	2		4		6	7	8	9		11			5					3	10				
1			4		6	7	5	9	8	11								3	10		2		
1			4		6	7	5		8	11								3	10		2		9
1			4		6	7	5	9	8	11								3	10		2		
1			4		6	7	5	9	8	11								3	10		2		
40	21	11	41	31	21	40	34	40	37	42	20	7	3	23	1	1	2	21	13	2	8	2	1
			1	3	1	5	13	28	13	10	1	1							4			1	
1			4	5	6	7	8	9	10	11				2				3					
1			4	5	6	7	8	9	10	11				2				3					
1			4	5	6	7	8	9	10	11				2				3					
1			4	5	6	7	8	9	10	11				2				3					
1			4	5	6	7	8	9	10	11				2				3					
5			5	5	5	5	5	5	5	5				5				5					
				1		3	2	4	3	3													

League Table

	P	W	D	L	F	A	Pts
Everton	42	26	4	12	116	64	56
Arsenal	42	22	10	10	90	48	54
Sheffield W	42	22	6	14	96	82	50
Huddersfield T	42	19	10	13	80	63	48
Aston Villa	42	19	8	15	104	72	46
W.B.A.	42	20	6	16	77	55	46
Sheffield U	42	20	6	16	80	75	46
Portsmouth	42	19	7	16	62	62	45
Birmingham C	42	18	8	16	78	67	44
Liverpool	42	19	6	17	81	93	44
Newcastle U	42	18	6	18	80	87	42
Chelsea	42	16	8	18	69	73	40
Sunderland	42	15	10	17	67	73	40
Manchester C	42	13	12	17	83	73	38
Derby Co	42	14	10	18	71	75	38
Blackburn R	42	16	6	20	89	95	38
Bolton W	42	17	4	21	72	80	38
Middlesbrough	42	15	8	19	64	89	38
Leicester C	42	15	7	20	74	94	37
Blackpool	42	12	9	21	65	102	33
Grimsby T	42	13	6	23	67	98	32
West Ham U	42	12	7	23	62	107	31

1932-33

Division One

Manager: Wilf Wild

Did you know that?

Match 3: Higgs's first and only game.
Match 8: Robertson's last game.
Match 12: Barrass's last League game.
Match 15: Race's last League game.
Match 24: Naylor's first and only game.
Match 24: Rowley's last game.
Match 28: Ridley's last game.
Match 42: McMullan's last game.

The early 1930s were mixed years for City's 'keepers. Langford was the first choice following injury to Barber, but a variety of 'keepers were tried both in the first team and reserves. Walmsley, Nicholls and Higgs were all tried, before Swift made his debut in 1933–34. Frank Higgs was unfortunate in that his only game ended in a 3–2 defeat at home. He went on to play for several clubs, with his longest spell coming at Carlisle in 1935–36.

Match No.	Date	Venue	Opponents	Result		Scorers	Attendance
1	Aug 27	A	Sunderland	L	2-3	Brook 2	27,056
2	31	H	Birmingham	W	1-0	Marshall	20,655
3	Sep 3	H	Middlesbrough	L	2-3	Marshall 2	20,211
4	7	A	Birmingham	L	0-3		13,463
5	10	H	Arsenal	L	2-3	Busby, Tilson	36,542
6	17	A	Everton	L	1-2	Toseland	32,852
7	24	H	Blackpool	W	5-1	Halliday 2, Toseland 2, Brook	25,175
8	Oct 1	A	Derby County	L	0-4		13,233
9	8	H	Blackburn Rovers	L	2-3	Halliday, Tilson	8,428
10	15	A	Leeds United	L	1-2	Tilson	16,898
11	22	A	Bolton Wanderers	L	1-2	Tilson	14,468
12	29	H	Liverpool	D	1-1	Marshall	11,957
13	Nov 5	A	Sheffield United	W	5-2	Race 2, Brook, Marshall, Toseland	12,658
14	12	H	Wolverhampton W.	W	4-1	Marshall 2, Brook, Comrie	20,525
15	19	A	Newcastle United	L	0-2		20,551
16	26	H	Aston Villa	W	5-2	Tilson 4, Brook	35,025
17	Dec 3	A	Leicester City	W	2-1	Brook, Tilson	13,517
18	10	H	Portsmouth	W	3-1	Tilson 2, Cowan	22,312
19	17	A	Chelsea	L	1-3	Tilson	26,240
20	24	H	Huddersfield Town	W	3-0	Brook, Tilson, Toseland	21,252
21	26	H	Sheffield Wednesday	D	2-2	Brook, Cowan	45,916
22	27	A	Sheffield Wednesday	L	1-2	Cowan	37,193
23	31	H	Sunderland	L	2-4	Tilson, Toseland	24,036
24	Jan 7	A	Middlesbrough	L	0-2		7,912
25	21	A	Arsenal	L	1-2	Tilson	32,456
26	Feb 1	H	Everton	W	3-0	Brook, Tilson, Toseland	10,986
27	4	A	Blackpool	L	0-1		13,399
28	11	H	Derby County	W	2-1	Herd, Toseland	33,611
29	23	A	Blackburn Rovers	L	0-1		8,931
30	Mar 8	H	Bolton Wanderers	W	2-1	Cowan, Herd	19,144
31	11	A	Liverpool	D	1-1	Herd	27,329
32	22	H	Sheffield United	W	1-0	Tilson	19,082
33	25	A	Wolverhampton W.	W	2-1	Brook, Herd	26,752
34	Apr 1	H	Newcastle United	L	1-2	Brook	34,686
35	5	H	Leeds United	D	0-0		16,789
36	8	A	Aston Villa	D	1-1	Marshall	20,998
37	14	H	West Bromwich Albion	W	1-0	Brook	42,086
38	15	H	Leicester City	W	4-1	Herd 2, Marshall, Toseland	26,092
39	17	A	West Bromwich Albion	L	0-4		18,988
40	22	A	Portsmouth	W	2-1	Brook, Herd	16,027
41	May 3	H	Chelsea	L	1-4	Brook	14,827
42	6	A	Huddersfield Town	L	0-1		5,482
							Appearances
							Goals

FA Cup

Rd	Date	Venue	Opponents	Result		Scorers	Attendance
R3	Jan 14	A	Gateshead	D	1-1	Toseland	9,123
rep	18	H	Gateshead	W	9-0	Tilson 3, Cowan 2, Barrass, Brook, Busby, McMullan	22,590
R4	28	H	Walsall	W	2-0	Brook 2	52,085
R5	Feb 18	A	Bolton Wanderers	W	4-2	Brook 3, Tilson	69,920
R6	4	A	Burnley	W	1-0	Tilson	48,717
SF	18	N	Derby County	W	3-2	McMullan, Tilson, Toseland	51,961
F	Apr 29	N	Everton	L	0-3		92,900
							Appearances
							Goals

SF at Leeds Road, Huddersfield. Final at Wembley Stadium

Langford L	Cann ST	Dale W	Busby MW	Cowan S	McMullan J	Toseland E	Marshall RS	Halliday D	Tilson SF	Brook EF	Gregory CF	Rowley HB	Higgs FJ	Syme RG	Nicholls JH	Barrass MW	Robertson G	Race H	Comrie M	Bray J	Corbett FW	Barnett LH	Naylor J	Ridley JG	Fletcher L	Herd A
1	2	3	4	5	6	7	8	9	10	11																
1	2	3	4		6	7	8	9		11	5	10														
	2	3	4		6	7	8	9		11	5	10	1													
1	2	3	4		6	7	8		10	11	5			9												
1	2	3	4	5	6	7	8		10	11				9												
	2	3	4	5	6	7	8		10	11				9	1											
	2	3		5	6	7	8	9	10	11					1	4										
	2	3		5		7	8	9	10	11					1	4	6									
	2	3		5	6	7	8	9	10	11					1			4								
	2	3	4		6	7	5	9	8	11					1				10							
	2	3	4		6	7	5	9	8	11					1				10							
	2	3	4	5		7	8			11		10			1	9				6						
	2	3	4	5		7	8			11		10			1			9		6						
	2	3	4	5		7	8			11					1			9	10	6						
	2	3	4	5		7	8		10	11					1			9		6						
		3	4	5		7	8		9	11					1				10	6	2					
		3	4	5		7	8		9	11					1				10	6	2					
1		3	4	5		7	8		9	11									10	6	2					
		3	4	5		7	8		9	11					1				10	6	2					
1			4	5		7	8		9	11									10	6	2	3				
1			4	5		7	8		9	11									10	6	2	3				
1		3	4	5		7	8		9	11									10	6	2					
1		3	4	5		7	8		9	11									10	6	2					
1		3	4	5		7			9	11		10							8		2		6			
1		3	4	5	10	7	8		9	11										6				2		
1		3	4	5	10	7			8	11										6				2	9	
1		3	4		10	7			9	11	5									6				2		8
1		3	4		10	7			9	11	5									6				2		8
1	2	3	4			7	8		9	11	5									6						10
1	2	3	4	5	10	7			9	11										6						8
1	2	3	4	5	10	7			9	11										6						8
1	2	3	4	5	10	7			9	11										6						8
1	2	3	4	5	10	7	8			11										6						9
1	2	3	4	5	10	7			9	11										6						8
1	2	3	4	5	10	7			9	11										6						8
1	2	3	4	5	10	7	8			11										6						9
1	2	3	4	5	10	7	8			11										6						9
1	2	3	4	5		7	8			11									10	6						9
1	2	3	4		10	7	8			11	5									6						9
1	2		4		10	7	5			11									8	6		3				9
1	2	3	4	5	10	7	8			11										6						9
		3	4	5	10	7	9			11					1					6		2				8
27	28	39	39	32	26	42	33	8	29	42	7	5	1	3	14	3	1	4	14	30	9	4	1	4	1	16
			1	4		9	9	3	17	15								2	1							7

Langford L	Cann ST	Dale W	Busby MW	Cowan S	McMullan J	Toseland E	Marshall RS	Halliday D	Tilson SF	Brook EF	Gregory CF	Rowley HB	Higgs FJ	Syme RG	Nicholls JH	Barrass MW	Robertson G	Race H	Comrie M	Bray J	Corbett FW	Barnett LH	Naylor J	Ridley JG	Fletcher L	Herd A
1		3	4	5	10	7			9	11								8		6				2		
1		3	4	5	10	7			9	11						8				6				2		
1		3	4	5	10	7	8		9	11										6				2		
1	2	3	4	5		7	8		9	11										6						10
1	2	3	4	5	10	7			9	11										6						8
1	2	3	4	5	10	7			9	11										6						8
1	2	3	4	5	10	7	8			11										6						9
7	4	7	7	7	6	7	3		6	7						1		1		7				3		4
			1	2	2	2			6	6						1										

League Table

	P	W	D	L	F	A	Pts
Arsenal	42	25	8	9	118	61	58
Aston Villa	42	23	8	11	92	67	54
Sheffield W	42	21	9	12	80	68	51
W.B.A.	42	20	9	13	83	70	49
Newcastle U	42	22	5	15	71	63	49
Huddersfield T	42	18	11	13	66	53	47
Derby Co	42	15	14	13	76	69	44
Leeds U	42	15	14	13	59	62	44
Portsmouth	42	18	7	17	74	76	43
Sheffield U	42	17	9	16	74	80	43
Everton	42	16	9	17	81	74	41
Sunderland	42	15	10	17	63	80	40
Birmingham C	42	14	11	17	57	57	39
Liverpool	42	14	11	17	79	84	39
Blackburn R	42	14	10	18	76	102	38
Manchester C	42	16	5	21	68	71	37
Middlesbrough	42	14	9	19	63	73	37
Chelsea	42	14	7	21	63	73	35
Leicester C	42	11	13	18	75	89	35
Wolverhampton W	42	13	9	20	80	96	35
Bolton W	42	12	9	21	78	92	33
Blackpool	42	14	5	23	69	85	33

1933-34

Division One

Manager: Wilf Wild

Did you know that?

Match 10: Halliday's last game.
Match 19: Langford's last game.
Match 20: Nicholl's last game.
Match 29: Gregory's last game.
Match 30: Corbett's last game.
Match 31: P. Percival's last game.
Match 36: Syme's last game.
Match 39: Cann and Payne's last game.
Match 40: Lloyd's last game.
Match 41: Comrie's last game.

The crowd of 84,569 remains the record provincial crowd for a first-team game by any club.

Match No.	Date	Venue	Opponents	Result		Scorers	Attendance
1	Aug 26	H	Sheffield Wednesday	L	2-3	Herd, Tilson	29,151
2	30	A	Birmingham	W	1-0	Tilson	20,084
3	Sep 2	A	Leicester City	D	0-0		24,682
4	6	H	Birmingham	W	1-0	Syme	19,388
5	9	A	Arsenal	D	1-1	Herd	43,412
6	16	H	Everton	D	2-2	Brook, Herd	48,826
7	23	A	Middlesbrough	L	1-2	Marshall	9,095
8	30	H	Blackburn Rovers	W	3-1	Brook, Cowan, Halliday	33,343
9	Oct 7	A	Newcastle United	D	2-2	Halliday, Herd	19,044
10	14	H	Leeds United	L	0-1		22,413
11	21	H	Aston Villa	W	1-0	Marshall	35,387
12	28	A	Sheffield United	D	1-1	Tilson	13,548
13	Nov 4	H	Sunderland	W	4-1	Brook 2, Marshall, Toseland	29,177
14	11	A	Stoke City	W	1-0	Toseland	23,908
15	18	H	Huddersfield Town	D	2-2	Tilson, Toseland	31,900
16	25	A	Portsmouth	L	0-2		15,179
17	Dec 2	H	Tottenham Hotspur	W	2-0	Brook, Herd	38,021
18	9	A	Chelsea	W	2-1	Gregory, Herd	18,048
19	16	H	Liverpool	W	2-1	Herd, Tilson	13,815
20	23	A	Wolverhampton W.	L	0-8		20,640
21	25	A	Derby County	L	1-4	Toseland	32,320
22	26	H	Derby County	W	2-0	Brook, Gregory	57,218
23	30	A	Sheffield Wednesday	D	1-1	Busby	27,074
24	Jan 1	H	West Bromwich Albion	L	2-7	Bray, Herd	27,781
25	6	H	Leicester City	D	1-1	Herd	21,496
26	20	H	Arsenal	W	2-1	Herd, Marshall	60,401
27	Feb 3	H	Middlesbrough	W	5-2	Brook 2, Tilson 2, Busby	22,082
28	7	A	Everton	L	0-2		17,134
29	10	A	Blackburn Rovers	L	0-3		14,076
30	24	A	Leeds United	L	1-3	Syme	15,791
31	Mar 7	A	Aston Villa	D	0-0		20,643
32	10	H	Sheffield United	W	4-1	Tilson 2, Busby, Herd	13,908
33	21	H	Newcastle United	D	1-1	Wright	11,964
34	24	H	Stoke City	W	4-2	Herd 2, Bray, Cowan	20,075
35	31	A	Huddersfield Town	L	0-1		20,817
36	Apr 2	A	West Bromwich Albion	L	0-4		22,232
37	7	H	Portsmouth	W	2-1	Busby, Herd	35,641
38	11	A	Sunderland	D	0-0		3,841
39	14	A	Tottenham Hotspur	L	1-5	Toseland	24,576
40	21	H	Chelsea	W	4-2	Tilson 3, Toseland	25,861
41	May 2	A	Liverpool	L	2-3	Heale, Herd	19,924
42	5	H	Wolverhampton W.	W	4-0	Herd 2, Cowan, Heale	33,368
							Appearances
							Goals

FA Cup

Round	Date	Venue	Opponents	Result		Scorers	Attendance
R3	Jan 13	H	Blackburn Rovers	W	3-1	Toseland 2, Brook	54,336
R4	27	A	Hull City	D	2-2	Brook, Herd	28,000
rep	31	H	Hull City	W	4-1	Tilson 2, Marshall, Toseland	49,042
R5	Feb 17	A	Sheffield Wednesday	D	2-2	Herd 2	72,841
rep	21	H	Sheffield Wednesday	W	2-0	Marshall, Tilson	68,614
R6	Mar 3	H	Stoke City	W	1-0	Brook	84,569
SF	17	N	Aston Villa	W	6-1	Tilson 4, Herd, Toseland	45,473
F	Apr 28	N	Portsmouth	W	2-1	Tilson 2	93,258
							Appearances
							Goals

SF at Leeds Road, Huddersfield. Final at Wembley Stadium

Nicholls JH	Barnett LH	Dale W	Busby MW	Cowan S	Bray J	Toseland E	Herd A	Tilson SF	McLuckie JS	Brook EF	Langford L	Syme RG	Marshall RS	Corbett VJS	Halliday D	Comrie M	Payne JF	Percival J	Dunne L	Gregory CF	Swift FV	Heale JA	Corbett FW	Percival P	Cann ST	Wright N	Lloyd N	Barkas S
1	2	3	4	5	6	7	8	9	10	11																		
	2	3	4	5		7	8	10	6	11	1	9																
	2	3	4	5		7	10		6	11	1	9	8															
	2	3	4	5		7	10		6	11	1	9	8															
	3		4	5		7	10		6	11	1	9	8	2														
	2	3	4	5		7	10		6	11	1	9	8															
	2	3	4	5		7	10		6	11	1		8		9													
	2	3	4	5		7	10		6	11	1		8		9													
	2	3	4	5		7	10		6	11	1		8		9													
	2	3	4	5		7	8		6		1				9	10	11											
	2	3		5	10	7	9		6	11	1		8					4										
	2	3	4	5		7	10	9	6	11	1		8															
	2	3	4	5		7	9	10	6	11	1		8															
	2	3	4	5		7	9	10	6	11	1		8															
	2	3	4	5		7	10	9	6	11	1		8															
	2			5		7	10	9	6	11	1		8					4	3									
	2	3	4		6	7	8	10		11	1		5							9								
	2	3	4		6	7	8	10		11	1		5							9								
	2	3	4		6	7	8	10		11	1		5							9								
1	2		4		6	7		10		11			5			8			3	9								
	2		4		6	7	8	10		11			5	3						9	1							
	2		10		6	7	8			11			5	3				4		9	1							
	2		10		6	7	8			11			5	3				4		9	1							
	2	3	10		6	7	8			11			5					4		9	1							
	2	3	4			7	8	10	6	11			5							9	1							
	2	3	4	5		7	10	9	6	11			8								1							
	2	3	4	5		7	8	9	6	11											1	10						
	2	3	4	5		7	8		6	11										9	1	10						
	2		4	5		7			6	11			8							9	1	10	3					
		3		5	4				6	11		9	8	2							1	10		7				
		3	4	5	6		8	9		11											1	10		7	2			
	3		4	5	6	7	10	9		11			8								1				2			
	2	3	4	5	6	7	8	9													1	10				11		
	2	3	4	5	6	7	9			11			8								1	10						
	2	3	4	5		7	9			11			8								1	10					6	
	3		4	5		7				11		9	8								1	10			2		6	
	2	3	4	5		7	9		6	11			8								1	10						
		3	4	5	11	7	9		6				8								1	10			2			
		3	4	5		7		9	6				8				11				1	10			2			
	2	3	4	5		7	10	9		11			8								1						6	
	2		4			7	9		6	11			5			8					1	10						3
	2		4	5		7	8	9	6	11											1	10						3
2	38	31	39	32	16	40	37	21	27	38	18	7	34	5	4	3	2	5	2	11	22	14	1	2	5	1	3	2
			4	3	2	6	17	12		8		2	4		2					2		2				1		

Nicholls JH	Barnett LH	Dale W	Busby MW	Cowan S	Bray J	Toseland E	Herd A	Tilson SF	McLuckie JS	Brook EF	Langford L	Syme RG	Marshall RS	Corbett VJS	Halliday D	Comrie M	Payne JF	Percival J	Dunne L	Gregory CF	Swift FV	Heale JA	Corbett FW	Percival P	Cann ST	Wright N	Lloyd N	Barkas S
	2	3	4	5		7	10	9	6	11			8								1							
	2	3	4	5		7	10	9	6	11			8								1							
	2	3	4	5		7	10	9	6	11			8								1							
		3	4	5		7	10	9	6	11			8	2							1							
	2	3	4	5		7	10	9	6	11			8								1							
	2	3	4	5	6	7	10	9		11			8								1							
	2	3	4	5	6	7	10	9		11			8								1							
	2	3	4	5	6	7	10	9		11			8								1							
	7	8	8	8	3	8	8	8	5	8			8	1							8							
						4	4	9		3			2															

League Table

	P	W	D	L	F	A	Pts
Arsenal	42	25	9	8	75	47	59
Huddersfield T	42	23	10	9	90	61	56
Tottenham H	42	21	7	14	79	56	49
Derby Co	42	17	11	14	68	54	45
Manchester C	42	17	11	14	65	72	45
Sunderland	42	16	12	14	81	56	44
W.B.A.	42	17	10	15	78	70	44
Blackburn R	42	18	7	17	74	81	43
Leeds U	42	17	8	17	75	66	42
Portsmouth	42	15	12	15	52	55	42
Sheffield W	42	16	9	17	62	67	41
Stoke C	42	15	11	16	58	71	41
Aston Villa	42	14	12	16	78	75	40
Everton	42	12	16	14	62	63	40
Wolverhampton W	42	14	12	16	74	86	40
Middlesbrough	42	16	7	19	68	80	39
Leicester C	42	14	11	17	59	74	39
Liverpool	42	14	10	18	79	87	38
Chelsea	42	14	8	20	67	69	36
Birmingham C	42	12	12	18	54	56	36
Newcastle U	42	10	14	18	68	77	34
Sheffield U	42	12	7	23	58	101	31

1934-35

Division One

Manager: Wilf Wild

Did you know that?

Match 16: McLuckie's last game.
Match 17: Barnett's last game.
Match 32: Dunne's last game.
Match 34: Fletcher's last game.
Match 35: Shadwell and Wright's last game.
Match 42: Cowan's last game.

The attendance of 79,491 for the Arsenal game was the record for a League fixture at the time. This figure has only been surpassed in two League games – 82,905 Chelsea v Arsenal in October 1935 and 83,260 Manchester United v Arsenal in 1948 at Maine Road.

Match No.	Date	Venue	Opponents	Result		Scorers	Attendance
1	Aug 25	A	West Bromwich Albion	D	1-1	Barkas	24,958
2	29	H	Liverpool	W	3-1	Brook, Marshall, Bradshaw (og)	25,567
3	Sep 1	H	Sheffield Wednesday	W	4-1	Herd 2, Brook, Marshall	44,704
4	5	A	Liverpool	L	1-2	Tilson	31,696
5	8	A	Birmingham	W	3-1	Brook, Herd, Tilson	24,895
6	15	H	Stoke City	W	3-1	Tilson 3	51,535
7	22	A	Leicester City	W	3-1	Herd 2, Busby	21,359
8	29	A	Middlesbrough	W	2-1	Herd, Fletcher	9,377
9	Oct 6	H	Blackburn Rovers	D	3-3	Brook 2, Heale	35,489
10	13	A	Arsenal	L	0-3		68,145
11	20	H	Derby County	L	0-1		44,393
12	27	A	Aston Villa	L	2-4	Herd, Tilson	38,136
13	Nov 3	H	Tottenham Hotspur	W	3-1	Heale, Herd, McLuckie	28,802
14	10	A	Sunderland	L	2-3	Brook 2	14,725
15	17	H	Huddersfield Town	D	0-0		36,176
16	24	A	Everton	W	2-1	Heale, Tilson	36,926
17	Dec 1	H	Grimsby Town	W	1-0	Toseland	31,642
18	8	A	Preston North End	W	4-2	Tilson 3, Brook	22,683
19	15	H	Chelsea	W	2-0	Heale, Tilson	28,797
20	22	A	Wolverhampton W.	L	0-5		27,099
21	25	A	Leeds United	W	2-1	Heale, Toseland	24,810
22	26	H	Leeds United	W	3-0	Heale 2, Brook	51,387
23	29	H	West Bromwich Albion	W	3-2	Brook 2, Herd	34,615
24	Jan 5	A	Sheffield Wednesday	L	0-1		32,057
25	19	H	Birmingham	D	0-0		31,644
26	26	A	Stoke City	L	0-2		24,460
27	Feb 2	H	Leicester City	W	6-3	Brook 2, Bray, Herd, Tilson, Toseland	24,224
28	9	H	Middlesbrough	W	6-2	Brook, Herd, Tilson, Toseland, Stuart (og), Warren (og)	29,431
29	23	H	Arsenal	D	1-1	Brook	79,491
30	Mar 2	A	Derby County	W	2-1	Dellow, Herd	27,020
31	4	A	Blackburn Rovers	L	0-1		11,328
32	9	H	Aston Villa	W	4-1	Dellow 2, Brook, Heale	33,367
33	16	A	Tottenham Hotspur	D	0-0		43,572
34	30	A	Huddersfield Town	L	0-3		18,597
35	Apr 6	H	Everton	D	2-2	Heale, Tilson	26,138
36	10	H	Sunderland	W	1-0	Heale	23,262
37	13	A	Grimsby Town	D	1-1	Herd	13,394
38	19	H	Portsmouth	L	2-4	Tilson 2	33,477
39	20	H	Preston North End	L	1-2	Herd	23,255
40	22	A	Portsmouth	L	2-4	Dellow, Tilson	20,510
41	27	A	Chelsea	L	2-4	Heale, Tilson	22,593
42	May 4	H	Wolverhampton W.	W	5-0	Heale 2, Brook, Marshall, Toseland	13,899
							Appearances
						Three own goals	Goals

FA Cup

R3	Jan 12	A	Tottenham Hotspur		0-1		48,983
							Appearances

Charity Shield

	Nov 28	A	Arsenal	L	0-4	Brook 3	10,888
							Appearances
							Goals

Swift FV	Dale W	Barkas S	Busby MW	Cowan S	Bray J	Toseland E	Marshall RS	Tilson SF	Herd A	Brook EF	Corbett FW	McLuckie JS	Fletcher L	Heale JA	Wright N	Barnett LH	Dellow RW	Dunne L	Percival J	Shadwell WJ
1	2	3	4	5	6	7	8	9	10	11										
1	2	3	4	5	6	7	8	9	10	11										
1	2	3	4	5	6	7	8	9	10	11										
1	2	3	4	5	6	7	8	9	10	11										
1	2	3	4	5	6	7	8	9	10	11										
1	2	3	4	5	6	7	8	9	10	11										
1	2	3	8	5	6	7		9	10	11	4									
1	2	3	4	5		7			8			6	9	10	11					
1		3	4	5	6	7		9	8	11				10		2				
1	2	3	4	5	6	7	8	9	10	11										
1		3	4	5	6	7	8	9	10	11						2				
1	2	3	4	5	6	7		9	8	11				10						
1	2	3	4	5	6			9	7	11		8		10						
1	2	3	4	5	6	7		9		11		8		10						
1	2	3	4	5	6	7	8			11		10		9						
1	2	3	4	5	6	7		9		11		8		10						
1	2		4	5	6	7		9	8	11				10		3				
1	2	3	4	5	6	7		9	8	11				10						
1	2	3	4	5	6	7		9	8	11				10						
1	2	3	4	5	6	7	10		8	11				9						
1	2	3	4	5	6	7	10		8	11				9						
1	2	3	4	5	6	7		9	10	11				8						
1	2	3	4	5	6	7		9	10	11				8						
1	2	3	4	5	6	7		9	10	11				8						
1	2	3	4	5	6	7		9	10	11				8						
1	2	3	4	5	6	7	8	9	10	11										
1	2	3	4	5	6	7	8	9	10	11										
1	2	3	4	5	6	7	8	9	10	11										
1	2	3	4	5	6	7	8	9	10	11										
1	2	3	4	5	6		8	9	10	11							7			
1	2	3	4	5	6		8		10	11				9			7			
1		3		5	6		8			11			9	10			7	2	4	
1	2	3		5	6				10	11			9	8			7		4	
1	2	3	4	5				10		11			9	8			7			6
1	2	3	4	5				9	10					8	11		7			6
1	2	3		5	6			9	10	11				8			7		4	
1	2	3		5	6			9	10	11				8			7		4	
1	2	3		5	6			9	10	11				8			7		4	
1	2	3		5	6	7		9	10	11				8					4	
1	2	3		5	6	7		9	10	11							8		4	
1	2	3		5	6	7		9	10	11				8					4	
1	2	3		5	6	7	8		10	11				9					4	
42	39	41	33	42	39	32	19	34	37	40	1	5	4	27	2	3	10	1	9	2
		1	1		1	5	3	18	14	17		1	1	13			4			

Swift FV	Dale W	Barkas S	Busby MW	Cowan S	Bray J	Toseland E	Marshall RS	Tilson SF	Herd A	Brook EF	Corbett FW	McLuckie JS	Fletcher L	Heale JA	Wright N	Barnett LH	Dellow RW	Dunne L	Percival J	Shadwell WJ
1	2	3	4	5	6	7		9	10	11				8						
1	1	1	1	1	1	1		1	1	1				1						
1	2	3	4	5	6	7		9		11		8		10						
1	1	1	1	1	1	1		1		1		1		1						
										3										

League Table

	P	W	D	L	F	A	Pts
Arsenal	42	23	12	7	115	46	58
Sunderland	42	19	16	7	90	51	54
Sheffield W	42	18	13	11	70	64	49
Manchester C	42	20	8	14	82	67	48
Grimsby T	42	17	11	14	78	60	45
Derby Co	42	18	9	15	81	66	45
Liverpool	42	19	7	16	85	88	45
Everton	42	16	12	14	89	88	44
W.B.A.	42	17	10	15	83	83	44
Stoke C	42	18	6	18	71	70	42
Preston N.E.	42	15	12	15	62	67	42
Chelsea	42	16	9	17	73	82	41
Aston Villa	42	14	13	15	74	88	41
Portsmouth	42	15	10	17	71	72	40
Blackburn R	42	14	11	17	66	78	39
Huddersfield T	42	14	10	18	76	71	38
Wolverhampton W	42	15	8	19	88	94	38
Leeds U	42	13	12	17	75	92	38
Birmingham C	42	13	10	19	63	81	36
Middlesbrough	42	10	14	18	70	90	34
Leicester C	42	12	9	21	61	86	33
Tottenham H	42	10	10	22	54	93	30

1935-36

Division One

Manager: Wilf Wild

Did you know that?

Match 24: Owen's last game.
Match 29: Corbett and Busby's last game.

The Blues were leading 1–0 at half-time in the match with Liverpool on 11 September, and then five second-half goals completely dumbfounded the Reds. The result was significant as Liverpool had defeated Everton 6–0 four days before the Maine Road meeting and went on to beat Grimsby 7–2 three days later. City had to wait until March before netting six again.

Match No.	Date	Venue	Opponents	Result		Scorers	Attendance
1	Aug 31	H	West Bromwich Albion	W	1-0	Herd	41,777
2	Sep 4	A	Liverpool	W	2-0	Brook, Tilson	32,449
3	7	A	Sunderland	L	0-2		38,224
4	11	H	Liverpool	W	6-0	Heale 2, Toseland 2, Busby, Herd	32,913
5	14	H	Birmingham	W	3-1	Bray, Tilson, Toseland	32,337
6	21	A	Arsenal	W	3-2	Herd, Tilson, Toseland	61,290
7	28	H	Portsmouth	D	0-0		40,672
8	Oct 5	H	Stoke City	L	1-2	Heale	38,825
9	12	A	Blackburn Rovers	L	1-4	Toseland	21,416
10	19	A	Preston North End	L	0-4		14,946
11	26	H	Brentford	W	2-1	Marshall, Owen	29,868
12	Nov 2	A	Derby County	L	0-3		28,776
13	9	H	Everton	W	1-0	Herd	39,883
14	16	A	Bolton Wanderers	D	3-3	Brook 2, Tilson	45,809
15	23	H	Sheffield Wednesday	W	3-0	Owen 2, McCullough	36,781
16	30	A	Middlesbrough	L	0-2		19,438
17	Dec 7	H	Aston Villa	W	5-0	Tilson 2, Toseland 2, Brook	40,588
18	14	A	Wolverhampton W.	L	3-4	Tilson 2, Brook	20,860
19	25	H	Chelsea	D	0-0		36,074
20	26	A	Chelsea	L	1-2	Herd	41,732
21	28	A	West Bromwich Albion	L	1-5	McLeod	31,070
22	Jan 1	H	Grimsby Town	L	0-3		32,470
23	4	H	Sunderland	L	0-1		48,732
24	15	H	Huddersfield Town	L	1-2	Brook	16,884
25	18	A	Birmingham	W	1-0	McLeod	23,165
26	Feb 1	A	Portsmouth	W	2-1	McLeod 2	19,363
27	8	A	Stoke City	L	0-1		27,960
28	19	H	Blackburn Rovers	W	2-0	McLeod 2	12,498
29	22	H	Preston North End	L	1-3	Brook	41,415
30	29	A	Everton	D	2-2	Tilson, Toseland	14,418
31	Mar 7	H	Middlesbrough	W	6-0	Herd 2, Brook, Doherty, Tilson, Toseland	20,094
32	11	H	Arsenal	W	1-0	Percival	32,750
33	14	A	Brentford	D	0-0		28,364
34	21	H	Bolton Wanderers	W	7-0	Brook 3, Doherty 2, Herd, Toseland	40,779
35	28	A	Sheffield Wednesday	L	0-1		20,840
36	Apr 4	H	Derby County	W	1-0	McLeod	25,806
37	10	H	Leeds United	L	1-3	Herd	38,773
38	11	A	Aston Villa	D	2-2	Marshall, Percival	41,638
39	13	A	Leeds United	D	1-1	Brook	17,175
40	18	H	Wolverhampton W.	W	2-1	Herd, Tilson	25,188
41	25	A	Huddersfield Town	D	1-1	Doherty	8,258
42	May 2	A	Grimsby Town	L	1-3	Brook	8,974
							Appearances
							Goals

FA Cup

Round	Date	Venue	Opponents	Result	Scorers	Attendance
R3	Jan 11	H	Portsmouth	3-1	Brook 3	53,340
R4	25	H	Luton Town	2-1	Herd, McLeod	65,978
R5	Feb 15	A	Grimsby Town	2-3	McLeod, Tilson	28,000
						Appearances
						Goals

Swift FV	Dale W	Barkas S	Busby MW	Donnelly R	Bray J	Toseland E	Herd A	Heale JA	Tilson SF	Brook EF	Owen W	Percival J	Cassidy JA	Marshall RS	McCullough K	McLeod JS	Corbett FW	Rodger C	Neilson R	Doherty PD	Rogers JH
1	2	3	4	5	6	7	8	9	10	11											
1	2	3	4	5	6	7	8	9	10	11											
1	2	3	4	5	6	7	8	10	9	11											
1	2	3	4	5	6	7	8	10	9	11											
1	2	3	4	5	6	7	8	10	9	11											
1	2	3	4	5	6	7	8	10	9	11											
1	2	3	4	5	6	7	8	10	9	11											
1	2	3	4	5	6	7	8	10	9	11											
1	2	3	4	5	6	7	8		10	11	9										
1	2	3	4	5		7	11				9	6	8	10							
1	2	3	4	5	6	7			10	11	9			8							
1	2	3	4	5	6	7			10	11	9				8						
1	2	3	4	5	6	7	10		9	11					8						
1	2	3	4	5	6	7	10		9	11					8						
1	2	3	4	5	6	7	10			11	9				8						
1	2	3	5		6	7	8		10	11	9				4						
1	2	3		5	6	7	10		9	11				8	4						
1	2	3		5	6	7	10		9	11				8	4						
1	2	3	4	5	6	7	10		9	11					8						
1	2	3		5	6	7	10			11	9			8	4						
1	2	3		5		7	10			11		4	8		6	9					
1	2	3		5	6	7				11		4		8	10	9					
1		3		5	6	7				11	9	4		10	8		2				
1	2	3			6	7	8			11	9	4						10	5		
1	2				6	7	10			11		4		8		9	3		5		
1	2	3			6	7			8	11		4		5		9		10			
1	2	3			6	7			10	11		4		8		9			5		
1	3		4		6	7			10	11		8		5		9	2				
1	2		4		6				8	11		7		5		9	3			10	
1	2	3			6	7	8		9	11		4		5						10	
1	2	3			6	7	8		9	11		4		5						10	
1	2	3			6	7	8		9	11		4		5						10	
1	2	3		5	6	7			9	11		4		8						10	
1	2	3			6	7	8		9	11		4		5						10	
1	2	3		5	6	7	10			11		4		8		9					
1	2	3		5		7	10					4		8		9		11			6
1	2	3		5	6	7	8		9	11		4						10			
1	2	3		5		7	10		9	11		4		8							6
1	2	3		5	6	7	10		9	11		4		8							
1	2	3		5	6	7	8		9	11		4								10	
1	2	3			6	7	8		9	11		4							5	10	
1	2	3		5	6	7	8		9	11		4								10	
42	41	39	19	30	38	41	33	8	32	40	9	23	2	21	12	9	4	4	4	9	2
			1		1	10	10	3	11	13	3	2		2	1	7				4	

Swift FV	Dale W	Barkas S	Busby MW	Donnelly R	Bray J	Toseland E	Herd A	Heale JA	Tilson SF	Brook EF	Owen W	Percival J	Cassidy JA	Marshall RS	McCullough K	McLeod JS	Corbett FW	Rodger C	Neilson R	Doherty PD	Rogers JH
1	2	3			6	7	8			11	9			5	4			10			
1	2	3			6	7	8		10	11		4		5		9					
1	2	3	5		6	7	8		10	11		4				9					
3	3	3	1		3	3	3		2	3	1	2		2	1	2		1			
							1		1	3						2					

League Table

	P	W	D	L	F	A	Pts
Sunderland	42	25	6	11	109	74	56
Derby Co	42	18	12	12	61	52	48
Huddersfield T	42	18	12	12	59	56	48
Stoke C	42	20	7	15	57	57	47
Brentford	42	17	12	13	81	60	46
Arsenal	42	15	15	12	78	48	45
Preston N.E.	42	18	8	16	67	64	44
Chelsea	42	15	13	14	65	72	43
Manchester C	42	17	8	17	68	60	42
Portsmouth	42	17	8	17	54	67	42
Leeds U	42	15	11	16	66	64	41
Birmingham C	42	15	11	16	61	63	41
Bolton W	42	14	13	15	67	76	41
Middlesbrough	42	15	10	17	84	70	40
Wolverhampton W	42	15	10	17	77	76	40
Everton	42	13	13	16	89	89	39
Grimsby T	42	17	5	20	65	73	39
W.B.A.	42	16	6	20	89	88	38
Liverpool	42	13	12	17	60	64	38
Sheffield W	42	13	12	17	63	77	38
Aston Villa	42	13	9	20	81	110	35
Blackburn R	42	12	9	21	55	96	33

1936-37

Division One

Manager: Wilf Wild

Did you know that?

Match 8: Cassidy's last game.
Match 12: Regan's last game.
Match 14: McLeod's last game.
Match 40: Donnelly's last game.

By drawing in their final match of the season City had gone 22 League games without defeat. This feat was matched in Division Two in 1946–47, and remains the club's best sequence.

Match No.	Date	Venue	Opponents	Result		Scorers	Attendance
1	Aug 29	A	Middlesbrough	L	0-2		23,081
2	Sep 2	H	Leeds United	W	4-0	Brook, Doherty, Herd, Tilson	24,726
3	5	H	West Bromwich Albion	W	6-2	Doherty 2, Herd 2, Brook, Heale	33,063
4	9	A	Leeds United	D	1-1	Heale	13,933
5	12	A	Manchester United	L	2-3	Bray, Heale	68,796
6	16	H	Birmingham	D	1-1	Doherty	20,280
7	19	A	Portsmouth	L	1-2	McLeod	24,600
8	26	H	Chelsea	D	0-0		30,004
9	Oct 3	A	Stoke City	D	2-2	Doherty, Heale	36,400
10	10	H	Charlton Athletic	D	1-1	Heale	33,664
11	17	H	Derby County	W	3-2	Doherty, Heale, Toseland	21,245
12	24	A	Wolverhampton W.	L	1-2	Doherty	20,888
13	31	H	Sunderland	L	2-4	Doherty, McLeod	39,444
14	Nov 7	A	Huddersfield Town	D	1-1	Brook	18,438
15	14	H	Everton	W	4-1	Rodger 2, Brook, Toseland	27,818
16	21	A	Bolton Wanderers	W	2-0	Brook, Herd	32,003
17	Dec 5	A	Arsenal	W	3-1	Rodger 2, Doherty	41,783
18	12	H	Preston North End	W	4-1	Toseland 2, Brook, Doherty	20,093
19	19	A	Sheffield Wednesday	L	1-5	Doherty	18,826
20	25	A	Grimsby Town	L	3-5	Brook, Doherty, Rodger	17,921
21	26	H	Middlesbrough	W	2-1	Brook, Rodger	56,227
22	28	H	Grimsby Town	D	1-1	Tilson	16,146
23	Jan 2	A	West Bromwich Albion	D	2-2	Herd, Tilson	18,137
24	9	H	Manchester United	W	1-0	Herd	64,862
25	23	H	Portsmouth	W	3-1	Brook, Herd, Toseland	19,595
26	Feb 3	A	Chelsea	D	4-4	Doherty 2, Bray, Tilson	11,620
27	6	H	Stoke City	W	2-1	Doherty, Tilson	34,767
28	13	A	Charlton Athletic	D	1-1	Herd	35,509
29	24	A	Derby County	W	5-0	Tilson 3, Brook, Rodger	12,572
30	27	H	Wolverhampton W.	W	4-1	Tilson 3, Herd	42,133
31	Mar 13	H	Huddersfield Town	W	3-0	Doherty 2, Brook	28,240
32	20	A	Everton	D	1-1	Percival	31,921
33	26	A	Liverpool	W	5-0	Brook 3, Doherty, Herd	34,088
34	27	H	Bolton Wanderers	D	2-2	Doherty, Herd	51,714
35	29	H	Liverpool	W	5-1	Herd 2, Brook, Neilson, Tilson	38,763
36	Apr 3	A	Brentford	W	6-2	Doherty 2, Brook, Herd, Tilson, Toseland	29,028
37	7	H	Brentford	W	2-1	Brook, Doherty	24,629
38	10	H	Arsenal	W	2-0	Doherty, Toseland	74,918
39	14	A	Sunderland	W	3-1	Doherty 2, Brook	14,827
40	17	A	Preston North End	W	5-2	Doherty 3, Donnelly, Herd	21,804
41	24	H	Sheffield Wednesday	W	4-1	Brook 2, Doherty, Tilson	50,985
42	May 1	A	Birmingham	D	2-2	Doherty, Tilson	17,325
							Appearances
							Goals

FA Cup

Round	Date	Venue	Opponents	Result	Scorers	Attendance
R3	Jan 16	A	Wrexham	3-1	Brook, Herd, Tilson	20,600
R4	30	H	Accrington Stanley	2-0	Doherty, Tilson	39,135
R5	Feb 20	A	Bolton Wanderers	5-0	Herd 2, Brook, Doherty, Tilson	60,979
R6	Mar 6	A	Millwall	0-2		42,474
						Appearances
						Goals

Swift FV	Dale W	Barkas S	Percival J	Neilson R	Bray J	Toseland E	Herd A	Tilson SF	Doherty PD	Brook EF	Clark GV	Marshall RS	Heale JA	Donnelly R	McCullough K	McLeod JS	Cassidy JA	Regan RH	Rodger C	Freeman RH	Rogers JH
1	2	3	4	5	6	7	8	9	10	11											
1	3		4		6	7	8	9	10	11	2	5									
1	3		4		6	7	8		9	11	2	5	10								
1	3		4		6	7	8		9	11	2		10	5							
1	2	3	4		6	7	8		10	11			9	5							
1	3		4		6	7			10	11	2	5	9		8						
1	3		8		6	7			10	11	2	5			4	9					
1	3		4		6	7			9	11	2	5	10				8				
1	3		4		6	7			10	9	2	5	8					11			
1	2	3	4		6	7			10	9		5	8					11			
1	2	3	4		6	7			10	9		5	8					11			
1	2	3	4		6	7			10	9		5	8					11			
1	2	3	4		6	7			10	11		5	8			9					
1	2	3	4		6	7	8		10	11		5				9					
1	2	3	4		6	7	8		10	11		5							9		
1	2	3	4		6	7	8		10	11		5							9		
1	2	3	4		6	7	8		10	11		5							9		
1	2	3	4		6	7	8		10	11		5							9		
1	2	3	4		6	7	8		10	11		5							9		
1	2	3	4		6	7	8		10	11		5							9		
1	2		4		6	7	8		10	11		5		3					9		
1			4		6	7	8	9	10	11	2	5		3							
1	2		4		6	7	8	9	10	11		5		3							
1	2	3	4		6	7	8	9	10	11		5									
1	2	3	4		6	7	8	9		11		5								10	
1	2	3	4		6	7	8	9	10	11		5									
1	2	3	4		6	7	8	9	10	11		5									
1	2	3	4		6	7	8	9	10	11		5									
1	2	3	4		6	7		9	8	11		5							10		
1		3	4		6	7	8	9	10	11	2	5									
1	2	3	4		6	7	8	9	10	11		5									
1	2	3	4		6	7	8	9	10	11		5									
1	2	3	4		6	7	8	9	10	11		5									
1	2	3	4		6	7	8	9	10	11		5									
1	2	3	4	5	6	7	8	9	10	11											
1	2	3	4		6	7	8	9	10	11		5									
1	2	3	4		6	7	8	9	10	11		5									
1	2	3	4		6	7	8	9	10	11		5									
1			4			7		9	8	11	2	5		3					10		6
1			4			7	8	9	10	11	2	5		3							6
1		3	4		6	7	8	9	10	11	2	5									
1		3	4		6	7	8	9	10	11	2	5									
42	36	30	42	2	40	42	32	23	41	42	13	38	10	7	2	3	1	4	9	1	2
			1	1	2	7	15	15	30	20			6	1		2			7		

Swift FV	Dale W	Barkas S	Percival J	Neilson R	Bray J	Toseland E	Herd A	Tilson SF	Doherty PD	Brook EF	Clark GV	Marshall RS	Heale JA	Donnelly R	McCullough K	McLeod JS	Cassidy JA	Regan RH	Rodger C	Freeman RH	Rogers JH
1		3	4		6	7	8	9	10	11	2	5									
1	2	3	4		6	7	8	9	10	11		5									
1	2	3	4		6	7	8	9	10	11		5									
1	2	3			6	7	8	9	10	11		5									4
4	3	4	3		4	4	4	4	4	4	1	4									1
							3	3	2	2											

League Table

	P	W	D	L	F	A	Pts
Manchester C	42	22	13	7	107	61	57
Charlton A	42	21	12	9	58	49	54
Arsenal	42	18	16	8	80	49	52
Derby Co	42	21	7	14	96	90	49
Wolverhampton W	42	21	5	16	84	67	47
Brentford	42	18	10	14	82	78	46
Middlesbrough	42	19	8	15	74	71	46
Sunderland	42	19	6	17	89	87	44
Portsmouth	42	17	10	15	62	66	44
Stoke C	42	15	12	15	72	57	42
Birmingham C	42	13	15	14	64	60	41
Grimsby T	42	17	7	18	86	81	41
Chelsea	42	14	13	15	52	55	41
Preston N.E.	42	14	13	15	56	67	41
Huddersfield T	42	12	15	15	62	64	39
W.B.A.	42	16	6	20	77	98	38
Everton	42	14	9	19	81	78	37
Liverpool	42	12	11	19	62	84	35
Leeds U	42	15	4	23	60	80	34
Bolton W	42	10	14	18	43	66	34
Manchester U	42	10	12	20	55	78	32
Sheffield W	42	9	12	21	53	69	30

1937-38

Division One

Manager: Wilf Wild

Did you know that?

Match 4: Allmark's first and only game.
Match 10: Clayton's last League game.
Match 17: Rodger's last game.
Match 21: McCullough's last game.
Match 21: Wardle's last League game.
Match 27: Rogers's last game.
Match 39: Dale and Marshall's last game.

This relegation season ended in a similar way to the famous 1983 relegation mach with Luton. Huddersfield's 78th-minute goal guaranteed their survival but relegated City in the final match. However, even at full-time the Blues were convinced they were safe. It was an absolute shock when the news came through that fellow strugglers Grimsby, Portsmouth, Birmingham and Stoke had all won. City would have been safe on goal average had any of those sides lost, or indeed had they defeated Huddersfield.

Match No.	Date	Venue	Opponents	Result		Scorers	Attendance
1	Aug 28	A	Wolverhampton W.	L	1-3	Herd	39,391
2	Sep 1	H	Everton	W	2-0	Doherty, Herd	27,603
3	4	H	Leicester City	W	3-0	Bray, Brook, Herd	37,687
4	8	A	Everton	L	1-4	Brook	27,290
5	11	A	Sunderland	L	1-3	Doherty	32,617
6	15	H	Huddersfield Town	W	3-2	Herd 2, Percival	19,968
7	18	H	Derby County	W	6-1	Brook 2, Doherty 2, Clayton, Percival	32,991
8	25	A	Portsmouth	D	2-2	Barr, Doherty	18,451
9	Oct 2	A	Arsenal	L	1-2	Clayton	68,353
10	9	H	Blackpool	W	2-1	Brook, Herd	38,846
11	16	H	Stoke City	D	0-0		44,095
12	23	A	Middlesbrough	L	0-4		18,442
13	30	H	Birmingham	W	2-0	Doherty 2	16,829
14	Nov 6	A	Preston North End	D	2-2	Brook, Doherty	33,107
15	13	H	Liverpool	L	1-3	Toseland	28,111
16	20	A	Chelsea	D	2-2	Brook, Herd	40,197
17	27	H	Grimsby Town	W	3-1	Percival 2, Herd	27,526
18	Dec 18	A	Leeds United	L	1-2	Doherty	22,144
19	25	H	Brentford	L	0-2		37,478
20	27	A	Brentford	L	1-2	Herd	33,887
21	Jan 1	H	Wolverhampton W.	L	2-4	Doherty, Herd	49,407
22	15	A	Leicester City	W	4-1	Doherty 3, Heale	17,332
23	29	A	Derby County	W	7-1	Heale 3, Doherty 2, Brook, Toseland	13,625
24	Feb 2	H	Sunderland	D	0-0		23,644
25	5	H	Portsmouth	W	2-1	Brook, Rogers	33,496
26	16	H	Arsenal	L	1-2	Heale	34,299
27	19	A	Blackpool	L	1-2	Tilson	19,764
28	26	A	Stoke City	L	2-3	Doherty, Toseland	28,023
29	Mar 9	H	Middlesbrough	L	1-6	Milsom	16,396
30	12	A	Birmingham	D	2-2	Brook, Doherty	23,078
31	16	A	West Bromwich Albion	D	1-1	Dunkley	10,747
32	19	H	Preston North End	L	1-2	Doherty	54,911
33	26	A	Liverpool	L	0-2		29,081
34	Apr 2	H	Chelsea	W	1-0	Pritchard	31,033
35	6	H	Charlton Athletic	W	5-3	Milsom 3, Bray, Pritchard	18,622
36	9	A	Grimsby Town	L	1-3	Doherty	11,413
37	15	H	Bolton Wanderers	L	1-2	Milsom	53,328
38	16	H	West Bromwich Albion	W	7-1	Brook 4, Herd 2, Doherty	33,076
39	18	A	Bolton Wanderers	L	1-2	Brook	29,872
40	23	A	Charlton Athletic	D	0-0		26,883
41	30	H	Leeds United	W	6-2	Doherty 3, Brook, Heale, Percival	26,732
42	May 7	A	Huddersfield Town	L	0-1		35,100
							Appearances
							Goals

FA Cup

	Date	Venue	Opponents		Result	Scorers	Attendance
R3	Jan 8	A	Millwall		2-2	Herd 2	38,110
R3	12	H	Millwall		3-1	Brook, Heale, Herd	39,559
R4	22	H	Bury		3-1	Toseland 2, Whitfield (og)	71,937
R5	Feb 12	A	Luton Town		3-1	Doherty, Heale, Nelson (og)	21,099
R6	Mar 5	A	Aston Villa		2-3	Doherty, Allen (og)	75,500
							Appearances
						Three own goals	Goals

Charity Shield

	Date	Venue	Opponents		Result	Scorers	Attendance
	Nov 4	H	Sunderland	W	2-0	Herd. Docherty	20,000
							Appearances
							Goals

Swift FV	Dale W	Barkas S	Percival J	Marshall RS	Bray J	Toseland E	Herd A	Tilson SF	Doherty PD	Brook EF	Allmark JJ	Clark GV	Rodger C	Clayton R	Barr AMcD	McCullough K	Gregg W	Wardle W	Rogers JH	Neilson R	Heale JA	Emptage AT	Milsom J	Pritchard HJ	McDowall LJ	Dunkley MEF
1	2	3	4	5	6	7	8	9	10	11																
1	2	3	4	5	6	7	8	9	10	11																
1	2	3	4	5	6	7	8	9	10	11																
1	2	3	4	5	6	7	8		10	11	9															
1		3	4	5	6	7	8		10	11		2	9													
1		3	4	5	6	7	8		10	11		2	9													
1		3	4	5	6	7	8		10	11		2		9												
1	3		4	5	6	7		9	8	11		2			10											
1	2	3	4	5	6	7			10	11				9		8										
1	2	3	4	5	6	7	8		10	11				9												
1	2	3	4	5	6	7	8	9	10	11																
1			4	5	6	7	8	9				2	10				3	11								
1		3	4	5	6	7	8	9	10	11		2														
1		3	4	5	6	7	8	9	10	11		2														
1		3	4	5	6	7	8		10	11		2	9													
1	2	3	4	5	6	7	8		10	11			9													
1	2	3	4	5		7	8		10				9					11	6							
1	2	3	4	5	6	7	8	9	10									11								
1	2		4	5	6	7	8	9	10								3	11								
1	3			5	6	7	8	9	10			2				4		11								
1		3		5	6	7	8	9	10			2				4		11								
1	3		4			7			10	11		2							6	5	9	8				
1	2	3	4	5		7			10	11									6		9	8				
1	2	3	4	5		7			10	11									6		9	8				
1		3	4	5		7			10	11		2							6		9	8				
1	2	3	4	5		7	8		10	11									6		9					
1	2	3	4	5		7	8	9	10	11									6							
1	2	3	4	5	6	7	8		10	11													9			
1	2	3	4		6	7	8		10	11										5			9			
1	3		4	5	6		8		10	11		2											9	7		
1	3		4		6		8		10	11		2											9		5	7
1	3		4		6		8		10	11		2											9		5	7
1	3		4				8		10	11		2								5			9		6	7
1	3		4		6		8		10	11		2											9	7	5	
1	3		4		6				10	11		2									8		9	7	5	
1	3		4		6		8		10	11		2											9	7	5	
1	2	3	4	5			8		10	11													9	7	6	
1	2	3	4	5			8		10	11													9	7	6	
1	2	3	4	5		7	8		10	11													9		6	
1		3	4				8		10	11		2								5	9			7	6	
1		3	4				8		10	11		2								5	9			7	6	
1		3	4				8		10	11		2								5			9	7	6	
42	30	30	40	31	28	30	35	13	41	36	1	22	6	3	1	3	2	6	7	6	8	4	13	9	12	3
			5		2	3	12	1	23	16				2	1				1		6		5	2		1

Swift FV	Dale W	Barkas S	Percival J	Marshall RS	Bray J	Toseland E	Herd A	Tilson SF	Doherty PD	Brook EF	Allmark JJ	Clark GV	Rodger C	Clayton R	Barr AMcD	McCullough K	Gregg W	Wardle W	Rogers JH	Neilson R	Heale JA
1	3	6	4			7	8		10			2		9				11		5	
1	3	6	4			7	8		10	11		2								5	9
1	3		4			7	8		10	11		2							6	5	9
1	2	3	4	5		7	8		10	11									6		9
1	2	3	4		6	7	8		10	11										5	9
5	5	4	5	1	1	5	5		5	4		3		1				1	2	4	4
						2	3		2	1											2

Swift FV	Dale W	Barkas S	Percival J	Marshall RS	Bray J	Toseland E	Herd A	Tilson SF	Doherty PD	Brook EF
1	2	3	4	5	6	7	8	9	10	11
1	1	1	1	1	1	1	1	1	1	1
						1		1		

League Table

	P	W	D	L	F	A	Pts
Arsenal	42	21	10	11	77	44	52
Wolverhampton W	42	20	11	11	72	49	51
Preston N.E.	42	16	17	9	64	44	49
Charlton A	42	16	14	12	65	51	46
Middlesbrough	42	19	8	15	72	65	46
Brentford	42	18	9	15	69	59	45
Bolton W	42	15	15	12	64	60	45
Sunderland	42	14	16	12	55	57	44
Leeds U	42	14	15	13	64	69	43
Chelsea	42	14	13	15	65	65	41
Liverpool	42	15	11	16	65	71	41
Blackpool	42	16	8	18	61	66	40
Derby Co	42	15	10	17	66	87	40
Everton	42	16	7	19	79	75	39
Huddersfield T	42	17	5	20	55	68	39
Leicester C	42	14	11	17	54	75	39
Stoke C	42	13	12	17	58	59	38
Birmingham C	42	10	18	14	58	62	38
Portsmouth	42	13	12	17	62	68	38
Grimsby T	42	13	12	17	51	68	38
Manchester C	42	14	8	20	80	77	36
W.B.A.	42	14	8	20	74	91	36

1938-39

Division One

Manager: Wilf Wild

Did you know that?

Match 4: Neilson's last game.
Match 6: Howe's last game.
Match 10: Barr's last game.
Match 12: Gregg's last game.
Match 38: Freeman's last game.
Match 42: McLeod's last game.

A 3–0 victory for Sheffield United against Coventry on 29 April meant City's faint hopes of promotion ended despite a 3–1 win over Chesterfield.

Match No.	Date	Venue	Opponents	Result		Scorers	Attendance
1	Aug 27	H	Swansea Town	W	5-0	Doherty 2, Herd 2, Howe	32,514
2	29	A	Chesterfield	W	3-0	Howe 2, Brook	15,769
3	Sep 3	A	Bradford Park Avenue	L	2-4	Brook, Herd	16,738
4	7	H	West Ham United	L	2-4	Herd, Howe	20,351
5	10	H	Luton Town	L	1-2	Howe	31,316
6	17	H	Millwall	L	1-6	Bray	29,130
7	24	A	Blackburn Rovers	D	3-3	Heale, Herd, McDowall	26,457
8	Oct 1	H	Fulham	L	3-5	McDowall 2, Barr	29,671
9	8	A	Sheffield Wednesday	L	1-3	Brook	25,372
10	15	A	Plymouth Argyle	D	0-0		24,335
11	22	H	Sheffield United	W	3-2	Brook, Milsom, Toseland	31,544
12	29	A	West Bromwich Albion	L	1-3	Milsom	22,274
13	Nov 5	H	Tottenham Hotspur	W	2-0	Doherty, Milsom	47,998
14	12	A	Southampton	W	2-1	Brook, Milsom	23,104
15	19	H	Coventry City	W	3-0	Doherty 2, Herd	40,408
16	26	A	Nottingham Forest	W	4-3	Brook 3, Herd	15,727
17	Dec 3	H	Newcastle United	W	4-1	Herd 2, Milsom 2	43,114
18	10	A	Burnley	D	1-1	Milsom	24,096
19	17	H	Norwich City	W	4-1	Doherty 2, Herd 2	19,500
20	24	A	Swansea Town	L	0-2		13,219
21	26	A	Tranmere Rovers	W	9-3	Milsom 4, Toseland 2, Doherty 2, Herd	13,378
22	27	H	Tranmere Rovers	W	5-2	Milsom 3, Doherty, Pritchard	45,700
23	31	H	Bradford Park Avenue	W	5-1	Herd 3, Milsom, Pritchard	33,741
24	Jan 14	A	Luton Town	L	0-3		16,163
25	28	H	Blackburn Rovers	W	3-2	Heale 2, Doherty	47,089
26	Feb 4	A	Fulham	L	1-2	Evans (og)	24,668
27	18	H	Plymouth Argyle	L	1-3	Brook	30,495
28	25	A	Sheffield United	L	0-1		31,628
29	Mar 4	H	West Bromwich Albion	D	3-3	Brook, Doherty, Herd	28,810
30	11	A	Tottenham Hotspur	W	3-2	Sproston 2, Freeman	27,426
31	13	A	Millwall	L	1-3	Doherty	13,740
32	18	H	Southampton	W	2-1	McLeod, McDowall	19,687
33	25	A	Coventry City	W	1-0	Heale	20,238
34	Apr 1	H	Nottingham Forest	W	3-0	Herd 2, Pritty (og)	24,758
35	7	A	Bury	W	5-1	Heale 2, Brook, Doherty, Herd	24,520
36	8	A	Newcastle United	W	2-0	Doherty, Heale	24,487
37	10	H	Bury	D	0-0		38,527
38	15	H	Burnley	W	2-0	Doherty 2	19,230
39	22	A	Norwich City	D	0-0		14,340
40	26	H	Sheffield Wednesday	D	1-1	Pritchard	29,555
41	29	H	Chesterfield	W	3-1	Heale, Herd, McLeod	13,969
42	May 6	A	West Ham United	L	1-2	Heale	21,547
							Appearances
						Two own goals	Goals

FA Cup

Round	Date	Venue	Opponents	Result	Scorers	Attendance
R3	Jan 12	A	Norwich City	5-0	Herd 2, Milsom 2, Doherty	20,901
R4	21	A	Sheffield United	0-2		49,795
						Appearances
						Goals

Swift FV	Clark GV	Eastwood E	McDowall LJ	Neilson R	Bray J	Dunkley MEF	Herd A	Howe F	Doherty PD	Brook EF	Toseland E	Milsom J	Percival J	Robinson JJ	Gregg W	Cardwell L	Heale JA	Pritchard HJ	Emptage AT	Barr AMcD	Sproston B	Westwood E	Freeman RH	McLeod EH	Blackshaw W
1	2	3	4	5	6	7	8	9	10	11															
1	2	3	4	5	6	7	8	9	10	11															
1	2	3	4	5	6	7	8	9	10	11															
1	2	3	4	5	6		10	9		11	7	8													
1	2	3	5		6		10	9		11	7	8	4												
	2		4		6	7	8	9		11				1	3	5	10								
1		2	10		6		8			11			4		3	5	9	7							
1		2	10		6					11			4		3	5		7	8	9					
1	2		6							11		9	4		3	5		7	8	10					
1	2		6				8			11	7		4		3	5	10			9					
1	2		6							11	7	9	4		3	5	10		8						
1	2		6							11	7	9	4		3	5	10		8						
1			6				8		10	11	7	9	4			5					2	3			
1			6				8		10	11	7	9	4			5					2	3			
1			6				8		10	11	7	9	4			5					2	3			
1			6				8		10	11	7	9	4			5					2	3			
1			6				8		10	11	7	9	4			5					2	3			
1			6				8		10	11	7	9	4			5					2	3			
1			6				8		10	11	7	9	4			5					2	3			
1			6				8		10	11	7	9	4			5					2	3			
1			6				8		10		7	9	4			5		11			2	3			
1			6				8		10		7	9	4			5		11			2	3			
1			6				8		10		7	9	4			5		11			2	3			
1	2		6				8		10	11	7	9	4			5						3			
1			6				8		10	11			4			5	9	7			2	3			
1			6				8		10	11			4			5	9	7			2	3			
1			6						10	11	7	9	4			5			8		2	3			
1			4		6	7			10	11		9				5			8		2	3			
1			4		6	7	8		10	11						5					2	3	9		
1			4		6	7	8		10	11						5					2	3	9		
1	2				6	7	9		10	11			4			5			8			3			
1	2		4		6	7	8			11						5	10					3		9	
1	2		4		6	7	8		10	11						5	9					3			
1	2		4		6	7	8		10	11						5	9					3			
1	2		4		6	7	8		10	11						5	9					3			
1	2		4		6	7	8		10	11						5	9					3			
1	2		4		6	7	8		10	11						5	9					3			
1			4		6	7	8		10							5		11			2	3	9		
1			4		6	7	8									5	9	11			2	3		10	
1					6		8						4			5	9	11	10		2	3			7
1	2				6		8						4			5	9	11				3		10	7
1	2				6								4			5	9	11	8			3		10	7
41	20	7	38	4	23	16	35	6	28	34	18	19	26	1	7	37	17	13	9	3	20	30	3	4	3
			4		1		20	5	17	11	3	15					9	3		1	2		1	2	

Swift FV	Clark GV	Eastwood E	McDowall LJ	Neilson R	Bray J	Dunkley MEF	Herd A	Howe F	Doherty PD	Brook EF	Toseland E	Milsom J	Percival J	Robinson JJ	Gregg W	Cardwell L	Heale JA	Pritchard HJ	Emptage AT	Barr AMcD	Sproston B	Westwood E	Freeman RH	McLeod EH	Blackshaw W
1	2		6				8		10	11	7	9	4			5						3			
1			6				8		10	11	7	9	4			5					2	3			
2	1		2				2		2	2	2	2	2			2					1	2			
							2		1			2													

League Table

	P	W	D	L	F	A	Pts
Blackburn R	42	25	5	12	94	60	55
Sheffield U	42	20	14	8	69	41	54
Sheffield W	42	21	11	10	88	59	53
Coventry C	42	21	8	13	62	45	50
Manchester C	42	21	7	14	96	72	49
Chesterfield	42	20	9	13	69	52	49
Luton T	42	22	5	15	82	66	49
Tottenham H	42	19	9	14	67	62	47
Newcastle U	42	18	10	14	61	48	46
W.B.A.	42	18	9	15	89	72	45
West Ham U	42	17	10	15	70	52	44
Fulham	42	17	10	15	61	55	44
Millwall	42	14	14	14	64	53	42
Burnley	42	15	9	18	50	56	39
Plymouth A	42	15	8	19	49	55	38
Bury	42	12	13	17	65	74	37
Bradford P.A.	42	12	11	19	61	82	35
Southampton	42	13	9	20	56	82	35
Swansea T	42	11	12	19	50	83	34
Nottingham F	42	10	11	21	49	82	31
Norwich C	42	13	5	24	50	91	31
Tranmere R	42	6	5	31	39	99	17

1939-40

Division One

Manager: Wilf Wild

Match No.	Date	Venue	Opponents	Result		Scorers	Attendance
1	Aug 26	A	Leicester City	L	3-4	Dunkley, Doherty, Brook	13021
2	30	H	Bury	D	1-1	Doherty	17753
3	Sep 2	H	Chesterfield	W	2-0	Milsom 2	16620
							Appearances
							Goals

Note: The Football League was suspended after the opening three games of the season.
These three matches were later expunged from official records.

War Regional League (Western Division)

1	Oct 21	A	Manchester U	W	4-0	Herd, Heale, Doherty, Brook	7,000
2	28	H	Wrexham	W	6-1	Doherty2, Pritchard 2, Heale, Brook	4,000
3	Nov 11	A	Everton	L	1-3	Heale	5,000
4	18	H	Stoke C	D	1-1	Percival	5,000
5	25	A	New Brighton	W	3-1	Herd, Doherty 2	3,500
6	Dec 2	H	Stockport C	D	6-6	Heale 5, Wright	5,774
7	9	H	Chester	W	4-1	Blackshaw 2, Heale, Doherty	3,000
8	23	A	Crewe A	W	2-1	Herd 2	5,000
9	Jan 6	H	Liverpool	L	3-7	Doherty 2, Rudd	5,000
10	Feb 10	H	Manchester U	W	1-0	Herd	5,000
11	24	A	Wrexham	L	2-3	Heale, Rudd	4,000
12	Mar 9	H	Everton	D	2-2	Heale, Rudd	5,000
13	16	A	Stoke C	L	1-2	Herd	5,000
14	23	H	New Brighton	L	2-3	Doherty, Westwood	6,000
15	30	A	Stockport C	D	1-1	Herd	7,000
16	Apr 6	A	Chester	W	3-0	Herd 2, Emptage	2,500
17	13	H	Tranmere R	W	5-1	Currier 2, Bray, Herd, Emptage	3,000
18	May 4	A	Tranmere R	W	6-1	Currier 4, Herd, Doherty	2,500
19	11	A	Port Vale	W	5-2	Currier 4, Bray	2,000
20	13	H	Crewe A	W	6-2	Herd 4, Burdett, Doherty	1,300
21	18	H	Port Vale	W	7-0	Herd 4, Currier, Doherty, Pritchard	2,000
22	25	A	Liverpool	L	2-3	Pritchard, Doherty	2,000
							Appearances
							Goals

League War Cup

R1	Apr 20	A	Manchester U	W	1-0	Worsley	21,874
R1	27	H	Manchester U	L	0-2		21,596
							Appearances
							Goals

Football League Jubilee Fund Match

	Aug 19	A	Manchester U	D	1-1		20,000
							Appearances
							Goals

Note: City finished 4th in the Western Division & the War Cup was played on a 2 legged basis

Swift FV	Sproston B	Westwood E	McDowall LJ	Cardwell L	Bray J	Dunkley MEF	Herd A	Heale JA	Doherty PD	Brook EF	Milsom J
1	2	3	4	5	6	7	8	9	10	11	
1	2	3	4	5	6	7	8	9	10	11	
1	2	3	4	5	6	7	8		10	11	9
3	3	3	3	3	3	3	3	2	3	3	1
						1			2	1	2

Swift FV	Sproston B	Westwood E	McDowall LJ	Cardwell L	Bray J	Dunkley MEF	Herd A	Heale JA	Milsom	Doherty	Brook	Clark	Barkass	Percival	Bray	Blackshaw	Pritchard	Rudd	Wright	Walsh	Emptage	Robinson	Neilson	Smith G	Davenport	Worsley	Currier	Towsland	Burdett	McIntosh	Smith L	Tilson
1				5	6		8	9		10	11	2	3	4			7															
1		3		5	6		8	9		10	11		2	4			7															
1				5	6		8	9		10	11	2	3	4														7				
		3		5	6		8	9		10			2	4		7				11		1										
1	2			5	6		8	9		10	11		3	4		7																
1	2	3		5	6			9		10				4		7			11					8								
1	2	3		5	6		8	9		10				4		7			11													
1	2	3		5	6		8	9		10				4		7			11													
1		3		5	6		8	9		10		2		4		7		11														
1				5	6		8	9		10		2	3	4		7														11		
	2			5	6		8	9		10			3	4				11			7	1										
		3		5			8	9		10		2		4				11		6	7	1										
1		3		5			8	9				2		4		7		11		6	10											
1		11		5	6		9			10		2	3	8			7			4												
1		3					8					2		4			7			6			5	10							11	9
1	2	9		5	6		8					3		4			7	11			10											
1	2			5	6		8					3		4			11				10		7				9					
1	2	11		5	6		8			10		3					7			4							9					
1				5	6		8			10		2					11			4	7				3		9					
1				5	3		8			10		2		4			11			6	7								9			
1	3			5	6		8			10		2		4			11				7						9					
1	2			5	6		8			10		3					9	11		4	7											
19	10	12		21	19		21	13		18	4	15	8	19		8	11	6	3	9	9	3	2	2	1		4	1	1	1	1	1
		1			2		19	11		3	2			1		2	4	3	1		2						11		1			

Swift FV	Sproston B	Westwood E	McDowall LJ	Cardwell L	Bray J	Dunkley MEF	Herd A	Heale JA	Milsom	Doherty	Brook	Clark	Barkass	Percival	Bray	Blackshaw	Pritchard	Rudd	Wright	Walsh	Emptage	Robinson	Neilson	Smith G	Davenport	Worsley	Currier	Towsland	Burdett	McIntosh	Smith L	Tilson
1	2	11		5	6		8		9			3								4						7	10					
1	2			5	6		8			10		3					11			4				9		7						
2	2	1		2	2		2		1	1		2					1			2				1		2	1					
																										1						

Swift FV	Sproston B	Westwood E	McDowall LJ	Cardwell L	Bray J	Dunkley MEF	Herd A	Heale JA	Milsom	Doherty	Brook
1	2	3	4	5	6	7	8		9	10	11
1	1	1	1	1	1	1	1		1	1	1

1940-41

North Regional League

Match No.	Date	Venue	Opponents	Result		Scorers	Attendance
1	Aug 21	H	Everton	D	0-0		4,000
2	Sep 7	A	Everton	L	0-1		3,000
3	14	H	New Brighton	W	5-2	Doherty 2, Herd 2, Currier	4,000
4	21	A	Leeds U	D	0-0		5,000
5	28	H	Manchester U	W	4-1	Doherty 2, Brown, Currier	10,000
6	Oct 5	A	Manchester U	W	2-0	Currier, McShane	10,000
7	12	H	Huddersfield T	W	3-1	Currier, Brown	4,000
8	19	A	Liverpool	W	4-0	Currier 4	7,000
9	26	H	Blackburn R	D	1-1	Brown	5,000
10	Nov 2	A	Doncaster R	W	4-0	Herd 2, Currier, Doherty	2,000
11	9	H	Liverpool	W	5-1	Herd 3, Pritchard, Currier	3,000
12	16	A	Blackburn R	D	2-2	Currier, Doherty	2,000
13	23	H	Preston NE	L	1-2	Brown	4,000
14	30	A	Preston NE	D	4-4	Brown 2, Currier, Doherty	2,500
15	Dec 7	A	Oldham A	L	0-1		3,000
16	14	A	Stockport C	W	9-1	Herd 4, Currier 3, Bray, Opp own-goal	1,200
17	21	H	Stockport C	W	7-2	Currier 3, Doherty 3, Emptage	3,000
18	25	A	Burnley	D	2-2	Currier, McShane	8,300
19	28	A	Huddersfield T	L	0-2		2,689
20	Jan 4	H	Rochdale*	W	9-1	Currier 5, Doherty 2, Mulraney, Pritchard	2,000
21	11	A	Rochdale*	W	6-1	Currier 5, Mulraney	1,000
22	18	H	Blackpool*	L	2-4	Boothway, Bray	1,000
23	25	A	Blackpool*	L	1-2	Currier	12,000
24	Feb 1	H	Oldham A	W	5-4	Walsh, Mutch, Currier, Doherty 2	2,000
25	8	A	Oldham A	W	5-2	Currier 2, Bray, Mulraney, Doherty	2,000
26	Apr 12	H	Leeds U	D	1-1	Boothway	3,000
27	14	H	Manchester U	L	1-7	Currier	7,000
28	19	H	Wrexham	W	5-0	Reid 2, Percival, Boothway, Pritchard	2,000
29	26	H	Blackpool	W	2-0	Currier, Pearson	4,000
30	May 3	A	Blackpool	D	1-1	Currier	6,000
31	10	A	Wrexham	D	0-0		3,000
32	17	A	Bolton W	D	1-1	Brooks	1,500
33	24	H	Bolton W	W	6-4	Currier 3, Herd, Carey, Pritchard	1,500
34	31	A	Bury	W	3-2	Herd 2, Dunkley	1,371
35	Jun 7	H	Bury	W	3-2	Currier 2, Walsh	3,000
							Appearances
						1 own-goal	Goals

* Matches also counted in the Lancashire Cup.

League War Cup

Round	Date	Venue	Opponents	Result		Scorers	Attendance
R1/1	Feb 15	A	Blackpool	W	4-1	Currier 2, Doherty	15,000
R1/2	22	H	Blackpool	L	0-1		8,967
R2/1	Mar 1	H	Blackburn R	W	5-2	Sproston 2, Herd 2, Boothway	6,000
R2/2	8	A	Blackburn R	W	4-2	Bray, Pritchard, Currier, Doherty	5,000
R3/1	15	A	Everton	D	1-1	Currier	12,000
R3/1	22	H	Everton	W	2-0	Herd, Currier	10,000
R4/1	29	H	Preston NE	L	1-2	Boothway	15,304
R4/2	Apr 5	A	Preston NE	L	0-3		14,000
							Appearances
							Goals

Note: City finished third in the North Regional League and the War Cup was played on a 2 legged basis

Swift FV	Robinson J	Sproston	Eastwood	Clark	Walsh	Neilson	Bray	Pritchard	Herd	Doherty	Emptage	Percival	Boothway	Dunkley	Fagan	Jackson	Pearson	Cardwell	Barkas	Currier	McShane	Turner	Brown	Mulraney	Walker	Mutch	Carey	Rudd	Watt	Keeling	Davenport	Boultier	Robinson P	Nuttall	Beaumont	Breedon	Henry	Reid	Westwood	Brooks	Thomson	Vose	Dickie
1		2		3	4		6	11	8	10	7				5					9																							
1		2		3	4		6		8	10	7				5					9				11																			
1		2		3	4		6		8	10	11				5					9										7													
	1		2		4		3		8	10	6				5					9	11																						
1		2	3		4		6		8	10					5					9	11		7																				
	1	2	3		4	5	6		8	10	7									9	11																						
	1	2	3		4	5	6		8	10										9	11		7																				
	1	2	3		4	5	6		8	10										9	11		7																				
1		2	5		4		6			10	7									9	11		8								3												
1		2	3		4	5	6		7	10										9	11		8																				
1		2	3		4	5	6	7	8		10									9	11																						
1		2	3		4	5	6	7	8	10										9	11																						
1			3		6	5		7			8	4								9	11	2	10																				
1			3		4		6	7		10								5		9	11	2	8																				
	1		2		6	5		7	10			4							3	9	11											8										
1			3		4	5	6	7	8	10										9	11	2																					
	1		5	3	6			7		10	8									9	11	2											4									
1				3	4	5	6	7		10										9	11	2		8																		
1					4	5	3	8		10	6									9		2													7	11								
1				2	4	5	3	7		10							6			9	11			8																		
	1			3	4	5	6	7		10										9	11	2		8																		
	1			3		5	6	7				4	10							9	11	2		8																		
1					4	5	6	7		10									3	9	11	2				8																
				3	6			11		10		4						5		9		2	7			8										1							
1				3	4	5	6	11		10										9		2		7		8																
1			5		6		3	11		10		4	9			2				8																		7						
	1		5		6		3	7				4	9			2				10						8		11														
	1		5	2	6		3	11				8	9							10			7																4					
	1		5		4		6	11						7			10			9			8		2														3				
	1		2		4	5	6	11			8		9	7						10					3																	
1			2		6	5	3	11				4	9	7						8									10														
	1		5	2	4		6		8				11	7						10					3															9			
	1		5				6	11	8			4		7		2				9					3		10																	
	1		5	3	4		6		8					7		2				9	11						10																	
1				2	4		6		8			10	11	7						9					3		5																	
19	15	11	23	14	33	18	31	24	17	22	11	10	8	7	5	4	2	2	2	35	20	11	10	6	5	4	3	1	1	1	1	1	1	1	1	1	1	1	1	1			
					2		3	4	14	15	1	1	3	1			1			42	2		6	3		1	1											2		1			

Swift FV	Robinson J	Sproston	Eastwood	Clark	Walsh	Neilson	Bray	Pritchard	Herd	Doherty	Emptage	Percival	Boothway	Dunkley	Fagan	Jackson	Pearson	Cardwell	Barkas	Currier	McShane	Turner	Brown	Mulraney	Walker	Mutch	Carey	Rudd	Watt	Keeling	Davenport	Boultier	Robinson P	Nuttall	Beaumont	Breedon	Henry	Reid	Westwood	Brooks	Thomson	Vose	Dickie
1		2		3	4	5	6	7	8	10										9								11																
1		2		3	4	5	6	7												9			8					11													10		
1		10		2	4	5	6	7	8				9						3										11														
1		5		2	4		6	7		10			9						3	8									11														
	1	5		2	4		6	7	8				9						3	10								11															
1		5		2	4		6		8	10									3	9	11		7																				
1		5		2	4		6		8				9						3	10	11		7																				
	1				6			7				4				2				9	11		8		3																		5	10
6	2	7		7	8	3	7	6	5	3		1	4			1			5	7	3		4		1			3	2												1	1	1
		2					1	1	3	3			2							5																							

1941-42

North Regional League

Match No.	Date	Venue	Opponents	Result		Scorers	Attendance
1	Aug 30	A	Tranmere R	L	2-5	Bray, Dunkley	3,500
2	Sep 6	H	Tranmere R	D	1-1	Doherty	3,000
3	13	H	Liverpool	L	3-4	Dunkley, Smith, Currier	3,000
4	20	A	Liverpool	L	2-4	Parlane, O'Donnell	5,000
5	27	A	Wrexham	W	5-3	Boothway 5	2,000
6	Oct 4	H	Wrexham	W	2-0	Boothway 2	2,000
7	11	H	Stoke C	W	4-3	Barkas 3, Boothway	3,000
8	18	A	Stoke C	L	0-5		3,000
9	25	H	New Brighton	D	2-2	Bray, Currier	2,000
10	Nov 1	A	New Brighton	L	2-3	Boothway 2	1,500
11	8	A	Stockport C	W	6-4	Boothway 3, Currier 2, Emptage	3,000
12	15	H	Stockport C	W	2-1	Herd 2	2,000
13	22	H	Everton	L	3-4	Boothway 3	2,500
14	29	A	Everton	L	0-9		8,000
15	Dec 6	A	Chester	W	3-1	Walsh 2, Fenton	1,200
16	13	H	Chester	W	7-2	Dunkley 2, Fenton 2, Boothway 2, Smith	3,000
17	20	H	Manchester U	W	2-1	Boothway 2	7,000
18	25	A	Manchester U	D	2-2	Boothway 2	16,000
							Appearances
							Goals

North Regional League (2nd period)

Match No.	Date	Venue	Opponents	Result		Scorers	Attendance
19	Dec 27	A	Blackburn R*	L	0-3		5,200
20	Jan 3	H	Blackburn R*	L	1-2	Currier	4,000
21	10	A	Burnley*	W	2-1	Bray, Fenton	4,000
22	17	H	Burnley*	W	5-0	Currier 2, Dunkley 2, Fenton	2,500
23	Feb 14	H	Rochdale*	W	5-0	Boothway 3, Walsh, Fenton	4,000
24	21	A	Wolves*	W	3-1	Boothway 2, Smith	6,000
25	28	H	Wolves*	W	4-1	Boothway 3, Fenton	5,000
26	Mar 14	H	Preston NE*	L	0-3		6,000
27	21	A	Rochdale*	L	1-3	Currier	3,200
28	28	A	Preston NE*	D	0-0		5,000
29	Apr 4	H	Blackpool**	W		Blackpool withdrew and City were awarded the victory	
30	6	A	Blackpool**	W		Blackpool withdrew and City were awarded the victory	
31	11	A	Southport**	W	4-1	Malam 2, Dellow, Currier	4,000
32	18	H	Southport**	W	3-0	Boothway 2, Dellow	5,700
33	25	A	Wolves**	L	0-2		15,000
34	May 2	H	Wolves**	W	1-0	Currier	14,715
35	9	H	Everton***	W	2-0	Dellow, Boothway	4,000
36	16	A	Everton***	L	1-6	Boothway	18,000
37	23	H	Manchester U	L	1-3	Stuart	6,000
							Appearances
							Goals

Note: City finished 17th in the First Championship and were not placed in the Second Championship as teams needed to have played 18 games or more. Blackpool's withdrawal left City short of the figure.

* Matches also counted towards the League War Cup Qualifying Round.

** Matches also counted towards the League War Cup knock out section (two legged basis).

*** Matches also counted in the Lancashire Cup.

Robinson J.	Clark	Robinson P.	Eastwood	Bray	Walsh	Dunkley	Parlane	Boothway	Wild	Pritchard	Barkas	Kirton	Doherty	Sproston	Hogan	Stuart	Swift	Westwood	Percival	Bardsley	Smith	Davenport D.	Walker	Currier	Carey W.	Charlesworth	Fenton	Dellow	Crompton	Neilson	Brown	Goodall	Kinghorn	O'Donnell	Hall	Devlin	Rudman	Davenport J.	Emptage	Herd	Goddard	Pearson	Rudd	Scales	Carey J.	Dodd	Malam	
	2			6	4	7		10		11													3	9					1	5	8																	
	2		5	6	4			11		7			10									8	3	9								1																
	2		5	6		7	8											11	4		10		3	9								1																
	2		5				8	9		7	6								4				3		1								10	11														
		4	5				8	9		7	3			6											1										2	10	11											
		4	5				8	9	11			7		6									3	10	1										2													
	2	4	5	6				9	11		10	7					1						3	8																								
	2		5	6	4			9	11			7					1					10	3	8																								
	2			6	4	7		9	11				10	5									3	8	1																							
	2		5	6	4	7		9	11		10												3	8	1																							
	2		5	6	4			9	11			7												10	1													3	8									
		4	5		6	7		9	11					2									3	10	1															8								
			4		6			9	11		3	7								8			2	10	1	5																						
	2		4		6	7		9	11				10										3		1	5	8																					
1	2	4	3	6	10			9	11			7														5	8																					
1	2		3	6	4	7		9													10					5	8														11							
1			2	6	4	7		9															3	10		5	8															11						
1			2	6	4			9			3		10							7			11	8		5																						
4	12	5	16	12	13	8	4	17	10	4	6	6	4	4			2	1	2	2	2	2	14	13	9	6	4		1	1	1	2	1	1	2	1	1	1	1	1	1	1						
				2	2	4	1	22			3		1								2			4			3							1					1	2								
1			4		6	7		9			3		10										2	11		5	8																					
1			2	6	4			9	11			7											3	10		5	8																					
1	2	4	5	6				9												8			3	10			7																11					
1	2		4	6		7								10									3	9		5	8																11					
1			2	6	4	7		9													10		3	11		5	8																					
		4	3		6			9						2						7	10			11		5	8																	1				
				6	4	7		9			3										10		2	11		5	8																	1				
				6	4	7		9										2			8		3	11		5																		1	10			
1	2	7	5		6			9												10			3	11																						4	8	
			2	6	4			9									1				8		3	11		5		7																				
1	2		3	6	4			9													10			11		5		7																			8	
1	2		4	6	8			9			3										10			11		5		7																				
1	2		5	6	4			9								11					10		3	8				7																				
1	2			6	4			9			3												11	10				7																				
1	2			3	4			9							10	11							5	8				7																		6		
1	2			6	4			9							10	11							5	8				7																				
1	2	4		6	8										10	11		3						9		5		7																				
13	10	4	11	14	15	5		15	1		4	1	1	2	3	4	1	2		3	8		13	17		11	7	8															2	3	1	2	2	
				1	1	2		12								1					1			6			4	3																			2	

1942-43

North Regional League

Match No.	Date	Venue	Opponents	Result		Scorers	Attendance
1	Aug 29	H	Blackpool	L	1-3	Dellow	6,000
2	Sep 5	A	Blackpool	L	2-5	Dellow, Boothway	5,000
3	12	A	Wrexham	L	2-4	Boothway, Stuart	3,500
4	19	H	Wrexham	W	5-1	Malam 3, Currier, Hogan	4,000
5	26	H	Bolton W	W	2-0	Malam, Currier	4,000
6	Oct 3	A	Bolton W	L	1-2	Boothway	3,000
7	10	A	Crewe A	L	3-5	Bray, Bardsley, Stuart	3,000
8	17	H	Crewe A	W	5-1	Maslam 3, Boothway 2	4,000
9	24	H	Liverpool	L	1-4	Currier	6,500
10	31	A	Liverpool	L	1-3	Stuart	12,401
11	Nov 7	A	Manchester U	L	1-2	H. Clark	9,301
12	14	H	Manchester U	L	0-5		5,674
13	21	H	Chester	W	4-2	Walsh, Williamson, Currier, Jones	3,000
14	28	A	Chester	D	1-1	Currier	2,500
15	Dec 5	A	Tranmere R	W	3-1	P.Robinson, Pearson, Jones	1,000
16	12	H	Tranmere R	W	4-1	Jones, Currier 2, Williamson	2,500
17	19	H	Everton	W	7-1	King 2, Currier 2, Cox, Stuart, P.Robinson	3,000
18	25	A	Everton	L	3-6	King, Currier 2	10,000
							Appearances
							Goals

North Regional League (Second Championship)

Match No.	Date	Venue	Opponents	Result		Scorers	Attendance
19	Dec 26	A	Bolton W*	W	4-2	King, Currier, Doherty, opp. og	8,000
20	Jan 2	H	Bolton W*	W	2-0	Currier, Herd	3,000
21	9		Stockport C*	W	7-1	Herd 2, Welsh 2, Cox, Currier, Stuart	5,000
22	16		Stockport C*	W	5-2	Currier 3, Williamson 2	2,500
23	23		Bury*	W	3-2	Williamson 2, Currier	4,500
24	30		Bury	W	3-2	Currier 3	5,649
25	Feb 6		Manchester U*	D	0-0		17,577
26	13		Manchester U*	D	1-1	Herd	16,366
27	20		Liverpool*	L	2-4	King, Stuart	21,863
28	27		Liverpool*	W	3-1	Herd 2, opp. og	14,795
29	Mar 6		Manchester U**	W	1-0	Currier	28,962
30	13		Manchester U**	W	2-0	Currier, Doherty	36,453
31	20		Blackburn R**	L	0-2		15,623
32	27		Blackburn R**	W	4-0	Boothway 2, King, Currier	24,690
33	Apr 3		Blackpool **	L	1-3	Boothway	25,000
34	10		Blackpool **	D	1-1	Currier	53,205
35	17		Chesterfield	W	2-1	Boothway 2	2,700
36	24		Chesterfield	D	1-1	Boothway	3,000
37	26		Huddersfield T	D	1-1	Currier	4,000
							Appearances
							Goals

Note: City finished 30th in the First Championship and were third in the Second Championship.

* Matches also counted towards the League War Cup Qualifying Round.

** Matches also counted towards the League War Cup knock out section (two legged basis).

Robinson J	Clarke G	Eastwood	Walsh	Bray	Clarke H	Boothway	Stuart	Scales	Robinson P	Barkas	Doherty	McDowell	Jackson	Swift	Pearson	Bardsley	Westwood	Kenny	Pritchard	Herd	Grant	Currier	Malam	Charlesworth	Jones C	King	Dellow	Williamson	Cox	Welsh	Hogan	Setters	Taylor	Cardwell	Barclay	Paton	Bellis	Cassidy
1	2		4	6		9	11										3					10	8	5			7											
1	2	3	4	6		9	11															10	8	5			7											
1	2		4	6		9	11			3												10	8	5			7											
	2	3	4	6			11	1														9	8	5			7				10							
	2	3	4	6			11							1								9	8	5			7				10							
1	2	3	4	6	7	9	11															10	8	5														
1	2	3	4	6	7		11									10						9	8	5														
	2	3	4	6	7	9	11	1														10	8	5														
	2	3	4	6	7		11	1			10											9	8	5														
	2	3	4		7		11	1			10											9	8	5	6													
		2	4	6	7		11	1		3												9	8	5	10													
	2	3	4	6		9	11	1															8	5	10	7												
	2	5	6				11	1	4				3									9			10	7		8										
	2	5	6				11	1	4	3					10							9		8								7						
	2	5	6				11	1	4	3			7		8							9			10													
	2	5	4	6				1		3												9			10	7		8					11					
	2	5	6				11		4					1				3				9				7		8	10									
	2	3	8	6			11	1	4		10											9				7								5				
5	17	16	18	13	6	6	17	11	5	5	3		2	2	2	1	1	1				17	12	12	7	5	5	3	1		2	1	1	1				
			1	1	1	5	4		2						1	1						11	7		3	3	2	2	1		1							

Robinson J	Clarke G	Eastwood	Walsh	Bray	Clarke H	Boothway	Stuart	Scales	Robinson P	Barkas	Doherty	McDowell	Jackson	Swift	Pearson	Bardsley	Westwood	Kenny	Pritchard	Herd	Grant	Currier	Malam	Charlesworth	Jones C	King	Dellow	Williamson	Cox	Welsh	Hogan	Setters	Taylor	Cardwell	Barclay	Paton	Bellis	Cassidy
	2	4	6	3			11	1			10					8						9				7								5				
	2	5	4	6			11	1		3						8				10		9													7			
	2	5	6	3			11	1	4											8		9							7	10								
1	2	5	6				11		4	3										8		9						10	7									
1	2	5	4	6						3							11			8		9						10								7		
1	2	5		6			11		4								3			10	8	9							7									
1	2	5		6			11		4	3												9			10			8	7									
1		5	4	6			11			3			2							8		9						10	7									
1	2	5	4	6			11						3							10	8	9				7												
	2	5	6	3					4					1						10	8	9				7			11									
1	2	5	4	6						3										8		9				7		10	11									
1	2	5	6						4		10	3									11	9						8	7									
1	2	5	6						4	3	10										7	9						8							11			
	2	5	6	11		9			4	3		10		1								8				7												
	2	5	4	6		9				3	10			1							11	7						8										
	2	5	6							3		4		1						8		9				7		10									11	
1	2	5	6	11		9			4	3		10										8				7												
1	2	5	6			9	11		4		10	3										8				7												
1	2	5	6			9						4	3			8			11			10																7
12	18	19	17	13		5	9	3	10	11	5	6	3	4		3	2		1	10	6	19			1	8		9	8	1				1	2	1	1	1
						6	2				2									6		15				3		4	1	2								

1943-44

North Regional League

Match No.	Date	Venue	Opponents	Result		Scorers	Attendance
1	Aug 28	A	Liverpool	L	1-4	Percival	13,600
2	Sep 4	H	Liverpool	W	2-1	Williamson, Boothway	10,229
3	11	A	Blackpool	L	2-6	Boothway, Baker	10,000
4	18	H	Blackpool	L	1-2	Doherty	17,500
5	25	A	Bolton W	L	1-4	Williamson	2,500
6	Oct 2	H	Bolton W	W	4-0	McDowell, Barclay, Burke, Williamson	3,000
7	9	A	Wrexham	W	1-0	Burke	4,500
8	16	A	Wrexham	W	4-1	Doherty 2, Barclay, Leech	4,000
9	23	H	Crewe A	W	2-0	King 2	5,000
10	30	A	Crewe A	W	2-0	Doherty 2	4,000
11	Nov 6	H	Manchester U	D	2-2	Burke, Boothway	15,157
12	13	A	Manchester U	L	0-3		8,958
13	20	A	Chester	W	2-1	Boothway, Barclay	3,500
14	27	H	Chester	W	3-0	King, Williamson, Leech	3,000
15	Dec 4	H	Tranmere R	D	2-2	Doherty 2	3,700
16	11	A	Tranmere R	W	6-0	Doherty 3, Heale 2, King	3,000
17	18	A	Everton	L	0-4		10,000
18	25	H	Everton	L	3-5	Williamson, Doherty 2	16,468
							Appearances
							Goals

North Regional League (Second Championship)

Match No.	Date	Venue	Opponents	Result		Scorers	Attendance
19	Dec 26	A	Bury*	W	4-0	Williamson 2, Heale, Doherty	7,000
20	Jan 1	H	Bury*	L	1-7	Heale	6,000
21	8	H	Oldham A*	D	0-0		6,000
22	15	A	Oldham A*	D	1-1	Williamson	6,000
23	22	A	Manchester U*	W	3-1	Boothway 2, Heale	12,372
24	29	H	Manchester U*	L	2-3	Williamson, Heale	18,569
25	Feb 5	H	Stockport C*	W	4-0	Williamson 2, Heale, Doherty	6,000
26	12	A	Stockport C*	L	3-4	Heale 2, Boothway	5,500
27	19	A	Halifax T*	W	5-3	Williamson 2, Heale 2, Doherty	4,000
28	26	H	Halifax T*	W	4-0	Doherty 3, Heale	7,000
29	Mar 4	H	Blackburn R**	W	3-0	Williamson 3	13,897
30	11	A	Blackburn R**	L	2-4	Doherty 2 (aet, 90 min score was 0-3)	8,000
31	18	H	Liverpool**	D	1-1	Heale	27,792
32	25	A	Liverpool**	W	3-2	Heale 2, Herd (aet, 90 min score was 2-2)	41,498
33	Apr 1	H	Birmingham**	W	1-0	Herd	27,137
34	8	A	Birmingham**	D	0-0		40,000
35	10	H	Manchester U	W	4-1	McDowall 3, Bardsley	18,990
36	15	A	Blackpool***	D	1-1	Doherty	25,000
37	22	H	Blackpool***	L	1-2	Doherty	60,000
38	10	A	Bradford	L	0-5		5,000
39	15	H	Bradford	W	2-1	Bootle, Doherty	5,000
							Appearances
							Goals

Note: City finished 17th in the First Championship and were 19th in the Second Championship.

* Matches also counted towards the League War Cup Qualifying Round.

** Matches also counted towards the League War Cup knock-out section (two legged basis).

*** Also counted as the League War Cup semi-final

Match 8 should have been a Home fixture but was played at Wrexham as England played Scotland at Maine Road on that day.

For games featuring extra-time, the additional time determined the War Cup result while the 90 minute score counted for League results.

Swift FV	Clark G	Bray	Walsh	Eastwood	McDowall	Barclay	Bardsley	Boothway	Doherty	Jackson	Chappell	Heale	Taylor	Leech	Sproston	Scales	Percival	Brown	Bootle	Worrall	Westwood	Robinson J.	Clarke H.	Robinson P.	Herd	Cox	Williamson	King	Burke	Thomson	Dodd	Porter	Baker	Powell	Williams	Beattie	Butler	Nielson	Bentham	Iddon	Hanson	Chishom	Eastwood R.	Paton	Pearson	Poole	Grant	
1		3	4	5	6	7	8	9	10	11																		8			10																		
1		3	4	5	2	11		9	10																			8	7			6																	
		6	4	5		11		9		2						1												8	7				3	10																
1		3	4					9	10	2																			7				5		6	8	11													
1	2	6	4																									9	7									11	3	5	8	10									
1	2	3	4	5	6	7		11	10																		8		9																				
1	2	3	4	5	6	7		11	10																		8		9																				
	2	3	4	5	6	7	8	11	10		1			9																																				
1	2	3	4	5	6		8	9	10												11							7																					
	2	3	4	5	6		8	9	10												11							7																					
1	2		4	5	6		8	11	3											10								7	9																				
		3	4	5	6	7	2	11	10		1																8		9																				
1		3	4	5	6	7		9							2					10								8														11								
1	2	3	4	5		11	6		10					9													8	7																					
	2	3	4	5	6				10		1		11	9														7															8							
1			4	5	6	11	8		10	2		9															7																3						
1				5	6	7	10			2		9	11				4										8																	3						
1	2	3	4	5	6	7			10			9															8																			11					
13	10	15	17	16	14	12	8	12	12	6	4	3	2	3	1	1	2			2	2						10	11	4	1	1	2	1	1	1	1	1	1	1	1	1	1	2	1				
					1	3		4	12			2		2			1										5	4	3				1																
1	2	3	4	5	6	7			10			9	11														8																						
			4	3	5	7	6			2	1	9	11															8																		10			
1	2	3	6	5	10							9			8		4									7																				11				
1	2	3	4	5	6							9			8													10	7																		11				
1	2		4	5	6			11	10			9							7		3						8																						
1	2	3		5	6			11	10			9											7	4			8																						
1		3	4	5	6			11	10			9					2		7								8																						
			4	5	6			9		2	1	10	11						7								8																			3		
	2	3	4	5	6				10		1	9							7								8																				11	
1	2	3	4	5					10			9							7								8																				11	
1	2	3	4	5	6	11		7	10						8												9																						
	2	3	4	5	6			11	10						8	1											9																						
	2		6	5				11	10	3		9							7			1		4				8																					
1	2		4	5	6				10			9					3		7						8																								
	2	3	4	5	6			11				9				1									8		10	7																					
1	2	3	4	5	6				10			9														11	8	7																					
	2	3	4	9	10	11	8									1		6	7																												
1	2	3	4	5	6				10			9														11	8	7																					
	2	3	4	5	6				10			9										1				11	8	7																					
	2	3	4	5	10			9					11		8			6				1	7																									
1	2	3	4	5	6				10			9	11		8				7																												
12	18	16	20	21	19	4	2	9	14	3	3	17	5		6	3	3	2	9		1	3	2	2	2	4	14	7																	2	1	1	2	
					3		1	3	11			13								1						2		11																						

1944-45

North Regional League

Match No.	Date	Venue	Opponents	Result		Scorers	Attendance
1	Aug 26	H	Tranmere R	W	4-1	Smith 3, Heale	6,000
2	Sep 2	A	Tranmere R	W	4-0	Sproston, Heale, Smith, Taylor	3,000
3	9	A	Liverpool	D	2-2	Williamson, Smith	24,009
4	16	H	Liverpool	D	2-2	Sproston, Smith	14,000
5	23	A	Stockport C	W	6-2	Williamson 3, McDowall, King, Smith	8,000
6	30	H	Stockport C	W	5-1	Smith 2, McDowall, Heale, King	12,000
7	Oct 7	H	Crewe A	D	1-1	Heale	16,000
8	14	A	Crewe A	W	6-1	Heale 2, Bootle 2, Walsh, Taylor	9,000
9	21	A	Wrexham	D	1-1	Bootle	8,854
10	28	H	Wrexham	W	2-1	McDowall 2	7,000
11	Nov 4	H	Everton	L	1-3	Heale	30,000
12	11	A	Everton	L	1-4	Smith	14,000
13	18	A	Manchester U	L	2-3	Smith 2	20,764
14	25	H	Manchester U	W	4-0	Williamson 2, Smith, Doherty	18,657
15	Dec 2	H	Bury	W	4-0	King 2, Bootle, Williamson	5,000
16	9	A	Bury	L	1-2	King	4,579
17	16	A	Chester	L	1-7	Bray	4,500
18	23	H	Chester	W	6-0	Owen 2, Doherty 2, Bootle, Smith	14,000
							Appearances
							Goals

North Regional League (Second Championship)

Match No.	Date	Venue	Opponents	Result		Scorers	Attendance
19	Dec 26	H	Blackpool	D	1-1	Smith	13,600
20	30	H	Bury*	W	3-2	Smith 2, Owen	10,000
21	Jan 6	A	Halifax Town*	D	1-1	Owen	6,000
22	13	H	Halifax Town*	L	2-3	Owen, Smith	10,000
23	27	A	Oldham A*	W	4-3	Dunkley, Williamson, Owen, Smith	1,432
24	Feb 3	A	Manchester U*	W	3-1	Herd 2, Dunkley	25,655
25	10	H	Manchester U*	W	2-0	Williamson, Smith	22,923
26	17	A	Huddersfield T*	L	1-3	King	12,937
27	24	H	Huddersfield T*	W	2-0	King, Williamson	24,000
28	Mar 3	A	Bury*	L	2-4	Smith, Taylor	10,875
29	10	H	Oldham A*	W	3-2	Williamson 2, King	13,000
30	17	A	Stockport C**	L	1-4	Williamson	4,000
31	24	H	Crewe A***	W	5-1	Williamson 4, King	22,560
32	31	A	Crewe A***	L	0-2		6,300
33	Apr 2	H	Stockport C**	L	1-5	Smith	18,000
34	7	A	Liverpool***	L	0-3		36,131
35	14	H	Liverpool***	L	1-3	Herd	24,905
36	21	H	Blackpool	L	0-1		9,500
37	28	A	Blackpool	L	0-4		5,000
							Appearances
							Goals

Note: City finished 10th in the First Championship and were 47th in the Second Championship.

* Matches also counted towards the League War Cup Qualifying Round.

** Matches also counted towards the League War Cup knock-out section (two legged basis).

*** Also counted as the Lancashire Cup.

Swift FV	McMillan	Clark	Bray	Walsh	Eastwood	McDowall	Bootle	Heale JA	Smith	Taylor	Sproston	Doherty	Owen	Hodgson	Brown	Barber	Linaker	Rudd	Robinson J	Robinson P	Dunkley	Grant	Bardsley	Herd	Meiklem	Williamson	King	Thorpe	Roxburgh	Jones	Ollerenshaw	Emptage	Cardwell	Westwood	Williams	Breedon	Jackson	Baillie	Barkas
1		2	3	4	5	6	7	9	10	11																8													
1		2	3	4	5	6	7	9	10	11	8																												
	1	2	3	4	5	6	7	9	10	11																8													
	1	2	3	4	5	6	7		10	11	8															9													
1		2		4	5	6			8	11	3	10														9	7												
	1	2	3	4		5		9	10	11					6											8	7												
1		2	6	4		5		9	10	11	3															8	7												
			3	4	5	6	7	9	8	11		10							1												2								
	1	2	3	4	5	10	7	9	8	11					6																								
	1		3	4	5	6	7	9	10	11				2												8													
1		2	3	4	5	6		9	10	11																8	7												
	1	2	3	4	5	6	7		10	11																9	8												
1		2		4	5	6	7		10	11	3															9						8							
1		2	3	4	5	6	7		8	11		10														9													
1			3	4	5	6	7		10	11	2															9	8												
	1	2	3	4	5	6	11		10							7										9	8												
	1	2	10	4	5	6	7		8				9	3											11														
1		2	3	4	5	6	11		7			10	9													9													
9	8	15	16	18	16	18	14	9	18	15	6	4	2	2	2	1			1						1	14	7				1	1							
			1	1		4	5	7	14	2	2	3	2													7	5												

Swift FV	McMillan	Clark	Bray	Walsh	Eastwood	McDowall	Bootle	Heale JA	Smith	Taylor	Sproston	Doherty	Owen	Hodgson	Brown	Barber	Linaker	Rudd	Robinson J	Robinson P	Dunkley	Grant	Bardsley	Herd	Meiklem	Williamson	King	Thorpe	Roxburgh	Jones	Ollerenshaw	Emptage	Cardwell	Westwood	Williams	Breedon	Jackson	Baillie	Barkas
1			3	4		6	7		8	11	2	10	9																				5						
		2	3	4	5	6	7		10	11			9						1				8																
1		2	3	4	5	6			10	11			9									8					7												
1		2	3	4	5	6			10	11			9													8	7												
1		2	3	4	5	6	11		10				9								7					8													
		2		4	5	6	11					10									7			8		9			1					3					
1		2	3	4	5	6	11		10		8										7					9													
1		2	3	4	5	6	7		10	11			9														8												
		2	3	4	5	6			10	11											7					9	8		1										
		2	3	4	5	6			10	11									1				8			9	7												
		2		4	5	6			10												7	11				9	8		1						3				
				4	5	6			10								7					11				9									3	1	2	8	
		2	3	4	5				10											6	7	11				9	8			1									
1		2	3	4	5				10											6	7	11				9	8												
1			3	5					10	11				2	6	9	7			4							8												
1		2	3	4	5	6			10												7			8		9	11												
		3		4	5	6			10		2										7			8		9	11			1									
		2	3	4	5	6	11		8							9		10			7							1											
		2	6	4	5	10	7		8				9					11										1											3
9		16	15	19	17	16	8		18	8	3	2	7	1	1	2	2	2	2	3	10	5	2	3		12	11	2	3	2			1	1	2	1	1	1	1
									8	1			4								2			3		10	4												

1945-46

Football League North

Match No.	Date	Venue	Opponents	Result		Scorers	Attendance
1	Aug 25	H	Middlesbrough	W	2-1	Dunkley, Pearson	25,000
2	Sep 1	A	Middlesbrough	D	2-2	Smith 2	14,000
3	8	A	Stoke C	L	0-2		15,000
4	12	H	Sheffield W	L	1-5	Sproston	8,000
5	15	H	Stoke C	L	0-2		15,000
6	22	H	Grimsby T	L	0-2		20,000
7	29	A	Grimsby T	W	2-0	Hart, Constantine	13,000
8	Oct 6	A	Blackpool	L	4-5	Constantine 3, Dunkley	20,000
9	13	H	Blackpool	L	1-4	King	32,730
10	20	H	Liverpool	W	1-0	Constantine	23,034
11	27	A	Liverpool	W	5-0	Herd 2, Pearson 2, Smith	34,941
12	Nov 3	A	Bury	W	3-1	Walsh, Smith, Pearson	12,216
13	10	H	Bury	W	4-1	Smith 2, Woodroffe, Pearson	24,600
14	17	H	Blackburn R	W	4-2	Constantine 2, Dunkley, Smith	22,177
15	24	A	Blackburn R	D	0-0		9,000
16	Dec 1	A	Bradford	W	3-2	Constantine 2, Smith	14,012
17	8	H	Bradford	W	6-0	Herd 2, Constantine 2, Wild, Dunkley	18,525
18	15	A	Burnley	L	0-1		10,000
19	22	H	Burnley	L	1-2	Constantine	21,000
20	25	H	Newcastle U	W	4-3	Dunkley, Constantine, Pearson, Smith	29,000
21	26	A	Newcastle U	D	1-1	Smith	54,495
22	29	A	Sheffield W	D	1-1	Wild	20,000
23	Jan 1	H	Huddersfield T	W	3-2	Herd 2, Constantine	25,490
24	12	A	Chesterfield	W	1-0	Herd	10,000
25	19	H	Chesterfield	W	1-0	Constantine	24,245
26	Feb 2	A	Barnsley	L	0-2		20,128
27	9	A	Everton	L	1-4	Constantine	40,000
28	16	H	Everton	L	1-3	Constantine	35,000
29	23	H	Bolton W	W	1-0	Constantine	25,000
30	Mar 9	A	Preston NE	L	1-3	Herd	12,000
31	13	H	Barnsley	L	2-3	Constantine 2	6,662
32	16	H	Preston NE	W	3-0	Smith 2, Constantine	20,000
33	23	H	Leeds U	L	5-1	Constantine 2, Herd, Smith, Emptage	20,000
34	27	A	Bolton W	L	1-3	Gemmell	12,000
35	30	A	Leeds U	W	3-1	Herd 2, Constantine	10,000
36	Apr 6	A	Manchester U	W	4-1	Smith 4	62,144
37	13	H	Manchester U	L	1-3	Smith	50,440
	19	H	Sunderland	L	0-2		31,209
	20	A	Sheffield U	W	3-2	Woodroffe, Constantine, Smith	40,000
	22	A	Sunderland	L	0-4		27,650
	27	H	Sheffield U	W	2-1	Dunkley, Smith	19,241
38	May 4	A	Huddersfield T	L	0-3		8,781
							Appearances
							Goals

FA Cup

Match No.	Date	Venue	Opponents	Result		Scorers	Attendance
R3/1	Jan 5	H	Barrow	W	6-2	Herd 3, Constantine 3	19,589
R3/2	10	A	Barrow	D	2-2	Dunkley, Hart	7,377
R4/1	26	A	Bradford	W	3-1	Smith 2, Herd	25,014
R4/2	30	H	Bradford	L	2-8	Constantine, Smith	15,026
							Appearances
							Goals

Note: City finished 10th in the Football League North and the FA Cup was re-introduced on a two legged basis.

Swift FV	Clark	Sproston	Barkas	Walsh	Cardwell	McDowall	Dunkley	Herd	Constantine	Smith	Emptage	Williams	Eastwood	Woodroffe	Wild	Westwood	Bray	Fagan	Linaker	Hart	Walker	Taylor	Daniels	Robinson P	Hodgson	Brown	Pimbey	Gemmell	Pearson	Murray	Moore	King	Bootle	Hilton	Campbell	Toseland	Laing	Cunliffe	Thorpe	McCormack	Pritchard	Roxburgh	Wilson	Capel	Hope			
1	3	2		4		6	7			10			5									11							9			8																
1	3	2		4		6	7	8		10			5									11							9																			
1	3	2		4		6		8		10			5														9						7	11														
	3	2		4						10			5						7	8			1			6	9		11																			
	2	8	3	4		10				9			5						7				1			6									11													
1		2	3	4		5		8	9	10							6		7			11																										
1	3	2		4		6			9	10						11			7	8	5																											
1	3	2		4		6	7	8	9	10						11					5																											
	2	5		4		6	7	8	9	10							3						1									11																
1	2	5	3	4		6	7		9	10							6												11																			
1	2		3	4		6		8	9	10			5	7															11																			
1	2	5	3	4		6	7	8	9	10																			11																			
1		2	3	4		6		8	9	10				7											5				11																			
1		2	3	4		6	7	8	9	10															5				11																			
1		2	3	4	5	6			9	10										8																7	11											
1		2	3	4	5	6	7	8	9	10					11																																	
1	2		3	4	5	6	7	8	9	10					11																																	
1	2		3	4	5	6	7	8	9	10					11																																	
1	2		3	4	5	6	7		9	10																			11	8																		
1	2		3	4	5	6	7		9	10																			11	8																		
1	2		3	6		5	7		9	10										8									11	4																		
1	2		3	4	5	6	7	8	9	10					11																																	
1	2			6	5		7	8	9	10		3												4														11										
1	2		3	4	5	6	7	8	9	10					11																																	
	2		3	4	5	6	7	8	9	10							11																						1									
1	2		3	4		6		8		10			5	7															11											9								
1	2		3	4		6	7	8	9	10											5																				11							
1	2	5	3	4		6	7	8	9	10																			11																			
1	2	5	3	4		6		8	9	10	7																		11																			
1	2	5	3	4		6	7	8	9	10						11																																
1	2		3	4		6	7	8	9	10						11		5																														
1			3	4		6	7	8	9	10	11	2						5																														
1			3	4		6	7	8	9	10	11	2						5																														
1			3	4		6	7	8		10	11	2						5										9																				
1			3		5	6	7	8	9	10	11	2																		4																		
1			3	4	5	6	7	8	9	10	11	2																																				
			3	4	5	6	7	8	9	10	11	2																														1						
1			3	4	5	6			9	10	8	2		7																	11																	
1		2	3	4	5	6			9	10	8			7																	11																	
		2	3	4	5	6			9	10	8			7																	11												1					
		2	3	4	5	6	7	8	9	10	11																															1						
1		2				6	7				8		5			3								4				9																10	11			
35	26	22	33	40	17	40	29	29	34	41	12	8	8	6	5	5	4	4	4	4	3	3	3	2	2	2	2	2	14	4	3	2	1	1	1	1	1	1	1	1	1	2	1	1	1			
		1		1			6	11	25	20	1			2	2					1								1	6			1																
1	2		3	6	5			8	9	10														4									11								7							
1	2		3	4	5	6	7		9	10										8																		11										
1	2		3	4	5	6	7	8	9	10																															11							
1	2		3	4	5	6	7	8	9	10																															11							
4	4		4	4	4	3	3	3	4	4										1				1									1					1			3							
							1	4	4	3										1																												

1946-47

Division One

Manager: Wilf Wild (until 1 December 1946)/Sam Cowan (from 2 December 1946 – 30 June 1947)

Did you know that?

Match 5: J. Robinson's last game.
Match 6: Hodgson's last game.
Match 10: Cardwell's last game.
Match 14: Hope's last game.
Match 16: Percival and Rudd's last game.
Match 19: Eastwood's last game.
Match 20: P. Robinson's last game.
Match 33: Constantine's last game.
Match 34: Woodroffe's last game.
Match 41: Oakes and McCormack's first and only game.
Match 42: Barkas and Dunkley's last game.

City's 22 League match unbeaten run from 16 November to 19 April matched the record set in 1936–37.

The final game remains the latest finish to the season and is also noteworthy for the debut of Roy Clarke, and the five goals scored by George Smith. Clarke is the only City man to make his League debut in June.

Match No.	Date	Venue	Opponents	Result		Scorers	Attendance
1	Aug 31	A	Leicester City	W	3-0	Jackson, McDowall, Walsh	28,017
2	Sep 4	H	Bury	W	3-1	Black, Dunkley, Smith	33,814
3	7	H	Chesterfield	D	0-0		49,046
4	14	A	Millwall	W	3-1	Constantine 3	24,182
5	18	A	Bury	D	2-2	Herd 2	10,724
6	21	H	Bradford Park Avenue	W	7-2	Black 3, Smith 2, Constantine, Sproston	40,087
7	28	A	Tottenham Hotspur	D	0-0		55,253
8	Oct 5	A	West Ham United	L	0-1		33,007
9	12	H	Sheffield Wednesday	W	2-1	Constantine, Herd	38,099
10	19	H	Swansea Town	D	1-1	Sproston	36,184
11	26	A	Newcastle United	L	2-3	Black, Westwood	65,798
12	Nov 2	H	West Bromwich Albion	W	5-0	Black 3, Dunkley, Herd	40,611
13	9	A	Birmingham City	L	1-3	Smith	37,747
14	16	H	Coventry City	W	1-0	Dunkley	27,359
15	23	A	Nottingham Forest	W	1-0	Smith	32,194
16	30	H	Southampton	D	1-1	Constantine	26,657
17	Dec 7	A	Newport County	W	3-0	Black, Constantine, Dunkley	13,641
18	14	H	Barnsley	W	5-1	Constantine 2, Smith 2, Charlesworth (og)	24,000
19	21	A	Burnley	D	0-0		31,210
20	25	H	Plymouth Argyle	W	4-3	Smith 2, Constantine, Herd	26,323
21	26	A	Plymouth Argyle	W	3-2	Constantine, Smith, Jones (og)	28,617
22	28	H	Leicester City	W	1-0	Constantine	45,709
23	Jan 1	H	Fulham	W	4-0	Black 2, Herd 2	49,449
24	4	A	Chesterfield	W	1-0	Jackson	21,079
25	18	H	Millwall	W	1-0	Capel	38,426
26	Feb 1	H	Tottenham Hotspur	W	1-0	Westwood	41,645
27	22	A	Swansea Town	W	2-1	Herd, Smith	22,497
28	Mar 1	A	Fulham	D	2-2	Herd, Smith	32,120
29	15	H	Birmingham City	W	1-0	Smith	55,655
30	22	A	Coventry City	D	1-1	Herd	26,579
31	29	H	Nottingham Forest	W	2-1	Smith, Wharton	24,763
32	Apr 4	H	Luton Town	W	2-0	Smith, Woodroffe	53,692
33	5	A	Southampton	W	1-0	Smith	24,197
34	7	A	Luton Town	D	0-0		22,976
35	19	A	Barnsley	W	2-0	Black, McDowall	26,346
36	May 3	H	Newcastle United	L	0-2		44,763
37	10	H	Burnley	W	1-0	Herd	69,463
38	14	A	Bradford Park Avenue	D	1-1	Smith	15,162
39	24	H	West Ham United	W	2-0	McDowall, Smith	33,771
40	26	A	Sheffield Wednesday	L	0-1		33,412
41	31	A	West Bromwich Albion	L	1-3	Black	19,168
42	Jun 14	H	Newport County	W	5-1	Smith 5	25,431
							Appearances
						Two own goals	Goals

FA Cup

R3	Jan 11	H	Gateshead	W	3-0	Capel, Jackson, Westwood	38575
R4	25	A	Bolton Wanderers	D	3-3	Black 2, Capel	41286
rep	29	H	Bolton Wanderers	W	1-0	Westwood	39355
R5	Feb 8	A	Birmingham City	L	0-5		50000
							Appearances
							Goals

Swift FV	Sproston B	Barkas S	Percival J	McDowall LJ	Walsh W	Dunkley MEF	Herd A	Jackson H	Black A	Smith GB	Hope JG	Woodroffe LC	Constantine J	Robinson JJ	Cardwell L	Hodgson R	Thurlow ACE	Westwood E	Eastwood E	Emptage AT	Rudd JJ	Robinson P	Fagan JF	Williams E	Capel TA	Wharton JE	Murray WJ	Rigby J	Oakes T	McCormack M	Clarke RJ
1	2	3	4	5	6	7	8	9	10	11																					
1	2	3	4	5	6	7	8	9	10	11																					
1	2	3	4	5	6	7		9	10	8	11																				
1	2	3	4	5	6		8	11	10			7	9																		
	2	3	4	6			8	11	10			7	9	1	5																
1	2	3	4		6				8	10	11	7	9			5															
	2	3	4	5	6				8	10	11	7	9				1														
1	2	3	4	5	6				8	10	11	7	9																		
1	2	3	4	5	6	7	8			10			9					11													
1	2	3	4		6	7	8		10				9		5			11													
1	2	3	4		6	7	8		9	10								11	5												
1	2		4			7	8		9	10	11							3	5	6											
1	2		4	6		7	8		9	10	11							3	5												
1	2		4	6		7			10		11		9					3	5	8											
1	2		4			7			8	10			9					3	5	6	11										
1	2		4			7			8	10			9					3	5	6	11										
1	2	3		6		7			8	10			9					11	5	4											
1	2	3		6		7	8			10			9					11	5	4											
1	2	3		6		7	8			10			9					11	5	4											
1	2	3		5			8			10		7	9					11		4		6									
1	2	3		5	6	7	8			10			9					11		4											
1	2	3		5	6	7	8			10			9					11		4											
1	2	3		5		7	8		9	10								11		6			4								
1		3		5		7		9		8								11		6			4	2	10						
1		3		5		7			9	8								11		6			4	2	10						
1	2	3		5		7			9	8								11		6			4		10						
1	2	3		5		7	8		9	10										6			4		11						
1	2	3		5		7	8		9	10										6			4		11						
1	2			5		7	8		9	10								11		6			4	3							
1	2	3		5		7	8		9	10										6			4			11					
1	2	3		5		7	8		9	10										6			4			11					
1	2	3		5					8	10		7	9							6			4			11					
1	2	3		5					8	10		7	9					11		6			4								
1	2	3		5					9	10		7						11		6			4				8				
1	2			5		7	8		9	10								11		6			4	3							
	2					7	8	9		10							1	11		6			4	3				5			
	2	3		5		7	8		9	10							1	11		6			4								
		3		5		7	8		9	10							1	11		6			4	2							
	2	3		5		7	8		9	10							1	11		6			4								
	2	3		5		7	8		9	10							1	11		6			4								
1				5			8		9	10								3		6			4	2					7	11	
1	2	3		5	6	7	8		9	10													4								11
35	38	33	16	35	13	32	28	7	34	38	7	9	18	1	2	1	6	28	9	29	2	1	20	7	5	3	1	1	1	1	1
	2			3	1	4	11	2	13	23		1	12					2							1	1					

Swift FV	Sproston B	Barkas S	Percival J	McDowall LJ	Walsh W	Dunkley MEF	Herd A	Jackson H	Black A	Smith GB	Hope JG	Woodroffe LC	Constantine J	Robinson JJ	Cardwell L	Hodgson R	Thurlow ACE	Westwood E	Eastwood E	Emptage AT	Rudd JJ	Robinson P	Fagan JF	Williams E	Capel TA	Wharton JE	Murray WJ	Rigby J	Oakes T	McCormack M	Clarke RJ
1	2	3		5		7		9		8								11		6			4		10						
1		3		5		7			9	8								11		6			4	2	10						
1		3		5		7			9	8								11		6			4	2	10						
1	2	3		5		7			9	8								11		6			4		10						
4	2	4		4		4		1	3	4								4		4			4	2	4						
								1	2									2							2						

League Table

	P	W	D	L	F	A	Pts
Manchester C	42	26	10	6	78	35	62
Burnley	42	22	14	6	65	29	58
Birmingham C	42	25	5	12	74	33	55
Chesterfield	42	18	14	10	58	44	50
Newcastle U	42	19	10	13	95	62	48
Tottenham H	42	17	14	11	65	53	48
W.B.A.	42	20	8	14	88	75	48
Coventry C	42	16	13	13	66	59	45
Leicester C	42	18	7	17	69	64	43
Barnsley	42	17	8	17	84	86	42
Nottingham F	42	15	10	17	69	74	40
West Ham U	42	16	8	18	70	76	40
Luton T	42	16	7	19	71	73	39
Southampton	42	15	9	18	69	76	39
Fulham	42	15	9	18	63	74	39
Bradford P.A.	42	14	11	17	65	77	39
Bury	42	12	12	18	80	78	36
Millwall	42	14	8	20	56	79	36
Plymouth A	42	14	5	23	79	96	33
Sheffield W	42	12	8	22	67	88	32
Swansea T	42	11	7	24	55	83	29
Newport Co	42	10	3	29	61	133	23

1947-48

Division One

Manager: Jock Thomson (from October 1947)

Did you know that?

Match 11: Capel's last game.
Match 16: Jackson's last game.
Match 30: Herd's last game.
Match 41: Oxford's first and only game.
Match 42: Wharton's last game.

Both Manchester derbies were played at Maine Road and both were watched by crowds in excess of 70,000. This is the only season when both fixtures had crowds above 70,000. The City home match remains the highest Manchester derby crowd of all time.

Match No.	Date	Venue	Opponents	Result		Scorers	Attendance
1	Aug 23	H	Wolverhampton W.	W	4-3	Black, Clarke, McMorran, Smith	65,809
2	27	A	Everton	L	0-1		53,622
3	30	A	Aston Villa	D	1-1	Clarke	50,614
4	Sep 3	H	Everton	L	0-1		46,462
5	6	H	Sunderland	W	3-0	Black, Clarke, McMorran	55,172
6	10	A	Derby County	D	0-0		31,275
7	13	A	Grimsby Town	L	0-1		16,766
8	17	H	Derby County	W	3-2	Capel, McMorran, Smith	38,481
9	20	H	Manchester United	D	0-0		71,364
10	27	H	Blackburn Rovers	L	1-3	Smith	47,544
11	Oct 4	A	Blackpool	D	1-1	Wharton	30,930
12	11	A	Preston North End	L	1-2	Black	35,947
13	18	H	Stoke City	W	3-0	Smith 2, Herd	45,017
14	25	A	Burnley	D	1-1	Fagan	41,454
15	Nov 1	H	Portsmouth	W	1-0	Smith	49,894
16	8	A	Middlesbrough	L	1-2	Black	36,548
17	15	H	Charlton Athletic	W	4-0	Black 3, McMorran	40,706
18	22	A	Bolton Wanderers	L	1-2	Linacre	28,883
19	29	H	Liverpool	W	2-0	McMorran, Smith	40,093
20	Dec 6	A	Arsenal	D	1-1	Black	41,274
21	13	H	Sheffield United	W	4-3	Smith 2, Black, McMorran	29,654
22	20	A	Wolverhampton W.	L	0-1		32,545
23	26	H	Huddersfield Town	D	1-1	Linacre	59,060
24	27	A	Huddersfield Town	D	1-1	Black	32,634
25	Jan 3	H	Aston Villa	L	0-2		52,689
26	17	A	Sunderland	W	1-0	Black	36,958
27	31	H	Grimsby Town	W	3-1	McMorran 2, Smith	36,971
28	Feb 14	A	Blackburn Rovers	L	0-1		30,975
29	21	H	Blackpool	W	1-0	Smith	31,445
30	Mar 6	A	Stoke City	L	0-3		30,326
31	13	H	Burnley	W	4-1	Clarke 2, Smith 2	32,213
32	20	A	Portsmouth	L	0-1		29,459
33	26	A	Chelsea	D	2-2	Black, Linacre	64,396
34	27	H	Middlesbrough	W	2-0	Black, McMorran	42,297
35	29	H	Chelsea	W	1-0	Black	31,643
36	Apr 3	A	Charlton Athletic	W	1-0	McMorran	34,792
37	7	A	Manchester United	D	1-1	Linacre	73,114
38	10	H	Bolton Wanderers	L	0-2		36,409
39	17	A	Liverpool	D	1-1	Black	39,348
40	21	H	Preston North End	L	0-3		20,902
41	24	H	Arsenal	D	0-0		23,391
42	May 1	A	Sheffield United	L	1-2	Black	16,938
							Appearances
							Goals

FA Cup

	Date	Venue	Opponents	Result		Scorers	Attendance
R3	Jan 10	H	Barnsley	W	2-1	Black, Smith	54,747
R4	24	H	Chelsea	W	2-0e	Linacre, Smith	45,059
R5	Feb 7	H	Preston North End	L	0-1		67,494
							Appearances
							Goals

Swift FV	Sproston B	Westwood E	Fagan JF	McDowall LJ	Emptage AT	Wharton JE	Black A	McMorran EJ	Smith GB	Clarke RJ	Walsh W	Capel TA	Thurlow ACE	Williams E	Herd A	Linacre W	Jackson H	Munro JF	Murray WJ	Hart JP	Oxford K
1	2	3	4	5	6	7	8	9	10	11											
1	2	3	4	5	6	7	8	9	10	11											
1	2	3	4	5	6	7	8	9	10	11											
1	2	3	4	5	6	7	8	9	10	11											
1	2	3	4	5	6	7	8	9	10	11											
1	2	3	4	5	6	7	8	9	10	11											
1	2	3	4	5	6	7	8	9	10	11											
1	2	3	5		6	7		9	8	11	4	10									
	2	3	5		6	7		9	8	11	4	10	1								
1	2	3	5		6	7		9	8	11	4	10									
1	2	3	4	5	6	11	8		10	7		9									
1		3	5		6	7	8	9	10	11	4			2							
	2	3	5		6	7	9		10	11	4		1		8						
1	2	3	5		6	11	9		10		4				8	7					
1	2	3	5		6		9		10	11	4				8	7					
1		3	5		6		8		10	11	4			2		7	9				
1		3	5		6	11	8	9	10		4			2		7					
1		3	5		6	11	8	9	10		4			2		7					
		3	4	5	6		8	9	10	11			1	2		7					
1	2	3	4	5	6		8	9	10	11						7					
1	2	3	4	5	6		8	9	10	11						7					
1	2	3	4	5	6		8	9	10	11						7					
1	2	3	5		6		8	9	10	11	4					7					
1	2	3	5		6		8	9	10	11	4					7					
1	2	3	5		6	11	8	9	10		4					7					
1	2	3	5		6	11	8	9	10		4					7					
	2	3	5		6	11	8	9	10		4		1			7					
1	2	3	4	5			9		10	11	6					7		8			
1	2	3	9	5	6				10	11	4					7			8		
1	2	3	5		6		8		10	11	4				9	7					
1	2	3	4	5	8		9		10	11	6					7					
1	2	3	4	5	8		9		10	11	6					7					
1	2	3	5		4		9		10	11	6					7		8			
1	2	3	5		4		8	9	10	11	6					7					
1	2	3	5		4		8	9	10	11	6					7					
1	2	3	5		8		10	9		11	6							7	4		
	2	3	5		10		8			11	6		1			9		7	4		
	2	3	5		10			9		11	6		1					7	4	8	
	2	3	5				8	9	10	11	6		1			7			4		
	2	3	5				8	9	10	11	6		1			7			4		
	2	3	5		6		8	9	10	11	4					7					1
1	2	3	5		6	7	8		10	11	4					9					
33	37	42	42	16	39	20	37	29	39	36	30	4	8	5	4	27	1	5	6	1	1
			1			1	16	10	13	5		1			1	4					

Swift FV	Sproston B	Westwood E	Fagan JF	McDowall LJ	Emptage AT	Wharton JE	Black A	McMorran EJ	Smith GB	Clarke RJ	Walsh W	Capel TA	Thurlow ACE	Williams E	Herd A	Linacre W	Jackson H	Munro JF	Murray WJ	Hart JP	Oxford K
1	2	3	5		6	11	8	9	10		4					7					
1	2	3	5		6	11	8	9	10		4					7					
1	2	3	5		6	11	8	9	10		4					7					
3	3	3	3		3	3	3	3	3		3					3					
							1		2							1					

League Table

	P	W	D	L	F	A	Pts
Arsenal	42	23	13	6	81	32	59
Manchester U	42	19	14	9	81	48	52
Burnley	42	20	12	10	56	43	52
Derby Co	42	19	12	11	77	57	50
Wolverhampton W	42	19	9	14	83	70	47
Aston Villa	42	19	9	14	65	57	47
Preston N.E.	42	20	7	15	67	68	47
Portsmouth	42	19	7	16	68	50	45
Blackpool	42	17	10	15	57	41	44
Manchester C	42	15	12	15	52	47	42
Liverpool	42	16	10	16	65	61	42
Sheffield U	42	16	10	16	65	70	42
Charlton A	42	17	6	19	57	66	40
Everton	42	17	6	19	52	66	40
Stoke C	42	14	10	18	41	55	38
Middlesbrough	42	14	9	19	71	73	37
Bolton W	42	16	5	21	46	58	37
Chelsea	42	14	9	19	53	71	37
Huddersfield T	42	12	12	18	51	60	36
Sunderland	42	13	10	19	56	67	36
Blackburn R	42	11	10	21	54	72	32
Grimsby T	42	8	6	28	45	111	22

1948-49

Division One

Manager: Jock Thomson

Did you know that?

Match 9: McMorran's last game.
Match 16: McDowall's last game.
Match 32: Greenwood's first and only game.
Match 36: Thurlow's last game.
Match 38: Godwin's last game.
Match 42: Hogan's last game.

The away game at Huddersfield became noted for its celebration of Frank Swift's career. This was scheduled to be Swift's last game and the player was given a triumphal parade by the supporters' club all the way back across the Pennines. Swift travelled with fans in the lead coach, while most of the vehicles were dressed with buntings, photos of Swift and colourful banners. No player had ever been given such a send-off before. Ironically, due to various issues Swift was asked to play a few games again the following season, so the great send-off was a little premature.

Match No.	Date	Venue	Opponents	Result		Scorers	Attendance
1	Aug 21	A	Burnley	L	0-1		33,621
2	25	H	Preston North End	W	3-2	McDowall, McMorran, Sproston	39,024
3	28	H	Stoke City	D	0-0		45,570
4	Sep 1	A	Preston North End	W	3-1	Black, Godwin, Linacre	38,700
5	4	A	Charlton Athletic	L	2-3	Godwin 2	43,756
6	8	H	Birmingham City	W	1-0	Black	29,956
7	11	H	Manchester United	D	0-0		67,616
8	15	A	Birmingham City	L	1-4	Smith	35,593
9	18	H	Portsmouth	D	1-1	McMorran	51,490
10	25	A	Newcastle United	D	0-0		49,729
11	Oct 2	H	Middlesbrough	W	1-0	Oakes	45,146
12	9	A	Sheffield United	W	2-0	Black, Oakes	27,668
13	16	H	Aston Villa	W	4-1	Smith 3, Oakes	41,240
14	23	A	Sunderland	L	0-3		46,979
15	30	H	Wolverhampton W.	D	3-3	Black, Linacre, Oakes	47,246
16	Nov 6	A	Bolton Wanderers	L	1-5	Smith	40,089
17	13	H	Liverpool	L	2-4	Black, Clarke	24,775
18	20	A	Blackpool	D	1-1	Smith	22,412
19	27	H	Derby County	W	2-1	Black, Clarke	45,341
20	Dec 4	A	Arsenal	D	1-1	Oakes	48,960
21	11	H	Huddersfield Town	W	3-1	Clarke 2, Emptage	34,833
22	18	H	Burnley	D	2-2	Smith, Attwell (og)	26,849
23	25	A	Everton	D	0-0		37,444
24	27	H	Everton	D	0-0		40,471
25	Jan 1	A	Stoke City	W	3-2	Smith 2, Clarke	27,616
26	15	H	Charlton Athletic	L	0-1		23,209
27	22	A	Manchester United	D	0-0		69,191
28	Feb 5	A	Portsmouth	L	1-3	Smith	34,949
29	19	H	Newcastle United	W	1-0	Black	51,740
30	26	A	Middlesbrough	W	1-0	Black	37,073
31	Mar 5	H	Sheffield United	W	1-0	Black	19,618
32	12	A	Aston Villa	L	0-1		41,952
33	19	H	Blackpool	D	1-1	Hart	38,973
34	26	A	Derby County	L	0-2		29,068
35	Apr 2	H	Bolton Wanderers	W	1-0	Black	27,241
36	9	A	Liverpool	W	1-0	Smith	31,389
37	15	H	Chelsea	W	1-0	Smith	36,554
38	16	H	Sunderland	D	1-1	Clarke	34,461
39	18	A	Chelsea	D	1-1	Munro	25,864
40	23	A	Wolverhampton W.	D	1-1	Black	51,789
41	27	H	Arsenal	L	0-3		41,321
42	May 7	A	Huddersfield Town	L	0-1		27,507
							Appearances
						One own goal	Goals

FA Cup

R3	Jan 8	A	Everton	L	0-1		63,459
							Appearances

Swift FV	Sproston B	Westwood E	Fagan JF	McDowall LJ	Walsh W	Linacre W	Black A	McMorran EJ	Smith GB	Clarke RJ	Oakes J	Godwin V	Williams E	Thurlow ACE	Emptage AT	Hart JP	Bootle W	Greenwood JJ	Munro JF	Phillips E	Gill R	Hogan WJJ	Jones WJB
1	2	3	4	5	6	7	8	9	10	11													
1	2	3	4	5	6	7	8	9	10	11													
1	2	3	4	5	6	9	8		10	11	7												
1	2	3	4	5	6	10	8			11	7	9											
1		3	4	5	6	10	8			11	7	9	2										
1		3	4	5	6	10	8			11	7	9	2										
1		3	4	5	6	10	8			11	7	9	2										
	2	3	4	5	6	10		9	8	11	7			1									
1	2	3	4	5	6	10		9	8	11	7												
	2	3	4	5	6	7	8		10	11		9		1									
1	2	3	4	5	6	10	8			11	7	9											
	2	3	4	5		10	8		9	11	7			1	6								
1	2	3	4	5	6	10	8		9	11	7												
1		3	4	5	6	10	8		9	11	7		2										
1		3	4	5	6	10	8		9	11	7		2										
1	2	3	4	5	6	10	8		9	11	7												
		3	5		4	10	8		9	11	7		2	1	6								
		3	5		4	10	8		9	11	7		2	1	6								
1		3	5		4	10	8		9	11	7		2		6								
1		3	5		4	10	8		9	11	7		2		6								
1		3	5		4	10	8		9	11	7		2		6								
1		3	5		4	10	8		9	11	7		2		6								
1		3	5		4	10			9	11	7		2		6	8							
1		3	5		4	10			9	11	7		2		6	8							
		3	5		4	10			9	11	7		2	1	6	8							
1		3	5		4	7	10		9	11			2		6	8							
1	2	3	5		4	7	9		10	11					6	8							
1	2	3	5		4	10			9	11	7				6	8							
1	2	3	5		4		10		9		7				6	8	11						
1	2	3	5		4	11	10		9		7				6	8							
1	2	3	5		4	11	10		9		7				6	8							
1	2	3	5			11	10		9		7				6	8		4					
1	2	3	5		4		10		9		7				6	8	11						
1	2	3	5		4	7	10		9		11				6	8							
1	2	3	5		4	7	8		10		11	9			6								
	2	3	5		4	7	10		9		11			1	6				8				
1	2	3	5		4	10	8		9	11	7				6								
1		3	5		4	10				11	7	9			6				8	2			
1		3	5		4	10	9			11	7				6				8	2			
1	2	3	5			10	8			11					6						4	7	9
1	2	3	5		4	10	8			11					6							7	9
1	2	3	5		4	10	8			11					6					9		7	
35	25	42	42	16	39	40	35	4	32	34	34	8	15	7	27	12	2	1	3	3	1	3	2
	1			1		2	11	2	12	6	5	3			1	1			1				

Swift FV	Sproston B	Westwood E	Fagan JF	McDowall LJ	Walsh W	Linacre W	Black A	McMorran EJ	Smith GB	Clarke RJ	Oakes J	Godwin V	Williams E	Thurlow ACE	Emptage AT	Hart JP	Bootle W	Greenwood JJ	Munro JF	Phillips E	Gill R	Hogan WJJ	Jones WJB
1		3	5		4	10			9	11	7		2		6	8							
1		1	1		1	1			1	1	1		1		1	1							

League Table

	P	W	D	L	F	A	Pts
Portsmouth	42	25	8	9	84	42	58
Manchester U	42	21	11	10	77	44	53
Derby Co	42	22	9	11	74	55	53
Newcastle U	42	20	12	10	70	56	52
Arsenal	42	18	13	11	74	44	49
Wolverhampton W	42	17	12	13	79	66	46
Manchester C	42	15	15	12	47	51	45
Sunderland	42	13	17	12	49	58	43
Charlton A	42	15	12	15	63	67	42
Aston Villa	42	16	10	16	60	76	42
Stoke C	42	16	9	17	66	68	41
Liverpool	42	13	14	15	53	43	40
Chelsea	42	12	14	16	69	68	38
Bolton W	42	14	10	18	59	68	38
Burnley	42	12	14	16	43	50	38
Blackpool	42	11	16	15	54	67	38
Birmingham C	42	11	15	16	36	38	37
Everton	42	13	11	18	41	63	37
Middlesbrough	42	11	12	19	46	57	34
Huddersfield T	42	12	10	20	40	69	34
Preston N.E.	42	11	11	20	62	75	33
Sheffield U	42	11	11	20	57	78	33

1949-50

Division One

Manager: Jock Thomson (until February 1950)

Did you know that?

Match 6: Swift's last game.
Match 8: Linacre's last game.
Match 16: Powell's last League game.
Match 23: Murray and Bootle's last game.
Match 27: Sproston's last game.
Match 28: Jones's last game.
Match 29: Munro's last game.
Match 34: Walsh's last game.
Match 35: Gill's last game.
Match 38: Black's last game.
Match 39: Williams's last game.

Prior to the final match City were one point behind Charlton with an outside chance of survival, but a crushing 3–1 defeat by an Everton side that was already safe guaranteed City's relegation. Charlton beat Derby 2–1 in any case.

Match No.	Date	Venue	Opponents	Result		Scorers	Attendance
1	Aug 20	H	Aston Villa	D	3-3	Smith 2, Black	43,196
2	24	A	Portsmouth	D	1-1	Munro	43,965
3	27	A	Charlton Athletic	L	1-3	Fagan	31,048
4	31	H	Portsmouth	W	1-0	Smith	32,732
5	Sep 3	A	Manchester United	L	1-2	Munro	51,108
6	7	H	Everton	D	0-0		27,331
7	10	H	Fulham	W	2-0	Clarke, Turnbull	42,308
8	17	A	Newcastle United	L	2-4	Clarke, Turnbull	58,412
9	24	H	Blackpool	L	0-3		57,931
10	Oct 1	A	Middlesbrough	D	0-0		38,515
11	8	A	Chelsea	L	0-3		45,153
12	15	H	Stoke City	D	1-1	Munro	31,267
13	22	A	Burnley	D	0-0		25,063
14	29	H	Sunderland	W	2-1	Murray, Turnbull	37,182
15	Nov 5	A	Liverpool	L	0-4		50,536
16	12	H	Arsenal	L	0-2		28,404
17	19	A	Bolton Wanderers	L	0-3		35,376
18	26	H	Birmingham City	W	4-0	Black 2, Clarke 2	30,617
19	Dec 3	A	Derby County	L	0-7		23,681
20	10	H	West Bromwich Albion	D	1-1	Black	29,660
21	17	A	Aston Villa	L	0-1		27,622
22	24	H	Charlton Athletic	W	2-0	Black, Clarke	32,208
23	26	A	Huddersfield Town	L	0-1		29,989
24	27	H	Huddersfield Town	L	1-2	Clarke	50,195
25	31	H	Manchester United	L	1-2	Black	63,593
26	Jan 14	A	Fulham	L	0-1		29,283
27	21	H	Newcastle United	D	1-1	Clarke	43,102
28	Feb 4	A	Blackpool	D	0-0		23,780
29	18	H	Middlesbrough	L	0-1		59,714
30	25	H	Chelsea	D	1-1	Hart	29,950
31	Mar 4	A	Stoke City	L	0-2		28,647
32	11	H	Bolton Wanderers	D	1-1	Black (p)	43,764
33	18	A	Birmingham City	L	0-1		29,967
34	29	H	Liverpool	L	1-2	Alison	22,661
35	Apr 1	A	Arsenal	L	1-4	Hart	39,420
36	8	H	Burnley	W	1-0	Westcott	31,298
37	10	H	Wolverhampton W.	W	2-1	Smith, Turnbull	36,839
38	11	A	Wolverhampton W.	L	0-3		44,735
39	15	A	Sunderland	W	2-1	Clarke, Oakes	40,404
40	22	H	Derby County	D	2-2	Smith 2	53,044
41	29	A	West Bromwich Albion	D	0-0		16,780
42	May 6	A	Everton	L	1-3	Clarke	29,627
							Appearances
							Goals

FA Cup

R3	Jan 7	H	Derby County	L	3-5	Black 2, Clarke	53,213
							Appearances
							Goals

Swift FV	Sproston B	Westwood E	Walsh W	Fagan JF	Emptage AT	Linacre W	Munro JF	Smith GB	Black A	Clarke RJ	Powell RWH	Williams E	Oakes J	Murray W	Turnbull RW	Phillips E	Cunliffe RA	Trautmann BC	Rigby J	Gill R	Bootle W	Alison J	Spurdle W	Hart JP	Jones WJL	Westcott D	Williamson J
1	2	3	4	5	6	7	8	9	10	11																	
		3	4	5	6	7	8	9	10	11	1	2															
		3	4	5	6	7	8	9	10	11	1	2															
1		3	4	5	6	7	8	9	10	11		2															
1		3	4	5	6	7	8	9	10			2	11														
1		3	4	5		7	8	9	10			2	11	6													
		3	4	5		10			8	11	1	2	7	6	9												
		3	4	5		10			8	11	1	2	7	6	9												
		3	4	5			8		10	11	1	2	7	6	9												
	2	3	4	5			8		10	11	1		7	6	9												
		3	4	5			8	10		11	1	2	7	6	9												
		3	4	5	6		8		10	11	1		7		9	2											
		3	4	5	6		8		10	11	1		7		9	2											
		3	4	5	6				10		1		7	8	9	2	11										
		3	4	5	6				10		1		7	8	9	2	11										
		3	4	5	6				10	11	1		7	8	9	2											
		3	4	5			7		8	10			11	6	9	2		1									
	2	11	6						8	10			7	4	9	3		1	5								
	2	11	6	5					8	10			7	4	9	3		1									
		3			6				8	10					9	2		1	5	4	7	11					
		3		4	6				8	10					9	2		1	5		7	11					
		3			6		8		10	11			7		9	2		1	5	4							
		3		4					10	11				6	9	2		1	5		7	8					
		3		4	8		7		9	11						2		1	5	6		10					
		3	6	5			7		8	11					9	2		1		4		10					
		3	6	5			7		8				11		9	2		1		4		10					
	2	3	6	5	10				8	11			7		9			1		4							
		3	6	5					10	11			7			2		1					4	8	9		
		3	4	5	6		7		10	11						2		1					8			9	
		3	6	5					10	11					7	2		1					4	8		9	
		3	6	5					10	11					7	2		1					4	8		9	
		3		5	6				8	11					7	2		1				10	4			9	
		3		5	6					11					8	2		1				7	4	10		9	
		3	4	5	6			10	8	11						2		1				7				9	
		3		5	6					11					9	2		1		4		7		10			8
		3		5	6			10		11					7	2		1					4	8		9	
		3		5	6			10		11					7	2		1					4	8		9	
				5	6			10	8	11		3			7	2		1					4			9	
				5	6			10		11		3	7			2		1					4			9	8
		3		5	6			10		11			7			2		1					4			9	8
		3		5	6			10		11			7			2		1					4	8		9	
		3		5	6			10		11					7	2		1					4	8		9	
4	5	40	27	39	27	8	17	15	33	37	12	11	22	13	29	30	2	26	6	7	3	10	13	9	1	13	3
				1			3	6	7	9			1	1	4							1		2		1	

Swift FV	Sproston B	Westwood E	Walsh W	Fagan JF	Emptage AT	Linacre W	Munro JF	Smith GB	Black A	Clarke RJ	Powell RWH	Williams E	Oakes J	Murray W	Turnbull RW	Phillips E	Cunliffe RA	Trautmann BC	Rigby J	Gill R	Bootle W	Alison J	Spurdle W	Hart JP	Jones WJL	Westcott D	Williamson J
		3	6	5					8	11	1		7		9	2				4		10					
		1	1	1					1	1	1		1		1	1				1		1					
									2	1																	

League Table

	P	W	D	L	F	A	Pts
Portsmouth	42	22	9	11	74	38	53
Wolverhampton W	42	20	13	9	76	49	53
Sunderland	42	21	10	11	83	62	52
Manchester U	42	18	14	10	69	44	50
Newcastle U	42	19	12	11	77	55	50
Arsenal	42	19	11	12	79	55	49
Blackpool	42	17	15	10	46	35	49
Liverpool	42	17	14	11	64	54	48
Middlesbrough	42	20	7	15	59	48	47
Burnley	42	16	13	13	40	40	45
Derby Co	42	17	10	15	69	61	44
Aston Villa	42	15	12	15	61	61	42
Chelsea	42	12	16	14	58	65	40
W.B.A.	42	14	12	16	47	53	40
Huddersfield T	42	14	9	19	52	73	37
Bolton W	42	10	14	18	45	59	34
Fulham	42	10	14	18	41	54	34
Everton	42	10	14	18	42	66	34
Stoke C	42	11	12	19	45	75	34
Charlton A	42	13	6	23	53	65	32
Manchester C	42	8	13	21	36	68	29
Birmingham C	42	7	14	21	31	67	28

1950-51

Division One

Manager: Les McDowall (from June 1950)

Did you know that?

Match 8: Turnbull's last game.
Match 13: Emptage's last game.
Match 25: Fagan's last game.
Match 27: Alison's last game.
Match 31: Oakes's last game.
Match 41: Haddington's last game.

City's draw on the final day of the season relegated Grimsby to Division Three (North), and guaranteed City's promotion. Main rivals Cardiff could only manage a point from their final game.

Match No.	Date	Venue	Opponents	Result		Scorers	Attendance
1	Aug 19	A	Preston North End	W	4-2	Smith 2, Clarke, Westcott	36,294
2	23	H	Cardiff City	W	2-1	Smith, Westcott	18,242
3	26	H	Bury	W	5-1	Westcott 3, Hart, Oakes	44,162
4	28	A	Cardiff City	D	1-1	Oakes	32,817
5	Sep 2	A	Queen's Park Rangers	W	2-1	Clarke, Smith	21,696
6	6	A	Grimsby Town	D	4-4	Westcott 2, Clarke, Spurdle	18,529
7	9	H	Chesterfield	W	5-1	Hart 2, Smith 2, Westcott	43,631
8	16	A	Leicester City	W	2-1	Smith, Turnbull	32,856
9	23	H	Luton Town	D	1-1	Paul	42,312
10	30	H	Coventry City	W	1-0	Spurdle	40,868
11	Oct 7	A	Doncaster Rovers	L	3-4	Smith 3	32,937
12	14	H	Brentford	W	4-0	Westcott 2, Clarke, Hart	39,646
13	21	A	Swansea Town	W	3-2	Cunliffe, Westcott, Westwood	22,762
14	28	H	Hull City	D	0-0		45,842
15	Nov 4	A	Leeds United	D	1-1	Haddington	30,764
16	11	H	West Ham United	W	2-0	Haddington, Westcott	41,473
17	18	A	Blackburn Rovers	L	1-4	Haddington	37,594
18	25	H	Southampton	L	2-3	Haddington, Westcott	39,091
19	Dec 2	A	Barnsley	D	1-1	Westcott	29,681
20	9	H	Sheffield United	W	5-3	Smith 2, Hart, Spurdle, Westcott	33,291
21	16	H	Preston North End	L	0-3		30,512
22	25	H	Birmingham City	W	3-1	Paul 2, Westcott	40,173
23	26	A	Birmingham City	L	0-1		32,092
24	Jan 13	A	Chesterfield	W	2-1	Clarke, Smith	12,384
25	20	H	Leicester City	D	1-1	Hart	30,297
26	27	A	Bury	L	0-2		25,439
27	Feb 3	A	Luton Town	D	2-2	Smith 2	12,087
28	17	A	Coventry City	W	2-0	Clarke, Spurdle	29,205
29	24	H	Doncaster Rovers	D	3-3	Westcott 2, Oakes	38,691
30	Mar 3	A	Brentford	L	0-2		24,288
31	14	H	Swansea Town	L	1-2	Cunliffe	10,361
32	17	A	Hull City	D	3-3	Westcott 2, Hart	26,840
33	24	H	Leeds United	W	4-1	Hart, Meadows, Smith, Westcott	35,149
34	26	H	Notts County	D	0-0		32,047
35	31	A	West Ham United	W	4-2	Smith 2, Hart, Westcott	21,533
36	Apr 4	H	Queen's Park Rangers	W	5-2	Hart 2, Westcott 2, Clarke	21,573
37	7	H	Blackburn Rovers	W	1-0	Hart	37,853
38	14	A	Southampton	L	1-2	Hart	24,579
39	21	H	Barnsley	W	6-0	Clarke 2, Smith 2, Hart, Meadows	39,838
40	28	A	Sheffield United	D	0-0		21,695
41	30	A	Notts County	D	0-0		13,873
42	May 5	H	Grimsby Town	D	2-2	Smith, Westcott	30,293
							Appearances
							Goals

FA Cup

R3	Jan 6	A	Birmingham City	L	0-2		30,057
							Appearances

Trautmann BC	Phillips E	Westwood E	Spurdle W	Rigby J	Paul R	Oakes J	Hart JP	Westcott D	Smith GB	Clarke RJ	Turnbull RW	Williamson J	Alison J	Emptage AT	Cunliffe RA	Haddington WR	Branagan KF	Gunning JM	Fagan JF	McCourt FJ	Meadows J
1	2	3	4	5	6	7	8	9	10	11											
1	2	3	4	5	6	7	8	9	10	11											
1	2	3	4	5	6	7	8	9	10	11											
1	2	3	4	5	6	7	8	9	10	11											
1	2	3	4	5	6	7	8	9	10	11											
1	2	3	4	5	6	7	8	9	10	11											
1	2	3	4	5	6	7	8	9	10	11											
1	2	3	4	5	6		8	9	10	11	7										
1	2	3	4	5	6	7		9	10	11		8									
1	2	3	4	5	6	7		9	10	11			8								
1	2	3	4	5	6	7		9	10	11			8								
1	2	3	4	5	6		8	9	10	11			7								
1	2	3	4	5			8	9	10				7	6	11						
1	2	3	4	5	6		8	9	10	11			7								
1	2	3	4	5	6			9	10	11			7			8					
1	2	3	4	5	6		7	9	10	11						8					
1	2	3	4	5	6		7	9	10	11						8					
1	2	3	4	5	6	7		9	10	11						8					
1	2	3	6	5	4	7		9	10	11						8					
1	3		6	5	4	11	8	9	10								2	7			
1	3		6		4	11	8	9	10								2	7	5		
1	3		6		4			9		11		8	10				2	7	5		
1	3		6		4			9		11		8	10				2	7	5		
1	3		6		4	7	8	9	10	11							2		5		
1		3	6		4	7	8	9	10	11							2		5		
1		3	6	5	4	7	8	9	10	11							2				
1		3	4	5	8			9	10	11			7				2			6	
1		3	8	5	4	7		9	10	11							2			6	
1		3	8	5	4	7		9	10	11							2			6	
1	2	3	8	5	4	7		9	10	11										6	
1	2	3		5	4	7		9	8	10					11					6	
1	2	3		5	4		8	9	10	11										6	7
1	2	3		5	4		8	9	10	11										6	7
1	2	3		5	4		8	9	10	11										6	7
1	2	3		5	4		8	9	10	11										6	7
1	2	3		5	4		8	9	10	11										6	7
1	2	3		5	4		8		10	11		9								6	7
1	2	3		5	4		8	9	10	11										6	7
1	2	3		5	4		8	9	10	11										6	7
1	2	3		5	4		8	9	10	11										6	7
1	2	3	10	5	4					11		9				8				6	7
1	2	3		5	4			9	10	11		8								6	7
42	37	37	31	37	41	21	27	40	39	39	1	6	9	1	2	6	10	4	5	16	11
		1	4		3	3	14	25	21	9	1				2	4					2

Trautmann BC	Phillips E	Westwood E	Spurdle W	Rigby J	Paul R	Oakes J	Hart JP	Westcott D	Smith GB	Clarke RJ	Turnbull RW	Williamson J	Alison J	Emptage AT	Cunliffe RA	Haddington WR	Branagan KF	Gunning JM	Fagan JF	McCourt FJ	Meadows J
1	3	11	6		4			9	10							8	2	7	5		
1	1	1	1		1			1	1							1	1	1	1		

League Table

	P	W	D	L	F	A	Pts
Preston N.E.	42	26	5	11	91	49	57
Manchester C	42	19	14	9	89	61	52
Cardiff C	42	17	16	9	53	45	50
Birmingham C	42	20	9	13	64	53	49
Leeds U	42	20	8	14	63	55	48
Blackburn R	42	19	8	15	65	66	46
Coventry C	42	19	7	16	75	59	45
Sheffield U	42	16	12	14	72	62	44
Brentford	42	18	8	16	75	74	44
Hull C	42	16	11	15	74	70	43
Doncaster R	42	15	13	14	64	68	43
Southampton	42	15	13	14	66	73	43
West Ham U	42	16	10	16	68	69	42
Leicester C	42	15	11	16	68	58	41
Barnsley	42	15	10	17	74	68	40
Q.P.R.	42	15	10	17	71	82	40
Notts Co	42	13	13	16	61	60	39
Swansea T	42	16	4	22	54	77	36
Luton T	42	9	14	19	57	70	32
Bury	42	12	8	22	60	86	32
Chesterfield	42	9	12	21	44	69	30
Grimsby T	42	8	12	22	61	95	28

1951-52

Division One

Manager: Les McDowall

Did you know that?

Match 6: Smith's last game.
Match 10: Phillips' last game.
Match 27: Westcott's last League game.
Match 30: Williams's first and only game.

Derek Williams was the second of three goalkeepers called Williams to play in Division One for the Blues. Charlie was City's star at the start of the 20th century, while Alex was City's popular number one immediately after Joe Corrigan in the 1980s. Mancunian Alex was later awarded an MBE for his dedicated community work in and around Manchester.

Match No.	Date	Venue	Opponents	Result		Scorers	Attendance
1	Aug 18	H	Wolverhampton W.	D	0-0		45,849
2	22	A	Huddersfield Town	L	1-5	Westcott	25,623
3	25	A	Sunderland	L	0-3		45,396
4	29	H	Huddersfield Town	W	3-0	Meadows, Hart, Westcott	34,212
5	Sep 1	H	Aston Villa	D	2-2	Paul Westcott	32,515
6	5	A	Portsmouth	L	0-1		30,018
7	8	A	Derby County	W	3-1	Meadows, Hart, Williamson	22,073
8	15	H	Manchester United	L	1-2	Hart	52,520
9	22	H	Arsenal	L	0-2		48,418
10	29	A	Blackpool	D	2-2	Hart, Westcott	33,858
11	Oct 6	A	Tottenham Hotspur	W	2-1	Clarke 2	58,163
12	13	H	Preston North End	W	1-0	Cunningham (og)	57,663
13	20	A	Burnley	D	0-0		30,977
14	27	H	Charlton Athletic	W	4-2	Meadows, Westcott, Broadis, Clarke	44,538
15	Nov 3	A	Fulham	W	2-1	Broadis, Revie	33,581
16	10	H	Middlesbrough	W	2-1	Meadows, Westcott	47,522
17	17	A	West Bromwich Albion	L	2-3	Hart , Rickaby (og)	31,982
18	24	H	Newcastle United	L	2-3	Meadows, Clarke	39,455
19	Dec 1	A	Bolton Wanderers	L	1-2	Meadows	43,405
20	8	H	Stoke City	L	0-1		20,488
21	15	A	Wolverhampton W.	D	2-2	Westcott, Clarke	28,526
22	22	H	Sunderland	W	3-1	Westcott 2 ,Clarke	28,626
23	25	A	Chelsea	W	3-0	Westcott, Broadis, Meadows	34,850
24	26	H	Chelsea	W	3-1	Meadows, Revie, Westcott	49,791
25	29	A	Aston Villa	W	2-1	Meadows, Williamson	37,319
26	Jan 1	H	Portsmouth	L	0-1		49,503
27	5	H	Derby County	W	4-2	Hart 2, Broadis, Clarke	37,663
28	19	A	Manchester United	D	1-1	McCourt	56,122
29	26	A	Arsenal	D	2-2	Hart, Phoenix	52,527
30	Feb 9	H	Blackpool	D	0-0		47,528
31	16	H	Tottenham Hotspur	D	1-1	Revie	39,080
32	Mar 1	A	Preston North End	D	1-1	Hart	34,353
33	12	H	Burnley	L	0-1		20,223
34	15	A	Charlton Athletic	D	0-0		24,143
35	22	H	Fulham	D	1-1	Hart	31,036
36	29	A	Middlesbrough	D	2-2	Hart, Revie	16,920
37	Apr 5	H	West Bromwich Albion	L	1-2	Revie	13,933
38	11	H	Liverpool	L	1-2	Clarke	35,396
39	12	A	Newcastle United	L	0-1		46,645
40	14	A	Liverpool	W	2-1	Williamson, Clarke	34,404
41	19	H	Bolton Wanderers	L	0-3		28,388
42	26	A	Stoke City	L	1-3	Branagan	24,807
							Appearances
						Two own goals	Goals

FA Cup

R3	Jan 12	H	Wolverhampton W.	D	2-2	Meadows, Revie	54,497
rep	16	A	Wolverhampton W.	L	1-4	Clarke	43,865
							Appearances
							Goals

Trautmann BC	Phillips E	Hannaway J	Paul R	Rigby J	McCourt FJ	Meadows J	Hart JP	Westcott D	Clarke RJ	Cunliffe RA	Smith GB	Williamson J	Spurdle W	Branagan KF	Broadis IA	Revie DG	Barnes KH	Phoenix RJ	Williams D	Westwood E	Gunning JM	Davies GE
1	2	3	4	5	6	7	8	9	10	11												
1	2	3	4	5	6	7	8	9	11		10											
1	2	3	4	5	6	7	8	9	11		10											
1	2	3	4	5	6	7	8	9	10	11												
1	2	3	4	5	6	7	8	9	10	11												
1	2	3	4	5	6	7		9	11		10	8										
1	2	3	4	5	6	7	8		11			9	10									
1	2	3	4	5	6	7	8	10	11			9										
1	2	3	4	5	6	7	8	10	11			9										
1	2	3	4	5	6	7	8	10	11			9										
1		3	4	5	6	7	8		11			9		2	10							
1		3	4	5	6	7	8		11			9		2	10							
1		3		5	6	7				11		9	4	2	10	8						
1		3	4	5	6	7		9	11					2	10	8						
1		3	4	5		7		9	11				6	2	10	8						
1		3	4	5	6	7		9	11					2	10	8						
1		3	4	5	6	7	8	9	11					2	10							
1		3	4	5	6	9	7		11					2	10	8						
1		3	4	5	6	9	7		11					2	10	8						
1		3	4	5	6	7			11			9		2	10	8						
1		3		5	6	7		9	11				4	2	10	8						
1		3		5	6	7		9	11				4	2	10	8						
1		3		5	6	7		9	11				4	2	10	8						
1		3		5	6	7		9	11				4	2	10	8						
1		3	4	5	6	7			11			9		2	10	8						
1		3	4	5	6	7		9	11					2	10	8						
1		3	6	5			7	9	11					2	10	8	4					
1		3		5	6	9	7		11				4	2	10	8						
1		3		5	6	9	7		11				4	2	8			10				
		3	4	5		7			11			9		2	10	8		6	1			
1		3	4	5		7	9		11					2	10	8		6				
1		3	5		4	7	9		11					2	8	10		6				
1			5				9		11					2	8	4		6		3	7	10
1			5		4		9		11					2	8	10		6		3	7	
1			5		4		9		11					2	8	10		6		3	7	
1		3	4	5		9	7		11					2	8	10		6				
1		3	4	5		7	9		11					2		8		6				10
1		3	4	5		7	9		11					2	8	10		6				
1			4	5		7			11			9		2	8	10		6		3		
1			4	5		7			11			9		2	8	10		6		3		
1			4	5		7			11			9		2	8			6		3		10
1			4	5	6		7		11			9		2	8			10		3		
41	10	35	35	38	31	37	26	19	41	4	3	15	9	32	31	26	1	14	1	7	3	3
			1		1	9	11	11	9			3		1	4	5		1				

Trautmann BC	Phillips E	Hannaway J	Paul R	Rigby J	McCourt FJ	Meadows J	Hart JP	Westcott D	Clarke RJ	Cunliffe RA	Smith GB	Williamson J	Spurdle W	Branagan KF	Broadis IA	Revie DG	Barnes KH	Phoenix RJ	Williams D	Westwood E	Gunning JM	Davies GE
1		3	6	5		7		9	11				4	2	10	8						
1		3	4	5		7		9	11				6	2	10	8						
2		2	2	2		2		2	2				2	2	2	2						
						1			1							1						

League Table

	P	W	D	L	F	A	Pts
Manchester U	42	23	11	8	95	52	57
Tottenham H	42	22	9	11	76	51	53
Arsenal	42	21	11	10	80	61	53
Portsmouth	42	20	8	14	68	58	48
Bolton W	42	19	10	13	65	61	48
Aston Villa	42	19	9	14	79	70	47
Preston N.E.	42	17	12	13	74	54	46
Newcastle U	42	18	9	15	98	73	45
Blackpool	42	18	9	15	64	64	45
Charlton A	42	17	10	15	68	63	44
Liverpool	42	12	19	11	57	61	43
Sunderland	42	15	12	15	70	61	42
W.B.A.	42	14	13	15	74	77	41
Burnley	42	15	10	17	56	63	40
Manchester C	42	13	13	16	58	61	39
Wolverh'pton W	42	12	14	16	73	73	38
Derby Co	42	15	7	20	63	80	37
Middlesbrough	42	15	6	21	64	88	36
Chelsea	42	14	8	20	52	72	36
Stoke C	42	12	7	23	49	88	31
Huddersfield T	42	10	8	24	49	82	28
Fulham	42	8	11	23	58	77	27

1952-53

Division One

Manager: Les McDowall

Did you know that?

Match 2: Smith's last game.
Match 22: Rigby's last game.
Match 24: Westwood's last game.
Match 29: Gunning's last game.
Match 29: Webster and Woosnam's first and only game.

The 1–0 away win at Liverpool in January was the first City away win since 14 April 1952 when they also defeated Liverpool.

Match No.	Date	Venue	Opponents	Result		Scorers	Attendance
1	Aug 23	A	Stoke City	L	1-2	Smith	37,666
2	27	H	Tottenham Hotspur	L	0-1		33,621
3	30	H	Manchester United	W	2-1	Broadis, Clarke	56,240
4	Sep 1	A	Tottenham Hotspur	D	3-3	Sowden 2, Meadows	41,113
5	6	H	Liverpool	L	0-2		43,065
6	8	A	Burnley	L	1-2	Meadows	27,083
7	13	A	Middlesbrough	L	4-5	Revie 2, Broadis, Meadows	30,924
8	17	H	Burnley	D	0-0		25,094
9	20	H	West Bromwich Albion	L	0-1		33,143
10	27	A	Newcastle United	L	0-2		48,961
11	Oct 4	H	Cardiff City	D	2-2	Branagan, Revie	33,551
12	11	A	Portsmouth	L	1-2	Williamson	33,573
13	18	H	Bolton Wanderers	L	1-2	Revie	42,369
14	25	A	Aston Villa	D	0-0		30,370
15	Nov 1	H	Sunderland	L	2-5	Hart, Williamson	33,210
16	8	A	Wolverhampton W.	L	3-7	Williamson 2, Davies	33,832
17	15	H	Charlton Athletic	W	5-1	Meadows 3, Clarke, Williamson	23,461
18	22	A	Arsenal	L	1-3	Meadows	38,161
19	29	H	Derby County	W	1-0	Hart	23,017
20	Dec 6	A	Blackpool	L	1-4	Williamson	19,496
21	13	H	Chelsea	W	4-0	Clarke, Hart, Meadows, Harris (og)	20,733
22	20	H	Stoke City	W	2-1	Hart, Williamson	13,669
23	26	A	Preston North End	L	2-6	Hart 2	37,093
24	Jan 3	A	Manchester United	D	1-1	Broadis	49,738
25	17	A	Liverpool	W	1-0	Hart	41,191
26	24	H	Middlesbrough	W	5-1	Spurdle 3, Revie, Williamson	26,822
27	Feb 7	A	West Bromwich Albion	L	1-2	Revie	27,783
28	14	H	Newcastle United	W	2-1	Meadows, Phoenix	24,998
29	21	A	Cardiff City	L	0-6		24,886
30	28	H	Portsmouth	W	2-1	Cunliffe, Meadows	38,726
31	Mar 7	A	Bolton Wanderers	L	0-1		39,585
32	14	H	Aston Villa	W	4-1	Spurdle 3, Anders	32,552
33	21	A	Sunderland	D	3-3	Broadis 2, Williamson	26,270
34	28	H	Wolverhampton W.	W	3-1	McCourt, Spurdle, Whitfield	27,127
35	Apr 3	H	Sheffield Wednesday	W	3-1	Broadis, Cunliffe, Whitfield	55,435
36	4	A	Charlton Athletic	W	2-1	Hart, McCourt	26,327
37	6	A	Sheffield Wednesday	D	1-1	Hart	43,233
38	11	H	Arsenal	L	2-4	Spurdle 2	50,018
39	18	A	Derby County	L	0-5		15,616
40	22	H	Preston North End	L	0-2		42,863
41	25	H	Blackpool	W	5-0	Spurdle 2, Cunliffe, McCourt, Williamson	35,507
42	29	A	Chelsea	L	1-3	Williamson	48,594
							Appearances
						One own goal	Goals

FA Cup

Round	Date	Venue	Opponents	Result	Scorers	Attendance
R3	Jan 10	H	Swindon Town	W	Hart 4, Broadis, Cunliffe, Williamson	28,953
R4	31	H	Luton Town	D	Broadis	38,411
rep	Feb 4	A	Luton Town	L	Spurdle	21,991
						Appearances
						Goals

Trautmann BC	Branagan KF	Westwood E	Paul R	Rigby J	McCourt FJ	Spurdle W	Revie DG	Smith FE	Broadis IA	Clarke RJ	Meadows J	Sowden W	Hannaway J	Hart JP	Phoenix RJ	Williamson J	Cunliffe RA	Davies GE	Gunning JM	Ewing D	Little R	Webster E	Woosnam PA	Whitfield K	Anders H
1	2	3	4	5	6	7	8	9	10	11															
1	2	3	4	5	6	7	8	9	10	11															
1	2	3	4	5		6	8		10	11	7	9													
1	2	3	4	5		6	8		10	11	7	9													
1	2		4	5		6	8		10	11	7	9	3												
1	2		4	5		6	8		10	11	7	9	3												
1		3	4	5		6	8		10	11	7	9	2												
1	2	3	4	5		6	8		10	11	7	9													
1	2	3	4	5		6	8		10	11	7	9													
1	2	3	4	5		6	10			11	7	9		8											
1	2	3	4	5		6	10			11	7	9		8											
1	2	3		5		4	10			11	7			8	6	9									
1	2	3				4	10		8		5			7	6	9	11								
1	2	3	5				4		9	11	7			8	6			10							
1	2	3	5				4			11	7			8	6	9		10							
1	2	3	5				4			11	7			8	6	9		10							
1	2	3	4	5			6		10	11	7			8		9									
1	2	3	4	5			6		10	11	7			8		9									
1	2	3	6	5			4			11	7			8		9		10							
1	2	3	6	5			4			11	7			8		9		10							
1	2	3		5		6	4		10	11	7			8		9									
1	2	3	6	5			4		10	11	7			8		9									
1	2	3	6				4		10	11	5			8		9			7						
1	2	3	6				4		10		7			8		9	11			5					
1	2		6				4		10					8		9	11		7	5	3				
1	2		6			8	4		10							9	11		7	5	3				
1	2		6			8	4		10							9	11		7	5	3				
1	2		6				4		8		9		3		10		11		7	5					
1	2						4		8		9		3				11		7	5		6	10		
1	2		4		6		10		8		7		3				11			5				9	
1	2		4		6				8		9		3			10	11			5					7
1	2		4		6	8			10				3				11			5				9	7
1	2		4		6	8			10				3			9	11			5					7
1	2		4		6	8			10				3				11			5				9	7
1	2		4		6	8			10				3				11			5				9	7
1	2		4		6	8			10				3	9			11			5					7
1	2		4		6	8			10				3	9			11			5					7
1	2		4		6	8			10				3	9			11			5					7
1	2		6			8	4						3	10			11			5				9	7
1	2		6			8	4		10				3				11			5				9	7
1	2		4		6	8			10				3			9	11			5					7
1	2		4		6	8			10				3			9	11			5					7
42	41	22	38	18	13	27	32	2	34	22	26	9	18	20	6	19	20	5	6	19	3	1	1	6	12
	1				3	11	6	1	6	3	10	2		9	1	11	3	1						2	1

Trautmann BC	Branagan KF	Westwood E	Paul R	Rigby J	McCourt FJ	Spurdle W	Revie DG	Smith FE	Broadis IA	Clarke RJ	Meadows J	Sowden W	Hannaway J	Hart JP	Phoenix RJ	Williamson J	Cunliffe RA	Davies GE	Gunning JM	Ewing D	Little R	Webster E	Woosnam PA	Whitfield K	Anders H
1	2		6				4		10					8		9	11		7	5	3				
1	2		6			8	4		10		7					9	11			5	3				
1	2		6			8	4		10		7					9	11			5	3				
3	3		3			2	3		3		2			1		3	3		1	3	3				
						1			2					4		1	1								

League Table

	P	W	D	L	F	A	Pts
Arsenal	42	21	12	9	97	64	54
Preston N.E.	42	21	12	9	85	60	54
Wolverh'pton W	42	19	13	10	86	63	51
W.B.A.	42	21	8	13	66	60	50
Charlton A	42	19	11	12	77	63	49
Burnley	42	18	12	12	67	52	48
Blackpool	42	19	9	14	71	70	47
Manchester U	42	18	10	14	69	72	46
Sunderland	42	15	13	14	68	82	43
Tottenham H	42	15	11	16	78	69	41
Aston Villa	42	14	13	15	63	61	41
Cardiff C	42	14	12	16	54	46	40
Middlesbrough	42	14	11	17	70	77	39
Bolton W	42	15	9	18	61	69	39
Portsmouth	42	14	10	18	74	83	38
Newcastle U	42	14	9	19	59	70	37
Liverpool	42	14	8	20	61	82	36
Sheffield W	42	12	11	19	62	72	35
Chelsea	42	12	11	19	56	66	35
Manchester C	42	14	7	21	72	87	35
Stoke C	42	12	10	20	53	66	34
Derby Co	42	11	10	21	59	74	32

1953-54

Division One

Manager: Les McDowall

Did you know that?

Match 9: Whitfield's last game.
Match 13: Davidson's last game.
Match 15: Sowden and Broadis's last game.
Match 31: McCourt's last game.

For three successive Wednesdays beginning 14 October 1953, City staged high-profile floodlit matches at Maine Road. These were the first floodlit games at Maine Road and were played against Hearts (6–3), Fenerbahce (5–1) and Celtic (1–1). In 2005 Hearts presented City with a signed shirt commemorating that landmark game and City's 125th anniversary since formation as St Mark's. Celtic also presented the Blues with a signed shirt marking the 125th anniversary.

Match No.	Date	Venue	Opponents	Result		Scorers	Attendance
1	Aug 19	A	Sheffield Wednesday	L	0-2		39,586
2	22	H	Wolverhampton W.	L	0-4		22,729
3	24	A	Aston Villa	L	0-3		21,194
4	29	A	Sunderland	W	5-4	Hart 2, Anders, Clarke, Whitfield	49,434
5	Sep 2	H	Aston Villa	L	0-1		24,918
6	5	H	Manchester United	W	2-0	Hart, Revie	53,097
7	9	A	Huddersfield Town	D	1-1	Little	24,341
8	12	H	Cardiff City	D	1-1	Montgomery (og)	31,915
9	16	H	Huddersfield Town	L	0-1		24,580
10	19	A	Arsenal	D	2-2	Hart, Spurdle	65,869
11	26	H	Portsmouth	W	2-1	Hart, Revie	35,688
12	Oct 3	A	Blackpool	L	0-2		35,666
13	10	A	Bolton Wanderers	L	2-3	Revie 2	34,443
14	17	H	Preston North End	L	1-4	Anders	43,295
15	24	A	Tottenham Hotspur	L	0-3		37,577
16	31	H	Burnley	W	3-2	Meadows 2, Cunliffe	32,353
17	Nov 7	A	Liverpool	D	2-2	Hart, Meadows	30,917
18	14	H	Newcastle United	D	0-0		34,150
19	21	A	Middlesbrough	W	1-0	Robinson (og)	22,099
20	28	H	West Bromwich Albion	L	2-3	Hart, Revie	40,753
21	Dec 5	A	Charlton Athletic	L	1-2	Meadows	17,813
22	12	H	Sheffield Wednesday	W	3-2	Davies, Little, Revie	27,710
23	19	A	Wolverhampton W.	L	1-3	Davies	27,606
24	25	A	Sheffield United	D	2-2	Hart, Revie	32,787
25	26	H	Sheffield United	W	2-1	Hart, Rawson (og)	35,786
26	Jan 2	H	Sunderland	W	2-1	McAdams, Revie	23,742
27	16	A	Manchester United	D	1-1	McAdams	48,216
28	23	A	Cardiff City	W	3-0	Anders, Clarke, Revie	22,516
29	Feb 6	H	Arsenal	D	0-0		39,503
30	13	A	Portsmouth	L	1-4	McAdams	30,013
31	24	H	Blackpool	L	1-4	Clarke	22,515
32	27	H	Bolton Wanderers	W	3-0	McAdams, Meadows, Revie (pen)	39,340
33	Mar 6	A	Preston North End	L	0-4		23,669
34	17	H	Tottenham Hotspur	W	4-1	Clarke, Hart, McAdams, Revie	9,984
35	20	A	Burnley	L	1-3	Hart	23,061
36	Apr 3	A	Newcastle United	L	3-4	Clarke, Hart (pen), McAdams	27,764
37	7	H	Liverpool	L	0-2		12,593
38	10	H	Middlesbrough	W	5-2	Clarke 2, Meadows 2, Revie	28,445
39	16	A	Chelsea	W	1-0	Meadows	59,794
40	17	A	West Bromwich Albion	L	0-1		38,567
41	19	H	Chelsea	D	1-1	Branagan	30,620
42	24	H	Charlton Athletic	W	3-0	McAdams 2, Spurdle	19,549
							Appearances
						Three own goals	Goals

FA Cup

	Date	Venue	Opponents	Result		Scorers	Attendance
R3	Jan 9	A	Bradford Park Avenue	W	5-2	McAdams 3, Clarke, Revie	22,194
R4	30	H	Tottenham Hotspur	L	0-1		50,576
							Appearances
							Goals

Trautmann BC	Branagan KF	Hannaway J	Revie DG	Ewing D	Paul R	Anders H	Hart JP	Williamson J	Broadis IA	Cunliffe RA	Clarke RJ	Little R	Spurdle W	Whitfield K	Davidson D	Sowden W	Hayes J	Meadows J	McTavish JR	Davies GE	Fagan F	McAdams WJ	McCourt FJ
1	2	3	4	5	6	7	8	9	10	11													
1	2	3	4	5	6	7	8	9	10		11												
1	2		4	5	6	7			10		11	3	8	9									
1	2		4	5	6	7	8				11	3	10	9									
1	2		4	5	6	7	8				11	3	10	9									
1	2		4	5	6	7	8				11	3	10	9									
1	2		4	5	6	7	8				11	3	10	9									
1	2		4	5	6	7	8				11	3	10	9									
1	2		4	5	6	7	8				11	3	10	9									
1	2		4	5	6		8	9	10		11	3	7										
1	2		4	5	6		8	9	10		11	3	7										
1	2		4	5	6	11	8	9	10			3	7										
1	2		4	5		11	8	9	10			3	7		6								
1	2		4	5	6	7	8		10		11	3				9							
1	2		4	5	6		8		10		11	3				9	7						
1	2		4	5	6		8			11	10	3					7	9					
1	2		4	5	6		8			11	10	3					7	9					
1	2		4	5	6		8			11	10	3					7	9					
1	2		10	5	6		8			11		3					7	9	4				
1	2		4	5	6	7	8			11	10	3						9					
1	2			5	6	7				11	10	3					8	9	4				
1	2		8	5	6						11	3					7	9	4	10			
1	2		4	5	6		8				11	3					7	9		10			
1	2		10	5	6	7	8				11	3						9	4				
1	2		10	5	6		8				11	3						9	4		7		
1	2		10	5	6						11	3						8	4		7	9	
1	2		10	5	6		8				11							3	4		7	9	
1	2		10	5	6	7	8				11							3	4			9	
1	2		10	5	6		8			11			7					3	4			9	
1	2		10	5	6		8			11			7					3	4			9	
1	2		10	5			8				11	3	7						4			9	6
1	2	3	10	5		7					11		6					9	4			8	
1	2	3		5	6	7		9			11		10						4			8	
1	2	3	10	5	6		8				11		7						4			9	
1	2		10	5	6	7	8				11							3	4			9	
1	2	3		5	4		8			11	10		6								7	9	
1	2		10	5	4						11	3	6					9			7	8	
1	2		10	5	6						11	3	7					9	4			8	
1	2		10	5	6						11	3	7					9	4			8	
1	2			5	6		10					3	7				8		4		11	9	
1	2		10	5	6						11	3	7				8		4			9	
1	2			5	6		10				11	3	7				8		4			9	
42	42	6	37	42	39	19	32	7	9	10	35	31	24	7	1	2	11	20	20	2	6	17	1
	1		12			3	12			1	7	2	2	1				8		2		8	

Trautmann BC	Branagan KF	Hannaway J	Revie DG	Ewing D	Paul R	Anders H	Hart JP	Williamson J	Broadis IA	Cunliffe RA	Clarke RJ	Little R	Spurdle W	Whitfield K	Davidson D	Sowden W	Hayes J	Meadows J	McTavish JR	Davies GE	Fagan F	McAdams WJ	McCourt FJ
1	2		10	5	6		8				11							3	4		7	9	
1	2		10	5	6	7	8				11							3	4			9	
2	2		2	2	2	1	2				2							2	2		1	2	
			1								1											3	

League Table

	P	W	D	L	F	A	Pts
Wolverh'pton W	42	25	7	10	96	56	57
W.B.A.	42	22	9	11	86	63	53
Huddersfield T	42	20	11	11	78	61	51
Manchester U	42	18	12	12	73	58	48
Bolton W	42	18	12	12	75	60	48
Blackpool	42	19	10	13	80	69	48
Burnley	42	21	4	17	78	67	46
Chelsea	42	16	12	14	74	68	44
Charlton A	42	19	6	17	75	77	44
Cardiff C	42	18	8	16	51	71	44
Preston N.E.	42	19	5	18	87	58	43
Arsenal	42	15	13	14	75	73	43
Aston Villa	42	16	9	17	70	68	41
Portsmouth	42	14	11	17	81	89	39
Newcastle U	42	14	10	18	72	77	38
Tottenham H	42	16	5	21	65	76	37
Manchester C	42	14	9	19	62	77	37
Sunderland	42	14	8	20	81	89	36
Sheffield W	42	15	6	21	70	91	36
Sheffield U	42	11	11	20	69	90	33
Middlesbrough	42	10	10	22	60	91	30
Liverpool	42	9	10	23	68	97	28

1954-55

Division One

Manager: Les McDowall

Did you know that?

Match 34: Anders's last game.
Match 35: Davies's last game.
Match 40: Williamson's last game.
Match 42: Meadows's last League game.

Despite only appearing in 59 League games Johnny Williamson, who scored in his final game (Match 40), is a very important player in City's history. It was Williamson who played the role of the deep-lying centre-forward in the reserves, which ultimately led to the first team's adoption of the 'Revie Plan' during 1954–55. In later years Williamson became a key figure in the former players' association and remains a popular matchday presence at the City of Manchester Stadium.

Match No.	Date	Venue	Opponents	Result		Scorers	Attendance
1	Aug 21	A	Preston North End	L	0-5		33,098
2	25	H	Sheffield United	W	5-2	Hart 2, Revie 2, Clarke	23,856
3	28	H	Burnley	D	0-0		38,201
4	30	A	Sheffield United	W	2-0	Hart, Revie	23,652
5	Sep 4	A	Leicester City	W	2-0	Hart, McAdams	32,975
6	8	H	Arsenal	W	2-1	Hart, Bowen (og)	38,146
7	11	H	Chelsea	D	1-1	Paul	36,230
8	14	A	Arsenal	W	3-2	Clarke, Hart, McAdams	33,898
9	18	A	Cardiff City	L	0-3		28,847
10	25	H	Manchester United	W	3-2	Fagan, Hart, McAdams	54,105
11	Oct 2	H	Everton	W	1-0	Clarke	45,737
12	9	A	Wolverhampton W.	D	2-2	Fagan 2	41,601
13	16	H	Aston Villa	L	2-4	Spurdle 2	36,384
14	23	A	Bolton Wanderers	D	2-2	McAdams, Revie	29,841
15	30	H	Huddersfield Town	L	2-4	Revie 2 (1p)	34,246
16	Nov 6	A	Sheffield Wednesday	W	4-2	Williamson 2, Clarke, Hart	18,270
17	13	H	Portsmouth	L	1-2	Fagan	24,564
18	20	A	Blackpool	W	3-1	McAdams 2, Williamson	21,734
19	27	H	Charlton Athletic	L	1-5	Davies	25,799
20	Dec 4	A	Sunderland	L	2-3	Hart 2	33,733
21	11	H	Tottenham Hotspur	D	0-0		27,052
22	18	H	Preston North End	W	3-1	Hart 2, Hayes	26,615
23	25	H	Newcastle United	W	3-1	Spurdle 2, Hayes	26,664
24	27	A	Newcastle United	L	0-2		52,872
25	Jan 1	A	Burnley	L	0-2		28,825
26	15	H	Leicester City	D	2-2	Clarke, Hayes	13,648
27	22	A	Chelsea	W	2-0	Clarke, Hayes	34,160
28	Feb 5	H	Cardiff City	W	4-1	Clarke, Fagan, Hayes, Revie	31,922
29	12	A	Manchester United	W	5-0	Fagan 2, Hayes 2, Hart	49,733
30	23	A	Everton	L	0-1		20,457
31	Mar 5	A	Tottenham Hotspur	D	2-2	Hart, Hayes	35,358
32	16	H	Bolton Wanderers	W	4-2	Hayes 3, Fagan	27,742
33	19	A	Huddersfield Town	D	0-0		31,065
34	30	H	Sheffield Wednesday	D	2-2	Davies, Hayes	14,825
35	Apr 2	A	Portsmouth	L	0-1		24,296
36	8	H	West Bromwich Albion	W	4-0	Fagan, Hayes, Johnstone, Spurdle	57,663
37	9	H	Sunderland	W	1-0	Revie	60,611
38	11	A	West Bromwich Albion	L	1-2	Spurdle	29,995
39	16	A	Charlton Athletic	D	1-1	Johnstone	25,064
40	20	H	Wolverhampton W.	W	3-0	Fagan, Meadows, Williamson	50,705
41	23	H	Blackpool	L	1-6	Fagan	44,839
42	30	A	Aston Villa	L	0-2		27,788
							Appearances
						One own goal	Goals

FA Cup

	Date	Venue	Opponents	Result	Scorers	Attendance
R3	Jan 8	A	Derby County	3-1	Barnes, Hayes, Revie (p)	23,409
R4	29	H	Manchester United	2-0	Hayes, Revie	74,723
R5	Feb 19	A	Luton Town	2-0	Clarke 2	23,104
R6	Mar 12	A	Birmingham City	1-0	Hart	58,000
SF	26	N	Sunderland	1-0	Clarke	58,498
F	May 7	N	Newcastle United	1-3	Johnstone	100,000
						Appearances
						Goals

SF at Villa Park. Final at Wembley Stadium

Trautmann BC	Leivers WE	Meadows J	McTavish JR	Ewing D	Paul R	Spurdle W	McAdams WJ	Revie DG	Hart JP	Clarke RJ	Little R	Barnes KH	Fagan F	Williamson J	Hayes J	Davies GE	Branagan KF	Savage JA	Johnstone R	Anders H	Hannaway J
1	2	3	4	5	6	7	8	9	10	11											
1		2		5	6	7	8	9	10	11	3	4									
1		2		5	6		8	9	10	11	3	4	7								
1		2		5	6		8	9	10	11	3	4	7								
1		2		5	6		8	9	10	11	3	4	7								
1		2		5	6		8	9	10	11	3	4	7								
1		2		5	6		8	9	10	11	3	4	7								
1		2		5	6		8	9	10	11	3	4	7								
1		2		5	6		8	9	10	11	3	4	7								
1		2		5	6		8	9	10	11	3	4	7								
1		2		5	6	8			10	11	3	4	7	9							
1		2		5	6			9	10	11	3	4	7	8							
1		2	6	5		7	8	9	10		3	4	11								
1		2		5	6		8	9	10	11	3	4	7								
1		2		5	6		8	9	10	11	3	4	7								
1		2		5	6	7	8		10	11	3	4		9							
1		2		5	6	7	10				3	4	11	9	8						
1		2		5	6		8		10	11	3	4	7	9							
1		2		5	6		8			11	3	4	7	9		10					
1		3		5	6	9	8		10	11		4	7				2				
1		3		5	6		8	9	10	11		4	7				2				
1				5	6			9	10	11	3	4	7		8		2				
1				5	6	7		9	10	11	3	4			8		2				
				5	6	7		9	10	11	3	4			8		2	1			
		5			6	7		9	10		3	4	11		8		2	1			
1	5				6			9	10	11	3	4	7		8		2				
1		2		5	6			9	10	11	3	4	7		8						
1		2		5	6			9	10	11	3	4	7		8						
1		2		5	6			9	10	11	3	4	7		8						
1		2		5	6			9	10	11	3	4	7		8						
1		2		5	6			9	10	11	3	4	7		8						
1		2		5	6				9	11	3	4	7		8				10		
1		2		5	6			9	10	11	3	4			7				8		
1				5	6						3	4	11	9	8	10	2			7	
1			4	5	6	7							11	9	8	10	2				3
1		2		5	6	7		9			3	4	11		8				10		
1		2		5	6	7		9			3	4	11		8				10		
1		2		5	6	7		9			3	4	11		8				10		
1		2		5	6	8		9		11	3	4	7						10		
1		8		5	6					11	3	4	7	9			2		10		
1		10		5	6	7		9			3	4	11		8		2				
1		2		5	6			9		11	3	4	7		8				10		
40	2	36	3	40	41	16	19	32	31	33	38	40	36	9	20	3	11	2	8	1	1
		1			1	6	6	8	14	7			11	4	13	2			2		

Trautmann BC	Leivers WE	Meadows J	McTavish JR	Ewing D	Paul R	Spurdle W	McAdams WJ	Revie DG	Hart JP	Clarke RJ	Little R	Barnes KH	Fagan F	Williamson J	Hayes J	Davies GE	Branagan KF	Savage JA	Johnstone R	Anders H	Hannaway J
1	5				6			9	10	11	3	4	7		8		2				
1		2		5	6			9	10	11	3	4	7		8						
1		2		5	6			9	10	11	3	4	7		8						
1		2		5	6			9	10	11	3	4	7		8						
1		2		5	6			9		11	3	4	7		8				10		
1		2		5	6	7		9			3	4	11		8				10		
6	1	5		5	6	1		6	4	5	6	6	6		6		1		2		
								2	1	3		1			2				1		

League Table

	P	W	D	L	F	A	Pts
Chelsea	42	20	12	10	81	57	52
Wolverh'pton W	42	19	10	13	89	70	48
Portsmouth	42	18	12	12	74	62	48
Sunderland	42	15	18	9	64	54	48
Manchester U	42	20	7	15	84	74	47
Aston Villa	42	20	7	15	72	73	47
Manchester C	42	18	10	14	76	69	46
Newcastle U	42	17	9	16	89	77	43
Arsenal	42	17	9	16	69	63	43
Burnley	42	17	9	16	51	48	43
Everton	42	16	10	16	62	68	42
Huddersfield T	42	14	13	15	63	68	41
Sheffield U	42	17	7	18	70	86	41
Preston N.E.	42	16	8	18	83	64	40
Charlton A	42	15	10	17	76	75	40
Tottenham H	42	16	8	18	72	73	40
W.B.A.	42	16	8	18	76	96	40
Bolton W	42	13	13	16	62	69	39
Blackpool	42	14	10	18	60	64	38
Cardiff C	42	13	11	18	62	76	37
Leicester C	42	12	11	19	74	86	35
Sheffield W	42	8	10	24	63	100	26

1955-56

Division One

Manager: Les McDowall

Did you know that?

Match 26: Cunliffe's last game.
Match 39: Murray's first and only game.
Match 40: Faulkner's last game.

Prior to his heroics in the 1956 Cup Final Trautmann had already been voted the Football Writers' player of the year. This was the second successive season a City player had won the award – Don Revie was 1955's star man.

Match No.	Date	Venue	Opponents	Result		Scorers	Attendance
1	Aug 20	H	Aston Villa	D	2-2	Cunliffe, Revie	37,999
2	27	A	Wolverhampton W.	L	2-7	Hayes, Revie (pen)	38,790
3	31	H	Arsenal	D	2-2	Hayes 2	36,955
4	Sep 3	H	Manchester United	W	1-0	Hayes	59,192
5	6	A	Arsenal	D	0-0		30,862
6	10	H	Cardiff City	W	3-1	Hayes 2, Johnstone	33,240
7	17	A	Huddersfield Town	D	3-3	Clarke, Fagan, Johnstone	26,443
8	24	H	Blackpool	W	2-0	Johnstone, Revie (pen)	63,925
9	Oct 1	A	Chelsea	L	1-2	Marsden	44,583
10	8	A	Sheffield United	D	1-1	Dyson	25,984
11	15	H	Preston North End	L	0-2		33,187
12	22	A	Birmingham City	L	3-4	Dyson (pen), Hayes, Faulkner	28,398
13	29	H	West Bromwich Albion	W	2-0	Cunliffe, Brookes (og)	25,081
14	Nov 5	A	Charlton Athletic	L	2-5	Cunliffe, Hayes	24,555
15	12	H	Tottenham Hotspur	L	1-2	Hayes	24,094
16	19	A	Everton	D	1-1	Faulkner	34,612
17	26	H	Newcastle United	L	1-2	Clarke	22,860
18	Dec 3	A	Burnley	D	2-2	Dyson, Hayes	26,217
19	10	H	Luton Town	W	3-2	Clarke, Hayes, Spurdle	15,499
20	17	A	Aston Villa	W	3-0	Dyson 2, Spurdle	19,215
21	24	H	Wolverhampton W.	D	2-2	Hayes, Spurdle	32,935
22	26	A	Bolton Wanderers	W	3-1	Dyson, Spurdle, Hartle (og)	43,947
23	27	H	Bolton Wanderers	W	2-0	Clarke, Paul	38,407
24	31	A	Manchester United	L	1-2	Dyson	61,194
25	Jan 2	H	Portsmouth	W	4-1	Johnstone 3, Hayes	43,163
26	14	A	Cardiff City	L	1-4	Johnstone	26,329
27	21	H	Huddersfield Town	W	1-0	Spurdle	21,976
28	Feb 4	A	Blackpool	W	1-0	Faulkner	17,012
29	11	H	Chelsea	D	2-2	Hayes 2	26,642
30	25	A	Preston North End	W	3-0	Johnstone 2, Hayes	22,464
31	Mar 7	H	Everton	W	3-0	Clarke, Johnstone, Spurdle	15,227
32	10	A	West Bromwich Albion	W	4-0	Johnstone 2, Dyson, Hayes	32,517
33	21	H	Charlton Athletic	L	0-2		13,998
34	24	A	Tottenham Hotspur	L	1-2	Hayes	31,622
35	30	A	Sunderland	W	3-0	Hayes, Revie, Aitken (og)	40,394
36	31	H	Birmingham City	D	1-1	Hayes	44,777
37	Apr 2	H	Sunderland	W	4-2	Dyson 2, Hayes 2	40,915
38	7	A	Newcastle United	L	1-3	Dyson	26,181
39	11	H	Sheffield United	W	3-1	Hayes, Faulkner, Spurdle	16,991
40	14	H	Burnley	L	1-3	Spurdle	29,087
41	21	A	Luton Town	L	2-3	Barnes, Clarke	18,074
42	28	A	Portsmouth	W	4-2	Dyson 2, Hart, Spurdle	24,684
							Appearances
						Three own goals	Goals

FA Cup

R3	Jan 11	H	Blackpool	W	2-1	Dyson, Johnstone	42,517
R4	28	A	Southend United	W	1-0	Hayes	29,500
R5	Feb 18	H	Liverpool	D	0-0		70,640
rep	22	A	Liverpool	W	2-1	Dyson, Hayes	57,528
R6	Mar 3	H	Everton	W	2-1	Hayes, Johnstone	76,129
SF	17	N	Tottenham Hotspur	W	1-0	Johnstone	69,788
F	May 5	N	Birmingham City	W	3-1	Dyson, Hayes, Johnstone	100,000

SF at Villa Park, Final at Wembley Stadium

Appearances
Goals

Trautmann BC	Paul R	Little R	Barnes KH	Ewing D	Spurdle W	Fagan F	Hayes J	Revie DG	Johnstone R	Cunliffe RA	Branagan KF	Clarke RJ	Phoenix RJ	Marsden K	Dyson J	Faulkner RV	Leivers WE	McTavish JR	Hannaway J	Murray H	Savage JA	Hart JP
1	2	3	4	5	6	7	8	9	10	11												
1	2	3	4	5	6	7	8	9	10	11												
1	6	3	4	5	7	11	8	9	10		2											
1	6	3	4	5	7	11	8	9	10		2											
1	6	3	4	5	7	11	8	9	10		2											
1	6	3	4	5		7	8	9	10		2	11										
1		3	4	5		7	8	9	10		2	11	6									
1		3	4	5		7	8	9	10		2	11	6									
1		3	4	5	7	11	8		9		2		6	10								
1	6	3	4	5	7	11	8				2		10		9							
1	6	3	4	5	7	11	8	9	10		2											
1		3	4	5		7	8			11	2		6		9	10						
1	6	3	4	5	7		8	9		11	2					10						
1		3	4	5	7		8	9	10	11	2		6									
1	6	3	4		7		8	9	10		2	11					5					
1	4	3				7	8		9		2	11				10	5	6				
1	4	3				7	8		9		2	11				10	5	6				
1	6	3	4	2	7		8		9			11			10		5					
1	6	3	4	2	7		8		9			11			10		5					
1	6	3	4	5	7		8		9			11			10		2					
1	6	3	4	5	7		8		9			11			10		2					
1	6	3	4	5	7		8		9			11			10		2					
1	6	3	4	5	7		8		9			11			10		2					
1	6	3	4	5	7		8		9			11			10		2					
1	6	3	4	5	7		8		9			11			10		2					
1	6	3	4	5	7		8		9	11					10		2					
1	6	3	4	5	7		8		9			11			10		2					
1	6	3	4	5	7		8	9				11				10	2					
1	6	3	4	5		11	8	9	7						10		2					
1	6	3	4	5	7	11	8		9						10		2					
1	6	3	4	5	7		8		9			11			10		2					
1	6	3	4	5	7		8		9			11			10		2					
1	6	3	4	5	7		8	9				11			10		2					
1	6	3	4	5	7		8		9			11			10		2					
1	6	3	4	5	7		8	9				11			10		2					
1	6	3	4	5	7		8	9				11			10		2					
1	6	3		5	7		8		9			11			10			4	2			
1	6	3	4	5	7		8		9			11			10				2			
1		3	4	5	7		8	9								10	2	6		11		
	6	3	4	5	7		8	9							11	10	2				1	
	6	3	4	5	7		8	9				11			10		2				1	
1	2	3	4	5	7		8	9							10			6				11
40	36	42	39	39	35	16	42	21	31	6	15	25	6	1	25	7	25	5	2	1	2	1
	1		1		9	1	23	4	12	3		6		1	13	4						1

Trautmann BC	Paul R	Little R	Barnes KH	Ewing D	Spurdle W	Fagan F	Hayes J	Revie DG	Johnstone R	Cunliffe RA	Branagan KF	Clarke RJ	Phoenix RJ	Marsden K	Dyson J	Faulkner RV	Leivers WE
1	6	3	4	5	7		8		9			11			10		2
1	6	3	4	5	7		8		9			11			10		2
1	6	3	4	5	7		8	9	11						10		2
1	6	3	4	5	7		8		9			11			10		2
1	6	3	4	5	7		8		9			11			10		2
1	6	3	4	5	7		8		9			11			10		2
1	6	3	4	5			8	9	7			11			10		2
7	7	7	7	7	6		7	2	7			6			7		7
							4		4						3		

League Table

	P	W	D	L	F	A	Pts
Manchester U	42	25	10	7	83	51	60
Blackpool	42	20	9	13	86	62	49
Wolverh'pton W	42	20	9	13	89	65	49
Manchester C	42	18	10	14	82	69	46
Arsenal	42	18	10	14	60	61	46
Birmingham C	42	18	9	15	75	57	45
Burnley	42	18	8	16	64	54	44
Bolton W	42	18	7	17	71	58	43
Sunderland	42	17	9	16	80	95	43
Luton T	42	17	8	17	66	64	42
Newcastle U	42	17	7	18	85	70	41
Portsmouth	42	16	9	17	78	85	41
W.B.A.	42	18	5	19	58	70	41
Charlton A	42	17	6	19	75	81	40
Everton	42	15	10	17	55	69	40
Chelsea	42	14	11	17	64	77	39
Cardiff C	42	15	9	18	55	69	39
Tottenham H	42	15	7	20	61	71	37
Preston N.E.	42	14	8	20	73	72	36
Aston Villa	42	11	13	18	52	69	35
Huddersfield T	42	14	7	21	54	83	35
Sheffield U	42	12	9	21	63	77	33

1956-57

Division One

Manager: Les McDowall

Did you know that?

Match 2: Thompson's last game.
Match 10: Spurdle's last game.
Match 13: Hannaway's last game.
Match 16: Revie's last game.
Match 41: Paul's last game.

The first City game filmed by the BBC at Maine Road was the 15 December 1956 meeting with Wolves. The game was noteworthy as it was the return match of Bert Trautmann.

Match No.	Date	Venue	Opponents	Result		Scorers	Attendance
1	Aug 18	A	Wolverhampton W.	L	1-5	Revie	43,406
2	22	H	Tottenham Hotspur	D	2-2	Clarke 2	32,718
3	25	H	Aston Villa	D	1-1	Clarke	24,326
4	29	A	Tottenham Hotspur	L	2-3	Johnstone, Paul	33,443
5	Sep 1	A	Luton Town	L	2-3	Hayes, McAdams	21,648
6	5	H	Leeds United	W	1-0	McAdams	34,185
7	8	H	Sunderland	W	3-1	McAdams, Revie, Hayes	35,753
8	12	A	Leeds United	L	0-2		35,068
9	15	A	Charlton Athletic	L	0-1		18,533
10	22	A	Manchester United	L	0-2		53,751
11	29	H	Blackpool	L	0-3		39,528
12	Oct 6	A	Arsenal	L	3-7	Clarke 2, Dyson	33,652
13	13	H	Burnley	L	0-1		35,981
14	20	A	Newcastle United	W	3-0	Fagan, Johnstone, Dyson	34,802
15	27	H	Sheffield Wednesday	W	4-2	Fagan, Hayes 2, Johnstone	29,259
16	Nov 3	A	Cardiff City	D	1-1	Dyson	23,820
17	10	H	Birmingham City	W	3-1	Johnstone 2, Hayes	21,005
18	17	A	West Bromwich Albion	D	1-1	Dyson	25,958
19	24	H	Portsmouth	W	5-1	Fagan, Hayes 2, Johnstone, Clarke	24,364
20	Dec 1	A	Preston North End	L	1-3	Walton (og)	25,433
21	8	H	Chelsea	W	5-4	Johnstone 3, Hayes 2	24,412
22	15	H	Wolverhampton W.	L	2-3	Johnstone 2	30,329
23	25	H	Bolton Wanderers	L	1-3	Fagan	19,731
24	26	A	Bolton Wanderers	L	0-1		20,856
25	29	H	Luton Town	W	3-2	Dyson 2, Clarke	27,253
26	Jan 12	A	Sunderland	D	1-1	Fagan	34,119
27	19	H	Charlton Athletic	W	5-1	Dyson 3, Johnstone, Fagan	22,108
28	Feb 2	H	Manchester United	L	2-4	Hayes, Clarke	63,872
29	4	A	Aston Villa	D	2-2	McClelland, Hayes	10,593
30	9	A	Blackpool	L	1-4	Johnstone	21,105
31	23	A	Sheffield Wednesday	D	2-2	Paul, Hayes	10,159
32	Mar 2	H	Newcastle United	L	1-2	Barnes	25,229
33	9	A	Chelsea	L	2-4	Fagan, Hayes	35,664
34	16	H	Cardiff City	W	4-1	Johnstone 3, Dyson	26,395
35	20	H	Arsenal	L	2-3	Barnes, Clarke	27,974
36	30	H	West Bromwich Albion	W	2-1	Paul, Fagan	26,361
37	Apr 6	A	Portsmouth	W	1-0	Dyson	24,949
38	13	H	Preston North End	L	0-2		31,305
39	19	H	Everton	L	2-4	Fagan, Clarke	28,009
40	20	A	Burnley	W	3-0	Hayes, Dyson, Clarke	16,746
41	22	A	Everton	D	1-1	McAdams	28,887
42	27	A	Birmingham City	D	3-3	Kirkman 2, McSeveney (og)	23,747
							Appearances
						Two own goals	Goals

FA Cup

	Date	Venue	Opponents	Result		Scorers	Attendance
R3	Jan 5	A	Newcastle United	D	1-1	Johnstone	57,890
rep	9	H	Newcastle United	L	4-5e	Johnstone 2, Fagan, Stokoe (og)	46,988
							Appearances
						One own goal	Goals

Charity Shield

	Date	Venue	Opponents	Result		Scorers	Attendance
	Oct 24	H	Manchester United	L	0-1		30,495
							Appearances

Thompson GH	Leivers WE	Little R	Barnes KH	Ewing D	Paul R	Hart JP	Hayes J	Revie DG	Johnstone R	Clarke RJ	Savage JA	McClelland JB	McAdams WJ	McTavish JR	Spurdle W	Dyson J	Fagan F	Hannaway J	Trautmann BC	Phoenix RJ	Marsden K	Sear RC	Kirkman AJ
1	2	3	4	5	6	7	8	9	10	11													
1	2	3	4	5	6	10	8	9	7	11													
	2	3	4	5	6	10	8	9	7	11	1												
	2	3	4	5	6	10	8		9	11	1	7											
	2	3	4	5	6		8	9	7	11	1		10										
	2	3		5	4		10	9		11	1		8	6	7								
	2	3		5	4		10	9		11	1		8	6	7								
	2	3		5	4		10	9		11	1		8	6	7								
	2	3		5	4			9			1		8	6	7	10	11						
	2		4	5	6			9		11	1		8		7	10		3					
	2		4	5	3		8	9		11	1			6		10	7						
	2		4	5	3		8		9	11	1			6		10	7						
	2			5	6		8	4	9	11	1					10	7	3					
	2	3		5	6		8	4	9	11	1					10	7						
	2	3		5	6		8	4	9	11	1					10	7						
	2	3		5	6		8	4	9	11	1					10	7						
	2	3	4	5	6		8		9	11	1					10	7						
	2	3	4	5	6		8		9	11	1					10	7						
	2	3	4	5	6		8		9	11	1					10	7						
	2	3	4	5	6		8		9	11	1					10	7						
	2	3	4	5			8		9	11	1			6		10	7						
	2	3	4	5	6		8		9	11						10	7		1				
	2	3	4	5	6		8		9	11						10	7		1				
	2	3	4	5	6		8		9	11						10	7		1				
	2	3	4	5	6		8		9	11						10	7		1				
	2	3	4	5	6				9	11			8			10	7		1				
	2	3	4	5	6		8		9			7				10	11		1				
	2	3	4	5	6		8		9	11						10	7		1				
	2	3	4	5	6		8		9	11		7				10			1				
	2	3	4	5	6		8		9	11						10	7		1				
	2	3	4	5	6		8			11			10			9	7		1				
	2	3	4	5	6		10			11			8			9	7		1				
	2	3	9	5	4		10			11			8	6			7		1				
	2	3	9		6				8	11						10	7		1	4	5		
	2	3	9		6				8	11						10	7		1	4	5		
	2	3	9		6				8	11						10	7		1	4	5		
	2	3	9		6				8	11						10	7		1	4	5		
	2	3	9		6				8	11						10	7		1	4	5		
	2	3	4		6		8		9	11						10	7		1		5		
	2	3			6		8		9	11						10	7		1	4	5		
	2	3			6		8			11			9			10	7		1	4	5		
	2			5			10			11		7	9						1	6	4	3	8
2	42	37	31	34	40	4	34	14	31	40	19	4	12	8	5	32	31	2	21	8	9	1	1
			2		3		14	2	16	11		1	4			12	9						2

Thompson GH	Leivers WE	Little R	Barnes KH	Ewing D	Paul R	Hart JP	Hayes J	Revie DG	Johnstone R	Clarke RJ	Savage JA	McClelland JB	McAdams WJ	McTavish JR	Spurdle W	Dyson J	Fagan F	Hannaway J	Trautmann BC	Phoenix RJ	Marsden K	Sear RC	Kirkman AJ
	2	3	4	5	6				9	11			8			10	7		1				
	2	3	4	5	6				9	11			8			10	7		1				
	2	2	2	2	2				2	2			2			2	2		2				
									3								1						

Thompson GH	Leivers WE	Little R	Barnes KH	Ewing D	Paul R	Hart JP	Hayes J	Revie DG	Johnstone R	Clarke RJ	Savage JA	McClelland JB	McAdams WJ	McTavish JR	Spurdle W	Dyson J	Fagan F	Hannaway J	Trautmann BC	Phoenix RJ	Marsden K	Sear RC	Kirkman AJ
	2	3		5	6		8	4	9	11	1					10	7						
	1	1		1	1		1	1	1	1	1					1	1						

League Table

	P	W	D	L	F	A	Pts
Manchester U	42	28	8	6	103	54	64
Tottenham H	42	22	12	8	104	56	56
Preston N.E.	42	23	10	9	84	56	56
Blackpool	42	22	9	11	93	65	53
Arsenal	42	21	8	13	85	69	50
Wolverh'pton W	42	20	8	14	94	70	48
Burnley	42	18	10	14	56	50	46
Leeds U	42	15	14	13	72	63	44
Bolton W	42	16	12	14	65	65	44
Aston Villa	42	14	15	13	65	55	43
W.B.A.	42	14	14	14	59	61	42
Birmingham C*	42	15	9	18	69	69	39
Chelsea*	42	13	13	16	73	73	39
Sheffield W	42	16	6	20	82	88	38
Everton	42	14	10	18	61	79	38
Luton T	42	14	9	19	58	76	37
Newcastle U	42	14	8	20	67	87	36
Manchester C	42	13	9	20	78	88	35
Portsmouth	42	10	13	19	62	92	33
Sunderland	42	12	8	22	67	88	32
Cardiff C	42	10	9	23	53	88	29
Charlton A	42	9	4	29	62	120	22

*Birmingham City & Chelsea finished in equal 12th position

1957-58

Division One

Manager: Les McDowall

Did you know that?

Match 8: Marsden's last game.
Match 11: Savage's last game.
Match 19: Clarke's last game.
Match 31: Taylor's first and only game.

The 1957–58 season became noteworthy as the Blues both scored and conceded 100 goals or more. Incredibly, high-scoring defeats, such as the 9–2 at West Bromwich Albion, were followed by great wins such as the 5–1 defeat of Spurs in September. Of all four divisions, only Leicester (112) and Rotherham (101) conceded more goals.

Considering the number of goals conceded City's fifth-place finish is an outstanding achievement.

Match No.	Date	Venue	Opponents	Result		Scorers	Attendance
1	Aug 28	A	Chelsea	W	3-2	Barlow, Hayes, McAdams	43,722
2	31	A	Manchester United	L	1-4	Barnes	63,347
3	Sep 4	H	Chelsea	W	5-2	Barlow 2, Fagan 2, McAdams	27,943
4	7	A	Nottingham Forest	L	1-2	Hayes	37,191
5	11	H	Preston North End	W	2-0	Fagan, Hayes	24,439
6	14	H	Portsmouth	W	2-1	Ewing, Johnstone	28,798
7	18	A	Preston North End	L	1-6	Fagan	22,034
8	21	A	West Bromwich Albion	L	2-9	Clarke, Fagan	26,080
9	28	H	Tottenham Hotspur	W	5-1	Hayes 2, Johnstone 2, Barlow	22,497
10	Oct 5	A	Birmingham City	L	0-4		28,059
11	9	H	Sheffield Wednesday	W	2-0	Barlow, McAdams	24,036
12	12	H	Leicester City	W	4-3	Hayes 2, Barlow, McAdams	29,884
13	19	A	Blackpool	W	5-2	Hayes 2, Barlow, Barnes, McAdams	28,322
14	26	H	Luton Town	D	2-2	Barlow, McAdams	30,654
15	Nov 2	A	Arsenal	L	1-2	McAdams	43,692
16	9	H	Bolton Wanderers	W	2-1	Hayes, McAdams	34,147
17	16	A	Leeds United	W	4-2	Hayes 2, Barnes, McAdams	23,855
18	23	H	Wolverhampton W.	L	3-4	Barnes 2, McAdams	45,121
19	30	A	Sunderland	L	1-2	McAdams	35,442
20	Dec 7	H	Everton	W	6-2	Barnes 3, McAdams 2, Hayes	20,912
21	14	A	Aston Villa	W	2-1	Hayes, Aldis (og)	24,767
22	21	A	Sheffield Wednesday	W	5-4	Hayes 2, Kirkman 2, Johnstone	22,042
23	25	A	Burnley	L	1-2	Fagan	27,666
24	26	H	Burnley	W	4-1	Barlow, Fagan, Hayes, Kirkman	47,285
25	28	H	Manchester United	D	2-2	Hayes, Foulkes (og)	70,483
26	Jan 11	H	Nottingham Forest	D	1-1	Johnstone	34,837
27	18	A	Portsmouth	L	1-2	Sambrook	26,254
28	Feb 1	H	West Bromwich Albion	W	4-1	McAdams 3, Barlow	38,702
29	8	A	Tottenham Hotspur	L	1-5	Hayes	37,539
30	22	A	Leicester City	L	4-8	Johnstone 2, Barnes, McAdams	31,017
31	Mar 1	H	Blackpool	W	4-3	Barlow, Barnes(p), McAdams, H Kelly (og)	30,621
32	5	H	Birmingham City	D	1-1	Barlow	30,655
33	8	A	Luton Town	W	2-1	Sambrook, Dunne (og)	16,019
34	15	H	Arsenal	L	2-4	Barlow, Hayes	31,645
35	22	A	Wolverhampton W.	D	3-3	Barlow 2, Stuart (og)	34,932
36	29	H	Leeds United	W	1-0	McAdams	21,962
37	Apr 5	A	Bolton Wanderers	W	2-0	Barlow 2	27,733
38	7	H	Newcastle United	W	2-1	Hayes, Warhurst	33,995
39	12	H	Sunderland	W	3-1	Hayes 2, Hart	31,166
40	14	A	Newcastle United	L	1-4	Warhurst	53,226
41	19	A	Everton	W	5-2	Hart 2, Barnes, Hayes, Sambrook	31,433
42	26	H	Aston Villa	L	1-2	Hayes	28,275
							Appearances
						Five own goals	Goals

FA Cup

R3	Jan 4	A	West Bromwich Albion	L	1-5	Hayes	49,669
							Appearances
							Goals

Trautmann BC	Leivers WE	Little R	Barnes KH	Ewing D	Warhurst R	Barlow CJ	Hayes J	Johnstone R	McAdams WJ	Clarke RJ	Fagan F	Savage JA	Sear RC	Marsden K	Branagan KF	McTavish JR	McClelland JB	Fidler DJ	Phoenix RJ	Fleet S	Kirkman AJ	Sambrook R	Taylor KV	Cheetham RAJ	Hart JP
1	2	3	4	5	6	7	8	9	10	11															
1	2	3	4	5	6	7	8	9	10	11															
1	2	3	4	5	6	7	8	9	10		11														
		3	4	5	6	7	8	9	10		11	1	2												
		3	4	5	6		7	8	9		11	1	2	10											
1	2	3	4	5	6		7	8	9		11			10											
		3	4	5	6	7	8		9		11	1	2	10											
		3	4	5			8		9	11	7	1		10	2	6									
			4	5	6	7	8	9	10		11	1	3		2										
			4	5	6	10	8	9		11		1	3		2		7								
	2	3	4	5	6	7	8	9	10		11	1													
1	2		4	5	6	7	8	9	10		11		3												
1	2		4	5	6	7	8	9	10		11		3												
1	2		4	5	6	7	8	9	10				3					11							
1	2		4	5	6	7	8	9	10		11		3												
1	2		4	5	6	7	8	9	10		11		3												
1	2	3	4	5	6	7	8		10	11									9						
	2		4	5	6	7	8	9	10		11		3							1					
1	2		4	5	6	7	8	9	10	11			3												
1	2		4	5	6	7	8	9	10		11		3												
1	2		4	5	6	7	8	9	10		11		3												
1	2	3	4	5	6	7	10	9			11										8				
1	2	3	4	5	6	7	10	9			11										8				
1	2	3	4	5	6	7	10				11								9		8				
1	2	3	4	5	6	7	10	9			11										8				
1	2		4	5	6	8	10	9					3				7					11			
1	2		4	5		8	10	9					3			6	7					11			
1	2		4	5	6	7	8	9	10				3									11			
1	2		4	5	6	7	8	9	10				3									11			
1	2	3	4	5	6	7	8	9	10		11														
1	2		4			7	8	9	10				3			6						11	5		
1	2			5	4	7	8	9	10				3			6						11			
1	2			5		7	8		10				3			6						11		4	9
1	2	3		5		7	8	9			10					6						11		4	
1	2		4	5	6	8		9	10		7		3									11			
1	2		4	5	6	8		9	10		7		3									11			
1	2		4	5	6	8	10	9			7		3									11			
1	2		4	5	6	8	10	9			7		3									11			
1	2		4	5	6	8	10				7		3									11			9
1	5		4		6	8	10				7		3		2							11			9
1	5		4		6	8	10				7		3		2							11			9
1	5		4		6	8	10				7		3		2							11			9
34	36	16	39	38	37	39	40	33	28	6	29	7	29	4	6	6	3	1	2	1	4	16	1	2	5
			11	1	2	17	25	7	19	1	7										3	3			3

Trautmann BC	Leivers WE	Little R	Barnes KH	Ewing D	Warhurst R	Barlow CJ	Hayes J	Johnstone R	McAdams WJ	Clarke RJ	Fagan F	Savage JA	Sear RC	Marsden K	Branagan KF	McTavish JR	McClelland JB	Fidler DJ	Phoenix RJ	Fleet S	Kirkman AJ	Sambrook R	Taylor KV	Cheetham RAJ	Hart JP
1			4	5	6	7	8	9		10	11		3		2										
1			1	1	1	1	1	1		1	1		1		1										
							1																		

League Table

	P	W	D	L	F	A	Pts
Wolverh'pton W	42	28	8	6	103	47	64
Preston N.E.	42	26	7	9	100	51	59
Tottenham H	42	21	9	12	93	77	51
W.B.A.	42	18	14	10	92	70	50
Manchester C	42	22	5	15	104	100	49
Burnley	42	21	5	16	80	74	47
Blackpool	42	19	6	17	80	67	44
Luton T	42	19	6	17	69	63	44
Manchester U	42	16	11	15	85	75	43
Nottingham F	42	16	10	16	69	63	42
Chelsea	42	15	12	15	83	79	42
Arsenal	42	16	7	19	73	85	39
Birmingham C	42	14	11	17	76	89	39
Aston Villa	42	16	7	19	73	86	39
Bolton W	42	14	10	18	65	87	38
Everton	42	13	11	18	65	75	37
Leeds U	42	14	9	19	51	63	37
Leicester C	42	14	5	23	91	112	33
Newcastle U	42	12	8	22	73	81	32
Portsmouth	42	12	8	22	73	88	32
Sunderland	42	10	12	20	54	97	32
Sheffield W	42	12	7	23	69	92	31

1958-59

Division One

Manager: Les McDowall

Did you know that?

Match 3: McClelland's last game.
Match 5: Little's last game.
Match 8: Warhurst's last game.
Match 26: Horridge's last game.
Match 27: Kirkman's last game.
Match 30: Fidler's last game.
Match 36: Lister's last game.
Match 39: Pennington's first and only game.

The goalless draw with Villa (Match 41) meant either side could still be relegated on the final day. Villa had a better goal average and so City needed to better their result. Villa's final match (v WBA) started 15 minutes before City's and they were leading until the 88th minute when WBA equalised. City's 3–1 win sent Villa, managed by Joe Mercer, down.

Match No.	Date	Venue	Opponents	Result		Scorers	Attendance
1	Aug 23	A	Burnley	W	4-3	Hayes 2, Johnstone 2	31,371
2	27	H	Bolton Wanderers	D	3-3	Barlow, Barnes, Sambrook	40,844
3	30	H	Preston North End	D	1-1	McClelland	42,576
4	Sep 3	A	Bolton Wanderers	L	1-4	Hayes	39,727
5	6	A	Leicester City	L	1-3	McAdams	29,053
6	10	H	Luton Town	D	1-1	Fagan	30,771
7	13	H	Everton	L	1-3	Barlow	35,437
8	17	A	Luton Town	L	1-5	Johnstone	18,160
9	20	A	Arsenal	L	1-4	Sambrook	47,681
10	27	H	Manchester United	D	1-1	Hayes	62,912
11	Oct 4	H	Leeds United	W	2-1	Barlow, Hayes	31,989
12	11	A	Wolverhampton W.	L	0-2		33,769
13	18	H	Portsmouth	W	3-2	Cheetham, Fagan, Hayes	31,330
14	25	A	Newcastle United	L	1-4	Hannah	54,837
15	Nov 1	H	Tottenham Hotspur	W	5-1	Barlow 3, Hannah, Hayes	30,601
16	8	A	Nottingham Forest	L	0-4		31,154
17	15	H	Chelsea	W	5-1	Barlow, Fagan, Hayes, Leivers, Sambrook	19,778
18	22	A	Blackpool	D	0-0		19,200
19	29	H	Blackburn Rovers	L	0-1		16,405
20	Dec 6	A	Aston Villa	D	1-1	Kirkman	21,684
21	13	H	West Ham United	W	3-1	Barlow 3	22,250
22	20	H	Burnley	L	1-4	Barnes	22,328
23	26	A	Birmingham City	L	1-6	Barlow	34,290
24	27	H	Birmingham City	W	4-1	Hayes 2, Barlow, Sambrook	29,276
25	Jan 3	A	Preston North End	L	0-2		21,268
26	31	A	Everton	L	1-3	Barlow	43,409
27	Feb 7	H	Arsenal	D	0-0		31,819
28	14	A	Manchester United	L	1-4	Johnstone	59,846
29	21	A	Leeds United	W	4-0	Barlow 2, Barnes, Fidler	18,515
30	28	H	Wolverhampton W.	L	1-4	Hayes	42,776
31	Mar 7	A	Portsmouth	W	4-3	Fagan, Hayes, McAdams, Sambrook	19,919
32	14	H	Newcastle United	W	5-1	Hayes 2, Sambrook 2, Barnes	25,417
33	21	A	Tottenham Hotspur	L	1-3	McAdams	34,493
34	28	H	Nottingham Forest	D	1-1	Barlow	28,146
35	30	H	West Bromwich Albion	L	0-2		25,551
36	31	A	West Bromwich Albion	L	0-3		31,887
37	Apr 4	A	Chelsea	L	0-2		32,554
38	11	H	Blackpool	L	0-2		27,118
39	18	A	Blackburn Rovers	L	1-2	Hayes	24,616
40	20	A	West Ham United	L	1-5	Barlow	23,516
41	25	H	Aston Villa	D	0-0		39,661
42	29	H	Leicester City	W	3-1	Hayes, McAdams, Sambrook	46,936
							Appearances
							Goals

FA Cup

	Date	Venue	Opponents	Result		Scorers	Attendance
R3	Jan 10	A	Grimsby Town	D	2-2	Barlow, Hayes	14,964
rep	24	H	Grimsby Town	L	1-2	Johnstone	35,840
							Appearances
							Goals

Trautmann BC	Leivers WE	Sear RC	Barnes KH	Ewing D	McTavish JR	Barlow CJ	Hayes J	Johnstone R	McAdams WJ	Sambrook R	McClelland JB	Little R	Fleet S	Warhurst R	Fagan F	Branagan KF	Shawcross FD	Hannah G	Cheetham RAJ	Lister HF	Horridge P	Kirkman AJ	Phoenix RJ	Fidler DJ	Pennington J
1	2	3	4	5	6	7	8	9	10	11															
1	2	3	4	5	6	7	8	9	10	11															
1	2	3	4	5	6	8	10	9		11	7														
1	2	3	4	5	6	7	10	9	8	11															
1		2	4	5	6	7	10	9	8	11		3													
	2	3	4	5		8	10		9	11			1	6	7										
1	2	3	4	5		8	10		9	11				6	7										
1	5	3	4			7	10	9	8					6	11	2									
1	2	3	4	5		7	10	9		11							6	8							
1	2	3	6	5		8	10			11					7			9	4						
1	2	3	6	5		7	8		10						11			9	4						
1	2	3	6	5		7	8								11			9	4	10					
1	2	3	6	5		7	10	8							11			9	4						
1	2	3	6	5		7	10	8							11			9	4						
1	2	3	6	5		8	10			11					7			9	4						
1	2	3	6	5		8	10			11					7			9	4						
1	2	3	6	5		8	10			11					7			9	4						
1	2		6	5		8	10			11					7			9	4		3				
1	2	3	6	5		8	10			11					7			9	4						
1		2	6	5		10	7			11								9	4		3	8			
1	2	3	6	5		8	7		10						11			9	4						
1	2	3	6	5		8	7		10	11								9	4						
1		3	6	5		8	10			11					7	2		9	4						
1		3	6	5		8	10		9	11					7	2							4		
1		3		5		8	10		9	11					7	2			6				4		
1	2		6	5		10		8	9	11								7			3		4		
1	2	3	4		5	10		9							7							8	6	11	
1	2		4		5	8	10	9		7						3							6	11	
1	2		4		5	9	10			7						3		8					6	11	
1	2		4		5	9	10			7						3		8					6	11	
1		3	4		5		10		9	11					7	2		8					6		
1	2		4		5		10		9	11					7	3		8					6		
1	2		4		5		10		9	11					7	3		8					6		
1	2	3	4		5	7	10		9	11								8					6		
1	2	3	4		5	7	10		9	11								8					6		
1		3	4	5			10		9	11					7	2				8			6		
1		3	4	5		9	10	8							7	2	11						6		
1	2	3	4	5		9	10	8							7		11						6		
1	2		4	5		9	10	8		11						3							6		7
1	2			5		7	10	8	9	11						3	6		4						
1	2		6		5	8	10	9		11					7	3			4						
1	2		6		5	7	10	8	9	11						3			4						
41	34	31	40	30	16	38	40	18	21	33	1	1	1	3	25	16	4	23	18	2	3	2	16	4	1
	1		4			17	16	4	4	8	1				4			2	1			1		1	

Trautmann BC	Leivers WE	Sear RC	Barnes KH	Ewing D	McTavish JR	Barlow CJ	Hayes J	Johnstone R	McAdams WJ	Sambrook R	McClelland JB	Little R	Fleet S	Warhurst R	Fagan F	Branagan KF	Shawcross FD	Hannah G	Cheetham RAJ	Lister HF	Horridge P	Kirkman AJ	Phoenix RJ	Fidler DJ	Pennington J
1		3	6	5		7	10	8	9	11						2							4		
1	2	3	6	5		7	10	8	9	11													4		
2	1	2	2	2		2	2	2	2	2						1							2		
						1	1	1																	

League Table

	P	W	D	L	F	A	Pts
Wolverh'pton W	42	28	5	9	110	49	61
Manchester U	42	24	7	11	103	66	55
Arsenal	42	21	8	13	88	68	50
Bolton W	42	20	10	12	79	66	50
W.B.A.	42	18	13	11	88	68	49
West Ham U	42	21	6	15	85	70	48
Burnley	42	19	10	13	81	70	48
Blackpool	42	18	11	13	66	49	47
Birmingham C	42	20	6	16	84	68	46
Blackburn R	42	17	10	15	76	70	44
Newcastle U	42	17	7	18	80	80	41
Preston N.E.	42	17	7	18	70	77	41
Nottingham F	42	17	6	19	71	74	40
Chelsea	42	18	4	20	77	98	40
Leeds U	42	15	9	18	57	74	39
Everton	42	17	4	21	71	87	38
Luton T	42	12	13	17	68	71	37
Tottenham H	42	13	10	19	85	95	36
Leicester C	42	11	10	21	67	98	32
Manchester C	42	11	9	22	64	95	31
Aston Villa	42	11	8	23	58	87	30
Portsmouth	42	6	9	27	64	112	21

1959-60

Division One

Manager: Les McDowall

Did you know that?

Match 3: Johnstone's last game.
Match 15: Phoenix's last game.
Match 15: Phoenix's last game.
Match 16: Kerr's last game.
Match 27: Fagan's last game.
Match 32: Dyson's last game.
Match 35: McTavish's last game.
Match 40: Leigh and McAdams's last game.
Match 42: Branagan's last game.

Bert Trautmann's 400th League appearance came on 9 March 1960 against Blackpool. At this time, Eric Brook remained City's record holder, but he would ultimately be passed by first Trautmann, then Alan Oakes, who made his debut during this season.

Match No.	Date	Venue	Opponents	Result		Scorers	Attendance
1	Aug 22	H	Nottingham Forest	W	2-1	Fagan, Johnstone	38,974
2	26	A	Fulham	L	2-5	Barlow, Colbridge	26,818
3	29	A	Sheffield Wednesday	L	0-1		34,093
4	Sep 2	H	Fulham	W	3-1	McAdams 2, Colbridge	37,482
5	5	H	Wolverhampton W.	L	4-6	McAdams 3, Barlow	43,650
6	9	A	Luton Town	W	2-1	Hannah, Hayes	13,122
7	12	A	Arsenal	L	1-3	McAdams	38,221
8	16	H	Luton Town	L	1-2	Colbridge	29,309
9	19	H	Manchester United	W	3-0	Hayes 2, Hannah	58,300
10	26	H	Blackburn Rovers	W	2-1	Hayes, McAdams	41,687
11	Oct 3	A	Blackpool	W	3-1	Barlow, Colbridge, Hayes	33,226
12	10	A	Preston North End	W	5-1	McAdams 3, Barlow, Cheetham	32,546
13	17	H	Leicester City	W	3-2	McAdams 2, Hayes	33,896
14	24	A	Burnley	L	3-4	Hannah 2, Colbridge	28,653
15	31	H	Tottenham Hotspur	L	1-2	Leivers	45,506
16	Nov 7	A	West Ham United	L	1-4	Hayes	25,243
17	14	H	Chelsea	D	1-1	Dyson	24,364
18	21	A	West Bromwich Albion	L	0-2		24,219
19	28	H	Newcastle United	L	3-4	McAdams 3	29,416
20	Dec 5	A	Birmingham City	L	2-4	Colbridge, Hayes	18,661
21	12	H	Leeds United	D	3-3	Barlow 2, McAdams	19,715
22	19	A	Nottingham Forest	W	2-1	Barlow, Burkitt (og)	13,506
23	26	A	Everton	L	1-2	Barlow	43,351
24	28	H	Everton	W	4-0	Barlow, Fagan, Hayes, McAdams	30,580
25	Jan 2	H	Sheffield Wednesday	W	4-1	McAdams 2, Barlow, Hayes	44,167
26	16	A	Wolverhampton W.	L	2-4	Barlow, Colbridge	27,864
27	23	H	Arsenal	L	1-2	McAdams	28,441
28	Feb 6	A	Manchester United	D	0-0		59,450
29	13	A	Blackburn Rovers	L	1-2	Barlow	23,731
30	27	H	Birmingham City	W	3-0	Hayes 2, Barlow	23,479
31	Mar 5	A	Leicester City	L	0-5		24,009
32	9	H	Blackpool	L	2-3	Barlow, Haydock	19,653
33	19	A	Leeds United	L	3-4	Barlow, Law, Gibson (og)	32,545
34	30	H	West Ham United	W	3-1	Barlow, Law, McAdams	29,572
35	Apr 2	A	Chelsea	L	0-3		34,044
36	9	H	West Bromwich Albion	L	0-1		24,342
37	15	H	Bolton Wanderers	W	1-0	Barlow	50,053
38	16	A	Tottenham Hotspur	W	1-0	McAdams	49,767
39	18	A	Bolton Wanderers	L	1-3	Barlow	35,591
40	23	H	Preston North End	W	2-1	Barlow, Colbridge	29,812
41	30	A	Newcastle United	W	1-0	Hayes	27,812
42	May 2	H	Burnley	L	1-2	Colbridge	65,981
							Appearances
						Two own goals	Goals

FA Cup

R3	Jan 9	H	Southampton	L	1-5	Barlow	42,065
							Appearances
							Goals

Trautmann BC	Leivers WE	Kerr A	Barnes KH	McTavish JR	Shawcross FD	Fagan F	Johnstone R	Barlow CJ	Hayes J	Colbridge C	Branagan KF	McAdams WJ	Cheetham RAJ	Hannah G	Sear RC	Phoenix RJ	Oakes AA	Dyson J	Sambrook R	Fleet S	Haydock WE	Law D	Ewing D	Leigh P
1	2	3	4	5	6	7	8	9	10	11														
1	2	3	4	5	6	7	8	9	10	11														
1		3	4	5	6		8	7	10	11	2	9												
1		3	6	5				7	10	11	2	9	4	8										
1		3	6	5				7	10	11	2	9	4	8										
1	2	6		5				7	10	11	3	9	4	8										
1	2	6		5				7	10	11	3	9	4	8										
1	2	3	6	5		10		7		11		9	4	8										
1	2		6	5				7	10	11		9	4	8	3									
1	2		6	5				7	10	11		9	4	8	3									
1	2	9	6	5				7	10	11			4	8	3									
1	2		6	5				7	10	11		9	4	8	3									
1	2		6	5				7	10	11		9	4	8	3									
1	2		6	5				7	10	11		9	4	8	3									
1	2			5	6	7		9	10	11				8	3	4								
1	2	9		5	6			7	10	11			4	8	3									
1	2			5				7	9	11			4	8	3		6	10						
1	2		6	5				7	10	11		9	4	8	3									
1	2		6	5		11		7	10			9	4	8	3									
1	2		6	5				7	10	11		9	4	8	3									
1			6	5		11		7	10		2	9	4	8	3									
1			6	5				7	8	11	2	9	4		3			10						
1			6	5				7	8	11	2	9	4		3			10						
1			6	5		7		8	10	11	2	9	4		3									
1			6	5		7		8	10	11	2	9			3		4							
1	2		4	5		7		8	10	11	3	9					6							
1	2		4	5		7		8	10	11	3	9					6							
1			4	5					10	11	2	9		8	3		6		7					
1			4	5				9	10	11	2			8	3		6		7					
	2		4	5				7	9	11	3			8			6	10		1				
1	2		4	5				7	9	11	3			8			6	10						
1	2		6	5				7	8	11	3		4					10			9			
1			4	5				7	10	11	2	9			3		6					8		
1	2		4	5				7	10	11	3	9					6					8		
1	2		4	5					10	11	3	9					6				7	8		
1	2		4		10				7	11		9		8	3		6						5	
1	2		4					7	10	11		9			3		6					8	5	
1	2		4					7	10	11		9			3		6					8	5	
1			4					7	10	11	2	9		8			6						5	3
1	2		4					7	10	11		9		8			6						5	3
1			4					8	9	7	2				3		6		11			10	5	
1			4					7	9	11	2			8	3		6					10	5	
41	28	10	37	35	6	10	3	39	41	40	23	30	21	26	25	1	18	6	3	1	2	7	7	2
	1					2	1	19	13	9		22	1	4				1			1	2		

Trautmann BC	Leivers WE	Kerr A	Barnes KH	McTavish JR	Shawcross FD	Fagan F	Johnstone R	Barlow CJ	Hayes J	Colbridge C	Branagan KF	McAdams WJ	Cheetham RAJ	Hannah G	Sear RC	Phoenix RJ	Oakes AA	Dyson J	Sambrook R	Fleet S	Haydock WE	Law D	Ewing D	Leigh P
1			4	5		7		10	8	11	2	9			3		6							
1			1	1		1		1	1	1	1	1			1		1							
								1																

League Table

	P	W	D	L	F	A	Pts
Burnley	42	24	7	11	85	61	55
Wolverh'pton W	42	24	6	12	106	67	54
Tottenham H	42	21	11	10	86	50	53
W.B.A.	42	19	11	12	83	57	49
Sheffield W	42	19	11	12	80	59	49
Bolton W	42	20	8	14	59	51	48
Manchester U	42	19	7	16	102	80	45
Newcastle U	42	18	8	16	82	78	44
Preston N.E.	42	16	12	14	79	76	44
Fulham	42	17	10	15	73	80	44
Blackpool	42	15	10	17	59	71	40
Leicester C	42	13	13	16	66	75	39
Arsenal	42	15	9	18	68	80	39
West Ham U	42	16	6	20	75	91	38
Everton	42	13	11	18	73	78	37
Manchester C	42	17	3	22	78	84	37
Blackburn R	42	16	5	21	60	70	37
Chelsea	42	14	9	19	76	91	37
Birmingham C	42	13	10	19	63	80	36
Nottingham F	42	13	9	20	50	74	35
Leeds U	42	12	10	20	65	92	34
Luton T	42	9	12	21	50	73	30

1960-61

Division One

Manager: Les McDowall

Did you know that?

Match 22: Haydock's last game.
Match 29: Fleet's last League game.
Match 36: Hart's last game.
Match 41: Barnes's last game.
Match 42: Law's last game.

In the FA Cup City were leading 6–2 against Luton when the match was abandoned due to fog. Denis Law had scored six goals at this point, and unfortunately all his goals were wiped from the records. In the replay Law scored again, but the game ended in defeat.

Match No.	Date	Venue	Opponents	Result		Scorers	Attendance
1	Aug 20	A	Nottingham Forest	D	2-2	Hayes, Law	30,133
2	24	H	Burnley	W	2-1	Barlow, Hayes	26,941
3	30	A	Burnley	W	3-1	Barlow, Colbridge, Law	29,547
4	Sep 3	H	Arsenal	D	0-0		36,656
5	7	H	Sheffield Wednesday	D	1-1	Law	35,180
6	10	A	Newcastle United	W	3-1	Hannah, Hayes, Law	25,904
7	14	A	Sheffield Wednesday	L	1-3	Wagstaffe	28,796
8	17	H	Cardiff City	W	4-2	Barlow 2, Hayes 2	30,932
9	24	A	West Bromwich Albion	L	3-6	Barlow, Hannah, Hayes	25,143
10	Oct 1	H	Birmingham City	W	2-1	Barlow, Law	27,665
11	10	A	Tottenham Hotspur	D	1-1	Colbridge	58,916
12	15	H	Leicester City	W	3-1	Barlow, Hayes, Sambrook	30,193
13	24	A	Everton	L	2-4	Barlow, Hayes	53,781
14	29	H	Blackburn Rovers	W	4-0	Hayes 2, Hannah, Law	33,641
15	Nov 5	A	Bolton Wanderers	L	1-3	Law	34,005
16	12	H	West Ham United	L	1-2	Barlow	33,751
17	19	A	Chelsea	L	3-6	Baker, Betts, Law	37,346
18	Dec 3	A	Aston Villa	L	1-5	Law	25,093
19	10	H	Wolverhampton W.	L	2-4	Baker, Law	30,078
20	17	H	Nottingham Forest	L	1-2	Betts	18,252
21	24	H	Fulham	W	3-2	Baker 2, Colbridge	18,469
22	26	A	Fulham	L	0-1		20,240
23	31	A	Manchester United	L	1-5	Barlow	61,621
24	Jan 14	A	Arsenal	L	4-5	Hayes 2, Barlow, Betts	36,220
25	21	H	Newcastle United	D	3-3	Barlow, Hayes, Law	19,746
26	Feb 4	A	Cardiff City	D	3-3	Hayes 2, Baker	15,218
27	11	H	West Bromwich Albion	W	3-0	Barlow 2, Betts	21,382
28	25	H	Tottenham Hotspur	L	0-1		40,278
29	Mar 4	H	Manchester United	L	1-3	Wagstaffe	50,479
30	11	H	Everton	W	2-1	Baker, Shawcross	29,751
31	18	A	Blackburn Rovers	L	1-4	Hayes	19,733
32	22	A	Birmingham City	L	2-3	Law 2	18,092
33	25	H	Bolton Wanderers	D	0-0		21,816
34	31	H	Preston North End	L	2-3	Law 2	31,164
35	Apr 1	A	Wolverhampton W.	L	0-1		25,365
36	3	A	Preston North End	D	1-1	Baker	25,358
37	8	H	Chelsea	W	2-1	Law, Bonetti (og)	27,720
38	15	A	West Ham United	D	1-1	Barlow	17,982
39	19	H	Blackpool	D	1-1	Law	28,269
40	22	H	Aston Villa	W	4-1	Law 2, Barlow, Hayes	25,235
41	26	A	Leicester City	W	2-1	Baker 2	22,248
42	29	A	Blackpool	D	3-3	Barlow, Hayes, Wagstaffe	20,838
							Appearances
						One own goal	Goals

FA Cup

	Date	Venue	Opponents	Result		Scorers	Attendance
R3	Jan 7	A	Cardiff City	D	1-1	Harrington (og)	30,000
rep	11	H	Cardiff City	D	0-0*		39,035
rep2	16	N†	Cardiff City	W	2-0*	Hayes, Law	24,168
R4	Feb 1	A	Luton Town	L	1-3	Law	15,783
							Appearances
						One own goal	Goals

* after extra time. † played at Highbury

League Cup

	Date	Venue	Opponents	Result		Scorers	Attendance
R2	Oct 18	H	Stockport County	W	3-0	Law 2, Hayes	21,065
R3	Nov 21	A	Portsmouth	L	0-2		10,386
							Appearances
							Goals

Trautmann BC	Betts JB	Sear RC	Barnes KH	Plenderleith JB	Oakes AA	Barlow CJ	Law D	Hannah G	Hayes J	Colbridge C	Wagstaffe D	Shawcross FD	Sambrook R	Baker GA	Leivers WE	Cheetham RAJ	Haydock WE	Ewing D	Fleet S	Hart JP
1	2	3	4	5	6	7	8	9	10	11										
1	2	3	4	5	6	7	8	9	10	11										
1	2	3	4	5	6	7	8	9	10	11										
1	2	3	4	5	6	7	8	9	10	11										
1	2	3	4	5	6	7	8	9	10		11									
1	2	3	4	5	6	7	8	9	10		11									
1	2	3	4	5	6	7	8	9	10		11									
1	2	3	4	5	6	7	8	9	10		11									
1	2	3	4	5	6	7	8	9	10		11									
1	2	3	4	5	6	7	8	9	10		11									
1	2	3	4	5		7	8	9	10	11		6								
1	2	3	4	5		7	8	9	10			6	11							
1	2	3	4	5		7	8	9	10	11		6								
1	2	3	4	5		7	8	9	10	11		6								
1	2	3	4	5		7	8	9		11		6		10						
1	2	3	4	5		7	8	9		11		6		10						
1	2	3	4	5		7	8	9		11		6		10						
1	2	3	4	5			8	9	7	11		6		10						
1	2	3	4	5			8	9	10	11		6		7						
1	3			5			8	9	10		11	6		7	2	4				
1	2	3	4	5				8	10	7	11	6		9						
1	2	3	4	5				8	10		11	6		9			7			
1	2	3	4	5		7	10	8	11			6		9						
1	3		4	5		7	8	9	10	11		6			2					
1	3		4	5		7	10	8	9	11		6			2					
1	3					7	8		10	11		6		9	2	4		5		
1	3			5	6	7	8		10	11		4		9	2					
	3			5	6	9	8		10	7	11	4			2				1	
	3			5	6	9	10	8		7	11	4			2				1	
1	3		4	5		7	8		10		11	6		9	2					
1	2	3	4	5		7	8		10		11	6		9						
1	2	3	4	5			9	8	10		11	6	7							
1	2	3	4	5		7	9	8	10			6	11							
1	2	3		5	6		8		10		11		7	9		4				
1	2	3			6				8		11	10	7	9		4		5		
1	2	3			6			7	10				11	9		4		5		8
1	2	3			6	7	8		10		11			9		4		5		
1	2	3			6	7		8	10		11			9		4		5		
1	2	3	4		6	7	8		10		11			9				5		
1	2	3	4		6	7	8		10		11			9				5		
1	2	3	4		6	7	8		10		11			9				5		
1	3			4	6	7	8		10		11			9	2			5		
40	42	33	31	34	22	33	37	30	38	19	22	24	6	22	9	7	1	9	2	1
	4					17	19	3	18	3	3	1	1	9						

Trautmann BC	Betts JB	Sear RC	Barnes KH	Plenderleith JB	Oakes AA	Barlow CJ	Law D	Hannah G	Hayes J	Colbridge C	Wagstaffe D	Shawcross FD	Sambrook R	Baker GA	Leivers WE	Cheetham RAJ	Haydock WE	Ewing D	Fleet S	Hart JP
1	3			4	6	7	8		10		11			9	2			5		
1	3		4	5		7	8	9	10			6	11		2					
1	3		4	5		7	8	9	10			6	11		2					
1	2	3	4	5		7	8	9	10	11		6								
4	4	1	3	4	1	4	4	3	4	1	1	3	2	1	3			1		
							2		1											

Trautmann BC	Betts JB	Sear RC	Barnes KH	Plenderleith JB	Oakes AA	Barlow CJ	Law D	Hannah G	Hayes J	Colbridge C	Wagstaffe D	Shawcross FD	Sambrook R	Baker GA	Leivers WE	Cheetham RAJ	Haydock WE	Ewing D	Fleet S	Hart JP
1	2	3	4	5		7	8	9	10			6	11							
1	2	3	4	5			8	9	7	11		6		10						
2	2	2	2	2		1	2	2	2	1		2	1	1						
							2		1											

League Table

	P	W	D	L	F	A	Pts
Tottenham H	42	31	4	7	115	55	66
Sheffield W	42	23	12	7	78	47	58
Wolverh'pton W	42	25	7	10	103	75	57
Burnley	42	22	7	13	102	77	51
Everton	42	22	6	14	87	69	50
Leicester C	42	18	9	15	87	70	45
Manchester U	42	18	9	15	88	76	45
Blackburn R	42	15	13	14	77	76	43
Aston Villa	42	17	9	16	78	77	43
W.B.A.	42	18	5	19	67	71	41
Arsenal	42	15	11	16	77	85	41
Chelsea	42	15	7	20	98	100	37
Manchester C	42	13	11	18	79	90	37
Nottingham F	42	14	9	19	62	78	37
Cardiff C	42	13	11	18	60	85	37
West Ham U	42	13	10	19	77	88	36
Fulham	42	14	8	20	72	95	36
Bolton W	42	12	11	19	58	73	35
Birmingham C	42	14	6	22	62	84	34
Blackpool	42	12	9	21	68	73	33
Newcastle U	42	11	10	21	86	109	32
Preston N.E.	42	10	10	22	43	71	30

1961-62

Division One

Manager: Les McDowall

Did you know that?

Match 13: Sambrook's last game.
Match 16: Baker's last game.
Match 18: Colbridge's last game.
Match 28: McDonald's last game.
Match 30: Ewing's last game.

Glyn Pardoe made his debut in Match 37 at the age of 15 years and 314 days. This made him the youngest player to appear for the first team in a League match.

Match No.	Date	Venue	Opponents	Result		Scorers	Attendance
1	Aug 19	H	Leicester City	W	3-1	Barlow, Hayes, Kennedy	28,899
2	23	A	Fulham	W	4-3	Cheetham 2, Betts (pen), Hayes	16,281
3	26	A	Ipswich Town	W	4-2	Dobing 2, Barlow, Hayes	21,473
4	30	H	Fulham	W	2-1	Baker, Hayes	36,775
5	Sep 2	H	Burnley	L	1-3	Baker	38,171
6	6	A	Everton	W	2-0	Baker, Dobing	38,023
7	9	A	Arsenal	L	0-3		41,488
8	16	H	Bolton Wanderers	W	2-1	Baker, Hayes	27,275
9	20	H	Everton	L	1-3	Hayes	35,102
10	23	A	Manchester United	L	2-3	Kennedy, Stiles (og)	56,345
11	30	A	West Bromwich Albion	D	2-2	Baker, Jones (og)	20,820
12	Oct 7	H	Cardiff City	L	1-2	Sambrook	20,143
13	14	A	Tottenham Hotspur	L	0-2		40,561
14	21	H	Nottingham Forest	W	3-0	Barlow, Dobing, Hayes	20,258
15	28	A	Wolverhampton W.	L	1-4	Barlow	22,821
16	Nov 4	H	West Ham United	L	3-5	Dobing 3	18,839
17	11	A	Sheffield United	L	1-3	Hannah	18,135
18	18	H	Chelsea	D	2-2	Barlow, Kennedy	16,583
19	25	A	Aston Villa	L	1-2	Dobing	26,617
20	Dec 2	H	Blackpool	L	2-4	Barlow, Dobing	15,971
21	9	A	Blackburn Rovers	L	1-4	Kennedy	13,892
22	16	A	Leicester City	L	0-2		15,196
23	23	H	Ipswich Town	W	3-0	Dobing, Hayes, Young	18,376
24	26	A	Birmingham City	D	1-1	Dobing	21,926
25	Jan 13	A	Burnley	L	3-6	Dobing, Hayes, Young	22,728
26	20	H	Arsenal	W	3-2	Young 2, Bacuzzi (og)	20,414
27	Feb 3	A	Bolton Wanderers	W	2-0	Hayes, Wagstaffe	18,454
28	10	H	Manchester United	L	0-2		49,959
29	21	H	West Bromwich Albion	W	3-1	Dobing, Oakes, Young	17,225
30	24	A	Cardiff City	D	0-0		19,347
31	Mar 3	H	Tottenham Hotspur	W	6-2	Dobing 3, Hayes, Young, Baker (og)	31,706
32	10	A	Nottingham Forest	W	2-1	Hayes, Young	20,199
33	17	H	Wolverhampton W.	D	2-2	Dobing 2	28,407
34	24	A	West Ham United	W	4-0	Dobing 3, Hayes	25,808
35	31	H	Sheffield United	D	1-1	Hayes	19,157
36	Apr 7	A	Chelsea	D	1-1	Hayes	18,629
37	11	H	Birmingham City	L	1-4	Smith (og)	21,941
38	14	H	Aston Villa	W	1-0	Young	18,564
39	20	H	Sheffield Wednesday	W	3-1	Dobing, Hayes, Kennedy	32,131
40	21	A	Blackpool	L	1-3	Leivers	19,954
41	23	A	Sheffield Wednesday	L	0-1		21,048
42	28	H	Blackburn Rovers	W	3-1	Young 2, Kennedy	22,259
							Appearances
						Five own goals	Goals

FA Cup

	Date	Venue	Opponents	Result		Scorers	Attendance
R3	Jan 6	A	Notts County	W	1-0	Young	25,015
R4	Jan 27	A	Everton	L	0-2		56,980
							Appearances
							Goals

League Cup

	Date	Venue	Opponents	Result		Scorers	Attendance
R1	Sep 11	A	Ipswich Town	L	2-4	Betts (pen), Compton (og)	14,926
							Appearances
						One own goal	Goals

Trautmann BC	Betts JB	Leivers WE	Cheetham RAJ	Ewing D	Kennedy R	Barlow CJ	Dobing PA	Baker GA	Hayes J	Wagstaffe D	Sear RC	Colbridge C	Hannah G	Oakes AA	Sambrook R	MacDonald R	Gomersall V	Young NJ	Dowd HW	Plenderleith JB	Aimson PE	Benson JH	Pardoe G	Shawcross FD
1	2	3	4	5	6	7	8	9	10	11														
1	2	3	4	5	6	7	8	9	10	11														
1	2	3	4	5	6	7	8	9	10	11														
1	2		4	5	6	7	8	9	10	11	3													
1	2	3	4	5	6	7	8	9	10	11														
1	2		4	5	6		8	9	10	11	3	7												
1	2		4	5	6	9	8		10	11	3	7												
1	2		4	5	6		8	7	10	11	3		9											
1	2		4	5	6		8	7	10	11	3		9											
1	2			5	4		8	9	10	11	3			6	7									
1	2			5	4		8	9	10	11	3			6	7									
1	2			5	4		8	9	10	11	3			6	7									
1	2			5	4		8	9	10	11	3			6	7									
1				5	4	9	8	7	10	11	3			6		2								
1	2			5	4	9	8	7	10	11	3			6										
1	2			5	4	9	8	7	10	11	3			6										
1	2	3		5	4	9	8		7	11			10	6										
1	2			5	4	9	8			11		7	10	6			3							
1	2			5	4	9	8			11	3		10	6				7						
1	2			5	4	9	8		10	11	3			6				7						
	2				4		8		10	11	3			6				7	1	5	9			
1	2	5	4		6		9		10	11	3		8					7						
1	2	5	4		6		9		10	11	3		8					7						
1	2	5	4		6		9		10	11	3		8					7						
		5	4		6		9		10	11	3		8			2		7	1					
1		5	4		6		9		10	11	3		8			2		7						
1		5	4		6		9		10	11			8			2	3	7						
1		5	4		6		9		10	11	3		8			2		7						
1		5			2	9	8		10	11	3			6				7				4		
1				5	2	9	8			11	3			6				7			10	4		
1		5			2	9	8		10	11	3			6				7				4		
1		5			2	9	8		10	11	3			6				7				4		
1		5			2	9	8		10	11	3			6				7				4		
1		5			2	9	8		10	11	3			6				7				4		
1		5			2	9	8		10	11	3			6				7				4		
1		5			2	9	8		10	11	3			6				7				4		
1		5			2		8		10	11	3			6				7				4	9	
1					2				10	11	3		8	6				7		5		4	9	
1		5			2		8		10	11	3			6				7				4	9	
1		5			2		8		10	11	3			6				7				4	9	
1		5			2		8		9	11	3			6				7				4		10
1	6	5			2		8		9	11	3							7				4		10
40	24	24	16	21	42	21	41	15	39	42	35	3	13	25	4	5	2	24	2	2	2	14	4	2
	1	1	2		6	6	22	5	16	1			1	1	1			10						

Trautmann BC	Betts JB	Leivers WE	Cheetham RAJ	Ewing D	Kennedy R	Barlow CJ	Dobing PA	Baker GA	Hayes J	Wagstaffe D	Sear RC	Colbridge C	Hannah G	Oakes AA	Sambrook R	MacDonald R	Gomersall V	Young NJ	Dowd HW	Plenderleith JB	Aimson PE	Benson JH	Pardoe G	Shawcross FD
1	2	5	4		6		9		10	11	3		8					7						
1		5	4		6		9		10	11	3		8			2		7						
2	1	2	2		2		2		2	2	2		2			1		2						
																		1						

Trautmann BC	Betts JB	Leivers WE	Cheetham RAJ	Ewing D	Kennedy R	Barlow CJ	Dobing PA	Baker GA	Hayes J	Wagstaffe D	Sear RC	Colbridge C	Hannah G	Oakes AA	Sambrook R	MacDonald R	Gomersall V	Young NJ	Dowd HW	Plenderleith JB	Aimson PE	Benson JH	Pardoe G	Shawcross FD
1	2		4	5	6	7	8		10	11	3		9											
1	1		1	1	1	1	1		1	1	1		1											
	1																							

League Table

	P	W	D	L	F	A	Pts
Ipswich T	42	24	8	10	93	67	56
Burnley	42	21	11	10	101	67	53
Tottenham H	42	21	10	11	88	69	52
Everton	42	20	11	11	88	54	51
Sheffield U	42	19	9	14	61	69	47
Sheffield W	42	20	6	16	72	58	46
Aston Villa	42	18	8	16	65	56	44
West Ham U	42	17	10	15	76	82	44
W.B.A.	42	15	13	14	83	67	43
Arsenal	42	16	11	15	71	72	43
Bolton W	42	16	10	16	62	66	42
Manchester C	42	17	7	18	78	81	41
Blackpool	42	15	11	16	70	75	41
Leicester C	42	17	6	19	72	71	40
Manchester U	42	15	9	18	72	75	39
Blackburn R	42	14	11	17	50	58	39
Birmingham C	42	14	10	18	65	81	38
Wolverh'pton W	42	13	10	19	73	86	36
Nottingham F	42	13	10	19	63	79	36
Fulham	42	13	7	22	66	74	33
Cardiff C	42	9	14	19	50	81	32
Chelsea	42	9	10	23	63	94	28

1962-63

Division One

Manager: Les McDowall (until May 1963)

Did you know that?

Match 27: Plenderleith's last game.
Match 38: Barlow's last game.
Match 42: Dobing and Harley's last game.

The worst winter since 1947 caused significant fixture problems for the Blues which, ultimately, contributed to City's relegation. During March eight League and Cup games were played, most occurring within three days of the previous fixture. Only two points were taken in the League during this period.

Similar spells followed in April and May and, apart from a four-game unbeaten spell in April, City never had chance to pull out of danger.

Match No.	Date	Venue	Opponents	Result		Scorers	Attendance
1	Aug 18	A	Wolverhampton W.	L	1-8	Showell (og)	26,986
2	22	H	Liverpool	D	2-2	Young 2	33,715
3	25	H	Aston Villa	L	0-2		29,524
4	29	A	Liverpool	L	1-4	Dobing	46,073
5	Sep 1	A	Tottenham Hotspur	L	2-4	Dobing, Harley	48,758
6	5	H	Ipswich Town	W	2-1	Harley 2	24,825
7	8	H	West Ham United	L	1-6	Barlow	24,069
8	11	A	Ipswich Town	D	0-0		18,849
9	15	A	Manchester United	W	3-2	Dobing, Harley, Hayes	49,455
10	22	A	Blackpool	D	2-2	Harley, Young	29,461
11	29	H	Blackburn Rovers	L	0-1		23,249
12	Oct 6	H	Leyton Orient	W	2-0	Hannah, Harley	19,706
13	13	A	Birmingham City	D	2-2	Harley, Young	21,114
14	20	H	Sheffield Wednesday	W	3-2	Harley 3	20,756
15	27	A	Burnley	D	0-0		30,504
16	Nov 3	H	Everton	D	1-1	Dobing	40,336
17	10	A	Bolton Wanderers	L	1-3	Oakes	21,700
18	17	H	Leicester City	D	1-1	Leivers	21,053
19	24	A	Fulham	W	4-2	Harley 2, Dobing, Hannah	17,671
20	Dec 1	H	Arsenal	L	2-4	Harley 2	25,454
21	8	A	West Bromwich Albion	L	1-2	Dobing	11,505
22	15	H	Wolverhampton W.	D	3-3	Dobing, Hannah, Hayes	14,170
23	Feb 23	A	Leyton Orient	D	1-1	Harley	12,464
24	Mar 2	H	Birmingham City	W	2-1	Gray, Harley	28,798
25	9	A	Sheffield Wednesday	L	1-4	Harley	17,424
26	23	A	Everton	L	1-2	Wagstaffe	46,101
27	26	H	Burnley	L	2-5	Harley 2	21,985
28	29	H	Fulham	L	2-3	Barlow, Gray	12,789
29	Apr 3	A	Sheffield United	L	1-3	Gray	16,710
30	6	A	Leicester City	L	0-2		27,092
31	12	H	Nottingham Forest	W	1-0	Gray	25,793
32	13	H	Bolton Wanderers	W	2-1	Dobing, Young	18,551
33	15	A	Nottingham Forest	D	1-1	Harley	15,017
34	20	A	Arsenal	W	3-2	Gray 2, Hayes	20,539
35	24	H	Sheffield United	L	1-3	Hayes	19,277
36	27	H	West Bromwich Albion	L	1-5	Harley	14,995
37	May 1	A	Blackburn Rovers	L	1-4	Oakes	12,894
38	4	H	Blackpool	L	0-3		19,062
39	8	A	Aston Villa	L	1-3	Dobing	20,418
40	11	H	Tottenham Hotspur	W	1-0	Harley	27,784
41	15	H	Manchester United	D	1-1	Harley	52,452
42	18	A	West Ham United	L	1-6	Oakes	16,602
							Appearances
						One own goal	Goals

FA Cup

Round	Date	Venue	Opponents	Result		Scorers	Attendance
R3	Mar 6	A	Walsall	W	1-0	Harley	11553
R4	13	H	Bury	W	1-0	Harley	41575
R5	16	H	Norwich City	L	1-2	Harley	31217
							Appearances
							Goals

League Cup

Round	Date	Venue	Opponents	Result		Scorers	Attendance
R2	Sep 24	H	Blackpool	D	0-0		12,064
rep	Oct 8	A	Blackpool	D	3-3e	Harley 2, Young	10,508
rep2	15	N	Blackpool	W	4-2	Harley 2, Dobing, Oakes	12,237
R3	24	A	Newport County	W	2-1	Hannah, Harley	14,000
R4	Nov 14	H	Luton Town	W	1-0	Harley	8,682
R5	Dec 11	A	Birmingham City	L	0-6		18,010
							Appearances
							Goals

Trautmann BC	Kennedy R	Betts JB	Benson JH	Leivers WE	Shawcross FD	Young NJ	Dobing PA	Pardoe G	Hayes J	Wagstaffe D	Plenderleith JB	Oakes AA	Barlow CJ	Harley A	Sear RC	Chadwick G	Dowd HW	Hannah G	Fleet S	Cheetham RAJ	Gray M	Batty M	Wood AEH
1	2	3	4	5	6	7	8	9	10	11													
1	3	2	4			7	8		10	11	5	6	9										
1	3	2	4		10	7	8			11	5	6		9									
1	3	2	4			7	8	10		11	5	6		9									
1	3	2	4			10	8		11		5	6	7	9									
1	3	2	4	5		10	8		11			6	7	9									
1	3	2	4	5		10	8		11			6	7	9									
1	4	2		5		7	8		10	11				9	3	6							
1	4	2		5		7	8		10	11				9	3	6							
1	4	2		5		7	8		10	11				9	3	6							
1	4	2		5		7	8		10	11				9	3	6							
	4	2	6	5		7	8			11				9	3		1	10					
	2		4	5		7	8			11		6		9	3		1	10					
	2		4	5		7	8		11			6		9	3		1	10					
	2		4	5		7	8		11			6		9	3		1	10					
	2		4	5		7	8		11			6		9	3		1	10					
	2		4	5		7	8			11		6		9	3		1	10					
	2		4	5		7	8			11		6		9	3		1	10					
	2		4	5		7	8			11		6		9	3		1	10					
1	2		4	5		7	8			11		6		9	3			10					
1	2		4	5		7	8			11		6		9	3			10					
		2	4	5			8		7	11		6		9	3		1	10					
	8	2	4	5			7					6		9	3		1	11		10			
	8	2	4	5			7	6		11				9	3		1				10		
	8	2	4	5			7	6		11				9	3		1				10		
	3	2	4	5		7	8			11		6		9			1				10		
	2		4			7	8			11	5	6		9	3		1				10		
	2			5			8			11		6	7	9	3		1			4	10		
	2		4	5			8					6	7	9	3		1			11	10		
	2			5		11	8					6	7	9	3		1			4	10		
	2			5		11	8					6	7	9	3		1			4	10		
	2					7	8			11		6		9	3		1			4	10	5	
	2					7	8		10	11		6		9	3		1			4			5
	2			5		11	7		8			6		9	3		1			4	10		
	2			5			7		8	11		6		9	3		1			4	10		
	2			5		7			8	11		6		9	3		1			4	10		
1	2			5	6		8	7		11		4		9	3						10		
1	3			2	6		8			11		4	7	9							10		5
	6			2			8		7	11		4		9	3		1				10		5
	2			5			8		7	11		4		9	3		1	10			6		
	2			5		7	8		10	11		4		9	3		1				6		
	2			5		7	8		10	11		4		9	3		1				6		
15	41	17	24	35	4	31	41	5	21	31	5	34	9	40	33	4	27	13		10	18	1	3
				1		5	9		4	1		3	2	23				3			6		

Trautmann BC	Kennedy R	Betts JB	Benson JH	Leivers WE	Shawcross FD	Young NJ	Dobing PA	Pardoe G	Hayes J	Wagstaffe D	Plenderleith JB	Oakes AA	Barlow CJ	Harley A	Sear RC	Chadwick G	Dowd HW	Hannah G	Fleet S	Cheetham RAJ	Gray M	Batty M	Wood AEH
	8	2	4	5			7	6		11				9	3		1	10					
	3	2	4	5		7	8			11		6		9			1	10					
	3	2	4	5			8		7	11		6		9			1	10					
	3	3	3	3		1	3	1	1	3		2		3	1		3	3					
														3									

Trautmann BC	Kennedy R	Betts JB	Benson JH	Leivers WE	Shawcross FD	Young NJ	Dobing PA	Pardoe G	Hayes J	Wagstaffe D	Plenderleith JB	Oakes AA	Barlow CJ	Harley A	Sear RC	Chadwick G	Dowd HW	Hannah G	Fleet S	Cheetham RAJ	Gray M	Batty M	Wood AEH
1	4	2		5		7	8		10	11				9	3	6							
	4	2	6	5		7	8			11				9	3		1	10					
	2		4	5		7	8		11			6		9	3		1	10					
	2		4	5		7	8		11			6		9	3		1	10					
	2		4	5		7	8			11		6		9	3		1	10					
		2	4	5		11	8		7			6		9	3			10	1				
1	5	3	5	6		6	6		4	3		4		6	6	1	4	5	1				
						1	1					1		6				1					

League Table

	P	W	D	L	F	A	Pts
Everton	42	25	11	6	84	42	61
Tottenham H	42	23	9	10	111	62	55
Burnley	42	22	10	10	78	57	54
Leicester C	42	20	12	10	79	53	52
Wolverh'pton W	42	20	10	12	93	65	50
Sheffield W	42	19	10	13	77	63	48
Arsenal	42	18	10	14	86	77	46
Liverpool	42	17	10	15	71	59	44
Nottingham F	42	17	10	15	67	69	44
Sheffield U	42	16	12	14	58	60	44
Blackburn R	42	15	12	15	79	71	42
West Ham U	42	14	12	16	73	69	40
Blackpool	42	13	14	15	58	64	40
W.B.A.	42	16	7	19	71	79	39
Aston Villa	42	15	8	19	62	68	38
Fulham	42	14	10	18	50	71	38
Ipswich T	42	12	11	19	59	78	35
Bolton W	42	15	5	22	55	75	35
Manchester U	42	12	10	20	67	81	34
Birmingham C	42	10	13	19	63	90	33
Manchester C	42	10	11	21	58	102	31
Leyton O	42	6	9	27	37	81	21

1963-64

Division One

Manager: George Poyser

Did you know that?

Match 10: Hodgkinson's last game.
Match 12: Hannah's last game.
Match 14: McAlinden's last game.
Match 17: Chadwick's last game.
Match 20: Cunliffe's last game.
Match 26: Aimson's last game.
Match 27: Panter's last game.
Match 30: Leivers and Frost's last game.
Match 33: Betts's last game.
Match 34: Benson's last game.
Match 37: Trautmann's last game.

The attendance for Match 34 was the lowest peacetime first-team crowd since the first season at Maine Road, and the average attendance was the lowest since about 1905.

Match No.	Date	Venue	Opponents	Result		Scorers	Attendance
	Aug 24	H	Portsmouth	L	0-2		21,822
2	28	A	Cardiff City	D	2-2	Hannah, Kevan	25,134
3	31	A	Rotherham United	W	2-1	Kevan 2	11,418
4	Sep 4	H	Cardiff City	W	4-0	Aimson 2, Kevan, Young	22,138
5	7	H	Leeds United	W	3-2	Hannah, Kevan, Young	29,186
6	10	A	Swindon Town	L	0-3		28,291
7	14	A	Sunderland	L	0-2		39,298
8	18	H	Swindon Town	D	0-0		23,103
9	21	H	Northampton Town	W	3-0	Oakes, Wagstaffe, Young	21,340
10	28	A	Bury	D	1-1	Hodgkinson	18,032
11	Oct 5	H	Charlton Athletic	L	1-3	Gray	16,138
12	9	H	Plymouth Argyle	D	1-1	Cunliffe	13,456
13	12	A	Grimsby Town	D	1-1	Walker (og)	9,754
14	19	H	Preston North End	L	2-3	Aimson, Kevan	23,153
15	26	A	Derby County	W	3-1	Aimson, Oakes, Young	15,675
16	Nov 2	H	Swansea Town	W	1-0	Oakes	16,770
17	9	A	Southampton	L	2-4	Kevan, Murray	17,142
18	23	A	Newcastle United	L	1-3	Gray	22,557
19	30	H	Huddersfield Town	W	5-2	Kevan 2, Murray 2, Gray	16,192
20	Dec 7	A	Leyton Orient	W	2-0	Kevan, Murray	9,610
21	14	A	Portsmouth	D	2-2	Kevan, Murray	13,206
22	21	H	Rotherham United	W	6-1	Murray 3, Kevan 2, Young	11,060
23	26	H	Scunthorpe United	W	8-1	Gray 3, Murray 3, Kevan 2	26,365
24	28	A	Scunthorpe United	W	4-2	Murray 2, Kevan, Wagstaffe	9,324
25	Jan 11	A	Leeds United	L	0-1		33,737
26	18	H	Sunderland	L	0-3		31,136
27	Feb 1	A	Northampton Town	L	1-2	Kevan	12,330
28	8	H	Bury	D	1-1	Dowd	14,698
29	15	A	Charlton Athletic	L	3-4	Frost, Gray, Kevan	18,870
30	22	H	Grimsby Town	L	0-4		11,411
31	29	A	Middlesbrough	D	2-2	Gray, Kevan	12,763
32	Mar 7	H	Derby County	W	3-2	Kevan 2, Murray	11,908
33	14	A	Plymouth Argyle	L	1-2	Kevan	11,761
34	17	H	Middlesbrough	W	1-0	Kevan	8,053
35	21	H	Southampton	D	1-1	Murray	13,481
36	27	H	Norwich City	W	5-0	Kevan 3, Murray, Wagstaffe	20,212
37	28	A	Preston North End	L	0-2		24,796
38	30	A	Norwich City	W	2-1	Murray, Shawcross	16,737
39	Apr 4	H	Newcastle United	W	3-1	Kevan 2, Murray	15,450
40	11	A	Huddersfield Town	W	2-0	Murray, Pardoe	13,520
41	18	H	Leyton Orient	W	2-0	Kevan, Murray	15,144
42	25	A	Swansea Town	D	3-3	Kevan, Murray, Pardoe	13,832
							Appearances
						One own goal	Goals

FA Cup

	Date	Venue	Opponents	Result		Scorers	Attendance
R3	Jan 4	A	Swindon Town	L	1-2	Oakes	18,065
							Appearances
							Goals

League Cup

	Date	Venue	Opponents	Result		Scorers	Attendance
R2	Sep 25	H	Carlisle United	W	2-0	Aimson, Kevan	8,265
R3	Oct 16	A	Hull City	W	3-0	Aimson, Kevan, Young	13,882
R4	Nov 27	H	Leeds United	W	3-1	Kevan 2, Gray	10,748
R5	Dec 17	A	Notts County	W	1-0	Kevan	7,330
SF1	Jan 15	A	Stoke City	L	0-2		21,019
SF2	Feb 5	H	Stoke City	W	1-0	Kevan	16,891
							Appearances
							Goals

Dowd HW	Betts JB	Sear RC	Benson JH	Wood AEH	Oakes AA	Young NJ	Gray M	Hannah G	Kevan DT	Hayes J	Gomersall V	Chadwick G	Cheetham RAJ	Aimson PE	Wagstaffe D	Leivers WE	Hodgkinson DJ	Cunliffe R	Pardoe G	Kennedy R	McAlinden RJ	Murray JR	Shawcross FD	Panter D	Ogley A	Frost RA	Trautmann BC	Batty M
1	2	3	4	5	6	7	8	9	10	11																	
1	2				6	7		8	10		3	4	5	9	11													
1	2				6	7		8	10		3	4	5	9	11													
1	2				6	7		8	10		3	4	5	9	11													
1	2				6	7		8	10		3	4	5	9	11													
1	2				6	7		8	10		3	4	5	9	11													
1	2	3			6	7	4	8	10				5	9	11													
1	2	3			6	7	4	8	10				5	9	11													
1		3			6	7	4		10	8		2	5	9	11													
1		3			6		4		10	8			5	9	11	2	7											
1	2	3			6	7	8		10				4	9	11	5												
1	2	3			6	7	4	8	9				5		11			10										
1	2	3			6	7	4		9				5		11			10	8									
1		3	6			7	8		10			2	5	9						4	11							
1		3			6	11	8		10				5	9		2			7	4								
1		3			6	11	8		10				5	9		2			7	4								
1		3			6	11	8		10			2	5						7	4		9						
1		3			6	7	8		10				5		11	2				4		9						
1		3		5	6	7	8		10						11	2				4		9						
1		3		5	6	7	8		10							2		11		4		9						
1		3		5	6	7	8		10						11	2				4		9						
1		3		5	6	7	8		10						11	2				4		9						
1		3		5	6	7	8		10						11	2				4		9						
1		3		5	6	7	8		10						11	2				4		9						
1		3		5	6	7	8								11	2			9	4			10					
1		3		5	6	7	8		10					9	11	2				4								
1	2	3			6	7	8		10						11	5				4				9				
1	2	3		5	6	7	8		10						11				9	4								
	2			5	6		8		10		3				11				9	4					1	7		
	2	3			6		8		10						11	5			9	4					1	7		
1	2	3	4		6	7	8		10				5		11				9									
1	2	3	4		6		8		10				5		11				7			9						
1	2	3	4		6	11	8		10				5						7			9						
1		3	4		6		8		10				5		11				7	2		9						
		3			6	7	4		10				5		11				8	2		9					1	
		3			6	7	4		10				5		11				8	2		9					1	
					6	7	4		10		3				11				8	2		9					1	5
		3			6	7	4								11				8	2		9	10		1			5
		3			6	7	4		10				5		11				8	2		9			1			
		3			6	7	4		10				5		11				8	2		9			1			
		3			6	7	4		10				5		11				8	2		9			1			
		3			6	7	4		10				5		11				8	2		9			1			
32	18	35	6	11	41	37	37	9	40	3	7	8	27	14	35	15	1	3	20	26	1	19	2	1	7	2	3	2
1					3	5	8	2	30					4	3		1	1	2			21	1			1		

Dowd HW	Betts JB	Sear RC	Benson JH	Wood AEH	Oakes AA	Young NJ	Gray M	Hannah G	Kevan DT	Hayes J	Gomersall V	Chadwick G	Cheetham RAJ	Aimson PE	Wagstaffe D	Leivers WE	Hodgkinson DJ	Cunliffe R	Pardoe G	Kennedy R	McAlinden RJ	Murray JR	Shawcross FD	Panter D	Ogley A	Frost RA	Trautmann BC	Batty M
1		3		5	6	7	8		10						11	2				4		9						
1		1		1	1	1	1		1						1	1				1		1						
					1																							

Dowd HW	Betts JB	Sear RC	Benson JH	Wood AEH	Oakes AA	Young NJ	Gray M	Hannah G	Kevan DT	Hayes J	Gomersall V	Chadwick G	Cheetham RAJ	Aimson PE	Wagstaffe D	Leivers WE	Hodgkinson DJ	Cunliffe R	Pardoe G	Kennedy R	McAlinden RJ	Murray JR	Shawcross FD	Panter D	Ogley A	Frost RA	Trautmann BC	Batty M
1		3			6				10	8		4	5	9	11	2	7											
1	2	3			6	7	8		10				5	9	11					4								
1		3		5	6	7	8		10						11	2				4		9						
1		3		5	6	7	8		10						11	2				4		9						
1		3		5	6	7	8							10	11	2				4				9				
1	2	3			6	7	8		10						11	5			9	4								
6	2	6		3	6	5	5		5	1		1	2	3	6	5	1		1	5		2		1				
						1	1		6					2														

League Table

	P	W	D	L	F	A	Pts
Leeds U	42	24	15	3	71	34	63
Sunderland	42	25	11	6	81	37	61
Preston N.E.	42	23	10	9	79	54	56
Charlton A	42	19	10	13	76	70	48
Southampton	42	19	9	14	100	73	47
Manchester C	42	18	10	14	84	66	46
Rotherham U	42	19	7	16	90	78	45
Newcastle U	42	20	5	17	74	69	45
Portsmouth	42	16	11	15	79	70	43
Middlesbrough	42	15	11	16	67	52	41
Northampton T	42	16	9	17	58	60	41
Huddersfield T	42	15	10	17	57	64	40
Derby Co	42	14	11	17	56	67	39
Swindon T	42	14	10	18	57	69	38
Cardiff C	42	14	10	18	56	81	38
Leyton O	42	13	10	19	54	72	36
Norwich C	42	11	13	18	64	80	35
Bury	42	13	9	20	57	73	35
Swansea T	42	12	9	21	63	74	33
Plymouth A	42	8	16	18	45	67	32
Grimsby T	42	9	14	19	47	75	32
Scunthorpe U	42	10	10	22	52	82	30

1964-65

Division One

Manager: George Poyser (until Easter 1965), Fred Tilson and Albert Alexander Jnr (caretakers until end of season)

Did you know that?

Match 9: Shawcross's last League game.
Match 14: Stobart's last game.
Match 22: Wagstaffe's last game.
Match 27: Kevan's last game.
Match 34: Batty's last game.
Match 36: Gratrix's last game.
Match 38: Hayes and Ogden's last game.

Although attendances were low during January and February there were several reasons for this. Naturally, poor performance was one factor, but also poor weather and a bus strike impacted crowds. Prior to the Swindon game (Match 26) there had been widespread reports that heavy snow was on its way – this didn't actually arrive until a few days after the match – and then the next home game (Match 28) took place in the midst of a bus strike which meant fans could only get to the game on foot or via cars. The attendance of 11,931 was actually greeted as a positive one in light of the difficulties fans faced.

Match No.	Date	Venue	Opponents	Result		Scorers	Attendance
1	Aug 22	A	Charlton Athletic	L	1-2	Kevan	19,299
2	26	H	Leyton Orient	W	6-0	Murray 3, Kevan, Oakes, Pardoe	21,085
3	29	H	Northampton Town	L	0-2		20,935
4	31	A	Leyton Orient	L	3-4	Gray, Kevan, Pardoe	11,512
5	Sep 5	H	Portsmouth	W	2-0	Kevan, Murray	16,527
6	9	H	Norwich City	L	0-2		16,191
7	12	A	Swindon Town	W	1-0	Kevan	17,353
8	16	A	Norwich City	L	1-4	Gray	22,443
9	19	H	Derby County	W	2-0	Kevan, Stobart	16,214
10	26	A	Swansea Town	L	0-3		10,862
11	Oct 3	H	Rotherham United	W	2-1	Gray, Kevan	15,211
12	10	A	Southampton	L	0-1		18,412
13	14	H	Newcastle United	W	3-0	Kevan, Oakes, Young	10,215
14	17	H	Huddersfield Town	L	2-3	Kevan 2	15,704
15	24	A	Coventry City	D	2-2	Young, Curtis (og)	28,733
16	31	H	Cardiff City	W	2-0	Murray 2	13,146
17	Nov 7	A	Preston North End	W	5-2	Kevan 3, Young 2	19,367
18	14	H	Ipswich Town	W	4-0	Kevan 2, Murray 2	16,835
19	21	A	Plymouth Argyle	L	2-3	Gray, Kevan	19,714
20	28	H	Bolton Wanderers	L	2-4	Ogden, Young	21,895
21	Dec 5	A	Middlesbrough	W	1-0	Kevan	13,873
22	19	A	Northampton Town	L	0-2		12,665
23	26	H	Bury	D	0-0		22,299
24	28	A	Bury	W	2-0	Kevan, Murray	11,279
25	Jan 2	A	Portsmouth	D	1-1	Young	12,500
26	16	H	Swindon Town	L	1-2	Oakes	8,015
27	30	A	Derby County	L	0-2		14,765
28	Feb 6	H	Swansea Town	W	1-0	Murray	11,931
29	13	A	Rotherham United	D	0-0		10,917
30	20	H	Southampton	W	3-1	Crossan, Kennedy, Young	10,470
31	27	A	Huddersfield Town	L	0-1		14,405
32	Mar 6	H	Middlesbrough	D	1-1	Ogden	14,231
33	12	A	Cardiff City	D	2-2	Connor, Gray	9,094
34	20	H	Preston North End	W	4-3	Murray 2, Connor, Crossan	12,884
35	27	A	Ipswich Town	L	1-4	Crossan	12,709
36	Apr 3	H	Plymouth Argyle	W	2-1	Oakes, Ogden	10,929
37	10	A	Bolton Wanderers	L	0-4		14,546
38	16	H	Crystal Palace	L	0-2		15,885
39	17	H	Coventry City	D	1-1	Connor	10,804
40	19	A	Crystal Palace	D	1-1	Pardoe	12,175
41	24	A	Newcastle United	D	0-0		35,600
42	28	H	Charlton Athletic	W	2-1	Murray, Young	8,409
							Appearances
						One own goal	Goals

FA Cup

R3	Jan 9	H	Shrewsbury Town	D	1-1	Kevan	16,131
rep	13	A	Shrewsbury Town	L	1-3	Gray	15,924
							Appearances
							Goals

League Cup

R2	Sep 23	H	Mansfield Town	L	3-5	Kevan, Murray, Young	8,789
							Appearances
							Goals

Dowd HW	Kennedy R	Gomersall V	Gray M	Cheetham RAJ	Oakes AA	Pardoe G	Stobart BH	Murray JR	Kevan DT	Connor DR	Bacuzzi RD	Shawcross FD	Wood AEH	Ogley A	Wagstaffe D	Gratrix R	Young NJ	Ogden T	Sear RC	Batty M	Crossan JA	Hayes J	Doyle M
1	2	3	4	5	6	7	8	9	10	11													
1	3		4	5	6	7	8	9	10	11	2												
1	3		4	5	6	7	8	9	10	11	2												
1	3		4	5	6	7	8	9	10	11	2												
1	3		8		6		7	9	10	11	2	4	5										
		3			6	8	9		10	11	2	4	5	1	7								
		3	8	5	6		9		10	11	2	4		1	7								
		3	8	5	6		9		10	11	2	4		1	7								
	3		8		6		7	9	10		2	4		1	11	5							
1	3		4		6		8	9	10		2				11	5	7						
	4	3	8		6		7	9	10		2		5	1	11								
	4	3	8		6		7	9	10		2			1		5	11						
	4	3	8		6		7	9	10		2			1		5	11						
	4	3	8		6		7	9	10		2			1		5	11						
	4	3	8		6			9	10		2			1	7	5	11						
	4	3	8		6			9	10		2			1	7	5	11						
	4	3	8		6			9	10		2			1	7	5	11						
	4	3			6	8		9	10		2			1	7	5	11						
	4	3	8		6			9	10		2			1	7	5	11						
	4	3	8		6				10		2			1	7	5	11	9					
1	4		8		6			9	10		2				7		11		3	5			
1	4		8		6			9	10		2				7		11		3	5			
1	4		8		6	7		9	10		2						11		3	5			
1	4		8		6	7		9	10		2		5				11		3				
1	4		8		6	7		9	10		2		5				11		3				
1	4				6	7		9	10	11	2					5		8	3				
1	4				6			9	10	11	2					5	7		3		8		
1	4	3	10		6			9		7	2						11			5	8		
1		3	10	4	6			9		7	2						11			5	8		
	4	3		6	10			9		7	2			1			11			5	8		
	4	3		6	10			9			2			1			11			5	8	7	
	4	3	10		6					7	2			1			11	9		5	8		
1	4	3	10							7	2						11	9		5	8		6
1	4	3			6			8		7	2						11	9		5	10		
1	4	3			6			8		7	2					5	11	9			10		
1	4	3		6	10					7	2					5	11	9			8		
1	4	3		6	10					7	2		5				11	9			8		
1	5	3			6					7	2						11	9			10	8	4
	5	3			6	10				7	2		9	1			11				8		4
	5	3			6	10				7	2		9	1			11				8		4
	5	3			6	10				7	2		9	1			11				8		4
	5	3			6	8		9		7	2			1			11				10		4
21	38	29	27	11	41	14	14	30	27	24	41	5	9	21	14	15	31	9	7	10	16	2	6
	1		5		4	3	1	13	18	3							8	3			3		

Dowd HW	Kennedy R	Gomersall V	Gray M	Cheetham RAJ	Oakes AA	Pardoe G	Stobart BH	Murray JR	Kevan DT	Connor DR	Bacuzzi RD	Shawcross FD	Wood AEH	Ogley A	Wagstaffe D	Gratrix R	Young NJ	Ogden T	Sear RC
1	4		8		6	7		9	10		2		5				11		3
1	4		8		6	7		9	10		2	11	5						3
2	2		2		2	2		2	2		2	1	2				1		2
			1						1										

Dowd HW	Kennedy R	Gomersall V	Gray M	Cheetham RAJ	Oakes AA	Pardoe G	Stobart BH	Murray JR	Kevan DT	Connor DR	Bacuzzi RD	Shawcross FD	Wood AEH	Ogley A	Wagstaffe D	Gratrix R	Young NJ
1	3		8	5	6			9	10		2	4			11		7
1	1		1	1	1			1	1		1	1			1		1
								1	1								1

League Table

	P	W	D	L	F	A	Pts
Newcastle U	42	24	9	9	81	45	57
Northampton T	42	20	16	6	66	50	56
Bolton W	42	20	10	12	80	58	50
Southampton	42	17	14	11	83	63	48
Ipswich T	42	15	17	10	74	67	47
Norwich C	42	20	7	15	61	57	47
Crystal Palace	42	16	13	13	55	51	45
Huddersfield T	42	17	10	15	53	51	44
Derby Co	42	16	11	15	84	79	43
Coventry C	42	17	9	16	72	70	43
Manchester C	42	16	9	17	63	62	41
Preston N.E.	42	14	13	15	76	81	41
Cardiff C	42	13	14	15	64	57	40
Rotherham U	42	14	12	16	70	69	40
Plymouth A	42	16	8	18	63	79	40
Bury	42	14	10	18	60	66	38
Middlesbrough	42	13	9	20	70	76	35
Charlton A	42	13	9	20	64	75	35
Leyton O	42	12	11	19	50	72	35
Portsmouth	42	12	10	20	56	77	34
Swindon T	42	14	5	23	63	81	33
Swansea T	42	11	10	21	62	84	32

1965-66

Division One

Manager: Joe Mercer

Did you know that?

Match 1: Gomersall's last game.
Match 26: Wood's last game.
Match 30: Bacuzzi's last game.
Match 37: Sear's last game.

Roy Cheetham became the first player to come on as substitute in the League for City when he replaced Mike Summerbee in Match 4. Glyn Pardoe was the first player to be named as substitute (Match 1).

Match No.	Date	Venue	Opponents	Result		Scorers	Attendance
1	Aug 21	A	Middlesbrough	D	1-1	Murray	17,982
2	25	H	Wolverhampton W.	W	2-1	Miller (og), Thomson (og)	25,572
3	28	H	Bristol City	D	2-2	Brand, Gibson (og)	19,349
4	30	A	Wolverhampton W.	W	4-2	Crossan, Doyle, Murray, Harris (og)	22,799
5	Sep 4	A	Coventry City	D	3-3	Young 2, Murray	29,467
6	11	H	Carlisle United	W	2-1	Pardoe 2	22,891
7	15	A	Norwich City	D	3-3	Pardoe 2, Crossan	15,622
8	18	A	Cardiff City	L	3-4	Gray, Murray, Pardoe	11,365
9	25	H	Derby County	W	1-0	Murray	20,834
10	Oct 2	A	Southampton	W	1-0	Young	21,504
11	9	A	Huddersfield Town	D	0-0		31,876
12	16	H	Crystal Palace	W	3-1	Pardoe 2, Young	24,765
13	23	A	Preston North End	W	3-0	Young 2, Brand	25,117
14	27	H	Norwich City	D	0-0		34,091
15	30	H	Charlton Athletic	D	0-0		23,102
16	Nov 6	A	Plymouth Argyle	L	0-1		16,211
17	13	H	Portsmouth	W	3-1	Murray 2, Pardoe	22,106
18	20	A	Bolton Wanderers	L	0-1		22,927
19	27	H	Ipswich Town	W	2-1	Crossan 2	19,416
20	Dec 4	A	Birmingham City	L	1-3	Summerbee	10,445
21	11	H	Leyton Orient	W	5-0	Young 3, Crossan, Summerbee	16,202
22	18	A	Crystal Palace	W	2-0	Doyle 2	12,817
23	Jan 1	H	Huddersfield Town	W	2-0	Crossan, Doyle	47,171
24	8	A	Portsmouth	D	2-2	Doyle, Summerbee	17,152
25	12	H	Rotherham United	W	3-1	Doyle 2, Crossan	25,526
26	15	H	Preston North End	D	0-0		26,668
27	29	H	Middlesbrough	W	3-1	Summerbee 2, Young	25,278
28	Feb 5	A	Bristol City	D	1-1	Young	25,723
29	19	H	Coventry City	W	1-0	Crossan	40,190
30	26	A	Carlisle United	W	2-1	Pardoe, Summerbee	13,510
31	Mar 12	H	Cardiff City	D	2-2	Connor, Young	29,642
32	19	A	Derby County	W	2-1	Bell, Young	22,553
33	Apr 2	H	Plymouth Argyle	D	1-1	Crossan	24,087
34	8	H	Bury	W	1-0	Summerbee	43,104
35	12	A	Bury	L	1-2	Summerbee	21,837
36	16	H	Bolton Wanderers	W	4-1	Connor, Crossan, Kennedy, Sear	29,459
37	23	A	Ipswich Town	D	1-1	Crossan	15,995
38	30	H	Birmingham City	W	3-1	Bell, Crossan, Young	28,409
39	May 4	A	Rotherham United	W	1-0	Bell	11,685
40	7	A	Leyton Orient	D	2-2	Bell, Sorrell (og)	6,109
41	13	A	Charlton Athletic	W	3-2	Connor, Crossan, Oakes	13,678
42	18	H	Southampton	D	0-0		34,653

Appearances
Sub appearances
Five own goals — Goals

FA Cup

	Date	Venue	Opponents	Result		Scorers	Attendance
R3	Jan 22	A	Blackpool	D	1-1	Crossan	23,937
rep	24	H	Blackpool	W	3-1	Crossan, Doyle, Summerbee	52,661
R4	Feb 12	H	Grimsby Town	W	2-0	Summerbee, Cockerill (og)	37,918
R5	Mar 5	H	Leicester City	D	2-2	Young 2	56,787
rep	9	A	Leicester City	W	1-0	Young	41,892
R6	26	H	Everton	D	0-0		63,034
rep	29	A	Everton	D	0-0*		60,349
rep2	Apr 5	N†	Everton	L	0-2		27,948

* after extra time. † played at Molineux

Appearances
Sub appearances
One own goal — Goals

League Cup

	Date	Venue	Opponents	Result		Scorers	Attendance
R2	Sep 22	H	Leicester City	W	3-1	Murray, Pardoe, King (og)	13,246
R3	Oct 13	H	Coventry City	L	2-3	Crossan, Pardoe	18,213

Appearances
Sub appearances
One own goal — Goals

Dowd HW	Bacuzzi RD	Gomersall V	Doyle M	Cheetham RAJ	Oakes AA	Summerbee MG	Crossan JA	Murray JR	Brand RL	Connor DR	Pardoe G	Sear RC	Kennedy R	Gray M	Young NJ	Heslop GW	Ogley A	Horne SF	Wood AEH	Bell C
1	2	3	4	5	6	7	8	9	10	11										
1	2		4	5	6	7	8	9	10	3	11									
1	2		4	5	6	7	8	9	10	3	11									
1	2		4	12	5	7	8	9		11	10	3	6							
1				2	6	7	8	9		3	10		5	4	11					
1	2		4	5		7	8		10	3	9			6	11					
1	2			12	6	7	8		10	3	9			4	11	5				
	2		4	5	6	7	8	9			10	3		12	11		1			
					6	7	8	9		3	10		2		11	5	1	4		
1					6	7		9	8	12	10	3	2		11	5		4		
1				4	6	7	8		10		9	3	2		11	5				
1				4	6	7	8		10		9	3	2		11	5				
1	12			4	6	7	8		10		9	3	2		11	5				
1				4	6	7	8		10		9	3	2		11	5				
1				4	6	7	8		10		9	3	2	12	11				5	
1				4	6	7	8			10	9	3	2		11	5				
1	3				6	7	8	9			10		2		11	5		4		
1	3				6	7	8	9			10		2		11	5		4		
1	3				6	7	8	9	10		12		2		11	5		4		
1	3				6	7	8		9		10		2	12	11	5		4		
1			4		6	7	8			11	9	3	2		10	5				
1			4		6	7	8			10	9	3	2		11	5				
1			4		6	7	8			10	9	3	2		11	5				
1			4		6	7	8			10	9	3	2		11	5				
			4		6	7	8		10		9	3	2		11	5	1			
	3		4		6	7	8		10		9		2		11	5	1		12	
1	2		4		6	7	8			11	9	3			10	5				
1			4		6	7	8			11	9	3	2		10	5				
1	3		4		6	7	8			10	9		2		11	5				
1	3		4	12	6	7	8			10	9		2		11	5				
1			9		6	7	8			10	4		2		11	5		3		
1					6	7	8			11	4		2		9	5		3		10
1			4		6	9	10			11	7		2			5		3		8
1					6	7	8		11	10	4		2			5		3		9
1					6	7	8			10	4	3	2		11	5				9
1			9		6	7	8			11	4	3	2			5				10
1					6	7	10			11	4	3	2		9	5				8
1					6	7	10			11	4		2		9	5		3		8
1					6	7	10			11	4		2		9	5		3		8
1					6	7			10	11	4		2		9	5		3		8
1					6	7	10			11	4		2		9	5		3		8
1			12		6	7	10			11	4		2		9	5		3		8
38	15	1	19	12	41	42	40	11	17	29	40	19	35	3	35	34	4	15	1	11
	1		1	3						1	1			3					1	
			7		1	8	13	7	2	3	9	1	1	1	14					4

Dowd HW	Bacuzzi RD	Gomersall V	Doyle M	Cheetham RAJ	Oakes AA	Summerbee MG	Crossan JA	Murray JR	Brand RL	Connor DR	Pardoe G	Sear RC	Kennedy R	Gray M	Young NJ	Heslop GW	Ogley A	Horne SF	Wood AEH	Bell C
1				4	6	7	8			11	9	3	2		10	5				
1			4		6	7	8			11	9	3	2		10	5				
1			4		6	7	8			11	9	3	2		10	5				
1			4		6	7	8			11	9		2		10	5		3		
1			4		6	7	8			10	9		2		11	5		3		
1			4		6	7	8			11	10		2		9	5		3		
1			4	7	6	9	8			11	10		2			5		3		
1			4		6	7	8			10	9		2		11	5		3		
8			7	2	8	8	8			8	8	3	8		7	8		5		
			1			2	2								3					

Dowd HW	Bacuzzi RD	Gomersall V	Doyle M	Cheetham RAJ	Oakes AA	Summerbee MG	Crossan JA	Murray JR	Brand RL	Connor DR	Pardoe G	Sear RC	Kennedy R	Gray M	Young NJ	Heslop GW	Ogley A	Horne SF	Wood AEH	Bell C
					6	7		9			10	3	2	8	11		1	4	5	
1				4	6	7	8		10		9	3	2		11	5				
1				1	2	2	1	1	1		2	2	2	1	2	1	1	1	1	
					1		1				2									

League Table

	P	W	D	L	F	A	Pts
Manchester C	42	22	15	5	76	44	59
Southampton	42	22	10	10	85	56	54
Coventry C	42	20	13	9	73	53	53
Huddersfield T	42	19	13	10	62	36	51
Bristol C	42	17	17	8	63	48	51
Wolverh'pton W	42	20	10	12	87	61	50
Rotherham U	42	16	14	12	75	74	46
Derby Co	42	16	11	15	71	68	43
Bolton W	42	16	9	17	62	59	41
Birmingham C	42	16	9	17	70	75	41
Crystal Palace	42	14	13	15	47	52	41
Portsmouth	42	16	8	18	74	78	40
Norwich C	42	12	15	15	52	52	39
Carlisle U	42	17	5	20	60	63	39
Ipswich T	42	15	9	18	58	66	39
Charlton A	42	12	14	16	61	70	38
Preston N.E.	42	11	15	16	62	70	37
Plymouth A	42	12	13	17	54	63	37
Bury	42	14	7	21	62	76	35
Cardiff C	42	12	10	20	71	91	34
Middlesbrough	42	10	13	19	58	86	33
Leyton O	42	5	13	24	38	80	23

1966-67

Division One

Manager: Joe Mercer

Did you know that?

Match 24: Gray's last game.
Match 34: Murray and Brand's last game.
Match 42: Crossan's last game.

The FA Cup quarter-final with Leeds was described by ABC TV, who filmed the match for ITV, as 'the most exciting match of the season'. Neutrals felt City should have won the match – certainly the goal was highly controversial and should have been disallowed. Despite the defeat, it was this game that made other First Division sides realise that City were back as serious challengers.

Match No.	Date	Venue	Opponents	Result		Scorers	Attendance
1	Aug 20	A	Southampton	D	1-1	Summerbee	19,900
2	24	H	Liverpool	W	2-1	Bell, Murray	50,923
3	27	H	Sunderland	W	1-0	Oakes	34,948
4	30	A	Liverpool	L	2-3	Gray, Murray	51,645
5	Sep 3	A	Aston Villa	L	0-3		15,552
6	7	H	West Ham United	L	1-4	Bell	31,989
7	10	H	Arsenal	D	1-1	Pardoe	27,946
8	17	A	Manchester United	L	0-1		62,085
9	24	A	Blackpool	W	1-0	Crossan	25,761
10	Oct 1	H	Chelsea	L	1-4	Young	31,989
11	8	H	Tottenham Hotspur	L	1-2	Summerbee	32,551
12	15	A	Newcastle United	L	0-2		16,523
13	29	A	Burnley	W	3-2	Crossan 2, Bell	25,596
14	Nov 5	H	Newcastle United	D	1-1	Young	26,137
15	12	A	Stoke City	W	1-0	Summerbee	27,765
16	19	H	Everton	W	1-0	Bell	39,572
17	26	A	Fulham	L	1-4	Young	14,579
18	Dec 3	H	Nottingham Forest	D	1-1	Kennedy	24,013
19	10	A	West Bromwich Albion	W	3-0	Crossan, Jones, Pardoe	17,299
20	17	H	Southampton	D	1-1	Bell	20,104
21	27	A	Sheffield Wednesday	L	0-1		33,366
22	31	A	Sunderland	L	0-1		28,826
23	Jan 2	H	Sheffield Wednesday	D	0-0		32,198
24	14	A	Arsenal	L	0-1		22,392
25	21	H	Manchester United	D	1-1	Stiles (og)	62,983
26	Feb 4	H	Blackpool	W	1-0	Bell	27,840
27	11	A	Chelsea	D	0-0		28,633
28	25	A	Tottenham Hotspur	D	1-1	Connor	33,832
29	Mar 4	H	Burnley	W	1-0	Bell	32,692
30	18	A	Leeds United	D	0-0		34,366
31	24	H	Leicester City	L	1-3	Crossan	35,396
32	25	H	West Bromwich Albion	D	2-2	Hince 2	22,780
33	28	A	Leicester City	L	1-2	Jones	17,361
34	Apr 1	A	Sheffield United	L	0-1		16,976
35	12	H	Stoke City	W	3-1	Bell 3	25,753
36	19	H	Aston Villa	D	1-1	Summerbee	26,252
37	22	H	Fulham	W	3-0	Bell, Crossan, Oakes	22,752
38	29	A	Everton	D	1-1	Coleman	33,239
39	May 2	A	Nottingham Forest	L	0-2		33,352
40	6	H	Sheffield United	D	1-1	Crossan	21,627
41	8	H	Leeds United	W	2-1	Crossan, Young	24,924
42	13	A	West Ham United	D	1-1	Bell	17,186
							Appearances
							Sub appearances
						One own goal	Goals

FA Cup

Round	Date	Venue	Opponents	Result		Scorers	Attendance
R3	Jan 28	H	Leicester City	W	2-1	Doyle, Pardoe	38,529
R4	Feb 18	A	Cardiff City	D	1-1	Coldrick (og)	37,205
rep	22	H	Cardiff City	W	3-1	Bell, Crossan, Young	41,616
R5	Mar 11	H	Ipswich Town	D	1-1	Young	47,075
rep	14	A	Ipswich Town	W	3-0	Summerbee 2, McNeill (og)	30,605
R6	Apr 8	A	Leeds United	L	0-1		48,887
							Appearances
						Two own goals	Goals

League Cup

Round	Date	Venue	Opponents	Result		Scorers	Attendance
R2	Sep 14	H	Bolton Wanderers	W	3-1	Bell, Murray, Pardoe	9,006
R3	Oct 5	A	West Bromwich Albion	L	2-4	Summerbee, Young	19,913
							Appearances
							Sub appearances
							Goals

Dowd HW	Book AK	Kennedy R	Pardoe G	Heslop GW	Oakes AA	Summerbee MG	Bell C	Murray JR	Connor DR	Young NJ	Crossan JA	Horne SF	Gray M	Doyle M	Cheetham RAJ	Ogley A	Jones CMN	Coleman AG	Hince PF	Brand RL
1	2	3	4	5	6	7	8	9	10	11										
1	2	3	4	5	6	7	8	9		11	10									
1	2	3	4	5	6	7	8	9	12	11	10									
1	2	3	4	5	6		8	9	7	11			10							
1	2	3	4	5	6	7	8	9		11	10									
1	2	3	4	5	6	9	8		7	11	10									
1	2	3	9	5	6	7	8		12	11	10	4								
1	2	3	10	5	6	9	8		7	11		4		12						
1	2		9	5	6	7	8		3	11	10	4								
1	2		9	5	6	7	8		3	11	10			4	12					
1	2		3	5	6	7	8	9		11	10	4								
1	2		3	5	6	7	8	9		11	10	4								
1	2		3	5	6	7	8	9		11	10	4								
1	2		3	5	6	7	8	9		11	10	4								
1	2	6	3	5		7	8		9	11	10	4								
1	2	5	3		6	9	8		7	11	10	4								
1	2	6	3	5		9	8		7	11	10	4								
	2	6	3	5			8		11	7	10	4				1	9			
	2	8	3	5	6		7			11	10	4				1	9			
	2	8	3	5	6	9	7				10	4				1	11			
	2	8	3	5	6	9	10			11	7	4				1				
	2	8		5	6	9	10		3	11	7	4				1				
	2	3		5	6		8		7	11	10	4	12			1	9			
	2	12	3	5	6	7	8			11	10	4	9			1				
	2		3	5	6	7	9		8	11		4		10		1				
	2		3	5	6	7	8			11	10	4		9		1				
	2		3	5	6	7	8			11	10	4		9		1				
	2		3	5	6		8		11	7	10	4		9		1				
	2	5	3		6	7	10		12	11	8	4		9		1				
	2	5	3		6		10			11	8	4		9		1		7		
	2	5	3		6		10		7	11	8	4		9		1				
	2		3	5	6		10			11	8	4				1			7	9
	2		3	5	6		10		7	11	8	4				1	12			9
			3		6		10	9	7		8	4		5	2	1				11
1	2		3	5	6	7	8		10		9	4						11		
1	2		3	5	6	7	8		12	10	9	4						11		
1	2		3	5	6	7	8		10		9	12		4				11		
1	2		3	5	6	7	8			10	9			4				11		
1	2		3	5	6	7	8			10	9			4				11		
1	2		3	5	6	7	8			10	9			4				11		
1	2		3	5	6	7	8			10	9			4				11		
1	2		3	5	6	7	8		4	10	9			12				11		
25	41	20	40	37	39	32	42	10	20	38	38	29	2	14	1	17	4	9	1	3
		1							4			1	1	2	1		1			
		1	2		2	4	12	2	1	4	8		1				2	1	2	

Dowd HW	Book AK	Kennedy R	Pardoe G	Heslop GW	Oakes AA	Summerbee MG	Bell C	Murray JR	Connor DR	Young NJ	Crossan JA	Horne SF	Gray M	Doyle M	Cheetham RAJ	Ogley A	Jones CMN	Coleman AG	Hince PF	Brand RL
	2		3	5	6		8		7	11	10	4		9		1				
	2		3	5	6	7	8			11	10	4		9		1				
	2		3	5	6	7	8			11	10	4		9		1				
	2	5	3		6		10		7	11	8	4		9		1				
	2	5	3		6	7	10			11	8	4		9		1				
1	2		3	5	6	7	8		9		10	4								11
1	6	2	6	4	6	4	6		3	5	6	6		5		5				1
			1			2	1			2	1			1						

Dowd HW	Book AK	Kennedy R	Pardoe G	Heslop GW	Oakes AA	Summerbee MG	Bell C	Murray JR	Connor DR	Young NJ	Crossan JA	Horne SF	Gray M	Doyle M	Cheetham RAJ	Ogley A	Jones CMN	Coleman AG	Hince PF	Brand RL
1	2	3	10	5	6	7	8	9		11		4			12					
1	2		9	5	6	7	8	12		11	10	4			3					
2	2	1	2	2	2	2	2	1		2	1	2			1					
								1							1					
			1			1	1	1		1										

League Table

	P	W	D	L	F	A	Pts
Manchester U	42	24	12	6	84	45	60
Nottingham F	42	23	10	9	64	41	56
Tottenham H	42	24	8	10	71	48	56
Leeds U	42	22	11	9	62	42	55
Liverpool	42	19	13	10	64	47	51
Everton	42	19	10	13	65	46	48
Arsenal	42	16	14	12	58	47	46
Leicester C	42	18	8	16	78	71	44
helsea	42	15	14	13	67	62	44
Sheffield U	42	16	10	16	52	59	42
Sheffield W	42	14	13	15	56	47	41
Stoke C	42	17	7	18	63	58	41
W.B.A.	42	16	7	19	77	73	39
Burnley	42	15	9	18	66	76	39
Manchester C	42	12	15	15	43	52	39
West Ham U	42	14	8	20	80	84	36
Sunderland	42	14	8	20	58	72	36
Fulham	42	11	12	19	71	83	34
Southampton	42	14	6	22	74	92	34
Newcastle U	42	12	9	21	39	81	33
Aston Villa	42	11	7	24	54	85	29
Blackpool	42	6	9	27	41	76	21

1967-68

Division One

Manager: Joe Mercer

Did you know that?

Match 2: Ogley's last game.
Match 9: Hince's last game.
Match 24: Horne and Clay's last game.
Match 28: Jones's last game.

The League Championship trophy remained at Old Trafford on the last day of the season. Shortly before the end of United's final match the trophy disappeared from the United boardroom where it had been all season. Journalist Alan Thompson went in search of it and was told by one United official that it had been collected earlier in the week; another said nobody had seen it all day, and finally another admitted it had just been locked in the 'vault'. Joe Mercer told journalists he'd be happy to walk all the way from Newcastle to collect it if he had to.

Match No.	Date	Venue	Opponents	Result		Scorers	Attendance
1	Aug 19	H	Liverpool	D	0-0		49,531
2	23	A	Southampton	L	2-3	Bell, Coleman	23,675
3	26	A	Stoke City	L	0-3		22,426
4	30	H	Southampton	W	4-2	Bell 2, Young 2	22,002
5	Sep 2	H	Nottingham Forest	W	2-0	Coleman, Summerbee	29,547
6	6	H	Newcastle United	W	2-0	Hince, Young	29,978
7	9	A	Coventry City	W	3-0	Bell, Hince, Summerbee	34,578
8	16	H	Sheffield United	W	5-2	Bowles 2, Bell, Summerbee, Young	31,922
9	23	A	Arsenal	L	0-1		41,567
10	30	H	Manchester United	L	1-2	Bell	62,942
11	Oct 7	A	Sunderland	L	0-1		27,885
12	14	H	Wolverhampton W.	W	2-0	Doyle, Young	36,476
13	21	A	Fulham	W	4-2	Summerbee 2, Lee, Young	22,108
14	28	H	Leeds United	W	1-0	Bell	39,713
15	Nov 4	A	Everton	D	1-1	Connor	47,144
16	11	H	Leicester City	W	6-0	Lee 2, Young 2, Doyle, Oakes	29,039
17	18	A	West Ham United	W	3-2	Lee 2, Summerbee	25,495
18	25	H	Burnley	W	4-2	Coleman 2, Summerbee, Young	37,098
19	Dec 2	A	Sheffield Wednesday	D	1-1	Oakes	38,207
20	9	H	Tottenham Hotspur	W	4-1	Bell, Coleman, Summerbee, Young	35,792
21	16	A	Liverpool	D	1-1	Lee	53,268
22	23	H	Stoke City	W	4-2	Lee 2, Coleman, Young	40,121
23	26	A	West Bromwich Albion	L	2-3	Lee, Summerbee	44,897
24	30	H	West Bromwich Albion	L	0-2		45,754
25	Jan 6	A	Nottingham Forest	W	3-0	Coleman, Summerbee, Young	39,581
26	20	A	Sheffield United	W	3-0	Bell, Doyle, Lee	32,142
27	Feb 3	H	Arsenal	D	1-1	Lee	42,392
28	24	H	Sunderland	W	1-0	Lee	28,624
29	Mar 2	A	Burnley	W	1-0	Lee	23,486
30	9	H	Coventry City	W	3-1	Bell, Summerbee, Young	33,310
31	16	H	Fulham	W	5-1	Young 2, Bell, Lee, Summerbee	30,773
32	23	A	Leeds United	L	0-2		51,818
33	27	A	Manchester United	W	3-1	Bell, Heslop, Lee	62,243
34	Apr 6	A	Leicester City	L	0-1		24,925
35	12	H	Chelsea	W	1-0	Doyle	47,132
36	13	H	West Ham United	W	3-0	Young 2, Doyle	38,755
37	16	A	Chelsea	L	0-1		36,466
38	20	A	Wolverhampton W.	D	0-0		39,632
39	25	H	Sheffield Wednesday	W	1-0	og	32,999
40	29	H	Everton	W	2-0	Book, Coleman	37,786
41	May 4	A	Tottenham Hotspur	W	3-1	Bell 2, Summerbee	51,242
42	11	A	Newcastle United	W	4-3	Young 2, Lee, Summerbee	46,492
							Appearances
							Sub appearances
						One own goal	Goals

FA Cup

	Date	Venue	Opponents	Result		Scorers	Attendance
R3	Jan 27	H	Reading	D	0-0		40,343
R3	31	A	Reading	W	7-0	Summerbee 3, Bell, Coleman, Heslop, Young	25,659
R4	Feb 17	H	Leicester City	D	0-0		51,009
R4	19	A	Leicester City	L	3-4	Bell, Lee, Summerbee	39,112
							Appearances
							Sub appearances
							Goals

League Cup

	Date	Venue	Opponents	Result		Scorers	Attendance
R2	Sep 13	H	Leicester City	W	4-0	Bowles 2, Book, Young	25,653
R3	Oct 11	H	Blackpool	D	1-1	Summerbee	27,633
rep	18	A	Blackpool	W	2-0	Summerbee, Craven (og)	23,405
R4	Nov 1	A	Fulham	L	2-3	Bell, Oakes	11,732
							Appearances
							Sub appearances
						One own goal	Goals

Ogley A	Book AK	Pardoe G	Connor DR	Heslop GW	Oakes AA	Summerbee MG	Bell C	Young NJ	Jones CMN	Coleman AG	Doyle M	Dowd HW	Cheetham RAJ	Hince PF	Bowles S	Mulhearn KJ	Horne SF	Corrigan TJ	Lee FH	Clay JH	Kennedy R
1	2	3	4	5	6	7	8	9	10	11											
1	2	3	4	5	6	7	8	9		11	10										
	2	3	9	5	6	7	8	11			10	1	4								
	2	3		5	6	9	8	10		11	12	1	4	7							
	2	3		5	6	9	8	10		11	4	1		7							
	2	3		5	6	9	8	10		11	4	1		7							
	2	3		5	6	9	8	10		11	4	1		7							
	2	3		5	6	9	8	10			4	1		7	11						
	2	3	12	5	6	9	8	10		11	4	1		7							
	2	3		5	6	9	8	10		11	4				7	1	12				
	2	3		5	6	9	8	10		11					7	1	4				
	2	3		5	6	9	8	10		11	4					1			7	12	
	2		3	5	6	9	8	10		11	4					1			7		
	2	3		5	6	9	8	10		11	4					1			7		
	2	3	10	5	6	9	8			11	4					1			7		
	2	3			6	9	8	10		11	4					1	5		7		
	2	3		5	6	9	8	10		11	4					1			7		
	2	3		5	6	9	8	10		11	4					1			7		
	2	3		5	6	9	8	10		11	4					1			7		
	2	3		5	6	9	8	10		11	4					1			7		
	2	3		5	6	9	8	10		11	4					1			7		12
	2	3		5	6	9	8	10		11	4					1			7		
	2	3		5	6	9		10		11			12		8	1	4		7		
	2	3		5	6	9		10		11						1	4		7	8	
	2	3	8	5	6	9		10		11	4					1			7		
	2	3	12	5	6	9	8	10		11	4					1			7		
	2	3		5	6	9	8	10		11	4					1			7		
	2	3	10	5	6		8		9	11	4					1			7		
	2	3		5	6	9	8	10		11	4					1			7		
	2	3		5	6	9	8	10		11	4					1			7		12
	2	3		5		9	8	10		11	4					1			7		6
	2	3		5	6	9	8	10		11	4					1			7		
	2	3	12	5	6	9	8	10		11	4					1			7		
	2	3	8	5	6	9		10		11	4					1			7		
	2	3		5	6	9		10		11	8					1			7		4
	2	3		5	6	9		10		11	8					1			7		4
	2	3	11	5	6	9		10			8					1			7		4
	2	3	11	5	6	9	8	10			4					1			7		
	2	3		5	6	9	8	10		11	4					1			7		
	2	3		5	6	9	8	10		11	4					1			7		
	2	3		5	6	9	8	10		11	4					1			7		
	2	3		5	6	9	8	10		11	4					1			7		
2	42	41	10	41	41	41	35	40	2	38	37	7	2	6	4	33	4		31	1	4
			3								1		1				1			1	2
	1		1	1	2	14	14	19		8	5			2	2				16		

Ogley A	Book AK	Pardoe G	Connor DR	Heslop GW	Oakes AA	Summerbee MG	Bell C	Young NJ	Jones CMN	Coleman AG	Doyle M	Dowd HW	Cheetham RAJ	Hince PF	Bowles S	Mulhearn KJ	Horne SF	Corrigan TJ	Lee FH	Clay JH	Kennedy R
	2	3		5	6	9	8	10		11	4					1			7		
	2	3	12	5	6	9	8	10		11	4					1			7		
	2	3		5	6	9	8	10		11	4					1			7		
	2	3		5	6	9	8	10		11	4					1			7		
	4	4		4	4	4	4	4		4	4					4			4		
			1																		
				1		4	2	1		1									1		

Ogley A	Book AK	Pardoe G	Connor DR	Heslop GW	Oakes AA	Summerbee MG	Bell C	Young NJ	Jones CMN	Coleman AG	Doyle M	Dowd HW	Cheetham RAJ	Hince PF	Bowles S	Mulhearn KJ	Horne SF	Corrigan TJ	Lee FH	Clay JH	Kennedy R
	2	3		5	6	9	8	10		11	4	1		7	12						
	2	3		5	6	9	8	10		11				7			4	1			
	2	3	12	5	6	9	8	10		11	4			7				1			
	2	3		5	6	9	8	10		11	4	1		7			12				
	4	4		4	4	4	4	4		4	3	2		4			1	2			
			1												1		1				
	1				1	2	1	1							2						

League Table

	P	W	D	L	F	A	Pts
Manchester C	42	26	6	10	86	43	58
Manchester U	42	24	8	10	89	55	56
Liverpool	42	22	11	9	71	40	55
Leeds U	42	22	9	11	71	41	53
Everton	42	23	6	13	67	40	52
Chelsea	42	18	12	12	62	68	48
Tottenham H	42	19	9	14	70	59	47
W.B.A.	42	17	12	13	75	62	46
Arsenal	42	17	10	15	60	56	44
Newcastle U	42	13	15	14	54	67	41
Nottingham F	42	14	11	17	52	64	39
West Ham U	42	14	10	18	73	69	38
Leicester C	42	13	12	17	64	69	38
Burnley	42	14	10	18	64	71	38
Sunderland	42	13	11	18	51	61	37
Southampton	42	13	11	18	66	83	37
Wolverh'pton W	42	14	8	20	66	75	36
Stoke C	42	14	7	21	50	73	35
Sheffield W	42	11	12	19	51	63	34
Coventry C	42	9	15	18	51	71	33
Sheffield U	42	11	10	21	49	70	32
Fulham	42	10	7	25	56	98	27

1968-69

Division One

Manager: Joe Mercer

Did you know that?

Match 2: Kennedy's last game.

Tony Book's absence through injury was severely felt during the first half of the season. City averaged 1.2 points per game for every match he played and only 0.815 for those without him. Had his points ratio been applied throughout the season City would have finished fifth, possibly higher depending on results.

Match No.	Date	Venue	Opponents	Result		Scorers	Attendance
1	Aug 10	A	Liverpool	L	1-2	Young	51,236
2	14	H	Wolverhampton W.	W	3-2	Summerbee 2, Lee	35,835
3	17	H	Manchester United	D	0-0		63,052
4	21	A	Leicester City	L	0-3		30,076
5	24	A	Queen's Park Rangers	D	1-1	Doyle	19,716
6	27	A	Arsenal	L	1-4	Bell	40,746
7	31	H	Ipswich Town	D	1-1	Bell	31,303
8	Sep 7	A	Stoke City	L	0-1		22,034
9	14	H	Southampton	D	1-1	Coleman	29,222
10	21	A	Sunderland	W	4-0	Lee 2, Bell, Summerbee	31,687
11	28	H	Leeds United	W	3-1	Bell 2, Young	46,431
12	Oct 5	A	Everton	L	0-2		55,399
13	9	H	Arsenal	D	1-1	Bell	33,830
14	12	H	Tottenham Hotspur	W	4-0	Lee 2, Coleman, Connor	38,019
15	19	A	Coventry City	D	1-1	Bruck (og)	30,666
16	26	H	Nottingham Forest	D	3-3	Bell, Young, Hindley (og)	32,937
17	Nov 2	A	Chelsea	L	0-2		40,700
18	9	H	Sheffield Wednesday	L	0-1		24,278
19	16	A	Newcastle United	L	0-1		36,420
20	23	H	West Bromwich Albion	W	5-1	Bell 2, Young 2, Doyle	24,667
21	30	A	West Ham United	L	1-2	Lee	33,082
22	Dec 7	H	Burnley	W	7-0	Bell 2, Young 2, Coleman, Doyle, Lee	31,009
23	14	A	Tottenham Hotspur	D	1-1	Lee	28,462
24	21	H	Coventry City	W	4-2	Young 2, Booth, Curtis (og)	27,700
25	26	H	Everton	L	1-3	Bell	53,549
26	Jan 11	H	Chelsea	W	4-1	Owen 2, Lee, Young	35,605
27	18	A	Sheffield Wednesday	D	1-1	Young	32,324
28	Mar 4	A	Burnley	L	1-2	Bell	18,360
29	8	A	Manchester United	W	1-0	Summerbee	63,264
30	11	A	Ipswich Town	L	1-2	Doyle	24,313
31	15	H	Queen's Park Rangers	W	3-1	Bowyer, Lee, Young	28,859
32	24	A	Nottingham Forest	L	0-1		24,612
33	29	H	Stoke City	W	3-1	Bell, Doyle, Owen	27,337
34	Apr 4	H	Leicester City	W	2-0	Summerbee 2	42,022
35	5	A	Leeds United	L	0-1		43,176
36	8	A	Wolverhampton W.	L	1-3	Lee	28,533
37	12	H	Sunderland	W	1-0	Young	22,842
38	16	A	West Bromwich Albion	L	0-2		22,717
39	19	A	Southampton	L	0-3		26,254
40	30	H	West Ham United	D	1-1	Pardoe	31,846
41	May 5	H	Newcastle United	W	1-0	Young	20,108
42	12	H	Liverpool	W	1-0	Lee	28,309
							Appearances
							Sub appearances
						Three own goals	Goals

FA Cup

	Date	Venue	Opponents	Result		Scorers	Attendance
R3	Jan 4	H	Luton Town	W	1-0	Lee	37,120
R4	25	A	Newcastle United	D	0-0		55,680
R4	29	H	Newcastle United	W	2-0	Owen, Young	60,844
R5	Feb 24	A	Blackburn Rovers	W	4-1	Coleman 2, Lee 2	42,315
R6	Mar 1	H	Tottenham Hotspur	W	1-0	Lee	48,872
SF	22	N	Everton	W	1-0	Booth	63,025
F	Apr 26	N	Leicester City	W	1-0	Young	100,000
SF at Villa Park, Final at Wembley Stadium							Appearances
							Goals

League Cup

	Date	Venue	Opponents	Result		Scorers	Attendance
R2	Sep 3	A	Huddersfield Town	D	0-0		23,426
rep	11	H	Huddersfield Town	W	4-0	Summerbee 2, Bell, Ellam (og)	26,948
R3	25	A	Blackpool	L	0-1		23,795
							Appearances
							Sub appearances
						One own goal	Goals

European Cup

	Date	Venue	Opponents	Result		Scorers	Attendance
R1/1	Sep 18	H	Fenerbahce	D	0-0		38,787
R1/2	Oct 2	A	Fenerbahce	L	1-2	Coleman	45,000
							Appearances
							Goals

Charity Shield

	Date	Venue	Opponents	Result		Scorers	Attendance
	Aug 3	H	West Bromwich Albion	W	6-1	Lee 2, Owen 2, Young, Lovett (og)	35,510
							Appearances
						One own goal	Goals

Mulhearn KJ	Connor DR	Pardoe G	Doyle M	Heslop GW	Oakes AA	Lee FH	Bell C	Summerbee MG	Owen R	Young NJ	Coleman AG	Kennedy R	Booth TA	Bowles S	Dowd HW	Bowyer I	Mann AF	Book AK	Corrigan TJ	Glennon CD	Mundy HJ	Towers MA
1	2	3	4	5	6	7	8	9	10	11	12											
1		3	4	5	6	7	8	9	10	11		2										
1		3	4	5	6	7	8	9	10	11		2										
1		3	4	5	6	7	8	9		10	11	2										
1	2	3	4	5	6	7	8	9		10	11											
1	2	3	4	5	6	7	8	9		10	11											
1	2	3	4	5	6	7	8	9		10	11											
1	3		4	5	6	7	8	9		10	11	2										
1	3		4	5	6	7	8	9	10		11	2										
1		3	4	5	6	7	8	9		10	11	2										
1	2	3	4	5	6	7	8	9		10	11											
	2	3	4	5	6	7	8	9		10	11				1							
	2	3	4		6	7	8	9		10	11		5		1							
	2	3	4		6	7	8	9		10	11		5		1							
	2	3	4		6	7	8	9		10	11		5		1							
	2	3	4		6	7	8	9		10	11		5		1							
		3	4		6	7	8	9	10		11	2	5		1							
		3	4	12	6	7	8	9		10	11	2	5		1							
		3	4		6	7	8	9	12	10		2	5		1	11						
	11	3	4		6	7	8	9		10		2	5		1							
	11	2	4		6	7	8	9		10			5		1		3					
	12	2	4		6	7	8	9		10	11		5		1		3					
		2	4		6	7	8		9	10	11		5		1		3					
		2	4		6	7	8		9	10	11		5		1		3					
		2	4		6	7	8	9	12	10	11		5		1		3					
		3	4		6	7	8		9	10	11		5	12	1			2				
		3	4		6	8		7	9	10	11		5		1			2				
		3	4		6		8	7	9	10	11		5		1			2				
		3	4		6	9	8	7	12	10	11		5		1			2				
	8	6	4					7	9	10	11		5			12	3	2	1			
		3	4		6	9	8	7	11	10			5		1	12		2				
	2	3		5			4	7	9	10			6	8		11			1	12		
		3	4		6		8	7	9	10			5		1	11		2				
		3	4		6	9	8	7		10	11		5		1	12		2				
	11	3	4		6	9	8	7		10			5					2	1		12	
		3	4		6	9	8	7		10	11		5		1			2				
		3	4	5	6	9	8	7	12	10	11				1			2				
	4			5	6	9	7	8	10	11					1		3	2				
	2	3	4			9	8	7		10	11		5		1		12					6
		3	4		6	9	8	7		10	11		5		1			2				
		3	4		6			7	8	10	11		5		1			2			9	
	11	3	4		6	9	8	7		10			5					2	1			
11	20	39	40	15	39	37	39	39	16	40	30	10	28	1	27	3	7	15	4		1	1
	1			1					4		1			1		3	1			1	1	
	1	1	5			12	14	6	3	14	3		1			1						

Mulhearn KJ	Connor DR	Pardoe G	Doyle M	Heslop GW	Oakes AA	Lee FH	Bell C	Summerbee MG	Owen R	Young NJ	Coleman AG	Kennedy R	Booth TA	Bowles S	Dowd HW	Bowyer I	Mann AF	Book AK	Corrigan TJ	Glennon CD	Mundy HJ	Towers MA
		2	4		6	7	8		9	10	11		5		1		3					
		3	4		6	8		7	9	10	11		5		1			2				
		3	4		6	8		7	9	10	11		5		1			2				
		3	4		6	9	8	7		10	11		5		1			2				
		3	4		6	9	8	7		10	11		5		1			2				
	11	3	4		6	9	8	7		10			5		1			2				
		3	4		6	9	8	7		10	11		5		1			2				
	1	7	7		7	7	5	6	3	7	6		7		7		1	6				
						4			1	2	2		1									

Mulhearn KJ	Connor DR	Pardoe G	Doyle M	Heslop GW	Oakes AA	Lee FH	Bell C	Summerbee MG	Owen R	Young NJ	Coleman AG	Kennedy R	Booth TA	Bowles S	Dowd HW	Bowyer I	Mann AF	Book AK	Corrigan TJ	Glennon CD	Mundy HJ	Towers MA
1	2	3	4		6	9	8	7	10		11		5									
1	3		4	5	6	9	8	7		10	11	2		12								
1	2	3	4	5	6	9	8	7		10	11											
3	3	2	3	2	3	3	3	3	1	2	3	1	1									
														1								
							1	2														

Mulhearn KJ	Connor DR	Pardoe G	Doyle M	Heslop GW	Oakes AA	Lee FH	Bell C	Summerbee MG	Owen R	Young NJ	Coleman AG	Kennedy R	Booth TA	Bowles S	Dowd HW	Bowyer I	Mann AF	Book AK	Corrigan TJ	Glennon CD	Mundy HJ	Towers MA
1		3	4	5	6	9	8	7		10	11	2										
1	2	3	4	5	6	9	8	7		10	11											
2	1	2	2	2	2	2	2	2		2	2	1										
											1											

Mulhearn KJ	Connor DR	Pardoe G	Doyle M	Heslop GW	Oakes AA	Lee FH	Bell C	Summerbee MG	Owen R	Young NJ	Coleman AG	Kennedy R	Booth TA	Bowles S	Dowd HW	Bowyer I	Mann AF	Book AK	Corrigan TJ	Glennon CD	Mundy HJ	Towers MA
1	2	3	4	5	6	7	8	9	10	11												
1	1	1	1	1	1	1	1	1	1	1												
						2			2	1												

League Table

	P	W	D	L	F	A	Pts
Leeds U	42	27	13	2	66	26	67
Liverpool	42	25	11	6	63	24	61
Everton	42	21	15	6	77	36	57
Arsenal	42	22	12	8	56	27	56
Chelsea	42	20	10	12	73	53	50
Tottenham H	42	14	17	11	61	51	45
Southampton	42	16	13	13	57	48	45
West Ham U	42	13	18	11	66	50	44
Newcastle U	42	15	14	13	61	55	44
W.B.A.	42	16	11	15	64	67	43
Manchester U	42	15	12	15	57	53	42
Ipswich T	42	15	11	16	59	60	41
Manchester C	42	15	10	17	64	55	40
Burnley	42	15	9	18	55	82	39
Sheffield W	42	10	16	16	41	54	36
Wolverh'pton W	42	10	15	17	41	58	35
Sunderland	42	11	12	19	43	67	34
Nottingham F	42	10	13	19	45	57	33
Stoke C	42	9	15	18	40	63	33
Coventry C	42	10	11	21	46	64	31
Leicester C	42	9	12	21	39	68	30
Q.P.R.	42	4	10	28	39	95	18

1969-70

Division One

Manager: Joe Mercer

Did you know that?

Match 5: Coleman's last game.
Match 16: Mundy's last game.
Match 24: Owen's last game.
Match 30: Bowles's last game.
Match 31: Mulhearn's last game.
Match 39: Glennon's last game.
Match 42: Dowd's last game.

Winning the ECWC in April 1970 meant City were the first English side to win a major European and domestic trophy in the same season. Leeds had won the Fairs Cup and League Cup in 1968, but the Fairs Cup Final was held over until 1968–69 while many major sides had boycotted the League Cup. In fact 1969–70 was the first to see all 92 sides enter the League Cup.

Match No.	Date	Venue	Opponents	Result		Scorers	Attendance
1	Aug 9	H	Sheffield Wednesday	W	4-1	Young 2, Bell, Lee	32,583
2	12	A	Liverpool	L	2-3	Bowyer, Smith (og)	51,959
3	16	A	Newcastle United	L	0-1		46,850
4	20	H	Liverpool	L	0-2		47,888
5	23	H	Everton	D	1-1	Bowyer	43,366
6	27	A	Sunderland	W	4-0	Bowyer 2, Bell, Oakes	21,515
7	30	A	Burnley	D	1-1	Bowyer	26,342
8	Sep 6	H	Chelsea	D	0-0		35,995
9	13	A	Tottenham Hotspur	W	3-0	Bell, Bowyer, Oakes	41,644
10	20	H	Coventry City	W	3-1	Bell 2, Lee	34,230
11	27	A	Stoke City	L	0-2		29,742
12	Oct 4	H	West Bromwich Albion	W	2-1	Bell, Young	34,329
13	8	H	Newcastle United	W	2-1	Lee, Young	32,172
14	11	A	Nottingham Forest	D	2-2	Lee 2	30,037
15	18	A	Derby County	W	1-0	Lee	40,788
16	25	H	Wolverhampton W.	W	1-0	Doyle	34,425
17	Nov 1	A	Ipswich Town	D	1-1	Lee	24,128
18	8	H	Southampton	W	1-0	Bell	27,069
19	15	H	Manchester United	W	4-0	Bell 2, Young, Sadler (og)	63,013
20	22	A	Arsenal	D	1-1	Bowyer	42,923
21	29	H	Leeds United	L	1-2	Lee	44,590
22	Dec 6	A	West Ham United	W	4-0	Bowyer 2, Doyle, Lee	27,485
23	13	H	Tottenham Hotspur	D	1-1	Oakes	29,216
24	20	A	Chelsea	L	1-3	Summerbee	34,791
25	23	A	Everton	L	0-1		51,864
26	Jan 6	H	Burnley	D	1-1	Lee	22,074
27	10	A	Coventry City	L	0-3		30,050
28	17	H	Stoke City	L	0-1		31,565
29	31	A	West Bromwich Albion	L	0-3		30,341
30	Feb 7	H	Nottingham Forest	D	1-1	Doyle	27,077
31	18	H	Arsenal	D	1-1	Bowyer	25,508
32	21	A	Wolverhampton W.	W	3-1	Summerbee 2, Bell	30,873
33	28	H	Ipswich Town	W	1-0	Lee	29,376
34	Mar 11	H	Crystal Palace	L	0-1		25,381
35	21	H	West Ham United	L	1-5	Lee	28,353
36	27	H	Derby County	L	0-1		42,316
37	28	A	Manchester United	W	2-1	Doyle, Lee	59,777
38	Apr 4	H	Sunderland	L	0-1		22,006
39	6	A	Crystal Palace	L	0-1		27,704
40	8	A	Southampton	D	0-0		24,384
41	18	A	Leeds United	W	3-1	Bell, Towers, Young	22,932
42	22	A	Sheffield Wednesday	W	2-1	Bowyer 2	43,893
							Appearances
							Sub appearances
						Two own goals	Goals

FA Cup

	Date	Venue	Opponents	Result		Scorers	Attendance
R3	Jan 3	A	Hull City	W	1-0	Young	30,271
R4	24	A	Manchester United	L	0-3		63,417
							Appearances
							Sub appearances
							Goals

League Cup

	Date	Venue	Opponents	Result		Scorers	Attendance
R2	Sep 3	A	Southport	W	3-0	Bell, Lee, Oakes	11,215
R3	24	H	Liverpool	W	3-2	Bowyer, Doyle, Young	28,019
R4	Oct 14	H	Everton	W	2-0	Bell, Lee	45,643
R5	29	H	Queen's Park Rangers	W	3-0	Bell 2, Summerbee	42,058
SF1	Dec 3	H	Manchester United	W	2-1	Bell, Lee	55,799
SF2	17	A	Manchester United	D	2-2	Bowyer, Summerbee	63,418
F	Mar 7	N	West Bromwich Albion	W	2-1e	Doyle, Pardoe	97,963
Final at Wembley Stadium							Appearances
							Sub appearances
							Goals

European Cup Winners Cup

	Date	Venue	Opponents	Result		Scorers	Attendance
R1/1	Sep 17	A	Athletic Bilbao	D	3-3	Booth, Young, Echeberria (og)	41,400
R1/2	Oct 1	H	Athletic Bilbao	W	3-0	Bell, Bowyer, Oakes	49,664
R2/1	Nov 12	A	Lierse	W	3-0	Lee 2, Bell	15,348
R2/2	26	H	Lierse	W	5-0	Bell 2, Lee 2, Summerbee	26,486
QF1	Mar 4	A	Academica Coimbra	D	0-0		8,206
QF2	18	H	Academica Coimbra	W	1-0	Towers	36,338
SF1	Apr 1	A	Schalke 04	L	0-1		27,429
SF2	15	H	Schalke 04	W	5-1	Young 2, Bell, Doyle, Lee	46,361
F	29	N	Gornik Zabrze	W	2-1	Lee, Young	7,968
Final at the Prater, Vienna							Appearances
							Sub appearances
						One own goal	Goals

Charity Shield

	Date	Venue	Opponents	Result		Scorers	Attendance
	Aug 2	A	Leeds United	L	1-2	Bell	39,859
							Appearances
							Sub appearances
							Goals

Corrigan TJ	Book AK	Pardoe G	Doyle M	Booth TA	Oakes AA	Summerbee MG	Bell C	Lee FH	Young NJ	Coleman AG	Bowyer I	Bowles S	Connor DR	Heslop GW	Owen R	Towers MA	Jeffries D	Mundy HJ	Mulhearn KJ	Mann AF	Donachie W	Carrodus F	Glennon CD	Dowd HW
1	2	3	4	5	6	7	8	9	10	11														
1	2	3	4	5	6	7	8	9		11	10													
1	2	3	4	5	6	7	8	9		11	10													
1	2	3	4	5		7	8	9		11	10	6												
1	2	3	4	5		7		9		11	10	6	8											
1	2	3	4	5	6	7	8	9			10	11												
1	2		4	5	6	7	8	9			10	11	3											
1	2	3	4	5	6	7	8	9			10	11												
1	2	3	4	5	6	7	8	9	10		11													
1	2	3	4		6	7	8	9	10		11			5										
1	2	3	4	5	6	7		9	10		11				8	12								
1	2	3	4	5	6	7	8	9	10		11						12							
1	2	3	4	5	6	7	8	9	10		11													
1	2	3	4	5	6	7	8	9	10		11													
1	2	3	4	5	6	7	8	9	10		11													
1	2	3	4	5	6	7	8		10		11							9						
1	2	3	4	5	6	7	8	9	10		11						12							
1	2	3	4	5	6	7	8	9			11					10								
1	2	3	4	5	6	7	8	9	10		11													
1	2	3	4	5	6	7	8	9	10		11													
	2	3	4	5	6	7	8	9	10		11								1					
1	2	3	4	5	6	7	8	9	10		11		12											
	2	3	4	5	6	7		9	10		11		8						1					
1	2			4	6	7			10		11	8	3	5	9									
1	2		8	4	6	7		9	10		11		3	5										
1	2	3	4	5	6	7	8	9			11	10		12										
1		3	4	5	6	7	8	9			11	10	2											
	2	3	4	5	6	7	8	9	10		11	12							1					
		3	4	5	6		8	9	10		11	7	2				12		1					
	2		4	5	6		8	9	10		11	7							1	3	12			
		2	4	5	6		8	10	11		9								1	3		7		
1	2	11	4	5	6	9	8	10												3		7		
1	2	11	4	5	6	9	8	10												3		7		
1		11	9	4	6		8	10					2	5			7			3				
1	2	11	4	5	6			8	10		9					7				3				
1	2	11	4	5	6			8	10								7			3			9	
1	2	11	4	5	6			9	10		8						7			3				
1	2	8	4	5	6				10								11			3	12	7	9	
1	2	3	4	5	6	12			11							10					8	7	9	
1	2	3	4	5	6	9	8	10	11							7								
	2	3	4	5	6		8		10		9			11		7								1
	2	3	4	5	6	9			10		12			11		8						7		1
34	38	38	41	41	40	32	31	36	29	5	33	10	8	6	2	6	4	1	6	9	1	6	3	2
						1					1	1	1	1		1	3				2			
			4		3	3	11	13	6		12					1								

Corrigan TJ	Book AK	Pardoe G	Doyle M	Booth TA	Oakes AA	Summerbee MG	Bell C	Lee FH	Young NJ	Coleman AG	Bowyer I	Bowles S	Connor DR	Heslop GW	Owen R	Towers MA	Jeffries D	Mundy HJ	Mulhearn KJ	Mann AF	Donachie W	Carrodus F	Glennon CD	Dowd HW
1	2	3	4	5	6	7	8	9	10		11													
	2	3	4	5	6	7	8	9	10		11					12			1					
1	2	2	2	2	2	2	2	2	2		2								1					
																1								
									1															

Corrigan TJ	Book AK	Pardoe G	Doyle M	Booth TA	Oakes AA	Summerbee MG	Bell C	Lee FH	Young NJ	Coleman AG	Bowyer I	Bowles S	Connor DR	Heslop GW	Owen R	Towers MA	Jeffries D	Mundy HJ	Mulhearn KJ	Mann AF	Donachie W	Carrodus F	Glennon CD	Dowd HW
1	2		4	5	6	7	8	9			10	11	3											
1	2	3	4		6	7	8	9	10	12	11			5										
1	2	3	4	5	6	7	8	9	10		11													
1	2	3	4	5	6	7	8	9	10		11													
1	2	3	4	5	6	7	8	9	10		11													
1	2	3	4	5	6	7		9	10		11		8											
1	2	11	4	5	6	9	8	10			12			7						3				
7	7	6	7	6	7	7	6	7	5		6	1	2	2						1				
										1	1													
		1	2		1	2	5	3	1		2													

Corrigan TJ	Book AK	Pardoe G	Doyle M	Booth TA	Oakes AA	Summerbee MG	Bell C	Lee FH	Young NJ	Coleman AG	Bowyer I	Bowles S	Connor DR	Heslop GW	Owen R	Towers MA	Jeffries D	Mundy HJ	Mulhearn KJ	Mann AF	Donachie W	Carrodus F	Glennon CD	Dowd HW
1	2	3	4	5	6	7	8	9	10		11													
1	2	3	4	5	6	7	8	9	10		11													
1	2	3	4	5	6	7	8	9	10		11			12										
	2	3	4	5	6	7	8	9			11					12	10		1					
1	2	7	4	5	6	9	8	10	11					12						3				
1	2	11	7	4	6		8	9	10					5		12				3			13	
1	2	3	4	11	6	7	8	9	10								5							
1	2	3	4	5	6	7	8	9	10					12		11						13		
1	2	3	4	5	6		8	9	10		12			7		11								
8	9	9	9	9	9	7	9	9	8		4			2		2	2		1	2				
											1			3		2						1	1	
			1	1	1	1	5	6	4		1					1								

Corrigan TJ	Book AK	Pardoe G	Doyle M	Booth TA	Oakes AA	Summerbee MG	Bell C	Lee FH	Young NJ	Coleman AG	Bowyer I	Bowles S	Connor DR	Heslop GW	Owen R	Towers MA	Jeffries D	Mundy HJ	Mulhearn KJ	Mann AF	Donachie W	Carrodus F	Glennon CD	Dowd HW
1	2	3	4	5	6	7	8	9	10	11			12											
1	1	1	1	1	1	1	1	1	1	1														
													1											
							1																	

League Table

	P	W	D	L	F	A	Pts
Everton	42	29	8	5	72	34	66
Leeds U	42	21	15	6	84	49	57
Chelsea	42	21	13	8	70	50	55
Derby Co	42	22	9	11	64	37	53
Liverpool	42	20	11	11	65	42	51
Coventry C	42	19	11	12	58	48	49
Newcastle U	42	17	13	12	57	35	47
Manchester U	42	14	17	11	66	61	45
Stoke C	42	15	15	12	56	52	45
Manchester C	42	16	11	15	55	48	43
Tottenham H	42	17	9	16	54	55	43
Arsenal	42	12	18	12	51	49	42
Wolverh'pton W	42	12	16	14	55	57	40
Burnley	42	12	15	15	56	61	39
Nottingham F	42	10	18	14	50	71	38
W.B.A.	42	14	9	19	58	66	37
West Ham U	42	12	12	18	51	60	36
Ipswich T	42	10	11	21	40	63	31
Southampton	42	6	17	19	46	67	29
Crystal Palace	42	6	15	21	34	68	27
Sunderland	42	6	14	22	30	68	26
Sheffield W	42	8	9	25	40	71	25

1970-71

Division One

Manager: Joe Mercer

Did you know that?

Match 40: White's first and only game.
Match 40: Mann's last game.
Match 41: Bowyer's last game.

The last match of the season was a strange affair. Pre-match ex-Blue and United manager Matt Busby was presented with a This Is Your Life book by Eamon Andrews, and the whole game was played as if it was an end-of-season friendly rather than a full-blooded derby. United's victory was their only win in 14 League derbies between Christmas 1967 and Easter 1976.

Match No.	Date	Venue	Opponents	Result		Scorers	Attendance
1	Aug 15	A	Southampton	D	1-1	Bell	24,599
2	19	A	Crystal Palace	W	1-0	Oakes	33,618
3	22	H	Burnley	D	0-0		36,599
4	26	H	Blackpool	W	2-0	Bell, Lee	37,598
5	29	A	Everton	W	1-0	Bell	50,724
6	Sep 5	H	West Bromwich Albion	W	4-1	Bell 2, Lee, Summerbee	30,549
7	12	A	Nottingham Forest	W	1-0	Doyle	28,896
8	19	H	Stoke City	W	4-1	Book, Lee, Young, Banks (og)	35,465
9	26	A	Tottenham Hotspur	L	0-2		42,490
10	Oct 3	H	Newcastle United	D	1-1	Doyle	33,159
11	10	A	Chelsea	D	1-1	Bell	51,903
12	17	H	Southampton	D	1-1	Lee	31,998
13	24	A	Wolverhampton W.	L	0-3		32,700
14	31	H	Ipswich Town	W	2-0	Bell, Lee	27,317
15	Nov 7	A	Coventry City	L	1-2	Bell	25,287
16	14	H	Derby County	D	1-1	Bell	31,817
17	21	H	West Ham United	W	2-0	Lee 2	28,485
18	28	A	Leeds United	L	0-1		43,511
19	Dec 5	H	Arsenal	L	0-2		33,036
20	12	A	Manchester United	W	4-1	Lee 3, Doyle	51,969
21	19	A	Burnley	W	4-0	Bell 2, Lee, Summerbee	19,917
22	26	H	Huddersfield Town	D	1-1	Bell	40,091
23	Jan 9	H	Crystal Palace	W	1-0	Book	27,442
24	12	A	Liverpool	D	0-0		45,985
25	16	A	Blackpool	D	3-3	Summerbee 2, Bell	29,356
26	30	H	Leeds United	L	0-2		43,317
27	Feb 6	A	Arsenal	L	0-1		46,162
28	20	A	West Ham United	D	0-0		30,168
29	26	A	Ipswich Town	L	0-2		20,686
30	Mar 6	H	Wolverhampton W.	D	0-0		24,663
31	13	A	Derby County	D	0-0		31,987
32	20	H	Coventry City	D	1-1	Lee (pen)	22,210
33	27	A	West Bromwich Albion	D	0-0		20,363
34	Apr 3	H	Everton	W	3-0	Booth, Doyle, Hill	26,885
35	9	H	Nottingham Forest	L	1-3	Doyle	33,772
36	10	A	Huddersfield Town	L	0-1		21,922
37	12	A	Newcastle United	D	0-0		29,148
38	17	H	Chelsea	D	1-1	Lee	26,120
39	24	A	Stoke City	L	0-2		13,497
40	26	H	Liverpool	D	2-2	Carter (pen), Ross (og)	17,961
41	May 1	H	Tottenham Hotspur	L	0-1		19,761
42	5	H	Manchester United	L	3-4	Hill, Lee, Mellor	43,623
							Appearances
							Sub appearances
						Two own goals	Goals

FA Cup

Match No.	Date	Venue	Opponents	Result		Scorers	Attendance
R3	Jan 2	H	Wigan Athletic	W	1-0	Bell	46,212
R4	23	A	Chelsea	W	3-0	Bell 2, Bowyer	50,176
R5	Feb 17	H	Arsenal	L	1-2	Bell	45,105
							Appearances
							Sub appearances
							Goals

League Cup

Match No.	Date	Venue	Opponents	Result		Scorers	Attendance
R2	Sep 9	A	Carlisle United	L	1-2	Lee	17,942
							Appearances
							Sub appearances
							Goals

European Cup Winners Cup

Match No.	Date	Venue	Opponents	Result		Scorers	Attendance
R1/1	Sep 16	H	Linfield (Belfast)	W	1-0	Bell	25,184
R1/2	30	A	Linfield (Belfast)	L	1-2	Lee	24,000
R2/1	Oct 21	A	Honved	W	1-0	Lee	14,000
R2/2	Nov 4	H	Honved	W	2-0	Bell, Lee	28,770
QF1	Mar 10	H	Gornik Zabrze	W	2-0		100,000
QF2	24	A	Gornik Zabrze	L	0-2	Doyle, Mellor	31,950
rep	31	N	Manchester City	W	3-1	Booth, Lee, Young	12,100
SF1	Apr 14	A	Chelsea	L	0-1		45,955
SF2	28	H	Chelsea	L	0-1		43,663
							Appearances
							Sub appearances
							Goals

R1 won on away goals rule
QF replay in Copenhagen

Anglo-Italian Cup

Match No.	Date	Venue	Opponents	Result		Scorers	Attendance
R1/1	Sep 2	A	Bologna	L	0-1		28,000
R1/2	23	H	Bologna	D	2-2	Heslop, Lee	25,843
							Appearances
							Sub appearances
							Goals

Corrigan TJ	Book AK	Pardoe G	Doyle M	Heslop GW	Oakes AA	Towers MA	Bell C	Summerbee MG	Lee FH	Hill F	Booth TA	Young NJ	Bowyer I	Jeffries D	Connor DR	Mann AF	Carrodus F	Healey R	Brennan M	Donachie W	Mellor I	Johnson JD	Carter SC	White HK
1	2	3	4	5	6	7	8	9	10	11														
1	2	3	4	5	6	7	8	9	10	11														
1	2	3	4	5	6	7	8	9	10	11														
1	2	3	4		6	11	8	7	9		5	10												
1	2	3	4		6	11	8	7	9		5	10												
1	2	3	4		6	11	8	7	9		5	10												
1	2	3	4		6	11	8	7	9		5	10												
1	2	3	4	12	6	11	8	7	9		5	10												
1	2	3	4	5	6	11	8	7	9			10	12											
1		3	4	5	6	11	8	7	9	10				12	2									
1	2	3	4	5	6	11	8	7	9	10														
1	2	3	4	5	6	11	8	7	9	10														
1	2	3	4	5		11	8	7	9	10				6										
1	2	3	4	5	6	11	8	7	9	10														
1		3	4	5	6	11	8		9	10			7			2								
1	2		4	5	6	11	8	7	9	10						3								
1	2	3	4	5	6	11	8	7	9					12		10								
1	2	3	4	5	6	11	8	7	9							10								
1	2	3	4	5	6	12	8	7	9					11		10								
1	2	3	4		6		8	7	9		5	10		11		12								
1	2		4		6		8	7	9		5	10		11		3								
1	2		4		6		8	7	9		5	10		11		3	12							
1	2		4		6		8	9		12	5	10		11		3	7							
1	2		4		6		8	9		10	5			11	12	3	7							
1	2		4		6		8	7	9		5	10	12	11		3								
1	2		4	7	6		8		9		5		12	11		3	10							
1			4	7	6		8		9	10	5		11	2		3								
1	2		4		6	3			9	8	5	10	11	7										
	2		4		6	3			9	11	5	10	8	7				1						
1	2		4		6	3		7	9		5	10	12	11			8							
	2		4		6	3	8	7	9		5	10		11				1	12					
			4			3	8		9		5	10		7	2			1		6	11			
			4			3	8		9	12	5	10		7	2			1		6	11			
			4			3	8		9	11	5	10		7	2			1		6		12		
	12		4			3	8		9	11	5	10		7	2			1		6				
1	2		4			7	8		9	11	5	10			3	12				6				
1			4			2	8				5				3	11			12	6	9	7	10	
1	2					4			9	12	5	10			3	11				6		7	8	
1	2					4			9	8	5	10			3	11				6		7		
				4		2					5		9			10	7	1		3	12	8	11	6
	2			5		4			9	8		10	11		3			1		6	7		12	
	2			5		4			9	11		10			3			1		6	8		7	
33	33	19	37	19	30	33	34	26	38	20	26	24	6	18	11	16	5	9		11	5	4	4	1
	1			1		1				3			4	2	1	2	1		2		1	1	1	
	2		5		1		13	4	14	2	1	1									1		1	

Corrigan TJ	Book AK	Pardoe G	Doyle M	Heslop GW	Oakes AA	Towers MA	Bell C	Summerbee MG	Lee FH	Hill F	Booth TA	Young NJ	Bowyer I	Jeffries D	Connor DR	Mann AF	Carrodus F	Healey R	Brennan M	Donachie W	Mellor I	Johnson JD	Carter SC	White HK
1	2		4		6		8	7	9		5	10		11		3	12							
1	2		4	7	6		8	9			5	12	10	11		3								
1	2		4	7	6		8		9		5	10	11			3								
3	3		3	2	3		3	2	2		3	2	2	2		3								
												1					1							
							4						1											

Corrigan TJ	Book AK	Pardoe G	Doyle M	Heslop GW	Oakes AA	Towers MA	Bell C	Summerbee MG	Lee FH	Hill F	Booth TA	Young NJ	Bowyer I	Jeffries D	Connor DR	Mann AF	Carrodus F	Healey R	Brennan M	Donachie W	Mellor I	Johnson JD	Carter SC	White HK
1	2	3	4		6	11	8	7	9		5	10	12											
1	1	1	1		1	1	1	1	1		1	1												
													1											
									1															

Corrigan TJ	Book AK	Pardoe G	Doyle M	Heslop GW	Oakes AA	Towers MA	Bell C	Summerbee MG	Lee FH	Hill F	Booth TA	Young NJ	Bowyer I	Jeffries D	Connor DR	Mann AF	Carrodus F	Healey R	Brennan M	Donachie W	Mellor I	Johnson JD	Carter SC	White HK
1	2	3	4		6	11	8	7	9		5	10												
1	2	3	4		6	11	8	7	9			10	12	5										
1		3	4	5		11	8	7	9	10	2			6										
1	2	3	4	5	6	11	8	7	9	10														
1	2		4		6	3	8	7	9		5	10		11										
			4			3	8		9		5	10	13	7	2	12		1		6	11			
			4			3	8		9	11	5	10		7	2			1		6				
1	2					4			9	8	5	10			3	11				6		7		
	2			5		4		7	8			10	9	6	3			1		13		11	12	
6	6	4	7	3	4	9	7	6	9	4	6	7	1	6	4	1		3		3	1	2		
													2			1				1			1	
			1				2		4		1	1									1			

Corrigan TJ	Book AK	Pardoe G	Doyle M	Heslop GW	Oakes AA	Towers MA	Bell C	Summerbee MG	Lee FH	Hill F	Booth TA	Young NJ	Bowyer I	Jeffries D	Connor DR	Mann AF	Carrodus F	Healey R	Brennan M	Donachie W	Mellor I	Johnson JD	Carter SC	White HK
1	2	3	4		6	11	8	7	9		5	10												
1	2	3	4	5	6	11	8	12	9	7		10												
2	2	2	2	1	2	2	2	1	2	1	1	2												
								1																
				1					1															

League Table

	P	W	D	L	F	A	Pts
Arsenal	42	29	7	6	71	29	65
Leeds U	42	27	10	5	72	30	64
Tottenham H	42	19	14	9	54	33	52
Wolverh'pton W	42	22	8	12	64	54	52
Liverpool	42	17	17	8	42	24	51
Chelsea	42	18	15	9	52	42	51
Southampton	42	17	12	13	56	44	46
Manchester U	42	16	11	15	65	66	43
Derby Co	42	16	10	16	56	54	42
Coventry C	42	16	10	16	37	38	42
Manchester C	42	12	17	13	47	42	41
Newcastle U	42	14	13	15	44	46	41
Stoke C	42	12	13	17	44	48	37
Everton	42	12	13	17	54	60	37
Huddersfield T	42	11	14	17	40	49	36
Nottingham F	42	14	8	20	42	61	36
W.B.A.	42	10	15	17	58	75	35
Crystal Palace	42	12	11	19	39	57	35
Ipswich T	42	12	10	20	42	48	34
West Ham U	42	10	14	18	47	60	34
Burnley	42	7	13	22	29	63	27
Blackpool	42	4	15	23	34	66	23

1971-72

Division One

Manager: Joe Mercer (until 7 October 1971), Malcolm Allison (Joe Mercer as General Manager)

Did you know that?

Match 7: Heslop's last game.
Match 10: Johnson's last game.
Match 6: Connor's last game.
Match 13: Young's last game.
Match 15: Carter's last game..

Had City managed to get at least a point against Ipswich, then the final match of the season would have been a play-off for the title. Malcolm Allison believed a thrilling performance by England 'keeper Gordon Banks in City's home game with Stoke in Match 36 was actually the moment City lost the title.

Match No.	Date	Venue	Opponents	Result		Scorers	Attendance
1	Aug 14	H	Leeds United	L	0-1		38,566
2	18	H	Crystal Palace	W	4-0	Lee 2 (1 pen), Booth, Davies	27,103
3	21	A	Chelsea	D	2-2	Lee 2 (1 pen)	38,425
4	24	A	Wolverhampton W.	L	1-2	Lee (pen)	26,683
5	28	H	Tottenham Hotspur	W	4-0	Bell, Lee, Davies, Summerbee	33,683
6	Sep 1	H	Liverpool	W	1-0	Mellor	45,143
7	4	A	Leicester City	D	0-0		25,238
8	11	H	Newcastle United	W	2-1	Bell, Lee	32,710
9	18	A	Nottingham Forest	D	2-2	Davies, Lee (pen)	21,488
10	25	H	Southampton	W	3-0	Bell, Davies, Lee	27,897
11	Oct 2	A	West Bromwich Albion	W	2-0	Connor, Lee	25,834
12	9	H	Everton	W	1-0	Lee (pen)	33,538
13	16	A	Leeds United	L	0-3		36,004
14	23	H	Sheffield United	W	2-1	Doyle, Lee	41,688
15	30	A	Huddersfield Town	D	1-1	Carter	20,153
16	Nov 6	H	Manchester United	D	3-3	Bell, Lee (pen), Summerbee	63,326
17	13	A	Arsenal	W	2-1	Bell, Mellor	47,433
18	20	A	West Ham United	W	2-0	Davies, Lee (pen)	33,694
19	27	H	Coventry City	W	4-0	Bell 2, Lee 2	31,003
20	Dec 4	A	Derby County	L	1-3	Lee (pen)	35,384
21	11	H	Ipswich Town	W	4-0	Bell, Lee, Davies, Mellor	26,900
22	18	H	Leicester City	D	1-1	Lee (pen)	29,524
23	27	A	Stoke City	W	3-1	Book, Lee, Towers	43,007
24	Jan 1	H	Nottingham Forest	D	2-2	Davies, Lee (pen)	38,777
25	8	A	Tottenham Hotspur	D	1-1	Davies	36,470
26	22	A	Crystal Palace	W	2-1	Lee, Blyth (og)	31,518
27	29	H	Wolverhampton W.	W	5-2	Lee 3, Booth, Towers	37,649
28	Feb 12	A	Sheffield United	D	3-3	Lee 2 (1 pen), Bell	38,184
29	19	H	Huddersfield Town	W	1-0	Booth	36,421
30	26	A	Liverpool	L	0-3		50,074
31	Mar 1	H	West Bromwich Albion	W	2-1	Bell 2	25,672
32	4	H	Arsenal	W	2-0	Lee 2 (1 pen)	44,213
33	11	A	Everton	W	2-1	Hill, T Wright (og)	44,649
34	18	H	Chelsea	W	1-0	Booth	53,322
35	25	A	Newcastle United	D	0-0		37,506
36	Apr 1	H	Stoke City	L	1-2	Lee	49,392
37	4	A	Southampton	L	0-2		27,374
38	8	H	West Ham United	W	3-1	Marsh 2, Bell	38,488
39	12	A	Manchester United	W	3-1	Lee 2, Marsh	56,362
40	15	A	Coventry City	D	1-1	Towers	34,302
41	18	A	Ipswich Town	L	1-2	Summerbee	24,464
42	22	H	Derby County	W	2-0	Lee (pen), Marsh	55,023
							Appearances
							Sub appearances
						Two own goals	Goals

FA Cup

	Date	Venue	Opponents	Result		Scorers	Attendance
R3	Jan 15	H	Middlesbrough	D	1-1	Lee (pen)	42,620
rep	18	A	Middlesbrough	L	0-1		37,917
							Appearances
							Goals

League Cup

	Date	Venue	Opponents	Result		Scorers	Attendance
R2	Sep 8	H	Wolverhampton W.	W	4-3	Bell 2, Davies, Lee (pen)	29,156
R3	Oct 5	A	Bolton Wanderers	L	0-3		40,000
							Appearances
							Sub appearances
							Goals

Texaco Cup

	Date	Venue	Opponents	Result		Scorers	Attendance
R1/1	Sep 15	H	Airdrieonians	D	2-2	Mellor, Doyle	15,033
R1/2	27	A	Airdrieonians	L	0-2		13,700
							Appearances
							Sub appearances
							Goals

Corrigan TJ	Book AK	Connor DR	Doyle M	Booth TA	Oakes AA	Summerbee MG	Heslop GW	Davies RW	Lee FH	Mellor I	Young NJ	Donachie W	Jeffries D	Bell C	Johnson JD	Towers MA	Hill F	Carter SC	Henson PM	Marsh RW	Healey R	Brennan M	Hanvey K
1	2	3	4	5	6	7	8	9	10	11	12												
1	2	3	4	5	6		8	9	10	11	7												
1	2	3	4	5	6		8	9	10	11	7	12											
1		3	4	5	6	7	8	9	10	11			2										
1		3	4	5		7	8	9	10	11		12	2	6									
1	2	3	4	5		7	8	9	10	11			12	6									
1	2		4	5		7	8	9	10	11			3	6									
1	2		4	5		7		9	10	11		3	8	6									
1	2		4	5		7		9	10	11		3	8	6									
1	2		4	5		7		9	10	11		3	8	6	12								
1	2	11	4	5		7		9	10			3	8			6							
1	2	3	4	5		7			10	11	9	8	12			6							
1	2		4	5		7		9	10	11	12	3	8			6							
1	2		4	5	6	7		9	10	11		3		8									
1	2		4	5	6	7		9	10	11		3		8				12					
1	2		4	5	6	7		9	10	11		3		8									
1	2		4	5	6	7		9	10	11		3	12	8									
1	2		4	5	6	7		9	10	11		3		8									
1	2		4	5	6	7		9	10	11		3		8									
1	2		4	5	6	7		9	10	11		3		8									
1	2		4	5	6	7		9	10	11		3		8									
1	2		4	5	6	7		9	10	11		3		8									
1	2		4	5	6	7		9	10			3		8		11							
1	2		4	5	6	7		9	10			3		8		11							
1	2		4	5	6	7		9	10			3		8		11							
1	2		4	5	6	7		9	10			3		8		11			12				
1	2		4	5	6	7		9	10			3		8		11	12						
1	2		4	5	6	7		9	10			3		8		11							
1	2		4	5	6	7		9	10			3				11	8						
1	2		4	5	6	7		9	10			3				11	8						
1	2		4	5	6	7		9	10			3		8		11	12						
1	2		4		6	7		9	10			3		8		11	5						
1	2		4		6	7		9	10	12		3		8		11	5						
1	2		4	5	6	7		9	10			3		8		12				11			
	2		4	5	6	7		9	10			3		8						11	1		
	2		4	5	6	7		9	10			3		8						11	1		
	2		4	5	6	11		9	7			3		8		12				10	1		
	2			5	6	11		9	7			3		8		4				10	1		
	2		4	5	6	7		9	10			3		8		11				12	1		
	2		4	5	6	7		9	10			3		8		11					1		
	2		4	5	12	7		9	6			3		8		11				10	1		
1	2		4	5		9			7			3	6	8		11				10			
35	40	8	41	40	31	40	7	40	42	21	3	35	9	33		19	4			7	7		
					1					1	2	2	3		1	2	2	1	1	1			
	1	1	1	4		3		8	33	3				12		3	1	1		4			

Corrigan TJ	Book AK	Connor DR	Doyle M	Booth TA	Oakes AA	Summerbee MG	Heslop GW	Davies RW	Lee FH	Mellor I	Young NJ	Donachie W	Jeffries D	Bell C	Johnson JD	Towers MA	Hill F	Carter SC	Henson PM	Marsh RW	Healey R	Brennan M	Hanvey K
1	2		4	5	6	7		9	10			3		8		11							
1	2		4	5	6	7		9	10			3		8		11							
2	2		2	2	2	2		2	2			2		2		2							
									1														

Corrigan TJ	Book AK	Connor DR	Doyle M	Booth TA	Oakes AA	Summerbee MG	Heslop GW	Davies RW	Lee FH	Mellor I	Young NJ	Donachie W	Jeffries D	Bell C	Johnson JD	Towers MA	Hill F	Carter SC	Henson PM	Marsh RW	Healey R	Brennan M	Hanvey K
1	2		4	5		7	8	9	10	11		3	12	6									
1	2		4	5		7		9	10			3	8			6	11						
2	2		2	2		2	1	2	2	1		2	1	1		1	1						
													1										
								1	1					2									

Corrigan TJ	Book AK	Connor DR	Doyle M	Booth TA	Oakes AA	Summerbee MG	Heslop GW	Davies RW	Lee FH	Mellor I	Young NJ	Donachie W	Jeffries D	Bell C	Johnson JD	Towers MA	Hill F	Carter SC	Henson PM	Marsh RW	Healey R	Brennan M	Hanvey K
13	2		4	5		7		9	12	11		3	6			8					1	10	
		2										3	6		8	4	11	7	10		1	9	5
	1	1	1	1		1		1		1		2	2		1	2	1	1	1		2	2	1
1									1														
			1							1													

League Table

	P	W	D	L	F	A	Pts
Derby Co	42	24	10	8	69	33	58
Leeds U	42	24	9	9	73	31	57
Liverpool	42	24	9	9	64	30	57
Manchester C	42	23	11	8	77	45	57
Arsenal	42	22	8	12	58	40	52
Tottenham H	42	19	13	10	63	42	51
Chelsea	42	18	12	12	58	49	48
Manchester U	42	19	10	13	69	61	48
Wolverh'pton W	42	18	11	13	65	57	47
Sheffield U	42	17	12	13	61	60	46
Newcastle U	42	15	11	16	49	52	41
Leicester C	42	13	13	16	41	46	39
Ipswich T	42	11	16	15	39	53	38
West Ham U	42	12	12	18	47	51	36
Everton	42	9	18	15	37	48	36
W.B.A.	42	12	11	19	42	54	35
Stoke C	42	10	15	17	39	56	35
Coventry C	42	9	15	18	44	67	33
Southampton	42	12	7	23	52	80	31
Crystal Palace	42	8	13	21	39	65	29
Nottingham F	42	8	9	25	47	81	25
Huddersfield T	42	6	13	23	27	59	25

1972-73

Division One

Manager: Malcolm Allison (until 30 March 1973), John Hart

Did you know that?

Match 8: Davies's last game.
Match 25: Hill's last game.
Match 30: Mellor and Brennan's last game.
Match 42: Jeffries's last game.

City wore four different styled kits during 1972–73. These were the traditional sky blue with white shorts; the Allison inspired red and black shirts with black shorts; a white shirt with diagonal blue and red stripe and white shorts; and a dark blue shirt with a diagonal red and white stripe and dark blue shorts.

Match No.	Date	Venue	Opponents	Result		Scorers	Attendance
1	Aug 12	A	Liverpool	L	0-2		55,383
2	16	H	Everton	L	0-1		38,676
3	19	H	Norwich City	W	3-0	Lee 2, Bell	31,171
4	23	A	Derby County	L	0-1		31,173
5	26	A	Chelsea	L	1-2	Mellor	30,845
6	29	A	Crystal Palace	L	0-1		24,731
7	Sep 2	H	Leicester City	W	1-0	Marsh	27,620
8	9	A	Birmingham City	L	1-4	Towers	32,983
9	16	H	Tottenham Hotspur	W	2-1	Marsh 2	31,755
10	23	A	Stoke City	L	1-5	Lee (pen)	26,448
11	30	H	West Bromwich Albion	W	2-1	Booth, Lee (pen)	27,332
12	Oct 7	H	Wolverhampton W.	D	1-1	Marsh	31,201
13	14	A	Coventry City	L	2-3	Marsh, Summerbee	24,541
14	21	H	West Ham United	W	4-3	Marsh 2, Summerbee, Towers	31,052
15	28	A	Arsenal	D	0-0		45,403
16	Nov 4	H	Derby County	W	4-0	Bell, Carrodus, Marsh, Todd (og)	35,829
17	11	A	Everton	W	3-2	Lee 2, Kenyon (og)	32,924
18	18	H	Manchester United	W	3-0	Bell 2, Buchan (og)	52,086
19	25	A	Leeds United	L	0-3		39,879
20	Dec 2	H	Ipswich Town	D	1-1	Lee	27,838
21	9	A	Sheffield United	D	1-1	Bell	19,208
22	16	H	Southampton	W	2-1	Marsh 2	24,725
23	23	A	Newcastle United	L	1-2	Mellor	28,274
24	26	H	Stoke City	D	1-1	Mellor	36,352
25	30	A	Norwich City	D	1-1	Towers	23,900
26	Jan 20	A	Leicester City	D	1-1	Bell	18,761
27	27	H	Birmingham City	W	1-0	Donachie	31,877
28	Feb 10	A	Tottenham Hotspur	W	3-2	Lee 2, Marsh	30,944
29	17	H	Liverpool	D	1-1	Booth	41,709
30	Mar 3	A	Wolverhampton W.	L	1-5	Marsh	25,047
31	6	A	Southampton	D	1-1	Lee	16,188
32	10	H	Coventry City	L	1-2	Booth	30,877
33	17	A	West Ham United	L	1-2	Doyle	30,156
34	24	H	Arsenal	L	1-2	Booth	32,031
35	27	H	Chelsea	L	0-1		23,973
36	31	H	Leeds United	W	1-0	Towers	35,772
37	Apr 7	A	Ipswich Town	D	1-1	Oakes	19,107
38	14	H	Sheffield United	W	3-1	Bell, Lee (pen), Marsh	27,232
39	18	H	Newcastle United	W	2-0	Booth, Marsh	25,320
40	21	A	Manchester United	D	0-0		61,676
41	25	A	West Bromwich Albion	W	2-1	Lee, Towers	21,480
42	28	H	Crystal Palace	L	2-3	Lee 2 (2 pens)	34,948
							Appearances
							Sub appearances
						Three own goals	Goals

FA Cup

	Date	Venue	Opponents	Result		Scorers	Attendance
R3	Jan 13	H	Stoke City	W	3-2	Bell, Marsh, Summerbee	38,648
R4	Feb 3	A	Liverpool	D	0-0		56,296
rep	7	H	Liverpool	W	2-0	Bell, Booth	49,572
R5	24	H	Sunderland	D	2-2	Towers, Montgomery (og)	54,478
rep	27	A	Sunderland	L	1-3	Lee	51,782
							Appearances
							Sub appearances
						One own goal	Goals

League Cup

	Date	Venue	Opponents	Result		Scorers	Attendance
R2	Sep 6	H	Rochdale	W	4-0	Marsh 2, Bell, Lee	17,222
R3	Oct 3	A	Bury	L	0-2		16,614
							Appearances
							Sub appearances
							Goals

UEFA Cup

	Date	Venue	Opponents	Result		Scorers	Attendance
R1/1	Sep 13	H	Valencia	D	2-2	Marsh, Mellor	21,698
R1/2	27	A	Valencia	L	1-2	Marsh	35,000
							Appearances
							Sub appearances
							Goals

Charity Shield

	Date	Venue	Opponents	Result		Scorers	Attendance
	Aug 5	A	Aston Villa	W	1-0	Lee	34,859
							Appearances
							Sub appearances
							Goals

Corrigan TJ	Book AK	Donachie W	Doyle M	Booth TA	Bell C	Summerbee MG	Lee FH	Davies RW	Marsh RW	Towers MA	Jeffries D	Barrett C	Mellor I	Oakes AA	Healey R	Carrodus F	Hill F	Brennan M	Pardoe G	Whelan AM
1	2	3	4	5	6	7	8	9	10	11										
1	2	3	4	5	6	7	8	9	**10**	11	12									
1		3	4	5	8	7	10	**9**		6	11	2	12							
1	12	3	4	5	8	7	**10**			6	11	2	9							
1		3	4	5	8	7	10			6	11	2	9							
1		3	4	5	8	7	9		10	6	11	2								
1	2	3		5	8	7		9	10	6	4		11							
1		3	4	5	8	7	10	**9**	11	6	2			12						
		3	4	5	**8**	7	10		9	11	2		12	6	1					
1		3	4	5	8		10		9	11	**2**		7	6		12				
	2	3		5	8	7	10		9	4		12	11	**6**	1					
	2	3	**4**	5	8		10		9			6	7		1		11	12		
	2	3	12	5	8	7	10		9	4	6				1		11			
	2	3	4	5	8	7	10		9	11	6				1					
1	2	3	4	5	8	7	10		9		6					11				
1		3	4		8	7	10		9		6	5				11			2	
1	2	3	4		8	7	10		9		6	5				11				
1	2	3	4		8	7	10		9	11	6	5								
1	2	3	4		8	7	10		9	11	6	5								
1	2	3	4		8		10		9	11	6	5				**7**	12			
1	2	3	4		8	7	10		9	11	6	5								
1	2	3	**4**		8	7	10		9	11	6	5					12			
1		3	4	5	8	7			9	11	6		10						2	
1			4	5		7			9	11	2	6	10				8		3	
1			4	5		7			9	11	2	6	10				8		3	
1	2	3	12	5	8	7	10		9	4	6					**11**				
1	2	3	4	5	8	7	10		9	11	6									
1	2	3	4	5	8	7	10		9	11	6									
1	2	3	4	5	8	7	10		9	11	6									
1	2	3	4	5	8				9	11	6		7					10		
1		3	4	5	8	7	10		9		6			11					2	
1		3	**4**	5	8	7	10		9		6			11		12			2	
1	2	3	4	5	8	7	10				**6**			11		12				9
1	2	3	4	5	8	7			9	11	6									10
1	2	3	4	5		7			9	11	6					8				10
	2	3	4	5	8	7	10		9	11				6	1					
	2	3	4	5	8	7	9			11	10			6	1					
	2	3	4	5	8	7	10		9	11				6	1					
	2	3	4	5	8	**7**	10		9	11				6	1	12				
	2	3	4	5	8	7	10		9	11				6	1					
	2	3	4	5	8	**7**	10		9	11				6	1	12				
	2	3	4		8	7	10		9	11	5			6	1					
30	29	40	38	34	39	38	35	5	37	35	33	14	10	13	12	6	4	1	6	3
	1		2								1	1	2	1		5	2	1		
		1	1	5	7	2	14		14	5			3	1		1				

Corrigan TJ	Book AK	Donachie W	Doyle M	Booth TA	Bell C	Summerbee MG	Lee FH	Davies RW	Marsh RW	Towers MA	Jeffries D	Barrett C	Mellor I	Oakes AA	Healey R	Carrodus F	Hill F	Brennan M	Pardoe G	Whelan AM
1	2	3	4	5	8	7	10		9		6		11							
1	2	3	4	5	8	7	10		9	11	6									
1	2	3	4	5	8	7	10		9	11	6									
1	2	3	**4**	5	8	7	10		9	11	6		12							
1	2	3	4	5	8		10		9	11	6		7							
5	5	5	5	5	5	4	5		5	4	5		2							
													1							
				1	2	1	1		1	1										

Corrigan TJ	Book AK	Donachie W	Doyle M	Booth TA	Bell C	Summerbee MG	Lee FH	Davies RW	Marsh RW	Towers MA	Jeffries D	Barrett C	Mellor I	Oakes AA	Healey R	Carrodus F	Hill F	Brennan M	Pardoe G	Whelan AM
1	2	3		5	**4**	7	10	9	8	6	11			12						
	2	3	4	5	8	**7**	10		9	11		6	12		1					
1	2	2	1	2	2	2	2	1	2	2	1	1			1					
													1	1						
					1		1		2											

Corrigan TJ	Book AK	Donachie W	Doyle M	Booth TA	Bell C	Summerbee MG	Lee FH	Davies RW	Marsh RW	Towers MA	Jeffries D	Barrett C	Mellor I	Oakes AA	Healey R	Carrodus F	Hill F	Brennan M	Pardoe G	Whelan AM
1		3	4	5	8		10		9	11	2		7	6	12					
	2		4	**5**	8	7	10		9	11		3	12	6	1					
1	1	1	2	2	2	1	2		2	2	1	1	1	2	1					
													1		1					
									2				1							

Corrigan TJ	Book AK	Donachie W	Doyle M	Booth TA	Bell C	Summerbee MG	Lee FH	Davies RW	Marsh RW	Towers MA	Jeffries D	Barrett C	Mellor I	Oakes AA	Healey R	Carrodus F	Hill F	Brennan M	Pardoe G	Whelan AM
1	2	**3**	4	5		7	8	9	10	11	12		13	6						
1	1	1	1	1		1	1	1	1	1				1						
											1		1							
							1													

League Table

	P	W	D	L	F	A	Pts
Liverpool	42	25	10	7	72	42	60
Arsenal	42	23	11	8	57	43	57
Leeds U	42	21	11	10	71	45	53
Ipswich T	42	17	14	11	55	45	48
Wolverh'pton W	42	18	11	13	66	54	47
West Ham U	42	17	12	13	67	53	46
Derby Co	42	19	8	15	56	54	46
Tottenham H	42	16	13	13	58	48	45
Newcastle U	42	16	13	13	60	51	45
Birmingham C	42	15	12	15	53	54	42
Manchester C	42	15	11	16	57	60	41
Chelsea	42	13	14	15	49	51	40
Southampton	42	11	18	13	47	52	40
Sheffield U	42	15	10	17	51	59	40
Stoke C	42	14	10	18	61	56	38
Leicester C	42	10	17	15	40	46	37
Everton	42	13	11	18	41	49	37
Manchester U	42	12	13	17	44	60	37
Coventry C	42	13	9	20	40	55	35
Norwich C	42	11	10	21	36	63	32
Crystal Palace	42	9	12	21	41	58	30
W.B.A.	42	9	10	23	38	62	28

1973-74

Division One

Manager: John Hart (until 22 October 1973), Ron Saunders (from 24 November 1973 – 11 April 1974), Tony Book (from 12 April 1974)

Did you know that?

Match 9: Book's last game.
Match 11: Healey's last game.
Match 30: Towers's last game.
Match 36: Whelan's last game.
Match 39: Carrodus's last game.
Match 42: Lee and Law's last League game.

Fans were promised the earth when Ron Saunders was appointed manager. New chairman Peter Swales told supporters in December 1973 that Saunders's appointment was destined to be a success, and added: 'Unless I am a poor judge of character, I say that City are in the strongest position they have ever been in. Far stronger than at the peak of the Mercer-Allison partnership.'

Saunders was dismissed before the season ended, and only one major trophy followed during the following two decades under the new chairman.

Match No.	Date	Venue	Opponents	Result		Scorers	Attendance
1	Aug 25	H	Birmingham City	W	3-1	Law 2, Bell	35,881
2	29	A	Derby County	L	0-1		31,295
3	Sep 1	A	Stoke City	D	1-1	Law	22,434
4	5	H	Coventry City	W	1-0	Marsh (pen)	31,180
5	8	H	Norwich City	W	2-1	Bell, Lee	31,209
6	11	A	Coventry City	L	1-2	Marsh	27,491
7	15	A	Leicester City	D	1-1	Bell	25,466
8	22	H	Chelsea	W	3-2	Lee 2 (1 pen), Towers	32,118
9	29	A	Burnley	L	0-3		24,147
10	Oct 6	H	Southampton	D	1-1	Marsh	27,727
11	13	A	Newcastle United	L	0-1		35,346
12	20	A	Sheffield United	W	2-1	Law, Dearden (og)	25,234
13	27	H	Leeds United	L	0-1		45,363
14	Nov 3	A	Wolverhampton W.	D	0-0		21,499
15	10	H	Arsenal	L	1-2	Lee	31,251
16	17	H	Queen's Park Rangers	W	1-0	Lee (pen)	30,486
17	24	A	Ipswich Town	L	1-2	Leman	19,210
18	Dec 8	A	West Ham United	L	1-2	Lee	20,790
19	15	A	Tottenham Hotspur	W	2-0	Bell, Booth	17,066
20	22	H	Burnley	W	2-0	Bell, Doyle	28,114
21	26	A	Everton	L	0-2		36,007
22	29	A	Norwich City	D	1-1	Law	23,978
23	Jan 1	H	Stoke City	D	0-0		35,009
24	12	H	Leicester City	W	2-0	Law, Marsh	27,488
25	19	A	Birmingham City	D	1-1	Law	31,401
26	Feb 2	H	Tottenham Hotspur	D	0-0		24,652
27	6	H	Derby County	W	1-0	Bell	22,845
28	9	A	Chelsea	L	0-1		20,206
29	23	A	Southampton	W	2-0	Law, Marsh	19,234
30	Mar 9	A	Leeds United	L	0-1		36,578
31	13	H	Manchester United	D	0-0		51,331
32	16	H	Sheffield United	L	0-1		26,220
33	23	A	Arsenal	L	0-2		25,577
34	27	H	Newcastle United	W	2-1	Lee 2	21,590
35	30	H	Wolverhampton W.	D	1-1	Lee	25,236
36	Apr 2	H	Everton	D	1-1	Tueart	22,918
37	6	H	Ipswich Town	L	1-3	Summerbee	22,269
38	9	A	Queen's Park Rangers	L	0-3		20,461
39	12	H	Liverpool	D	1-1	Lee	43,284
40	16	A	Liverpool	L	0-4		50,781
41	20	H	West Ham United	W	2-1	Bell, Booth	29,700
42	27	A	Manchester United	W	1-0	Law	56,803
							Appearances
							Sub appearances
						One own goal	Goals

FA Cup

	Date	Venue	Opponents	Result		Scorers	Attendance
R3	Jan 5	A	Oxford United	W	5-2	Law 2, Summerbee 2, Marsh	13,435
R4	27	A	Nottingham Forest	L	1-4	Carrodus	41,472
							Appearances
							Sub appearances
							Goals

League Cup

	Date	Venue	Opponents	Result		Scorers	Attendance
R2	Oct 2	A	Walsall	D	0-0		12,943
rep	22	H	Walsall	D	0-0		19,428
rep2	30	N	Walsall	W	4-0	Lee 3 (2 pens), Bell	13,646
R3	Nov 6	A	Carlisle United	W	1-0	Lee	14,472
R4	21	A	York City	D	0-0		15,360
rep	Dec 5	H	York City	W	4-1	Marsh 3, Lee (pen)	17,972
R5	19	A	Coventry City	D	2-2	Booth, Leman	12,661
rep	Jan 16	H	Coventry City	W	4-2	Lee 2 (1 pen), Law, Summerbee	25,409
SF1	23	A	Plymouth Argyle	D	1-1	Booth	30,390
SF2	30	H	Plymouth Argyle	W	2-0	Bell, Lee	40,117
F	Mar 2	N	Wolverhampton W.	L	1-2	Bell	100,000
							Appearances
							Sub appearances
							Goals

R2 replay 2 at Old Trafford
Final at Wembley Stadium

Charity Shield

	Date	Venue	Opponents	Result		Scorers	Attendance
	Aug 18	H	Burnley	L	0-1		23,988
							Appearances

Corrigan TJ	Book AK	Donachie W	Doyle M	Booth TA	Oakes AA	Summerbee MG	Bell C	Law D	Lee FH	Marsh RW	Carrodus F	Pardoe G	Towers MA	Healey R	Leman D	Whelan AM	MacRae KA	Lester MJA	Barrett C	Daniels BJ	Horswill MF	Tueart D	Henson PM
1	2	3	4	5	6	7	8	9	10	11	12												
1		3	4	5	6	7	8	9	10	11		2											
1		3	4	5	6	7	8	9	10	11	12	2											
1		3	4	5	6	7	8	9	12	11	10	2											
1		3	4	5		7	8	9	10	11	12	2	6										
1		3	4	5		7	8		10	11	9	2	6										
1	2	3	4	5	6	7	8		10	11			9										
1	2	3	4	5	6	7	8		10	9			11										
1	2	3	4	5	6	7	8		10	9			11										
		3	4	5	6	7	8			9		2	11	1	10	12							
		3	4	5	6	7	8	9	10	12		2	11	1									
		3	4	5	6	7	8	9	10	11		2					1						
		3	4	5	6	7	8	9	10			2	11		12		1						
		3	4	5	6	9	8	12	10		7	2	11				1						
		3		5	6	7	8	9	10		11	2			12		1	4					
		3		5		7	8	9	10	11		2	6				1		4				
		3	4	5		9	8			11		2	6		10		1		7				
		3	4	5		7	8		10	9		2	6		11		1						
		3	4	5		7	8	9		10		2	6		11		1		12				
		3	4	5		7	8		10	9		2	6		11		1						
		3	4	5		7	8	12	10	9		2	6		11		1						
		3	4	5			8	10		9	7		6		11		1		2				
1		3	4	5		7	8	10		9			6		11				2				
		3	4	5		7	8	10	11	9			6		12		1		2				
		3	4	5		7	8	10	9	11		12	6				1		2				
		3	4	5	10		8				11	7	6		9		1		2				
		3	4	5	10		8				11	7	6				1		2	9			
		3	4	5	6	7	8				11	10	12				1		2	9			
		3	4	5		7	8	10		11	9	2	6				1						
1		3	4	5		7	8	10	9	11		2	6										
1		3	4	5	10	7	8				9	2									6	11	
1		3	4	5	10	7	8				9				12				2		6	11	
		3	4	5	10	7	8		9			2					1				6	11	
		3	4	5	10	7	8		9			2				12	1				6	11	
		3	4	5	10	7	8		9		11	2					1				6		
		3	4		10	7			9		8	2				12	1		5		6	11	
		3	4		10	7	8				9	2					1		5		6	11	
		3	4	5	6	7	8	10	9		11	2					1				12		
		3		5	6	7	8	10	9		11	2					1		4				
		3	4	5	6	7	8	10	9			2					1		11	12			
1		3	4	5	6	7	8	10	9										2			11	
1		3	4	5	6	7	8	10	9										2			11	12
15	4	42	39	40	28	39	41	22	29	23	16	31	23	2	9		25	1	16	2	7	8	
								2	1	1	3	1	1		4	3			1	1	1		1
			1	2		1	7	9	10	5			1		1							1	

Corrigan TJ	Book AK	Donachie W	Doyle M	Booth TA	Oakes AA	Summerbee MG	Bell C	Law D	Lee FH	Marsh RW	Carrodus F	Pardoe G	Towers MA	Healey R	Leman D	Whelan AM	MacRae KA	Lester MJA	Barrett C	Daniels BJ	Horswill MF	Tueart D	Henson PM
1		3	4	5		7	8	9	10	11			6						2				
		3	4	5		7	8		9	11	10		6		12		1		2				
1		2	2	2		2	2	1	2	2	1		2				1		2				
															1								
						2		2		1	1												

Corrigan TJ	Book AK	Donachie W	Doyle M	Booth TA	Oakes AA	Summerbee MG	Bell C	Law D	Lee FH	Marsh RW	Carrodus F	Pardoe G	Towers MA	Healey R	Leman D	Whelan AM	MacRae KA	Lester MJA	Barrett C	Daniels BJ	Horswill MF	Tueart D	Henson PM
	2	3	4	5	6	7	8		10	9			11	1									
	12	3	4	5	6	7	8	10	9	11		2					1						
		3	4	5	6	9	8		10		7	2	11				1						
		3	4	5	6	9	8		10		7	2	11				1						
		3	4	5		9	8		10	11		2	6				1		7				
		3	4	5		7	8		10	9		2	6		11		1						
		3	4	5		7	8		10	9		2	6		11		1						
		3	4	5		7	8	10	9	11			6				1		2				
		3	4	5		7	8	10	9	11			6		12		1		2				
		3	4	5	10	7	8		9		11		6		12		1		2				
		3	4	5		7	8	10	9	11		2	6				1						
	1	11	11	11	5	11	11	4	11	8	3	7	10	1	2		10		4				
	1														2								
				2		1	3	1	8	3					1								

Corrigan TJ	Book AK	Donachie W	Doyle M	Booth TA	Oakes AA	Summerbee MG	Bell C	Law D	Lee FH	Marsh RW
1	2	3	4	5	6	7	8	9	10	11
1	1	1	1	1	1	1	1	1	1	1

League Table

	P	W	D	L	F	A	Pts
Leeds U	42	24	14	4	66	31	62
Liverpool	42	22	13	7	52	31	57
Derby Co	42	17	14	11	52	42	48
Ipswich T	42	18	11	13	67	58	47
Stoke C	42	15	16	11	54	42	46
Burnley	42	16	14	12	56	53	46
Everton	42	16	12	14	50	48	44
Q.P.R.	42	13	17	12	56	52	43
Leicester C	42	13	16	13	51	41	42
Arsenal	42	14	14	14	49	51	42
Tottenham H	42	14	14	14	45	50	42
Wolverh'pton W	42	13	15	14	49	49	41
Sheffield U	42	14	12	16	44	49	40
Manchester C	42	14	12	16	39	46	40
Newcastle U	42	13	12	17	49	48	38
Coventry C	42	14	10	18	43	54	38
Chelsea	42	12	13	17	56	60	37
West Ham U	42	11	15	16	55	60	37
Birmingham C	42	12	13	17	52	64	37
Southampton	42	11	14	17	47	68	36
Manchester U	42	10	12	20	38	48	32
Norwich C	42	7	15	20	37	62	29

1974-75

Division One

Manager: Tony Book

Did you know that?

Match 22: Henson's last game.
Match 26: Oakes surpassed Trautmann's 508 League appearances.
Match 29: Horswill's last game.
Match 32: Pardoe's last game.
Match 34: Clarke's last game.
Match 35: Summerbee's last game.
Match 42: Daniels's last game.

Although both Francis Lee and Denis Law played their last League game on the final day of 1973–74 they both appeared and scored in first-team competition during 1974–75. They both featured in the Texaco Cup, with their last game being the meeting with Oldham on 10 August 1974. Lee scored in that game, while Law netted four days earlier at Sheffield United. So, in fact, Law's last first-team goal was not in the Manchester derby of 1974, but at Bramall Lane. It is a myth that Law retired from club football immediately after relegating United.

Match No.	Date	Venue	Opponents	Result		Scorers	Attendance
1	Aug 17	H	West Ham United	W	4-0	Marsh 2, Doyle, Tueart	30,240
2	21	H	Tottenham Hotspur	W	1-0	Hartford	31,549
3	24	A	Arsenal	L	0-4		27,469
4	28	A	Tottenham Hotspur	W	2-1	Bell, Booth	20,079
5	31	H	Leeds United	W	2-1	Bell, Summerbee	37,919
6	Sep 7	A	Coventry City	D	2-2	Marsh, Oakes	15,555
7	14	H	Liverpool	W	2-0	Marsh, Tueart	45,194
8	21	A	Middlesbrough	L	0-3		30,256
9	24	A	Carlisle United	D	0-0		17,495
10	28	H	Queen's Park Rangers	W	1-0	Marsh	30,647
11	Oct 5	H	Chelsea	D	1-1	Bell	32,412
12	12	A	Burnley	L	1-2	Tueart (pen)	23,512
13	16	H	Arsenal	W	2-1	Tueart 2	26,658
14	19	H	Luton Town	W	1-0	Summerbee	30,649
15	26	A	Ipswich Town	D	1-1	Bell	25,177
16	Nov 2	A	Everton	L	0-2		43,905
17	9	H	Stoke City	W	1-0	Marsh	36,966
18	16	A	Birmingham City	L	0-4		35,143
19	23	H	Leicester City	W	4-1	Daniels 2, Bell, Tueart	31,628
20	30	A	Newcastle United	L	1-2	Marsh	37,684
21	Dec 7	H	Sheffield United	W	3-2	Bell, Hammond, Marsh	29,675
22	14	A	West Ham United	D	0-0		33,479
23	21	H	Wolverhampton W.	D	0-0		29,326
24	26	A	Liverpool	L	1-4	Bell	46,062
25	28	H	Derby County	L	1-2	Bell	40,188
26	Jan 11	A	Sheffield United	D	1-1	Booth	25,109
27	18	H	Newcastle United	W	5-1	Tueart 3 (1 pen), Bell, Hammond	32,021
28	Feb 1	A	Stoke City	L	0-4		32,262
29	8	H	Everton	W	2-1	Bell, Tueart	44,718
30	22	H	Birmingham City	W	3-1	Bell, Royle, Tueart	33,240
31	Mar 1	A	Leeds United	D	2-2	Donachie, Oakes	47,489
32	8	A	Leicester City	L	0-1		23,059
33	15	A	Queen's Park Rangers	L	0-2		22,102
34	19	H	Carlisle United	L	1-2	Barnes	24,047
35	22	H	Coventry City	W	1-0	Tueart (pen)	25,903
36	28	H	Middlesbrough	W	2-1	Bell, Marsh	37,772
37	29	A	Wolverhampton W.	L	0-1		21,716
38	Apr 1	A	Derby County	L	1-2	Bell	32,966
39	12	A	Chelsea	W	1-0	Hartford	26,249
40	19	H	Burnley	W	2-0	Bell, Tueart	30,723
41	23	H	Ipswich Town	D	1-1	Bell	29,391
42	26	A	Luton Town	D	1-1	Tueart	20,768
							Appearances
							Sub appearances
							Goals

FA Cup

R3	Jan 4	H	Newcastle United	L	0-2		37,625
							Appearances
							Sub appearances

League Cup

R2	Sep 10	H	Scunthorpe United	W	6-0	Bell 3, Barrett, Doyle, Marsh	14,790
R3	Oct 9	A	Manchester United	L	0-1		55,225
							Appearances
							Sub appearances
							Goals

Texaco Cup

Gp	Aug 3	A	Blackpool	D	1-1	Tueart	12,342
Gp	6	A	Sheffield United	L	2-4	Summerbee, Law	9,358
Gp	10	H	Oldham Athletic	W	2-1	Lee, Tueart	13,880
							Appearances
							Sub appearances
							Goals

MacRae KA	Barrett C	Donachie W	Doyle M	Clarke JD	Oakes AA	Henson PM	Bell C	Marsh RW	Hartford RA	Tueart D	Booth TA	Summerbee MG	Keegan GA	Hammond G	Pardoe G	Horswill MF	Barnes PS	Leman D	Daniels BJ	Corrigan TJ	Royle J	Lee FH	Law D
1	2	3	4	5	6	7	8	9	10	11													
1	2	3	4	5	6	7	8	9	10	11													
1	2	3	4	5	6	7	8	9	10	11													
1	2	3	4		6		8	9	10	11	5	7											
1	2	3	4		6		8	9	10	11	5	7											
1	2	3	4		6		8	9	10	11	5	7											
1	2	3	4	5	6	12	8	9	10	11		7											
1	2	3	4	5	6		8	9	10	11		7											
1	5	3	4		6	12	8	9	10	11		7		2									
1	5	3	4		6		8	9	10	11		7		2									
1	5		4		6		8	9	10	11		7		2	3	12							
1			4	5	6	7	8			11		9		2	3		10						
1		3	4	5	6	10	8	9		11		7		2				12					
1		3	4	5	6	10	8	9				7		2			11						
1	11	3	4	5	6	10	8	9				7		2									
1	11	3	4	5	6	12	8	9	10			7		2									
1	5	3	4		6		8	9	10	11		7		2									
1	5	3	4		6	10	8	9		11		7		2									
1		3	5		6	4	8	9	10	11				2					7				
1	12	3	5		6	4	8	9	10	11				2					7				
1		3	5		6	4	8	9	10	11		12		2					7				
1		3	5		6	4	8	9	10	11				2		7			12				
	2	3	6	5			8	9	10	11						4			7	1			
		3	6	5			4	9	10	11		7				2				1	8		
		3	5		6		4	9	10	11				2		7				1	8		
		3	4		6		8	9		11	5	7		2						1	10		
		3	4		6		8	9		11	5	7		2						1	10		
1		3	4		6		8		10	11	5	7		2							9		
1		3	4		6		8	9		11	5	7			2	12					10		
1		3	4		6		8	9		11	5	7			2						10		
1		3	4		6		8	9		11	5	7			2						10		
1		3	4		6		8	9	12	11	5	7			2						10		
		2	4		3		8	9	6	11	5	7								1	10		
		3	2	5	6		8		4	11		7	12				10			1	9		
		3	4		6		8			11	5	7	10	2						1	9		
		3	4		6		8	9		11	5		7	2						1	10		
	5	3	4		6		8		10	11			7	2					12	1	9		
		3	4		6		8	9	7	11	5			2						1	10		
		3	4		6		8	10	7	11	5			2					12	1	9		
		3	4		6		8	9	7	11	5			2					10	1			
		3	4		6		8	9	7	11	5			2					10	1			
		3	4		6		8	9	7	11	5		12	2					10	1			
27	17	40	42	13	40	12	42	37	29	39	18	26	3	26	6	4	3		7	15	16		
	1					3			1			1	2			2		1	3				
		1	1		2		15	9	2	14	2	2		2			1		2		1		

MacRae KA	Barrett C	Donachie W	Doyle M	Clarke JD	Oakes AA	Henson PM	Bell C	Marsh RW	Hartford RA	Tueart D	Booth TA	Summerbee MG	Keegan GA	Hammond G	Pardoe G	Horswill MF	Barnes PS	Leman D	Daniels BJ	Corrigan TJ	Royle J	Lee FH	Law D
		3	5		6	12	8	9	10	11				2		4	7			1			
		1	1		1		1	1	1	1				1		1	1			1			
						1																	

MacRae KA	Barrett C	Donachie W	Doyle M	Clarke JD	Oakes AA	Henson PM	Bell C	Marsh RW	Hartford RA	Tueart D	Booth TA	Summerbee MG	Keegan GA	Hammond G	Pardoe G	Horswill MF	Barnes PS	Leman D	Daniels BJ	Corrigan TJ	Royle J	Lee FH	Law D
1	2	3	4	5	6	10	8	9		11		7	12										
1			4	5	6		8	9	10	11		7		2	3		12						
2	1	1	2	2	2	1	2	2	1	2		2		1	1								
													1				1						
	1		1				3	1															

MacRae KA	Barrett C	Donachie W	Doyle M	Clarke JD	Oakes AA	Henson PM	Bell C	Marsh RW	Hartford RA	Tueart D	Booth TA	Summerbee MG	Keegan GA	Hammond G	Pardoe G	Horswill MF	Barnes PS	Leman D	Daniels BJ	Corrigan TJ	Royle J	Lee FH	Law D
	2	3	4		6		8	10		11	5	7								1		9	
	2	3	4		6	12	8	10		11	5	7								1			9
1	2	3	4		6		8	9		11	5								12			7	10
1	3	3	3		3		3	3		3	3	2								2		2	2
						1													1				
										2		1										1	1

League Table

	P	W	D	L	F	A	Pts
Derby Co	42	21	11	10	67	49	53
Liverpool	42	20	11	11	60	39	51
Ipswich T	42	23	5	14	66	44	51
Everton	42	16	18	8	56	42	50
Stoke C	42	17	15	10	64	48	49
Sheffield U	42	18	13	11	58	51	49
Middlesbrough	42	18	12	12	54	40	48
Manchester C	42	18	10	14	54	54	46
Leeds U	42	16	13	13	57	49	45
Burnley	42	17	11	14	68	67	45
Q.P.R.	42	16	10	16	54	54	42
Wolverh'pton W	42	14	11	17	57	54	39
West Ham U	42	13	13	16	58	59	39
Coventry C	42	12	15	15	51	62	39
Newcastle U	42	15	9	18	59	72	39
Arsenal	42	13	11	18	47	49	37
Birmingham C	42	14	9	19	53	61	37
Leicester C	42	12	12	18	46	60	36
Tottenham H	42	13	8	21	52	63	34
Luton T	42	11	11	20	47	65	33
Chelsea	42	9	15	18	42	72	33
Carlisle U	42	12	5	25	43	59	29

1975-76

Division One

Manager: Tony Book

Did you know that?

Match 3: Telford's last game.
Match 12: Marsh and Leman's last game.
Match 27: Barrett's last game.
Match 38: Hammond's last game.
Match 42: Oakes's last game.

An iron fence divided the Kippax terracing into a home and an away section for the first time in September 1975. Match 10 was the first to see it used, although the Blues chose only to segregate fans for high-profile matches. During 1975–76 the only League matches chosen for this added measure were matches 23, 28, and 30.

Match No.	Date	Venue	Opponents	Result		Scorers	Attendance
1	Aug 16	H	Norwich City	W	3-0	Tueart 2, Bell	29,103
2	20	H	Leicester City	D	1-1	Birchenall (og)	28,538
3	23	A	Coventry City	L	0-2		21,115
4	27	A	Aston Villa	L	0-1		35,712
5	30	H	Newcastle United	W	4-0	Royle 2, Tueart 2 (2 pens)	31,806
6	Sep 6	A	West Ham United	L	0-1		29,752
7	13	H	Middlesbrough	W	4-0	Marsh 2, Royle, Tueart	30,353
8	20	A	Derby County	L	0-1		28,076
9	24	H	Stoke City	W	1-0	Marsh	28,915
10	27	H	Manchester United	D	2-2	Royle, Nicholl (og)	46,931
11	Oct 4	A	Arsenal	W	3-2	Hartford, Marsh, Royle	24,928
12	11	H	Burnley	D	0-0		35,003
13	18	A	Tottenham Hotspur	D	2-2	Bell, Watson	30,554
14	25	H	Ipswich Town	D	1-1	Bell	30,644
15	Nov 1	A	Sheffield United	D	2-2	Barnes, Booth	24,670
16	8	H	Birmingham City	W	2-0	Bell 2	28,329
17	15	A	Everton	D	1-1	Booth	32,077
18	22	H	Tottenham Hotspur	W	2-1	Oakes, Tueart	31,457
19	29	A	Wolverhampton W.	W	4-0	Hartford 2, Barnes, Tueart	20,867
20	Dec 6	H	Queen's Park Rangers	D	0-0		36,066
21	13	H	Coventry City	W	4-2	Barnes, Booth, Oakes, Tueart	27,256
22	20	A	Norwich City	D	2-2	Royle, Tueart	19,100
23	26	H	Leeds United	L	0-1		48,077
24	27	A	Liverpool	L	0-1		53,386
25	Jan 10	A	Middlesbrough	L	0-1		22,358
26	17	H	West Ham United	W	3-0	Royle 2 (1 pen), Oakes	32,147
27	31	A	Leicester City	L	0-1		21,723
28	Feb 7	H	Aston Villa	W	2-1	Booth, Hartford	32,331
29	14	A	Birmingham City	L	1-2	Hartford	22,445
30	21	H	Everton	W	3-0	Hartford, Royle, Tueart (pen)	33,148
31	Mar 6	H	Sheffield United	W	4-0	Hartford 2, Royle, Tueart	33,510
32	13	A	Burnley	D	0-0		24,329
33	20	H	Wolverhampton W.	W	3-2	Doyle, Keegan, Tueart (pen)	32,761
34	27	A	Queen's Park Rangers	L	0-1		29,883
35	Apr 2	A	Stoke City	D	0-0		18,799
36	7	A	Ipswich Town	L	1-2	Keegan	21,306
37	10	H	Derby County	W	4-3	Tueart 2, Royle, Power	42,061
38	14	A	Newcastle United	L	1-2	Royle	21,095
39	17	A	Leeds United	L	1-2	Bell	33,514
40	19	H	Liverpool	L	0-3		50,439
41	24	H	Arsenal	W	3-1	Booth 2, Hartford	31,003
42	May 4	A	Manchester United	L	0-2		59,517
							Appearances
							Sub appearances
						Two own goals	Goals

FA Cup

	Date	Venue	Opponents	Result		Scorers	Attendance
R3	Jan 3	H	Hartlepool	W	6-0	Booth 2, Tueart 2 (1 pen), Hartford, Oakes	26,863
R4	28	A	Stoke City	L	0-1		38,072
							Appearances
							Sub appearances
							Goals

League Cup

	Date	Venue	Opponents	Result		Scorers	Attendance
R2	Sep 10	A	Norwich City	D	1-1	Watson	18,332
rep	17	H	Norwich City	D	2-2e	Royle, Tueart (pen)	29,667
rep2	29	N	Norwich City	W	6-1	Tueart 3 (2 pens), Doyle, Royle, Butler (og)	6,238
R3	Oct 8	H	Nottingham Forest	W	2-1	Bell, Royle	26,536
R4	Nov 12	H	Manchester United	W	4-0	Tueart 2, Hartford, Royle	50,182
R5	Dec 3	H	Mansfield Town	W	4-2	Hartford, Oakes, Royle, Tueart	30,022
SF1	Jan 13	A	Middlesbrough	L	0-1		35,000
SF2	21	H	Middlesbrough	W	4-0	Barnes, Keegan, Oakes, Royle	44,426
F	Feb 28	N	Newcastle United	W	2-1	Barnes, Tueart	99,999
R2 replay 2 at Stamford Bridge							Appearances
Final at Wembley Stadium							Sub appearances
						One own goal	Goals

Anglo-Scottish Cup

	Date	Venue	Opponents	Result		Scorers	Attendance
Gp	Aug 2	A	Blackpool	L	0-1		11,091
Gp	6	A	Blackburn Rovers	L	0-1		10,612
Gp	9	H	Sheffield United	W	3-1	Royle, Marsh, Leman	11,167
							Appearances
							Sub appearances
							Goals

Corrigan TJ	Hammond G	Donachie W	Doyle M	Watson DV	Oakes AA	Hartford RA	Bell C	Marsh RW	Royle J	Tueart D	Telford WA	Clements KH	Power PC	Leman D	Barnes PS	Booth TA	MacRae KA	Keegan GA	Barrett C	Owen GA	Docherty M	Henry A
1	2	3	4	5	6	7	8	9	10	11												
1	2	3	4	5	6	7	8	9	10	11												
1	2	3	4	5	6	7	8	10	9	11	12											
1		3	4	5	6	7	8	9		11		2	10									
1		3	4	5	6	7	8	10	9	11		2										
1		3	4	5	6	7	8	10		11		2		9								
1		3	4	5	6	7	8	10	9	11		2										
1		3	4	5	6	7	8	10	9	11		2										
1		3	4	5	6	7	8	10	9	11		2										
1		3	4	5	6	7	8	10	9	11		2		12								
1		3	4	5	6	7	8	10	9	11		2	12									
1		3	4	5	6	7	8	9	10			2		12	11							
1		3	4	9	6	10	8			11		2			7	5						
1		3	4	9	6	10	8			11		2			7	5						
		3	4	5	6	10	8			11		2			7	9	1					
1		3	4	5	6	10	8		9	11		2			7							
1		3	4	5	6	10			9	11		2	12		7	8						
1		3	4	5	6	10			9	11		2	8		7							
1		3	4	5	6	10			9	11		2	8		7							
1		3	4	5	6	10			9	11		2			7	8						
1	2	3	4	5	6	10			9	11			12		7	8						
1		3	4	5	6	10			9	11		2			7	8						
1		3	4	5	6	10			9	11		2	12		7	8						
1		3	4	5	6	10			9	11		2	7			8		12				
1		3	4	5	6	10			9				11			8		7	2			
1		3	4		6	10			9			5	7		11			8	2			
1		3	4	5	6	10			9	11			7		12	8			2			
1		3	4	5	6	10			9	11		2			7	12		8				
1		3	4	5	6	10			9			2			11	8		7				
1		3	4	5	6	10			9	11					7	8		2				
1		3	4	5	6	10			9	11					7	8		2				
1		3	4	5	6	10			9	11					7	8		2				
1		3	4			10			9	11		5			7	8		2		6		
1		3	4		6	10			9	11		12			7	5		2		8		
1	2	3	4		6				9	11			10		7	5		8				
1	2	3	4			10			9	11			6		7	5		8				
1	12	3	4		6		8		9	11			10		7	5		2				
1	2				3				9	11		4	10		7	5		8		6		
1		2	4		3	10	8		9	11			7			5		6				
1		2	4		3	10	8		9	11			12		7	5		6				
1		3	4			10	8		9	12			6		7	5		2		11		
1			4		12	10			9	11		2	8		7	5		6			3	
41	7	40	41	31	38	39	20	12	37	37		26	14	1	27	25	1	17	3	4	1	
	1				1					1	1	1	5	2	1	1		1				
			1	1	3	9	6	4	12	14			1		3	6		2				

Corrigan TJ	Hammond G	Donachie W	Doyle M	Watson DV	Oakes AA	Hartford RA	Bell C	Marsh RW	Royle J	Tueart D	Telford WA	Clements KH	Power PC	Leman D	Barnes PS	Booth TA	MacRae KA	Keegan GA	Barrett C	Owen GA	Docherty M	Henry A
1		3	4	5	6	10			9	11		2	7			8						
1		3	4		6	10			9	11			8		7	5		12	2			
2		2	2	1	2	2			2	2		1	2		1	2			1			
																		1				
					1	1				2						2						

Corrigan TJ	Hammond G	Donachie W	Doyle M	Watson DV	Oakes AA	Hartford RA	Bell C	Marsh RW	Royle J	Tueart D	Telford WA	Clements KH	Power PC	Leman D	Barnes PS	Booth TA	MacRae KA	Keegan GA	Barrett C	Owen GA	Docherty M	Henry A
1		3	4	5	6	7	8	10	9	11		2										
1		3	4	5	6	7	8	10	9	11		2			12							
1		3	4	5	6	7	8	10	9	11		2										
1		3	4	5	6	7	8	10	9			2			11							
1		3	4	5	6	10	8		9	11		2			7	12						
1		3	4	5	6	10			9	11		2	12		7	8						
1		3	4		6	10			9	11			8		7	5			2			
1		3	4		6	10			9			5	7		11			8	2			
1		3	4	5	6	10			9	11					7	8		2				
9		9	9	7	9	9	5	4	9	7		7	2		6	3		2	2			
													1		1	1						
			1	1	2	2	1		6	8					2			1				

Corrigan TJ	Hammond G	Donachie W	Doyle M	Watson DV	Oakes AA	Hartford RA	Bell C	Marsh RW	Royle J	Tueart D	Telford WA	Clements KH	Power PC	Leman D	Barnes PS	Booth TA	MacRae KA	Keegan GA	Barrett C	Owen GA	Docherty M	Henry A
1		2	4	5	3	10		9	8	11				12		6						7
1		2	4	5	3	10		9	8	11						6		7				
1	2	3		5	6	10		9	8	11	7			12		4						
3	1	3	2	3	3	3		3	3	3	1					3		1				1
														2								
								1	1					1								

League Table

	P	W	D	L	F	A	Pts
Liverpool	42	23	14	5	66	31	60
Q.P.R.	42	24	11	7	67	33	59
Manchester U	42	23	10	9	68	42	56
Derby Co	42	21	11	10	75	58	53
Leeds U	42	21	9	12	65	46	51
Ipswich T	42	16	14	12	54	48	46
Leicester C	42	13	19	10	48	51	45
Manchester C	42	16	11	15	64	46	43
Tottenham H	42	14	15	13	63	63	43
Norwich C	42	16	10	16	58	58	42
Everton	42	15	12	15	60	66	42
Stoke C	42	15	11	16	48	50	41
Middlesbrough	42	15	10	17	46	45	40
Coventry C	42	13	14	15	47	57	40
Newcastle U	42	15	9	18	71	62	39
Aston Villa	42	11	17	14	51	59	39
Arsenal	42	13	10	19	47	53	36
West Ham U	42	13	10	19	48	71	36
Birmingham C	42	13	7	22	57	75	33
Wolverh'pton W	42	10	10	22	51	68	30
Burnley	42	9	10	23	43	66	28
Sheffield U	42	6	10	26	33	82	22

1976-77

Division One

Manager: Tony Book

Did you know that?

Match 7: Docherty's last game.
Match 10: Lester's last game.
Match 42: Conway's last game.

When third-placed City defeated title challengers Ipswich in Match 32 Watson scored a wonderful goal. Afterwards Ipswich manager Bobby Robson told Tony Book: 'If we don't win it, I hope you do.' Sadly the 4–0 defeat at Derby gave Liverpool the edge, and when City's season ended Liverpool were already champions with one game left to play (which they lost at Bristol City).

City wore an all-blue kit for the first time in history this season. Sadly, while wearing all blue City failed to win a major trophy and were relegated in 1983. White shorts were re-introduced by Billy McNeill in 1985 following promotion.

Match No.	Date	Venue	Opponents	Result		Scorers	Attendance
1	Aug 21	A	Leicester City	D	2-2	Royle, Tueart	22,612
2	25	H	Aston Villa	W	2-0	Tueart, Watson	41,007
3	28	H	Stoke City	D	0-0		39,878
4	Sep 4	A	Arsenal	D	0-0		35,097
5	11	H	Bristol City	W	2-1	Barnes, Tueart	35,891
6	18	A	Sunderland	W	2-0	Royle, Tueart	37,348
7	25	H	Manchester United	L	1-3	Tueart	48,861
8	Oct 2	H	West Ham United	W	4-2	Tueart 2, Hartford, Owen	37,795
9	5	A	Everton	D	2-2	Hartford, Power	31,370
10	16	H	Queen's Park Rangers	D	0-0		40,751
11	23	A	Ipswich Town	L	0-1		25,113
12	30	A	Norwich City	W	2-0	Kidd, Royle	22,586
13	Nov 6	H	Newcastle United	D	0-0		39,949
14	20	H	West Bromwich Albion	W	1-0	Tueart	36,656
15	27	A	Birmingham City	D	0-0		29,722
16	Dec 4	H	Derby County	W	3-2	Kidd 2, Tueart	34,179
17	7	A	Middlesbrough	D	0-0		18,484
18	11	A	Tottenham Hotspur	D	2-2	Kidd, Power	24,608
19	18	H	Coventry City	W	2-0	Kidd, Tueart	32,427
20	27	A	Leeds United	W	2-0	Kidd 2	48,698
21	29	H	Liverpool	D	1-1	Royle	50,020
22	Jan 22	H	Leicester City	W	5-0	Kidd 4, Doyle	37,609
23	Feb 5	A	Stoke City	W	2-0	Royle, Tueart	27,141
24	12	H	Arsenal	W	1-0	Royle	45,368
25	16	A	Newcastle United	D	2-2	Kidd, Tueart	28,954
26	19	A	Bristol City	L	0-1		27,018
27	Mar 1	H	Norwich City	W	2-0	Tueart 2 (2 pens)	36,021
28	5	A	Manchester United	L	1-3	Royle	58,595
29	9	H	Sunderland	W	1-0	Tueart	44,439
30	12	A	West Ham United	L	0-1		24,974
31	22	A	Queen's Park Rangers	D	0-0		17,619
32	Apr 2	H	Ipswich Town	W	2-1	Kidd, Watson	42,780
33	8	H	Leeds United	W	2-1	Kidd 2	47,727
34	9	A	Liverpool	L	1-2	Kidd	55,283
35	11	H	Middlesbrough	W	1-0	Hartford	37,735
36	16	A	West Bromwich Albion	W	2-0	Kidd, Tueart	24,889
37	19	H	Birmingham City	W	2-1	Kidd 2	36,203
38	30	A	Derby County	L	0-4		29,127
39	May 4	A	Aston Villa	D	1-1	Tueart	36,190
40	7	H	Tottenham Hotspur	W	5-0	Barnes, Booth, Hartford, Kidd, Tueart	37,919
41	10	H	Everton	D	1-1	Kidd	38,004
42	14	A	Coventry City	W	1-0	Conway	21,370

Appearances
Sub appearances
Goals

FA Cup

R3	Jan 8	H	West Bromwich Albion	D	1-1	Kidd	38,195
rep	11	A	West Bromwich Albion	W	1-0	Royle	27,218
R4	29	A	Newcastle United	W	3-1	Owen, Royle, D Craig (og)	45,300
R5	Feb 26	A	Leeds United	L	0-1		47,731

Appearances
One own goal Goals

League Cup

R2	Sep 1	A	Aston Villa	L	0-3		34,585

Appearances
Sub appearances

UEFA Cup

R1/1	Sep 15	H	Juventus	W	1-0	Kidd	36,955
R1/2	29	A	Juventus	L	0-2		55,000

Appearances
Sub appearances
Goals

Corrigan TJ	Docherty M	Donachie W	Doyle M	Watson DV	Power PC	Conway JP	Kidd B	Royle J	Hartford RA	Tuart D	Barnes PS	Booth TA	Henry A	Keegan GA	Lester MJA	Clements KH	Owen GA
1	2	3	4	5	6	7	8	9	10	11							
1	2	3	4	5	6	7	8	9	10	11							
1	2	3	4	5	6	8		9	10	11	7						
1	2	3	4	5	7	8		9	10	11		6					
1	2	3	4	5		6	8	9	10	11	7						
1	2	3	4	5	7	**6**	8	9	10	11			12				
1	2	3	4	5	6		8	9	10	11		12		**7**			
1		3	4	5			8	9	10	11	7					2	6
1		3	4	5	7		8	9	10	11						2	6
1		3	4	5	7		8	**9**	10	11					12	2	6
1		3	4	5	7		8	9	10	11						2	6
1		3	4	5	6		8	9	10	11						2	7
1		3	4	5	**6**		8	9	10	11	12					2	7
1		3	4	5	12	6	8	**9**	10	11						2	7
1		3	4	5	6		8	9	10	11						2	7
1		3	4	5	6		8	9	10	11	12					**2**	7
1		3	4	5	6	7	8	9	10	11						2	
1		3	4	5	6		8	9	10	11						2	7
1		3	4	5	6		8	9	10	11						2	7
1		3	4	5	6		8	9	10	11						2	7
1		3	4	5	6		8	9	10	11						2	7
1		3	4	5	6		8	9	10	**11**	12					2	7
1		3	4	5	6		8	9	10	11						2	7
1		3	4	5	6		8	9	10	11						2	7
1		3	4	5	6		8	9	10	11						2	7
1		3	4	5	6		8	9	10	11						2	7
1		3	4	5	6		8	9	10	11						2	7
1		3	4	5	**6**		8	9	10	11	12					2	7
1		3	4				8	9	10	11	7	5				2	6
1		3	**4**	5		6	8	9	10	11	7					2	12
1		3		5		6	8	9	10	11	7	4				2	
1		3		5			8	9	10		7	4	12	6		2	**11**
1		3	4	5			8	9	10	11	7	6				2	
1		3	4	5	11		8	**9**	10		12	6		7		2	
1		3		5			9		10	11	7	4		8		2	6
1		3		5			9		10	11	7	4		8		2	6
1		3		5			9		10	11	7	4		8		2	6
1		3	6	5	12		8	**9**			7	4		11		2	10
1		3		5		12	**8**	9		11	7	4		10		2	6
1		3		5		12	8	**9**	10	11	7	4				2	6
1		3		5			8	9	10	11	7	4				2	6
1		3		5	11	8		9	10		7	4				2	6
42	7	42	33	41	27	11	39	39	40	38	16	14		8		35	30
					2	2					5	1	2		1		1
			1	2	2	1	21	7	4	18	2	1					1

Corrigan TJ	Docherty M	Donachie W	Doyle M	Watson DV	Power PC	Conway JP	Kidd B	Royle J	Hartford RA	Tuart D	Barnes PS	Booth TA	Henry A	Keegan GA	Lester MJA	Clements KH	Owen GA
1		3	4	5	6		8	9	10	11						2	7
1		3	4	5	6		8	9	10	11						2	7
1		3	4	5	6		8	9	10	11						2	7
1		3	4	5	6	7	8	9	10	11						2	
4		4	4	4	4	1	4	4	4	4						4	3
							1	2									1

Corrigan TJ	Docherty M	Donachie W	Doyle M	Watson DV	Power PC	Conway JP	Kidd B	Royle J	Hartford RA	Tuart D	Barnes PS	Booth TA	Henry A	Keegan GA	Lester MJA	Clements KH	Owen GA
1	2	3	4	5	**6**	8		9	10	11	7	12					
1	1	1	1	1	1	1		1	1	1	1						
												1					

Corrigan TJ	Docherty M	Donachie W	Doyle M	Watson DV	Power PC	Conway JP	Kidd B	Royle J	Hartford RA	Tuart D	Barnes PS	Booth TA	Henry A	Keegan GA	Lester MJA	Clements KH	Owen GA
1	2	3	4	5	12	6	8	9	10	11	**7**						
1	2	3	4	5			8	9	10	11		6		**7**	12		
2	2	2	2	2		1	2	2	2	2	1	1		1			
					1										1		
							1										

League Table

	P	W	D	L	F	A	Pts
Liverpool	42	23	11	8	62	33	57
Manchester C	42	21	14	7	60	34	56
Ipswich T	42	22	8	12	66	39	52
Aston Villa	42	22	7	13	76	50	51
Newcastle U	42	18	13	11	64	49	49
Manchester U	42	18	11	13	71	62	47
W.B.A.	42	16	13	13	62	56	45
Arsenal	42	16	11	15	64	59	43
Everton	42	14	14	14	62	64	42
Leeds U	42	15	12	15	48	51	42
Leicester C	42	12	18	12	47	60	42
Middlesbrough	42	14	13	15	40	45	41
Birmingham C	42	13	12	17	63	61	38
Q.P.R.	42	13	12	17	47	52	38
Derby Co	42	9	19	14	50	55	37
Norwich C	42	14	9	19	47	64	37
West Ham U	42	11	14	17	46	65	36
Bristol C	42	11	13	18	38	48	35
Coventry C	42	10	15	17	48	59	35
Sunderland	42	11	12	19	46	54	34
Stoke C	42	10	14	18	28	51	34
Tottenham H	42	12	9	21	48	72	33

1977-78

Division One

Manager: Tony Book

Did you know that?

Match 13: Royle's last game.
Match 26: Tueart's last League game.
Match 37: Doyle's last game.

City's fourth-placed finish was watched by Maine Road's second highest average attendance of all time.

Match No.	Date	Venue	Opponents	Result		Scorers	Attendance
1	Aug 20	H	Leicester City	D	0-0		45,963
2	24	A	Aston Villa	W	4-1	Tueart 3, Booth	40,121
3	27	A	West Ham United	W	1-0	Royle	25,278
4	Sep 3	H	Norwich City	W	4-0	Channon 2, Hartford, Power	41,269
5	10	H	Manchester United	W	3-1	Kidd 2, Channon	50,856
6	17	A	Queen's Park Rangers	D	1-1	Royle	24,668
7	24	H	Bristol City	W	2-0	Barnes, Owen	41,897
8	Oct 1	A	Everton	D	1-1	Hartford	43,286
9	4	A	Coventry City	L	2-4	Barnes, Tueart	19,650
10	8	H	Arsenal	W	2-1	Barnes, Tueart (pen)	43,177
11	15	A	Nottingham Forest	L	1-2	Kidd	35,572
12	22	H	Wolverhampton W.	L	0-2		42,730
13	29	H	Liverpool	W	3-1	Channon, Kidd, Royle	49,207
14	Nov 5	A	Ipswich Town	L	0-1		24,575
15	12	H	Leeds United	L	2-3	Barnes, Channon	42,651
16	19	A	West Bromwich Albion	D	0-0		26,953
17	26	H	Chelsea	W	6-2	Tueart 3, Barnes, Channon, G Wilkins (og)	34,354
18	Dec 3	A	Derby County	L	1-2	Power	26,888
19	10	H	Birmingham City	W	3-0	Channon, Owen, Tueart	36,671
20	17	A	Leeds United	L	0-2		37,380
21	26	H	Newcastle United	W	4-0	Tueart 3, Kidd	45,811
22	27	A	Middlesbrough	W	2-0	Hartford, Owen	27,319
23	31	H	Aston Villa	W	2-0	Barnes, Kidd	46,074
24	Jan 2	A	Leicester City	W	1-0	Owen (pen)	24,041
25	14	H	West Ham United	W	3-2	Barnes, Booth, Kidd	43,627
26	21	A	Norwich City	W	3-1	Kidd 2, Owen	20,009
27	Feb 11	H	Queen's Park Rangers	W	2-1	Bell, Channon	39,860
28	17	A	Bristol City	D	2-2	Booth, Kidd	25,416
29	25	H	Everton	W	1-0	Kidd	46,817
30	Mar 4	A	Arsenal	L	0-3		34,103
31	15	A	Manchester United	D	2-2	Barnes, Kidd	58,398
32	18	A	Wolverhampton W.	D	1-1	Bell	20,583
33	25	H	Middlesbrough	D	2-2	Channon 2	37,944
34	29	A	Newcastle United	D	2-2	Palmer 2	20,256
35	Apr 1	H	Ipswich Town	W	2-1	Channon, Palmer	34,975
36	11	H	Nottingham Forest	D	0-0		43,428
37	15	H	West Bromwich Albion	L	1-3	Kidd	36,521
38	22	A	Birmingham City	W	4-1	Kidd 2, Owen (pen), Power	25,294
39	25	H	Coventry City	W	3-1	Hartford, Kidd, Owen (pen)	32,412
40	29	H	Derby County	D	1-1	Channon	39,175
41	May 1	A	Liverpool	L	0-4		44,528
42	5	A	Chelsea	D	0-0		20,999

Appearances
Sub appearances
One own goal — Goals

FA Cup

	Date	Venue	Opponents	Result		Scorers	Attendance
R3	Jan 7	A	Leeds United	W	2-1	Barnes, Tueart	38,516
R4	31	A	Nottingham Forest	L	1-2	Kidd	38,509

Appearances
Sub appearances
Goals

League Cup

	Date	Venue	Opponents	Result		Scorers	Attendance
R2	Aug 31	A	Chesterfield	W	1-0	Kidd	17,500
R3	Oct 25	A	Luton Town	D	1-1	Barnes	16,443
rep	Nov 1	H	Luton Town	D	0-0e	28,254	1
rep2	9	N	Luton Town	W	3-2e	Channon, Kidd, Tueart (pen)	13,043
R4	29	A	Ipswich Town	W	2-1	Kidd, Tueart	22,645
R5	Jan 18	H	Arsenal	D	0-0		42,000
rep	24	A	Arsenal	L	0-1		57,748

R3 replay 2 at Old Trafford

Appearances
Sub appearances
Goals

Other

	Date	Venue	Opponents	Result		Scorers	Attendance
R1/1	Sep 14	H	Widzew Lodz	D	2-2	Barnes, Channon	33,695
R1/2	28	A	Widzew Lodz	D	0-0		40,000

Lost on the away goals rule

Appearances
Sub appearances
Goals

Corrigan TJ	Clements KH	Donachie W	Doyle M	Watson DV	Booth TA	Owen GA	Channon MR	Royle J	Hartford RA	Tueart D	Kidd B	Barnes PS	Power PC	Keegan GA	Henry A	Bell C	Palmer RN
1	2	3	4	5	6	7	8	9	10	11							
1	2	3	4	5	6		8	9	10	11	7						
1	2	3	4	5	6		8	9	10	11	7						
1	2	3		5	6	4	8		10		9	7	11				
1	2	3		5	6	4	8		10		9	7	11				
1	2	3		5	6	4	8	9	10		7	11					
1	2		3	5	6	4	8		10		9	7	11				
1	2	3		5	**6**	4		12	10	11	9	7	8				
1	2	3		5	6			9	10	11	4	7	8				
1	2	3		5	6	4			10	11	9	7	8				
1	12	3	5		6	4	8		10	**11**	9	7	2				
1	12	3	2	5	6	4	8				9	7	11		**10**		
1	2	3	4	5		6	8	9			10	7	11				
1	2	3	4	5		6	8		10		9	7	11				
1	2	3	4	5			8		10	11	9	7	6				
1	2	3		5	4		8		10	11	9	7	6				
1	2	3		5	4		8		10	11	9	7	6				
1	2	3		5	4		8		10	11	9	7	6				
1	2	3		5	4	7	8		10	11	9		6				
1	2	3		5	4	7	8		**10**	11	9		6	12			
1	2	3		5	4	8			10	11	9	7	**6**			12	
1	2	3		5	4	6			10		9	7				8	11
1	2	3		5	4	6			10	11	9	7				8	
1	2	3	12	5	4	6			10		9	**7**				8	11
1	**2**	3		5	4	6	12		10	11	9	7				8	
1	2	3		5	4	6			10	11	9	7				8	
1	2	3		5	4	6	7		10		9	11				8	
1	2	3		5	4	6	7		10		9	11				8	
1	2	3		5	4		7		10		9	11	6			8	
1	2	3		5	4		7		10		9	11	6			8	
1	2	3		5	4	6	7		10		9	11				8	
1	2	3		5	4	6	7				9	11	10			8	
1	2	3		5	4	6	7				**9**	11	10	12		8	
1	2	3	4	5	8	6	7					11	10				9
1	2	3	4	5	8	6	7		10			11					9
1	2		4	5	8	6	7		10		9	11	3				
1	2		4	5	**8**	6	7		10		9	11	3				12
1	2	3		5	**4**	6	7		10		9		11			8	
1	2	3		5	4	6	7		10		9		11			8	
1	2	3		5	4	**6**	7		10		9	12	11			8	
1	2	3		5	4	6	7		10		9		11			8	
1	2	3		5	4	6	8		10		9	7	11				
42	40	39	13	41	39	33	33	6	37	17	39	33	29		1	16	4
	2		1				1	1				1		2		1	1
					3	7	12	3	4	12	16	8	3			2	3

Corrigan TJ	Clements KH	Donachie W	Doyle M	Watson DV	Booth TA	Owen GA	Channon MR	Royle J	Hartford RA	Tueart D	Kidd B	Barnes PS	Power PC	Keegan GA	Henry A	Bell C	Palmer RN
1	2	3		5	4	6			10	11	9	7				8	
1	2	3		5	4	**6**	12		10	11	9	7				8	
2	2	2		2	2	2			2	2	2	2				2	
							1										
										1	1	1					

Corrigan TJ	Clements KH	Donachie W	Doyle M	Watson DV	Booth TA	Owen GA	Channon MR	Royle J	Hartford RA	Tueart D	Kidd B	Barnes PS	Power PC	Keegan GA	Henry A	Bell C	Palmer RN
1	2	3	4	5	6	10	8	9		**11**	7	12					
1	2	3		5	6	4	8				9	7	11	10			
2	3	4		5		8	9	10		6	7	11					
1	2	3	4	5			8		10	11	9	7	6				
1	2	3		5	4		8		10	11	9	7	6				
1	2	3		5	4	6			10	11	9	7				8	
1	2	3		5	4	6	12		10	11	9	**7**				8	
7	7	7	3	6	6	4	5	2	5	5	7	6	4	1		2	
							1					1					
							1			2	3	1					

Corrigan TJ	Clements KH	Donachie W	Doyle M	Watson DV	Booth TA	Owen GA	Channon MR	Royle J	Hartford RA	Tueart D	Kidd B	Barnes PS	Power PC	Keegan GA	Henry A	Bell C	Palmer RN
1	2	3		5	6	4	8	12	10		9	7		**11**			
1	12		**2**	5	6	4		9	10	11	8	7	3				
2	1	1	1	2	2	2	1	1	2	1	2	2	1	1			
	1							1									
							1					1					

League Table

	P	W	D	L	F	A	Pts
Nottingham F	42	25	14	3	69	24	64
Liverpool	42	24	9	9	65	34	57
Everton	42	22	11	9	76	45	55
Arsenal	42	21	10	11	60	37	52
Manchester C	42	20	12	10	74	51	52
W.B.A.	42	18	14	10	62	53	50
Coventry C	42	18	12	12	75	62	48
Aston Villa	42	18	10	14	57	42	46
Leeds U	42	18	10	14	63	53	46
Manchester U	42	16	10	16	67	63	42
Birmingham C	42	16	9	17	55	60	41
Derby Co	42	14	13	15	54	59	41
Norwich C	42	11	18	13	52	66	40
dlesbrough	42	12	15	15	42	54	39
Wolverh'pton W	42	12	12	18	51	64	36
Chelsea	42	11	14	17	46	69	36
Bristol C	42	11	13	18	49	53	35
Ipswich T	42	11	13	18	47	61	35
Q.P.R.	42	9	15	18	47	64	33
West Ham U	42	12	8	22	52	69	32
Newcastle U	42	6	10	26	42	78	22
Leicester C	42	5	12	25	26	70	22

1978-79

Division One

Manager: Tony Book

Did you know that?

Match 16: Clements's last game.
Match 17: Keegan's last game.
Match 28: Kidd's last game.
Match 33: R. Futcher's last game.
Match 36: Barnes's last game.
Match 41: Owen's last game.
Match 42: Watson, Bell and Hartford's last game.

The 1978–79 season is seen by many as the turning point in City's fortunes. A season that promised much, including the possibility of glory in Europe, ended with the lowest finish since 1966–67 and the departure of several popular international players.

Match No.	Date	Venue	Opponents	Result		Scorers	Attendance
1	Aug 19	A	Derby County	D	1-1	Kidd	26,480
2	22	H	Arsenal	D	1-1	Kidd	39,506
3	26	H	Liverpool	L	1-4	Kidd	46,710
4	Sep 2	A	Norwich City	D	1-1	Channon	18,069
5	9	H	Leeds United	W	3-0	Palmer 2, Watson	40,125
6	16	A	Chelsea	W	4-1	R Futcher 3, Channon	29,727
7	23	H	Tottenham Hotspur	W	2-0	R Futcher, Owen	43,471
8	30	A	Manchester United	L	0-1		55,301
9	Oct 7	A	Birmingham City	W	2-1	R Futcher, Kidd	18,378
10	14	H	Coventry City	W	2-0	Owen 2 (2 pens)	36,723
11	21	A	Bolton Wanderers	D	2-2	Owen, Palmer	32,249
12	28	H	West Bromwich Albion	D	2-2	Channon, Hartford	40,521
13	Nov 4	A	Aston Villa	D	1-1	Owen (pen)	32,724
14	11	H	Derby County	L	1-2	Owen (pen)	37,376
15	18	A	Liverpool	L	0-1		47,765
16	25	H	Ipswich Town	L	1-2	Hartford	38,256
17	Dec 9	H	Southampton	L	1-2	Power	33,450
18	16	A	Queen's Park Rangers	L	1-2	Channon	12,902
19	23	H	Nottingham Forest	D	0-0		37,012
20	26	A	Everton	L	0-1		46,996
21	30	A	Bristol City	D	1-1	R Futcher	25,693
22	Jan 13	A	Leeds United	D	1-1	Kidd	36,303
23	20	H	Chelsea	L	2-3	R Futcher, Power	31,876
24	Feb 3	A	Tottenham Hotspur	W	3-0	Barnes, Channon, Kidd (pen)	32,037
25	10	H	Manchester United	L	0-3		46,151
26	24	A	Coventry City	W	3-0	Channon 2, Kidd	20,043
27	27	H	Norwich City	D	2-2	Owen 2 (1 pen)	29,852
28	Mar 3	H	Bolton Wanderers	W	2-1	Channon, Owen (pen)	41,127
29	24	A	Arsenal	D	1-1	Channon	34,914
30	27	A	Wolverhampton W.	D	1-1	Channon	19,998
31	31	A	Ipswich Town	L	1-2	Silkman	19,569
32	Apr 4	A	West Bromwich Albion	L	0-4		21,940
33	7	H	Wolverhampton W.	W	3-1	Channon, Palmer, Silkman	32,298
34	14	H	Everton	D	0-0		39,711
35	17	A	Middlesbrough	L	0-2		19,676
36	21	H	Queen's Park Rangers	W	3-1	Owen 2, Silkman	30,694
37	24	H	Middlesbrough	W	1-0	Deyna	28,264
38	28	A	Southampton	L	0-1		19,744
39	May 1	H	Birmingham City	W	3-1	Deyna 2, Power	27,366
40	5	H	Bristol City	W	2-0	Deyna, Hartford	29,739
41	9	A	Nottingham Forest	L	1-3	Lloyd (og)	21,104
42	15	H	Aston Villa	L	2-3	Deyna 2	30,028
							Appearances
							Sub appearances
						One own goal	Goals

FA Cup

	Date	Venue	Opponents	Result		Scorers	Attendance
R3	Jan 15	H	Rotherham United	D	0-0		26,029
rep	17	A	Rotherham United	W	4-2	Kidd 2, Barnes, Owen	13,758
R4	27	A	Shrewsbury Town	L	0-2		14,215
							Appearances
							Sub appearances
							Goals

League Cup

	Date	Venue	Opponents	Result		Scorers	Attendance
R2	Aug 29	H	Grimsby Town	W	2-0	Palmer, Moore (og)	21,481
R3	Oct 4	A	Blackpool	D	1-1	Channon	18,868
R3	10	H	Blackpool	W	3-0	Owen 2 (1 pen), Booth	26,213
R4	Nov 8	A	Norwich City	W	3-1	Channon 2, Barnes	19,413
R5	Dec 12	A	Southampton	L	1-2	Nicholl (og)	21,500
							Appearances
							Sub appearances
						Two own goals	Goals

UEFA Cup

	Date	Venue	Opponents	Result		Scorers	Attendance
R1/1	Sep 13	A	Twente (Enschede)	D	1-1	Watson	12,000
R1/2	27	H	Twente (Enschede)	W	3-2	Bell, Kidd, Wildschut (og)	29,330
R2/q	Oct 18	H	Standard Liege	W	4-0	Kidd 2 (1 pen), Hartford, Palmer	27,489
R2/2	Nov 1	A	Standard Liege	L	0-2		25,000
R3/1	23	A	AC Milan	D	2-2	Kidd, Power	40,000
R3/2	Dec 6	H	AC Milan	W	3-0	Booth, Hartford, Kidd	38,026
QF1	Mar 7	H	Borussia Monchengladbach	D	1-1	Channon	39,005
QF2	20	A	Borussia Monchengladbach	L	1-3	Deyna	30,000
							Appearances
							Sub appearances
						One own goal	Goals

Corrigan TJ	Clements KH	Donachie W	Futcher P	Watson DV	Power PC	Channon MR	Keegan GA	Kidd B	Hartford RA	Barnes PS	Booth TA	Owen GA	Futcher R	Palmer RN	Viljoen C	Henry A	Bell C	Deyna K	Ranson R	MacRae KA	Reid NS	Silkman B	Bennett DA
1	2	3	4	5	6	7	8	9	10	11													
1	2	3	6	5	4	7	8	9	10	11													
1	2	3	6		4	7	8	9	10		5	11											
1	2	3	6		4	7			10	11	5	8	9										
1	2	3	6	5	4	7			10	11		8		9									
1		2	6	5	3	7			**10**	11		8	9		4	12							
1	2	3	6	5	11	7			10			8	9		4								
1	2	3	6	5	4	7		9	10	11		8											
1	2	3		5		7		6	10	**11**	4	8	9			12							
1	2	3		5				6	10	11	4	8	9	7									
1	2	3		5				9	10	11	4	8	12	**7**	6								
1	2	3	6			7		9	10		5	8	12	11	**4**								
1	2	3	6			7		9	10		5	8		11	4								
1	2	3		5		7		9	10	11	4	6					8						
1	2	3		5		**7**		9	10	11	4	6	12	8									
1	**2**	3		5	6			9	10	11	4	7		12				8					
1		3		5	6	7	2	**9**	10	11	4	12			8								
1		3	2	5	6	7			10	11	4	8	12					**9**					
1		3	6	5	4	7			10	11		8	9						2				
1		3	6	5	4	7			**10**	11		8	9	12					2				
1		3	6	5	4	7			10	11		8	9						2				
1		3	6	**5**	4	7		12	10	11		8	9						2				
1		2	6		3	7		9	10	11	**5**	4	12					8					
1		2	6	**5**	3	7		9	10	11		4					8	12					
1		2	6	5	3	7		9	10	11		4					8						
1		2	6		3	7		9	10	11	5	4			8								
1		2	6		3	7		9	10	11	5	4			8								
1		2		5	3	7		9	10	11	6	4			8								
1		2		5	3	7			10		6	11			8	9		4					
1				5	3	7			10	11		4	**9**	12	8	6			2				
1				5	**3**	7			10	11		4	12			6			2		8	9	
1		**2**	6		3	7			10		5			11	8	4					12	9	
1		3	6			**7**			10		5	8	12	11		4					2	9	
1			2	5	3				10	11	**4**			7	8	6						9	12
1			6	5	3				10	11				**7**	8	4		12	2			9	
1		2		5	3				10	11		7			4		6	8				9	
1		3		5	11	7						8				4	6	10			2	9	
1		3		5	11	7						8				4	6	10			2	9	
1		3		5	11	7						8				4	6	10			2	9	
1		3		5	11	7			10							4	6	8			2	9	
1		3		5		7			10			11				4	6	8			2	9	
1		3		**5**		7			10					12	8	4	6	11	2			9	
42	15	38	24	33	32	36	4	19	39	29	20	34	10	10	16	13	10	11	8		7	12	
								1				1	7	4		2		2			1		1
				1	3	11		7	3	1		11	7	4				6				3	

Corrigan TJ	Clements KH	Donachie W	Futcher P	Watson DV	Power PC	Channon MR	Keegan GA	Kidd B	Hartford RA	Barnes PS	Booth TA	Owen GA	Futcher R	Palmer RN	Viljoen C	Henry A	Bell C	Deyna K	Ranson R	MacRae KA	Reid NS	Silkman B	Bennett DA
1		3	5		4	7		8	10	11			9				6		2				
		2	6	5	3	7		9	10	11		4						8		1			
1		2	6	5	3	7		9	10	11		4					12	**8**					
2		3	3	2	3	3		3	3	3		2	1				1	2	1	1			
																	1						
								2		1		1											

Corrigan TJ	Clements KH	Donachie W	Futcher P	Watson DV	Power PC	Channon MR	Keegan GA	Kidd B	Hartford RA	Barnes PS	Booth TA	Owen GA	Futcher R	Palmer RN	Viljoen C	Henry A	Bell C	Deyna K	Ranson R	MacRae KA	Reid NS	Silkman B	Bennett DA
1	2		6		3	7	4		10		5	8	**9**	11	12								
1	2	3		5	6	7		9	10	**11**	4	8		12									
1	2	3		5				6	10	11	4	8	9	7									
1	2	3		5		7		9	10	11	4	8	12		**6**								
1		2		5	3	7		9	10	12	4	6					8	**11**					
5	4	4	1	4	3	4	1	4	5	3	5	5	2	2	1		1	1					
										1			1	1	1								
						3				1	1	2		1									

Corrigan TJ	Clements KH	Donachie W	Futcher P	Watson DV	Power PC	Channon MR	Keegan GA	Kidd B	Hartford RA	Barnes PS	Booth TA	Owen GA	Futcher R	Palmer RN	Viljoen C	Henry A	Bell C	Deyna K	Ranson R	MacRae KA	Reid NS	Silkman B	Bennett DA
1	2		6	5	3	7			10	11		8		9	4								
1	2		6	5	3	7		9	10	11		8			**4**		12						
1	2	3		5			12	9	10	11	4			7	**6**		8						
1	2	3		5		7		9	10		4	6		11			8						
1	2	3		5	6		12	9	10		4			11	**7**		8						
1		3		5	6	7	2	9	10	11	4				8								
1		2		5	3	7		9	10	11	6				8						4		
1		2		5	3	7			10	11	6				4	9		12			**8**		
8	5	6	2	8	6	6	1	6	8	6	6	3		4	7	1	3				2		
							2										1	1					
				1	1	1		5	2		1			1			1	1					

League Table

	P	W	D	L	F	A	Pts
Liverpool	42	30	8	4	85	16	68
Nottingham F	42	21	18	3	61	26	60
W.B.A.	42	24	11	7	72	35	59
Everton	42	17	17	8	52	40	51
Leeds U	42	18	14	10	70	52	50
Ipswich T	42	20	9	13	63	49	49
Arsenal	42	17	14	11	61	48	48
Aston Villa	42	15	16	11	59	49	46
Manchester U	42	15	15	12	60	63	45
Coventry C	42	14	16	12	58	68	44
Tottenham H	42	13	15	14	48	61	41
Middlesbrough	42	15	10	17	57	50	40
Bristol C	42	15	10	17	47	51	40
Southampton	42	12	16	14	47	53	40
Manchester C	42	13	13	16	58	56	39
Norwich C	42	7	23	12	51	57	37
Bolton W	42	12	11	19	54	75	35
Wolverh'pton W	42	13	8	21	44	68	34
Derby Co	42	10	11	21	44	71	31
Q.P.R.	42	6	13	23	45	73	25
Birmingham C	42	6	10	26	37	64	22
Chelsea	42	5	10	27	44	92	20

1979-80

Division One

Manager: Tony Book (until July 1979, continuing as General Manager until 8 October 1980), Malcolm Allison

Did you know that?

Match 4: Channon's last game.
Match 14: Silkman's last game.
Match 22: Shinton's last game.
Match 26: Lee's last game.
Match 30: Donachie's last game.
Match 32: Viljoen's last game.
Match 40: Robinson's last game.
Match 42: Futcher's last game.

Michael Robinson, City's number 9 for much of the season, later became an anchorman for football on Spanish TV. In fact, for the Germany 2006 World Cup Robinson was the main host, performing a similar role to the BBC's Gary Lineker throughout the finals.

Match No.	Date	Venue	Opponents	Result		Scorers	Attendance
1	Aug 18	H	Crystal Palace	D	0-0		40,681
2	21	A	Middlesbrough	L	0-3		24,002
3	25	H	Brighton & Hove Alb.	W	3-2	Channon, Power, Robinson (pen)	34,557
4	Sep 1	A	Tottenham Hotspur	L	1-2	MacKenzie	30,901
5	8	H	Southampton	L	0-1		34,920
6	15	A	West Bromwich Albion	L	0-4		22,183
7	22	H	Coventry City	W	3-0	Robinson 2, MacKenzie	30,869
8	29	A	Leeds United	W	2-1	Deyna, Power	29,592
9	Oct 6	A	Arsenal	D	0-0		35,068
10	10	H	Middlesbrough	W	1-0	Deyna	29,384
11	13	H	Nottingham Forest	W	1-0	Deyna	41,683
12	20	A	Norwich City	D	2-2	Bennett 2	18,200
13	27	H	Liverpool	L	0-4		48,128
14	Nov 3	A	Crystal Palace	L	0-2		29,639
15	10	H	Manchester United	W	2-0	Henry, Robinson	50,067
16	17	A	Bolton Wanderers	W	1-0	Daley	25,515
17	24	A	Bristol City	L	0-1		18,549
18	Dec 1	H	Wolverhampton W.	L	2-3	Deyna, Palmer	33,894
19	8	A	Ipswich Town	L	0-4		18,244
20	15	H	Derby County	W	3-0	Henry, Robinson, Webb (og)	27,664
21	22	A	Everton	W	2-1	Daley, Henry	26,314
22	26	H	Stoke City	D	1-1	Power	36,286
23	29	A	Brighton & Hove Alb.	L	1-4	Lee	28,040
24	Jan 12	H	Tottenham Hotspur	D	1-1	Robinson (pen)	34,837
25	19	A	Southampton	L	1-4	Power	21,422
26	Feb 2	H	West Bromwich Albion	L	1-3	Lee	32,904
27	9	A	Coventry City	D	0-0		17,185
28	16	H	Leeds United	D	1-1	Power	34,392
29	23	A	Nottingham Forest	L	0-4		27,255
30	27	A	Aston Villa	D	2-2	Power, Robinson (pen)	29,139
31	Mar 1	H	Norwich City	D	0-0		32,348
32	11	A	Liverpool	L	0-2		40,443
33	15	H	Arsenal	L	0-3		33,792
34	22	A	Manchester United	L	0-1		56,387
35	29	H	Bolton Wanderers	D	2-2	Tueart 2	33,500
36	Apr 2	H	Everton	D	1-1	Deyna	33,437
37	5	A	Stoke City	D	0-0		20,639
38	7	H	Aston Villa	D	1-1	Power	32,943
39	12	A	Wolverhampton W.	W	2-1	Reeves, Tueart (pen)	23,850
40	19	H	Bristol City	W	3-1	Deyna, Robinson, Tueart	32,745
41	26	A	Derby County	L	1-3	Tueart	22,572
42	May 3	H	Ipswich Town	W	2-1	Henry, Reeves	31,678
							Appearances
							Sub appearances
						One own goal	Goals

FA Cup

R3	Jan 5	A	Halifax Town	L	0-1		12,599
							Appearances

League Cup

R2/1	Aug 28	A	Sheffield Wednesday	D	1-1	Viljoen	24,095
R2/2	Sep 4	H	Sheffield Wednesday	W	2-1	Henry 2	24,074
R3	Sep 26	H	Sunderland	D	1-1	Robinson	26,181
R3	Oct 3	A	Sunderland	L	0-1		33,559
							Appearances
							Sub appearances
							Goals

Bennett DA	Booth TA	Caton TS	Channon MR	Corrigan TJ	Daley SJ	Deyna K	Donachie W	Futcher P	Henry A	Lee FS	Mackenzie S	Palmer RN	Power PC	Ranson R	Reeves KP	Reid NS	Robinson MJ	Shinton RT	Silkman B	Stepanovic D	Sugrue PA	Tuart D	Viljoen C
	5	4		1		10			11		7		6	**2**			9		8	3			12
	5	4		1		**10**			11		7		6	2			9		8	3			12
	5	4	11	1							7		6	2			9		8	3			10
	5	4	11	1					12		7		6	2			9		8	3			**10**
		4		1	10		5		12	11	7		6	2			**9**		8	3			
		4		1	10		5	12		11	7		**6**	2			9		8	3			
11		5		1	8		3	6			7		10	2			9			4			
		5		1	8	11	3	6			7		10	2			9			4			
12		5		1	8	11		6			7		10	2			9	3		**4**			
		5		1	8	11		6			7		10	2			9	4		3			
4		5		1		11		6			7		10	2		3	9						8
4		5		1		11		6			**7**		10	2		3	9			12			8
4		5		1		11		6			7		3	2		10	9						8
4		5		1	8			6	12		7		3	2		**10**	9		11				
4	6	5		1	8	11	3		7				10	2			9						
4		5		1	8	11	3		7				10	2			9			6			
4		5		1	8	11	3		7				10	2			9			6			
7	4	5		1	8	11	3		10	12		9		2						**6**			
4	6	5		1	8				7			11	3	2			9						10
4	6	5		1	8		3		7				11	2			9	10					
4	6	5		1	8		3		7				11	2			9	10					
4	6	5		1	8		3		7				11	2			9	10					
4	6	5		1	8		3		7	11			9	2		10							
6		5		1	8		2		**7**	11	12		3			4	9						10
	6	5		1	8		3			11		12	7	2		4	9						**10**
	6	5		1	8		3		7	11			10	2		4	9						
11	6	5		1	8		3		4		7		10	2			9						
11	6	5		1	**8**		3		4		7	9	10	2		12							
11	6	5		1			3		7			9	10	2		4	8						
11	6	5		1	8		3		7				10	2		4	9						
11	**6**	5		1	8	12			7				3	2		4	9					10	
11		5		1	8	9			7				3	2		4						10	6
11	6	5		1		9			7				3	2	8	4	12					**10**	
11	4	5		1	8				7			12	6	2	9	3						10	
	4	5		1	8				7			11	6	2	9	3						10	
	4	5		1	8	9			7				6	2	11	3						10	
	4	5		1	8	9			7				6	2	11	3						10	
	4	5		1	8	9			7				6	2	11	3						10	
		5		1	8	9		4	7				6	2	11	3						10	
		5		1	8	9		4	7				6	2		3	11					10	
		5		1	8	**9**		4	7		12		6	2	11	3						10	
12		5		1	8	9		4	**6**		7		3		11	2					10		
23	24	42	2	42	33	21	19	12	29	6	17	5	41	40	9	22	29	5	7	13	1	11	9
2						1		1	3	1	2	2				1	1			1			2
2			1		2	6			4	2	2	1	7		2		8					5	

Bennett DA	Booth TA	Caton TS	Channon MR	Corrigan TJ	Daley SJ	Deyna K	Donachie W	Futcher P	Henry A	Lee FS	Mackenzie S	Palmer RN	Power PC	Ranson R	Reeves KP	Reid NS	Robinson MJ	Shinton RT	Silkman B	Stepanovic D	Sugrue PA	Tuart D	Viljoen C
6		5		1	8				7				3	2		4	9	11					10
1		1		1	1				1				1	1		1	1	1					1

Bennett DA	Booth TA	Caton TS	Channon MR	Corrigan TJ	Daley SJ	Deyna K	Donachie W	Futcher P	Henry A	Lee FS	Mackenzie S	Palmer RN	Power PC	Ranson R	Reeves KP	Reid NS	Robinson MJ	Shinton RT	Silkman B	Stepanovic D	Sugrue PA	Tuart D	Viljoen C
	5	4	11	1							7		6	2			9		8	3			10
	5	4		1			10		11		7		6	2			9		8	3			
11		5		1	8		3	6			7		10	2			9			4			
		5		1	8	11	3	6			7	12	10	**2**			9			4			
1	2	4	1	4	2	1	3	2	1		4		4	4			4		2	4			1
												1											
									2								1						1

League Table

	P	W	D	L	F	A	Pts
Liverpool	42	25	10	7	81	30	60
Manchester U	42	24	10	8	65	35	58
Ipswich T	42	22	9	11	68	39	53
Arsenal	42	18	16	8	52	36	52
Nottingham F	42	20	8	14	63	43	48
Wolverh'pton W	42	19	9	14	58	47	47
Aston Villa	42	16	14	12	51	50	46
Southampton	42	18	9	15	65	53	45
Middlesbrough	42	16	12	14	50	44	44
W.B.A.	42	11	19	12	54	50	41
Leeds U	42	13	14	15	46	50	40
Norwich C	42	13	14	15	58	66	40
Crystal Palace	42	12	16	14	41	50	40
Tottenham H	42	15	10	17	52	62	40
Coventry C	42	16	7	19	56	66	39
Brighton & H.A.	42	11	15	16	47	57	37
Manchester C	42	12	13	17	43	66	37
Stoke C	42	13	10	19	44	58	36
Everton	42	9	17	16	43	51	35
Bristol C	42	9	13	20	37	66	31
Derby Co	42	11	8	23	47	67	30
Bolton W	42	5	15	22	38	73	25

1980-81

Division One

Manager: Malcolm Allison (until 8 October 1980), Tony Book as caretaker, John Bond (from 17 October 1980)

Did you know that?

Match 2: Stepanovic's last game.
Match 6: MacRae's last game.
Match 10: Palmer's last game.
Match 11: Deyna's last game.
Match 15: Daley's last game.
Match 39: Sugrue's last game.
Match 40: Buckley's last game.
Match 42: Bennett and MacKenzie's last game.

According to John Bond, Gerry Gow was signed without a medical as the Blues feared he would have failed one!

Match No.	Date	Venue	Opponents	Result		Scorers	Attendance
1	Aug 16	A	Southampton	L	0-2		23,320
2	20	H	Sunderland	L	0-4		33,271
3	23	H	Aston Villa	D	2-2	Ranson, Tueart (pen)	30,017
4	30	A	Middlesbrough	D	2-2	Mackenzie, Reeves	15,761
5	Sep 6	H	Arsenal	D	1-1	Tueart (pen)	32,233
6	13	A	Nottingham Forest	L	2-3	Bennett, Henry	23,184
7	20	H	Stoke City	L	1-2	Tueart	29,507
8	27	A	Manchester United	D	2-2	Palmer, Reeves	55,918
9	Oct 4	H	Liverpool	L	0-3		41,102
10	8	A	Leeds United	L	0-1		19,404
11	11	A	West Bromwich Albion	L	1-3	Daley	19,382
12	18	H	Birmingham City	L	0-1		30,041
13	22	H	Tottenham Hotspur	W	3-1	Daley, Mackenzie, Reeves	28,788
14	25	A	Brighton & Hove Alb.	W	2-1	Tueart 2	18,378
15	Nov 1	H	Norwich City	W	1-0	Power	33,056
16	8	A	Leicester City	D	1-1	Tueart	19,104
17	12	A	Sunderland	L	0-2		23,387
18	15	H	Southampton	W	3-0	Bennett, Gow, Reeves	32,661
19	22	H	Coventry City	W	3-0	Bennett, Power, Reeves	30,047
20	29	A	Crystal Palace	W	3-2	Gow 2, Reeves	17,156
21	Dec 6	H	Ipswich Town	D	1-1	Gow	35,215
22	13	A	Tottenham Hotspur	L	1-2	Boyer	23,883
23	20	H	Leeds United	W	1-0	Reeves	31,866
24	26	A	Everton	W	2-0	Gow, Power	36,222
25	27	H	Wolverhampton W.	W	4-0	Hutchinson 2, McDonald, Reeves	37,817
26	Jan 10	A	Coventry City	D	1-1	Mackenzie	18,257
27	17	H	Middlesbrough	W	3-2	Hutchinson, McDonald, Reeves	30,774
28	31	A	Aston Villa	L	0-1		33,682
29	Feb 7	H	Nottingham Forest	D	1-1	Power	40,524
30	21	H	Manchester United	W	1-0	Mackenzie	50,114
31	24	A	Arsenal	L	0-2		24,790
32	Mar 14	H	West Bromwich Albion	W	2-1	McDonald, Tueart	36,581
33	18	A	Stoke City	L	1-2	McDonald	15,993
34	21	A	Birmingham City	L	0-2		16,160
35	28	H	Brighton & Hove Alb.	D	1-1	Mackenzie	30,122
36	31	H	Leicester City	D	3-3	Reeves 2, Henry	26,141
37	Apr 4	A	Norwich City	L	0-2		17,685
38	18	A	Wolverhampton W.	W	3-1	Bennett 2, Tueart	17,371
39	20	H	Everton	W	3-1	Bennett, Mackenzie, Reeves	34,434
40	25	A	Ipswich Town	L	0-1		22,644
41	May 2	H	Crystal Palace	D	1-1	Bennett	31,017
42	19	A	Liverpool	L	0-1		24,462
							Appearances
							Sub appearances
							Goals

FA Cup

	Date	Venue	Opponents	Result		Scorers	Attendance
R3	Jan 3	H	Crystal Palace	W	4-0	Reeves 2 (1 pen), Boyer, Power	39,347
R4	24	H	Norwich City	W	6-0	Bennett, Gow, McDonald, Mackenzie, Power, Reeves	38,919
R5	Feb 14	A	Peterborough United	W	1-0	Booth	27,780
R6	Mar 7	A	Everton	D	2-2	Gow, Power	52,791
rep	11	H	Everton	W	3-1	McDonald 2, Power	52,532
SF	Apr 11	N	Ipswich Town	W	1-0e	Power	46,537
F	May 9	N	Tottenham Hotspur	D	1-1e	Hutchinson	100,000
rep	14	N	Tottenham Hotspur	L	2-3	Mackenzie, Reeves (pen)	92,500
							Appearances
							Sub appearances
							Goals

SF at Villa Park, Birmingham
Final and replay at Wembley Stadium

League Cup

	Date	Venue	Opponents	Result		Scorers	Attendance
R2/1	Aug 27	A	Stoke City	D	1-1	Henry	13,176
R2/2	Sep 3	H	Stoke City	W	3-0	Bennett 2, Henry	21,356
R3	23	A	Luton Town	W	2-1	Bennett, Henry	10,030
R4	Oct 29	H	Notts County	W	5-1	Tueart 4, Bennett	26,363
R5	Dec 3	H	West Bromwich Albion	W	2-1	Bennett, Henry	35,011
SF1	Jan 14	H	Liverpool	L	0-1		48,045
SF2	Feb 10	A	Liverpool	D	1-1	Reeves	46,711
							Appearances
							Sub appearances
							Goals

Corrigan TJ	Ranson R	Caton TS	Reid NS	Booth TA	Henry A	Tueart D	Daley SJ	Sugrue PA	Power PC	Reeves KP	Stepanovic D	Mackenzie S	Palmer RN	MacRae KA	Bennett DA	Deyna K	Buckley G	McDonald RW	Hutchison T	Gow G	Boyer PJ	Williams A	Kinsey S	May AMP
1	2	3	4	5	6	7	8	9	10	11														
1		3	2	5	6	7	8	9	10	11	4													
1	2	5	3	4		7	8	9	10	11		6	12											
	2	5	3	4	6		8		10	11		9		1	7									
		5	2	4	6	7	8		3	11		9		1	10									
		5	2	4	6	7	8		3	11		9		1	10									
1		5	2	4	6	7	8		3			9	12		10	11								
1	2	5	3	4	6		8	12	7	11			9		10									
1	2	5	3	4	6		8		7	11		9	10											
1	2	5	3	4	6		8		7	11		9	10			12								
1	2	5	3	4	6		8		7	11		9				10								
1	2	6	4	5	7		8		3	11		9			10									
1	12	6	2	5	4	7	8		3	11		9					10							
1	2	6	4			7	8		5	11		9						3	10					
1	2	6	4			7	12		5			9			11			3	10	8				
1	2	6	4			7			5	11		9			12			3	10	8				
1	2		4	6		7			5	11		9			12			3	10	8				
1	2		4	6					5	11		9			7			3	10	8				
1	2		4	6	12				5	11		9			7			3	10	8				
1	2		4	6					5	11		9			7			3	10	8				
1	2		4	6		7			5	11		9						3	10	8	12			
1	2		4	6					5	11		9			12			3	10	8	7			
1	2		4	6	12				5	11		9						3	10	8	7			
1	2	6	4						5	11		9						3	10	8	7			
1	2	6	4						5	11		9						3	10	8	7			
1	2	6	4						5	11		9						3	10	8	7			
1	2	6	4						5	11		9			12			3	10	8	7			
1		6		4	2				5	11		9			7			3	10	8				
1		6		4	2	7			5	11		9						3	10	8				
1			4	6	2				5	11		9			7			3	10	8				
1	2	6	4			12			5	11		9			7			3	10	8				
	2	6	4		10	7			5	11		9					12	3		8		1		
1	2	12	4	6	10	7			5	11		9					8	3						
1	2	6		4	8	7			5	11		9			12			3	10					
1	2	6	4		8	7			5	11		9			12			3	10					
1	2	6	4		8				5	11		9			7			3	10					
1	2		4	6	8				5	11		9			7			3	10					
1		6		4	2	8			5	11		9			7		12	3					10	
1			4	6	2	8		11	5	12		9			7		10	3						
1	2		4	6	3	8			5	11		9			7		10							12
1	2	6			4				5	11		9			7			3	10	8				
	2		4	6		11			5			9			7			3	10	8		1		
37	32	29	37	30	25	21	14	4	42	38	1	39	3	3	20	2	4	28	24	20	6	2	1	
	1	1			2	1	1	1		1			2		6	1	2				1			1
	1				2	8	2		4	12		6	1		7			4	3	5	1			

Corrigan TJ	Ranson R	Caton TS	Reid NS	Booth TA	Henry A	Tueart D	Daley SJ	Sugrue PA	Power PC	Reeves KP	Stepanovic D	Mackenzie S	Palmer RN	MacRae KA	Bennett DA	Deyna K	Buckley G	McDonald RW	Hutchison T	Gow G	Boyer PJ	Williams A	Kinsey S	May AMP
1	2	6	4						5	11		9						3	10	8	7			
1		6		4	2				5	11		9			12			3	10	8	7			
1			4	6	2				5	11		9			7			3	10	8				
1	2	6	4			7			5	11		9						3	10	8				
1	2	6	4			7			5	11		9						3	10	8				
1	2	6	4						5	11		9			7			3	10	8				
1	2	6	4		12				5	11		9			7			3	10	8				
1	2	6	4			12			5	11		9			7			3	10	8				
8	6	7	7	2	2	2			8	8		8			4			8	8	8	2			
					1	1									1									
				1					5	4		2			1			3	1	2	1			

Corrigan TJ	Ranson R	Caton TS	Reid NS	Booth TA	Henry A	Tueart D	Daley SJ	Sugrue PA	Power PC	Reeves KP	Stepanovic D	Mackenzie S	Palmer RN	MacRae KA	Bennett DA	Deyna K	Buckley G	McDonald RW	Hutchison T	Gow G	Boyer PJ	Williams A	Kinsey S	May AMP
1	2	5	3	4	6	7	8		10	11		9	12											
	2	5	3	4	6		8		10	11		9		1	7									
1	2	5	3	4	6		8		10	11			9		7									
1	2	5	4		6	7		12	3	11		9			10		8							
1	2		4	5	6	7			3	11		9			8						10			
1	2	5	4		6	7			3	11		9			8						10			
1	2	5	4	6	12	7			3	11		9			10		8							
6	7	6	7	5	6	5	3		7	7		6	1	1	6		2				2			
					1			1					1											
					4	4				1					5									

League Table

	P	W	D	L	F	A	Pts
Aston Villa	42	26	8	8	72	40	60
Ipswich T	42	23	10	9	77	43	56
Arsenal	42	19	15	8	61	45	53
W.B.A.	42	20	12	10	60	42	52
Liverpool	42	17	17	8	62	42	51
Southampton	42	20	10	12	76	56	50
Nottingham F	42	19	12	11	62	44	50
Manchester U	42	15	18	9	51	36	48
Leeds U	42	17	10	15	39	47	44
Tottenham H	42	14	15	13	70	68	43
Stoke C	42	12	18	12	51	60	42
Manchester C	42	14	11	17	56	59	39
Birmingham C	42	13	12	17	50	61	38
Middlesbrough	42	16	5	21	53	61	37
Everton	42	13	10	19	55	58	36
Coventry C	42	13	10	19	48	68	36
Sunderland	42	14	7	21	52	53	35
Wolverh'pton W	42	13	9	20	43	55	35
Brighton & H.A.	42	14	7	21	54	67	35
Norwich C	42	13	7	22	49	73	33
Leicester C	42	13	6	23	40	67	32
Crystal Palace	42	6	7	29	47	83	19

1981-82

Division One

Manager: John Bond

Did you know that?

Match 2: Henry's last game.
Match 5: Booth's last game.
Match 7: Gow's last game.
Match 21: O'Neill's last game.
Match 24: Hutchison's last game.
Match 32: Elliot's first and only game.
Match 41: Reid and Francis' last game.
Match 42: Ryan and Jackson's last game.

City defeated Stoke on penalties in the League Cup second-round tie. Incredibly it was only when Corrigan saved the 20th spot-kick that the game ended with the Blues winning by nine penalties to eight.

Match No.	Date	Venue	Opponents	Result		Scorers	Attendance
1	Aug 29	H	West Bromwich Albion	W	2-1	Hutchinson, Tueart	36,187
2	Sep 1	A	Notts County	D	1-1	McDonald	14,493
3	5	A	Stoke City	W	3-1	Francis 2, Boyer	25,256
4	12	H	Southampton	D	1-1	Reeves	42,003
5	19	A	Birmingham City	L	0-3		20,109
6	23	H	Leeds United	W	4-0	Reeves 2, Tueart 2	35,077
7	26	H	Tottenham Hotspur	L	0-1		39,085
8	Oct 3	A	Brighton & Hove Alb.	L	1-4	Reeves	18,284
9	10	H	Manchester United	D	0-0		52,037
10	17	A	Arsenal	L	0-1		25,466
11	24	H	Nottingham Forest	D	0-0		34,881
12	31	A	Everton	W	1-0	Tueart	31,305
13	Nov 7	H	Middlesbrough	W	3-2	Francis, Reeves, Tueart (pen)	32,025
14	21	H	Swansea City	W	4-0	Reeves 2, Tueart 2 (1 pen)	34,744
15	28	A	Ipswich Town	L	0-2		20,614
16	Dec 5	H	Aston Villa	W	1-0	Tueart	32,487
17	12	A	Coventry City	W	1-0	Tueart	12,420
18	19	H	Sunderland	L	2-3	Francis 2	29,462
19	26	A	Liverpool	W	3-1	Bond (pen), Hartford, Reeves	37,929
20	28	H	Wolverhampton W.	W	2-1	Francis, Hartford	40,298
21	Jan 9	H	Stoke City	D	1-1	Francis	31,941
22	30	H	Birmingham City	W	4-2	Francis 2, Reeves 2	28,438
23	Feb 2	A	West Ham United	D	1-1	Bond (pen)	26,552
24	6	A	Southampton	L	1-2	McDonald	22,643
25	13	H	Brighton & Hove Alb.	W	4-0	Francis, McDonald, Reeves, Stevens (og)	30,038
26	20	A	Tottenham Hotspur	L	0-2		46,181
27	27	A	Manchester United	D	1-1	Reeves	57,830
28	Mar 6	H	Arsenal	D	0-0		30,288
29	10	A	Leeds United	W	1-0	Reeves	20,797
30	13	A	Nottingham Forest	D	1-1	Caton	20,929
31	20	H	Everton	D	1-1	Bond	33,002
32	27	A	Middlesbrough	D	0-0		11,709
33	Apr 3	H	West Ham United	L	0-1		30,875
34	10	H	Liverpool	L	0-5		40,112
35	12	A	Wolverhampton W.	L	1-4	McDonald	14,819
36	17	A	Swansea City	L	0-2		19,212
37	21	A	West Bromwich Albion	W	1-0	Francis	11,632
38	24	H	Ipswich Town	D	1-1	Hartford	30,329
39	May 1	A	Aston Villa	D	0-0		22,150
40	5	H	Notts County	W	1-0	Power	24,443
41	8	H	Coventry City	L	1-3	Francis	27,580
42	15	A	Sunderland	L	0-1		26,167
							Appearances
							Sub appearances
						One own goal	Goals

FA Cup

	Date	Venue	Opponents	Result		Scorers	Attendance
R3	Jan 2	H	Cardiff City	W	3-1	Francis 2, McDonald	31,547
R4	23	H	Coventry City	L	1-3	Bond (pen)	31,276
							Appearances
							Sub appearances
							Goals

League Cup

	Date	Venue	Opponents	Result		Scorers	Attendance
R2/1	Oct 7	H	Stoke City	W	2-0	Hartford, Smith (og)	23,146
R2/2	28	A	Stoke City	L	0-2		17,373
R3	Nov 11	H	Northampton Town	W	3-1	Tueart 2, McDonald	21,139
R4	Dec 2	A	Barnsley	L	0-1		33,792

R2 won on penalties, a.e.t.

Appearances
Sub appearances
One own goal — Goals

Corrigan TJ	Ranson R	McDonald RW	Reid NS	Power PC	Caton TS	O'Neill MHM	Tueart D	Boyer PJ	Hutchison T	Reeves KP	Henry A	Williams A	Gow G	Francis TJ	Bond KJ	Booth TA	Wilson CEA	Hartford RA	Hareide AF	Kinsey S	Ryan JG	Jackson GA	Elliott A	May AMP
1	2	3	4	5	**6**	7	8	9	10	11	12													
	2	3	4	5	6	7		9	10	**11**	12	1	8											
1	2	3	4	**6**	5	7		12	10	11			8	9										
1	2	3	4		6	7		5	10	11			8	9										
1			4		3	7	6	12	10	**11**			8	9	2	5								
1	2	3	4	**5**	6	12	7		10	11			8	9										
1	2	3	4		6	5	7	**9**	10	11			8		12									
1	2	3	4		6	8	7	9	10	11					5									
1	2		4	5	6	8	7		9	11					3			10						
1	2		4	5	6	8	7		9	11					3			10						
1	2		4	5	6	**8**	7		9	11					3			10	12					
1	2	3	4	10	6		7	9	12	11					5				**8**					
1	2	3	4	**11**	6		7		12	8				9	5			10						
1	2	3	4		**6**		7		11	8				9	5			10	12					
1	2	3	4			6	7		11	8				9	5			10						
1	2	3	4		6		7		11	8				9	5			10						
1	2	3	4		6		7		11	8				9	5			10						
1	2	3	4		6		**7**		11	8				9	5			10	12					
1	2	3	4		6				11	8				9	5			10		7				
1	2		4		6				11	8				9	5		3	10		7				
1		3	4		6	7			11	8				9	5			10			2			
1	2	3		11	6					8				9	5			10		7	4			
1	2	3		11	6					8				9	5			10	12	7	**4**			
1	2	3		11	6				**10**	8				9	5				12	7	4			
1	2	3	4	11	6					8				9	**5**			10		12	7			
1	2	3	4	11	6					8				9	**5**			10			7	12		
1	2	3	4	11	6					8								10	5		7	9		
1	2	3	4	11	6					8				**9**				10	5		7	12		
1	2	3	4	11	6					8					5				9		7	10		
1	2	3	4	**11**	6					8					5			10	9	12	7			
1	2	3	4		6					8				9	5			10	11		7			
1	2		4		6					8				9			3		11	7		**5**	10	12
1	2	3	4	5	6					8								10	9		7	11		
1	2	3	4		6					8					5		11	10		9	7			
1	2	3								8				9	5			10	4	11	7	**6**		12
	2	3	4		6					8		1		9	5			10	12	11				**7**
1	2	3	4	6						8				9	5			10	12	**11**	7			
1	**2**	3		4	6					8				9	5			10		11	7			12
1		3	4	11	6			9		8					5			10		12	7			**2**
1		3	4	11	6			9		8					5			10		7	2			
		3	4	11	6			7		8		1		9	5			10						2
1		3		5	6			9		8					4		12	10		**7**	2	11		
39	36	36	36	25	39	12	15	10	20	42		3	6	26	32	1	3	30	9	13	19	6	1	3
						1		2	2		2				1		1		7	3		2		3
		4		1	1		9	1	1	13				12	3			3						

Corrigan TJ	Ranson R	McDonald RW	Reid NS	Power PC	Caton TS	O'Neill MHM	Tueart D	Boyer PJ	Hutchison T	Reeves KP	Henry A	Williams A	Gow G	Francis TJ	Bond KJ	Booth TA	Wilson CEA	Hartford RA	Hareide AF	Kinsey S	Ryan JG	Jackson GA	Elliott A	May AMP
1	2	3	4		6				11	9			8	7	5			10						
1		3	4	11	6				7	8			**2**	9	5			10		12				
2	1	2	2	1	2				2	2			2	2	2			2						
																				1				
		1												2	1									

Corrigan TJ	Ranson R	McDonald RW	Reid NS	Power PC	Caton TS	O'Neill MHM	Tueart D	Boyer PJ	Hutchison T	Reeves KP	Henry A	Williams A	Gow G	Francis TJ	Bond KJ	Booth TA	Wilson CEA	Hartford RA	Hareide AF	Kinsey S	Ryan JG	Jackson GA	Elliott A	May AMP
1	2		4		6	8	7		11	9					5		3	10						
1	2		4	5	6	**8**	7		11	9					3			10	12					
1	2	3	4		6	**11**	7		12	8				9	5			10						
1	2	3	4		6		7	9	11	8					5			10						
4	4	2	4	1	4	3	4	1	3	4				1	4		1	4						
									1										1					
		1					2											1						

League Table

	P	W	D	L	F	A	Pts
Liverpool	42	26	9	7	80	32	87
Ipswich T	42	26	5	11	75	53	83
Manchester U	42	22	12	8	59	29	78
Tottenham H	42	20	11	11	67	48	71
Arsenal	42	20	11	11	48	37	71
Swansea C	42	21	6	15	58	51	69
Southampton	42	19	9	14	72	67	66
Everton	42	17	13	12	56	50	64
West Ham U	42	14	16	12	66	57	58
Manchester C	42	15	13	14	49	50	58
Aston Villa	42	15	12	15	55	53	57
Nottingham F	42	15	12	15	42	48	57
Brighton & H.A.	42	13	13	16	43	52	52
Coventry C	42	13	11	18	56	62	50
Notts Co	42	13	8	21	61	69	47
Birmingham C	42	10	14	18	53	61	44
W.B.A.	42	11	11	20	46	57	44
Stoke C	42	12	8	22	44	63	44
Sunderland	42	11	11	20	38	58	44
Leeds U	42	10	12	20	39	61	42
Wolverh'pton W	42	10	10	22	32	63	40
Middlesbrough	42	8	15	19	34	52	39

1982-83

Division One

Manager: John Bond (until 29 January 1983),
John Benson (from 5 February 1983 – June 1983)

Did you know that?

Match 3: McDonald spent 87 minutes in net after injury to Corrigan.
Match 7: Boyer's last game.
Match 9: Hareide and Jones's last game.
Match 28: Park's last game.
Match 32: Corrigan and Hildersley's last game.
Match 33: Golac's last game.
Match 37: Cross's last game.
Match 39: Bodak's last game.
Match 42: McDonald, Tueart and Reeves's last game.

The 1982–83 season was the first to see a sponsor's name on City's shirts. Saab were the first sponsors.

Match No.	Date	Venue	Opponents	Result		Scorers	Attendance
1	Aug 28	A	Norwich City	W	2-1	Cross, Power	21,781
2	Sep 1	H	Stoke City	W	1-0	Cross	27,847
3	4	H	Watford	W	1-0	Tueart	29,617
4	7	A	Notts County	L	0-1		9,369
5	11	A	Tottenham Hotspur	W	2-1	Baker 2	32,483
6	18	H	Aston Villa	L	0-1		28,650
7	25	A	West Ham United	L	1-4	Boyer	23,883
8	Oct 2	H	Coventry City	W	3-2	Baker, Caton, Cross	25,105
9	9	A	Everton	L	1-2	Cross	25,162
10	16	H	Sunderland	D	2-2	Cross, Reeves	25,053
11	23	A	Manchester United	D	2-2	Cross, Tueart	57,334
12	30	H	Swansea City	W	2-1	Hartford, Tueart	25,021
13	Nov 6	H	Southampton	W	2-0	McDonald, Reeves	25,115
14	13	A	Ipswich Town	L	0-1		19,362
15	20	H	Birmingham City	D	0-0		23,174
16	27	A	Nottingham Forest	L	0-3		18,845
17	Dec 4	H	Arsenal	W	2-1	Caton 2	23,057
18	11	A	Luton Town	L	1-3	Cross	11,013
19	18	H	Brighton & Hove Alb.	D	1-1	Bond	20,615
20	27	A	Liverpool	L	2-5	Caton, Cross	43,695
21	28	H	West Bromwich Albion	W	2-1	Kinsey, Robertson (og)	25,172
22	Jan 1	A	Birmingham City	D	2-2	Bodak, Bond	16,362
23	3	A	Watford	L	0-2		20,049
24	15	H	Norwich City	W	4-1	Cross 2, Bond, Hartford	22,000
25	22	A	Aston Villa	D	1-1	Hartford	20,415
26	Feb 5	H	Tottenham Hotspur	D	2-2	Cross, Tueart (pen)	26,357
27	12	A	Coventry City	L	0-4		9,604
28	19	H	Notts County	L	0-1		21,199
29	26	A	Sunderland	L	2-3	Caton, Reeves	15,496
30	Mar 2	H	Everton	D	0-0		22,253
31	5	H	Manchester United	L	1-2	Reeves	45,400
32	12	A	Swansea City	L	1-4	McDonald	9,884
33	19	A	Southampton	L	1-4	Reeves	17,241
34	26	H	Ipswich Town	L	0-1		21,845
35	Apr 2	A	West Bromwich Albion	W	2-0	Cross, Reeves	13,764
36	4	H	Liverpool	L	0-4		35,647
37	9	A	Stoke City	L	0-1		15,373
38	16	H	West Ham United	W	2-0	McDonald, Tueart (pen)	23,015
39	23	A	Arsenal	L	0-3		16,810
40	30	H	Nottingham Forest	L	1-2	Baker	23,583
41	May 7	A	Brighton & Hove Alb.	W	1-0	Reeves	17,777
42	14	H	Luton Town	L	0-1		42,843
							Appearances
							Sub appearances
						One own goal	Goals

FA Cup

	Date	Venue	Opponents	Result		Scorers	Attendance
R3	Jan 8	A	Sunderland	D	0-0		21,518
rep	12	H	Sunderland	W	2-1	Cross, Hartford	22,356
R4	29	A	Brighton & Hove Alb.	L	0-4		16,804
							Appearances
							Sub appearances
							Goals

League Cup

	Date	Venue	Opponents	Result		Scorers	Attendance
R2/1	Oct 5	A	Wigan Athletic	D	1-1	Tueart	12,194
R2/2	27	H	Wigan Athletic	W	2-0	Power 2	16,083
R3	Nov 10	H	Southampton	D	1-1	Tueart (pen)	17,463
rep	24	A	Southampton	L	0-4		13,298
							Appearances
							Goals

Corrigan TJ	Ranson R	McDonald RW	Baker GE	Bond KJ	Caton TS	Hareide AF	Reeves KP	Cross D	Hartford RA	Power PC	Tueart D	Williams A	Jones CH	Boyer PJ	Simpson PD	Reid NS	Davies IC	Kinsey S	May AMP	Bodak PJ	Park T	Golac I	Hildersley R	Lomax GW
1	2	3	4	5	6	7	8	9	10	11														
1	2	3	4	5	6	7	8	9	10	11														
1	2	3	4	5	6	7	8	9	10	11	12													
	2	3	4	5	6	7	8	9	10	11	12	1												
	2	3	4	5	6	7	8		10	11	12	1	9											
	2	3	4	5	6	7	8		10	11	12	1	9											
	2	3	4	5	6	7	8		10	11	12	1		9										
	2		4	5	6		8	9	10	3	7	1			11									
	2		5		6	10	8	9		3	7	1	11		12	4								
1	2				6		8	9	10	5	7				12	4	3	11						
1	2	3	11	4	6		8	9	10	5	7													
1	2	3	11	4	6		8	9	10	5	7													
1	2	3	11	4	6		8	9	10	5	7													
1	2	3	11	4	6		8	9	10	5	7					12								
1	2	3	11	4	6		8	9	10	5	7													
1	2	3		10	6		8	9		5	7					4			11					
1	2	3	11	4	6		8	9	10	5	7													
1	2	3		11	6		8	9	10	5	7					4								
1	2	3		4	6		8	9	10	5	7								12	11				
1	2	3		4	6		8	9	10	5	7									11				
1	2	3		6			8	9	10		7					4		5		11				
1	2	3		6			8	9	10		7					4		5		11				
1	2	3		6			8		10	5	7					4		9		11				
1	2			3			8	9	10	5	7					4		6		11				
1	2			3	6		8	9	10	5	7					4		11						
1	2	3		5	6		8	9	10		7					4				11				
	2	3		5	6		8	9	10			1				4			7	11	12			
1	2			5	6		8	9	10		7						4		3	11	12			
1	2	3	9	5	6		8		10		7								4	11				
1	2	3	9	5	6		8		10		7					4				11				
1	2	3	11	5	6		8	9	10		7					4				12				
1		3	11	5	6		8	9			7					4			12			2	10	
			11	5	6		8	9		10	7	1				4			12			3		2
	2		11	5	6		8	9	10	3	12	1				4				7				
	2		11	5	6		8	9	10	3		1				4		7						
	2		11	5	6		8	9	10	3		1				4		7	12					
	2	3		5	6		8	9	10	11		1				4		7						
	2	3		5	6		8		10	11	7	1				4		9						
	2	3	8	5	6				10	11	7	1				4		9		12				
	2	3	8	5	6				10	11	7	1				4		9						
	2	3	9	5	6		8		10	11	7	1				4								
	2	3	9	5	6		8		10	11	7	1				4		12						
25	40	32	27	40	38	8	40	31	38	33	30	17	3	1	1	24	2	12	4	12		2	1	1
											6				2	1		1	4	2	2			
		3	4	3	5		7	12	3	1	5			1				1		1				

Corrigan TJ	Ranson R	McDonald RW	Baker GE	Bond KJ	Caton TS	Hareide AF	Reeves KP	Cross D	Hartford RA	Power PC	Tueart D	Williams A	Jones CH	Boyer PJ	Simpson PD	Reid NS	Davies IC	Kinsey S	May AMP	Bodak PJ	Park T	Golac I	Hildersley R	Lomax GW
1	2			3	6		8	9	10	5	12					4		11		7				
1	2	12		3			8	9	10	5	7					4		6		11				
1	2			3	6		8	9	10	5	7					4		11		12				
3	3			3	2		3	3	3	3	2					3		3		2				
		1									1									1				
								1	1															

Corrigan TJ	Ranson R	McDonald RW	Baker GE	Bond KJ	Caton TS	Hareide AF	Reeves KP	Cross D	Hartford RA	Power PC	Tueart D	Williams A	Jones CH	Boyer PJ	Simpson PD	Reid NS	Davies IC	Kinsey S	May AMP	Bodak PJ	Park T	Golac I	Hildersley R	Lomax GW
	2		4	5	6		8	9	10	3	7	1		11										
1	2	3	11	4	6		8	9	10	5	7													
1	2	3	11	4	6		8	9	10	5	7													
1	2	3	11	7	6		8	9	10	5						4								
3	4	3	4	4	4		4	4	4	4	3	1		1		1								
										2	2													

League Table

	P	W	D	L	F	A	Pts
Liverpool	42	24	10	8	87	37	82
Watford	42	22	5	15	74	57	71
Manchester U	42	19	13	10	56	38	70
Tottenham H	42	20	9	13	65	50	69
Nottingham F	42	20	9	13	62	50	69
Aston Villa	42	21	5	16	62	50	68
Everton	42	18	10	14	66	48	64
West Ham U	42	20	4	18	68	62	64
Ipswich T	42	15	13	14	64	50	58
Arsenal	42	16	10	16	58	56	58
W.B.A.	42	15	12	15	51	49	57
Southampton	42	15	12	15	54	58	57
Stoke C	42	16	9	17	53	64	57
Norwich C	42	14	12	16	52	58	54
Notts Co	42	15	7	20	55	71	52
Sunderland	42	12	14	16	48	61	50
Birmingham C	42	12	14	16	40	55	50
Luton T	42	12	13	17	65	84	49
Coventry C	42	13	9	20	48	59	48
Manchester C	42	13	8	21	47	70	47
Swansea C	42	10	11	21	51	69	41
Brighton & H.A.	42	9	13	20	38	68	40

1983-84

Division Two

Manager: Billy McNeill MBE

Did you know that?

Match 10: Davies's last game.
Match 12: Davidson's last game.
Match 16: Caton's last game.
Match 17: Walsh's last game.
Match 31: Dalziel's last game.
Match 32: Hartford's last game.
Match 40: Johnson's last game.
Match 42: Ranson's last game.

City's meeting with Chelsea (Match 40) was the first Second Division match shown live on television. The BBC showed the match live on a Friday night.

Match No.	Date	Venue	Opponents	Result		Scorers	Attendance
1	Aug 27	A	Crystal Palace	W	2-0	May, Parlane	13,207
2	29	A	Cardiff City	L	1-2	Tolmie	8,895
3	Sep 3	H	Barnsley	W	3-2	Tolmie 2, Parlane	25,105
4	7	H	Fulham	D	0-0		23,673
5	10	A	Portsmouth	W	2-1	Parlane, Tolmie (pen)	19,852
6	17	H	Blackburn Rovers	W	6-0	Parlane 3, Baker, May, Tolmie	25,433
7	24	A	Leeds United	W	2-1	Baker, Parlane	21,918
8	Oct 1	H	Grimsby Town	W	2-1	Caton, Tolmie	25,060
9	8	H	Swansea City	W	2-1	Davidson, Parlane	23,567
10	15	A	Charlton Athletic	L	0-1		7,639
11	22	H	Middlesbrough	W	2-1	Parlane, Tolmie	24,466
12	29	A	Newcastle United	L	0-5		33,675
13	Nov 5	A	Shrewsbury Town	W	3-1	Caton, Kinsey, May	9,471
14	12	H	Brighton & Hove Alb.	W	4-0	Baker 2, Parlane, Tolmie	24,562
15	19	A	Carlisle United	L	0-2		8,745
16	26	H	Derby County	D	1-1	Parlane	22,689
17	Dec 3	A	Chelsea	W	1-0	Tolmie	29,142
18	10	H	Sheffield Wednesday	L	1-2	Bond	41,862
19	17	A	Cambridge United	D	0-0		5,204
20	26	H	Oldham Athletic	W	2-0	Kinsey, Parlane	35,898
21	27	A	Huddersfield Town	W	3-1	Baker, Kinsey, Lomax	23,497
22	31	A	Barnsley	D	1-1	Parlane	17,148
23	Jan 2	H	Leeds United	D	1-1	Tolmie (pen)	34,441
24	14	H	Crystal Palace	W	3-1	Baker, Kinsey, Power	20,144
25	21	A	Blackburn Rovers	L	1-2	Tolmie (pen)	18,201
26	Feb 4	A	Grimsby Town	D	1-1	Parlane	11,987
27	11	H	Portsmouth	W	2-1	Reid, Tolmie (pen)	23,138
28	18	H	Newcastle United	L	1-2	Kinsey	41,767
29	25	A	Middlesbrough	D	0-0		9,343
30	Mar 3	H	Shrewsbury Town	W	1-0	Reid	20,083
31	10	A	Brighton & Hove Alb.	D	1-1	Hartford	14,111
32	17	A	Fulham	L	1-5	McNab	9,684
33	24	H	Cardiff City	W	2-1	Baker, Johnson	20,140
34	31	H	Charlton Athletic	L	0-1		19,147
35	Apr 7	A	Swansea City	W	2-0	Kinsey, Parlane	6,261
36	14	H	Carlisle United	W	3-1	May, Parlane, Smith	20,760
37	20	A	Oldham Athletic	D	2-2	Bond (pen), McCarthy	20,320
38	23	H	Huddersfield Town	L	2-3	Bond 2 (2 pens)	23,247
39	28	A	Derby County	L	0-1		14,470
40	May 4	H	Chelsea	L	0-2		21,713
41	7	A	Sheffield Wednesday	D	0-0		37,080
42	12	H	Cambridge United	W	5-0	Baker, Kinsey, May, Power, Tolmie	20,787
							Appearances
							Sub appearances
							Goals

FA Cup

R3	Jan 7	A	Blackpool	L	1-2	Hetzke (og)	15,377
							Appearances
						One own goal	Sub appearances

League Cup

R2/1	Oct 5	A	Torquay United	D	0-0		6,439
R2/2	25	H	Torquay United	W	6-0	Parlane 3, Tolmie 2 (1 pen), Hoyland	14,021
R3	Nov 9	A	Aston Villa	L	0-3		23,922
							Appearances
							Sub appearances
							Goals

Williams A	Ranson R	May AMP	Bond KJ	Power PC	Caton TS	McNab N	Reid NS	Parlane DJ	Hartford RA	Tolmie J	Kinsey S	Baker GE	Davies IC	Davidson D	Sullivan D	Walsh MT	Hoyland JW	Wilson CEA	Lomax GW	Dalziel G	McCarthy MJ	Smith GD	Johnson DE
1	2	3	4	5	6	7	8	9	10	11													
1	2	3	4	5	6	7	8	9	10	11	12												
1	2	3	4	5	6	7	8	9		11		10											
1	2	3	4	5	6	7	8	9		11		10											
1	2	7	4	5	6		8	9		11		10	3										
1	2	3	4	5	6	7	8	9		11		10		12									
1	2	8		5	6	7	4	9		11		10	3	12									
1	2	8		5	6	7	4	9		11		10	3										
1	2	8		5	6	7	4	9		11		10	3	12									
1	2	8		5	6	7	4	9		11		10	3	12									
1	2	3		5	6	7		9		11		10		8		4							
1	2	3		5	6	7		9		11	12	10		8		4							
1	2	3		5	6	7	4	9		11	8	10											
1	2	8		5	6	7	4	9		11		10						3					
1	2	8	12	5	6	7	4	9		11		10						3					
1	2	8	4	5	6	7		9		11						12	10	3					
1		3	4	5		7		9	10	11	12					6			2	8			
1	2	6	4	5		7		9	10	11	12								3	8			
1		3	4	5		7		9	10	11		8							2		6		
1		3	4	5		7		9		11	10	8							2		6		
1		3	4	5		7		9		11	10	8							2		6		
1	12	3	4	5		7		9		11	10	8							2		6		
1		3	4	5		7		9		11		8							2	10	6		
1		3	4	5		7		9		11	10	8							2		6		
1		3	4	5		7		9		11	10	8							2		6		
1		3	4	5		7		9		11	10	8							2		6		
1		3	4	5		7	12	9		11	10	8							2		6		
1		3	4	5		7	2	9		11	10	8							12		6		
1	2	9	4	5		7	8	12		11	10								3		6		
1		3	4	5		7	2	9		11	10	8								12	6		
1		3	11	5			4		10		9	8							2	7	6		
1		3	4	5		7	2	9	10	11		8									6		
1	2	3	4	5		7		9		12		10									6	8	11
1	2	3	4	5		7		9		11	12	10									6		8
1		5	4					9		11	10	8						3	2		6	7	
1		5	4					9		11	10	8						3	2		6	7	12
1		5	4					9		12	10	8						3	2		6	7	11
1	2	5	4					9		12	10	8						3			6	7	11
1	2	5	4			10		9		11	12	8						3			6	7	
1	2	7	4	5				9		11		8						3			6	10	12
1	2	7	4	5				9		11		8						3			6	10	
1	2	7	4	5				9		11	12	8						3			6	10	
42	25	42	33	37	16	33	18	40	7	38	16	36	5	2		3	1	11	16	4	24	9	4
	1		1				1	1		3	7			4		1			1	1			2
		5	4	2	2	1	2	16	1	13	7	8		1					1		1	1	1

Williams A	Ranson R	May AMP	Bond KJ	Power PC	Caton TS	McNab N	Reid NS	Parlane DJ	Hartford RA	Tolmie J	Kinsey S	Baker GE	Davies IC	Davidson D	Sullivan D	Walsh MT	Hoyland JW	Wilson CEA	Lomax GW	Dalziel G	McCarthy MJ	Smith GD	Johnson DE
1		10	4	5		7		9		11		8				3			2	12	6		
1		1	1	1		1		1		1		1				1			1		1		
																				1			

Williams A	Ranson R	May AMP	Bond KJ	Power PC	Caton TS	McNab N	Reid NS	Parlane DJ	Hartford RA	Tolmie J	Kinsey S	Baker GE	Davies IC	Davidson D	Sullivan D	Walsh MT	Hoyland JW	Wilson CEA	Lomax GW	Dalziel G	McCarthy MJ	Smith GD	Johnson DE
1	2	8		5	6		4	9		11		10	3		7								
1	2	3		5	6	7		9		11		10		8		4	12						
1	2	3		5	6	7	4	9		11	8	10				12							
3	3	3		3	3	2	2	3		3	1	3	1	1	1	1							
																1	1						
								3		2							1						

League Table

	P	W	D	L	F	A	Pts
Chelsea	42	25	13	4	90	40	88
Sheffield W	42	26	10	6	72	34	88
Newcastle U	42	24	8	10	85	53	80
Manchester C	42	20	10	12	66	48	70
Grimsby T	42	19	13	10	60	47	70
Blackburn R	42	17	16	9	57	46	67
Carlisle U	42	16	16	10	48	41	64
Shrewsbury T	42	17	10	15	49	53	61
Brighton & H.A.	42	17	9	16	69	60	60
Leeds U	42	16	12	14	55	56	60
Huddersfield T	42	14	15	13	56	49	57
Fulham	42	15	12	15	60	53	57
Charlton A	42	16	9	17	53	64	57
Barnsley	42	15	7	20	57	53	52
Cardiff C	42	15	6	21	53	66	51
Portsmouth	42	14	7	21	73	64	49
Middlesbrough	42	12	13	17	41	47	49
Crystal Palace	42	12	11	19	42	52	47
Oldham A	42	13	8	21	47	73	47
Derby Co	42	11	9	22	36	72	42
Swansea C	42	7	8	27	36	85	29
Cambridge U	42	4	12	26	28	77	24

1984-85

Division Two

Manager: Billy McNeill MBE

Did you know that?

Match 3: Bond's last game.
Match 10: Parlane's last game.
Match 16: Sinclair's last game.
Match 25: Cunningham's last game.
Match 27: McNaught's last game.
Match 40: Hoyland's last game.
Match 42: Lomax's last game.

Despite losing at Oxford (Match 33) City were still top of Division Two, but only two points in the following four games caused the Blues to slip. Tension was extremely high as the season neared its end, then City's last day victory gave them the third promotion position.

Match No.	Date	Venue	Opponents	Result		Scorers	Attendance
1	Aug 25	A	Wimbledon	D	2-2	Parlane, Smith	8,365
2	27	H	Grimsby Town	W	3-0	Bond (pen), Parlane, Smith	21,137
3	Sep 1	H	Fulham	L	2-3	Parlane 2	21,071
4	4	A	Wolverhampton W.	L	0-2		13,255
5	8	A	Carlisle United	D	0-0		6,261
6	15	H	Huddersfield Town	W	1-0	Baker	20,201
7	22	A	Cardiff City	W	3-0	Cunningham, Phillips, Wilson	6,089
8	29	H	Crystal Palace	W	2-1	Kinsey, Smith	20,251
9	Oct 6	H	Oxford United	W	1-0	Kinsey	24,755
10	13	A	Shrewsbury Town	L	0-1		8,563
11	20	A	Middlesbrough	L	1-2	Kinsey	7,735
12	27	H	Blackburn Rovers	W	2-1	May, Lowey (og)	23,797
13	Nov 3	A	Brighton & Hove Alb.	D	0-0		14,009
14	10	H	Birmingham City	W	1-0	Phillips	25,369
15	17	A	Sheffield United	D	0-0		16,645
16	24	H	Portsmouth	D	2-2	Kinsey, Smith	23,700
17	Dec 1	A	Oldham Athletic	W	2-0	Melrose, Smith	14,026
18	8	H	Notts County	W	2-0	Melrose, Smith	20,109
19	15	A	Charlton Athletic	W	3-1	Melrose, Phillips, Smith	5,568
20	22	A	Fulham	L	2-3	Baker (pen), Melrose	6,758
21	26	H	Barnsley	D	1-1	Melrose	27,131
22	29	H	Wolverhampton W.	W	4-0	Baker, Phillips, Smith, Wilson	22,022
23	Jan 1	A	Leeds United	D	1-1	Melrose	22,649
24	12	A	Huddersfield Town	W	2-0	Smith, Wilson	15,640
25	19	H	Wimbledon	W	3-0	Baker, Phillips, Smith	23,303
26	Feb 2	A	Crystal Palace	W	2-1	Phillips, Wilson	7,668
27	9	H	Carlisle United	L	1-3	Phillips	21,374
28	23	H	Brighton & Hove Alb.	W	2-0	Phillips, Smith	20,217
29	Mar 2	A	Blackburn Rovers	W	1-0	Kinsey	22,137
30	9	H	Middlesbrough	W	1-0	Phillips	22,399
31	16	H	Shrewsbury Town	W	4-0	Kinsey, May, Power, Smith	20,828
32	19	A	Birmingham City	D	0-0		18,004
33	23	A	Oxford United	L	0-3		13,096
34	30	H	Cardiff City	D	2-2	Kinsey, Simpson	20,047
35	Apr 6	A	Barnsley	D	0-0		12,930
36	8	H	Leeds United	L	1-2	Tolmie	33,553
37	13	A	Grimsby Town	L	1-4	Simpson	8,364
38	20	H	Sheffield United	W	2-0	Clements, Tolmie	21,132
39	27	A	Portsmouth	W	2-1	Phillips, Simpson	22,249
40	May 4	H	Oldham Athletic	D	0-0		28,933
41	6	A	Notts County	L	2-3	Simpson 2	17,812
42	11	H	Charlton Athletic	W	5-1	Phillips 2, May, Melrose, Simpson	47,285
							Appearances
							Sub appearances
						One own goal	Goals

FA Cup

R3	Jan 5	A	Coventry City	L	1-2	Power	15,642
							Appearances
							Sub appearances
							Goals

League Cup

R2/1	Sep 25	H	Blackpool	W	4-2	Cunningham 2, McCarthy, Wilson	13,344
R2/2	Oct 9	A	Blackpool	W	3-1	Tolmie 2, Smith	10,966
R3	31	H	West Ham United	D	0-0		20,510
rep	Nov 6	A	West Ham United	W	2-1	Cunningham, Kinsey	17,461
R4	21	A	Chelsea	L	1-4	Smith	26,364
							Appearances
							Sub appearances
							Goals

Williams A	Phillips DO	Power PC	Bond KJ	McCarthy MJ	Wilson CEA	McNab N	Baker GE	Parlane DJ	Cunningham AE	Smith GD	Tolmie J	May AMP	Reid NS	Kinsey S	Lomax GW	Beckford DRL	Melrose JM	Sinclair GJ	Simpson PD	McNaught K	Clements KH	Hoyland JW	Player name
1	2	3	4	5	6	7	8	9	10	**11**	12												
1	2	3	4	5	6	7	8	11	9	10													
1	2	3	4	5	6	7	8	11	9	**10**	12												
1	6	3		5	10	**7**	8	11	9		12	2	4										
1	7	3		5	6		8	11	9		**10**	2	4	12									
1	6	3		5	10		8	**11**	9	7		2	4	12									
1	6	3		5	10		**8**		9	7	12	2	4	11									
1	6	3		5	10		8		**9**	7	12	2	4	11									
1	6	3		5	10		8		9	**7**	12	2	4	11									
1	6	3		5	10	12	8	11	**9**	7		2	4										
1	6	3		5	10		8		9	**7**		2	4	11		12							
1	6	3		5	10		8		9	7		2	4	11									
1	6	3		5	10		**8**		9	7		2	4	11		12							
1	6	3		5	10	8			9	7		2	4	**11**			12						
1	6	3			10	8			9	7		5	4		2		**11**		12				
1	6	3			10		8		9	12		5	4	11			7	**2**					
1	6	3		5	10		8			7		2	4	11			9						
1	6	3		5	10		8			7		2	4	11			9						
1	6	3		5	10		8			7		2	4	11			9						
1	6	3		5	10		8			7		2	4	11			9						
1	6	3		5	10		8		12	**7**		2		11			9			4			
1	6	3		5	10		8			7		2		11			9			4			
1	6	3		5	10		8			7		2		11			9			4			
1	6	3		5	10		8			7		2		11			9			4			
1	6	3		5	10		8		12	7		2		11			**9**			4			
1	6	3		5	10		8			7		2		11			9			4			
1	6	3		**5**	10		8			7		2	12	11			9			4			
1	6	3		5		10	8			7	11	2	4				9						
1	6	3		5		10	**8**			7	12	2	4	11			9						
1	6	3		5		10				7		8	4	11			9				2		
1	6	3		5		10				7	12	**8**	4	11			9				2		
1	6	3		5		10				7		8	4	11			9				2		
1	**6**	3		5		10				7	12	8	4	11			9				2		
1	6	3		5		12					10	**8**	4	11			9		7		2		
1	6	10		5			8					2	4	11	3		**9**		7		12		
1	6	10		5			**8**				12	2	4	11	3	9			7				
1	6	10		5							9	**2**	8	11	3	12			7		4		
1	6	3		5		12					10	8	4	11			**9**		7		2		
1	6	3		5						10	9	8	4	11					7		2		
1	6	3		5		10						8	4	11	12				7		2	**9**	
1	6	9		5		10						8	4	11	3				7		2		
1	6	3				8					10	4		11	2		9		7		5		
42	42	42	3	39	27	15	29	7	16	31	7	39	31	33	6	1	23	1	9	7	11	1	
						3			2	1	10		1	2	1	3	1		1		1		
	12	1	1		4		4	4	1	12	2	3		7			7		6		1		

Williams A	Phillips DO	Power PC	Bond KJ	McCarthy MJ	Wilson CEA	McNab N	Baker GE	Parlane DJ	Cunningham AE	Smith GD	Tolmie J	May AMP	Reid NS	Kinsey S	Lomax GW	Beckford DRL	Melrose JM	Sinclair GJ	Simpson PD	McNaught K	Clements KH	Hoyland JW	Player name
1	6	3		5	10		8		12	**7**		4		11	2		9						
1	1	1		1	1		1			1		1		1	1		1						
									1														
		1																					

Williams A	Phillips DO	Power PC	Bond KJ	McCarthy MJ	Wilson CEA	McNab N	Baker GE	Parlane DJ	Cunningham AE	Smith GD	Tolmie J	May AMP	Reid NS	Kinsey S	Lomax GW	Beckford DRL	Melrose JM	Sinclair GJ	Simpson PD	McNaught K	Clements KH	Hoyland JW	Player name
1	6	3		5	10		8		9	**7**	12		4	11	2								
1	6	3		5	10		8		9	7	12	2	4	**11**									
1	6	3		5	10		8		9	**7**		2	4	11		12							
1	6	3		5	10	8			9	7		2	4	11									
1	6	3			10	8			9	7		5	4	11				2					
5	5	5		4	5	2	3		5	5		4	5	5	1			1					
											2					1							
				1					3	2	2			1									1

League Table

	P	W	D	L	F	A	Pts
Oxford U	42	25	9	8	84	36	84
Birmingham C	42	25	7	10	59	33	82
Manchester C	42	21	11	10	66	40	74
Portsmouth	42	20	14	8	69	50	74
Blackburn R	42	21	10	11	66	41	73
Brighton & H.A.	42	20	12	10	54	34	72
Leeds U	42	19	12	11	66	43	69
Shrewsbury T	42	18	11	13	66	53	65
Fulham	42	19	8	15	68	64	65
Grimsby T	42	18	8	16	72	64	62
Barnsley	42	14	16	12	42	42	58
Wimbledon	42	16	10	16	71	75	58
Huddersfield T	42	15	10	17	52	64	55
Oldham A	42	15	8	19	49	67	53
Crystal Palace	42	12	12	18	46	65	48
Carlisle U	42	13	8	21	50	67	47
Charlton A	42	11	12	19	51	63	45
Sheffield U	42	10	14	18	54	66	44
Middlesbrough	42	10	10	22	41	57	40
Notts Co	42	10	7	25	45	73	37
Cardiff C	42	9	8	25	47	79	35
Wolverh'pton W	42	8	9	25	37	79	33

1985-86

Division One

Manager: Billy McNeill MBE

Did you know that?

Match 6: Smith's last League game.
Match 8: Williams's last game.
Match 11: Tolmie's last League game.
Match 23: Melrose's last game.
Match 31: Johnson's last game.
Match 10: Kinsey's last game.
Match 40: Power's last game.
Match 41: Siddall's last game.
Match 42: Phillips's and Lillis's last game.

The League Cup away game with Bury was played at Old Trafford as Bury hoped to attract a larger crowd than Gigg Lane could accommodate. The attendance was 11,377 – around 3,000 more than Gigg Lane's capacity – but playing the game at Old Trafford was not the attraction Bury had hoped.

Match No.	Date	Venue	Opponents	Result		Scorers	Attendance
1	Aug 17	A	Coventry City	D	1-1	McIlroy	14,521
2	21	H	Leicester City	D	1-1	Lillis (pen)	25,528
3	24	H	Sheffield Wednesday	L	1-3	Simpson	26,934
4	26	A	West Bromwich Albion	W	3-2	Lillis, Simpson, Wilson	12,088
5	31	H	Tottenham Hotspur	W	2-1	Simpson, Miller (og)	27,789
6	Sep 3	A	Birmingham City	L	0-1		11,714
7	7	A	Southampton	L	0-3		14,308
8	14	H	Manchester United	L	0-3		48,773
9	21	H	West Ham United	D	2-2	Lillis, Melrose	22,001
10	28	A	Oxford United	L	0-1		9,453
11	Oct 5	H	Chelsea	L	0-1		20,104
12	12	A	Watford	L	2-3	Lillis, McNab	15,559
13	19	A	Queen's Park Rangers	D	0-0		10,471
14	26	H	Everton	D	1-1	Simpson	28,807
15	Nov 2	A	Arsenal	L	0-1		22,229
16	9	H	Ipswich Town	D	1-1	Lillis (pen)	20,853
17	16	A	Nottingham Forest	W	2-0	Simpson, Wilson	15,140
18	23	H	Newcastle United	W	1-0	Lillis	25,179
19	30	A	Luton Town	L	1-2	Lillis (pen)	10,096
20	Dec 7	A	Leicester City	D	1-1	Davies	10,259
21	14	H	Coventry City	W	5-1	Davies 2, Simpson 2, Lillis	20,075
22	21	A	Sheffield Wednesday	L	2-3	Lillis, McNab	23,177
23	26	H	Liverpool	W	1-0	Wilson	35,584
24	28	H	Birmingham City	D	1-1	McNab	24,955
25	Jan 1	A	Aston Villa	W	1-0	Lillis	14,215
26	11	H	Southampton	W	1-0	Phillips	21,674
27	18	A	Tottenham Hotspur	W	2-0	Davies, Lillis	17,009
28	Feb 1	H	West Bromwich Albion	W	2-1	Davies, Power	20,540
29	8	H	Queen's Park Rangers	W	2-0	Davies, Simpson	20,414
30	11	A	Everton	L	0-4		29,811
31	Mar 1	H	Oxford United	L	0-3		20,099
32	8	A	Chelsea	L	0-1		17,573
33	15	H	Watford	L	0-1		18,899
34	22	A	Manchester United	D	2-2	Wilson, Albiston (og)	51,274
35	29	H	Aston Villa	D	2-2	McNab, Wilson	20,935
36	31	A	Liverpool	L	0-2		43,316
37	Apr 5	H	Arsenal	L	0-1		19,590
38	12	A	Ipswich Town	D	0-0		13,740
39	19	H	Nottingham Forest	L	1-2	Davies	19,715
40	26	A	Newcastle United	L	1-3	Davies	23,479
41	28	A	West Ham United	L	0-1		27,153
42	May 3	H	Luton Town	D	1-1	Davies	20,361
							Appearances
							Sub appearances
						Two own goals	Goals

FA Cup

Round	Date	Venue	Opponents	Result		Scorers	Attendance
R3	Jan 4	A	Walsall	W	3-1	Simpson 2, Davies	10,779
R4	25	H	Watford	D	1-1	Davies	31,632
rep	Feb 3	A	Watford	D	0-0e	19,347	
rep2	6	H	Watford	L	1-3	Kinsey	27,260
							Appearances
							Sub appearances
							Goals

League Cup

Round	Date	Venue	Opponents	Result		Scorers	Attendance
R2/1	Sep 25	A	Bury	W	2-1	Melrose, Wilson	11,377
R2/2	Oct 8	H	Bury	W	2-1	Lillis, Melrose	9,799
R3	30	H	Arsenal	L	1-2	Davies	18,279
							Appearances
							Sub appearances
							Goals

Full Members Cup

Round	Date	Venue	Opponents	Result		Scorers	Attendance
Gp	Oct 14	H	Leeds United	W	6-1	Davies 3, Baker, Lillis, Power	4,029
Gp	22	A	Sheffield United	W	2-1	Phillips, Baker	3,420
NSF	Nov 4	H	Sunderland	D	0-0e	6,642	
NF1	26	A	Hull City	L	1-2	Phillips	5,213
NF2	Dec 11	H	Hull City	W	2-0	Phillips, Melrose	10,180
F	Mar 23	N	Charlton Athletic	L	4-5	Lillis 2 (1 pen), Kinsey, Rougvie (og)	68,000

Nov 4: Won 4-3 on penalties
Final at Wembley Stadium

	Appearances
	Sub appearances
One own goal	Goals

Williams A	Phillips DO	Power PC	Clements KH	Johnson NM	Wilson CEA	Lillis MA	McNab N	Kinsey S	McIlroy SB	Simpson PD	McCarthy MJ	May AMP	Tolmie J	Beckford DRL	Smith GD	Melrose JM	Nixon EW	Baker GE	Davies GJ	Reid NS	Moulden PAJ	Redmond S	Siddall BA	Barrett ED
1	2	3	4	5	6	7	8	9	10	11														
1	2	3	4		6	7	8	9	10	11	5													
1	**6**	3	4			7	8	9	10	11	5	2	12											
1	6		4		3	7	8	9	10	11	5	2												
1	6		4		3	7	8	9	10	11	5	2												
1	6		4		3		8	9	10	11	5	2		**7**	12									
1	6		4		3	7	8	9	**10**	11	5	2				12								
1	6	8	4		3	7		**9**	10	11	5	2				12								
	6	8	4		3	7			10	11	5	2				9	1							
	6	3	4		8	7		12	**10**		5	2	11			9	1							
	6	3	4		8	7	10			11	5	2	12			**9**	1							
	6	3	4			7	10			11	5	2					1	8	9					
	6	11		4		7	10				5	3					1	8	9	2				
	6	3	4			7	10			11	5						1	8	9	2				
	6	8	4			7	10			**11**	5	3				12	1		9	2				
	6	8	4			7	10			11	5	3					1		9	2				
	6	3	4		11	7	10			12	5	8					1		**9**	2				
	6	3	4		11	7	10			12	5	8					1		**9**	2				
	6	3		4	**11**	7	10				5	8					1	12	9	2				
	6	3	4			7	10			11	5	**8**				12	1		9	2				
	6	3	4			7	10			11	**5**	8				12	1		9	2				
	6	3	4		8	**7**	10			11		5				12	1		9	2				
	6	3	4		11		10				5	8				7	1		9	2				
	6	3	4		**11**	7	10			12	5	8					1		9	2				
	6	3	4			7	10			11	5	8					1			2	9			
	6	3	4			7	10			11	5	8					1		9	2				
	6	3	4			7	10			11	5	8					1		9	2				
	6	3	4			7	10			11	5	8					1		9	2				
	6	3				7				11	5	8					1	10	9	2		4		
	6	3				7	10			11	5	12					1	**8**	9	2		4		
	6	3	4	5		7	10			11							1	8	9	2				
	6	3	4			7	10			11	5	8					1		9	2				
	6	3	4			7	10			11	5	8					1		**9**	2	12			
	6	3	**4**		11	7	10	9		12		8					1			2		5		
	6	3			11	7	10	9		12	5	8					1			2		4		
	6	3			11	7		9		10	5	8								2		4	1	
	6	3			8		10	9		11	5								7	2		4	1	
		3			9	10	8				5	7		11				6		2		4	1	
		3			12	7	10			11	5	8						6	**9**	2		4	1	
		3			11	7	10			12	5	8						6	9	2		4	1	
	2				6	7	10		8	**11**	5	3		12					9	4			1	
	6				11	7	10		8	12	5	3					1		9	**4**				2
8	39	36	30	4	24	39	37	12	12	30	38	36	1	2		4	28	9	26	30	1	9	6	1
					1			1		7		1	2	1	1	6		1			1			
	1	1			5	11	4		1	8						1			9					

Williams A	Phillips DO	Power PC	Clements KH	Johnson NM	Wilson CEA	Lillis MA	McNab N	Kinsey S	McIlroy SB	Simpson PD	McCarthy MJ	May AMP	Tolmie J	Beckford DRL	Smith GD	Melrose JM	Nixon EW	Baker GE	Davies GJ	Reid NS	Moulden PAJ	Redmond S	Siddall BA	Barrett ED
	6	3	4			7	10			11	5	8					1		**9**	2	12			
	6	3	4			7	10			11	5	8					1		9	2				
6	3	4			7	10	12		**11**	5	8					1		9	2					
	6	3	4			7	**10**	12		11	5	8					1		9	2				
	4	4	4			4	4			4	4	4					4		4	4				
								2													1			
								1		2									2					

Williams A	Phillips DO	Power PC	Clements KH	Johnson NM	Wilson CEA	Lillis MA	McNab N	Kinsey S	McIlroy SB	Simpson PD	McCarthy MJ	May AMP	Tolmie J	Beckford DRL	Smith GD	Melrose JM	Nixon EW	Baker GE	Davies GJ	Reid NS	Moulden PAJ	Redmond S	Siddall BA	Barrett ED
	6	3	4		8	7			10	11	5	2				9	1							
	6	3	4			7	10			11	5	2				9	1	8						
	6	3	4			7	10			11	5					12	1	**8**	9	2				
	3	3	3		1	3	2		1	3	3	2				2	3	2	1	1				
																1								
					1	1										2			1					

Williams A	Phillips DO	Power PC	Clements KH	Johnson NM	Wilson CEA	Lillis MA	McNab N	Kinsey S	McIlroy SB	Simpson PD	McCarthy MJ	May AMP	Tolmie J	Beckford DRL	Smith GD	Melrose JM	Nixon EW	Baker GE	Davies GJ	Reid NS	Moulden PAJ	Redmond S	Siddall BA	Barrett ED
		3	4	5		7	10			11		6	13			12	1	8	**9**	2				
	6	3		5		7	10		**11**	12		2					1	8	9	4				
6	10	4	5		7				11		3			12	**8**	1			9	2	13			
	6	3	4		11		10			12	5	8				**7**	1		9	2				
	6	3	4			7			10	**11**	5	8				12	1		9	2				
	6	3			11	7	10	9		13	5	8					1	12		**2**		4		
	5	6	4	3	2	5	4	1	2	3	3	6				2	6	2	5	6		1		
										3			1		1	2		1			1			
	3	1				3		1								1		2	3					

League Table

	P	W	D	L	F	A	Pts
Liverpool	42	26	10	6	89	37	88
Everton	42	26	8	8	87	41	86
West Ham U	42	26	6	10	74	40	84
Manchester U	42	22	10	10	70	36	76
Sheffield W	42	21	10	11	63	54	73
Chelsea	42	20	11	11	57	56	71
Arsenal	42	20	9	13	49	47	69
Nottingham F	42	19	11	12	69	53	68
Luton T	42	18	12	12	61	44	66
Tottenham H	42	19	8	15	74	52	65
Newcastle U	42	17	12	13	67	72	63
Watford	42	16	11	15	69	62	59
Q.P.R.	42	15	7	20	53	64	52
Southampton	42	12	10	20	51	62	46
Manchester C	42	11	12	19	43	57	45
Aston Villa	42	10	14	18	51	67	44
Coventry C	42	11	10	21	48	71	43
Oxford U	42	10	12	20	62	80	42
Leicester C	42	10	12	20	54	76	42
Ipswich T	42	11	8	23	32	55	41
Birmingham C	42	8	5	29	30	73	29
W.B.A.	42	4	12	26	35	89	24

1986-87

Division One

Manager: Billy McNeill MBE (until 20 September 1986), Jimmy Frizzell

Did you know that?

Match 6: Barrett's last League game.
Match 9: Christie's last game.
Match 5: Davies's last game.
Match 10: Hopkins's last game.
Match 20: McIlroy's last game.
Match 26: Beckford's last game.
Match 32: Grealish's last game.
Match 33: Reid's last game.
Match 37: Barnes's last League game.
Match 38: Baker's last game.
Match 42: Wilson, McCarthy, Langley and May's last game.

Play-offs to determine one of the promotion places were introduced this season, and Chairman Peter Swales was one of their strongest supporters. The first season the team finishing 20th in Division One would not be automatically relegated and would compete in the play-offs against Second Division sides. Swales admitted in an interview early in the season that he wouldn't mind being involved in the mini-tournament as a means of generating more income. Sadly, that comment seemed to be the kiss of death and City weren't good enough to reach 20th place, never mind safety.

Match No.	Date	Venue	Opponents	Result		Scorers	Attendance
1	Aug 23	H	Wimbledon	W	3-1	Baker 2, Christie	20,756
2	25	A	Liverpool	D	0-0		39,989
3	30	A	Tottenham Hotspur	L	0-1		23,164
4	Sep 3	H	Norwich City	D	2-2	Christie 2	19,122
5	6	H	Coventry City	L	0-1		18,320
6	13	A	Oxford United	D	0-0		8,250
7	20	H	Queen's Park Rangers	D	0-0		17,774
8	27	A	Luton Town	L	0-1		9,371
9	Oct 4	H	Leicester City	L	1-2	Hopkins	18,033
10	11	A	Newcastle United	L	1-3	Simpson	21,897
11	18	A	Chelsea	L	1-2	Varadi	12,990
12	26	H	Manchester United	D	1-1	McCarthy	32,440
13	Nov 1	A	Southampton	D	1-1	Baker	14,352
14	8	H	Aston Villa	W	3-1	Moulden 2, Varadi	22,875
15	15	H	Charlton Athletic	W	2-1	Moulden, Simpson	20,578
16	22	A	Arsenal	L	0-3		29,008
17	29	H	Everton	L	1-3	Moulden	27,097
18	Dec 6	A	Nottingham Forest	L	0-2		19,129
19	13	H	West Ham United	W	3-1	Varadi 2, White	19,067
20	21	A	Coventry City	D	2-2	Redmond 2	12,689
21	26	H	Sheffield Wednesday	W	1-0	Simpson	30,193
22	28	A	Charlton Athletic	L	0-5		7,697
23	Jan 1	A	Watford	D	1-1	Varadi	15,514
24	3	H	Oxford United	W	1-0	McNab (pen)	20,724
25	17	H	Liverpool	L	0-1		35,336
26	24	A	Wimbledon	D	0-0		5,672
27	Feb 14	A	Norwich City	D	1-1	Brightwell	15,623
28	21	H	Luton Town	D	1-1	Lake	17,507
29	28	A	Queen's Park Rangers	L	0-1		10,715
30	Mar 7	A	Manchester United	L	0-2		48,619
31	14	H	Chelsea	L	1-2	McNab	19,819
32	21	H	Newcastle United	D	0-0		23,060
33	28	A	Leicester City	L	0-4		10,743
34	Apr 4	A	Aston Villa	D	0-0		18,241
35	11	H	Southampton	L	2-4	Moulden, Stewart	18,193
36	15	H	Tottenham Hotspur	D	1-1	McNab (pen)	21,460
37	18	H	Watford	L	1-2	McNab (pen)	18,541
38	20	A	Sheffield Wednesday	L	1-2	Varadi	19,769
39	25	H	Arsenal	W	3-0	Varadi 2, Stewart	18,072
40	May 2	A	Everton	D	0-0		37,548
41	4	H	Nottingham Forest	W	1-0	Varadi	21,405
42	9	A	West Ham United	L	0-2		18,413
							Appearances
							Sub appearances
							Goals

FA Cup

R3	Jan 10	A	Manchester United	L	0-1		54,297
							Appearances
							Sub appearances

League Cup

R2/1	Sep 23	A	Southend United	D	0-0		6,182
R2/2	Oct 8	H	Southend United	W	2-1	McNab, Simpson	9,373
R3	Oct 28	A	Arsenal	L	1-3	Simpson	21,604
							Appearances
							Sub appearances
							Goals

Full Members Cup

R2	Nov 4	H	Wimbledon	W	3-1	Moulden 2, Clements	4,914
R3	26	H	Watford	W	1-0	Moulden	6,393
R4	Jan 31	H	Ipswich Town	L	2-3	Varadi 2	11,027
							Appearances
							Sub appearances
							Goals

Suckling PJ	May AMP	Wilson CEA	Clements KH	McCarthy MJ	Redmond S	Davies GJ	McNab N	Christie TJ	Baker GE	Brightwell IR	Simpson PD	Barrett ED	Hopkins RA	Beckford DRL	Moulden PAJ	White D	Varadi I	Gidman J	Grealish AP	Reid NS	McIlroy SB	Barnes PS	Lake PA	Stewart PA	Langley KJ	Nixon EW
1	2	3	4	5	6	7	8	9	10	11	12															
1	2	3	4	5	6	7	8	9		11	10	12														
1	2	3	4	5	6	7	8	9	12	11	10															
1	2	3		5	6	10	8	9	4		11		7													
1	3	11	2	5	6	10	8	9	4	12			7													
1	5	3	4		6		8	9		11		2	7	10												
1	2	3	4	5	6		8	9		10	11		7		12											
1	2	3	4	5	6		8	9			11		7	10		12										
1	2	3		5	4		8	9			11		6		10	7										
1	2	3	4	5	6		8			10	11		9			7										
1	2	3	4	5	6		8		12	10	11					7	9									
1		3	4	5	6		8			12	11					7	9	2	10							
1		3	4	5			8		6		11				12	7	9	2	10							
1		3	4	5			8		7		11				10		9	2	6							
1		3	4	5			8		7		11				10	12	9	2	6							
1		3	4	5			8		7		11				10	9		2	6							
1		3	4	5			8		7		11				10	9	12	2	6							
1		3	4	5			8		7						10	11	9	2	6	12						
1		3	4	5	12		8				11				10	7	9	2	6							
1		3	4	5	6		8								10	7	9			2	11					
1		3	4		6		8				11				10	7	9	2		5						
1		3	4		6		8				11				10	7	9	2		5						
1		3	4	5	6		8				11				10		9	2	7							
1		3	4	5	6		8				11				10	12	9	2	7							
1		3	4	5	6		8							10		11	9	2				7				
1	2	3	4	5	6		8				12			10			9					11	7			
1		3	4	5	6		8			7						12	9	2				11	10			
1		3	4	5	6		8			7					12		9	2				11	10			
1		3	4	5			8		6	7							9	2		10		11				
1		3	4	5	12		8		7	6	11				10		9			2						
1		3	4	5			8		6	12					10	7	9	2				11				
1		3	4	5	11		8				12					7	9	2	6					10		
1		11		5	4		8				12					7	9	2		3				10	6	
1		3	4	5			8			11						7	9	2						10	6	
1		3	4	5			8				12				11	7	9	2						10	6	
1		3	4	5			8				7						9	2				11		10	6	
1	2	3	4	5			8				7				12		9					11		10	6	
		3	2	5	4		8		6	12	11					7	9							10		1
	7	3	2	5	4		8				11						9							10	6	1
	7	3	2	5	4		8				11						9							10	6	1
	7	3	2	5	4		8				11						9							10	6	1
	7	3	2	5	4		8				11				9	12								10	6	1
37	17	42	39	39	28	5	42	9	13	12	27	1	7	4	16	19	29	22	11	6	1	8	3	11	9	5
					2				2	4	5	1			4	5	1			1						
				1	2		4	3	3	1	3		1		5	1	9						1	2		

Suckling PJ	May AMP	Wilson CEA	Clements KH	McCarthy MJ	Redmond S	Davies GJ	McNab N	Christie TJ	Baker GE	Brightwell IR	Simpson PD	Barrett ED	Hopkins RA	Beckford DRL	Moulden PAJ	White D	Varadi I	Gidman J	Grealish AP	Reid NS	McIlroy SB	Barnes PS	Lake PA	Stewart PA	Langley KJ	Nixon EW
1		3	4	5	6		8		13	12	11					7	9	2	10							
1		1	1	1	1		1				1					1	1	1	1							
									1	1																

Suckling PJ	May AMP	Wilson CEA	Clements KH	McCarthy MJ	Redmond S	Davies GJ	McNab N	Christie TJ	Baker GE	Brightwell IR	Simpson PD	Barrett ED	Hopkins RA	Beckford DRL	Moulden PAJ	White D	Varadi I	Gidman J	Grealish AP	Reid NS	McIlroy SB	Barnes PS	Lake PA	Stewart PA	Langley KJ	Nixon EW
1	2	3		5	6			9	8	10	11	4	7		12	13										
1		3	2	5	4	9	8				11		6		10	7										
1		3	4	5	10		8		12	6	11					7	9	2								
3	1	3	2	3	3	1	2	1	1	2	3	1	2		1	2	1	1								
									1						1	1										
							1				2															

Suckling PJ	May AMP	Wilson CEA	Clements KH	McCarthy MJ	Redmond S	Davies GJ	McNab N	Christie TJ	Baker GE	Brightwell IR	Simpson PD	Barrett ED	Hopkins RA	Beckford DRL	Moulden PAJ	White D	Varadi I	Gidman J	Grealish AP	Reid NS	McIlroy SB	Barnes PS	Lake PA	Stewart PA	Langley KJ	Nixon EW
1	2	3	4	5	6						11				8	7	9		10							
1	12	3		5	4		8		7		11				10		9	2	6							
1		3	4	5			8				7						9	2	6			11	10			
3	1	3	2	3	2		2		1		3				2	1	3	2	3			1	1			
	1																									
			1												3		2									

League Table

	P	W	D	L	F	A	Pts
Everton	42	26	8	8	76	31	86
Liverpool	42	23	8	11	72	42	77
Tottenham H	42	21	8	13	68	43	71
Arsenal	42	20	10	12	58	35	70
Norwich C	42	17	17	8	53	51	68
Wimbledon	42	19	9	14	57	50	66
Luton T	42	18	12	12	47	45	66
Nottingham F	42	18	11	13	64	51	65
Watford	42	18	9	15	67	54	63
Coventry C	42	17	12	13	50	45	63
Manchester U	42	14	14	14	52	45	56
Southampton	42	14	10	18	69	68	52
Sheffield W	42	13	13	16	58	59	52
Chelsea	42	13	13	16	53	64	52
West Ham U	42	14	10	18	52	67	52
Q.P.R.	42	13	11	18	48	64	50
Newcastle U	42	12	11	19	47	65	47
Oxford U	42	11	13	18	44	69	46
Charlton A	42	11	11	20	45	55	44
Leicester C	42	11	9	22	54	76	42
Manchester C	42	8	15	19	36	57	39
Aston Villa	42	8	12	22	45	79	36

1987-88

Division Two

Manager: Mel Machin

Did you know that?

Match 10: Mimm's last game.
Match 25: Suckling's last game.
Match 28: Adcock's last game.
Match 35: Clements's last game.
Match 41: Gidman's last game.
Match 42: Lennon's first and only game.
Match 43: Stowell's last game.
Match 44: Nixon and Stewart's last game.

All four goalkeepers used in first-team games were to play their last City match during this season.

Match No.	Date	Venue	Opponents	Result		Scorers	Attendance
1	Aug 15	H	Plymouth Argyle	W	2-1	Stewart, Varadi	20,046
2	22	A	Oldham Athletic	D	1-1	Varadi	16,008
3	31	A	Aston Villa	D	1-1	Scott	16,282
4	Sep 5	H	Blackburn Rovers	L	1-2	Scott	20,372
5	12	A	Shrewsbury Town	D	0-0		6,280
6	16	H	Millwall	W	4-0	Gidman, Scott, Stewart, White	15,430
7	19	H	Stoke City	W	3-0	Varadi 3	19,322
8	26	A	Leeds United	L	0-2		25,270
9	29	A	Hull City	L	1-3	Stewart (pen)	9,650
10	Oct 3	H	Leicester City	W	4-2	Stewart 2, Varadi 2	16,481
11	10	H	Sheffield United	L	2-3	Brightwell, White	18,377
12	17	A	Ipswich Town	L	0-3		12,624
13	21	A	Bradford City	W	4-2	Stewart 2, Lake, White	14,819
14	24	H	Barnsley	D	1-1	Varadi	17,063
15	31	A	Swindon Town	W	4-3	White 2, Simpson, Varadi	11,536
16	Nov 4	H	Middlesbrough	D	1-1	Hinchcliffe	18,434
17	7	H	Huddersfield Town	W	10-1	Adcock 3, Stewart 3, White 3, McNab	19,583
18	14	A	Reading	W	2-0	Stewart 2	10,272
19	21	H	Birmingham City	W	3-0	White 2, Stewart	22,690
20	28	A	West Bromwich Albion	D	1-1	Adcock	15,425
21	Dec 1	A	Bournemouth	W	2-0	Stewart, White	9,499
22	5	H	Crystal Palace	L	1-3	Lake	23,161
23	12	A	Millwall	W	1-0	Adcock	10,477
24	19	H	Oldham Athletic	L	1-2	Stewart	22,518
25	26	H	Leeds United	L	1-2	White	30,153
26	28	A	Stoke City	W	3-1	Stewart 2, Brightwell	18,020
27	Jan 2	H	Shrewsbury Town	L	1-3	Lake (pen)	21,455
28	16	A	Plymouth Argyle	L	2-3	McNab, Stewart	13,291
29	23	H	Aston Villa	L	0-2		24,668
30	Feb 6	A	Blackburn Rovers	L	1-2	Varadi	13,508
31	13	H	Bournemouth	W	2-0	Stewart, Varadi	16,161
32	27	A	Leicester City	L	0-1		13,852
33	Mar 2	H	Hull City	W	2-0	Varadi 2	16,040
34	5	H	Ipswich Town	W	2-0	Morley, Varadi	17,402
35	8	A	Sheffield United	W	2-1	Morley, White	13,906
36	19	H	Swindon Town	D	1-1	Stewart	17,022
37	26	A	Barnsley	L	1-3	Varadi	9,061
38	Apr 2	A	Huddersfield Town	L	0-1		7,835
39	4	H	Reading	W	2-0	Stewart 2 (1 pen)	15,172
40	9	A	Middlesbrough	L	1-2	Thompstone	19,443
41	23	H	Bradford City	D	2-2	Brightwell, Morley	20,338
42	30	A	Birmingham City	W	3-0	Brightwell 2, Varadi	8,014
43	May 2	H	West Bromwich Albion	W	4-2	Stewart 2 (2 pens), Morley, Varadi	16,490
44	7	A	Crystal Palace	L	0-2		17,550
							Appearances
							Sub appearances
							Goals

FA Cup

Round	Date	Venue	Opponents	Result		Scorers	Attendance
R3	Jan 9	A	Huddersfield Town	D	2-2	Brightwell, Gidman	18,102
rep	12	H	Huddersfield Town	D	0-0e	24,565	1
rep2	25	A	Huddersfield Town	W	3-0	Hinchcliffe, Varadi, White	21,510
R4	30	A	Blackpool	D	1-1	Lake	10,835
rep	Feb 3	H	Blackpool	W	2-1	Simpson, Stewart	26,503
R5	20	H	Plymouth Argyle	W	3-1	Moulden, Scott, Simpson	29,206
R6	Mar 13	H	Liverpool	L	0-4		44,047
							Appearances
							Sub appearances
							Goals

League Cup

Round	Date	Venue	Opponents	Result		Scorers	Attendance
R2/1	Sep 22	H	Wolverhampton W.	L	1-2	Adcock	8,551
R2/2	Oct 6	A	Wolverhampton W.	W	2-0	Gidman, Hinchcliffe	13,843
R3	27	H	Nottingham Forest	W	3-0	Varadi 2, Stewart	15,168
R4	Nov 17	H	Watford	W	3-1	White 2, Stewart	20,357
R5	Jan 20	A	Everton	L	0-2		40,014
							Appearances
							Sub appearances
							Goals

Full Members Cup

Round	Date	Venue	Opponents	Result		Scorers	Attendance
R1	Nov 10	H	Plymouth Argyle	W	6-2	Hinchcliffe, Adcock 3, Stewart, Lake	5,051
R2	Dec 16	H	Chelsea	L	0-2		6,402
							Appearances
							Sub appearances
							Goals

Nixon EW	Gidman J	Hinchcliffe AG	Clements KH	Brightwell IR	Redmond S	White D	Stewart PA	Varadi I	Scott IJ	McNab N	Simpson PD	Adcock AC	Lake PA	Barnes PS	Mimms RA	Seagraves M	Suckling PJ	Moulden PAJ	Morley TW	Stowell M	Beckford JN	Thompstone IP	Lennon NF
1	2	3	4	**5**	6	7	8	9	10	11	12	13											
1	2	3	4	5	6	7	8	9	10	11													
1	2	3	4	5	6	7	8		10	11		9											
1	2	3	4	5	6	**7**	8		10	11	12	9											
1	2	3		**5**	6	7	8	9	10	11	12		4										
1	2	3			6	7	8	9	10	11	5		4										
1	2	3			6	7	8	9	10	11	5		4										
	2	3			6	7	8	9	10	11	5	13	**4**		1	12							
	2	3		11	6	**7**	8	9	10	12	5		13		1	4							
	2	3		11	6	12	8	9	**10**	7			5		1	4							
1	2	3	12	11	6	9	8		10	7	13		5			**4**							
1		3	4	5	6	2	8	12		7	10		9			**11**							
1	2	3	4	5	6	12	8	9		10	11		**7**										
1	2	3	4	5	6	12	8	9	**7**	10	11												
1	2	3	4	5	6	7	8	9		10	**11**		12										
1	2	3	4	5	6	7	8	9		**10**	11	12	13										
1	2	3	4		6	7	8			10	11	9	5										
1	2		4	3	6	7	8		12	10	**11**	9	5										
1	2	3	4		6	7	8			10	11	9	5										
1	2	3	4	13	6	7	8	12		10	**11**	9	5										
1	2	3	4		6	7	8	12		10	11	**9**	5										
1	2	3	4		6	7	8			10	11	9	5										
1	2	3			6	7	8			10	11	9	5			4							
	2	3	4		6	**7**	8	12	10		11	9	5				1						
		3	4	2	6	7	8	9	10		11		5				1						
1		3	4	2	6	7	8	**9**	12	10	11		5										
1		3	4	2	6	7		9	12	10	**11**	8	5			13							
1	2	3	4	**5**	6	7	8	12		10	13	9	11										
1	2	3	4	**5**	6	7	8	12			11		9						10				
		3		2	6	7	8	9		4	11		5						10	1			
	2	3			6	7	8	9	10	4	11		5							1			
	2	3			6	7	8	9	10	**5**	11					4			12	1			
			2	3	6	7	8	9	**10**	4	11		5						12	1			
		3	2	4	6	7		9	10		11		5						8	1			
		3	2	4	6	7		9	10		11		**5**			12		13	8	1			
		3		2	6	7	8	9		10	11		4						5	1			
		3		2	6	7	8	9		10	**11**		4			12		13	5	1			
	2	3		5	6	7	8	9			12		**10**			4		13	11	1			
	2	3		5	6	7	8			10	11					4			9	1			
	2	3		5	6	7					11					4		8	**10**	1	9	12	
	12	3		5	6	7	8			10			**2**			4		13	9	1	11		
		3		5	6	12	8	11		10						4			9	1	7		**2**
		3		5	6	2	8	11		10						4			9	1	7		
1		3		**5**	6	2	8		12	10	13					4		11	9		7		
25	30	42	24	32	44	40	40	26	19	36	31	12	30		3	13	2	2	13	14	5		1
	1		1	1		4		6	4	1	7	3	3			4		4	2			1	
	1	1		5		13	24	17	3	2	1	5	3						4			1	

Nixon EW	Gidman J	Hinchcliffe AG	Clements KH	Brightwell IR	Redmond S	White D	Stewart PA	Varadi I	Scott IJ	McNab N	Simpson PD	Adcock AC	Lake PA	Barnes PS	Mimms RA	Seagraves M	Suckling PJ	Moulden PAJ	Morley TW	Stowell M	Beckford JN	Thompstone IP	Lennon NF
1	2	3	4	5	6	**7**		9	11	10	12	8						13					
2	3	4	**5**	6	7	8	13	11	10	12	9												
1	2	3	4	12	6	7	8	9		10	11		**5**										
1	2	3	4	12	6	7	8			10	11		5					**9**					
1	2	3	4		6	7	8	9		10	11		5										
1	2	3			6	7	8	**9**	10	5	11					4		12					
	2	3		4	6	7	8	9		10	11		5							1			
6	7	7	5	3	7	7	6	5	3	7	5	2	4			1		1		1			
				2				1			2							2					
	1	1		1		1	1	1	1		2		1					1					

Nixon EW	Gidman J	Hinchcliffe AG	Clements KH	Brightwell IR	Redmond S	White D	Stewart PA	Varadi I	Scott IJ	McNab N	Simpson PD	Adcock AC	Lake PA	Barnes PS	Mimms RA	Seagraves M
1	2	3			6	7		9	10	11	**5**	8	4	12		
1	2	3		11	6		8	**9**	10	7		12	5			4
1	2	3	4	5	6	7	8	9		10	11					
1	2		4	3	6	7	8	12		10	11	**9**	5			
1	2	3	**4**	5	6	7	8	13	12	10	11		9			
5	5	4	3	4	5	4	4	3	2	5	4	2	4			1
								2	1			1		1		
	1	1				2	2	2				1				

Nixon EW	Gidman J	Hinchcliffe AG	Clements KH	Brightwell IR	Redmond S	White D	Stewart PA	Varadi I	Scott IJ	McNab N	Simpson PD	Adcock AC	Lake PA	Barnes PS	Mimms RA	Seagraves M
1	**2**	3	4	12	6	7	8		13	10	11	9	5			
1	2	3			6	**7**	8	13	12	10	11	9	5			4
2	2	2	1		2	2	2			2	2	2	2			1
				1				1	2							
		1					1					3	1			

League Table

	P	W	D	L	F	A	Pts
Millwall	44	25	7	12	72	52	82
Aston Villa	44	22	12	10	68	41	78
Middlesbrough	44	22	12	10	63	36	78
Bradford C	44	22	11	11	74	54	77
Blackburn R	44	21	14	9	68	52	77
Crystal Palace	44	22	9	13	86	59	75
Leeds U	44	19	12	13	61	51	69
Ipswich T	44	19	9	16	61	52	66
Manchester C	44	19	8	17	80	60	65
Oldham A	44	18	11	15	72	64	65
Stoke C	44	17	11	16	50	57	62
Swindon T	44	16	11	17	73	60	59
Leicester C	44	16	11	17	62	61	59
Barnsley	44	15	12	17	61	62	57
Hull C	44	14	15	15	54	60	57
Plymouth A	44	16	8	20	65	67	56
Bournemouth	44	13	10	21	56	68	49
Shrewsbury T	44	11	16	17	42	54	49
Birmingham C	44	11	15	18	41	66	48
W.B.A.	44	12	11	21	50	69	47
Sheffield U	44	13	7	24	45	74	46
Reading	44	10	12	22	44	70	42
Huddersfield T	44	6	10	28	41	100	28

1988-89

Division Two

Manager: Mel Machin

Did you know that?

Match 2: Simpson's last League game.
Match 3: Varadi's last game.
Match 10: Williams' first and only game.
Match 38: Scott's last game.
Match 39: Bradshaw's last game.
Match 44: Biggins's last game.
Match 46: Moulden's last game.

Against both Walsall (Match 36) and Crystal Palace (Match 44) Nigel Gleghorn replaced Andy Dibble in nets due to injury during the game. Against Palace Gleghorn had earlier netted a goal, and in the Walsall game he was the undisputed star as City had been 2–0 down when he went in nets and ended the game 3–3. The points in both games were vital in City's promotion challenge.

Match No.	Date	Venue	Opponents	Result		Scorers	Attendance
1	Aug 27	A	Hull City	L	0-1		11,653
2	29	H	Oldham Athletic	L	1-4	Lake	22,594
3	Sep 3	H	Walsall	D	2-2	McNab (pen), Morley	17,104
4	10	A	Leeds United	D	1-1	McNab (pen)	23,677
5	17	H	Brighton & Hove Alb.	W	2-1	Brightwell, Moulden	16,033
6	20	A	Chelsea	W	3-1	Brightwell 2, Moulden	8,071
7	24	A	Barnsley	W	2-1	Morley, White	9,300
8	Oct 1	H	Blackburn Rovers	W	1-0	Biggins	22,111
9	5	H	Portsmouth	W	4-1	Biggins, Lake, Moulden, White	17,202
10	8	A	Ipswich Town	L	0-1		15,799
11	15	A	Plymouth Argyle	W	1-0	Gayle	10,158
12	22	H	Birmingham City	D	0-0		20,205
13	26	A	West Bromwich Albion	L	0-1		14,258
14	29	H	Sunderland	D	1-1	Hinchcliffe	22,398
15	Nov 5	A	Leicester City	D	0-0		14,080
16	12	H	Watford	W	3-1	Biggins 2, Moulden	21,142
17	19	A	Bournemouth	W	1-0	Moulden	9,874
18	26	H	Oxford United	W	2-1	Morley, Redmond	20,145
19	Dec 3	A	Crystal Palace	D	0-0		12,274
20	10	H	Bradford City	W	4-0	Brightwell 2, Moulden 2	20,129
21	17	H	Shrewsbury Town	D	2-2	Hinchcliffe 2 (1 pen)	19,613
22	26	A	Stoke City	L	1-3	Gleghorn	24,059
23	31	A	Swindon Town	W	2-1	Beckford, Gayle	10,776
24	Jan 2	H	Leeds United	D	0-0		33,034
25	14	A	Oldham Athletic	W	1-0	Megson	19,536
26	21	H	Hull City	W	4-1	Biggins 2, Moulden, White	20,485
27	Feb 4	A	Portsmouth	W	1-0	Gleghorn	13,187
28	11	H	Ipswich Town	W	4-0	Biggins 2, Gayle, Morley	22,145
29	18	A	Birmingham City	W	2-0	Gleghorn, McNab	11,707
30	25	H	Plymouth Argyle	W	2-0	Biggins, McNab (pen)	22,451
31	Mar 1	H	West Bromwich Albion	D	1-1	Moulden	25,109
32	4	A	Watford	L	0-1		15,747
33	11	H	Leicester City	W	4-2	Morley 3, Spearing (og)	22,266
34	14	A	Sunderland	W	4-2	White 2, Gleghorn, Morley	16,167
35	18	H	Chelsea	L	2-3	McNab (pen), Taggart	40,070
36	25	A	Walsall	D	3-3	Moulden 2, Oldfield	7,562
37	27	H	Stoke City	W	2-1	Hinchcliffe (pen), Oldfield	28,303
38	Apr 1	A	Brighton & Hove Alb.	L	1-2	Morley	12,072
39	4	A	Shrewsbury Town	W	1-0	Morley	8,271
40	8	H	Swindon Town	W	2-1	Hinchcliffe (pen), Oldfield	22,663
41	15	A	Blackburn Rovers	L	0-4		16,927
42	22	H	Barnsley	L	1-2	Lake	21,274
43	29	A	Oxford United	W	4-2	Brightwell, Gleghorn, White, Greenall (og)	7,762
44	May 1	H	Crystal Palace	D	1-1	Gleghorn	33,456
45	6	H	Bournemouth	D	3-3	Moulden 2, Morley	30,564
46	13	A	Bradford City	D	1-1	Morley	12,479
							Appearances
							Sub appearances
						Two own goals	Goals

FA Cup

	Date	Venue	Opponents	Result		Scorers	Attendance
R3	Jan 7	H	Leicester City	W	1-0	McNab (pen)	23,838
R4	28	A	Brentford	L	1-3	Gleghorn	12,000
							Appearances
							Sub appearances
							Goals

League Cup

	Date	Venue	Opponents	Result		Scorers	Attendance
R2/1	Sep 28	H	Plymouth Argyle	W	1-0	White	9,454
R2/2	Oct 12	A	Plymouth Argyle	W	6-3	Gleghorn 2, Biggins, Lake, McNab (pen), Moulden	8,794
R3	Nov 2	H	Sheffield United	W	4-2	Moulden 3, Morley	16,609
R4	29	A	Luton Town	L	1-3	White	10,178
							Appearances
							Sub appearances
							Goals

Full Members Cup

	Date	Venue	Opponents	Result		Scorers	Attendance
R2	Dec 13	A	Blackburn Rovers	L	2-3e	Gleghorn, Hendrie (og)	5,763
							Appearances
							Sub appearances
						One own goal	Goals

Dibble AG	Lake PA	Hinchcliffe AG	Gayle BW	Brightwell IR	Redmond S	White D	Biggins W	Morley TW	McNab N	Gleghorn NW	Varadi I	Simpson PD	Seagraves M	Moulden PAJ	Beckford JN	Williams W	Hughes ME	Bradshaw C	Scott IJ	Megson GJ	Taggart GP	Oldfield DC	Cooper PD
1	2	3	4	5	6	7	8	9	10	11	12												
1	2	3	4	5	6	7	8	9	10		12	11	13										
1	7	3	4	5	6	12		9	10	11	8		2	13									
1	11	3	4	5	6	7		9	10				2	8									
1	11	3	4	5	6	7		9	10				2	8									
1	11	3	4	5	6	7		9	10				2	8									
1	11	3	4	5	6	7		9	10				2	8									
1	11	3	4		6	7	5	9	10				2	8									
1	11	3	4		6	7	5	9	10				2	8									
1	11	3	4		6	7	5	9	10				2	8		12							
1		3	4		6	7	5	9	10	2				8	12		11						
1	11	3	4	13	6	7	5	9	10	2			12	8									
1		3	4	5	6	7	11	9	10	2				8				12					
1		3	4	5	6	7	11		10	8			2		12			9					
1		3	4	5	6	7	11	9	10				2	8									
1		3	4	5	6	7	11	9	10				2	8									
1		3	4	5	6	7	11	9	10				2	8									
1	3		4	5	6	7	11	9	10	13			2	8	12								
1	3		4	5	6	7	11	9	10	13			2	8				12					
1	12	3	4	5	6	7		9	10	11			2	8	13								
1	10	3	4	5	6	7	12	9		11			2	8									
1	10	3	4	5	6	7	11	9		8			2	13	12								
1	8	3	4	5	6	7	11		10	12			2		9								
1	8	3	4	5	6	7	11	13	10	12			2		9								
1	9	3	4	13	6	7	11		10	12			2	8						5			
1	9	3	4		6	7	11		10				2	8						5			
1	2		4		6	7	11	8	10	9										5	3		
1	2		4		6	7	11	8	10	9										5	3		
1	2		4		6	7	11	8	10	9										5	3		
1	2	12	4		6	7	11	8	10	9				13						5	3		
1	2	12	4		6	7	11	8	10	9				13						5	3		
1	2	3	4		6	7	11	8	10	9				12						5			
1	2	3	4		6		11	8	10	9				7	13					5	12		
1		3	4		6	7		8	10	9										5	2	11	
1	2		4		6	7		8	10	9				12						5	3	11	
1	2		4		6	7			10	9				8				12		5	3	11	
	2	3	4		6	7		11	10	12				8						5		9	1
	4	3		2	6	7		11		12				8					10	5	13	9	1
	2	3	4		6	7	11	8		9								12		5		10	1
	2	3	4		6	7	11	9	10					8						5		12	1
		3	4		6	7	11	8	10					12						5	2	9	1
	2	3	4		6	7	12		10	11				8						5		9	1
1	2	3		5	6	7		9	10	11				8						4			
1	2	3		5	6	7	13	9	10	11				8						4		12	
	2	3		5	6	7		9	10	11				8						4		12	1
	2	3		5	6	7		9	10	11				8						4			1
38	37	37	41	24	46	44	29	39	42	25	1	1	21	29	2		1	1	1	22	9	8	8
	1	2		2		1	3	1		7	2		2	7	6	1		4			2	3	
	3	5	3	6	1	6	9	12	5	6				13	1					1	1	3	

Dibble AG	Lake PA	Hinchcliffe AG	Gayle BW	Brightwell IR	Redmond S	White D	Biggins W	Morley TW	McNab N	Gleghorn NW	Varadi I	Simpson PD	Seagraves M	Moulden PAJ	Beckford JN	Williams W	Hughes ME	Bradshaw C	Scott IJ	Megson GJ	Taggart GP	Oldfield DC	Cooper PD
1	8	3	4	5	6	7	11		10				2	9					12				
1	9	3	4		6	7	11	8	10	12			2					13		5			
2	2	2	2	1	2	2	2	1	2				2	1						1			
										1								1	1				
									1	1													

Dibble AG	Lake PA	Hinchcliffe AG	Gayle BW	Brightwell IR	Redmond S	White D	Biggins W	Morley TW	McNab N	Gleghorn NW	Varadi I	Simpson PD	Seagraves M	Moulden PAJ	Beckford JN	Williams W	Hughes ME	Bradshaw C	Scott IJ	Megson GJ	Taggart GP	Oldfield DC	Cooper PD
1	11	3	4	5	6	7	2	9	10			12		8	13								
1	11	3	4		6	7	5	9	10	2				8	12								
1		3	4	5	6		11	9	10	12			2	8	7								
1			4		6	7	11	9	10	3			2	8	12				5				
4	2	3	4	2	4	3	4	4	4	2			2	4	1				1				
										1		1			3								
	1					2	1	1	1	2				4									

Dibble AG	Lake PA	Hinchcliffe AG	Gayle BW	Brightwell IR	Redmond S	White D	Biggins W	Morley TW	McNab N	Gleghorn NW	Varadi I	Simpson PD	Seagraves M	Moulden PAJ	Beckford JN	Williams W	Hughes ME	Bradshaw C	Scott IJ	Megson GJ	Taggart GP	Oldfield DC	Cooper PD
1	2	3		5	6	7		9	10	99			4	8				12					
1	1	1		1	1	1		1	1				1	1									
										1								1					
										1													

League Table

	P	W	D	L	F	A	Pts
Chelsea	46	29	12	5	96	50	99
Manchester C	46	23	13	10	77	53	82
Crystal Palace	46	23	12	11	71	49	81
Watford	46	22	12	12	74	48	78
Blackburn R	46	22	11	13	74	59	77
Swindon T	46	20	16	10	68	53	76
Barnsley	46	20	14	12	66	58	74
Ipswich T	46	22	7	17	71	61	73
W.B.A.	46	18	18	10	65	41	72
Leeds U	46	17	16	13	59	50	67
Sunderland	46	16	15	15	60	60	63
Bournemouth	46	18	8	20	53	62	62
Stoke C	46	15	14	17	57	72	59
Bradford C	46	13	17	16	52	59	56
Leicester C	46	13	16	17	56	63	55
Oldham A	46	11	21	14	75	72	54
Oxford U	46	14	12	20	62	70	54
Plymouth A	46	14	12	20	55	66	54
Brighton & H.A.	46	14	9	23	57	66	51
Portsmouth	46	13	12	21	53	62	51
Hull C	46	11	14	21	52	68	47
Shrewsbury T	46	8	18	20	40	67	42
Birmingham C	46	8	11	27	31	76	35
Walsall	46	5	16	25	41	80	31

1989-90

Division One

Manager: Mel Machin (until 26 November 1989), Howard Kendall (from 8 December 1989)

Did you know that?

Match 2: Gleghorn's last game.
Match 9: Cooper's last game.
Match 13: Fashanu's last game.
Match 15: Gayle's last game.
Match 15: Fleming and McNab's last League game.
Match 16: Taggart's last game.
Match 17: A. Ward's last League game.
Match 19: Bishop & Morley's last game.
Match 21: Oldfield's last game.
Match 38: Hinchcliffe's last game.

Former £1 million player Justin Fashanu made two League appearances during the season as he fought to regain the form he had enjoyed during his career at Norwich and Nottingham Forest. Sadly, it was a struggle and he soon moved on to a variety of clubs, including West Ham and Torquay, before his shock death in 1998.

Match No.	Date	Venue	Opponents	Result		Scorers	Attendance
1	Aug 19	A	Liverpool	L	1-3	Hinchcliffe	35,628
2	23	H	Southampton	L	1-2	Gleghorn	25,416
3	26	H	Tottenham Hotspur	D	1-1	White	32,004
4	30	A	Coventry City	L	1-2	White	16,129
5	Sep 9	H	Queen's Park Rangers	W	1-0	Allen	23,420
6	16	A	Wimbledon	L	0-1		6,922
7	23	H	Manchester United	W	5-1	Oldfield 2, Bishop, Hinchcliffe, Morley	43,246
8	30	H	Luton Town	W	3-1	Bishop, Brightwell, Oldfield	23,863
9	Oct 14	A	Arsenal	L	0-4		40,393
10	22	H	Aston Villa	L	0-2		23,354
11	28	A	Chelsea	D	1-1	Allen	21,917
12	Nov 4	H	Crystal Palace	W	3-0	Allen, Morley, White	23,768
13	11	A	Derby County	L	0-6		19,239
14	18	H	Nottingham Forest	L	0-3		26,238
15	25	A	Charlton Athletic	D	1-1	Allen	8,857
16	Dec 2	H	Liverpool	L	1-4	Allen (pen)	31,641
17	9	A	Southampton	L	1-2	Allen	15,832
18	17	A	Everton	D	0-0		21,491
19	26	H	Norwich City	W	1-0	Allen	29,534
20	30	H	Millwall	W	2-0	White 2	28,084
21	Jan 1	A	Sheffield Wednesday	L	0-2		28,756
22	13	A	Tottenham Hotspur	D	1-1	Hendry	26,384
23	20	H	Coventry City	W	1-0	White	24,345
24	Feb 3	A	Manchester United	D	1-1	Brightwell	40,216
25	10	H	Wimbledon	D	1-1	Hendry	24,126
26	24	H	Charlton Athletic	L	1-2	White	24,030
27	Mar 3	A	Nottingham Forest	L	0-1		22,644
28	10	H	Arsenal	D	1-1	White	29,087
29	17	A	Luton Town	D	1-1	Allen (pen)	9,765
30	21	H	Chelsea	D	1-1	Quinn	24,670
31	Apr 1	A	Aston Villa	W	2-1	Reid, M Ward	24,797
32	7	A	Millwall	D	1-1	M Ward	10,267
33	11	A	Queen's Park Rangers	W	3-1	Allen, Hendry, M Ward	8,437
34	14	H	Sheffield Wednesday	W	2-1	Heath, Quinn	33,022
35	16	A	Norwich City	W	1-0	Heath	18,914
36	21	H	Everton	W	1-0	Quinn	32,144
37	28	H	Derby County	L	0-1		29,542
38	May 5	A	Crystal Palace	D	2-2	Allen (pen), Quinn	20,056
							Appearances
							Sub appearances
							Goals

FA Cup

	Date	Venue	Opponents	Result		Scorers	Attendance
R3	Jan 6	H	Millwall	D	0-0		25,038
rep	9	A	Millwall	D	1-1e	Hendry	17,616
rep2	15	A	Millwall	L	1-3	Lake	17,771
							Appearances
							Sub appearances
							Goals

League Cup

	Date	Venue	Opponents	Result		Scorers	Attendance
R2/1	Sep 19	A	Brentford	L	1-2	Oldfield	6,065
R2/2	Oct 4	H	Brentford	W	4-1	Morley 2, Oldfield, White	17,874
R3	25	H	Norwich City	W	3-1	Allen, Bishop, White	20,126
R4	Nov 22	H	Coventry City	L	0-1		23,355
							Appearances
							Sub appearances
							Goals

Full Members Cup

	Date	Venue	Opponents	Result		Scorers	Attendance
R2	Nov 29	A	Nottingham Forest	L	2-3	White, Oldfield	9,279
							Appearances
							Sub appearances
							Goals

Dibble AG	Lake PA	Hinchcliffe AG	Bishop IW	Gayle BW	Redmond S	Oldfield DC	Allen CD	Morley TW	McNab N	Gleghorn NW	White D	Fleming GJ	Cooper PD	Brightwell IR	Beckford JN	Fashanu JS	Hendry ECJ	Seagraves M	Taggart GP	Ward A	Harper A	Reid P	Megson GJ	Ward MW	Clarke W	Heath AP	Quinn NJ
1	2	3	4	5	6	7	8	9	10	11	12																
1	2	3	4	5	6	7	8	9	10	11	12	13															
	11	3	4	5	6		8	9	10		7	2	1														
		3	4	5	6		9	8	10		7	2	1	11													
	11	3	4	5	6		9	8	10		7	2	1	12													
	11	3	4	5	6	9		8	10		7	2	1	12													
	11	3	4	5	6	9		8			7	2	1	10	12												
	11	3	4	5	6	9		8	12		7	2	1	10													
	11	3	4	5	6	9	12	8			7	2	1	10													
1	11	3	4	5	6	9	13	8			7	2		10		12											
1	11	3	4	5	6	12	9	8	10		7	2															
1	11	3	4	5	6		9	8	10		7	2															
1		3	4	5	6	8	9		10		7	2		11	13	12											
1		3	4		6	8	9		10		7	2			11		5										
1		3	4	8	6	12	9	11	10		7	2					5										
1	11		4		6	12	9	10			7			8			5	2	3								
1	11	3	4		6	10	9	8			7						5	2		12							
1		3	12		6	13	9	8			7			11			5				2	4	10				
1	11	3	8		6		13	9			7			12			5				2	4	10				
1	11	3			6		9				7			12			5				2	4	10	8			
1	11	3			6	13	9				7			12			5				2	4	10	8			
1	11	3			6		9				7			12			5				2	4	10	8	13		
1	11	3			6						7			12	13		5				2	4	10	8	9		
1	11	3			6						7			4	12		5				2		10	8	9		
1	11	3			6		12				7			4			5				2		10	8	9		
1	11	3			6						7			13			5				2	4	10	8	9	12	
1	11	3			6						7			13			5				2	4	10	8	12	9	
1	11	3			6		12				7						5				2	4	10	8		9	
1	4	3			6		9				7			13			5				2		10	8	12	11	
1	2				6		9				7						5				3	4	11	8			10
1	2				6		9				7			12			5				3	4	11	8		13	10
1	2				6		9				7			12			5				3	4	11	8		13	10
1	2				6		9				7			12			5				3	4	11	8		13	10
1	2				6		9				7			12			5				3	4	11	8		13	10
1		13			6		9							2			5				3	4	11	8	12	7	10
1		13			6						7			2			5				3	4	11	8	12	9	10
1	11				6		12				7			2			5				3	4		8		9	10
1	11	12			6		13				7			2			5				3	4		8		9	10
31	31	28	18	14	38	10	23	17	11	2	35	13	7	14	1		25	2	1		21	18	19	19	4	7	9
		3	1			5	7		1		2	1		14	4	2				1					5	5	
		2	2			3	10	2		1	8			2			3					1		3		2	4

Dibble AG	Lake PA	Hinchcliffe AG	Bishop IW	Gayle BW	Redmond S	Oldfield DC	Allen CD	Morley TW	McNab N	Gleghorn NW	White D	Fleming GJ	Cooper PD	Brightwell IR	Beckford JN	Fashanu JS	Hendry ECJ	Seagraves M	Taggart GP	Ward A	Harper A	Reid P	Megson GJ	Ward MW	Clarke W	Heath AP	Quinn NJ
1	11	3			6		9				7						5			12	2	4	10	8			
1	11	3			6		9				7						5				2	4	10	8			
1	11	3			6		9				7						5			12	2	4	10	8			
3	3	3			3		3				3						3				3	3	3	3			
																				2							
	1																1										

Dibble AG	Lake PA	Hinchcliffe AG	Bishop IW	Gayle BW	Redmond S	Oldfield DC	Allen CD	Morley TW	McNab N	Gleghorn NW	White D	Fleming GJ	Cooper PD	Brightwell IR	Beckford JN	Fashanu JS	Hendry ECJ	Seagraves M	Taggart GP	Ward A	Harper A	Reid P	Megson GJ	Ward MW	Clarke W	Heath AP	Quinn NJ
	11	3	4	5	6	9		8	10		7	2	1														
	11	3	4	5	6	9		8			7	2	1	10													
1	11	3	4	5	6		9	8	10		7	2															
1	11	3	4	8	6	13	9		10		7	2		12			5										
2	4	4	4	4	4	2	2	3	3		4	4	2	1			1										
						1								1													
			1			2	1	2			2																

Dibble AG	Lake PA	Hinchcliffe AG	Bishop IW	Gayle BW	Redmond S	Oldfield DC	Allen CD	Morley TW	McNab N	Gleghorn NW	White D	Fleming GJ	Cooper PD	Brightwell IR	Beckford JN	Fashanu JS	Hendry ECJ	Seagraves M	Taggart GP	Ward A	Harper A	Reid P	Megson GJ	Ward MW	Clarke W	Heath AP	Quinn NJ
1	11	9	4	5	6	12		8	10		7	2		13					3								
1	1	1	1	1	1			1	1		1	1							1								
						1								1													
						1					1																

League Table

	P	W	D	L	F	A	Pts
Liverpool	38	23	10	5	78	37	79
Aston Villa	38	21	7	10	57	38	70
Tottenham H	38	19	6	13	59	47	63
Arsenal	38	18	8	12	54	38	62
Chelsea	38	16	12	10	58	50	60
Everton	38	17	8	13	57	46	59
Southampton	38	15	10	13	71	63	55
Wimbledon	38	13	16	9	47	40	55
Nottingham F	38	15	9	14	55	47	54
Norwich C	38	13	14	11	44	42	53
Q.P.R.	38	13	11	14	45	44	50
Coventry C	38	14	7	17	39	59	49
Manchester U	38	13	9	16	46	47	48
Manchester C	38	12	12	14	43	52	48
Crystal Palace	38	13	9	16	42	66	48
Derby Co	38	13	7	18	43	40	46
Luton T	38	10	13	15	43	57	43
Sheffield W	38	11	10	17	35	51	43
Charlton A	38	7	9	22	31	57	30
Millwall	38	5	11	22	39	65	26

1990-91

Division One

Manager: Howard Kendall (until 5 November 1990), Peter Reid

Did you know that?

Match 37: Ward's last game.
Match 38: Harper and Beckford's last game.

City's fifth-place finish was not only the best since 1977–78, it was also the first time the Blues had finished above the Reds during that spell.

Match No.	Date	Venue	Opponents	Result		Scorers	Attendance
1	Aug 25	A	Tottenham Hotspur	L	1-3	Quinn	33,501
2	Sep 1	H	Everton	W	1-0	Heath	31,456
3	5	H	Aston Villa	W	2-1	Pointon, Ward (pen)	30,199
4	8	A	Sheffield United	D	1-1	White	21,895
5	15	H	Norwich City	W	2-1	Brennan, Quinn	26,247
6	22	A	Chelsea	D	1-1	Ward (pen)	20,924
7	29	A	Wimbledon	D	1-1	Allen	6,227
8	Oct 6	H	Coventry City	W	2-0	Harper, Quinn	26,198
9	20	A	Derby County	D	1-1	Ward (pen)	17,654
10	27	H	Manchester United	D	3-3	White 2, Hendry	36,427
11	Nov 3	A	Sunderland	D	1-1	White	23,021
12	11	H	Leeds United	L	2-3	Ward (pen), White	27,782
13	17	A	Luton Town	D	2-2	Redmond, White	9,564
14	24	A	Liverpool	D	2-2	Quinn, Ward (pen)	37,849
15	Dec 1	H	Queen's Park Rangers	W	2-1	Quinn 2	25,080
16	15	H	Tottenham Hotspur	W	2-1	Redmond, Ward (pen)	31,263
17	22	H	Crystal Palace	L	0-2		25,321
18	26	A	Southampton	L	1-2	Quinn	13,572
19	29	A	Nottingham Forest	W	3-1	Quinn 2, Clarke	24,937
20	Jan 1	H	Arsenal	L	0-1		30,579
21	13	A	Everton	L	0-2		22,764
22	19	H	Sheffield United	W	2-0	Ward 2	25,741
23	Feb 2	A	Norwich City	W	2-1	Quinn 2	15,195
24	9	H	Chelsea	W	2-1	Megson, White	25,116
25	Mar 2	A	Queen's Park Rangers	L	0-1		12,746
26	5	H	Luton Town	W	3-0	Quinn 2, Allen (pen)	20,404
27	9	H	Liverpool	L	0-3		35,150
28	16	H	Wimbledon	D	1-1	Ward (pen)	21,089
29	23	A	Coventry City	L	1-3	Allen	13,195
30	30	H	Southampton	D	3-3	Allen, Brennan, White	23,163
31	Apr 1	A	Crystal Palace	W	3-1	Quinn 3	18,001
32	6	H	Nottingham Forest	W	3-1	Quinn, Redmond, Ward (pen)	25,169
33	10	A	Leeds United	W	2-1	Hill, Quinn	28,757
34	17	A	Arsenal	D	2-2	Ward (pen), White	38,409
35	20	H	Derby County	W	2-1	Quinn, White	24,037
36	23	A	Aston Villa	W	5-1	White 4, Brennan	24,168
37	May 4	A	Manchester United	L	0-1		45,286
38	11	H	Sunderland	W	3-2	Quinn 2, White	39,194
							Appearances
							Sub appearances
							Goals

FA Cup

Round	Date	Venue	Opponents	Result		Scorers	Attendance
R3	Jan 6	A	Burnley	W	1-0	Hendry	20,331
R4	26	A	Port Vale	W	2-1	Allen, Quinn	19,132
R5	Feb 16	A	Notts County	L	0-1		18,979
							Appearances
							Sub appearances
							Goals

League Cup

Round	Date	Venue	Opponents	Result		Scorers	Attendance
R2/1	Sep 26	A	Torquay United	W	4-0	Allen, Beckford, Harper, Hendry	5,249
R2/2	Oct 10	H	Torquay United	D	0-0		12,204
R3	30	H	Arsenal	L	1-2	Allen	26,825
							Appearances
							Sub appearances
							Goals

Full Members Cup

Round	Date	Venue	Opponents	Result		Scorers	Attendance
R2	Dec 19	H	Middlesbrough	W	2-1	White, Quinn	6,406
R3	Jan 22	A	Sheffield United	W	2-0	Ward 2	5,106
R4	Feb 20	A	Leeds United	L	0-2		11,898
							Appearances
							Sub appearances
							Goals

Coton AP	Brightwell IR	Pointon NG	Harper A	Hendry ECJ	Reid P	White D	Lake PA	Quinn NJ	Heath AP	Ward MW	Redmond S	Allen CD	Dibble AG	Brennan MR	Beckford JN	Megson GJ	Margetson MW	Clarke W	Hill AR	Hughes ME
1	2	3	4	5	6	7	8	9	10	11	12	13								
1	2	3	4	5	6	7	8	9	10	11										
	2	3		5	6	7	8	9	10	11	12		1	4						
1	2	3	8	5	6	7		9	10	11	4	12								
1	2	3	8	5	6	7		9	10	11	4	12		13						
1	2	3	8	5	6	7		9	10	11	4	12		13						
1	2	3	4	5		7		9	8	11	6	12		10	13					
1	2	3	10	5	4	7		9	8	11	6	12		13						
1	13	3	2	5	4	7		9	8	11	6	12				10				
1	12	3	2	5	4	7		9	8	11	6					10				
1		3	2	5	4	7		9	8	11	6	12				10				
1	13	3	2	5	4	7		9	8	11	6	12				10				
1	2	3	4	5		7		9	8	11	6			12		10				
	2	3		5	4	7		9	8	11	6	12	1			10				
	2	3		5	4	7		9	8	11	6		1			10				
1	2	3		5	4	7		9	8	11	6					10		12		
1	2	3		5	4	7		9	8	11	6					10		12		
1	2	3	12	5	4	7		9		11	6					10		8		
1	2	3		5	4	7		9	8	11	6					10		12		
1	2	3		5	4	7		9		11	6					10		8		
1	2	3	13	5	4	7		9	8	11	6	12				10				
1	2	3		5	4	7		9		11	6	8				10				
1	2	3	4	5		7		9	12	11	6	8				10				
1	2	3	4	5		7		9	12	11	6	8				10				
1	2	3	13	5	4	7		9	8	11	6	12				10				
1	2	3	13	5	4	7		9	11		6	8				10			12	
1	2	3	12	5	4	7		9		11	6	8				10				
1	2		10	5	4	7		9	12	11	6	8							3	
1	2		10		4	7		9	5	11	6	8		3						
1	2		10		4	7		9	5	11	6	8		3						
1	2	3	10		4	7		9	5	11	6			8						
1	2	3	10		4	7		9	5	11	6			8						12
1	2	3	10			7		9	5	11	6			8					4	
1	2	3	10			7		9	5	11	6			8					4	
1		3	10	5	12	7		9	4	11	6			8					2	
1		3	10	5		7		9	4	11	6			8					2	
		3	10	5	12	7		9	4	11	6			8			1	13	2	
		3	10	5		7		9	4		6			8	12		1	11	2	
33	30	35	25	32	28	38	3	38	31	36	35	8	3	12		19	2	3	7	
	3		5		2				3		2	12		4	2			4	1	1
		1	1	1		16		20	1	11	3	4		3		1		1	1	

Coton AP	Brightwell IR	Pointon NG	Harper A	Hendry ECJ	Reid P	White D	Lake PA	Quinn NJ	Heath AP	Ward MW	Redmond S	Allen CD	Dibble AG	Brennan MR	Beckford JN	Megson GJ	Margetson MW	Clarke W	Hill AR	Hughes ME
1	2	3	9	5	4	7				11	6	12				10		8		
1	2	3	4			7		9	8	11	6	12		5		10				
1	2	3	4	5		7		9	12	11	6	8				10				
3	3	3	3	2	1	3		2	1	3	3	1		1		3		1		
									1			2								
				1				1				1								

Coton AP	Brightwell IR	Pointon NG	Harper A	Hendry ECJ	Reid P	White D	Lake PA	Quinn NJ	Heath AP	Ward MW	Redmond S	Allen CD	Dibble AG	Brennan MR	Beckford JN	Megson GJ	Margetson MW	Clarke W	Hill AR	Hughes ME
1	2	3	4	5				9	11	7	6	8		10	12					
1	2	3	4	5				9	12	11	6	8		7		10	13			
1	13	3	2	5	4	7		9	8	11	6	12				10				
3	2	3	3	3	1	1		3	2	3	3	2		2		2				
	1								1			1			1		1			
			1	1								2			1					

Coton AP	Brightwell IR	Pointon NG	Harper A	Hendry ECJ	Reid P	White D	Lake PA	Quinn NJ	Heath AP	Ward MW	Redmond S	Allen CD	Dibble AG	Brennan MR	Beckford JN	Megson GJ	Margetson MW	Clarke W	Hill AR	Hughes ME
1	2	3	4	5		7		9		11	6			10				8		
1	12	3	4	5		7		9	13	11	6	8				10			2	
1	2	3	4	5		7		9	12	11	6	8				10				
3	2	3	3	3		3		3		3	3	2		1		2		1	1	
	1								2											
						1		1		2										

League Table

	P	W	D	L	F	A	Pts
Arsenal*	38	24	13	1	74	18	83
Liverpool	38	23	7	8	77	40	76
Crystal Palace	38	20	9	9	50	41	69
Leeds U	38	19	7	12	65	47	64
Manchester C	38	17	11	10	64	53	62
Manchester U**	38	16	12	10	58	45	59
Wimbledon	38	14	14	10	53	46	56
Nottingham F	38	14	12	12	65	50	54
Everton	38	13	12	13	50	46	51
Tottenham H	38	11	16	11	51	50	49
Chelsea	38	13	10	15	58	69	49
Q.P.R.	38	12	10	16	44	53	46
Sheffield U	38	13	7	18	36	55	46
Southampton	38	12	9	17	58	69	45
Norwich C	38	13	6	19	41	64	45
Coventry C	38	11	11	16	42	49	44
Aston Villa	38	9	14	15	46	58	41
Luton T	38	10	7	21	42	61	37
Sunderland	38	8	10	20	38	60	34
Derby Co	38	5	9	24	37	75	24

*Arsenal had two points deducted for disciplinary reasons.

**Manchester United had one point deducted for disciplinary reasons.

1991-92

Division One

Manager: Peter Reid

Did you know that?

Match 12: Hoekman's last game.
Match 15: Hendry's last game.
Match 18: Allen's last game.
Match 32: Heath's last game.
Match 35: Redmond's last game.
Match 38: Brennan's last game.
Match 39: Hughes's last game.
Match 40: Pointon, Clarke and Megson's last game.

City defeated champions-to-be Leeds 4–0 in April 1992 and followed this up with another 4–0 victory over them in November 1992.

Match No.	Date	Venue	Opponents	Result		Scorers	Attendance
1	Aug 17	A	Coventry City	W	1-0	Quinn	17,946
2	21	H	Liverpool	W	2-1	White 2	37,332
3	24	H	Crystal Palace	W	3-2	Brennan 2 (2 pens), White	28,053
4	28	A	Norwich City	D	0-0		15,376
5	31	A	Arsenal	L	1-2	I Brightwell	35,009
6	Sep 4	H	Nottingham Forest	W	2-1	Hill, Quinn	29,146
7	7	A	Leeds United	L	0-3		28,986
8	14	H	Sheffield Wednesday	L	0-1		29,453
9	17	H	Everton	L	0-1		27,509
10	21	A	West Ham United	W	2-1	Hendry, Redmond (pen)	25,678
11	28	H	Oldham Athletic	L	1-2	White	31,271
12	Oct 6	A	Notts County	W	3-1	Allen 2 (1 pen), Sheron	11,878
13	19	A	Tottenham Hotspur	W	1-0	Quinn	30,502
14	26	H	Sheffield United	W	3-2	Hughes, Quinn, Sheron	25,495
15	Nov 2	A	Southampton	W	3-0	Quinn, Sheron, Gittens (og)	12,685
16	16	H	Manchester United	D	0-0		38,180
17	23	A	Luton Town	D	2-2	Curle, Quinn	10,031
18	30	H	Wimbledon	D	0-0		22,429
19	Dec 7	A	Aston Villa	L	1-3	White	26,265
20	14	H	Queen's Park Rangers	D	2-2	Curle, White	21,437
21	21	A	Liverpool	D	2-2	White 2	36,743
22	26	H	Norwich City	W	2-1	Quinn, White	28,164
23	28	H	Arsenal	W	1-0	White	32,325
24	Jan 1	A	Chelsea	D	1-1	Sheron	18,196
25	11	A	Crystal Palace	D	1-1	Curle (pen)	14,766
26	18	H	Coventry City	W	1-0	White	23,005
27	Feb 1	H	Tottenham Hotspur	W	1-0	White	30,123
28	8	A	Sheffield United	L	2-4	Curle (pen), Hill	25,839
29	15	H	Luton Town	W	4-0	White 2, Heath, Hill	22,137
30	22	A	Wimbledon	L	1-2	Sheron	5,802
31	29	H	Aston Villa	W	2-0	Quinn, White	28,268
32	Mar 7	A	Queen's Park Rangers	L	0-4		10,791
33	15	H	Southampton	L	0-1		24,265
34	21	A	Nottingham Forest	L	0-2		24,115
35	28	H	Chelsea	D	0-0		23,663
36	Apr 4	H	Leeds United	W	4-0	Brennan, Hill, Quinn, Sheron	30,239
37	7	A	Manchester United	D	1-1	Curle (pen)	46,781
38	11	A	Sheffield Wednesday	L	0-2		32,138
39	18	H	West Ham United	W	2-0	Clarke, Pointon	25,601
40	20	A	Everton	W	2-1	Quinn 2	20,536
41	25	H	Notts County	W	2-0	Quinn, Simpson	23,426
42	May 2	A	Oldham Athletic	W	5-2	White 3, Mike, Sheron	18,588
							Appearances
							Sub appearances
						One own goal	Goals

FA Cup

R3	Jan 4	A	Middlesbrough	L	1-2	Reid	21,174
							Appearances
							Sub appearances
							Goals

League Cup

R2/1	Sep 25	H	Chester City	W	3-1	White 2, Quinn	10,987
R2/2	Oct 8	N	Chester City	W	3-0	Allen, Brennan, Sheron	4,146
R3	29	H	Queen's Park Rangers	D	0-0		15,512
R3	Nov 20	A	Queen's Park Rangers	W	3-1	Heath 2, Quinn	11,033
R4	Dec 3	A	Middlesbrough	L	1-2	White	17,286
							Appearances
							Sub appearances
							Goals

Full Members Cup

R2	Oct 23	A	Sheffield Wednesday	L	2-3	Hendry 2	7,951
							Appearances
							Sub appearances
							Goals

Margetson MW	Hill AR	Pointon NG	Reid P	Curle K	Redmond S	White D	Brightwell IR	Quinn NJ	Megson GJ	Brennan MR	Heath AP	Coton AP	Hendry ECJ	Hughes ME	Sheron MN	Dibble AG	Allen CD	Hoekman D	Quigley MAJ	McMahon S	Brightwell DJ	Simpson F	Clarke W	Vonk MC	Mike AR	Mauge RC
1	2	3	**4**	5	6	7	8	9	10	11	12															
	2	3	**4**	5	6	7	8	9	10	11	12	1														
	2	3	4	5	6	7	8	9	**10**	11	12	1	13													
	2	3	4	5	6	7	8		10	11	9	1														
	2	3	**4**	5	6	7	8	9	10	11	12	1	13													
	2	3	4	5	6	7	8	9	10	11		1														
	2	3	4	5	6	7	8	9	10	**11**	12	1														
	2	3	4	5	6	7	8	9	10	**11**	12	1														
	2	3	**4**	5	6	7		9	10		8	1	13	11	12											
	2	3		5	6	7	4	9	10		8	1	12	**11**												
	2	3		5	6	7	4	9	10		8		13	11	12	1										
		3	4		6	7	5		10	**2**	8	1		11	9		12	13								
	2	3	4	5	6		10	9			8	1		11	7											
	2	3	4	5	6		10	9			8	1		11	7											
	2	3	4	5	6		10	**9**			8	1	12	11	7											
	2	3	4	5	6	**7**	10	9			8	1		11	12		13									
1	2	3		5	6	**7**	10	9	4		8			11	12											
	2	3		5	6	7	10	9	**4**		8	1		11	12		13									
	2	3		5		7	10	9	4		8	1		**11**	6				12							
	2	3		5	6	7	10	9	4		8	1		11												
		3	4	5	6	7	2	9			8	1		11	10											
		3	4	5	6	7	2	9	12		8	1		11						**10**						
	2	3	4	5	6	7	10	9	12		8	1		11												
		3	4	5	6	7	2	9	10		**8**			11	12	1			13							
		3	4	5	6	7	2	9	10		8	1		**11**	12				13							
	2	**3**	4	5	6	7	8					1		11	9				12	10						
	2	3	**4**	5	6	7	8					1		11	9				12	10						
	2	3	4	5	6	7	8	9	13		12	1		**11**						10						
	2	3	**4**	5	6	7	8	9			12	1		11	13					10						
	2	3	4	5	6	7	**8**	9			11	1			12					10	13					
	2	3	4	5		7	12	9				1		**11**	8					10	6					
	2	3	4	5		7		9			11	1			**8**					10	6	12				
	2	3	4	5		7	12	9				1		11	8					10	**6**	13				
1	2		**4**	5	6	7	3	9							8					10		11	12	13		
	2	3			6	7	**4**			9		1			8					11		10	12	5		
	2	3		5		7	12	**9**		4		1			8					11		10		6		
	2	3	13	5		7	12	9		**4**		1			8					11		10		6		
	2	3	13	5		7	9			4		1			8					11		**10**	12	6		
	2	3		5		7	4					1		9	8					11		10	12	6		
		3	4	5		7	2	9	13			1			**8**					11		10	12	6		
	2			5		7	3	9				1			8					11		4		6	10	
	2			5		7	3	9				1			8					11		4		6	10	
3	36	39	29	40	31	39	36	35	18	13	20	37		24	20	2				18	3	9		8	2	
			2				4		4		8		6		9		3	1	5		1	2	5	1		
	4	1		5	1	18	1	12		3	1		1	1	7		2					1	1		1	

Margetson MW	Hill AR	Pointon NG	Reid P	Curle K	Redmond S	White D	Brightwell IR	Quinn NJ	Megson GJ	Brennan MR	Heath AP	Coton AP	Hendry ECJ	Hughes ME	Sheron MN	Dibble AG	Allen CD	Hoekman D	Quigley MAJ	McMahon S	Brightwell DJ	Simpson F	Clarke W	Vonk MC	Mike AR	Mauge RC
		3	4	5	6	7	**2**	9	13		8	1		11	12					10						
		1	1	1	1	1	1	1			1	1		1						1						
									1						1											
			1																							

Margetson MW	Hill AR	Pointon NG	Reid P	Curle K	Redmond S	White D	Brightwell IR	Quinn NJ	Megson GJ	Brennan MR	Heath AP	Coton AP	Hendry ECJ	Hughes ME	Sheron MN	Dibble AG	Allen CD	Hoekman D	Quigley MAJ	McMahon S	Brightwell DJ	Simpson F	Clarke W	Vonk MC	Mike AR	Mauge RC
	2	3		5	6	7	4	9	10		8	1		11												
	2	3			6		5		**10**	4	8	1		11	7		9	12								
	2	3	4	5	6		10				8	1	13	11	**7**		9	12								
	2	3		5	6		10	9	4		8	1		11	7											
	2	**3**		5	6	7	10	9		4	8	1		11	13		12									
	5	5	1	4	5	2	5	3	3	2	5	5		5	3		2									
													1		1		1	2								
						3		2		1	2				1		1									

Margetson MW	Hill AR	Pointon NG	Reid P	Curle K	Redmond S	White D	Brightwell IR	Quinn NJ	Megson GJ	Brennan MR	Heath AP	Coton AP	Hendry ECJ	Hughes ME	Sheron MN	Dibble AG	Allen CD	Hoekman D	Quigley MAJ	McMahon S	Brightwell DJ	Simpson F	Clarke W	Vonk MC	Mike AR	Mauge RC
1		3		5	6		10			9	8		4	11	7			**2**								12
1		1		1	1		1			1	1		1	1	1			1								
																										1
													2													

League Table

	P	W	D	L	F	A	Pts
Leeds U	42	22	16	4	74	37	82
Manchester U	42	21	15	6	63	33	78
Sheffield W	42	21	12	9	62	49	75
Arsenal	42	19	15	8	81	46	72
Manchester C	42	20	10	12	61	48	70
Liverpool	42	16	16	10	47	40	64
Aston Villa	42	17	9	16	48	44	60
Nottingham F	42	16	11	15	60	58	59
Sheffield U	42	16	9	17	65	63	57
Crystal Palace	42	14	15	13	53	61	57
Q.P.R.	42	12	18	12	48	47	54
Everton	42	13	14	15	52	51	53
Wimbledon	42	13	14	15	53	53	53
Chelsea	42	13	14	15	50	60	53
Tottenham H	42	15	7	20	58	63	52
Southampton	42	14	10	18	39	55	52
Oldham A	42	14	9	19	63	67	51
Norwich C	42	11	12	19	47	63	45
Coventry C	42	11	11	20	35	44	44
Luton T	42	10	12	20	38	71	42
Notts Co	42	10	10	22	40	62	40
West Ham U	42	9	11	22	37	59	38

1992-93

Premiership

Manager: Peter Reid

Did you know that?

Match 2: Lake's last game.
Match 42: Ranson's last game.

The FA Cup quarter-final was later viewed as the beginning of the end of Chairman Peter Swales's reign. The match with Spurs ended in embarrassing defeat, in front of an enormous television audience. In addition, the opening of the surprisingly small-capacity Umbro Stand at the Platt Lane end of the ground suggested City's ambitions were somewhat limited. This season was the last complete season of Swales's time as chairman.

Match No.	Date	Venue	Opponents	Result		Scorers	Attendance
1	Aug 17	H	Queen's Park Rangers	D	1-1	White	24,471
2	19	A	Middlesbrough	L	0-2		15,369
3	22	A	Blackburn Rovers	L	0-1		19,433
4	26	H	Norwich City	W	3-1	White 2, McMahon	23,182
5	29	H	Oldham Athletic	D	3-3	Quinn, Vonk, White	27,288
6	Sep 1	A	Wimbledon	W	1-0	White	4,714
7	5	A	Sheffield Wednesday	W	3-0	White 2, Vonk	27,169
8	12	H	Middlesbrough	L	0-1		25,244
9	20	H	Chelsea	L	0-1		22,420
10	28	A	Arsenal	L	0-1		21,504
11	Oct 3	H	Nottingham Forest	D	2-2	Holden, Simpson	22,571
12	17	A	Crystal Palace	D	0-0		14,005
13	24	H	Southampton	W	1-0	Sheron	20,089
14	31	A	Everton	W	3-1	Sheron 2, White	20,247
15	Nov 7	H	Leeds United	W	4-0	Brightwell, Hill, Sheron, White	27,255
16	21	A	Coventry City	W	3-2	Curle (pen), Quinn, Sheron	14,556
17	28	H	Tottenham Hotspur	L	0-1		25,496
18	Dec 6	A	Manchester United	L	1-2	Quinn	35,408
19	12	A	Ipswich Town	L	1-3	Flitcroft	17,005
20	19	H	Aston Villa	D	1-1	Flitcroft	23,525
21	26	H	Sheffield United	W	2-0	White 2	27,455
22	28	A	Liverpool	D	1-1	Quinn	43,037
23	Jan 9	A	Chelsea	W	4-2	Sheron 2, White, Sinclair (og)	15,939
24	16	H	Arsenal	L	0-1		25,041
25	26	A	Oldham Athletic	W	1-0	Quinn	14,903
26	30	H	Blackburn Rovers	W	3-2	Curle (pen), Sheron, White	29,122
27	Feb 6	A	Queen's Park Rangers	D	1-1	Sheron	13,003
28	20	A	Norwich City	L	1-2	Sheron	16,386
29	23	H	Sheffield Wednesday	L	1-2	Quinn	23,619
30	27	A	Nottingham Forest	W	2-0	Flitcroft, White	25,956
31	Mar 10	H	Coventry City	W	1-0	Flitcroft	20,092
32	13	A	Leeds United	L	0-1		30,840
33	20	H	Manchester United	D	1-1	Quinn	37,136
34	24	A	Tottenham Hotspur	L	1-3	Sheron	27,247
35	Apr 3	H	Ipswich Town	W	3-1	Holden, Quinn, Vonk	20,680
36	9	A	Sheffield United	D	1-1	Pemberton (og)	18,231
37	12	H	Liverpool	D	1-1	Flitcroft	28,098
38	18	A	Aston Villa	L	1-3	Quinn	33,108
39	21	H	Wimbledon	D	1-1	Holden	19,524
40	May 1	A	Southampton	W	1-0	White	16,730
41	5	H	Crystal Palace	D	0-0		21,167
42	8	H	Everton	L	2-5	Curle (pen), White	25,180
							Appearances
							Sub appearances
						Two own goals	Goals

FA Cup

	Date	Venue	Opponents	Result		Scorers	Attendance
R3	Jan 2	H	Reading	D	1-1	Sheron	20,533
rep	13	A	Reading	W	4-0	Flitcroft, Holden, Quinn, Sheron	12,065
R4	23	A	Queen's Park Rangers	W	2-1	Vonk, White	18,652
R5	Feb 13	H	Barnsley	W	2-0	White 2	32,809
R6	Mar 7	H	Tottenham Hotspur	L	2-4	Phelan, Sheron	34,050
							Appearances
							Sub appearances
							Goals

League Cup

	Date	Venue	Opponents	Result		Scorers	Attendance
R2/1	Sep 23	H	Bristol Rovers	D	0-0		9,967
R2/2	Oct 7	A	Bristol Rovers	W	2-1e	Holden, Quinn	7,823
R3	28	H	Tottenham Hotspur	L	0-1		18,399
							Appearances
							Sub appearances
							Goals

Brightwell DJ	Brightwell IR	Coton AP	Curle K	Dibble AG	Flitcroft GW	Hill AR	Holden RW	Ingebrigtsen K	Kerr DW	Lake PA	Margetson MW	McMahon S	Mike AR	Phelan TM	Quigley MAJ	Quinn NJ	Ranson R	Reid P	Sheron MN	Simpson F	Vonk MC	White D
	3	1	5			2	**10**			8		11				9			12	4	6	7
	3	1	5			2	10			**8**		11				9			12	4	6	7
	3	1	5			2	10					11				9			8	4	6	7
	2	1	5				10					11		3		9			8	4	6	7
	2	1	5		13		10					**11**		3		9		12	8	4	6	7
	2	1	5		8		11					12		3		9		**4**		10	6	7
	2	1	5		8		11					12		3				**4**	9	10	6	7
	2	1	5		8		11						12	3				4	9	10	**6**	7
	2	1	5		8	6	11						12	3				**4**	9	10		7
	2	1	5		8	6	**11**					12		3		9		4		10		7
	2	1	5			6	11					**4**		3		9		12	8	10		7
	2	1	5		8	6	11					4		3		9				10		7
	2	1	5			6	11					4		3		9			8	10		7
	2	1	5		13	6	11					4		3		9		12	8	**10**		7
	2	1	5			6	11					4		3		9			8	10		7
12	**2**	1	5			6	11					4		3		9			8	10		7
2		1	5		12	6	11					4		3		9			8	**10**		7
	2	1	5		13	6	11					4		3		9		12	8	**10**		7
	2	1	5		10	**6**	11					4		3		9		8	12			7
	2	1	5		10	6	11					4		3		9		**8**	12			7
	2	1	5		10	6	11					4		3		9			8			7
	2	1	5		10	6	11					4		3		9		12	**8**			7
6		1	5		10		11					4		3		9	2		8			7
6		1	5		10		11							3		9	2		8	4		7
		1			10		11					4		3		9	2		8	6	5	7
		1	5				11	12				4		3		9	2		8	**10**	6	7
			5	1			11	12				4		3		**9**	2	13	8	10	6	7
		1	5		10	12	11	4						**3**	13	9	2		8		6	7
12		1	5		10	3							**11**		4	9	2		8		6	7
		1			10	5	11							3	12	9	2		**8**	4	6	7
		1	5		10	2	11							3		9			8	4	6	7
		1	5		10	2	11							3		**9**	8		12	4	6	7
		1	5		10	2	11							3		9		4	8		6	7
		1	5		**10**	2	11	13						3	12	9		4	8		6	7
		1	5		10		11	12						3		9	2	4	8		6	**7**
		1			10		11	5						3		9	2	4	8		6	7
		1	5		10		11	12						3	13	9	2	4	**8**		6	7
12		1	5		10		**11**							3		9	2	4		8	6	7
13		1	5		10		12							3		9	2	**4**	8	11	6	7
3		1	5		10		**11**					4				9	2		8	12	6	7
		1	5		10		11		12			4		3		9	2		**8**		6	7
			5	13	10		11				1	**4**		3		9	2		8	12	6	7
4	21	40	39	1	28	23	40	2		2	1	24	1	37	1	39	17	14	33	27	26	42
4				1	4	1	1	5	1			3	2		4			6	5	2		
	1		3		5	1	3					1				9			11	1	3	16

Brightwell DJ	Brightwell IR	Coton AP	Curle K	Dibble AG	Flitcroft GW	Hill AR	Holden RW	Ingebrigtsen K	Kerr DW	Lake PA	Margetson MW	McMahon S	Mike AR	Phelan TM	Quigley MAJ	Quinn NJ	Ranson R	Reid P	Sheron MN	Simpson F	Vonk MC	White D
12	**2**	1	5		10	6	11					4		3		9			8			7
6		1	5		10		11							3		9		**4**	8	2	12	7
		1			10		11					4		3		9	2		8	6	5	7
		1	5		10	12	11							3		9		**2**	8	4	6	7
		1	5		10	2	11							3		9			8	4	6	7
1	1	5	4		5	2	5					2		5		5	1	2	5	4	3	5
1						1															1	
					1		1							1		1			3		1	3

Brightwell DJ	Brightwell IR	Coton AP	Curle K	Dibble AG	Flitcroft GW	Hill AR	Holden RW	Ingebrigtsen K	Kerr DW	Lake PA	Margetson MW	McMahon S	Mike AR	Phelan TM	Quigley MAJ	Quinn NJ	Ranson R	Reid P	Sheron MN	Simpson F	Vonk MC	White D
	2	1	5	-	8	6	11							3		9		4		10		7
	2	1	5	-	13	6	11					**4**		3		9		12	8	10		7
	2	1	5	-		6	11					4		3		9			8	10		7
	3	3	3		1	3	3					2		3		3		1	2	3		3
					1													1				
							1									1						

League Table

	P	W	D	L	F	A	Pts
Manchester U	42	24	12	6	67	31	84
Aston Villa	42	21	11	10	57	40	74
Norwich C	42	21	9	12	61	65	72
Blackburn R	42	20	11	11	68	46	71
Q.P.R.	42	17	12	13	63	55	63
Liverpool	42	16	11	15	62	55	59
Sheffield W	42	15	14	13	55	51	59
Tottenham H	42	16	11	15	60	66	59
Manchester C	42	15	12	15	56	51	57
Arsenal	42	15	11	16	40	38	56
Chelsea	42	14	14	14	51	54	56
Wimbledon	42	14	12	16	56	55	54
Everton	42	15	8	19	53	55	53
Sheffield U	42	14	10	18	54	53	52
Coventry C	42	13	13	16	52	57	52
Ipswich T	42	12	16	14	50	55	52
Leeds U	42	12	15	15	57	62	51
Southampton	42	13	11	18	54	61	50
Oldham A*	42	13	10	19	63	74	49
Crystal Palace	42	11	16	15	48	61	49
Middlesbrough	42	11	11	20	54	75	44
Nottingham F	42	10	10	22	41	62	40

1993-94

Premiership

Manager: Peter Reid (until 26 August 1993),
Brian Horton (from 28 August 1993)

Did you know that?

Match 4: Reid's last game.
Match 10: Holden's last game.
Match 21: White and Quigley's last game.
Match 24: Groenendijk's last League game.
Match 25: Ingebrigtsen's last game.
Match 30: Shutt's last game.
Match 37: Sheron's last game.
Match 40: Karl's last game.
Match 42: Rocastle's last game.

The Chelsea game was the last to be played in front of the old Kippax terracing. It is estimated that the entire attendance for that game would have been stood on the Kippax during the 1934 record crowd.

Match No.	Date	Venue	Opponents	Result		Scorers	Attendance
1	Aug 14	H	Leeds United	D	1-1	Flitcroft	32,366
2	17	A	Everton	L	0-1		26,025
3	21	A	Tottenham Hotspur	L	0-1		24,535
4	24	H	Blackburn Rovers	L	0-2		25,185
5	27	H	Coventry City	D	1-1	Sheron	21,537
6	Sep 1	A	Swindon Town	W	3-1	Mike, Quinn, Vonk	16,067
7	11	H	Queen's Park Rangers	W	3-0	Flitcroft, Quinn, Sheron	24,445
8	20	A	Wimbledon	L	0-1		8,533
9	25	A	Sheffield United	W	1-0	Sheron	20,067
10	Oct 4	H	Oldham Athletic	D	1-1	Sheron	21,401
11	16	A	Arsenal	D	0-0		29,567
12	23	H	Liverpool	D	1-1	White	30,403
13	Nov 1	A	West Ham United	L	1-3	Curle (pen)	16,605
14	7	H	Manchester United	L	2-3	Quinn 2	35,155
15	20	A	Norwich City	D	1-1	Quinn	16,626
16	22	A	Chelsea	D	0-0		10,128
17	27	H	Sheffield Wednesday	L	1-3	Sheron	23,416
18	Dec 4	A	Leeds United	L	2-3	Griffiths, Sheron	33,820
19	8	H	Everton	W	1-0	Griffiths	20,513
20	11	H	Tottenham Hotspur	L	0-2		21,566
21	18	A	Blackburn Rovers	L	0-2		19,479
22	28	H	Southampton	D	1-1	Phelan	24,712
23	Jan 1	A	Newcastle United	L	0-2		35,585
24	15	H	Arsenal	D	0-0		25,642
25	22	A	Liverpool	L	1-2	Griffiths	41,872
26	Feb 5	H	Ipswich Town	W	2-1	Flitcroft, Griffiths	28,188
27	12	H	West Ham United	D	0-0		29,118
28	19	A	Coventry City	L	0-4		11,739
29	22	A	Aston Villa	D	0-0		19,254
30	26	H	Swindon Town	W	2-1	Rocastle, Horlock (og)	26,360
31	Mar 5	A	Queen's Park Rangers	D	1-1	Rocastle	13,474
32	12	H	Wimbledon	L	0-1		23,981
33	19	H	Sheffield United	D	0-0		25,448
34	26	A	Oldham Athletic	D	0-0		16,462
35	29	A	Ipswich Town	D	2-2	Rosler, Walsh	12,871
36	Apr 2	H	Aston Villa	W	3-0	Beagrie, Rosler, Walsh	26,075
37	4	A	Southampton	W	1-0	Karl	16,377
38	9	H	Newcastle United	W	2-1	D Brightwell, Walsh	33,774
39	16	H	Norwich City	D	1-1	Rosler	28,020
40	23	A	Manchester United	L	0-2		44,333
41	30	H	Chelsea	D	2-2	Rosler, Walsh	33,594
42	May 7	A	Sheffield Wednesday	D	1-1	Rosler	33,589
							Appearances
							Sub appearances
							Goals

FA Cup

R3	Jan 8	H	Leicester City	W	4-1	Ingebrigtsen 3, Kernaghan	22,613
R4	29	A	Cardiff City	L	0-1		20,486
							Appearances
							Sub appearances
							Goals

League Cup

R2/1	Sep 22	H	Reading	D	1-1	White	9,280
R2/2	Oct 6	A	Reading	W	2-1	Lomas, Quinn	10,052
R3	26	H	Chelsea	W	1-0	White	16,713
R4	Dec 1	A	Nottingham Forest	D	0-0		22,195
rep	15	H	Nottingham Forest	L	1-2	Vonk	14,117
							Appearances
							Sub appearances
							Goals

Coton AP	Hill AR	Phelan TM	McMahon S	Curle K	Vonk MC	White D	Sheron MN	Simpson F	Flitcroft GW	Holden RW	Reid P	Brightwell DJ	Groenendijk A	Quinn NJ	Mike AR	Edghill RA	Kernaghan AN	Lomas SM	Dibble AG	Griffiths CB	Ingebrigtsen K	Kerr DW	Quigley MAJ	Rocastle DC	Foster JC	Shutt CS	Rosler U	Walsh PAM	Karl S	Brightwell IR	Beagrie PS
1	2	3	4	5	6	7	8	**9**	10	11	12	13																			
1	2	3	4		6	7	8		10	11	12	5	**9**																		
1	2	3	**4**		6	7	8		10	11	9	5		12																	
1	2	3	**4**	5	6		8		10	11	12	13	7	9																	
1		3	4	5	6	7	8		10	11			2	9																	
1			4	5	6	7	8	12	10	11		3	**2**	9	13																
1		3	4	5		**7**	8		10	11		6	2	9	12																
1			4	5			8	7	10			3	**11**	9	12	2	6														
1			4	5			8			11		3	7	9		2	6	10													
		3	4	5			8		10	**11**			7	9	12	2	6	13	1												
1		3	4	5			8	7	10					9		2	6	11													
1		3	4	5		7	8	**11**	10					9		2	6	12													
1		3	4	5	12	7	8		10					9		2	6	**11**		13											
1		3	4	5	11	7	8		10					9		2	6														
1		3	4	5		7	**8**	10						9		2	6	11		12											
1		3	4	5	2	7	**8**	10						9			6	11		12											
1		3	4	5	2	7	8	10						**9**	12		6	11													
1		3	4	5	2	7	8	**9**							10		6	11		12	13										
1		3	4	5	6	7	8		10									11		**9**	12	2									
1		3		5	6	7	**8**		10			12						11		9	13	2	4								
1		3		5	6	7	8									2	4	11		9	12		**10**								
1		3		5	10		8	12				6				2	4	11		**9**	13			7							
1					10		**8**	9				3				2	6	11			12			4	5	7					
1		11			10		12		13			**5**	6			2	4	3		9	8			7							
1		11			10				7			6				2	5	3		9	8			4							
1		11		5	6		8		10							2		3		9				4		7					
1		3	4	**5**	6		8		10							2	12	13		9				7		11					
1		3	4		6		8	12							13	2	5	**10**		9				7		11					
1	12	**3**	4		6		8	9								2	5	10						7		11					
	13	3	4		6		8	11	**10**							2	5		1	9				7		12					
	11	3	4		6		8								12	2	5		1	**9**				7			10				
1	11	3	4		6			**9**							12	2	5							7			8	10	13		
1	2	11	4		6							3					5			12				7			**8**	10	9		
1	2		4	5	6		12					3												7			**9**	10		8	11
	2		4	5	6							3							1					7			9	10		8	11
	2		4	5	6		12					3							1					7			**9**	10		8	11
	2		4	5	6		12					3							1					7			9	**10**	13	8	11
	2		4	5	6							3						12	1					7			9	10	**8**		11
	2		4	5	6							3						12	1					7			9	10	**8**		11
	2		4	5	6							3							1					7			9	10	**8**	12	11
	2		4		6							3				5			1					7			9	10		8	11
		3	4		**6**				12							2	5	13	1					7			9	10		8	11
31	15	30	35	29	34	16	29	12	19	9	1	19	9	14	1	22	23	17	11	11	2	2	2	21	1	5	12	11	4	6	9
	2				1		4	3	2		3	3		1	8		1	6		5	6					1			2	1	
		1		1	1	1	6		3			1		5	1					4				2			5	4	1		1

Coton AP	Hill AR	Phelan TM	McMahon S	Curle K	Vonk MC	White D	Sheron MN	Simpson F	Flitcroft GW	Holden RW	Reid P	Brightwell DJ	Groenendijk A	Quinn NJ	Mike AR	Edghill RA	Kernaghan AN	Lomas SM	Dibble AG	Griffiths CB	Ingebrigtsen K	Kerr DW	Quigley MAJ	Rocastle DC	Foster JC	Shutt CS	Rosler U	Walsh PAM	Karl S	Brightwell IR	Beagrie PS
1		11			10		13					3	6			2	4	12		9	8			7	**5**						
1		3		5	6		12		10				11				4	2	13	9	**8**			7							
2		2		1	2				1			1	2			1	2	1		2	2			2	1						
							2											1	1												
																	1				3										

Coton AP	Hill AR	Phelan TM	McMahon S	Curle K	Vonk MC	White D	Sheron MN	Simpson F	Flitcroft GW	Holden RW	Reid P	Brightwell DJ	Groenendijk A	Quinn NJ	Mike AR	Edghill RA	Kernaghan AN	Lomas SM	Dibble AG	Griffiths CB	Ingebrigtsen K	Kerr DW	Quigley MAJ	Rocastle DC	Foster JC	Shutt CS	Rosler U	Walsh PAM	Karl S	Brightwell IR	Beagrie PS
1			4	5		**7**	8	13	10			3	11	9	12	2	6														
		3	4	5			8	7	10					9		2	6	11	1												
1		3	4	5	12	7	**8**		10					9		2	6	11													
1		3	4	5	2	7	8	9							10		6	11													
1		3	4	5	6	7	8		10							2	9	11													
4		4	5	5	2	4	5	2	4			1	1	3	1	4	5	4	1												
					1			1							1																
					1	2								1				1													

League Table

	P	W	D	L	F	A	Pts
Manchester U	42	27	11	4	80	38	92
Blackburn R	42	25	9	8	63	36	84
Newcastle U	42	23	8	11	82	41	77
Arsenal	42	18	17	7	53	28	71
Leeds U	42	18	16	8	65	39	70
Wimbledon	42	18	11	13	56	53	65
Sheffield W	42	16	16	10	76	54	64
Liverpool	42	17	9	16	59	55	60
Q.P.R.	42	16	12	14	62	61	60
Aston Villa	42	15	12	15	46	50	57
Coventry C	42	14	14	14	43	45	56
Norwich C	42	12	17	13	65	61	53
West Ham U	42	13	13	16	47	58	52
Chelsea	42	13	12	17	49	53	51
Tottenham H	42	11	12	19	54	59	45
Manchester C	42	9	18	15	38	49	45
Everton	42	12	8	22	42	63	44
Southampton	42	12	7	23	49	66	43
Ipswich T	42	9	16	17	35	58	43
Sheffield U	42	8	18	16	42	60	42
Oldham A	42	9	13	20	42	68	40
Swindon T	42	5	15	22	47	100	30

1994-95

Premiership

Manager: Brian Horton (until 16 May 1995)

Did you know that?

Match 8: McMahon's last game.
Match 13: Mike's last game.
Match 14: Tracey's last game.
Match 30: Griffiths's last game.
Match 35: D. Brightwell and Vonk's last game.
Match 36: Hill's last game.
Match 39: Coton's last game.
Match 42: Burridge, Gaudino, Simpson and Thomas's last game.

John Burridge became the oldest player to appear in the Premier League while with City. His age on the day of Match 42, his last game, was 43 years and five months.

Match No.	Date	Venue	Opponents	Result		Scorers	Attendance
1	Aug 20	A	Arsenal	L	0-3		38,368
2	24	H	West Ham United	W	3-0	Beagrie, Rosler, Walsh	19,150
3	27	H	Everton	W	4-0	Rosler 2, Walsh 2	19,867
4	31	A	Chelsea	L	0-3		21,740
5	Sep 10	H	Crystal Palace	D	1-1	Walsh	19,971
6	17	A	Sheffield Wednesday	D	1-1	Walsh	26,585
7	24	H	Norwich City	W	2-0	Rosler, Quinn	21,031
8	Oct 1	A	Leeds United	L	0-2		30,938
9	8	H	Nottingham Forest	D	3-3	Quinn 2, Lomas	23,150
10	15	A	Queen's Park Rangers	W	2-1	Flitcroft, Walsh	13,631
11	22	H	Tottenham Hotspur	W	5-2	Walsh 2, Flitcroft, Lomas, Quinn	25,473
12	29	A	Coventry City	L	0-1		15,802
13	Nov 5	H	Southampton	D	3-3	Walsh 2, Beagrie	21,589
14	10	A	Manchester United	L	0-5		43,738
15	20	A	Leicester City	W	1-0	Quinn	19,006
16	26	H	Wimbledon	W	2-0	Flitcroft, Rosler	21,131
17	Dec 3	A	Ipswich Town	W	2-1	Flitcroft, Rosler	13,754
18	12	H	Arsenal	L	1-2	Simpson	20,500
19	17	A	West Ham United	L	0-3		17,286
20	26	H	Blackburn Rovers	L	1-3	Quinn	23,387
21	28	A	Liverpool	L	0-2		38,122
22	31	H	Aston Villa	D	2-2	Rosler 2	22,513
23	Jan 2	A	Newcastle United	D	0-0		34,437
24	14	H	Coventry City	D	0-0		20,232
25	25	H	Leicester City	L	0-1		21,007
26	Feb 4	A	Southampton	D	2-2	Flitcroft, Kernaghan	14,902
27	11	H	Manchester United	L	0-3		26,368
28	22	H	Ipswich Town	W	2-0	Quinn, Rosler	21,430
29	25	H	Leeds United	D	0-0		22,892
30	Mar 4	A	Norwich City	D	1-1	Simpson	16,266
31	8	H	Chelsea	L	1-2	Gaudinho	21,880
32	15	A	Everton	D	1-1	Gaudinho	28,485
33	18	H	Sheffield Wednesday	W	3-2	Rosler 2, Walsh	23,355
34	21	A	Wimbledon	L	0-2		5,268
35	Apr 1	A	Crystal Palace	L	1-2	Rosler	13,451
36	11	A	Tottenham Hotspur	L	1-2	Rosler	27,410
37	14	H	Liverpool	W	2-1	Gaudinho, Summerbee	27,055
38	17	A	Blackburn Rovers	W	3-2	Curle (pen), Rosler, Walsh	27,851
39	29	H	Newcastle United	D	0-0		27,389
40	May 3	A	Aston Villa	D	1-1	Rosler	30,133
41	6	A	Nottingham Forest	L	0-1		28,882
42	14	H	Queen's Park Rangers	L	2-3	Curle (pen), Quinn	27,850
							Appearances
							Sub appearances
							Goals

FA Cup

	Date	Venue	Opponents	Result		Scorers	Attendance
R3	Jan 8	A	Notts County	D	2-2	Beagrie, Brightwell	12,376
rep	18	H	Notts County	W	5-2	Rosler 4, Gaudinho	14,261
R4	28	H	Aston Villa	W	1-0	Walsh	21,177
R5	Feb 19	A	Newcastle United	L	1-3	Rosler	33,219
							Appearances
							Sub appearances
							Goals

League Cup

	Date	Venue	Opponents	Result		Scorers	Attendance
R2/1	Sep 20	A	Barnet	L	0-1		3,120
R2/2	Oct 5	H	Barnet	W	4-1	Quinn 2, Summerbee, Walsh	11,545
R3	25	A	Queen's Park Rangers	W	4-3	Beagrie, Curle (pen), Lomas, Summerbee	11,701
R4	Nov 30	H	Newcastle United	D	1-1	Rosler	25,162
rep	Dec 21	A	Newcastle United	W	2-0	Rosler, Walsh	30,156
R5	Jan 11	A	Crystal Palace	L	0-4		16,668
							Appearances
							Sub appearances
							Goals

Coton AP	Hill AR	Phelan TM	McMahon S	Curle K	Vonk MC	Summerbee NJ	Walsh PAM	Rosler U	Flitcroft GW	Beagrie PS	Quinn NJ	Brightwell IR	Lomas SM	Edghill RA	Foster JC	Mike AR	Griffiths CB	Dibble AG	Tracey SP	Brightwell DJ	Kernaghan AN	Simpson F	Kerr DW	Gaudino M	Burridge J	Thomas SL
1	2	3	4	5	6	7	8	9	10	11	12	13														
1		3	4	5	6	7	8	9	10	11	12	2	13													
1			4	5	6	7	8	9	10	11	12	2	3													
1			4	5	6	7	8	9	10	11	12	2	3													
1		3	4	5	6	7	8		10	11	9	2														
1	5		4		6	7	8	9		11	12	3	10	2												
1	12	3		5		7	8	9	4	11	10	6	13	2												
1	2	3	12		6	7			4	11	9	5	10			8	13									
	5	3				7	8		4	11	9	6	10	2				1								
13	12	3		5		7	8		4	11	9	6	10	2				1								
		3		5		7	8		4	11	9	6	10	2				1								
	2	3			6	7	8		4	11	9	5	10						1							
	2	3			6	7	8		4	11	9	5	10			12			1							
		3			6	7	8		4	11	9	5	10	2					1							
	2			5		7	8	12	4	11	9	6	10					1		3						
	2			5		7	8	12	4	11	9	6	10					1		3	13					
				5		7	8	10	4	11	9	6		2				1		3	12	13				
				5		7	8	10	4	11	9	6	3					1			12	13	2			
					12	7	8	11	4		9	6	10		13			1		3	5		2			
		12				7		10	4	11	9	6	3		2			1			5			8		
		3			12	7	8	9	4	11		6	2					1			5			10		
		3				7	8	9	4	11		6	10		2			1			5					
		3			6	7	8	9	4	11			10		2			1			5	12				
		3		5		2	8	9	10	11								1		6	4	12		7		
				5	6	2	8	9	10	11	12	4						1		3				7		
1				5	6	2	8	9	10	11		7						13		3	4			12		
1				5		2	8	9	10	11	12	6								3	4			7		
1		3		5		2	8	9	10	11	12	6									4	13		7		
1	2	3		5	6	7					10	8									4	11		9		
1	12	3		5	6	2	8				9	10					13				4	11		7		
1		3		5		2	8	9		11	12	6									4	10		7		
1		3		5	6		8	9		11	10	2			12							4		7		
1		3		5	6	2	8	9	10	11												4		7		
1		3		5	6	12	8	9	10	11	13				2							4		7		
1				5	6	12	8	9	10	11					2					3	4			7		
1	4	3		5		7	8	9	10		12			2	6									11		
1		3		5		7	8	9	4	12	10			2	6						13			11		
1				5		7	8	9	4	12	10			3	2						6	11				
1		3		5		7	8	9	4	12	10			2							6	11		14	13	
		3		5		7	8	9	4	12	10			2							6	11		13	1	
				5		2	8		10	11	9			3							4	6		7	1	12
				5		7	8	9	4		10			2	3						6	12		11	1	13
22	10	26	6	31	19	39	39	29	37	33	24	29	18	14	9	1		14	3	9	18	10	2	17	3	
1	3	1	1		2	2		2		4	11	1	2		2	1	2	1			4	6		3	1	2
				2		1	12	15	5	2	8		2								1	2		3		

Coton AP	Hill AR	Phelan TM	McMahon S	Curle K	Vonk MC	Summerbee NJ	Walsh PAM	Rosler U	Flitcroft GW	Beagrie PS	Quinn NJ	Brightwell IR	Lomas SM	Edghill RA	Foster JC	Mike AR	Griffiths CB	Dibble AG	Tracey SP	Brightwell DJ	Kernaghan AN	Simpson F	Kerr DW	Gaudino M	Burridge J	Thomas SL
		3				7	8	9	10	11	12	6	4		2			1		13	5					
				5		2	8	9	10	11	12	6						1		3	4	13		7		
1				5	6	2	8	9	10	11	12	4								3				7		
				5		2		8	10	11	9	6			12	13		1		3	4			7		
1		1		3	1	4	3	4	4	4	1	4	1		1			3		3	3			3		
											3				1	1				1		1				
							1	5		1										1				1		

Coton AP	Hill AR	Phelan TM	McMahon S	Curle K	Vonk MC	Summerbee NJ	Walsh PAM	Rosler U	Flitcroft GW	Beagrie PS	Quinn NJ	Brightwell IR	Lomas SM	Edghill RA	Foster JC	Mike AR	Griffiths CB	Dibble AG	Tracey SP	Brightwell DJ	Kernaghan AN	Simpson F	Kerr DW	Gaudino M	Burridge J	Thomas SL
1	5		4		6	7	8	9		11	13	3	10	2	12											
	5	3				7	8		4	11	9	6	10	2			12	1								
		3		5		7	8		4	11	9	6	10	2				1								
	2			5		7	8	12	4	11	9	6	10					1		3						
					12	7	8	9	4	11	13	6	3		2			1			5			10		
		3		5		2	8	7	10	11	9		4					1		12	6			13		
1	3	3	1	3	1	6	6	3	5	6	4	5	6	3	1			5		1	2			1		
					1			1			2				1		1			1				1		
				1		2	2	2		1	2		1													

League Table

	P	W	D	L	F	A	Pts
Blackburn R	42	27	8	7	80	39	89
Manchester U	42	26	10	6	77	28	88
Nottingham F	42	22	11	9	72	43	77
Liverpool	42	21	11	10	65	37	74
Leeds U	42	20	13	9	59	38	73
Newcastle U	42	20	12	10	67	47	72
Tottenham H	42	16	14	12	66	58	62
Q.P.R.	42	17	9	16	61	59	60
Wimbledon	42	15	11	16	48	65	56
Southampton	42	12	18	12	61	63	54
Chelsea	42	13	15	14	50	55	54
Arsenal	42	13	12	17	52	49	51
Sheffield W	42	13	12	17	49	57	51
West Ham U	42	13	11	18	44	48	50
Everton	42	11	17	14	44	51	50
Coventry C	42	12	14	16	44	62	50
Manchester C	42	12	13	17	53	64	49
Aston Villa	42	11	15	16	51	56	48
Crystal Palace	42	11	12	19	34	49	45
Norwich C	42	10	13	19	37	54	43
Leicester C	42	6	11	25	45	80	29
Ipswich T	42	7	6	29	36	93	27

1995-96

Premiership

Manager: Alan Ball

Did you know that?

Match 3: Walsh's last game.
Match 4: Kerr's last game.
Match 10: Phelan's last game.
Match 22: Ekelund's last League game.
Match 31: Flitcroft's last game.
Match 32: Mazzarelli's last game.
Match 38: Curle and Quinn's last game.

Alan Ball won the manager of the month award for November after City only dropped one point during the month.

Match No.	Date	Venue	Opponents	Result		Scorers	Attendance
1	Aug 19	H	Tottenham Hotspur	D	1-1	Rosler	30,827
2	23	A	Coventry City	L	1-2	Rosler	16,568
3	26	A	Queen's Park Rangers	L	0-1		14,212
4	30	H	Everton	L	0-2		28,432
5	Sep 10	H	Arsenal	L	0-1		23,984
6	16	A	Newcastle United	L	1-3	Creaney	36,501
7	23	H	Middlesbrough	L	0-1		25,865
8	30	A	Nottingham Forest	L	0-3		25,620
9	Oct 14	A	Manchester United	L	0-1		35,707
10	21	H	Leeds United	D	0-0		26,390
11	28	A	Liverpool	L	0-6		39,267
12	Nov 4	H	Bolton Wanderers	W	1-0	Summerbee	28,397
13	18	A	Sheffield Wednesday	D	1-1	Lomas	24,422
14	22	H	Wimbledon	W	1-0	Quinn	23,617
15	25	H	Aston Villa	W	1-0	Kinkladze	28,027
16	Dec 2	A	Leeds United	W	1-0	Creaney	33,249
17	9	A	Middlesbrough	L	1-4	Kinkladze	29,469
18	18	H	Nottingham Forest	D	1-1	Rosler	24,287
19	23	H	Chelsea	L	0-1		28,668
20	26	A	Blackburn Rovers	L	0-2		28,915
21	Jan 1	H	West Ham United	W	2-1	Quinn 2	26,024
22	13	A	Tottenham Hotspur	L	0-1		31,438
23	20	H	Coventry City	D	1-1	Rosler	25,710
24	31	A	Southampton	D	1-1	Rosler	15,172
25	Feb 3	H	Queen's Park Rangers	W	2-0	Clough, Symons	27,509
26	10	A	Everton	L	0-2		37,354
27	24	H	Newcastle United	D	3-3	Quinn 2, Rosler	31,115
28	Mar 2	H	Blackburn Rovers	D	1-1	Lomas	29,078
29	5	A	Arsenal	L	1-3	Creaney	34,519
30	12	A	Chelsea	D	1-1	Clough	17,078
31	16	H	Southampton	W	2-1	Kinkladze 2	29,550
32	23	A	West Ham United	L	2-4	Quinn 2	24,017
33	30	A	Bolton Wanderers	D	1-1	Quinn	21,050
34	Apr 6	H	Manchester United	L	2-3	Kavelashvili, Rosler	29,688
35	8	A	Wimbledon	L	0-3		11,844
36	13	H	Sheffield Wednesday	W	1-0	Rosler	30,898
37	27	A	Aston Villa	W	1-0	Lomas	39,336
38	May 5	H	Liverpool	D	2-2	Rosler (pen), Symons	31,436
							Appearances
							Sub appearances
							Goals

FA Cup

	Date	Venue	Opponents	Result		Scorers	Attendance
R3	Jan 6	A	Leicester City	D	0-0		20,640
rep	17	H	Leicester City	W	5-0	Creaney, Kinkladze, Lomas, Quinn, Rosler	19,980
R4	Feb 7	A	Coventry City	D	2-2	Flitcroft, Busst (og)	18,709
rep	14	H	Coventry City	W	2-1	Clough, Quinn	22,419
R5	18	A	Manchester United	L	1-2	Rosler	42,692
							Appearances
							Sub appearances
						One own goal	Goals

League Cup

	Date	Venue	Opponents	Result		Scorers	Attendance
R2/1	Sep 19	A	Wycombe Wanderers	D	0-0		7,443
R2/2	Oct 4	H	Wycombe Wanderers	W	4-0	Rosler 2, Curle (pen), Quinn	11,474
R3	25	A	Liverpool	L	0-4		29,394
							Appearances
							Sub appearances
							Goals

Immel E	Edghill RA	Phelan TM	Lomas SM	Symons CJ	Brightwell IR	Summerbee NJ	Walsh PAM	Rosler U	Flitcroft GW	Kinkladze G	Quinn NJ	Kernaghan AN	Foster JC	Brown MR	Ingram R	Kerr DW	Curle K	Beagrie PS	Creaney GT	Margetson MW	Ekelund RM	Phillips MJ	Frontzeck M	Clough NH	Hiley SP	Mazzarelli G	Kavelashvili M
1	2	3	4	5	6	7	8	9	10	11	12																
1	2	3	4	5	6	7	8	9	10	11	12	13															
1		3	4	5		7	8	9	10	11	12	6	2	13													
1		3		5		7		9	10	11	8	12	2	6	4	13											
1	2	3		5	6	7		9	10	11	12						4	8									
1	2	3	13	5	6	12		9	10	7							4	11	8								
1	2	3	10	5	6	12		9		11				7			4	13	8								
1			10	5	3	12		9		7			2	6			4	11	8								
1	2	3	6	5		12		9	10	7	8						4	11	13								
1	2	3	6	5	12	7		9	10	11	8						4		13								
1	2		6	5	3	7		9	10	11	8			13			4		12								
1	3		6	5		7		9	10	11	8		2	13			4		12								
1	2		6	5	3	7		9	10	11	8						4										
1	2		6	5	3	7		9	10	11	8						4		12								
1	2		6	5	3	7		9	10	11	8						4										
1	2		6	5	3	7		9	10	11	8						4		12								
1			6	5	2	7				11	9			8	3		4		10								
1			10	5	2	7		9		11	8	6		12	3		4										
1				5	2	7		9		11	8			6	3		4		10		12						
1				5	3	2		9	10	11	8			6			4		12		7						
1			7	5	3	2		9	10	11	8			6			4				12	13					
1			6	5		2		9	10	11	8			12	3		4				7						
1			7	5	3	2		9	10	11	8			6			4					12					
1			6	5	12	2		9	10	11	8						4					13	3	7			
1			6	5	12	2		9	10	11							4		13			7	3	8			
1			6	5		2		9	10		12			7			4		13			11	3	8			
1			6	5		2		9		11	10			7			4							8	3		
1			6	5		2		9	10	11	8						4					12	3	7	13		
1			6	5		2		9	10	11		4							8			12	3	7	13		
1			8	5	6	2		9	10	11		4											3	7		12	
1			8	5	6	2		9	10	11	12						4						3	7	13		
1			10	5	6	2		9		11	12			7			4						3	8	13	14	
1			10	5	6	2				11	8			7			4						12	9	3		
1				5	6	2		12		11	8			7			4					13	3	9			10
1			6	5	2	7		12		11	8						4					13	3	9			10
1			6	5	2			9		11	12			7			4					13	3	8			10
1			10	5	6	2		9		11	8			3			4							7			
1			10	5	6	2		9		11	8			3			4					12		7			13
38	13	9	32	38	26	33	3	34	25	37	24	4	4	16	5		32	4	6		2	2	11	15	2		3
			1		3	4		2			8	2		5		1		1	9		2	9	1		4	2	1
			3	2		1		9		4	8								3					2			1

Immel E	Edghill RA	Phelan TM	Lomas SM	Symons CJ	Brightwell IR	Summerbee NJ	Walsh PAM	Rosler U	Flitcroft GW	Kinkladze G	Quinn NJ	Kernaghan AN	Foster JC	Brown MR	Ingram R	Kerr DW	Curle K	Beagrie PS	Creaney GT	Margetson MW	Ekelund RM	Phillips MJ	Frontzeck M	Clough NH	Hiley SP	Mazzarelli G	Kavelashvili M
1			11	5	3	2		9	10		8			6			4				7						
1			7	5		2		9	10	11	8			6	3		4		12		13						
1			7	5	3	2		9	10	11				6			4							8			
1			3	5		2		9	10	11	8			6			4		12					7			
1			6	5		2		9		11	8			10			4		12				3	7			
5			5	5	2	5		5	4	4	4			5	1		5				1		1	3			
																			3		1						
			1					2	1	1	2								1					1			

Immel E	Edghill RA	Phelan TM	Lomas SM	Symons CJ	Brightwell IR	Summerbee NJ	Walsh PAM	Rosler U	Flitcroft GW	Kinkladze G	Quinn NJ	Kernaghan AN	Foster JC	Brown MR	Ingram R	Kerr DW	Curle K	Beagrie PS	Creaney GT	Margetson MW	Ekelund RM	Phillips MJ	Frontzeck M	Clough NH	Hiley SP	Mazzarelli G	Kavelashvili M
1	2	3	10	5	6	12		9		7	8						4	11									
1	2		6	5	3	12		9	10	7	8			13			4	11		14							
1	2		6	5	3	7		9		11	8		10	12			4										
3	3	1	3	3	3	1		3	1	3	3		1				3	2									
						2								2						1							
								2			1						1										

League Table

	P	W	D	L	F	A	Pts
Manchester U	38	25	7	6	73	35	82
Newcastle U	38	24	6	8	66	37	78
Liverpool	38	20	11	7	70	34	71
Aston Villa	38	18	9	11	52	35	63
Arsenal	38	17	12	9	49	32	63
Everton	38	17	10	11	64	44	61
Blackburn R	38	18	7	13	61	47	61
Tottenham H	38	16	13	9	50	38	61
Nottingham F	38	15	13	10	50	54	58
West Ham U	38	14	9	15	43	52	51
Chelsea	38	12	14	12	46	44	50
Middlesbrough	38	11	10	17	35	50	43
Leeds U	38	12	7	19	40	57	43
Wimbledon	38	10	11	17	55	70	41
Sheffield W	38	10	10	18	48	61	40
Coventry C	38	8	14	16	42	60	38
Southampton	38	9	11	18	34	52	38
Manchester C	38	9	11	18	33	58	38
Q.P.R.	38	9	6	23	38	57	33
Bolton W	38	8	5	25	39	71	29

1996-97

Division One

Manager: Alan Ball (until 26 August 1996), Asa Hartford (caretaker 26 August – 7 October 1996), Steve Coppell (from 7 October – 8 November 1996), Phil Neal (caretaker 8 November – 29 December 1996), Frank Clark (from 30 December 1996)

Did you know that?

Match 4: Immel and Hiley's last game.
Match 5: Phillips's last League game.
Match 9: Foster's last game.
Match 19: Frontzeck's last game.
Match 21: Wassell and Dibble's last game.
Match 24: Rodger's last game.
Match 34: Lomas's last game.
Match 37: Ingram's last game.
Match 40: Kavelashvili's last game.
Match 41: Atkinson's last game.
Match 42: Clough's last game.

Both Asa Hartford and Phil Neal were caretaker managers longer than Steve Coppell was City's permanent choice.

Match No.	Date	Venue	Opponents	Result		Scorers	Attendance
1	Aug 16	H	Ipswich Town	W	1-0	Lomas	29,126
2	20	A	Bolton Wanderers	L	0-1		18,257
3	24	A	Stoke City	L	1-2	Rosler	21,120
4	Sep 3	H	Charlton Athletic	W	2-1	Creaney, Rosler (pen)	25,963
5	7	H	Barnsley	L	1-2	Clough	26,464
6	10	A	Port Vale	W	2-0	Dickov, Rosler	10,770
7	14	A	Crystal Palace	L	1-3	Kavelashvili	18,205
8	21	H	Birmingham City	W	1-0	Kinkladze (pen)	26,757
9	28	A	Sheffield United	L	0-2		20,867
10	Oct 12	A	Queen's Park Rangers	D	2-2	Brightwell, Kinkladze (pen)	16,265
11	15	A	Reading	L	0-2		11,724
12	19	H	Norwich City	W	2-1	Clough, Dickov	28,269
13	27	H	Wolverhampton W.	L	0-1		27,296
14	29	A	Southend United	W	3-2	Kinkladze 2 (1 pen), Rosler	8,274
15	Nov 2	A	Swindon Town	L	0-2		14,792
16	13	H	Oxford United	L	2-3	Brightwell, Dickov	23,079
17	16	A	Portsmouth	L	1-2	Rodger	12,844
18	19	H	Huddersfield Town	D	0-0		23,314
19	23	H	Tranmere Rovers	L	1-2	Summerbee	26,531
20	27	H	West Bromwich Albion	W	3-2	Kinkladze 2 (2 pens), Rosler	24,200
21	Dec 1	A	Wolverhampton W.	L	0-3		23,911
22	7	H	Bradford City	W	3-2	Dickov, Whitley, Kinkladze (pen)	25,035
23	21	A	Oldham Athletic	L	1-2	Kinkladze	12,992
24	26	H	Port Vale	L	0-1		30,344
25	28	A	Barnsley	L	0-2		17,159
26	Jan 11	H	Crystal Palace	D	1-1	Tuttle (og)	27,395
27	18	A	Huddersfield Town	D	1-1	Lomas	18,358
28	29	H	Sheffield United	D	0-0		26,551
29	Feb 2	A	Oxford United	W	4-1	Kinkladze 2, Rosler, Gilchrist (og)	8,820
30	8	H	Southend United	W	3-0	Rosler 2, Kinkladze	26,261
31	22	H	Swindon Town	W	3-0	Horlock, Rosler, Summerbee	27,262
32	Mar 1	A	Bradford City	W	3-1	Rosler 2 (1 pen), Horlock	17,609
33	5	H	Portsmouth	D	1-1	Horlock	26,051
34	8	H	Oldham Athletic	W	1-0	Rosler	30,729
35	11	A	Birmingham City	L	0-2		20,084
36	15	A	Grimsby Town	D	1-1	Kavelashvili	9,041
37	18	A	Tranmere Rovers	D	1-1	O'Brien (og)	12,019
38	22	H	Stoke City	W	2-0	Atkinson, Lomas	28,497
39	Apr 5	A	Charlton Athletic	D	1-1	Brannan	14,815
40	9	H	Bolton Wanderers	L	1-2	Kinkladze	28,026
41	12	A	West Bromwich Albion	W	3-1	Rosler 2, Horlock	19,909
42	16	H	Grimsby Town	W	3-1	Summerbee 2, Atkinson	23,334
43	19	H	Queen's Park Rangers	L	0-3		27,580
44	22	A	Ipswich Town	L	0-1		15,736
45	25	A	Norwich City	D	0-0		14,080
46	May 3	H	Reading	W	3-2	Dickov, Heaney, Rosler	27,260
							Appearances
							Sub appearances
						Three own goals	Goals

FA Cup

	Date	Venue	Opponents	Result		Scorers	Attendance
R3	Jan 25	A	Brentford	W	1-0	Summerbee	27,260
R4	Feb 5	H	Watford	W	3-1	Heaney, Rosler, Summerbee	12,019
R5	15	H	Middlesbrough	L	0-1		24,031
							Appearances
							Sub appearances
							Goals

League Cup

	Date	Venue	Opponents	Result		Scorers	Attendance
R2/1	Sep 17	A	Lincoln City	L	1-4	Rosler	7,599
R2/2	24	H	Lincoln City	L	0-1		14,242
							Appearances
							Sub appearances
							Goals

Immel E	Brightwell IR	Frontzeck M	Lomas SM	Symons CJ	Brown MR	Summerbee NJ	Phillips MJ	Kavelashvili M	Kinkladze G	Rosler U	Hiley SP	Creaney GT	Clough NH	Kernaghan AN	Dickov P	Foster JC	Dibble AG	Whitley, Jeff	Ingram R	Crooks LR	Wassall DPJ	McGoldrick EJP	Rodger SL	Margetson MW	Heaney NA	Wright TJ	Beagrie PS	Horlock K	Beesley P	Greenacre CM	Branman GD	Atkinson DR
1	2	3	4	5	6	7	8	9	10	11	12	13																				
1	2	3	4	5	6	12	13	9	10	11	7		8																			
1	2		4	5	6	7	12	9	10	11			8	3	13																	
1			4	5	6	7			10	11	3	13	8	12	9	2																
		3	4	5		7	12		10	11		13	6		9	2	1	8	14													
		3	4	5	2			12	10	11			7		9		1	8	6	13												
	12	3	4	5	2			13	10	11			7		9		1	8	6		14											
		3	4	5		7			10	11			8		9		1	12			6	2										
			4		12	7		13	10	11			8		9	5	1		3		6	2										
	2		4	5		7		12	10	11			8		9		1				6	3										
	2	12	4	5		7		13	10	11			8		9		1				6	3										
	2		4	5		7			10	11			8		9		1	12			6	3										
		3	4	5		2		12	10	11			8		9		1	7	13		6											
		3		5	12	7			10	11			8		9		1	2	13		6		4									
		12		5		7		13	10	11			8		9		1	4			6	2	3									
	4			5		7		12	10	11			8		9		1	13			6	2	3									
	3		4	5		7		12	10	11			8		13			14			6	2	9	1								
	3		4	5		7		9	10	11			12		13			14			6	2	8	1								
	3	12	4	5		7		11	10	13			14		9			8			6	2		1								
	3		4	5		7			10	11					9			12		2	6			1	8							
	3		4	5		7			10	11			12		9		13	8		2	6			1								
	6		4	5		7		12	10	11					9			14		13		2	3	1	8							
	6		4	5		7		12	10	11					9			8		13		2	3	1								
	6		4	5	8	7		12	10	11		13			9			14				2	3	1								
	6		4	5	12	7			10	11								8		3		2		1	9							
	6		4	5		7		12	10	11		8						13	3	14		2		1	9							
	6		4	5		7			10	11								12	3	8		2			9	1						
	2		4	5		7			10	11				6					3			8			9	1	12					
	2		4	5		7			10	11				6					3			8			12	1		9				
			4	5		7			10	11								12	3	2					8	1		9	6			
	2		4	5		7				11					9							8			10	1		3	6	12		
	2		4	5		7				11					9				12			8		1	10			3	6	13		
	2		4	5	12	7				11					9				10			8				1		3	6	13		
	2		4	5		7				11					9				10	12		8				1		3	6			
	2		4	5		7		12		11					9				10	13		8				1		3	6			
	2		4			7		9	10	11				5								8				1		3		12	6	
	2		4	5		7			10	11									9			8			12	1		3			6	
	2		4	5		7		12	10	11												3				1		9			6	8
	2			5		7		12	10	11				4								3				1		9			6	8
	2			5		7			10	11				9					4			8				1		3			6	12
	2			5		7		12	10	11			13	9					14			4		1				3			6	8
	2			5		7			10	11			4	9						12				1	13			3			6	8
	2			5		7			10	11				9								4		1	12			3			6	8
	2			5		7		12	10											11		4		1	9			3			6	8
	2			5		7							9		12			10		11		4		1				3			6	8
	2			5		7				11			12		9			8		10		4		1	13			3			6	
4	36	8	35	44	7	43	1	6	39	43	2	1	18	9	25	3	12	12	13	8	14	33	8	17	10	13		18	6		11	7
	1	3			4	1	3	18		1	1	4	5	1	4		1	11	5	7	1				5		1			4		1
	2		3			4		2	12	15			2		5			1					1		1			4			1	2

Immel E	Brightwell IR	Frontzeck M	Lomas SM	Symons CJ	Brown MR	Summerbee NJ	Phillips MJ	Kavelashvili M	Kinkladze G	Rosler U	Hiley SP	Creaney GT	Clough NH	Kernaghan AN	Dickov P	Foster JC	Dibble AG	Whitley, Jeff	Ingram R	Crooks LR	Wassall DPJ	McGoldrick EJP	Rodger SL	Margetson MW	Heaney NA	Wright TJ	Beagrie PS	Horlock K	Beesley P	Greenacre CM	Branman GD	Atkinson DR
	2			5		7				11			12		9			8		10		4		1	13			3			6	
	2		4	5		7			10	11				6					3			8		1	9							
			4	5		7			10	11		12		6					3	2		8		1	9							
	2		2	3		3			2	3				2	1			1	2	2		3		3	2			1			1	
												1	1												1							
						2				1															1							

Immel E	Brightwell IR	Frontzeck M	Lomas SM	Symons CJ	Brown MR	Summerbee NJ	Phillips MJ	Kavelashvili M	Kinkladze G	Rosler U	Hiley SP	Creaney GT	Clough NH	Kernaghan AN	Dickov P	Foster JC	Dibble AG	Whitley, Jeff	Ingram R	Crooks LR	Wassall DPJ	McGoldrick EJP	Rodger SL	Margetson MW	Heaney NA	Wright TJ	Beagrie PS	Horlock K	Beesley P	Greenacre CM	Branman GD	Atkinson DR
			4	5	2	7				11			10		9		1	8	3	12	6											
		3	4	5	12	7	13	14	10	11			8		9		1				6	2										
		1	2	2	1	2			1	2			2		2		2	1	1		2	1										
					1		1	1												1												
										1																						

League Table

	P	W	D	L	F	A	Pts
Bolton W	46	28	14	4	100	53	98
Barnsley	46	22	14	10	76	55	80
Wolverh'pton W	46	22	10	14	68	51	76
Ipswich T	46	20	14	12	68	50	74
Sheffield U	46	20	13	13	75	52	73
Crystal Palace	46	19	14	13	78	48	71
Portsmouth	46	20	8	18	59	53	68
Port Vale	46	17	16	13	58	55	67
Q.P.R.	46	18	12	16	64	60	66
Birmingham C	46	17	15	14	52	48	66
Tranmere R	46	17	14	15	63	56	65
Stoke C	46	18	10	18	51	57	64
Norwich C	46	17	12	17	63	68	63
Manchester C	46	17	10	19	59	60	61
Charlton A	46	16	11	19	52	66	59
W.B.A.	46	14	15	17	68	72	57
Oxford U	46	16	9	21	64	68	57
Reading	46	15	12	19	58	67	57
Swindon T	46	15	9	22	52	71	54
Huddersfield T	46	13	15	18	48	61	54
Bradford C	46	12	12	22	47	72	48
Grimsby	46	11	13	22	60	81	46
Oldham A	46	10	13	23	51	66	43
Southend U	46	8	15	23	42	86	39

1997-98

Division One

Manager: Frank Clark (until 17 February 1998),
Joe Royle (from 18 February 1998)

Did you know that?

Match 2: Kernaghan's last game.
Match 11: Summerbee's last game.
Match 15: Morley's last game.
Match 16: Kelly's first and only game.
Match 17: Creaney's last game.
Match 19: McGoldrick's last game.
Match 25: Scully's last game.
Match 31: Van Blerk and Conlon's last game.
Match 34: Brightwell's last game.
Match 35: Beesley's last game.
Match 37: Briscoe and Beardsley's last game.
Match 44: Rosler's last game.
Match 46: Margetson, Symons, Kinkladze, and Brannan's last game.

The 1997–98 season saw the arrival of the new club badge and the redevelopment of the City Social Club into the City Superstore.

Match No.	Date		Venue	Opponents	Result		Scorers	Attendance
1	Aug	9	H	Portsmouth	D	2-2	Rosler, Wiekens	30,474
2		15	A	Sunderland	L	1-3	Kinkladze (pen)	35,568
3		22	H	Tranmere Rovers	D	1-1	Horlock	26,336
4		30	A	Charlton Athletic	L	1-2	Wiekens	14,014
5	Sep	3	A	Nottingham Forest	W	3-1	Brannan 2, Dickov	23,552
6		12	A	Bury	D	1-1	Morley	11,216
7		20	H	Norwich City	L	1-2	Bradbury	27,252
8		27	H	Swindon Town	W	6-0	Dickov 2, Bradbury, Horlock, Kinkladze, Casper (og)	26,646
9	Oct	4	A	Ipswich Town	L	0-1		14,587
10		18	H	Reading	D	0-0		26,488
11		22	H	Stoke City	L	0-1		25,333
12		26	A	Queen's Park Rangers	L	0-2		14,451
13		29	H	Crewe Alexandra	W	1-0	Greenacre	27,384
14	Nov	1	A	Oxford United	D	0-0		8,584
15		4	H	Port Vale	L	2-3	Dickov, Wiekens	24,554
16		7	H	Huddersfield Town	L	0-1		24,425
17		15	A	Sheffield United	D	1-1	Horlock	23,850
18		22	H	Bradford City	W	1-0	Vaughan	29,746
19		29	A	Stockport County	L	1-3	Brannan	11,351
20	Dec	2	A	West Bromwich Albion	W	1-0	Dickov	17,904
21		6	H	Wolverhampton W.	L	0-1		28,999
22		13	A	Birmingham City	L	1-2	Shelia	21,014
23		20	H	Middlesbrough	W	2-0	Dickov, Rosler (pen)	28,097
24		26	A	Crewe Alexandra	L	0-1		5,759
25		28	H	Nottingham Forest	L	2-3	Dickov, Shelia	31,839
26	Jan	10	A	Portsmouth	W	3-0	Kinkladze, Rosler, Russell	13,512
27		17	H	Sunderland	L	0-1		31,715
28		28	H	Charlton Athletic	D	2-2	Symons, Dickov (pen)	24,058
29		31	A	Tranmere Rovers	D	0-0		12,830
30	Feb	7	A	Norwich City	D	0-0		15,274
31		14	H	Bury	L	0-1		28,885
32		18	H	Ipswich Town	L	1-2	Symons	27,156
33		21	A	Swindon Town	W	3-1	Rosler 2, Bradbury	12,987
34		24	A	Reading	L	0-3		11,513
35		28	H	West Bromwich Albion	W	1-0	Rosler	28,460
36	Mar	3	A	Huddersfield Town	W	3-1	Briscoe, Tskhadadze, Wiekens	15,694
37		7	H	Oxford United	L	0-2		28,690
38		14	A	Port Vale	L	1-2	Wiekens	13,122
39		21	H	Sheffield United	D	0-0		28,496
40		28	A	Bradford City	L	1-2	Jeff Whitley	17,099
41	Apr	4	H	Stockport County	W	4-1	Bradbury 2, Goater, Jobson	31,855
42		11	A	Wolverhampton W.	D	2-2	Horlock, Pollock	24,458
43		13	H	Birmingham City	L	0-1		29,569
44		17	A	Middlesbrough	L	0-1		30,182
45		25	H	Queen's Park Rangers	D	2-2	Bradbury, Kinkladze	32,040
46	May	3	A	Stoke City	W	5-2	Goater 2, Bradbury, Dickov, Horlock	26,664
								Appearances
								Sub appearances
							One own goal	Goals

FA Cup

R3	Jan	3	H	Bradford City	W	2-0	Brown, Rosler	23686
R4		25	H	West Ham United	L	1-2	Kinkladze	26495
								Appearances
								Sub appearances
								Goals

League Cup

R1/1	Aug	12	A	Blackpool	L	0-1		8,084
R1/2		26	H	Blackpool	W	1-0e	Horlock	12,563
Lost on penalties								Appearances
								Sub appearances
								Goals

Margetson MW	Brightwell IR	Vaughan AJ	Wiekens G	Symons CJ	Beesley P	Brannan GD	Horlock K	Bradbury LM	Kinkladze G	Rosler U	Summerbee NJ	Dickov P	Kernaghan AN	Van Blerk J	McGoldrick EJP	Scully ADT	Edghill RA	Morley DT	Conlon BJ	Heaney NA	Brown MR	Whitley, Jeff	Greenacre CM	Wright TJ	Kelly R	Creaney GT	Russell CS	Shelia M	Whitley, Jim	Crooks LR	Tskhadadze K	Beardsley PA	Briscoe LS	Jobson RI	Pollock J	Goater LS	Bishop IW
1	2	3	4	5	6	7	8	9	10	11	12	13																									
1	2	3	4	5		7	8	9	10	11	12		6	13																							
1	2	3	4	5	6	7	8	9	10	11	12																										
1	2		4	5		7	8	9		11	10			3	6	12																					
1	2		4	5		7	8	9	10		11	12		3			6																				
1			4	5		11	8	9	10		7			3		12	6	2																			
1	2		4	5		11	8	9	10		7	12		3		13	6																				
1	2		4	5	3	11	8	9	10			7				12	6		13																		
1	2		4	5	3	11	8	9	10	12		7				13	6																				
1	2		4	5		7	8		10		12	11		3	13		6			9																	
1	2			5		7	8		10		12	11		3	4		6		13	9																	
1	2		3	5		7	8		10			11			4		6				9	12	13														
		2	3	5		7	8					11		13		14	6		12		9	4	10	1													
		2	3	5		7	8					11		9			6	12				4	10	1													
		2	3	5		7	8		10			11				4	6	12	9					1													
1		2	3	5		7	8		10			11				12	6		13		14	4			9												
1		5	4	3		6	7		10			12			8		2				13					9	11										
1		3	6	5		7	8		10			9			4		2				12						11										
1		3	6	5		7	8		10			9			4		2				12						11										
1		3	6	5		7	8		10	12		9		13			2				4						11										
1		3	6	5		7				12		9		10			2				4	8					11										
1	12		6	5		7				11		9		10			2				4						8	3									
			6	5		7			10	11		9					2				4			1			8	3									
	12		6	5		7			10	11		9		13			2				4			1			8	3									
	2	5	6			7			10	11		9		13		12					4			1			8	3									
	2			5					10	11		9					6				4			1			8	3	7								
	2		7	5		12			10	11		9		13			6		14		4			1			8	3									
	2			5				12	10	11		9		13			6				4			1			8	3	7	14							
	2			5				9	10	11				12			6				4			1			8	3		7							
	2			5				9	10	11				12			6				4			1			8		13	7	3						
	2			5	12			9		11				10			6		13					1			8		4	7	3						
				5	14			12	10	11							2					7		1			8	4	6	13	3	9					
			12	5				13	10	11											8	2		1			9	4	7		6	14	3				
	2		4	5				9		11		12									8	13		1			14		7		6	10	3				
			4	5	12			9		11											8	2		1					7		6	10	3				
			7	5				9		11											8	2		1			13	4	12		6	10	3				
			7	5				9		11		12									13	2		1			14	4	8		6	10	3				
1			4	5		8			10	11		12					3			9	13	2					14		7					6			
1			10	5		12		9		11		13					3					2							7		6			4	8		
1			12	5				13		11							3					2					14		7		6			4	8	9	10
1		6	5					11									3					2							7					4	8	9	10
1		6	5				3	11		12							2				13						14		7					4	8	9	10
1		6	5			12	3	11		13							2				14								7					4	8	9	10
1		6		5		12	3	11		13							2				10	4							7						8	9	14
1		6		5		4	3	11	10			12					2										13		7						8	9	14
1		6	4	5		12	3	11	13			10					2					14							7						8	9	
28	19	19	35	42	4	27	25	23	29	23	4	21	1	10	6	1	36	1	1	3	18	14	2	18	1	1	17	12	17	3	10	5	5	6	8	7	4
	2		2		3	5		4	1	6	5	9		9	1	8		2	6		8	3	1				7		2	2		1					2
		1	5	2		3	5	7	4	6		9						1				1	1				1	2			1		1	1	1	3	

Margetson MW	Brightwell IR	Vaughan AJ	Wiekens G	Symons CJ	Beesley P	Brannan GD	Horlock K	Bradbury LM	Kinkladze G	Rosler U	Summerbee NJ	Dickov P	Kernaghan AN	Van Blerk J	McGoldrick EJP	Scully ADT	Edghill RA	Morley DT	Conlon BJ	Heaney NA	Brown MR	Whitley, Jeff	Greenacre CM	Wright TJ	Kelly R	Creaney GT	Russell CS	Shelia M	Whitley, Jim
	2		6			7			10	11		9		14							4	5	13	1			8	3	12
	2			5					10	11		9					6				4			1			8	3	7
	2		1	1		1			2	2		2					1				2	1		2			2	2	1
														1									1						1
									1	1											1								

Margetson MW	Brightwell IR	Vaughan AJ	Wiekens G	Symons CJ	Beesley P	Brannan GD	Horlock K	Bradbury LM	Kinkladze G	Rosler U	Summerbee NJ	Dickov P	Kernaghan AN	Van Blerk J	McGoldrick EJP
1	2	3	4			7	8	9	10	11	6		5		
1	2	3	4	5		7	8	9	10	11	6	13		14	12
2	2	2	2	1		2	2	2	2	2	2		1		
												1		1	1
							1								

League Table

	P	W	D	L	F	A	Pts
Nottingham F	46	28	10	8	82	42	94
Middlesbrough	46	27	10	9	77	41	91
Sunderland	46	26	12	8	86	50	90
Charlton A	46	26	10	10	80	49	88
Ipswich T	46	23	14	9	77	43	83
Sheffield U	46	19	17	10	69	54	74
Birmingham C	46	19	17	10	60	35	74
Stockport Co	46	19	8	19	71	69	65
Wolverh'pton W	46	18	11	17	57	53	65
W.B.A.	46	16	13	17	50	56	61
Crewe A	46	18	5	23	58	65	59
Oxford U	46	16	10	20	60	64	58
Bradford	46	14	15	17	46	59	57
Tranmere R	46	14	14	18	54	57	56
Norwich C	46	14	13	19	52	69	55
Huddersfield T	46	14	11	21	50	72	53
Bury	46	11	19	16	42	58	52
Swindon T	46	14	10	22	42	73	52
Port Vale	46	13	10	23	56	66	49
Portsmouth	46	13	10	23	51	63	49
Q.P.R.	46	10	19	17	51	63	49
Manchester C	46	12	12	22	56	57	48
Stoke C	46	11	13	22	44	74	46
Reading	46	11	9	26	39	78	42

1998-99

Division Two

Manager: Joe Royle

Did you know that?

Match 2: Tskhadadze's last game.
Match 10: Greenacre's last game.
Match 14: Bradbury's last game.
Match 15: Shelia's last game.
Match 20: Branch's last game.
Match 25: Russell's last game.
Match 41: Robins's last game.
Match 42: Mason's last game.

By playing at Wembley this season, the Blues became only the second side (Arsenal were first) to play at the old Wembley stadium in every decade of its existence, except the war-dominated 1940s.

Match No.	Date	Venue	Opponents	Result		Scorers	Attendance
1	Aug 8	H	Blackpool	W	3-0	Goater, Bradbury, Tskhadadze	32,134
2	14	A	Fulham	L	0-3		14,284
3	22	H	Wrexham	D	0-0		27,677
4	29	A	Notts County	D	1-1	Goater	10,316
5	Sep 2	H	Walsall	W	3-1	Goater 2, Dickov	24,291
6	8	H	Bournemouth	W	2-1	Allsop, Dickov	26,696
7	12	A	Macclesfield Town	W	1-0	Goater	6,381
8	19	H	Chesterfield	D	1-1	Bradbury	27,500
9	26	A	Northampton Town	D	2-2	Dickov, Goater	7,557
10	29	A	Millwall	D	1-1	Bradbury	12,726
11	Oct 3	H	Burnley	D	2-2	Goater, Allsop	30,722
12	12	H	Preston North End	L	0-1		28,779
13	17	A	Wigan Athletic	W	1-0	Goater	6,700
14	20	A	Lincoln City	L	1-2	Holmes (og)	7,338
15	24	H	Reading	L	0-1		24,365
16	31	H	Colchester United	W	2-1	Horlock (pen), Morrison	24,820
17	Nov 7	A	Oldham Athletic	W	3-0	Horlock 2, Morrison	12,976
18	10	A	Wycombe Wanderers	L	0-1		8,129
19	21	H	Gillingham	D	0-0		26,529
20	28	A	Luton Town	D	1-1	Morrison	9,070
21	Dec 12	H	Bristol Rovers	D	0-0		24,976
22	19	A	York City	L	1-2	Russell	7,527
23	26	A	Wrexham	W	1-0	Wiekens	9,048
24	28	H	Stoke City	W	2-1	Dickov, Taylor	30,478
25	Jan 9	A	Blackpool	D	0-0		9,752
26	16	H	Fulham	W	3-0	Goater, Taylor, Horlock	30,251
27	23	A	Walsall	D	1-1	Pollock	9,517
28	29	A	Stoke City	W	1-0	Wiekens	13,679
29	Feb 6	H	Millwall	W	3-0	Dickov, Cooke, Horlock	29,862
30	13	A	Bournemouth	D	0-0		10,946
31	20	H	Macclesfield Town	W	2-0	Goater, Taylor	31,086
32	27	A	Chesterfield	D	1-1	Crooks	8,245
33	Mar 6	H	Northampton Town	D	0-0		27,999
34	9	A	Burnley	W	6-0	Horlock, Morrison, Goater 3, Allsop	17,251
35	13	H	Oldham Athletic	L	1-2	Taylor	30,321
36	16	H	Notts County	W	2-1	Brown, Cooke	26,502
37	20	A	Colchester United	W	1-0	Goater	6,554
38	27	A	Reading	W	3-1	Cooke 2, Goater	20,055
39	Apr 3	H	Wigan Athletic	W	1-0	Cooke	31,058
40	5	A	Preston North End	D	1-1	Brown	20,857
41	10	H	Lincoln City	W	4-0	Dickov 3, Horlock	26,298
42	14	H	Luton Town	W	2-0	Dickov, Vaughan	26,130
43	17	A	Gillingham	W	2-0	Cooke, Horlock	10,400
44	24	H	Wycombe Wanderers	L	1-2	Goater	29,337
45	May 1	A	Bristol Rovers	D	2-2	Goater, Cooke	8,033
46	8	H	York City	W	4-0	Dickov, Horlock, Jeff Whitley, Allsop	32,471
							Appearances
							Sub appearances
						One own goal	Goals

Play-offs

SF1	May 15	A	Wigan Athletic	D	1-1	Dickov	6,762
SF2	19	H	Wigan Athletic	W	1-0	Goater	31,305
F	30	N	Gillingham	W	2-2	Horlock, Dickov	76,935
	Final won 3-1 on penalties a.e.t. Played at Wembley Stadium						Appearances
							Sub appearances
							Goals

FA Cup

R1	Nov 13	H	Halifax Town	W	3-0	Russell 2, Goater	11,106
R2	Dec 4	A	Darlington	D	1-1	Dickov	7,250
rep	15	H	Darlington	W	1-0e	Brown	8,595
R3	Jan 2	A	Wimbledon	L	0-1		11,226
							Appearances
							Sub appearances
							Goals

League Cup

R1/1	Aug 11	A	Notts County	W	2-0	Tskhadadze, Allsop	5,795
R1/2	19	H	Notts County	W	7-1	Mason, Dickov 2, Bradbury, Goater 2, Jim Whitley	10,063
R2/1	Sep 16	A	Derby County	D	1-1	Tiatto	22,986
R2/2	23	H	Derby County	L	0-1		19,622
							Appearances
							Sub appearances
							Goals

Auto Windcreens Shield

R1	Dec 8	H	Mansfield Town	L	1-2	Allsop	3,007
							Appearances
							Sub appearances
							Goals

Weaver NJ	Edghill RA	Horlock K	Tskhadadze K	Wiekens G	Vaughan AJ	Mason GR	Pollock J	Goater LS	Dickov P	Bradbury LM	Allsopp D	Whitley, Jim	Whitley, Jeff	Fenton NL	Conlon BJ	Tiatto DA	Brown MR	Wright TJ	Crooks LR	Greenacre CM	Sheila M	Russell CS	Morrison AC	Branch PM	Bishop IW	Taylor GK	Cooke TJ	Robins MG	Rimmer SA	Heaney NA	Bailey A
1	2	3	4	5	6	7	8	9	10	11	12	13																			
1	2	3	4	5	6	7	8	9	10		13	11	12																		
1	3			5	6	7	8	9	10	11	12	2		4																	
1	3	11		5	6	7	8	9	10	12		2		4																	
1	2			5	6	7	8	9	10	11	12			4		3	13														
1	2	3		5	6	7	8	9	10	12	11			4		13															
1	2	8		5	6	7		9	10	11	13	12		4		3															
	2			5	6	7	8	9	10	11	12			4		3		1	13												
1	2	3		5	6		8	9	12	11	10	7		4		14			13												
1	2	3		5	6		8	9		11	12	7		4		13				10											
1	2	10		5	6	8		9		11	12	7		4		3															
1	2	3		5	6			9	10	11	12	7		4		13	8														
1		10		5		7		9		11		8	12	4		3			2		6										
1		10		5				9	12	11	13	8	7	4		3			2		6										
1		10		5		7		9	11		12	2	13	4		3			8		6	14									
1	2	11		5	3	8		9	12		7								6				4	10	13						
1	2	11		5	3	8		9									12		6				4	10	7						
1	2	11		5	3	8		9	13		12						14		6				4	10	7						
1				5	3	6	7	9	12								13		2			11	4	10	8						
1	2			5	3	7		9								12	13		6			11	4		8	10					
1	2			5		6	8	9	7		13	12				14			3			11	4			10					
1	3	2			5		8				13	12		4			7		6			11			10	9					
1	3	6		4	5		8	12	13			14					7		2			11			10	9					
1	3	6		4	5		8	12	11								7		2						10	9					
1		6		4	3		8	10	11								7		2			12	5			9					
1	3	6		4	5		8	10				12					7		2							9	11				
1	3	6		4	5		8	10				12					7		2							9	11				
1	3	6		4	5		8	10	12			13					7		2						14	9	11				
1	3	6		4	5		8	10	12								7		2				13			9	11				
1	3	6		4	12		8	10	13								7		2				5			9	11				
1	3	6		4			8	10	12								7		2				5		13	9	11				
1	3			4		8		10	12		13			5		14	7		2						6	9	11				
1	3	6		4				10	12								7		2				5		8	9	11				
1	3	6		4	12			10			13						7		2				5		8	9	11				
1	2	6		4	3		12	10	13							14	7						5		8	9	11				
1	3	6		4			12		10		13						7		2				5		8	9	11				
1	3			4	6			10					12				7		2				5		8	9	11				
1				4	3		6	10	9		12						7		2				5		8	13	11				
1	3	12		4	5		6	10	9		13						7		2						8		11				
1	3	8			4		6	10									7		2				5		12	9	11	13			
1		6			4			10	9				12			3	7		2				5		8	13	11	14			
1	3	6			4	12		10	9								7		2				5		8	13	11				
1		6		4	3			10	9				12				7		2				5		8	13	11				
1	2	6		4	3			10	9		12						7						5		8	13	11				
1	3	6		4	12			10	9								7		2				5		8	13	11				
1	3	6		4	5				9		12		13			14	7		2						8	10	11				
45	38	36	2	42	35	18	24	41	22	11	3	10	1	15		8	26	1	32	1	3	5	21	4	21	20	21				
		1			3	1	2	2	13	2	21	8	7			9	5		2			2	1		4	6		2			
		9	1	2	1		1	17	10	3	4						2		1			1	4			4	7				

Weaver NJ	Edghill RA	Horlock K	Tskhadadze K	Wiekens G	Vaughan AJ	Mason GR	Pollock J	Goater LS	Dickov P	Bradbury LM	Allsopp D	Whitley, Jim	Whitley, Jeff	Fenton NL	Conlon BJ	Tiatto DA	Brown MR	Wright TJ	Crooks LR	Greenacre CM	Sheila M	Russell CS	Morrison AC	Branch PM	Bishop IW	Taylor GK	Cooke TJ	Robins MG	Rimmer SA	Heaney NA	Bailey A
1	3	6		4	5			10	9		12		8				7		2							13	11				
1	3	6		4	5		13	10	9				8				7		2							12	11				
1	3	6		4	13			10	9				8				7		2				5		12	14	11				
3	3	3		3	2			3	3				3				3		3				1				3				
					1		1				1														1	3					
		1						1	2																						

Weaver NJ	Edghill RA	Horlock K	Tskhadadze K	Wiekens G	Vaughan AJ	Mason GR	Pollock J	Goater LS	Dickov P	Bradbury LM	Allsopp D	Whitley, Jim	Whitley, Jeff	Fenton NL	Conlon BJ	Tiatto DA	Brown MR	Wright TJ	Crooks LR	Greenacre CM	Sheila M	Russell CS	Morrison AC	Branch PM	Bishop IW	Taylor GK	Cooke TJ	Robins MG	Rimmer SA	Heaney NA	Bailey A
1		6		5	3	8	13	9	10								12		2			11	4		7						
1	2			5	3	7	8	9	12										6			11	4			10					
1	3	6		5			8	9	13							12	7		2			11	4		14	10					
1		6		4	3		8	10	11			2					7					12	5			9					
4	2	3		4	3	2	3	4	2			1					2		3			3	4		1	3					
							1		2							1	1					1			1						
								1	1								1					2									

Weaver NJ	Edghill RA	Horlock K	Tskhadadze K	Wiekens G	Vaughan AJ	Mason GR	Pollock J	Goater LS	Dickov P	Bradbury LM	Allsopp D	Whitley, Jim	Whitley, Jeff	Fenton NL	Conlon BJ	Tiatto DA	Brown MR	Wright TJ	Crooks LR	Greenacre CM	Sheila M	Russell CS	Morrison AC	Branch PM	Bishop IW	Taylor GK	Cooke TJ	Robins MG	Rimmer SA	Heaney NA	Bailey A
1	2	3	4	5	6	7	8		10	11	12	9																			
1	2	3		5	6	7	8	9	10	11	13	12		4	14																
1	2			5	6		8	9	10	11		7	13	4		3	12														
	2	3		5	6	7	8	9	13	11	12	10		4				1													
3	4	3	1	4	4	3	4	3	3	4		3		3		1		1													
									1		3	1	1		1		1														
			1			1		2	2	1	1	1				1															

Weaver NJ	Edghill RA	Horlock K	Tskhadadze K	Wiekens G	Vaughan AJ	Mason GR	Pollock J	Goater LS	Dickov P	Bradbury LM	Allsopp D	Whitley, Jim	Whitley, Jeff	Fenton NL	Conlon BJ	Tiatto DA	Brown MR	Wright TJ	Crooks LR	Greenacre CM	Sheila M	Russell CS	Morrison AC	Branch PM	Bishop IW	Taylor GK	Cooke TJ	Robins MG	Rimmer SA	Heaney NA	Bailey A
					6		8				9	12	2	4		3	7	1								10			5	11	13
					1		1				1		1	1		1	1	1								1			1	1	
												1																			1
											1																				

League Table

	P	W	D	L	F	A	Pts
Fulham	46	31	8	7	79	32	101
Walsall	46	26	9	11	63	47	87
Manchester C	46	22	16	8	69	33	82
Gillingham	46	22	14	10	75	44	80
Preston N.E.	46	22	13	11	78	50	79
Wigan A	46	22	10	14	75	48	76
Bournemouth	46	21	13	12	63	41	76
Stoke C	46	21	6	19	59	63	69
Chesterfield	46	17	13	16	46	44	64
Millwall	46	17	11	18	52	59	62
Reading	46	16	13	17	54	63	61
Luton T	46	16	10	20	51	60	58
Bristol R	46	13	17	16	65	56	56
Blackpool	46	14	14	18	44	54	56
Burnley	46	13	16	17	54	73	55
Notts Co	46	14	12	20	52	61	54
Wrexham	46	13	14	19	43	62	53
Colchester U	46	12	16	18	52	70	52
Wycombe	46	13	12	21	52	58	51
Oldham A	46	14	9	23	48	66	51
York C	46	13	11	22	56	80	50
Northampton T	46	10	18	18	43	57	48
Lincoln C	46	13	7	26	42	74	46
Macclesfield	46	11	10	25	43	63	43

1999-2000

Division One

Manager: Joe Royle

Did you know that?

Match 2: Vaughan's last league game.
Match 20: Cooke's last game.
Match 22: G. Taylor's last game.
Match 31: Jim Whitley's last game.
Match 34: Peacock's last game.
Match 42: Mills's last game.
Match 46: Pollock and R. Taylor's last game.
Match 46: Jobson's last League game.

After the final game of the season, supporters staged an unofficial homecoming in city centre Manchester just as they had in 1904 when the Blues became the first Manchester side to win the FA Cup.

Match No.	Date	Venue	Opponents	Result		Scorers	Attendance
1	Aug 8	H	Wolverhampton W.	L	0-1		31,755
2	14	A	Fulham	D	0-0		16,754
3	21	H	Sheffield United	W	6-0	Horlock 2 (2 pens), Kennedy, Goater, Dickov, G Taylor	30,110
4	28	A	Bolton Wanderers	W	1-0	Kennedy	19,623
5	30	H	Nottingham Forest	W	1-0	Goater	31,857
6	Sep 11	H	Crystal Palace	W	2-1	Jobson, G Taylor	31,541
7	18	A	Walsall	W	1-0	Goater	7,260
8	26	A	Ipswich Town	L	1-2	Goater	19,453
9	28	A	Norwich City	L	0-1		15,130
10	Oct 2	H	Port Vale	W	2-1	Bishop 2	31,608
11	16	A	Tranmere Rovers	D	1-1	Horlock (pen)	13,208
12	19	A	Birmingham City	W	1-0	Jobson	22,126
13	23	H	Blackburn Rovers	W	2-0	Edghill, Jeff Whitley	33,027
14	27	H	Ipswich Town	W	1-0	Horlock	32,799
15	30	A	Port Vale	W	2-1	Snijders (og), Granville	10,250
16	Nov 3	H	Portsmouth	W	4-2	Jeff Whitley, G Taylor 2, Pollock	31,660
17	6	A	Queen's Park Rangers	D	1-1	Horlock	19,002
18	20	A	Charlton Athletic	W	1-0	Goater	20,048
19	24	H	Barnsley	W	3-1	G Taylor, Goater, Horlock	32,686
20	27	H	Huddersfield Town	L	0-1		32,936
21	Dec 3	A	Wolverhampton W.	L	1-4	Goater	21,635
22	7	H	Stockport County	L	1-2	Wiekens	32,686
23	18	H	Swindon Town	W	3-0	Pollock, R Taylor, Goater	31,751
24	26	A	West Bromwich Albion	W	2-0	Granville, Goater	19,481
25	28	H	Grimsby Town	W	2-1	Horlock 2	32,607
26	Jan 3	A	Crewe Alexandra	D	1-1	Crooks	10,066
27	16	H	Fulham	W	4-0	Goater 3, Horlock (pen)	30,057
28	22	A	Sheffield United	L	0-1		23,962
29	Feb 5	A	Nottingham Forest	W	3-1	R Taylor, Goater 2	25,846
30	12	H	Norwich City	W	3-1	Goater, Kennedy 2	32,681
31	18	A	Huddersfield Town	D	1-1	Goater	18,173
32	26	H	Walsall	D	1-1	Goater	32,438
33	Mar 4	A	Crystal Palace	D	1-1	R Taylor	21,052
34	8	H	Queen's Park Rangers	L	1-3	Jeff Whitley	31,353
35	11	A	Barnsley	L	1-2	Goater	22,650
36	19	H	Charlton Athletic	D	1-1	Goater	32,139
37	21	A	Stockport County	D	2-2	Pollock, Jobson	11,212
38	25	H	West Bromwich Albion	W	2-1	Kennedy, Goater	30,072
39	Apr 1	A	Swindon Town	W	2-0	Goater, Kennedy	12,397
40	5	H	Bolton Wanderers	W	2-0	Horlock, Dickov	32,927
41	8	H	Crewe Alexandra	W	4-0	Prior, Dickov 2, Kennedy	32,433
42	15	A	Grimsby Town	D	1-1	Prior	8,166
43	22	H	Tranmere Rovers	W	2-0	Goater, Jeff Whitley	32,842
44	24	A	Portsmouth	D	2-2	Prior, R Taylor	18,956
45	28	H	Birmingham City	W	1-0	R Taylor	32,062
46	May 7	A	Blackburn Rovers	W	4-1	Goater, Dailly (og), Kennedy, Dickov	29,913
							Appearances
							Sub appearances
						Two own goals	Goals

FA Cup

R3	Dec 12	A	Chester City	W	4-1	Goater 2, Bishop, Doughty (og)	5,469
R4	Jan 9	H	Leeds United	L	2-5	Goater, Bishop	29,240
							Appearances
							Sub appearances
						One own goal	Goals

League Cup

R1/1	Aug 11	H	Burnley	W	5-0	Goater, Kennedy 2, Horlock (pen), G Taylor	11,074
R1/2	24	A	Burnley	W	1-0	Cooke	3,647
R2/1	Sep 15	H	Southampton	D	0-0		17,476
R2/2	21	A	Southampton	L	3-4e	Dickov, Goater 2	10,960
							Appearances
							Sub appearances
							Goals

Weaver NJ	Edghill RA	Granville DP	Wiekens G	Morrison AC	Horlock K	Cooke TJ	Whitley, Jeff	Dickov P	Goater LS	Kennedy M	Crooks LR	Taylor GK	Tiatto DA	Bishop IW	Allsopp D	Pollock J	Vaughan AJ	Jobson RI	Brown MR	Wright-Phillips SC	Fenton NL	Peacock LA	Taylor RA	Wright TJ	Grant AJ	Whitley, Jim	Mills RL	Prior SJ
1	2	3	4	5	6	7	8	9	10	11	12	13																
1			4	5	6		8	9	10	11	2		3	7			12											
1	2		4	5	6	7	8	9	10	11		12	3	13				14										
1	2		4		6	7	8	9	10	11	14	13	3	12				5										
1	2			5	6	7	8	9	10	11	12	14	3	13				4										
1	2			5	6	7	8	9	10	11	14	12	3	13				4										
1	2		4		6		8	9	10	11	12		3	7				5										
1		13	4		6	12	8	9	10	11	2		3	7				5										
1		3		5	6	13	8	9	10	11	2	12		7	14			4										
1		3		5	6	13	8	9	10	11	2			7	12			4										
1	12	3		5	6		8	9		11	2	10		7				4										
1	2	3		5	6		8	9		11	12	10		7	13			4										
1	2	3		5	6		8	9	10	11	13	12		7				4										
1	2	3		5	6		8	9	10	11	13	12	14	7				4										
1	2	3	14	5		7	8			11	6	9		12		10		4		13								
1	2	3	4		6	12	8			11		9	14	7		13		5		10								
1	2	3			6	12	8			11	4	9	14	7				5		10		13						
1	2	3	4		6	12	8		10			9	11			7		5										
1	2	3	4		6		8		10		13	9	11			7		5				12						
1	2	3	4		6	12	8		10			9	11			7		5				13						
1	2	3	4		6		8		10	11			12	7		13		5					9					
1	2	3	4		6		8		10	11		13		7		12		5					9					
	2	3	4		6				10	11			12	7		8		5				13	9	1				
1	2	3	4				8	12	10	11			12	7		6		5				9			13			
1	2	3	4		6			12	10		14		11	7		8		5				9			13			
1		3	4		6		14	12	10		2		13	8		11		5					9		7			
1	2	3	4		6				10	11			12	8				5					9		7			
1	2				6			12	10	11	4		3	8				5					9		7			
1	2	12	4		6		8	14	10	11			3	7		13		5					9					
1	2	3	4		6		8	9	10	11				7	12	13		5										
1	2	3	4		6		8	9	10	11			12	7				5								13		
1	2	3	4		6		8	9	10	11	14			7				5					12		13			
1	2	3	4				8			11			6			7		5		12		10	9					
1	2	3	4		14		8	13	10	11			6	12		7		5				9						
1	2	3	4				8	13	10	11			6	12		7		5									9	
1	2	12	4				8		10	11			3	7		6		5					9					
1	2	3	4				8	12	10	11				7		6		5					9					
1	2	3					8	12	10	11			6			7		5					9		13			4
1	2		13				8	9	10	11			3	12		6		5							7			4
1	2	13	7		6		8	9	10	11			3					5									12	4
1	2		7		6		8	9	10	11			3	12				5										4
1	2		7		6		8	9	10	11			3	12				5									13	4
1	2		7		6		8	9	10	11			3	13		14		5					12					4
1	2	14	7		13		8	12	10	11			3			6		5					9					4
1	2	12	7		6		8	13	10	11			3			14		5					9					4
1	2	14			6		8	13	10	11			3	12		7		5					9					4
45	40	28	32	12	36	6	41	22	40	41	9	8	26	25		17		43		2		4	14	1	4		1	9
	1	7	2		2	7	1	12			11	9	9	12	4	7	1	1		2		4	2		4	1	2	
	1	2	1		10		4	5	23	8	1	5		2		3		3					5					3

Weaver NJ	Edghill RA	Granville DP	Wiekens G	Morrison AC	Horlock K	Cooke TJ	Whitley, Jeff	Dickov P	Goater LS	Kennedy M	Crooks LR	Taylor GK	Tiatto DA	Bishop IW	Allsopp D	Pollock J	Vaughan AJ	Jobson RI	Brown MR	Wright-Phillips SC	Fenton NL	Peacock LA	Taylor RA	Wright TJ	Grant AJ	Whitley, Jim	Mills RL	Prior SJ
1	2	3	4		6		12		10	11				7		8		5				9						
1	2	3	4		6		12	9	10	11				8				5				13			7			
2	2	2	2		2			1	2	2				2		1		2				1			1			
							2															1						
									3					2														

Weaver NJ	Edghill RA	Granville DP	Wiekens G	Morrison AC	Horlock K	Cooke TJ	Whitley, Jeff	Dickov P	Goater LS	Kennedy M	Crooks LR	Taylor GK	Tiatto DA	Bishop IW	Allsopp D	Pollock J	Vaughan AJ	Jobson RI	Brown MR	Wright-Phillips SC	Fenton NL	Peacock LA	Taylor RA	Wright TJ	Grant AJ	Whitley, Jim	Mills RL	Prior SJ
1			4	5	6	7	8	9	10	11	2	14	3	13	12													
1	2		4			7				11	3	9		8	12	6	13	5	10	14								
1	2			5	6	7	8		10	11	12	9	3	14	13			4										
1	2				6	14	8	9	10	11	4		3	7	13			5			12							
4	3		2	2	3	3	3	2	3	4	3	2	3	2		1		3	1									
						1					1	1		2	4		1			1	1							
					1	1		1	3	2		1																

League Table

	P	W	D	L	F	A	Pts
Charlton Athletic	46	27	10	9	79	45	91
Manchester City	46	26	11	9	78	40	89
Ipswich Town	46	25	12	9	71	42	87
Barnsley	46	24	10	12	88	67	82
Birmingham City	46	22	11	13	65	44	77
Bolton Wanderers	46	21	13	12	69	50	76
Wolverhampton W	46	21	11	14	64	48	74
Huddersfield Town	46	21	11	14	62	49	74
Fulham	46	17	16	13	49	41	67
Queen's Park Rangers	46	16	18	12	62	53	66
Blackburn Rovers	46	15	17	14	55	51	62
Norwich City	46	14	15	17	45	50	57
Tranmere Rovers	46	15	12	19	57	68	57
Nottingham Forest	46	14	14	18	53	55	56
Crystal Palace	46	13	15	18	57	67	54
Sheffield United	46	13	15	18	59	71	54
Stockport County	46	13	15	18	55	67	54
Portsmouth	46	13	12	21	55	66	51
Crewe Alexandra	46	14	9	23	46	67	51
Grimsby Town	46	13	12	21	41	67	51
West Bromwich Albion	46	10	19	17	43	60	49
Walsall	46	11	13	22	52	77	46
Port Vale	46	7	15	24	48	69	36
Swindon Town	46	8	12	26	38	77	36

2000-01

Premiership

Manager: Joe Royle

Did you know that?

Match 8: Wright, Weah, and Crooks's last game.
Match 13: Allsopp's last game.
Match 22: Bishop's last League game.
Match 25: Morrison's last League game.
Match 31: Ostenstad's last game.
Match 35: Kanchelskis's last game.
Match 37: Prior's last game.
Match 38: Kennedy and Dunfield's last game.

City's top scorer Paulo Wanchope was in and out of favour throughout the season.

Match No.	Date	Venue	Opponents	Result		Scorers	Attendance
1	Aug 19	A	Charlton Athletic	L	0-4		20,039
2	23	H	Sunderland	W	4-2	Wanchope 3, Haaland	34,410
3	26	H	Coventry City	L	1-2	Horlock	34,140
4	Sep 5	A	Leeds United	W	2-1	Howey, Wiekens	40,055
5	9	A	Liverpool	L	2-3	Weah, Horlock (p)	44,692
6	17	H	Middlesbrough	D	1-1	Wanchope	32,053
7	23	A	Tottenham Hotspur	D	0-0		36,065
8	30	H	Newcastle United	L	0-1		34,497
9	Oct 14	H	Bradford City	W	2-0	Dickov, Haaland	34,229
10	23	A	Southampton	W	2-0	Dickov, Tiatto	15,056
11	28	A	Arsenal	L	0-5		38,049
12	Nov 4	H	Leicester City	L	0-1		34,279
13	11	A	West Ham United	L	1-4	Prior	26,022
14	18	H	Manchester United	L	0-1		34,429
15	25	H	Ipswich Town	L	2-3	Wanchope, Howey	33,741
16	Dec 3	A	Chelsea	L	1-2	Dickov	34,971
17	9	H	Everton	W	5-0	Wanchope, Howey, Goater, Dickov, Naysmith (og)	34,516
18	16	A	Aston Villa	D	2-2	Haaland, Wanchope	29,281
19	23	A	Sunderland	L	0-1		45,686
20	26	H	Derby County	D	0-0		34,321
21	30	H	Charlton Athletic	L	1-4	Huckerby (pen)	33,280
22	Jan 1	A	Coventry City	D	1-1	Wanchope	21,991
23	13	H	Leeds United	L	0-4		34,288
24	20	A	Derby County	D	1-1	Howey	31,174
25	31	H	Liverpool	D	1-1	Tiatto	34,629
26	Feb 3	A	Middlesbrough	D	1-1	Vickers (og)	31,792
27	10	H	Tottenham Hotspur	L	0-1		34,399
28	24	A	Newcastle United	W	1-0	Goater	51,981
29	Mar 3	H	Southampton	L	0-1		33,990
30	17	A	Bradford City	D	2-2	Wiekens, Goater	19,117
31	31	H	Aston Villa	L	1-3	Goater	34,243
32	Apr 8	A	Everton	L	1-3	Whitley	36,561
33	11	H	Arsenal	L	0-4		33,444
34	14	A	Leicester City	W	2-1	Goater, Wanchope	20,224
35	21	A	Manchester United	D	1-1	Howey	67,535
36	28	H	West Ham United	W	1-0	I Pearce (og)	33,737
37	May 7	A	Ipswich Town	L	1-2	Goater	24,888
38	19	H	Chelsea	L	1-2	Howey	34,479
							Appearances
							Sub appearances
						Three own goals	Goals

FA Cup

Round	Date	Venue	Opponents	Result		Scorers	Attendance
R3	Jan 6	H	Birmingham City	W	3-2	Morrison, Huckerby, Goater (pen)	19,380
R4	27	H	Coventry City	W	1-0	Goater	24,637
R5	Feb 18	A	Liverpool	L	2-4	Kanchelskis, Goater	36,531
							Appearances
							Sub appearances
							Goals

League Cup

Round	Date	Venue	Opponents	Result		Scorers	Attendance
R2/1	Sep 20	H	Gillingham	D	1-1	Weah	17,408
R2/2	26	A	Gillingham	W	4-2e	Weah 2, Dickov, Kennedy	6,520
R3	Nov 1	A	Aston Villa	W	1-0	Horlock (pen)	24,138
R4	29	H	Wimbledon	W	2-1	Wanchope, Goater	19,513
R5	Dec 19	H	Ipswich Town	L	1-2e	Goater	31,252
							Appearances
							Sub appearances
							Goals

Weaver NJ	Edghill RA	Tiatto DA	Prior SJ	Howey SN	Horlock K	Wiekens G	Haaland A-IR	Wanchope WPC	Weah GMOO	Kennedy M	Wright-Phillips SC	Grant AJ	Dickov P	Ritchie PS	Whitley, Jeff	Granville DP	Bishop IW	Crooks LR	Jobson RI	Wright TJ	Dunne RP	Goater LS	Charvet LJ	Allsopp D	Morrison AC	Huckerby DC	Kanchelskis A	Ostenstad E	Nash CJ	Dunfield T
1	2	3	4	5	6	7	8	9	10	11	12																			
1	2	3	4	5	6	7	8	9	10	11																				
1	2	3	4	5	6	7	8	9	10	11		12	13																	
1		10	4	5	6	7	2	9		11	12			3	8	13														
1			4	5	6	7	2	9	12	11			10	3	8															
1		12	4	5	6	7	2	9	10	11			14	3	8		13													
1		11	4	5	6	7	2	9	14	13			10	3	8			12												
		3	4		6	7	2	9	10	12			11	5	8		13	14		1										
1		6	4	5		7	2	9		11			10	3	8		12													
1		11	4	5		7	6	9					10	3	8						2	12								
1		11	4	5		7	6			12			9	3	8							10	2							
1		11	4	5		7	6	9		12			10	3	8		13						2							
1			4	5		7	6	9		11	10			3	8						12		2	13						
1		3	4	5		7	6			11	10		9		8		12					13	2							
1		12	4	5			6	14		11	8		9		13		7				2	10	3							
1		3	4	5	6	13	7	9			11		12		8							10	2							
1		3		5	6	13	7	9		14	11		12		8						4	10	2							
1		3		5	6	13	7	9		12	11				8						4	10	2							
1		3		5	6		7			11	10		12		8		13				4	9	2							
1		3		5	6	12	8	9			11						7				4	10	2							
1		3		5	6	7	8				11		9			14	12				4	10	2			13				
1	2	11		5			8	9			13					3	7				4	12			6	10				
1	2	11		5			7	9			14	12	13		8	3					4	10			6					
1		11	4	5		7	6	9			12			3	8	14					2	13				10				
1		11		5		7	6							13	8	3					2	10			4	9	12			
1		11		5		2	6				13	12			8	3					4	10				9	7			
1		11		5		2	6					13			8	3					4	10				9	7	12		
1		11		5		2	6					8			13	3					4	10	12			9	7			
1		11		5		2	6					8				3					4	10	12			9	7	13		
1		11		5		6				14		8			12	3					4	10	2			9	7	13		
1		11	5			14	6			12					8	3					4	10	2			13	7	9		
1		11		5		2	6	9		12			10		8	3					4					13	7			
		7		5		2	6	9		11					8	3					4	10	13			12			1	
			14	5		7	6	9		11		13			8	3					4	10	2				12		1	
			13	5		7	6	9				11	10		8	3					4	14	2				12		1	
		7		5		2	6	13		11			9		8	3					4	10	12			14			1	
		11	14	5		6		9		13		7	10		8	3					4	12	2						1	
	2			5		6		9		11			7		8	3					4	10							1	12
31	6	31	18	36	14	29	35	25	5	15	9	5	15	11	28	16	3			1	24	20	16		3	8	7	1	6	
		2	3			5		2	2	10	6	5	6	1	3	3	7	2			1	6	4	1		5	3	3		1
		2	1	6	2	2	3	9	1				4		1							6				1				

Weaver NJ	Edghill RA	Tiatto DA	Prior SJ	Howey SN	Horlock K	Wiekens G	Haaland A-IR	Wanchope WPC	Weah GMOO	Kennedy M	Wright-Phillips SC	Grant AJ	Dickov P	Ritchie PS	Whitley, Jeff	Granville DP	Bishop IW	Crooks LR	Jobson RI	Wright TJ	Dunne RP	Goater LS	Charvet LJ	Allsopp D	Morrison AC	Huckerby DC	Kanchelskis A	Ostenstad E	Nash CJ	Dunfield T
1	2	11	14	5		7	8						12			3	13				4	10			6	9				
1			4			13	11	9				7		6	8	3					2	14	12		5	10				
1		11	6			2	8					12				3					4	10			5	9	7			
3	1	2	2	1		2	3	1				1		1	1	3					3	2			3	3	1			
			1			1						1	1				1					1	1							
																						3			1	1	1			

Weaver NJ	Edghill RA	Tiatto DA	Prior SJ	Howey SN	Horlock K	Wiekens G	Haaland A-IR	Wanchope WPC	Weah GMOO	Kennedy M	Wright-Phillips SC	Grant AJ	Dickov P	Ritchie PS	Whitley, Jeff	Granville DP	Bishop IW	Crooks LR	Jobson RI	Wright TJ	Dunne RP	Goater LS	Charvet LJ	Allsopp D	Morrison AC	Huckerby DC	Kanchelskis A	Ostenstad E	Nash CJ	Dunfield T
1			4				5	9	10	11	6		13	3	8	12	7	2	14											
1		11			6	7	4		10	12			9	3	8	14	13	2	5											
1		11	4	5	6	7	2			12	14		9	3	8		13					10								
1		3	4	5	6	12	2	9		13	11				8		7					10								
1		3	4		6	7	2	9		12	11				8	13	14					10			5					
5		4	4	2	4	3	5	3	2	1	3		2	3	5		2	2	1			3			1					
						1				4	1		1			3	3		1											
					1			1	3	1			1									2								

League Table

	P	W	D	L	F	A	Pts
Manchester United	38	24	8	6	79	31	80
Arsenal	38	20	10	8	63	38	70
Liverpool	38	20	9	9	71	39	69
Leeds United	38	20	8	10	64	43	68
Ipswich Town	38	20	6	12	57	42	66
Chelsea	38	17	10	11	68	45	61
Sunderland	38	15	12	11	46	41	57
Aston Villa	38	13	15	10	46	43	54
Charlton Athletic	38	14	10	14	50	57	52
Southampton	38	14	10	14	40	48	52
Newcastle United	38	14	9	15	44	50	51
Tottenham Hotspur	38	13	10	15	47	54	49
Leicester City	38	14	6	18	39	51	48
Middlesbrough	38	9	15	14	44	44	42
West Ham United	38	10	12	16	45	50	42
Everton	38	11	9	18	45	59	42
Derby County	38	10	12	16	37	59	42
Manchester City	38	8	10	20	41	65	34
Coventry City	38	8	10	20	36	63	34
Bradford City	38	5	11	22	30	70	26

2001-02

Division One

Manager: Kevin Keegan OBE

Did you know that?

Match 2: Whitley's last game.
Match 3: Charvet's last game.
Match 6: Grant's last game.
Match 11: Toure's first and only League game.
Match 18: Colosimo's last game.
Match 20: Mike's last game.
Match 25: Granville's last game.
Match 26: Etuhu's last game.
Match 27: Haaland's last League game.
Match 30: Dickov's last game.
Match 33: Killen's last game.
Match 34: Edghill's last game.
Match 35: Ritchie's last game
Match 42: Mears's first and only game.
Match 46: Pearce's last game.

For the first time in four years fans could relax on the final day of the season. In previous years the Blues needed to either avoid relegation or push for promotion on the final day. This time City were already champions.

Match No.	Date	Venue	Opponents	Result		Scorers	Attendance
1	Aug 11	H	Watford	W	3-0	Goater, Berkovic, Pearce	33,939
2	18	A	Norwich City	L	0-2		18,745
3	25	H	Crewe Alexandra	W	5-2	Wanchope 2, Pearce (pen), Goater 2	32,844
4	27	A	Burnley	W	4-2	Goater 3, Wanchope	19,603
5	Sep 8	A	West Bromwich Albion	L	0-4		23,524
6	15	H	Birmingham City	W	3-0	Goater 2, Dunne	31,714
7	19	A	Coventry City	L	3-4	Benarbia, Horlock, Hall (og)	18,804
8	22	A	Sheffield Wednesday	W	6-2	Benarbia, Goater 2, Granville, Wanchope 2 (1 pen)	25,731
9	25	H	Walsall	W	3-0	Benarbia, Goater, Wanchope (pen)	31,525
10	29	H	Wimbledon	L	0-4		32,989
11	Oct 13	H	Stockport County	D	2-2	Benarbia, Goater	34,214
12	16	H	Sheffield United	D	0-0		32,454
13	21	A	Preston North End	L	1-2	Huckerby	21,013
14	23	H	Grimsby Town	W	4-0	Goater, Howey, Huckerby 2	30,797
15	28	A	Nottingham Forest	D	1-1	Goater	28,226
16	31	A	Barnsley	W	3-0	Goater, Pearce, Huckerby	15,159
17	Nov 3	H	Gillingham	W	4-1	Goater 3, Huckerby	33,067
18	17	A	Portsmouth	L	1-2	Huckerby	19,103
19	24	H	Rotherham United	W	2-1	Negouai, Benarbia	34,223
20	Dec 1	A	Grimsby Town	W	2-0	Huckerby (pen), Goater	7,960
21	4	A	Millwall	W	3-2	Goater, Huckerby, Wright-Phillips	13,026
22	8	A	Crystal Palace	L	1-2	Goater	22,080
23	11	H	Wolverhampton W.	W	1-0	Horlock	33,639
24	16	H	Bradford City	W	3-1	Mettomo, Horlock, Wright-Phillips	30,749
25	26	H	West Bromwich Albion	D	0-0		34,407
26	29	H	Burnley	W	5-1	Wanchope 3, Berkovic, Huckerby	34,250
27	Jan 1	A	Sheffield United	W	3-1	Goater, Berkovic, Wright-Phillips	26,291
28	13	H	Norwich City	W	3-1	Berkovic 2, Wanchope (pen)	31,794
29	20	A	Watford	W	2-1	Wanchope, Helguson (og)	17,074
30	30	H	Millwall	W	2-0	Goater 2	30,238
31	Feb 3	A	Wimbledon	L	1-2	Benarbia	10,664
32	10	H	Preston North End	W	3-2	Wright-Phillips, Howey, Wanchope	34,220
33	23	A	Walsall	D	0-0		7,618
34	27	H	Sheffield Wednesday	W	4-0	Horlock, Huckerby, Berkovic, Goater	33,682
35	Mar 3	H	Coventry City	W	4-2	Huckerby, Tiatto, Wright-Phillips 2	33,335
36	5	A	Birmingham City	W	2-1	Jensen, Horlock	24,160
37	8	A	Bradford City	W	2-0	Huckerby, Macken	18,168
38	12	A	Crewe Alexandra	W	3-1	Benarbia, Huckerby, Goater	10,092
39	16	H	Crystal Palace	W	1-0	Horlock	33,637
40	19	A	Stockport County	L	1-2	Macken	9,537
41	23	A	Rotherham United	D	1-1	Benarbia	11,426
42	30	H	Nottingham Forest	W	3-0	Huckerby 3 (1 pen)	34,345
43	Apr 1	A	Wolverhampton W.	W	2-0	Wright-Phillips 2	28,015
44	6	H	Barnsley	W	5-1	Huckerby 3, Macken 2	33,628
45	13	A	Gillingham	W	3-1	Horlock, Goater, Huckerby	9,494
46	21	H	Portsmouth	W	3-1	Howey, Goater, Macken	34,657
							Appearances
							Sub appearances
						Two own goals	Goals

FA Cup

	Date	Venue	Opponents	Result		Scorers	Attendance
R3	Jan 5	H	Swindon Town	W	2-0	Wanchope, Horlock	21,581
R4	27	A	Ipswich Town	W	4-1	Berkovic, Goater 2, Huckerby	21,199
R5	Feb 17	A	Newcastle United	L	0-1		51,020
							Appearances
							Sub appearances
							Goals

League Cup

	Date	Venue	Opponents	Result		Scorers	Attendance
R2	Sep 11	A	Notts County	W	4-2e	Goater, Huckerby, Dickov, Shuker	6,532
R3	Oct 10	H	Birmingham City	W	6-0	Huckerby 4, Goater, Luntala (og)	13,912
R4	Nov 28	A	Blackburn Rovers	L	0-2		17,907
							Appearances
							Sub appearances
						One own goal	Goals

Nash CJ	Charvet LJ	Granville DP	Dunne RP	Howey SN	Pearce S	Wiekens G	Berkovic E	Wanchope WPC	Goater LS	Tiatto DA	Whitley, Jeff	Huckerby DC	Dickov P	Weaver NJ	Horlock K	Wright-Phillips SC	Grant AJ	Edghill RA	Colosimo S	Shuker CA	Benarbia A	Etuhu DP	Toure A	Mettomo L	Negouai C	Mike LJ	Killen C	Ritchie PS	Haaland A-IR	Jensen N	Jihai S	Macken JP	Mears T
1	2	3	4	5	6	7	8	9	10	11	12	13	14																				
1	2	3	4	5	6	7	8	9	10	11	12			13	14																		
	2	3	4	5	6	7		9	10	11		14		1	12	8	13																
		3	4	5	6			9	10	11				1	8		7	2															
		3	4	5	6	12			10	11		9	13	1	8		7	2	14														
		3	4	5	6			9	10	11		13	14	1	12			2			7	8											
		3		5	6	4		9	10	11				1	13			2	12		7	8											
		3	12	5	6	4		9	10	11		13		1	14			2			7	8											
		3	4	5	6	2		9	10	11		13		1	14					12	7	8											
		3	4	5	6	2			10	11		9		1	13				14		7	8	12										
		3	4	5	6	2	12		10	11		9		1		14					7	8		13									
			2	5	6		12		10	11				1	3	9			13		7	8		4									
		3	2		6	5	12		10	11		9	13	1					14		7	8		4									
			2	5	6		12		10	11		9	13	1	3	14					7	8		4									
		12	2	5	6	11			10			9		1	3						7	8		4									
		14	2	5	6		8		10	3		9	13	1		11				12	7			4									
			2	5	6		8		10	3		9		1	13	11			12		7	14		4									
			2	5	6				10			9		1	3	11					7			4	8	12							
			2	5	6	12				3		9		1	13	11					7			4	8	10	14						
1			2			5	8		10	3		9			6	11					7			4									
1		12	2			5	8		10	3		9			6	11					7			4									
1			2			5	8		10	3		9			6	11					7			4	12								
1		12	2			5	8		10	3		9			6	11					7			4	13			14					
1			2			5		12	10			9			6	11		3			7	8		4				14	13				
1				5		6	8	9	10	3					11	12		2			7			4				14	13				
1			12	5		6	8	9	10	3		13			11	14		2			7			4									
1			6	5			8	9	10	3		14			11	7		2						4				12	13				
1			4	5	6		8	9	10	3		13			11	2					7						14	12					
1			4		6	5	8	9	10	3		13			11	2					7									12			
			4		6	5	8		10			9	12	1	11	2					7									3			
			4		6	5	8		10			9		1	11	2		12			7				13					3			
			4	5	6	13	8	9		12		10		1	11	2					7							14		3			
			4	5	6		8		10	11		9		1	7	2											12			3			
			4	5	6		8		10	11		9		1	7	2		12										13		3			
				5	6		8		10	3		9		1	11	2					7			4				14		12	13		
12			4	5	6				10	11		9		1	8	2					7			13						3			
1			4		6	5			10	11		9			8	2					7									3		12	
1			4		6	5			10	11		9			8	2					7									3			
1			4		6	5			10	11		9			8	2					7									3	12	13	
1			4	5	6	8			9						11	2					7			12						3		10	
1			4	5	6		8		10			9			11	2					7									3	12		
1			4	5	6				10			9			11	8					7			12						3	2	13	14
1			4	5	6							9			11	8					7									3	2	10	
1			4	5	6	12				11		9			8	2					7			13						3	14	10	
1			4	5	6				9	11		12			8	2					7			14						3	13	10	
1			4	5	6	12	14		10	11		9			8	2					7									3		13	
22	3	12	41	34	38	24	20	14	42	36		30		24	33	31	2	9			38	11		17	2	1				16	2	4	
1		4	2			5	5	1		1	2	10	7	1	9	4	1	2	6	2		1	1	6	3	1	3	8	3	2	5	4	1
		1	1	3	3		6	12	28	1		20			7	8					8			1	1					1		5	

Nash CJ	Charvet LJ	Granville DP	Dunne RP	Howey SN	Pearce S	Wiekens G	Berkovic E	Wanchope WPC	Goater LS	Tiatto DA	Whitley, Jeff	Huckerby DC	Dickov P	Weaver NJ	Horlock K	Wright-Phillips SC	Grant AJ	Edghill RA	Colosimo S	Shuker CA	Benarbia A	Etuhu DP	Toure A	Mettomo L	Negouai C	Mike LJ	Killen C	Ritchie PS	Haaland A-IR	Jensen N	Jihai S	Macken JP	Mears T
1			4	5	12		8	9	14			10			3	11		2			7							6	13				
			4		6	5	8		10			9		1	11	2					7									3			
			4	5			8	9		11		10		1	7	2		12							13			6		3			
1			3	2	1	1	3	2	1	1		3		2	3	3		1			2							2		2			
					1				1									1							1				1				
							1	1	2			1			1																		

Nash CJ	Charvet LJ	Granville DP	Dunne RP	Howey SN	Pearce S	Wiekens G	Berkovic E	Wanchope WPC	Goater LS	Tiatto DA	Whitley, Jeff	Huckerby DC	Dickov P	Weaver NJ	Horlock K	Wright-Phillips SC	Grant AJ	Edghill RA	Colosimo S	Shuker CA	Benarbia A	Etuhu DP	Toure A	Mettomo L	Negouai C	Mike LJ	Killen C	Ritchie PS	Haaland A-IR	Jensen N	Jihai S	Macken JP	Mears T
			4	5	3		8	9	10	11		13	14	1	6		7		2	12													
		3	4	5	6	2	13		10	11		9		1		14					7	8		12									
1		12	2		6	5	11					9			3	10					7		14	4	8			13					
1		1	3	2	3	2	2	1	2	2		2		2	2	1	1		1		2	1		1	1								
		1					1					1	1			1				1			1	1				1					
									2			5	1							1													

League Table

	P	W	D	L	F	A	Pts
Manchester City	46	31	6	9	108	52	99
West Bromwich Albion	46	27	8	11	61	29	89
Wolverhampton W	46	25	11	10	76	43	86
Millwall	46	22	11	13	69	48	77
Birmingham City	46	21	13	12	70	49	76
Norwich City	46	22	9	15	60	51	75
Burnley	46	21	12	13	70	62	75
Preston North End	46	20	12	14	71	59	72
Wimbledon	46	18	13	15	63	57	67
Crystal Palace	46	20	6	20	70	62	66
Coventry City	46	20	6	20	59	53	66
Gillingham	46	18	10	18	64	67	64
Sheffield United	46	15	15	16	53	54	60
Watford	46	16	11	19	62	56	59
Bradford City	46	15	10	21	69	76	55
Nottingham Forest	46	12	18	16	50	51	54
Portsmouth	46	13	14	19	60	72	53
Walsall	46	13	12	21	51	71	51
Grimsby Town	46	12	14	20	50	72	50
Sheffield Wednesday	46	12	14	20	49	71	50
Rotherham United	46	10	19	17	52	66	49
Crewe Alexandra	46	12	13	21	47	76	49
Barnsley	46	11	15	20	59	86	48
Stockport County	46	6	8	32	42	102	26

2002-03

Premiership

Manager: Kevin Keegan OBE

Did you know that?

Match 8: Shuker's last game.
Match 15: Mettomo's last League game.
Match 22: Huckerby's last League game.
Match 28: Howey's last game.
Match 29: Nash's last game.
Match 32: Wieken's last League game.
Match 38: Schmeichel, Benarbia, Foe, Jensen, Goater, Belmadi and Horlock's last game.

Foe scored the last City first-team goal at Maine Road. Sadly the player was to die of a heart attack while playing international football during the close season. Tributes to Foe appeared at the City of Manchester Stadium in the Memorial Garden, Museum and Walk of Pride.

Match No.	Date	Venue	Opponents	Result		Scorers	Attendance
1	Aug 17	A	Leeds United	L	0-3		40,195
2	24	H	Newcastle United	W	1-0	Huckerby	34,776
3	28	A	Aston Villa	L	0-1		33,494
4	31	H	Everton	W	3-1	Anelka 2, Radzinski (og)	34,835
5	Sep 10	A	Arsenal	L	1-2	Anelka	37,878
6	15	H	Blackburn Rovers	D	2-2	Anelka, Goater	34,130
7	21	A	West Ham United	D	0-0		35,550
8	28	H	Liverpool	L	0-3		35,131
9	Oct 5	A	Southampton	L	0-2		31,009
10	19	H	Chelsea	L	0-3		34,953
11	26	A	Birmingham City	W	2-0	Jihai, Anelka	29,316
12	Nov 2	A	West Bromwich Albion	W	2-1	Anelka, Goater	27,044
13	9	H	Manchester United	W	3-1	Anelka, Goater 2	34,649
14	16	H	Charlton Athletic	L	0-1		33,455
15	23	A	Middlesbrough	L	1-3	Anelka	31,510
16	30	H	Bolton Wanderers	W	2-0	Howey, Berkovic	34,860
17	Dec 9	A	Sunderland	W	3-0	Jihai, Foe, Goater	36,511
18	14	A	Charlton Athletic	D	2-2	Foe 2	26,434
19	23	H	Tottenham Hotspur	L	2-3	Howey, Benarbia	34,563
20	26	H	Aston Villa	W	3-1	Benarbia, Foe 2	33,991
21	28	A	Fulham	W	1-0	Anelka	17,937
22	Jan 1	A	Everton	D	2-2	Anelka, Foe	40,163
23	11	H	Leeds United	W	2-1	Jensen, Goater	34,884
24	18	A	Newcastle United	L	0-2		52,152
25	29	H	Fulham	W	4-1	Wright-Phillips, Benarbia, Anelka, Foe	33,260
26	Feb 1	H	West Bromwich Albion	L	1-2	Gilchrist (og)	34,765
27	9	A	Manchester United	D	1-1	Goater	67,646
28	22	H	Arsenal	L	1-5	Anelka	34,960
29	Mar 1	A	Blackburn Rovers	L	0-1		28,647
30	16	H	Birmingham City	W	1-0	Fowler	34,596
31	22	A	Chelsea	L	0-5		41,105
32	Apr 5	A	Bolton Wanderers	L	0-2		26,949
33	12	H	Middlesbrough	D	0-0		34,793
34	18	A	Tottenham Hotspur	W	2-0	Sommeil, Barton	36,075
35	21	H	Sunderland	W	3-0	Foe 2, Fowler	34,357
36	27	H	West Ham United	L	0-1		34,815
37	May 3	A	Liverpool	W	2-1	Anelka 2 (1 pen)	44,220
38	11	H	Southampton	L	0-1		34,957
							Appearances
							Sub appearances
						Two own goals	Goals

FA Cup

R3	Jan 5	H	Liverpool	L	0-1		28,586
							Appearances
							Sub appearances

League Cup

R2	Oct 1	H	Crewe Alexandra	W	3-2	Walker (og), Berkovic, Huckerby	21,820
R3	Nov 5	A	Wigan Athletic	L	0-1		15,007
							Appearances
							Sub appearances
						One own goal	Goals

Nash CJ	Wright-Phillips SC	Jensen N	Jihai S	Howey SN	Distin S	Benarbia A	Berkovic E	Anelka N	Foe M-V	Horlock K	Huckerby DC	Dunne RP	Shuker CA	Schmeichel PB	Tiatto DA	Goater LS	Bischoff M	Mettomo L	Wiekens G	Macken JP	Belmadi D	Sommeil D	Fowler RB	Barton JA	Jordan SR
1	2	3	4	5	6	7	8	9	10	11	13	12	14												
	2	3	4	5	6	7	8	9	11	12	10			1											
	2	3	4	5	6	7	8	9	11		10			1	12	13									
	2	3	4	5	6	7	8	9	11	12	10			1	13	14									
	2	3	4	5	6	7	8	9	11	13	10			1		12									
	2	3	4		6	7	8	9	11				10	1	12	13	5								
	2	3	4	5	6	7	8	9	10	11	12			1											
	2	3	4	5	6		8	9	7	11	10		13	1		12									
	10	2	4	5	6	7	8	9	11	3	13			1				12							
	2	3	4	5	6	7	8	9	11		12			1		10									
1		3	2	5	6		8	9	7	12	13	4			11	10									
1		3	2	5	6		8	9	7	12		4			11	10									
	12	3	2				8	9	7	13		4		1	11	10		6	5						
	2	3	5			14	8	9	7	12	13	4		1	11	10		6							
	2	3	5			13	8	9		7	12	4		1	11	10		6							
			2	5	6	12	8	9	7	11		4		1	3	10									
			2	5	6		8	9	7	11		4		1	3	10									
			2	5	6	12	8	9	7	11		4		1	3	10									
			2	5	6	12	8	9	7	11	13	4		1	3	10									
	2	12		5	6	13	8	9	7	11	14	4		1	3	10									
	13	2	12	5	6	7	8	9	11	3	10	4		1					14						
	10	3	2	5	6	7		9	8	11	12	4		1											
	12	3	2	5	6	13	8	9	7	11		4		1		10									
1		3	2	5	6	7		9	8	11		4				10				13	12				
1	12	3		5	6	7		9	8	11		2				13					10	4			
1	12	3		5	6	7		9	8	11		2				14					13	4	10		
1	12	3	2	5	6	14	8	9	7	11						13						4	10		
1	12	3	2	5		13	8	9	7			4									11	6	10		
1	13	3	2		6	12	8	9	7	11						14			5			4	10		
	2	3	12		6	7		9	8	11				1					5			4	10		
	2	3	14		6	7		9	8	11				1		12			5		13	4	10		
	7				6	13	8	9		3		2		1					5	14		4	10	11	12
	2	3			6	12	8	9	7			5		1		13				14		4	10	11	
	2	3			6	7		9	8			5		1						12		4	10	11	
	2	3			6	7		9	8			5		1							12	4	10	11	
	2	3			6	7		9	8			5		1		14				12	13	4	10	11	
	2	3			6	7		9		11		5		1								4	10	8	
	2	3			6	7		9	8	14		5		1		10					13	4	12	11	
9	23	32	25	24	34	21	27	38	35	22	6	24	1	29	10	14	1	3	5		2	14	12	7	
	8	1	3			12				8	10	1	2		3	12		1	1	5	6		1		1
	1	1	2	2		3	1	14	9		1					7						1	2	1	

Nash CJ	Wright-Phillips SC	Jensen N	Jihai S	Howey SN	Distin S	Benarbia A	Berkovic E	Anelka N	Foe M-V	Horlock K	Huckerby DC	Dunne RP	Shuker CA	Schmeichel PB	Tiatto DA	Goater LS	Bischoff M	Mettomo L	Wiekens G	Macken JP	Belmadi D	Sommeil D	Fowler RB	Barton JA	Jordan SR
	10	3	2		6	7	12	9	8	11	14			1		13		4	5						
	1	1	1		1	1		1	1	1				1				1	1						
							1				1					1									

Nash CJ	Wright-Phillips SC	Jensen N	Jihai S	Howey SN	Distin S	Benarbia A	Berkovic E	Anelka N	Foe M-V	Horlock K	Huckerby DC	Dunne RP	Shuker CA	Schmeichel PB	Tiatto DA	Goater LS	Bischoff M	Mettomo L	Wiekens G	Macken JP	Belmadi D	Sommeil D	Fowler RB	Barton JA	Jordan SR
	13	2	4	5		7	8	9	11	3	12			1		10		6							
1	7	3	2	5	6	8		9	11	13	14	4				10			12						
1	1	2	2	2	1	2	1	2	2	1		1		1		2		1							
	1									1	2								1						
							1				1														

League Table

	P	W	D	L	F	A	Pts
Manchester United	38	25	8	5	74	34	83
Arsenal	38	23	9	6	85	42	78
Newcastle United	38	21	6	11	63	48	69
Chelsea	38	19	10	9	68	38	67
Liverpool	38	18	10	10	61	41	64
Blackburn Rovers	38	16	12	10	52	43	60
Everton	38	17	8	13	48	48	59
Southampton	38	13	13	12	43	46	52
Manchester City	38	15	6	17	47	54	51
Tottenham Hotspur	38	14	8	16	51	62	50
Middlesbrough	38	13	10	15	48	44	49
Charlton Athletic	38	14	7	17	45	56	49
Birmingham City	38	13	9	16	41	49	48
Fulham	38	13	9	16	41	50	48
Leeds United	38	14	5	19	58	57	47
Aston Villa	38	12	9	17	42	47	45
Bolton Wanderers	38	10	14	14	40	51	44
West Ham United	38	10	12	16	42	59	42
West Bromwich Albion	38	6	8	24	29	65	26
Sunderland	38	4	7	27	21	65	19

2003-04

Premiership

Manager: Kevin Keegan OBE

Did you know that?

Match 13: Berkovic's last League game.
Match 21: Seaman's last game.
Match 21: Ellegaard's last League game.
Match 22: Tiatto's last game.
Match 29: Van Buyten's last game.
Match 37: Elliott's last game.
Match 38: Tarnat and Wanchope's last game.

Two goalkeepers – Seaman and Ellegaard – played their last City League games on the same day (Match 21). Ellegaard replaced Seaman on the day and did go on to make Cup appearances, but never appeared in the League again for the Blues.

Match No.	Date	Venue	Opponents	Result		Scorers	Attendance
1	Aug 17	A	Charlton Athletic	W	3-0	Jihai, Anelka (pen), Sibierski	25,780
2	23	H	Portsmouth	D	1-1	Sommeil	46,287
3	25	A	Blackburn Rovers	W	3-2	Tarnat, Anelka, Barton	23,361
4	31	H	Arsenal	L	1-2	Lauren (og)	46,436
5	Sep 14	H	Aston Villa	W	4-1	Tarnat, Anelka 3 (2 pens)	46,687
6	20	A	Fulham	D	2-2	Knight (og), Wanchope	16,124
7	28	H	Tottenham Hotspur	D	0-0		46,842
8	Oct 4	A	Wolverhampton W.	L	0-1		29,386
9	18	H	Bolton Wanderers	W	6-2	Wright-Phillips 2, Distin, Anelka 2, Reyna	47,101
10	25	A	Chelsea	L	0-1		41,040
11	Nov 1	A	Southampton	W	2-0	Fowler, Wanchope	31,952
12	9	H	Leicester City	L	0-3		46,966
13	22	A	Newcastle United	L	0-3		52,159
14	30	H	Middlesbrough	L	0-1		46,824
15	Dec 7	A	Everton	D	0-0		37,871
16	13	A	Manchester United	L	1-3	Wright-Phillips	67,645
17	22	H	Leeds United	D	1-1	Sibierski	47,126
18	26	A	Birmingham City	L	1-2	Fowler	29,520
19	28	H	Liverpool	D	2-2	Anelka (pen), Fowler	47,201
20	Jan 7	H	Charlton Athletic	D	1-1	Fowler	44,307
21	10	A	Portsmouth	L	2-4	Anelka, Sibierski	20,120
22	17	H	Blackburn Rovers	D	1-1	Anelka	47,090
23	Feb 1	A	Arsenal	L	1-2	Anelka	38,103
24	8	H	Birmingham City	D	0-0		46,967
25	11	A	Liverpool	L	1-2	Wright-Phillips	43,257
26	21	A	Bolton Wanderers	W	3-1	Fowler 2, Charlton (og)	27,301
27	28	H	Chelsea	L	0-1		47,304
28	Mar 14	H	Manchester United	W	4-1	Wright-Phillips, Fowler, Sinclair, Macken	47,284
29	22	A	Leeds United	L	1-2	Anelka	36,998
30	27	H	Fulham	D	0-0		46,522
31	Apr 4	A	Aston Villa	D	1-1	Distin	37,602
32	10	H	Wolverhampton W.	D	3-3	Wright-Phillips, Anelka, Sibierski	47,248
33	12	A	Tottenham Hotspur	D	1-1	Anelka	35,282
34	17	H	Southampton	L	1-3	Anelka	47,152
35	24	A	Leicester City	D	1-1	Tarnat	31,457
36	May 1	H	Newcastle United	W	1-0	Wanchope	47,226
37	8	A	Middlesbrough	L	1-2	Wanchope	34,734
38	15	H	Everton	W	5-1	Wright-Phillips, Anelka, Wanchope 2, Sibierski	47,284
							Appearances
							Sub appearances
						Three own goals	Goals

FA Cup

	Date	Venue	Opponents	Result		Scorers	Attendance
R3	Jan 3	H	Leicester City	D	2-2	Anelka 2 (1 pen)	30,617
rep	14	A	Leicester City	W	3-1	Anelka, Sibierski, Macken	18,916
R4	25	H	Tottenham Hotspur	D	1-1	Anelka	28,840
rep	Feb 4	A	Tottenham Hotspur	W	4-3	Wright-Phillips, Distin, Bosvelt, Macken	30,400
R5	14	A	Manchester United	L	2-4	Tarnat, Fowler	67,228
							Appearances
							Sub appearances
							Goals

League Cup

	Date	Venue	Opponents	Result		Scorers	Attendance
R3	Oct 28	A	Queen's Park Rangers	W	3-0	Wright-Phillips 2, Macken	16,773
R4	Dec 3	A	Tottenham Hotspur	L	1-3	Fowler	31,727
							Appearances
							Sub appearances
							Goals

UEFA Cup

	Date	Venue	Opponents	Result		Scorers	Attendance
Q1/1	Aug 14	H	TNS Llansantffraid	W	5-0	Wright-Phillips, Jihai, Sommeil, Anelka, Sinclair	34,103
Q1/2	28	N	TNS Llansantffraid	W	2-0	Huckerby, Negouai	10,000
R1/1	Sep 24	H	Lokeren	W	3-2	Anelka (pen), Fowler, Sibierski	29,067
R1/2	Oct 15	A	Lokeren	W	1-0	Anelka (pen)	10,000
R2/1	Nov 6	H	Groclin Dyskobolia	D	1-1	Anelka	32,506
R2/2	27	A	Groclin Dyskobolia	L	0-0		5,500
							Appearances
							Sub appearances
							Goals

Q1 second leg played at the Millennium Stadium, Cardiff
R2 lost on the away goals rule

Seaman DA	Wright-Phillips SC	Tarnat M	Jihai S	Sommeil D	Distin S	Barton JA	Sibierski A	Anelka N	Fowler RB	Sinclair TL	Wanchope WPC	Tiatto DA	Barkovic E	Bosvelt P	McManaman S	Reyna C	Dunne RP	Macken JP	Ellegaard KS	James DB	Van Buyten D	Elliott S	Jordan SR	Weaver NJ	Bischoff M	Wiekens G	Flood WR	Huckerby DC	Negouai C	Whelan G	Arason A
1	2	3	4	5	6	7	8	9	10	11	12	13																			
1	2	3	4	5	6	7	8	9	10	11	12		13																		
1	2	3	4	5	6	7	10	9		11				8																	
1	2	3	4	5	6	7	10	9	13	11		12	14	8																	
1	2	3	4	5	6	7	12	9		11	10				8	13															
1	2		4	5	6	7	12	9	14	11	10	3		13	8																
1	7	3	2	5	6		12	9	13	11	10			4	8	14															
1	7	3	2	5	6		11	9	13	12	10			4		8															
1	7	3	2	5	6	8	12	9	10			13			11	4	14														
1	7	3	2	5	6	8	13	9	10	11	12					4															
1		3	2		6	8	12		10	7	9				11	4	5														
		3	2		6	7	4	9	13		10		8	12	11		5		1												
1		3	2		6	8	14	9	10	11			12	4	7		5	13													
	7		2	6	3	8	13	9	12	11	10					4	5		1												
1	7		2	6	3	4		9	10	11	13				8		5		12												
1	7		2	6	3	4		9	10	11	12				8		5														
1	7		2	6	3	8	14	9	10		13				11	4	5	12													
1	7		2	6	3	8	12	9	10	13					11	4	5														
1	7	3		2	6		13	9	10	12				8	11	4	5	14													
1	14	3		2	6	12	11	9	10	7				8		4	5	13													
1		3		2	6	8	11	9	10	7				4			5		12												
	12	3	2		6	8	11	9		7		13		4			5	10		1											
	7	3	2		6	10		9	12	11				8	13	4	5			1											
	2	3	12		6	13	11		10					7	14	8	5	9		1	4										
	2	3			6	12	13		10					7	11	8	5	9		1	4										
	2	3	12		6		8		10	7					11	4	5	9		1		13	14								
	2	3			6		8		10	12					11	7	5	9		1	4										
	2	3	14		6		8		10	13				12	11	7	5	9		1	4										
	2	3	12		6	8	11	9	10					7			5			1	4										
	7	3	2		6		11	9	10	14	12			8		4	5	13		1											
	7	3	2		6			13	12	14	9			8	11	4	5	10		1											
	7	3	2		6	12	8	9	10		13			4	11		5			1											
	7	3	2		6		8	9	10	13	12			4	11		5			1											
	7	3	2		6		8	9	10	12	13			4	11	14	5			1											
	7	3	2		6	8	12	9		11	10			4			5			1											
	7	3	2		6	8		9		11	10			4		12	5	13		1											
	7	3	2		6	8	12	9			10			4		11	5	13		1		14									
	7	3	2		6	8	14	9			10			4		11	5	12		1			14								
19	32	32	29	18	38	24	18	31	23	20	12	1	1	22	20	19	28	7	2	17	5										
	2		4			4	15	1	8	9	10	4	3	3	2	4	1	8	2			2	2								
	7	3	1	1	2	1	5	16	7	1	6					1		1													

Seaman DA	Wright-Phillips SC	Tarnat M	Jihai S	Sommeil D	Distin S	Barton JA	Sibierski A	Anelka N	Fowler RB	Sinclair TL	Wanchope WPC	Tiatto DA	Barkovic E	Bosvelt P	McManaman S	Reyna C	Dunne RP	Macken JP	Ellegaard KS	James DB	Van Buyten D	Elliott S	Jordan SR	Weaver NJ	Bischoff M	Wiekens G	Flood WR	Huckerby DC	Negouai C	Whelan G	Arason A
1	7		2	6	3	13	12	9	10	14				8	11	4	5														
		3		2	6	8	11	9		7				4			5	10	1												
	13	3	2		6		11	9	10	7				8		4	5	12	1												
	7	3	2		6	8	14	9	10	11				4	13		5	12													1
	2	3			6	7	10		9						11	8	5				4										1
1	3	4	3	2	5	3	3	4	4	3				4	2	3	5	1	2		1										2
	1					1	2			1					1			2													
	1	1			1		1	4	1					1				2													

Seaman DA	Wright-Phillips SC	Tarnat M	Jihai S	Sommeil D	Distin S	Barton JA	Sibierski A	Anelka N	Fowler RB	Sinclair TL	Wanchope WPC	Tiatto DA	Barkovic E	Bosvelt P	McManaman S	Reyna C	Dunne RP	Macken JP	Ellegaard KS	James DB	Van Buyten D	Elliott S	Jordan SR	Weaver NJ	Bischoff M	Wiekens G	Flood WR	Huckerby DC	Negouai C	Whelan G	Arason A
1	7	3	2		6	8	13	9	10	11			14	4			5	12													
	7	3		2	6	8		9	10	11					12	4	5		1												
1	2	2	1	1	2	2		2	2	2				1		1	2		1												
							1						1		1			1													
	2								1									1													

Seaman DA	Wright-Phillips SC	Tarnat M	Jihai S	Sommeil D	Distin S	Barton JA	Sibierski A	Anelka N	Fowler RB	Sinclair TL	Wanchope WPC	Tiatto DA	Barkovic E	Bosvelt P	McManaman S	Reyna C	Dunne RP	Macken JP	Ellegaard KS	James DB	Van Buyten D	Elliott S	Jordan SR	Weaver NJ	Bischoff M	Wiekens G	Flood WR	Huckerby DC	Negouai C	Whelan G	Arason A
1	2	3	4	5	6	12		9	10	11	13	14	8	7																	
	12					14						3	8	7			2	10						1	4	5	6	9	11	13	
1	12		2	5	6		8	9	10			3		7	11	4	13														
1	7	3	2	5	6	13		9		11	10			4	8	12															
1	7	3	2		6	8		9	10		14	13		12	11	4	5														
1	7		2	6	3	4		9	10	11	13				8	14	5	12													
5	4	3	5	4	5	2	1	5	4	3	1	2	2	4	4	2	3	1						1	1	1	1	1	1		
	2					3					3	2		1		2	1	1												1	
	1		1	1			1	4	1	1																		1	1		

League Table

	P	W	D	L	F	A	Pts
Arsenal	38	26	12	0	73	26	90
Chelsea	38	24	7	7	67	30	79
Manchester United	38	23	6	9	64	35	75
Liverpool	38	16	12	10	55	37	60
Newcastle United	38	13	17	8	52	40	56
Aston Villa	38	15	11	12	48	44	56
Charlton Athletic	38	14	11	13	51	51	53
Bolton Wanderers	38	14	11	13	48	56	53
Fulham	38	14	10	14	52	46	52
Birmingham City	38	12	14	12	43	48	50
Middlesbrough	38	13	9	16	44	52	48
Southampton	38	12	11	15	44	45	47
Portsmouth	38	12	9	17	47	54	45
Tottenham Hotspur	38	13	6	19	47	57	45
Blackburn Rovers	38	12	8	18	51	59	44
Manchester City	38	9	14	15	55	54	41
Everton	38	9	12	17	45	57	39
Leicester City	38	6	15	17	48	65	33
Leeds United	38	8	9	21	40	79	33
Wolverhampton W.	38	7	12	19	38	77	33

2004-05

Premiership

Manager: Kevin Keegan OBE (11 March 2005),
Stuart Pearce

Did you know that?

Match 19: Negouai's last game.
Match 21: Anelka's last game.
Match 33: Bosvelt's last game.
Match 37: Macken's last game.
Match 38: S. Wright-Phillips's last game.

David James played as an outfield player for the latter stages of the game wearing a specially prepared number one shirt, while Nicky Weaver came on as goalkeeper.

Match No.	Date	Venue	Opponents	Result		Scorers	Attendance
1	Aug 14	H	Fulham	D	1-1	Fowler	44,026
2	21	A	Liverpool	L	1-2	Anelka	42,831
3	24	A	Birmingham City	L	0-1		28,551
4	28	H	Charlton Athletic	W	4-0	Anelka 2, Sinclair, S Wright-Phillips	43,593
5	Sep 11	H	Everton	L	0-1		47,006
6	18	A	Crystal Palace	W	2-1	Anelka 2 (1 pen)	25,052
7	25	H	Arsenal	L	0-1		47,015
8	Oct 2	A	Southampton	D	0-0		28,605
9	16	H	Chelsea	W	1-0	Anelka (pen)	45,047
10	24	A	Newcastle United	L	3-4	S Wright-Phillips 2, Fowler	52,316
11	Nov 1	H	Norwich City	D	1-1	Flood	42,803
12	7	A	Manchester United	D	0-0		67,863
13	13	H	Blackburn Rovers	D	1-1	Sibierski	45,504
14	20	A	Portsmouth	W	3-1	S Wright-Phillips, Sibierski, Bosvelt	20,101
15	27	H	Aston Villa	W	2-0	Macken, S Wright-Phillips	44,530
16	Dec 6	A	Middlesbrough	L	2-3	Fowler, B Wright-Phillips	29,787
17	11	H	Tottenham Hotspur	L	0-1		45,805
18	18	A	Bolton Wanderers	W	1-0	Barton	27,274
19	26	A	Everton	L	1-2	Fowler	40,530
20	28	H	West Bromwich Albion	D	1-1	Anelka	47,177
21	Jan 1	H	Southampton	W	2-1	Bosvelt, S Wright-Phillips	42,895
22	4	A	Arsenal	D	1-1	S Wright-Phillips	38,086
23	15	H	Crystal Palace	W	3-1	S Wright-Phillips 2, Fowler	44,010
24	22	A	West Bromwich Albion	L	0-2		25,348
25	Feb 2	H	Newcastle United	D	1-1	Fowler (pen)	45,752
26	6	A	Chelsea	D	0-0		42,093
27	13	H	Manchester United	L	0-2		47,111
28	28	A	Norwich City	W	3-2	Sibierski, Fowler 2	24,302
29	Mar 7	H	Bolton Wanderers	L	0-1		43,050
30	19	A	Tottenham Hotspur	L	1-2	Reyna	35,681
31	Apr 2	A	Charlton Athletic	D	2-2	Dunne, Fowler	26,436
32	9	H	Liverpool	W	1-0	Musampa	47,203
33	16	A	Fulham	D	1-1	Reyna	21,796
34	20	H	Birmingham City	W	3-0	Fowler, Dunne, Sibierski (pen)	42,453
35	23	A	Blackburn Rovers	D	0-0		24,646
36	30	H	Portsmouth	W	2-0	Distin, Fowler	46,454
37	May 7	A	Aston Villa	W	2-1	S Wright-Phillips, Musampa	39,645
38	15	H	Middlesbrough	D	1-1	Musampa	47,221
							Appearances
							Sub appearances
							Goals

FA Cup

R3	Jan 8	A	Oldham Athletic	L	0-1		13,171
							Appearances
							Sub appearances

League Cup

R2	Sep 21	H	Barnsley	W	7-1	Barton, Macken 2, Flood, S Wright-Phillips, Sibierski 2	19,578
R3	Oct 27	H	Arsenal	L	1-2	Fowler	21,708
							Appearances
							Sub appearances
							Goals

James DB	Mills DJ	Thatcher BD	Bosvelt P	Dunne RP	Distin S	Wright-Phillips SC	Reyna C	Anelka N	Fowler RB	Sibierski A	Macken JP	Barton JA	Sinclair TL	Jihai S	McManaman S	Flood WR	Jordan SR	Onuoha C	Wright-Phillips BE	Negouai C	Musampa K	Croft LD	Sommeil D	Weaver NJ	D'Laryea J	Waterreus R
1	2	3	4	5	6	7	8	9	**10**	11	12	13														
1	2	3	**4**	5	6	7	8	9	10	11		13	12													
1	5	3	*4*		6	7	8	9	10	**11**	13	14	12	2												
1	2	3		5	6	7	8	9	10		13	**4**	11		12											
1	2	3		5	6	7	8	9	**10**	14	12	4	*11*	13												
1	2	3		5	6	7	8	9		11	**10**	4		12												
1	2		**8**	5	6	7		9		11	10	4		3	12	13										
1	2	3	8	5	6	7		9			10	4		11												
1	2	3	8	5	6	7		9	13	11	10			**4**	12											
1	2	3	4	5	6	7		**9**	12	8	10				11	13										
1	2		4	**5**	6	10		9	13	8					11	7	3	12								
1	2		4	5	6	10		9		8					11	7	3									
1	2		4	5	6	10	12	9		8					11	**7**	3									
1			8	5	6	7		**9**	12	11	10	4					3	2								
1	2		8	5	**6**	7			10	11	9	4					3	12								
1	2		8	5	6	7			10	11	**9**	4				13	3		12							
1	2		8	5	6	7		13	10	11	**9**	4					3		12							
1	2		8	5	6	7		9	10	11		4					3									
1	**2**		4	5	6	7		9	10	11	8						3	12		13						
1	2		8	5	6	7		9	10	11		4					**3**	12								
1	2	3	8	5	6	7		**9**	*10*	11	12	4			14			13								
1		3	8	5	6	7			10	11	9	**4**				12		2	13							
1	2	3	8	5	6	7			*10*	**11**	9	4			12			14	13							
1	2		8	5	6	7			10	11	**9**	4			13		3		12							
1	2	3	8	5	6	7			10		**9**	4							12		11					
1	2	3	8	5	6	7			9	**10**		4			12						11					
1	2	3		5	6	7			9	10	12	**4**			8				13		11					
1	2		8	5	6	7			9	10		4					3				11					
1	2		4	5	6		8		9	*10*					12	**7**			13		11	14	3			
1	**12**		8	5	6		7		9	*10*	13	4				*14*	3	**2**			11					
1				5	6		7		10	8	9	4					3	2			11					
1	12		8	5	6		7		9	*10*		4					3	**2**	14		11	13				
1			8	5	6	12	7		**9**	10		4					3	2	13		11					
1				5	6	7	8		**9**	10		4					3	2	12		11	13				
1				5	6	7	8		9	10		4					3	2	13		**11**	12				
1	14	12		5	6	7	8		9	10		4					**3**	2			*11*	13				
1	2	3			6	7	8			**10**	9	4						5	12		11	13				
1	2	3			6	7	*8*		9	**10**		4						5	12		11	13		14		
38	29	17	28	35	38	33	16	18	28	34	16	28	2	4	5	4	19	11			14		1			
	3	1				1	1	1	4	1	7	3	2	2	8	5		6	14	1		7		1		
			2	2	1	10	2	7	11	4	1	1	1			1			1		3					

James DB	Mills DJ	Thatcher BD	Bosvelt P	Dunne RP	Distin S	Wright-Phillips SC	Reyna C	Anelka N	Fowler RB	Sibierski A	Macken JP	Barton JA	Sinclair TL	Jihai S	McManaman S	Flood WR	Jordan SR	Onuoha C	Wright-Phillips BE	Negouai C	Musampa K	Croft LD	Sommeil D	Weaver NJ	D'Laryea J	Waterreus R
1	2	3	8	5	6	7				11	9	4			13	12			10							
1	1	1	1	1	1	1				1	1	1							1							
															1	1										

James DB	Mills DJ	Thatcher BD	Bosvelt P	Dunne RP	Distin S	Wright-Phillips SC	Reyna C	Anelka N	Fowler RB	Sibierski A	Macken JP	Barton JA	Sinclair TL	Jihai S	McManaman S	Flood WR	Jordan SR	Onuoha C	Wright-Phillips BE	Negouai C	Musampa K	Croft LD	Sommeil D	Weaver NJ	D'Laryea J	Waterreus R
	5	*3*	8		**6**	9				11	10	4		2		7	14		13				12			1
	2	3			6	9			10	8			11			7	14	5	13	*12*					4	1
	2	2	1		2	2			1	2	1	1	1	1		2		1							1	2
																	2		2	1			1			
						1			1	2	2	1				1										

League Table

	P	W	D	L	F	A	Pts
Chelsea	38	29	8	1	72	15	95
Arsenal	38	25	8	5	87	36	83
Manchester United	38	22	11	5	58	26	77
Everton	38	18	7	13	45	46	61
Liverpool	38	17	7	14	52	41	58
Bolton Wanderers	38	16	10	12	49	44	58
Middlesbrough	38	14	13	11	53	46	55
Manchester City	38	13	13	12	47	39	52
Tottenham Hotspur	38	14	10	14	47	41	52
Aston Villa	38	12	11	15	45	52	47
Charlton Athletic	38	12	10	16	42	58	46
Birmingham City	38	11	12	15	40	46	45
Fulham	38	12	8	18	52	60	44
Newcastle United	38	10	14	14	47	57	44
Blackburn Rovers	38	9	15	14	32	43	42
Portsmouth	38	10	9	19	43	59	39
West Bromwich Albion	38	6	16	16	36	61	34
Crystal Palace	38	7	12	19	41	62	33
Norwich City	38	7	12	19	42	77	33
Southampton	38	6	14	18	45	66	32

2005-06

Premiership

Manager: Stuart Pearce

Did you know that?

Match 23: Fowler's last game.
Match 37: Riera's last game.
Match 38: Musampa and Sommeil's last game.

Match No.	Date	Venue	Opponents	Result		Scorers	Attendance
1	Aug 13	H	West Bromwich Albion	D	0-0		42,983
2	20	A	Birmingham City	W	2-1	Barton, Cole	26,366
3	23	A	Sunderland	W	2-1	Vassell, Sinclair	33,357
4	27	H	Portsmouth	W	2-1	Reyna, Cole	41,022
5	Sep 10	A	Manchester United	D	1-1	Barton	67,839
6	18	H	Bolton Wanderers	L	0-1		43,137
7	24	A	Newcastle United	L	0-1		52,280
8	Oct 2	H	Everton	W	2-0	Mills, Vassell	42,681
9	16	H	West Ham United	W	2-1	Cole 2	43,647
10	22	A	Arsenal	L	0-1		38,189
11	31	H	Aston Villa	W	3-1	Vassell 2, Cole	42,069
12	Nov 5	A	Fulham	L	1-2	Croft	22,241
13	19	H	Blackburn Rovers	D	0-0		44,032
14	26	H	Liverpool	L	0-1		47,105
15	Dec 4	A	Charlton Athletic	W	5-2	Cole 2, Sinclair, Barton, Vassell	25,289
16	10	A	West Bromwich Albion	L	0-2		25,472
17	17	H	Birmingham City	W	4-1	Sommeil, Barton (pen), Sibierski, Wright-Phillips	41,343
18	26	A	Wigan Athletic	L	3-4	Sibierski, Barton, Cole	25,017
19	28	H	Chelsea	L	0-1		46,587
20	31	A	Middlesbrough	D	0-0		28,022
21	Jan 4	H	Tottenham Hotspur	L	0-2		40,808
22	14	H	Manchester United	W	3-1	Sinclair, Vassell, Fowler	47,192
23	21	A	Bolton Wanderers	L	0-2		26,466
24	Feb 1	H	Newcastle United	W	3-0	Riera, Cole, Vassell	42,413
25	4	A	Everton	L	0-1		37,827
26	12	H	Charlton Athletic	W	3-2	Dunne, Samaras, Barton	41,347
27	26	A	Liverpool	L	0-1		44,121
28	Mar 5	H	Sunderland	W	2-1	Samaras 2	42,200
29	11	A	Portsmouth	L	1-2	Dunne	19,556
30	18	H	Wigan Athletic	L	0-1		42,444
31	25	A	Chelsea	L	0-2		42,321
32	Apr 2	H	Middlesbrough	L	0-1		40,256
33	8	A	Tottenham Hotspur	L	1-2	Samaras	36,167
34	15	A	West Ham United	L	0-1		34,305
35	25	A	Aston Villa	W	1-0	Vassell	26,422
36	29	H	Fulham	L	1-2	Dunne	41,128
37	May 4	H	Arsenal	L	1-3	Sommeil	41,875
38	7	A	Blackburn Rovers	L	0-2		25,731
							Appearances
							Sub appearances
							Goals

FA Cup

	Date	Venue	Opponents	Result		Scorers	Attendance
R3	Jan 7	H	Scunthorpe United	W	3-1	Fowler 3 (1 pen)	27,779
R4	28	H	Wigan Athletic	W	1-0	Cole	30,811
R5	Feb 19	A	Aston Villa	D	1-1	Richards	23,847
rep	Mar 14	H	Aston Villa	W	2-1	Samaras, Vassell	33,006
R6	20	H	West Ham United	L	1-2	Musampa	39,357
							Appearances
							Sub appearances
							Goals

League Cup

	Date	Venue	Opponents	Result		Scorers	Attendance
R2	Sep 21	A	Doncaster Rovers	L	1-1	Vassell (pen)	8,228
Lost 0-3 on penalties a.e.t.							Appearances
							Sub appearances
							Goals

James DB	Mills DJ	Thatcher BD	Barton JA	Sommeil D	Jordan SR	Sinclair TL	Reyna C	Cole AA	Vassell D	Musampa K	Croft LD	Wright-Phillips BE	Sibierski A	Dunne RP	Jihai S	Onuoha C	Distin S	Fowler RB	Ireland SJ	Hussein Y	Richards M	Riera A	Samaras G	Miller I	Mills M	Flood WR
1	2	3	4	5	6	7	8	9	10	11	13	12	14													
1	2	3	4		6	7	8	9	10	11		14	13	5	12											
1	2	3	4		6	7	8	9	10	11				5	13	12										
1	2	3	4			7	8	9	10	11				5	12	6										
1	2	3	4			7	8	9	10	11			13	5	12		6	14								
1	2	3	4			7	8		9	11			10	5	12		6		13							
1		3	4				8		9	11	13		10	5	7	2	6		12							
1	2		4		3			9	10	11	12		7	5	13		6		8							
1	2		4		3		7	9	10	11	12				13	5	6		8							
1	2		4	5	3		7		9	11	12		10		14		6		8		13					
1	2		4	5	3			9	10	11	7	14	13		12		6		8							
1	2		4		3			9	10	11	7	14	12	5	13		6		8							
1	2				5	12		9	10	11	6	13		3	7		4		8							
1	2		7		5	12		9	10	11	6	14		3	13		4		8							
1		5	7	2		6	8	9	10		12	14		3	11		4		13							
1		5	7	2		6	8	9	10		13	14		3	11		4		12							
1		5	7	2		6	8		10			12	11		9	3	4	13	14							
1		5	7	3		6	8	12	10				11	13	9	2	4									
1		5	7			6		9	10		13	12	11	3	8	2	4		14							
1			7		5	6		9	10			13	11	3	8	2	4		12							
1		5	7	12		6		9	10		13	14		3	8	2	4		11							
1			7		5	6		9	10	13				3	2	12	4	14	8			11				
1			7		5	6		9	10		14		12	3	2		4	13	8			11				
1			7		5	6		9	10	8			13	3	2		4				14	11	12			
1			7		5	6		12	10	8		13	14	3	2		4					9	11			
1			7	5		6		11	10	8			13	3			4		14		2	9	12			
1	2		7		5	6				8	14	12	11	3			4		13			9	10			
1					5	6	7		10	8		13		3	12		4		14		2	9	11			
1			7		5	6	9		10	8	12	13		3	2				14		4		11			
1	2	3		5		6	7				14	11	10		9		4		8				12	13		
1	2	6		5					10	11	13			3			4		8		9	12			14	7
1	2	5				6			10	12	13		7	3					8		4	9	11			14
1	2	5				6	9		10	8			13	3			4				7	12	11			
1		5		12		6	7		10	8			13	3			4				2	9	11			14
1			7	5		6	8		10	14			12	3	13		4				2	9	11			
1			7	5		6	8		10				11	3			4				2	9	12			13
1			7	5		6	8		10		12			3	2						4	9	11			13
1			7	5		6	8		10	9	13	14		3			4				2	12	11			
38	18	18	31	14	18	29	22	20	36	24	4	1	12	31	16	8	31		13		11	12	10			1
				2		2		2		3	17	17	12	1	13	2		4	11		2	3	4	1	1	4
	1		6	2		3	1	9	8		1	1	2	3				1				1	4			

James DB	Mills DJ	Thatcher BD	Barton JA	Sommeil D	Jordan SR	Sinclair TL	Reyna C	Cole AA	Vassell D	Musampa K	Croft LD	Wright-Phillips BE	Sibierski A	Dunne RP	Jihai S	Onuoha C	Distin S	Fowler RB	Ireland SJ	Hussein Y	Richards M	Riera A	Samaras G	Miller I	Mills M	Flood WR
1			7		5	6					12	13	11	3	8	2	4	10	9							
1			7		5	6		10	11	13		12	14	3	2		4		8			9				
1			7		5				10	6	12	13	8	3			4				2	9	11			
1			7		5	6			11	8		13	12	3	2						4	9	10			
1			7	12	5				10	8	13	11		3	6		4		14		2	9				
5			5		5	3		1	4	3		1	2	5	4	1	4	1	2		3	4	2			
				1						1	3	4	2						1							
								1	1	1								3			1		1			

James DB	Mills DJ	Thatcher BD	Barton JA	Sommeil D	Jordan SR	Sinclair TL	Reyna C	Cole AA	Vassell D	Musampa K	Croft LD	Wright-Phillips BE	Sibierski A	Dunne RP	Jihai S	Onuoha C	Distin S	Fowler RB	Ireland SJ	Hussein Y	Richards M	Riera A	Samaras G	Miller I	Mills M	Flood WR
1		3			13		8		9		12		10	5	4	2	6		7	11						
1		1					1		1				1	1	1	1	1		1	1						
					1						1															
									1																	

League Table

	P	W	D	L	F	A	Pts
Chelsea	38	29	4	5	72	22	91
Manchester United	38	25	8	5	72	34	83
Liverpool	38	25	7	6	57	25	82
Arsenal	38	20	7	11	68	31	67
Tottenham Hotspur	38	18	11	9	53	38	65
Blackburn Rovers	38	19	6	13	51	42	63
Newcastle United	38	17	7	14	47	42	58
Bolton Wanderers	38	15	11	12	49	41	56
West Ham United	38	16	7	15	52	55	55
Wigan Athletic	38	15	6	17	45	52	51
Everton	38	14	8	16	34	49	50
Fulham	38	14	6	18	48	58	48
Charlton Athletic	38	13	8	17	41	55	47
Middlesbrough	38	12	9	17	48	58	45
Manchester City	38	13	4	21	43	48	43
Aston Villa	38	10	12	16	42	55	42
Portsmouth	38	10	8	20	37	62	38
Birmingham City	38	8	10	20	28	50	34
West Bromwich Albion	38	7	9	22	31	58	30
Sunderland	38	3	6	29	26	69	15

City Factfile

Year formed: 1880 as St Mark's (West Gorton), 1887 as Ardwick AFC, 1894 as Manchester City FC
Turned professional: 1887 as Ardwick FC
Limited company: 1894

Football League Record
1891 Alliance League
1892 Founder members of Division Two
1992 Founder members of the Premier League

Division One: 1899–1902; 1903–09; 1910–26; 1928–38; 1947–50; 1951–63; 1966–83; 1985–87; 1989–92
Division Two: 1892–99; 1902–03; 1909–10; 1926–28; 1938–47; 1950–51; 1963–66; 1983–85; 1987–89.
Premier League: 1992–1996; 2000–2001; 2002–present day
'New' Division One: 1996–1998; 1999–2000; 2001–02
'New' Division Two: 1998–99

Club honours

Football League

Division One
Champions: (twice) 1936–37, 1967–68.
Runners-up: (three times) 1903–04, 1920–21, 1976–77

'New' Division One
Champions: (once) 2001–02.
Runners-up: (once) 1999–2000

Division Two
Champions: (six times) 1898–99, 1902–03, 1909–10, 1927–28, 1946–47, 1965–66.
Runners-up: (three times) 1895–96, 1950–51, 1988–89

'New' Division Two
Play-off winners: (once) 1998–99

FA Cup
Winners: (four times) 1904, 1934, 1956, 1969
Runners-up: (four times) 1926, 1933, 1955, 1981

Football League Cup
Winners: (twice) 1970, 1976
Runners-up: 1974**European competition**
European Cup: 1968–69
European Cup-Winners' Cup: 1969–70 (Winners), 1970–71
UEFA Cup: 1972–73, 1976–77, 1977–78, 1978–79, 2003–04

FA Charity Shield
Winners: (three times) 1937–38, 1968–69, 1972–73
Runners-up: 1934–35, 1956–57, 1969–70, 1973–74

Full Members' Cup
Runners-up: 1985–86

FA Youth Cup
Winners: 1986.
Runners-up: 1979, 1980, 1989, 2006

Reserves League
Champions: 1977–78, 1986–87, 1999–2000

Seasonal Record

Season	Division	Pos	Games	HOME W	D	L	F	A	AWAY W	D	L	F	A	No. of Players Used	Top League Goalscorers	Total
1891-92	Alliance	12	22	5	3	3	28	21	1	3	7	11	30	26	Morris	10
1892-93	FL Div2	5	22	6	3	2	27	14	3	0	8	18	26	24	Weir	8
1893-94	FL Div2	13	28	6	1	7	32	20	2	1	11	15	51	35	Morris	7
1894-95	FL Div2	9	30	9	3	3	56	28	5	0	10	26	44	22	Finnerhan	14
1895-96	FL Div2	2	30	12	3	0	37	9	9	1	5	26	29	29	Meredith	12
1896-97	FL Div2	6	30	10	3	2	39	15	2	5	8	19	35	28	Meredith	10
1897-98	FL Div2	3	30	10	4	1	45	15	5	5	5	21	21	21	Gillespie	18
1898-99	FL Div2	Champions	34	15	1	1	64	10	8	5	4	28	25	18	Meredith	29
1899-1900	FL Div1	7	34	10	3	4	33	15	3	5	9	17	29	21	Meredith	14
1900-1	FL Div1	11	34	12	3	2	32	16	1	3	13	16	42	25	Cassidy	14
1901-2	FL Div1	18	34	10	3	4	28	17	1	3	13	14	41	28	Gillespie	15
1902-3	FL Div2	Champions	34	15	1	1	64	15	10	3	4	31	14	22	Gillespie	28
1903-4	FL Div1	2	34	10	4	3	35	19	9	2	6	36	26	28	Gillespie	18
1904-5	FL Div1	3	34	14	3	0	46	17	6	3	8	20	20	24	Turnbull	19
1905-6	FL Div1	5	38	11	2	6	46	23	8	3	8	27	31	25	Thornley	21
1906-7	FL Div1	17	38	7	7	5	29	25	3	5	11	24	52	28	Thornley	13
1907-8	FL Div1	3	38	12	5	2	36	19	4	6	9	26	35	24	Thornley	14
1908-9	FL Div1	19	38	12	3	4	50	23	3	1	15	17	46	28	Thornley	18
1909-10	FL Div2	Champions	38	15	2	2	51	17	8	6	5	30	23	27	G. Dorsett	13
1910-11	FL Div1	17	38	7	5	7	26	26	2	8	9	17	32	29	Wynn	9
1911-12	FL Div1	15	38	10	5	4	39	20	3	4	12	17	38	28	Wynn	17
1912-13	FL Div1	6	38	12	3	4	34	15	6	5	8	19	22	22	Wynn	14
1913-14	FL Div1	13	38	9	3	7	28	23	5	5	9	23	30	26	Browell	13
1914-15	FL Div1	5	38	9	7	3	29	15	6	6	7	20	24	27	Howard	18
1919-20	FL Div1	7	42	14	5	2	52	27	4	4	13	19	35	37	Barnes & Browell	22
1920-21	FL Div1	2	42	19	2	0	50	13	5	4	12	20	37	29	Browell	31
1921-22	FL Div1	10	42	13	7	1	44	21	5	2	14	21	49	32	Browell	21
1922-23	FL Div1	8	42	14	6	1	38	16	3	5	13	12	33	26	Barnes	21
1923-24	FL Div1	11	42	11	7	3	34	24	4	5	12	20	47	28	Barnes	20
1924-25	FL Div1	10	42	11	7	3	44	29	6	2	13	32	39	23	Roberts	31
1925-26	FL Div1	21	42	8	7	6	48	42	4	4	13	41	58	26	Browell & Roberts	21
1926-27	FL Div2	3	42	15	3	3	65	23	7	7	7	43	38	25	Johnson	25
1927-28	FL Div2	Champions	42	18	2	1	70	27	7	7	7	30	32	29	Roberts	20
1928-29	FL Div1	8	42	12	3	6	63	40	6	6	9	32	46	23	Johnson	38
1929-30	FL Div1	3	42	12	5	4	51	33	7	4	10	40	48	23	Tait	27
1930-31	FL Div1	8	42	13	2	6	41	29	5	8	8	34	41	23	Brook	16
1931-32	FL Div1	14	42	10	5	6	49	30	3	7	11	34	43	24	Halliday	28
1932-33	FL Div1	16	42	12	3	6	47	30	4	2	15	21	41	27	Tilson	17
1933-34	FL Div1	5	42	14	4	3	50	29	3	7	11	15	43	29	Herd	18
1934-35	FL Div1	4	42	13	5	3	53	25	7	3	11	29	42	21	Tilson	18
1935-36	FL Div1	9	42	13	2	6	44	17	4	6	11	24	43	22	Brook	13
1936-37	FL Div1	Champions	42	15	5	1	56	22	7	8	6	51	39	22	Doherty	30
1937-38	FL Div1	21	42	12	2	7	49	33	2	6	13	31	44	27	Doherty	23
1938-39	FL Div2	5	42	13	3	5	56	35	8	4	9	40	37	26	Herd	20
1946-47	FL Div2	Champions	42	17	3	1	49	14	9	7	5	29	21	32	Smith	23
1947-48	FL Div1	10	42	13	3	5	37	22	2	9	10	15	25	22	Black	16
1948-49	FL Div1	7	42	10	8	3	28	21	5	7	9	19	30	24	Smith	12
1949-50	FL Div1	21	42	7	8	6	27	24	1	5	15	9	44	28	Clarke	9
1950-51	FL Div2	2	42	12	6	3	53	25	7	8	6	36	36	22	Westcott	25
1951-52	FL Div1	15	42	7	5	9	29	28	6	8	7	29	33	23	Hart	12
1952-53	FL Div1	20	42	12	2	7	45	28	2	5	14	27	59	26	Spurdle	11
1953-54	FL Div1	17	42	10	4	7	35	31	4	5	12	27	46	24	Hart & Revie	12

Average Home League Attend.	Highest Home League Attend.	Game
6,800	12,000	Lincoln City 28/11/91
3,000	6,000	Small Heath 22/10/92 Darwen 17/12/92
4,000	6,000	Liverpool 16/9/93
6,000	14,000	Newton Heath 3/11/94
10,000	30,000	Liverpool 3/4/96
8,000	20,000	Newton Heath 3/10/96
8,000	20,000	Burnley 20/11/97
10,000	25,000	Newton Heath 26/12/98
16,000	26,000	Newcastle Utd 14/10/99
18,300	25,000	Derby County 27/10/00 Sunderland 25/12/00
17,000	30,000	The Wednesday 28/3/02
16,000	30,000	Manchester United 10/4/03
20,000	30,000	Aston Villa 17/10/03 Middlesbrough 1/1/04
20,000	40,000	Newcastle Utd 28/1/05 Everton 21/4/05
18,000	38,000	Bolton W 25/11/05
22,150	40,000	Manchester United 1/12/06 Newcastle United 16/2/07
23,000	40,000	Manchester United 18/4/08
20,000	40,000	Manchester United 19/9/08
18,275	40,000	Oldham Athletic 26/3/10
26,000	40,000	Liverpool 24/9/10 Manchester United 21/1/11
24,625	40,000	Blackburn Rovers 2/12/11 Tottenham Hotspur 5/4/12
24,000	40,000	Newcastle United 12/10/12
27,000	40,000	Blackburn Rovers 11/10/13
21,000	40,000	Oldham Athletic 5/4/15
25,240	40,000	Liverpool 27/3/20
31,020	47,500	Burnley 26/3/21
25,000	35,000	Birmingham City 14/4/22 Bolton W 3/12/21 Oldham A 8/10/21 Blackburn R 24/9/21 Aston Villa 27/8/21
24,000	40,000	Liverpool 17/3/23
27,400	58,159	Sheffield Utd 25/8/23
29,000	58,000	Huddersfield Town 18/10/24
32,000	62,994	Manchester United 12/9/25
30,848	49,384	Bradford City 7/5/27
37,468	59,500	Preston North End 25/2/28
31,715	61,007	Manchester United 1/9/28
33,339	68,704	Aston Villa 26/12/29
26,849	56,750	Arsenal 25/12/30
24,173	46,756	Arsenal 19/9/31
24,254	45,916	Sheffield Wednesday 26/12/32
30,058	60,401	Arsenal 20/11/34
34,824	79,491	Arsenal 23/2/35
33,577	48,732	Sunderland 4/1/36
35,872	74,918	Arsenal 10/4/37
32,670	54,911	Preston North End 19/3/38
31,291	47,998	Tottenham H 5/11/38
39,283	69,463	Burnley 10/5/47
42,725	78,000	Manchester United 20/9/47
38,699	67,616	Manchester United 11/9/48
39,381	63,704	Manchester United 31/12/49
35,016	45,842	Hull City 28/10/50
38,302	57,663	Preston NE 13/10/51
34,663	56,140	Manchester United 30/8/52
30,155	53,097	Manchester United 5/9/53

				HOME					AWAY					No. of		
Season	Division	Pos	Games	W	D	L	F	A	W	D	L	F	A	Players Used	Top League Goalscorers	Total
1954-55	FL Div1	7	42	11	5	5	45	36	7	5	9	31	33	22	Hart	14
1955-56	FL Div1	4	42	11	5	5	40	27	7	5	9	42	42	23	Hayes	23
1956-57	FL Div1	18	42	10	2	9	48	42	3	7	11	30	46	24	Johnstone	16
1957-58	FL Div1	5	42	14	4	3	58	33	8	1	12	46	67	26	Hayes	25
1958-59	FL Div1	20	42	8	7	6	40	32	3	2	16	24	63	26	Barlow	17
1959-60	FL Div1	15	42	11	2	8	47	34	6	1	14	31	50	25	McAdams	21
1960-61	FL Div1	13	42	10	5	6	41	30	3	6	12	38	60	21	Law	19
1961-62	FL Div1	12	42	11	3	7	46	38	6	4	11	32	43	25	Dobing	22
1962-63	FL Div1	21	42	7	5	9	30	45	3	6	12	28	57	23	Harley	23
1963-64	FL Div2	6	42	12	4	5	50	27	6	6	9	34	39	29	Kevan	30
1964-65	FL Div2	11	42	12	3	6	40	24	4	6	11	23	38	24	Kevan	18
1965-66	FL Div2	Champions	42	14	7	0	40	14	8	8	5	36	30	21	Young	14
1966-67	FL Div1	15	42	8	9	4	27	25	4	6	11	16	27	21	Bell	12
1967-68	FL Div1	Champions	42	17	2	2	52	16	9	4	8	34	27	21	Young	19
1968-69	FL Div1	13	42	13	6	2	49	20	2	4	15	15	35	23	Bell & Young	14
1969-70	FL Div1	10	42	8	6	7	25	22	8	5	8	30	26	25	Lee	13
1970-71	FL Div1	11	42	7	9	5	30	22	5	8	8	17	20	25	Lee	14
1971-72	FL Div1	4	42	16	3	2	48	15	7	8	6	29	30	22	Lee	33
1972-73	FL Div1	11	42	12	4	5	36	20	3	7	11	21	40	21	Lee & Marsh	14
1973-74	FL Div1	14	42	10	7	4	25	17	4	5	12	14	29	24	Lee	10
1974-75	FL Div1	8	42	16	3	2	40	15	2	7	12	14	39	22	Bell	15
1975-76	FL Div1	8	42	14	5	2	46	18	2	6	13	18	28	22	Tueart	14
1976-77	FL Div1	2	42	15	5	1	38	13	6	9	6	22	21	18	Kidd	21
1977-78	FL Div1	4	42	14	4	3	46	21	6	8	7	28	30	18	Kidd	16
1978-79	FL Div1	15	42	9	5	7	34	28	4	8	9	24	28	23	Channon & Owen	11
1979-80	FL Div1	17	42	8	8	5	28	25	4	5	12	15	41	24	Robinson	8
1980-81	FL Div1	12	42	10	7	4	35	25	4	4	13	21	34	25	Reeves	12
1981-82	FL Div1	10	42	9	7	5	32	23	6	6	9	17	27	25	Reeves	13
1982-83	FL Div1	20	42	9	5	7	26	23	4	3	14	21	47	25	Cross	12
1983-84	FL Div2	4	42	13	3	5	43	21	7	7	7	23	27	23	Parlane	16
1984-85	FL Div2	3	42	14	4	3	42	16	7	7	7	24	24	23	Phillips & Smith	12
1985-86	FL Div1	15	42	7	7	7	25	26	4	5	12	18	31	25	Lillis	11
1986-87	FL Div1	21	42	8	6	7	28	24	0	9	12	8	33	27	Varadi	9
1987-88	FL Div2	9	44	11	4	7	50	38	8	4	10	30	22	23	Stewart	24
1988-89	FL Div2	2	46	12	8	3	48	28	11	5	7	29	25	24	Moulden	13
1989-90	FL Div1	14	38	9	4	6	26	21	3	8	8	17	31	28	Allen	10
1990-91	FL Div1	5	38	12	3	4	35	25	5	8	6	29	28	21	Quinn	20
1991-92	FL Div1	5	42	13	4	4	32	14	7	6	8	29	34	26	White	18
1992-93	FA Prem *	9	42	7	8	6	30	25	8	4	9	26	26	23	White	16
1993-94	FA Prem	16	42	6	10	5	24	22	3	8	10	14	27	32	Sheron	6
1994-95	FA Prem	17	42	8	7	6	37	28	4	6	11	16	36	27	Rosler	15
1995-96	FA Prem	18	38	7	7	5	21	19	2	4	13	12	39	27	Rosler	9
1996-97	New One	14	46	12	4	7	34	25	5	6	12	25	35	33	Rosler	15
1997-98	New One	22	46	6	6	11	28	26	6	6	11	28	31	38	Dickov	9
1998-99	New Two	3	46	13	6	4	38	14	9	10	4	31	19	28	Goater	18
1999-2000	New One	2	46	17	2	4	48	17	9	9	5	30	23	24	Goater	23
2000-01	FA Prem	18	38	4	3	12	20	31	4	7	8	21	34	30	Wanchope	9
2001-02	New One	Champions	46	19	3	1	63	19	12	3	8	45	33	34	Goater	28
2002-03	FA Prem	9	38	9	2	8	28	26	6	4	9	19	28	26	Anelka	14
2003-04	FA Prem	16	38	5	9	5	31	24	4	5	10	24	30	24	Anelka	16
2004-05	FA Prem	8	38	8	6	5	24	14	5	7	7	23	25	25	Fowler	11
2005-06	FA Prem	15	38	9	2	8	26	20	4	2	13	17	18	26	Cole	9

Average Home League Attend.	Highest Home League Attend.	Game
35,217	60,611	Sunderland 9/4/55
32,198	63,925	Blackpool 24/9/55
30,005	63,872	Manchester United 2/2/57
32,765	70,483	Manchester United 28/12/57
32,568	62,812	Manchester United 27/9/58
35,637	65,981	Burnley 2/5/60
29,409	50,479	Manchester United 4/3/61
25,626	49,959	Manchester United 10/2/62
24,683	52,452	Manchester United 15/5/63
18,201	31,136	Sunderland 18/1/64
14,753	22,299	Bury 26/12/64
27,739	47,171	Huddersfield Town 1/1/66
31,209	62,983	Manchester United 21/1/67
37,223	62,942	Manchester United 30/9/67
33,750	63,052	Manchester United 17/8/68
33,930	63,013	Manchester United 15/11/69
31,041	43,636	Manchester United 5/5/71
38,573	63,326	Manchester United 6/11/71
32,351	52,086	Manchester United 18/11/72
30,756	51,331	Manchester United 13/3/74
32,898	45,194	Liverpool 14/9/74
34,281	50,439	Liverpool 19/4/76
40,058	50,020	Liverpool 29/12/76
41,687	50,856	Manchester United 10/9/77
36,203	46710	Liverpool 26/8/78
35272	50,067	Manchester United 10/11/79
33,587	50,114	Manchester United 21/2/81
34,063	52,037	Manchester United 10/10/81
26,789	45,400	Manchester United 5/3/83
25,604	41,862	Sheffield Wednesday 10/12/83
24,220	47,285	Charlton Athletic 11/5/85
24,229	48,773	Manchester United 14/9/85
21,922	35,336	Liverpool 17/1/87
19,471	30,153	Leeds United 26/12/87
23,500	40,070	Chelsea 18/3/89
27,975	43,246	Manchester United 23/9/89
27,874	39,194	Sunderland 11/5/91
27,691	38,180	Manchester United 16/11/91
24,698	37,136	Manchester United 20/3/93
26,709	35,155	Manchester United 7/11/94
22,725	27,850	QPR 14/5/95
27,869	31,436	Liverpool 5/5/96
26,753	30,729	Oldham Athletic 8/3/97
28,196	32,040	QPR 25/4/98
28,261	32,471	York City 8/5/99
32,088	33,027	Blackburn Rovers 23/10/99
34,058	34,629	Liverpool 31/1/01
33,059	34,657	Portsmouth 21/4/02
34,564	35,131	Liverpool 28/09/02
46,830	47,304	Chelsea 28/02/04
45,192	47,221	Middlesbrough 15/5/05
42,856	47,192	Manchester Utd 14/1/06

Against Other Clubs

Opponents	P	W	D	L	F	A
AFC Bournemouth	6	4	2	0	10	4
Arsenal	156	40	37	79	179	262
Aston Villa	134	50	36	48	204	204
Barnsley	28	13	10	5	62	30
Birmingham City	126	58	21	47	199	189
Blackburn Rovers	100	34	24	42	151	156
Blackpool	58	24	18	16	112	94
Bolton Wanderers	100	39	22	39	153	157
Bootle	2	1	0	1	10	5
Bradford City	32	18	5	9	67	42
Bradford Park Avenue	12	6	1	5	29	21
Brentford	8	4	1	3	15	10
Brighton & Hove Albion	14	7	4	3	24	17
Bristol City	22	6	6	10	31	30
Bristol Rovers	2	0	2	0	2	2
Burnley	84	35	22	27	157	120
Burton Swifts	14	5	4	5	33	26
Burton United	2	2	0	0	7	0
Burton Wanderers	6	1	3	2	6	16
Bury	44	21	12	11	95	68
Cambridge United	2	1	1	0	5	0
Cardiff City	38	15	16	7	77	59
Carlisle United	8	3	2	3	9	10
Charlton Athletic	52	20	13	19	92	83
Chelsea	122	39	36	47	157	169
Chesterfield	10	7	3	0	21	7
Colchester United	2	2	0	0	3	1
Coventry City	64	31	16	17	105	77
Crewe Alexandra	14	9	2	3	33	16
Crystal Palace	42	18	12	12	57	46
Darlington	2	1	1	0	9	2
Darwen	12	8	0	4	40	22
Derby County	88	39	17	32	140	130
Doncaster Rovers	4	2	1	1	12	9
Everton	146	56	38	52	211	201
Fulham	42	19	10	13	87	68
Gainsborough Trinity	10	7	1	2	31	8
Gillingham	4	3	1	0	9	2
Glossop North End	8	6	1	1	20	9
Grimsby Town	52	25	10	17	101	92
Huddersfield Town	68	21	25	22	95	81
Hull City	12	5	4	3	21	15
Ipswich Town	58	19	14	25	72	73
Leeds City	2	2	0	0	6	1
Leeds United	94	40	17	37	140	124
Leicester City	88	40	23	25	163	127
Leyton Orient/Clapton Orient	14	10	2	2	44	17
Lincoln City	20	13	0	7	51	27

Opponents	P	W	D	L	F	A
Liverpool	140	37	32	71	188	257
Loughborough Town	8	6	1	1	24	7
Luton Town	36	13	12	11	56	51
Macclesfield Town	2	2	0	0	3	0
Manchester United	134	35	48	51	180	194
Middlesbrough	108	42	25	41	154	164
Middlesbrough Ironopolis	2	1	0	1	6	3
Millwall	12	8	2	2	23	14
New Brighton Tower	2	1	1	0	2	1
Newcastle United	142	45	33	64	192	220
Newport County	2	2	0	0	8	1
Northampton Town	6	1	2	3	6	8
Northwich Victoria	4	3	1	0	12	4
Norwich City	50	24	19	7	83	49
Nottingham Forest	90	37	26	27	139	124
Notts County	58	29	12	17	89	62
Oldham Athletic	42	21	9	12	68	49
Oxford United	12	5	2	5	14	16
Plymouth Argyle	14	6	3	5	22	21
Portsmouth	70	33	15	22	129	104
Port Vale	22	17	1	4	55	22
Preston North End	82	38	15	29	147	131
Queen's Park Rangers	40	14	14	12	48	47
Reading	12	6	2	4	18	12
Rotherham Town	6	5	0	1	14	8
Rotherham United	8	6	2	0	17	6
Scunthorpe United	2	2	0	0	12	3
Sheffield United	108	44	31	33	186	169
Sheffield Wednesday	96	30	24	42	150	159
Shrewsbury Town	8	4	2	2	12	7
Southampton	68	22	21	25	90	91
Southend United	2	2	0	0	6	2
South Shields	4	2	1	1	7	4
Stockport County	10	5	2	3	22	14
Stoke City	78	32	17	29	102	97
Sunderland	112	50	19	43	192	175
Swansea City/Town	20	12	2	6	44	33
Swindon Town	16	11	2	3	33	16
Tottenham Hotspur	114	44	30	40	170	150
Tranmere Rovers	8	3	4	1	20	10
Walsall	20	11	7	2	48	25
Watford	10	4	1	5	13	12
West Bromwich Albion	124	50	26	48	206	206
West Ham United	76	33	11	32	120	127
Wigan Athletic	4	2	0	2	5	5
Wimbledon	20	5	7	8	18	23
Wolverhampton W.	102	38	23	41	194	202
Wrexham	2	1	1	0	1	0
Wycombe Wanderers	2	0	0	2	1	3
York City	2	1	0	1	5	2

City in the Football League

	P	W	D	L	F	A
Premier League/old Div One	3126	1164	778	1184	4730	4724
old Div Two/new Div One	970	488	212	270	1913	1281
old Div Three/new Div Two	46	22	16	8	69	33
Test Matches/Play Offs	7	2	3	2	9	18
TOTAL	4149	1676	1009	1464	6721	6056

Position

Highest: **1st** twice – 1936–37, 1967–68

Lowest: **47th** (third in 'new' Division Two (= League One/original Division Three) 1998–99 – low point of 56th in December 1998 during the only season outside top two divisions.

Points

Most: **62** – 1946–47 (2 points for a win), **99** – 2001–02 (3 points for a win)

Most in top flight: **58** – 1967–68 (2 points for a win), **70** – 1991–92 (3 points for a win)

Most at home: **40** – 1920–21 (2 points for a win), **60** – 2001–02 (3 points for a win)

Most at home in top flight: **40** – 1920–21 (2 points for a win), **43** – 1991–92 (3 points for a win)

Most away: **25** – 1946–47 (2 points for a win), **39** – 2001–02 (3 points for a win)

Most away in top flight: **22** (four times) – 1936–37, 1950–51, 1967–68, 1971–72 (2 points for a win), **28** – 1992–93 (3 points for a win)

Fewest: **18** – 1893–94 (2 points for a win), **34** – 2000–02 (3 points for a win)

Fewest in top flight: **28** – 1901–02 (2 points for a win), **34** – 2000–02 (3 points for a win)

Fewest at home: **13** – 1893–94 (2 points for a win), **15** – 2000–02 (3 points for a win)

Fewest away: **5** (three times) – 1893–94, 1900–01, 1901–02 (2 points for a win), **9** – 1986–87 (3 points for a win)

Wins

Most: **31** – 2001–02

Most in top flight: **26** – 1967–68

Most at home: **19** (twice) – 1920–21, 2001–02

Most at home in top flight: **19** – 1920–21

Most away: **12** – 2001–02

Most away in top flight: **9** – 1903–04, 1967–68

Fewest: **8** (four times) – 1893–94, 1949–50, 1986–87, 2000–01

Fewest at home: **4** – 2000–01

Fewest away: **0** – 1986–87

Defeats

Fewest: **5** (four times) – 1895–96, 1898–99, 1902–03, 1965–66

Fewest in top flight: **7** (twice) – 1936–37, 1976–77

Fewest at home: **0** (four times) – 1895–96, 1904–05, 1920–21, 1965–66

Fewest away: **4** (three times) – 1898–99, 1902–03, 1998–99

Most: **22** (three times) – 1958–59, 1959–60, 1997–98

Most at home: **12** – 2000–01

Most away: **16** – 1958–59

Draws
Most: **18** – 1993–94
Most in top flight: **18** – 1993–94
Most at home: **10** – 1993–94
Most at home in top flight: **10** – 1993–94
Most away: **10** – 1998–99
Most away in top flight: **9** (three times) – 1947–48, 1976–77, 1986–87
Fewest: **2** – 1893–94
Fewest at home: **1** (three times) – 1893–94, 1898–99, 1902–03
Fewest away: **0** (twice) – 1892–93, 1894–95

Goals in a season
Most scored: **108** (twice) – 1926–27, 2001–02
Most scored in top flight: **107** – 1936–37
Most scored at home: **70** – 1927–28
Most scored away: **51** – 1936–37
Fewest scored: **33** – 1995–96
Fewest scored at home: **20** – 2000–01
Fewest scored away: **8** – 1986–87
Fewest conceded: **29** – 1902–03
Fewest conceded at home: **9** – 1895–96
Fewest conceded away: **14** – 1902–03
Most conceded: **102** – 1962–63
Most conceded at home: **45** – 1962–63
Most conceded away: **67** – 1957–58

Individual matches
Highest score for: **11–3** v Lincoln City (h) 23 March 1895
Highest score for away: **9–3** v Tranmere Rovers 26 December 1938
Highest score against: **2–10** v Small Heath (a) 17 March 1893
Biggest winning margin: **10** – 10–0 v Darwen (h) 18 February 1899
Biggest losing margin: **8** – 2–10 v Small Heath (a) 17 March 1893, 1–9 v Everton (a) 3 September 1906, 0–8 v Burton Wanderers (a) 26 December 1894, 0–8 v Wolverhampton Wanderers (a) 23 December 1933
Highest aggregate score: **14** – 11–3 v Lincoln City (h) 23 March 1895
Highest scoring draw: **4–4** (three times) – v Everton (h) 19 September 1925, v Chelsea (a) 3 February 1937, v Grimsby Town (a) 6 September 1950

Sequences
Consecutive wins: **9** – 8 April 1912 to 28 September 1912
Consecutive home wins: **16** – 13 November 1920 to 27 August 1921
Consecutive away wins: **6** – 7 March 1903 to 26 September 1903
Consecutive games unbeaten: **22** – 26 December 1936 to 1 May 1937, 16 November 1946 to 19 April 1947
Consecutive games unbeaten at home: **41** – 25 December 1919 to 19 November 1921
Consecutive games unbeaten away: **15** – 26 December 1998 to 18 September 1999
Consecutive defeats: **8** – 23 August 1995 to 14 October 1995
Consecutive home defeats: **5** – 5 December 1987 to 23 January 1988
Consecutive away defeats: **14** – 5 November 1892 to 13 January 1894
Consecutive games without a win: **17** – 26 December 1979 to 7 April 1980

Consecutive home games without a win: **9** – 26 December 1979 to 7 April 1980
Consecutive away games without a win: **34** – 11 February 1986 to 17 October 1987
Consecutive draws: **6** – 5 April 1913 to 6 September 1913
Consecutive home draws: **6** – 18 October 1924 to 20 December 1924
Consecutive away draws: **7** – 8 September 1990 to 24 November 1990

Top 20 goalscorers in the League

158	Eric Brook
158	Tommy Johnson
145	Billy Meredith
142	Joe Hayes
126	Billy Gillespie
122	Tommy Browell
120	Horace Barnes
117	Colin Bell
116	Frank Roberts
112	Francis Lee
110	Fred Tilson
107	Alec Herd
92	Irvine Thornley
86	Dennis Tueart
86	Neil Young
84	Shaun Goater
79	David White
78	Colin Barlow
75	George Smith
74	Peter Doherty

Eric Brook

Joe Hayes

Tommy Johnson

City in the FA Cup

City first competed in the FA Cup in the 1890–91 season, winning the club's first ever tie 12–0 at home to Liverpool Stanley.

	P	*W*	*D*	*L*	*F*	*A*
HOME	132	76	28	28	286	138
AWAY	176	70	35	71	268	266
TOTAL	308	146	63	99	554	404

Best performances
Winners: 1904, 1934, 1956, 1969
Finalists: 1926, 1933, 1955, 1981
Semi-finalists: 1924, 1932

Highest winning margins
At Hyde Road: 12 – 12–0 v Liverpool Stanley, 4 October 1890
At Maine Road: 9 (twice) – 10–1 v Swindon Town, 29 January 1930, 9–0 v Gateshead, 18 January 1933
At City of Manchester: 2 – 3–1 v Scunthorpe United, 7 January 2006
Away: 7 – 7–0 v Reading, 31 January 1968

Note: The victories over Swindon and Gateshead remain their highest FA Cup defeats.

Highest aggregate score
11–4 v Crystal Palace (h) 20 February 1926

Note: This remains Crystal Palace's heaviest FA Cup defeat.

Highest victory in a semi-final
6–1 v Aston Villa (Leeds Road, Huddersfield) 17 March 1934

Note: This shares the record as the highest score in a semi-final.

Heaviest defeat
2–8 v Bradford Park Avenue, 30 January 1946, 0–6 v Preston NE, 30 January 1897

Longest run without defeat
8 (three times) – round 3 1933–34 to 1934 Final, round 3 1955–56 to round 3 1956–57, round 3 1968–69 to round 3 1969–70

Longest run without a win
8 – round 3 1956–57 to round 3 replay 1960–61

FA Cup goalscorers with 10 or more goals

22	Fred Tilson
19	Eric Brook
17	Tommy Browell

17	Alec Herd
14	Frank Roberts
14	Ernie Toseland
11	Mike Summerbee
10	Neil Young
10	Bobby Marshall

Most appearances
44 – Mike Doyle, 1962–78

Most FA Cup Final appearances while with City
3 – Sam Cowan 1926, 1933, 1934

Highest individual scores
5 (twice) – Frank Roberts v Crystal Palace (h) 1925–26, Bobby Marshall v Swindon Town (h) 1929–30

Note: Denis Law did score 6 v Luton Town (a) in 1960–61, but the match was abandoned.

The following are national records for FA Cup games involving City or played at Maine Road:

Oldest player in FA Cup
49 years 8 months, Billy Meredith (City) v Newcastle United 1923–24

Youngest FA Cup Final goalkeeper
19 years 220 days, Peter Shilton (Leicester), City v Leicester City, 1969 FA Cup Final

Note: When Frank Swift kept goal for City in the 1934 Final he held the record as the youngest. He was 20 years and 123 days.

Record crowd apart from Final
84,569 – v Stoke City (h), 1933–34

Record crowd for a midweek FA Cup tie (excluding Final)
80,480 – Derby County v Birmingham City, 1946 semi-final replay at Maine Road

First player to score in consecutive FA Cup Finals at Wembley
Bobby Johnstone, 1955 and 1956

Fastest FA Cup Final goals
Joe Hayes's goal in the 1956 Final is currently recorded as the 12th fastest FA Cup Final goal of all time, while Jackie Milburn's goal against City in 1955 is recorded as the third fastest.

Interestingly, the fastest goal ever in an FA Cup Final is now acknowledged to have been scored by Bob Chatt for Aston Villa against WBA in 1895. This is of interest to City fans as Chatt was City's coach for many years during the early years of the 20th century.

City in the League Cup

City first competed in the League Cup in the 1960–61 season, winning the club's first-ever tie 3–0 at home to Stockport County.

	P	*W*	*D*	*L*	*F*	*A*
HOME	83	54	16	13	194	70
AWAY	89	33	20	36	123	132
TOTAL	172	87	36	49	317	202

Best performances
Winners: 1970, 1976
Finalists: 1974
Semi-finalists: 1964, 1981

Highest winning margins
At Maine Road: 6 (four times) – 6–0 v Scunthorpe United, 10 September 1974, 6–0 Torquay United, 25 October 1983, 7–1 Notts County, 19 August 1998, 6–0 Birmingham City, 10 October 2001
At City of Manchester: 6 – 7–1 Barnsley, 21 September 2004
Away: 4 – 4–0 Torquay United, 26 September 1990
At a neutral venue: 5 – 6–1 Norwich City, 29 September 1975 (Stamford Bridge)

Highest aggregate score
9 – 6–3 Plymouth Argyle, 12 October 1988

Highest victory in a semi-final
4–1 on aggregate v Middlesbrough, 1975–76

Heaviest defeat
0–6 v Birmingham City, 11 December 1962

Longest run without defeat
10 – round 2 1st leg 1973–74 to semi-final 2nd leg 1973–74 (lost Final)

Longest run without a win
4 – round 3 1995–96 to round 1 1st leg 1997–98

Top five League Cup goalscorers

18	Colin Bell and Dennis Tueart
14	Francis Lee
11	David White
9	Shaun Goater

Most appearances
44 (plus 2 as sub) – Tommy Booth, 1965–81

Most League Cup Final appearances while with City
3 – Tommy Booth and Mike Doyle 1970, 1974, 1976

Highest individual scores
4 (twice) – Dennis Tueart v Notts County (h) 1980–81, Darren Huckerby v Birmingham City 2001–02

City in other cups

FA Charity Shield

1934–35

28 Nov v Arsenal (a) 0–4

Swift; Dale, Barnett, Busby, Cowan, Bray, Toseland, McLuckie, Tilson, Heale, Brook

Att: 10,888

1937–38

3 Nov v Sunderland (h) 2–0

Herd, Doherty

Swift; Dale, Barkas, Percival, Marshall, Bray, Toseland, Herd, Tilson, Doherty, Brook

Att: 20,000

1956–57

24 Oct v Manchester United (h) 0–1

Savage; Leivers, Little, Revie, Ewing, Paul, Fagan, Hayes, Johnstone, Dyson, Clarke

Att: 30,495

1968–69

3 Aug v West Bromwich Albion (h) 6–1

Lee 2, Owen 2, Young, Lovett (og)

Mulhearn; Connor, Pardoe, Doyle, Heslop, Oakes, Lee, Bell, Summerbee, Owen, Young

Att: 35,510

1969–70

2 Aug v Leeds United (a) 1–2

Bell

Corrigan; Book, Pardoe, Doyle, Booth, Oakes, Summerbee, Bell, Lee (Connor), Young, Coleman

Att: 39,535

1972–73

5 Aug v Aston Villa (a) 1–0

Lee (pen)

Corrigan; Book, Donachie (Jeffries), Doyle, Booth, Bell, Summerbee, Lee, Davies (Mellor), Marsh, Towers

Att: 34,859

1973–74

18 Aug v Burnley (h) 0–1

Corrigan; Book, Donachie, Doyle, Booth, Oakes, Summerbee, Bell, Law, Lee, Marsh

Att: 23,988

Texaco Cup

1971–72

15 Sep R1 leg 1 v Airdrieonians (h) 2–2

Doyle (pen), Mellor

Healey (Corrigan); Book, Donachie, Doyle (Lee), Booth, Jeffries, Summerbee, Towers, Davies, Brennan, Mellor

Att: 15,029

27 Sep R1 leg 2 v Airdrieonians (a) 0–2 (agg 2–4)

Healey; Connor, Donachie, Jeffries, Hanvey, Towers, Carter, Johnson, Brennan, Hill, Henson

Att: 13,700

1974–75

3 Aug Gp 1 v Blackpool (a) 1–1

Tueart

Corrigan; Barrett, Donachie, Doyle, Booth, Oakes, Summerbee, Bell, Lee, Marsh, Tueart

Att: 12,342

6 Aug Gp 1 v Sheffield United (a) 2–4

Summerbee, Law

Corrigan; Barrett, Donachie, Doyle, Booth, Oakes, Summerbee, Bell (Henson), Marsh, Law, Tueart

Att: 9,358

10 Aug Gp 1 v Oldham Athletic (h) 2–1

Tueart, Lee

MacRae; Barrett, Donachie, Doyle, Booth, Oakes, Lee, Bell, Marsh, Law (Daniels), Tueart

Att: 13,880

City failed to qualify.

Anglo-Scottish Cup

1975–76

2 Aug Gp 1 v Blackpool (a) 0–1
Corrigan; Donachie, Oakes, Doyle (Leman), Watson, Booth, Henry, Royle, Marsh, Hartford, Tueart
Att: 11,091

6 Aug Gp 1 v Blackburn Rovers (a) 0–1
Corrigan; Donachie, Oakes, Doyle, Watson, Booth, Keegan, Royle, Marsh, Hartford, Tueart
Att: 10,612

9 Aug Gp 1 v Sheffield United (h) 3–1
Booth, Marsh, Leman
Corrigan; Hammond, Donachie, Booth, Watson, Oakes, Telford (Leman), Royle, Marsh, Hartford, Tueart
Att: 11,167

Auto Windscreens Shield

(Originally named Associate Members' Cup)
1998–99

8 Dec R1 v Mansfield Town (h) 1–2
Allsop
Wright; Jeff Whitley, Tiatto, Fenton, Rimmer, Vaughan, Brown, Pollock (Jim Whitley), Allsop, Taylor (Bailey), Heaney
Att: 3,007

NOTE: The Texaco Cup was a competition for English, Scottish and Northern Irish sides. In 1975–76 the Irish element was dropped and the competition became the Anglo-Scottish Cup. In 1981 the Scottish clubs pulled out, by which time the senior English clubs had chosen not to take part. The competition evolved into a knock-out style trophy for sides from the bottom two divisions and was renamed the Associate Members' Cup (sides in the top two divisions were Full Members of the Football League, hence the title of the 1985–86 competition City reached the final of). Since 1984–85 the tournament has been sponsored and City re-entered the competition in 1998–99 when they were members of the 'new' Division Two (third tier of football).

Tennent-Caledonian Cup

1976–77

2 Aug v Southampton (n) 1–1
Tueart
Corrigan; Docherty, Donachie, Doyle, Watson, Hartford, Barnes (Power), Keegan, Royle, Kidd (Lester), Tueart
Att: 30,000
(after each side had scored 11 penalties Southampton won by toss of coin)

Play-off for third place
3 Aug v Partick Thistle (n) 4–1
Kidd 2, Hartford, Tueart
Corrigan; Docherty, Donachie, Doyle, Watson, Hartford, Leman, Power, Royle, Kidd, Tueart
Att: 35,000

Note: This was a four-club tournament played in Scotland.

Anglo-Italian Cup

1970–71

2 Sep R1 leg 1 v Bologna (a) 0–1
Corrigan; Book, Pardoe, Doyle, Booth, Oakes, Young, Bell, Lee, Towers, Summerbee
Att: 28,000

Sep 23 R1 leg 2 v Bologna (h) 2–2 (agg 2–3)
Heslop, Lee
Corrigan; Book, Pardoe, Doyle, Heslop, Oakes, Hill, Bell, Lee, Young, Towers (Summerbee).
Att: 25,843

Full Members' Cup

(Renamed following sponsorship as the Simod Cup and the Zenith Data Systems Cup)

1985–86

14 Oct Gp 3 v Leeds United (h) 6–1
Davies 3, Baker, Lillis, Power
Nixon; Reid, Power, Clements, Johnson, May, Lillis, Baker, Davies (Melrose), McNab, Simpson (Tolmie)
Att: 4,029

22 Oct Gp 3 v Sheffield United (a) 2–1
Phillips, Baker
Nixon; May, Power, Reid, Johnson, Phillips, Lillis, Baker, Davies, McNab, McIlroy (Simpson).
Att: 3,420

4 Nov Northern SF v Sunderland (h) 0–0
Nixon; Reid, May, Clements, Johnson, Phillips, Lillis, Melrose (Smith), Davies (Moulden), Power, Simpson.
Att: 6,642
(City won 4–3 on penalties)

26 Nov Northern Final leg 1 v Hull City (a) 1–2
Phillips
Nixon; Reid, Power, Clements, McCarthy, Phillips, Melrose (Simpson), May, Davies, McNab, Wilson.
Att: 5,213

11 Dec Northern Final leg 2 v Hull City (h) 2–0 (agg 3–2)
Phillips, Melrose
Nixon; Reid, Power, Clements, McCarthy, Phillips, Lillis, May, Davies, McIlroy, Simpson (Melrose).
Att: 10, 180

23 Mar Final v Chelsea (Wembley) 4–5
Lillis 2 (1 pen), Kinsey, Rougvie (og)
Nixon; Reid (Baker), Power, Redmond, McCarthy, Phillips (Simpson), Lillis, May, Kinsey, McNab, Wilson.
Att: 68,000

1986–87

4 Nov R2 v Wimbledon (h) 3–1
Moulden 2, Clements
Suckling; May, Wilson, Clements, McCarthy, Redmond, White, Moulden, Varadi, Grealish, Simpson
Att: 4,914

26 Nov R3 v Watford (h) 1–0
Moulden
Suckling; Gidman (May), Wilson, Redmond, McCarthy, Grealish, Baker, McNab, White, Moulden, Simpson
Att: 6,393

31 Jan R4 v Ipswich Town (h) 2–3
Varadi 2
Suckling; Gidman, Wilson, Clements, McCarthy, Grealish, Simpson, McNab, Varadi, Lake, Barnes.
Att: 11,027

1987–88

10 Nov R1 v Plymouth Argyle (h) 6–2
Hinchcliffe, Adcock 3, Stewart, Lake
Nixon; Gidman (Scott), Hinchcliffe, Clements, Lake, Redmond, White, Stewart, Adcock, McNab (Brightwell), Simpson.
Att: 5,051

16 Dec R2 v Chelsea (h) 0–2
Nixon; Gidman, Hinchcliffe, Seagraves, Lake, Redmond, White (Scott), Stewart, Adcock (Varadi), McNab, Simpson.
Att: 6,406

1988–89
Round 2
13 Dec v Blackburn Rovers (a) 2–3
Gleghorn, Hendry (og)
Dibble; Lake, Hinchcliffe, Seagraves, Brightwell, Redmond, White, Moulden, Morley, McNab (Bradshaw), Gleghorn
Att: 5,793

1989–90
29 Nov R2 v Nottingham Forest (a) 2–3
White, Oldfield
Dibble; Fleming, Taggart, Bishop, Gayle, Redmond, White, Morley, Hinchcliffe (Brightwell), McNab (Oldfield), Lake
Att: 9,279

1990–91
19 Dec R2 v Middlesbrough (h) 2–1
White, Quinn
Coton; Brightwell, Pointon, Harper, Hendry, Redmond, White, Clarke, Quinn, Brennan, Ward
Att: 6,406

22 Jan R3 v Sheffield United (a) 2–0
Ward 2
Coton; Hill, Pointon, Harper, Hendry, Redmond, White (Brightwell), Allen (Heath), Quinn, Megson, Ward
Att: 5,106

20 Feb R4 v Leeds United (a) 0–2 (aet)
Coton; Brightwell, Pointon, Harper, Hendry, Redmond, White, Allen (Heath), Quinn, Megson, Ward
Att: 11,898

1991–92
23 Oct 23 R2 v Sheffield Wednesday (a) 2–3
Hendry 2
Margetson; Quigley (Mauge), Pointon, Hendry, Curie, Redmond, Sheron, Heath, Brennan, Brightwell, Hughes
Att: 7,951

City in Europe

City first competed in the European Cup in the 1968–69 season and that season Manchester made history by becoming the first English city to have two sides competing in the European Cup.

Best performances
Winners of ECWC: 1970
Semi-finalists of ECWC: 1971

Highest winning margins
5 (twice) – 5–0 v SK Lierse, ECWC (h), 26 November 1969 and 5–0 v Total Network Solutions, UEFA Cup (h), 14 August 2003

Highest victory in a semi-final
5–2 on aggregate v Schalke 04, ECWC, 1969–70

Heaviest defeat
1–3 v Borussia Moenchengladbach, UEFA Cup, 20 March 1979

Longest run without defeat
6 – round 1 1st leg ECWC 1969–70 to round 3 2nd leg 1969–70

Top five European goalscorers

10	Francis Lee
8	Colin Bell
6	Brian Kidd
5	Neil Young
4	Nicolas Anelka

Most appearances
27 Joe Corrigan 1967–83

European Cup

1968–69
18 Sep R1 leg 1 v Fenerbahce (h) 0–0
Mulhearn; Kennedy, Pardoe, Doyle, Heslop, Oakes, Lee, Bell, Summerbee, Young, Coleman
Att: 38,787

2 Oct 2 R1 leg 2 v Fenerbahce (a) 1–2 (agg 1–2)
Coleman
Mulhearn; Connor, Pardoe, Doyle, Heslop, Oakes, Lee, Bell, Summerbee, Young, Coleman
Att: 45,000

European Cup-Winners' Cup

1969–70
17 Sep R1 leg 1 v Atletico Bilbao (a) 3–3
Young, Booth, Echebarria (og)
Corrigan; Book, Pardoe, Doyle, Booth, Oakes, Summerbee, Bell, Lee, Young, Bowyer
Att: 45,000

1 Oct R1 leg 2 v Atletico Bilbao (h) 3–0 (agg 6–3)
Oakes, Bell, Bowyer
Corrigan; Book, Pardoe, Doyle, Booth, Oakes, Summerbee, Bell, Lee, Young, Bowyer
Att: 49,665

12 Nov R2 leg 1 v SK Lierse (a) 3–0
Lee 2, Bell
Corrigan; Book, Pardoe, Doyle (Heslop), Booth, Oakes, Summerbee, Bell, Lee, Young, Bowyer
Att: 18,000

26 Nov R2 leg 2 v SK Lierse (h) 5–0 (agg 8–0)
Bell 2, Lee 2, Summerbee
Mulhearn; Book, Pardoe, Doyle, Booth, Oakes (Towers), Summerbee, Bell, Lee, Jeffries, Bowyer
Att: 26,486

City in 1967–68 with the team that first won qualification into Europe.

4 Mar R3 leg 1 v Academica Coimbra (a) 0–0
Corrigan; Book (Heslop), Mann, Doyle, Booth, Oakes, Pardoe, Bell, Summerbee, Lee, Young
Att: 8.000

18 Mar R3 leg 2 v Academica Coimbra (h) 1–0 (agg 1–0)
Towers
Corrigan; Book, Mann, Booth, Heslop (Towers), Oakes, Doyle, Bell (Glennon), Lee, Young, Pardoe
Att: 36,338

1 Apr SF leg 1 v Schalke 04 (a) 0–1
Corrigan; Book, Pardoe, Doyle, Jeffries, Oakes, Booth, Bell, Lee, Young, Summerbee
Att: 38,000

15 Apr SF leg 2 v Schalke 04 (h) 5–1 (agg 5–2)
Doyle, Young 2, Lee, Bell
Corrigan; Book, Pardoe, Doyle (Heslop), Booth, Oakes, Towers, Bell, Lee, Young, Summerbee (Carrodus)
Att: 46,361

29 Apr Final v Gornik Zabrze (Vienna) 2–1
Young, Lee (pen)
Corrigan; Book, Pardoe, Doyle (Bowyer), Booth, Oakes, Heslop, Bell, Lee, Young, Towers
Att: 12,000

1970–71
16 Sep R1 leg 1 v Linfield (h) 1–0
Bell
Corrigan; Book, Pardoe, Doyle, Booth, Oakes, Summerbee. Bell, Lee, Young, Towers
Att: 25,184

30 Sep R1 leg 2 v Linfield (a) 1–2 (agg 2–2*)
Lee
Corrigan; Book, Pardoe, Doyle, Jeffries, Oakes, Summerbee, Bell, Lee (Bowyer), Young, Towers
Att: 21,000
* City won on away-goals rule

21 Oct R2 leg 1 v Honved (a) 1–0
Lee
Corrigan; Book, Pardoe, Doyle, Heslop, Jeffries, Summerbee, Bell, Lee, Hill, Towers
Att: 10,000

4 Nov R2 leg 2 v Honved (h) 2–0 (agg 3–0)
Bell, Lee
Corrigan; Book, Pardoe, Doyle, Heslop, Oakes, Summerbee, Bell, Lee, Hill, Towers
Att: 28,770

10 Mar R3 leg 1 v Gornik Zabrze (a) 0–2
Corrigan; Book, Towers, Doyle, Booth, Oakes, Summerbee, Bell, Lee, Young, Jeffries
Att: 100,000

24 Mar R3 leg 2 v Gornik Zabrze (h) 2–0 (agg 2–2)
Mellor, Doyle
Healey; Connor, Towers, Doyle, Booth, Donachie, Jeffries, Bell, Lee, Young (Mann), Mellor (Bowyer)
Att: 31,950

31 Mar R3 replay v Gornik Zabrze (Copenhagen) 3–1
Young, Booth, Lee
Healey; Connor, Towers, Doyle, Booth, Donachie, Jeffries, Bell, Lee, Young, Hill
Att: 12,100

14 Apr SF leg 1 v Chelsea (a) 0–1
Corrigan; Book, Connor, Towers, Booth, Donachie, Johnson, Hill, Lee, Young, Mann
Att: 45,595

28 Apr SF leg 2 v Chelsea (h) 0–1 (agg 0–2)
Healey; Book, Connor, Towers, Heslop, Jeffries, Summerbee (Carter), Lee, Bowyer, Young, Johnson (Donachie)
Att: 43,663

UEFA Cup

1972–73

13 Sep R1 leg 1 v Valencia CF (h) 2–2
Mellor, Marsh
Corrigan; Jeffries, Donachie, Doyle, Booth, Oakes, Mellor, Bell, Marsh, Lee, Towers
Att: 21,698

27 Sep R1 leg 2 v Valencia CF (a) 1–2 (agg 3–4)
Marsh
Healey; Book, Barrett, Doyle, Booth (Mellor), Oakes, Summerbee, Bell, Marsh, Lee, Towers
Att: 54,000

1976-77

15 Sep R1 leg 1 v Juventus (h) 1–0
Kidd
Corrigan; Docherty, Donachie, Doyle, Watson, Conway, Barnes (Power), Kidd, Royle, Hartford, Tueart
Att: 36,955

29 Sep R1 leg 2 v Juventus (a) 0–2 (agg 1–2)
Corrigan; Docherty, Donachie, Doyle, Watson, Booth, Keegan (Lester), Kidd, Royle, Hartford, Tueart
Att: 55,000

1977–78

14 Sep R1 leg 1 v Widzew Lodz (h) 2–2
Barnes, Channon
Corrigan; Clements, Donachie, Owen, Watson, Booth, Barnes, Channon, Kidd, Hartford, Keegan (Royle)
Att: 33,695

28 Sep R1 leg 2 v Widzew Lodz (a) 0–0 (agg 2–2*)
Corrigan; Doyle (Clements), Power, Owen, Watson, Booth, Barnes, Kidd, Royle, Hartford, Tueart
Att: 40,000
*City lost on away-goals rule

1978–79
13 Sep R1 leg 1 v FC Twente (a) 1–1
Watson
Corrigan; Clements, Power, Viljoen, Watson, Futcher, Channon, Owen, Palmer, Hartford, Barnes
Att: 12,000

27 Sep R1 leg 2 v FC Twente (h) 3–2 (agg 4–3)
Wildschut (og), Kidd, Bell
Corrigan; Clements, Power, Viljoen (Bell), Watson, Futcher, Channon, Owen, Kidd, Hartford, Barnes
Att: 29,330

18 Oct R2 leg 1 v Standard Liege (h) 4–0
Hartford, Kidd 2 (1 pen), Palmer
Corrigan; Clements, Donachie, Booth, Watson, Viljoen (Keegan), Palmer, Bell, Kidd, Hartford, Barnes
Att: 27,487

1 Nov R2 leg 2 v Standard Liege (a) 0–2 (agg 4–2)
Corrigan; Clements, Donachie, Booth, Watson, Owen, Channon, Bell, Kidd, Hartford, Palmer
Att: 25,000

23 Nov R3 leg 1 v Milan AC (a) 2–2
Kidd, Power
Corrigan; Clements, Donachie, Booth, Watson, Power, Viljoen (Keegan), Bell, Kidd, Hartford, Palmer.
Att: 40,000

6 Dec R3 leg 2 v Milan AC (h) 3–0 (agg 5–2)
Booth, Hartford, Kidd
Corrigan; Keegan, Donachie, Booth, Watson, Power, Channon, Viljoen, Kidd, Hartford, Barnes
Att: 38,026

7 Mar R4 leg 1 v Borussia Monchengladbach (h) 1–1
Channon
Corrigan; Donachie, Power, Reid, Watson, Booth, Channon, Viljoen, Kidd, Hartford, Barnes
Att: 39,005

20 Mar R4 leg 2 v Borussia Monchengladbach (a) 1–3 (agg 2–4)
Deyna
Corrigan; Donachie, Power, Viljoen, Watson, Booth, Channon, Reid (Deyna), Henry, Hartford, Barnes
Att: 30,000

2003–04
14 Aug QR leg 1 v Total Network Solutions (h) 5–0
Sinclair, Wright-Phillips, Jihai, Sommeil, Anelka
Seaman; Jihai, Tarnat (Tiatto), Sommeil, Distin, Bosvelt (Barton), Wright-Phillips, Berkovic, Anelka, Fowler (Wanchope), Sinclair
Att: 34,103

28 Aug QR leg 2 v Total Network Solutions (a – Millennium Stadium) 2–0
Negouai, Huckerby
Weaver; Flood, Tiatto, Dunne, Wiekens, Bischoff, Bosvelt (Whelan), Negouai, Huckerby, Macken (Wright-Phillips), Berkovic (Barton)
Att: 10,123

24 Sept R1 leg 1 v Lokeren (h) 3–2
Sibierski, Fowler, Anelka
Seaman; Jihai, Tiatto (Dunne), Sommeil, Distin, Bosvelt (Wright-Phillips), Sibierski, Reyna, Anelka, Fowler, McManaman
Att: 29,067

15 Oct R1 leg 2 v Lokeren (a) 1–0
Anelka (pen)
Seaman; Jihai, Tarnat, Sommeil, Distin, Bosvelt, Wright-Phillips, McManaman, Anelka, Wanchope (Reyna), Sinclair (Barton)
Att: 10,000

6 Nov R2 leg 1 v Groclin (h) 1–1
Anelka
Seaman; Jihai, Tarnat, Dunne, Distin, Barton, Wright-Phillips, Reyna (Bosvelt), McManaman (Tiatto), Anelka, Fowler (Wanchope)
Att: 32,506

27 Nov R2 leg 2 v Groclin (a) 0–0
Seaman; Jihai, Dunne, Sommeil, Distin, Barton, Wright-Phillips (Reyna), McManaman, Anelka (Macken), Fowler (Wanchope), Sinclair
Att: 5,500

Player Factfile

Record transfers

The following records are the figures reported at the time by Manchester City. In both cases the media and other sources have quoted the figures as lower amounts (approximately £3 million lower in both cases), but the total value of a transfer is often difficult to assess. Debates over whether the records should include taxes and other amounts such as agent's fees complicate matters, while the selling club will often try to overstate the amount received if a popular player is sold. Buying clubs will often give the total amount paid to sign a player, including taxes, if they want to appear as big spenders and on other occasions will give only the figure paid directly to the selling club (if they want to give the impression they've driven a tough bargain).

Record fee received
£23 million from Chelsea for Shaun Wright-Phillips, August 2005
Previous highest was £7 million from Fenerbahce for Nicolas Anelka, January 2005

Record transfer fee paid
£13 million to Paris St Germain for Nicolas Anelka, June 2002
Previous highest was £3 million to Portsmouth for Lee Bradbury, July 1997

National awards

Footballer of the year
Don Revie 1954–55
Bert Trautmann 1955–56
Tony Book 1968–69 (shared with Derby County's Dave Mackay)

PFA Young Player of the Year
Peter Barnes 1975–76

PFA Merit Award
Denis Law 1975
Sir Matt Busby 1980
Joe Mercer OBE 1982
Tommy Hutchison 1992
Niall Quinn 2002

Player of the year

The Official Supporter's Club first organised their player of the year award to commemorate the 1966-67 season. These players are the ones the fans love to see.

1966–67	Tony Book
1967–68	Colin Bell
1968–69	Glyn Pardoe
1969–70	Francis Lee
1970–71	Mike Doyle
1971–72	Mick Summerbee
1972–73	Mick Summerbee
1973–74	Mike Doyle
1974–75	Alan Oakes
1975–76	Joe Corrigan
1976–77	Dave Watson
1977–78	Joe Corrigan
1978–79	Asa Hartford
1979–80	Joe Corrigan
1980–81	Paul Power
1981–82	Tommy Caton
1982–83	Kevin Bond
1983–84	Mick McCarthy
1984–85	Paul Power
1985–86	Kenny Clements
1986–87	Neil McNab
1987–88	Steve Redmond
1988–89	Neil McNab
1989–90	Colin Hendry
1990–91	Niall Quinn
1991–92	Tony Coton
1992–93	Garry Flitcroft
1993–94	Tony Coton
1994–95	Uwe Rösler
1995–96	Georgiou Kinkladze
1996–97	Georgiou Kinkladze
1997–98	Michael Brown
1998–99	Gerhard Wiekens

1999–2000	Shaun Goater
2000–01	Danny Tiatto
2001–02	Ali Benarbia
2002–03	Eyal Berkovic
2003–04	Shaun Wright-Phillips
2004–05	Richard Dunne
2005–06	Richard Dunne

Youngest League player
Glyn Pardoe – 15 years 314 days v Birmingham City, 11 April 1962

Most capped player while with City
Colin Bell – 48 for England

World Cup players while with City
The following players have travelled to the World Cup while with City.

1970	Francis Lee and Colin Bell (both England)
1974	Willie Donachie and Denis Law (both Scotland)
1978	Willie Donachie and Asa Hartford (both Scotland)
1982	Asa Hartford (Scotland), Trevor Francis and Joe Corrigan (both England)
1986	Sammy McIlroy (N. Ireland)
1990	Niall Quinn (Rep. of Ireland)
1994	Alan Kernaghan and Terry Phelan (both Rep. of Ireland)
2002	Niclas Jensen (Denmark), Sun Jihai (China), Lucien Mettomo (Cameroon), Paulo Wanchope (Costa Rica) and Richard Dunne (Rep. of Ireland)
2006	David James (England) and Claudio Reyna (US)

The following City managers have travelled to the World Cup as players with other clubs.
Peter Reid
Alan Ball
Kevin Keegan
Stuart Pearce

Most clean sheets in the League
22 (out of 42 games) – Joe Corrigan, 1976–77
22 (out of 45 games) – Nicky Weaver, 1998–99*
21 (out of 42 games) – Alex Williams, 1984–85
* Weaver appeared in 45 matches of a 46 game season.

Substitutions
First substitute used
Roy Cheetham (replaced Mike Summerbee) – 30 August 1965, Wolverhampton Wanderers (a), Division Two
First substitute used in FA Cup
Dave Connor (replaced Tony Coleman) – 31 January 1968, Reading (a)

First substitute used in League Cup
Roy Cheetham (replaced Jimmy Murray) – 14 September 1966, Bolton Wanderers (h)

First substitute used in European Cup
None used in the two games played.

First substitute used in ECWC
George Heslop (replaced Mike Doyle) – 12 November 1969, SK Lierse (a)

First substitute used in UEFA Cup
Ian Mellor (replaced Tommy Booth) – 27 September 1972, Valencia (a)

Debuts
First League debut
Dave Russell – 3 September 1892, Bootle (h), Division Two

Technically every player appearing in the club's first League game was making his League debut, but Dave Russell was the only one not to have appeared in the previous season's Alliance League campaign, and therefore has been assumed to be the club's first League debutant.

Last debut at Hyde Road
George Utley – 28 October 1922, Preston NE, Division One

First debut at Maine Road
Alex Donaldson – 25 August 1923, Sheffield United, Division One

Last debut at Maine Road
Robbie Fowler – 1 February 2003, West Bromwich Albion, Premier League

First debut at City of Manchester Stadium
David Seaman, Michael Tarnat, Paul Bosvelt and Trevor Sinclair – 14 August 2003, Total Network Solutions, UEFA Cup

Penalties

First League penalty taken
3 September 1892, Bootle (h), Division Two. Taken by Dave Russell (missed).

First League penalty taken at Maine Road
25 August 1923, Sheffield United, Division One. Taken by Frank Roberts (missed).

Last League penalty taken at Maine Road
21 April 2002, Portsmouth, 'New' Division One. Taken by Stuart Pearce (missed).

First League penalty taken at City of Manchester Stadium
14 September 2003 (46 mins), Aston Villa, Premier League. Taken by Nicolas Anelka (scored).

Own-goals

First own-goal scored
7 October 1893, Burslem Port Vale (h), Division Two. Scored by a Port Vale player for City.

First own-goal scored for the opposition
21 October 1893, Newcastle United (h), Division Two. Scored by an unknown Ardwick player for Newcastle.

First own-goal scored at Maine Road
5 February 1927, Reading, Division Two. Scored by Dai Evans for City.

Last own-goal scored at Maine Road
1 February 2003 (22 mins), West Bromwich Albion, Premier League. Scored by Phil Gilchrist for City.

First League own-goal scored at City of Manchester Stadium
31 August 2003 (10 mins), Arsenal, Premier League. Scored by Arsenal's Bisan Lauren for City.

Frank Roberts had the distinction of taking the first penalty at Maine Road, against Sheffield United in 1923.

ATTENDANCES

City's all-time highest attendances

The following details City's 70,000 plus attendances (games are at Maine Road unless otherwise stated):

100,000 (ECWC round 3 at Gornik, Poland 1971)*
100,000 (FA Cup Final v Tottenham Hotspur at Wembley 1981)
100,000 (League Cup Final v Newcastle United at Wembley 1976)
100,000 (FA Cup Final v Leicester City at Wembley 1969)
100,000 (FA Cup Final v Birmingham City at Wembley 1956)
100,000 (FA Cup Final v Newcastle United at Wembley 1955)
97,963 (League Cup Final v WBA at Wembley 1970)
97,886 (League Cup Final v Wolverhampton Wanderers at Wembley 1974)
93,258 (FA Cup Final v Portsmouth at Wembley 1934)
92,950 (FA Cup Final v Everton at Wembley 1933)
92,500 (FA Cup Final replay v Tottenham Hotspur at Wembley 1981)
91,547 (FA Cup Final v Bolton Wanderers at Wembley 1926)
84,569 (FA Cup v Stoke 1934)**
79,491 (v Arsenal 1935)***
78,000 (v Manchester United 1947)
76,166 (FA Cup v Cardiff 1924)****
76,129 (FA Cup v Everton 1956)
75,540 (FA Cup at Aston Villa 1938)
74,918 (v Arsenal 1937)
74,789 (FA Cup v Huddersfield 1926)
74,723 (FA Cup v United 1955)
73,668 (FA Cup v Stoke 1928)
72,841 (FA Cup at Sheffield Wednesday 1934)*****
71,937 (FA Cup v Bury 1938)
71,690 (v Manchester United, away at Maine Road 1948)
70,640 (FA Cup v Liverpool 1956)
70,483 (v United 1957)
70,000 (v Aston Villa 1929)

*The Gornik official attendance in 1971 was recorded as 100,000 by the *Manchester Evening News*. This does seem a high figure, but it is actually some 10,000 less than the capacity at the time, and Gornik did stage other European games in front of 100,000 plus crowds. It seems more likely the attendance was around 105,000, but it is now impossible to prove the actual figure.
**This remains a record for a provincial match.
***This was the League's record attendance at the time.
****The attendance against Cardiff in 1924 was a record for any football match in Manchester at the time (including all games at Old Trafford and two FA Cup Finals)
*****This remains Hillsborough's record. City also held the attendance record at Burnden Park – 69,912 v Bolton, 1933.

Maine Road also staged the following neutral games played in front of 70,000 plus crowds:

83,260	(Manchester United v Arsenal, 1948)*
82,771	(Manchester United v Bradford, FA Cup fourth round 1949)
81,565	(Manchester United v Yeovil, FA Cup fifth round 1949)
80,480	(Birmingham City v Derby County, FA Cup semi-final 1946)
75,598	(Manchester United v Borussia Dortmund, European Cup first round 1956)**
75,213	(Sheffield Wednesday v Preston NE 1954)
75,000	(Bolton W v Everton, FA Cup semi-final 1953)
74,800	(Blackburn R v Bolton W, FA Cup semi-final 1958)
74,213	(Manchester United v Preston NE, FA Cup sixth round 1948)
74,135	(Sheffield W v Blackburn R, FA Cup semi-final 1960)
72,000	(Burnley v Liverpool, FA Cup semi-final 1947)
72,000	(Liverpool v Everton, FA Cup semi-final 1950)
71,623	(Manchester United v Bolton Wanderers 1948)
70,787	(Manchester United v Newcastle United 1948)
70,434	(Manchester United v Bradford, FA Cup fourth round replay 1949)
70,000	(Manchester United v Atletico Bilbao, Euro Cup quarter-final 1957)
70,000	(Birmingham City v Blackpool, FA Cup semi-final 1951)
70,000	(England v Scotland, Burnden Park disaster match 1946)

*This remains the record League attendance.
**This is United's highest home crowd in European football.
Note: No other English League ground has staged so many attendances over 80,000. Also, at the time of going to press no other English League ground has staged so many attendances over 70,000 plus, although the increase in size of Old Trafford to around 75,000 means that record will disappear during 2006–07.

Progressive attendance records

*c.*4,000	3 September 1892	Bootle
*c.*6,000	22 October 1892	Small Heath
*c.*14,000	3 November 1894	Newton Heath
*c.*20,000	7 December 1895	Newton Heath
*c.*30,000	3 April 1896	Liverpool
*c.*35,000	5 March 1904	Middlesbrough (FA Cup)
*c.*40,000	28 January 1905	Newcastle
41,709	1 February 1913	Sunderland (FA Cup, abandoned)
*c.*50,000	26 March 1921	Burnley (unofficial)
58,159	25 August 1923	Sheffield United
76,166	8 March 1924	Cardiff City (FA Cup)
84,569	3 March 1934	Stoke City (FA Cup)

Attendances – City's last

84,000 plus	84,569	3 March 1934 v Stoke
76,000 plus	76,129	3 March 1956, v Everton
70,000 plus	70,483	28 December 1957 v United
65,000 plus	65,981	2 May 1960 v Burnley
60,000 plus	63,326	6 November 1971 v United
54,000 plus	54,478	24 February 1973 v Sunderland FA Cup
50,000 plus	52,037	10 October 1981 v United
48,000 plus	48,773	14 September 1985 v United
47,000 plus	47,192	14 January 2006 v United*

* At the time of publication.

ABANDONED MATCHES

Abandoned matches are usually simply wiped from the records with little or no thought of the implications, but many of the matches listed below did have significant consequences for the players taking part.

Kare Ingebrigtsen's only League goal for the Blues was scratched from the records by referee David Elleray in the 1994 meeting with Ipswich, while in 1969 Newcastle debutant Arthur Horsfield saw his first goal cancelled by referee David Corbett.

In August 1960 the highest crowd to watch an abandoned City match, 51,927, saw goals from Joe Hayes and Denis Law for City with Dennis Violet and Alex Dawson netting for the Reds prior to the game being abandoned. Had Hayes's goal been allowed to stand that would have made him the all-time record derby goalscorer with 11 (he currently shares the record of 10 derby goals with Francis Lee, one more than Bobby Charlton).

The meeting with Birmingham in 1958 was the first game played in Manchester following the Munich disaster. Few Mancunians were in the mood for a match, and with poor weather contributing to the misery of the period a significantly lower crowd (23,461) than usual attended – it was 20,000 down on the average for the six previous home matches.

One interesting statistic is that Billy Meredith has played in six abandoned City matches, while Denis Law has seen seven of his first-team goals scratched from the records. In addition to his 1960 derby goal, he netted six against Luton in the FA Cup. He did also score for City in the abandoned tour match with Torino in June 1961 – a month before he was transferred to the Italian side.

Officially, the 1–0 City win at Old Trafford in April 1974 was abandoned, although the result was allowed to stand. This game became recognised as the match which saw Denis Law back-heel a goal to help United into Division Two. It was abandoned four minutes from time after a second pitch invasion – and some supporters on the Stretford End had also started a fire.

Abandoned Matches

Date	Against	Score	Scorers	Attendance
Division Two				
14/12/1895	Burslem Port Vale	1-0	McBride	3,000 (H)
Abandoned at half-time				
Replay 17/02		1-0	Finnerhan	3,000
Division Two				
21/12/1895	Burslem Port Vale	0-0		2,000 (A)
Abandoned after 65 mins				
Replay 10/02		1-0	Davies	5,000
Division Two				
31/12/1898	Grimsby Town	0-0		300 (A)
Replay 11/04		2-1	Meredith, Gillespie	5,000

Date	Against	Score	Scorers	Attendance
Division One				
21/12/1901	Stoke	0-2		6,000 (A)
Abandoned after 75 mins				
Replay 13/01		0-3		5,000
FA Cup 1st round				
25/01/1902	Preston NE	1-1	Henderson	10,000 (A)
Abandoned in extra-timeReplay at Hyde Road				
Replay 29/01		0-0		7,000
Division Two				
25/10/1902	Barnsley	5-0	Meredith, Gillespie, Drummond, Threlfall, Own-goal	16,000 (H)
Abandoned after 85 mins				
Replay 24/11		3-2	Gillespie (2), Meredith	8,000
Division Two				
10/01/1903	Small Heath	0-0		35,000 (H)
Abandoned after 40 mins				
Replay 23/02		4-0	Meredith (2), Gillespie, Threlfall	20,000
FA Cup 2nd round				
01/02/1913	Sunderland*	0-2*		41,709 (H)
Abandoned due to crowd congestion after 58 mins. Replay at Sunderland*				
Replay 05/02		0-2		27,974
Division One				
09/02/1921	Everton	0-0		30,000 (H)
Replay 23/02		2-0	Browell (2)	33,000
Division One				
28/11/1936	Brentford	0-0		20,000 (H)
Abandoned after 40 mins				
Replay 07/04		2-1	Doherty, Brook	24,629
FA Cup 3rd round				
07/01/1956	Blackpool	1-1	Dyson	32,577 (H)
Abandoned after 56 mins				
Replay 11/01		2-1	Johnstone, Dyson	42,517
Division One				
15/02/1958	Birmingham City	1-1	McAdams	23,461 (H)
Abandoned after 40 mins				
Replay 05/03		1-1	Barlow	30,565

NOTE: * The Sunderland Cup match has been incorrectly recorded as 0–0 and abandoned in extra-time in earlier City books. It was actually abandoned after Sunderland scored their second goal.

Date	Against	Score	Scorers	Attendance
Division One				
27/08/1960	Manchester Utd	2-2	Law, Hayes	51,927 (H)
Abandoned after 56 mins Heavy rain				
Replay 04/03 1-3		Wagstaffe	50,479	
FA Cup 4th round				
28/01/1961	Luton Town	6-2	Law (6)	23,727 (A)
Abandoned 69 mins		Fog		
Replay 01/02 1-3		Law	15,783	
Division One				
22/12/1962	Aston Villa	1-0	Dobing	21,264 (A)
Abandoned 48 mins				
Replay 08/05 1-3		Dobing	17,707	
Division Two				
09/09/1965	Norwich City	1-1	Young	13,235 (H)
Abandoned at half-timeWaterlogged pitch				
Replay 27/10 0-0			34,091	
Division One				
01/02/1969	Newcastle Utd	1-1	Owen	30,160 (H)
Abandoned 41 mins				
Replay 05/05 1-0		Young	20,108	
Premier League				
03/01/1994	Ipswich Town	2-0	Ingebrigtsen, Vonk	20,306 (H)
Abandoned after 39 minsWaterlogged pitch				
Replay 05/02 2-1	Griffiths, Flitcroft		28,188	
League Cup 5th round				
12/12/2000	Ipswich Town	1-1	Dickov	23,260 (H)
Abandoned after 23 minsWaterlogged pitch				
Replay 19/12 1-2		Goater	31,252	

CAREER RECORDS

The career records detailed within this table include games played in the League, FA Cup, League Cup, European and Play-offs/Test Matches. The Other columns details games played in the Charity Shield, Full Members' Cup, Auto Windscreens Shield, Anglo-Scottish Cup, Anglo-Italian Cup and Texaco Cup. It does not include games in the Tennent-Caledonian Cup, Alliance League, wartime games, abandoned or expunged games (for example the three games in the abandoned 1939–40 season).

		Career		League			FA Cup			League Cup			European			Play-offs			Other			TOTAL		
Surname	Born	Start	Finish	Ap	Sub	Gls	Ap	Sub	Gls	Ap	Sub	Gls	Ap	Sub	Gls	Ap	Sub	Gls	Ap	Sub	Gls	Ap	Sub	Gls
Abbott JA	Patricroft	1913		3	0	2	0	0	0	0	0	0	0	0	0	0	0	0	0	0	0	3	0	2
Adcock AC	Bethnal Green	1987		12	3	5	2	0	0	2	1	1	0	0	0	0	0	0	2	0	3	18	4	9
Aimson PE	Macclesfield	1961	1963	16	0	4	0	0	0	3	0	2	0	0	0	0	0	0	0	0	0	19	0	6
Albinson G	Manchester	1921		3	0	0	0	0	0	0	0	0	0	0	0	0	0	0	0	0	0	3	0	0
Alison J	Peebles	1949	1950	19	0	0	1	0	0	0	0	0	0	0	0	0	0	0	0	0	0	20	0	0
Allan J	Glasgow	1926	1927	8	0	1	1	0	0	0	0	0	0	0	0	0	0	0	0	0	0	9	0	1
Allen AJ	Moston	1919	1923	52	0	0	4	0	0	0	0	0	0	0	0	0	0	0	0	0	0	56	0	0
Allen CD	Stepney	1989	1991	31	22	16	4	2	1	5	2	4	0	0	0	0	0	0	2	0	0	42	26	21
Allmark JJ	Liverpool	1937		1	0	0	0	0	0	0	0	0	0	0	0	0	0	0	0	0	0	1	0	0
Allsopp D	Melbourne, Australia	1998	2000	3	26	4	0	0	0	0	7	1	0	0	0	0	1	0	1	0	1	4	34	6
Anders H	St Helens	1952	1954	32	0	4	1	0	0	0	0	0	0	0	0	0	0	0	0	0	0	33	0	4
Anelka N	Versailles, France	2002	2004	87	2	37	5	0	4	4	0	0	5	0	4	0	0	0	0	0	0	101	2	45
Angus H		1892		2	0	0	0	0	0	0	0	0	0	0	0	0	0	0	0	0	0	2	0	0
Angus WJ	Blythswood	1892		7	0	3	1	0	0	0	0	0	0	0	0	0	0	0	0	0	0	8	0	3
Appleton F	Hyde	1925	1927	2	0	0	1	0	0	0	0	0	0	0	0	0	0	0	0	0	0	3	0	0
Arason AG	Reykjavik, Iceland	2003		0	0	0	2	0	0	0	0	0	0	0	0	0	0	0	0	0	0	2	0	0
Armitt GGH		1892		1	0	0	0	0	0	0	0	0	0	0	0	0	0	0	0	0	0	1	0	0
Ashworth SB	Fenton	1903		18	0	0	4	0	0	0	0	0	0	0	0	0	0	0	0	0	0	22	0	0
Atkinson DR	Shrewsbury	1996		7	1	2	0	0	0	0	0	0	0	0	0	0	0	0	0	0	0	7	1	2
Austin SW	Arnold	1924	1930	160	0	43	12	0	4	0	0	0	0	0	0	0	0	0	0	0	0	172	0	47
Bacon A	Birdholme	1928		5	0	1	0	0	0	0	0	0	0	0	0	0	0	0	0	0	0	5	0	1
Bacuzzi RD	Islington	1964	1965	56	1	0	2	0	0	1	0	0	0	0	0	0	0	0	0	0	0	59	1	0
Bailey A	Macclesfield	1998		0	0	0	0	0	0	0	0	0	0	0	0	0	0	0	0	1	0	0	1	0

Surname	Born	Career Start	Finish	League Ap	Sub	Gls	FA Cup Ap	Sub	Gls	League Cup Ap	Sub	Gls	European Ap	Sub	Gls	Play-offs Ap	Sub	Gls	Other Ap	Sub	Gls	TOTAL Ap	Sub	Gls
Baker GA	New York, USA	1960	1961	37	0	14	1	0	0	1	0	0	0	0	0	0	0	0	0	0	0	39	0	14
Baker GE	Southampton	1982	1986	114	3	19	2	1	0	13	1	0	0	0	0	0	0	0	3	1	2	132	6	21
Baker J		1893		3	0	1	0	0	0	0	0	0	0	0	0	0	0	0	0	0	0	3	0	1
Baldwin W		1906	1907	2	0	0	0	0	0	0	0	0	0	0	0	0	0	0	0	0	0	2	0	0
Banks W	Riccarton	1905	1911	25	0	1	1	0	0	0	0	0	0	0	0	0	0	0	0	0	0	26	0	1
Bannister C	Burton-on-Trent	1896		18	0	2	0	0	0	0	0	0	0	0	0	0	0	0	0	0	0	18	0	2
Bannister E	Buxton	1907		1	0	0	0	0	0	0	0	0	0	0	0	0	0	0	0	0	0	1	0	0
Bannister J	Leyland	1902	1905	45	0	21	2	0	1	0	0	0	0	0	0	0	0	0	0	0	0	47	0	22
Barber LF	Wombwell	1927	1930	92	0	0	7	0	0	0	0	0	0	0	0	0	0	0	0	0	0	99	0	0
Barkas S	Wardley Colliery	1933	1946	175	0	1	20	0	0	0	0	0	0	0	0	0	0	0	1	0	0	196	0	1
Barlow CJ	Manchester	1957	1962	179	0	78	8	0	2	2	0	0	0	0	0	0	0	0	0	0	0	189	0	80
Barnes H	Wadsley Bridge	1914	1924	217	0	120	18	0	5	0	0	0	0	0	0	0	0	0	0	0	0	235	0	125
Barnes KH	Birmingham	1951	1960	258	0	18	23	0	1	2	0	0	0	0	0	0	0	0	0	0	0	283	0	19
Barnes PS	Manchester	1972	1979																					
		1987	1988	116	7	15	7	0	2	16	5	4	9	0	1	0	0	0	1	0	0	149	12	22
Barnett LH	Bramley	1930	1934	84	0	0	8	0	0	0	0	0	0	0	0	0	0	0	1	0	0	93	0	0
Barr AMcD	Ballymena	1937	1938	4	0	2	0	0	0	0	0	0	0	0	0	0	0	0	0	0	0	4	0	2
Barrass MW	Seaham Harbour	1926	1932	162	0	14	10	0	1	0	0	0	0	0	0	0	0	0	0	0	0	172	0	15
Barrett C	Stockport	1972	1975	50	3	0	3	1	0	8	0	1	1	0	0	0	0	0	3	0	0	65	4	1
Barrett ED	Rochdale	1985	1986	2	1	0	0	0	0	1	0	0	0	0	0	0	0	0	0	0	0	3	1	0
Barrett F	Dundee	1901		5	0	0	3	0	0	0	0	0	0	0	0	0	0	0	0	0	0	8	0	0
Barton JA	Huyton	2002	2005	90	7	9	9	1	0	3	0	1	2	3	0	0	0	0	0	0	0	104	11	10
Batty M	Manchester	1962	1964	13	0	0	0	0	0	0	0	0	0	0	0	0	0	0	0	0	0	13	0	0
Beagrie PS	North Ormesby	1993	1996	46	6	3	4	1	1	8	0	1	0	0	0	0	0	0	0	0	0	58	7	5
Beardsley PA	Longbenton	1997		5	1	0	0	0	0	0	0	0	0	0	0	0	0	0	0	0	0	5	1	0
Beckford DRL	Manchester	1984	1986	7	4	0	0	0	0	0	1	0	0	0	0	0	0	0	0	0	0	7	5	0
Beckford JN	Manchester	1987	1990	8	12	1	0	0	0	1	4	1	0	0	0	0	0	0	0	0	0	9	16	2
Beeby AR	Ashbourne	1911		11	0	0	0	0	0	0	0	0	0	0	0	0	0	0	0	0	0	11	0	0
Beesley P	Liverpool	1996	1997	10	3	0	0	0	0	0	0	0	0	0	0	0	0	0	0	0	0	10	3	0
Bell C	Hesleden	1965	1978	393	1	117	33	1	9	40	0	18	23	1	8	0	0	0	9	0	1	498	3	153
Bell PN	Ferryhill	1926	1927	42	0	7	0	0	0	0	0	0	0	0	0	0	0	0	0	0	0	42	0	7
Belmadi D	Champigny, France	2002		2	6	0	0	0	0	0	0	0	0	0	0	0	0	0	0	0	0	2	6	0
Benarbia A	Oran, Algeria	2001	2002	59	12	11	3	0	0	4	0	0	0	0	0	0	0	0	0	0	0	66	12	11
Bennett A		1893		12	0	6	0	0	0	0	0	0	0	0	0	0	0	0	0	0	0	12	0	6

Surname	Born	Career Start	Career Finish	League Ap	League Sub	League Gls	FA Cup Ap	FA Cup Sub	FA Cup Gls	League Cup Ap	League Cup Sub	League Cup Gls	European Ap	European Sub	European Gls	Play-offs Ap	Play-offs Sub	Play-offs Gls	Other Ap	Other Sub	Other Gls	TOTAL Ap	TOTAL Sub	TOTAL Gls
Bennett DA	Manchester	1978	1980	43	9	9	5	1	1	7	0	5	0	0	0	0	0	0	0	0	0	55	10	15
Bennett ET	Barton Regis	1926	1928	19	0	0	1	0	0	0	0	0	0	0	0	0	0	0	0	0	0	20	0	0
Benson JH	Arbroath	1961	1963	44	0	0	3	0	0	5	0	0	0	0	0	0	0	0	0	0	0	52	0	0
Bentley J	Knutsford	1911		1	0	0	0	0	0	0	0	0	0	0	0	0	0	0	0	0	0	1	0	0
Benzie R	Greenock	1924	1926	13	0	0	0	0	0	0	0	0	0	0	0	0	0	0	0	0	0	13	0	0
Berkovic E	Haifa, Israel	2001	2003	48	8	7	3	1	1	3	2	1	2	0	0	0	0	0	0	0	0	56	11	9
Betts JB	Barnsley	1960	1963	101	0	5	8	0	0	8	0	1	0	0	0	0	0	0	0	0	0	117	0	6
Bevan FETW	Poplar	1901	1902	8	0	1	1	0	0	0	0	0	0	0	0	0	0	0	0	0	0	9	0	1
Biggins W	Sheffield	1988		29	3	9	2	0	0	4	0	1	0	0	0	0	0	0	0	0	0	35	3	10
Bischoff M	Denmark	2002	2003	1	0	0	0	0	0	0	0	0	1	0	0	0	0	0	0	0	0	2	0	0
Bishop IW	Liverpool	1989	1990																					
		1998	2000	71	26	4	3	2	2	8	5	1	0	0	0	0	1	0	1	0	0	83	34	7
Black A	Stirling	1946	1949	139	0	47	7	0	5	0	0	0	0	0	0	0	0	0	0	0	0	146	0	52
Blackshaw W	Ashton-under-Lyne	1938		3	0	0	0	0	0	0	0	0	0	0	0	0	0	0	0	0	0	3	0	0
Blair J	Dumfries	1906	1909	76	0	0	5	0	1	0	0	0	0	0	0	0	0	0	0	0	0	81	0	1
Blair T	Glasgow	1921		38	0	0	3	0	0	0	0	0	0	0	0	0	0	0	0	0	0	41	0	0
Blew HE	Wrexham	1906		1	0	0	0	0	0	0	0	0	0	0	0	0	0	0	0	0	0	1	0	0
Bodak PJ	Birmingham	1982		12	2	1	2	1	0	0	0	0	0	0	0	0	0	0	0	0	0	14	3	1
Bond KJ	West Ham	1981	1984	108	2	11	6	0	1	8	0	0	0	0	0	0	0	0	0	0	0	122	2	12
Book AK	Bath	1966	1973	242	2	4	28	0	0	19	1	1	17	0	0	0	0	0	6	0	0	312	3	5
Booth F	Hyde	1902	1906																					
		1911	1912	98	0	18	9	0	1	0	0	0	0	0	0	0	0	0	0	0	0	107	0	19
Booth TA	Middleton	1968	1981	380	2	25	27	0	5	44	2	3	25	0	3	0	0	0	11	0	1	487	4	37
Bootle W	Ashton-under-Lyne	1945	1949	5	0	0	1	0	0	0	0	0	0	0	0	0	0	0	0	0	0	6	0	0
Bosvelt P	Doetinchem, Holland	2003	2004	50	3	2	5	0	1	2	0	0	4	1	0	0	0	0	0	0	0	61	4	3
Bottomley W	Mossley	1908	1914	98	0	2	5	0	0	0	0	0	0	0	0	0	0	0	0	0	0	103	0	2
Bowles S	Manchester	1967	1969	15	2	2	0	0	0	1	2	2	0	0	0	0	0	0	0	0	0	16	4	4
Bowman WW	Waterloo, Ontario, Canada	1892	1898	47	0	3	2	0	0	0	0	0	0	0	0	0	0	0	0	0	0	49	0	3
Bowyer I	Little Sutton	1968	1970	42	8	13	4	0	1	6	2	2	5	3	1	0	0	0	0	0	0	57	13	17
Boyer PJ	Nottingham	1980	1982	17	3	3	2	0	1	4	0	0	0	0	0	0	0	0	0	0	0	23	3	4
Bradbury LM	Cowes	1997	1998	34	6	10	0	0	0	6	0	1	0	0	0	0	0	0	0	0	0	40	6	11
Bradford LJ	Eccles	1925		5	0	1	0	0	0	0	0	0	0	0	0	0	0	0	0	0	0	5	0	1
Bradshaw C	Sheffield	1988		1	4	0	0	1	0	0	0	0	0	0	0	0	0	0	0	1	0	1	6	0
Branagan KF	Salford	1950	1959	196	0	3	12	0	0	0	0	0	0	0	0	0	0	0	0	0	0	208	0	3

		Career		League			FA Cup			League Cup			European			Play-offs			Other			TOTAL		
Surname	Born	Start	Finish	Ap	Sub	Gls	Ap	Sub	Gls	Ap	Sub	Gls	Ap	Sub	Gls	Ap	Sub	Gls	Ap	Sub	Gls	Ap	Sub	Gls
Branch PM	Liverpool	1998		4	0	0	0	0	0	0	0	0	0	0	0	0	0	0	0	0	0	4	0	0
Brand RL	Edinburgh	1965	1966	20	0	2	1	0	0	1	0	0	0	0	0	0	0	0	0	0	0	22	0	2
Brannan GD	Prescot	1996	1997	38	5	4	1	0	0	2	0	0	0	0	0	0	0	0	0	0	0	41	5	4
Bray J	Oswaldtwistle	1929	1939	257	0	10	20	0	0	0	0	0	0	0	0	0	0	0	2	0	0	279	0	10
Brennan J	Manchester	1910	1921	56	0	0	4	0	0	0	0	0	0	0	0	0	0	0	0	0	0	60	0	0
Brennan M	Salford	1970	1972	1	3	0	0	0	0	0	0	0	0	0	0	0	0	0	2	0	0	3	3	0
Brennan MR	Rossendale	1990	1991	25	4	6	1	0	0	4	0	1	0	0	0	0	0	0	2	0	0	32	4	7
Brightwell DJ	Lutterworth	1988	1994	35	8	1	5	2	1	2	1	0	0	0	0	0	0	0	0	0	0	42	11	2
Brightwell IR	Lutterworth	1986	1997	285	36	18	19	4	1	29	2	0	0	0	0	0	0	0	4	3	0	337	45	19
Briscoe LS	Pontefract	1997		5	0	1	0	0	0	0	0	0	0	0	0	0	0	0	0	0	0	5	0	1
Broad TH	Stalybridge	1903	1920	42	0	0	2	0	0	0	0	0	0	0	0	0	0	0	0	0	0	44	0	0
Broadhurst C	Moston	1926	1928	33	0	25	3	0	1	0	0	0	0	0	0	0	0	0	0	0	0	36	0	26
Broadis IA	Poplar	1951	1953	74	0	10	5	0	2	0	0	0	0	0	0	0	0	0	0	0	0	79	0	12
Brook EF	Mexborough	1927	1939	450	0	158	41	0	19	0	0	0	0	0	0	0	0	0	2	0	0	493	0	177
Brooks GH	Radcliffe	1910	1911	3	0	1	0	0	0	0	0	0	0	0	0	0	0	0	0	0	0	3	0	1
Broomfield HC	Audlem	1908		4	0	0	0	0	0	0	0	0	0	0	0	0	0	0	0	0	0	4	0	0
Browell T	Walbottle	1913	1925	222	0	122	25	0	17	0	0	0	0	0	0	0	0	0	0	0	0	247	0	139
Brown HR		1910		2	0	0	0	0	0	0	0	0	0	0	0	0	0	0	0	0	0	2	0	0
Brown JP	Liverpool	1908	1909	6	0	0	0	0	0	0	0	0	0	0	0	0	0	0	0	0	0	6	0	0
Brown MR	Hartlepool	1995	1999	67	22	2	10	1	2	2	4	0	0	0	0	3	0	0	1	0	0	83	27	4
Buchan J	Perth	1904	1910	155	0	8	9	0	2	0	0	0	0	0	0	0	0	0	0	0	0	164	0	10
Buckley FC	Urmston	1907	1908	11	0	0	0	0	0	0	0	0	0	0	0	0	0	0	0	0	0	11	0	0
Buckley G	Manchester	1980		4	2	0	0	0	0	2	0	0	0	0	0	0	0	0	0	0	0	6	2	0
Burgess C	Church Lawton	1908	1910	32	0	0	0	0	0	0	0	0	0	0	0	0	0	0	0	0	0	32	0	0
Burgess H	Openshaw	1903	1905	85	0	2	9	0	0	0	0	0	0	0	0	0	0	0	0	0	0	94	0	2
Burridge J	Workington	1994		3	1	0	0	0	0	0	0	0	0	0	0	0	0	0	0	0	0	3	1	0
Busby MW	Orbiston	1929	1935	202	0	11	24	0	3	0	0	0	0	0	0	0	0	0	1	0	0	227	0	14
Cairns J		1893		1	0	0	0	0	0	0	0	0	0	0	0	0	0	0	0	0	0	1	0	0
Calderwood JC	Busby	1922	1925	35	0	0	2	0	0	0	0	0	0	0	0	0	0	0	0	0	0	37	0	0
Callaghan T	Birmingham	1907		2	0	0	0	0	0	0	0	0	0	0	0	0	0	0	0	0	0	2	0	0
Calvey M	Blackburn	1894		7	0	5	0	0	0	0	0	0	0	0	0	0	0	0	0	0	0	7	0	5
Cann ST	Torquay	1929	1933	42	0	0	4	0	0	0	0	0	0	0	0	0	0	0	0	0	0	46	0	0
Capel TA	Chorlton	1946	1947	9	0	2	4	0	2	0	0	0	0	0	0	0	0	0	0	0	0	13	0	4
Cardwell L	Blackpool	1938	1946	39	0	0	6	0	0	0	0	0	0	0	0	0	0	0	0	0	0	45	0	0

Surname	Born	Career Start	Career Finish	League Ap	League Sub	League Gls	FA Cup Ap	FA Cup Sub	FA Cup Gls	League Cup Ap	League Cup Sub	League Cup Gls	European Ap	European Sub	European Gls	Play-offs Ap	Play-offs Sub	Play-offs Gls	Other Ap	Other Sub	Other Gls	TOTAL Ap	TOTAL Sub	TOTAL Gls
Carrodus F	Manchester	1969	1973	33	9	1	1	1	1	3	0	0	0	1	0	0	0	0	0	0	0	37	11	2
Carroll F	Bessbrook	1920	1923	18	0	0	2	0	0	0	0	0	0	0	0	0	0	0	0	0	0	20	0	0
Carson A		1892	1893	9	0	3	0	0	0	0	0	0	0	0	0	0	0	0	0	0	0	9	0	3
Carter SC	Great Yarmouth	1970	1971	4	2	2	0	0	0	0	0	0	0	1	0	0	0	0	1	0	0	5	3	2
Cartwright JE	Lower Walton	1913	1920	38	0	3	9	0	2	0	0	0	0	0	0	0	0	0	0	0	0	47	0	5
Cassidy J	Dalziel	1899	1900	31	0	14	1	0	0	0	0	0	0	0	0	0	0	0	0	0	0	32	0	14
Cassidy JA	Lurgan	1935	1936	3	0	0	0	0	0	0	0	0	0	0	0	0	0	0	0	0	0	3	0	0
Caton TS	Liverpool	1979	1983	164	1	8	12	0	0	21	0	0	0	0	0	0	0	0	0	0	0	197	1	8
Chadwick G	Oldham	1962	1963	12	0	0	0	0	0	2	0	0	0	0	0	0	0	0	0	0	0	14	0	0
Channon MR	Orcheston	1977	1979	71	1	24	3	1	0	10	1	4	7	0	2	0	0	0	0	0	0	91	3	30
Chapelhow H		1909		7	0	0	0	0	0	0	0	0	0	0	0	0	0	0	0	0	0	7	0	0
Chaplin JF	Dundee	1910		15	0	0	2	0	0	0	0	0	0	0	0	0	0	0	0	0	0	17	0	0
Chapman T	Newtown	1895		26	0	3	0	0	0	0	0	0	0	0	0	2	0	0	0	0	0	28	0	3
Chappell T		1897	1898	8	0	0	0	0	0	0	0	0	0	0	0	0	0	0	0	0	0	8	0	0
Charvet LJ	Beziers, France	2000	2001	19	4	0	0	1	0	0	0	0	0	0	0	0	0	0	0	0	0	19	5	0
Cheetham RAJ	Eccles	1957	1967	127	5	4	4	0	0	6	1	0	0	0	0	0	0	0	0	0	0	137	6	4
Christie J		1904	1906	10	0	0	0	0	0	0	0	0	0	0	0	0	0	0	0	0	0	10	0	0
Christie TJ	Cresswell, North'land	1986		9	0	3	0	0	0	1	0	0	0	0	0	0	0	0	0	0	0	10	0	3
Clare T	Congleton	1897		1	0	0	0	0	0	0	0	0	0	0	0	0	0	0	0	0	0	1	0	0
Clark GV	Gainsborough	1936	1945	55	0	0	9	0	0	0	0	0	0	0	0	0	0	0	0	0	0	64	0	0
Clarke JD	Hemsworth	1974		13	0	0	0	0	0	2	0	0	0	0	0	0	0	0	0	0	0	15	0	0
Clarke RJ	Newport	1946	1957	349	0	73	20	0	6	0	0	0	0	0	0	0	0	0	1	0	0	370	0	79
Clarke W	Wolverhampton	1989	1991	7	14	2	1	0	0	0	0	0	0	0	0	0	0	0	1	0	0	9	14	2
Clay JH	Stockport	1967		1	1	0	0	0	0	0	0	0	0	0	0	0	0	0	0	0	0	1	1	0
Clayton R	Retford	1937		3	0	2	1	0	0	0	0	0	0	0	0	0	0	0	0	0	0	4	0	2
Clements KH	Middleton	1971	1979																					
		1985	1987	220	5	1	17	0	0	26	0	0	6	1	0	0	0	0	7	0	1	276	6	2
Clifford H	Carfin	1895		4	0	1	0	0	0	0	0	0	0	0	0	0	0	0	0	0	0	4	0	1
Clough NH	Sunderland	1995	1996	33	5	4	3	0	1	2	0	0	0	0	0	0	0	0	0	0	0	38	5	5
Codling RJ	Durham	1910		5	0	0	0	0	0	0	0	0	0	0	0	0	0	0	0	0	0	5	0	0
Colbridge C	Hull	1959	1961	62	0	12	2	0	0	1	0	0	0	0	0	0	0	0	0	0	0	65	0	12
Cole AA	Nottingham	2005		20	2	9	1	0	1	0	0	0	0	0	0	0	0	0	0	0	0	21	2	10
Coleman AG	Great Crosby	1966	1969	82	1	12	10	0	3	7	1	0	2	0	1	0	0	0	1	0	0	102	2	16
Colosimo S	Melbourne, Australia	2001		0	6	0	0	0	0	1	0	0	0	0	0	0	0	0	0	0	0	1	6	0

Surname	Born	Career Start	Career Finish	League Ap	League Sub	League Gls	FA Cup Ap	FA Cup Sub	FA Cup Gls	League Cup Ap	League Cup Sub	League Cup Gls	European Ap	European Sub	European Gls	Play-offs Ap	Play-offs Sub	Play-offs Gls	Other Ap	Other Sub	Other Gls	TOTAL Ap	TOTAL Sub	TOTAL Gls
Comrie M	Denny	1932	1933	17	0	1	0	0	0	0	0	0	0	0	0	0	0	0	0	0	0	17	0	1
Conlin J	Durham	1906	1910	161	0	28	14	0	2	0	0	0	0	0	0	0	0	0	0	0	0	175	0	30
Conlon BJ	Drogheda	1997	1998	1	6	0	0	0	0	0	1	0	0	0	0	0	0	0	0	0	0	1	7	0
Connor DR	Wythenshawe	1962	1972																					
		1974	1975	130	11	10	12	1	0	5	1	0	5	0	0	0	0	0	2	1	0	154	14	10
Constantine JJ	Ashton-under-Lyne	1945	1946	18	0	12	4	0	4	0	0	0	0	0	0	0	0	0	0	0	0	22	0	16
Conway JP	Dublin	1976		11	2	1	1	0	0	1	0	0	1	0	0	0	0	0	0	0	0	14	2	1
Cooke TJ	Marston Green	1998	1999	27	7	7	0	0	0	3	1	1	0	0	0	3	0	0	0	0	0	33	8	8
Cookson S	Manchester	1919	1927	285	0	0	21	0	1	0	0	0	0	0	0	0	0	0	0	0	0	306	0	1
Cooper PD	Brierley Hill	1988	1989	15	0	0	0	0	0	2	0	0	0	0	0	0	0	0	0	0	0	17	0	0
Corbett FW	Birmingham	1932	1935	15	0	0	0	0	0	0	0	0	0	0	0	0	0	0	0	0	0	15	0	0
Corbett VJS	Birmingham	1933		5	0	0	1	0	0	0	0	0	0	0	0	0	0	0	0	0	0	6	0	0
Corrigan TJ	Sale	1967	1982	476	0	0	37	0	0	52	0	0	27	0	0	0	0	0	10	1	0	602	1	0
Coton AP	Tamworth	1990	1994	162	1	0	12	0	0	16	0	0	0	0	0	0	0	0	3	0	0	193	1	0
Coupe D		1909		1	0	0	0	0	0	0	0	0	0	0	0	0	0	0	0	0	0	1	0	0
Coupland CA	Grimsby	1925	1926	24	0	2	3	0	0	0	0	0	0	0	0	0	0	0	0	0	0	27	0	2
Cowan S	Chesterfield	1924	1934	369	0	19	37	0	5	0	0	0	0	0	0	0	0	0	1	0	0	407	0	24
Cowan WD	Edinburgh	1926		22	0	11	1	0	0	0	0	0	0	0	0	0	0	0	0	0	0	23	0	11
Cowie A	Lochee	1898		11	0	3	0	0	0	0	0	0	0	0	0	0	0	0	0	0	0	11	0	3
Cox W	Southampton	1900		1	0	0	0	0	0	0	0	0	0	0	0	0	0	0	0	0	0	1	0	0
Crawshaw RL	Manchester	1919	1921	25	0	6	1	0	0	0	0	0	0	0	0	0	0	0	0	0	0	26	0	6
Creaney GT	Coatbridge	1995	1997	8	13	4	0	4	1	0	0	0	0	0	0	0	0	0	0	0	0	8	17	5
Croft LD	Wigan	2002	2005	4	24	1	0	3	0	0	1	0	0	0	0	0	0	0	0	0	0	4	28	1
Crooks LR	Wakefield	1996	2000	52	24	2	5	0	0	5	2	0	0	0	0	3	0	0	0	0	0	65	26	2
Cross D	Heywood	1982		31	0	12	3	0	1	4	0	0	0	0	0	0	0	0	0	0	0	38	0	13
Crossan JA	Derry	1964	1966	94	0	24	14	0	3	2	0	1	0	0	0	0	0	0	0	0	0	110	0	28
Cumming JF	Alexandria	1913	1914	35	0	3	6	0	0	0	0	0	0	0	0	0	0	0	0	0	0	41	0	3
Cunliffe R	Manchester	1963		3	0	1	0	0	0	0	0	0	0	0	0	0	0	0	0	0	0	3	0	1
Cunliffe RA	Garswood	1945	1955	44	0	9	4	0	1	0	0	0	0	0	0	0	0	0	0	0	0	48	0	10
Cunningham AE	Kingston, Jamaica	1984		16	2	1	0	1	0	5	0	3	0	0	0	0	0	0	0	0	0	21	3	4
Curle K	Bristol	1991	1995	171	0	11	14	0	0	18	0	2	0	0	0	0	0	0	1	0	0	204	0	13
Dale W	Manchester	1931	1937	237	0	0	32	0	0	0	0	0	0	0	0	0	0	0	2	0	0	271	0	0
Daley SJ	Barnsley	1979	1980	47	1	4	1	0	0	5	0	0	0	0	0	0	0	0	0	0	0	53	1	4
Dalziel G	Motherwell	1983		4	1	0	0	1	0	0	0	0	0	0	0	0	0	0	0	0	0	4	2	0

Surname	Born	Career Start	Career Finish	League Ap	League Sub	League Gls	FA Cup Ap	FA Cup Sub	FA Cup Gls	League Cup Ap	League Cup Sub	League Cup Gls	European Ap	European Sub	European Gls	Play-offs Ap	Play-offs Sub	Play-offs Gls	Other Ap	Other Sub	Other Gls	TOTAL Ap	TOTAL Sub	TOTAL Gls
Daniels AWC	Mossley	1922	1925	31	0	1	1	0	0	0	0	0	0	0	0	0	0	0	0	0	0	32	0	1
Daniels BJ	Salford	1973	1974	9	4	2	0	0	0	0	0	0	0	0	0	0	0	0	0	1	0	9	5	2
Dartnell H		1899	1900	4	0	0	0	0	0	0	0	0	0	0	0	0	0	0	0	0	0	4	0	0
Davidson AL	Beith	1899	1900	7	0	1	0	0	0	0	0	0	0	0	0	0	0	0	0	0	0	7	0	1
Davidson D	Govan Hill	1953		1	0	0	0	0	0	0	0	0	0	0	0	0	0	0	0	0	0	1	0	0
Davidson D	Elgin	1983		2	4	1	0	0	0	1	0	0	0	0	0	0	0	0	0	0	0	3	4	1
Davidson R	West Calder	1902	1903	32	0	0	0	0	0	0	0	0	0	0	0	0	0	0	0	0	0	32	0	0
Davies F	Birkenhead	1906	1909	6	0	0	0	0	0	0	0	0	0	0	0	0	0	0	0	0	0	6	0	0
Davies GE	Ardwick	1951	1954	13	0	5	0	0	0	0	0	0	0	0	0	0	0	0	0	0	0	13	0	5
Davies GJ	Merthyr Tydfil	1985	1986	31	0	9	4	0	2	2	0	1	0	0	0	0	0	0	5	0	3	42	0	15
Davies IC	Bristol	1982	1983	7	0	0	0	0	0	1	0	0	0	0	0	0	0	0	0	0	0	8	0	0
Davies J	Chirk	1891 1900	1899 1901	35	0	13	3	0	0	0	0	0	0	0	0	2	0	1	0	0	0	40	0	14
Davies R	Chirk	1911		6	0	0	0	0	0	0	0	0	0	0	0	0	0	0	0	0	0	6	0	0
Davies RW	Caernarfon	1971	1972	45	0	8	2	0	0	3	0	1	0	0	0	0	0	0	2	0	0	52	0	9
Dearden R		1902	1905	21	0	0	0	0	0	0	0	0	0	0	0	0	0	0	0	0	0	21	0	0
Dellow RW	Crosby	1934		10	0	4	0	0	0	0	0	0	0	0	0	0	0	0	0	0	0	10	0	4
Dennison J		1903		1	0	2	0	0	0	0	0	0	0	0	0	0	0	0	0	0	0	1	0	2
Dennison R	Arnold	1925		8	0	4	2	0	0	0	0	0	0	0	0	0	0	0	0	0	0	10	0	4
Deyna K	Starograd, Poland	1978	1980	34	4	12	2	0	0	2	0	0	0	1	1	0	0	0	0	0	0	38	5	13
Dibble AG	Cwmbran	1988	1996	113	3	0	8	1	0	14	0	0	0	0	0	0	0	0	2	0	0	137	4	0
Dickov P	Livingston	1996 2006	2001	105	51	33	5	4	1	9	4	5	0	0	0	3	0	2	0	0	0	122	59	41
Distin S	Paris, France	2002	2005	141	0	3	11	0	1	6	0	0	5	0	0	0	0	0	0	0	0	163	0	4
Ditchfield JC		1895	1896	12	0	1	0	0	0	0	0	0	0	0	0	3	0	0	0	0	0	15	0	1
D'Laryea JA	Manchester	2004		0	0	0	0	0	0	1	0	0	0	0	0	0	0	0	0	0	0	1	0	0
Dobing PA	Manchester	1961	1962	82	0	31	5	0	0	7	0	1	0	0	0	0	0	0	0	0	0	94	0	32
Docherty M	Preston	1975	1976	8	0	0	0	0	0	1	0	0	2	0	0	0	0	0	0	0	0	11	0	0
Doherty PD	Magherafelt	1935	1939	119	0	74	11	0	5	0	0	0	0	0	0	0	0	0	1	0	1	131	0	80
Donachie W	Glasgow	1969	1979	347	4	2	21	0	0	40	0	0	13	1	0	0	0	0	10	0	0	431	5	2
Donaldson AP	Barrhead	1923		7	0	0	0	0	0	0	0	0	0	0	0	0	0	0	0	0	0	7	0	0
Donnelly R	Craigneuk	1935	1936	37	0	1	0	0	0	0	0	0	0	0	0	0	0	0	0	0	0	37	0	1
Doran JF	Belfast	1922		3	0	1	0	0	0	0	0	0	0	0	0	0	0	0	0	0	0	3	0	1
Dorsett G	Brownhills	1904	1911	193	0	62	18	0	3	0	0	0	0	0	0	0	0	0	0	0	0	211	0	65

		Career		League			FA Cup			League Cup			European			Play-offs			Other			TOTAL		
Surname	Born	Start	Finish	Ap	Sub	Gls	Ap	Sub	Gls	Ap	Sub	Gls	Ap	Sub	Gls	Ap	Sub	Gls	Ap	Sub	Gls	Ap	Sub	Gls
Dorsett JAH	Brownhills	1910	1919	132	0	17	6	0	0	0	0	0	0	0	0	0	0	0	0	0	0	138	0	17
Dougal G		1897	1900	75	0	13	2	0	0	0	0	0	0	0	0	0	0	0	0	0	0	77	0	13
Douglas W	Dundee	1892	1893	36	0	0	5	0	0	0	0	0	0	0	0	0	0	0	0	0	0	41	0	0
Dowd HW	Salford	1961	1969	181	0	1	22	0	0	16	0	0	0	0	0	0	0	0	0	0	0	219	0	1
Doyle M	Manchester	1964	1977	441	7	32	44	0	2	43	0	4	23	0	2	0	0	0	12	0	1	563	7	41
Drummond J	Bellshill	1901	1903	28	0	5	0	0	0	0	0	0	0	0	0	0	0	0	0	0	0	28	0	5
Dunfield T	Vancouver, Canada	2000		0	1	0	0	0	0	0	0	0	0	0	0	0	0	0	0	0	0	0	1	0
Dunkley MEF	Kettering	1937	1946	51	0	5	7	0	1	0	0	0	0	0	0	0	0	0	0	0	0	58	0	6
Dunne L	Dublin	1933	1934	3	0	0	0	0	0	0	0	0	0	0	0	0	0	0	0	0	0	3	0	0
Dunne RP	Dublin	2000	2005	183	6	6	17	0	0	7	0	0	3	1	0	0	0	0	0	0	0	210	7	6
Dyer F	Bishopbriggs	1893	1897	36	0	3	1	0	0	0	0	0	0	0	0	0	0	0	0	0	0	37	0	3
Dyson J	Oldham	1955	1959	63	0	26	9	0	3	0	0	0	0	0	0	0	0	0	1	0	0	73	0	29
Eadie WP	Greenock	1906	1913	185	0	6	19	0	0	0	0	0	0	0	0	0	0	0	0	0	0	204	0	6
Eastwood E	Heywood	1938	1946	16	0	0	0	0	0	0	0	0	0	0	0	0	0	0	0	0	0	16	0	0
Edelston JH	Appley Bridge	1920		6	0	0	0	0	0	0	0	0	0	0	0	0	0	0	0	0	0	6	0	0
Eden J		1911		1	0	0	0	0	0	0	0	0	0	0	0	0	0	0	0	0	0	1	0	0
Edge A	Stoke-on-Trent	1893		1	0	0	0	0	0	0	0	0	0	0	0	0	0	0	0	0	0	1	0	0
Edghill RA	Oldham	1993	2001	178	3	1	8	1	0	17	0	0	0	0	0	3	0	0	0	0	0	206	4	1
Edmondson JH	Accrington	1902	1905	38	0	0	2	0	0	0	0	0	0	0	0	0	0	0	0	0	0	40	0	0
Egan TW	Chirk	1893		7	0	0	0	0	0	0	0	0	0	0	0	0	0	0	0	0	0	7	0	0
Ekelund RM	Glostrup, Denmark	1995		2	2	0	1	1	0	0	0	0	0	0	0	0	0	0	0	0	0	3	3	0
Ellegaard KS	Copenhagen, Denmark	2003		2	2	0	2	0	0	1	0	0	0	0	0	0	0	0	0	0	0	5	2	0
Elliott A	Ashton-under-Lyne	1981		1	0	0	0	0	0	0	0	0	0	0	0	0	0	0	0	0	0	1	0	0
Elliott SW	Dublin	2003		0	2	0	0	0	0	0	0	0	0	0	0	0	0	0	0	0	0	0	2	0
Elwood JH	Belfast	1923	1926	31	0	0	1	0	0	0	0	0	0	0	0	0	0	0	0	0	0	32	0	0
Emptage AT	Grimsby	1937	1950	136	0	1	8	0	0	0	0	0	0	0	0	0	0	0	0	0	0	144	0	1
Espie J	Hamilton	1895		1	0	0	0	0	0	0	0	0	0	0	0	0	0	0	0	0	0	1	0	0
Etherington RD	Croston	1921	1922	12	0	0	0	0	0	0	0	0	0	0	0	0	0	0	0	0	0	12	0	0
Etuhu DP	Kano, Nigeria	2001		11	1	0	0	0	0	1	0	0	0	0	0	0	0	0	0	0	0	12	1	0
Ewing D	Logierait	1952	1961	279	0	1	22	0	0	1	0	0	0	0	0	0	0	0	1	0	0	303	0	1
Eyres S	Droylsden	1906		1	0	1	0	0	0	0	0	0	0	0	0	0	0	0	0	0	0	1	0	1
Fagan F	Dublin	1953	1959	153	0	34	11	0	1	0	0	0	0	0	0	0	0	0	1	0	0	165	0	35
Fagan JF	Liverpool	1946	1950	148	0	2	10	0	0	0	0	0	0	0	0	0	0	0	0	0	0	158	0	2
Fairclough A	St Helens	1913	1919	5	0	1	0	0	0	0	0	0	0	0	0	0	0	0	0	0	0	5	0	1

Surname	Born	Career Start	Career Finish	League Ap	League Sub	League Gls	FA Cup Ap	FA Cup Sub	FA Cup Gls	League Cup Ap	League Cup Sub	League Cup Gls	European Ap	European Sub	European Gls	Play-offs Ap	Play-offs Sub	Play-offs Gls	Other Ap	Other Sub	Other Gls	TOTAL Ap	TOTAL Sub	TOTAL Gls
Fairclough P	St Helens	1914	1919	5	0	0	0	0	0	0	0	0	0	0	0	0	0	0	0	0	0	5	0	0
Farrell T	Earlestown	1906		3	0	0	0	0	0	0	0	0	0	0	0	0	0	0	0	0	0	3	0	0
Fashanu JS	Hackney	1989		0	2	0	0	0	0	0	0	0	0	0	0	0	0	0	0	0	0	0	2	0
Faulkner RV	Manchester	1955		7	0	4	0	0	0	0	0	0	0	0	0	0	0	0	0	0	0	7	0	4
Fayers FL	King's Lynn	1920	1922	73	0	5	4	0	0	0	0	0	0	0	0	0	0	0	0	0	0	77	0	5
Felton W	Heworth	1928	1931	73	0	0	10	0	0	0	0	0	0	0	0	0	0	0	0	0	0	83	0	0
Fenton NL	Preston	1998	1999	15	0	0	0	0	0	3	1	0	0	0	0	0	0	0	1	0	0	19	1	0
Ferguson A		1894		2	0	0	0	0	0	0	0	0	0	0	0	0	0	0	0	0	0	2	0	0
Fidler DJ	Stockport	1957	1958	5	0	1	0	0	0	0	0	0	0	0	0	0	0	0	0	0	0	5	0	1
Finnerhan P	Northwich	1894	1896	85	0	27	0	0	0	0	0	0	0	0	0	4	0	1	0	0	0	89	0	28
Finnigan RP	Wrexham	1926		8	0	0	0	0	0	0	0	0	0	0	0	0	0	0	0	0	0	8	0	0
Fisher A	Glasgow	1906		5	0	2	0	0	0	0	0	0	0	0	0	0	0	0	0	0	0	5	0	2
Fleet S	Urmston	1957	1962	5	0	0	0	0	0	1	0	0	0	0	0	0	0	0	0	0	0	6	0	0
Fleming GJ	Derry	1989		13	1	0	0	0	0	4	0	0	0	0	0	0	0	0	1	0	0	18	1	0
Fletcher E	Tunstall	1911	1925	301	0	2	25	0	0	0	0	0	0	0	0	0	0	0	0	0	0	326	0	2
Fletcher L	Overton, Cheshire	1932	1934	5	0	1	0	0	0	0	0	0	0	0	0	0	0	0	0	0	0	5	0	1
Flitcroft GW	Bolton	1991	1995	109	6	13	14	0	2	11	1	0	0	0	0	0	0	0	0	0	0	134	7	15
Flood WR	Dublin	2003	2005	5	9	1	0	1	0	2	0	1	1	0	0	0	0	0	0	0	0	8	10	2
Foe M-V	Nkolo, Cameroon	2002		35	0	9	1	0	0	2	0	0	0	0	0	0	0	0	0	0	0	38	0	9
Ford A	Newcastle	1921		4	0	0	0	0	0	0	0	0	0	0	0	0	0	0	0	0	0	4	0	0
Forrester T	Stoke-on-Trent	1892	1893	10	0	2	0	0	0	0	0	0	0	0	0	0	0	0	0	0	0	10	0	2
Foster CL	Rotherham	1927		3	0	0	0	0	0	0	0	0	0	0	0	0	0	0	0	0	0	3	0	0
Foster HA		1896	1897	7	0	1	1	0	0	0	0	0	0	0	0	0	0	0	0	0	0	8	0	1
Foster JC	Blackley	1993	1996	17	2	0	2	1	0	2	1	0	0	0	0	0	0	0	0	0	0	21	4	0
Fowler RB	Liverpool	2002	2005	63	17	21	5	0	4	3	0	2	4	0	1	0	0	0	0	0	0	75	17	28
Francis TJ	Plymouth	1981		26	0	12	2	0	2	1	0	0	0	0	0	0	0	0	0	0	0	29	0	14
Freeman RH	Droitwich	1936	1938	4	0	1	0	0	0	0	0	0	0	0	0	0	0	0	0	0	0	4	0	1
Frontzeck M	Moenchengladbach, Germany	1995	1996	19	4	0	1	0	0	1	0	0	0	0	0	0	0	0	0	0	0	21	4	0
Frost RA	Stockport	1963		2	0	1	0	0	0	0	0	0	0	0	0	0	0	0	0	0	0	2	0	1
Frost S	Poplar	1901	1905	103	0	4	9	0	0	0	0	0	0	0	0	0	0	0	0	0	0	112	0	4
Furr GM	Barnet	1909		3	0	0	0	0	0	0	0	0	0	0	0	0	0	0	0	0	0	3	0	0
Futcher P	Chester	1978	1979	36	1	0	3	0	0	3	0	0	2	0	0	0	0	0	0	0	0	44	1	0
Futcher R	Chester	1978		10	7	7	1	0	0	2	1	0	0	0	0	0	0	0	0	0	0	13	8	7
Garner W	Manchester	1912	1914	5	0	0	0	0	0	0	0	0	0	0	0	0	0	0	0	0	0	5	0	0

Surname	Born	Career Start	Career Finish	League Ap	League Sub	League Gls	FA Cup Ap	FA Cup Sub	FA Cup Gls	League Cup Ap	League Cup Sub	League Cup Gls	European Ap	European Sub	European Gls	Play-offs Ap	Play-offs Sub	Play-offs Gls	Other Ap	Other Sub	Other Gls	TOTAL Ap	TOTAL Sub	TOTAL Gls
Gartland P	Seaham	1914		1	0	0	0	0	0	0	0	0	0	0	0	0	0	0	0	0	0	1	0	0
Gaudino M	Brule, Germany	1994		17	3	3	3	0	1	1	1	0	0	0	0	0	0	0	0	0	0	21	4	4
Gaughan WB	Stoke D'Abernon	1914		10	0	0	0	0	0	0	0	0	0	0	0	0	0	0	0	0	0	10	0	0
Gayle BW	Kingston	1988	1989	55	0	3	2	0	0	8	0	0	0	0	0	0	0	0	1	0	0	66	0	3
Gibbons S	Darlaston	1927	1929	10	0	0	1	0	0	0	0	0	0	0	0	0	0	0	0	0	0	11	0	0
Gibson TD	Glasgow	1926		2	0	2	0	0	0	0	0	0	0	0	0	0	0	0	0	0	0	2	0	2
Gidman J	Liverpool	1986	1987	52	1	1	8	0	1	6	0	1	0	0	0	0	0	0	4	0	0	70	1	3
Gill R	Manchester	1948	1949	8	0	0	1	0	0	0	0	0	0	0	0	0	0	0	0	0	0	9	0	0
Gillespie WJ	Strathclyde	1896	1904	218	0	126	13	0	6	0	0	0	0	0	0	0	0	0	0	0	0	231	0	132
Gillies A	Scotland	1895		3	0	0	0	0	0	0	0	0	0	0	0	2	0	0	0	0	0	5	0	0
Gleghorn NW	Seaham	1988	1989	27	7	7	0	1	1	2	1	2	0	0	0	0	0	0	1	0	1	30	9	11
Glennon CD	Manchester	1968	1969	3	1	0	0	0	0	0	0	0	0	1	0	0	0	0	0	0	0	3	2	0
Goater LS	Hamilton, Bermuda	1997	2002	164	20	84	9	3	9	13	0	9	0	0	0	3	0	1	0	0	0	189	23	103
Godfrey J	Waleswood	1919		9	0	1	0	0	0	0	0	0	0	0	0	0	0	0	0	0	0	9	0	1
Godwin V	Blackburn	1948		8	0	3	0	0	0	0	0	0	0	0	0	0	0	0	0	0	0	8	0	3
Golac I	Kuprivnica, Yugoslavia	1982		2	0	0	0	0	0	0	0	0	0	0	0	0	0	0	0	0	0	2	0	0
Gomersall V	Manchester	1961	1965	39	0	0	0	0	0	0	0	0	0	0	0	0	0	0	0	0	0	39	0	0
Goodchild AJ	Southampton	1911	1926	204	0	0	13	0	0	0	0	0	0	0	0	0	0	0	0	0	0	217	0	0
Goodwin EW	Chester-le-Street	1919	1920	20	0	3	1	0	2	0	0	0	0	0	0	0	0	0	0	0	0	21	0	5
Gorringe FC	Salford	1927		1	0	2	0	0	0	0	0	0	0	0	0	0	0	0	0	0	0	1	0	2
Gould W	Burton-on-Trent	1909	1910	8	0	2	0	0	0	0	0	0	0	0	0	0	0	0	0	0	0	8	0	2
Gow G	Glasgow	1980	1981	26	0	5	10	0	2	0	0	0	0	0	0	0	0	0	0	0	0	36	0	7
Grant AJ	Liverpool	1999	2001	11	10	0	2	1	0	1	0	0	0	0	0	0	0	0	0	0	0	14	11	0
Granville DP	Islington	1999	2001	56	14	3	5	0	0	1	4	0	0	0	0	0	0	0	0	0	0	62	18	3
Gratrix R	Salford	1964		15	0	0	0	0	0	0	0	0	0	0	0	0	0	0	0	0	0	15	0	0
Gray A	Tredegar	1926	1928	68	0	0	2	0	0	0	0	0	0	0	0	0	0	0	0	0	0	70	0	0
Gray G	Bolton	1919	1920	3	0	0	0	0	0	0	0	0	0	0	0	0	0	0	0	0	0	3	0	0
Gray M	Renfrew	1962	1966	87	4	21	3	0	1	7	0	1	0	0	0	0	0	0	0	0	0	97	4	23
Grealish AP	Paddington	1986		11	0	0	1	0	0	0	0	0	0	0	0	0	0	0	3	0	0	15	0	0
Greenacre CM	Halifax	1996	1998	3	5	1	0	1	0	0	0	0	0	0	0	0	0	0	0	0	0	3	6	1
Greenwood JJ	Manchester	1948		1	0	0	0	0	0	0	0	0	0	0	0	0	0	0	0	0	0	1	0	0
Gregg W	Woodhouse	1937	1938	9	0	0	0	0	0	0	0	0	0	0	0	0	0	0	0	0	0	9	0	0
Gregory CF	Doncaster	1931	1933	21	0	2	0	0	0	0	0	0	0	0	0	0	0	0	0	0	0	21	0	2
Gregory J	Romiley	1905		3	0	0	0	0	0	0	0	0	0	0	0	0	0	0	0	0	0	3	0	0

Surname	Born	Career Start	Career Finish	League Ap	League Sub	League Gls	FA Cup Ap	FA Cup Sub	FA Cup Gls	League Cup Ap	League Cup Sub	League Cup Gls	European Ap	European Sub	European Gls	Play-offs Ap	Play-offs Sub	Play-offs Gls	Other Ap	Other Sub	Other Gls	TOTAL Ap	TOTAL Sub	TOTAL Gls
Grieve RB	Greenock	1906	1908	44	0	18	2	0	1	0	0	0	0	0	0	0	0	0	0	0	0	46	0	19
Griffiths CB	Welshpool	1993	1994	11	7	4	2	0	0	0	1	0	0	0	0	0	0	0	0	0	0	13	8	4
Groenendijk A	Leiden, Holland	1993		9	0	0	2	0	0	1	0	0	0	0	0	0	0	0	0	0	0	12	0	0
Gunn J		1896		21	0	4	1	0	0	0	0	0	0	0	0	0	0	0	0	0	0	22	0	4
Gunning JM	Helensburgh	1950	1952	13	0	0	2	0	0	0	0	0	0	0	0	0	0	0	0	0	0	15	0	0
Haaland A-IR	Stavanger, Norway	2000	2001	35	3	3	3	1	0	5	0	0	0	0	0	0	0	0	0	0	0	43	4	3
Haddington WR	Scarborough	1950		6	0	4	1	0	0	0	0	0	0	0	0	0	0	0	0	0	0	7	0	4
Hall JE	Boldon	1914		1	0	0	0	0	0	0	0	0	0	0	0	0	0	0	0	0	0	1	0	0
Hall WJ		1906		11	0	0	0	0	0	0	0	0	0	0	0	0	0	0	0	0	0	11	0	0
Halliday D	Dumfries	1930	1933	76	0	47	6	0	4	0	0	0	0	0	0	0	0	0	0	0	0	82	0	51
Hallows H		1900		1	0	0	0	0	0	0	0	0	0	0	0	0	0	0	0	0	0	1	0	0
Hamblett G		1906		1	0	0	0	0	0	0	0	0	0	0	0	0	0	0	0	0	0	1	0	0
Hamill M	Belfast	1920	1923	118	0	1	10	0	1	0	0	0	0	0	0	0	0	0	0	0	0	128	0	2
Hammond G	Sudbury	1974	1975	33	1	2	1	0	0	1	0	0	0	0	0	0	0	0	1	0	0	36	1	2
Hannah G	Liverpool	1958	1963	114	0	15	9	0	0	8	0	1	0	0	0	0	0	0	0	0	0	131	0	16
Hannaway J	Bootle	1951	1956	64	0	0	2	0	0	0	0	0	0	0	0	0	0	0	0	0	0	66	0	0
Hanney TP	Bradfield	1913	1919	68	0	1	10	0	0	0	0	0	0	0	0	0	0	0	0	0	0	78	0	1
Hanvey K	Manchester	1971		0	0	0	0	0	0	0	0	0	0	0	0	0	0	0	1	0	0	1	0	0
Hareide AF	Hareide, Norway	1981	1982	17	7	0	0	0	0	0	1	0	0	0	0	0	0	0	0	0	0	17	8	0
Hargreaves J		1893		8	0	0	0	0	0	0	0	0	0	0	0	0	0	0	0	0	0	8	0	0
Harley A	Glasgow	1962		40	0	23	3	0	3	6	0	6	0	0	0	0	0	0	0	0	0	49	0	32
Harper A	Liverpool	1989	1990	46	4	1	6	0	0	3	0	1	0	0	0	0	0	0	3	0	0	58	4	2
Harper J		1895	1897	32	0	0	1	0	0	0	0	0	0	0	0	1	0	0	0	0	0	34	0	0
Harper WG	Bothwell	1923		4	0	0	0	0	0	0	0	0	0	0	0	0	0	0	0	0	0	4	0	0
Harrison JR	Rhyl	1929		2	0	1	0	0	0	0	0	0	0	0	0	0	0	0	0	0	0	2	0	1
Hart JP	Golborne	1945	1960	169	0	67	9	0	6	0	0	0	0	0	0	0	0	0	0	0	0	178	0	73
Hartford RA	Clydebank	1974	1979																					
		1981	1984	259	1	29	17	0	2	29	0	3	12	0	2	0	0	0	3	0	0	320	1	36
Harvey H	Birmingham	1899	1900	7	0	1	0	0	0	0	0	0	0	0	0	0	0	0	0	0	0	7	0	1
Haydock WE	Salford	1959	1960	3	0	1	0	0	0	0	0	0	0	0	0	0	0	0	0	0	0	3	0	1
Hayes J	Kearsley	1953	1964	331	0	142	24	0	9	8	0	1	0	0	0	0	0	0	1	0	0	364	0	152
Heale JA	Bristol	1933	1939	84	0	39	5	0	2	0	0	0	0	0	0	0	0	0	1	0	0	90	0	41
Healey R	Manchester	1970	1973	30	0	0	0	0	0	2	0	0	4	0	0	0	0	0	2	0	0	38	0	0
Heaney NA	Middlesbrough	1996	1998	13	5	1	2	0	1	0	0	0	0	0	0	0	0	0	1	0	0	16	5	2

Surname	Born	Career		League			FA Cup			League Cup			European			Play-offs			Other			TOTAL		
		Start	Finish	Ap	Sub	Gls	Ap	Sub	Gls	Ap	Sub	Gls	Ap	Sub	Gls	Ap	Sub	Gls	Ap	Sub	Gls	Ap	Sub	Gls
Heath AP	Stoke-on-Trent	1989	1991	58	17	4	2	1	0	7	1	1	0	0	0	0	0	0	1	2	0	68	21	5
Hedley F	Monkseaton	1929		2	0	2	0	0	0	0	0	0	0	0	0	0	0	0	0	0	0	2	0	2
Heinemann GH	Stafford	1928	1930	21	0	0	3	0	0	0	0	0	0	0	0	0	0	0	0	0	0	24	0	0
Henderson J		1901		5	0	1	0	0	0	0	0	0	0	0	0	0	0	0	0	0	0	5	0	1
Henderson J	Kelty	1914	1919	5	0	0	0	0	0	0	0	0	0	0	0	0	0	0	0	0	0	5	0	0
Hendren EH	Turnham Green	1908		2	0	0	0	0	0	0	0	0	0	0	0	0	0	0	0	0	0	2	0	0
Hendry ECJ	Keith	1989	1991	57	6	5	5	0	2	4	1	1	0	0	0	0	0	0	4	0	2	70	7	10
Henry A	Houghton-le-Spring	1975	1981	68	11	6	3	1	0	7	1	6	1	0	0	0	0	0	1	0	0	80	13	12
Henry WA	Glasgow	1911	1919	143	0	1	14	0	0	0	0	0	0	0	0	0	0	0	0	0	0	157	0	1
Henson PM	Manchester	1971	1974	12	4	0	0	1	0	1	0	0	0	0	0	0	0	0	1	1	0	14	6	0
Herd A	Bowhill	1932	1947	257	0	107	30	0	17	0	0	0	0	0	0	0	0	0	1	0	1	288	0	125
Hesham FJ	Manchester	1896	1900	3	0	0	0	0	0	0	0	0	0	0	0	0	0	0	0	0	0	3	0	0
Heslop GW	Wallsend	1965	1971	159	3	1	17	0	1	12	0	0	7	3	0	0	0	0	2	0	1	197	6	3
Hicks GW	Salford	1923	1928	123	0	40	12	0	8	0	0	0	0	0	0	0	0	0	0	0	0	135	0	48
Higgs FJ	Willington Quay	1932		1	0	0	0	0	0	0	0	0	0	0	0	0	0	0	0	0	0	1	0	0
Hildersley R	Kirkcaldy	1982		1	0	0	0	0	0	0	0	0	0	0	0	0	0	0	0	0	0	1	0	0
Hiley SP	Plymouth	1995	1996	4	5	0	0	0	0	0	0	0	0	0	0	0	0	0	0	0	0	4	5	0
Hill AR	Maltby	1990	1994	91	7	6	2	1	0	11	0	0	0	0	0	0	0	0	1	0	0	105	8	6
Hill F	Sheffield	1970	1972	28	7	3	0	0	0	1	0	0	4	0	0	0	0	0	2	0	0	35	7	3
Hill P		1906	1907	38	0	0	2	0	0	0	0	0	0	0	0	0	0	0	0	0	0	40	0	0
Hill R	Scotland	1895	1896	21	0	9	0	0	0	0	0	0	0	0	0	1	0	0	0	0	0	22	0	9
Hillman J	Tavistock	1901	1905	116	0	0	8	0	0	0	0	0	0	0	0	0	0	0	0	0	0	124	0	0
Hince PF	Manchester	1966	1967	7	0	4	0	0	0	4	0	0	0	0	0	0	0	0	0	0	0	11	0	4
Hinchcliffe AG	Manchester	1987	1989	107	5	8	12	0	1	11	0	1	0	0	0	0	0	0	4	0	1	134	5	11
Hindmarsh JL	Whitburn	1913	1914	28	0	1	7	0	1	0	0	0	0	0	0	0	0	0	0	0	0	35	0	2
Hitchcock E		1908		1	0	0	0	0	0	0	0	0	0	0	0	0	0	0	0	0	0	1	0	0
Hoad SJ	Eltham	1911	1914	64	0	1	4	0	1	0	0	0	0	0	0	0	0	0	0	0	0	68	0	2
Hodgkinson DJ	Weston-super-Mare	1963		1	0	1	0	0	0	1	0	0	0	0	0	0	0	0	0	0	0	2	0	1
Hodgson R	Birkenhead	1946		1	0	0	0	0	0	0	0	0	0	0	0	0	0	0	0	0	0	1	0	0
Hoekman D	Nijmegen, Holland	1991		0	1	0	0	0	0	0	2	0	0	0	0	0	0	0	0	0	0	0	3	0
Hogan WJJ	Salford	1948		3	0	0	0	0	0	0	0	0	0	0	0	0	0	0	0	0	0	3	0	0
Holden RW	Skipton	1992	1993	49	1	3	5	0	1	3	0	1	0	0	0	0	0	0	0	0	0	57	1	5
Holford T	Hanley	1907	1913	172	0	34	11	0	4	0	0	0	0	0	0	0	0	0	0	0	0	183	0	38
Holmes WM	Darley Hillside	1896	1904	156	0	4	10	0	0	0	0	0	0	0	0	0	0	0	0	0	0	166	0	4

Surname	Born	Career Start	Career Finish	League Ap	League Sub	League Gls	FA Cup Ap	FA Cup Sub	FA Cup Gls	League Cup Ap	League Cup Sub	League Cup Gls	European Ap	European Sub	European Gls	Play-offs Ap	Play-offs Sub	Play-offs Gls	Other Ap	Other Sub	Other Gls	TOTAL Ap	TOTAL Sub	TOTAL Gls
Hope JG	Glasgow	1946		7	0	0	0	0	0	0	0	0	0	0	0	0	0	0	0	0	0	7	0	0
Hopkins RA	Hall Green	1986		7	0	1	0	0	0	2	0	0	0	0	0	0	0	0	0	0	0	9	0	1
Hopkins W		1892	1893	23	0	0	1	0	0	0	0	0	0	0	0	0	0	0	0	0	0	24	0	0
Horlock K	Erith	1996	2002	184	20	37	9	0	1	15	1	3	0	0	0	3	0	1	0	0	0	211	21	42
Horne A	Birmingham	1927	1928	11	0	2	0	0	0	0	0	0	0	0	0	0	0	0	0	0	0	11	0	2
Horne SF	Clanfield	1965	1967	48	2	0	11	0	0	4	1	0	0	0	0	0	0	0	0	0	0	63	3	0
Horridge P	Manchester	1958		3	0	0	0	0	0	0	0	0	0	0	0	0	0	0	0	0	0	3	0	0
Horswill MF	Annfield Plain	1973	1974	11	3	0	1	0	0	0	0	0	0	0	0	0	0	0	0	0	0	12	3	0
Hosie J	Glasgow	1900	1902	39	0	3	3	0	0	0	0	0	0	0	0	0	0	0	0	0	0	42	0	3
Howard FJ	Walkden	1912	1919	79	0	40	11	0	3	0	0	0	0	0	0	0	0	0	0	0	0	90	0	43
Howe F	Bredbury	1938		6	0	5	0	0	0	0	0	0	0	0	0	0	0	0	0	0	0	6	0	5
Howey SN	Sunderland	2000	2002	94	0	11	3	0	0	6	0	0	0	0	0	0	0	0	0	0	0	103	0	11
Hoyland JW	Sheffield	1983	1984	2	0	0	0	0	0	0	1	1	0	0	0	0	0	0	0	0	0	2	1	1
Huckerby DC	Nottingham	2000	2003	44	25	22	6	1	2	2	3	6	1	0	1	0	0	0	0	0	0	53	29	31
Hughes E	Wrexham	1912	1919	77	0	2	11	0	1	0	0	0	0	0	0	0	0	0	0	0	0	88	0	3
Hughes J		1893		2	0	0	0	0	0	0	0	0	0	0	0	0	0	0	0	0	0	2	0	0
Hughes ME	Larne	1988	1991	25	1	1	1	0	0	5	0	0	0	0	0	0	0	0	1	0	0	32	1	1
Humphreys R	Oswestry	1910		3	0	0	0	0	0	0	0	0	0	0	0	0	0	0	0	0	0	3	0	0
Hunter R		1900	1901	7	0	0	0	0	0	0	0	0	0	0	0	0	0	0	0	0	0	7	0	0
Hurst DJ	Cockermouth	1901		15	0	0	0	0	0	0	0	0	0	0	0	0	0	0	0	0	0	15	0	0
Hussein Y	Doha, Qatar	2005		0	0	0	0	0	0	1	0	0	0	0	0	0	0	0	0	0	0	1	0	0
Hutchinson GW		1894		7	0	0	0	0	0	0	0	0	0	0	0	0	0	0	0	0	0	7	0	0
Hutchison T	Cardenden	1980	1981	44	2	4	10	0	1	3	1	0	0	0	0	0	0	0	0	0	0	57	3	5
Hynds T	Hurlford	1901	1905	158	0	9	13	0	0	0	0	0	0	0	0	0	0	0	0	0	0	171	0	9
Immel E	Marburg Lahn, Germany	1995	1996	42	0	0	5	0	0	3	0	0	0	0	0	0	0	0	0	0	0	50	0	0
Ingebrigtsen K	Rosenborg, Norway	1992	1993	4	11	0	2	0	3	0	0	0	0	0	0	0	0	0	0	0	0	6	11	3
Ingham TW	Chorlton-cum-Hardy	1921		2	0	1	0	0	0	0	0	0	0	0	0	0	0	0	0	0	0	2	0	1
Ingram R	Manchester	1995	1996	18	5	0	4	0	0	1	0	0	0	0	0	0	0	0	0	0	0	23	5	0
Ireland SJ	Cork	2005		13	11	0	2	1	0	1	0	0	0	0	0	0	0	0	0	0	0	16	12	0
Jackson BH	Manchester	1907	1910	91	0	0	10	0	0	0	0	0	0	0	0	0	0	0	0	0	0	101	0	0
Jackson GA	Swinton	1981		6	2	0	0	0	0	0	0	0	0	0	0	0	0	0	0	0	0	6	2	0
Jackson H	Blackburn	1946	1947	8	0	2	1	0	1	0	0	0	0	0	0	0	0	0	0	0	0	9	0	3
James DB	Welwyn Garden City	2003	2005	93	0	0	6	0	0	1	0	0	0	0	0	0	0	0	0	0	0	100	0	0
James FE	Brownhills	1909		2	0	0	0	0	0	0	0	0	0	0	0	0	0	0	0	0	0	2	0	0

		Career		League			FA Cup			League Cup			European			Play-offs			Other			TOTAL		
Surname	Born	Start	Finish	Ap	Sub	Gls	Ap	Sub	Gls	Ap	Sub	Gls	Ap	Sub	Gls	Ap	Sub	Gls	Ap	Sub	Gls	Ap	Sub	Gls
Jarvis HE	Manchester	1919	1920	2	0	0	0	0	0	0	0	0	0	0	0	0	0	0	0	0	0	2	0	0
Jeffries D	Longsight	1969	1972	64	9	0	7	0	0	2	1	0	9	0	0	0	0	0	2	1	0	84	11	0
Jensen N	Copenhagen, Denmark	2001	2002	48	3	2	3	0	0	2	0	0	0	0	0	0	0	0	0	0	0	53	3	2
Jobling LW	Sunderland	1912		2	0	0	0	0	0	0	0	0	0	0	0	0	0	0	0	0	0	2	0	0
Jobson RI	Holderness	1997	2000	49	1	4	2	0	0	4	1	0	0	0	0	0	0	0	0	0	0	55	2	4
Johnson DE	Liverpool	1983		4	2	1	0	0	0	0	0	0	0	0	0	0	0	0	0	0	0	4	2	1
Johnson JD	Cardiff	1970	1971	4	2	0	0	0	0	0	0	0	2	0	0	0	0	0	1	0	0	7	2	0
Johnson NM	Rotherham	1985		4	0	0	0	0	0	0	0	0	0	0	0	0	0	0	3	0	0	7	0	0
Johnson TCF	Dalton-in-Furness	1919	1929	328	0	158	26	0	8	0	0	0	0	0	0	0	0	0	0	0	0	354	0	166
Johnstone R	Selkirk	1954	1959	124	0	42	14	0	9	0	0	0	0	0	0	0	0	0	1	0	0	139	0	51
Jones A	Llandudno	1893		2	0	1	0	0	0	0	0	0	0	0	0	0	0	0	0	0	0	2	0	1
Jones CH	Jersey	1982		3	0	0	0	0	0	0	0	0	0	0	0	0	0	0	0	0	0	3	0	0
Jones CMN	Altrincham	1966	1967	6	1	2	0	0	0	0	0	0	0	0	0	0	0	0	0	0	0	6	1	2
Jones D	Trefonen	1898	1901	114	0	1	4	0	0	0	0	0	0	0	0	0	0	0	0	0	0	118	0	1
Jones RS	Wrexham	1894		18	0	0	0	0	0	0	0	0	0	0	0	0	0	0	0	0	0	18	0	0
Jones RTW	Montgomeryshire	1901		8	0	2	4	0	0	0	0	0	0	0	0	0	0	0	0	0	0	12	0	2
Jones WL	Chirk	1903	1914	281	0	69	20	0	5	0	0	0	0	0	0	0	0	0	0	0	0	301	0	74
Jones WJB	Liverpool	1948	1949	3	0	0	0	0	0	0	0	0	0	0	0	0	0	0	0	0	0	3	0	0
Jordan SR	Warrington	1998	2005	37	3	0	5	0	0	0	3	0	0	0	0	0	0	0	0	0	0	42	6	0
Kanchelskis A	Kirowograd, Ukraine	2000		7	3	0	1	0	1	0	0	0	0	0	0	0	0	0	0	0	0	8	3	1
Karl S	Hohenm-Oelsen, Germany	1993		4	2	1	0	0	0	0	0	0	0	0	0	0	0	0	0	0	0	4	2	1
Kavelashvili M	Tbilisi, Georgia	1995	1996	9	19	3	0	0	0	0	1	0	0	0	0	0	0	0	0	0	0	9	20	3
Keary A	Liverpool	1911		8	0	1	0	0	0	0	0	0	0	0	0	0	0	0	0	0	0	8	0	1
Keegan GA	Little Horton	1974	1978	32	5	2	0	1	0	4	1	1	3	2	0	0	0	0	1	0	0	40	9	3
Kelly PJ	Kilcoo	1920	1922	25	0	1	4	0	2	0	0	0	0	0	0	0	0	0	0	0	0	29	0	3
Kelly R	Athlone	1994	1997	1	0	0	0	0	0	0	0	0	0	0	0	0	0	0	0	0	0	1	0	0
Kelly WB	Newcastle	1911	1912	10	0	0	0	0	0	0	0	0	0	0	0	0	0	0	0	0	0	10	0	0
Kelso T	Renton	1906	1911	138	0	3	13	0	0	0	0	0	0	0	0	0	0	0	0	0	0	151	0	3
Kennedy M	Dublin	1999	2000	56	10	8	2	0	0	5	4	3	0	0	0	0	0	0	0	0	0	63	14	11
Kennedy R	Motherwell	1961	1968	216	3	9	18	0	0	16	0	0	1	0	0	0	0	0	0	0	0	251	3	9
Kernaghan AN	Otley	1993	1997	55	8	1	7	0	1	8	0	0	0	0	0	0	0	0	0	0	0	70	8	2
Kerr A	Lugar	1959		10	0	0	0	0	0	0	0	0	0	0	0	0	0	0	0	0	0	10	0	0
Kerr DW	Dumfries	1992	1995	4	2	0	0	0	0	0	0	0	0	0	0	0	0	0	0	0	0	4	2	0
Kevan DT	Ripon	1963	1964	67	0	48	3	0	1	6	0	7	0	0	0	0	0	0	0	0	0	76	0	56

Surname	Born	Career Start	Career Finish	League Ap	League Sub	League Gls	FA Cup Ap	FA Cup Sub	FA Cup Gls	League Cup Ap	League Cup Sub	League Cup Gls	European Ap	European Sub	European Gls	Play-offs Ap	Play-offs Sub	Play-offs Gls	Other Ap	Other Sub	Other Gls	TOTAL Ap	TOTAL Sub	TOTAL Gls
Kidd B	Manchester	1976	1978	97	1	44	9	0	4	11	0	3	10	0	6	0	0	0	0	0	0	127	1	57
Killen CJ	Wellington, New Zealand	1998	2001	0	3	0	0	0	0	0	0	0	0	0	0	0	0	0	0	0	0	0	3	0
Kinkladze G	Tbilisi, Georgia	1995	1997	105	1	20	9	0	2	6	0	0	0	0	0	0	0	0	0	0	0	120	1	22
Kinsey S	Manchester	1980	1985	87	14	15	4	3	1	6	0	1	0	0	0	0	0	0	1	0	1	98	17	18
Kirkman AJ	Bolton	1956	1958	7	0	6	0	0	0	0	0	0	0	0	0	0	0	0	0	0	0	7	0	6
Knowles F	Hyde	1919		2	0	0	0	0	0	0	0	0	0	0	0	0	0	0	0	0	0	2	0	0
Lake PA	Denton	1986	1992	106	4	7	9	0	2	10	0	1	0	0	0	0	0	0	5	0	1	130	4	11
Lambie WA	Larkhall	1892		3	0	1	0	0	0	0	0	0	0	0	0	0	0	0	0	0	0	3	0	1
Lamph T	Gateshead	1919		11	0	0	0	0	0	0	0	0	0	0	0	0	0	0	0	0	0	11	0	0
Langford L	Alfreton	1930	1933	112	0	0	13	0	0	0	0	0	0	0	0	0	0	0	0	0	0	125	0	0
Langley KJ	St Helens	1986	1987	9	0	0	0	0	0	0	0	0	0	0	0	0	0	0	0	0	0	9	0	0
Law D	Aberdeen	1959	1974	66	2	30	5	0	4	6	0	3	0	0	0	0	0	0	3	0	1	80	2	38
Lawrence V	Arbroath	1911	1912	20	0	0	2	0	0	0	0	0	0	0	0	0	0	0	0	0	0	22	0	0
Lee FH	Westhoughton	1967	1974	248	1	112	24	0	7	26	0	14	22	0	10	0	0	0	8	1	5	328	2	148
Lee FS	Manchester	1979		6	1	2	0	0	0	0	0	0	0	0	0	0	0	0	0	0	0	6	1	2
Leigh P	Wythenshawe	1959		2	0	0	0	0	0	0	0	0	0	0	0	0	0	0	0	0	0	2	0	0
Leivers WE	Bolsover	1954	1963	250	0	4	20	0	0	11	0	0	0	0	0	0	0	0	1	0	0	282	0	4
Leman D	Newcastle	1973	1975	10	7	1	0	1	0	2	2	1	0	0	0	0	0	0	0	2	1	12	12	3
Lennon NF	Lurgan	1987		1	0	0	0	0	0	0	0	0	0	0	0	0	0	0	0	0	0	1	0	0
Leonard P	Scotland	1897	1898																					
		1899	1900	16	0	5	1	0	0	0	0	0	0	0	0	0	0	0	0	0	0	17	0	5
Leslie AJ	Methil	1923		1	0	0	0	0	0	0	0	0	0	0	0	0	0	0	0	0	0	1	0	0
Lester MJA	Manchester	1973	1976	1	1	0	0	0	0	0	0	0	0	1	0	0	0	0	0	0	0	1	2	0
Lewis W	Bangor	1896		12	0	4	1	0	0	0	0	0	0	0	0	0	0	0	0	0	0	13	0	4
Leyland J	Northwich	1920	1921	3	0	0	0	0	0	0	0	0	0	0	0	0	0	0	0	0	0	3	0	0
Lievesley EF	Netherthorpe	1919	1921	2	0	0	0	0	0	0	0	0	0	0	0	0	0	0	0	0	0	2	0	0
Lillis MA	Manchester	1977	1985	39	0	11	4	0	0	3	0	1	0	0	0	0	0	0	5	0	3	51	0	15
Linacre W	Chesterfield	1947	1949	75	0	6	4	0	1	0	0	0	0	0	0	0	0	0	0	0	0	79	0	7
Lister HF	Manchester	1958		2	0	0	0	0	0	0	0	0	0	0	0	0	0	0	0	0	0	2	0	0
Little R	Manchester	1952	1958	168	0	2	18	0	0	0	0	0	0	0	0	0	0	0	1	0	0	187	0	2
Little T	Dumfries	1894	1895	16	0	5	0	0	0	0	0	0	0	0	0	0	0	0	0	0	0	16	0	5
Livingstone GT	Dumbarton	1903	1905	81	0	19	7	0	1	0	0	0	0	0	0	0	0	0	0	0	0	88	0	20
Lloyd N	Salford	1933		3	0	0	0	0	0	0	0	0	0	0	0	0	0	0	0	0	0	3	0	0
Lomas SM	Hanover, Germany	1993	1996	102	9	8	10	1	1	15	0	2	0	0	0	0	0	0	0	0	0	127	10	11

Surname	Born	Career Start	Career Finish	League Ap	League Sub	League Gls	FA Cup Ap	FA Cup Sub	FA Cup Gls	League Cup Ap	League Cup Sub	League Cup Gls	European Ap	European Sub	European Gls	Play-offs Ap	Play-offs Sub	Play-offs Gls	Other Ap	Other Sub	Other Gls	TOTAL Ap	TOTAL Sub	TOTAL Gls
Lomax GW	Droylsden	1982	1984	23	2	1	2	0	0	1	0	0	0	0	0	0	0	0	0	0	0	26	2	1
Lyall J	Dundee	1909	1910	40	0	0	4	0	0	0	0	0	0	0	0	0	0	0	0	0	0	44	0	0
Lyon WJ	Clachnacuddin	1903		6	0	0	0	0	0	0	0	0	0	0	0	0	0	0	0	0	0	6	0	0
McAdams WJ	Belfast	1953	1959	127	0	62	7	0	3	0	0	0	0	0	0	0	0	0	0	0	0	134	0	65
McAlinden RJ	Salford	1963		1	0	0	0	0	0	0	0	0	0	0	0	0	0	0	0	0	0	1	0	0
McBride J	Renton	1894	1896	70	0	1	1	0	0	0	0	0	0	0	0	4	0	1	0	0	0	75	0	2
McCabe A		1895		1	0	0	0	0	0	0	0	0	0	0	0	0	0	0	0	0	0	1	0	0
McCarthy MJ	Barnsley	1983	1986	140	0	2	7	0	0	10	0	1	0	0	0	0	0	0	6	0	0	163	0	3
McClelland JB	Bradford	1956	1958	8	0	2	0	0	0	0	0	0	0	0	0	0	0	0	0	0	0	8	0	2
McCloy P	Uddingston	1925	1929	147	0	0	10	0	0	0	0	0	0	0	0	0	0	0	0	0	0	157	0	0
McConnell T		1896		2	0	0	0	0	0	0	0	0	0	0	0	0	0	0	0	0	0	2	0	0
McCormack M	Glasgow	1946		1	0	0	0	0	0	0	0	0	0	0	0	0	0	0	0	0	0	1	0	0
McCourt FJ	Portadown	1950	1953	61	0	4	0	0	0	0	0	0	0	0	0	0	0	0	0	0	0	61	0	4
McCourt J	Bellshill	1924		4	0	0	0	0	0	0	0	0	0	0	0	0	0	0	0	0	0	4	0	0
McCullough K	Larne	1935	1937	17	0	1	1	0	0	0	0	0	0	0	0	0	0	0	0	0	0	18	0	1
MacDonald R	Kilpatrick	1961		5	0	0	1	0	0	0	0	0	0	0	0	0	0	0	0	0	0	6	0	0
McDonald RW	Aberdeen	1980	1982	96	0	11	10	1	4	5	0	1	0	0	0	0	0	0	0	0	0	111	1	16
McDowall LJ	Gunga Pur, India	1937	1948	117	0	8	9	0	0	0	0	0	0	0	0	0	0	0	0	0	0	126	0	8
McDowell A		1893		4	0	0	0	0	0	0	0	0	0	0	0	0	0	0	0	0	0	4	0	0
McGoldrick EJP	Islington	1996	1997	39	1	0	3	0	0	1	1	0	0	0	0	0	0	0	0	0	0	43	2	0
McGuire P	Manchester	1912	1914	15	0	0	0	0	0	0	0	0	0	0	0	0	0	0	0	0	0	15	0	0
McIlroy SB	Belfast	1985	1986	13	0	1	0	0	0	1	0	0	0	0	0	0	0	0	2	0	0	16	0	1
Macken JP	Manchester	2001	2004	27	24	7	2	2	2	1	1	3	1	1	0	0	0	0	0	0	0	31	28	12
Mackenzie S	Romford	1979	1980	56	2	8	8	0	2	10	0	0	0	0	0	0	0	0	0	0	0	74	2	10
McLeod EH	Glasgow	1938		4	0	2	0	0	0	0	0	0	0	0	0	0	0	0	0	0	0	4	0	2
McLeod JS	Gorbals	1935	1936	12	0	9	2	0	2	0	0	0	0	0	0	0	0	0	0	0	0	14	0	11
McLuckie JS	Stonehouse, Lanarkshire	1933	1934	32	0	1	5	0	0	0	0	0	0	0	0	0	0	0	1	0	0	38	0	1
McMahon J		1902	1905	100	0	1	9	0	0	0	0	0	0	0	0	0	0	0	0	0	0	109	0	1
McMahon S	Liverpool	1991	1994	83	4	1	3	0	0	8	0	0	0	0	0	0	0	0	0	0	0	94	4	1
McManaman S	Bootle	2003	2004	25	10	0	2	2	0	0	1	0	4	0	0	0	0	0	0	0	0	31	13	0
McMorran EJ	Larne	1947	1948	33	0	12	3	0	0	0	0	0	0	0	0	0	0	0	0	0	0	36	0	12
McMullan J	Denny	1925	1932	220	0	10	22	0	2	0	0	0	0	0	0	0	0	0	0	0	0	242	0	12
McNab N	Greenock	1983	1989	216	5	16	15	0	1	20	0	2	0	0	0	0	0	0	10	0	0	261	5	19
McNaught K	Kirkcaldy	1984		7	0	0	0	0	0	0	0	0	0	0	0	0	0	0	0	0	0	7	0	0

Surname	Born	Career Start	Career Finish	League Ap	League Sub	League Gls	FA Cup Ap	FA Cup Sub	FA Cup Gls	League Cup Ap	League Cup Sub	League Cup Gls	European Ap	European Sub	European Gls	Play-offs Ap	Play-offs Sub	Play-offs Gls	Other Ap	Other Sub	Other Gls	TOTAL Ap	TOTAL Sub	TOTAL Gls
McOustra W		1901	1906	65	0	6	0	0	0	0	0	0	0	0	0	0	0	0	0	0	0	65	0	6
MacRae KA	Glasgow	1973	1980	56	0	0	2	0	0	13	0	0	0	0	0	0	0	0	1	0	0	72	0	0
McReddie W	Lochee	1894	1895	31	0	12	0	0	0	0	0	0	0	0	0	0	0	0	0	0	0	31	0	12
McTavish JR	Glasgow	1953	1959	93	0	0	3	0	0	0	0	0	0	0	0	0	0	0	0	0	0	96	0	0
McVickers J		1892	1893	26	0	0	3	0	0	0	0	0	0	0	0	0	0	0	0	0	0	29	0	0
Maley W	Newry	1895		1	0	0	0	0	0	0	0	0	0	0	0	0	0	0	0	0	0	1	0	0
Mann AF	Burntisland	1968	1970	32	3	0	4	0	0	1	0	0	3	1	0	0	0	0	0	0	0	40	4	0
Mann GW		1894	1896	59	0	7	1	0	0	0	0	0	0	0	0	4	0	0	0	0	0	64	0	7
Mansfield E		1908		1	0	0	0	0	0	0	0	0	0	0	0	0	0	0	0	0	0	1	0	0
Margetson MW	Neath	1990	1997	51	0	0	3	0	0	2	2	0	0	0	0	0	0	0	1	0	0	57	2	0
Marsden K	Darley Dale	1955	1957	14	0	1	0	0	0	0	0	0	0	0	0	0	0	0	0	0	0	14	0	1
Marsh RW	Hatfield	1971	1975	116	2	36	8	0	2	16	0	6	2	0	2	0	0	0	8	0	1	150	2	47
Marshall RS	Hucknall	1927	1937	325	0	70	30	0	10	0	0	0	0	0	0	0	0	0	1	0	0	356	0	80
Mason GR	Edinburgh	1998		18	1	0	2	0	0	3	0	1	0	0	0	0	0	0	0	0	0	23	1	1
Mauge RC	Islington	1991		0	0	0	0	0	0	0	0	0	0	0	0	0	0	0	0	1	0	0	1	0
May AMP	Bury	1980	1986	141	9	8	6	0	0	10	0	0	0	0	0	0	0	0	7	1	0	164	10	8
Mazzarelli G	Uster, Switzerland	1995		0	2	0	0	0	0	0	0	0	0	0	0	0	0	0	0	0	0	0	2	0
Meadows J	Breightmet	1950	1954	130	0	30	11	0	1	0	0	0	0	0	0	0	0	0	0	0	0	141	0	31
Mears T	Stockport	2001		0	1	0	0	0	0	0	0	0	0	0	0	0	0	0	0	0	0	0	1	0
Meehan P	Broxburn	1900		6	0	0	0	0	0	0	0	0	0	0	0	0	0	0	0	0	0	6	0	0
Megson GJ	Manchester	1988	1991	78	4	2	7	1	0	5	0	0	0	0	0	0	0	0	2	0	0	92	5	2
Mellor I	Sale	1970	1972	36	4	7	2	1	0	1	1	0	2	1	2	0	0	0	1	1	1	42	8	10
Melrose JM	Glasgow	1984	1985	27	7	8	1	0	0	2	1	2	0	0	0	0	0	0	2	2	1	32	10	11
Meredith WH	Chirk	1894	1923	366	0	146	23	0	5	0	0	0	0	0	0	4	0	1	0	0	0	393	0	152
Mettomo L	Douala, Cameroon	2001	2002	20	7	1	1	0	0	2	1	0	0	0	0	0	0	0	0	0	0	23	8	1
Middleton H		1892	1893	36	0	4	3	0	0	0	0	0	0	0	0	0	0	0	0	0	0	39	0	4
Mike AR	Manchester	1991	1994	5	11	2	0	1	0	1	1	0	0	0	0	0	0	0	0	0	0	6	13	2
Mike LJ	Manchester	1999	2001	1	1	0	0	0	0	0	0	0	0	0	0	0	0	0	0	0	0	1	1	0
Milarvie R	Pollokshields	1892	1895	50	0	9	4	0	1	0	0	0	0	0	0	0	0	0	0	0	0	54	0	10
Millar J		1895		2	0	0	0	0	0	0	0	0	0	0	0	2	0	0	0	0	0	4	0	0
Millar J		1902		8	0	2	0	0	0	0	0	0	0	0	0	0	0	0	0	0	0	8	0	2
Miller I	Manchester	2005		0	1	0	0	0	0	0	0	0	0	0	0	0	0	0	0	0	0	0	1	0
Mills DJ	Norwich	2004	2005	47	3	1	1	0	0	2	0	0	0	0	0	0	0	0	0	0	0	50	3	1
Mills M	Swindon			0	1	0	0	0	0	0	0	0	0	0	0	0	0	0	0	0	0	0	1	0

Surname	Born	Career Start	Career Finish	League Ap	League Sub	League Gls	FA Cup Ap	FA Cup Sub	FA Cup Gls	League Cup Ap	League Cup Sub	League Cup Gls	European Ap	European Sub	European Gls	Play-offs Ap	Play-offs Sub	Play-offs Gls	Other Ap	Other Sub	Other Gls	TOTAL Ap	TOTAL Sub	TOTAL Gls
Mills RL	Mexborough	1999		1	2	0	0	0	0	0	0	0	0	0	0	0	0	0	0	0	0	1	2	0
Milne J		1892	1893	18	0	3	1	0	0	0	0	0	0	0	0	0	0	0	0	0	0	19	0	3
Milsom J	Bedminster	1937	1939	32	0	20	2	0	2	0	0	0	0	0	0	0	0	0	0	0	0	34	0	22
Mimms RA	York	1987		3	0	0	0	0	0	0	0	0	0	0	0	0	0	0	0	0	0	3	0	0
Mitchell JF	Manchester	1922	1925	99	0	0	10	0	0	0	0	0	0	0	0	0	0	0	0	0	0	109	0	0
Moffatt J	Paisley	1903	1905	20	0	4	2	0	0	0	0	0	0	0	0	0	0	0	0	0	0	22	0	4
Moffatt R	Dumfries	1895	1902	156	0	7	7	0	0	0	0	0	0	0	0	0	0	0	0	0	0	163	0	7
Mooney F		1892		9	0	4	0	0	0	0	0	0	0	0	0	0	0	0	0	0	0	9	0	4
Morgan H	Lanarkshire	1901		12	0	1	3	0	1	0	0	0	0	0	0	0	0	0	0	0	0	15	0	2
Morley DT	St Helens	1997		1	2	1	0	0	0	0	0	0	0	0	0	0	0	0	0	0	0	1	2	1
Morley TW	Nottingham	1987	1989	69	3	18	1	0	0	7	0	3	0	0	0	0	0	0	2	0	0	79	3	21
Morris H	Chirk	1891	1893																					
		1895	1896	44	0	21	4	0	0	0	0	0	0	0	0	4	0	0	0	0	0	52	0	21
Morris H	Giffnock	1922	1923	57	0	0	4	0	0	0	0	0	0	0	0	0	0	0	0	0	0	61	0	0
Morrison AC	Inverness	1998	2000	36	1	4	7	0	1	3	0	0	0	0	0	1	0	0	0	0	0	47	1	5
Moulden PAJ	Farnworth	1985	1988	48	16	18	2	3	1	5	1	3	0	0	0	0	0	0	3	1	3	58	21	25
Mulhearn KJ	Liverpool	1967	1969	50	0	0	5	0	0	3	0	0	3	0	0	0	0	0	1	0	0	62	0	0
Mulligan JA	Bessbrook	1921	1922	3	0	0	0	0	0	0	0	0	0	0	0	0	0	0	0	0	0	3	0	0
Mundy HJ	Wythenshawe	1968	1969	2	1	0	0	0	0	0	0	0	0	0	0	0	0	0	0	0	0	2	1	0
Munn S	Greenock	1897	1899	20	0	0	0	0	0	0	0	0	0	0	0	0	0	0	0	0	0	20	0	0
Munro JF	Garmouth	1947	1949	25	0	4	0	0	0	0	0	0	0	0	0	0	0	0	0	0	0	25	0	4
Murphy W	St Helens	1919	1925	209	0	30	11	0	1	0	0	0	0	0	0	0	0	0	0	0	0	220	0	31
Murray H	Drybridge	1955		1	0	0	0	0	0	0	0	0	0	0	0	0	0	0	0	0	0	1	0	0
Murray JR	Elvington	1963	1966	70	0	43	3	0	0	5	1	3	0	0	0	0	0	0	0	0	0	78	1	46
Murray WJ	Burnley	1946	1949	20	0	1	0	0	0	0	0	0	0	0	0	0	0	0	0	0	0	20	0	1
Musampa K	Kinshasa, DR Congo	2004	2005	38	3	3	3	1	1	0	0	0	0	0	0	0	0	0	0	0	0	41	4	4
Nash CJ	Bolton	2000	2002	37	1	0	1	0	0	2	0	0	0	0	0	0	0	0	0	0	0	40	1	0
Nash J	Uxbridge	1894		17	0	1	0	0	0	0	0	0	0	0	0	0	0	0	0	0	0	17	0	1
Naylor J	High Crompton	1932		1	0	0	0	0	0	0	0	0	0	0	0	0	0	0	0	0	0	1	0	0
Negouai C	Fort de France, Martinique	2001	2004	2	4	1	0	1	0	1	1	0	1	0	1	0	0	0	0	0	0	4	6	2
Neilson R	Blackhall	1935	1938	16	0	1	4	0	0	0	0	0	0	0	0	0	0	0	0	0	0	20	0	1
Nelson JH	Manchester	1910		8	0	0	0	0	0	0	0	0	0	0	0	0	0	0	0	0	0	8	0	0
Newton WAA	Romiley	1919		2	0	0	0	0	0	0	0	0	0	0	0	0	0	0	0	0	0	2	0	0
Nicholls JH	Bilston	1932	1933	16	0	0	0	0	0	0	0	0	0	0	0	0	0	0	0	0	0	16	0	0

Surname	Born	Career Start	Career Finish	League Ap	League Sub	League Gls	FA Cup Ap	FA Cup Sub	FA Cup Gls	League Cup Ap	League Cup Sub	League Cup Gls	European Ap	European Sub	European Gls	Play-offs Ap	Play-offs Sub	Play-offs Gls	Other Ap	Other Sub	Other Gls	TOTAL Ap	TOTAL Sub	TOTAL Gls
Nixon EW	Manchester	1985	1987	58	0	0	10	0	0	8	0	0	0	0	0	0	0	0	8	0	0	84	0	0
Norgrove F	Hyde	1903	1911	94	0	1	4	0	0	0	0	0	0	0	0	0	0	0	0	0	0	98	0	1
Oakes AA	Winsford	1959	1975	561	3	26	41	0	2	46	1	5	17	0	1	0	0	0	11	0	0	676	4	34
Oakes J	Hamilton	1948	1950	77	0	9	2	0	0	0	0	0	0	0	0	0	0	0	0	0	0	79	0	9
Oakes T	Manchester	1946		1	0	0	0	0	0	0	0	0	0	0	0	0	0	0	0	0	0	1	0	0
O'Brien J		1893		2	0	0	0	0	0	0	0	0	0	0	0	0	0	0	0	0	0	2	0	0
Ogden T	Culcheth	1964		9	0	3	0	0	0	0	0	0	0	0	0	0	0	0	0	0	0	9	0	3
Ogley A	Darton	1963	1967	51	0	0	5	0	0	1	0	0	0	0	0	0	0	0	0	0	0	57	0	0
Oldfield DC	Perth, Australia	1988	1989	18	8	6	0	0	0	2	1	2	0	0	0	0	0	0	0	1	1	20	10	9
O'Neill MHM	Kilrea	1981		12	1	0	0	0	0	3	0	0	0	0	0	0	0	0	0	0	0	15	1	0
Onuoha C	Warri, Nigeria	2004	2005	19	8	0	1	0	0	2	0	0	0	0	0	0	0	0	0	0	0	22	8	0
Orr W	Ayrshire	1901	1902	36	0	0	4	0	0	0	0	0	0	0	0	0	0	0	0	0	0	40	0	0
Ostenstad E	Haugesund, Norway	2000		1	3	0	0	0	0	0	0	0	0	0	0	0	0	0	0	0	0	1	3	0
Owen GA	St Helens	1975	1978	101	2	19	7	0	2	9	0	2	5	0	0	0	0	0	0	0	0	122	2	23
Owen R	Farnworth	1968	1969	18	4	3	3	0	1	1	0	0	0	0	0	0	0	0	1	0	2	23	4	6
Owen W	Llanfairfechan	1935		9	0	3	1	0	0	0	0	0	0	0	0	0	0	0	0	0	0	10	0	3
Oxford K	Oldham	1947		1	0	0	0	0	0	0	0	0	0	0	0	0	0	0	0	0	0	1	0	0
Palmer RN	Manchester	1977	1980	22	9	9	0	0	0	3	3	1	4	0	1	0	0	0	0	0	0	29	12	11
Panter D	Blackpool	1963		1	0	0	0	0	0	1	0	0	0	0	0	0	0	0	0	0	0	2	0	0
Pardoe G	Winsford	1961	1974	303	2	17	30	0	1	26	0	4	15	0	0	0	0	0	4	0	0	378	2	22
Park TC	Liverpool	1982		0	2	0	0	0	0	0	0	0	0	0	0	0	0	0	0	0	0	0	2	0
Parlane DJ	Helensburgh	1983	1984	47	1	20	1	0	0	3	0	3	0	0	0	0	0	0	0	0	0	51	1	23
Patterson W		1896		1	0	0	0	0	0	0	0	0	0	0	0	0	0	0	0	0	0	1	0	0
Paul R	Ton Pentre	1950	1956	270	0	9	23	0	0	0	0	0	0	0	0	0	0	0	1	0	0	294	0	9
Payne JF	Southall	1931	1933	4	0	1	0	0	0	0	0	0	0	0	0	0	0	0	0	0	0	4	0	1
Peacock LA	Paisley	1999		4	4	0	1	1	0	0	0	0	0	0	0	0	0	0	0	0	0	5	5	0
Pearce S	Shepherds Bush	2001		38	0	3	1	1	0	3	0	0	0	0	0	0	0	0	0	0	0	42	1	3
Pearson F	Manchester	1903	1905	7	0	2	1	0	0	0	0	0	0	0	0	0	0	0	0	0	0	8	0	2
Pearson H		1921		1	0	0	0	0	0	0	0	0	0	0	0	0	0	0	0	0	0	1	0	0
Pennington J	Golborne	1958		1	0	0	0	0	0	0	0	0	0	0	0	0	0	0	0	0	0	1	0	0
Percival J	Pittington	1933	1946	161	0	8	12	0	0	0	0	0	0	0	0	0	0	0	1	0	0	174	0	8
Percival P	Reddish	1933		2	0	0	0	0	0	0	0	0	0	0	0	0	0	0	0	0	0	2	0	0
Phelan TM	Manchester	1992	1995	102	1	1	8	0	1	11	0	0	0	0	0	0	0	0	0	0	0	121	1	2
Phillips DO	Wegburg, Germany	1984	1985	81	0	13	5	0	0	8	0	0	0	0	0	0	0	0	5	0	3	99	0	16

Surname	Born	Career Start	Career Finish	League Ap	League Sub	League Gls	FA Cup Ap	FA Cup Sub	FA Cup Gls	League Cup Ap	League Cup Sub	League Cup Gls	European Ap	European Sub	European Gls	Play-offs Ap	Play-offs Sub	Play-offs Gls	Other Ap	Other Sub	Other Gls	TOTAL Ap	TOTAL Sub	TOTAL Gls
Phillips E	North Shields	1948	1951	80	0	0	2	0	0	0	0	0	0	0	0	0	0	0	0	0	0	82	0	0
Phillips JR	Weston Rhyn	1925		1	0	0	0	0	0	0	0	0	0	0	0	0	0	0	0	0	0	1	0	0
Phillips MJ	Exeter	1995	1996	3	12	0	0	0	0	0	1	0	0	0	0	0	0	0	0	0	0	3	13	0
Phoenix RJ	Stretford	1951	1959	53	0	2	2	0	0	0	0	0	0	0	0	0	0	0	0	0	0	55	0	2
Pickford E		1893		8	0	3	0	0	0	0	0	0	0	0	0	0	0	0	0	0	0	8	0	3
Platt JW		1896		1	0	0	0	0	0	0	0	0	0	0	0	0	0	0	0	0	0	1	0	0
Plenderleith JB	Bellshill	1960	1962	41	0	0	4	0	0	2	0	0	0	0	0	0	0	0	0	0	0	47	0	0
Pointon NG	Church Warsop	1990	1991	74	0	2	4	0	0	8	0	0	0	0	0	0	0	0	4	0	0	90	0	2
Pollock J	Stockton	1997	1999	49	9	5	4	1	0	5	0	0	0	0	0	0	1	0	1	0	0	59	11	5
Porteous TS	Newcastle	1895		5	0	0	0	0	0	0	0	0	0	0	0	0	0	0	0	0	0	5	0	0
Powell RWH	Knighton	1949		12	0	0	1	0	0	0	0	0	0	0	0	0	0	0	0	0	0	13	0	0
Power PC	Manchester	1975	1985	358	7	26	28	0	6	37	1	2	7	1	1	0	0	0	6	0	1	436	9	36
Pringle CR	Nitshill	1922	1927	197	0	1	19	0	0	0	0	0	0	0	0	0	0	0	0	0	0	216	0	1
Prior SJ	Rochford	1999	2000	27	3	4	2	1	0	4	0	0	0	0	0	0	0	0	0	0	0	33	4	4
Pritchard HJ	Meriden	1937	1945	22	0	5	3	0	0	0	0	0	0	0	0	0	0	0	0	0	0	25	0	5
Quigley MAJ	Manchester	1991	1993	3	9	0	0	0	0	0	0	0	0	0	0	0	0	0	1	0	0	4	9	0
Quinn NJ	Dublin	1989	1995	183	20	66	13	3	4	20	2	6	0	0	0	0	0	0	3	0	1	219	25	77
Race H	Evenwood	1930	1932	10	0	3	1	0	0	0	0	0	0	0	0	0	0	0	0	0	0	11	0	3
Ramsey JD		1908		1	0	0	0	0	0	0	0	0	0	0	0	0	0	0	0	0	0	1	0	0
Rankin B	Glasgow	1906		2	0	0	0	0	0	0	0	0	0	0	0	0	0	0	0	0	0	2	0	0
Ranson R	St Helens	1976	1984																					
		1993		198	2	1	13	0	0	22	0	0	0	0	0	0	0	0	0	0	0	233	2	1
Ray R	Newcastle-under-Lyme	1896	1900																					
		1902	1903	82	0	3	6	0	0	0	0	0	0	0	0	0	0	0	0	0	0	88	0	3
Read TH	Manchester	1895	1901	115	0	2	4	0	0	0	0	0	0	0	0	0	0	0	0	0	0	119	0	2
Redmond S	Liverpool	1985	1991	231	4	7	17	0	0	24	0	0	0	0	0	0	0	0	11	0	0	283	4	7
Reeves KP	Burley	1979	1982	129	1	34	13	0	4	15	0	1	0	0	0	0	0	0	0	0	0	157	1	39
Regan EJ		1893		21	0	0	1	0	0	0	0	0	0	0	0	0	0	0	0	0	0	22	0	0
Regan RH	Falkirk	1936		4	0	0	0	0	0	0	0	0	0	0	0	0	0	0	0	0	0	4	0	0
Reid JE	Hebburn	1919		3	0	1	0	0	0	0	0	0	0	0	0	0	0	0	0	0	0	3	0	1
Reid NS	Urmston	1977	1982																					
		1982	1987	211	6	2	17	0	0	20	0	0	2	0	0	0	0	0	6	0	0	256	6	2
Reid P	Huyton	1989	1993	90	13	1	7	0	1	3	1	0	0	0	0	0	0	0	0	0	0	100	14	2
Revie DG	Middlesbrough	1951	1956	162	0	37	15	0	4	0	0	0	0	0	0	0	0	0	1	0	0	178	0	41

Surname	Born	Career Start	Finish	League Ap	Sub	Gls	FA Cup Ap	Sub	Gls	League Cup Ap	Sub	Gls	European Ap	Sub	Gls	Play-offs Ap	Sub	Gls	Other Ap	Sub	Gls	TOTAL Ap	Sub	Gls
Reyna C	Livingston, USA	2003	2005	57	5	4	3	0	0	2	0	0	2	2	0	0	0	0	0	0	0	64	7	4
Richards M	Birmingham	2005		11	2	0	3	0	1	0	0	0	0	0	0	0	0	0	0	0	0	14	2	1
Ridding W	Heswall	1929	1931	9	0	4	0	0	0	0	0	0	0	0	0	0	0	0	0	0	0	9	0	4
Ridley JG	Bardon Mill	1927	1932	174	0	0	10	0	0	0	0	0	0	0	0	0	0	0	0	0	0	184	0	0
Riera A	Manacor, Spain	2005		12	3	1	4	0	0	0	0	0	0	0	0	0	0	0	0	0	0	16	3	1
Rigby J	Golborne	1946	1952	100	0	0	2	0	0	0	0	0	0	0	0	0	0	0	0	0	0	102	0	0
Rimmer SA	Liverpool	1998		0	0	0	0	0	0	0	0	0	0	0	0	0	0	0	1	0	0	1	0	0
Ritchie PS	Kirkcaldy	2000	2001	11	9	0	3	0	0	3	1	0	0	0	0	0	0	0	0	0	0	17	10	0
Roberts CL	Halesowen	1930		8	0	2	0	0	0	0	0	0	0	0	0	0	0	0	0	0	0	8	0	2
Roberts F	Sandbach	1922	1928	216	0	116	21	0	14	0	0	0	0	0	0	0	0	0	0	0	0	237	0	130
Robertson D		1893		7	0	3	0	0	0	0	0	0	0	0	0	0	0	0	0	0	0	7	0	3
Robertson G	Failsworth	1927	1932	14	0	0	1	0	0	0	0	0	0	0	0	0	0	0	0	0	0	15	0	0
Robertson J	Dundee	1895		3	0	2	0	0	0	0	0	0	0	0	0	0	0	0	0	0	0	3	0	2
Robins MG	Ashton-under-Lyne	1998		0	2	0	0	0	0	0	0	0	0	0	0	0	0	0	0	0	0	0	2	0
Robinson JJ	Oswaldtwistle	1938	1946	2	0	0	0	0	0	0	0	0	0	0	0	0	0	0	0	0	0	2	0	0
Robinson LG		1896		3	0	2	0	0	0	0	0	0	0	0	0	0	0	0	0	0	0	3	0	2
Robinson MJ	Leicester	1979		29	1	8	1	0	0	4	0	1	0	0	0	0	0	0	0	0	0	34	1	9
Robinson P	Manchester	1945	1946	1	0	0	1	0	0	0	0	0	0	0	0	0	0	0	0	0	0	2	0	0
Robinson RB		1893		4	0	2	0	0	0	0	0	0	0	0	0	0	0	0	0	0	0	4	0	2
Robinson WS	Prescot	1903		1	0	0	0	0	0	0	0	0	0	0	0	0	0	0	0	0	0	1	0	0
Robson D		1890	1896	86	0	1	5	0	0	0	0	0	0	0	0	4	0	0	0	0	0	95	0	1
Rocastle DC	Lewisham	1993		21	0	2	2	0	0	0	0	0	0	0	0	0	0	0	0	0	0	23	0	2
Rodger C	Ayr	1935	1937	19	0	7	1	0	0	0	0	0	0	0	0	0	0	0	0	0	0	20	0	7
Rodger SL	Shoreham	1996		8	0	1	0	0	0	0	0	0	0	0	0	0	0	0	0	0	0	8	0	1
Rogers JH	Normanton	1935	1937	11	0	1	3	0	0	0	0	0	0	0	0	0	0	0	0	0	0	14	0	1
Rosler U	Attenburg, Germany	1993	1997	141	11	50	14	0	9	10	1	5	0	0	0	0	0	0	0	0	0	165	12	64
Ross D	Over Darwen	1906	1911	61	0	19	4	0	0	0	0	0	0	0	0	0	0	0	0	0	0	65	0	19
Ross JD	Edinburgh	1898	1901	67	0	21	2	0	1	0	0	0	0	0	0	0	0	0	0	0	0	69	0	22
Rowan A		1894	1895	45	0	23	0	0	0	0	0	0	0	0	0	3	0	1	0	0	0	48	0	24
Rowley HB	Bilston	1931	1932	18	0	4	0	0	0	0	0	0	0	0	0	0	0	0	0	0	0	18	0	4
Royle J	Norris Green	1974	1977	98	1	23	6	0	2	12	0	6	3	1	0	0	0	0	3	0	0	122	2	31
Royle S	Stockport	1921		1	0	0	0	0	0	0	0	0	0	0	0	0	0	0	0	0	0	1	0	0
Rudd JJ	Dublin	1946		2	0	0	0	0	0	0	0	0	0	0	0	0	0	0	0	0	0	2	0	0
Russell CS	Jarrow	1997	1998	22	9	2	5	1	2	0	0	0	0	0	0	0	0	0	0	0	0	27	10	4

		Career		League			FA Cup			League Cup			European			Play-offs			Other			TOTAL		
Surname	Born	Start	Finish	Ap	Sub	Gls	Ap	Sub	Gls	Ap	Sub	Gls	Ap	Sub	Gls	Ap	Sub	Gls	Ap	Sub	Gls	Ap	Sub	Gls
Russell D	Beith	1892		17	0	3	2	0	0	0	0	0	0	0	0	0	0	0	0	0	0	19	0	3
Ryan JG	Lewisham	1981		19	0	0	0	0	0	0	0	0	0	0	0	0	0	0	0	0	0	19	0	0
Saddington H		1893		6	0	0	0	0	0	0	0	0	0	0	0	0	0	0	0	0	0	6	0	0
Salt GO		1910		1	0	0	0	0	0	0	0	0	0	0	0	0	0	0	0	0	0	1	0	0
Samaras G	Greece	2005		10	4	4	2	0	1	0	0	0	0	0	0	0	0	0	0	0	0	12	4	5
Sambrook R	Wolverhampton	1957	1961	62	0	13	4	0	0	1	0	0	0	0	0	0	0	0	0	0	0	67	0	13
Savage JA	Bromley	1954	1957	30	0	0	0	0	0	0	0	0	0	0	0	0	0	0	1	0	0	31	0	0
Schmeichel PB	Gladsaxe, Denmark	2002		29	0	0	1	0	0	1	0	0	0	0	0	0	0	0	0	0	0	31	0	0
Scotson J		1900	1901	8	0	3	1	0	0	0	0	0	0	0	0	0	0	0	0	0	0	9	0	3
Scott IJ	Radcliffe	1987	1988	20	4	3	3	1	1	3	1	0	0	0	0	0	0	0	0	2	0	26	8	4
Scott S	Macclesfield	1919	1920	15	0	0	1	0	0	0	0	0	0	0	0	0	0	0	0	0	0	16	0	0
Scully ADT	Dublin	1997		1	8	0	0	0	0	0	0	0	0	0	0	0	0	0	0	0	0	1	8	0
Seagraves M	Bootle	1987	1989	36	6	0	3	0	0	3	0	0	0	0	0	0	0	0	2	0	0	44	6	0
Seaman DA	Rotherham	2003		19	0	0	1	0	0	1	0	0	5	0	0	0	0	0	0	0	0	26	0	0
Sear RC	Rhostyllen	1956	1965	248	0	1	14	0	0	17	0	0	0	0	0	0	0	0	0	0	0	279	0	1
Shadwell WJ	Bury	1934		2	0	0	0	0	0	0	0	0	0	0	0	0	0	0	0	0	0	2	0	0
Sharp S	Manchester	1919	1927	176	0	0	6	0	1	0	0	0	0	0	0	0	0	0	0	0	0	182	0	1
Sharples J	Blackburn	1894	1896	39	0	20	1	0	0	0	0	0	0	0	0	0	0	0	0	0	0	40	0	20
Shawcross FD	Stretford	1958	1964	47	0	2	5	0	0	3	0	0	0	0	0	0	0	0	0	0	0	55	0	2
Shelia M	Tbilisi, Georgia	1997	1998	15	0	2	2	0	0	0	0	0	0	0	0	0	0	0	0	0	0	17	0	2
Sheron MN	St Helens	1990	1993	82	18	24	5	3	3	9	1	1	0	0	0	0	0	0	1	0	0	97	22	28
Shinton RT	West Bromwich	1979		5	0	0	1	0	0	0	0	0	0	0	0	0	0	0	0	0	0	6	0	0
Shuker CA	Liverpool	1999	2002	1	4	0	0	0	0	0	1	1	0	0	0	0	0	0	0	0	0	1	5	1
Shutt CS	Sheffield	1993		5	1	0	0	0	0	0	0	0	0	0	0	0	0	0	0	0	0	5	1	0
Sibierski A	Lille, France	2003	2005	64	28	11	6	4	1	3	1	2	1	0	1	0	0	0	0	0	0	74	33	15
Siddall BA	Ellesmere Port	1985		6	0	0	0	0	0	0	0	0	0	0	0	0	0	0	0	0	0	6	0	0
Silkman B	Stepney	1978	1979	19	0	3	0	0	0	2	0	0	0	0	0	0	0	0	0	0	0	21	0	3
Simpson A	Salford	1921		1	0	0	0	0	0	0	0	0	0	0	0	0	0	0	0	0	0	1	0	0
Simpson F	Bradford-on-Avon	1991	1994	58	13	4	4	1	0	5	1	0	0	0	0	0	0	0	0	0	0	67	15	4
Simpson PD	Carlisle	1982	1988	99	22	18	10	2	4	10	1	2	0	0	0	0	0	0	8	3	0	127	28	24
Sinclair JG	Paisley	1984		1	0	0	0	0	0	1	0	0	0	0	0	0	0	0	0	0	0	2	0	0
Sinclair TL	Dulwich	2003	2005	51	13	5	6	1	0	3	0	0	3	0	1	0	0	0	0	0	0	63	14	6
Slater P	Adlington	1900	1903	20	0	0	3	0	0	0	0	0	0	0	0	0	0	0	0	0	0	23	0	0
Smelt T	Rotherham	1927		2	0	1	0	0	0	0	0	0	0	0	0	0	0	0	0	0	0	2	0	1

		Career		League			FA Cup			League Cup			European			Play-offs			Other			TOTAL		
Surname	Born	Start	Finish	Ap	Sub	Gls	Ap	Sub	Gls	Ap	Sub	Gls	Ap	Sub	Gls	Ap	Sub	Gls	Ap	Sub	Gls	Ap	Sub	Gls
Smith FE	Draycott	1952		2	0	1	0	0	0	0	0	0	0	0	0	0	0	0	0	0	0	2	0	1
Smith GB	Fleetwood	1945	1951	166	0	75	13	0	5	0	0	0	0	0	0	0	0	0	0	0	0	179	0	80
Smith GD	Kilwinning	1983	1985	40	2	13	1	0	0	5	0	2	0	0	0	0	0	0	0	1	0	46	3	15
Smith HE		1894		18	0	0	0	0	0	0	0	0	0	0	0	0	0	0	0	0	0	18	0	0
Smith JW	Derby	1910	1911	18	0	6	2	0	1	0	0	0	0	0	0	0	0	0	0	0	0	20	0	7
Smith R	Walkden	1923		6	0	0	0	0	0	0	0	0	0	0	0	0	0	0	0	0	0	6	0	0
Smith W	Buxton	1897	1901	144	0	5	9	0	3	0	0	0	0	0	0	0	0	0	0	0	0	153	0	8
Smith W	Stockport	1897	1899	54	0	22	3	0	0	0	0	0	0	0	0	0	0	0	0	0	0	57	0	22
Smith WE	Leicester	1906	1919	232	0	0	23	0	0	0	0	0	0	0	0	0	0	0	0	0	0	255	0	0
Sommeil D	Pointe-a-Pitre, Guadeloupe	2002	2005	47	2	4	2	1	0	1	1	0	4	0	1	0	0	0	0	0	0	54	4	5
Sowden W	Manchester	1952	1953	11	0	2	0	0	0	0	0	0	0	0	0	0	0	0	0	0	0	11	0	2
Spittle A		1893		1	0	1	0	0	0	0	0	0	0	0	0	0	0	0	0	0	0	1	0	1
Spottiswood JD	Carlisle	1913		6	0	0	0	0	0	0	0	0	0	0	0	0	0	0	0	0	0	6	0	0
Sproston B	Elworth	1938	1949	125	0	5	6	0	0	0	0	0	0	0	0	0	0	0	0	0	0	131	0	5
Spurdle W	St Peter Port, Guernsey	1949	1956	160	0	32	12	0	1	0	0	0	0	0	0	0	0	0	0	0	0	172	0	33
Steel A	Newmilns	1905	1907	30	0	1	2	0	0	0	0	0	0	0	0	0	0	0	0	0	0	32	0	1
Steele F		1892	1893	17	0	1	1	0	0	0	0	0	0	0	0	0	0	0	0	0	0	18	0	1
Stenson J		1893		2	0	0	0	0	0	0	0	0	0	0	0	0	0	0	0	0	0	2	0	0
Stepanovic D	Rekovac, Yugoslavia	1979	1980	14	1	0	0	0	0	4	0	0	0	0	0	0	0	0	0	0	0	18	1	0
Stewart G	Wishaw	1906	1910	93	0	11	9	0	2	0	0	0	0	0	0	0	0	0	0	0	0	102	0	13
Stewart PA	Manchester	1986	1987	51	0	26	6	0	1	4	0	2	0	0	0	0	0	0	2	0	1	63	0	30
Stobart BH	Doncaster	1964		14	0	1	0	0	0	0	0	0	0	0	0	0	0	0	0	0	0	14	0	1
Stones H	Manchester	1892	1893	12	0	0	0	0	0	0	0	0	0	0	0	0	0	0	0	0	0	12	0	0
Stowell M	Preston	1987		14	0	0	1	0	0	0	0	0	0	0	0	0	0	0	0	0	0	15	0	0
Suckling PJ	Leyton	1986	1987	39	0	0	1	0	0	3	0	0	0	0	0	0	0	0	3	0	0	46	0	0
Sugden FA	Gorton	1919		6	0	0	0	0	0	0	0	0	0	0	0	0	0	0	0	0	0	6	0	0
Sugrue PA	Coventry	1979	1980	5	1	0	0	0	0	0	1	0	0	0	0	0	0	0	0	0	0	5	2	0
Sullivan D	Glasgow	1983		0	0	0	0	0	0	1	0	0	0	0	0	0	0	0	0	0	0	1	0	0
Summerbee MG	Cheltenham	1965	1974	355	2	47	34	0	11	36	0	8	16	0	1	0	0	0	8	1	1	449	3	68
Summerbee NJ	Altrincham	1994	1997	119	12	6	12	0	2	11	2	2	0	0	0	0	0	0	0	0	0	142	14	10
Sun J	Dalian, China	2001	2005	76	27	3	8	0	0	5	0	0	5	0	1	0	0	0	0	0	0	94	27	4
Swann JW	Broughton	1909		1	0	0	0	0	0	0	0	0	0	0	0	0	0	0	0	0	0	1	0	0
Swift FV	Blackpool	1932	1949	338	0	0	35	0	0	0	0	0	0	0	0	0	0	0	2	0	0	375	0	0
Syme RG	South Queensferry	1931	1933	11	0	2	0	0	0	0	0	0	0	0	0	0	0	0	0	0	0	11	0	2

Surname	Born	Career		League			FA Cup			League Cup			European			Play-offs			Other			TOTAL		
		Start	Finish	Ap	Sub	Gls	Ap	Sub	Gls	Ap	Sub	Gls	Ap	Sub	Gls	Ap	Sub	Gls	Ap	Sub	Gls	Ap	Sub	Gls
Symons CJ	Basingstoke	1995	1997	124	0	4	9	0	0	6	0	0	0	0	0	0	0	0	0	0	0	139	0	4
Taggart GP	Belfast	1988	1989	10	2	1	0	0	0	0	0	0	0	0	0	0	0	0	1	0	0	11	2	1
Tait D		1896		4	0	2	0	0	0	0	0	0	0	0	0	0	0	0	0	0	0	4	0	2
Tait T	Hetton-le-Hole	1927	1930	61	0	43	3	0	3	0	0	0	0	0	0	0	0	0	0	0	0	64	0	46
Tarnat M	Hilden, Germany	2003		32	0	3	4	0	1	2	0	0	3	0	0	0	0	0	0	0	0	41	0	4
Taylor GK	Weston-super-Mare	1998	1999	28	15	9	3	0	0	2	1	1	0	0	0	0	3	0	1	0	0	34	19	10
Taylor HG	Fegg Hayes	1912	1920	91	0	27	10	0	1	0	0	0	0	0	0	0	0	0	0	0	0	101	0	28
Taylor KV	Manchester	1957		1	0	0	0	0	0	0	0	0	0	0	0	0	0	0	0	0	0	1	0	0
Taylor RA	Norwich	1999		14	2	5	0	0	0	0	0	0	0	0	0	0	0	0	0	0	0	14	2	5
Telford WA	Carlisle	1975		0	1	0	0	0	0	0	0	0	0	0	0	0	0	0	1	0	0	1	1	0
Thatcher BD	Swindon	2004	2005	35	1	0	1	0	0	3	0	0	0	0	0	0	0	0	0	0	0	39	1	0
Thomas SL	Bury	1994		0	2	0	0	0	0	0	0	0	0	0	0	0	0	0	0	0	0	0	2	0
Thompson F	Egerton	1921	1926	33	0	0	4	0	0	0	0	0	0	0	0	0	0	0	0	0	0	37	0	0
Thompson GH	Maltby	1956		2	0	0	0	0	0	0	0	0	0	0	0	0	0	0	0	0	0	2	0	0
Thompson J	Chadderton	1920		2	0	0	0	0	0	0	0	0	0	0	0	0	0	0	0	0	0	2	0	0
Thompstone IP	Bury	1987		0	1	1	0	0	0	0	0	0	0	0	0	0	0	0	0	0	0	0	1	1
Thornley I	Glossop	1903	1911	195	0	92	9	0	1	0	0	0	0	0	0	0	0	0	0	0	0	204	0	93
Threlfall F	Preston	1899	1904	67	0	8	6	0	0	0	0	0	0	0	0	0	0	0	0	0	0	73	0	8
Thurlow ACE	Depwade	1946	1948	21	0	0	0	0	0	0	0	0	0	0	0	0	0	0	0	0	0	21	0	0
Tiatto DA	Melbourne, Australia	1997	2003	112	28	3	3	1	0	10	0	1	2	2	0	0	0	0	1	0	0	128	31	4
Tilson SF	Barnsley	1927	1937	245	0	110	28	0	22	0	0	0	0	0	0	0	0	0	2	0	0	275	0	132
Tolmie J	Glasgow	1983	1985	46	15	15	1	0	0	3	2	4	0	0	0	0	0	0	0	1	0	50	18	19
Tompkinson H		1894		6	0	1	0	0	0	0	0	0	0	0	0	0	0	0	0	0	0	6	0	1
Tonge J		1896	1899	4	0	0	1	0	0	0	0	0	0	0	0	0	0	0	0	0	0	5	0	0
Toseland E	Northampton	1928	1938	368	0	61	41	0	14	0	0	0	0	0	0	0	0	0	2	0	0	411	0	75
Toure AK	St Brieuc, France	2001		0	1	0	0	0	0	0	1	0	0	0	0	0	0	0	0	0	0	0	2	0
Towers MA	Manchester	1968	1973	117	5	10	8	1	1	14	0	0	13	2	1	0	0	0	5	0	0	157	8	12
Townley WJ	Blackburn	1896		3	0	0	0	0	0	0	0	0	0	0	0	0	0	0	0	0	0	3	0	0
Tracey SP	Woolwich	1994		3	0	0	0	0	0	0	0	0	0	0	0	0	0	0	0	0	0	3	0	0
Trautmann BC	Bremen, Germany	1949	1963	508	0	0	33	0	0	4	0	0	0	0	0	0	0	0	0	0	0	545	0	0
Tskhadadze K	Rustavi, Georgia	1997	1998	12	0	2	0	0	0	1	0	1	0	0	0	0	0	0	0	0	0	13	0	3
Tueart D	Newcastle	1973	1982	216	8	86	13	2	3	27	0	18	3	0	0	0	0	0	6	0	2	265	10	109
Turnbull A	Hurlford	1902	1905	110	0	53	9	0	7	0	0	0	0	0	0	0	0	0	0	0	0	119	0	60
Turnbull RW	Newbiggin	1949	1950	30	0	5	1	0	0	0	0	0	0	0	0	0	0	0	0	0	0	31	0	5

Surname	Born	Career Start	Career Finish	League Ap	League Sub	League Gls	FA Cup Ap	FA Cup Sub	FA Cup Gls	League Cup Ap	League Cup Sub	League Cup Gls	European Ap	European Sub	European Gls	Play-offs Ap	Play-offs Sub	Play-offs Gls	Other Ap	Other Sub	Other Gls	TOTAL Ap	TOTAL Sub	TOTAL Gls
Turner WA	Cheshire	1892		1	0	0	0	0	0	0	0	0	0	0	0	0	0	0	0	0	0	1	0	0
Tyler HE	Ecclesall	1919	1920	44	0	0	3	0	0	0	0	0	0	0	0	0	0	0	0	0	0	47	0	0
Utley G	Elsecar	1922		1	0	0	0	0	0	0	0	0	0	0	0	0	0	0	0	0	0	1	0	0
Van Blerk J	Sydney, Australia	1997		10	9	0	0	1	0	0	1	0	0	0	0	0	0	0	0	0	0	10	11	0
Van Buyten D	Chimay, Belgium	2003		5	0	0	1	0	0	0	0	0	0	0	0	0	0	0	0	0	0	6	0	0
Varadi I	Paddington	1986	1988	56	9	26	6	1	1	4	2	2	0	0	0	0	0	0	2	1	2	68	13	31
Vassell D	Birmingham	2005		36	0	8	4	0	1	1	0	1	0	0	0	0	0	0	0	0	0	41	0	10
Vaughan AJ	Manchester	1997	1999	54	4	2	3	0	0	6	1	0	0	0	0	2	1	0	1	0	0	66	6	2
Viljoen C	Johannesburg, SA	1978	1979	25	2	0	1	0	0	2	1	1	7	0	0	0	0	0	0	0	0	35	3	1
Vonk MC	Alkmaar, Holland	1991	1994	87	4	4	6	1	1	3	2	1	0	0	0	0	0	0	0	0	0	96	7	6
Wagstaffe D	Manchester	1960	1964	144	0	8	6	0	0	11	0	0	0	0	0	0	0	0	0	0	0	161	0	8
Walker J	Alexandria	1894		19	0	1	0	0	0	0	0	0	0	0	0	0	0	0	0	0	0	19	0	1
Wall LJ	Shrewsbury	1910	1913	41	0	2	0	0	0	0	0	0	0	0	0	0	0	0	0	0	0	41	0	2
Wallace A	Darwen	1894		6	0	1	0	0	0	0	0	0	0	0	0	0	0	0	0	0	0	6	0	1
Wallace W	Blaydon	1912	1913	43	0	9	3	0	0	0	0	0	0	0	0	0	0	0	0	0	0	46	0	9
Walmsley C	Burnley	1931		2	0	0	0	0	0	0	0	0	0	0	0	0	0	0	0	0	0	2	0	0
Walsh MT	Blackley	1983		3	1	0	1	0	0	1	1	0	0	0	0	0	0	0	0	0	0	5	2	0
Walsh PAM	Plumstead	1993	1995	53	0	16	3	0	1	6	0	2	0	0	0	0	0	0	0	0	0	62	0	19
Walsh W	Dublin	1945	1949	109	0	1	9	0	0	0	0	0	0	0	0	0	0	0	0	0	0	118	0	1
Wanchope WPC	Heredia, Costa Rica	2000	2003	51	13	27	3	0	1	4	0	1	1	3	0	0	0	0	0	0	0	59	16	29
Ward AS	Manchester	1989		0	1	0	0	2	0	0	0	0	0	0	0	0	0	0	0	0	0	0	3	0
Ward MW	Huyton	1989	1990	55	0	14	6	0	0	3	0	0	0	0	0	0	0	0	3	0	2	67	0	16
Wardle W	Houghton-le-Spring	1937		6	0	0	1	0	0	0	0	0	0	0	0	0	0	0	0	0	0	7	0	0
Warhurst R	Sheffield	1957	1958	40	0	2	1	0	0	0	0	0	0	0	0	0	0	0	0	0	0	41	0	2
Warner J	Woolwich	1920	1925	76	0	15	2	0	0	0	0	0	0	0	0	0	0	0	0	0	0	78	0	15
Wassall DPJ	Edgbaston	1996		14	1	0	0	0	0	2	0	0	0	0	0	0	0	0	0	0	0	16	1	0
Waterreus R	Kerkrade, Holland	2004		0	0	0	0	0	0	2	0	0	0	0	0	0	0	0	0	0	0	2	0	0
Watson DV	Stapleford	1975	1978	146	0	4	9	0	0	18	0	1	12	0	1	0	0	0	3	0	0	188	0	6
Watson LP	Southport	1901		1	0	0	00	0		0 0	0		00	0	0	0	0	0	0	0		1 0	0	
Weah GMOO	Monrovia, Liberia	2000		5	2	1	0	0	0	2	0	3	0	0	0	0	0	0	0	0	0	7	2	4
Weaver NJ	Sheffield	1998	2004	145	2	0	11	0	0	14	0	0	1	0	0	3	0	0	0	0	0	174	2	0
Webb C	Higham Ferrers	1907	1908	22	0	3	0	0	0	0	0	0	0	0	0	0	0	0	0	0	0	22	0	3
Webb GW	Poplar	1912		2	0	0	0	0	0	0	0	0	0	0	0	0	0	0	0	0	0	2	0	0
Webster E	Manchester	1952		1	0	0	0	0	0	0	0	0	0	0	0	0	0	0	0	0	0	1	0	0

		Career		League			FA Cup			League Cup			European			Play-offs			Other			TOTAL		
Surname	Born	Start	Finish	Ap	Sub	Gls	Ap	Sub	Gls	Ap	Sub	Gls	Ap	Sub	Gls	Ap	Sub	Gls	Ap	Sub	Gls	Ap	Sub	Gls
Weir D	Aldershot	1892		14	0	8	2	0	3	0	0	0	0	0	0	0	0	0	0	0	0	16	0	11
Westcott D	Wallasey	1949	1951	72	0	37	3	0	0	0	0	0	0	0	0	0	0	0	0	0	0	75	0	37
Westwood E	Manchester	1938	1952	248	0	3	12	0	2	0	0	0	0	0	0	0	0	0	0	0	0	260	0	5
Wharton JE	Bolton	1946	1947	23	0	2	3	0	0	0	0	0	0	0	0	0	0	0	0	0	0	26	0	2
Whelan AM	Salford	1972	1973	3	3	0	0	0	0	0	0	0	0	0	0	0	0	0	0	0	0	3	3	0
Whelan GD	Dublin	2003		0	0	0	0	0	0	0	0	0	0	1	0	0	0	0	0	0	0	0	1	0
White D	Urmston	1986	1993	273	12	79	22	0	4	24	1	11	0	0	0	0	0	0	9	0	2	328	13	96
White HK	Timperley	1970		1	0	0	0	0	0	0	0	0	0	0	0	0	0	0	0	0	0	1	0	0
Whitehead JW	Church	1897	1898	24	0	7	2	0	0	0	0	0	0	0	0	0	0	0	0	0	0	26	0	7
Whitfield K	Spennymoor	1952	1953	13	0	3	0	0	0	0	0	0	0	0	0	0	0	0	0	0	0	13	0	3
Whitley J	Ndola, Zambia	1996	2001	96	27	8	2	2	0	9	1	0	0	0	0	3	0	0	1	0	0	111	30	8
Whitley J	Ndola, Zambia	1997	1999	27	11	0	2	1	0	3	1	1	0	0	0	0	0	0	0	1	0	32	14	1
Whittaker JH	Bolton	1904	1906																					
		1907	1908	6	0	1	0	0	0	0	0	0	0	0	0	0	0	0	0	0	0	6	0	1
Whittle D		1892	1893	30	0	3	3	0	1	0	0	0	0	0	0	0	0	0	0	0	0	33	0	4
Wiekens G	Tolhuiswyk, Holland	1997	2003	167	15	10	11	1	0	13	2	0	1	0	0	3	0	0	0	0	0	195	18	10
Wilkinson J	Darlington	1906	1910	31	0	2	0	0	0	0	0	0	0	0	0	0	0	0	0	0	0	31	0	2
Willey W		1893		1	0	0	0	0	0	0	0	0	0	0	0	0	0	0	0	0	0	1	0	0
Williams A	Manchester	1980	1985	114	0	0	2	0	0	9	0	0	0	0	0	0	0	0	0	0	0	125	0	0
Williams CA	Welling	1894	1901	221	0	1	7	0	0	0	0	0	0	0	0	4	0	0	0	0	0	232	0	1
Williams D	Mold	1951		1	0	0	0	0	0	0	0	0	0	0	0	0	0	0	0	0	0	1	0	0
Williams E	Salford	1946	1949	38	0	0	3	0	0	0	0	0	0	0	0	0	0	0	0	0	0	41	0	0
Williams F	Manchester	1896	1901	125	0	38	5	0	0	0	0	0	0	0	0	0	0	0	0	0	0	130	0	38
Williams WR	Littleborough	1988		0	1	0	0	0	0	0	0	0	0	0	0	0	0	0	0	0	0	0	1	0
Williamson J	Manchester	1949	1954	59	0	18	3	0	1	0	0	0	0	0	0	0	0	0	0	0	0	62	0	19
Wilson CEA	Manchester	1981	1986	107	2	9	2	0	0	10	0	2	0	0	0	0	0	0	5	0	0	124	2	11
Wilson J	Ayrshire	1897		1	0	0	0	0	0	0	0	0	0	0	0	0	0	0	0	0	0	1	0	0
Wilson W	Middlesbrough	1921	1926	48	0	0	5	0	0	0	0	0	0	0	0	0	0	0	0	0	0	53	0	0
Wood AEH	Macclesfield	1962	1965	24	1	0	4	0	0	4	0	0	0	0	0	0	0	0	0	0	0	32	1	0
Wood J		1907	1908	28	0	6	5	0	3	0	0	0	0	0	0	0	0	0	0	0	0	33	0	9
Woodcock W	Ashton-under-Lyne	1920	1921	15	0	2	0	0	0	0	0	0	0	0	0	0	0	0	0	0	0	15	0	2
Woodroffe LC	Portsmouth	1946		9	0	1	0	0	0	0	0	0	0	0	0	0	0	0	0	0	0	9	0	1
Woosnam M	Liverpool	1919	1924	86	0	4	7	0	0	0	0	0	0	0	0	0	0	0	0	0	0	93	0	4
Woosnam PA	Caersws	1952		1	0	0	0	0	0	0	0	0	0	0	0	0	0	0	0	0	0	1	0	0

		Career		League			FA Cup			League Cup			European			Play-offs			Other			TOTAL		
Surname	Born	Start	Finish	Ap	Sub	Gls	Ap	Sub	Gls	Ap	Sub	Gls	Ap	Sub	Gls	Ap	Sub	Gls	Ap	Sub	Gls	Ap	Sub	Gls
Wright N	Ushaw Moor	1933	1934	3	0	1	0	0	0	0	0	0	0	0	0	0	0	0	0	0	0	3	0	1
Wright TJ	Belfast	1996	2000	34	0	0	2	0	0	1	0	0	0	0	0	0	0	0	1	0	0	38	0	0
Wright-Phillips BE	Lewisham	2004	2005	1	31	2	2	4	0	0	2	0	0	0	0	0	0	0	0	0	0	3	37	2
Wright-Phillips SC	Greenwich	1999	2004	130	23	26	8	1	1	9	4	3	4	2	1	0	0	0	0	0	0	151	30	31
Wrightson FL	Shildon	1929	1931	22	0	4	0	0	0	0	0	0	0	0	0	0	0	0	0	0	0	22	0	4
Wynn GA	Treflach	1909	1919	119	0	54	8	0	5	0	0	0	0	0	0	0	0	0	0	0	0	127	0	59
Yates J	Sheffield	1892	1893	20	0	9	1	0	0	0	0	0	0	0	0	0	0	0	0	0	0	21	0	9
Young AS	Slamannan	1911		13	0	2	2	0	0	0	0	0	0	0	0	0	0	0	0	0	0	15	0	2
Young J		1905		1	0	0	0	0	0	0	0	0	0	0	0	0	0	0	0	0	0	1	0	0
Young NJ	Manchester	1961	1971	332	2	86	32	0	10	28	0	6	17	0	5	0	0	0	4	0	1	413	2	108
Yuill JG		1906	1908	3	0	1	0	0	0	0	0	0	0	0	0	0	0	0	0	0	0	3	0	1

World War One

	League		Subsid		TOTAL	
Allen A.J.	4	0	0	0	4	0
Armstrong	0	0	4	0	4	0
Barnes H.	57	56	16	17	73	73
Blackwell E.	2	0	0	0	2	0
Bottomley W.	31	0	1	0	32	0
Brennan J.	75	3	19	1	94	4
Brierley H.	11	0	0	0	11	0
Broad J.	1	0	0	0	1	0
Broad T.	36	2	10	0	46	2
Browell T.	27	14	6	4	33	18
Brown A.E.	2	0	0	0	2	0
Capper	1	5	0	0	1	5
Cartwright J.E.	45	7	15	2	60	9
Callow	4	0	0	0	4	0
Clegg J.	0	0	2	0	2	0
Connor	1	0	0	0	1	0
Cope	6	1	0	0	6	1
Corcoran	0	0	1	0	1	0
Crowther	1	0	0	0	1	0
Cruse	4	2	0	0	4	2
Cunningham	5	2	3	0	8	2
Davies A.	18	1	0	0	18	1
Dorsett J.H.	7	3	0	0	7	3
Duffy	1	0	0	0	1	0
Elliott	0	0	2	0	2	0
Fairclough A.	4	7	2	1	6	8
Fairclough P.	85	12	17	1	102	13
Fielding	1	0	0	0	1	0
Fletcher E.	106	0	27	3	133	3
Gartland P.	23	0	9	0	32	0
Geddes R.	1	0	0	0	1	0
Goddard H.	3	3	0	0	3	3
Goodchild A.J.	106	0	24	0	130	0
Hanney E.T.	3	0	0	0	3	0
Hargreaves R.	1	0	1	0	2	0
Henderson J.	23	0	10	0	33	0
Henry W.A.	23	0	2	0	25	0
Hoad S.J.	3	1	0	0	3	1
Hoare G.	1	1	0	0	1	1
Howard F.J.	7	4	0	0	7	4
Howarth J.T.	4	0	0	0	4	0
Howe G.A.	1	0	0	0	1	0
Hughes E.	55	2	10	0	65	2
James	1	0	0	0	1	0
Johnson A.	1	0	0	0	1	0
Johnson T.C.F.	5	4	0	0	5	4
Jones F.	0	0	1	0	1	0
Jones W.L.	29	4	8	2	37	6

	League		Subsid		TOTAL	
Kelly	1	0	0	0	1	0
Kenyon	4	3	0	0	4	3
Kite P.	1	0	0	0	1	0
Knowles F.	1	0	0	0	1	0
Lee M.	0	0	1	0	1	0
Lewis T.E.	0	0	1	0	1	0
Lievesley E.F.	10	8	1	0	11	8
Lingard	3	0	0	0	3	0
Lloyd	1	0	0	0	1	0
Lomas W.	32	22	13	1	45	23
McIlvenney F.	0	0	2	1	2	1
McRay	1	0	0	0	1	0
Malone	0	0	1	0	1	0
Mann	0	0	2	1	2	1
Meredith W.H.	85	5	22	2	107	7
Miller	4	0	0	0	4	0
Moses	11	4	0	0	11	4
Murphy W.	20	2	3	0	23	2
Nelson	6	2	0	0	6	2
Newton H.	1	0	4	1	5	1
Newton W.A.A.	11	1	3	0	14	1
Ollerenshaw E.	2	0	1	0	3	0
Osmond J.E.	2	0	0	0	2	0
Parker F.	21	0	3	0	24	0
Petrie C.	1	0	0	0	1	0
Roberts	1	0	0	0	1	0
Royle S.	2	1	5	3	7	4
Scott S.	9	0	1	0	10	0
Sharp S.	0	0	2	0	2	0
Skeldon	1	0	0	0	1	0
Smith A.W.	7	2	0	0	7	2
Smith W.E.	5	0	3	0	8	0
Spruce	2	0	0	0	2	0
Sugden F.A.	27	0	12	0	39	0
Tavo J.D.	2	1	0	0	2	1
Taylor H.G.	24	9	8	5	32	14
Thompson J.	15	6	6	1	21	7
Thorpe	2	2	0	0	2	2
Tomkins	2	0	0	0	2	0
Tomlinson	1	0	0	0	1	0
Tyler H.E.	80	7	14	0	94	7
Voysley	2	0	0	0	2	0
Waldon H.	2	1	0	0	2	1
Watson	17	4	0	0	17	4
Woodcock W.	1	0	1	1	2	1
Wood house	0	0	1	0	1	0
Wray J.	6	1	2	0	8	1
Wynn G.A.	24	7	6	2	30	9

WORLD WAR TWO

	League		War Cup		TOTAL	
Bacuzzi J.	1	0	0	0	1	0
Baillie M.	1	0	0	0	1	0
Baker H.V.	1	1	0	0	1	1
Barber E.	3	0	0	0	3	0
Barclay C.E.	13	3	5	0	18	3
Bardsley L.	13	2	8	0	21	2
Barkas S.	56	3	19	0	75	3
Beattie A.	2	0	0	0	2	0
Beaumont L.	1	0	0	0	1	0
Bellis A.	0	0	1	0	1	0
Bentham S.	1	0	0	0	1	0
Blackshaw W.	8	2	0	0	8	2
Boothway J.	49	39	27	18	76	57
Bootle W.	20	6	12	0	32	6
Boulter L.	1	0	0	0	1	0
Bray J.	121	9	56	2	177	11
Breedon J.	2	0	0	0	2	0
Brook E.F.G.	4	2	0	0	4	2
Brooks H.	1	1	0	0	1	1
Brown A.R.J.	11	6	4	0	15	6
Brown E.	7	0	0	0	7	0
Burdett T.	1	1	0	0	1	1
Burke R.J.	4	3	0	0	4	3
Butler M.P.	1	0	0	0	1	0
Butt L.	0	0	1	0	1	0
Campbell J.	1	0	0	0	1	0
Capel T.A.	1	0	0	0	1	0
Cardwell L.	42	0	3	0	45	0
Carey J.J.	3	1	1	0	4	1
Carey W.J.	9	0	0	0	9	0
Carter D.F.	0	0	1	0	1	0
Cassidy L.	1	0	0	0	1	0
Chappell F.G.	4	0	3	0	7	0
Charlesworth S.	19	0	10	0	29	0
Chisholm K.M.	1	0	0	0	1	0
Clark G.V.	120	0	60	0	180	0
Clark H.	7	1	1	0	8	1
Constantine J.	34	25	0	0	34	25
Cox F.J.A.	1	1	12	1	13	2
Crompton J.	1	0	0	0	1	0
Cunliffe R.A.	1	0	0	0	1	0
Currier J.	75	69	38	15	113	84
Daniels D.	'3	0	0	0	3	0
Davenport D. W.	2	0	0	0	2	0
Davenport J.	3	0	0	0	3	0
Dellow R.W.	8	3	5	2	13	5

	League		War Cup		TOTAL	
Devlin J.	1	0	0	0	1	0
Dickie P.	0	0	1	0	1	0
Dodd L.	2	0	1	0	3	0
Doherty P.D.	66	45	23	15	89	60
Dunkley M.E.F.	45	11	15	4	60	15
Eastwood E.	104	0	59	0	163	0
Eastwood R.	2	0	0	0	2	0
Emptage A.T.	33	5	1	0	34	5
Fagan J.F.	10	0	0	0	10	0
Fenton B.R.V.	4	3	7	4	11	7
Gemmell E.	2	1	0	0	2	1
Goddard W.G.	1	0	0	0	1	0
Goodall E.L	2	0	0	0	2	0
Grant W.	1	0	12	0	13	0
Hall B.A.C.	2	0	0	0	2	0
Hanson A.J.	1	0	0	0	1	0
Hart J.P.	4	1	0	0	4	1
Heale J.A.	26	20	16	13	42	33
Henry G.R.	1	0	0	0	1	0
Herd A.	68	46	22	14	90	60
Hilton J.	1	0	0	0	1	0
Hodgson R.	5	0	0	0	5	0
Hogan W.J.	5	1	0	0	5	1
Hope J.G	1	0	0	0	1	0
Iddon H.	1	0	0	0	1	0
Jackson L.	14	0	6	0	20	0
Jones C.W.	7	3	1	0	8	3
Jones J.T.	0	0	2	0	2	0
Jones L.J.	0	0	1	0	1	0
Keeling A.J.	1	0	0	0	1	0
Kenny F.	1	0	0	0	1	0
King F.A.B.	28	13	23	7	51	20
Kinghorn W.J.D.	1	0	0	0	1	0
Kirton T.W.	6	0	1	0	7	0
Laing R.	1	0	0	0	1	0
Leech F.	3	2	0	0	3	2
Linaker J.E.	6	0	0	0	6	0
McCormack C.J.	1	0	0	0	1	0
McDowall L.J.	82	8	32	0	114	8
McIntosh J.M.	1	0	0	0	1	0
McMillan J.	8	0	0	0	8	0
McShane H.	20	2	3	0	23	2
Malam A.	12	7	2	2	14	9
Meiklem R.C.	1	0	0	0	1	0
Milsom J.	0	0	1	0	1	0
Moore B.	3	0	0	0	3	0

	League		War Cup		TOTAL	
Mulraney A.	6	3	0	0	6	3
Murray W.	4	0	0	0	4	0
Mutch G.	4	1	0	0	4	1
Neilson R.	22	0	3	0	25	0
Nuttall E.	1	0	0	0	1	0
O'Donnell H.	1	1	0	0	1	1
Ollerenshaw J.	1	0	0	0	1	0
Owen F.L.	4	2	5	4	9	6
Paton J.	3	0	2	0	3	2
Paton T.J.	0	0	1	0	1	0
Parlane J.	4	1	0	0	4	1
Pearson S.	5	2	1	0	6	2
Pearson W.G.	14	6	0	0	14	6
Percival J.	33	3	4	0	37	3
Pimbley D.W.	2	0	0	0	2	0
Poole B.	0	0	1	0	1	0
Porter W.	2	0	0	0	2	0
Powell I.V.	1	0	0	0	1	0
Pritchard H.J.	41	8	7	1	48	9
Reid J.D.	1	2	0	0	1	2
Robinson J.J.	35	0	25	0	60	0
Robinson P.	17	2	15	0	32	2
Roxburgh A.W.	2	0	3	0	5	0
Rudd J.J.	9	3	5	0	14	3
Rudman K.	1	0	0	0	1	0
Scales G.	13	0	8	0	21	0
Sellers W.E.	1	0	0	0	1	0
Smith G.B.	68	38	22	7	90	45

	League		War Cup		TOTAL	
Smith L.G.F.	1	0	0	0	1	0
Sproston B.	57	3	17	2	74	5
Stuart D.	21	5	9	2	30	7
Swift F.V.	102	0	31	0	133	0
Taylor J.	25	2	9	1	34	3
Thomson A.	1	0	0	0	1	0
Thomson J.	0	0	1	0	1	0
Thorpe W.F.	3	0	0	0	3	0
Tilson .S.	1	0	0	0	1	0
Toseland E.	2	0	0	0	2	0
Turner H.	11	0	0	0	11	0
Vose G.	0	0	1	0	1	0
Walker C.E.	21	0	12	0	33	0
Walker S.	3	0	0	0	3	0
Walsh W.	162	7	67	1	229	8
Watt A.	1	0	0	0	1	0
Welsh D.	0	0	1	2	1	2
Westwood E.	23	1	6	0	29	1
Wild A.	15	2	1	0	16	2
Williams E.	9	0	1	0	10	0
Williams J.	1	0	0	0	1	0
Williamson W.M.	28	15	34	24	62	39
Wilson F.	1	0	0	0	1	0
Woodroffe L.C.	6	2	0	0	6	2
Worrell J.	2	0	0	0	2	0
Worsley H.	0	0	2	1	2	1
Wright T.B.	3	1	0	0	3	1